Developments in international labour statistics

Developments in international labour statistics

Edited by Ralph Turvey
Formerly Chief Statistician, ILO

Prepared for the International Labour Office

 Pinter Publishers
London and New York

Copyright © International Labour Organisation 1990

First published in Great Britain in 1990 by
Pinter Publishers Limited
25 Floral Street, London WC2E 9DS

British Library Cataloguing in Publication Data

A CIP catalogue record for this book is available from the
British Library
ISBN 0 86187 818 3

Library of Congress Cataloging in Publication Data

Developments in international labour statistics / edited by Ralph
   Turvey ; prepared for the International Labour Office
      p.   cm.
   ISBN 0-86187-818-3
   1. Labor supply—Statistical methods.   2. Labor supply-
-Statistics.   I. Turvey, Ralph.   II. International Labour Office.
HD5711.D48   1989
331.1'01'5195—dc20   89–39047
                                                              CIP

Photoset in North Wales by
Derek Doyle & Associates, Mold, Clwyd
Printed and bound in Great Britain by
Biddles Ltd.

Contents

List of figures

List of tables

Notes on Contributors

Richard Anker Member of the Employment and Development Department, ILO. Holds a Ph.D. in economics from the University of Michigan, United States. Has written exclusively on labour, development and population issues.

K. M. Bashir Retired Chief, Statistics of Conditions of Work Section, Bureau of Statistics, ILO. Now Executive Director of the Kerala Statistical Institute and Chairman of the Vakkom Moulevi Foundation Trust, Trivandrum, India.

Michael Blakemore Lecturer in Quantitative Geography, University of Durham, United Kingdom.

Igor Chernyshev Member of the ILO Bureau of Statistics since 1986, where he is in the Employment and Unemployment Statistics Section. Previously worked with the Central Statistical Office of the Ukrainian SSR. Holds a Master's degree in economics and statistics from the Kiev State University. Deals with the problem of internationally comparable employment and unemployment statistics.

Marie-Thérèse Dupré Member of the Employment and Unemployment Statistics Section, Bureau of Statistics, ILO.

Vladimir Gouriev Deputy Chairman of the State Committee for Statistics of the USSR. Holds a Master's degree in statistics from the Moscow Institute of the National Economy. Contributed to the development of Soviet social and labour statistics.

Eivind Hoffman Chief of the Employment and Unemployment Statistics Section, Bureau of Statistics, ILO. Holds a graduate degree in economics from the University of Oslo, Norway. Worked in the Department of Research at the Norwegian Central Bureau of Statistics and headed the Division of Labour Market Statistics. Before joining the ILO in 1984, headed the group for research on spatial data at the Norwegian Computer Centre. Has published papers on the problems of data collection and co-ordination in labour statistics and other areas.

Ralf Hussmanns Joined the ILO Bureau of Statistics in 1987, where he is in the Employment and Unemployment Statistics Section. Co-author of the forthcoming ILO publication *Surveys of economically active population, employment, unemployment and underdevelopment: A manual on concepts and methods.* Previously worked as a researcher with the Federal Institute for Population Research in Wiesbaden, Federal Republic of Germany, and then with the Federal Statistical Office.

Lars Lyberg Head of the Secretariat for International Research, previously Head of the Statistical Research Unit, in Statistics Sweden, where he has worked since 1967. Chief Editor of *The Journal of Official Statistics.* Holds a doctorate from Stockholm University. Has made contributions in the field of coding, telephone survey methodology and nonsampling errors.

Farhad Mehran Chief Statistician, ILO. Holds a Harvard Ph.D. degree. Taught at Rutgers University, United States, and the College of Statistics, Teheran and was Deputy Director of the Iranian Statistical Office before joining the ILO in 1979. He has published many papers on labour force surveys and related topics and on income distribution.

Robert Nelson System Manager of NOMIS, Department of Geography, University of Durham, United Kingdom.

Richard Platek Director responsible for the methodology of social surveys with Statistics Canada until 1986. Holds a D.Sc in statistics. He has published a number of works on survey design, imputation, questionnaire design and non-sampling errors.

Thomas J. Plewes Associate Commissioner for Employment and Unemployment Statistics, Bureau of Labor Statistics, United States. Holds a Master's degree in economics from George Washington University, Washington, D.C. Responsible for establishment and household survey data on the labour force, hours and earnings.

M. V. S. Rao Technical Advisor, National Household Survey Capability Programme, Statistical Office of the United Nations. Holds a Master's degree in mathematics from Andhra University, India. Formerly Adviser for Employment and Manpower Planning, Planning Commission, India, and then ILO Regional Adviser on Household Surveys in Bangkok.

Mirjana Scott Member of the Employment and Unemployment Statistics Section, Bureau of Statistics, ILO. Graduated in economics and statistics from the University of Belgrade. Since 1984 has worked on the revision of the International Standard Classification of Occupations, having previously worked on international cost of living comparisons for the International Civil Service Commission, United Nations.

John Stokkan Planner in the Vest-Agder county administration, Norway. Previously Senior Executive Officer and then planner in the Norwegian Central Bureau of Statistics, working especially with employment statistics.

Karen Taswell Joined the ILO Bureau of Statistics in 1975. Graduate of the

University of Kent at Canterbury, United Kingdom. Responsible for the recent revision of the October Inquiry and for the introduction of labour cost statistics in the *Year Book of Labour Statistics*.

J. N. Tewari Retired as Chief Executive Officer, National Sample and Survey Organisation, and Joint Secretary, Department of Statistics, Government of India.

Alan Townsend Reader in Geography, University of Durham. Has written extensively on the geography of industry and employment in the United Kingdom.

Ralph Turvey Formerly Chief Statistician, ILO. Holds a London D.Sc.(Econ.) degree. Author of several books on public enterprise economics and macro-economics. Taught at the London School of Economics, was visiting professor at Chicago, was Joint Deputy Chairman of the National Board for Prices and Incomes in the United Kingdom and worked as a consultant for various governments and the World Bank before joining the ILO in 1975. Awarded a Research Fellowship with Statistics Canada 1989–90.

Introduction

by R. Turvey

Labour statistics answer such questions as: How do men's wages compare with those of women? How fast is self-employment in services growing? How does youth unemployment compare with adult unemployment? In which industries are fatalities from industrial accidents increasing? What has been happening to labour costs? Are inter-industry differences in hours of working becoming smaller or larger?

When such questions cannot be answered, or where the answers are unreliable, there is need for assistance and advice about the collection of labour statistics. When they are asked about other countries and can be answered, the statistics from these other counties have to be made available internationally. And when comparisons between countries are requested, then some uniformity of concepts, classifications and methods is essential if the comparisons are to have meaning.

These needs explain the work of the ILO Bureau of Statistics. Thus it has three main functions. The first is to make countries' major labour statistics mutually available through the medium of the ILO *Year Book of Labour Statistics*, the ILO *Bulletin of Labour Statistics* and the United Nations' *Monthly Bulletin of Statistics*. The five volumes of *Statistical Sources and Methods* published by the ILO provide authoritative methodological descriptions of these statistics, country by country.

The second function is to provide guidance to national statisticians and to promote the international comparability of labour statistics by the promulgation of international recommendations on labour statistics.[1] The third, which is closely related, is to assist the statisticians of member countries in their efforts to develop and enhance their programmes for national data collection of labour statistics. This involves advisory visits, participation in seminars and the publication of ILO manuals. At the time of writing, *An Integrated System of Wages Statistics* is available, while manuals on consumer prices indices, occupational classification and household labour force surveys will soon be published.

The papers printed here, four of them not previously published, have

1

been written by members of the Bureau of Statistics as part of its work in performing these functions, or have been obtained from colleagues in national statistical offices in the course of collaboration with them. Such collaboration, usually informal and always very friendly, involves an international network of labour statisticians of which the Bureau forms but one part.

The contacts within this network are not as frequent or extensive as could be wished, and the papers that have been published are scattered throughout past numbers of the *Bulletin of Labour Statistics*. Furthermore, many users of labour statistics – university, union and employer researchers – are not aware that for a whole decade the *Bulletin* has carried articles on methodology as well as the statistics which form its main content. Hence this collection of papers has been designed to make some of our work more widely accessible. However, it includes no papers from the *Bulletin* on consumer price indices, since some of these are reprinted in the *Manual on Consumer Price Indices* (Geneva, ILO, 1989).

The topics treated in these papers reflect the range of work of the Bureau of Statistics as it has evolved over a whole decade, though they by no means cover all its activities. All the topics in one way or another are dedicated to the idea that the quantitative description of employment, wages, hours and so on is an intellectually rewarding and a socially and economically useful activity. Statisticians do not want to be in the public eye, but they do want their output to be widely understood and extensively used. They aim at objectivity, timeliness and accuracy. These papers are dedicated to these qualities.

Note

1. These have recently been made conveniently available in *Current International Recommendations on Labour Statistics*, 1988 edition (Geneva, ILO), which is also available in French and Spanish.

Part One: The ICLS

1 Thirteenth International Conference of Labour Statisticians

Highlights of the conference

The Thirteenth International Conference of Labour Statisticians (ICLS) met in Geneva from 18 to 29 October 1982. The main objectives of this conference were to revise existing or adopt new international standards in the field of labour statistics, in particular, with respect to statistics of the labour force, employment, unemployment and underemployment, and statistics of occupational injuries, and to obtain professional views and guidance from national labour statisticians in respect of the ILO's statistical activities.

The meeting was attended by delegates from 62 countries, representatives of the Employers' and Workers' groups of the ILO Governing Body, and representatives of the United Nations Statistical Office, the Economic Commission for Europe, the United Nations Conference on Trade and Development, the International Research and Training Institute for the Advancement of Women, the World Health Organisation, the World Bank, the Organisation for Economic Co-operation and Development, the Statistical Office of the European Communities, the Arab Labour Organisation, the International Confederation of Free Trade Unions, the World Confederation of Labour, the International Organisation of Employers, and the International Social Security Association.

The Conference elected Mrs J. L. Norwood (United States) as Chairman of the conference, Mrs C. Jusidman (Mexico), Mr E. Ouaba (Benin) and Mr K. C. Seal (India) as Vice-Chairmen, Mr D. A. Worton (Canada) as Rapporteur, and Mr B. Grais (France) as Chairman of the Committee on Labour Force, Employment, Unemployment and Underemployment.

The following items formed the agenda of the conference:
I.   General Report.
II. Labour force, employment, unemployment and underemployment.

5

III. Occupational injuries.
IV. Revision of the ILO October Inquiry on Occupational Wages.
V.   International coding of labour statistics.
VI. Paid holidays.

The conference had before it six reports dealing with the respective items on the agenda.

General Report

The General Report (Report II) reviewed the work of the Bureau of Statistics in recent years in the collection and dissemination of labour statistics, in standard setting, and in the provision of technical advice and assistance. The report also dealt with possibilities for the future work of the Bureau of Statistics.

Under this agenda item the conference discussed, *inter alia*, the desirability of more frequent International Conferences of Labour Statisticians; statistics of labour migration, social security, prices, wages, hours of work and consumer price indices; the scope and coverage of the ILO *Year Book* and *Bulletin of Labour Statistics*; revision of the International Standard Classification of Occupations (ISCO 1968); the revision and updating of past resolutions; the seasonal adjustment of series; the ILO's labour force estimates and projections; the examination of new subjects, and the organisation of training seminars.

With regard to ISCO, the majority of countries expressed their support, in principle, of a revision, as the present version no longer adequately served the purposes for which it was originally intended. Since the next round of population censuses, for which the United Nations guidelines recommended the use of the latest revision of ISCO, was scheduled to take place in the 1990s, it was deemed advisable that a revised ISCO be available by 1987 in order that countries could make the necessary arrangements for its implementation.

In view of the general support shown for a revision of the present ISCO, a Working Group was set up under the chairmanship of Mr L. Herberger (Federal Republic of Germany). The text of the report of the Working Group, contained its views on the need for a revision of ISCO, the factors to be taken into account in revising ISCO, its recommendations for actions to be taken by the ILO and the list of participants in the Working Group.

The conference unanimously approved the Working Group's recommendations for ILO action.

Labour force, employment, unemployment and underemployment

The conference considered the second agenda item on the basis of Report II; 'Labour Force, Employment, Unemployment and Underemployment', which dealt with the history and substance of present international recommendations relating to statistics of the labour force, employment and unemployment (the 1954 resolution), as well as the measurement and analysis of underemployment and under utilisation of manpower (the 1966 resolution); the new conditions, concerns and practices which had developed during the long currency of these recommendations and which rendered them unsuitable in certain respects as a basis for national practices in developing countries, in industrialised market economies, and in centrally planned economies, as well as for international comparisons; and proposals for the reorientation, amplification and extension of the recommendations.

The elements of these proposals were consolidated into a draft resolution for updating the 1954 and 1966 resolutions. The major points of departure from the 1954 and 1966 resolutions were: the use of two approaches for measuring the economically active population, one based on the current activity status and the other on the usual activity status; the distinction between the paid labour force and its self-employed counterpart; the provision of an alternative, extended definition of unemployment; and, for the measurement of underemployment, the separation of the measurement of visible from that of invisible underemployment, in which the latter would be replaced by a study of the relationships between employment and income.

The conference devoted two plenary sessions to a general review of the draft resolution contained in Report II before referring it to the Committee on Labour Force, Employment, Unemployment and Underemployment for more detailed study. The draft resolution, as modified by the committee, was reviewed by the plenary session and, following the approval of further amendments, was then adopted by the conference.

Occupational injuries

This topic was considered by the conference on the basis of Report III, 'Occupational Injuries', which dealt with the purpose of international recommendations on statistics of occupational injuries; terminologies involved; sources of data and methods of collection; units of enumeration; classification of occupation injuries; and various comparative measures. It also included the resolution concerning statistics of employment injuries adopted by the Tenth International Conference of Labour Statisticians in 1962, and a proposed draft resolution which consolidated recommended improvements of the statistics of occupational injuries in the light of conditions, concerns and practices that had evolved during the intervening 20 years.

The conference considered in detail the draft resolution on occupational injury statistics submitted by the ILO. Many specific points were raised including the treatment or classification of accidents involving more than one employee, or several industries; accidents at the workplace not directly related to or influenced by the work itself; diseases or injuries resulting from multiple causes, and the treatment of commuting accidents where these are not distinguished from work accidents. In the light of proposals made by delegates, it decided on a number of amendments. Taking into account the definitions with regard to employment injuries contained in ILO Convention No. 121, it recommended standard methodology, definitions and concepts relating to occupational injuries, and guiding rules for the classification and presentation of such statistics. The amended resolution was adopted by the conference.

Revision of the ILO October Inquiry on Occupational Wages

This item was considered by the conference on the basis of Report IV; 'Revision of the ILO October Inquiry on Occupational Wages' and conference document D.4, *Descriptions of Selected Occupations for the Revised ILO October Inquiry on Occupational Wages.* Report IV described the origin and development of the Inquiry, and the reasons and methods used for its revision. It also presented a revised list of occupations which were described in document D.4 as well as a draft questionnaire for the collection of data from national statistical offices. In presenting this topic to the conference, the ILO sought co-operation and support for the implementation of the revision, as well as guidance in respect of the selected occupations and procedures for compiling data through the Inquiry.

Many countries expressed their support, in principle, of the revision of the October Inquiry. They recognised the desirability of extending the occupational and industrial coverage and the types of data to be collected, as well as the need for obtaining wages and hours data separately for men and women. However, concern was expressed about the difficulties which would be encountered by national statistical offices in providing information for the expanded list of occupations in the revised Inquiry.

The major concerns expressed by the conference related to the lack of clarity as to the objectives of the revised October Inquiry and the uses to which the results should be put. A Working Group was set up under the chairmanship of Mr J. T. McCracken (United States) to examine the various issues raised in the Report and by the conference.

The Working Group made several recommendations concerning, *inter alia*, the collection and publication of qualitative information on the results of the Inquiry in order to avoid its misinterpretation; and the publication of an international directory of statistics on wages, consumer prices and related topics. In addition, the ILO was urged to increase efforts to improve the international comparability of the published data, and it was recommended that this work be assigned high priority for the future programme of the ILO Bureau of Statistics, and be considered as an item to be placed on the agenda of the next ICLS.

International coding of labour statistics

This item was considered by the conference on the basis of Report V, 'International Coding of Labour Statistics'. Report V presented a preliminary outline concerning the possible development of a computerised schema for the retrieval of information about available national statistical data which could be analogous with systems for the retrieval of bibliographic references. The purpose of presenting this report to the conference was to seek confirmation or otherwise that the idea of an international coding schema was a useful one and, if so, to consider how the present formulation might be developed further.

The conference expressed general support for the underlying rationale of the proposal and there appeared to be widespread confidence that the technical details could be worked out. It was suggested that with further research and study this item might be considered at the next ICLS.

Paid holidays

This item was discussed by the conference on the basis of Report VI, 'Paid Holidays'. The report comprised a summary of *ad hoc* research carried out by the Bureau of Statistics into the availability of national statistics of paid holidays, as well as the different methodologies and concepts used in their compilation. The report had been prepared for the conference not with the aim of proposing any resolution on statistics of paid holidays, but more as a background research paper of methodological interest, and to draw attention to the subject. The conference agreed that Report VI should be revised to take account of corrections and additions proposed by the conference with the aim of publishing the resulting paper[1] to provide methodological information for those interested in, or concerned with statistics of paid holidays.

Note

1. R. Turvey, 'Statistics of paid vacations' in this volume.

2 Fourteenth International Conference of Labour Statisticians

Highlights of the conference

The Fourteenth International Conference of Labour Statisticians (ICLS) met in Geneva from 28 October to 6 November 1987. Its objectives were, first, to revise the existing international recommendations relating to consumer price indices, statistics of industrial disputes and the International Standard Classification of Occupations (ISCO), and, second, to discuss three topics with the aim of guiding the future work of the ILO Bureau of Statistics; employment in the informal sector; statistics of absence from work; and the implications of employment creation schemes for the measurement of employment and unemployment.

The meeting was attended by delegates from 71 countries, representatives of the employer and worker groups on the ILO Governing Body and representatives from a number of other international organisations.

The conference elected Mr Y. Miura (Japan) as Chairman of the conference, Ms R. Grosskoff (Uruguay) as Vice-Chairman and Mr N. Davis (United Kingdom) as Rapporteur. A committee on consumer price indices was set up, which elected Mr I. Castles (Australia) as Chairman and Ms B. Slater (Canada) as Rapporteur. A Working Group on employment promotion schemes was also set up, whose chairman was Mr L. Herberger (Federal Republic of Germany).

The work of the Bureau of Statistics

The conference discussed the work of the Bureau of Statistics in the light of a chapter in the General Report. It was recognised that shortage of resources rather than a lack of initiative was the main limitation upon its activities. Delegates expressed approval of the Bureau's plans to study productivity statistics; non-standard forms of employment; household income and expenditure surveys; employment and unemployment flows and durations; and the classification of status in employment.

The work of the regional advisers was discussed, as was the improvement of the Bureau's database and the proposed restructuring of the *Year Book of Labour Statistics* to facilitate inter-country comparisons. This is a major project which will take some years to accomplish. The excellent co-operation with the statistical offices of other international organisations was recognised.

The recent Labour Statistics Convention, 1985 (no. 160), and its accompanying Recommendation (no. 170) were recognised as being extremely useful, and countries were encouraged to ratify this Convention, particularly those countries which had ratified the now superseded Convention no. 63 concerning statistics of wages and hours of work.

Employment in the informal sector

This was the first time the ICLS discussed this topic. Accordingly, the chapter on it in the General Report formed the subject of an extended discussion. Drawing a distinction between concealed activities and employment in the informal sector, the conference decided to deal only with the latter. It was recognised that informal sector statistics are needed for many purposes, such as the formulation of employment and income-generation policies, promotion of self-employment activities, improvement of national accounts and other types of statistics.

The discussion centred upon the most appropriate measurement unit (the economic unit, the individual worker or the occupation); the choice of criteria for defining employment in the informal sector (scale of operation, level of organisation, level of technology, etc.); the scope and coverage of the sector (inclusion or exclusion of non-market production); the need for subclassifications (e.g. to identify outworkers, household enterprises, ambulant activities, street outlets); and feasible strategies for data collection (household-based or establishment-based sources or a combination of the two).

No formal conclusions were reached on these issues, the whole point of the discussion being to exchange ideas and to stimulate further work, but a resolution was passed urging the ILO to continue to work on this subject and to include it on the agenda of the Fifteenth International Conference of Labour Statisticians.

Statistics of absence from work

The chapter on this subject in the General Report was extensively discussed. Absence in general, rather than absenteeism in particular, was agreed to be the appropriate topic. The possibilities of classifying reasons for absence were felt to fall short of what might be desired, though it was stressed that household surveys might provide a wider range of information than could be obtained from establishment surveys.

It was considered that these statistics would generally have to be limited to regularly paid employees and, to the extent that they were obtained from establishments, might have to exclude small establishments. However, the desirability of combining statistics from different sources was stressed. The conference wanted the Bureau to continue to work on this subject, with particular attention being given to sources of data and collection methods that might be used.

Employment promotion schemes

A Working Group was formed to discuss this topic which concerned the implications of employment promotion schemes for the measurement of employment and unemployment. Conclusions were reached on the principles to be followed in classifying participants in job-training schemes into the broad categories 'employed', 'unemployed' and 'not in the labour force'. In addition, recommendations were made on the relevance of the concept of 'visible underemployment' and on the usefulness of compiling employment-training balance sheets from various sources. An article based on the chapter of the General Report, has subsequently been published.[1]

Consumer price indices

These formed the subject of Report II submitted to the conference and were discussed in a separate committee, where the draft resolution included in the report was examined in detail and extensively amended during eight sessions.

The use of probability sampling rather than purposive sampling of items and outlets in price collection attracted considerable attention. Because it is costly, its use is currently limited to very few countries, but its desirability in principle was recognised, though purposive sampling will remain the best approach in most circumstances.

The conference subsequently adopted the resolution as amended by the committee. It supersedes the earlier resolutions on the subject of 1947 and 1962. The conference also adopted a brief resolution expressing the desire (heartily shared by the Bureau of Statistics) that the ILO should be better equipped to provide technical advice and to improve the exchange of experience among government statisticians.

Industrial disputes

Report III discussed this topic and proffered a draft resolution to supersede that of 1926. The importance of strike statistics was agreed, and discussion focused on the scope and coverage of the topic, the reasons for collecting the statistics and measurement issues. Many amendments were submitted and it proved impossible to accommodate them all in the time available. Hence the conference readily agreed upon a fairly short resolution denominated 'Interim resolution concerning statistics of strikes and lock-outs' in which the terms 'strikes' and 'lock-outs' were defined for statistical purposes and brief indications were given concerning their measurement and classification. The conference then unanimously adopted another resolution recommending the Bureau of Statistics to convene a number of technical meetings and/or establish a Working Group to assist it with further work. This was naturally welcomed by the Bureau, though the absence of any of the necessary provisions for it in the programme and budget was noted.

International Standard Classification of Occupations

An updated and improved International Standard Classification of Occupations, ISCO-88, was adopted to replace ISCO-68. The resolution contains the new system of major, submajor, minor and unit groups. Persons are classified according to their job relation and jobs are classified with respect to the type of work performed.

The resolution urges countries to discuss with the ILO the way in which their national classifications can be related to ISCO. It notes that the Bureau of Statistics will provide guidelines on the application of occupational classification and a manual on the development of national classifications and dictionaries.

Note

1. R. G. Doss, M. T. Dupré and F. Mehran, 'Employment promotion schemes and the statistical measure of unemployment' *International Labour Review*, volume 127. no. 1, 1988.

Part Two: Labour Accounting

3 A labour accounting system

R. Turvey and E. Hoffmann

The idea of constructing a labour accounting system which in some way
paralleled a national accounting system was put forward internationally at
a joint ILO/ECE meeting on Manpower Statistics in 1983 and has
subsequently been discussed at two informal work sessions. Among the
participants from national statistical offices, Mr Verhage and Mr Leunis of
the Netherlands should be mentioned as having contributed a number of
papers. Systematic national work has been carried out in the Netherlands,
the Federal Republic of Germany and Norway.

An accounting system is an interrelated set of definitions, classifications
and measurement conventions which are useful for organising quantitative
description, planning and analysis. In the present case, four major types of
planning and analysis can be listed: productivity and production functions;
the role of the labour market in personal income generation and
distribution; the dynamics of labour markets; and macroeconomics.

Figure 3.1 displays the conceptual framework that has been developed in
a process of iterative discussion since 1983. It centres on jobs. These link a
person to a post. Persons derive some of their characteristics[1] from the
households to which they belong. Posts derive some of their characteristics
from the employers to which they belong. (A self-employed person is his or
her own employer.)

The classifications used for categorising employers, posts, households
and persons should either be the international standard classifications or
should be capable of mapping onto them.

Although the framework includes unemployment, it is universal, since it
applies perfectly well to countries where unemployment is zero. There is a
question, however, whether the framework should not be extended by
distinguishing (filled) posts whose abolition would damage achievement of
the employer's output target from those which would not. Such labour
hoarding or unproductive employment would thus be incorporated into
the system as a measure of labour surplus.

17

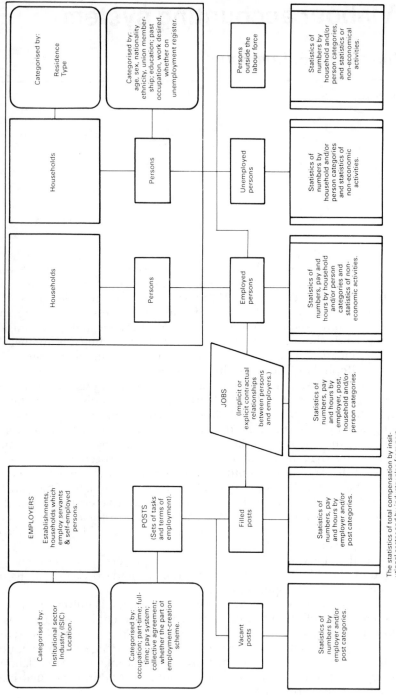

The statistics of total compensation by insitutional sector and by industry also from part of the System of National Accounts.

EMPLOYERS
Establishments, households which employ servants & self-employed persons.

Categorised by:
Institutional sector Industry (ISIC) Location.

POSTS
(Sets of tasks and terms of employment).

Categorised by: occupation; part-time; full-time; pay system; collective agreement; whether the part of employment-creation scheme.

Filled posts

Vacant posts

Statistics of numbers, pay and hours by employer and/or post categories.

Statistics of numbers by employer and/or post categories.

JOBS
(Implicit or explicit contractual relationships between persons and employers.)

Statistics of numbers, pay and hours by employer, post, household and/or person categories.

Households

Categorised by:
Residence Type

Households

Persons

Persons

Categorised by:
age, sex, nationality ethnicity, union membership; education; past occupation, work desired, whether on unemployment register.

Employed persons

Unemployed persons

Persons outside the labour force

Statistics of numbers, pay and hours by household and/or person categories and statistics of non-economic activities.

Statistics of numbers by household and/or person categories and statistics of non-economic activities.

Statistics of numbers by household and/or person categories, and statistics or non-economical activities.

The direct link with national accounting is, first, the use of common classifications and definitions, including the definition of economic activity in terms of the production boundary in the national accounts. Second, it is that the total compensation of employed persons comes into both systems. The numbers employed, their full-time equivalents or hours worked or paid for by industry, which form part of the labour accounting system, may also be shown in satellite tables of the national accounts. In addition to this co-ordination in *principle*, co-ordination in *practice* involves using consistent estimates. Furthermore there are certain similarities, such as:

- Imputing a wage to self-employment is like imputing a value to own-account production.
- Labour cost, gross pay and net pay need to be distinguished in the same way as market value and factor cost.
- Value aggregates can be broken down either into quantity and unit value or into value at constant prices (or wages) and a price (or wage) deflator.[2]
- Many of the estimates have to be made on the basis of statistics from several, sometimes conflicting, sources.

In the case of the labour accounting system, the framework, in the six boxes at the bottom of Figure 3.1 where classifying variables are specified, defines the universe of possible labour accounting tables. Since this is enormous, it seems useful to propose a small set of model tables. Those suggested (Tables 3.1–3.8) go beyond what is currently practicable in most countries in three important respects, but are worth aiming at. First, good data on vacancies are rare. Yet how can labour problems be understood without a measure of labour shortages? If as much effort as has gone into measuring unemployment over the last 40 years had gone into measuring vacancies, we should have a measure of them. This is urgent work. Second, imputing wages to the self-employed is no more difficult than imputing rents to owner-occupied houses, so a similar remark applies. Third, the division between economic and non-economic activities has been changing so much that concentrating only on the market activities can give a misleading picture.

Notes

1. The characteristic 'Work desires' for persons without a job would indicate the type of job desired (including whether it is part-time or full-time), while for persons with a job it would indicate whether a change of job is desired.
2. For a criticism of earnings indices that measure trends in unit values rather resembling price indices, see R. Turvey 'What kinds of earnings indices are useful?' in this volume.

Table 3.1	MALES		FEMALES		Registered male unemployed	Registered female unemployed
	Full time	Part time	Full time	Part time		
Employed	x	x	x	x	x	x
Unemployed	x	x	x	x	x	x
Not in LF	x		x		x	x

Table 3.2	UNEMPLOYED MALES		UNEMPLOYED FEMALES		VACANT POSTS	
	Full time	Part time	Full time	Part time	Full time	Part time
Occupation	x	x	x	x	x	x
,,	x	x	x	x	x	x
,,	x	x	x	x	x	x
,,	x	x	x	x	x	x

Employees only

Table 3.3	MALES			FEMALES		
	From Employed	From Unempl.	From n.i. LF	From Employed	From Unempl.	From n.i. LF
MALES						
To Employed	x	x	x			
To Unempl.	x	x	x			
To not in LF	x	x	x			
FEMALES						
To Employed				x	x	x
To Unempl.				x	x	x
To not in LF				x	x	x

Table 3.4	FILLED POSTS				VACANT POSTS	
	Employees		Self-employed		Employees	
	Part time	Full time	Part time	Full time	Part time	Full time
Industry	x	x	x	x	x	x
,,	x	x	x	x	x	x
,,	x	x	x	x	x	x

Table 3.5	Cumulative number of posts filled	Cumulative number of post vacated or terminated
Industry	x	x
,,	x	x
,,	x	x
,,	x	x

Employees only

Table 3.6	Annual Data:		Employees only		Self-employed Imputed	
	Labour Cost	Total Compens.	Hours Paid For	Actual Hours	Total Compens.	Actual Hours
Industry	x	x	x	x	x	x
,,	x	x	x	x	x	x
,,	x	x	x	x	x	x
,,	x	x	x	x	x	x

Table 3.7	Labour Cost per Job	Earnings per Job	Labour Cost per Act.hour	Earnings per Actual Hour	Earnings per Actual Hour
Industry	x	x	x	x	x
,,	x	x	x	x	x
,,	x	x	x	x	x
,,	x	x	x	x	x
		Full-time jobs			Part-time

Table 3.8	Earnings per full-time Job		Hours Paid for per full-time Job	
	MALES	FEMALES	MALES	FEMALES
Occupation	x	x	x	x
,,	x	x	x	x
,,	x	x	x	x
,,	x	x	x	x
		per week or equivalent week		

DEFINITIONAL RELATIONSHIPS
Including some variables which are not in Tables 3.1–3.8

Number of filled posts = Employed persons
    − Correction for shared posts
    + Correction for multiple job-holders

Filled posts at end = Filled posts at beginning
    + Cumulative number filled
    − Cumulative number vacated or terminated

Vacant posts at end = Vacant posts at beginning
    + Cumulative number of posts vacated
    + Cumulative new posts created
    − Cumulative number of posts filled

Employed at the end = Employed at the beginning
    + Gross changes to employment from not in the labour force
    + Gross changes to employment from unemployment
    − Gross changes from employment to not in the labour force
    − Gross changes from employment to unemployment
    + net balance of migration of employed and deaths of employed.

A similar final term enters the similar relationships for unemployed and for persons not in the labour force.

DATA ON NON-ECONOMIC ACTIVITIES.
These should be in terms of number of persons and or total hours, separately for persons employed, unemployed and not in the labour force, and might relate to two types of activity which could be performed by someone else. The first consists of activities performed for the benefit of one's own household, frequently activities which could be performed by a servant or paid for. The second consists of activities performed for the benefit of others, i.e. voluntary work.

4 Labour statistics in the centrally planned economy countries of the Council for Mutual Economic Assistance (CMEA)[1]

(Technical note prepared by the Bureau of Statistics, International Labour Office)

In May 1978, the Standing Commission on Statistics of the Council for Mutual Economic Assistance (CMEA) adopted new standards for the compilation of the principal series on labour statistics. These new standards refer in particular to:

(a) the number of persons in the industrial labour force (wage earners and salaried employees);
(b) wages and salaries;
(c) the utilisation of working time.

Number of persons in the industrial labour force

With regard to this point, the criteria of standardisation refer to:

(i)   the *number of registered* wage earners and salaried employees;
(ii) the *average number* of wage earners and salaried employees;
(iii) the principal *socio-economic classifications*;
(iv) the statistics of labour force *turnover*.

It is to be noted that 'industrial labour force' (wage earners and salaried employees) is to be understood as referring to all categories of persons engaged in undertakings, organisations and institutions. That concept covers mainly; wage earners, apprentices, engineers and technicians, agronomist and veterinary technical personnel, salaried employees,

22

services and security staff.

Numbers of registered wage earners and salaried employees

The number of registered persons in the labour force of an undertaking, an organisation or an institution covers not only the permanent workers (full-time and part-time) but also seasonal workers and temporary workers with a contract for at least one day. Registration is made on the day of recruitment. In accordance with the legislation in force, the registers are kept up to date for each 'calendar day' and must include all persons present at work and those who are absent for whatever reason, among others (or) in particular: sick leave; work stoppage for technical reasons; annual holidays and compensatory leave; maternity leave (women on supplementary maternity leave are included in the number of persons registered but may also be entered on a separate list); official reasons (for example, a representative of public interest); temporary detachment to other undertakings (especially agricultural or construction undertakings) or to attend specialised and vocational training courses in educational and training centres provided that the worker continues to be paid by the undertaking or organisation or institution that has detached him; study leave for attendance (in the evening or by correspondence) at training courses given by institutions of higher or secondary education irrespective of whether or not the worker continues to be paid during his absence; participation in training courses financed by the undertaking.

The number of persons registered includes also: persons working at home for an enterprise which provides them with the working material; full-time students working for pay during their periods of leisure, as well as retired persons at work receiving both a pension and full pay or part pay. It is to be noted that the last two categories may be the subject of a separate count.

Workers temporarily seconded by the principal undertaking to other undertakings or organisations or institutions, as well as workers temporarily seconded to the principal undertaking, are registered only with the undertakings or organisations or institutions which remunerate them during the period of temporary detachment.

The following categories are not included in the number of persons registered: persons performing their compulsory military service; students seeking practical production experience in an undertaking or an organisation or an institution but who are not recruited for the purpose of engaging in an activity or holding a particular job; workers who have been sent by their undertaking or organisation or institutions to institutions of specialised higher or secondary education for full-time attendance at courses and who receive from their employer an education grant for that purpose; persons who are detached from their undertaking for technical assistance work abroad during a long period if they no longer receive pay from their undertaking during their absence.

Lastly, in order to avoid double counting, multi-job holders are registered only by the undertaking or organisation or institution in which they exercise their principal activity. In the other undertakings or organisations or institutions in which the activities of such persons are of a complementary or marginal character relatively to the principal activity, such persons are listed separately. In order to ascertain the number of multi-job holders, special *ad hoc* surveys are made in the USSR and in most of the planned economy countries of Europe.

Average numbers of wage earners and salaried employees

On the basis of the daily registration of these workers, the average number of those registered in the course of a given month is calculated. The calculation is made by aggregating the numbers registered on each day of the month and by dividing the resulting total by the number of days in the calendar month in question. The number recorded for a holiday (Saturday, Sunday, public holiday) is the same as the one for the preceding working day.

Average numbers other than monthly averages (quarterly, half-yearly or annual averages) are calculated by aggregating the monthly average numbers and by dividing the resulting total by the number of months in the period considered (for example, three or six or twelve months).

It is to be noted that, for the calculation of the average numbers, part-time workers are previously converted into full-time workers on the basis of the normal hours of work as prescribed in their labour contracts.

Principal socio-economic classifications

For the purpose of the socio-economic classifications, an initial distinction is drawn between, on the one hand, the number of persons engaged in the *material production sector* and, on the other hand, the numbers engaged in the *non-material production sector*.

That distinction is consistent with the Classification by Economic Sector adopted at the 26th Session of the Standing Commission on Statistics of the CMEA. Furthermore, wage earners and salaried employees in the material production sector are classified by *type of activity* as: persons engaged in *basic* activities; and persons engaged in *non-basic* activities. The first category includes workers participating directly in production, technical and managerial personnel, the inspection personnel and the personnel in charge of accounts, supplies, equipment and maintenance of the basic production. The second category is composed of the auxiliary or subsidiary staff who, although at the charge of the undertaking or the organisation or the institution, are not normally concerned in its basic activities.

As for the workers engaged on basic activities for the various sectors of an undertaking's material production, they may be classified by *qualification*, as: manual workers; apprentices; engineers and technicians; salaried employees; and services and security personnel.

Labour turnover

In the CMEA, the elements of movement in the labour force that are recorded concern the entries to and departures from an undertaking or organisation or institution in the course of a given period. The statistics refer to the material production sector as well as to the non-material production sector. In the case of the material production sector, data are given separately, for the whole of the personnel engaged in basic activities and for wage earners.

Entrants are registered according to the method of recruitment, namely by: organised competition; placement by the ministries or departments concerned (graduates of universities, technical institutes and professional schools); transfer from other undertakings or organisations or institutions; and direct recruitment by the undertaking. The last category includes new entrants not covered by the first three methods of recruitment, as well as persons resuming their activity in an undertaking after having performed their compulsory military service.

It is to be noted that transfers from one category of workers to another within an undertaking (for example, from the category of 'apprentices' to that of 'manual workers' or from the category of 'manual workers' to that of 'salaried employees' and vice versa) are not counted among the entrants but are listed separately.

As for *departures* from an undertaking or organisation or institution, they are classified according to the circumstances, as follows: persons transferred to other undertakings, or organisations or institutions; persons whose labour contract comes to an end (temporary, seasonal, etc., contracts); persons leaving the undertaking in order to attend training courses in specialised establishments or who are called up to perform their compulsory military service, as well as persons who retire; persons who leave the undertaking of their own free will (for personal reasons, owing to dissatisfaction with their occupation, due to difficult working conditions, etc.); and persons who are discharged for absenteeism or other breaches of labour discipline (persons who leave their employment without informing the management, as well as those who do so before the expiration of their contract, are included among persons discharged for absenteeism).

The Standing Commission on Statistics of the CMEA recommends that, in addition to data on entries and departures, data should be collected that would enable the *stability* of employment in an undertaking or organisation or institution to be measured. In the case of the industrial sector, construction and a few other sectors of production, that stability is measured on the basis of the number of persons who worked uninterruptedly in the same undertaking or organisation or institution during the whole year. That number is obtained as follows: number of workers registered on 1 January in a given year; *less* departures during the year of workers who were registered on 1 January of the year in question (departures of persons recruited in the course of the year are not taken into account); *less* workers entered on the register but who have been transferred to other undertakings or organisations or institutions or who have been transferred within their undertaking from a basic activity to a non-basic activity.

On the basis of the three categories of labour force data indicated above, namely, the data on entries, the data on departures and the data on workers registered during the whole year as well as the average number of persons at work in the undertaking or organisation or institution during the period considered, the following rates are calculated: rate of *turnover* (separately for entries and exits); rate of *stability* of employment; and rate of *fluidity*. It is to be noted that the last-mentioned rate concerns only voluntary separations or separations due to discharge for unwarranted absenteeism or breach of labour discipline.

Wages and salaries (wage earners and salaried employees)

Total amounts

In the CMEA, wages and salaries are a part of the national income which is distributed among the labour force according to the quantity and quality of their labour. Note that in addition to wages and salaries, they receive additional payments and allowances from public consumption funds.

Wages and salaries include all payments made by undertakings, institutions and organisations to permanent, temporary and seasonal workers for work performed, by which they are registered.

In particular, gross wages and salaries relating to a given period of a month, quarter or year, include remuneration for time worked including overtime, piece-work, bonuses, remuneration according to the law for hours not worked (particularly holidays, sick leave and maternity), and extra payments for dirty, dangerous or unpleasant work and supplements for night work. Wages and salaries also include authors' royalties and payments to workers giving apprenticeship courses or themselves receiving training. On the other hand, wages and salaries do not include exceptional bonuses, travel expenses, the cost of special clothing or footwear, and social insurance payments.

Average wages and salaries

Average wages and salaries are calculated for the whole economy and by sector. They refer to all payments for work, including non-recurrent bonuses and, for the economy-wide calculation, to all workers (including supernumerary workers) whether or not they are on the registered labour force of the undertakings, institutions and organisations concerned.

Utilisation of working time

In view of the importance which the centrally planned economies attach to the utilisation of working time and, in particular, to an evaluation of the degree of utilisation or non-utilisation for production, the Standing Commission on Statistics of the CMEA recommends the collection of statistics on *working time actually utilised* for production and on *time not utilised*, especially in the case of basic activities in the industrial, construction and transport sectors. As yardsticks, the Commission recommends the worked man-day and the worked man-hour.

The number of worked man-days is obtained by aggregating the days of actual presence of the workers concerned at the place of work, whatever may be the number of hours actually worked in the course of a day or the period considered. The days of official missions (within the country or abroad), as well as the days worked in other undertakings or organisations or institutions by persons detached from the undertaking or organisation or institution concerned, are reckoned among the man-days worked. These man-days include also public holidays that can be worked with a special authorisation and are counted, therefore, as overtime.

As for the number of man-days not worked, this is obtained by aggregating all the whole days of absence due to: work stoppages, maternity leave, illness, legally authorised reasons, reasons authorised by the undertaking or organisation or institution, causes neither authorised nor warranted. Absences on public holidays and annual leave are counted separately.

The sum of the man-days worked and not worked represents the total number of available working days. The ratio of the various components listed above to the total number of working days available provides detailed information on the utilisation of the available time.

A more exact measurement of time actually worked can be obtained by substituting the man-hours worked for the man-days worked. In that case, account can also be taken of the hours that are not worked by the persons present at the workplace.

Conclusion

Standards in the field of statistics of employment, of wages and salaries and of utilisation of working time as summarised above on the basis of a document[2] communicated by the Secretariat of the Council for Mutual Economic Assistance indicate clearly enough the methods employed by the centrally planned economy members of the European Economic Commission. Taken as a whole, the definitions, criteria and methods of collection of data differ from the practice followed in market economy countries as well as from the recommendations adopted in this field by International Conferences of Labour Statisticians.

Notes

1. Bulgaria, Cuba, Czechoslovakia, German Democratic Republic, Hungary, Mongolia, Poland, Romania, USSR and Vietnam.
2. Secretariat of the CMEA, *Methodological principles relating to the basic indicators of labour statistics in the member countries of the CMEA* (in Russian), Moscow, June 1978.

5 Compilation of balance sheets of labour resources in the USSR: methodological principles[1]

V. Gouriev

The contents of the 'labour resources' category

The starting-point for preparing a balance sheet of labour resources (BSLR) is the determination of the population of working age. In the USSR the lower working age limit is 16, and the upper limit is 59 for males and 54 for females.

These working age limits provide an indication of the potential labour resources. In reality, a certain part of the population of working age is not included among the labour resources, namely the physically disabled and persons of working age who retire on special terms, i.e. those previously employed in industries and occupations where, due to the nature of the work performed, the retirement age is lower than 59 for males and 54 for females. At the same time, a certain part of the population of retirement age may continue to remain employed, although receiving a retirement pension, and therefore this category is included among the labour resources.[2]

In addition, young persons of 15 years of age who are employed in social production are included in the total labour resources category. According to labour legislation and under agreements with trade union officials, these 15-year-olds may be employed as an exception. They are mostly engaged seasonally on collective farms during harvest periods, generally performing light agricultural tasks.

Thus, the total labour resources include able-bodied population of working age; persons of retirement age who receive a pension but who continue to remain employed; and seasonally employed 15-year-olds.

General methodological concepts of BSLR compilation

The BSLR is one of the principal tools of planning. It provides information on the availability and distribution of labour resources according to type of activity, branch of national economy and social group. The BSLR reflects the distribution of labour resources in *(a)* the public sector of the economy (wage earners and salaried employees of governmental, co-operative and public organisations, institutions and enterprises, and collective farmers participating in the economic activity of collective farms); *(b)* other economically active population of working age (artisans who are not members of a co-operative, etc.); *(c)* students aged 16 and over attending educational institutions full-time and who do not work; and *(d)* able-bodied population of working age engaged in personal subsidiary agricultural plot activities or in household duties (i.e. those not employed in the public sector of the economy and not in full-time study).

In general, the BSLR can be presented according to Table 5.1. *Section A* of this table presents the supply and composition of total available labour resources; *section B* shows the utilisation of labour resources by sector and/or type of activity.

Table 5.1 Balance sheet of labour resources

Labour resource categories	Total, of which:	
	in urban areas	in rural areas

Section A: Labour resources
Total of which:
1. Able-bodied population of working age
2. Employed population of non-working age, of which:
   (a) retired persons who work;
   (b) 15-year-olds who work

Section B: Utilisation of labour resources
1. Total number of persons employed in the public sector of the national economy (excluding full-time students and persons engaged in personal subsidiary agricultural plot activities or in household duties),
   of which:
   (a) wage earners and salaried employees of governmental, co-operative and public organisations, institutions and enterprises;
   (b) collective farmers;
   (c) others who are not members of co-operatives (artisans, etc.)
2. Students of working age who only study and do not work
3. Able-bodied population of working age engaged in personal subsidiary agricultural plot activities or in household duties

Indexes of labour resources availability and composition: principles of computation

As stated earlier, the starting-point of the BSLR compilation is the estimation of the size of population of working age (see section A of Table 5.1). The main component of this population, the able-bodied population of working age, for a particular area is computed as in Table 5.2.

Table 5.2 The able-bodied population of working age

| Categories | Total, of which: | |
	in urban areas	in rural areas
1. Number of persons of working age (16–59 for males, 16–54 for females)		
2. Number of disabled former wage earners and salaried employees of working age who do not work		
3. Number of disabled former collective farmers of working age who do not work		
4. Number of persons who receive pensions on special terms (before standard age of retirement) and who do not work		
5. In- and out-flow of the number of wage earners and salaried employees who live in one area and commute to another area to work		
6. In- and out-flow of the number of students who live in one area but commute to educational institutions in another		
7. Total able-bodied population of working age in the particular area (row 1 − row 2 − row 3 − row 4 and ± row 5 ± row 6)		

Data obtained from demographic registers and surveys, labour reports and surveys and censuses of population are used to calculate the size of the able-bodied population of working age. Censuses of population provide the size of the population of working age at the date of the census. In order to take account of the changes incurred during the period between the census date and the date on which the BSLR is drawn up, data on the size of the population of working age obtained during the census are modified: by deleting the number of persons who have attained retirement age; by deleting the number of persons of working age who died; by adding the number of persons who have attained age; and by adding or deleting changes in the population of working age due to net migration.

When the population of working age has thus been determined, it is necessary to re-estimate the able-bodied population of working age. This is calculated as the difference between the size of the total population of working age and the size of the population of working age who do not participate in economic activity due to the fact that they become disabled before reaching retirement.

Data on the total able-bodied population of working age are used not only for planning the volume of production, rates and ratios of economic development, the structure of capital investments, and the location of production units, but also for analysing important socio-demographic issues.

Indexes of labour resource utilisation: principles of computation by type of activity and by sector of national economy

Section B of the BSLR (see Table 5.1) provides indexes on the distribution of the labour resources according to type of activity.

The structure of labour resource utilisation reflects the nature of labour resources distribution by sector and/or type of activity. In order to measure the degree of labour resource utilisation in the public sector of the national economy, an index of utilisation is computed; this is the ratio of the total number of employed persons in the national economy (excluding persons engaged in personal subsidiary agricultural plot activities or in household duties but including full-time students of working age) to the total number of available labour resources (section A of Table 5.1).

Problems of labour resource utilisation are of great importance from the sectoral point of view, especially those concerning the ratio of labour resources employed in the non-productive sectors.[2]

Indexes of this BSLR section are computed on the basis of data drawn from periodic reports of organisations, institutions and enterprises, on the number of their employed, and from reports of collective farms on the number of collective farmers. The number of persons of working age who are full-time students and who do not work are obtained from reports of educational institutions on such student enrolement.

Labour reserves: principles of computation

Urban and rural populations of working age who are able to work and who are engaged in personal subsidiary agricultural plot activities or in household duties constitute the labour reserve. Persons engaged in personal subsidiary agricultural plot activities are those able-bodied persons of working age who farm personal plots and keep private livestock. Persons engaged in household duties are those able-bodied persons of working age who either bring up children, look after the old and the ill non-working members of the household, or do not work for other reasons. In rural areas, those household members engaged in personal subsidiary agricultural plot activities are often also engaged in household duties.

The size of the able-bodied population of working age engaged in personal subsidiary agricultural plot activities and in household duties can be computed as the difference between the total labour resources (section A of Table 5.1) and the total labour resources employed in the national economy, including full-time students aged 16 and over attending educational institutions. This figure represents the untapped reserve of labour.

In addition, it is important to determine the age structure of this labour reserve. Such information is necessary for formulating social measures designed to promote more active utilisation of the non-active population in public social production (e.g. by the development of crèche and kinder-garten networks, the expansion of services, the extensions of privileges for working women with children, etc.). These issues are studied by means of special surveys.

The Central Statistical Board of the USSR received detailed information on the size and sex/age composition of persons engaged in personal subsidiary agricultural plot activities and in household duties from a socio-demographic sample survey of the population, which took place in 1985. Data from this survey provided information on the able-bodied population of working age who were not engaged in social production and not attending educational institutions, according to age, educational level, occupation, major source of livelihood, and reason for not being employed in social production. This survey also identified those who would like to be employed in social production, and also elicited information on the condi-tions under which they could be engaged (e.g. part-time job, short working week, possibilities for working at or near home, provision of vocational training, etc.).

As regards women engaged in personal subsidiary agricultural plot activities and in household duties, information was also collected on children who lived with them, stating the age of each child under 16.

The computation of the number of students has two aims: to determine the scope and magnitude of attendance at educational institutions, taking into consideration the necessity of full satisfaction of participants' educatio-nal intentions; and to determine the impact of this category of population on the future size and composition of employment in social production.

Journey to work

Some words should also be said regarding the movement of population from one administrative region to another, such as from place of residence to place of work or of education, from urban to rural areas and vice versa, from one district to another, etc. The need for information concerning such in- and out-flows of students and workers derives from the fact that a large part of the population lives in one place but works or studies in another. Such accounting practices are important for estimating the labour resources in a given administrative region. Special single-tail surveys are conducted in order to provide information on in- and out-flows of wage earners and salaried employees.

Information is also needed on the inter-area movements of workers and students in order to compile BSLRs at the levels of union republics and provinces (*oblast*), including subdivisions for urban and rural areas, and to develop measures for improved utilisation of labour at its place of permanent residence.

Conclusions

In the statistical practices of the USSR, balance sheets of labour resources (BSLRs) are compiled each year for territories, large cities, union republics and the USSR as a whole, as of 1 January and 1 July. Using these, BSLRs are also compiled to reflect annual averages.

BSLRs are compiled for the middle and end of the year in order to provide information on the composition and utilisation of labour resources during the periods of minimum and maximum employment, and also to ascertain the seasonal variations of labour resource utilisation. In general, it is typical of the USSR situation that 1 July falls in the period of maximum employment (mainly due to agriculture) and that 1 January falls within the period of minimum employment. This information on seasonal variations of labour resource utilisation is useful for developing measures for a more even utilisation of labour resources during the yearly cycle.

The system of BSLR indexes in operation in the USSR allows BSLRs to be drawn up in respect of all major categories and types of activity, and particularly for urban and rural areas, which is especially important for determining the composition of the rural population not employed in the public sector of the social economy, both as a whole and by regions and republics. BSLRs provide the basic statistical data required for such important tasks as ensuring full employment of the population, that is, satisfaction of population employment needs, and ensuring a supply of workers with appropriate trades, occupations, skills and qualifications for the various branches of the national economy.

Notes

1. Translated from Russian
2. For additional information on definitions, criteria and methods of collection of data, see technical note on 'Labour statistics in the centrally planned economy countries of the CMEA' and Chapter 6 in this volume.

Bibliography

Chizhova, L. S., *Formirovanie struktury rabochey sily s ucehtom pola i vozrasta*, Moscow, Economika, 1976 (Formation of labour force composition by age and sex).

Kasimovsky, E. V., *Trudovye resursy. Formirovanie i ispol'zovanie*, Moscow, Economika, 1975 (Labour resources. Formation and utilisation).

Kostin, L. A., *Trudovye resursy v odinnadtzatoy pyatiletke*, Moscow, Economika, 1981 (Labour resources in the period of the 11th Five-Year Plan).

Metodicheskie ukazaniya Gosplana SSSR k razrabotke gosudarstvennykh planov economicheskogo i social'noo razvitiya SSSR, Moscow, Economika, 1980, pp. 542–56 (State plans of economic and social development of the USSR. Methodological principles formulated by the State Planning Committee of the USSR).

Nazarov, M. G., Parteshko, N. S. and Rumyantnev, V. N., *Statistika truda*, Moscow, Finansy i Statistika, 1981 (Labour statistics).

Ryabushkin, T. V. and Dadashev A. Z., *Trudovye resursy i effectivnost' proizvodstva*, Moscow, Znanie, 1981 (Labour resources and production effectiveness).

Sonin, M. Ya., *Vosprioizvodstvo rabochey sily SSSR i balans truda*, Moscow, Gosplanizdat, 1959 (Reproduction of labour force in the USSR and balance sheets of labour).

6 ILO-comparable annual employment and unemployment estimates: basic programme and application to countries with a centrally planned economy

I. Chernyshev

Introduction

In 1987 the ILO Bureau of Statistics launched a programme with a view to publishing for as many countries as possible annual data of employment and unemployment, including regional totals, in a standardised format, adjusted as much as possible to conform to international recommendations adopted by the 13th International Conference of Labour Statisticians in 1982.[1]

The ultimate ambition of the ILO with respect to this project is to cover all industrialised countries (both with a centrally planned and a market economy), newly industrialised countries and those developing countries with a developed statistical infrastructure.

The achievement of this objective depends upon the availability of national information and the extent to which the adjustments necessary for harmonisation prove to be feasible.

At present, there are four major regular programmes of international comparisons of labour force statistics covering a number of countries. They are carried out by the Organisation for Economic Co-operation and development (OECD), the United States Bureau of Labor Statistics (BLS), the Statistical Office of the European Communities (EUROSTAT) and by the Council for Mutual Economic Assistance (CMEA).

Although these programmes have the common goal of making international comparisons, the only published data which are common to the first three are *unemployment rates*. The CMEA publishes the average number of persons engaged in the national economy as a whole and in the principal sectors of economic activity. Though the first three agencies seek to measure essentially the same concept, the resulting unemployment rates are not identical in all cases, because of different statistical treatment of various labour force categories. For example, the BLS makes its international comparisons by adjusting the national figures to the US definitions, which are slightly different from the ILO concept. The labour statistics computed by the CMEA follow the concepts and definitions established within the Eastern European economies which in a number of cases do not follow the ILO treatment of manpower resources.

Because it is not in the spirit of an international organisation to proceed completely independently of existing programmes, the ILO Bureau of Statistics has decided in making its own international comparisons to utilise as much as possible the information collected by these four programmes. In 1985 the Bureau commissioned an external collaborator to undertake a preliminary study of the international comparisons made for Western countries with market economies.[2] This has provided the background material enabling the Bureau of Statistics to obtain internationally comparable estimates by introducing adjustments in conformity with the ILO standards, carried out on the basis of national and international labour statistics.

The Bureau of Statistics has since undertaken a further study of the four major programmes and has also made case studies of the methodology used to compile labour force data in eight countries of Eastern Europe with a centrally planned economy (Bulgaria, Czechoslovakia, German Democratic Republic, Hungary, Poland, Romania, USSR and Yugoslavia) and in five newly industrialised countries or territories of the Far East and South East Asia (Hong Kong, Indonesia, Republic of Korea, Philippines and Singapore).

The adjustment procedures have been worked out and approved by national experts. It is now planned to extend the analysis to annual estimates for Argentina, Brazil, China, India, Malaysia, Mexico, Pakistan and Thailand.

The next section of this paper describes the four programmes mentioned above. This is followed by an outline of the general principles, adjustment procedures and tabulation plan to be applied by the ILO and a list of the countries to be covered. The work of the national statistical bodies in countries with a centrally planned economy for the collection and publication of labour force data is then described. Information is provided about the methodology used and about the differences between the Western and Eastern European approaches to employment measurement. This is followed by a description of the data sources used in a number of Eastern European countries, as well as proposed methods of adjustment necessary to arrive at comparable estimates of annual averages of employment corresponding to the ILO recommendations.

As for the industrialised market economies and for newly industrialised and developing countries, the ILO will publish a separate document containing methodological descriptions and adjustment procedures for employment and unemployment.*

International experience and the ILO efforts

The *BLS*, beginning with its series of 'Unemployment rates approximating US concept', appears to have been the first of the four programmes. It started in late 1961 and currently covers ten countries with a market economy: Canada, United States, Japan, France, Federal Republic of Germany, Italy, Netherlands, Sweden, United Kingdom and Australia.

At the initial stage the studies were confined to international comparisons of *unemployment* only. The national unemployment rates of eight and later the above ten countries were adjusted to US concepts. More recently the programme has been expanded to include comparisons of employment trends by economic sector and breakdowns of unemployment rates by age and sex. The Bureau also began to study two additional labour market indicators – participation rates and employment–population ratios.[3] Although the US labour force definitions are slightly different from the ILO international standards (e.g. unpaid family workers are included in labour force totals if they worked 15 hours a week, whereas according to the ILO definitions all unpaid family workers should be included irrespective of the number of hours worked), the conceptual approach to adjustment procedures is very close to the one the ILO Bureau of Statistics will follow, which makes for a close co-operation between the two agencies.

The *OECD* programme covers fourteen countries: Australia, Belgium, Canada, Finland, France, Federal Republic of Germany, Italy, Japan, Netherlands, Norway, Spain, Sweden, United Kingdom and the United States. Ten of these fourteen countries are also covered by the BLS programme. However, the methods of adjustment used by the OECD are different from those used by the BLS.

The information available to the ILO indicates that the OECD secretariat normally selects from among the national unemployment series which it obtains, the one that most closely approximates unemployment measured according to the ILO recommendations. This selection is made in consultation with the national labour force statisticians. Thus, the OECD uses official data as compiled by the statistical agencies of member countries and, except in the case of the United Kingdom, no adjustments are made. For the United Kingdom figures, the OECD applies the BLS adjustment procedures.

The OECD programme only publishes *standardised unemployment rates* (SURs) (whereas the BLS programme publishes all the data obtained, i.e. labour force, employment and unemployment). These rates are calculated with a standard denominator – namely the total labour force which consists of total (civilian and military) employment plus unemployment.[4]

* ILO, *ILO-comparable employment and unemployment estimates*, STAT Working Papers, forthcoming.

The *EUROSTAT* programme covers the twelve countries of the European Economic Community: Belgium, Denmark, France, Federal Republic of Germany, Greece, Ireland, Italy, Luxembourg, the Netherlands, Portugal, Spain and the United Kingdom. Seven of these twelve countries are also covered by the OECD programme and five by the BLS programme.

The method differs in a fundamental way from the OECD and BLS programmes. It involves a general Community-wide labour force survey. On the basis of proposals from EUROSTAT, a Working Party on Labour Force Sample Survey determines the content of the Survey, the list of questions and the common coding of individual replies, as well as the principal definitions to be applied in the analysis of the results.[5] The national statistical services are then responsible for preparing the questionnaire, selecting the sample, conducting the direct interviews among households, and forwarding the results to EUROSTAT according to the standardised coding scheme.[6]

Thus, the programme gets member countries to compile comparable data directly, rather than adjusting national data. This approach is clearly admirable, though it may not be always possible to secure exactly the same sequence of questions in each country's questionnaire forms.[7] As it is well known that even the order of questions, as well as their wording, may have an effect on the replies received, there cannot be a guarantee that precisely the same information will be obtained from each country in response to a particular question. In addition, for practical reasons, only a part of the armed forces are covered and are thus included in the denominator of the unemployment rate; in particular all conscripts are excluded.

The *CMEA* programme encompasses ten countries: Bulgaria, Cuba, Czechoslovakia, German Democratic Republic, Hungary, Mongolia, Poland, Romania, USSR and Vietnam. Since its inception in 1949 the standardisation and classification of all sectors of the national economy and unification of statistical indicators have been among the Council's priorities.

To achieve the objectives set out in the field of statistics a CMEA Standing Commission for Co-operation in the Field of Statistics was set up in 1962, its main task being the unification of the system of statistical indicators and of the methodology used for statistical treatment and measurement of a wide range of economic categories, an increase in the information exchange between the member states, and the creation and development of a unified Automated System of State Statistics. The Commission meets twice a year for discussion of questions of unification and international comparability of national data, and for adoption of rules, recommendations and resolutions. Labour statistics has been a special subject at almost all sessions.

The first set of international instruments on labour statistics was approved in January 1963 at the second session of the Commission but they turned out to be rather limited in their capacity to arrive at comparable estimates for a number of important labour force indicators. Hence, in view of the increased requirements for more comparable information on labour statistics, the Standing Commission undertook a revision of the 1963 rules, and approved certain amendments and additions at its 23rd session in July 1974. However, further work was needed and the 31st session of the CMEA Standing Commission for Co-operation in the Field of Statistics in May 1978 adopted a document entitled *Methodological rules for computing the principal labour statistics indicators in CMEA member countries*.[8] It contains recommendations for CMEA member states on how to achieve international comparability of the primary labour statistics indicators and states: 'The revised and approved methodological rules on labour statistics represent a further step on the way to achieving international comparability of labour statistics and will make for greater accuracy in calculating the development and levels of labour productivity in CMEA member countries.'[9]

The CMEA Secretariat has an agreement with the national statistical services of its members whereby they provide it with a prearranged set of labour statistics. It is assumed that these data have been compiled and readjusted according to the CMEA International Standards. Thus, the strategy is similar to that adopted by EUROSTAT.

The labour force data published by the CMEA clearly have a high degree of comparability and consistency. However, for the following reasons these data cannot be used by the ILO Bureau of Statistics as the source for its programme of comparable annual estimates. First, the Council for Mutual Economic Assistance publishes in its *Statistical Year Book* the annual averages and numbers as of the end of the year of wage earners and salaried employees engaged in the national economy. (The category 'wage earners and salaried employees' includes all categories of persons employed in enterprises, institutions and organisations, i.e. manual workers, apprentices, engineering and technical staff, agro-zootechnical and veterinary staff, office workers, junior service personnel and security staff.[10]) These figures, with the exception of data for the German Democratic Republic, are different from those that CMEA member countries forward to the ILO for the ILO *Year Book*.[11]

Second, the data on the average number of wage earners and salaried employees in the principal sectors of the national economy do not correspond to the International Standard Industrial Classification of All Economic Activities of the United Nations (ISIC). The Conference of European Statisticians in 1985 approved a 'Correspondence table between the International Standard Industrial Classification of All Economic Activities of the United Nations (ISIC) and the Classification of Branches of the National Economy of the Council for Mutual Economic Assistance (CBNE)'. Most of the ILO member countries with a centrally planned economy apart from the Byelorussian SSR, the Ukrainian SSR and the USSR supply the ILO with employment figures broken down according to ISIC divisions. However, the CMEA Secretariat neither publishes a table with data converted into ISIC categories nor publishes comparisons with non-member states.

Third, there are considerable conceptual differences between the ILO and the CMEA approach to the treatment and measurement of the labour force, as will be described in the following pages.

Adjustment principles and procedures

The aim of the ILO efforts is to produce internationally comparable series which would reflect the national labour policy, reveal the general situation on the labour market and, at the same time, show harmonised data brought to the common denominator of the 1982 ILO definitions.

Unlike the CMEA, EUROSTAT, OECD and the US Department of Labor, whose data relate only to a limited number of countries, the Bureau seeks to cover a much wider range.

Labour force statistics are rather a delicate subject for governments: even a decimal difference in employment and unemployment figures could sometimes cause embarrassment. For this reason the Bureau of Statistics will only adjust important deviations of national data from the ILO guidelines. To do this it will take the national data and, where necessary, make piecemeal additions or deductions for each country in accordance with the 1982 ILO international definitions, provided that the information for the adjustment is available. This work will be carried out in consultation with national statisticians. It will be important to avoid publication of data different from those published by the OECD and EUROSTAT (both of which seek to follow the ILO guidelines). To achieve this, the ILO will also collaborate with the secretaries of these organisations in order to work out a common adjustment procedure which will avoid differences in the figures published.

Countries to be covered

The present aim of the ILO Bureau of Statistics is to publish in the course of 1990 in the *Bulletin of Labour Statistics* pilot tables with internationally comparable estimates of annual average employment and unemployment for the following countries.

> *Countries with a market economy*: Australia, Austria, Belgium, Canada, Denmark, Finland, France, Federal Republic of Germany, Greece, Ireland, Italy, Japan, Luxembourg, Netherlands, Norway, Portugal, Spain, Sweden, United Kingdom, United States.
> *Countries with a centrally planned economy*: Bulgaria, Czechoslovakia, German Democratic Republic, Hungary, Poland, USSR, Yugoslavia.
> *Newly industrialised countries or territories*: Hong Kong, Indonesia, Republic of Korea, Philippines, Singapore.

Subsequently it is hoped to extend the work to cover the following countries:

> *Countries with a market economy*: Iceland, New Zealand, Switzerland.
> *Countries with a centrally planned economy*: China, Romania.
> *Newly industrialised countries*: Argentina, India, Brazil, Malaysia, Pakistan, Mexico, Thailand.
> *Developing countries*: Kenya.

Tabulation plan

With the goodwill and assistance of national statistical services it is hoped to publish annual comparable estimates of employment and unemployment according to the following breakdowns:

Population (total and by sex)
Labour force (total and by sex)
Civilian labour force (total and by sex)
Employment (total and by sex)
Employment (by age groups)
Civilian employment (total and by sex)
Unemployment (total and by sex)
Unemployment (by age groups)
Unemployment rates (total and by sex).

As is shown, the Bureau intends to publish tables by age. Unfortunately, at the initial stage these tables will contain data which will not be fully comparable as it seems that adjustments in this respect will pose certain problems because of current lack of data. However, it is expected that at a later date it will be possible to produce comparable estimates.

The Office would also like to publish a table with annual estimates of employment by industry for the nine one-digit ISIC-68 divisions.

A suggested table is shown in Table 6.1.

Table 6.1   Employment, by industry*

	1979	1980	1981	1982	1983	1984	1985	1986	1987
1. Agriculture, hunting, forestry, and fishing	...	...	...	...	...	...	...	...	...
2. Mining and quarrying	...	...	...	...	...	...	...	...	...
3. Manufacturing	...	...	...	...	...	...	...	...	...
4. Electricity, gas and water	...	...	...	...	...	...	...	...	...
5. Construction	...	...	...	...	...	...	...	...	...
6. Wholesale and retail trade, and restaurants and hotels	...	...	...	...	...	...	...	...	...
7. Transport, storage and communication	...	...	...	...	...	...	...	...	...
8. Financing, insurance, real estate, business service	...	...	...	...	...	...	...	...	...
9. Community, social, and personal services	...	...	...	...	...	...	...	...	...
10. Activities not adequately defined	...	...	...	...	...	...	...	...	...

* ISIC-68 major divisions.

Format and calendar of publication

The Bureau intends to present the annual estimates in a separate chapter of the *Year Book of Labour Statistics*. This chapter might have the following structure:

Chapter X. Comparable annual employment and unemployment estimates

It is intended to include requests for the necessary data as an integral part of the general *ILO Year Book* questionnaire. National statistical agencies will thus be spared the burden of filling in an additional questionnaire, and the information requested will correspond to the same bench-mark and population covered by their response to this questionnaire.

The final version of the tables will depend on the tabulation plan of the *Year Book*, which is currently under revision.

Countries with a centrally planned economy: Organisation of work of the national statistical bodies for the collection, processing and publishing of labour force data

The organisation and collection of statistics in countries with a centrally planned economy is almost the only sector of the national economy which is not influenced by recent trends towards decentralisation. The reason is neither the historical background nor the reluctance of bureaucrats, but that centralisation is seen as a necessary feature of statistical organisation in countries with a centrally planned economy.

In all the countries of Eastern Europe with a centrally planned economy there is one state institution which is responsible for the collection, processing and publication of labour force data which cover the whole national economy, the *State Committee for Statistics* or the *Central Statistical Office*. It maintains very close co-operation with the *State Labour Committee/ Ministry* and with the corresponding department(s) of the *State Planning Committee*. The former is responsible for policy-making in the field of labour, wages and social programmes and the latter is responsible for all kinds of labour force projections and planning of labour force utilisation.

The Central Statistical Committee has complete responsibility for the development of a uniform statistical reporting system on the labour force to meet the needs of governmental management and planning bodies. It is also responsible for determining the methodology of labour force data collection, computation and analysis.

Labour statistics, as a rule, are collected and analysed by a separate department which deals with manpower resources and wages. This department collaborates closely with all sectoral departments which also furnish it with some labour force data.

This type of set-up exists, in general, in the national statistical services of all the countries with a centrally planned economy though some differences do exist. For example, in Hungary in addition to a labour force section in the Department of Economics every sectoral department has a small unit (one or two persons) which deals with labour force issues in its sector of the national economy.

In practice the following sequence of work is carried out in a Department of Labour Force Statistics and Wages for the collection and processing of labour force data. Once or twice a year it forwards to the regional statistical offices several sets of labour force questionnaires to be sent on to all enterprises, organisations, institutions and agricultural units of the region. It is compulsory for these economic units to fill in these questionnaires and return them to district statistical offices. The reported data may be monthly, quarterly or annual averages, depending on the sector of the national economy. The data are then processed at the district statistical offices and sent as aggregative totals to the regional offices where they are also processed and sent to the Central Statistical Office in the form of aggregate totals. There, the same procedure takes place and the national averages are calculated. Thus it is possible to have up-to-date information on labour force distribution and utilisation by age and sex structure, occupation and sector within two weeks at national level and within five to ten days at administrative level.

On the basis of the data supplied, the experts of the Department of Labour Force Statistics and Wages write analytical reports and make recommendations to the government on efficient utilisation of the manpower resources of the country. The department provides data for the national statistical year book or produces its own periodical publications on labour statistics.

The general state of labour statistics, methodology used and differences between the Western and Eastern approaches to employment measurement

As a rule, the most complete time series of labour statistics of the countries of Eastern Europe are published in national statistical year books, which usually have a special chapter dealing with labour force indicators, or in a separate labour force compendium.

The data vary from country to country but there is a standard set of tables which may be found in practically every official statistical publication on the labour force. They are: average number of wage earners and salaried employees in the national economy; average number of wage earners and salaried employees according to administrative and territorial divisions of the country; average number of wage earners and salaried employees according to sectors of the national economy; average number of wages earners and salaried employees according to productive and non-productive spheres of the national economy (see below); average number of women engaged in the national economy and according to sectors of the national economy; average annual growth rates of the number of wage earners and salaried employees according to sectors of the national economy; and employment by level of education, etc. This list reveals one of the differences between the methodology used for labour statistics computation by countries with a centrally planned economy and those with a market economy. The difference is that the first group of countries calculates mainly average employment over a period while the second group calculates numbers at a point in time (a day or a week).

The CMEA members have chosen this approach because the size of the registered labour force of an enterprise, organisation or institution fluctuates considerably within a given reporting (reference) period (month, quarter, year), as some workers leave and others are taken on. In order to take these changes into account the average is used, which, it is said, is the most reliable measurement. Consequently a daily count of those employed on the basis of registers or other similar documents which give details of recruitment, departure and transfers of personnel is kept.

The average number for a reporting period of one month is computed by adding up the number of wage earners and salaried employees on the working list (payroll) for each calendar day of the reporting month, i.e. from the 1st to the 30th or 31st, including days off and holidays, and dividing this cumulative total by the number of calendar days in the reporting month.

The registered number of wage earners and salaried employees on a non-working day is assumed to be equal to that on the preceding working day. The average quarterly number of workers and employees is determined by adding up the average numbers for the months of the quarter in question and dividing the total by three. The average annual number of wage earners and salaried employees is similarly calculated on the basis of a simple arithmetic average. Persons working part-time are converted into those working full-time on the basis of the number of working hours specified in their contracts of employment.[12]

In general all centrally planned economies use this methodology in full accordance with the CMEA international recommendations.

Another difference between the methodologies is the industrial classification used. This difference originates partly from the differences between the System of National Accounts (SNA) and the System of Balances of the National Economy or the Material Product System (MPS) and partly from differences in the detailed breakdown of industries.

In SNA, production includes all market and governmental activities resulting in the production of industrial goods and non-material services, while in MPS, economic (material) production is restricted to production of material goods and material services. The 1975 'Classification by kind of economic activities of the CMEA country members' distinguishes between the material and non-material spheres, where the material sphere includes manufacturing, construction, agriculture, forestry, transport and communication, trade and other related sectors, but not health, physical culture and social security, education, arts, science, etc. Certain activities which provide material services are also allocated to various industries of material production, for example dyeing, cleaning and laundries are classified under industrial activities; veterinary services are classified under agriculture, etc.[13] Thus in the centrally planned economies all persons employed are divided into persons engaged in the sphere of material production and those engaged in the non-productive sphere.[14]

A third difference is found in the treatment of the concept of 'economically active population'. Countries with a centrally planned economy do not use the term 'economically active population' in their official publications, though Yugoslavia[15] is an exception and Hungary utilises the notion of 'active wage earners'.[16]

Planned economies treat the category 'economically active population' in a wider sense than it is treated in the market economies.

The ILO recommendation states: 'The economically active population comprises all persons of either sex who furnish the supply of labour for the production of economic goods and services as defined by the United Nations systems of national accounts and balances, during a specified time-reference period',[17] and divides it into the two categories employed and unemployed. 'Employed' are considered to be persons above a specific age who are engaged in the production of goods and services, and those 'unemployed' include persons above a specific age who are without work, currently available for work and seeking work. Members of the armed forces should also be included among persons in paid employment.[18] Hence the criterion which defines whether a person is economically active is activity – whether he or she is actually working or actively looking for work.

In the planned economies on the other hand, 'economically active population' comprises: all persons of working age able to work apart from full-time students and the armed forces; persons below or above working age who are engaged in a socialised production; and persons engaged in their individual farming plots.[19]

Thus inclusion or exclusion of the category 'armed forces' in the economically active population is one of the main differences between the two concepts, though here, too, there are some exceptions – in Hungary armed forces are included in the 'economically active population', as, in Poland, are those performing their military service who were previously employed.

In official statistical publications of countries with a centrally planned economy one may come across the term 'labour resources'. This concept is broader than that of 'economically active population'. Labour resources consist of 'economically active population' *plus* 'armed forces' *less* 'non-working invalids of the first and second group' less 'persons on early retirement and receiving beneficiary pensions' (miners, workers and employees of the chemical industry, etc.).[20] Invalids of the first group include persons who have completely lost their ability to work and who need everyday care (help, supervision); invalids of the second group also include persons who have completely lost their ability to work but who do not need such everyday care (invalids of the first and second group can perform some kind of work if there is a possibility to provide them with special facilities).[21]

The employed population is treated in planned economies as functional labour resources or 'labour resources in use'. This category corresponds to that of 'civilian employment' used in market economies.

The fourth difference is that the market economies mainly use establishment surveys or labour force survey data for employment estimates, apart from establishment censuses. These surveys are conducted at intervals and are normally sample surveys. The centrally planned economies, on the other hand, use current statistical reports. Their completion is compulsory for all economic units; they cover *all* enterprises, farms, organisations and institutions and they are continuous.

Data sources and adjustment techniques

In spite of the differences outlined in the previous section there is a sound possibility of carrying out international comparisons which include the countries with a centrally planned economy. This conclusion is based on the following:

1. As is stated in the 'Specific Instruction' on employment and unemployment attached to the ILO *Questionnaire for the Year Book of Labour Statistics*, all the statistics should, as far as possible, represent *annual averages* and relate to the whole country.[22] Thus, it is not that important how countries arrive at their averages, what is important is that those averages should be reliable and consistent.

2. As has already been emphasised, practically all ILO member countries with a centrally planned economy provide the ILO with employment data broken down according to ISIC divisions. The Bureau hopes that the remaining three will follow suit in the near future.

3. The ILO programme mainly aims at computing and publishing employment and, where relevant, unemployment estimates. Most of the

centrally planned economies claim that they have no unemployment as such. Those acknowledging the presence of this phenomenon follow the ILO concept of economically active population.

The ILO Bureau of Labour Statistics will do its best to achieve international comparability of employment and, where relevant, unemployment data, by adjusting data to conform with the ILO recommendations. This comparison will be done in respect of civilian employment only.

4. No issue arises as to which methodology is the most apt to obtain reliable and consistent data. The work will of necessity be limited to countries which have a highly developed statistical infrastructure permitting them to compile, process and publish labour statistics generally corresponding to the standards set out in ILO Convention No. 160 on Labour Statistics.

The ILO Bureau of Statistics has worked out adjustment procedures for labour force data of the countries with a centrally planned economy in order to calculate annual estimates which correspond to the ILO definitions. Here are examples of such procedures in respect of Czechoslovakia and Poland.

Czechoslovakia

Czechoslovakia has the following sources of employment statistics: statistical employment reports, which are compulsory for all state and co-operative enterprises, farms and organisations, and all types of educational establishments, as well as special surveys and population census data. Geographically, the reporting system covers the whole country. Persons covered in statistical employment reports are all those aged 15 years and over who are engaged in the national economy. The armed forces are excluded. The organisation responsible for the data collection is the Federal Statistical Office.

Concepts and definitions

Economically active population. This comprises all persons of working age (i.e. males aged 15–59 years and females aged 15–54 years) or older who are engaged in the national economy. Persons performing their military service, full-time students, paid apprentices and trainees, and non-working invalids of the first and second group are excluded.

Employment. The main requirement for a person to be classified as employed is a formal contract, in written or verbal form, for at least one day, or performance of some formal work for pay or profit.

Accordingly, the employed population consists of all persons aged 15 years and over who are in the following categories:

1. At work, that is persons who worked for pay during the reference period.

2. Having a job, but temporarily absent due to:
(i)   illness;
(ii)   injury;

(iii)   absence without leave;
(iv)   holidays;
(v)   bad weather;
(vi)   technical breakdown;
(vii)   compensatory leave;
(viii) maternity leave;
(ix)   official reasons;
(x)   study leave;
(xi)   professional qualifications improvement.

Categories 1 and 2 include:

(a)   full- and part-time workers;
(b)   persons who performed some work for pay or profit during the reference period, including:
        (i) those of compulsory schooling age;
        (ii) those retired and receiving a pension;
(c)   persons engaged in private agricultural units;
(d)   persons engaged in private productive and service activities;
(e)   full- and part-time students working full- or part-time;
(f)   homeworkers[23];
(g)   freelance workers;
(h)   piece-workers, casual, temporary and part-time workers;
(i)   domestic servants;
(j)   priests of all religions.

Evaluation of the average number of persons engaged in the national economy

The average number of persons employed in the state industrial enterprises and construction is determined on the basis of monthly statistical employment reports drawn up and submitted to statistical bodies by all relevant enterprises and construction units.

The average number of persons employed in all state and co-operative enterprises, farms and organisations as well as the average number of priests of all religions and homeworkers is determined on the basis of quarterly and annual statistical employment reports drawn up and submitted to statistical bodies by all economic units and churches.

The registered number of persons in the labour force of an enterprise or organisation covers not only the permanent workers (full- and part-time) but also seasonal workers, temporary and piece-workers with a contract for at least one day. Registration is carried out on the day of recruitment.

On the basis of the daily registration of those employed, the average number of persons registered in the course of a given month is calculated. The calculation is made by aggregating the number registered on each day of the month and by dividing the resulting total by the number of days in the calendar month in question.

Average numbers other than monthly averages are calculated by aggregating the monthly average numbers and by dividing the resulting total by the number of months in the period considered.

Part-time workers are included in the annual averages.

The average number of freelance workers and domestic servants is estimated on the basis of information contained in administrative records which are kept by the national insurance agencies. The data are reported once a year to statistical bodies and then submitted by the latter to the Federal Statistical Office, which calculates the national averages as the simple arithmetic average of two consecutive years.

The average number of persons engaged in private activities is determined on the basis of an annual survey conducted at the end of the reference year. The averages are calculated as a simple arithmetic average of two consecutive years.

Workers of Czechoslovak nationality in joint ventures, employed within the territory of the country, persons employed in international organisations, national embassies and consulates as well as members of the diplomatic corps working abroad are not included in total employment. Their number is very insignificant and cannot influence the total employment averages. Beginning in 1991, these categories will be included in national data.

Persons working at more than one workplace are registered at each workplace and are included in the labour reports of both enterprises or other economic units. This double counting is eliminated in figures calculated for the construction of the national labour force balances. The ratio of such persons in the total labour force is approximately 3 per cent.

Evaluation of the average number of persons not engaged in the national economy

The average number of persons on maternity leave (the first 28 weeks of leave) with a formal job attachment is determined on the basis of quarterly and annual statistical labour reports drawn up by all economic units and submitted to statistical bodies.

The average number of persons temporarily engaged in housework[24] is determined on the basis of quarterly and annual statistical reports drawn up by all economic units and sent to statistical bodies.

Not economically active population

This comprises all persons of non-working age who are not engaged in the national economy, non-working invalids of the first and second group, pensioners, persons engaged in housework, armed forces and full-time students.

According to the Czechoslovak concept, the category 'paid apprentices and trainees' is also included in the not economically active population.

The average number of paid apprentices and trainees is taken from an annual statistical report of enterprises sent to statistical bodies.

Reference

The data on the total and average number of persons engaged in the national economy is published by the Federal Statistical Office of Czechoslovakia in *Statisticka rocenka* (annual publication).

Conclusions

The coverage of 'population engaged in the national economy' and of 'economically active' is not the same. Czechoslovakia excludes, while according to the definitions adopted by the 13th International Conference of Labour Statisticians the ILO includes, 'armed forces', 'persons on maternity leave' (maintaining a formal job attachment), 'persons temporarily engaged in housework' (with a formal job attachment) and 'paid apprentices and trainees' in the category 'employed'.

Adjustment

First of all, it is necessary to mention that the Federal Statistical Office agreed to provide the ILO Bureau of Statistics with the total employment data which excludes double counting. Taking into account that most ILO member countries compile and send to the ILO annual averages, it would be appropriate to apply to the provided data a simple arithmetic average method for every two consecutive years. This method is also used by the Federal Statistical Office to calculate the average number of persons engaged in private activities. This methodology has been discussed with the national experts and approved by them.

Second, an agreement has been made with the Federal Statistical Office to provide the Bureau with the data on 'persons on maternity leave', 'persons temporarily engaged in housework' and 'paid apprentices and trainees' on a regular basis.

With regard to data on the armed forces, these are for confidential use only and cannot be sent to the ILO separately.

Table 6.2 shows the adjustments which should be made to make the data comparable according to the definitions adopted by the 13th International Conference of Labour Statisticians in 1982. The data shown in the table were sent to the Bureau on the basis of the agreement mentioned above.

Table 6.2   Czechoslovakia: Adjustment of employment data (thousands)

Item	1985*	1986*
Reported civilian employment (excluding double counting)	7 468	7 516
Plus: armed forces	...	...
Plus: persons on maternity leave	101	100
Plus: persons temporarily engaged in housework	250	249
Plus: paid apprentices and trainees	112	112
Adjusted civilian employment	7 931	7 977
Adjusted average civilian employment		7 954

* As of 31 December

Poland

Poland has several sources of employment statistics: compulsory monthly reports from industrial, construction, transport, communications, internal and foreign trade units and quarterly and annual unified reports which cover all sectors of the national economy (material and non-material production) as well as population census and micro-census data for rural population involved in private agriculture. Geographically, the reporting system covers the whole country. Persons covered are all those aged 18 years and over as well as younger persons (15–17 years) who are engaged in the national economy; excluded are persons performing their military service. The organisation responsible for the data collection is the Central Statistical Office.

Concepts and definitions

Economically active population. This comprises all persons of working age, i.e. males aged 18–64 and females aged 18–59 years as well as persons under (15–17 years) or over the working age who are engaged in the national economy. Also included are persons performing their military service and persons imprisoned provided that they previously performed some formal work for pay or profit. Excluded are persons performing their military service and persons imprisoned if they were not previously employed, non-working nuns and monks, non-working invalids of the first and second group, paid apprentices and trainees, mothers on childcare leave and full-time students.

Employment. The main requirement for a person to be classified as employed is a formal contract for at least one day or performance of some formal work for pay or profit. Also considered as employed are persons who temporarily have no work, because they are changing their job, persons on unpaid leave of up to three months, persons working seasonally, provided that the work is performed at least three months a year, as well as persons working abroad in foreign enterprises. In defining employment, no criterion of working hours per day was adopted. When a person performs more than one job, he/she is enumerated at the place of the main working activity.

Accordingly, the employed population consists of all persons aged 18 years and over (or in some cases 15 years and over) who are in the following categories:

1. At work, that is persons who worked for pay or profit during the reference period.

2. Having a job, but temporarily absent due to:
(i)   illness;
(ii)   injury;
(iii)   absence without leave;
(iv)   holidays;

(v)   bad weather;
(vi)   technical breakdown;
(vii) compensatory leave;
(viii) maternity leave;
(ix)   labour-management dispute;
(x)   official reasons.

Categories 1 and 2 include:

1. *In the socialised economy*:
(a) persons employed in non-agricultural and in agricultural activities on the basis of a labour contract (excluding employees in budgetary units of departments of national defence and internal affairs);
(b) homeworkers[25];
(c) franchise holders[26];
(d) members of agricultural farms in a state collective system (including paid and unpaid working members of their families);
(e) persons working on plots of land of the members of agricultural co-operative farms and plots of employees of the state agricultural farms;
(f) persons who performed some work for pay or profit during the reference period including:
   (i) those of an age of compulsory schooling;
   (ii) those retired and receiving a pension;
(g) part-time students working full or part time.

2. *In the non-socialised economy outside agriculture*:
(a) owners and co-owners of handicraft, trade and service establishments (including members of their families);
(b) marine fishermen (including members of their families);
(c) persons employed on the basis of an employment agreement in handicraft trade and service establishments;
(d) persons employed in religious organisations;
(e) persons taking care of residential buildings (caretakers, domestic servants);
(f) priests of all religions and working nuns and monks[27];
(g) employees of foreign small trade enterprises (since 1981) working in the country;
(h) cart drivers working on their own account.

3. *In the non-socialised economy in agriculture*:
(a) persons working in private agricultural holdings and agricultural plots;
(b) owners of livestock not possessing agricultural land.

Evaluation of the average number of persons engaged in the national economy

The average number of persons engaged in industry, construction, transport, communications, internal and external trade is determined on the basis of compulsory monthly unified reports from the corresponding units.

The average number of persons engaged in all sectors of material and non-material production is determined on the basis of quarterly and annual unified reports on the labour force. The average number of those employed is given in terms of full-time employment. However, there are some exceptions: the compulsory reports do not cover part-time workers employed in science, education, cultural services, health and social welfare, tourism, recreation, sports and political organisations and trade unions. These data are available on the basis of special reports for the construction of labour force balances. From 1989 these categories will be included in average employment.

The number of persons engaged in private agriculture is determined on the basis of a general population census and a micro-census; the latter is conducted every five years. During the period following the micro-census, the data are estimated on the basis of general time series. The last micro-census was conducted in 1984.

The average number of persons engaged in state and co-operative agriculture is determined on the basis of quarterly reports drawn up by the relevant agricultural units.

On the basis of the daily registration of those employed, the average number of persons registered in the course of a given month is calculated. The calculation is made by aggregating the number registered on each day of the month and by dividing the resulting total by the number of days in the calendar month in question. The number recorded for a holiday (Saturday, Sunday, public holiday) is the same as the one for the preceding working day.

Average numbers other than monthly averages (quarterly, half-yearly or annual averages) are calculated by aggregating the monthly average numbers and dividing the resulting total by the number of months in the period considered.

For the calculation of average numbers, part-time workers are previously converted into full-time workers on the basis of the normal hours of work as prescribed in their labour contracts.

Not economically active population

This comprises all persons of non-working age who are not engaged in the national economy, non-working invalids of the first and second group, persons performing their military service and persons imprisoned provided that they were not previously employed, non-working nuns and monks, mothers on child-care leave with a formal job attachment, paid apprentices and trainees, full-time students, persons engaged in housework and persons living on income from leasing.

The number of students is determined on the annual information sent to the statistical bodies by the relevant educational establishments.

The average number of paid apprentices and trainees engaged with a contract in vocational training is determined on the basis of compulsory quarterly reports from industrial and other units engaged in material production.

Reference

The data on the average number of persons engaged in the national economy are published by the Central Statistical Office of Poland in the *Statistical Yearbook* and *Yearbook on Labour Force*.

Conclusions

The coverage of the population engaged in the national economy and of that economically active is not the same. Poland excludes, whilst according to the definitions adopted by the 13th International Conference of Labour Statisticians the ILO includes, 'armed forces' (irrespective of whether they were or were not previously employed), 'paid apprentices and trainees', 'mothers on child-care leave' (with a formal job attachment), 'non-working nuns and monks' and 'persons living on income from leasing' in the category 'employed'.

Adjustment

According to the agreement reached by the Bureau with the Central Statistical Office of Poland, the latter will provide data on mothers on child-care leave with a formal job attachment and on paid apprentices and trainees on a regular basis. As regards the armed forces, these data are for confidential use only and cannot be provided to the ILO. As for persons living on income from leasing and on non-working nuns and monks, their number is very insignificant.

Table 6.3 shows the major adjustments which should be made to make the data comparable according to the definitions adopted by the 13th International Conference of Labour Statisticians in 1982.

Table 6.3   Poland: Adjustment of employment data (thousands)

Item	1986
Reported average civilian employment	17 236.5
Plus: armed forces	...
Plus: non-working nuns and monks	4.7*
Plus: paid apprentices and trainees	533.1
Plus: mothers on child-care leave	821.2
Adjusted average civilian employment	18 615.5

* Data from the 1978 population and household census.

The data shown in the table were sent to the Bureau on the basis of the agreement mentioned above.

Notes

1. See Chapter 1 of this volume.
2. A. Wainewright. *A proposed ILO programme: Report on preliminary work for*

industrialised countries, Nov. 1985.

3. A. Neef, 'International comparisons of employment and unemployment', paper presented to the Federal Statistics Users Conference, Washington, DC, 14 October 1981.
4. *Standardised unemployment rates: Sources and methods*, OECD, Paris, July 1985.
5. *Labour force sample surveys: Methods and definitions*, EUROSTAT, Luxembourg, 1985.
6. Ibid.
7. C. Sorrentino, *The uses of the European Community labour force surveys for international unemployment comparisons*, US Department of Labor, Bureau of Labor Statistics, March 1987.
8. *Methodological rules for computing the principal labour statistics indicators in CMEA member countries*, Council for Mutual Economic Assistance, Standing Commission on Statistics, Moscow, CMEA, June 1978.
9. Ibid.
10. Ibid.
11. See *Year Book of Labour Statistics, 1987*, Geneva, ILO, 1987; and *Statisticheskij Yezhegodnic Stran-Chlenov Sovieta Economicheskoj Vzaimopomoshchi* (Statistical yearbook of the member countries of the Council for Mutual Economic Assistance), Moscow, CMEA, 1987.
12. See Chapter 4 of this volume.
13. *Classification by kind of economic activities of the CMEA country members*, Moscow, CMEA, 1975.
14. See also M. T. Dupré, R. Hussmanns and F. Mehran, 'The concept and boundary of economic activity for the measurement of the economically active population' in this volume.
15. *Statistical Yearbook of the Socialist Federal Republic of Yugoslavia*, 1984, Belgrade, 1985.
16. *Statistical Yearbook, 1983*, Hungarian Central Statistical Office, Budapest, 1984.
17. ILO, 'Thirteenth International Conference of Labour Statisticians, Resolution concerning statistics of the economically active population, employment, unemployment and underemployment', *Bulletin of Labour Statistics*, 1983-3, p. xi.
18. Ibid., p. xii.
19. *Demografcheskij Entsiklopedicheskij Slovar'* (Encyclopedia of Demography), Moscow, 1986, p. 536.
20. Ibid., p. 480.
21. Ibid., p. 145
22. ILO, *Questionnaires for the Year Book of Labour Statistics* (Geneva, ILO), 1987, Part II and Part III.
23. Persons who have signed a contract for work at home with a unit of the socialised economy.
24. Persons on maternity leave who, maintaining a formal job attachment, decide to stay at home after the first 28 weeks of their leave and prolong it until the child reaches the age of two.
25. See n. 23.
26. These include agents paid out of commission funds and agents running retail sales outlets, restaurants and bars and service establishments on a contract basis (including members of their families and persons employed by the agents).
27. The number of non-working nuns and monks is insignificant (about 0.02 per cent).

Part Three: Measuring the Labour Force

7 Salient features of the new international standards on statistics of the economically active population[1]

M. V. S. Rao and F. Mehran

In October 1982, the Thirteenth International Conference of Labour Statisticians (ICLS) adopted a new resolution concerning statistics of the economically active population, employment, unemployment and under-employment. The resolution now forms the new international standards on these topics, replacing standards adopted in 1954 by the Eighth ICLS in its resolution concerning statistics of the labour force, employment and unemployment and parts of standards adopted in 1966 by the Eleventh ICLS in its resolution concerning measurement and analysis of underemployment and underutilisation of manpower.

The new international standards are essentially aimed at providing technical guidelines to all countries and particularly those with less developed statistics, and at enhancing the international comparability of the statistics on these topics. They set forth the objectives and scope of statistics of economically active population, the basic concepts and definitions, the principal classifications, certain particular topics of data collection, and guidelines on the evaluation and dissemination of the results.

The 1982 resolution calls on the ILO to prepare a manual detailing the application of the new international standards, describing such aspects as methodology of data collection, tabulations and analysis. As part of its preliminary work on preparing the manual, the ILO Bureau of Statistics has organised two methodological surveys in Kerala (India) and Costa Rica in order to test the application of the new international standards. The Kerala survey was conducted during a one-year period from 9 February 1983 to 12 March 1984 and involved about 4600 household interviews. The Costa Rica survey was conducted during a six-month period from 20 June to 20 December 1983 and involved about 2000 household interviews.

A separate small-scale study (on about 80 households) concerning the measurement of the relationship of employment and income in household enterprises was conducted in May 1984 in Costa Rica.

The purpose of this paper is to highlight some of the salient features of the new international standards, contrast them with the earlier standards and report on how they were formulated in the two ILO methodological surveys. The main features discussed in this paper are the concept and boundary of economic activity, the definitions of economically active population, employment and unemployment, the categorisation of the population not economically active, the measurement of underemployment and the relationship between income and employment.

The concept and boundary of economic activity

With the new international standards, the concept of economic activity has been clearly and unequivocally defined at the international level. While the 1954 resolution referred merely to 'work for pay or profit', the definition of 'economically active population' given in the new international standards is explicitly linked to the United Nations Systems of National Accounts and Balances to which the production of economic goods and services has been defined. It includes 'all production and processing of primary products, whether for the market, for barter or for own consumption, the production of all other goods and services for the market and, in the case of households which produce such goods and services for the market, the corresponding production for own consumption'. This definition is schematically summarised in Table 7.1.

Table 7.1   Scope of economic activity*

	For market (or barter) only	For both market (or barter) and own consumption	For own consumption only
Production and processing of primary products†	X	X	X
Other production of economic goods and services	X	X	

* An X means the corresponding activity is considered as an economic activity.
† 'Agriculture, hunting, forestry and fishing' as well as 'Mining and quarrying' – ISIC (1968) Major Divisions 1 and 2 and corresponding processing activities.

One implication of this definition is that unpaid household work is considered as 'economic activity' if it is related not only to a household enterprise producing wholly or partly for the market, but also to any agriculture or allied activity, even if the production is wholly for own or household consumption. Thus, primary production activities such as producing vegetables, eggs and milk for own consumption or cutting firewood and building poles for own use as well as activities of processing primary products such as making butter, ghee and cheese for own consumption or weaving textiles, baskets and mats for own use are considered as economic activities. On the other hand, non-primary production or processing activities such as storing crops, carrying water, dressmaking and tailoring for own use or rearing children, cooking, washing and similar housekeeping activities remain outside the boundary of economic activity if performed wholly for own consumption or use.

Economically active population

The new resolution permits the measurement of the 'economically active population' in different ways. The new resolution refers, significantly, in its very title to the 'economically active population', rather than the 'labour force', which was the main concern of the 1954 resolution. The term 'labour force' as defined by the 1954 resolution and used in statistical literature over the last quarter of a century has come to be associated with a particular approach to the measurement of employment and unemployment and recognised as the sum of the employed and unemployed population measured in relation to a brief reference period such as one week or one day. The new resolution, on the other hand, uses the term 'economically active population' as a generic term and identifies, in particular, two useful measures of the 'economically active population' without excluding other possibilities: the 'usually active population' measured in relation to a long reference period such as a year; and the 'currently active population' measured in relation to a short reference period such as one week or one day. The latter is conceptually equated to the 'labour force' in the sense defined by the 1954 resolution.

The usually active population is intended to be measured when the aim is to obtain data reflecting the dominant pattern of activity and where there is a significant seasonal pattern of activities and the data collection programme does not permit repeated measurements in the course of a year. Since a year encompasses an entire agricultural and climatic cycle, when the usually active population is measured the length of the reference period should preferably be one year. The measurement of the 'usually active population' may also provide supplementary information in surveys in which the 'currently active population' is the principal measurement objective. The difference between usual and current status is of particular analytical and policy relevance and may be used to determine persons who are usually active but are not in the labour force during the current reference period. This category of persons includes: those who were economically active for a major part of the preceding year but are no longer active at the time of the survey (e.g. retired); those who are economically active in the busy season but are not active in the off-season (if the survey is made in the off-season); those who may be in and out of the labour force occasionally depending on the exigencies of work, or casual workers who may be usually active but for some reason or another are not in the reference week.

The definition of the 'usually active population' is linked to that of the 'currently active population'. The 'usually active population' is defined as comprising all persons, above a specified age, whose main activity status as determined in terms of number of weeks or days during a long specified period (such as the preceding 12 months or the preceding calendar year) was 'employed' or 'unemployed'. The 'currently active population' is defined as comprising all persons 'employed' or 'unemployed' during a specified brief period, either one week or one day. As the definitions of employment and unemployment, detailed below, are based on activity during a reference week or day, the 'usually active population' is conceived as a summary measure based on the variable status of the individual with reference to the weeks or days that together constitute the long specified reference period, whether the preceding 12 months or the preceding calendar year. Thus, if the current activity status is determined in terms of a reference week, the usual activity status is to be determined as that status which prevailed over most of the weeks during the reference year. If the current activity status is determined in terms of a reference day, the usual activity status is to be determined as that activity which prevailed over most of the days during the reference year.

In practice, most countries would not be able to study through censuses or surveys the status of each individual over each of the 52 weeks or over each of the 365 days and then determine the usual status over the year. One could only expect to determine the usual status of each individual through a retrospective question on the status which prevailed over most of the weeks or most of the days during the reference year. The usual status could be substantially different depending on whether it is the status which prevailed over most of the weeks or most of the days.

The sequence of questionnaire items used in a phase of the Kerala Methodological Survey to determine the 'usual status' of the respondent using a day as the unit of measurement is reproduced below. The questionnaire items are designed to compare the reported usual status (Q10) as stated by the respondent himself (herself) with the derived usual status as determined from responses on four subsequent probing questions (Q11 – Q14). The design also permits a person to be classified as 'usually employed' if he or she was 'employed' during most of the days of the reference year or as 'usually unemployed' if he or she was 'unemployed' during most of the days of the reference year. The 'usually active population' would include, besides the above two categories, persons who might have been 'employed' for a certain number of days, and 'unemployed' for a certain number of days, each of which was less than half the total, but the two together accounted for most of the days during the year. Those persons could also be sub-divided as employed and unemployed according to the main activity, i.e. depending on whether the person was mainly employed or mainly unemployed during the period he or she was active.

Usual activity

10 What was his/her main activity status last year (i.e., the last 365 days)
  Employed (i.e., working or with a job or enterprise if not working) 1 → 12
  Unemployed (i.e., not employed, seeking and/or available for work) 2
  Student 3
  Homemaker 4
  Pensioner 5
  Rentier 6
  Permanently unable to work 7 (End)
  Other (specify) 8

11 Last year, was (s)he also employed in any subsidiary economic activity, in addition to the main activity mentioned above?
  Yes 1 ↓ No 2 → 13

12 How long has (s)he been employed (at all economic activities if more than one) last year? Most of the year (i.e., 183 days or more) 1 → 16
  Part of the year (i.e., 1 to 182 days)
  number of days employed 2 ↓

  (Do not ask if code 2 in 10)
13 Was (s)he unemployed at any time last year?
  Yes 1 ↓ No 2 → 20

14 How long has (s)he been unemployed last year?
  Most of the year (i.e., 183 days or more) 1 → 15
  Part of the year (i.e., 1 to 182 days) 2
  number of days unemployed ...... ↓

Employment

The new international definition of employment is based on activity during a specified brief reference period, either one week or one day, and is to a large extent similar to the earlier definition of employment adopted by the Eighth ICLS (1954). The new definition, however, introduces certain elaborations, which make it possible to measure employment more accurately.

First, it draws a basic distinction between 'paid employment' and 'self-employment' and develops appropriate criteria for each category. 'Paid employment' includes wages and salary earners. Employers, own-account workers, members of producer co-operatives and unpaid family workers are categorised as self-employed. The definition includes under 'paid employment':

(a1) *at work*: persons who during the reference period performed some work for wage or salary, in cash or kind; and

(a2) *with job but not at work*: persons who, having already worked in their present job, were temporarily not at work during the reference period, but had a formal attachment to their job.

Under 'self-employment', it includes:

(b1) *at work*: persons who during the reference period performed some work for profit or family gain, in cash or kind;

(b2) *with an enterprise but not at work*: persons with an enterprise, which may be a business enterprise, a farm, or a service undertaking, who were temporarily not at work during the reference period for any specific reason.

Further, it explicitly specifies the length of time that a person should be at work for classification as employed. The resolution lays down that for operational purposes, the notion of 'some work' in (a1) and (b1) above may be interpreted as work for at least one hour.

It introduces the new concept of 'formal job attachment' to clarify the old category 'with a job but not at work' and to resolve the problem of the statistical treatment of persons laid off. The main point is the following. Since, in times of economic downturn, firms in different countries resort to lay-offs or to reductions in daily or weekly hours of work, depending on the unemployment compensation systems in force, the statistical treatment of persons laid off should be in harmony with that of persons affected by reductions in daily or weekly hours of work. However, under the 1954 definition, persons affected by reductions in daily or weekly hours are classified as employed, while persons laid off are classified as unemployed. It has therefore been suggested that, for purposes of international comparisons, persons laid off, appropriately defined, should be classified not necessarily as unemployed, but as employed, unemployed or out of the labour force according to the strength of their attachment to their job and the existence or not of job-search activity. In particular, a person laid off who has a formal job attachment with his or her employer should be considered as employed. The nature of the job attachment is to be determined in the light of national circumstances, according to one or more of the following criteria; the continued receipt of wage or salary; an assurance of return to work following the end of the contingency, or an agreement as to the date of return; the elapsed duration of absence from the job which, wherever relevant, may be that duration for which workers can receive compensation benefits without obligation to accept other jobs. In the case of self-employment, no constraint has been laid on the circumstances in which a self-employed person can be regarded as 'with an enterprise but not at work'. It would be sufficient if the temporary absence from work can be attributed to any specific reason.

Another new feature of the recent international definition of employment is the elimination of the minimum time criterion adopted in the past for unpaid family workers. Thus, according to the new definition, unpaid family workers, if at all at work during the reference period, would be considered as in self-employment irrespective of the number of hours worked. Countries which prefer, however, to set a minimum time criterion for the inclusion of unpaid family workers among the employed, have been given the freedom to do so, but are required to identify and classify separately those who worked less than the prescribed time.

The new definition makes also explicit recognition of another category of unpaid family workers who, though they do not assist in a household enterprise, are engaged in the production of economic goods and services for their own and household consumption. In accordance with the concept of economic activity mentioned earlier, this category of unpaid workers are those persons who were engaged in production or processing activities of primary products wholly for own or household consumption during the reference period. For measurement purposes, however, they are to be classified as 'employed' only if the production comprises 'an important contribution to the total consumption of the household'. The qualifying clause leaves some flexibility and needs to be interpreted appropriately in the light of national circumstances.

Finally, the new definition makes clear that apprentices who received pay in cash or in kind should be considered to be in paid employment and classified as at work on the same basis as other persons in paid employment; that students, home-makers and others mainly engaged in non-economic activities during the reference period, but who were at the same time in paid employment or self-employment as defined should be considered as employed on the same basis as other categories of employed persons, and be identified separately wherever possible; and that members of armed forces should be included among persons in paid employment,

A major issue tested in the ILO methodological surveys in connection with the application of the new international definition of employment was the compliance with the concept of economic activity set forth in the resolution and, in particular, the coverage of unpaid family workers engaged in primary production or processing for own consumption. One criticism of conventional questionnaires used in many developing countries is their alleged failure to identify all economically active persons, by leaving out in particular those who are active in unpaid work and who are reported as not having worked to conventional labour force questionnaires, because the respondent or the investigator wrongly regarded those activities as falling outside the boundary of economic activity.

In order to test this issue an activity list was incorporated in the methodological surveys in Kerala (India) and Costa Rica, providing an explicit means for checking for possible economic activities that may have been missed in earlier conventional questions on work for pay, profit or family gain. The activity list used in the Kerala survey and specifically oriented to the Kerala situation is reproduced below.

20	Did (s)he do any work for pay, profit or family gain during the LAST 7 DAYS?
	Yes 1 → 23 No 2 ↓

21 Check again whether the person did any work during the last 7 days in the production or processing of any primary products, whether for the market, barter or household consumption, or in any other household or non-household economic activities, such as

	Code
Growing/attending:	
coconuts	11
paddy	12
tapioca	13
other vegetables or fruits	14
other crops	15
Engaged in activities related to:	
livestock and livestock products	16
poultry and poultry products	17
Other agriculture/mining activities	
including hunting/forestry/fishing	18
Hand pounding	31
Curing and preserving fish	32
Making copra and crushing	33
Other food processing activities	34
Retting coconut husk/making coir fiber	35
Making and repairing fishing nets	37
Making baskets/mats/other handicrafts	38
Spinning/weaving/dressmaking/tailoring	39
Other manufacturing activities	40
Construction/repair/maintenance of	
farm buildings	51
own dwellings	52
Other construction activities	53
Engaged in tea shops/street vending/etc.	61
Assisting in sales of agriculture products and other retail trades	62
Carrying loads to market/for storage	71
Other transport activities	72
Operating informal chit funds	81
Other financial activities	82
Giving tuition to students	91
Repair services (tools, shoes, etc.)	92
Collection of firewood, fetching water and other services	93

In determining whether a person has been engaged in one of the above activities during the reference week the basic guiding principles which were to be observed by the investigators were:

(a) Whether the activity was related at least partly to the production of goods or services for the market (for pay, profit, sale or barter).

(b) In the case of primary products, if it was not for the market but wholly for own or household consumption, whether the production comprised an *important contribution* to the total consumption of the household. It was stated that what is an 'important contribution to the total consumption of the household' should be determined on the basis of the relative share of the produce in the total household consumption of that production group. For example, code 15 may be circled if at least 10 per cent of the vegetable and fruits consumed by the household was provided from the vegetables and fruits produced on own account at home.

Unemployment

The new international definition of unemployment, though to a large extent similar to the earlier 1954 definition, introduces certain modifications and amplifications which improves its relevance to situations in developing countries as well as developed countries.

First, a standard definition of unemployment is laid down embodying three basic criteria:

(a) 'without work' during the reference period, i.e. not in paid employment or self-employment as defined;
(b) 'currently available for work', i.e. available for paid employment or self-employment during the reference period; and
(c) 'seeking work', i.e. having taken specific steps in a specified recent period (which could be longer than the reference period) to seek paid employment or self-employment.

This definition does not make reference to any institutional or legal criteria such as receipt of unemployment insurance benefit or registration at a public placement office, but takes account of the person's actual situation during the reference period.

The first criterion – being without work – is complementary to the definition of employment. Thus, a person who has been working during the reference period, even if it happens to be an occasional work or work of very short duration, will not be considered as unemployed, even if the person was, at the same time, seeking some alternative or additional employment. Similarly, a person who was not at work during the reference period but held a job (or enterprise) from which he or she was absent, will not be considered as unemployed if he or she had maintained a formal attachment to the job. On the other hand, a person without a formal job attachment (e.g. a long absence from work without pay and no specific date for return to work) could be considered as unemployed if the other criteria of employment are satisfied.

The second criterion – current availability for work – when used in conjunction with the third criterion – seeking work – is meant to exclude from the count of the unemployed, persons, such as students, who were seeking a job to begin at a later date, for example, after completion of the school year, or persons who had sought work some time during the reference period for job-seeking but were no longer available for work during the basic reference period.

The third criterion – seeking work – requires a specific work-search activity for classification as unemployed. A mere declaration of intention does not suffice. The specific steps may include registration at a public or private employment exchange; application to employers; checking at work-sites, farms, factory gates, markets or other assembly places; placing or answering newspaper advertisements; seeking the assistance of friends or relatives; looking for land, building, machinery or equipment to establish own enterprise; arranging for financial resources, applying for permits and licences, etc. Some of the steps detailed above indicate interest in paid employment, some others in self-employment, while still others could be for either paid employment or self-employment.

After setting forth the three basic criteria of the standard definition of unemployment, the resolution goes on to say: 'In situations where the conventional means of seeking work are of limited relevance, where the labour market is largely unorganized or of limited scope, where labour force is largely self-employed, the standard definition of unemployment may be applied by relaxing the criterion of seeking work.' This relaxation is apparently aimed at the less developed countries where the criterion of seeking work does not capture the extent of unemployment in its totality. With that relaxation, which permits in extreme cases complete suppression of that criterion, the two basic criteria which remain applicable are 'without work' and 'currently available for work'.

It is, however, cautioned that 'In the application of the criterion of current availability for work, especially in situations where the "seeking-work" criterion is relaxed, appropriate tests should be developed to suit national circumstances. Such tests may be based on notions such as present desire for work, previous work experience, willingness to take up work for wage or salary on locally prevailing terms, or readiness to undertake self-employment activity, given the necessary resources and facilities.' These criteria are expected to ensure objectivity in the expression of current availability.

Countries adopting the standard definition of unemployment, without the suggested relaxation, are required to identify persons not classified as unemployed because they were not seeking work, but were available for work all the same, and classify them separately under population not currently active. This provision applies in particular to the so-called 'discouraged workers'.

The resolution deals with two special situations and provides special solutions. First, 'Notwithstanding the criterion of seeking work embodied in the standard definition of unemployment, persons without work and currently available for work, who had made arrangements to take up paid employment or undertake self-employment activity at a date subsequent to the reference period should be considered unemployed.' In this case the 'seeking-work' criterion is completely set aside, as in the 1954 definition.

Second, 'Persons temporarily absent from their job with no formal job attachment, who were currently available for work and seeking work, should be regarded as unemployed in accordance with the standard definition of unemployment. Countries may, however, depending on national circumstances and policies, prefer to relax the seeking work criterion in the case of persons temporarily laid off. In such cases, persons temporarily laid off who were not seeking work but classified as unemployed should be identified as a separate category.' The 1954 definition treated temporary or indefinite lay-off without pay as unemployment, irrespective of any other consideration. The new definition is, however, more restrictive in so far as it treats only those cases in which no other formal attachment (such as a commitment to recall) exists as unemployed, provided that the person is currently available for work and seeking work.

The new definition also makes clear, as in the case of employment, that students, home-makers and others mainly engaged in non-economic activities during the reference period who satisfy the criteria laid down in the definition of unemployment should be regarded as unemployed on the same basis as other categories of unemployed persons and be identified separately.

In testing the application of the new definition of unemployment in the ILO methodoligical surveys, the formulation of the criterion of 'current availability for work' was a main preoccupation. After some experimentation, the procedure adopted in the questionnaire was to ascertain 'availability' on the basis of the degree to which the person reported to be available for work could specify the particulars of the work that he or she was available for, the ultimate test being whether the person had taken any specific steps to secure such work. The sequence of questions used for ascertaining 'availability' for work in the Kerala survey (phase two) is shown below.

Availability for work

---

40 Was (s)he available for work during the last 7 days?
      Yes   1   │   No │ 2
      It depended   3   ↓   ↓

---

41 (a) Available for:		41 (b) Reason for non-availability:	
Regular employment		Attending school	1
full-time	1	Engaged in household duties	2
part-time	2	Retired/old age	3
Temporary or casual		Other (specify)	4
employment	3		

---

42 Describe the type of occupation (s)he was available for.

43 (a) Was (s)he willing to take up work for wage or salary on locally prevailing
    terms last 7 days?
    Yes ↓   1   No 2

    minimum acceptable:
    daily wage   Rs
    monthly salary   Rs

    (b) Was (s)he willing to take up self-employment given the necessary
    resources and facilities?
    Yes   1   No 2

44 (a) Was (s)he willing to take up work outside home?
    Yes ↓   1   No 2 → 45

    (b) Was (s)he willing to take up work outside locality/village?
    Yes   1   No 2

Seeking work

45 (a) What specific steps has (s)he taken during the last year to seek paid or
    self-employment?
        (Mark all steps taken)   Months
    Registered with public or private
        employment exchange   1
    Applied to prospective employers   2
    Checked at work sites/farms/factory gates/markets/other
    assembly places   3
    Placed/answered advertisements   4
    Sought assistance of friends/relatives   5
    Looked for land/building/machinery/
        equipment for setting up own
        enterprise   6
    Arranged for financial resources   7
    Applied for permit/licence   8
    Other step (specify)   9
    No step taken   0

Population not economically active

As the definition of the economically active population permits different
measures, among which two – the usually active and the currently active –
have been specifically identified, the new resolution provides for two
alternative measures of the population not economically active. The
'population not currently active', equated to the old concept of persons not
in the labour force, comprises all persons not employed or unemployed
during the brief reference period and hence not currently active. This
group is to be classified by reasons for inactivity listed as: (a) attendance at

educational institutions; (b) engagement in household duties; (c) retirement or old age; and (d) other reasons such as infirmity or disablement. The 'population not usually active' comprises all persons whose main activity status during the longer specified period was neither employed nor unemployed. This group is divided into (a) students, (b) home-makers, (c) income recipients (pensioners, rentiers, etc.); and (d) others (recipients of public aid or private support, children not attending school, etc.) as in the United Nations Principles and Recommendations for Population Censuses.

The reason for the distinction made in the classification of the population not currently active and the population not usually active is that in the case of current activity, students, home-makers, etc. are to be regarded as employed or unemployed and hence currently active, if they had any such activity, even as a minor activity, during the brief reference period. In such a system, only students, home-makers, etc., who had no economic activity at all would be classified as not currently active. Logically, one could only classify them by reason for inactivity, it being understood that the persons classified as not active because of attendance at educational institutions do not include all the students, and the persons classified as not active because of engagement in household duties do not include all the home-makers. In the case of those usual active, on the other hand, as the activity status is based on a long reference period through the determination of main activity over the period, it is assumed that, by and large, persons who are mainly engaged in studies, household duties, etc., will turn out to be not usually active, and could therefore be categorised as students, home-makers, etc. It is possible, however, that persons mainly engaged in studies, household duties, etc., but usually participating in economic activity as a part-time activity would still be classified as usually active and to that extent the persons categorised as students, homemakers, etc., would not include all persons who were mainly students, home-makers, etc.

A point to be noted here is that the classification of persons not economically active as students, home-makers, etc., has often tended to preclude the classification of such persons as economically active even if they had worked part-time or had worked at different occasions over a period. The new resolution ensures, through specific reminders attached to the definitions of employment and unemployment, and through the classification of currently inactive persons by reason for inactivity rather than categorisation as students, home-makers, etc., that to the extent they are economically active they are classified as such.

The resolution also suggests that wherever necessary separate functional sub-categories be introduced to identify, as components of the population not usually active, persons engaged in unpaid community and volunteer services; and other persons engaged in marginal activities which fall outside the boundary of economic activities.

Underemployment

In addition to revising the definitions of employment and unemployment

and economically active population, the new international standards
provide guidance on the measurement of underemployment, replacing
part of the earlier international standards adopted by the Eleventh ICLS in
1966 (paragraphs 4-9 and 13 of the Eleventh ICLS Resolution III). The
new international standards maintain that: 'Underemployment exists when
a person's employment is inadequate in relation to specified norms or
alternative employment, account being taken of his or her occupational
skill (training and working experience)'. Further, it continues to distinguish
two principal forms of underemployment – visible and invisible – and
reiterates the characteristics of each. Visible underemployment 'is
primarily a statistical concept directly measurable by labour force and other
surveys, reflecting an insufficiency in the volume of employment'. Invisible
underemployment 'is primarily an analytical concept reflecting a
misallocation of labour resources or a fundamental imbalance as between
labour and other factors of production. Characteristic symptoms might be
low income, underutilisation of skill, low productivity. Analytical studies of
invisible underemployment should be directed to the examination and
analysis of a wide variety of data, including income and skill levels
(disguised underemployment) and productivity measures (potential
underemployment).'

The new resolution, however, suggests that, for operational reasons, the
statistical measurement of underemployment be limited to visible
underemployment. This reflects the great difficulties encountered in
measuring invisible underemployment in countries where they have done
so in their survey programmes in the last two decades or so. One difficulty
concerns the unreliability of the income data that are relevant for the
purpose of measurement of invisible underemployment, particularly as it
concerns self-employed workers, and the other is the problem of
interpreting low income as a symptom of labour underutilisation. It has
been argued that, although under ideal conditions income may be
regarded as reflecting productivity, owing to institutional factors, price
fluctuations and other non-ideal conditions, income may not be a
satisfactory proxy for productivity. For example, the low income received
by a full-time domestic help may be due more to the institutional set-up
than to low productivity. Similarly, the variations in the income received by
a self-employed worker may be due to a larger extent to price fluctuations
than to productivity. Thus, a low income, it is argued, may not necessarily
mean an inadequate utilisation of labour in such situations.

As in the past, the new international standards distinguish two elements
of the measurement of visible underemployment: the number of persons
visibly underemployed; and the quantum of visible underemployment.
According to the new resolution, 'persons visibly underemployed comprise
all persons in paid or self-employment, whether at work or not at work,
involuntarily working less than the normal duration of work determined
for the activity, who were seeking or available for additional work during
the reference period'. Thus, in essence, the criteria set forth for identifying
visibly underemployed persons are: (a) work less than the normal duration;
(b) involuntary reason for the low working hours and (c) seeking or

availability for additional work during the reference period. What is normal duration of work may vary from one activity to another and 'should be determined in the light of national circumstances as reflected in national legislation to the extent it is applicable, and usual practice in other cases, or in terms of a uniform conventional norm'.

In developing the measurement of the quantum of visible underemployment, the new resolution departs from its predecessor and outlines a new methodology. It states that: 'The quantum of visible underemployment may be measured by aggregating the time available for additional employment during the reference period in respect of each person visibly underemployed. The time available for additional employment may be computed in units of working days, half-days, hours as may be convenient in national circumstances, depending on the nature of data collected.'

The new resolution recognises the concept of 'time lost' used in some countries from the viewpoint of production as an approximation to the quantum of visible underemployment and suggests: 'It may be useful to measure separately the part of the quantum of visible underemployment that corresponds to "time lost" defined as the difference between hours usually employed and hours actually employed.' The new resolution also permits countries which wish to apply the criterion of 'seeking' to the measurement of the quantum of visible underemployment to do so by taking into account the duration of work sought.

The measurements outlined above reflect the current visible underemployment within the brief reference period selected for the determination of the current activity status. As in the case of current employment and current unemployment, current underemployment may also be regarded as a current variable, the variations in which can usefully be studied over time. The quantum of current visible underemployment can, however, be regarded not only as a current variable, but also as an additive element, which, if aggregated over time, e.g. over the season or over the year, can provide an estimate of the total quantum of visible underemployment over the period.

Measured in labour time unemployed, rather than as labour force unemployed, current unemployment can also be regarded as an additive element, which can be aggregated over time, e.g. over the year, to provide estimates of the total quantum of current unemployment. It can also be combined with the corresponding estimate of the quantum of current visible underemployment to provide a composite estimate of the quantum of current unemployment and visible underemployment. The new resolution therefore introduces the new concept of a composite estimate as follows: 'A composite estimate of the quantum of current unemployment and visible underemployment may be compiled on the basis of the labour-time disposition of all persons in the labour force, by accounting for the total labour-time potentially available for each person in the labour force in terms of time employed, time available for employment and time not available for employment during the reference period. It can be measured for simplicity either in units of working days or half-days, or, more fully, in hours, where feasible.'

The concept of labour-time disposition has been well tried out in some of the developing countries of Asia and found useful to supplement the data on employment and unemployment collected by the labour force approach. It has also been tested in the ILO methodological surveys in Kerala (India) and Costa Rica in connection with the application of the new international standards. The procedure adopted is the following. With the week as a reference period, a daily record of the time disposition in units of days or half-days is obtained for the whole week in respect of each person found to be in the labour force, using the schedule below:

DAILY economic activity Enter 2 for full-day activity; 1 for half-day activity	Mo	Tu	We	Th	Fr	Sa	Su	Total
At work								
With job or enterprise but not at work								
Without job or enterprise, not at work, but available for work								
Without job or enterprise, not at work, and not available for work								
Total	2	2	2	2	2	2	2	14

The days or half-days in each category are counted for the whole week to provide: the number of days or half-days at work (w); the number of days or half-days with a job or enterprise but not at work (v); the number of days or half-days without a job or enterprise – not at work, but available for work (u); and the number of days or half-days not available for work. For each person in the labour force, the sum of w and v represents the number of days or half-days employed; u the number of days or half-days available for employment, i.e. the combined time of underemployment and unemployment; and, x the number of days or half-days not currently active. Corresponding estimates W, V, U and X for the total labour force are built up by the usual methods of estimation. Finally, a composite rate of current unemployment and visible underemployment is computed as $U/(U + V + W)$ and expressed as a percentage. Wherever feasible, the numbers w, v, u and x can well be ascertained directly in respect of each person in the labour force without the imposition of a daily record. Or they can be computed analytically on the basis relevant survey items.[2]

Analytical concepts

Building upon the basic concepts and definitions adopted of the economically active population, employment, unemployment and under-employment, the new international standards introduce certain illustrative concepts and measure useful for labour force analysis.

Activity participation rates

While the crude activity participation rate relates the economically active population to the total population, a more appropriate participation rate relating the economically active population to the population above the specified minimum age is suggested for analysis. Specific activity rates can also be compiled by age/sex groups. It will indeed be useful to compile activity rates both on the basis of usual activity and current activity.

Employment–population ratio

Generally the employed population is expressed as a proportion of the economically active population. However, for certain purposes, such as planning and monitoring progress in development, where maximization of employment is a development objective, the employment–population ratio, i.e. the proportion of the working-age population that is employed, is more useful. It has been considered in certain countries as a measure of the economy's ability to provide employment to a growing population and used as supplementary information in the analysis of unemployment and activity rates. The employment–population ratio has a number of properties. Neither the numerator nor the denominator involves counts of the unemployed, the labour force aspect that is most difficult to measure. Also, since both numerator and denominator are based on large quantities, sampling errors are reduced and detailed disaggregation is possible. Further, the ratio is less affected by short-term or cyclical factors and therefore may provide a suitable measure of long-term or structural trends.

General and sectional unemployment rates

The general unemployment rate is to be compiled by calculating the unemployed population as a percentage of the economically active population. The new resolution proposes two sectional unemployment rates to supplement the general unemployment rate: one dealing with persons seeking and/or available for paid employment, and the other dealing with persons seeking and/or available for self-employment. For the former, the number of persons seeking and/or available for paid employment may be related to the sum of the number in paid employment and the number seeking and/or available for paid employment. For the other sectional rate, the number of persons seeking and/or available for self-employment may be related to the sum of the number in self-employment and the number seeking and/or available for self-employment. Some persons may in fact be seeking and/or available for paid employment only. Some others may be seeking and/or available for self-employment only. Some may be seeking and/or available for either. The third ambivalent category may be tagged on either to paid employment or to self-employment depending on the policy emphasis and the nature of the ameliorative action envisaged. Thus two mutually exclusive rates can be compiled dealing with persons seeking and/or available for paid employment only; and persons seeking and/or available for self-employment, with or without the alternative of paid employment. Alternatively, the two rates may deal with persons seeking and/or available for self-employment only; and persons seeking and/or available for paid employment, with or without the alternative of self-employment.

Visible underemployment rate

This refers to the number of persons visibly underemployed as a proportion of the total number of persons employed. The proportion may be compiled for each branch of economic activity and for each occupational group, preferably for each season in countries where the intensity of employment is subject to seasonal variation.

Composite rate of unemployment and visible underemployment

Finally, a composite rate of unemployment and visible underemployment is suggested which 'may be compiled as the ratio of unemployed labour-time available for employment to the total labour-time employed or available for employment'. In terms of the symbolic presentation suggested above for labour-time disposition, it can be computed as $U(U+V+W)$ and expressed as a percentage.

In this connection, the new international standards suggest that the technique of labour-time disposition, 'if carried out through a series of current surveys covering a representative sample of reference periods spread over a year, can be used for the estimation of labour-time employed or unemployed over the year. The estimate may be expressed in terms of person-days or person-hours, or if so desired, converted into standard full-time person-years.' The estimation procedure would obviously depend on the sampling procedure adopted for the survey. The conversion of person-days into standard full-time person-years involves the adoption of a norm depending on national practices concerning holidays, leave with pay and prevalent rates of absence from work for other reasons.

Employment and income relationship

Having stated that for operational reasons the statistical measurement of underemployment may be limited to visible underemployment, and thus, in effect, discouraging the measurement of invisible underemployment on operational grounds, the new international standards go on to suggest the measurement of the relationship of employment and income and its analysis in relation to other economic and social variables. This broader perspective is aimed in particular at analysing the income-generating capacity of different economic activities, and identifying the number and characteristics of persons who are unable to maintain their economic well-being on the basis of the employment opportunities available to them.

It also recognises the impracticability of obtaining meaningful data on income through current labour force surveys and suggests that: 'In order to obtain comprehensive measures of the relationship between employment and income, the measurement of employment, income from employment, and household income should refer to the work experience of the population over a long reference period, preferably a year, taking into account not only the principal occupation but also secondary occupations and other sources of income.'

In this connection, the new international standards introduce the concept of 'work experience' over a long reference period, preferably a year. This involves identifying every person who has done any work at all over the year, and ascertaining the duration and intensity of work during the year, not only on the principal occupation but also on other secondary occupations, together with the corresponding data on income from such employment. From the viewpoint of economic well-being data are required not only on income from employment, but also on income from other sources.

References are also made to relevant definitions of income, income from employment and household income. It is further suggested that: 'The statistics on employment and income should be analysed, to the extent possible, in conjunction with duration of work, household size, number of earners, assets and other demographic, social and economic characteristics of the individual and the household.' It is thus no longer a problem of identifying and enumerating persons who are invisibly underemployed by the income criterion, but analysis of employment and income in relation to other economic and social aspects.

As part of the ILO methodological surveys, attempts have been made in both the Kerala and Costa Rica surveys to study the feasibility of measuring the relationship between employment and income in household surveys. The main measurement objective was to obtain information on 'employment' and 'income from employment' in a way that permits us to measure the income content of employment for different economic activities (objective (a) cited at the beginning of this section).[3] An important aspect was, therefore, to study the feasibility of obtaining data on employment and data on income from employment that fully correspond to each other.

For this purpose it was found necessary from the outset to make a basic distinction between employment in own household enterprise, on the one hand, and paid employment or self-employment in a non-household enterprise, on the other. The reason for this distinction was the impossibility of direct measurement of the share of income of each household member engaged in the household enterprise. In household enterprises, working members of the household are joint contributors of labour with varying duration and intensity of work and the income derived from such joint activities cannot be readily assigned to each individual. The primary income of these workers is more meaningfully measured as part of income from employment of the household as a whole.

It was also found necessary to distinguish between two categories of self-employment activity.

(i) *Self-employment providing services*: This refers to own-account employment in which the own-account worker is paid for his or her services directly by the recipient of the services. Examples are: doctors, lawyers, barbers, taxi-drivers, repairmen, newspaper vendors, lottery ticket sellers, etc. The net income received by this category of persons is generally mostly in return for the labour input. The part due to the utilisation of equipment and fixed capital is negligible.

(ii) *Other self-employment*: This refers to the employment of employers and own-account workers not classified as self-employment providing services. Examples are managers of businesses, shop-keepers, tailors selling clothing, fishermen, etc. The net income received by this category of persons is generally in return for their capital and equipment as well as labour input and, therefore, cannot be directly matched with the reported amount of employment.

The design of the methodological surveys on this topic was particularly complex. In addition to the problem of employment and income from household enterprises and self-employment, it involved tackling a number of other problems, particularly, the choice of reference periods for different types of activity, the measurement of productive assets in the case of the second category of self-employment, etc.

Other provisions

The new international standards also provide some guidance on data collection, analysis and classifications, data requirements on special topics of concern, evaluation and dissemination. The guidelines on data analysis suggest, in particular, that 'the population above the age specified for the measurement of the economically active population should be cross-classified by usual activity status and current activity status' so that one may study the extent to which persons usually active are currently inactive and vice versa, and the extent to which persons usually employed are currently unemployed or vice versa. This would indicate in particular the extent to which persons who are usually students or home-makers are currently active. It would also facilitate study of the extent to which persons usually engaged in an activity (e.g. agriculture) are currently engaged in other activities (e.g. manufacturing or construction).

The guidelines on data requirements on special topics refer, among others, to children and youths, women, families and households, time use, the urban informal sector, rural non-agricultural activities, disabled and handicapped persons, etc. Attention is drawn, in particular, to the requirement of data on the extent to which children and youths are simultaneously at school and at work, sex biases in statistics and the problems of measurement of women's participation in economic activity, analysis of multiple and marginal activities through time-use studies, etc. The resolution also endorses the balance sheets of labour resources compiled in centrally planned economies.

Conclusion

The new international standards on statistics of the economically active population, employment, unemployment and underemployment present a number of new features, some of special significance to the developing countries and some to the developed countries. While retaining the basic approach to the measurement of labour force, employment and unemployment, it provides for modifications, amplifications, relaxations and extensions of those basic features, which in their rigidity or ambiguity were found inapplicable or ineffective in the situations in many countries. Some of the new features have been well tested in certain countries, some have been or are being tried out, but some others are new. Countries intending to adopt the new standards may, however, be well advised to try them out in pilot studies before adopting them on a large scale. As mentioned earlier, the ILO is preparing a manual on statistics of the economically active population, employment, unemployment and underemployment, describing the application of the new international standards on these topics and detailing such aspects as methodology of data collection, tabulations and analysis. ILO assistance and advisory services are available for the implementation of the new international standards.

Notes

1. This paper draws in large part on M. V. S. Rao, 'New International Standards for Statistics of the Economically Active Population', *Quarterly Bulletin of Statistics for Asia and the Pacific*, vol. XII, no. 4, December 1982, and in part on ILO Bureau of Statistics, 'Recent Changes in the International Standards for Statistics of the Economically Active Population', paper presented to the OECD Working Party on Employment and Unemployment Statistics, Organisation for Economic Co-operation and Development, Paris, 24-25 October 1983.
2. See, for example, Curtis L. Gilroy, 'Supplemental measures of labour force underutilisation', *Monthly Labor Review*, May 1975, pp. 13-23.
3. Objective (b) was pursued only to the extent that the survey questionnaires covered information on total household income including income from sources other than employment (property and transfer income), but these only for control and cross-classification purposes.

8 International standards on the measurement of economic activity, employment, unemployment and underemployment[1]

R. Hussmanns

Introduction

Statistics of the economically active population, employment, unemployment and underemployment serve a large variety of purposes. They provide measures of labour supply, labour input, the structure of employment and the extent to which the available labour time and human resources are actually utilised or not. Such information is essential for macro-economic and human resources development planning and policy formulation. When collected at different points in time, the data provide the basis for monitoring current trends and changes in the labour market and employment situation, which may be analysed in connection with other economic and social phenomena so as to evaluate macro-economic policies. The unemployment rate, in particular, is widely used as an overall indicator of the current performance of a nation's economy.

Statistics of the economically active population, employment, unemployment and underemployment are also an essential base for the design and evaluation of government programmes geared to employment creation, vocational training, income maintenance, poverty alleviation and similar objectives. The measurement of the relationships between employment, income and other socio-economic characteristics provides information on the adequacy of employment of different sub-groups of the population, the income-generating capacity of different types of economic activities, and the number and characteristics of persons unable to ensure their economic well-being on the basis of the employment opportunities available to them. Information on employment and income, disaggregated by branches of economic activity, occupations and socio-demographic characteristics, is needed for collective bargaining, for assessment of the social effects of structural adjustment policies on different subgroups of the population, and for the analysis of race, sex or age inequalities in work opportunities and participation and their changes over time.

So as to provide guidance to countries in developing their national statistical programmes and promote international comparability, the International Labour Organisation promulgates international standards on the various topics of labour statistics. These standards are set by the International Conference of Labour Statisticians (ICLS) which convenes about every five years. The standards presently in force concerning statistics of the economically active population, employment, unemployment and underemployment have been adopted by the Thirteenth ICLS in 1982 (ILO 1983).

This chapter is intended to describe one by one the basic concepts and definitions laid down in the 1982 international standards. Where relevant, particular issues are discussed that may arise in survey applications concerning measurement problems and the appropriate statistical treatment of particular categories of workers, such as self-employed persons, unpaid family workers, casual workers, seasonal workers, apprentices and trainees, persons on lay-off and persons engaged in production for own and household consumption, who are sometimes on the borderline between labour force categories.

The concept and boundary of economic activity

A clear understanding of the concept and boundary of economic activity is a fundamental requirement for the correct application of the definitions of the economically active population, employment and unemployment in labour force surveys. The exact boundary between economic and non-economic activities is a matter of convention, but unless a precise dividing line is drawn, the statistical treatment of many situations encountered in practice remains ambiguous and will raise questions about the reliability of the resulting statistics.

The concept of economic activity adopted by the Thirteenth ICLS (1982) for the measurement of the economically active population is defined in terms of the production of goods and services as set forth by the United Nations System of National Accounts (SNA). The international standards specify that 'the economically active population comprises all persons of either sex who furnish the supply of labour for the production of economic goods and services, as defined by the United Nations systems of national accounts and balances, during a specified time-reference period'. Thus, persons are to be considered as economically active if (and only if) they contribute or are available to contribute to the production of goods and services falling within the SNA production boundary. The use of a definition of economic activity which is based on the SNA serves to ensure that the activity concepts of employment statistics and production statistics are consistent, thus facilitating the joint analysis of the two bodies of statistics.

SNA production boundary

According to the present SNA,[2] the production of goods and services comprises:

(a) the production of goods and services normally intended for sale on the market at a price that is designed to cover their costs of production;

(b) the production of other goods and services which are not normally sold on the market at a price intended to cover their cost of production, such as government services and private non-profit services to households, domestic services rendered by one household to another and other items;

(c) specified types of production for own consumption and fixed capital formation for own use, including:

(i) primary products (e.g. milk, cereals, fruit, cotton, wood);

(ii) the processing of primary products by their producer to make such goods as butter, flour, wine, cloth or furniture, whether or not any of these products are sold by their producer on the market;

(iii) other goods and services, if they are *also* produced for the market by the same household;

(iv) fixed assets, such as own-account construction of dwellings, farm buildings, roads, tools and similar items which have an expected life of use of one year or more;

(v) the total rent of owner-occupied dwellings (representing an imputed monetary value rather than an activity, this item has no relevance for employment statistics).

For convenience, the activities corresponding to *(a)* and *(b)* may be designated as market activities or market production, and those corresponding to *(c)* as non-market economic activities or non-market production. The aggregate constitutes the scope of economic activity for the measurement of the economically active population. All other activities are called non-economic activities.

Market activities

Though market production and non-market production are defined in terms of the end use of the product rather than on the basis of the paid or unpaid nature of the production, market activities typically involve some form of remuneration to those who participate in them. Such remuneration may be in the form of pay or profit. Pay includes cash payment as well as payment-in-kind, whether received in the same period as when the work is done or not. Cash payment includes wages or salaries at time or piece rates, fees or tips, bonuses or gratuities, etc. Payment-in-kind may be in the form of food, fuel, housing or other goods and services.

Payment-in-kind as the sole means of remuneration is not uncommon in some countries, e.g. for agricultural workers receiving a share of the harvest or for apprentices and trainees working in exchange for board and lodging.

Profit refers to the remuneration for activities performed by persons who operate their own farm, business enterprise or service undertaking with or without hired employees. An activity may be undertaken for profit even if currently no profit is made during the reference period of the survey. Work for profit also includes the activities of family members undertaken in connection with the operation of a household enterprise producing for the market, even though these persons typically work for family gain and do not receive any direct payment for the work done. Similarly, market activities include also work performed for productive purposes on the basis of an exchange labour arrangement between households, and the production of goods or services for barter among households, even when no cash payment is received.

Non-market economic activities

The rationale for the inclusion of certain types of non-market production in the present SNA definition while excluding others lies in the importance of the activities for the subsistence of the population in many countries, and in the frequent existence of close market parallels, i.e. identical or very similar goods and services are usually also available on the market. Throughout the world, the production and processing of primary products of agriculture, hunting, forestry, fishing, mining and quarrying for own use represent a major part of consumption for many persons and their families.

Similarly, in a number of countries construction of houses, wells and other items to be considered as investment goods is undertaken to a significant extent on an own-account basis. Furthermore, since a shift may take place from production for own consumption to market production as economic development proceeds, it is essential to account for both types of activity, so as to obtain a comparable measure of the economically active population at different periods or for different countries.

There are also practical considerations involved in the delineation of the SNA production boundary. So as to cover market production completely, it is necessary to include some non-market production as well, as it is in practice often impossible to measure the market component separately when the same persons are engaged in both types of production. A similar argument applies for the inclusion of processing of primary products for own consumption which cannot be separated from the production of such products when carried out by the same households. This is the main reason why at present processing of goods for own consumption is considered an economic activity only if it involves the processing of *primary* products and is carried out by the producers of such items. Thus, using cotton fabric (a processed product) to sew clothes is excluded the same as spinning cotton fibres (a primary product) bought at the market, whereas spinning cotton fibres produced by oneself is included.

Non-economic activities

Being based on the SNA definition of production of goods and services, the concept of economic activity for the measurement of the economically active population excludes production for own consumption of items other than those mentioned above under *(c)*, such as the processing of primary products by those who do not produce them, the production of other goods and services by households who do not sell any part of them in the market, and current repairs and maintenance of constructions, etc., carried out by households for themselves.

Moreover, the SNA production boundary excludes volunteer services rendered to the community or private non-profit organisations, and unpaid domestic activities such as teaching and nursing of own children or cooking food and washing clothes for one's own children or cooking food and washing clothes for one's own household. The fact that such activities fall at present outside the boundary of economic activity does not, however, mean that such activities, which are mainly carried out by women, should not be statistically measured at all, as it is widely recognised that they provide a major contribution to the welfare of populations and the development of countries. In fact, the 1982 international standards contain a provision to identify persons engaged in unpaid community and volunteer services, and other persons engaged in marginal activities which fall outside the boundary of economic activities, separately among the population not economically active.

Measurement

In measuring the economically active population in household surveys, it is essential that careful attention be paid in questionnaire design and interviewer instructions so as to translate the notion of economic activity into appropriate questions, because the interviewers' and respondents' own subjective understanding of economic activity may differ from what the concept intends to include. This requirement is fundamental, as it sets the frame for all subsequent information collected in the course of the interview. A misunderstanding of whether or not certain activities are to be considered as economic may thus have irremediable impacts on the entire interview and on the survey results. Such problems may particularly arise in situations where a substantial part of the economically active population is engaged in activities other than regular full-time full-year paid employment or self-employment, such as part-time employment, casual work, work remunerated in kind, home-based work, unpaid family work and production for own consumption. In such situations, additional probing questions or an activity list may prove useful to reduce under-reporting.

The currently active population

The 1982 international standards distinguish between two measures of the economically active population: the currently active population (labour force), measured in relation to a short reference period such as one week or one day, and the usually active population, measured in relation to a long reference period such as a year.

The currently active population (or the labour force) comprises all persons above a specified minimum age (e.g. 15 years) who, during a specified brief period of one week or one day, fulfil the requirements for inclusion among the employed or the unemployed as described in later sections of this paper. The currently active population is the most widely used measure of the economically active population. Being based on a short reference period, it is used for measuring the current employment and unemployment situation of the economy and the current employment characteristics of the population. When measurement is repeated at sufficiently frequent intervals, current changes over time can be monitored.

Labour force framework

The measurement of the currently active population is based on the labour force framework. The essential feature of the labour force framework is that individuals are categorised according to their activities during a specified short reference period by using a specific set of priority rules. The result is a classification of the population into three mutually exclusive and exhaustive categories: employed, unemployed and not in the labour force (or not currently active). The first two categories make up the currently active population (or labour force), which gives a measure of the number of persons furnishing the supply of labour at a given moment in time.

Priority rules

So as to ensure that each person is classified into one and only one of the three basic categories of the framework, the following set of priority rules is adopted. The first step consists of identifying among persons above the specified minimum age those who, during the specified short reference period, were either at work or temporarily absent from work (the 'employed' category); the next step is to identify among the remaining persons those who were seeking and/or available for work (the 'unemployed' category). The third category, persons not in the labour force or not currently active, i.e. those without work who were not seeking and/or not available for work, then falls out residually. Persons below the age specified for measuring the economically active population are added to the population not currently active. In this scheme, precedence is given to employment over unemployment and to unemployment over economic inactivity. A person who is both working and seeking work is classified as employed, and a student who is attending school and also seeking work is classified as unemployed. One corollary of the priority rules is that employment always takes precedence over other activities, regardless of the amount of time devoted to it during the reference period, which in extreme cases may be only one hour. A related feature of the labour force framework is that the concept of unemployment is limited to the situation of a total lack of work.

Activity principle

Another characteristic of the labour force framework is that a person's labour force status should be determined on the basis of what the person was actually doing during the specified reference period (the activity principle). The purpose of the activity principle is to make measurement of the labour force as objective as possible. Thus only persons who were engaged in an economic activity or who were seeking and/or available for such an activity are to be considered for inclusion in the labour force. There are only few exceptions to this activity principle, such as the inclusion among the employed of persons temporarily absent from work, or the inclusion among the unemployed of persons without work who are not seeking work because they have already found a job to start at a date subsequent to the reference period.

Applicability of the labour force framework

The labour force framework is best suited to situations where the dominant type of employment is regular full-time paid employment. In these situations, a working person falls unambiguously in the employed category, a person seeking and/or available for such employment falls into the unemployed category, and others fall outside the labour force. In practice, however, the employment situation in a given country will to a greater or lesser extent differ from this pattern. Some deviations may be unimportant or can be handled by proper application of the underlying concepts and definitions, but others may require more elaborate considerations. For example, there might be situations falling on the borderline between labour force categories (e.g. persons on temporary lay-off, unpaid family workers during the off-season, persons on training schemes), raising questions about their appropriate statistical treatment. Others, while clearly falling into one category or another, contribute to the heterogeneity of that category, thus raising difficulties in the interpretation of the resulting statistics and calling for further differentiations (e.g. distinction between adequately employed and inadequately employed). There may even be situations which raise questions about the very meaningfulness of categories, such as the virtual non-existence of unemployment in the sense of total lack of work in certain countries. Some of these issues will be discussed along with the definitions of employment, unemployment and underemployment in later sections of this paper.

The current activity measurement provides a snap-shot picture of the economically active population at a given point in time. In situations where the dominant pattern of employment is year-round, with little or no seasonal variation and relatively few movements into and out of the labour force or its main components, such a snapshot picture is probably sufficient to provide an adequate representation of the employment situation for the whole year. However, where significant seasonal patterns of activity or substantial labour force movements exist, the employment picture obtained for one short reference period may not be representative of others. In such situations, measurement should be made over a longer period of time, either by repeating or staggering the current activity measurement over time so as to cover the desired longer period, or by using the longer period itself as the reference period for measurement. In principle, the two approaches will give different results, due to differences in measurement concepts and methods. The first approach requires increasing the frequency of labour force surveys or spreading the sample over time, while the second approach calls for retrospective measurement on the basis of a long reference period with an appropriate conceptual framework. A framework introduced in 1982 as an international standard is that of the 'usually active population'.

The usually active population

The usually active population comprises all persons above a specified age (e.g. 15 years) whose main activity status as determined in terms of number of weeks or days during a long specified period (such as the preceding 12 months or the preceding calendar year) was employed or unemployed. Residually, the population not usually active comprises all persons whose main activity status during the reference period was neither employed nor unemployed, including persons below the age specified for measuring the economically active population.

The measurement of the usually active population is based on the activity status of individuals, assessed on the basis of a 'main activity' criterion over a long reference period, as opposed to assessment of activity status on the basis of the priority criterion used for measurement of the currently active population in the labour force framework. Another fundamental difference between the two measurement frameworks concerns subdivisions. In the ususal activity framework, individuals are first classified as usually active or not usually active, and then the usually active may be further subdivided as employed or unemployed according to the main activity during the active period. In the labour force framework, however, individuals are first identified as employed or unemployed, and then the two categories are summed to obtain the currently active population.

Illustration

To illustrate the usual activity framework, consider the example of a person who, during the course of a year, was employed for 13 weeks, unemployed for 18 weeks and not economically active during the remaining 21 weeks. This person would first be classified as usually active as the extent of economic activity over the year (31 weeks) exceeded the extent of inactivity, and would then be classified as unemployed as the extent of unemployment exceeded that of employment. This is despite the fact that among the three activity statuses 'employed', 'unemployed' and 'not active', the person was not active for the largest number of weeks. The example shows that, for the measurement of the usually active population and its components, data on the duration of employment and unemployment over the year may also be needed. This is because the main activity status of individuals is to be determined on the basis of the amount of time that these individuals were employed or unemployed during the reference period, measured in terms of weeks or days of employment or unemployment.

Measurement

Accurate measurement of the usually active population and its components is in practice not a simple task. Unless panel surveys for statistical follow-up of individuals are used, it involves retrospective questioning on the employment and unemployment experience of individuals during a whole year. Since retrospective measurement over such a long reference period may be subject to substantial recall errors, particularly in situations of frequent changes in activity status, it is important to adopt measurement procedures to reduce these errors to the extent possible. This may be done, for example, by structuring the reference year in terms of calendar months or jobs held.

The definitions of one week or one day of employment or unemployment should, in principle, be the same as those used in the labour force framework. This provides a conceptual link between the definitions of the usually active population and the currently active population. In survey applications, however, the procedure for measuring weeks or days of employment or unemployment will be somewhat different from the measurements in the current activity framework because of practical limitations due to the use of a long reference period.

Employment

The international definition of employment, as given in the 1982 standards, is formulated in terms of the labour force framework, i.e. with respect to a short reference period. The definition distinguishes between paid employment (including apprentices and members of the armed forces) and self-employment (including members of producers' co-operatives, unpaid family workers and persons engaged in non-market production). It provides separate criteria for the measurement of these two types of employment. According to the definition, the 'employed' comprise all persons above the age specified for measuring the economically active population (e.g. 15 years) who, during a specified short period of either one week or one day, were in the following categories:

(a) paid employment:
(i) *at work*: persons who, during the reference period, performed some work (i.e. at least one hour) for wage or salary, in cash or in kind;
(ii) *with a job but not at work*: persons who, having already worked in their present job, were temporarily not at work during the reference period and had a formal attachment to their job;
(b) self-employment:
(i) *at work*: persons who, during the reference period, performed some work (i.e. at least one hour) for profit or family gain, in cash or in kind;
(ii) *with an enterprise but not at work*: persons with an enterprise (which may be a business enterprise, a farm or a service undertaking) who were temporarily not at work during the reference period for any specific reason.

The concept of work for the measurement of employment corresponds to the concept of economic activity as derived from the United Nations System of National Accounts. This means that the notion of 'work for pay, profit or family gain' in the definition of employment should be interpreted as any activity falling within the SNA production boundary.

The one-hour criterion

For measuring the number of persons employed, employment is broadly defined in the labour force framework. The international standards stipulate that, for operational purposes, the notion of 'some work' should be interpreted as work for at least one hour during the reference period. This means that engagement in an economic activity for as little as one hour is sufficient for being classified as employed on the basis of the labour force framework. There are several interrelated reasons for the use of the one-hour criterion in the international definition of employment. One is to make this definition as extensive as possible, in order to cover all types of employment that may exist in a given country, including short-time work, casual labour, stand-by work and other types of irregular employment. Another reason is to ensure that at an aggregate-level total labour input corresponds to total production. This is particularly needed when joint analysis of employment and production statistics is intended. The one-hour criterion is in line with the priority rules of the labour force framework which gives precedence to any employment activity over any other activity, and which defines unemployment as a situation of total lack of work. The definitions of employment and unemployment being interrelated in that framework, raising the minimum number of hours worked in the definition of employment would have the effect that unemployment would no longer only refer to a situation of total lack of work.

The one-hour criterion has been reviewed by the 14th ICLS in 1987 and, while agreeing to retain it, the Conference emphasised that the resulting employment data should be further classified by hours of work (ILO 1988). Such additional information permits distinction among different subgroups of the employed and is helpful to a sound interpretation of the statistics. The broadness of the definition of employment emphasises also the importance of the recommendations of the 1982 international standards on the measurement of underemployment and the analysis of the relationships between employment and income.

Temporary absence from work

The international definition of employment includes among the employed certain persons who were not at work during the reference period. These are persons who were temporarily absent from work for reasons such as illness or injury, holiday or vacation, strike or lock-out, educational or training leave, maternity or parental leave, temporary reduction in economic activity, temporary disorganisation or suspension of work due to bad weather, mechanical or electrical breakdown, shortage of raw materials or fuels, etc., or other temporary absence with or without leave. In general, the notion of temporary absence from work refers to situations in which a period of work is interrupted by a period of absence. This implies that persons should only be considered as temporarily absent from work (and thus as employed) if they have already worked at their present activity and are expected to return to their work after the period of absence. However, there could be exceptional cases where persons might be considered as being temporarily absent from work even though they have not yet worked in their job, e.g. persons who happen to be sick on the day when they are to start a new job.

Temporary absence from paid employment

The international definition of employment specifies certain criteria for assessing temporary absence from work which differ between paid employment and self-employment. In the case of paid employment, the criteria are based on the notion of 'formal job attachment', to be determined in the light of national circumstances according to one or more of the following criteria: (i) the continued receipt of wage or salary; (ii) an assurance of return to work following the end of the contingency, or an agreement as to the date of return: and (iii) the elapsed duration of absence from the job, which may be that duration for which workers can receive compensation benefits without obligations to accept other jobs. This third criterion implies that the absence should be of a fairly short duration to be considered temporary, although the international standards could not specify any precise time limit that would meaningfully apply to all types of absence.

Regarding absence from work, a borderline situation may be that of persons temporarily laid off, i.e. persons whose contract of employment or whose activity has been suspended by the employer for a specified or unspecified period. They should be considered as temporarily absent from work and classified as employed only if they maintain a formal job attachment. Persons laid off without formal job attachment should be classified as unemployed or not economically active, depending on their job-search activity and/or current availability for work. Borderline situations may also arise in the case of non-regular employees. Casual workers working on a daily or weekly basis for an employer do not have a formal job attachment and, when not at work during the reference day or week, should not be classified as employed. Other non-regular employees, such as seasonal workers, should be classified as employed when not at work, if they have a formal job attachment during the reference period.

Temporary absence from self-employment

Given the large diversity in working patterns of self-employed persons, the notion of temporary absence from self-employment is less elaborate than that for paid employment. According to the international standards, persons with an enterprise, who were temporarily not at work during the reference period for any specific reason, should be considered employed. A corollary to the criterion of formal attachment for paid workers does not exist in the case of self-employed persons. In practice, the decision as to whether or not a self-employed person is to be considered absent from work (and therefore as employed) should be based on the continued existence of the enterprise during the absence of its operator. The decision as to whether the absence is to be considered temporary or not could be based on its duration, to be determined according to national circumstances.

For casual own-account workers, such as side-street shoeshine boys or itinerant newspaper vendors, it may be assumed that their enterprise does not continue to exist when they are away from work. Thus, casual own-account workers when not at work should not be considered as 'with an enterprise but not at work' and should not be classified as employed.

Regarding employers and own-account workers engaged in seasonal activities, one may assume that, during the busy season, the enterprise itself continues to exist when the operator is absent, and in this case the operator should be classified as employed when temporarily absent from work. During the off-season, however, one cannot always assume that an enterprise continues to exist. For example, enterprises like fruit kiosks, ice-cream shops and beach restaurants are generally not in operation during the off-season, and therefore the operators of such enterprises should not be classified as employed when they are not at work during the off-season. There are, however, other enterprises which continue to exist during the off-season, e.g. farms which are operated all year round though the bulk of their activities are carried out seasonally. In such cases, a self-employed person not at work during the off-season could be classified as employed (with an enterprise but not at work) provided the duration of absence from work falls within an acceptable limit.

Unpaid family workers, though participating in the activities of a family enterprise, are not considered to have an enterprise of their own. Accordingly, unpaid family workers cannot be 'with an enterprise but not at work'. Therefore, unpaid family workers not at work should not be included among the employed. They would be considered as unemployed or not economically active depending on their search or availability for work during the reference period.

Particular groups

The international standards refer explicitly to some particular groups of workers to be included among the employed: unpaid family workers at work, persons engaged in the production of goods and services for own and household consumption, paid apprentices, working students and home-makers, and members of the armed forces.

Unpaid family workers

An unpaid family worker is a person who works without pay in an economic enterprise operated by a related person living in the same household. Where it is customary for young persons, in particular, to work without pay in an economic enterprise operated by a related person who does not live in the same household, the requirement of 'living in the same household' may be eliminated (UN 1980). In the previous international standards, adopted at the 1954 ICLS, unpaid family workers were required to have worked at least one-third of normal working hours to be classified as employed. This special provision was abandoned at the 1982 ICLS, so that according to the present international standards unpaid family workers at work are to be considered as employed irrespective of the number of hours worked during the reference period, the same as other categories of workers. Referring to countries that, for special reasons, prefer to set a minimum time criterion for the inclusion of unpaid family workers among the employed, the international standards specify that they should identify and separately classify those who worked less than the prescribed time.

Persons engaged in non-market production

Another category of unpaid workers to be considered for inclusion among the employed are persons engaged in the production of goods and services for own and household consumption, if such activities fall into the production boundary of the SNA. The international standards mention, however, that these persons, should be considered employed if such production comprises an important contribution to the total consumption of the household. This provision conforms to the practice in many countries of excluding negligible non-market economic activities from national accounting statistics. Though its implementation in labour force surveys may be difficult, the important contribution provision also serves to exclude from the economically active population persons who may, for example, be growing some vegetables in their backyards but whose subsistence does not significantly depend on it.

Apprentices and trainees

Concerning apprentices, the international standards state explicitly that those who receive pay in cash or in kind should be considered in paid employment and be classified as 'at work' or 'not at work' on the same basis as other persons in paid employment. Regarding apprentices who are not paid, no specific statement is made in the international standards, and the appropriate statistical treatment should therefore follow from the general principles.

Apprentices who fulfil the conditions for inclusion among unpaid family workers should be classified as employed when at work for at least one hour during the reference period. In the case of other unpaid apprentices, their inclusion among the employed may be determined on the basis of whether or not they are associated with the productive activities of an enterprise. If such apprentices contribute to the production of goods and services, they should be classified as employed. Otherwise, they should be classified as unemployed or not economically active, depending on their job-search activity or availability for work.

In addition to apprenticeships, there are various other types of training scheme, organised directly by enterprises to train or retrain their staff, or subsidised by the government as a way to promote employment. Such training schemes are so varied in nature, modalities of contract, modes of payment, duration of training, etc., that specific guidelines on the classification of the trainees into labour force categories cannot be formulated. The appropriate statistical treatment should be determined on a scheme-by-scheme basis. Having discussed the issue, the 14th ICLS agreed on the following general guidelines (ILO 1988).

In principle, trainees can be classified as employed if their activity can be considered as work, or if they have a formal job attachment. When training takes place within the context of an enterprise, it can be assumed that the trainees are associated with the production of goods and services of the enterprise for at least one hour during the reference period. In that case they should be considered as 'at work' and be classified as employed, irrespective of whether or not they receive a wage or salary from the employer.

When the training does not take place within the context of an enterprise (e.g. training outside the enterprise, or inside the enterprise but without association with the production activity of the enterprise), the statistical treatment should depend on whether or not the trainees were employed by the enterprise before the training period (including cases classified as employed as mentioned above).

If employed by the enterprise before the training period, the trainees should be considered as employed but not at work while on training, if they maintain a formal job attachment. Examples are training schemes where periods of training in a specialised institution alternate with periods of work in the enterprise. To establish whether or not a formal job attachment exists, the criterion of 'assurance of return to work' (to be interpreted as assurance of return to work with the same employer) should be considered to be the essential one. In situations where such assurance of return to work does not exist, formal job attachment should be assessed on the basis of the criterion of 'continued receipt of wage or salary'. This criterion should be considered as satisfied if the employer paid directly all or a significant part of the wage or salary. The third criterion, 'elapsed duration of absence', might also be used in particular situations, e.g. in connection with long-term training schemes.

If the trainees were not employed by the enterprise before the training period, they cannot be considered as 'with a job but not at work' and the notion of formal job attachment does not apply. Consequently, if the training scheme provides a definite commitment to employment at the end of the training, the statistical treatment might follow that of persons who have made arrangements to take up employment at a date subsequent to the reference period, and who are to be classified as unemployed if currently available for work (see the following section). Otherwise, the trainees should be classified as unemployed or not economically active depending upon their job search activity or availability for work.

Students, home-makers, etc.

With respect to other groups particularly mentioned, the 1982 international standards specify that students, home-makers and others mainly engaged in non-economic activities during the reference period, who at the same time were in paid employment or self-employment, should be considered as employed on the same basis as other categories of employed person (and be identified separately, where possible). This is fully in line with the priority rules of the labour force framework.

Members of the armed forces

Another group of persons singled out in the international standards for inclusion among the employed are members of the armed forces. The statistics should include both the regular and temporary members of the armed forces as specified in the most recent revision of the International Standard Classification of Occupations (ISCO). It follows logically that persons performing civilian services as an alternative to compulsory military service, wherever such possibility exists, should also be classified as employed.

Unemployment

The international standard definition of unemployment is based on three criteria which have to be met simultaneously. According to this definition the 'unemployed' comprise all persons above the age specified for measuring the economically active population who during the reference period were:

(a) 'without work', i.e. were not in paid employment or self-employment as specified by the international definition of employment;
(b) 'currently available for work', i.e. were available for paid employment or self-employment during the reference period; and
(c) 'seeking work', i.e. had taken specific steps in a specified recent period to seek paid employment or self-employment.

In formulating these criteria, the international standards do not refer to any institutional or legal provisions, such as the receipt of unemployment insurance benefits or the registration at a public placement office. The international definition of unemployment is intended to refer exclusively to a person's particular activities during a specified reference period.

Without work

The 'without work' criterion serves to draw the distinction line between employment and non-employment and to ensure that employment and unemployment are mutually exclusive, with precedence given to employment. Thus, a person is to be considered as without work if he or she did not work at all during the reference period (not even for one hour) nor was temporarily absent from work in the sense described in the previous section of this paper. The other two criteria of the standard definition of unemployment, 'current availability for work' and 'seeking work', serve to distinguish among the non-employed population those who are unemployed from those who are not economically active.

Seeking work

In accordance with the activity principle of the labour force framework, the seeking-work criterion is formulated in terms of active search for work. A person must have taken specific steps in a specified recent period to obtain work in order to be considered as seeking work. A general declaration of being in search of work is not sufficient. This formulation of the criterion is meant to provide an element of objectivity for measurement. The recent period specified for job search activities need not be the same as the basic survey reference period of one week or one day, but might be longer, such as one month or the past four weeks. The purpose of extending the job search period somewhat backwards in time is to take account of the prevailing time-lags involved in the process of obtaining work after the initial step to find it was made, time-lags during which persons may take no further initiative to find work. This may particularly be the case of persons who can only apply for employment with one potential employer (e.g. judges) and are awaiting the reply to their application.

The examples of active steps to seek work listed in the international standards include: registration at a public or private employment exchange; application to employers; checking at worksites, farms, factory gates, market or other assembly places; placing or answering newspaper advertisements; seeking the assistance of friends or relatives; looking for land, building, machinery or equipment to establish own enterprise; arranging for financial resources; applying for permits and licences, etc. Some of these examples refer to rather formal methods of seeking work (e.g. registration at an employment exchange), while others are more informal (e.g. seeking the assistance of friends or relatives). Concerning 'registration at a public or private employment exchange', the 14th ICLS specified that this should be considered an active step to seek work only when it is for the purpose of obtaining a job offer, as opposed to cases where registration is merely an administrative requirement for the receipt of certain social benefits (ILO 1988).

Note that the examples given above cover steps referring not only to paid employment but also to self-employment. This is because the notion of seeking work is independent from the type and duration of employment sought, including self-employment, part-time employment, temporary, seasonal or casual work, and, in general, any type of work considered as economic activity.

Seeking self-employment

The notion of seeking self-employment requires particular attention, as for self-employed persons the dividing line between seeking work activities and the self-employment activities themselves is often difficult to draw. In many situations, activities such as looking for potential clients or orders, or advertising the goods or services produced, are an essential component of the self-employment activity itself. One may also need to clarify, when new enterprises are set up, at what point the process of seeking self-employment turns to become a self-employment activity itself. For example, it is not obvious whether the activities of buying an initial stock or acquiring the necessary equipment for opening a shop should still be regarded as a search activity or already as self-employed work. Having discussed the subject, the 14th ICLS noted that the distinction between seeking self-employment and the self-employment activity itself could be based on the point when the enterprise starts to exist formally, e.g. when the enterprise is registered. Thus, activities taking place before the registration of the enterprise would be regarded as search activities while activities after registration would be considered as self-employment itself. In situations where enterprises are not necessarily required formally to register in order to operate, it was suggested to draw the dividing line at the point when the enterprise is ready to receive the first order, when financial resources have become available, or when the necessary infrastructure is in place (ILO 1988).

Current availability for work

According to the international standards, persons should be available for work during the reference period to be considered unemployed. Availability for work means that, given a work opportunity, a person should be able and ready to work. When used in the context of the standard definition of unemployment, a purpose of the availability criterion is to exclude persons who are seeking work to begin at a later date. Such may be the case of students who, at the time of the survey, are seeking work to be taken up after completion of the school year. In this situation the availability criterion serves as a test of the current readiness to start work. The availability criterion also serves to exclude other persons who cannot take up work due to certain impediments, such as family responsibilities, illness, or commitments to community services.

While the availability criterion is formulated in the international standards as availability during the reference week or day of the survey, in practice many countries prefer to use a slightly longer period, e.g. the two weeks following the interview. This is to account for the fact that not everyone who is seeking work can be expected or is expected to take up a job immediately it is offered. Persons may be temporarily sick at that moment, or may have to make arrangements concerning childcare, transport facilities, etc., before being able to start work. Furthermore, it may be usual practice that enterprises do not expect newly recruited employees to start work before the forthcoming first or fifteenth of the month.

Future starts

The international standards specify one particular category of workers for whom an exception is made from the general rule that all three criteria (without work, currently available for work, seeking work) have to be satisfied simultaneously for being considered as unemployed under the standard definition. These are persons without work who have made arrangements to take up paid employment or undertake self-employment activity at a date subsequent to the reference period ('future starts'). Such persons, if currently available for work, are to be considered as unemployed, whether or not they continue to seek work. Between the alternative of considering them as unemployed or employed (with a job or enterprise but not at work), the international standards have opted for unemployment. This is because these persons, being currently available for work, would presumably already have started work had the job begun earlier and as such form part of the currently underutilised labour resources. Furthermore, their classification as temporarily absent from work would not be in line with the requirement that a person temporarily absent from work must have worked already in the job in question.

Relaxation of the standard definition of unemployment

Seeking work is essentially a process of search for information on the labour market. In this sense, it is particularly meaningful as a definitional criterion in situations where the bulk of the working population is oriented towards paid employment and where channels for exchange of labour market information exist and are widely used. While in industrialised countries these conditions are largely satisfied, this may not be the case in many developing countries where most workers are self-employed, often in household enterprises, and where labour exchanges and similar institutional arrangements are not fully developed and are often limited to certain urban sectors or particular categories of workers. In rural areas and in agriculture, because of the size of the localities and the nature of the activities, most workers have more or less complete knowledge of the work opportunities in their areas at particular periods of the year, making it often unnecessary to take active steps to seek work. Even in industrialised countries and in urban labour markets of developing countries, there may exist similar situations in which particular groups of workers do not actively seek work because they believe that no work corresponding to their skill is available in their area or at particular times in the business cycle.

Relaxation of the seeking-work criterion

Because it was felt that the standard definition of unemployment, with its emphasis on the seeking-work criterion, might be somewhat restrictive and might not fully capture the prevailing employment situations in many countries, the 1982 international standards introduced a provision which allows for the relaxation of the seeking-work criterion in certain situations. This provision is confined to situations where 'the conventional means of seeking work are of limited relevance, where the labour market is largely unorganised or of limited scope where labour absorption is at the time inadequate, or where the labour force is largely self-employed' (ILO 1983).

Formulating a definition of unemployment under the relaxation provision does not necessarily mean that the seeking-work criterion should be completely relaxed for all categories of workers. The relaxation may be only partial. One would then include among the unemployed, in addition to persons satisfying the standard definition, certain groups of persons without work who are currently available for work but who are not seeking work for particular reasons.

An example of partial relaxation of the seeking-work criterion, explicitly mentioned in the international standards, refers to persons temporarily laid off by their employer without maintaining a formal job attachment, i.e. to lay-offs not to be classified as employed (with a job but not at work). Under the standard definition of unemployment, such persons should be considered unemployed only if they are currently available for work and seeking work. For countries which, depending on national circumstances and policies, prefer to relax the seeking-work criterion in the case of persons temporarily laid off, the international standards contain a provision to include such persons, if currently available for work but not seeking work, as a separate subcategory among the unemployed. Other examples, not specifically mentioned in the international standards, would be seasonal workers awaiting the busy season and the so-called 'discouraged workers'.

Availability for work under the relaxation provision

Where the labour market situation justifies the relaxation of the seeking-work criterion, unemployment would be defined, for the persons concerned, in terms of the remaining two criteria, i.e. without work and current availability for work. The availability criterion, in particular, becomes then a crucial element for measurement and should be fully tested.

Where the seeking-work criterion is relaxed, a person without work would be considered unemployed if, given a work opportunity, he or she is able and ready to work. The meaning of the conditional element 'given a work opportunity' is more ambiguous when the seeking-work criterion is relaxed than when it is not. When the seeking work criterion is applied, the conditional element is linked to the type of work sought by the job-seeker, as most active steps to seek work imply that the job-seeker has some idea of the type of work he or she has been looking for. However, when the seeking-work criterion is relaxed, this link is cut and the notion of 'given a work opportunity' is much less clear. The context to which current availability refers should then be specified by indicating the particulars of the potential work opportunities in terms of remuneration, working time, location, occupation, etc.

The international standards recognise that apart from special circumstances (e.g. school attendance, family responsibilities, infirmity or disablement) availability for work depends essentially on the nature of potential work opportunities. They recommend that in 'the application of the criterion of current availability for work, especially in situations where the "seeking-work" criterion is relaxed, appropriate tests should be developed to suit national circumstances. Such tests may be based on notions such as present desire for work, previous work experience, willingness to take up work for wage or salary on locally prevailing terms, or readiness to undertake self-employment activity, given the necessary resources and facilities.'

Underemployment

Unemployment is defined in the labour force framework as an extreme situation of total lack of work. Less extreme situations of partial lack of work are all embodied within the concept of employment, broadly defined as engagement in an economic activity for at least one hour during the reference period. It is for identifying such situations of partial lack of work and for complementing the statistics on employment and unemployment that the concept of underemployment has been introduced. According to the international standards, underemployment exists 'when a person's employment is inadequate, in relation to specified norms or alternative employment, account being taken of his or her occupation skill (training and working experience)'.

The measurement of underemployment has particular relevance in developing countries, notably in agricultural activities. In many developing countries, because of high prevalence of self-employment, limited coverage of workers by unemployment insurance or social security systems and other reasons, the level of measured unemployment is consistently low. This has been explained by the fact that only few people can afford to be unemployed for some period of time, whereas the bulk of the population must engage themselves in some economic activity, however little or inadequate that may be. In such circumstances, the employment situation cannot be fully described by unemployment data alone and the statistics should be supplemented with data on underemployment.

While the measurement of underemployment has mostly been recommended for describing the employment situation in developing countries, its relevance for industrialised countries is also increasingly felt. This is because in many countries, due to the recent changes in the employment situation and the rise of various forms of precarious employment, new situations have emerged that can be regarded as underemployment. In fact, the 1987 ICLS agreed on the usefulness of the concept of underemployment in relation to the employment situation of participants in certain categories of employment promotion schemes, though mentioning that the concept may need further elaboration in this context.

Visible and invisible underemployment

The international standards distinguish between two principal forms of underemployment: visible underemployment and invisible underemployment. Visible underemployment reflects an insufficiency in the volume of employment and is thus a statistical concept which is directly measurable by surveys. Invisible underemployment is primarily an analytical concept reflecting a misallocation of labour resources or a fundamental imbalance between labour and other factors of production. The characteristic symptoms of invisible underemployment, as indicated in the international standards, might be low income, underutilisation of skill, or low productivity.

A comprehensive study of invisible underemployment involves analysis of a wide variety of data, including income and skill levels (disguised underemployment) and productivity measures (potential underemployment). Data requirements for the measurement of invisible underemployment are thus very demanding and involve a number of unresolved difficulties (e.g. evaluating the quality of jobs against the skills of the incumbents, linking data on the productivity of establishments to data on the characteristics of individual workers). Recognising the formidable measurement problems involved, the 1982 international standards state that 'for operational reasons, the statistical measurement of underemployment may be limited to visible underemployment'.

Visible underemployment

The international standards consider two elements in the measurement of visible underemployment: the number of persons visibly underemployed; and the quantum of visible underemployment. The first element gives results in terms of number of persons, and the second element is measured in terms of time units such as working days, half-days or hours.

Persons visibly underemployed

According to the international standards, persons visibly underemployed comprise 'all persons in paid or self-employment, whether at work or not at work, involuntarily working less than the normal duration of work determined for the activity, who were seeking or available for additional work during the reference period'. Thus, the definition sets forth three criteria for identification of the visibly underemployed: working less than normal duration; doing so on an involuntary basis; and seeking or being available for additional work during the reference period. For considering a person as visibly underemployed, all three criteria must be satisfied simultaneously.

The concept applies to all employed persons, not only to persons in paid employment but also to persons in self-employment, and not only to those currently at work but also to those temporarily absent from work. The underemployed being a subgroup of the employed, the concept does not apply to the population not economically active. By definition, an economically inactive person cannot be underemployed.

Working less than normal duration

Assessment of this criterion involves comparing the number of hours worked by a particular worker during the reference period with the number of hours that workers normally work in the corresponding activity. Visible underemployment being a characteristic of a person and not of an activity, special provisions have to be made for multiple job-holders so as to account for all of their activities.

There are essentially two approaches for identifying work of less than normal duration in a survey. One approach is to ask respondents directly whether or not they worked less than normal duration. The other approach is to obtain information on both normal and individual hours of work and compare the two. The first approach may be suitable where the working hours of the bulk of the population are contractually regulated and survey respondents know about these regulations. Otherwise, the second approach should be used.

Determination of normal duration of work

The international standards specify that, for the purpose of classifying persons as visibly underemployed, normal duration of work for an activity should be determined 'as reflected in national legislation to the extent it is applicable, and usual practice in other cases, or in terms of a uniform conventional norm'. Assessment of normal hours of work in surveys raises certain difficulties. In its strict sense, the notion is essentially limited to regular paid employees, whose working time is regulated by national legislation, collective agreements or at least by a written or verbal employment contract. However, such regulations may vary from one branch of economic activity to another, and even for a given branch they may differ among establishments or according to the occupation, age and other characteristics of the worker. This means that normal hours of work would have to be assessed on an individual basis.

Moreover, similar provisions for casual workers, multiple job-holders and self-employed persons do not generally exist, so that in such cases the normal duration of work would have to be determined on the basis of usual practices. Even this may, however, be difficult in cases where the hours of work usually spent in a given activity are highly variable among workers. This may particularly be the case in agricultural and seasonal activities.

The international standards suggest therefore, as an alternative method, to use a uniform conventional norm (e.g. 30, 35, 40 hours) for the normal duration of work. Such a norm is to be defined in the light of national circumstances and to be applied to all activities and all categories of workers. In assessing visible underemployment, special provisions have then to be made for workers who, though reporting working hours below the uniform norm, are nevertheless to be considered as fully employed, since full-time work in their activity does not involve more hours of work (teachers, judges, etc.).

Involuntary nature

Having identified that a person is working less than normal duration, one has to assess whether this situation is involuntary or not. This may be determined in surveys by asking for the reason why a person worked less than normal duration. The importance of this second criterion of the international definition of persons visibly underemployed results from the fact that there are many different reasons for working less than normal duration. In certain situations, persons are forced to do so for economic reasons, i.e. they are faced with a slack period, material shortages, etc., or they cannot find more work. However, there are also situations where persons decide voluntarily to work less. This is the case of many working women with children, young persons combining studies with employment, or elderly workers voluntarily participating in phased retirement schemes. Moreover, for the purpose of measuring visible underemployment, the notion of 'involuntary reason' should be interpreted in the sense of 'due to the economic situation' so as to exclude other involuntary reasons like illness, disablement, etc.

Seeking or available for additional work

Finally, to be considered as visibly underemployed, a person involuntarily working less than normal duration must be seeking or available for additional work during the reference period. The purpose of this criterion is twofold: first, the criterion serves to reinforce the probe on the involuntary nature of short-time work; second, it is used to maintain consistency with the activity principle embedded in the labour force framework.

The notion of additional work should be interpreted in a broad sense. It is meant to refer to all work arrangements and types of work that could increase a person's total working hours. Additional work may thus mean: working more hours at the present job; obtaining a job of the same or a different type in addition to the present one; replacing the present job by another one of the same or a different type, but with more hours; or combinations of these. In the case of self-employment, additional work should be interpreted so as to cover not only an increase in the number of working hours but also an increase in the number of clients or orders.

Quantum of visible underemployment

According to the 1982 international standards, quantum of visible underemployment refers to the aggregate 'time available for additional employment during the reference period in respect of each person visibly underemployed ... computed in units of working days, half-days or hours as may be convenient in national circumstances, depending on the nature of the data collected'.

The international standards particularly mention two methods for measuring the time available for additional employment, without excluding other possibilities. The first method is based on a direct inquiry on the duration of work sought, i.e. on the number of additional days, half-days or hours of work sought or available for during the reference period up to the normal duration of work. Difficulties may, however, arise in the case of workers not remunerated on time rates, such as many self-employed persons, piece-rate workers, home-based workers and workers remunerated by the task. Such persons may not think in terms of duration of work sought but rather in terms of the amount of extra orders they could accept, the number of additional clients they could cope with, etc.

The second method, called labour-time disposition, is more precise but also more complex. It consists of compiling, on a day-by-day basis, for each person concerned, a balance sheet of the total labour time potentially available, broken down into time employed (or, more precisely, time worked), time available for employment and time not available for employment during the reference period. When compiled for all persons in the labour force, the labour-time disposition approach also permits derivation of a composite estimate of the quantum of current unemployment and visible underemployment. It should also be mentioned that the approach offers many other possibilities for data analysis. In particular, many different work patterns can be revealed, e.g. full-time/full-week, full-time/part-week, part-time/full-week and part-time/part-week employment.

Employment and income relationships

Inadequacy of employment may result from a number of different factors, among which insufficient volume of employment (in terms of time worked) and low remuneration are the two most obvious ones. Statistics on unemployment and visible underemployment provide insight only on the first of these factors. They do not provide any information on the adequacy of the incomes obtained from employment and on related social aspects. The limitation of the concepts of unemployment and visible underemployment becomes evident, for example, in the case of persons who, though fully employed in terms of hours, have low earnings and therefore seek extra or different work. Another example applies to the situation of self-employed persons, where a lack of demand may result in low intensity of work and low income rather than in a reduction of time spent at work. This is because there is a tendency for such persons to spread their work over time rather than to work short-time when the demand for their products or services is low. Such situations are as important for employment policies as are unemployment and visible underemployment.

So as to indicate the need for supplementing statistics of employment, unemployment and invisible underemployment with statistics that would provide insights on the income aspect of employment inadequacy, the 1982 international standards recommend that countries develop data collection programmes for the analysis of the relationships between employment and income. In particular, data should be compiled for the purpose of analysing the income-generating capacity of different economic activities, and identifying the number and characteristics of persons who are unable to maintain their economic well-being on the basis of the employment opportunities available to them. However, the relationships between employment and income are complex, and up to now relatively little national or international experience exists regarding statistics on these topics. Thus, there is still much work to be done in the future.

Notes

1. This paper is based on various chapters drafted by Farhad Mehran and the author for a Manual on Surveys of the Economically Active Population, being prepared by the ILO Bureau of Statistics. The paper is a revised version of papers presented to the Caribbean Round Table on Employment Planning and Policy Issues, Grenada, 3-5 August, 1988, and to the ESCAP/ILO Seminar on Employment and Unemployment Statistics, Bangkok, 16-20 January 1989.
2. The SNA is currently under review; the revised version (planned for 1990) will entail, among others, some slight modifications in the delineation of the production boundary.

References

International Labour Office (1983) 'Thirteenth International Conference of

Labour Statisticians, Resolution concerning statistics of the economically active population, employment, unemployment and underemployment' (text also in French and Spanish), *Bulletin of Labour Statistics*, 1983:3, pp. xi-xv.

International Labour Organisation (1988) *Fourteenth International Conference of Labour Statisticians, Geneva, 28 October-6 November 1987, Report of the Conference*, (ICLS/14/D.14), ILO, Geneva, 1988.

United Nations (1980) *Principles and Recommendations for Population and Housing Censuses*, Statistical Papers Series M no. 67(ST/ESA/STAT/SER.M/67), New York, 1980.

9 The concept and boundary of economic activity for the measurement of the economically active population

M. T. Dupré, R. Hussmanns and F. Mehran

Introduction

The 'economically active population' comprises all persons of either sex who furnish the supply of labour for the production of economic goods and services as defined by the United Nations systems of national accounts and balances, during a specified time-reference period. According to these systems, the production of economic goods and services includes all production and processing of primary products, whether for the market, for barter or for own consumption the production of all other goods and services for the market and, in the case of households which produce such goods and services for the market, the corresponding production for own consumption (ILO 1983).

A clear understanding of the concept and boundary of economic activity is a fundamental requirement for the correct application of the definitions of employment, unemployment and economically active population in surveys of households or individuals. The exact boundary between economic and non-economic activities is to some extent a matter of convention, but unless a precise line is drawn the exact statistical treatment of many situations encountered in practice cannot be resolved and, as a consequence, the resulting statistics are likely to be subject to more controversy and to higher response errors than there would otherwise be.

The concept of economic activity adopted by the 13th ICLS in 1982 (ILO 1983) for the measurement of the economically active population is defined in terms of production of economic goods and services as set forth by the United Nations System of National Accounts (SNA) (United Nations, 1968a). Thus persons should be counted as economically active if (and only if) they contribute or are available to contribute to the production of economic goods and services falling within the SNA production boundary. The use of a uniform definition of economic activity serves to ensure that the activity concepts of employment statistics and production statistics are consistent, thus facilitating the joint analysis of the two bodies of statistics.

Economic activity as defined by the present SNA[1] covers production for sale (market production) and certain types of production for own consumption (non-market production), including production and processing of primary products for own consumption, own-account construction and other production of fixed assets for own use. It excludes unpaid domestic activities, volunteer community services and certain other types of unpaid activities.

The purpose of this section is to explain these terms for use in surveys of economically active populations. The next section begins with the SNA definition of economic activity in terms of production of economic goods and services, then explains in some detail its two components: market production and non-market production. Examples of particular activities are given, indicating which should be considered as economic activity and which not. The treatment of illegal activities is also analysed. This is followed by an examination of some important activities which, though according to the present definition falling outside the boundary of economic activity, are nevertheless recognised as providing a major contribution to output and to the welfare of the population. Two particular sets of such activities (domestic activities and volunteer community services) are examined in more detail. Finally, we review national practices in measuring economic activity in surveys, and suggest the use of an activity list as one possibility to cope with some of the cognitive issues involved.

Economic activities

Production of economic goods and services

The production of economic goods and services as specified in the SNA comprises:

(a) Production of goods and services normally intended for sale on the market at a price that is designed to cover their cost of production (UN, 1986a, para. 6.2 and p. 232).

(b) Production of other goods and services which are not normally sold on the market at a price intended to cover their cost of production. These items correspond to government services and private non-profit services to households, to domestic services rendered by one household to another and other items (UN, 1986a, para. 6.2 and p. 235).

(c) Specified types of production for own consumption and fixed capital formation for own use (UN, 1986a, paras. 6.19 and 6.23) including:
(i) primary products, that is, the characteristic products of agriculture, fishing, forestry and logging and mining and quarrying;

(ii) the processing of primary commodities by the producers of these items in order to make such goods as butter, cheese, flour, wine, oil, cloth or furniture whether or not any of these products are sold by their producer on the market;

(iii) production of other commodities *only* if they are *also* produced for the market by the same household;

(iv) fixed assets, that is, own-account construction of structures, roads and similar works as well as tools, instruments, containers and similar items which have an expected life of use of one year or more; and

(v) the total rent of owner-occupied dwellings.

This definition of production of economic goods and services excludes by default production for own consumption of other items, such as the processing of primary commodities by those who do not produce them; the production of other commodities by households who do not sell any part of them on the market; and repair and maintenance of constructions and other structures carried out by households for themselves. It also excludes unpaid domestic activities such as cooking food for own consumption, sewing or mending clothes for own use, teaching or looking after own children.

The rationale for the inclusion of certain types of non-market production and the exclusion of others in the present SNA definition lies in the importance of the activities in many countries and the frequent existence of 'close' market parallels, i.e. the existence of identical or very similar goods and services which are usually also available on the market (United Nations, 1986a). There are also practical considerations involved. When the same persons are engaged in both market and non-market production, it is, in practice, often impossible to measure the two components separately, and therefore in setting the SNA production boundary either both components should have been included or both should have been excluded. Since the SNA definition was meant to cover market production completely, it was necessary to include the non-market component as well. A similar argument applies for the particular treatment of processing of primary products for own consumption which cannot be separated from the production of those products by the same households.

The concept of economic activity for the measurement of the economically active covers all activities corresponding to *(a)*, *(b)* and *(c)* defined above, except for *(c)(v)*. This last item represents a monetary value rather than an activity. For convenience the activities corresponding to *(a)* and *(b)* are designated here as market production (or market activities), while those corresponding to *(c)(i)-(c)(iv)* are called non-market production (or non-market activities). The aggregate of market production and non-market production constitutes the set of economic activities. All other activities are called non-economic activities. The distinction between market and non-market production is convenient not only to highlight the fact that economic activity includes certain types of non-market production but also because the methods to be used for identifying the economic activity of individuals in surveys may differ according to the type of production. The scope of economic activity in terms of the different types of production is shown schematically in Figure 9.1.

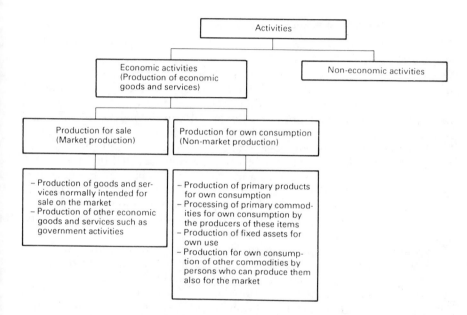

Figure 9.1 The scope of economic activity in terms of the SNA concept of production of economic goods and services

In centrally planned economies using the material product system, the concept of production is confined to material production, that is production of goods and services related to the production, repair, transportation and distribution of goods (usually referred to as material services). It excludes all other services of the SNA concept (for details see United Nations, 1977). In measuring the economically active population, however, employment in both the productive and the non-productive spheres is covered. The statistics are generally compiled showing the two categories separately (United Nations, 1986b).

Production for sale (market production)

Production for sale, or market production, includes activities of workers employed in factories, firms, farms, shops, service undertakings, family businesses and other economic units engaged in production of goods and services intended for sale on the market. It also includes activities of employees of government and other social and cultural institutions, even though their output may not normally be sold on the market (or if so at a price which is often not intended to cover their cost of production). In general, market production covers all activities given in the International Standard Classification of All Economic Activities (ISIC 1968), i.e. agriculture, hunting, forestry and fishing; mining and quarrying; manufacturing; electricity, gas and water; construction; wholesale and retail trade, restaurants and hotels; transport, storage and communication; financing, insurance, real estate and business services; and community, social and personal services (United Nations, 1968b).

Typically, market production involves some form of remuneration to those who contribute to it. Remuneration may be in the form of pay or profit. Pay includes cash payment or payment in kind, whether payment is received in the period the work is done or not. Cash payment may be in the form of direct wages or salaries at time or piece rates, fees or tips, bonuses or gratuities, or other forms of payment. Payment in kind may be in the form of food, drink, fuel, housing and rental allowances, or other goods and services. Payment in kind as the sole means of remuneration is not uncommon in some countries, particularly for agricultural workers receiving a share of the harvest or for certain types of apprentice working just for bed and board.

Production for profit is another form of market production. It includes, for example, activities of farmers, traders, craft workers, shopkeepers, doctors, lawyers and the like who are operating their own farm or business with or without employees and with or without sales or clients during the specified time-period set for the inquiry, even if no profit is actually made. It similarly includes the activities of family members undertaken in connection with the operation of a household enterprise producing for the market, even if no direct payments are received for the work done.

Production for own consumption (non-market production)

The four relevant types of non-market production included in the SNA boundary of production are explained below.

Primary production for own consumption comprises characteristic products of agriculture, hunting, forestry and fishing and mining and quarrying. It corresponds to activities of major divisions 1 and 2 of ISIC 1968. Throughout the world many farmers, hunters, fishermen and other persons feed themselves and their families with the crops they grow, the cattle they raise, the animals they hunt and the fish they catch. Many also use the stones they collect or the wood they cut for shelter and heating. Primary commodities produced by households for their own use form a major part of household consumption in many countries and the corresponding output is generally included in their national accounts and balances. Furthermore, since a shift takes place from production for own consumption to market production as economic development proceeds, it is essential to account for these household activities in the employment statistics as well, so as to obtain a comparable measure of the economically active population at different periods or for different countries. Examples of primary production for own consumption which according to the SNA should be included as economic activity are listed in the first column of Table 9.1.

Processing of primary commodities for own consumption covers activities such as milling grain, slaughtering, preparing and preserving meat, making butter, cheese and other dairy products, spinning and tanning, making baskets and mats, constructing wooden furniture and fixtures, etc. They mostly correspond to major groups 31, 32 and 33 of the major division 3 (Manufacturing) of ISIC 1968. In a number of countries many households undertake a substantial amount of primary processing of this kind for their own use. Whether they sell any of these items or not, such activities are conventionally considered as economic activity and, where significant, generally accounted for in the national accounts and balances. It should be emphasised that these various activities are considered as economic activity only if they involve the processing of *primary* products. Thus, pounding maize (a primary product) to make cornflour is included, but using flour (a processed product) to bake bread is excluded. Similarly, spinning cotton fibres (a primary product) is included, but using cloth (a processed product) for sewing is excluded. Further examples are given in the second column of Table 9.1 It should further be noted that the SNA includes only the processing of primary commodities *by the producers of these items*, which means that the processing for own consumption of primary commodities by those who do not produce them is excluded. Thus, crushing oil-seeds bought at the market is not included, but crushing oil-seeds produced by oneself is.

Production of fixed assets for own use covers essentially own-account construction (ISIC major division 5). It includes the building of houses, roads, wells and other private facilities. In the case of a number of countries house-building, in particular, is undertaken to a significant

Table 9.1 Examples of non-market production covered by the SNA concept of production of economic goods and services

All to be included		Mainly to be excluded (unless produced also for the market)	
Primary production	*Processing primary products**	*Fixed capital formation*	
– growing field crops, fruit and vegetables	– threshing and milling grain	– construction of dwellings	– repairing and maintaining dwellings and garden shelters
– producing eggs, milk	– making butter, ghee and cheese	– construction of farm buildings	– storing crops if not part of the production process itself
– hunting animals and birds	– slaughtering livestock	– building boats and canoes	
– catching fish, crabs and shellfish	– curing hides and skins	– clearing land for cultivation	– dress-making and tailoring
– cutting firewood and erecting poles	– preserving meat and fish		– handicrafts not involving primary products and not being fixed capitals (e.g. metal hollow-ware, rubber shoes)
– collecting thatching and weaving materials	– making beer, wine and spirits		
	– crushing oil-seeds		
– mining salt	– weaving baskets and mats		– midwife services
– cutting peat	– making clay pots and plates		– funeral services

Source: Based on 'Conceptual Framework of the Revised SNA', joint paper prepared by the Statistical Offices of the UNO, OECD, ECE, IMF and the World Bank for the Inter-Secretariat Working Group on National Accounts, EEC, Geneva, 3-7 March 1986.
* These articles are only included if they involve the processing of *primary* products by the producers of these items. Pounding maize (a primary product) to make cornflour is included in gross output, but using flour (a processed product) to bake bread is excluded.

extent on an own-account basis and contributes to the housing stock of the nation. On the same basis, own-account production of tools, instruments, containers and similar items which have a significant expected life of use (i.e. long enough to be classified as investment goods, say, one year or more) is, in principle, also considered as economic activity. Examples are given in the third column of Table 9.1. It should be mentioned that own-account construction does not generally include repairs. It may, however, include certain types of improvement such as the extension of a farmhouse, construction of a second floor, or major renovation of the dwelling.

Production of other non-primary products for own consumption covers mostly manufacturing but can also include trade, transportation, communication and all other services. These activities carried out for own consumption are considered as economic activity only if they are conducted in conjunction with market production. Thus, when a shoemaker, who normally produces for the market, makes shoes for the family, that activity is considered as non-market production, and, hence, as part of economic activity. This type of non-market production affects the measurements of output, of value added, of income, etc., but does not generally have an impact on the measurement of the economically active population. This is because persons producing both for the market and for own consumption will in any case be included among the economically active on the basis of their market production, irrespective of the additional production for their own consumption. The non-market part of production can, however, affect the measurement of hours worked and related concepts.

It can be noted from the above descriptions that non-market production (as well as market production) is defined in terms of the end use of the product and not on the basis of the paid or unpaid nature of the production. For example, growing vegetables for own consumption is non-market production not because the activity is unpaid but because the product is not intended for sale on the market. Also, it should be noted that the use of the term 'non-market' does not mean that no market transaction at all is taking place in the production process. An example of non-market production involving market transactions is the activity of a person who buys seeds in the market for growing vegetables, but retains the output for his own consumption.

Examples of particular activities

In many countries a substantial part of the population is working as paid employees in enterprises or government, or running a farm or a business producing goods and services for sale on the market. There are also many individuals, particularly in rural areas in developing countries, working on land producing agricultural and allied products for their own consumption. In the light of the definition of economic activity given earlier, it is clear that all these activities are economic and the persons involved are part of the economically active population. However, there are many borderline situations where it is not immediately obvious whether certain types of activity should be considered as economic activity and the persons involved considered as economically active.

List A below gives some examples of particular activities which should be considered as economic activity in line with the SNA concepts of production of economic goods and services described earlier (market or non-market production). A second list (list B) gives examples of other activities which should not be considered as economic activity for the measurement of the economically active population. The two lists supplement the examples of Table 9.1 which concerns non-market production.

The following are examples of situations which *should be considered as economic activity* in line with the SNA concept of production of economic goods and services:

A1. vending newspapers or lottery tickets in the street; cleaning car windshields for tips at traffic lights;

A2. managing one's own business or farm even though not involved in producing the output;

A3. repairing work equipment by a self-employed person for future operation, e.g. a fisherman repairing his boat or net for future outings;

A4. buying or installing equipment and ordering supplies in preparation for opening a new business;

A5. work in a household enterprise without pay but with a share in the earnings of the enterprise;

A6. unpaid family work in an economic enterprise operated by a related person living in the same household; including work such as cleaning and grading cash-crops;

A7. outwork, the practice prevalent in some enterprises where part of the work is put out to different households to do at home for payment on a piece-rate basis, e.g. the master weaver putting out jobs to different households, or the *bidi* manufacturer in India getting the *bidis* (local leaf-wrapped cigarettes) produced through distribution of work to different households;

A8. exchange work, the practice in some countries of exchanging labour between households for productive purposes, such as the work performed by a farm operator or members of his family on the farm of another farmer on an exchange labour arrangement;

A9. production of goods or services for barter, e.g. the practice among some nomadic households of exchanging sheep's milk, butter or other home-made products for clothing or footwear produced by other households;

A10. work for an employer or landlord or money-lender under obligation (mostly a debt) without pay or with less than normal pay till the debt is reimbursed;

A11. paid domestic services, including babysitting, teaching children in other persons' homes in exchange for cash payment or bed and board or other types of payment-in-kind such as clothing;

A12. cooking food specially for labourers working in one's farm when food is provided as part of the labourers' wages;

A13. apprenticeship and on-the-job training for which some pay is received in exchange for goods or services produced during training;

A14. paid religious activity of members of religious orders;

A15. military duties of career military personnel as well as conscripts and others engaged in equivalent civilian service.

The following are examples of situations which *should not be considered as economic activity*, i.e. falling outside the SNA production boundary:

B1. work done without pay for a related member of the household who does not own a farm or business but is himself or herself a salaried employee, such as typing for a spouse who is a lawyer employed in a corporation;

B2. work without pay for an unrelated member of the household, e.g. work in a grocery store owned by a lodger;

B3. work without pay for a relative not living in the same household, e.g. helping out in the tea-shop of an uncle who lives in another household (however, as suggested in United Nations, 1980, where it is customary for young persons, in particular, to work without pay in an economic enterprise operated by a related person who does not live in the same household, such work may be considered as economic activity);

B4. unpaid domestic activities such as housework, mowing the lawn, painting the house;

B5. on-the-job training when the financial compensation received is not related to the goods or services produced but is simply an allowance to enable the person to take the training, e.g. student nurses, armed forces reserves;

B6. volunteer work without pay for organisations such as the local hospital, the parent and school association, or unpaid community work for local road surfacing, etc.;

B7. work in prison farms or workshops even if some form of compensation for work is received; payments to prisoners and the costs of feeding and housing them are all regarded as part of government intermediate consumption in the SNA;

B8. investing in a business but contributing no part either to management or actual operation, e.g. holding shares or stocks in a company.

Lists A and B above are not exhaustive. Many other particular situations may present themselves in practice, e.g. employment-training schemes now being developed in most European countries; various types of unpaid apprenticeship common in many African countries. In each case their inclusion or exclusion from the scope of economic activity should be examined with reference to the details of the SNA definition of production of economic goods and services, in the context of the measurement of the economically active population and of the prevailing national circumstances.

Treatment of illegal activities

The SNA concept of economic activity does not distinguish between the legal and *illegal* nature of the activities. Two types of illegal activity should, however, be differentiated. The first type includes activities which are by themselves legal, but conducted in an illegal fashion, such as the work of an illegal immigrant in a citrus farm, work in the construction industry without a work permit, selling legal merchandise without a licence, working off-the-book for tax evasion or for fear of losing unemployment insurance benefits or because the employer wants to avoid social security payments or other labour legislations. These activities should, in principle, be considered as economic activity. In practice, however, their measurement may be extremely difficult and their effects on employment and unemployment statistics are difficult to assess (McDonald, 1984).

The second type of illegal activity refers to activities which are illegal in themselves, such as prostitution through soliciting in some countries, loan-sharking, pushing drugs. The appropriate statistical treatment of these activities is not conceptually clear. The present SNA does not refer to the legality of an activity in deciding whether or not it should be included in gross output. In a recent international examination of this issue, a conclusion was that '*in principle* the production of illegal goods and services is included in gross output, but whether a country should *in practice* include any particular type of illegal production would depend on its relative importance and on the possibilities of making plausible estimates' (United Nations, 1986c). The issue is to be discussed further as part of the forthcoming revision of the SNA.

Non-economic activities

Quasi-economic activities

While the SNA definition of production of economic goods and services covers a wide range of activities, many other activities still remain outside its scope. Examples are unpaid activities such as domestic activities, child care, dressmaking for own use, do-it-yourself repair, storing crops, carrying water for own domestic use, volunteer help in hospitals, free delivery of food to the elderly at their homes. It is recognised that most of these activities, though not considered as economic for the measurement of the economically active population, contribute to the output and welfare of the society. In fact, many of them are just at the outside boundary of economic activities and their exclusion is essentially a matter of convention. For instance, in rural households where fresh food is prepared daily, the dividing line between food processing (an activity included within the boundary) and cooking for the family (an excluded activity) is difficult to draw. Furthermore, while cooking for one's own family is excluded from the scope of economic activity, cooking food for labourers working on one's farm is included on the ground that food is provided as part of the labourers' wages.

In general, these activities include all non-market production of non-primary goods and services which are not already considered as part of economic activity. For convenience they may be referred to as 'quasi-economic activities'. The discussion below is limited to two particular sets of such activities, namely domestic activities and volunteer community services.

Unpaid domestic activities

The current debate on data collection regarding domestic activities is essentially centred around three main issues: the exact scope and definition of domestic activities; how these activities should be identified and measured in practice; and what monetary value should be imputed to them for statistical and other purposes (such as national income accounting, matrimonial property settlements and compensation issues following losses in household production services due to wrongful injury or death). Without entering into details, it may be useful to point out here some of the main points for possible application in household surveys.

Domestic activities may be defined in a number of ways. One is based on the so-called 'third-person' criterion. According to this criterion domestic activities are distinguished from other unpaid activities of the household (e.g. study, leisure) by the fact that the latter can only be performed by the household member in question, whereas the former may, conceivably, be done by someone else (a third person) without diminishing its indirect utility. Thus, doing school work at home or playing the piano at home for pleasure are not domestic activities in this sense, but washing the dishes or repairing the oven are. For a more precise formulation of the definition, see Hawrylyshyn (1977).

The identification and measurement of domestic activities is commonly made on the basis of time-use surveys, according to which individuals are asked about their daily activities over a certain period, using various methods of data collection. For a discussion of time-use surveys in connection with labour force surveys, see Hoffmann (1981).

Methods used for monetary imputation of domestic activities are generally based on input evaluations using, for example, the wage of a fictitious substitute household worker or an average wage for equivalent market services or the wage forgone by the household member or a flat wage such as the minimum wage. Certain monetary imputations are sometimes also based on output evaluations, for example using the price of an equivalent market product or other price imputations. For a discussion of the various methodologies as well as numerical estimates of monetary evaluations of domestic activities in various countries, see Goldschmidt-Clermont (1982; 1985).

Volunteer community services

In most countries volunteer workers contribute to private non-profit organisations for supplying various social services to their community such as child and elderly welfare, education and medical related services. Sometimes emergency services such as sea rescue and fire services are also organised on a voluteer basis. Furthermore, in many developing countries, particularly in rural areas, household members often provide work on a volunteer basis for community development, such as filling ditches, cleaning tanks, and flood prevention.

In general, the purpose of voluntary work is to provide a service to others. In a study conducted in Australia it has been defined as 'any work undertaken without coercion for an organisation either in an unpaid capacity or for a token payment' (Paterson, 1982). Embedded in this definition are three basic elements: the activity is essentially unpaid; it is carried out freely without coercion; and it is performed for an organisation as opposed to a family member, a friend, etc. Data on voluntary work have been obtained through surveys of welfare agencies and specially designed household surveys. Methods to estimate the value of voluntary work include the use of the earning rates of the paid employees of the welfare organisations or the market value of similar services provided by profit-making establishments or a fictitious rate uniformly applied to all types of voluntary work. For more detailed discussion on voluntary community work in different countries see, among others, Gidron (1980) and Le Net and Werquin (1985) and references therein.

Measurement

National practices

In measuring the economically active population in household surveys, the concept of economic activity described in this section must be conveyed in an operational way to the respondents in order to obtain accurate data. This is a fundamental requirement as it sets the frame for the classification of the economically active population and for all subsequent information collected in the course of the interview. A misunderstanding at this level may have an irremediable impact on the entire interview and on the survey results. It is therefore essential that careful attention be paid in survey design and operation to how to convey correctly the notion of economic activity in practice. Most surveys try to achieve this by formulating one or more carefully designed pre-coded questions in the survey questionnaire and by providing interviewers, through oral or written training, with explanations of the scope of economic activity for the measurement of the economically active population, illustrated with various examples of activities which are to be included and of those which are not.

A review of some 30 questionnaires of national labour force surveys indicates that almost invariably the leading question on economic activity is formulated around the key word 'work'. Typically, the term 'work' is qualified by further specifications such as gainful work; work for pay, profit, or family gain; work for money or share of output; work in a job, business or farm; work as employee or self-employed.

In many cases, the leading question is followed by explanatory notes or by one or more additional probing questions. The most common notes or probes concern unpaid family work, casual labour and other types of economic activities which experience has shown respondents may omit in their response to the initial question. Certain questionnaires include very specific probing questions relevant to national conditions. Three examples used in three different countries are:

Are you or any member of your household self-employed, e.g. as a farmer, owner of a shop or workshop? Did you do any work without pay in this business during last week? (Norway, Labour Force Sample Survey, 2nd Quarter 1986);

Do you have land or a cattlepost where you work? (Botswana, Labour Force Survey, 1984/85);

Did you carry out or help to carry out any activity last week, paid or unpaid, at home or outside, in the street or on the main road, even if it was only for a *few* hours? For example, did you help in a store, a side-street stand, a greengrocers, sell food, vegetables, newspapers, lottery tickets, cosmetics or artisanal goods, sow soil, reap produce, or breed animals *for sale*; did you wash, iron, or sew clothes *for others*, make cakes, cheese or cloth *for sale*, take care of children or elderly people *for pay*? (Argentina-Paraguay, Project 'Mano de obra y tipo de hogar', 1985).

A review of the interviewers' instructions in different countries shows that, with respect to the leading and probing questions on economic activity, training manuals essentially contain three types of guidelines: an explanation of the concept of work and economic activity; a warning that the respondents or the interviewers' understanding of the concept may be different from the concept it is intended to measure; and a list of supplementary examples of borderline activities which are to be included or excluded for the purpose of the survey. One of the most thorough training manuals reviewed (United States Bureau of the Census, 1980) contained as many as 22 pages of guidelines on this topic.

Cognitive issues

Respondents' and interviewers' subjective understanding of the notion of 'work' and 'economic activity' is unlikely to be as encompassing as that envisaged by survey definitions. This may be further influenced by cultural perceptions of sex roles. There is, for instance, a general tendency in certain cultures to consider women primarily as housewives and thereby to ignore any economic activity they may have performed. There is also the problem that certain activities commonly performed by women, particularly agricultural and related activities performed for own consumption, are on the borderline of economic activity as defined by the SNA, and as such are liable to misinterpretation, not only by interviewers or proxy-respondents but also by female respondents themselves. These cognitive issues often lead to an underreporting of economic activity in surveys, found to be particularly important in the case of women (Agarwal, 1984; Ware, 1986).

Recent research (Schwarz, 1987) indicates that the subjective under-standing of terms like 'economic activity' or 'work for pay or profit' depends on the form and probably the amount of remuneration; on one's own employment history; and, when the respondent is reporting for another person in the household, on the employment history of the target person. Proper understanding of how people comprehend these terms (as well as others used in the surveys, such as absence from work, seeking work) may have important implications on questionnaire design and survey operations. Such cognitive issues are receiving increasing attention from those conducting national household surveys of the economically active population. The following gives some examples based on studies conducted in the United States, India and Costa Rica.

In response to a question on 'paid work performed last week' asked in an experimental study conducted in the United States and analysed in Schwarz (1987), a small sample of college students reported, among other responses, to having donated blood, mowed a neighbour's lawn, done babysitting. Later, other students and a sample of university employees were asked which of these activities they considered as paid work. The results showed that not everyone considered these activities as 'paid work'. But, the college students were more likely to include these activities in the 'paid work' category than were the university employees, indicating how the notion of 'paid work' may be influenced by the respondent's employment status. It was also found that the number of student respondents who classified these activities as 'paid work' dropped sharply when it was qualified that the payment was in kind and not in cash. This indicates that respondents, in general, may be inclined to consider payment in kind as an exchange of favours rather than as compensation for the work done. A conclusion drawn from this study was that leading questions in national surveys formulated in terms like 'paid work' tend to be understood as referring only to regular forms of employment, omitting casual work and work remunerated in kind, and thus causing overall underreporting of economic activity. A suggestion was made to improve the comprehension of the concept of economic activity in surveys of OECD member countries by reformulating the question about 'paid work' in terms of 'any activity for which money or goods were received' (Schwarz, 1987, p. 6),

The measurement problem is even more acute in countries where regular forms of employment are less widespread and particularly in measuring women's economic activities in rural areas. Some evidence is provided by the results of an ILO-sponsored study conducted in three districts of Uttar Pradesh, India (Anker *et al.*, 1987). One of the purposes of the study was to analyse the effect of different approaches in collecting information of economic activities of women in rural areas. A sample of 1,621 households was divided into a hierarchy of subsamples according to a specific survey design, combining three different questionnaire formats, assignment of male versus female interviewers, and rules for choosing proxy versus self-respondents. The first questionnaire format was based on questions centred around key phrases such as 'main activity', 'secondary activity', 'any work for earnings'. The second was based on an activity schedule asking every respondent to report engagement in any of the 14

Activity list, ILO survey in Costa Rica (Original in Spanish)

Q20. Please indicate whether you worked last week
    Yes 1 → Q21   No 2 ↓

Q30. Even if you did not work last week, did you hold any job or have your own enterprise/business?

Q31. Yes, a paid employment   No 3 ↓   1

    Yes, an own enterprise or business 1

Q40. Did you carry out any of the following activities during the last week?   Code

	Code
Prepare the land, sow/plant, cultivate (weed, water, etc.) or harvest sugar cane, coffee, beans, yucca, fruits, vegetables, others	11
Look after cattle, poultry, etc., or produce milk, eggs, etc.	12
Other activities related to agriculture, mining, hunting, fishing, forestry	13
Work in the industrial processing of food products	35
Manufacture baskets, carpets/mats, other handicrafts	37
Manufacture thread, cloth, men's or women's clothing	38
Other manufacturing activities	39

Work in the construction, repair, maintenance of:

Barn	51
Own house/dwelling	52
Other activities related to construction	53
Help in the sale/distribution of meals/beverages	61
Help in the sale of agricultural products or in other retail trade establishments	62
Transport loads for marketing/storage	71
Other activities related to transport	72
Repair tools, shoes, etc	92
Collect firewood, fetch water, other services	93

Q41. *Interviewer check item*
    If at least one activity   If no activity
    marked ↓   marked → Q50

Q42. Please fill in the codes (up to 4 activities), tick the appropriate box and insert the total number of hours.
    Then go to Q50.

Code	All or part for sale	All for consumption by own household	Number of hours
☐ ☐	☐ 1	☐ 2	_____
☐ ☐	☐ 1	☐ 2	_____
☐ ☐	☐ 1	☐ 2	_____
☐ ☐	☐ 1	☐ 2	_____

Source: Dirección General de Estadística y Censos/República de Costa Rica, Organización Internacional del Trabajo, *Encuesta Metodológica sobre la Medición del Empleo, el Desempleo, el Subempleo y el Ingreso*, Costa Rica, 1983, Questionnaire.

Activity list, ILO survey in Kerala

Q20. Did(s)he do any work for pay, profit or family gain during the last 7 days? Yes 1 → Q23   No 2 ↓

Q21. Check again whether the person did any work during the last 7 days in the production or processing of any primary products, whether for the market, barter or household consumption, or in any other household or non-household economic activities, such as (circle codes as appropriate)

	Code
Growing/attending to	
coconuts	11
paddy	12
tapioca	13
other vegetables or fruits	14
other crops	15
Engagement in activities related to:	
livestock and livestock products	16
poultry and poultry products	17
Other agriculture/mining activities including hunting/forestry/ fishing	18
Hand pounding	31
Curing and preserving fish	32
Making copra and crushing	33
Other food processing activities	34
Retting coconut husk/making coir fibre	35
Making and repairing fishing nets	37
Making baskets/mats/other handicrafts	38
Spinning/weaving/dressmaking/tailoring	39
Other manufacturing activities	40
Construction/repair/maintenance of:	
farm buildings	51
own dwellings	52
Other construction activities	53
Engagement in tea shops/street vending/etc.	61
Assisting in sales of agriculture products and other retail trades	62
Carrying loads to market/for storage	71
Other transport activities	72
Operating informal chit funds	81
Other financial activities	82
Giving tuition to students (private tutoring)	91
Repair services (tools, shoes, etc.)	92
Collection of firewood, fetching water and other services	93

Source: Kerala Statistical Institute, International Labour Office, Methodological Survey on the Measurement of Employment, Unemployment, Underemployment and Income, Trivandrum 1983, Questionnaire C.

activities listed in the schedule. The third questionnaire format combined key-worded questions with activity schedule. The results concerning question comprehension indicated sharp increases in reported activities when the activity schedule was used as opposed to the key-worded format (measured activity rate of 88.3 per cent as compared to 15.7 per cent in the most extreme situation). The results concerning the effects of male versus female interviewers and proxy versus self-response were not as conclusive, and found to be dependent on the questionnaire format itself.

Similar but much less drastic results were obtained in two other ILO methodological surveys conducted in Costa Rica and Kerala, India, in 1983-4. In these surveys only respondents who gave a negative answer to the leading question on 'work for pay, profit or family gain' were probed by using activity lists as shown below.

Out of the 2,055 persons in the Costa Rica survey who initially reported not having worked for pay, profit or family gain, 102 were found, when probes with the activity list were made, to have nevertheless performed some economic activity during the reference week. This represented a 4.2 per cent increase in the reported total number of persons engaged in economic activity as a result of using the activity list. A preliminary estimate for the corresponding percentage increase in the Kerala survey was 5.4 per cent. In addition to probing, the activity list, being an integral part of the questionnaire, had no doubt the indirect effect of reminding the interviewer throughout the whole interview of the range of activities to be considered as economic. (This may explain to some extent the relatively small effect of the activity list observed in the Costa Rica and Kerala surveys (see above) as compared with the Uttar Pradesh result cited earlier.)

Conclusions

The SNA concept of economic activity is complex and therefore, not always easy to convey to respondents in surveys. However, measurement should not be very difficult in the case of persons working in regular full-time, full-year paid employment or self-employment. Any one of the conventional leading questions on 'work' or 'economic activity' used in well-established surveys should suffice to elucidate accurate response from persons working in such conditions. But, the more the work status deviates from these 'core' situations, the more the cognitive problems discussed in this section may become important. Persons engaged in economic activities such as part-time work, casual work, unpaid family labour, non-market production may not comprehend the leading question as referring to their situation. Many activities may thus go unreported. The underreporting may be reduced by supplementing the conventional leading question with appropriate probing questions. What is appropriate depends on national conditions and in particular on the extent and nature of non-core work situations prevailing in the country. Where such situations are widespread and varied, probing questions formulated in terms of an activity list may prove useful. The activity list should as a minimum cover the most important activities in the country which otherwise are suspected to go unreported. The length and content of appropriate activity lists may thus vary from one country to another.

The use of an activity list in the questionnaire cannot, of course, replace good training of interviewers and clear explanations of the scope of economic activity in the instruction manual. The definitions and the lists of examples brought together in this article may be useful as a basis for organising the training material and drafting the part of the instruction manual dealing with the concept and boundary of economic activity.

Note

1. The SNA is currently being reviewed by the United Nations Statistical Office and other national and international organisations (IARIW, 1986). The revised version is planned for 1990.

References

Agarwal, B. (1985) 'Work participation of rural women in Third World: Some data and conceptual biases', *Economic and Political Weekly*, nos. 51 and 52, Bombay, 21–28 December, pp. A-155, A-164.

Anker, R., Khan, M. E., and Gupta, R. B. (1987) 'Biases in measuring the labour force: Results of a methods test survey in Uttar Pradesh, India', *International Labour Review*, no. 2, March–April.

Gidron, B. (1980) 'Les Travailleurs bénévoles dans l'économie sociale', *Travail et Société*, no. 4, October, pp. 385–94.

Goldschmidt-Clermont, L. (1982) *Unpaid work in the household*, ILO, Geneva.

Goldschmidt-Ciermont, L. (1985) 'Domestic activities in Africa, Asia, Latin America and Oceania – A review of economic evaluation', unpublished report, ILO, Geneva.

Hawrylyshyn, O. (1977) 'Towards a definition of non-market activities', *Review of Income and Wealth*, series 23, no. 1, March, pp. 79–96.

Hoffmann, E. (1981), 'Accounting for time in labour force surveys' in this volume.

International Association for Research on Income and Wealth (1986) 'Special Issue on the Review of the United Nations System of National Accounts', *Review of Income and Wealth*, June.

International Labour Office (1983) 'Thirteenth International Conference of Labour Statisticians, 'Resolution concerning statistics of the economically active population, employment, unemployment and underemployment' (text also in French and Spanish), *Bulletin of Labour Statistics*, no. 3, pp. xi–xvi.

ILO (1983–4) 'Methodological survey on the measurement of employment, unemployment, underemployment and income in Kerala, India' in 'Instructions to Field Staff', Subrounds 3 and 4, Questionnaire C, unpublished document, Bureau of Statistics, Geneva, September 1983.

Le Net, M. and Werquin, J. (1985) 'Le Volontariat: aspects sociaux, économiques et politiques en France et dans le monde', *Notes et Etudes Documentaires*, La Documentation Française, Paris.

McDonald, R. J. (1984) 'The "underground economy" and BLS statistical data', by Richard J. McDonald, *Monthly Labor Review*, Washington, DC. January, pp. 4–18.

Paterson, H. M. (1982) 'Voluntary work in Australia', *Australian Bulletin of Labour* March, pp. 95–103.

Schwarz, N. (1987) 'Cognitive issues in labour force surveys in a multinational context'. Paper prepared for the Organisation for Economic Co-operation and Development Working party on employment and unemployment statistics, Paris, 14-16 April.

Trigueros, R. M. (1986) (1983–4) 'La encuesta metodológica de la OIT para la medición del empleo, del desempleo y del subempleo en Costa Rica' *Bulletin of Labour Statistics*, no. 1, pp. ix–xx.

UN (1968a), *A system of national accounts*, Statistical Office of the United Nations, Studies in methods, series F, no. 2, rev. 3, New York (paragraphs 5.13, 6.19 to 6.23).

UN (1968b), *International Standard Industrial Classification of all Economic Activities*, Statistical Papers, series M. no. 4, rev. 2, New York.

UN (1977), *Comparisons of the system of national accounts and the system of balances of the national economy*, Part One: *Conceptual relationships: Studies in methods*, series F, no. 20, New York (paragraphs 3.10–3.13).

UN (1980) *Principles and recommendations for population and housing censuses*. series M, no. 67, New York (paragraph 2.206).

UN (1986a) *Handbook of national accounting, Accounting for production: Sources and methods*. Series F. no. 39, New York (paragraph 2).

UN (1986b) *Draft basic methodological principles governing the compilation of the system of statistical balances of the national economy*. Provisional ST/ESA/STAT/SER.F/17/rev. 1 (Vol. 1), New York (Chapter 5).

UN (1986c) *Conceptual framework of the revised SNA*, joint paper prepared by the statistical offices of the United Nations, OECD, EEC, IMF and the World Bank for the Inter-Secretariat Working Group on National Accounts, Geneva, 3–7 March.

United States Bureau of the Census (1980) *Current population survey: Interviewer's reference manual*, CPS-250, Washington, DC.

Ware, H. (1986) 'Improving statistics and indicators on women using household surveys', draft working paper prepared for the International Research and Training Institute for the Advancement of Women (INSTRAW), Santo Domingo, and the Statistical Office of the United Nations, New York.

10 Female labour force participation in developing countries: A critique of current definitions and data collection methods

R. Anker

Introduction

It is generally recognised that data on female labour force participation are inaccurate, or at any rate incomplete. The problem is particularly acute in developing countries, where women are frequently presented as economically inactive members of society even though their labour (especially among the poor) is essential for their families' survival. A number of conferences, commissions and committees have pointed out the shortcomings of female labour force data and recommended that they be improved – in other words, that the important economic role played by women be reflected in statistics (e.g. UN/ESCAP, 1982; UN, 1980); the ILO has received its share of criticism (Dixon, 1982; Fong, 1980; Boserup, 1975).

This paper discusses the difficulties involved in obtaining accurate labour force data for Third World women, from the point of view of interviewers, respondents and labour statisticians and economists. Suggestions are then made regarding alternative definitions of the labour force and survey questionnaire structures in order to circumvent some of these problems; preliminary results from a field study are presented in order to illustrate these points.

The interview setting

The respondent

In many ways, the Third World is an ideal setting for censuses and surveys: respondents, though often relatively uneducated, are co-operative and non-response rates tend to be low.

There are also difficulties, of course. First, respondents are often overly anxious to please, answering questions in the way they believe the interviewer would like. This biases answers towards socially accepted norms. In countries where a family's social status is negatively affected by a female member working for a non-family member, it is generally believed that respondents tend to understate the labour force activity of female household members.

Second, as in developed countries, the respondent and the person about whom information is collected are not always the same. Proxy respondents may not possess detailed knowledge on the activities of other household members. But surveys are not generally concerned with whether those interviewed are self-respondents or proxy respondents. A common procedure in large surveys and censuses is to interview the 'head of the household' (usually assumed to be male) if present. None the less, many respondents are women, especially in countries where the men are likely to be working away from home. The male–female ratio varies with the time of year when interviews take place (especially where agriculture is an important male activity), with the extensiveness of female-headed households, with the time of day and the day of the week, and with the degree to which it is socially acceptable for males to interview females.

A third factor relates specifically to the sex of the respondent. Although statistical evidence is sketchy, it is generally believed that in developing countries male respondents are more likely than female respondents to understate the labour force activity of female household members (Pittin, 1982; UN, 1980, Baster, 1981; Dixon, 1982).

Fourth, interviews are often conducted in the presence of other persons (besides the respondent and interviewer), which undoubtedly affects results. In Third World countries, it is common for others, especially older persons, to make interjections, but even when they keep silent, answers are conditioned by their presence – especially, one would assume, on sensitive issues and with regard to low-status activities, which might include many of those performed by women.

The interviewer

Interviewers in large-scale surveys and censuses frequently stay in a village one or two days, often living and working in difficult conditions. They also tend to be from a higher social class than respondents and as a result may sometimes act in a condescending manner, biasing results by steering respondents towards what they (the interviewers) consider the correct answer. For Third World labour force data, this often implies an underestimate of female labour force activity.

Another problem in collecting such data in developing countries is that male interviewers (who form the majority) are commonly believed to be more likely than female interviewers to hold the preconception of women as 'housewives'; if this is so, it would cause a downward bias in reported female labour force activity rates (Baster, 1981; Recchini de Lattes and Wainerman, 1979; UN, 1980). Although there is little statistical evidence to indicate whether this belief is well founded, the fact remains that in many Third World countries male interviewers tend to interview male respondents (or female respondents in the presence of men), which, if the argument presented in the previous section on the sex of the respondent is valid, must bias the results.

It was doubtless with considerations such as these in mind that the authors of a recent document for the United Nations Economic and Social Council Commission on the Status of Women (1982) noted that 'most technical studies on the improvement of statistics and indicators on women have emphasised the importance of women's participation in statistical collection activities'.

Typical questions used in censuses and labour force surveys

Questionnaires on labour force participation typically include a filter question whose main aim is to divide persons into two categories – active and inactive (comprising those out of the labour force and those unemployed). It should be noted that no consideration is given in this paper to unemployment or its measurement.

Examples of typical short, census-type labour force questions are given below. They are taken from India and the Philippines. Italics have been introduced for emphasis – to demonstrate how these questions depend on one key word or phrase.

If you consider your total time and activities, what do you spend *most of your time* on? (*Refer here to usual or main activity*.)
(1) Working
(2) Housekeeping
....
(University of the Philippines, National Demographic Survey, 1973.)

Are you *working* as 'cultivator', 'agricultural labourer', working at 'household industries' or working under any other category other than the three mentioned? (1961 Indian Census.)

What is your *main activity*?
Secondary work (What is your other activity?) (1971 Indian Census.)

Worked any time at all last year? If 'Yes' did you *work* for major part of the last year?
Main activity last year?
Any other *work* any time last year? (1981 Indian Census.)

Let us consider for a moment how respondents would answer questions such as those given above, in particular, how they would interpret key words or phrases such as 'main activity', 'job', 'work' (assuming that these words have been translated meaningfully into the local language). Until this is understood, all other considerations are unimportant, since respondents are being asked to provide information on labour force activity based largely on these 'key' words or phrases.

An indication of the difficulty respondents face in coping with these key words is provided by survey data from Kenya. In a 1974 national sample survey of approximately 3,000 households, it was found that the reported labour force activity rate for married women aged 20-49 varied from about 20 per cent to about 90 per cent in response to questions using the words 'job' or 'work' respectively (Anker and Knowles, 1978). It seems that these respondents regarded a 'job' as wage or salary employment, while 'work' was considered to include time-consuming activities required for family survival. Similarly, the well-known fluctuations of female labour force rates between the 1961, 1971 and 1981 Indian censuses may well be largely due to the use of different key words (see above for questions employed), particularly the relatively low rate reported in the 1971 Indian Census where many women considered their 'main activity' to be 'housewife'; to many Indian women who were full-time earners, being a housewife was a more important activity (see Anker, 1983, for analyses of female labour force data from the Indian censuses and the World Fertility Surveys).

Definition of labour force activity

The difficulty faced by respondents in answering general key-word-based labour force questions becomes even more obvious when one considers the ambiguities involved in the internationally accepted definition of labour force activity – that is, what words such as 'work', 'job' and 'main activity' are *supposed* to mean.

The following two internationally accepted definitions of persons engaged in labour force activity show how the concept has changed over the past 30 years: 'persons who performed some work *for pay or profit* during a specified brief period' (ILO, 1954; emphasis added); 'all persons of either sex who furnish the supply of labour for the production of *economic goods and services* as defined by the United Nations systems of national accounts and balances' (ILO, 1983; emphasis added).

The keyword or phrase in these definitions is 'economic', or 'pay or profit'. Only those activities that are 'economic' in nature are considered labour force activities. But use of the word 'economic' begs the issue: it is still necessary to know how 'economic' is defined.

ILO recommendations defer to the United Nations system of national income accounts statistics (SNA).[1] Thus, activities that – according to the United Nations – result in goods or services which are included in the SNA, i.e. included in GNP statistics and hence related to wage or salary employment and/or entrepreneurial profit, are considered to be 'economic' (and therefore labour force) activities; other activities are considered to be 'non-economic' (and therefore non-labour force) activities. *In principle,* however, both the United Nations and the ILO recommend that activities oriented to own consumption, such as subsistence agriculture, home construction and improvement, milking animals and processing food, should also be considered labour force activities, as the following passages show:

> According to these systems [of national income accounts], the production of economic goods and services should include all *production and processing of primary products,* whether for the market, *for barter* or *for own consumption* (ILO, 1982).

> *All production of primary products* should, in principle, be included in gross output [in national income], whether for own-account consumption, for barter or for sale for money. It is also desirable to include in gross output (i) the output by producers of other commodities which are consumed in their households and which they also produce for the market and (ii) the *processing of primary commodities* by the producers of these items in order to make such goods as butter, cheese, flour, wine, oil, cloth or furniture *for their own use* though they may not sell any of these manufactures (UN, 1968; emphasis added).

According to the above recommendations, many of the activities in which Third World women are engaged should be regarded as 'economic' in nature and therefore as labour force activities. Examples are animal husbandry (tending, milking, etc.) and activities for own consumption such as processing food for storage (pickling, grinding meal, flour-making) and sewing clothes for family use.

At present, the distinction between economic (i.e. labour force) and non-economic (i.e. non-labour force) activities is often illogical or impracticable. The following three examples illustrate this. The making of footwear for own use is supposed to be an economic/labour force activity only if the material used is a primary product such as wood (and not if the material is synthetic such as rubber). Processing of food for preservation such as pickling, making butter or cheese, husking of rice, slaughtering of animals, and grinding of grain are supposed to be economic/labour force activities but cooking for the family is not; in practice, the dividing line between cooking and these other activities is often difficult to draw, especially where fresh food is prepared daily. Construction and improvement of one's house are supposed to be economic/labour force activities, whereas repairing it is not. Yet, where mud houses are common, it is difficult to distinguish between repair, improvement and construction, since such houses require frequent maintenance, often of an extensive nature. This is particularly important in countries such as India, where women spend several hours a day every few weeks resurfacing their mud floors and walls.

In addition, only certain subsistence-type activities are generally considered to be labour force activities in *national practice.* Thus, unpaid gathering of wood and fruit for family use, processing food for family use, or milking animals for family use are usually not considered to be labour force activities.[2] In an effort to correct for these anomalies, national statistical organisations have been known to create new categories. In Fiji, for example, persons had to tend more than ten chickens for this activity to be considered a labour force activity (Blacker, 1978.); in India, the 32nd round of the National Sample Survey created a new non-labour force activity described as 'Attended domestic duties and was also engaged in free collection of goods, sewing, tailoring, weaving, etc., for household use' (Government of India, 1980).

One possible explanation for anomalies such as these (and one which we subscribe to) is a straightforward sex bias in national practice. Notice that activities where women are active (such as animal husbandry, unpaid gathering, and food processing for the family) are usually not considered to be labour force activities. It is almost as if the criteria were determined on the basis of existing knowledge of male and female activity patterns.

Given the ambiguities and arbitrariness involved and the often artificial distinction between economic and non-economic activities, some have questioned the appropriateness of these distinctions for rural areas (e.g. Myrdal, 1968; Beneria, 1982; ILO, 1972). Similarly, a United Nations Asia and Pacific Centre for Women and Development (1977) report concluded that 'accurate figures of women's economic contribution are almost impossible to [obtain] in most parts of the region [Asia and the Pacific]. In the non-market sector where most women work, the distinction between economic and non-economic activities [is] seldom clear and mostly arbitrarily applied. The work activities of many women have only a weak attachment to the traditionally defined workforce.' The truth is that among the Third World poor virtually all adults and most children engage in 'economic activities' to help the family to meet its basic needs; much of this work occurs outside of the marketplace. Among the poor, it is not so much whether men, women and children are or are not economically active, but how hard they are working and what they are doing. To retain the mistaken notion that many persons must be excluded from the labour force for its measurement to be a meaningful statistic belies the actual situation in many parts of the Third World.

There is clearly a need for *several* measures of the labour force – measures that indicate the type (e.g. paid, not paid) and level (e.g. part-time, full-time) of labour force activity based on different definitions of 'economic activity'. Only in this way will it be possible for planners to have accurate and useful labour force data.

There cannot be *one* correct definition of labour force activity, in our opinion, as a simplistic distinction between labour force and non-labour force activities must be ambiguous and arbitrary for subsistence activities. In addition, not all aspects of labour supply and labour markets can be covered by one definition, and there is great variation in the accuracy with which data on various segments of the labour force are reported.

In the light of such considerations, four possible labour force definitions are proposed below, at increasing levels of inclusion.[3] Each of these definitions provides different information on the labour market and on the various forms of contribution to national income.

(i) *Paid labour force* (persons in wage or salary employment for which they are paid in cash or kind). This category corresponds fairly closely to the employment status category of 'employees' in current use; it is also in line with the recommendations of the Thirteenth International Conference of Labour Statisticians (ILO 1983) and those of Boserup. Data for the 'paid labour force' measure are believed to be relatively accurate even now, so that most questionnaires are generally satisfactory for collecting information on this segment of the labour force. This implies that it would be reasonable to make cross-national comparisons using currently available data on the 'paid labour force'.

(ii) *Market-oriented labour force* (persons in paid employment plus persons engaged in activities on a family farm or in a family enterprise or business that sells some or all of its products). This group could include employers, own-account workers, unpaid family workers and members of producer co-operatives. Data on the 'market-oriented labour force' are useful to economic planners because they cover persons not engaged in subsistence activities who are directly affected by many government policies in such fields as subsidisation, pricing and availability of intermediate inputs.

(iii) *Standard labour force* (persons engaged in activities whose products or services should be included in the national income accounts statistics according to United Nations recommendations). This definition of the labour force corresponds to that recommended by the Thirteenth International Conference of Labour Statisticians (ILO, 1983a). The 'standard labour force' would comprise all persons engaged in the production of goods and services, irrespective of whether these goods or services are sold. Thus, certain important anomalies in current measurement practices would be eliminated. For example, all activities associated with primary products, such as food 'production' and food 'processing', including animal tending and milking, threshing in the home compound, processing and preparing food for preservation and storage, and unpaid gathering of food or fruit, would be considered labour force activities whether or not market-related exchanges occur. Also included would be activities which add to the profit of a family enterprise, such as preparation of meals for hired labourers, since they are a form of payment.

(iv) *Extended labour force* (in addition to the above, persons engaged in activities *not* included in the most recent United Nations recommendations on the SNA but which none the less contribute to meeting their family's basic needs for goods and services that are generally purchased in developed countries). The 'extended labour force' would include activities such as gathering and preparing fuel (e.g. gathering sticks and wood, drying crop refuse, preparing cow dung cakes), and making clothes. Water fetching might also be included in countries where this requires long distances to be traversed.[4]

In this section we have reviewed labour force definitions and indicated some of the difficulties in applying them. We have also suggested four labour force definitions with increasing levels of inclusion – beginning with the 'paid labour force' and ending with a fairly broad definition of the 'extended labour force'. Each provides planners with a different perspective on the labour force, on economic activity, on the possible effects of government policies, on the meeting of basic needs, on the sectoral distribution of output, on international comparability, and on women's status. It is our feeling that governments should be encouraged to collect sufficient information to allow them to estimate the labour force in several different ways, so as to meet their diverse planning needs and to have at their disposal labour force measures which are comparable over time and with those from other countries.

Before proceeding further, it is important to keep in mind that many members of the labour force (however defined) are part-time participants. Many are active only in periods of peak labour demand (e.g. seasonally); others are active for only an hour or so each day. This implies that just as it is misleading – and patently illogical – to exclude many persons from the labour force on the ground that overall labour force activity rates can be statistically meaningful only if they are substantially less than 100 per cent, it would also be misleading to lump together all persons without considering the level of their activity. For this reason, along with more accurate measures of labour force activity (based on a simple in/out dichotomy), we feel it is important to divide the labour force – however defined – into subcategories based on time criteria (e.g. part-time and full-time).

Suggestions for improved labour force survey questionnaires

Given the ambiguities and difficulties involved in defining and measuring labour force activity, it is hardly surprising that respondents do not provide accurate data in response to simple key-word-type questions. How can respondents be expected to know all the nuances behind words such as 'work', 'main activity', 'job' and 'pay or profit', when these are often obscure even to those designing the questions and using the data? Worse still, translation of these key words into local languages often results in words that have a wage-earning connotation.

Consequently, it is our feeling that use of simple key-word questions for collecting labour force data must almost of necessity result in data that are virtually impossible to understand or classify. *Specific* questions about major labour force activities are required; only in that way will it be possible for users to be certain that respondents (and interviewers) will provide the desired data, however 'labour force' may be defined.

There are two possible approaches: either to follow a key-word-type filter question with more specific questions about certain activities which respondents may not have regarded as 'work' or to ask about these activities right from the start (Anker, 1980; Hoffmann, 1981; ILO, 1981; Acharya, 1982). There are major advantages in using an activity schedule: no a priori assumptions are made about what is, and what is not, a labour force activity; respondents are not required to reply to ambiguous, possibly socially 'loaded' questions but only to indicate whether or not each activity is or is not performed. Further advantages of an activity-type questionnaire (or a follow-up activity section to key-word questions) are that with this information (a) labour force participation can be defined after the survey

has been completed – in different ways for different purposes and definitions; (b) it is possible to indicate how fully individuals are integrated into
the economy and possibly the extent of underemployment, which is especially important for women, since the many activities performed by them can
easily be added together.

Detailed activity/time-use-type questionnaires do have their own set of
difficulties. They tend to be complicated to administer (therefore requiring unusually well-trained and well-supervised interviewers) and costly in
terms of interviewing time and data processing (therefore greatly increasing
survey cost or reducing sample size); moreover, the information collected is
often too detailed to use except in aggregated form. These difficulties make
detailed activity/time use questionnaires inappropriate for national surveys
or censuses, although they are useful instruments for smaller in-depth
studies concerned with micro-level relationships; they are also useful as a
validity check in post-enumeration inquiries for large surveys and censuses
(ILO, 1983; Jain and Chand, 1982).

What is required for national surveys and censuses, it seems to us, is a
questionnaire that incorporates the advantages of the detailed activity/time
questionnaire approach (such as its directness, the absence of in-built
assumptions regarding definition of labour force activity and the absence of
ambiguous key words), but is easy to use and process as well as requiring
relatively little interview time. With these considerations in mind, a simplified activity/time schedule that met most of these criteria was developed and
used in a 1981 rural survey in India where 716 currently married women
aged 25–50 years were interviewed.

Twelve major activities, all of which could be considered labour force
activities, were specified. For each activity performed, additional information was collected (more details on nature of activity; amount of time spent
on it per day/season; whether performed for family or others; whether
performed at home or inside or outside the village; whether income was
received and/or products were sold).

To give an idea of whether a simplified activity/time schedule of this kind
can provide reasonably accurate and usable data, Tables 10.1 and 10.2
present data from the survey. Table 10.1 presents data from the two groups
interviewed – Barias (middle-to-low-caste) and Patidars (high-caste) – on the
percentage of sample women reporting that they performed each of 12
specified activities. The main activities in which sample women were
engaged were fetching water (89.4 per cent of women), gathering sticks
(74.9 per cent), making cow dung cakes (50.0 per cent), agricultural work for
others (36.6 per cent) and tending animals, mainly milk buffalo (36.0 per
cent). The general activity pattern was similar for both castes with the
exception of agricultural work for others, which was common for Baria
(low-income) women and unusual for Patidar (high-income) women, and
livestock activities, which were more common for Patidar women than for
Baria women (because Patidar families could more easily afford milk
buffalo).

Table 10.1   Percentage of married women aged 25–50 years engaged in each of 12 activities

Activity	Barias	Patidars	Total
1. Agriculture for others	47.6	3.4	36.6
2. Agriculture for family	14.9	9.0	13.4
3. Cooking for hired labourers	1.7	2.2	1.8
4. Processing food for storage for family	7.1	1.1	5.6
5. Animal husbandry	32.5	46.6	36.0
6. Handicraft	0.7	1.1	0.8
7. Non-agriculture wage or salary	1.5	0.6	1.3
8. Family business, petty trading	2.0	0.6	1.7
9. Other cash earning	4.3	1.7	3.6
10. Gathering sticks	82.5	51.7	74.9
11. Fetching water	89.0	90.4	89.4
12. Making cow dung cakes for fuel	55.5	33.7	50.0

Source: Unpublished data, Baroda resurvey, 1981.

When these data are combined to provide overall measures of labour force activity (see bottom half of Table 10.2), we find that 41.2 per cent of sample women are reported to be in the paid labour force (LF$_A$); 48.6 per cent in the labour force defined more or less according to current national practices (LF$_B$); 69.6 per cent in the labour force as defined according to SNA criteria (LF$_C$); and 85.6 or 93.2 per cent according to two broader definitions of an extended labour force (LF$_D$ and LF$_E$). It is interesting that labour force activity rates increase most when livestock activities are included (moving from LF$_B$ to LF$_C$) and when activities related to provision of fuel or water are included (moving from LF$_C$ to LF$_D$ or LF$_E$); changes are particularly marked for Patidar women. These data are consistent with the generally held belief that most rural women in India make economic contributions, in particular in poorer (lower-caste) groups where they are often out of the house working in the fields as landless labourers or as owner-cultivators.

It is instructive to compare the resulting labour force activity rates with those reported by sample women (LF$_1$ and LF$_2$) in response to a typical simple keyword question: 'Have you ever done any work other than housekeeping during the past year?' These data are presented in Table 10.2. Note that both the activity schedule and the keyword question were asked on the same questionnaire, with the latter asked first, which may have reduced observed differences between the two sets of results. As expected, activity rates are higher when based on an activity schedule than on one simple keyword question – although there is little difference in the measurement of the 'paid labour force': there seems to be little ambiguity about whether a paid activity is 'work'.

For Patidars, while results are similar for LF$_1$ and LF$_A$ (4.5 per cent compared to 7.3 per cent), the absolute level of the difference in the reported female labour force activity rate rises to 9.6 percentage points (15.2 versus 5.6 per cent) when LF$_B$ (labour on the family farm or in the family business) is compared with LF$_2$, to 47.8 per cent when other subsistence-type activities usually included in national income accounts

Table 10.2 Comparison of reported female labour force (LF) activity rates based on a simple keyword question and a simple activity schedule

Question/definition used	Barias	Patidars	Total
*Simple keyword question**			
LF$_1$ (agriculture for others + other wage activities)	54.4	4.5	39.5
LF$_2$ (LF$_1$ + all other 'work' activities)	60.1	5.6	43.4
Simple activity schedule			
LF$_A$ (paid)	52.4	7.3	41.2
LF$_B$ (according to current national practice)†	59.7	15.2	48.6
LF$_C$ (according to current ILO definition)†	74.9	53.4	69.6
LF$_D$ (LF$_C$ + gathering sticks and/or making cow dung cakes)	91.1	69.1	85.6
LF$_E$ (LF$_D$ + fetching water)	93.3	92.7	93.2

* Women reporting that they had worked in the past 12 months were asked what type of work they had done. This latter information was used to distinguish between LF$_1$ and LF$_2$.
† Main difference between LF$_B$ and LF$_C$ is the inclusion in LF$_C$ of women engaged in livestock activities for family.
Source: as Table 10.1.

statistics (LF$_C$) are considered, and to 63.5 or 87.1 per cent when more extended labour force definitions (LF$_D$ or LF$_E$) are used. Differences for the Barias are similar in nature to those for the Patidars, although much smaller in size, since approximately half the sample Baria women are reported to be in the paid labour force under either definition.[5]

The implications of the comparisons by question type shown in Table 10.2 are clear. When wage or salary work is considered, responses are similar for both types of question. For subsistence activities, where the dividing line between economic and non-economic activities is ambiguous and often arbitrary, results by question type differ greatly. These results thus confirm the need for explicit questions on activities performed rather than exclusive reliance on key-word questions.

Summary

This paper has been concerned with the measurement of female labour force activity, and particularly with why it is so often underreported in surveys and censuses conducted in the Third World. A review of typical fieldwork techniques and questionnaires revealed that both interviewers and respondents frequently are male and suggested that their perception of women as 'housewives' may be a factor in explaining the low female activity rates reported. It was also demonstrated that questions on labour force participation are often ambiguous and basically rely on one key word or phrase such as 'work', or 'job' or 'main activity'. This ambiguity also exists at the level of international definitions of the labour force, particularly in the arbitrary division of subsistence activities into 'labour force' and 'non-labour force' activities. Moreover, national statistical practices frequently deviate from international recommendations.

The many definitional and practical difficulties involved in accurately measuring the labour force and the diversity of economic planning requirements suggest the need for *several* labour force definitions. This paper has proposed four, with increasing levels of inclusion – 'paid labour force', 'market-oriented labour force', 'standard labour force' (current definition), and 'extended labour force'. Collecting sufficient information to calculate several labour force measures is strongly recommended, since there cannot be one correct labour force definition; the best measure depends on what aspect of the labour market one is interested in and how the data will be used.

To obtain accurate labour force data, the use of an activity schedule is suggested, respondents being questioned on the specific activities they perform. Such an activity schedule can be used on a stand-alone basis or as a follow-up section to one or two general keyword questions. In this way, no a priori assumptions are made about what is and what is not a labour force activity; respondents are not required to reply to ambiguous socially loaded questions; the labour force can be easily defined after the survey in different ways for different purposes; and many of the numerous economic activities performed by women can be taken into account. The usefulness of this approach is confirmed by the results of a sample survey conducted among rural women in India in 1981, which revealed a far higher level of female non-wage activity for the family than did a simple 'key-word' question.

The difficulties of collecting accurate data on female labour force activity and the need for guidelines for improving their accuracy have led the ILO to conduct experimental field studies. In rural areas of India and Egypt, replicate (i.e. statistically identical) samples of male and female respondents, male and female interviewers, keyword and activity-type questionnaires were used in order to observe how reported female activity rates vary according to the type of questions asked, the type of interviewer and respondent, and the definition of labour force activity employed. Results from these studies (Anker, *et al.*, 1987; 1988; Anker and Anker, 1988) reinforce the conclusions drawn above about the uncontestable need to use detailed, specific type questions or an activity schedule. On the other hand, results from these studies lend little support to the assertion that male respondents and male interviewers significantly underreport the labour force activity of women, although it was found that Egyptian men reported significantly less paid labour force activity than Egyptian women.

Survey designers, economists and labour statisticians have all too often blissfully ignored the difficulties involved in collecting information on the female labour force. Yet, as this paper has tried to show, respondents cannot be expected to provide accurate labour force data unless interviewers and survey designers ensure that the questions relating to labour force activity are very specific. Nor can labour force data be used intelligently without a precise understanding of what they actually reflect. Only by improving fieldwork techniques and questionnaire design can the statistical invisibility of much of the economic and labour force activity of women be eliminated.

Notes

1. The resolution of the Thirteenth International Conference of Labour Statisticians (ILO 1983) states that 'persons engaged in the production of economic goods and services for own and household consumption should be considered as in self-employment [and therefore as labour force participants] *if such production comprises an important contribution to the total consumption of the household*' (emphases added). It is to be hoped that this 'clarification' (what, indeed, is an 'important' contribution?) will not have the effect of excluding subsistence activities from classification as labour force activities.
2. National practices on inclusion in national statistics of the value of subsistence activities vary considerably. In an investigation of 70 developing countries, 71 per cent were reported to include the imputed value of forestry activities, 39 per cent food processing, 50 per cent handicrafts, and 7 per cent water carrying (Blades, 1975).
3. The proposed definitions differ in how they distinguish between economic and non-economic activity. They do not address labour supply issues related to unemployment such as willingness to work, looking for work and availability for work – other important dimensions of potential labour supply in which planners are interested (see Standing, 1981, for a good discussion of these points).
4. The activities included would be country-specific and would therefore need to be listed with the data. The main pursuits *not* included in 'extended labour force' activities are leisure and daily maintenance activities such as rest, sleep, talking, eating, personal hygiene and recreation, besides day-to-day household services not usually purchased in industrial countries, such as cleaning and child care – although arguably many of these activities would also be included as labour force activities if one took a wider view of the economic value of household activities (see Beneria, 1982; Goldschmidt-Clermont, 1982).
5. Cross-tabulations (not reported here) indicate that much of the observed undercount in female labour force activity associated with the key-word question is also associated with part-time activity. Whereas 75 (40) per cent of women in LF_B (LF_C) *and not* in LF_2, were estimated to be working for an average of approximately two hours a day or less on the activity schedule, the percentage was only 13 (2) for women reported to be in the labour force on *both* the key-word question and the activity schedule (i.e. LF_2 and LF_B, and LF_2 and LF_C, respectively).

Bibliography

Acharya, M. (1982) *Time use data and the living standards measurement study*. LSMS Working Paper No. 18. Washington, World Bank.

Anker, R. (1980) *Research on women's role and demographic change: Survey questionnaires for households, women, men and communities, with background explanations*. Geneva, ILO.

Anker, R. (1983) 'The effect on reported levels of female labour force participation in developing countries of questionnaire design, sex of interviewer and sex/proxy status of respondent: Description of a methodological field experiment', mimeographed World Employment Programme research working paper; restricted. Geneva, ILO.

Anker, R. and Anker, M (1988) 'Improving the measurement of women's participation in the Egyptian labour force: Results of a methodological study', mimeographed World Employment Programme research working paper;

restricted. Geneva, ILO.

Anker, R., Khan, M. E. and Gupta, R. B., 1987. 'Biases in measuring the labour force: Results of a methods test survey in Uttar Pradesh, India', *International Labour Review*.

Anker, R., Khan, M. E. and Gupta, R. B. 1988: 'Women in the labour force: A methods test in India for improving its measurement', *Women, Work and Development Series*, no. 16, ILO, Geneva.

Anker, R., and Knowles, J. C. (1978) 'A micro-analysis of female labour force participation in Africa' in G. Standing and G. Sheehan (eds), *Labour force participation in low-income countries*. Geneva, ILO, pp. 137–63.

Baster, No. (1981) 'The measurement of women's participation in development: The use of census data', Discussion Paper no. 159. Brighton, University of Sussex, Institute of Development Studies.

Benería, L. (1982) 'Accounting for women's work', in L. Benería (ed.), *Women and development. The sexual division of labour in rural societies. A study prepared for the International Labour Office within the framework of the World Employment Programme.* New York, Praeger, pp. 119–47.

Blacker, J. G. C. (1978) 'A critique of the international definitions of economic activity and employment status and their applicability in population censuses in Africa and the Middle East', *Population Bulletin of the United Nations Economic Commission for Western Asia*, June. pp. 47–54.

Blades, D. W. (1975) *Non-monetary (subsistence) activities in the national accounts of developing countries*. Development Centre Studies, Paris, OECD.

Boserup, E. (1975) 'Employment of women in developing countries' in L. Tabah (ed.) *Population growth and economic development in the Third World*. Liège, Ordina, Vol. 1, pp. 79–107.

Dixon, R. B. (1982) 'Women in agriculture: Counting the labour force in developing countries', *Population and Development Review*, September, pp. 539–66.

Fong, M. (1980) 'Victims of old-fashioned statistics', in *Ceres*, May–June. pp. 28–32.

Goldschmidt-Clermont, L. (1982) *Unpaid work in the household*. Geneva, ILO.

Government of India, Ministry of Planning, Department of Statistics (1980) 'Employment–Unemployment situation India during the seventies: A comparative study based on the results of the NSS 27th and 32nd round surveys', in *Sarvekshana*, Journal of the National Sample Survey Organisation, Jan.

Hoffmann, E. (1981) 'Accounting for time in labour force surveys', in *Bulletin of Labour Statistics*, no. 1, pp. ix–xxv.

International Labour Office (1954) 'Eighth International Conference of Labour Statisticians, resolution concerning statistics of the labour force, employment and unemployment', *Official Bulletin*, 31 Dec. 1954, p. 320.

ILO (1972) *Employment, incomes and inequality. A strategy for increasing productive employment in Kenya*. Report of an inter-agency team financed by the United Nations Development Programme and organised by the International Labour Office. Geneva.

ILO (1981) 'An alternative approach for collection and presentation of labour force data', background paper for Meeting of Experts on Household Surveys, 6–10 April. Geneva, Doc. MEHS/1981/D.4; mimeographed.

ILO (1982) 'Revision of the international guidelines on labour statistics', paper prepared for OECD Working Party on Employment and Unemployment Statistics, 14–16 June.

ILO (1983) 'Thirteenth International Conference of Labour Statisticians, Resolution concerning statistics of the economically active population, employment, unemployment and underemployment, Bulletin of Labour Statistics, no. 3, pp. xi–xvi.

Jain, D., and Chand, M. (1982) 'Report on a time allocation study – its methodological implications', paper prepared for a Technical Seminar on Women's Work and Employment, 9–11 April. New Delhi, Institute of Social Studies Trust.

Myrdal, G. (1968) *Asian drama. An inquiry into the poverty of nations*, Vol. III. New York, Pantheon.

Pittin, R. (1982) *Documentation of women's work in Nigeria: Problems and solutions*, mimeographed World Employment Programme research working paper; restricted. Geneva, ILO.

Recchini de Lattes, A. and Wainerman, C. H. (1979) *Data from censuses and household surveys for the analysis of female labour in Latin America and the Caribbean: Appraisal of deficiencies and recommendations for dealing with them.* Santiago, Chile, Economic Commission for Latin America. Doc. E/CEPAL/L.206.

Standing, G. (1981) *Labour force participation and development*, 2nd edn, Geneva, ILO.

United Nations (1968) *A system of national accounts.* Studies in Methods, series F, no. 2, rev. 3. New York.

UN (1980) *Sex-based stereotypes, sex biases and national data systems.* ST/ESA/STAT/99. New York.

UN Asian and Pacific Centre for Women and Development (1977) *The critical needs of women.* Report, Part I, Expert Group Meeting on the Identification of the Basic Needs of Women of Asia and the Pacific and on the Formulation of a Programme of Work, Tehran, 4–10 December.

UN Economic and Social Commission for Asia and the Pacific (1982). Regional Seminar on Strategies for Meeting Basic Socio-economic Needs and for Increasing Women's Participation in Development to Achieve Population Goals, 27 April–3 May 1982, Pattaya, Thailand, in *Population Headliners.* Bangkok. May.

UN Economic and Social Council, Commission on the Status of Women (1982). *Review and appraisal of progress achieved in the implementation of the World Plan of Action and the Programme of Action for the second half of the United Nations Decade for Women during the period 1980–1981.* New York. Doc. E/CN.6/1982/7.

11 Observation and recall method for collecting data on women's activities: an experiment in India

J. N. Tewari

Introduction

The 13th International Conference of Labour Statisticians recorded that 'in order to obtain more accurate statistics on women's participation in economic activities, measurement methods should be carefully reviewed to ensure unbiased coverage of men and women. Sex biases in the form of underestimation of women's participation in economic activity may result, for example, from incomplete coverage of unpaid economic activities, failure of respondents and enumerators to take account of women's multiple activities and use of proxy respondents. Where necessary, research should be carried out in order to identify the extent, nature and sources of the possible biases, if any, and to develop appropriate methods of reducing them.'[1] One of the methods for data collection as an alternative to the presently in vogue method of household interview through trained investigators is the observation method. It eliminates at least the respondent's failure and biases. Underestimation of women's participation in economic activity results partly from the failure of the respondents to take full account of the activities undertaken by women. This happens, on the one hand, because of recall lapse of the respondent, and on the other, because of the multiple and sometimes concurrent activities of the women and their work style in which they are intermittently in and out of gainful activity many times in a day/week. Their work style does not conform to a fixed pattern on a weekly or even daily basis, and because of this the activities are more likely to be forgotten by the respondent in the recall method. To get an exhaustive and accurate list of activities undertaken by women, therefore, the alternative method of observation can be employed. This article attempts to bring out possibilities and directions in which improvement in the method of data collection on women's activities can be brought about through the observation and the observation-cum-recall method and their possible role in labour force surveys.

The observation method needs to be distinguished from the conventional interview method where respondents report the activities undertaken by them in the personal interview with the enumerator. Here it is the enumerator who will observe the household member for a specified time and take snapshot readings of the activities being performed by the respondent. Thus, the observation does not depend on the responses of the respondent. In the conventional method, which could be briefly termed the 'recall method', responses are not only subjective but are also subject to recall/lapse, its degree, of course, depending upon the length of the recall period. In the observation method one relies only on the observations made by the appointed observer; his snapshot readings of the activities of the individual respondent as watched at the time he visits or during the period he remains in the household of the respondent, not on his questioning of the respondent. Thus, while subjective bias and recall/lapse are the shortcomings of the interview method, the difficulty of the observation method is managing observation of the subject throughout 24 hours in the day to get a complete picture. Complete day observation is neither physically possible by the observer, nor would be permissible by the respondent in a free and democratic set-up. With observation being limited to a truncated day (say 6 a.m. to 9 or 10 p.m.) one way to handle the situation scientifically is to have a judicious mixture of both the observation and recall methods in the field survey and a proper estimational procedure to derive the final estimate by linking the two estimates based on both the observational data and the recall data. For the observational data, a detailed sampling plan of the hours of the day when specific respondents are to be observed will have to be worked out. Generally, such a detailed sampling time plan for collection of observation data and an estimation procedure for linking the two sets of data results are missing in the experiments being conducted in this field. In such a sampling plan care has also to be taken that early morning hours and late night hours of the truncated day are duly represented in the observation, so that the results represent the true picture. This will be more relevant when activities falling into the extended concept are found to be relatively more in vogue in these odd hours. The above precaution by the survey authority is necessary as the odd hours are inconvenient both for the observer himself and for the subject observed, with regard to making himself/herself available for observation.

It is relevant here to mention that in India, at the initiative of the Planning Commission, a methodological study on time allocation between activities was sponsored by the Ministry of Social Welfare, Government of India, and taken up by the National Council of Applied Economic Research (NCAER) in 1983 in the rural areas of a few states. The National Sample Survey Organisation (NSSO), the Central Statistical Organisation and the NCAER collaborated in the plan of the study. The NCAER conducted the survey on a small subsample of the National Sample Survey

(NSS) 38th Round Survey on employment, unemployment and consumer expenditure (1983). The survey was expected to measure time use through different methodologies – snapshot readings, observation-cum-recall, recall of previous day and recall of the seventh day as in the NSS method. The report has recently been prepared by the NCAER.

Method of data collection (the NCAER study)

From a NSS sample village, data were collected from ten households. Data collection from a sample household was spread over five days. The first-day interview started in the morning, split into two stages, the first stage for general information and information on time disposition during the preceding seven days (NSS method) and the second stage for data by the 'recall of previous day' method (from 2 p.m. to night). The reference day of the 'recall of previous day' method corresponded to the seventh day recall of the 'time disposition during the week' method of the NSS.

On the second day data were collected through the snapshot reading method. For the purpose of snapshot readings the day was divided as follows into five sets of timings, each set with a duration of three hours:

Set of timings – Team A
1. 6 a.m.–9 a.m.
3. Noon–3 p.m.
5. 6 p.m.–9 p.m.
Set of timings – Team B
2. 9 a.m.–Noon
4. 3 p.m.–6 p.m.

The first five households were covered by team A. These investigators started taking snapshots from 6 a.m. and went for three alternative sets of timings (i.e. 1, 3, 5 above) to each of the five households. Within a set of timing each household was contacted twice, i.e. at an interval of one-and-a-half hours. Thus, on the first day of snapshot reading, six snaps were taken from members of each of the first five households. Team B went to the rest of the five households for snapshot readings during the other set of timings (i.e. 2, 4) starting from 9 a.m. The household members were contacted twice during each of the two alternative sets of timings. In all, four snapshots were taken in each of the remaining five households and the activities of all members were recorded. Similarly, on the third and fourth days, the activities of each member of the sample households were recorded by the following sets of timing.

Day of interview	Investigating team	Serial no. of households canvassed	Set of timing for snapshot reading	No. of snapshots taken from each member of the household
Second	A	1–5	6 a.m.–9 a.m. Noon–3 p.m. 6 p.m.–9 p.m.	6
	B	6–10	9 a.m.–Noon 3 p.m.–6 p.m.	4
Third	A	1–5	9 a.m.–Noon 3 p.m.–6 p.m.	4
	B	6–10	6 a.m.–9 a.m. Noon–3 p.m. 6 p.m.–9 p.m.	6
Fourth	A	1–5	6 a.m.–9 a.m. 6 p.m.–9 p.m.	6
	B	6–10	9 a.m.–Noon 3 p.m.–6 p.m.	4

Thus, a minimum of four and a maximum of six snaps for each person were taken in a day for three consecutive days from 6 a.m. to 9 p.m. and the day was divided into two sets of timings as shown below:

Set 1
(i)   6 a.m.–7.30 a.m.
(ii) 7.30 a.m.–9.00 a.m.
(iii) Noon–1.30 p.m.
(iv) 1.30 p.m.–3.00 p.m.
(v)   6.00 p.m.–7.30 p.m.
(vi) 7.30 p.m.–9.00 p.m.

Set 2
(i)   9.00 a.m.–10.30 a.m.
(ii) 10.30 a.m.–Noon
(iii) 3.00 p.m.–4.30 p.m.
(iv) 4.30 p.m.–6.00 p.m.

The set of timings followed on the first day to observe a person's activity was also followed on the third day and the other set of timings on the second day. Thus, if a person was observed on the first day with the first set of timings he would be observed six times on the first day, four times on the second day and again six times on the third day and a total of 16 snapshots in all, i.e. 16 independent observations of the activities would be obtained. Similarly, if a person was observed on the first day with the second set of timings, then he would be observed four times on the first day, six times on the second day and four times on the third day and thus, a total of 14 independent observations of activities during the period 6 a.m. to 9 p.m. would be obtained. A total of 42 or 48 independent observations of activities (snapshot readings) for each person were obtained during the three-day period (6 a.m. to 9 p.m.).

On the fifth day data were collected through the observation-cum-recall method (which is discussed below on pages 147-9).

Estimation methods and presentation of results

Through the above procedure of data collection the study attempted in its main report a comparison of estimates obtained by the different methods (mentioned on page 143) for two variables: percentage of persons engaged in and average time spent on economic activities. For the second variable, the number of hours worked in economic activities as obtained by the NCAER method was first converted into person-days following the NSS method, i.e. half-day for less than four hours and full day for four hours or more. The average number of hours spent in economic activities per day was estimated by dividing the total number of person-days by the number of persons and then assuming an eight-hour day. In addition, the actual number of hours worked (average per person per day) was also presented (see Table 11.1).[2] It will be observed that in the case of children and adult females actual time spent in economic activities based on recall for previous day as well as observation-cum-recall is higher than what is revealed by the seventh day recall. And more importantly, when actual hours are converted for comparability with the NSS in almost all cases the difference widens further.

The report does not give any error calculations, nor does it perform any tests of significance, but it does observe that the overall percentage of employment for adult males does not differ significantly whichever method is employed. However, there are marked differences in the case of male children of 5–14 years and females, based on the two methods (i.e. recall for previous day and observation-cum-recall), and the report therefore observes that the NSS method of estimation does not fully take into account the time spent in economic activities, especially by women and children. Of the three methodologies, snapshot reading is confined to 15 hours during the day, i.e. from 6 a.m. to 9 p.m., whereas with the other two methodologies the time spent in economic activities extends over all hours. In fact, it was found that people do engage in economic activities between 9 p.m. and 6 a.m. Furthermore, 'snap reading also suffers from two other limitations: (i) it does not provide an estimate based on the flow of activities during the day; and (ii) quite often the persons concerned are not found at the expected location and their activities, at that time, have to be recorded on the basis of responses from spouses, parents, other relatives or neighbours'. Incidentally, this also dilutes the snapshot reading method. The report concludes 'it would therefore seem that of the three methodologies snap reading may not be as appropriate as the other two. Between recall for previous day and observation-cum-recall, the latter is likely to be more accurate simply because the recall period is shorter.' If one looks at the figures in Table 11.2, it would seem that in recalling for the previous day people tend perhaps to overstate the time spent in economic activities, though the extent of this is marginal.

Table 11.1   Average time spent on economic activity (01–71), estimated by different methods (Round 1)

State	24 Hours					15 hours		
	Recall for seventh day	Recall for previous day		Observation-cum-recall		Recall for previous day	Observation-cum-recall	Snap reading
	(NSS method*)	Actual	NSS method*	Actual	NSS method*			
Age group 5–14								
				Males				
Kerala	0.16	0.13	0.21	0.37	0.72	0.13	0.36	0.59
Maharashtra	0.89	1.21	1.34	0.87	0.94	1.20	0.86	0.89
				Females				
Kerala	0.12	0.26	0.43	0.34	0.68	0.19	0.22	0.23
Maharashtra	0.53	0.72	0.87	0.33	0.44	0.72	0.33	0.70
Age group 15–19								
				Males				
Kerala	5.21	5.61	5.37	5.64	5.25	5.50	5.28	5.48
Maharashtra	6.60	7.40	6.69	6.33	5.90	7.15	6.21	5.99
				Females				
Kerala	1.61	2.31	3.24	2.06	3.11	2.22	1.96	2.30
Maharashtra	4.14	3.83	4.30	2.76	3.35	3.80	2.76	2.68

* It refers to the number of person-days divided by the number of persons, assuming an 8-hour day.

Table 11.2 Average time spent on economic activity (01.71), estimated by different methods (15 hours) (Round 1)

State	Male			Female		
	Recall for previous day	Observation-cum-recall	Snap reading	Recall for previous day	Observation-cum-recall	Snap reading
Age group 5–14						
Kerala	0.13	0.36	0.59	0.19	0.22	0.23
Maharashtra	1.20	0.86	0.89	0.72	0.33	0.70
Age group 15–59						
Kerala	5.50	5.20	5.40	2.22	1.96	2.30
Maharashtra	7.15	6.21	5.99	3.80	2.76	2.60

On the NSS method of measurement the report observes that it 'does not fully take into account the actual time spent especially by children and females on various economic activities'. The multiplicity of activities and their discontinuous flow during an average day, besides the use of male interviewers, seem to be, according to the report, the underlying reasons.

The NCAER study presents a detailed picture of the working day of a woman compared with that of a man by giving data on the percentage of time spent in a day (24 hours) in economic activities and household chores (Table 11.3) based on recall for the previous day for adults (15–59 years) and observes that 'tradition requires women to undertake household chores in order to release men for participation in economic activities. Logically, the exertion of women and children on household chores is relevant for accomplishment of economic activities but convention does not have it that way.' In reality, if account is taken of household chores, 'the working day of a woman is a fifth to a third more than the working day of a man', 'the working day of a man, on an average, is somewhat less than eight hours while the working day of a woman exceeds in all cases nine hours'.

Table 11.3   Percentage of total time spent in a day on economic activities and household chores

	Bihar	Kerala	Maharashtra	Uttar Pradesh
Male	33.23	20.27	32.02	30.15
Female	40.61	37.06	39.91	38.19

Table 11.4 reveals the detailed distribution of time spent in a day (24 hours) on total economic activity, total non-economic activity, household work, leisure, etc. But it is based only on one set of data, previous-day recall. The state volumes, however, give comparative data on average hours spent per person on different activities by the different methods, as can be seen in Table 11.5 for household work and leisure. Household work covered items such as washing clothes and utensils, cooking, house cleaning, child care, as well as sewing, knitting and coir-making. Free collection related to the collection of items such as fuel wood, dung, fodder, building materials and craft raw materials. Leisure covered also eating, sleeping, recreation, attending social and religious functions and meetings. In the case of leisure, snapshot reading gives minimum estimates, but because account has to be taken of the period between 9 p.m. and 6 a.m. (which was excluded in snapshot readings) the true comparative picture over the three methods is not known. The missing period may or may not be devoted to leisure (and sleep). What is needed for critical analysis is comparable estimates by the three methods for time spent on activities from 6 a.m. to 9 p.m. only.

The estimate of household work based on observation-cum-recall generally falls between those given by the other two methods. The divergences in the different estimates may, theoretically, result from two different factors – first, recall effect which operates in the first two methods and increases with the recall period, and second, a disparity in the

Table 11.4   Percentage distribution of time spent in a day (24 hours) by major activity based on recall for previous day (Round 1)

State	Total work	Total economic activity	Household	Leisure	Studies	Sick/child delivery, etc.	In search of job	Others
Kerala								
Male	23.50	76.42	3.37	57.07	5.15	0.44	1.40	9.50
Female	10.01	89.99	27.50	54.71	3.67	0.15	0.19	4.42
Maharashtra								
Male	30.01	69.19	1.79	60.75	0.93	0.23	—	5.49
Female	15.99	84.01	22.50	54.70	0.53	1.45	—	4.74

Table 11.5   Average hours spent per person on household work and leisure by females of 15–59 years (Round 2: June–August 1983)

Method	Household work			Leisure		
	Kerala	Maharashtra	Uttar Pradesh	Kerala	Maharashtra	Uttar Pradesh
Recall for previous day	6.25	5.01	4.47	13.24	12.21	13.15
Observation-cum-recall	6.32	5.34	4.51	13.56	12.27	12.59
Snap reading	6.65	6.18	5.82	3.79	4.28	3.49

number of actual observations (relevant for the last two methods). To decipher the number of observations effected it would have been helpful if the study had tabluated the data in such a way as to provide estimates based only on the 'observation' data set made in the second method. Then these estimates could be legitimately compared with the estimates based on the snapshot reading method and would thus have helped in deciding if in the observation-cum-recall method observation for just a day is good enough. As things stand at present, the provisional tables of the NCAER study do not give any data separately for the observation set in the second method. In fact, the way the household returns have been filled in and the questionnaire on observation-cum-recall designed, it is not possible to decipher for which activity information has been collected by observation and for which by same-day recall. On data collection by this method the report records that 'on the fifth day, data on time allocation for different activities were collected through a combination of the observation and recall method. Each one of the sample households was visited by the investigators five times with an approximately equal time interval starting from 6 a.m. All the members present *were observed and their activities recorded.* They were also asked to recall all the activities (and their duration) starting from 4 a.m. that day until the time of observation.' The last visit to the household was in the night and at that time, according to the report, '*the activities to be performed till 4 a.m. of the next day were recorded through the inquiry method.* The data from children and female members were collected by female investigators from the adult members of the household.' Thus, while the snapshot reading method is really observation in the full sense of the term the second method does not involve two data sets collected independently and then combined statistically. It appears more a method of same-day recall where the household was visited five times in a day within the period, say 6 a.m. to 9 p.m. Perhaps a more fruitful approach of the observation-cum-recall method would have been the adoption for data collection of an interpenetrating sample so as to obtain independent data sets through one-day observation and same-day recall and further preparing a combined estimate based on the two data sets statistically. An observation-cum-recall method so devised could be considered as a compromise solution in a large-scale survey on the labour force, particularly because the snapshot reading method is more time consuming and requires more resources. It is, however, important to determine the number of minimum days (one, two or three) for which 'observation' must be resorted to in the second method.

Another careful comparison which needs to be attempted for proper analysis and inference on the methodological issue is to compare the NCAER results of these three methods with the estimates obtained from the NSS 38th Round 1983 survey data, based on the 'previous day' reference period. For strict comparison with NSSO, the usually released NSS 'Current status' estimates based on the person-days concept with a reference period of the preceding seven days should not be used. Correct comparison will necessitate the tabluation of data for the restricted reference period by the NSSO. (Even the usual tables of the NSS 38th

Round 1983 are only partially released and they relate to the period January to June 1983 as against the reference period of May to October 1983 of the NCAER.[3]) Further, the NSS estimates based on person-days will have to be transformed into man-hours by assuming a yardstick of the 'working day'. For this purpose using a uniform yardstick, say eight hours per day, for the different rounds of the survey spread over May to October 1983 may not be so legitimate.

In spite of the above limitations one may like to look at the data available on labour time spent on and percentage of persons engaged in domestic duties from the two studies – the NSS 38th Round and the NCAER (Table 11.6). The latter are based on the 'recall for previous day' method and for Round 1 (May to July 1983) for the age group 15–59. The NCAER report gives data for the age groups 5–14, 15–59, 60 and above, not for the composite group 5 and above, while the NSSO has yet to release its data for the above three age groups. But the NCAER study gives the number of reported persons in the age groups. Using them as weights the comparable figures for the percentage of females (5 and above) engaged in 'domestic duties only' are shown in Table 11.7. The NSS figures are significantly higher, which supports the general conclusion of the NCAER, i.e. that the NSSO does not capture fully the gainful work done by females. No doubt before making this deduction, one has to consider whether this large difference could be attributed to differences in reference periods and sample size of the two studies.

Table 11.6 NSS and NCAER data on domestic duties

State	NCAER Round 1 Rural (15–59 age group)				NSS 38th Round Rural	
	Average time spent per person/day (hours)		Percentage of persons		Percentage of persons 5 years and above	
	Male	Female	Male	Female	Male	Female
Kerala						
Engaged in domestic duties only	0.75	6.32	0.70	30.10	3.01	36.87
Engaged in domestic duties and free collection	0.10	0.38	0.26	—	0.23	6.69
Maharashtra						
Engaged in domestic duties only	0.42	5.41	—	24.80	2.61	28.46
Engaged in domestic duties and free collection	0.01	0.01	—	—	0.62	5.88

Table 11.7 Percentage of females (5 and above) engaged in domestic duties only

Source	Kerala	Maharashtra	Uttar Pradesh
NSS 38th Round	36.87	28.46	32.20
NCAER	21.31	19.26	14.22

Conclusions

From an estimational angle the distinguishing feature of the snapshot reading or observation method is that it gives the activity picture at a point of time, not a time flow of activity. In order to convert this into a time-flow concept the NCAER study obtained the distribution of activities at half-hour intervals for the total observation period 6 a.m. to 9 p.m. and then, in the wording of the report, 'standardised it assuming that the total number of observations would be distributed equally in each such time interval as the observations were randomly distributed over the entire period of time. The standardised frequencies of activities were added to get a distribution for the entire period of 15 hours (6 a.m. to 9 p.m.) and on this basis the duration of each activity was obtained for an average day of 15 hours during the survey period.' The standardisation operation as implied could be formalised as below (though the report is not explicit). The basic tabulation for the observation method provided the distribution of the number of household members reporting specific activity groups by 30 time-interval groups. The original frequencies for the different activity-time interval group cells are standardised, i.e. adjusted by $p/30$ where p is the proportion of total number of persons reported in a specific time interval group (for all activities taken together) and there are 30 time intervals. Average time spent on a particular activity per person per day was estimated at 15 multiplied by the total number of adjusted frequencies for the particular activity (all time interval groups taken together), per person in the sample, where 15 hours in a day are taken as total time spent on activities.

Perhaps, as a methodological study, the NCAER report should also have presented the estimates derived through unstandardised frequencies in the case of the snapshot reading method. Then it would have been possible to comment on the order of the difference brought about in the estimates through the standardisation process. It may also be noted that for the observation-cum-recall method no standardisation was adopted in the estimation, presumably because this method amounted to 'recall the same day' and observations at a particular point of time were not involved.

In conclusion, this paper makes certain suggestions on the ways in which the method of data collection on women's activities in the labour force surveys of the developing and underdeveloped countries could be improved. It focuses on the recent methodological study undertaken in India by the NCAER, on its approach, its method of data collection through the observation and the observation-cum-recall methods, its estimation and tabulation. It also reviews some of the problems and pitfalls in the experiment which limit the usefulness of the NCAER study. Certain additional tabulations both by the NSSO and the NCAER are indicated to achieve better comparative analysis and more fruitful inference on the efficiency of the observation-cum-recall method. It is suggested that in the composite method the design and execution of field work should be planned so as to obtain two independent data sets – one collected through the observation method and the other through the recall method on interpenetrating samples (which was not done in the NCAER study). Further experimentation may be done to determine the optimum number of 'observation' days (whether one, two or three) and the procedure to combine the two methods into a composite one. More work is also needed to analyse quantitatively the benefits and costs of introducing the changes in the method. The trade-off between the gain from additional information on women's activities brought out through these changes (in quality and quantity) and the loss of the advantage of the present and the modified approaches, methodological studies need to be planned in more depth. Their design and execution could perhaps take advantage of the experience of the Indian experiment discussed here, in refining further the survey technology in this field.

Notes

1. Resolutions adopted in the 13th International Conference of Labour Statisticians, Geneva, 18–29 October 1982, para. 30 (2).
2. Data presented in the tables are still provisional. They are presented for illustration.
3. 'Key results of the last three quinquennial NSS inquiries on employment and unemployment: NSS 38th Round', *SarvEkshana*. Journal of the National Sample Survey Organisation, India, April 1986.

12 Accounting for time in labour force surveys

E. Hoffmann[1]

Introduction

Since 1979 there has been a fairly widespread debate among statisticians working in the area of labour market statistics and between the statisticians and the major users of such statistics, dealing with a number of issues related to the labour force surveys. Some of the more prominent issues can be summarised as follows:

(a) Shall everyone who satisfies the relevant ILO criteria be classified as unemployed, or as employed, as the case may be?
(b) Shall some persons who do not satisfy the relevant ILO criteria be classified as in some sense 'unemployed'?
(c) Are labour force surveys – as presently designed – able to cover adequately all kinds of employment, including second jobs and the 'grey' or 'black' labour market?
(d) Can we be reasonably sure that all employed persons have the same interpretation of which activities to regard as part of actual hours worked – for example as a basis for giving the number of hours worked?
(e) How shall we deal with productive activities outside the market place?
(f) How shall we deal with previous employment, previous unemployment and non-work activities in the past?
(g) How shall we deal with the differences between the actual hours worked during the survey week and the usual work hours?

Some of these questions, in particular (a), (c), (d) and (e) would be easier to handle if we could find ways to improve the present labour force surveys to obtain (aims):

(i) a more uniform way of dealing with activities which are ambiguous in relation to the work/non-work dichotomy, and with groups of persons whose activities make them borderline cases in the division between the three major groups: 'employed persons', 'unemployed persons' and 'persons outside the labour force';

(ii) a better basis for changing the definitions of the three major groups by moving persons engaged in certain activities – or having certain other characteristics – across the border lines, when the problem to be analysed so demands;

(iii) a better basis for using the labour force surveys as a tool for describing and analysing participation in activities in a way parallel with employment.

The purpose of this paper is to argue that one way to improve labour force surveys along these lines is to regard the surveys as a special variant of surveys on the use of time and to utilise the approaches and experiences of the general time-use surveys in the design of the labour force surveys – in particular in the design of the questionnaire. In the following sections the merits of this approach are indicated with respect to the issues and aims mentioned above. Watts and Skidmore have independently introduced the same idea of a time survey approach to labour market statistics, based on a concern with obtaining data for a wider range of productive activities (see issue *(e)* and aim (iii) above).

The labour force survey as a simplified time-use survey

The general time-use survey is designed to obtain an account of all activities of the respondents during the reference period in a way which records the nature of the activities, their duration and their location within the reference period. In some cases additional information on simultaneous activities (e.g. work and radio listening) and other aspects of the activities are recorded as well. The most common reference period is one day.

The labour force survey is designed to obtain information primarily related to one set of activities, namely work for pay or profit. The surveys typically record the total duration of these activities, the context (i.e. the industry) of the activities and the skill utilised (i.e. the occupation). Other activities are either not recorded (for those working for pay or profit) or covered in a summary manner (for those not working). Additional questions are also included, to separate the unemployed from other non-employed persons and for other purposes. These questions may deal with past activities or acts, usual activities and expectations, hopes and wishes about the future. The reference period is typically one week.

We can regard the labour force survey as a simplified time-use survey, which concentrates on the activities of primary interest (work for pay or profit) and almost totally neglect other activities. The advantage of this is that we have a survey which can be administered frequently to a large number of respondents, each interview taking only a few minutes even with the additional questions already mentioned, questions which it would possibly not have been economically or technically possible to include as part of a full-scale time-use survey. The extension of the reference period to one week rather than one day only must also be regarded as an advantage. The disadvantage is the loss of information about other activities during the reference period, and possibly also a loss of internal control arising from the logical need for the total time spent at all activities to cover exactly the total time available. This disadvantage is of little consequence as long as the survey is solely or mainly intended as a basis for estimating the number of employed persons and the number of unemployed persons among those not employed.

However, it now seems that both the more summary descriptions of the current labour market and its development, and the more sophisticated analysis of the labour market, would benefit from information about other activities undertaken by the respondent during the reference period. An example of this is the discussion about whether students are to be excluded from the unemployed, or to be excluded from the employed even though they satisfy the ordinary requirements for being included. In addition, complaints are heard in some countries that the labour force surveys give inadequate information about participation in other activities. There are, for example, indications that the increased participation in paid work during the 1970s, especially among married women, has been accompanied by a decrease in the total number of hours spent at productive activities in private households. The increased labour force participation may even have caused this decrease as these unpaid activities will suffer from competition with paid activities, in an increasingly well-educated population. The demographic and social development during the same period seems not to have caused any corresponding decline in the demand for such activities (and their corresponding services). The consequence has then been an increase in the demand for such services from the market (e.g. improved household appliances, new textiles and new easy-to-prepare food products) and from the publicly provided social services. These developments have in many countries been seriously underestimated. This might have been avoided if, during the 1970s, information on the development of the total number of hours allocated to these activities in private households had been available.

There is also strong evidence that the recording of hours worked is much more accurate in first-use surveys than in conventional labour force surveys, cf. Niemi (1983).

Suggestions for changes in the labour force surveys

There are, of course, many ways to extend the Labour Force Survey (LFS) into a more General Activities Survey (GAS). One way would be to substitute a GAS for the present LFS. Another way would be to utilise a combination of GAS and LFS for each respondent, for example so that each respondent were given one GAS during a sequence of surveys demanded of him; alternatively all respondents might be given a GAS once a year. We could also have a complete time-use survey (TUS) added on to an ordinary LFS programme every third or fifth year, trying to co-ordinate the two programmes as much as possible.

The design of the questionnaire in the GAS will of course largely depend upon which of these programmes one wishes to implement and upon the resources available for the whole programme, as well as what is felt to be the most urgent need for data on the labour market and other activities. The suggestions below, which must be regarded as the first trial shot in a long series of deliberations, are intended for a programme along the lines of the first or second of those sketched above, because these are the ones which seem to represent something new and untried.

The suggestions are also based upon the one-week reference period, as this is the reference period of most of the present LFSs. This means that it is necessary to keep the survey short enough to make it possible to administer it frequently to a large number of respondents, and that a high response rate is required. It should be possible to use either a mail survey, a personal interview survey or a telephone survey and the necessary coding and control work should be kept as low as possible to minimise processing time and costs. It is doubtful whether the suggestions below meet all these requirements, which have to be kept in mind during discussion of them.

The requirements outlined above call for a fairly highly structured questionnaire, more so than one would want in a general TUS for example. This again means that we need a limited and exhaustive list of activities to be covered by the survey. The following list is suggested as a point of departure for discussions (details and explanations are indicated in the Appendix):

Activity 1.   Work for pay or profit in main occupation.
Activity 2.   Work for pay or profit in secondary occupation.
Activity 3.   Preparatory and/or 'tidying up' activities related to 1 or 2 above.
Activity 4.   Journey to place of work.
Activity 5.   Housework for own family/household.
Activity 6.   Maintenance (not related to income-producing work).
Activity 7.   Work with children or other persons in own family/household.
Activity 8.   Purchase of goods and services for private consumption.
Activity 9.   Other household work.
Activity 10. Travelling other than 4 above.
Activity 11. Personal care and sleep.
Activity 12. Meals.
Activity 13. Education – schooling and studies.
Activity 14. Sport and outdoor recreation; culture and entertainment; socialising; radio and television; reading; other leisure.
Activity 15. Leadership and/or other active participation in social, political and/or humanitarian activities.

This list is a slightly revised and condensed version of those activities specified as 'Classification II' in the Norwegian TUS classification of activities (see Appendix 12). This TUS is fairly typical of TUSs in the 1970s. As indicated below, it may be argued that the questionnaire should list these activities in a slightly different order; the presentation above is to facilitate comparisons with the list in the appendix.

Any list like this will of course lead to a number of ambiguities in how some detailed activities are to be classified, but it seems probable that these are activities where the actual choice is not very important for the use of the data, as long as the choice pattern will be stable over time.

Remarks concerning the activities listed above

Activities 1 and 2 are of course the core activities which the ordinary LFSs try to cover, and the wish is often expressed to be able to distinguish between the two. Experiences with LFSs indicate that as long as the possible engagement in second jobs is not mentioned explicitly in the questionnaire, we must expect that such jobs are not included in the answers given by some respondents when stating the number of hours worked. This is an argument for making explicit inquiries about such jobs. In addition it is suspected that many of the respondents who have undertaken work resulting in income which is not reported to the authorities (in order to avoid taxes and social security contributions or to avoid losing certain social security benefits) do not respond in a truthful manner to the questions of the LFS. By asking the respondent to give a full account of the use of time during the reference period, it may be possible to bring some additional respondents in this group into giving a truthful account of their activities. It must be recognised, however, that the most crucial factor in obtaining truthful answers in this area is our ability to get the respondent to have confidence that his answers will be kept totally secret from authorities who might use them to his disadvantage.

Activities 3 and 4 are borderline activities which may or may not be included in the hours of work given in the ordinary LFSs, depending upon the circumstances of the respondent. They may, in particular, cause problems in comparing the total hours of work of self-employed persons with those of employees and in making comparisons between certain occupations or industries. Some groups of employed persons, for example those without a fixed place of work or self-employed persons in agriculture, will probably have a tendency to include in the total number of hours worked activities which employees in manufacturing or public service, for example, will not include (such as travel to the place of work, certain preparatory or maintenance activities). The inclusion or non-inclusion of meals and other interruptions in the work process in hours of work is another example of possible systematic differences between different groups of employed persons according to their particular working situations and work patterns. All this makes it an advantage to have them specified separately (activity 3 is also intended to include the reading of professional literature, etc.).

Activities 5 to 9 are activities which are in one sense substitutes for market or publicly supplied services and also compete for time with income-producing activities. This is also the case with activity 15. The inclusion of information on these activities seems to be of particular importance both for the reasons indicated earlier and as necessary background information in the analysis of the dynamics of the labour market, whether this analysis utilises the panel design of many LFSs or whether it is based on the ordinary time series from the surveys.

Activity 10 is intended to supplement activity 4.

Activity 13 is of interest in its own right and also because it has been suggested that persons being educated should not be regarded as employed or unemployed.

Activity 14 is of course a catch-all for what are usually regarded as leisure-type activities.

Referring to activities 5 to 9, 13 and 15 together, the following observations, bearing on question *(a)* in the introduction to this paper, seem to be of relevance:

(a) According to the standard ILO criteria the participation in paid work always takes priority over activities undertaken during the reference period when defining groups of persons, regardless of the duration of the activities. It has been argued that for some purposes it may be better to give priority to some other activities – at least if they are in some sense the dominant ones in the total time use during the period – e.g. that full-time students (or housewives) working for payment only a few hours at night or during weekends should be classified as students (or housewives) rather than as employed persons.

(b) Only a minority among those unemployed according to the ILO criteria are engaged in job-hunting on a full-time basis. Many of them will be engaged in other activities which they find meaningful and which also may be regarded as productive from a social point of view. In a broader perspective one may therefore wish to be able to pay particular attention to those unemployed persons who are not engaged in such activities above a minimum level and their number. It has, of course, also been suggested in the debate that some of them are not 'proper' unemployed (e.g. students).

It may prove to be an advantage to shorten the list of activities even further, for example, by combining all activities 5 to 9 into one 'Work for own household' activity, and activities 10, 11 and 14 into 'free-time' activities.

Sticking closely to the format of the ordinary LFS questionnaire we can use this list of activities by just presenting it to the respondent (displaying it on a card in the case of a personal interview) and asking which of these activities he has participated in during the reference week and for how many hours. The total number of hours available during one week is of course 168, and this could conceivably be used as a total consistency control for the answers given. However, experts on the TUSs seem to agree that the quality of the responses in this case will be highly dubious. (This sentiment is, of course, also relevant to any evaluation of the quality of the hours of work responses in ordinary LFSs.)

Another strategy would be to present the respondent with the following table (activities are indicated by key words only):

Activities	Days						
	Mo	Tu	We	Th	Fr	Sa	Su
1. Primary work							
2. Secondary work							
3. Preparatory work, etc.							
4. Journey to work							
5. Housework							
6. Maintenance							
7. Work with children							
8. Purchases							
9. Other household work							
15. Community work							
13. Education							
10. Other travelling							
14. Leisure							
12. Meals							
11. Personal care/sleep							
	24	24	24	24	24	24	24

The respondent would be asked to estimate the number of hours spent on each activity during each of the various days of the week, for example by using a display card much in the same way as indicated above. Presumably it would be an advantage for the respondent to receive it (with instructions) at the beginning of the reference week. This is basically the same approach as the previous one, but by breaking the week up into days the consistency requirement may become realistic and the quality of the duration estimates improve accordingly. If we believe that it is not realistic to ask each respondent to account for a whole week, then we may ask them to account for only one day, but distribute these days throughout the whole reference week – maintaining a reference week for the survey if not for the individual.

Perhaps the most realistic procedure both with this strategy, and with the first one, is to use the activity list simply as a check list of activities undertaken, and only ask for the total number of hours for certain key activities – not requiring a total account for the time use. Then we will, of course, lose the possibility for consistency control, and the departure from the ordinary LFS will be relatively small.

Most TUSs are based on the experience that it seems to be easier to remember sequences of different episodes and record them in a sort of time diary. This seems to be the preferred and recommended way to conduct the TUS. The respondent may in our case be given the following table and then asked to indicate on each day the intervals of time allotted to each episode, using either the precoded activities which are given above or using her own words which are then later coded according to the standard list of activities.

Time intervals	Days						
	Mo	Tu	We	Th	Fr	Sa	Su
Open intervals or Fixed intervals: 00-01 01-02 03-24							

Being the least structured of the alternatives presented, these schemes would entail the heaviest processing costs (and the longest processing time). Fixed interval diaries tend to underestimate the total time spent on short episodes – especially when they are repeated many times during the reference period. Precoding techniques seem to be better suited to studies concentrating on a few activities, as we are in this case. With this strategy we could also distribute one-day accounting periods over the reference week, as indicated above.

Concluding remarks

In order to serve the same functions as the present Labour Force Surveys, the General Activities Survey must also include questions about usual activities, past acts and experiences as well as present and future expectations and hopes which are necessary to identify those respondents who are temporarily absent from work (and their reasons for being absent), those who can be classified as unemployed, as discouraged workers or as completely outside the labour market, in order to deal with issues *(b)*, *(f)* and *(g)* mentioned in the introduction to this paper. Some questions about present activities now commonly included in the LFSs will be covered (and greatly expanded) by the complete activity accounting suggested above, but by and large the GAS questionnaire will probably be longer in terms of interview time than the corresponding LFS questionnaire. However, there is no reason to believe that it need be much longer and it will provide both much more information and greater flexibility for the analysis of the labour market and its development.

Of course most of the purposes which it has been indicated that a GAS may serve can also be served in an adequate way by additional questions within the existing LFS framework. If one is concerned with only one or two of them, then this will probably be the best course to take. If, however, one is concerned with a number of the issues, then the GAS approach may well have definite advantages in terms of the consistency and completeness of the information it can provide. The actual design of a GAS can of course only be decided after experiments with different questionnaire designs, trial surveys and discussions with researchers and data users. As recognised above, the question of response rates and costs will inevitably be decisive in determining whether or not a GAS is a realistic alternative or supplement to our present LFSs.

Note

1. This paper was originally prepared, for the OECD Working Party on Employment and Unemployment Statistics, by Mr E. Hoffmann of the Central Bureau of Statistics, Norway, as Consultant to the OECD Secretariat. It is published by permission of the Organisation for Economic Co-operation and Development, although it does not necessarily represent the views of the OECD.

The author wishes to state that the ideas presented in this article are the result of discussions with colleagues at the Central Bureau of Statistics of Norway about the future design of the Norwegian Labour Force Survey (LFS). Special thanks are due to Mr Petter Jakob Bjerve, Director of the Bureau, who suggested the need to use a time-use surveys (TUS) approach to solve problems in comparing actual work hours between different industries, and to Mrs Susan Lingsom, who has shared her experiences with TUSs with him, and whose paper (1979) was extensively used in the preparation of this document.

References

International Labour Office (1979) 'Problems of the statistical definition of the labour force, employment and unemployment in the ECE countries', paper prepared by the Bureau of Statistics of the ILO for the Joint ECE/ILO Meeting on Manpower Statistics (16–20 July 1979), document ILO:CES/AC.51/2.

Lingsom, Susan (1979) 'Advantages and disadvantages of alternative time diary techniques: A working paper', Interne notater IN 79/4 (Statistisk Sentralbyrå, Oslo, 20 July 1979).

National Commission on Employment and Unemployment Statistics (1979) *Counting the labor force* (Washington, DC, 1979).

Niemi, Iris (1983): 'Systematic Bias in Hours Worked?' *Statistisk Tidskrift* (Statistical Review), 1983:4.

Watts, H. W. and Skidmore, F. (1978) *The implications of changing family patterns and behavior for labor force and hardship measurement*, Background Paper no. 16 (National Commission on Employment and Unemployment Statistics, Washington, DC, June 1978).

Appendix 12

Classification of activities in the Norwegian time-use survey

Classification I	Classification II	Classification III
Income-producing work, journey to work, etc.	Income-producing work	Ordinary work in main occupation
		Overtime in main occupation
		Agriculture, forestry and fishing on own property/boat
		Work in secondary occupation
Income-producing work, journey to work, etc. (continued)	Time in connection with work	Meals at the workplace
		Time spent at place of work either before or after work hours
		Other pauses
	Journey to work	Journey to work
Household work and family care	Housework	Food preparation, setting of table, serving
		Dish washing
		House cleaning
		Washing and ironing
		Mending of clothes
		Heating, wood chopping, water fetching
		Private production of food
	Maintenance	Care of garden, lot, and animals
		Construction, larger remodelling
		Painting, smaller remodelling
		Maintenance and repair of dwelling and household equipment
		Maintenance and repair of other equipment
	Work with children	Childcare and helping children
		Help with schoolwork
		Other work with children
	Purchase of goods and services	Purchase of grocery goods
		Purchase of clothes, shoes
		Purchase of durable goods
		Other and unspecified purchase
		Personal care outside the home
		Medical treatment
		Visit to public offices and institutions
		Other errands
	Other household work and family care	Help to other households, collective projects
		Other household work and family care
	Travel in connection with household work and family care	Travel in connection with household work and family care
Personal needs	Personal care/sleep	Bedrest in connection with illness
		Personal hygiene and dressing
		Night sleep
		Other rest or sleep
	Meals	Meals
		Coffee and tea drinking
		Other refreshments

Classification of activities in the Norwegian time-use survey

Classification I	Classification II	Classification III
Education	Education	Full-time instruction
		Part-time instruction
		Homework and study in connection with instruction
		Reading of professional literature, other studies
		Pauses, time spent at place of education before or after school hours
		Travel in connection with education
Leisure	Sport and outdoor recreation	Competitive sport, training
		Skiing
		Hiking in the woods
		Walking
		Swimming, sunning
		Boat trips
		Other trips
	Entertainment	Restaurant or café visit
		Sports events (spectator)
		Cinema
		Theatre, concert, opera
		Museum, art exhibition
		Other entertainment
	Socialising	Play with children
		Conversation with children, reading to children
		Other socialising with children
		Visits with family or friends
		Parties
		Other gatherings
		Games, dance
		Conversations
		Other socialising
	Radio and television	Listening to radio
		Watching television
	Reading	Reading newspapers
		Reading books
		Reading magazines, journals
		Unspecified reading

	Other leisure	Leadership in voluntary public service, other political activities
		Participation in labour or professional organisations
		Participation in humanitarian organisations
		Participation in religious organisations
		Participation in other organisatons
		Meeting, lecture with unspecified purpose
		Participation in mass, prayers or other religious activity
		Handwork
		Carpentry
		Playing a musical instrument
		Other hobbies
		Letter writing
		Listening to records, tapes
		Relaxing
	Travel in connection with leisure time activities	Travel in connection with leisure time activities
Other, unknown,	Other, unknown	Other, unknown

13 Incomplete data in labour force and related surveys

R. Platek[1]

Introduction

Survey practitioners have long been able to design surveys to take into account the sample variability and the cost of gathering the survey data by means of a judicious choice of cost-effective sample designs and estimation procedures subject to survey requirements. They have also addressed the problem of non-sampling errors, such as response errors and errors due to non-response, both associated with data collection. There are many ways of dealing with response errors. For example, they may be avoided or minimised by a proper design and wording of questionnaires and in the field by means of a well-organised, carefully trained and well-controlled data gathering organisation. Non-response can also be reduced at the data collection stage by persistent efforts of well-trained interviewers and by motivation of non-respondents to become respondents. Most practising statisticians and data analysts recognise non-response as an important indication of quality of data since it affects the estimates by introducing a possible bias and an increase in sampling variance.

At the design stage, survey designers anticipating non-response may increase the sample size above the original specifications to take into account the fact that certain units will not respond. While this procedure is quite effective in reducing the variance, it may not reduce the bias resulting from non-response, since the relationship between the bias and the size of non-response depends on both the magnitude of non-response and the characteristics of both respondents and non-respondents.

Also, a reduction of non-response in the field does not necessarily ensure a reduction of non-response bias. In fact, if the procedures for the reduction of non-response are not well thought out and appropriately executed, the bias could be even increased. In most surveys, however, the elimination or reduction of non-response is very important and beneficial.

Apart from (unit) non-response, there are records which contain item non-response and invalid responses. One way of dealing with incomplete data (unit non-response, item non-response, invalid responses) is through methods of imputation and adjustment of weights at the processing and estimation stage. However, the most desirable way to control the effect of non-response is through well-designed data collection operations which will maintain non-response at an acceptable level and at a reasonable cost.

This paper deals mainly with non-response in household surveys, its sources, various methods of reducing it and/or adjusting for it in the final estimate. There will also be some discussion touching upon item non-response and invalid responses together with the methodology for dealing with them. Most of the examination of non-response problems and the application of some of the imputation procedures dealt with in this paper are based on experience in the Canadian Labour Force Survey and surveys associated with it.

Non-response

Non-response may be defined as a failure to obtain a complete report from a reporting unit which legitimately falls into the sample in a particular survey, and it may be one of two kinds: unit non-response, where survey questionnaire is not obtained for a designated unit; or, item non-response, where survey questionnaire is obtained for a unit, but responses for one or more questions are not obtained.

The causes and the size of non-response are related to: type of survey; data collection methods; and sample design. But even for a given design the magnitude of non-response will be affected by such factors as the type of area and the category of non-response. An illustration of the effects of these various factors on the size of non-response is given in the following section, based mostly on the data from the Labour Force Survey (LFS) as this is a large, continuing, monthly sample of dwellings having sophisticated control mechanisms and reporting systems. In the LFS, households within the selected dwellings are interviewed once a month for six consecutive months. In one particular month 56,000 dwellings throughout Canada are contacted by approximately 1,100 interviewers. Information is collected by the interviewers on the demographic characteristics and the labour force activities of the civilian non-institutional populaton 15 years of age and over who are members of households belonging to these dwellings. All interviews must be completed during the week following the survey reference week.

Non-response in the Labour Force Survey

Even though the LFS is a well-established and well-controlled survey, non-response is a continuing concern. A detailed record is kept of total non-response which may be broken down into a number of components, each of which has different causes and requires a different treatment.

One can recognise the following components: households temporarily absent[2]; no one at home[3]; refusal; no interviewer available; bad weather conditions; and other miscellaneous (e.g. language, illness).

Behaviour of non-response over time

In Table 13.1 a few trends in the behaviour of non-response rates in the LFS should be pointed out. The overall non-response rate always increases sharply during the months of July and to a lesser degree in August. This is mostly due to respondents being 'temporarily absent' on vacation. The size of non-response is mainly determined by 'temporarily absent' and 'no one at home'. The refusal rates have been fairly steady over a number of years with some downward trend recently and they appear to be slightly higher in summer months. One significant trend is that the Revised Labour Force Survey in 1975 had a relatively high non-response rate. This was probably due to the hiring of an almost completely new staff of interviewers along with heavy burdens on the field supervisors due to new procedures, new samples and very heavy training loads. As the survey settled down and supervisors were able to devote more attention to response rate, the non-response was reduced to more acceptable levels.

Table 13.1 LFS non-response rates* by component at the Canada level

Year	Month											
	Jan.	Feb.	Mar.	Apr.	May	June	July	Aug.	Sep.	Oct.	Nov.	Dec.
Overall												
1973	7.3	7.2	6.8	7.9	7.0	8.4	15.1	10.9	6.5	5.7	5.2	6.6
A 1974	6.0	6.0	6.4	8.3	7.0	6.8	10.4	8.8	5.6	5.5	4.3	4.6
1975	4.3	4.7	4.6	4.7	4.7	5.8	7.6	6.3	4.3	4.5	4.3	5.3
1975	10.2	9.3	8.7	7.5	7.9	8.9	13.2	11.0	7.5	7.5	7.0	7.6
B 1976	7.9	7.7	7.3	8.8	9.2	8.6	11.7	9.2	5.8	5.9	6.0	5.3
1977	6.1	5.9	5.8	4.5	5.8	5.7	8.4	5.6	4.6	4.3	4.3	4.2
1978	5.0	5.2	5.7	5.3	5.7	5.1	7.9	5.9	4.7	4.6	5.0	4.5
1979	5.4	5.8	5.8	5.1	5.1	5.2	7.5	5.9	4.9	4.5	4.2	4.8
1980	5.3	5.4	5.2	5.3	5.9	6.1	7.6	5.9	4.7	4.3	4.2	4.4

* calculated as the percentage of non-respondent households out of all sampled households.
A rates taken from the old Labour Force Survey.
B rates taken from the new Labour Force Survey.

Non-response and tenure in the survey

Table 13.2 provides an example of LFS non-response rates according to number of times a given household has been in the survey followed by a brief discussion of various components of total non-response rates. On the basis of the results shown on Table 13.2 the following comments can be made. First, the total non-response rate was highest during the first month, clearly because interviewers had more difficulty in finding people at home, having not yet determined the best time to call, as one may observe in the higher 'no one at home' rate, for example. The rate then decreased sharply in the second month and continued to decrease through the third and fourth months.

Table 13.2 Non-response rates (per cent) according to tenure of households in the LFS (1979-80)

Number of months in Survey	Non-response rates			
	Total non-response	Refusal	No one at home	Temporarily absent
1	8.04	1.43	2.96	2.94
2	5.09	1.21	1.44	1.99
3	4.71	1.32	1.10	1.90
4	4.65	1.46	1.09	1.79
5	4.62	1.51	0.99	1.77
6	4.45	1.52	0.78	1.73

Second, the 'refusal rate' decreased in the second month, increased gradually through the third, fourth and fifth months and levelled off in the sixth month. The initial decrease probably represents the effect of supervisory intervention; the subsequent increase is likely due to the effect of cumulative response burden.

Third, the 'no one at home' rate decreased sharply from the first month to the second month by roughly 50 per cent. It continued to decrease from the second month to the third month but decreased very gradually through the fourth and fifth months. A larger decrease then occurred in the sixth month. The behaviour of the 'no one at home' rate over the six month tenure of households in the survey is most probably due to the fact that the longer a household is in the survey the more familiar the interviewer becomes with when the respondent is most likely to be at home.

Fourth, the 'temporarily absent' rate decreased through all six months, particularly from the first to the second month. The 'temporarily absent' rate should not be expected to depend on how long a household remains in the survey, and it seems almost certain that interviewers may have confused 'no one at home' and 'temporarily absent' types of non-response.

Non-response by type of area

Whereas the total non-response rate at the Canada level averaged 5.4 per cent during 1979 and 1980, non-response varied from region to region and urban-rural areas for many reasons such as geography, respondent characteristics and attitudes in each area, weather conditions and regional office procedures.

The results for 1980 by type of area shown in Table 13.3 indicate that the total non-response rate was higher in large urban areas (SRUs) than other areas (NSRUs) (self-representing units are cities whose population exceeds 15,000 persons or whose unique characteristics demanded their establishment as SRUs; non-self-representing units are the areas outside

SRUs and contain rural and small urban centres). Averaged over twelve months 'temporarily absent' rates were the same in both areas. However, 'temporarily absent' rates were higher (by as much as 30 per cent) in SRUs than in NSRUs during the months of May, June, July, August and September, while NSRU 'temporarily absent' rates were higher (by as much as 35 per cent) during the remaining months of the year. This phenomenon may have been due to the fact that people in rural areas move to larger centres with a warmer climate during the winter and that families living in cities usually take summer vacations. Although the 'temporarily absent' rates averaged over the year were the same for SRUs and NSRUs, the 'no one at home' rate in SRUs was almost 29 per cent higher than the corresponding rate in NSRUs. The 'refusal' rate was approximately 40 per cent higher in SRUs than in NSRUs.

Table 13.3 Non-response rates (per cent) by type of area (monthly average: 1980)

Type of area	Proportion of sample	Total non-response	Refusal	No one at home	Temporarily absent
NSRU	48.03	4.9	1.2	1.4	1.8
urban	17.58	5.2	1.1	1.4	2.2
rural	30.45	4.8	1.3	1.4	1.6
SRU	51.08	5.7	1.8	1.8	1.8
built-up	36.34	5.6	1.7	1.7	1.8
fringe	10.47	4.8	1.6	1.2	1.6
apartment	4.27	9.9	2.5	4.0	2.6

Within NSRUs the total non-response rate was higher in the urban portion due to higher 'temporarily absent' rates among NSRU urban households. The 'no one at home' rates in the urban and rural portions were the same, but the 'refusal' rates were 20 per cent higher in NSRU rural areas than in NSRU urban areas.

Within SRUs, built-up areas had a higher total non-response rate than fringe areas due to higher 'no one at home' and 'temporarily absent' components.

Thus, it appears that people living in the core areas of cities tend to be more difficult to contact than people living in the fringe areas; the differences, however, were not large.

SRU apartments had a higher total non-response rate than any other area shown in Table 13.3. In fact, the total non-response rate in the SRU apartment sample was almost twice the rate in the SRU non-apartment sample (consisting of both built-up and fringe areas). The 'refusal', 'no one at home' and 'temporarily absent' components were also highest among apartments.

The 'no one at home' rate was almost three times higher in the apartment sample than in the non-apartment sample. This large difference may be due to the different lifestyles of apartment and non-apartment dwellers. Apartment households usually consist of single persons or very small families who tend to be more mobile and difficult to find at home, while non-apartment households are more likely to contain larger families with children. Another problem with apartments is that interviewers often find it difficult to gain entrance into apartment buildings.

Whereas the 'temporarily absent' rate was usually twice as high for apartments as non-apartments, the difference was less noticeable during July and August than in the other ten months. This probably resulted from the fact that it is easier for single persons and families without children to take their vacations during autumn, winter and spring than it is for families with school-age children.

The 'refusal' rate was almost always higher in the apartment sample than in the non-apartment sample, although the difference in the 'refusal' rates between the two samples was not as great as the differences observed for the 'no one at home' and 'temporarily absent' rates. Recent results however, indicate that the gap in the level of 'refusal' rates between apartments and non-apartments is gradually widening, to the extent that the 'refusal' rate in the apartment sample is now almost double the corresponding rate in the non-apartment sample.

The significance of examining non-response rates according to breakdowns such as SRU and NSRU is that this approach helps establish relationships among the various types of area in terms of the behaviour of non-response rates. For instance, the overall non-response rate is always expected to be higher in SRUs than in NSRUs, and any deviation from this relationship is considered unusual. The same holds true for the 'no one at home' and 'refusal' rates in SRUs and NSRUs. Another example is the two-to-one ratio of the total non-response rate in the apartment sample to the corresponding rate in the non-apartment sample. If non-response rates ever increase beyond average or expected levels, then knowledge of these relationships is useful for the purpose of analysing the situation and taking remedial action.

Incidence of non-response for interviewer assignments

As expected, non-response rates varied among interviewers. Many interviewers, in fact, achieved 100 per cent response rates, while a few interviewers did no better than 75 per cent. It is interesting to look at the distribution of interviewers according to the level of their total non-response rates as shown on Table 13.4

Table 13.4 Distribution of interviewers according to non-response rates (Monthly average: 1978)

Total non-response rate(%)	Number of interviewers	Percentage of total interviewers
0.0	159	15.0
0.1 to 5.0	434	40.8
5.1 to 10.0	333	31.3
10.1 to 15.0	98	9.2
15.1 to 20.0	29	2.7
over 20.0	10	0.9
Total	1 063	100.0

The data in Table 13.4 are based on all interviewers who enumerated assignments with at least 20 housholds and represent an average over the twelve months of 1978. The table indicates that 56 per cent of interviewers achieved non-response rates of 5% or better.

The 13 per cent of interviewers with non-response rates higher than 10% accounted for 31 per cent or almost one-third of all non-responses. It is also interesting to observe that 59 per cent of interviewers did not record any 'no one at home' non-responses and that 54 per cent encountered no refusals. Furthermore, 71 per cent and 70 per cent of interviewers achieved 'no one at home' rates and 'refusal' rates, respectively, of 2% or better. These percentages reflect the success of the ongoing training programmes, monitoring and controls as well as interviewing techniques and procedures which are all aimed at maximising response levels in the LFS.

LFS procedures to control non-response

Assignment planning

Interviewers are instructed to enumerate all dwellings in their assignments while keeping expenditure (time and travel) to a minimum. Their assignments must be completed before the end of the six-day survey week. Interviewers work only on the LFS during this time and, although supplementary surveys are frequently carried out simultaneously with the LFS, priority is given to completing the LFS within the specified time limits.

Generally speaking, an interviewer's workload depends on the type of area enumerated and whether telephone interviews are permitted. Usually rural assignments consist of approximately 40 to 50 dwellings. Urban assignments are larger: 70 to 80 dwellings in the case of telephone assignments.[4] It is suggested that interviewers make up to three or four calls to every dwelling and at least one call before the fourth day of survey week. Interviewers usually complete first-month interviews and non-responses from the previous month as early as possible during survey week. During subsequent visits interviewers attempt to contact households at the 'best time to call' (determined at the time of the first contact with a household). If unsuccessful, they make calls at different times on different days.

In telephone assignments interviewers telephone frequently at different times and follow-up unsuccessful attempts to telephone with a personal visit. If the household is not at home on the first visit, the interviewer leaves a brochure describing the survey.

First contact

Through improved training methods and policies, interviewers are becoming more knowledgeable on how to gain respondent co-operation and conduct interviews effectively. During training, interviewing techniques such as appearance, introduction, asking the questions, handling delicate situations and ending the interview are emphasised. Very important in this training is the interviewer's introduction and presentation of the survey.

It is very important that the respondent be informed about the nature and purpose of the survey. For this reason, in cases where a mailing address is known, an introductory letter together with a brochure describing the LFS is sent to the household prior to the first interview. Thus, when the interviewer visits, the respondent usually already knows something about the survey; this helps the interviewers with their introduction. If mailing is not possible, then the interviewer presents the letter at the time of the first visit. In all cases, interviewers must ensure that every household has material explaining the survey.

Every interviewer must carry a Statistics Canada identification card and present it to the respondent at the beginning of the interview. This helps gain the respondent's confidence and ensures that the respondent clearly understands who the interviewer is and whom he/she represents. The interviewer gives a short explanation of the survey, and assures the respondent that the information which is being collected will be kept confidential and used only for statistical purposes. In subsequent interviews the interviewer tries to contact the person who was interviewed last month (particularly important in the case of telephone interviews), but if this is not possible then another responsible member of the household is interviewed.

Proxy interviews

Because of time and cost constraints it is virtually impossible to obtain non-proxy responses from every individual. For this reason proxy interviews are accepted in the LFS. Generally only one member of a household is interviewed, and this member responds on behalf of all other members. Occasionally, separate interviews are required for household members such as roomers or boarders. On average it has been found that proxy interviews account for approximately 50 per cent of all respondents. Furthermore, because proxy interviews are accepted, it is possible to obtain complete responses for all household members in virtually 100 per cent of responding households. In fact, there are less than 0.2 per cent of all households where interviews (proxy or non-proxy) are obtained for some, but not all, members of the household. The acceptance of suitable proxy respondents is, therefore, an effective means of reducing non-response.

Refusal follow-ups

Refusal households are followed up whenever feasible. In most cases this involves a personal visit by a senior interviewer or a regional office representative. In areas where this type of follow-up is not possible, a letter may be sent. Households are usually provided with additional information about the survey and how the data will be used. The importance of the survey and the co-operation of the respondent are emphasised. The result is that 20 to 30 per cent of these refusal households can be successfully interviewed the following month. In the case of households which cannot be persuaded to respond, interviewers are told not to visit them again unless there is a complete change in household composition.

Telephone interviewing

The telephone interviewing procedure which is used in the LFS involves a combination of personal visits and telephone calls and is carried out only in large urban areas. Interviewers must conduct all first-month interviews in person, and telephone interviews can only be carried out in subsequent months if the respondent agrees to be interviewed by telephone. Experience has shown that approximately 75 per cent of households are interviewed by telephone in assignments where the telephone interviewing procedure is allowed.

Although the primary reason for using telephone interviewing in the LFS is to reduce costs, telephone interviewing seems worthwhile from the point of view of non-response since it allows interviewing to be completed on time regardless of weather conditions: it is especially suitable for single persons, small family households and apartment dwellers who are difficult to find at home and who can often be reached only during the evening (it is easier for an interviewer to phone at night than to make a personal visit), it allows interviewing to be conducted more readily at the convenience of the respondent (if one time is not suitable, then another can be easily arranged); and it has the potential of reducing non-response by allowing more opportunity and time for call-backs.

However, the telephone interviewing procedure does not appear to have a direct impact on the reduction of non-response rates. This was indicated by the results of a telephone interviewing experiment carried out during 1972 and 1973. The experiment showed that respondents who agree to be interviewed by telephone are very unlikely to be non-respondents during subsequent interviews. Those households which do not agree to telephone interviewing or which cannot be telephoned (for reasons such as no telephone available, party line telephone, unlisted telephone number, complete change in household composition, language or hearing problems, etc.) can be expected to contribute nearly 50 per cent of all non-response, even though this group of households accounts for only 10 to 20 per cent of all households in telephone assignments. Therefore, if more effort is directed towards these households then presumably the non-response rate can be reduced. According to the present interviewing procedures, interviewers are instructed to complete as many telephone interviews as possible during the first day or two of survey week and to try to contact newly selected households and non-responses from the previous month as early as possible during survey week. In this way, least priority is given to contacting the households which cannot be interviewed by telephone for reasons other than first month interviews.

This suggests that non-response may be reduced among those

households which can be interviewed by telephone, but that more non-response may be occurring among those households which are not telephoned.

Monitoring non-response

For dwellings where no contact can be made interviewers identify the reason for the non-interview and record this reason on the Household Record Docket.[5] Interviewers also complete a non-interview report explaining as fully as possible why no interview took place. Following the interviewer's coding of the non-interview the regional office decides what action should be taken the following month. This action is then preprinted on the following month's Household Record Docket indicating whether the interviewer should attempt to interview the household again or whether he/she should not conduct an interview unless there is a complete change in household composition.

The performance of interviewers is continually monitored and reviewed. Regional offices have a monthly report on non-response rates at the interviewer level. This report can be produced in each region as soon as survey week has been completed, and it allows supervisors to take immediate action in specific circumstances when interviewers have unusually high non-response rates. The objective is to remedy these situations in time for the next survey and to maintain non-response rates at a satisfactory level.

In the LFS there are also regular programmes of observation and reinterview. The observation programme is carried out for the purpose of evaluating and improving the performance of interviewers. Every month about one-tenth of the interviewers are selected for observation including interviewers scheduled for systematic observation as well as new interviewers and interviewers whose performance suggests they need observation. The observer, usually a senior interviewer, accompanies the interviewer into the field during survey week and evaluates the interviewer in nearly all aspects of his/her work. This observation provides an excellent opportunity to train or retrain interviewers in the use of proper interviewing procedures. Among specific areas evaluated are the interviewer's knowledge of non-interview procedures and his/her ability to minimise the number of non-responses in his/her assignment.

The reinterview programme is conducted in the week immediately following survey week by a senior interviewer or supervisor. Households which were enumerated during survey week are contacted again, and reinterviews proceed with the reinterviewer repeating the same questions previously asked by the interviewer. Any observed differences between the two sets of responses are attributable to several sources including the respondent, the interviewer, the reinterviewer, shortcomings in the instructions or training provided to interviewers, and the wording and sequence of the questions. Although the primary purpose of the reinterview programme is to measure response errors, it also allows the opportunity to check the quality of an interviewer's work including his/her handling of non-interviews. Checking with the respondent, for example, indicates whether or not the interviewer varied the time of his/her contact and made several call-backs. The reinterview programme, therefore, is a complement to the observation programme since it helps identify interviewer weakness and needs for further training.

Non-response by type of surveys

The major factors influencing the non-response rates are the sensitivity and complexity of subject matter (a nutrition survey we carried out, for example, imposed an additional respondent burden by requiring clinical tests). It has been our experience that the effort of the LFS to increase

Table 13.5 Non-response rate by type of survey

Name of survey	Year	Collection method	Non-response rate*	Supplement to LFS
Survey of Consumer Finance (Income)	1972	Drop-off-pick up	28.3	Yes
Survey of Consumer Finance (Income)	1973	Drop-off-pick up	18.1	No
Survey of Consumer Finance (Income)	1974	Drop-off-pick up	25.7	Yes
Survey of Consumer Finance (Income)	1975	Drop-off-pick up	20.2	No
Survey of Consumer Finance (Income)	1976	Drop-off-pick up	27.1	Yes
Survey of Consumer Finance (Income)	1977	Personal	20.3	No
Survey of Consumer Finance (Income)	1978	Drop-off-pick up	34.4	Yes
Survey of Consumer Finance (Income)	1979	Drop-off-pick up	28.1	No
Selected leisure activities	1978	Drop-off-pick up	13.0	Yes
Nutrition survey	1972	Personal	50.0†	No
Household facilities	1978	Personal	9.1	Yes
Household facitilies	1979	Personal	11.5	Yes
Household facilities	1980	Personal	15.9	Yes
Travel Survey	1979	Personal	7.3	Yes
Smoking habits	1979	Personal	8.0	Yes
Study of housing	1979	Personal	20.0	No
Travel Survey	1979	Telephone	10.0	Yes
Smoking habits	1979	Telephone	10.0	Yes
Victimisation	1979	Telephone	15.0	No
1976 graduate	1979	Telephone	14.5	No
Travel survey (1977)	1977	Drop-off-mailback	16.0	Yes
Methodology test	1977	Drop-in-mailback	18.0	Yes

* Non-response rates $= \frac{n_2}{N} \times 100$ where N is total sample and n_2 is the number of units which did not respond.
† Includes 25 per cent who refused to come to clinic.

response rates also benefits supplementary surveys. However, a combined effect of sensitive questions, complexity and the length of questionnaire may impose too much burden on the respondent, resulting in a higher non-response, even though the survey may be a supplement to the LFS. This is, in fact, the case with the Survey of Consumer Finance (income). However, during the years when SCF is an independent sample, the burden is at least a 'one-shot' affair and the respondent may co-operate, resulting in lower non-response rates than when it is a supplement.

A second but also important factor is the method of data collection. Usually personal interviews will have lower non-response rates than any other method of interviewing for approximately the same degree of sensitivity of the subject matter. For example, our travel surveys, when conducted using personal interviews, resulted in a lower non-response rate (7.3 per cent) than when using telephone (10 per cent) or drop off-mailback (16 per cent) methods of data collection (see Table 13.5). Similarly, the survey on smoking habits had a non-response rate of 8 per cent for personal and 10 per cent for telephone interviewing, respectively. In the latter case it should be noticed that both surveys were conducted as supplements to the LFS.

Survey design and non-response

The preceding section provided a detailed account of non-response and a number of operations dealing with it in the Labour Force Survey. The subsequent sections will discuss considerations related to non-response at such stages in surveys as sample design, data collection, edit and imputation.

Although the actual non-response occurs during data collection, its size can be greatly influenced at the planning stage by examining the possible effect that various design factors may have on non-response.

Careful and appropriate preparation for data collection with respect to methods of interviewing and motivation of respondents and interviewers will considerably affect the magnitude of non-response.

At the processing and estimation stage an attempt is made to minimise the effect of non-response on the final estimates by imputing for missing values.

Sample design (planning and development)

At the planning stage, an awareness of the effect of non-response on the mean square error (MSE) of survey data may lead to a survey design which would influence the size of non-response. One of the important factors in planning a survey is a decision on the tolerance level of non-response and an experienced survey designer can estimate fairly accurately the level of response for a particular survey that can be expected under various survey conditions. For example, for national estimates with a large sample size, the effect of non-response on sampling and response variance is likely to be unimportant and the bias is the likely predominant component of MSE. However, for subnational estimates the variances are likely to be large, so bias might be relatively less important.

The survey cost is another important item which will affect many factors in survey development including non-response. It is important to balance the other factors against the cost so as to achieve a non-response rate sufficiently low to serve the goals of the survey. It should also be realised that, within reasonable limits, it is sometimes better to accept a somewhat smaller sample than originally planned and to transfer the resources to appropriate data collection, follow-up and estimation procedures. This would be particularly advantageous if the survey designer suspected large differences between respondents and non-respondents in their characteristics.

In survey planning and development a number of factors should be taken into account in arriving at the final design. A group of factors with particular bearing as potential source and cause for non-response includes: sample frame; method of interviewing; selection, training and control of staff; length of questionnaire and wording; sensitivity of questions; type of area in which the survey is taken; feasibility and cost of call-backs; and publicity. If careful attention is paid to these factors at the design stage, serious non-response problems may be avoided.

Data collection

In discussing approaches to minimising non-response, one can distinguish between two types. One type, such as 'no one at home' or 'temporarily absent' is in fact a 'no contact' problem and is primarily operationally oriented. Refusal is an interviewer problem, where contact has been made with the respondent but an acceptable response is not obtained.

The 'no contact' type of problem is of course usually attacked with operational solutions. In a telephone or personal interview the time and patterns of calling on the respondent are important. The size of assignment and the time allotted to data collection must be adequate. In a mail survey, ensuring correct addresses on the mailing list, efficient follow-up procedures and convenient materials are all essential. The size of non-response due to 'no one at home' or 'temporarily absent' provides an important indication of the operational problems.

The existence of refusals presents a different set of problems. It should be conceded at the outset that refusal rates are not always as straightforward as one might expect. An interviewer may prefer to record a refusal as a 'no one at home' or a respondent may simply not answer the door as a means of refusing and thus is recorded as 'no one at home'. In a mail survey one is not always certain that the respondent received the questionnaire and if he/she has received it whether he/she simply neglected to mail it. Thus, the distinction between refusals and other causes is not easily established.

The invalid response presents still a different set of problems since an inexperienced interviewer may not realise that the data is invalid or illogical until an edit routine has discovered it. Also, the interviewer may carelessly code the response in an incorrect location on the questionnaire resulting in invalid data which must be discarded. The problem seems to be to motivate the appropriate respondent to produce a valid response.

With respect to motivation, let us look upon the respondent as being neutral towards the survey and consider the influence which may motivate him either to respond or not to respond. Such factors as difficulty in understanding questions, use of respondent time, privacy, indifference, difficulties in recalling information, embarrassing or personal questions are all examples of motivation not to respond. On the other hand, examples of motivation to respond are an interest in the survey, willingness to help out, duty, understanding of the importance of survey results, etc.

The problem becomes how to accentuate the positive motivation and reduce the negative motivation until the balance swings in favour of response. The key element is the respondent and anything which affects his/her ability and motivation to respond must be of interest and concern to a survey designer.

Motivation of respondent

It is a matter of common experience that in everyday life when one asks a question, one normally receives an answer. What, then, motivates a respondent not to respond to a survey? Invasion of privacy, respondent burden and general hostility or distrust of government are the three major reasons. In dealing with these problems, it is important to consider them from the respondents' point of view and not from some preconceived notions on the part of the sponsor or survey designer. Certain questionnaires may be perceived by the respondents as burdensome if they do not understand why they are being asked or how the survey is related to them. Under different conditions, however, the same questions may be perceived as very interesting and the respondent is motivated to participate in the survey. The general means by which respondent motivation can be sought may be divided into two parts, public relations and respondent relations.

Public relations are activities directed to the general public, and can take many forms. One long-range objective is to create a climate in the general public which will tend to motivate it in the direction of co-operation with surveys. The image of the survey organisation as perceived by the respondent can be an important factor in his/her motivation to respond. The extent and manner of data dissemination can be used to impress upon the public the importance of the role of the statistical agency. The statistical agency must be alert to possibilities for favourable comment via the media and also to the necessity for timely and appropriate handling of criticism. A public relations approach, in addition to maintaining a favourable image, may be used to publicise specific activities and request co-operation in carrying them out. Ill-conceived publicity may in fact have a negative effect. As a general rule, publicity campaigns are most suitable for population census operations where everyone is affected, and there is a need to motivate the population as a whole. Where the ratio of sample size to population is small, it is usually more cost effective (in the context of a single survey) to avoid direct publicity and to concentrate on respondent relations.

Respondent relations

A working definition of respondent relations might be that it comprises any action directed toward the individual respondent which may affect his/her attitude and motivation with regard to the survey. As was previously stated, the problems of most concern are invasion of privacy, respondent burden, and general hostility or distrust. In regard to hostility or distrust, public relations and the agency's image have already been mentioned. Identification of the interviewer and sponsor or agency conducting the survey is very important. Unwelcome callers have been known to use the pretext of a survey to establish contact or gain entry. It is important that the interviewer present official identification and that the survey materials convey an appearance of being official.

Introductory letters, examples of the uses of the data, and brochures describing the objectives and authority for the survey, are often excellent means of avoiding hostility and distrust.

Invasion of privacy is usually related to the content of the questionnaire although the reaction of different respondents is quite variable. Many procedures exist for minimising the effect on the respondent and the specific procedure should be tailored to the specific situation. In some cases, it may be best to allow the respondent to reply in a completely anonymous fashion. This can be accomplished by self-enumeration with no identification whatsoever on the questionnaire. Quite often, though, it is essential to have some area code or sample designation for weighting and estimation purposes and in that even care must be taken that respondent does not perceive this as a means of identifying his/her replies. Of course, it should be clear that whereas anonymous surveys might be beneficial to response from the point of view of privacy concerns, these benefits might be more than offset by the fact that such surveys permit no follow-up of non-respondents.

In addition to the assurance of privacy, some forms of compensating the respondents for their time and effort have been practised by some survey-taking organisations.

Field operations

Substitution in the field

One method of dealing with non-response at the data collection stage is to substitute other previously unselected units in the field. It must be emphasised, however, that this is still non-response, and substitution is a means of imputation. Two basic types of substitution are used: selection of a random substitute; and, selection of a specifically designated substitute.

With a random substitution method, an additional population unit is selected on a probability basis to replace each non-respondent. For many random substitution procedures, potential substitutes are selected prior to the data collection in order to avoid any delays and problems that could exist if the substitutes were selected after the data collection is begun.

In a procedure that uses specially designated substitutes (for example, a next-door neighbour), the intent is to find a substitute similar in characteristics to those of the non-respondent. Unfortunately, this could lead to a sampling bias, especially if the neighbour lives outside the sample frame. While any original unit may be selected with known probability according to the sample design, substitution of other previously unselected respondents to replace uncooperative respondents in some uncontrolled manner or even in a controlled manner will alter the inclusion probabilities. A sampling bias of unknown magnitude could be introduced (since the selection probabilities are not known). While the sampling variance may be reduced because of an increase in the effective sampling size, there would probably be no reduction in either the response or non-response bias. Even if the inclusion probabilities could be calculated, the non-response bias would, in effect, remain unchanged since the uncooperative or difficult-to-contact units continue to have a reduced or zero chance of inclusion. The key question regarding the worth of substitution procedures is whether or not the use of substitution provides better proxy values for non-respondents than those provided by alternative imputation procedures. Undoubtedly, there are some advantages and disadvantages to the use of substitution procedures. The first advantage is that they are a convenient way of balancing the sample with respect to sample size. The other is the reduction of the sampling variance due to increase in the effective sample size (although this advantage can also be achieved by selecting a sample where size is inflated by the expected non-response).

One of the major disadvantages of the use of substitution is a tendency to use it rather than making every effort to obtain responses from original units. Thus the use of substitution procedures requires that appropriate control should be taken to ensure that maximum effort is made to obtain responses from the original sample units. Another disadvantage is that there is a tendency to ignore the level and the frequency of substitution when the survey response rate is calculated.

Callbacks

In many surveys, callbacks are extensively used in order to reduce non-response and the resulting biases. The callbacks may take a variety of forms depending on the type of survey. In mail or interview surveys callbacks may take the form of a letter, a telephone call or a personal interview. In telephone surveys and in interview surveys repeated calls are the normal form of callbacks. There is a need to study various types of callbacks with respect to quality of data, cost and respondent reaction to them.

Respondent rule

In order to avoid any ambiguity as to the eligibility of respondents in a given survey a procedure referred to as 'respondent rule' should be defined and followed in the field.

For surveys which involve a designated respondent, two rules are most often used.

(a) Where a designated respondent is to be interviewed and he/she is capable of responding but unavailable, repeated callbacks are made until contact is established.

(b) If the designated respondent is not present or not capable of responding (because of deafness, illness, etc.) a proxy respondent is chosen. Variants of this rule involve different definitions of permissible proxy respondents.

For surveys in which responses for each eligible household member are required, one of several possible respondent rules is followed:

(a) Every member of the household is to respond personally (self-response).

(b) One member of the household may answer for every member of the household (proxy response).

(c) A mixture of self-response and proxy response, depending on the respondents' availability at the time of interview, or some specific respondent rule, e.g. persons unrelated to the head of the household must respond for themselves.

Methodological investigations of the effects of using various respondent rules have focused on two basic areas. The first involves the differences in the number of callbacks needed to contact the desired respondent (proposed by Cochran, 1977); the second involves differences in the quality of the data obtained which can be evaluated through a programme of reinterviewing of the original respondents.

The use of proxy respondents diminishes the number of callbacks, thus reducing the cost of survey and improving timeliness of obtaining the data. On the other hand, there may be a disadvantage to the use of proxies in that the data provided by proxy respondents may be less accurate than those obtained from self-responses. The use of a particular respondent rule should be very carefully examined in relation to the type and quality of the data required, cost involved in obtaining the data and timeliness for publications. Those considerations will vary from survey to survey depending on the survey topic, budget and field organisation.

Edit and imputation

Regardless of the efficiency of interviewers in controlling non-response and despite an increase in the sample size and other considerations discussed earlier, there will be a point beyond which non-response cannot be taken care of at a reasonable cost. Consequently, at the estimation stage, some compensation through edit and imputation must be carried out explicitly or implicitly to attempt to reduce bias due to non-response.

At the processing and estimation stage, survey data are usually classified according to total non-response, partial non-response and invalid response.

There are various ways of dealing with incomplete or invalid responses, and each of them results in assigning a value for the missing or invalid data unless a decision is made to publish 'raw' data. The procedure of assigning the value is called imputation, and some imputed value is assumed to refer to the characteristic of the non-respondent. Thus a 'clean' data set is produced, that is, a value is given to each unit in survey. Before proceeding to discuss various imputation methods let us examine conceptual issues of imputation.

As the information flows from data collection to tabulation, the various types of response can be identified and are presented as follows in Figure 13.1. The chart is, of course, a highly simplified diagram of the process and it is produced only for the purpose of the discussion of this paper.

Figure 13.1   Flow chart pertaining to each sampled unit

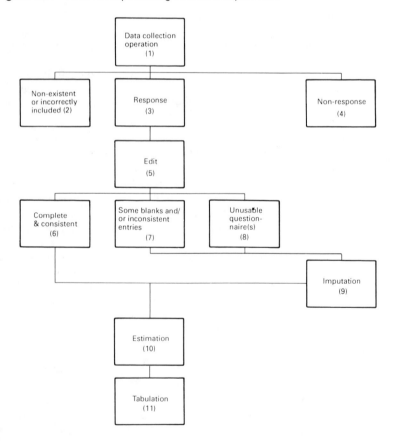

From Figure 13.1, it can be seen that, apart from (4) those containing non-responses, two of the three groups of questionnaires following the edit stage require further action prior to estimation. These are (8) unusable questionnaires, and (7) those containing some blanks and/or inconsistent entries. An unusable questionnaire could be classified as total non-response or it could be associated with a respondent household with some blank or inconsistent entries. In either case, however, further action denoted by (9) imputation would be required. Complete non-respondents are usually weighted up in some manner, except in census surveys. The deficient questionnaires, on the other hand, fall into two categories such as (7) inconsistent entries or illegitimate blanks.

The inconsistent entries can be either logical impossibilities or they can be plausible but highly unlikely. It seems natural that if the entries are logical impossibilities and they can be detected as such, they ought to be adjusted even though they may not affect the data to any great extent. The adjustment would eliminate a great deal of embarrassment to subject-matter analysts associated with the published reports.

In the case of plausible but highly unlikely entries, one is faced with a difficult choice between leaving what might seem to be an unnatural distribution or removing some of the extreme values of the distributon which may actually represent the real-life situation. Ideally, one ought to opt for one or other choice on the basis of experience with error mechanisms and the nature of the substantive distribution based on the knowledge of subject matter. In any case, one has to be able to identify the problem cases, i.e. one has to have suitable edit rules whenever one encounters impossible or highly unlikely events and a method of dealing with them (i.e. imputation).

There is a fundamental distinction between editing and imputation. Let us consider the set of all possible code combinations on a questionnaire. Editing can be defined as the division of this set into two mutually exclusive subsets – those combinations which are judged acceptable, and those which are unacceptable – the latter including questionnaires with invalid blanks and inconsistent entries. Thus, editing is basically a diagnosis and operationally it must be defined by a set of rules. Imputation, on the other hand, is more in the nature of treatment of data.

Imputation may be defined as the assignment of data to empty fields (including total non-response) or a replacement of invalid data in fields following a certain set of rules. There is no known unbiased method of imputing but some methods may be more suitable than others.

It is possible that, rather than imputing for non-response at the time when survey tabulations are prepared, tabulations could be presented with the amount of non-response reported. In this case, the users would have a choice among various methods of imputation from tabulated data. At first glance, this approach would appear to have some advantages giving the users the opportunity of selecting their own method of imputation. There are, however, some serious disadvantages. Conflicting estimates would be produced by various users due to the different imputation methods employed and problems in the consistency and integration of data would be created. Also, the data collection agency is usually in a better position, due to its proximity to the sources of the data, to make imputation decisions. For these reasons, imputation is normally carried out by data collecting agencies rather than by individual users. The whole philosophy of imputation is based upon the expectation that an appropriate procedure, whether for non-response or for blanks resulting from edit failure, will provide a more logical relationship between cross-classified data and will also lower the MSE of estimates.

The simplest situation occurs when there is only one possible value which can be imputed for a field in such a way that after the imputation the record will be consistent. This is what is called deterministic imputation. For example, if wife is coded 'male' then there is only one possible value to impute for sex to make it consistent with the other information. Sometimes, there may be more than one value which would make the record consistent. If this is the case, one would choose a particular value which is more predominant in proportion to total frequency or more plausible. A good example of this kind can be found in the Labour Force Survey where, in the autumn to spring months, for 15- and 16-year-old persons, if there is no Labour Force characteristic entered, one imputes that they are 'attending school', although it is not at all impossible that they do not attend school. So long as the proportion of such cases is sufficiently small, the effect of this imputation will be a slight increase in bias, but there will be some reduction in variance.

In other situations where one could reasonably impute a whole range of values, one needs some other criteria. One possible criterion would be to minimise the MSE of the resulting estimates. The question, however, arises: the MSE of which estimates? With the continuously increasing demand for data tabulated in a number of different and unforeseen ways one really does not know which MSE one ought to minimise. Futhermore, one would not know all the kinds of aggregates to which a particular record may contribute in different kinds of tabulations. Consequently, one might prefer to use some other criterion which would produce the most appropriate entry for a field in a particular record in relation to the other information in the record. In other words, how can one best predict the value of one field on the basis of knowing the other fields on the record? A good example of this kind of imputation is the use of the previous month's data in the Labour Force Survey: for a particular person, one could hardly find a better imputed value, particularly in those cases where demographic characteristics change slowly. If one does not have information based on the past, one would have to resort to such methods of imputation as regression or hot deck.

Methodology of Imputation

For a number of years various procedures of imputation for missing data due to non-response have been used in household surveys and censuses. The use of a particular procedure has been, to my knowledge, mostly justified on the ground of expedience, intuition and experience. It was often assumed that the probabilities of units responding were uniform and the non-response bias was largely ignored.

Although variations in response rates have been detected among units according to their characteristics, the effect of individual units responding or not responding upon the bias and variance of the estimates has usually been insufficiently examined.

To facilitate a detailed examination of the effect, Platek and Gray (1979) have developed methodology with respect to the bias and variance pertaining to several imputation procedures. The development of the expression of bias and variance of the estimates is based on a fundamental concept that a unit, if selected, responds with a certain response probability. This is an extension of the approach taken by Platek, Singh and Tremblay (1978) with respect to censuses.

The definitions of various imputation procedures involve the following: the use of cells for imputation, these cells being either balancing areas or weighting classes; or adjustments in weights using estimated response probabilities within the cells.

Balancing areas are frequently referred to as 'design-dependent balancing areas' for imputation purposes. A balancing area is a geographic area in which a deficient sample arising from missing data is enlarged to the prescribed level by means of imputation for the missing data. Commonly, a balancing area is a stratum, but it could be other design-dependent areas, such as a primary sampling unit, cluster, group, stratum, several strata or even the entire sample. The balancing areas may be delineated before or after the survey is taken.

Weighting classes are defined by post-strata (strata defined after sampling) formed on the basis of information pertaining to respondents and non-respondents in the sample. The information may be obtained from those partial non-respondents for whom some characteristics are known even though the particular characteristic being estimated is not known for these units as in the case of item non-response, for example. The characteristics used in the post-strata could also be obtained from external sources. From the operational point of view, a weighting class is very similar to a balancing area except that the units having similar characteristics are grouped into classes or post-strata without regard to their geographic location in the sample frame.

The choice of characteristics and the size of balancing areas or weighting classes are important, as the variance and bias of an estimate derived from the sample would depend upon the homogeneity of characteristics between the respondents and non-respondents within the balancing areas or weighting classes.

The *weighting method* of imputation, as applied in practice to complete non-response, is one in which the sample weights or inverse inclusion probabilities are inflated by the inverse of the response rate in a cell. Implicitly, the imputed value for the missing data of each non-respondent is the mean of all responding values in the cell, with some adjustments for selection probabilities in the case of sampling with unequal probabilities.

In the *duplication method* of imputation, the deficiency in the sample in a cell due to non-response is made up by duplicating all or a subsample of respondents. There are several ways of duplicating units. One of these and the simplest to treat from the point of view of methodological development is the random selection of units for duplication without replacement. Here, some or all responding units are duplicated the minimum number of times required in order to compensate for the deficient sample in the cell. An example of a duplication method is a hot deck procedure.

The *hot deck procedure* is a common method of adjusting data sets for missing values. In general, it is a duplication process – one reported value from the sample is duplicated to represent a missing value.

The primary reason for using a hot deck or a cold deck procedure is to attempt to reduce non-response bias. The essential difference between the two procedures lies in the way the information for missing data is specified. A cold deck procedure is deterministic: a predetermined value is substituted for each item non-response, the particular value being chosen as a function of the values on the questionnaire which are not missing. A hot deck procedure is probabilistic: the value substituted for item non-response is the value of that item which was encountered in the last 'acceptable' record, which is similar to the current one with respect to the reported values on the questionnaire.

As a method of imputation, hot deck procedures have some attractive features, including the following: the procedures result in a relatively easy way of constructing post-strata; matching of records does not present any special problems; no strong model assumptions need be made in order to estimate the individual values for missing items.

In evaluating hot deck procedures one would like to know how the bias and reliability of the principal estimates are affected by the size of classification groups (often referred to as weighting classes), the frequency of missing data, the choice of matching items, etc. Some theoretical work relating to hot decks has been done: see Fellegi and Holt (1976); Bailar and Bailar (1978); and Cox and Folsom (1978).

In the *historical data substitution method* historical or external sources such as census, earlier survey or administrative data are substituted for a unit to replace missing data caused by non-response. The following two cases may be considered: where historical or external source data are available for all units which have failed to respond; and where the external source data are available for some but not all units, and imputation by another method, e.g. 'weighting', must also be applied.

The third and least satisfactory case, because it merely shifts the problem to the users, is that of ignoring non-response. In this case, by implication, zero value is substituted for missing values.

Other imputation methods include substitution of historical data, regression and multiple imputation. Regression and multiple imputation methods are not discussed in this paper.

Application of imputation to the Labour Force Survey

The imputation procedures that are in common use in sample surveys and censuses in Canada include weight adjustment, duplication, substitution of historical or external data and hot decks.

In the monthly Labour Force Survey of Canada, imputation for complete household non-response is carried out according to the following criteria: (i) for about one-third of the non-respondents substitution of last month's values where they are applicable (with suitable transformations in some fields to update last month's data); or (ii) inflation by the inverse 'response' rate in balancing units 'response' in this case including substituted values for those non-respondents who actually responded in the preceding survey with applicable data). In the case of (ii), the imputation for the remaining two-thirds of the non-respondents is implicitly the mean of all respondents in the balancing unit (primary sampling units (PSUs), small urban and rural portions of PSUs, or subunits in large cities).

Imputation for item non-response or edit rejects is carried out in one of three ways, depending upon the item or items with missing or faulty data and depending upon the response status and characteristics of the unit in the previous survey:

(i) the proper response that has been omitted can be unambiguously deduced from the remainder of the questionnaire (a decision table would ensure a unique and consistent response);
(ii) the substitution of the item response of the previous survey if it is available and if it is appropriate according to a decision table;
(iii) the application of a hot deck procedure whereby a similar record is obtained in the same PSU, same path taken (one of six possible) in the sequence of questions, and same age-sex group. Here, collapsing of weighting classes may be required to find a similar type record; usually age-sex categories rather than PSUs or paths taken are grouped together for imputation purposes when necessary.

Procedures used in other household surveys lean heavily on the methods used in the Labour Force Survey and the Survey of Consumer Finances. The latter defines several imputation strata and the method of stratification is primarily based on a technique developed by Sonquist and Morgan (1964).

Notes

1. This paper has been made available for publication through the courtesy of the ECE Statistical Division. The views expressed are the author's personal views and do not necessarily reflect the views of the ECE Statistical Division or the ILO Bureau of Statistics. An earlier and expanded version of this paper was presented at the Meeting on Problems relating to Household Surveys (Statistical Methodology), convened by the Statistical Commission and Commission for Europe (Conference of European Statisticians, Geneva, 1–4 June 1981).

2. Absent for the entire survey week.
3. The occupant could not be contacted after several attempts.
4. In large cities, the first interview is in person and the subsequent interview is carried out by telephone, providing the respondent has a telephone and is willing to co-operate. The usual telephone assignment is 70–80 households.
5. The Household Record Docket provides a record of all persons (i.e. household members) found in a selected dwelling for the period that the dwelling is in the Labour Force Survey and contains information which helps interviewers plan their assignments and conduct interviews.

References

Bailar, B. and Bailar, J. (1978), 'Comparison of two Procedures for Imputing Missing Values', *Proceedings of the American Statistical Association*, Section on Survey Methods.

Cochran, W. G. (1977) *Sampling Techniques*, John Wiley and Sons.

Cox, B. and Folsom, R. (1978) 'An Empirical Investigation of Alternative Item Non-response Adjustments', Research Triangle Institute.

Fellegi, I. P., and Holt, D. (1976) 'A Systematic Approach to Automatic Edit and Imputation', *Journal of the American Statistical Association*, Volume 71, p. 17.

Platek, R. and Gray, G. B. (1979) 'Methodology of Adjustments for Non-response', invited paper presented at the 42nd Session of International Statistical Institute, Manila, Philippines.

Platek, R., Singh, M. P. and Tremblay, V. (1978) 'Adjustment for Non-response in Surveys' *Survey Sampling and Measurement* N. Krishnan Namboodiri, Ed., Academic Press, New York.

Sonquist, J. N. and Morgan, J. A. (1964) 'The Detection of Interaction Effects', Monograph no. 35, Survey Research Centre, Institute for Social Research, University of Michigan.

14 Labour force flow statistics – an examination of objectives, collecting methods and measurement issues[1]

F. Mehran

Introduction

There is an increasing concern in the field of social and demographic statistics to measure flows as well as stocks of populations. Examples of flow data are the flows of the working-age population into and out of the labour force, transitions of the youth population from learning to earning activities, flows of adult women into and out of different marital statuses, etc. Such flow data are generally difficult to compile and often subject to greater measurement errors than the corresponding stock data.

The purpose of this paper is to review the objectives and methods of compiling statistics on labour force flows and to examine some of the measurement issues.

Measurement objectives

Labour force flow statistics are needed to supplement labour force stock data, particularly for formulating and monitoring labour market policies. Labour market policies, for the most part, are primarily designed to affect flows of the target population, whether by encouraging, preventing or redirecting them. Employment creation policies, for example, are generally intended to move people out of unemployment and into employment. Similarly, programmes for creating part-time employment and development of day-care centres are generally designed to ease the flow of persons outside the labour force, particularly women, into the labour force. On the other hand, work-sharing programmes, wage subsidy schemes and similar plans are often instituted in order to prevent the flow of employed persons into unemployment. Many other programmes such as apprenticeship development, vocational training, etc., are basically aimed at redirection flows, for instance redirecting the flow of youth into employment rather than unemployment when first entering the labour force.

Labour force stock data alone do not provide the necessary information to examine in detail the flows intended by the various programmes mentioned above and others. A decline in the number of unemployed persons observed by comparing changes in the stock data on unemployment at two points in time, for example, could be interpreted, in the absence of flow data, as due either to persons ceasing to seek work and withdrawing from the labour force or to persons finding jobs following job-search activity. Similarly, an observed decline in the number of employed persons may be due to persons losing or leaving their jobs and becoming unemployed or to persons temporarily or indefinitely withdrawing from economic activity. Distinguishing between these possibilities and analysing their extent require flow data in addition to stock data, showing separately the number of unemployed and employed persons at the given time according to their labour force status at an earlier point of time.

In addition to providing further information for guiding the formulation and monitoring of labour market policies, labour force flow statistics serve a variety of particular purposes. Retrospectively, they may be used to analyse the dynamism of the labour market and the determinants of unemployment and labour force participation. Prospectively, they may be used to estimate transition probabilities and provide bases for making labour market projections and forecasting.[2]

Disaggregated statistics on flows within and between the basic components may also be useful, for example for analysing movements into and out of occupations, or movements into and out of different categories of non-economic activity, i.e. studies, household duties, retirement, etc.

In general, the basic measurement objective is to obtain statistics on the entries of the following tabulation:

| | | Labour force status at current date | | |
		E(t)	U(t)	N(t)
Labour force status	E(t−1)	EE	EU	EN
at previous date	U(t−1)	UE	UU	UN
	N(t−1)	NE	NU	NN

The meaning of the entries is as follows: *EE* represents the number of persons who were employed both at the current and previous dates, *EU* is the number of persons employed at the previous date who became unemployed, *EN* is the number of previously employed persons who withdrew from the labour force, etc.

Methods of data collection

Flow data may be obtained using specially designed procedures, for example on the basis of retrospective questions in conventional survey questionnaires or on longitudinal data. They may also be derived by exploiting the rotation sampling schemes often incorporated in surveys primarily designed to obtain stock data or by combining various sets of data obtained from administrative and other sources.

Retrospective questions

A restrospective question may concern one date in the past, for example the activity status one year before as in France's two annual employment surveys, or it may concern an event in the past, for example when a currently unemployed or currently inactive person was last employed. The latter type of restrospective question, however, is generally unsuitable for deriving flow data of the kind discussed here.

Although convenient and relatively inexpensive, the derivation of labour force flow data from retrospective questions has a number of limitations. First, various types of error due to memory lapses may occur. In the case of 'date-type' retrospective questions, there is a tendency to omit declaring changes in status, while in the case of the 'event-type' questions there is a tendency to bring the date closer to the present than it actually was. Errors of memory are aggravated when proxy responses are used.

Another problem is the difficulty of maintaining the same definition for ascertaining the current status and the past status. Generally, the determination of the current activity status of surveyed individuals as employed, unemployed and not in the labour force is based on the responses to a sequence of structured questions which may involve up to ten or twelve questions. It is clearly not feasible to use a similar sequence to determine the activity status in the distant past. A simpler procedure must be used and, therefore, what one is measuring for the past is not necessarily the same as one is measuring for the present.

If X'_{t-1} represents the 'true' activity status of the surveyed individual at time $t-1$ and $X'_{t-1,t}$ is the restrospective activity status at time $t-1$ measured at time t, the measurement error is equal to $X_{t-1}-X'_{t-1,t}$ which may be decomposed into two parts, $(X_{t-1}-X_{t-1,t}) + (X_{t-1,t}-X'_{t-1,t})$, where the first part represents the error due to memory and the second that due to differences of definitions. In order to minimise the definitional error, attempts are made so that the current and past activity statuses reflect, to the extent possible, the same concepts and definitions. It is, in fact, with this point in mind that in the French surveys mentioned earlier the flow data are compiled on the basis of the census definition of activity status rather than the more complicated survey or international definitions.[3]

A further difficulty with the retrospective method is the problem of disaggregation. If the flow data are to be disaggregated by components, for example in order to measure the movements from part-time to full-time employment or vice versa, more refined retrospective questions should be formulated, thus aggravating recall and other errors. Also, if the flow data are to be compiled separately for different population categories, for example for single women, married women, etc., additional retrospective questions should be incorporated, as the characteristics in question (marital status in this case) may not have been constant during the measurement period.

Longitudinal data

Longitudinal surveys in the sense used here are surveys especially designed to study the behaviour of identified social groups over time. In a longitudinal survey, a panel of households and individuals is selected and followed through time, and relevant statistical information collected at regular or irregular intervals.[4] Longitudinal surveys permit more accurate measurement of flows than retrospective questions. They also provide more flexibility in the choice of supplementary variables for behavioural studies of employment and unemployment movements and allow measurements of long-term as well as shorter-term flows. They are, however, expensive to operate and require well-developed statistical and administration machinery and data processing capability. Some of the difficulties are the relatively low response rates (refusals), the difficulty of following up households which have changed residence (attrition) or newly formed households (split-offs), and the conditioning effects due to repeated interviews. Longitudinal surveys are also not suitable for obtaining timely national flow data on a regular basis.

Matching census data

Another method for deriving long-term flow statistics is matching records of successive population censuses. It involves complex processing effort and the results should be interpreted with care since the resulting statistics do not account for any flow that may have occurred during the successive census dates. The method may be more meaningful for deriving occupational flow statistics or on other relatively stable characteristics. It may be also more convenient to work on a sample basis using reverse matching procedures than on a complete count.

Rotation sampling schemes

Labour force flow statistics may also be obtained by exploiting the rotation sampling schemes of labour force surveys with rotation samples. In order to increase the accuracy in the measurement of levels and changes and to limit conditioning effects from repeated interviews, many periodic labour force sample surveys incorporate a rotation scheme in their sampling design. In a rotation sampling scheme the sampling units at successive occasions are partially replaced according to a prescribed pattern. This means that a fraction of sampled households and persons remain in the sample at different points of time. Thus, by examining the labour force status of each person in the matched sample at different points of time, it is possible to derive labour force flow statistics of the form shown in the tabulation on page 190.

Because they are obtained from labour force surveys, the flow data are based on the same concepts and definitions as the stock data. Further, the accuracy of the data are not subject to recall errors as is the case with the retrospective method. The cost and organisation demand of the rotation method are lower than that involved in longitudinal surveys. Moreover, the time-lag of data production may be controlled more easily and can be set to minimal.

The rotation method, however, is unsuitable for deriving long-term flow data and involves a number of measurement and processing issues which need to be resolved.

The type and sampling accuracy of the flow statistics depend primarily on the rotation scheme adopted in the survey design. Table 14.1 summarises the rotation scheme of current labour force sample surveys in eight countries – Australia, Canada, Finland, France, Italy, Spain, Sweden and the United States. In the Finnish survey, for example, newly sampled persons in a given quarter remain in the sample for six consecutive quarters after which they are removed from the sample. In each quarter one-sixth of the sampled persons are thus renewed. In the French survey, the base of rotation is one year and in the survey-month of each year (March or October) one-third of the sampled households are renewed and retained in the sample for three consecutive years. In the United States survey (Current Population Survey) the base of rotation is a month. Newly sampled households remain in the sample for four consecutive months, leave the sample for the next eight months, and subsequently return to the sample for four more consecutive months. The base and rotation pattern of the surveys of the other countries are summarised in Table 14.1.

Table 14.1 Rotation sampling schemes of labour force sample surveys in eight countries

Country	Base of rotation	Pattern of rotation
Australia	Month	8–
Canada	Month	6–
Finland	Quarter	6–
France	Year	3–
Italy	Quarter	2–2–2
Spain	Quarter	6–
Sweden	Quarter	8–
USA	Month	4–8–4

In general, the base and pattern of rotation jointly determine the different flow periods for which flow statistics may be derived and the relative sample size of the corresponding matched samples. Table 14.2 shows these and other characteristics of the rotation schemes of the labour force sample surveys of the eight countries cited above. It can be observed, for example, that the Finnish survey may provide quarterly and yearly flow data, on the basis of five-sixths and one-third of the national sample, respectively. The French survey, on the other hand, gives only yearly flow data, based on two-thirds of the sample. Because of its particular rotation scheme, the United States survey may provide monthly, quarterly and yearly flow data. The monthly flow data are based on three-quarters of the monthly sample, the quarterly flow data on one-quarter and the yearly flow data on one-half of the sample.

Table 14.2 Some characteristics of the rotaton sampling schemes of labour force sample surveys in eight countries

Country	Percentage of sampled households common in two successive:			Number of times a sampled household is interviewed	Length of time for complete renewal of sample (in months)
	Months	Quarters	Years		
Australia	87½	62½	0	8	8
Canada	83⅓	50	0	6	6
Finland	0	83⅓	33⅓	6	18
France	0	0	66 2/3	3	36
Italy	0	50	50*	4	18
Spain	0	83⅓	33⅓	6	18
Sweden	0	87½	50	8	24
USA	75	25	50	8	16

* The actual percentage is in practice lower than 50 (it is about 41) due to annual rotations of 'communes' in addition to quarterly rotation of households.

While statistics based on various flow periods may be obtained by adopting appropriate rotation schemes, excessive repeated interviews spanning a long period may be difficult to manage and may affect the accuracy of responses. Therefore, the number of times a sampled household or person is interviewed and the maximum length of time over which the household or person should be traced are important factors in the choice of rotation schemes. The right-hand columns of Table 14.2 give information on these factors for the eight selected countries.

Register-based statistics

Flow statistics may also be derived from *register-based* data. The method, in general, consists of matching records of a system of registers and other sources, referring to the same unit at different points of time. The matching may be performed at the aggregate or at the individual unit level, using an exact or statistical match.

One example of labour force flow statistics obtained from register-based data is the Danish statistics of gross flows.[5] The Danish register-based labour market statistics are based on a system of several administrative registers and various other sources linked to each other through a Central Population Register and a Central Register of Enterprises and

Establishments. In the Central Population Register each resident individual has a unique 'person number', assigned to persons born before 1968 and allocated at birth to persons born in 1968 or later. By using the person number as an identifier in the system, it is possible to ascertain the labour force status and characteristics of each person at selected points in time and thus produce flow statistics for the population covered in two consecutive surveys.

Another example of register-based statistics is the Continuous Work History Sample (CWHS) constructed on the basis of several statistical sample files from information contained in the administrative files of the Social Security Administration of the Unitied States.[6] The CWHS system consists of a sample of records of individuals with employment covered by social security. A particular file in the system (1 per cent, 1937 to date, CWHS file) contains a 1 per cent sample of social security members issued through cut-off date of file reflecting entire work experience in covered employ-ment. The basic data elements include, in particular, the number and pattern of years employed, first and last years employed, pattern of quarters employed (last two years), number of quarters of coverage (1937 to date) pattern of quarters of coverage (1957 to date). The file contains also information on insurance status and benefit status. From these elements statistics on flows into and out of employment (and perhaps unemployment) may be derived on a regular basis.

Among advantages of register-based statistics are: reductions in data collection cost; reductions in response burden and non-response, both increasingly serious problems in establishment and household surveys in some countries; and amenability to fine geographic and other disaggre-gations, useful for deriving small area flow statistics or flow statistics between occupations and branches of economic activity. Register-based statistics should also be subject to less measurement errors than conventional survey-based statistics. Furthermore, errors in register-based statistics, when they occur, are often easier to identify when, for example, they involve a whole establishment or a whole branch of economic activity.

Along with these advantages, register-based statistics have also certain limitations. One is the problem of adapting concepts and definitions of administration systems to statistical needs. Because the data are vulnerable to changes in administrative systems, changes in administrative regulations or practices may affect the statistics and lead to overstatement of the true flows. Another problem concerns privacy considerations which may limit the merging of registers to enhance their information contents for wide coverage and cross-classification purposes. There is also the problem of timing. Because the basic data are collected and processed by administrative agencies, the statistician may not be able to control the timing of the data.

Partial methods and combinations

Particular types of flow statistics may be derived from establishment surveys, unemployment insurance registers and a variety of other sources, such as employment exchange records and vacancy statistics. Sometimes they may be used in combination to construct integrated sets of flow statistics.

Labour turnover statistics derived from establishment surveys, for example, provide data on the gross movement of wage and salary workers into and out of employment with respect to individual establishments during a specified period. For a given establishment the statistics consist of the numbers of employees employed at the beginning and at the end of the period, together with the number employed at the end of the period who were not employed at the beginning of the period.

On the other hand, unemployment insurance registers may be used to provide data on the gross movements of insured workers into and out of unemployment during a given period. Statistics on in-flows may be derived from the number of newly registered unemployed and out-flows on the basis of the number of persons leaving the register in the given period.

Flow data derived from statistics of labour turnover or unemployment insurance or other similar sources provide only partial information on the elements of the basic flow matrix (page 190). First, their coverage is limited to particular groups of workers covered by unemployment insurance). Second, because the labour force status of the workers prior to hiring and after separation from the establishment or prior to registration and after leaving the unemployment register are not generally known, the derived statistics do not provide full information on the off-diagonal elements of the flow matrix.

When using fragmented statistics to derive a complete set of flow statistics the different sources must be combined using appropriate procedures to adjust for differences in coverage, definitions and time references. An example of the construction of a flow matrix (with 15 rows and columns) based on statistics derived from a variety of sources is the Labour Force Account for the Federal Republic of Germany.[7]

Some measurement issues

Each one of the various methods described in the preceding section involves a number of measurement issues which need to be resolved. Here only problems concerning rotation sampling schemes are discussed. Some of these are in common with the other methods of compiling flow statistics. The selected measurement issues discussed below concern: increased sampling errors; maintenance of unbiased coverage and tolerable non-response rates; the question of inconsistency of responses over time and classification errors; the problem of matching two or more samples and the treatment of the unmatched portions; the appropriate weighting factors; and consistent estimation for stocks and flows. Some of these issues concern both flow and stock data but are more serious in the case of flow data. Other issues are particular to flow data. Each of them is briefly described in turn below.

Sampling

The sampling variances of flow statistics based on rotation sampling are necessarily higher than those for the corresponding stock statistics for at least two reasons. First, when matching sampled households or persons from two different periods the size of the matched sample always becomes at least one rotation group smaller than in either of the two original samples (see Table 14.2). Second, for a given characteristic there are more elements to estimate for the flow statistics than there are for the stock data. In the case of labour force categories specified in the matrix on page 190, the flow statistics involve nine elements, while the stock data consist of three elements.

Non-response and matching failures are other reasons which may further decrease the effective sample size of the matched sample and thus contribute to increased sampling variability.

In addition to sampling variability, flow statistics may be subject to sampling biases, due to the fact that the matched sample may not adequately represent the population universe during the flow period.

Coverage

While the scope of regular labour force sample surveys is generally the civilian non-institutional population, the coverage of the corresponding flow statistics is restricted to that portion of the survey population which did not change address during the flow period. This restrictive coverage arises because in regular labour force sample surveys interviewers are instructed to go to a sample address, not to a household or to a specific person living at an address.[8] Thus if a person or household in a given rotation group changes address between survey periods, the interviewer will in effect be contacting at subsequent surveys persons who replace the household or person (if any). The original household or person will not be traced to a new address. Thus, the matched sample will in effect cover only the civilian non-institutional population with fixed address during the successive survey periods. To the extent that geographical movements are related to labour market conditions, the restrictive coverage introduces biases in the flow statistics.

Non-response

Apart from coverage errors, there is the issue of non-response. The problem of non-response is doubly important in respect of flow statistics. This is because a sampled household or person must respond at *both* of the two successive surveys for it to be considered in the matched sample. Thus, the non-response rate is necessarily higher with flow statistics than it is with stock statistics (about twice as high).[9] A non-response rate of 10 per cent in a labour force survey represents an effective non-response rate of about 20 per cent for the flow statistics.

Moreover, there are indications that non-response is higher among households in rotation groups first entering the sample than others. This has been suggested as an explanation of rotation group biases observed in the stock data of many sample surveys using rotation sampling. If this is the case, the rotation group bias due to differential non-response rates will be affecting the flow data as well and, perhaps, to an even higher extent.

Response

Response errors may lead to the classification of a person into an erroneous labour force category. Classification errors that tend to cancel in the case of stock data may get compounded when measuring flows. A simple example illustrates the point.[10] Table 14.3 shows 'true' and 'observed' labour force statuses of ten hypothetical persons at two consecutive survey dates. The corresponding flow matrix is shown in Table 14.4, where the true flow and stock values are given in parentheses under each entry.

Table 14.3   True and observed labour force statuses of ten hypothetical persons at two consecutive survey dates

Persons	$t-1$		t	
	true	observed	true	observed
1	E	E	E	E
2	N	N	N	E
3	E	N	E	E
4	U	E	U	E
5	E	U	U	U
6	E	E	E	U
7	N	E	E	N
8	E	E	E	E
9	N	N	N	N
10	N	N	N	N

Table 14.4   True and observed flows for data from Table 14.3

	$E(t)$	$U(t)$	$N(t)$	
$E(t-1)$	3	1	1	5(5)
	(4)	(1)	(0)	
$U(t-1)$	–	1	–	1(1)
		(1)		
$N(t-1)$	2	–	2	4(4)
	(1)		(3)	
	5	2	3	
	(5)	(2)	(3)	

It can be observed from Table 14.4 that while the classification errors cancel each other in the stock data for both survey dates, the 'observed' values differ significantly from the 'true' values in the flow matrix.

Flow statistics may record spurious flows due to misclassification and, therefore, tend to overstate the true flows by a considerable amount. A study of the possible effects of response variance on the month-to-month gross flow statistics derived from the United States Current Population Survey indicates that the response variance (measured by the gross difference rate between original and reinterview data) may be as great as the actual gross flow that one is trying to estimate.[11]

One method of controlling the response error is the use of detailed reinterviews, particularly after the second visit and when changes of status have been reported.

Another possibility is to develop mathematical formulas that describe the structure of the expected errors in terms of parameters which can be estimated using subjective or informed judgements. The formulas, together with the estimated parameters, can then be used to correct the measured flow data.

Matching

The procedure of matching for the purpose of flow statistics involves linkage of data for the same person from two or more data files.[12] Thus for given data files from surveys at two points of time, matching cannot be performed for persons entering the sample for the first time or leaving the sample, for members of households or other persons who moved during the two periods, and for non-respondents in either or both surveys. In addition, matching failure may occur by erroneous matches, i.e. linking records that correspond to different persons, or by erroneous non-match, i.e. failure to link records that do correspond to the same person.

In the United States Current Population Survey, where 75 per cent of the sample are common between two successive survey months and, therefore, are potential matches, generally about 90 per cent of the potential matches are successful matches. Thus, the month-to-month flow statistics are in fact based on about 67½ per cent of all persons in the survey. In the Australian survey, the potential month-to-month matches make up 87½ per cent of the sample, about 90 per cent are successful matches and the resulting matched data represent about 80 per cent of all persons in the survey.

These examples relate to matching of two data files for successive surveys one month apart. With more data files or non-successive surveys or longer flow periods, the matching procedure will no doubt be more difficult and will have a higher failure rate. Some indications of this can be inferred from experimental results obtained from the United States Current Population Survey.[13]

There are also indications that the failure rate may differ from one labour force category to another. Analysis of the gross flow statistics from the Australian Survey shows that the failure rate is higher for the unemployed (about 26 per cent) and persons not in the labour force (about 24 per cent) than for the employed (about 20 per cent).[14]

Another issue concerns the treatment of non-matches. In the United

States survey or the Canadian survey the non-matched records are recorded (presumably by imputation procedures) and the final flow statistics cover all persons in the survey. In the Australian survey, on the other hand, the non-matches are left out and the flow statistics represent only persons in the matched sample. Leaving the non-matches outside the flow matrix leads perhaps to more factual statistics, but raises difficulties for the users of the statistics.

In order to reduce the matching problem and secure a unique identifier, the basic household or individual identifier may be complemented with a check-digit obtained by a series of arithmetic operations made on the digits of the basic identifier. One example of such a method is the 'Modulus 10 algorithm' used in the Canadian labour force survey.

Weighting

The derivation of estimates for stock data from sample surveys is generally obtained by multiplying and aggregating sample results by a weighting factor, which, in elementary cases, is simply the reciprocal of the sampling fraction. In more complicated estimation procedures the sampling fraction is adjusted for non-response and the aggregation is further improved using ratio or composite estimates. These estimates take into account the relationships between two or more variables or the correlation between present and past values.

The adaptation of these procedures to flow statistics is not straightforward. Associated to each observed flow there are two weight factors: one based on the current survey and one on the preceding survey. How these should be combined to derive the appropriate weighting factor for the flow data is not clear. The Canadian survey, for example, uses a particular combination according to which the minimum of the two weights and their positive or negative differences are allocated to the flow data depending on whether the observed flow is stationary, an in-flow or an out-flow. The procedure tends significantly to overestimate population in-flows and out-flows and, therefore, attempts are being made to use independently derived estimates of population in-flow and out-flow to adjust the in-flow and out-flow results.

Related to the weighting issue, there is the problem of ensuring consistency between flow and stock data. Unless appropriate care is taken, aggregating the flow statistics (row-wise or column-wise) may not necessarily give the corresponding stock statistics. Accordingly, in the Italian survey, before final tabulation the flow statistics are adjusted to stock totals using the RAS method. The method applies at the macro level only and therefore raises difficulties when attempting to achieve consistency at various levels of disaggregation.

Conclusions

Although the collection of labour force flow statistics involves many issues not yet adequately resolved, it is clear that the data offer an important and unique information base for understanding the operation of labour markets. Among the major sources of such data, the rotation samples of conventional labour force surveys with rotation sampling schemes and the register-based statistics in countries with comprehensive and statistically usable population and administrative registers seem to provide two adequate and relatively inexpensive means of collecting regular and timely flow statistics. With either source, certain measurement issues, in particular, the problem of matching individual data from one survey or register to another as well as the problem of maintaining consistency between aggregate stock and flow data should receive priority considerations. For international comparison purposes, the format of presentation of flow statistics should be standardised and suitable summary flow statistics should be developed to enable comparison of the extent of labour market mobility in different countries.

Notes

1. Revised version of a paper prepared for the Second Joint ECE/ILO Meeting on Manpower Statistics, Geneva, 16–20 May 1983. The revised version incorporates elements of the conclusions drawn at the meeting.
2. An international effort in this direction is the Nordic Project on Gross Flows on the Labour Market, being developed by the Nordic Labour Market Committee (NAUT).
3. INSEE, *Enquête sur l'emploi d'octobre 1981, résultats détaillés.* Collections de l'INSEE, D-89, Paris, June 1982, p.120.
4. Examples of longitudinal surveys in the United States from which labour force flow data may be derived are described in *Longitudinal surveys and labor market analysis.* National Commission on Employment and Unemployment Statistics, Background Paper no. 6, Washington DC. June 1978.
5. S. Egmose and S. Hostrup Petersen, 'Gross flow analyses on the basis of registers', paper presented at the Second Joint ECE/ILO Meeting on Manpower Statistics, Geneva, 16–20 May 1983.
6. Office of Federal Statistical Policy and Standards, *Report on statistical uses of administrative records.* Statistical Policy Working Paper 6, Washington, DC, 1980, pp. 19 and 23–6.
7. Lutz Reyher and Hans-Uwe Bach, 'Arbeitskräfte-Gesamtrechnung-Bestände und Bewegungen am Arbeitsmarkt', *MittAB*, 4/80. A description in English is given in L. Reyher 'Stocks and flows determining the labour market'. Institut für Arbeitsmarkt- und Berufsforschung (IAB), Seminar-Documentation: *The measurement of employment and unemployment for Community purposes.* Statistical Office of the European Communities, Luxembourg, 7–10 Dec. 1981.
8. This problem should not arise in surveys using population registers as sampling frames (e.g. the Finnish and Swedish ones referred to earlier).
9. In general, if q is the non-response rate in each of two successive surveys, the effective non-response rate for the flow statistics, assuming independence, is $1-(1-q)^2$ which is about equal to $2q$ when q is small.
10. Adapted from I. Marcredie, 'Estimation of gross flows from the Canadian Labour Force Survey', paper presented at the Seminar on the Measurement of Employment and Unemployment for Community Purposes, Statistical Office

of the European Communities, Luxembourg, 7–10 Dec. 1981.

11. Henry Woltman, 'Possible effects of response variance on the estimate of gross change from month to month in the CPS', in *Using the current population survey as a longitudinal data base*. United States Department of Labor, Bureau of Labor Statistics, Report 608, Aug. 1980, pp. 11–13.

12. In the literature of matching techniques this is called 'exact' matching as opposed to 'statistical' matching. In a statistical match the linkage of data for similar units is sufficient. For details reference is made to *Report on exact and statistical matching techniques*. Statistical Policy Working Paper 5, United States Office of Federal Statistical Policy and Standards, Washington, DC, 1980.

13. Robert J. McIntire, 'The mechanics of matching CPS microdata: Problems and solutions' in *Using the current population survey as a longitudinal data base* pp. 5–6.

14. Australian Bureau of Statistics, *The labour force, Australia, May 1982*, Catalogue no. 62030, Canberra, 20 Aug. 1982, p. 31.

15 Statistics concerning the urban informal sector

K. M. Bashir

The reports of the ILO employment missions[1] to various developing countries have focused attention on, among other things, the lack of statistical data and information relating to the urban informal sector for purposes of planning and policy-making. They nevertheless pointed out the important role played by the informal sector in providing employment opportunities to a substantial part of the urban labour force in many developing countries. The Kenya employment mission report in particular stressed the role of the urban 'informal sector' in employment promotion.

In 1974, the ILO initiated a series of research studies to build up a body of knowledge on the urban informal sector, useful for planning and policy purposes. These studies have been carried out through exploratory sample surveys in selected urban centres of different developing countries.

The present paper describes the main features of these exploratory surveys with particular reference to certain issues and problems that have emerged in the process. The solutions of these issues and problems are important for further development of informal sector statistics and their incorporation in the regular statistical programmes of the developing countries. The paper does not attempt to present an ILO position nor does it contain any proposals for adoption. Furthermore, the paper does not report the findings based on these surveys.[2]

Background

The ILO/UNDP employment mission to Kenya used in its report the term 'informal sector', and elaborated the characteristics of the informal and formal sectors.[3] Since then the term has gained considerable currency in connection with development planning and policies.

One of the important findings of the earlier studies under the World Employment Programme was that a substantial proportion of urban workers was employed in small, own-account, mostly unregistered enterprises and had significantly lower earnings than those employed in public services and large industrial and commercial establishments of the formal sector. It was also observed that a large share of the additions to the urban labour force, resulting especially from rural-urban migration, tended to be absorbed in such small enterprises.

On closer examination it seemed that such small, own-account enterprises were subject to severe constraints which prevented them in one way or another from realising their full growth potential. In other words, these enterprises were apparently unable to exploit the opportunities afforded by the general economic development fully and satisfactorily to their advantage. The enterprises, unlike those in the formal sector, generally appeared to have limited or no access to modern technology, credit facilities from formal financial institutions, facilities for skill development, infrastructure facilities and facilities for marketing their products. Consequently, they were forced to rely on other means, often detrimental to their interest, for their survival. Furthermore, such enterprises seemed to be often subjected to restrictive public policies, notably with regard to their location, which directly or indirectly inhibited their growth; as a result they tend to be concentrated in slum and squatter areas, with many of them operating under illegal conditions. These preliminary findings led to the conclusion that the World Employment Programme would need to focus more attention than in the past on a target group defined in terms of such small, own-account enterprises. This target group has been called the informal sector.

The formal/informal sector dichotomy of the urban economy differs from the conventional division into modern and traditional sectors; the latter division usually refers to the technology employed by the enterprise in the production of goods and services and its mode of organisation. The term 'traditional' implies that the economic activities under reference are carried out generation after generation without any significant changes in the mode of production, whereas many of the economic activities in the urban informal sector are new and arise from urbanisation.

List of surveys

Table 15.1 gives a list of 38 urban informal sector surveys undertaken in various countries since 1973, with or without the support of the ILO.[4] The list includes 18 surveys in 13 African countries, 15 surveys in 13 Latin American countries and five surveys in four Asian countries. As these surveys were exploratory and carried out by different research workers and agencies, they differed in objectives, scope, coverage and methods of collection and compilation of data.

Table 15.1 Urban informal sector surveys carried out in developing countries since 1973

Country	Areas covered	Year
Africa		
1. Kenya	1. Nairobi	1975
	2. Selected cities	1977
2. Ghana	3. Kumasi*	1975
	4. Accra, Nsawam, Abusi	1976
3. Nigeria	5. Lagos*	1976
	6. Kano*	1976
	7. Onitsha*	1977
	8. Lagos	1977
4. Senegal	9. Dakar*	1974
5. Upper Volta	10. Ouagadougou*	1976
6. Sierra Leone	11. Freetown*	1976
7. Rwanda	12. Kigali*	1977
8. Mauritania	13. Nouakchott*	1977
9. Cameroon	14. Yaoundé*	1978
10. Togo	15. Lomé*	1977-8
11. Mali	16. Bamako*	1978
12. Tunisia	17. Tunis	1977
13. Zambia	18. Lusaka (Chawama)	1974
America		
1. Brazil	1. Campinas*	1976
	2. Belo Horizonte	1978
	3. Recife	1977
2. Argentina	4. Córdoba*	1976
3. Dominican Republic	5. Santo Domingo	1973
4. El Salvador	6. San Salvador*	1974
5. Mexico	7. Mexico City	1977
6. Paraguay	8. Asunción*	1973
7. Peru	9. All cities	1974
8. Venezuela	10. All cities	1975
9. Colombia	11. Bogotá*	1974
10. Haiti	12. Port-au-Prince	1976
11. Jamaica	13. Kingston*	1975
12. Nicaragua	14. Managua	
13. Chile	15. Nunoa*	1976
Asia		
1. India	1. Calcutta*	1974
2. Indonesia	2. Jakarta*	1975
	3. Bandung, Surabaya, Semarang	1977
3. Philippines	4. Manila*	1976
4. Sri Lanka	5. Colombo*	1976-7

* ILO-sponsored surveys.

The ILO has sponsored 23 informal sector surveys in 21 countries. Table 15.2 shows readily available information on the main features of 17 of these surveys. The details in the table include the name of the collaborating agency (or individual) at the national level, the period of fieldwork of the survey, specific objectives of the survey, scope and coverage, universe covered, sample design and sample size, method of data collecton, field organisation, questionnaire used, reference period for

15.2 Characteristics of informal sector surveys

Country, city, collaborating agency at national level	Specific survey objectives	Scope and coverage: (i) geographical (ii) industrial (iii) other	Definition of universe covered	Sampling: (i) sample design (ii) sampling frame (iii) sampling unit (iv) sample size	Method of data collection, field organisation, type of questionnaire	Reference period of data collection (i) income, (ii) wages, (iii) hours of work, (iv) output/value added
1	2	3	4	5	6	7
India, Calcutta Dr A. N. Bose January–March 1974	(a) To investigate employment potential and mechanism for realising potential of slum industry. (b) To uncover specific difficulties of units, with regard to government help, credit, marketing, etc.	(i) Slum areas of Calcutta and Howrah cities. (ii) Manufacturing: 56 types grouped into 12 broad industry groups.	Informal sector industrial units in slum areas.	(i) Purposive selection of 11 geographic zones of Calcutta and Howrah cities. Random selection of units from each zone, number proportional to concentration of units in each zone. (ii) – (iii) Informal sector industrial units. (iv) 649 units employing 4,443 persons.	Questionnaire interviews	
Senegal, Dakar C. Gerry Institut Africain pour le Développement Économique et la Planification (IDEP) June–July 1974	(a) To determine relations between characteristically different modes of productive activity, i.e. between small producers and others, distribution of products, skills from industry, state support, competition for markets, etc. (b) To determine characteristics of small producers	(i) 3 areas of Dakar, selected as representative of the different occupational categories and spatial relationships with principal sources of raw material supply and markets. (ii) Carpentry, furniture and fittings; shoemaking, repairing, etc.; tailoring, embroidery, etc.; vehicle repairs, metal working and allied trades. (iii) 'Petty' producers and distributors	No clear definition was applied; the priority was to understand how the ensemble of productive and distributive activities related to one another.	(i) Informed random sampling. 3 main sample areas selected as representative. Occupational groupings selected as those most widely found among petty producers. Enterprises selected at random by interviewer. (ii) Census of activities and infrastructure conducted by NEDECO team, with IBRD and Senegal Office de l'Habitat à Loyer Modéré. (iii) Petty enterprises. (iv) 78 furniture makers, 74 shoemakers, 71 tailors/embroiderers, 62 vehicle repairers/metal workers.	(a) Long-questionnaire survey: personal interview with head of enterprise. (b) Short-questionnaire survey of casual workers: questionnaires completed by workers arriving at or leaving temporary workplace. (c) Personal interviews of varying types and lengths including illegal activities and casual workers. Interviewers: from School of Architecture.	

Country, city, collaborating agency at national level	Specific survey objectives	Scope and coverage: (i) geographical (ii) industrial (iii) other	Definition of universe covered	Sampling: (i) sample design (ii) sampling frame (iii) sampling unit (iv) sample size	Method of data collection, field organisation, type of questionnaire	Reference period of data collection (i) income, (ii) wages, (iii) hours of work, (iv) output/value added
1	2	3	4	5	6	7
Colombia, Bogotá O. Marulanda Oficina de investigaciones Socio-Económicas y Legales (OFISEL) October–December 1974	(a) To locate informal sector-type households. (b) To obtain information on the household characteristics. (c) To obtain information on the establishments in which household members work.	(i) Bogotá (ii) – (iii) Non-institutional household population of low and medium socio-economic strata.	Non-intitutional population of Bogotá in low socio-economic strata.	(i) 2-stage cluster sampling; systematic selection of areas; simple random sampling of clusters. (ii) – (iii) Households. (iv) 800 households; 562 responded.	Questionnaire for each household and each worker in the household. 20 enumerators and 5 supervisors.	(i) Per day, week or month; (ii) per day, week or month; (iii) per day and during previous week.
Indonesia, Jakarta Indonesia Population Studies Centre, National Institute of Economic and Social Research, Indonesian Institute of Sciences, LEKNAS July–September 1975	To collect quantitative information about the informal sector of Jakarta ● household information (size, composition, place of residence, etc.); ● information on household members participating in informal sector (age, sex, education, occupation, etc); ● information on informal sector enterprises (size, activity, structural background, physical background, legal constraints, history, operational characteristics, etc.).	(i) Jakarta. (ii) Manufacturing, construction, transport, trade and services.	Heads of informal sector enterprises: economic units that produce goods or services, whether using capital or not, having a fixed or variable location, with 10 or fewer workers, including head of enterprise.	(i) Systematic random selection of area units; representative random sample of heads of enterprises selected within each area unit. (ii) List of heads of enterprises identified from all households in selected area units. (iii) Heads of informal sector enterprises. (iv) 5,000 heads of informal sector enterprises (actual sample: 4,367).	Personal interviews during which enumerators completed 3 pre-coded questionnaires for ● households; ● informal sector enterprises; ● informal sector participants.	(i) Preceding day or week; (ii) last working day, week, month or year; (iii) each day; (iv) sales for preceding day or week.

Country, city, collaborating agency at national level	Specific survey objectives	Scope and coverage: (i) geographical (ii) industrial (iii) other	Definition of universe covered	Sampling: (i) sample design (ii) sampling frame (iii) sampling unit (iv) sample size	Method of data collection, field organisation, type of questionnaire	Reference period of data collection, (i) income, (ii) wages, (iii) hours of work, (iv) output/value added
1	2	3	4	5	6	7
Ghana, Kumasi G. Aryee Department of Housing and Planning Research, University of Science and Technology, Kumasi October 1975	(a) To determine the employment potential of the informal sector. (b) To determine the extent working, tailoring and seamstressing, of interdependence of relationships between formal and informal sectors and the factors which influence relationships.	(i) Kumasi (ii) Manufacturing: blacksmithing, metal woodcarving, cane weaving, carpet and doormat-making, footwear and other leatherware; motor repair and maintenance. (iii) Informal sector enterprises.	Small-scale non-factory enterprises, with not more than 10 wage-earning journeymen (skilled labour). Organisation similar to traditional artisan system: owner-craftsman centre of all operations, controlling all aspects from production to sales.	(i) Systematic stratified random sampling. enterprises stratified according to activity, and sample selected at random within each branch according to size and homogeneity of each branch. (ii) Census of small-scale enterprises (Aug–Sept. 1975). (iii) Informal sector enterprises. (iv) 324 units (10.1 % of sample frame).	Personal interviews to complete questionnaire. 5 interviewers.	(i) Previous day, week or month. (ii) Per day, week or month; previous day, week or month. (iii) Per day (and days per week). (iv) Output: previous day. week or month.
Sierra Leone, Freetown D. Fowler January and February 1976	(a) To determine the characteristics of the self-employed. (b) To determine the extent to which self-employed correspond to concept of informal sector.	(i) Inner Freetown area, divided into 5 areas, each with open markets and all activities investigated. (ii) Manufacturing, construction, commerce, transport and services. (iii) Self-employed enterprises.	Self-employed persons aged 10 years and over.	(i) Stratified random sampling. City divided into 5 areas, based on intimate knowledge of density of enterprises to be studied. Sample selected at random from each of the five activities in each area. (ii) No sampling frame, but sample size selected in each area proportionate to size of population from 1963 population census. (iii) Self-employed enterprises. (iv) 1,000 enterprises.	Personal interview (enumerator filled out questionnaire) supplemented by intensive discussions with and observation of a few typical enterprises. Supervisors checked the work of interviewers. Regular daily meeting during fieldwork to resolve problems.	(i) Average income per day, week or month. (ii) – (iii) Usual opening hours per day.

Country, city, collaborating agency at national level	Specific survey objectives	Scope and coverage: (i) geographical (ii) industrial (iii) other	Definition of universe covered	Sampling: (i) sample design (ii) sampling frame (iii) sampling unit (iv) sample size	Method of data collection, field organisation, type of questionnaire	Reference period of data collection (i) income, (ii) wages, (iii) hours of work, (iv) output/value added
1	2	3	4	5	6	7
Argentina, Córdoba C. Sánchez H. Palmieri F. Ferrero Group of private contractors 1976	To determine the size, structural and functional characteristics of the informal sector with a view to forming policy proposals.	(i) Córdoba. (ii) Selected manufacturing, trade and service activities: private sector. (iii)(a) Households. (b) Establishments with 0-5 employed persons, and fixed location.	(i) Household survey: to identify self-employed without fixed locations. (2) Establishment survey: establishments with 0-5 employed persons. Informal sector: activities such as unskilled manual work and sales activities with easy entry. Quasi-informal sector: activities requiring skills and some capital accumulation, semi-skilled and sales activities with some oligopolistic incomes, and self-employed professionals.	(i) Household survey: multi-stage random sampling with replacement. Each household in segment of 5 dwellings retained in sample, 1,500 households. (2)(i) Establishment survey: multi-stage stratified random sampling with optimal allocation. Stratification by activity and size of establishment. (ii) – (iii) Establishments. (iv) 1,500 establishments with 0–50 persons employed.	(a) Precoded questionnaire completed during personal interview with household. (b) Precoded questionnaires for establishment and individuals, completed during personal interviews.	(a) Household survey: (i) – (ii) Per month. (iii) During one specified week. (iv) – (b) Establishment survey: (i) Previous month. (ii) Highest/lowest wages paid to male/female worker: day before, previous week, previous month. (iii) – (iv) –
Philippines, Manila G. Jorado J. Castro University of the Philippines School of Economics, National Manpower and Youth Council March–May 1976	(a) To describe informal sector enterprises in terms of organisational and operational characteristics, linkages with rest of economy, etc. (b) To discover impact of these characteristics and linkages on enterprise's productivity, employment and income-generating power. (c) To explore policy measures to enhance participation of enterprises in productivity, income and employment goals.	(i) Greater Manila Area. (ii) Manufacturing construction, commerce, trade and services. (iii) Informal sector enterprises and owners.	Enterprises employing 10 or fewer persons.	(i) Proportional random sampling. All enterprises distributed according to area and industry, and sample selected as each 20th enterprise on list after random start. (ii) 1972 Census of Establishments, updated with results from 1975 Census of Establishments. (iii) Enterprises employing 10 or fewer persons. (iv) 3,507 enterprises.	Questionnaire interviews. Precoded questionnaires for: ● enterprises; ● heads of enterprises; ● households of heads; ● members of workforce.	(i) Per day, week or month (average). (ii) Per day (average, minimum and maximum). (iii) Average per day. (iv) Sales: preceding day or week.

Country, city, collaborating agency at national level	Specific survey objectives	Scope and coverage: (i) geographical (ii) industrial (iii) other	Definition of universe covered	Sampling: (i) sample design (ii) sampling frame (iii) sampling unit (iv) sample size	Method of data collection, field organisation, type of questionnaire	Reference period of data collection (i) income, (ii) wages, (iii) hours of work, (iv) output/value added
1	2	3	4	5	6	7
Mauritania, Nouakchott G. Nihan Census of informal sector activities: January–February 1977 Sample survey: June–July 1977	See Rwanda survey	(i) Nouakchott. (ii) Woodworking, metalworking, building and mechanical and electrical repairs. (iii) Modern informal sector enterprises.	See Rwanda survey	(i) Stratified random sampling. A census of all activities provided the sampling frame, which comprised all enterprises engaged in the selected activities. Two independent random samples were selected so that tests of homogeneity could be made. The enterprises were stratified by activity: production, service sand construction, and two samples selected from each. (ii) Census of all informal sector enterprises. (iii) Enterprises conducting activities in a permanent or semi-permanent location, such that the workshop or workplace exhibits characteristics which exclude the possibility of it belonging to the modern sector. (iv) 151 enterprises: 45.1% of total.	See Rwanda survey	See Rwanda survey
Togo, Lomé G. Nihan, E. Demol and C. Jondon Ministry of Planning and Economic Development Census of informal sector activities: October–November 1977 Sample survey: April–May 1978	See Rwanda survey	(i) Lomé. (ii) Woodworking, metalworking, building, and mechanical and electrical repairs. (iii) Modern informal sector enterprises.	See Rwanda survey	(i) Stratified random sampling. Enterprises stratified by activity. (ii) Census of all informal sector enterprises. (iii) Enterprises. (iv) 280 enterprises: 15% of total.	See Rwanda survey	See Rwanda survey

Country, city, collaborating agency at national level	Specific survey objectives	Scope and coverage: (i) geographical (ii) industrial (iii) other	Definition of universe covered	Sampling: (i) sample design (ii) sampling frame (iii) sampling unit (iv) sample size	Method of data collection, field organisation, type of questionnaire	Reference period of data collection (i) income, (ii) wages, (iii) hours of work, (iv) output/value added
1	2	3	4	5	6	7
Mali, Bamako G. Nihan, M. Carton, H. Sidiké Ministère du Travail et de la Fonction publique Census of informal sector enterprises: February–March 1978 Sample survey: May–June 1978	See Rwanda survey	(i) City of Bamako. (ii) Woodworking, metalworking, building, and mechanical and electrical repairs. (iii) Modern informal sector enterprises.	See Rwanda survey	(i) Stratified random sampling. Enterprises stratified by activity, and selection made from each activity. (ii) Census of informal sector enterprises. (iii) Enterprises. (iv) 226 enterprises: 20% of total.	See Rwanda survey	See Rwanda survey
Cameroon, Yaoundé G. Nihan 1978	See Rwanda survey	(i) City of Yaoundé. (ii) Production, services, clothing and leatherwear. (iii) Modern informal sector enterprises.	See Rwanda survey	(i) Stratified random sampling. Enterprises stratified by activity and sample selected from each. (ii) Census of informal sector enterprises. (iii) Enterprises. (iv) Production and services: 179 enterprises, 15% of total. Clothing and leather: 111 enterprises: 7.5% of total.	See Rwanda survey	See Rwanda survey

Country, city, collaborating agency at national level	Specific survey objectives	Scope and coverage (i) geographical (ii) industrial (iii) other	Definition of universe covered	Sampling: (i) sample design (ii) sampling frame (iii) sampling unit (iv) sample size	Method of data collection, field organisation, type of questionnaire	Reference period of data collection (i) income, (ii) wages, (iii) hours of work, (iv) output/value added
1	2	3	4	5	6	7
Sri Lanka, Colombo Marga Institute, Sri Lanka Centre for Development Studies, Colombo 1976-1977	(a) A quantitative analysis of various aspects of the informal sector, its geographical distribution in the city and its sectoral composition. (b) To uncover the network of social relationships which underpin informal sector economic activities and to throw light on such aspects as conditions which regulate access to informal sector employment in different trades, factors affecting upward mobility, and constraints on economic expansion in different segments of activity.	(i) Colombo city. (ii) All informal sector activities: private sector, excluding public sector employment, all employment in large-scale commercial and industrial enterprises and large-scale, self-employment enterprises. Trade, commerce, manufacturing and processing, services, transport construction, cultivation and sale of leafy vegetables, sea fishing by operators living in northern coastal wards of the city.	Informal sector enterprises and activities: employing less than 5 persons, where in employment informal in character, often in family enterprise; investment in buildings and equipment low and technology labour-intensive; management systems simple with minimum of documented controls; technical know-how and operating skills required for informal sector activities obtained outside formal education system.	(i) Stratified random sampling. City stratified into 11 homogeneous strata with regard to housing pattern, occupational pattern, infrastructure facilities, demographic data, degree of commercial and industrial activity in each ward. One ward selected from each stratum, purposively. A pocket of informal sector activities was selected from each ward at random complete enumeration. (ii) No sampling frame. (iii) Pocket of informal sector activities – all enterprises within pocket. (iv) 1,200 enterprises.	Three phases: I: Basic data on socio-economic and cultural pattern of city assembled from available sources. II: Selection and enumeration of enterprises to give estimates of actual size of sector and number of participants. III: Measurement of characteristics of units and participants using two questionnaires. Questionnaires edited and data tabulated by hand.	(i) Per day, week or month. (ii) Per month or day. (iii) Normal hours of work per day, number of days per week that enterprise operates. (iv) Output, income, profit, working capital per day, week or month.

Country, city, collaborating agency at national level	Specific survey objectives	Scope and coverage: (i) geographical (ii) industrial (iii) other	Definition of universe covered	Sampling: (i) sample design (ii) sampling frame (iii) sampling unit (iv) sample size	Method of data collection, field organisation, type of questionnaire	Reference period of data collection (i) income, (ii) wages, (iii) hours of work, (iv) output/value added
1	2	3	4	5	6	7
Rwanda, Kigali G. Nihan 1977	(a) To discover the potential for training, employment and economic development of the informal sector with a view to determining the capacity for absorption, among other things, of young unemployed migrants. (b) To identify the problems of the informal sector through an approach founded on empirical research principles. (c) To make concrete recommendations to the governments in order to develop, specifically for the young, educated unemployed, the potential for employment and training in an economic sector largely ignored up to the present time. (d) To develop a programme of action in collaboration with the responsible nationals in charge of economic and employment policy.	(i) Kigali – one quarter. (ii) Woodworking, metal working, building and mechanical and electrical repairs.	'Modern' informal sector: Activities with permanent or semi-permanent location, with characteristics such as to exclude them from the modern sector: type of construction, internal structure (organisation and management of workplace). The criteria defining the informal sector enterprises concern the composition of the labour force of the enterprise, the level of training of the labour force, the level of capitalisation and production of the enterprise, the rate of growth of the force, the productivity of capital and labour, the method of management, respect of legislation, access to banking facilities and modern sector assistance.	(i) Exhaustive survey of informal sector enterprises in one quarter of the city.	Precoded questionnaire, completed during personal interviews with heads of enterprises. Interviewers were selected from non-official sources to avoid misunderstanding of purpose of survey. Fieldwork was closely supervised.	(i) Per normal week. (ii) Per normal week. (iii) Per normal week. (iv) Sales last week per normal week.

Country, city, collaborating agency at national level	Specific survey objectives	Scope and coverage: (i) geographical (ii) industrial (iii) other	Definition of universe covered	Sampling: (i) sample design (ii) sampling frame (iii) sampling unit (iv) sample size	Method of data collection, field organisation, type of questionnaire	Reference period of data collection (i) income, (ii) wages, (iii) hours of work, (iv) output/value added
1	2	3	4	5	6	7
Brazil, Campinas M. Berlink J. Boro L. Cintra Instituto de Filosofia et Ciências Humanas, Universidade Etadual de Campiras July–August 1976	(a) To build up a body of knowledge about the informal sector useful for policy making.	(i) Campinas. (ii) Industry (metallurgy, carpentry and woodworking, tailors and seamstresse), commerce, and services. (iii) Autonomous (working alone or with associates or with unpaid family labour) and small enterprises with wage earners.	Own-account workers who use their own labour force or unpaid family labour and small enterprises employing from 1 to 10 wage earners.	(i) Stratified proportional random sampling. City divided into 40 areas. Each interviewer instructed to select 5 units of industrial activities, 10 of commercial activities and 10 of services, in each area, in most random manner possible and with widest geographic distribution possible. (ii) No sampling frame. (iii) Units: self-employed and small enterprises. (iv) 500 units (proportion based on data of employed population in Campinas in 1975).	20 interviewers: students from University. Each responsible for 2 geographic areas. Questionnaire completed by interviewer during private interview.	–
Nigeria, Lagos O. Fapahunda Federal Office of Statistics, Human Resources Research Unit, University of Lagos July–October 1976	(a) To study the informal sector with a view to mounting appropriate action-oriented programmes to improve the quality of life of people working in the informal sector, and to discover ways of generating employment and increasing productivity, and to encourage a more equitable distribution of income.	Informal sector enterprises employing not more than 10 workers, whose owners were not highly educated. The owner, at most, would possess school certificate standard of formal education and have no access to the formal sector.	(i) Greater Lagos: Lagos, Ikoyi and Victoria is Ebute-Metta, Yoba, Abule Ijesta, Apapa, Surulere, Itive, Ide-Oro, Mushin, Oshodi/Ilupeju, Ikeja, Agege, Ajegunle, Bariga/Somolu, Ilada/Maroko.Badia. (ii) All activities. (iii) Informal sector enterprises.	(i) 2-stage stratified random sampling. Greater Lagos divided into 200 enumeration areas according to mapping for 1973 census. In each enterprises selected at random from each area. (ii) No sample frame. (iii) Informal sector enterprises. (iv) 2,074 enterprises (103.7% achievement on proposed sample size).	Precoded questionnaire completed by enumerators during personal interviews. Enumerators from Human Resources Research Unit of University and Federal Office of Statistics, supervisors from FOS.	(i) Per month. (ii) Per month. (iii) Hours of operation per day. (iv) Value of inputs per week (usual), weekly sales from production.

Country, city, collaborating agency at national level	Specific survey objectives	Scope and coverage: (i) geographical (ii) industrial (iii) other	Definition of universe covered	Sampling: (i) sample design (ii) sampling frame (iii) sampling unit (iv) sample size	Method of data collection, field organisation, type of questionnaire	Reference period of data collection (i) income, (ii) wages, (iii) hours of work, (iv) output/value added
1	2	3	4	5	6	7
Nigeria, Kano M. Filani and Mabagunje Federal Office of Statistics; Ministry of Economic Planning, Department of Geography, University of Ibadan September–October 1976	(a) To evaluate the size and range of employment opportunities available to migrants in the informal sector. (b) To examine the scope offered by this sector for their entrepreneurial development. (c) To investigate relationship between enhanced employment opportunities and improvement in their housing and general environmental conditions. (d) To assess the ethnic dimension of the above. (e) To identify policy options which can facilitate the attainment of a mutual goal of employment promotion and environmental improvement.	Informal sector enterprises: all one-man enterprises and all enterprises employing not more than 10 persons engaged in manufacturing, construction, commerce trading or services.	(i) Kano. (ii) Manufacturing, construction, commerce trading or services. (iii) Informal sector enterprises.	(i) Stratified random sampling. (ii) All enterprises of all sizes enumerated to form frame (earlier survey). Enterprises stratified by size and sample taken from each size-stratum, with replacement where possible in cases of non-response. (iii) Enterprises. (iv) 772 enterprises: 11.7% of total selected. Actual sample: 505 establishments (65.4% of sample selected).	37 enumerators, 7 supervisors and 20 translators. Most enumerators from FOS. Questionnaire completed by enumerators during personal interviews. In cases of non-response or refusal to respond, enumerators were asked to substitute another establishment engaged in same activity in same area. Precoded questionnaire.	(i) Income not directly requested. (ii) Wages per day, week or month. (iii) Hours of work per day. (iv) Sales last week or month, preceding week or month.

collection of data on income, wages, hours of work and output or value added.

Objectives of the surveys

The main objectives of the surveys was to generate information, both quantitative and qualitative, relevant for policy formulation and assistance to the informal sector enterprises with a view to promoting employment and earnings in this sector. The informal sector surveys were generally designed to answer policy-oriented questions of immediate relevance rather than to provide global estimates of one or more variables, for example value added in this sector.

The specific objectives of these surveys were in general:

(a) to identify the enterprises of economic activities which should be included in the informal sector;

(b) to seek information about the potential for raising the incomes of those dependent on these enterprises and for promoting employment, i.e. the extent to which the characteristics of the enterprise, its problems and constraints are useful in explaining the individual incomes, besides the personal characteristics of the individuals themselves;

(c) to reveal which kinds of informal sector activity have expanded in recent years and to identify those activities which have potential for further growth;

(d) to throw light on the circumstances leading to the establishment of informal sector enterprises and the conditions which regulate the access to informal sector employment in different trades;

(e) to find out about the markets in which informal sector enterprises participate: capital market (access to credit, interest rates, etc.); product market (imperfections); access to infrastructure facilities and better technology;

(f) to find out the structure of goods and services produced in this sector: the demand for goods and services, the elasticity of demand, etc.;

(g) to find out the nature of restrictions imposed by public authorities as they affect different kinds of enterprises and the extent to which they damage their interests;

(h) to determine the extent of interdependence between the formal and informal sectors of the urban economy.

The universe covered

As already stated, the urban informal sector was considered as a subsector of the urban economy consisting of both the formal and the informal sector economic units engaged in the production of goods and services. Generally speaking, the formal sector economic units were defined to include government (department, agencies, enterprises, etc.) and private registered establishments, the common feature of these units being that they have formal relationships with the rest of the economy and the world and easy access to various markets and resources including technology and skills. The residual economic units which mostly consisted of small own-account enterprises and other small (unincorporated) enterprises, were therefore treated as belonging to the informal sector, with one important exception. The informal sector units engaged in agriculture, though relatively few in number in urban areas, were excluded from the informal sector universe on grounds of policy orientation and nature of assistance required by them. Exceptions to this included cases where individuals sought self-employment opportunities through vegetable production, horticulture and fishing.

The informal sector universe, identified above at the conceptual level, needed further refinement from an operational point of view. One of the major considerations facilitating the identification of the informal sector units was based on the nature of the industrial activity in which the economic unit was engaged. The enterprises falling under the International Standard Industrial Classification of All Economic Activities (ISIC) headings of mining and quarrying, electricity, gas and water, and finance, insurance, real estate and related services, generally belonged to the formal sector in the sense described earlier. Thus, economic units engaged in the above activities were also excluded from the universe in question.

The universe actually covered by these surveys, however, differed somewhat from the above, as can be seen from Table 15.2, depending on the individual researchers' objectives and constraints. Some surveys focused exclusively on manufacturing activity while in other cases the universe included construction, transport, trade and services as well.

An enterprise or economic unit, for the purpose of the informal sector surveys, was broadly defined to include all those engaged in the production of goods and services whether they employed only one person (i.e. sole proprietorship) or more; whether or not they used any fixed capital; whether or not they had a fixed location for conducting business. Thus, a self-employed construction worker, a self-employed transport worker and a self-employed service worker (e.g. a shoeshine boy on the pavement) were all treated as individual enterprises even though they owned little or no capital, they produced only services and they did not have a fixed location for their economic activities. This definition placed emphasis on the economic unit which produced goods and services and not on the individual associated with the economic activity as such. For example, a self-employed construction worker or plumber working alone was a one-man enterprise, but a construction worker or plumber employed for wages by an employer was an employee of the construction enterprise concerned. Similarly, a domestic servant, a self-employed watchman and a self-employed watch repairer working alone each constituted an individual enterprise engaged in the production of services. Some of these surveys included activities which are generally considered socially undesirable (e.g.

prostitution) or illegal; those engaged in these activities were thus treated as enterprises producing goods or services in return for a payment. The unit of enumeration (enterprise or economic unit) generally adopted in these surveys was thus broader than the definition of establishment given in the ISIC.

Sample design

The sampling unit adopted in the informal sector surveys was in general the enterprise since the basic objective of these surveys was to learn about the problems and potentials of small enterprises. The household approach was used in some surveys as a means to identify the informal sector enterprises. The general approach in these surveys was to construct a sampling frame consisting of the eligible units in a given geographical area, which in some surveys comprised the whole urban centre while in others selected sectors of the town or city.

Many problems were encountered in applying the definition of the informal sector universe in the field at the stage of construction of the sampling frame. It was therefore necessary to devise a set of *diagnostic* criteria which more or less reflected the definition of the universe, yet was easy to apply in the field, with very little information about the enterprise or even based on visual observation. These suggested criteria are reproduced in Table 15.3. In applying these criteria, the general approach was to include in the universe not only enterprises that clearly belonged to the informal sector but also those whose status was doubtful. Such a flexible procedure was adopted in order to provide the possibility of further screening at the tabulation stage or even for the tabulation of the results using alternative definitions.

Table 15.3 Criteria for identifying informal sector enterprises generally followed in various surveys

---

1. Manufacturing. A manufacturing enterprise may be included in the informal sector if it satisfies one or more of the following conditions:

(a)   It employs 10 persons or less (including part-time and casual workers).
(b)   It operates on an illegal basis, contrary to governmental regulations.
(c)   Members of the household of the head of the enterprise work in it.
(d)   It does not observe fixed hours/days of operation.
(e)   It operates in semi-permanent or temporary premises, or in a shifting location.
(f)   It does not use any electricity in the manufacturing process.
(g)   It does not depend on formal financial institutions for its credit needs.
(h)   Its output is normally distributed direct to the final consumer.
(i)   Almost all those working in it have fewer than six years of formal schooling.

2. Construction. A construction enterprise may be included in the informal sector if it satisfies one or more of the following conditions:

(a)   Any of 1 *(a)* to *(c)* or *(i)* above
(b)   It does not own power-operated construction machinery and equipment.
(c)   It is engaged in the construction of semi-permanent or temporary buildings only.

3. Transport. An enterprise providing services related to transport, storage and communications may be included in the informal sector if it satisfies one or more of the following conditions:

(a)   Any of 1 *(a)* to *(e)*, *(g)* or *(i)* above. Condition 1 *(e)* does not apply to transport activity *per se*.

(b)   It does not use any mechanical power.

4. Trade. A trading enterprise may be included in the informal sector if it satisfies one or more of the following conditions:

(a)   Any of 1 *(a)* to *(e)* above.

(b)   It deals in second-hand goods, or sells prepared foods.

5. Services. A service enterprise may be included in the informal sector if it satisfies one or more of conditions 1 *(a)* to *(e)* above.

Source: Reproduced from S. V. Sethuraman, 'The Urban Informal Sector: Concept, measurement and policy', *International Labour Review*, Vol. 114, No. 1 (July–August 1976).

Method of data collection

The fieldwork of the surveys varied from one month to three months. Information was collected in the prescribed questionnaires through personal interviews by investigators. Most of the information sought in the questionnaire was precoded in order to minimise the necessity for coding after the fieldwork; this meant that the data could be transferred almost directly to punch cards for computer processing. Interviewers for most of these surveys were recruited from unofficial sources such as universities.

The reference period for data collection varied according to the items in question. For items such as wages paid, value of goods produced, value of goods sold, value of services provided, earnings, household income, etc., the reference period was optional – the last working day, last week or last month, depending on the ability of the respondent to provide the information. For hours worked, the reference period was a day or a week. In the case of rent, the reference period was generally a month. Information on interest rates and taxes was collected on a yearly basis in some of the surveys.

Data collected

The questionnaires used were primarily designed to collect information on the enterprise though they also sought to collect additional information on the head of the enterprise. Some information was also collected on other working members of the household of the head of the enterprise, in certain surveys.

Information sought about the enterprise included:

(i)   physical background: fixed/variable location; permanent/temporary structure; access to economic infrastructure and public utilities;

(ii) structural background: description of the main and subsidiary activities, linkages with other economic units and their nature; structure of the market;

(iii) legal constraints such as licence requirements and registration, government restrictions on business operation and location;

(iv) history of the enterprise: initial difficulties in establishing the enterprise, age of the enterprise, changes in physical location and structure of the premises, changes in goods and services produced, changes in demand, conditions, employment and technology used, business expansion;

(v) operational characteristics: capacity utilisation, extent of underemployment among labour, structure of employment (full-time, part-time and casual), use of unpaid family labour, availability of skilled and unskilled labour, sources of supply of labour, age, sex and educational level of employees, sources of skill acquisition, the extent of labour turnover and reward for experience, training facilities and terms, wages paid, extent of cash and kind payment, value of capital employed, sources of funds for acquisition of capital, extent to which building, machinery and the like are hired and the cost of doing so, total revenue, value of inventories, taxes paid, etc.

Besides the above information, enterprises were asked about imperfections in factor and product markets, difficulties in securing the necessary inputs, including credit, and in marketing their products.

The information requested concerning the head of the enterprise related to: his or her personal characteristics: sex, age, formal or non-formal education, experience, occupational history, migration status, parents' occupations, sources of non-formal education and training, preference for self-employment as opposed to wage employment, job satisfaction, changes in earnings over time, extent of employment and desire for more work, attitudes towards possible government policies, such as training, alternative occupation, alternative location for the enterprise, etc.

The information sought with regard to the household of the head of the enterprise included: proximity of residence to place of work, other members of the household participating in the activities of the enterprise, extent to which other members of the household participate in the labour force, particularly in the informal sector, extent to which others contribute to household income, extent of unemployment and details about the residential structure in which the household was located, and access to utilities.

Selected issues

The experience gained by the ILO through the urban informal sector surveys suggests many problems in the collection of data on small enterprises through sample surveys, the foremost among them being the absence of a sampling frame. Though a few countries have made an effort in recent years to compile a frame consisting of small enterprises employing one or more persons, there are several difficulties in compiling such a frame.

The scope and size of the urban informal sector depend on the definition used. In this connection the criteria suggested in Table 15.3 for demarcating the informal sector need scrutiny. It is quite possible that for certain countries, one may find additional a priori information on the basis of which the scope of the informal sector can be further narrowed. For example, if the bulk of the urban poor are to be found in a few specific occupations or activities, the informal sector can be defined to include just those occupations or activities. Such information is usually not available. It is therefore of interest whether regular statistical surveys of small-scale and household enterprises can provide such information.

The difficulty in obtaining a sample frame of informal sector enterprises stems first from the problem of determining what is an eligible unit. Perhaps a more fundamental difficulty lies in the nature of the enquiry itself; the smaller the economic unit, the greater the probability of its exclusion from the official records, particularly in many developing countries. On top of this, the smaller units seem to have a higher birth and death rate, which makes it almost impossible for the authorities concerned to maintain a list of such units. In so far as some of these very small units are also engaged in illegal activities or in illegal locations (e.g. public pavement), the authorities have frequently excluded them from consideration for statistical purposes. Another reason for not maintaining an up-to-date list of such units could be that many of the small units lack a fixed location for conducting their business (e.g. a variety of repair service workers who go from house to house in search of business, a cobbler who manufactures and repairs footwear, etc.). Likewise, some small units tend to switch from one activity to another depending on the opportunities available. As a result it is extremely difficult to construct a frame of small enterprises; even if such a frame is compiled it is likely to become out of date quickly owing to the significant rate of their growth, as suggested by the ILO studies on the urban informal sector.

One of the issues for consideration is whether there are more efficient alternatives to the construction of such a frame. In this regard, one may want to consider the desirability of constructing three or four sub-frames as follows: one, including small enterprises with one or more hired workers; one consisting of own-account workers operating within established premises devoted exclusively to economic activities; one consisting of production units operating within the household premises; and one made up of the residual units including mainly those without fixed location. The advantage of this approach seems to lie in the different degrees of variability over time of the frames so constructed. For example, it is quite likely that the first two frames mentioned need reconstruction at less frequent intervals than the last frame; if this is true, then it would imply a significant saving in cost by eliminating the need to recompile these frames at more frequent intervals than is really necessary. Incidentally, the availability of four different sub-frames for the same universe would also facilitate the selection of a sample from each of the four sub-universes and application of four different types of questionnaire if necessary.

An extension of the above is to consider other (alternative) schemes for subdividing the universe; for example, sub-frames could be developed by types of activity or by types of occupation instead of by types of unit as suggested above. The most appropriate scheme for compiling the frame of small enterprises will of course be the one which minimises the task of recompilation, subject to other operational considerations.

Turning to data collection, the ILO experience shows that it is possible to collect meaningful and useful data from even very small enterprises. From the regular statistical programme's point of view one of the issues for consideration is the possibility of combining policy-oriented qualitative questions with quantitative questions on employment, output, value added, etc. It may be preferable to focus periodic surveys by the central statistical authorities on basic quantitative data and to supplement this information by qualitative in-depth interviews conducted on a sub-sample basis by economic research institutions. There is a need to clarify the methods and procedures for obtaining the value of assets used for business purposes only (as opposed to those used for household purposes); for assessing the value of self-constructed machinery and equipment or second-hand equipment; and for assessing the value of inputs retrieved from discarded or waste materials (e.g. used metals, paper, etc.). There is also the question of how to treat the value of land occupied illegally. Finally, since the ILO informal sector studies have generally shown that small enterprises play a key role in transmitting skills by providing on-the-job training, there is a question of valuation of the skills thus developed.

Informal sector enterprises seldom keep records and accounts. This creates a formidable problem for assessing the required data accurately. The method usually adopted to get around this problem is to use a short reference period. However, a short reference period may not adequately reflect seasonal and other variations in employment, income and output.

In so far as at least some of the small enterprises operate under illegal conditions or are unregistered or unlicensed, the difficulties in obtaining reliable information through government agencies are even greater. However, this difficulty is relatively less when the surveys are carried out by independent research institutions rather than by official statistical agencies of the governments. Official statistical surveys cannot generally cover many characteristics of the informal sector which are critical for an understanding of its basic nature; for example, they may not be able to detect the existence of a black market price or an illegally high rate of interest.

One of the important problems encountered in the ILO surveys was the difficulty of sorting out the prevailing occupations and activities in the informal sector into the ISIC activity and occupational codes of the International Standard Classification of Occupations because some of the informal sector occupations and activities seem to be unique to developing countries.

Finally, the ILO surveys have also raised an issue concerning the international comparability of the data collected through small-scale and household industries surveys not only because of the differences in survey methodology but also because of the differences in the universe covered. Whatever the criteria may be, the definition of 'small' industrial unit is bound to be a relative concept, depending on the country in question. If the data are to be comparable between countries then it would seem necessary to consider tabulations based on two alternative definitions, one for national and another for international comparison purposes.

Conclusion

The studies carried out by the World Employment Programme of the ILO have shown that between 25 and 50 per cent of the urban employed in the countries surveyed are engaged in informal sector activities. There is also evidence that this sector has contributed to a steady rise in employment. The sector's potential for growth has to be taken into account in future economic development and manpower planning and policies. This calls for regular and systematic collection, compilation and publication of comprehensive statistics concerning the informal sector. The time has arrived to consider the feasibility of incorporating the collection and compilation of statistics concerning the informal sector within the regular statistical programmes of the developing countries.

Notes

1. ILO employment mission reports: Colombia: *Towards full employment, A Programme for Colombia*, Geneva, 1970; Sri Lanka: *Matching employment opportunities and expectations, A programme of action for Ceylon*, Geneva, 1971; Kenya: *Employment, incomes and equality, A strategy for increasing productive employment in Kenya*, Geneva, 1972; Iran: *Employment and income policies for Iran*, Geneva, 1973; Ethiopia: *Employment and unemployment in Ethiopia*, Report of the Exploratory Employment Policy Mission, Geneva, 1973; Philippines: *Sharing in development, A programme of employment, equity and growth for the Philippines*, Geneva, 1974; Dominican Republic; *Generación de empleo productivo y crecimiento económico: El caso de la República Dominicana*, Geneva, 1975; Sudan: *Growth, employment and equity, A comprehensive strategy for the Sudan*, Geneva, 1976.
2. Many of these survey studies have been issued as research working papers under the World Employment Programme (WEP 2-19 series).
3. ILO: *Employment, incomes and equality: A strategy for increasing productive employment in Kenya*, op. cit. p. 6.
4. The list is only preliminary; perhaps a few other similar surveys, completed or in the process of completion, are not shown in this list.

Part Four: Standard classifications

16 The revised International Standard Classification of Occupations (ISCO-88) a short Presentation

E. Hoffmann and M. Scott

Introduction

The 14th International Conference of Labour Statisticians adopted in November 1987 a revised International Standard Classification of Occupations (ISCO-88) based on a proposal prepared by the Bureau of Statistics of the International Labour Office (ILO). This paper describes the main features and purposes of occupational classifications in general and those of ISCO-88 in particular.

Founded in 1919 together with the League of Nations, the International Labour Organisation (ILO) is a specialised agency of the United Nations. One of its tasks is to develop international standards and guidelines to help countries improve their labour administration as well as the quality and reliability of their labour statistics, and to improve international comparability of statistical data. To these ends the need for an international standard classification of occupations was first discussed in 1921. However, it was only in 1958 that ISCO was issued for the first time. A new, revised edition of ISCO was published in 1968 and the result of the second and most recent revision of ISCO will be published in 1989 as ISCO-88.

The purpose of this paper is to outline the main areas of use of an international standard classification of occupations; to present the main considerations and features of ISCO-88; and to describe further work on ISCO-88 to be carried out by the Bureau of Statistics of the ILO. In Appendix 16 a brief description of each ISCO-88 major group is given with a list of sub-major and minor groups.

What is an occupational classification?

An occupational classification is a tool for organising all jobs in an establishment, an industry or a country into a clearly defined set of groups. It will normally consist of two components: a descriptive component, which may be just a set of titles of occupations and occupational groups, but which usually consists of descriptions of the tasks and duties as well as other aspects of the jobs which belong to each of the defined groups, in which case we have a dictionary of occupations; and the classification system itself, which gives the guidelines on how jobs are to be classified into the most detailed groups of occupations and how these detailed groups are to be further aggregated to broader groups.

Occupational classifications can be compared to a system of maps for a country, say Switzerland: the top level of aggregation corresponds to a small-scale road map for the main motorways and highways; the next level corresponds to a set of larger-scale maps for say each of the main regions, also showing cantonal and local roads; and so on. At the most detailed level will be the detailed technical maps used by the municipal engineers to plan sidewalks, traffic lights, road extensions, etc. These very detailed technical maps can be compared to the detailed job descriptions which are used by enterprises for their wage systems and which in many countries will not be the concern of national authorities.

What are occupational classifications used for?

National occupational classifications and dictionaries are usually designed to serve several purposes. Although the detailed occupational descriptions and the classification structure must be seen as an integrated whole, different user areas have different degrees of interest in the various elements. Broadly speaking, the detailed occupational descriptions are being used mainly by client-oriented users (i.e. those responsible for job placement, vocational training and guidance, migration control, etc.) and should be designed primarily to meet the needs of such users, but should also include descriptive elements necessary for applying relevant aggregation schemes. The classification structure, grouping the detailed occupations together in progressively more aggregate groups, should be designed mainly to facilitate statistical description and analysis of the labour market and the social structure, supporting public debate and the formulation of policies.

Legislators and public sector administrators use occupational statistics in support of the formulation of government policies and to monitor progress with respect to the application of such policies, including those of manpower planning and the planning of educational and vocational training. *Managers* need occupational statistics for planning working conditions and deciding on manpower policies at the enterprise and industry level. *Psychologists* study the relationship between occupations and the personality and interests of workers. *Epidemiologists* use occupation in their study of work-related differences in morbidity and mortality. *Sociologists* use occupation as an important variable in the study of social differences in lifestyles and behaviour. *Economists* use occupation in the analysis of differences in the distribution of earnings and incomes over time and between groups. Depending on the purpose of the study, 'occupation' may be regarded as the main variable or it may serve as a background variable in the empirical analysis. Used as a background variable, it may serve as a proxy for other variables such as socio-economic groups or working conditions, or it may be used as one element in the construction of other variables, such as social class or socio-economic status.

ISCO is intended to facilitate international communication on the subject of occupations and occupational groups, narrowly or broadly defined, both for client-oriented and for statistical users. ISCO should therefore lend itself to the different uses at the national level, while taking into account the special consideration which must follow from its international nature.

Internationally comparable statistics on occupational groups are used mainly to:

(a) compare the *distribution* of the employed population or some other variable (e.g. wages, hours of work, work accidents, income, consumption, reading habits) over occupational groups in two or more countries;

(b) compare data on broadly or narrowly defined *individual sets of occupations* in two or more countries, for example, to compare the average wages of computer programmers in country A with those in country B, or to compare the number of industrial designers in the two countries;

(c) merge data from different countries referring to comparable groups, for example, to obtain enough observations to study the incidence of particular work-related accidents or diseases among workers in broadly or narrowly defined occupational groups, believed to have similar exposure to particular working conditions or harmful substances.

Experience shows that, at the international level, most users of occupational statistics need data at the higher level of aggregation – usually for type (a) descriptions. Important exceptions are international studies of earnings, work hazards and injuries and other conditions of work – such studies often require that detailed occupational groups be defined, sometimes in cross-classification with industry and/or status in employment.

It is important to note that while the statistical use of type (a) above requires that the occupational classification cover all jobs, the focus in other types of use (statistical or client-oriented) is on specific occupations or groups of occupations. The sum total of all users' interests in these types of use could conceivably also cover all occupations, but in practice only a subset of occupations is involved.

The main client-oriented applications of an international standard classification of occupations are in the international recruitment of workers and in the administration of short- or long-term migration of workers between countries. An internationally developed and agreed set of descriptions for detailed occupational categories which can serve as a common 'language' for the countries and parties involved in such programmes may greatly increase the effectiveness of the communication necessary for their execution.

When countries need a model as a basis for developing or revising their national classifications, or when a substitute for a national classification is needed in countries that have not developed their own, then an international standard classification may be a good alternative, and this has been kept in mind both in the original development and in the subsequent revisions of ISCO.

Key characteristics of ISCO-88

The recent revision of ISCO aimed to produce an international classification which would: have a firm and clear conceptual basis, to strengthen its usefulness as a descriptive and analytical tool and to make it easy to update with new occupations; reflect the labour markets of developing as well as of industrialised countries; better reflect women's position in the labour market; reflect occupational consequences of different technologies; and incorporate new occupations and reflect shifts in the relative importance of occupational groups.

In the present context a *job* is defined as a set of tasks and duties which are (or can be assigned to be) carried out by one person. Most occupational classifications classify, i.e. group together in *occupations* and more aggregate groups, jobs by similarity of the type of work done. *Persons* are classified by occupations through their relationship to a past, a present or a future job. In ISCO-88 occupations are grouped together and further aggregated mainly on the basis of *the similarity of skills* required to fulfil the tasks and duties of the jobs. Two dimensions of the skill concept are used in the definition of ISCO-88 groups: *skill level*, which is a function of the range and complexity of the tasks involved, where the complexity of tasks has priority over the range; and *skill specialisation*, which reflects type of knowledge applied, tools and equipment used, materials worked on, or with, and the nature of the goods and services produced. It should be emphasised that the focus in ISCO-88 is on the skills required to carry out the tasks and duties of an occupation – and not on whether a worker having a particular occupation is more or less skilled than another worker in the same occupation.

Only a few broad skill-level categories can usefully be identified for international comparisons. The use of the International Standard Classification of Education (ISCED) to define skill levels does not mean that skills can only be obtained by formal education or training. Most skills may, and often are acquired through experience and through informal training, although formal training plays a larger role in some countries than in others and a larger role at the higher skill levels than at the lower – see below. For the purpose of the ISCO classification system, the decisive factor for determining how an occupation should be classified is the nature of the skills that are required to carry out the tasks and duties of the corresponding jobs – not the way these skills are acquired.

Skill specialisation can be indicated both broadly and more narrowly and is related to subject matter areas, production processes, equipment used, material worked with, products and services produced, etc. Therefore words describing subject matter, production processes, etc., have to be used as labels for the core sets of skills with which occupations are concerned. The same type of words is used to describe the groups in an industrial classification of production activities. For some workers it will therefore be possible to predict the industry in which they are working with a fairly high degree of success, knowing how they are classified by occupation. This is not because ISCO is using industry as a classification criterion, but because skills are linked to products, materials, etc., which are the determinants of industry. The conceptual difference between the two types of classification should not be forgotten, even though it may be partly hidden by the correlation between them and by the terminology used.

ISCO-88 defines four levels of aggregation, consisting of 10 major groups, 28 sub-major groups (subdivisions of major groups), 113 minor groups (subdivisions of sub-major groups), and 377 unit groups (subdivisions of minor groups). Unit groups in most cases will consist of a number of detailed *occupations*. For example, as a separate occupation *nuclear physicist* belongs to ISCO-88 unit group 2111 *Physicists and astronomers*, which belongs to minor group 211 *Physicists, chemists and related professionals*, which is part of sub-major group 21 *Physical, mathematical and engineering science professionals* of the major group 2 *Professionals*. The structure of ISCO-88 is shown in Table 16.1, and the major groups are briefly described in Appendix 16.

Table 16.1   ISCO-88 major groups, number of sub-groups and skill level

Major Group	Sub-major groups	Minor groups	Unit groups	ISCO skill level
1 Legislators, senior officials and managers	3	7	25	–
2 Professionals	4	18	55	4
3 Technicians and associate professionals	4	20	74	3
4 Clerks	2	6	22	2
5 Service workers and shop and market sales workers	2	9	23	2
6 Skilled agricultural and fishery workers	2	6	16	2
7 Craft and related workers	4	16	67	2
8 Plant and machine operators and assemblers	3	20	68	2
9 Elementary occupations	3	10	26	1
0 Armed forces	1	1	1	–
Totals	28	113	337	

Eight of the ten ISCO-88 major groups are delineated with reference to the four broad skill levels defined for ISCO, cf. Table 16.1. These four ISCO skill levels have been given operational definitions in terms of the educational levels and categories of the ISCED. Five of the eight major groups, i.e. 4, 5, 6, 7 and 8, are considered to be at the same skill level and are distinguished by reference to broad skill specialisation groups. Skill-level references were not made in the definitions of the two major groups entitled *Legislators, senior officials and managers* and *Armed forces* respectively, because other aspects of the type of work were considered more important as similarity criteria, i.e. policy-making and management functions, and military duties, respectively. As a result there are significant skill-level differences within each of these two major groups. However, the sub-major and minor groups of major group 1 have been designed to include occupations at similar skill levels.

To cope with the issue of different skill requirements for jobs with similar purposes due to differences in technologies used, a distinction is made at the major group level between (a) occupations that are essentially craft-oriented (i.e. major group 6 'Skilled agricultural and fishery workers' and 7 'Craft and related workers'), and (b) occupations that are essentially oriented towards the operation of tools, machinery and industrial plants (i.e. major group 8 'Plant and machine operators and assemblers').

Occupations which are craft-oriented consist of skilled jobs directly involved in the *production* of goods where the tasks and duties require an understanding of and experience with the natural resources and raw materials used and how to achieve the desired techniques and practices, but they may also use more technologically advanced tools and machines, provided that this does not change the basic skills and understanding required. Modern machines and tools may be used to reduce the amount of physical effort and/or time required for specific tasks, or to increase the quality of the products. The tasks and duties of jobs in *occupations which are oriented towards the operation of tools, machinery and industrial plants* require an understanding of what to do with the machines to make them work properly, of how to identify malfunctioning and of what to do when something goes wrong. The skills required are oriented towards the machines and what they are doing rather than to the transformation process or its results. Occupations where the tasks and duties consist of assembling products from component parts according to strict rules and procedures are considered to belong to the same major group as the machine-oriented occupations. Jobs which only require low or elementary skills and little or no judgement are classified to occupations in major group 9.

The 14th ICLS decided that for international comparisons it should be possible to reflect in ISCO the important differences which exist between countries, and sometimes within a country, in the required skill levels of jobs which traditionally have been seen as belonging to the same occupational group. Such differences are linked to the actual tasks which are carried out as, although similar in nature, they may vary significantly in the degree of judgement, responsibility and planning required. These differences in tasks will have resulted in national differences in skill levels and qualifications required for entering the occupations. The 14th ICLS therefore decided that ISCO-88 should make it possible for countries to classify some occupational groups either to major group 2 *Professions* or to major group 3 *Technicians and associate professionals*, depending on national circumstances. This possibility was created for primary, pre-primary and special teaching occupations, nursing and midwifery occupations, social work occupations and some artistic occupations.

As in ISCO-68, jobs in the armed forces should be classified in a separate major group 0 *Armed forces*, even if the jobs involved tasks and duties similar to those of civilian counterparts.

All occupations which consist of jobs in which the workers have mainly legislative, administrative or managerial tasks and duties should be classified to major group 1 *Legislators, senior officials and managers*. In ISCO-68 they were partly classified to major group 2 (Administrative and managerial workers) and partly to other major groups.

'Working proprietors' are to be classified according to whether their tasks and duties are mainly similar to those of managers and supervisors or to those of other workers in the same area of work. This is because the status of 'working proprietor' is seen as related not to type of work performed but to 'status in employment' – corresponding to the 'self-employed' and 'employer' categories of the International Classification of Status in Employment (ICSE). One self-employed plumber may have mainly managerial tasks but another may do mainly the same work as a salaried plumber, depending, for example, on the size of the firm. In the former case the job should be classified with managers and in the latter case with plumbers.

Both 'apprentices' and 'trainees' should be classified according to their actual tasks and duties as, if needed, these two groups may be separately identified through the 'status in employment' classification. ISCO-68 recommended that apprentices should be classified to the occupation for which they are being trained, but that trainees be classified according to their actual tasks and duties.

The problem of classifying jobs which have a broad range of tasks and duties should be handled by the application of some *priority rules*, i.e. some tasks and duties are given priority in determining the occupational category to which a job should be classified. For example, in cases where the tasks and duties are associated with different stages of the process of producing and distributing goods and services, the tasks and duties related to the *production* stages should take priority over associated tasks and duties, such as those related to the sale and marketing of the same goods, their transportation or the management of the production process (unless either of these tasks and duties dominates): the worker who bakes bread and pastries and then sells them should be classified as 'baker', not as 'sales assistant'; the worker who operates a particular type of machinery and also instructs new workers in how to operate the machine should be classified with the machine operators; the taxi driver who drives his/her own car and also keeps the accounts should be classified with motor-vehicle drivers. In cases where the tasks and duties performed require skills usually obtained through different levels of training and experience, jobs should be classified in accordance with those tasks and duties which require the highest level of skill: there are a number of jobs whose tasks and duties most of the time require a set of relatively easily obtained skills, but where the workers are also expected to have skills which require more training or experience which enables them to cope with unexpected and infrequent situations, for instance, to avoid accidents or injuries. It is recognised that a certain amount of judgement and adjustment to national circumstances will be necessary in the choice and application of these priority rules.

Many users of the 1968 ISCO found that its top aggregation level of nine groups meant that the differences within each group were too large for the groups to be useful for description and analysis. However, the next level of aggregation, with 83 groups, represented too much detail for many types of analysis, as well as for international reporting of occupational distributions, especially if the data are obtained through sample surveys. ISCO-88 therefore includes the 'sub-major groups' as a new level in the aggregation system, between the former major and minor groups – see Table 16.1.

Comparison with ISCO-68

In all areas of statistics it is important to achieve a balance between continuity of time series and needed adjustments and improvements in definitions, in methods of data collection and in classification systems. In developing ISCO-88, continuity was aimed for at the unit group level. The revision did, nevertheless, result in the splitting of a significant number of ISCO-68 unit groups. The numerical importance of these splits remains to be investigated.

The unit group level is the most detailed level specified in the ISCO-88 structure. The previous versions of ISCO also specified a detailed set of occupational categories, although they were not discussed or approved by the ICLS. Those of the detailed ISCO-68 descriptions which are still relevant will be made available to the users of ISCO-88 in a companion volume.

The emphasis on skill level and skill specialisation as the main similarity criteria for the delineation of occupational groups in ISCO-88 is not such a dramatic change from ISCO-68 as it may seem. That skill was implicitly used in ISCO-68 can be seen through a closer analysis of its classification system. For example, the group 0/1 (Professional, Technical and Related Workers) contains occupations with tasks and duties which require, for the most part, highly trained or skilled workers. Occupations of comparable skill requirements are otherwise only found in major group 2 *Administrative and managerial workers*. Each of the other major groups in ISCO-68 covers different broad areas of skill specialisation. For example, most of the occupations in major group 3 *Clerical and related workers* mainly require skills needed to deal with data and information, while most of the occupations in major groups 4 and 5 'Sales workers' and *Service workers* can be said mainly to require skills needed in dealing with people. Similarly the distinctions between different minor and unit groups within a major group can be seen as distinctions between different skill specialisations. Skill level is explicitly discussed in the introduction to ISCO-68 in relation to minor group 9-9 (Labourers not elsewhere classified). The conclusion that skill implicitly plays an important role in both ISCO-58 and ISCO-68 is also supported by the following quotation from the Introduction to ISCO-58: 'combinations (of occupations) may be based on materials worked on, workplace, environment, the specialised equipment used (if any) and similar relationships. The particular skills, knowledge and abilities of the workers concerned have an intimate connection with such factors.'

ISCO-88 consists of ten major groups (ISCO-68 nine), followed by 28 sub-major groups, 113 (83) minor groups and 377 (286) unit groups. When coding ISCO-68 groups to ISCO-88 we find that 55 per cent of the ISCO-68 unit groups (157 out of 284) have been left unchanged or have had their scopes only slightly expanded or reduced. Fourteen of the new unit groups have been created by combining two or three ISCO-68 unit groups – using a total of 31. The coding also shows that 96 ISCO-68 unit groups were split – and that the parts were coded to 174 different ISCO-88 unit groups. Twenty-four of the split groups were 'not elsewhere classified' groups. A total of 32 ISCO-88 unit groups contain no reference to any ISCO-68 unit groups or occupations categories. See ILO (1987, 1988; 1989) for further information about ISCO-88.

Further work on ISCO-88

A publication presenting ISCO-88 will be available in English, French and Spanish at the end of 1989. In addition to presenting the main principles and the treatment of special groups of jobs, it will include descriptions of all ISCO-88 groups and updated and revised versions of the 'Expanded alphabetical list of titles' in ISCO-68 which contained 3,706 entries in the English volume, 2,743 in the French volume and 3,046 in the Spanish. The updating of these lists will use information obtained from national dictionaries of occupations in the three languages, as well as information obtained from experts in relevant areas. All entries in the updated lists will be coded to the unit groups of ISCO-88 and new entries will also be coded to ISCO-68. Descriptions of still relevant ISCO-68 occupational categories will be included in an appendix but they will not all be updated.

A manual on the development and use of national occupational classifications and dictionaries will cover both client-oriented and statistical applications. Work on the manual has been carried out parallel to the work on the revision of ISCO and it is expected that it will be published at the same time as the ISCO-88 publication mentioned above, i.e. at the end of 1989.

Both the introductory text of the ISCO-88 publication and the manual will discuss much more explicity than has been done in the past the collection and processing of occupational information using administrative forms and statistical census and survey questionnaires. The aim is to contribute to better and more uniform occupational statistics, both for those using ISCO-88 directly and for those using other classifications for possible later linkage to ISCO-88 groups. This will improve the usefulness of occupational data both nationally and for international comparisons and communication. The need for well-designed and tested occupational questions will be emphasised, as well as the fact that experience and experiments have shown that the best results are obtained when asking for both the occupational title of a job and for a brief description of the main tasks and duties. Guidance will be given on how to train coders, control the coding process and ensure that coders receive feedback on their performance. The importance of a good index of occupational responses and the way such indexes should be created and used will be explained. It will be recommended that coding always should be carried out at the most detailed level supported by the information given by the respondent. Available evidence indicates that this strategy involves small marginal costs, in terms of coding errors and time used per response, compared to that of coding at a predetermined aggregate level. It will also be recommended that the coding should distinguish between responses which are incomplete and the 'not elsewhere classified' categories for particular occupations.

The work programme and budget of the Bureau of Statistics will provide for the minimum amount of resources necessary for the ILO to maintain competence in the field of occupational classification. These limited resources will mainly be used to provide technical advice on links between ISCO-88 and other occupational classifications, national and international; revise existing and develop new detailed occupational descriptions for priority areas; and set up and run a small documentation centre and information service on national occupational classifications and their links to ISCO, and on activities relevant to the development of occupational classifications and their use.

References

ILO (1987) *Revision of the International Standard Classification of Occupations*, Report IV to the Fourteenth International Conference of Labour Statisticians: Part I, *Background, principles and draft resolution*; Part II, *Draft definitions*, ILO, Geneva.

ILO (1988) *Fourteenth International Conference of Labour Statisticians, Report of the Conference*, ILO Geneva.

ILO (1989) *The Revised International Standard Classification of Occupations (ISCO-88)*. ILO, Geneva. (Forthcoming).

Appendix 16
THE ISCO-88 MAJOR GROUPS

1. *Legislators, senior officials and managers*

This major group covers occupations whose main tasks consist of planning, formulating and deciding on policies, laws, rules and regulations of national, state, regional or local governments or legislative assemblies, or of planning, formulating, organising, co-ordinating, controlling and directing policies and operations of enterprises and organisations. The core content of this group is the same as that of major group 2, 'Administrative and managerial workers' in ISCO-68, but occupations with similar tasks classified under other ISCO-68 major groups have been added. This major group has been divided into three sub-major groups, seven minor groups and 25 unit groups– reflecting differences in tasks associated with different areas of authority and different types of enterprise and organisation.

Sub-major and minor groups

11 Legislators and senior officials
   111 Legislators
   112 Senior government officials
   113 Traditional chiefs and heads of villages
   114 Senior officials of special-interest organisations

12 Corporate managers[1]
   121 Directors and chief executives
   122 Specialised managers

13 General managers[2]
   131 General managers

1. This group is intended to include persons who – as directors, chief executives or specialised managers – manage enterprises requiring a total of three or more managers.
2. This group is intended to include persons who manage enterprises on their own behalf, or on behalf of the proprietor, with the assistance of no more than one other manager and/or some non-managerial help.

2. *Professionals*

This major group covers occupations whose main tasks require a high level of professional knowledge and experience in engineering, natural sciences, social sciences, humanities and related fields. The main tasks consist of engaging in the practical application of scientific and artistic concepts and theories, increasing the existing stock of knowledge by means of research and creativeness, and teaching about the foregoing in a systematic manner. All occupations classified under this major group were classified under major group 0/1 'Professional, technical and related workers' in ISCO-68. This major group has been divided into four sub-major groups, 18 minor groups and 55 unit groups – reflecting differences in tasks associated with different fields of knowledge and specialisation.

Sub-major and minor groups

21 Physical, mathematical and engineering science professionals
    211   Physicists, chemists and related professionals
    212   Mathematicians, statisticians and related professionals
    213   Computing professionals
    214   Architects, engineers and related professionals

22 Life science and health professionals
    221   Life science professionals
    222   Health professionals (except nursing)
    223   Nursing and midwifery professionals

23 Teaching professionals
    231   College, university and higher education teaching professionals
    232   Secondary education teaching professionals
    233   Primary and pre-primary education teaching professionals
    234   Special education teaching professionals
    235   Other teaching professionals

24 Other professionals
    241   Business professionals
    242   Legal professionals
    243   Archivists, librarians and related information professionals
    244   Social and related science professionals
    245   Writers and creative and performing artists
    246   Religion professionals

3. *Technicians and associate professionals*

This major group covers occupations whose main tasks require the experience and knowledge of principles and practices necessary to assume operational responsibility and to give technical support to *Professionals* in engineering, natural sciences, social sciences, humanities and related fields. The core content of this major group consists of occupations which were classified under major group 0/1 'Professional, technical and related workers' in ISCO-68. Occupations with skill requirements at a similar level, which were classified under other ISCO-68 major groups, especially major groups 3 'Clerical and related workers' and 4 'Sales workers', are also classified under this major group. This major group has been divided into four sub-major groups, 20 minor groups and 74 unit groups – reflecting differences in tasks associated with different fields of knowledge and different areas of specialisation.

Sub-major and minor groups

31 Physical science and engineering associate professionals
    311   Physical science and engineering technicians
    312   Computer assistants and computer equipment controllers
    313   Optical and electronic equipment controllers
    314   Ship and aircraft controllers and technicians
    315   Building, fire, safety and health and quality inspectors

32 Life science and health associate professionals
    321   Life science technicians and related workers
    322   Modern health associate professionals (except nursing)
    323   Nursing and midwifery associate professionals

324 Traditional medical practitioners and faith healers

33 Teaching associate professionals
   331 Primary education teaching associate professionals
   332 Pre-primary education teaching associate professionals
   333 Special education teaching associate professionals
   334 Other teaching associate professionals

34 Other associate professionals
   341 Finance and sales associate professionals
   342 Business service agents and trade brokers
   343 Administrative associate professionals
   344 Government associate professionals
   345 Police inspectors and detectives
   346 Social work associate professionals
   347 Artistic, entertainment and sports associate professionals
   348 Non-ordained religion associate professionals.

4. *Clerks*

This major group covers occupations whose main tasks require the knowledge and experience necessary to record, organise, store and retrieve information, compute numerical, financial and statistical data, and perform a number of client-oriented clerical duties, especially in connection with money-handling operations, travel arrangements, business information and appointments. The core content of this group consists of occupations that were classified under major group 3 'Clerical and related workers' in ISCO-68. This major group has been divided into two sub-major groups, six minor groups and 22 unit groups – reflecting differences in tasks associated with different areas of specialisation.

Sub-major and minor groups

41 Office clerks
   411 Secretaries and keyboard and operating clerks
   412 Numerical clerks
   413 Material-recording and transport clerks
   414 Library, mail and related clerks
   419 Other office clerks

42 Customer services clerks
   421 Cashiers, tellers and related clerks
   422 Client information clerks

5. *Service workers and shop and market sales workers*

This major group covers occupations whose main tasks require the knowledge and experience necessary to provide protective services, personal services related to travel, housekeeping, catering and personal care, or to sell and demonstrate goods for wholesale or retail shops and similar establishments. The core content of this group consists of occupations that were classified under major group 4 'Sales workers' or 5 'Service workers' in ISCO-68. This major group has been divided into two sub-major groups, nine minor groups and 23 unit groups – reflecting differences in tasks associated with different areas of specialisation.

Sub-major and minor groups

51   Personal and protective services workers
      511   Travel attendants and related workers
      512   Housekeeping and restaurant services workers
      513   Personal care and related workers
      514   Other personal services workers
      515   Astrologers, fortune-tellers and related workers
      516   Protective services workers

52   Salespersons, demonstrators and models
      521   Shop salespersons and demonstrators
      522   Stall and market salespersons
      523   Fashion and other models

6. *Skilled agricultural and fishery workers*

This major group covers occupations whose tasks require the knowledge and experience necessary to grow and harvest crops, breed, feed or hunt animals, gather wild fruit and plants, catch or breed fish, or cultivate or gather other forms of aquatic life. The core content of this group consists of occupations that were classified under major group 6 'Agricultural, animal husbandry and forestry workers, fishermen and hunters' in ISCO-68. This major group has been divided into two sub-major groups, six minor groups and 16 unit groups – reflecting differences in tasks associated with different areas of specialisation, and differences in market orientation.

Sub-major and minor groups

61   Market-oriented skilled agricultural and fishery workers
      611   Market gardeners and crop growers
      612   Market-oriented animal producers
      613   Market-oriented crop and animal producers
      614   Forestry and related workers
      615   Fishery workers, hunters and trappers

62   Subsistence agricultural and fishery workers
      621   Subsistence agricultural, fishery and related workers

7. *Craft and related workers*

This major group covers occupations whose tasks require the knowledge and experience necessary to extract and treat raw materials, manufacture and repair goods, and construct, maintain and repair roads, structures and machinery. The main tasks of these occupations require experience with and understanding of the work situation, the materials worked with and the requirements of the structures, machinery and other items produced. The core content of this group consists of occupations that were classified under major group 7/8/9 'Production and related workers, transport equipment operators and labourers' in ISCO-68. This major group has been divided into four sub-major groups, 16 minor groups and 67 unit groups – reflecting differences in tasks associated with different areas of specialisation.

Sub-major and minor groups

71 Extraction and building trades workers
   711 Miners and shotfirers, stone cutters and carvers
   712 Building frame and related trades workers
   713 Building finishers and related trades workers
   714 Painters, building structure cleaners and related workers

72 Metal, machinery and electricity trades workers
   721 Metal moulders, welders, sheet-metal workers, structural metal preparers. amd related workers
   722 Blacksmiths, tool-makers and related workers
   723 Machinery mechanics and fitters
   724 Electrical and electronic equipment mechanics and fitters

73 Precision, handicraft, printing and related trades workers
   731 Precision workers in metal and related materials
   732 Potters, glass-makers and related workers
   733 Handicraft workers in wood, textile, leather and similar materials
   734 Printing and related trades workers

74 Other craft and related workers
   741 Food products processing trades and related workers
   742 Wood treaters, cabinet-makers, and related trades workers
   743 Textiles and garments trades workers
   744 Pelt, leather and shoemaking trades workers

8. Plant and machine operators and assemblers

This major group covers occupations whose main tasks require the knowledge and experience necessary to operate vehicles and other mobile equipment, to tend, control and monitor the operation of industrial plant and machinery, on the spot or by remote control, or to assemble products from component parts according to strict rules and procedures. The tasks of these occupations require mainly experience with and understanding of the machinery worked with. The core content of this group consists of occupations that were classified under major group 7/8/9 'Production and related workers, transport equipment operators and labourers' in ISCO-68. This major group has been divided into three sub-major groups, 20 minor groups and 68 unit groups – reflecting differences in tasks associated with different areas of specialisation.

Sub-major and minor groups

81 Industrial plant operators
   811 Mining and mineral-processing plant operators
   812 Metal-processing plant operators
   813 Glass and ceramics kiln and related plant operators
   814 Wood-processing and paper-making plant operators
   815 Chemical processing plant operators
   816 Power-generating and related plant operators
   817 Automated assembly-line and industrial robot operators

82 Stationary machine operators and assemblers
   821 Metal and mineral products processing machine operators
   822 Chemical products machine operators

823   Rubber and plastics products machine operators
824   Wood products machine operators
825   Printing, binding and paper products machine operators
826   Textile, fur and leather products machine operators
827   Food and related products processing machine operators
828   Assemblers
829   Other stationary machine operators and assemblers

83   Drivers and mobile machinery operators
831   Railway engine drivers and related workers
832   Motor vehicle drivers
833   Agricultural, earthmoving, lifting and other mobile materials-handling equipment operators
834   Ships' deck crews and related workers

9. *Elementary occupations*

This major group covers occupations which require the knowledge and experience necessary to perform mostly simple and routine tasks, involving the use of simple hand-held tools and in some cases certain physical effort, and, with few exceptions, only limited personal initiative or judgement. The core content of this group consists of occupations that were classified under minor group 9-9 'Labourers not elsewhere classified' in ISCO-68. Occupations with skill requirements at a similar level classified under other ISCO-68 minor and major groups, especially major groups 5 'Service workers' and 6 'Agricultural, animal husbandry and forestry workers, fishermen and hunters' are also classified under this major group. This major group has been divided into three sub-major groups, ten minor groups and 26 unit groups – reflecting differences in tasks associated with different areas of work.

Sub-major and minor groups

91   Sales and services elementary occupations
911   Street vendors and related workers
912   Shoe-cleaning and other street services elementary occupations
913   Domestic and related helpers, cleaners and launderers
914   Building caretakers and window cleaners
915   Messengers, porters, doorkeepers and related workers
916   Garbage collectors and related labourers

92   Agricultural, fishery and related labourers
921   Agricultural, fishery and related labourers

93   Labourers in mining, construction, manufacturing and transport
931   Mining and construction labourers
932   Manufacturing labourers
933   Transport labourers and freight handlers

0. *Armed forces*

This major group covers the same occupations as those covered in the group 'Members of the armed forces' in ISCO-68, which was defined as follows:

Members of the armed forces are those personnel who are serving in the armed forces, including women's auxiliary services, whether on a voluntary or involuntary basis, and who are not free to accept civilian employment. Included are regular members of the army, navy, air force and other military services, as well as temporary members enrolled for full-time training or other service for a period of three months or more. Excluded are persons in civilian employment, such as administrative staff of government establishments concerned with defence questions; police (other than military police); customs inspectors and members of other armed civilian services; members of military reserves not currently on full-time active service; and persons who have been temporarily withdrawn from civilian life for a short period of military training.

Sub-major and minor groups

01   Armed forces
   011   Armed forces

17 Issues concerning a possible revision of the International Classification of Status in Employment (ICSE)[1]

E. Hoffmann

Introduction

The *International Classification of Status in Employment* (ICSE) comprises the following major groups:

(a) employers;
(b) own-account workers;
(c) employees;
(d) unpaid family workers;
(e) members of producers' co-operatives; and
(f) persons not classifiable by status.

Definitions as given in the UN Census Recommendations are reproduced in Appendix 17 (see also UNSO, 1986).

In addition, the recommendations concerning the statistics of the economically active population, employment, unemployment and under-employment adopted by the 13th International Conference of Labour Statisticians (ICLS) imply a set of rules for collapsing the five substantive groups into two groups: 'Employers, own-account workers and members of producers' co-operatives should be considered as in self-employment', and 'unpaid family workers at work should be considered as in self-employment'. This means that groups (a), (b), (d) and (e) may be said to form one group, with (c) forming the other. (Note that in this article the term 'self-employed' will be used to indicate the combination of groups (a) and (b).)

Although widely used in population censuses (cf. the next section), labour force surveys and other official statistics, concern has been expressed about the validity and relevance of ICSE in its present form, with the claim that the classification is of little use to developing countries and increasingly irrelevant for developed countries. The main elements in this concern seems to be the following:

(a) The classification has no clear basis, i.e. no clear statement about what it is that a 'status in employment' variable should measure.

(b) The borderlines between some of the groups are unclear. Some are drawn in a way which makes the classification less useful as a tool for description and analysis, and as an element in the definition of socio-economic groups, than it would have been if they had been drawn differently.

(c) The classification is incomplete as long as distinctions between important and relevant subgroups are not made.

After having briefly reviewed the history of the ICSE and national practices concerning its use, this paper will try to review these issues in more detail. A summary of issues for further work and discussion, as well as some tentative proposals, are then presented. Hopefully, this can provide a basis for deciding whether to prepare proposals for a revised ICSE.

Background and national practices[2]

The first international step towards a classification of workers by status in employment was taken in 1938 by the Committee of Statistical Experts of the League of Nations, which recommended the following classification of 'personal status' of the gainfully occupied population, in addition to classification by occupation and industry:

(a) employers (persons working on their own account with paid assistants in their occupations);

(b) persons working on their own account either alone or with the assistance of members of their families;

(c) members of families aiding the head of their families in his occupation; and

(d) persons in receipt of salaries or wages.

The Sixth ICLS (1947), in its resolution concerning statistics of employment, unemployment and the labour force, recommended that such statistics should include the following groups:

(a) workers for public or private employers;

(b) employers;

(c) workers who work on their own account without employees; and

(d) unpaid family workers.

In 1948 the Population Commission of the United Nations recommended that, in censuses, the economically active population be classified according to status into these status-in-employment (SE) groups, and in 1950 it adopted standard definitions for them.

In 1957 the Ninth ICLS had before it a detailed report recommending important subdivisions to the main groups of the classification. However, the Conference did not agree on the proposed conceptual basis for ICSE or the proposed subdivisions. Agreement was, however, reached concerning the usefulness of adding a group covering 'members of co-operative production units' to the four existing groups. 'Members of producers' co-operatives' was then added in the recommendations concerning population censuses approved by the Statistical Commission of the United nations in 1958. Since then only minor editorial revisions to the descriptions of the groups constituting the classification have been made. The draft resolution prepared for, but not adopted by, the Ninth ICLS in 1957, still contains the most detailed descriptions available of the five substantive groups in the ICSE – see ILO (1957a).

The UN Expert Group on the 1990 Round of Population Censuses, meeting in November 1985, recommended that no changes should be made to the classification outlined at the beginning of this paper, but that it should be recognised that countries might wish to specify 'apprentices' as a subgroup of 'employees'. Consequently, the ICSE has been left virtually unchanged for 30 to 40 years.

The first four major groups contained in the international recommendations have been widely used by almost all countries in their population censuses during the past three decades or more. Many countries collect, classify and present census data separately for 'employers' and 'own-account workers', but several countries in Europe, North America and Oceania have combined these two groups in their censuses. In certain countries, such as India, the two groups have been shown separately for the non-agricultural labour force only, while the agricultural workers have been classified into 'owner-holders', 'tenant-holders' and 'share-croppers'.

Differences have been observed in national census practices in respect of 'unpaid family workers'. Leaving aside the differences in the definition used by countries to identify unpaid family workers as members of the labour force, in some censuses the unpaid family workers have been included in the major group 'employees'. In other censuses they have been treated as partners and therefore as 'self-employed' or 'own-account workers'. It is the latter procedure which is consistent with the recommendations of the 13th ICLS (see above).

In addition to the original four major groups used by nearly all countries, a number of countries have distinguished other major groups. These include, in addition to the internationally recommended group of 'members of producers' co-operatives', the 'armed forces'; (b) 'unemployed'; and 'unknown status'.

A number of countries have subdivided one or more of the four major groups into several subgroups. This practice commonly has concerned the 'employees' group which has been subdivided by some countries into 'salaried employees', and 'wage earners'; and by some others into 'public employees', and 'private employees'. The criteria used by countries to distinguish between salaried employees and wage earners have varied, and have included the method of payment, the level of skill and the legal basis of eligibility for social security and similar programmes. Other groups which have been treated either as a separate group or as a subgroup include 'apprentices', 'domestic servants', 'persons earning commission', 'the clergy', 'elected office-holders', and so on.

In some cases the subdivision of ICSE groups has overlapped the classification by industry or by occupation. Often, at least in the early decades, the overlapping seemed to have occurred because countries had just included either an industry classification or an occupational classification (sometimes a hybrid of the two) in the censuses and, consequently, the status in employment classification tended to be combined with industry or occupation characteristics that were not included elsewhere.

The conclusion in UNSO (1985), p. 3), was that ISIC, ISCO and ISCE must be clearly defined and their classification principles and criteria must be distinct and not overlapping. Hopefully, this paper will contribute to this aim as well as to an improved understanding of the basis of the status in employment classification. The rest of this paper will try to outline the main issues which need to be discussed before deciding whether the present ICSE should be revised. Possible answers to questions raised will be indicated – at this stage more to stimulate discussion than to present preferred positions.

Issues in the discussion of the ICSE

Why measure 'status in employment'?

On this question, ILO (1957a, p. 6), says: 'It is principally to supplement the information necessary for the study of the economic and social structure of the labour force that various countries establish statistics on the distribution of labour according to status.' It was recognised that in addition to being used to present the number of workers by status in employment, the SE variable would also be used as a background variable for statistical descriptions of workers' behaviour and their conditions of work and living. The variable also serves as a component in the definition of socio-economic groups, which are often thought to be more valid for the description and analysis of social structures and behaviour than the SE variable on its own.

The interest in data on socio-economic groups as such has increased significantly in recent years as several developments, especially in the industrialised countries, have led many observers to question the dominance of the employment status situations of the 'standard'[3] own-account workers and employees, or at least to the expectation that employment in the exceptions to these 'standard' situations is increasing sharply. Córdova (1986) discusses these concerns from the point of view of labour legislation. Concern with the validity of the present ICSE groups is important in Standing (1983), where the discussion is oriented towards the situation in developing countries.

What should the status in employment variable measure?

In the context of international statistical co-operation there has been no in-depth discussion of the three issues listed in the introduction to this paper since proposals relating to concerns *(a)* and *(c)* were discussed at the Ninth ICLS in 1957 – where agreement could not be reached. It is disquieting that we have so little explicit agreement concerning *what* the SE variable is measuring, despite its widespread use in official statistics. However, this need not be a cause for rejection of its validity. Presumably one had a valid intuitive understanding of temperature and also methods for indicating temperature differences before a good and correct understanding of the nature of such differences had been reached. However, proposals for changing or extending the present ICSE, i.e. proposals for dealing with concerns *(b)* and *(c)*, should preferably be based on a clear understanding of what we are trying to measure and the use to be made of the SE variable.

ILO (1957a) says that:

The distinction between the four major groups recommended by the various international agencies, and actually used in most countries, appears to be based on two main criteria: the position of each individual to that of other persons and the mode of remuneration of the work. ... Any classification of individuals according to status will have to be based mainly on these two criteria.

However, it is clear from the discussion as reported in ILO (1957b, p. 30), that this understanding of SE did not receive the support of the Ninth ICLS. The Conference adopted neither the proposal by the secretariat concerning a general statement on the basis for the classification, nor the proposals for further subdivision of the major groups – proposals which were based on this understanding of the SE variable. In the report from the discussion it is said that:

agreement was far from complete as to the basis on which a classification according to status should be established, and ... the determination of such a basis would be particularly arduous in view of the great differences in the approach of the various countries to this problem.

Although 'a definition of status in terms of the type of payment received for work performed' was supported in the discussion, it was also said that 'the status criterion is based on the relationship of a person in his job to the enterprise or establishment within which the job is performed, and from this point of view the method of payment is not the basic criterion'. It was suggested by some participants that the classification should be based on the ownership of means of production. Another suggestion was that it should be based on the relations between persons in industry and in the national economy.

Going outside the context of international statistical co-operation, observations relevant to the question of what the SE variable should measure can be found in discussions of the measurement of 'social status', 'social class' and 'socio-economic groups'. Standing (1983) tries to address the issue directly, with special emphasis on situations found in developing countries. The literature should be reviewed systematically before formulating a concrete statement on what the SE variable is measuring. The suggestion on page 256 below must be seen as tentative.

Self-employed, employers and own-account workers

The term 'self-employed' is commonly used to cover those who work either as 'employers' or as 'own-account workers', the difference between these two groups being that the former have one or more hired employees working for them. Own-account workers may work with one or more unpaid family workers, i.e. with members of the same household. The common defining characteristic of persons in both groups is that they 'operate their own economic enterprise or engage independently in a profession or trade', cf. UNSO (1986). In ILO (1957a) it is emphasised that 'managers, directors and other salaried officials of economic enterprises who do not own the businesses in which they work, even though they may perform the same functions as employers' should be classified as employees, and most countries consequently restrict their definition of self-employed persons to those who operate *unincorporated* businesses.

As pointed out in OECD (1986), this means that the observed number of self-employed workers, on the one hand and the number of employees, on the other, are affected by the legal situation concerning incorporation of companies, as often, especially in *small* incorporated enterprises, the manager and his/her family own all or a controlling part of the enterprise. It may therefore better reflect social and economic realities to regard such managers as self-employed, although their legal status is that of employees. In addition, it has been argued by many statistical users, especially those interested in socio-economic and social class classifications, that it would be an advantage if persons having the authority to hire and fire workers on behalf of an enterprise, should at least be distinguished from other employees, as for some purposes it may be desirable to group them with employers. These points should be explored in a revision of the ICSE.

Should the definition of employers refer to the situation which exists in the reference period, or to some 'normal' or 'regular' situation? What should we mean by 'regular' in this context? If reference is made to the actual situation and the self-employed worker has had employees for part of the reference period, then some sort of priority rule must be applied – either an absolute one or one based on the duration of the contract. Many self-employed workers have only other household members working for them regularly, but they may engage casual workers, own-account workers, persons employed by temporary work agencies or seconded from other employers, for limited periods of time or for specific tasks, without entering into an employment contract with such workers. A revised ICSE should give guidelines on how to classify the users of such workers.

Rao (1985) recommends that the duration of the employment contract should determine whether it is regarded as regular or not, and that only those self-employed workers who have entered into a regular employment contract with an employee should be regarded as 'employers'. This would give a relatively simple rule for dividing the self-employed between the 'establishment sector' and the 'household sector', a division which is useful in the planning and execution of statistical surveys. With this approach, self-employed workers who engaged other workers without making them employees may warrant a separate group.

It has been argued that for many users of statistics the distinction between 'employers' and 'own-account workers' is not very interesting in itself and that a separate variable to indicate the scale of operations of the self-employed would be more valid, using for example the total number of workers involved, as employees, as unpaid family workers or as persons engaged on an *ad hoc* basis.

Own-account workers and employees

The definition of 'employer' is dependent upon that of 'employee', and vice versa, in a way which makes the borderline between the two groups unproblematic except for the managers who own incorporated businesses (see above). The difference between 'own-account workers' and 'employees' is more problematic. To distinguish between these two groups is to answer the question: 'What is the difference between, on the one hand an own-account worker who either produces and sells goods or sells services to one or more customers, and, on the other, an employee who sells labour, to an employer, to be used for the production and sale of goods or services?' Before trying to indicate how this question may be answered, it may be useful to have a closer look at the main features of the employment situations representing the core or the essence of these two groups, and the departures from these situations which seem to be most important for our discussion. The discussion will draw mainly upon ILO (1957a; 1957b), Standing (1983)and Córdova (1986).

The core employee situations are those where the workers are:

(a) working full-time for one employer (i.e. another person or an establishment);
(b) working at a place of work where the employer is responsible and has authority;
(c) working at hours determined by the employer;
(d) working with raw materials, other inputs and means of production provided by the employer;
(e) remunerated by a wage or salary;
(f) taking instructions from the employer;
(g) governed by an individual explicit or implicit contract or agreement of employment with the employer;
(h) expecting to go on working for the employer until reaching a specified age, unless the relationship is terminated by either party following certain agreed or specified procedures.

This is the framework within which labour law, collective bargaining and social security systems developed, to specify workers' rights and obligations in relation to the employer and the state.

The core *own-account worker* situations are those where the workers are:

(a) working alone full-time as professionals or craftsmen producing goods or services for sale to others;
(b) working at a place of work where they are responsible and have authority;
(c) working hours determined by themselves;
(d) owning or renting the means of production, having purchased raw materials and other inputs;
(e) remunerated by the profits of the sale of the produced goods and services;
(f) taking instructions only from purchasers of the goods and services produced;
(g) selling the goods and services to a large number of customers or to the same customer only for a limited period.

Comparing these descriptions with the ICSE definitions we find that the core groups do not correspond to any ICSE groups (or combinations of such groups). It may be seen as a desirable feature of a revised ICSE that it would be possible to identify those belonging to the core groups by using ICSE categories – alone or in combination with other variables commonly included in population censuses or labour force surveys.

Some of the more important departures from the core employee situations are the following:

(a) some 'employees' work regularly less than full-time over the day, week or month for the same employer and/or may regularly have more than one employer;
(b) some 'employees' work at home or at another place outside the employer's responsibility and authority (e.g. workers placed through temporary work agencies or seconded);
(c) some 'employees' work at hours set by themselves – within certain limits;
(d) some 'employees' work with raw materials, other inputs or means of production which they (partly) have to provide themselves (e.g. homeworkers);
(e) some 'employees' are not instructed by their employer but by third parties (e.g. by the user of workers placed through temporary work agencies or seconded);
(g) some 'employees' have a contract or agreement with the employer only as members of a group (e.g. members of work gangs);
(h) (i) some 'employees' have employment contracts or agreements only for a limited, specified period – contracts which may or may not be renewed (e.g. workers on short-term contracts, seasonal workers, casual workers, workers on call);
(ii) some contracts or agreements of employment can legally only be terminated before time by the employer (extreme cases: slaves and bonded labour).

Explicit or implicit contracts involving departures from the core employee situation will be entered into by the employers to reduce direct and indirect labour costs, to increase work efficiency, to increase flexibility of operation, to increase control of workers and/or to reduce obligations to the employees which the employers would have had if the work contracts had been in accordance with the core situation regulated by labour law. The employees will enter into employment contracts with departures from the core situation in order to have less time committed to work or greater flexibility in their work situations, to obtain higher remuneration and/or because they feel that they have no choice.

Some of the more important departures from the core own-account worker situations are the following:

(a) (i) The workers are not professionals or craftsmen but have some other skilled or unskilled occupations (e.g. as farmers, drivers, itinerant handicraft workers, salespersons);
(ii) the workers do not work alone, but with others on an equal basis (e.g. as partners, members of producers' co-operatives);
(b) the workers work at places of work where the customers are responsible and have authority;
(c) the hours of work are determined by the customers/clients;
(d) the terms of rental of means of production and/or the terms for financing purchases of raw materials and other inputs place restrictions on how the work should be carried out (e.g. franchises, share-croppers, tenant-holders);
(e) the product and proceeds of sales are shared with others – because of contractual obligations following from (d), or as part of partnership/co-operative agreements;
(f) instructions have to be taken from the owners of the means of production or the providers of raw materials and other inputs – often following from (d) (e.g. franchises, share-croppers);
(g) the goods and services produced are sold to only one customer and/or subject to conditions imposed by commitments following from (d).

The main differences between the core situations outlined above are related to the type and extent of economic risk carried by the workers, and the extent and type of control of the work and the enterprise exercised by the worker. The departures from the core situations seem mainly to increase the risks carried by the employee and reduce the control of the own-account worker. When present alone or in combination, the departures tend to blur the distinction between the two core situations. Some of the departures can be handled by the use of other variables commonly included in population censuses or labour force surveys, notably hours of work (actual as well as normal) and occupation. For others the ICSE has created separate groups (i.e. members of producers' co-operatives, unpaid family workers) or given directions concerning how they should be handled in simple cases (e.g. homeworkers). However, the need remains to find a criterion, or a set of criteria, which should be used for determining whether a particular work situation represents that of an own-account worker or that of an employee, and for subdividing the two groups further. If the above observations are basically correct, then economic risk and control would seem to be good candidates for such criteria.

In order to implement distinctions based on economic risk, it would be necessary to find indicators of risk involvement appropriate to the desired distinction. One possibility consistent with the concept of 'own-account work' would be to link the distinction between risk categories to means of remuneration; for example, on the one hand, whether the remuneration of the worker is totally dependent on the returns from the sale of the products or services being produced and, on the other, whether part of the remuneration is determined on the basis of time worked or amount produced but otherwise independent of the receipts or profits from sales.

In order to implement distinctions based on control, it would be necessary to establish more precisely what we mean by 'control'; the relevant areas of control (place of work; means of production, raw materials and other inputs; and output) and the relevant types and degree of control (legal, financial, cultural).

Household production and unpaid family workers

Rao (1985) argues that there are definite advantages to distinguishing between two types of productive economic unit, namely the *establishment* units which, as individual employers, enterprises and institutions, carry out economic activities with the assistance of paid employees, and the *household* units in which an own-account worker carries out such activities with the possible assistance of household members. It would be consistent with this suggestion to have a separate status-in-employment group combining the 'own-account workers' and the 'unpaid family workers' in a group for 'household account workers'. This group would meet the criticism that to classify one member of the household production unit as an 'own-account worker' and others as 'unpaid family workers' is misleading and discriminatory. On the other hand, customs and laws in many countries place different household members in very different positions with respect to ownership of business assets, rights to enter into business to ownership of business assets, rights to enter into business contracts or to receive and dispose of business incomes, and responsibility for business liabilities. Such differences may warrant the retention of a distinction between different members of the same household production unit. This would involve finding a way to define the 'head' or 'manager' of the household production unit, as well as finding a more appropriate term than 'unpaid family workers' for the other members of the household production unit.

Members of producers' co-operatives and partners

Many countries, where there are relatively few members of producers' co-operatives, tabulate them together with 'own-account workers' or the broader group 'self-employed'. This is consistent with the present ICSE rules for classifying 'partners', who are to be classified with 'employers' or 'own-account workers', although a partner's relationship to his/her partners has strong similarities to those existing in producers's co-operatives. Only small consequences for the statistics are likely to follow from a change in the treatment of partners to achieve greater conceptual consistency, as the number of partners is likely to be small in most countries – both relative to the number of self-employed in countries where this is a significant group and relative to the number of members of producers' co-operatives where this group is significant. However, the conceptual issues and realities should be clarified.

Population and reference period

The last basic issue to be mentioned is the following: To what population should a SE classification apply? The background document for the Ninth ICLS concluded that 'status in employment' means 'the status of the *individual in respect of his employment* (ILO 1957a, p. 22; emphasis added). Similarly, in UNSO (1985, p. 6), it is said that the ICSE applies to 'the position of the individual in respect of his or her job'. This would mean that the ICSE should apply only to *employed persons*. In UNSO (1986, para. 67), it is said that 'Status in employment refers to the status of an *economically active person* with respect to his or her employment, that is, whether he or she is employed (*or was, if unemployed*) during the time reference period established for data on economic characteristics' (emphasis added). Looking at national practices, we find that some countries classify only the employed population by SE group, while others classify the whole economically active population, and we find that a number of countries have also included categories for persons outside the labour force (such as 'students', 'housewives', 'pensioners') under the heading 'status in employment'.

A worker may have more than one job during the reference period and, as a consequence, work as an 'employee' in one job and be self-employed in others. This means that, just as with occupation and industry, *persons* must be classified to a specific SE group on the basis of their relationship to a job – past, present or future. Mutiple jobholders may therefore have several statuses in employment, and it is necessary to have rules for selecting the 'primary status' of persons and/or rules for defining multiple-status groups. The design of such rules will be important for those users who are primarily interested in persons as the units of observations and analysis.

Data collection considerations

A classification by status in employment which only distinguishes between a small number of classes is much easier to handle from a data collection point of view than one which makes distinctions between a large number of different groups – *if* the groups defined correspond closely to existing and easily recognisable work situations. The industrialised market-oriented and socialist economies, where the core employee situations, the core own-account worker situations and/or member of producers' co-operative situations dominate, seem traditionally to have satisfied this condition, and precoded responses could be used on questionnaires or interviewers. However, the situation for a large proportion of workers in developing countries never did correspond to the core situations, making it difficult to fit their actual work situations into the defined groups, especially as the basis for the classification has not been clearly stated and no subgroups have been defined. In addition, it has been strongly suggested that borderline situations are becoming increasingly important in industrialised countries, undermining the validity of the simple classification and data collection procedures which have seemed adequate in the past. In revising the ICSE it must be recognised, however, that the creation of a more valid, but also more complex, 'status in employment' variable is likely to require more complex and costly data-collection procedures. Internationally as well as nationally there may therefore be a trade-off between a valid, complex variable which will be used only in a limited number of specialised surveys and a simpler, less valid variable which will be used in censuses and most surveys.

Points and proposals for discussion

This chapter will try to outline points for future work and discussions on a possible revision of the ICSE. The work would have to be both 'top-down' and 'bottom-up' to ensure adequate definition of what it is that the ICSE should try to measure, clear criteria for delineation of the groups defined at the different levels in the classification, as well as the definition of groups which are both analytically and descriptively useful and possible to reflect with the data collection instruments available. The focus in the 'top-down' work should initially be to determine the variable(s) underlying the present ICSE and its groups and propose adjustments to group definitions as well as suggest how these groups could be further subdivided to make the ICSE a more valid reflection of the underlying variable(s). The focus in the 'bottom-up' work should initially be to determine the group that one would want to distinguish at the most detailed level in the classification and the value sets of the underlying variables necessary to make these distinctions.

The primary unit classified by ICSE should be the job, and persons should be classified in an ICSE group through their relationship to a job. For employed persons with more than one job in the reference period, the ICSE group should be determined by the same job which is used to classify them by industry and occupation. In addition, there may be a need for well-defined rules to defined multiple-status categories. Non-employed persons may be classified by reference to a past or future job as appropriate, but they should then be tabulated separately. Internationally comparable data should be restricted to the employed population because no international guidelines exist concerning the choice of relevant reference period for past or future jobs. (For convenience, the terminology used in the following, as well as in the previous paragraphs, will imply that there is a one-to-one relationship between jobs and persons.)

Based on the discussion in the previous section the following paragraphs outline suggestions for discussion relating to the definition of what the 'status in employment' variable tries to measure and the basis for defining groups for the variable.

The following is proposed as a definition of the ICSE variable.

The status in employment variable is designed to describe jobs in terms of how they are related to economic units and to economic risks through different types of control and dependence relationships, as reflected by systems of pay and remuneration and in written and verbal contracts concerning conditions of employment and ownership and use of means of production and raw materials.

One suggestion for a revised ICSE based on this definition would be to organise the classification in three different levels. At the top level it seems reasonable to retain a basic distinction between 'employees', on the one hand, and 'self-employed' workers, on the other. This distinction has a long tradition, is reflected in the way we commonly view the labour market, and the core contents of the two groups are likely to be unaffected by the particular ways chosen to resolve borderline issues. Whether to have separate groups, at this level, for members of producers' co-operatives' and 'unpaid family workers' would need to be discussed further. In particular, the present definition of 'unpaid family workers' may need to be modified in the light of the definitions developed for self-employed workers. Explicit recognition should be made of the possibility of combining this group with that of own-account workers to form a joint group 'household-account workers' when appropriate, based on national circumstances and analytical needs. The conditions to be satisfied for doing so should be discussed further.

Discussion will be needed on the basis of resolving the borderline issues for drawing the distinction between 'employees' and 'self-employed', and the respective roles to be played by indicators of 'control with work situation' and 'economic risks'. The present ICSE seems to draw this dividing line primarily with reference to the type of economic risk the jobs are subject to, as reflected by whether the remuneration is wholly dependent upon profits or whether part of it is in the form of a wage or salary based on the numbers of hours worked or number of items produced or customers/clients served, or some other criterion not directly linked to receipts of sales or profits. The treatments of managers in limited companies in which they or their families have controlling shares, strongly suggests this. It would therefore be consistent with the present ICSE to say that if a part of the remuneration for the job is result-independent, then the worker should be classified as an 'employee'; if not, then as 'self-employed'. However, it must be discussed whether this risk criterion is sufficient to obtain the distinction desired, as well as whether the form of remuneration is a valid indicator of risk. Should the result-independent part of the remuneration be above a certain proportion? Should some contractual obligations or rights substitute for or supplement the remuneration indicator? Should reference be made to direct or indirect ownership of means of production?

At the next level of aggregation it may be suggested that it should be possible to distinguish between:

(a) regular employees;
(b) casual employees;
(c) own-account workers without paid help;
(d) own-account workers with *ad hoc* paid help but without regular employees;
(e) employers with regular employees;
(f) members of producers' co-operatives;
(g) unpaid family workers.

Here 'economic risk', as indicated by type of employment contract, can be said to have been used to distinguish between the two suggested types of employee. Rao (1985) suggests that 'persons employed on a continuous basis on contracts, written or verbal, extending over periods of one month or more at a time may be regarded as regular employees'. Whether this is a necessary and sufficient criterion should be carefully discussed, as the criterion used to distinguish 'regular' from 'casual' employees will also influence the suggested subdivision of self-employed workers into '*own-account workers* without paid help', '*users of casual labour* – own-account workers with *ad hoc* paid help, but without regular employees' and '*employers with regular employees*', to reflect broad differences of control relationship and responsibilities for workers other than household members. The category 'user of casual labour' should include those who engage own-account workers for specific tasks, those who use workers seconded from their regular employers and those who use workers from temporary employment agencies, as well as those engaging casual employees.

If identified as a separate group at the first or second level of aggregation, the content of the concept 'producers' co-operative' should be made more explicit – even if the present definition of 'members of producers' co-operatives' does not seem to need any substantial changes. The definition should provide guidance on whether 'partners' should be included in this group and on how to classify workers in incorporated enterprises where the workers own the shares, either outright as individuals or through a trust or foundation established for that purpose. Explicit reference should be made to the possibility of including those classified in this group among the self employed or among the employees, as appropriate in the national context, if they are few in numbers.

At a possible third level in the classification, the further subdivision of self-employed workers should reflect the degree to which they are subject to the control of other economic factors, as well as the type of control. Such control is related to the ownership and acquisition of means of production, raw materials and other inputs used by the self-employed workers and to the terms under which services and products are produced and sold. The forms and means of such controls will vary according to historical, social and economic circumstances of countries, as well as with the type of work. Further work should try to establish patterns which are common across countries and areas of work in order to propose further subdivision of 'employers', 'users of labour' and 'own-account workers'. It seems likely that such subdivisions will be basically similar for these categories, although some for the resulting groups may not be as relevant for one as for the others. At this stage it seems reasonable that such subdivisions should include groups for and definitions of 'owner-holders' (in agriculture and other industries), 'franchise-holders', 'tenant-labour' and 'share-croppers'. Relevant distinctions should also be made between 'contract workers', 'consultants' and 'freelance workers' and should make it possible to define a separate group for those own-account workers whose situation corresponds to the 'core' situation outlined on page 251.

In the same way it should be possible at the third level of a revised ICSE to define a separate group for those employees who are in the 'core' situation outlined on page 250, and to distinguish between different situations for those outside the core group. This could result in separate groups for 'apprentices/trainees' and for employees seconded to other economic units from their employers, e.g. temporary work agencies. Duration and type of employment contract, as well as type of remuneration, are factors which should be taken into account when defining different subgroups of employees at this level. One should also consider the possibility of a separate group for those employees who, on behalf of the enterprise in which they work, exercise the powers and carry the responsibilities of the enterprise as an employer. This group may include controlling shareholders working as managers.

Concluding remarks

As outlined in the previous paragraphs, it seems obvious that definitions of groups at the third level may be quite complex and, on a statistical questionnaire, may need several questions in order to be implemented. In operational terms, the work with a revised ICSE at this level may therefore take the form of defining several different variables and rules for how these variables should be combined to arrive at desired groups. For the definition of subgroups of employees, examples of such variables may be 'type of remuneration' (in kind/tips/commissions/piece rate/etc.), 'length of contract', 'type of contract'. For self-employed workers, examples may be 'type of tenancy', 'length of contract', 'type of contract', 'terms of sales' and 'scale (size) of operations'. 'Place of work' (at home/at a separate place) may be relevant to the subdivision of both employees and self-employed workers.

It seems likely that most of the work with a revision of the ICSE would be related to obtaining appropriate categories at the most detailed level. However, proposals for groups at all levels in a revised ICSE should be based on a close study of the literature on actual work contract arrangements and on tenancy systems in industrialised and developing countries. National statistical practices as well as legal, economic, sociological and anthropological studies must be reviewed. Definitions used in a revised ICSE must try to take into account that contractual and legal rights and responsibilities do *influence* actual situations and behaviour, but that the contractual and legal provisions often do not adequately *reflect* actual situations and behaviour. Due attention must also be paid to the effectiveness of fruitful simplifications.

Notes

1. This chapter was prepared as a paper for discussion and comment. The author is responsible for remaining shortcomings, as he has benefited from, but not completely followed, the comments of colleagues. The article does not necessarily reflect the position of the International Labour Office or its Bureau of Statistics.
2. Information on the background of ICSE was adapted from UNSO (1985), pp. 5–7).
3. The terms 'typical' and 'normal' employment status situations have also been used by some authors. As the numerical dominance of these situations may be questioned, the term 'core' may perhaps be better than either of them. This term may also indicate the role these situations serve as convenient points of reference for other situations.

References

Córdova, E. (1986) 'From full-time wage employment to atypical employment: A major shift in the evolution of labour relations?' *International Labour Review*, Nov.–Dec.

ILO (1957a) *'International classification according to status'*, report prepared for the Ninth International Conference of Labour Statisticians, Geneva, 1957.

ILO (1957b) *Ninth International Conference of Labour Statisticians 1957*, Geneva.

OECD (1986) 'Definition of self-employment; Cyclical sensitivity of self-employment', Note C in *OECD Employment Outlook*, Paris.

Rao, M. V. S. (1985) 'Household economic activities: Definition, concepts, survey, methods, data analysis and evaluation', paper prepared for the SIAP/ESCAP Expert Group Meeting on Developing Statistics of Household Economic Activities, 23–28 September, Bangkok, Economic and Social Commission for Asia and the Pacific, STAT/SHEA/5.

Standing, G. (1983) 'A labour status approach to labour statistics', Population and Labour Policies Programme Working Paper no. 139, Geneva.

UNSO (1985) 'International Classification of Status in Employment (ICSE): Its contents and proposed revisions for adoption in the future population and housing censuses', Expert Group on the 1990 World Population and Housing Census Programme, New York 11–15 November.

UNSO (1986) *Draft supplementary principles and recommendations for population and housing censuses*, United Nations Secretariat, ST/ESA/STAT/SER.M/67/Add.1, New York, 11 Aug.

Appendix 17

Principles and Recommendations for Population and Housing Censuses: Status in employment

Status in employment refers to the status of an economically active person with respect to his or her employment, that is, whether he or she is employed (or was, if unemployed) as an employer, own-account worker, employee, unpaid family worker or a member of a producer's co-operative, etc. during the time-reference period established for data on economic characteristics.

(a) *Employer*: a person who operates his or her own economic enterprise or engages independently in a profession or trade, and hires one or more employees. Some countries may wish to distinguish among employers according to the number of persons they employ.

(b) *Own-account worker*: a person who operates his or her own economic enterprise or engages independently in a profession or trade, and hires no employees.

(c) *Employee*: a person who works for a public or private employer and receives remuneration in wages, salary, commission, tips, piece-rates or pay in kind.

(d) *Unpaid family worker*: usually a person who works without pay in an economic enterprise operated by a related person living in the same household. Where it is customary for young persons, in particular, to work without pay in an economic enterprise operated by a related person who does not live in the same household, the requirement of 'living in the same household' may be eliminated. If there are a significant number of unpaid family workers in enterprises of which the operators are members of a producers' co-operative who are classified in category (e), these unpaid family workers should be classified in a separate sub-group.

(e) *Member of producers' co-operative*: a person who is an active member of a producers' co-operative, regardless of the industry in which it is established. Where this group is not numerically important, it may be excluded from the classification and members of producers' co-operatives should be classified under other headings, as appropriate.

(f) *Persons not classifiable by status*: experienced workers whose status is unknown or inadequately described and unemployed persons not previously employed (i.e. new entrants). A separate group for new entrants may be included if information for this group is not already available elsewhere.

18 Notes on the French 'New Classification of Occupations and Socio-occupational Categories'

M. Scott

Introduction

A revision of the 1968 version of the International Standard Classification of Occupations (ISCO) has recently been undertaken by the Bureau of Statistics of the International Labour Organisation (ILO). The revision aims at producing a tool which will be, above all, useful for various international statistical comparisons. It will be accompanied by a Manual on Occupational Classifications to serve as a guide for member countries on how to set up or revise a national occupational classification.

As part of the preparatory work for the revision of ISCO, studies of a number of national occupational classifications have been carried out. One of them, the French New Classification of Occupations and Socio-occupational Categories (PCS) is examined in some detail in this paper.

The primary aim of the paper is to describe the main conceptual and structural characteristics of the PCS. In this way, it is hoped to make other national institutions concerned with these issues aware of the taxonomic options adopted by the French in constructing a new occupational classification, while endeavouring, at the same time, to ensure continuity with the existing one.

As will be seen from the bibliographical notes at the end of this paper, exclusively French sources were used. In order to avoid possible ambiguities about the meaning of the various and sometimes unfamiliar terms employed, the original wording in French has been retained in a number of instances. This paper is also available in French in a mimeographed version, on request.

The preparatory phase

The PCS is the latest French classification of occupations and of socio-occupational categories. It is the result of a complete recasting of a number of classifications previously used, which included: 'Classification of Individual Activities', 'Code of Occupations', 'Job Classification', 'Classification of Related Occupations', and the 'Code of Socio-occupational Categories'.

The complexity of the previous system, due to too many different classifications, its age and, therefore, inevitable inadequacy in coping with more recent occupations, made an overall revision essential.

The revision led to a classification which, while retaining the broad lines of the above mentioned 'Code of Socio-occupational Categories', at the same time succeeded in integrating, at a more disaggregated level, distinctions between different occupations.

The PCS was conceived and constructed by the French National Institute for Statistics and Economic Studies (INSEE). However, the task was made easier by the available information on the content of some 11,000 jobs which the Centre for Studies and Research on Qualifications (CEREQ) collected in the course of its work on the 'French Job Directory' (*Répertoire français des emplois*); also by comprehensive information on occupations collected by the National Office for Information on Education and Occupations (ONISEP) while compiling its 'Guide to Occupations' (*Guide des métiers*); and the description of occupations contained in the 'Operational Directory of Occupations' (*Répertoire opérationnel des métiers et emplois*), prepared by the National Agency for Employment (ANPE). In addition, various ministries concerned with job classifications, professional associations and employees' unions, survey officials, and researchers were regularly consulted at a score of meetings convened by the National Statistical Council between June 1979 and December 1981.

The PCS was used for the first time in connection with the 1982 Employment Survey.

Conceptual framework of the PCS

The conceptual framework necessary for designing and constructing the new PCS has been mainly based on the following assumptions and principles:

1. That taxonomic problems, and in particular those connected with the construction of socio-occupational classifications, are best dealt with if such a classification is built as 'a reasoned empirical system' (*système empirique raisonné*).
2. That, for the purposes of constructing a socio-occupational classification, society should be thought of and analysed in spatial terms, as a social space populated by persons who are simultaneously *holders* of occupations and *bearers* of different social attributes. A map of that

social space – drawn on the basis of empirical evidence and statistical work done over the last 30 years – would reveal its 'topography' in terms of 'density' of different occupations, contours of existing social groups, characteristics specific to different 'areas'; in short, all the elements of the 'local logic' (*logique locale*).

3. That the existing 'social topography' should be the most important element in determining the choice of criteria and other means used to delimit the social space in such a way as would allow it to be represented through socio-occupational categories. The representation, of course, should aim to be total – the categories must be mutually exclusive and in their totality, exhaustive.

These assumptions and principles are discussed in more detail below.

Classification as a 'Reasoned Empirical System'

It was found, on the basis of the conclusions derived from analysis of different classifications used up to the present time, that distinctions could be made between 'natural classification' – where taxonomists tried to classify according to a 'natural order of things' – and 'logical classifications' – where taxonomists tried to classify according to predetermined, systematically applied criteria. The conclusion was that neither of these was satisfactory. Natural classifications are actually often structured according to certain beliefs, such as natural nutrition needs, or according to users' needs, such as the development of school systems or of vocational training systems, etc., or even according to a particular ideology. This was the case of the Tolosan 1788 industrial classification, where the physiocrat-taxonomist classified the functioning of the production process on the basis of natural resources, dividing industries into three categories producing mineral, vegetable and animal objects.

Logical classifications aiming at the systematic application of predetermined criteria also have weak points. A good example is provided by the United States *Dictionary of Occupational Titles* (*DOT*), which is based on three main criteria – relationship to data, to people, and to objects – applied to fixed scales of ratings. If an attempt were to be made to group and aggregate occupations as rated by *DOT*, it would be seen that in a number of instances boundaries between different occupations were non-existent – for instance gamekeepers, taxi-operators and head cooks would belong together – and that the ranking of a given occupation relative to others in the same domain of specialisation would often be unjustified. Thus a theoretical physicist would be listed below all other physicists in his profession because of a low rating of his relationship to objects.

In the above sense, the PCS is neither a natural nor a logical classification. It is a classification whose structure is the result of actual observations of the French socio-economic scene combined with selective application of a number of general criteria, or a classification that could be called 'a reasoned empirical system'.

Society as social space and its occupants

Empirical evidence

Looking at social space by reference to the statistical information gathered over the past 30 years, the authors of the PCS found that they were confronted with a multi-dimensional and heterogeneous social reality, which was constantly undergoing changes, but which at the same time showed some distinct socio-occupational divisions.

They realised that there already existed in social consciousness certain categories, however vaguely defined and badly delineated, of persons having certain occupations and therefore *presumed to possess* certain social attributes (sex, age, education, lifestyle, etc). People considered themselves, and were considered by others, as belonging to a certain social milieu and/or category.

They further observed that some occupations enjoyed more 'typical' social images than others. They were, in a way, playing the role of an archetype representing others of the same kind. Such typical occupations were usually those whose terms of reference were precisely defined (*logique de l'appellation contrôlée*), sometimes even by law, as in the case of physicians. Or they were occupations which have, over the years, benefited from the efforts of organised social representation, as is the case of *cadres*, who organised as a group on the assumption of the existence of a common interest, similar bargaining positions, etc. It is generally recognised that the term *cadres* is non-translatable. It denotes a heterogeneous socio-occupational group – which encompasses a range as wide as, for instance, foremen and general directors. The origin of the group goes back to the 1930s, while its official recognition, in the form of Collective Agreements, took place after the Second World War. It could be said that the common denominator for *cadres* consists of the education or training needed and applied in the exercise of control and management functions.

The authors also noted that holders of certain occupations were constantly trying to influence, mainly through organised representation, the position and image of their particular occupation in relation to all others. For that reason the holders were always interested in occupational and other classifications. The authors also became aware that they themselves were at the same time observers and participants in the same social scene – the unavoidable position of any social researcher.

To summarise: the empirical evidence showed that in the social scene there existed a strong link between an occupation and the attributed qualities of its holder; and between occupational archetypes and different social groups.

Statistical evidence

Statistical evidence gathered over the past 30 years enabled the PCS authors to draw a map of social space outlining its 'topography' in terms of 'density' of different occupations, and contours of already existing social groups. However, in order to achieve this it was imperative to use different statistical criteria and different sets of variables for observation and analyses of each zone of social space.

As a consequence of unequal distribution of numerous social attributes, each social group and milieu – or, in terms of a map, each zone of social grace – has its specific mixture of social attributes together with a specific structure of their links and relationships, the so-called 'local logic'. For instance, some social groups have inherited modest material means and high esteem for scholarly achievement. Other groups may be far less cultivated but be rich in economic capital. Some members of the latter group may wish their children to have higher education but for no other reasons than those connected with the declining prospects of their family business.

This local logic cannot reveal itself if we measure different social phenomena at the level of society, using a unidimensional scale of values. The units of observation must be smaller and analytical tools (i.e. variables) must be chosen so as to enable the authors of the PCS to discover the whole constellation of characteristics particular to each group, and also to draw frontiers between the groups, proceeding to valid analyses of their respective differences and similarities.

Local logic is an important concept in the design of the PCS, and it might not be amiss to try to explain it further by means of an analogy, based on an example given by V. Zito, in his book on *Varieties of sociological inquiry* (New York, Praeger, 1975).

Let us imagine that we were shown a drawing of two geometrical figures and asked to compare them and say what similarities and differences we could find. Let us further imagine that by looking at the drawing we concluded that the figures were two squares of the same size. However, in order to determine whether this was indeed so, we would certainly take a ruler to measure their sides, and a protractor to measure their internal angles, and, having satisfied ourselves that all sides were equal and all internal angles were of 90 degrees, we would say that the figures were two squares and that there was no difference between the two squares. Now let us further imagine that the same drawing was shown to us but this time the two squares were coloured in different shades of blue. On the basis of the tools that we have used so far we would still claim that there were no differences between the two squares. In order to determine the difference – already perceived by our eyes – we would have to use a *new tool* – an instrument capable of measuring different shades of a colour. With these three tools we would be in a position to measure all three characteristics – length, angles and colouring – of our units of observation. In PCS terms this would mean that if our sets of tools (i.e. variables) are not pertinent, if they do not vary from one zone of social space to another, there is a danger that we may miss some of the purely local characteristics and their specific patterns, in short the local logic. Since it is through the discovered characteristics and through their patterns, that we describe, define, differentiate and analyse each zone of social space, this would mean running the risk of arriving at wrong conclusions.

Some basic decisions

The above findings, based on sociological and statistical information about existing occupations, social groups, local characteristics, etc., served as points of departure for the following decisions made by the authors of the PCS:

(a) To sever the link between an occupation and its holder would mean the risk of disregarding social attributes of the holder. Therefore it was concluded that the basic units to be classified by the PCS should be at the same time persons and occupations.

(b) Socio-occupational categories should be delineated in such a way as to recognise contours of social groups whose existence was made evident by relevant statistical analyses. The way to achieve this was to use existing socio-statistical evidence to identify typical socio-occupational cases – able to represent each zone of the densely populated social space – and then build up around them clusters of all other similar cases.

(c) The classification should bring into play a number of hierarchically arranged general criteria, which do not, however, have to be applied in a systematic manner throughout the entire structure of the PCS.

(d) An occupational classification should take into consideration both the nature and limitations of the primary material to be classified. The fact is that information on occupation is obtained through occupational or job titles, as recorded by respondents to population censuses or special surveys. In addition, analysis of coding practices shows that, even when the questionnaire asks for a short description of the main tasks and duties performed, in most cases the actual coding is done on the basis of occupation/job title provided by the respondent. Furthermore, these titles, being often based on the existing grading systems of collective and other agreements, provide less information on occupation/job content than on the social position of the respondent, as perceived by himself and by society.

Design and structure of the PCS

General criteria

The main division within the PCS is between those in paid employment (*salariés*) and those in self-employment (*indépendants*). However, this division is not systematic. There are a number of exceptions, in particular in the case of liberal professions, creative and performing artists, teachers, health and social welfare, etc.

The self-employed

The definition of 'self-employed' is somewhat broader than that agreed upon by the ILO Conference of Labour Statisticians, and other international bodies. In terms of the PCS the self-employed are:

(i)   Own-account workers, with or without employees.

(ii) Those who direct, manage or lead a company or a society 'in their own right' – meaning that they do not have to act through delegation. Therefore, president-directors, presidents, top managers and main administrators, of enterprises, shareholding societies, etc., are all classified as self-employed. If a person is simultaneously self-employed and in paid employment (a physician, for instance), then self-employment takes precedence.

(iii) Except in the case of liberal professions, unpaid family workers helping a person classified as self-employed find themselves in the same category as the person they are helping. Paid family workers are classified like any other persons in paid employment.

Self-employed persons are generally classified on the basis of *economic activity* and *size of the enterprise*. A big exception is the liberal professions, in the case of which size of enterprise is not taken into consideration. For instance, a lawyer is classified without regard to the number of persons he happens to employ.

Farmers are classified according to the size of their holdings into small, medium and large farmers. Other self-employed are classified according to the number of their employees. The dividing line between 'tradesman' and 'craftsman', on the one hand, and 'managers of business' on the other is set at ten employees. However, there is an exception here: if there are fewer than ten employees, but the activity of the enterprise is of financial importance (bank, housing agency, etc.) its owner or chief will be classified as a 'manager of business'.

It was found that the activity of the enterprise usually agrees with the declared occupation – especially when small enterprises are in question. However, if there is a difference then economic activity of the enterprise takes precedence over occupation. For instance, if a self-employed person declares his occupation to be 'delivery driver', while his enterprise is 'wholesale wine merchant' (*commerce de vins en gros*) then the person will be classified as a wine merchant and not as a delivery driver.

The employees

For purposes of classification of wage and salary earners (*salariés*), categories were delineated according to a number of general criteria whose application, however, was not carried out in a systematic manner.

Wage earners (including paid family workers), with the exception of those in agriculture, were first divided into skilled and unskilled manual workers. Then – except for drivers, skilled freight-handlers, ware-housemen and transport equipment operators – these two groups were further divided into industrial and artisanal workers depending on whether the workers performed only certain tasks of a particular job, or the whole range of tasks, as in the case of the latter. Further delimitation was determined on the basis of grades, occupational titles and categories existing in the current collective agreements concluded between trade unions and the employers' federation. However, there are a number of differences between occupational categories of these collective agreements and the PCS, notably regarding classification of drivers, warehousemen, laboratory hands, chemist-aids, biology-aids, etc.

Salary earners (including paid family workers) were first delineated according to whether they were civil servants, employed by central and local governments (*salariés de l'Etat et des collectivités locales*), or worked in industrial and commercial firms and enterprises. For PCS purposes, however, nationalised banks, social security establishments and similar institutions were considered as enterprises or firms, and their salaried employees classified accordingly.

In the case of civil servants further delimitations were made, on the whole on the basis of the current civil service grading system (categories A, B, C, D). There were some exceptions, usually concerning public health occupations. As for the wage and salary earners of industrial and commercial enterprises and firms, allowing for exceptions, further delimitations were mainly based on occupational names and categories existing in the current collective agreements between trade unions and the employers' federation.

In addition to the above criteria, in some instances specialisation and function were used in order to differentiate, in a given zone of social space, cases belonging to neighbouring categories: clerical and service staff from manual workers, engineers from administrative and commercial *cadres*, administration clerks from commercial clerks, industrial workers from artisanal workers, etc. In principle specialisation for this purpose means that of the individual and not of the enterprise. We should also add that in the case of civil servants the formal grading system took precedence over function. For instance INSEE civil servants may have the functions of a programmer, research assistant, or documentalist assistant, etc. but if they are in the same grade of the civil service grading system, they will find themselves in the same PCS category.

The fact that the self-employed are further classified according to the size of enterprise (or farm), while wage and salary earners are further classified according to the existing grading systems – that of the civil service, or those applied in industrial and commercial firms and enterprises according to the collective agreements – means two things. First, in the structure of the PCS there is an implicit hierarchical (vertical) classification. Second, in the last instance this hierarchy is determined on the basis of two different criteria; in the case of the self-employed the amount of capital is decisive while in the case of wage and salary earners it is their level of qualifications which is of primary importance.

To summarise: in order to decide which socio-occupational category is relevant in a particular case, or, in other words, how a given case should be *coded*, the following information is needed:

1. As far as possible, precise information on actual occupation, trade and job (*la profession, le métier, l'emploi*).

2. Status: employer, self-employed, associate, unpaid or paid family worker, employee.
3. Economic activity of the firm or enterprise.
4. Number of employees in the enterprise (in the case of the self-employed, chiefs of enterprises, associates and unpaid family workers).
5. Nature of the employer (for wage and salary earners): government (including local governments) or private firm.
6. Occupational classification – in the sense of collective agreements (for wage and salary earners):
   — unskilled and semi-skilled workers;
   — skilled and highly skilled workers;
   — salary earners;
   — technician, designer;
   — foreman;
   — engineer or *cadre*;
   — and any useful additional information, such as class, step, grading, index, etc.
7. Grade (for civil service).
8. Function (for engineers, *cadres*, foremen, and technicians): only the following functions are to be distinguished:
   — administrative, financial or accounting;
   — commercial or technico-commercial functions;
   — production, manufacturing, or construction functions;
   — upkeep, maintenance, new works, or emergency repair functions;
   — studies, testing, methods, research, data-processing functions.
9. For farmers: size and type of production.

The PCS and its categories

On the basis of the similarity criterion, and by taking as a point of departure terms officially used for different occupations – which in a number of instances also denoted 'typical cases' – the authors of the PCS succeeded in building clusters of related occupations. This cluster-building or assimilation process was, in terms of the similarity principle, most consistent when the central type was a clear-cut case to the point of being an 'archetype' – a physician, for instance.

In order to establish similarity not only of occupations to be clustered but also of all the social attributes that, as a rule, accompany given occupations (the notion of *logique locale*), a number of different variables were used such as: amount and origin of inherited capital and revenue; level and kind of education received; conditions of work (including position in the work process); stability of job; demographic behaviour; consumption and saving habits; cultural and leisure activities; political and religious opinions; etc.

When applying this procedure, the structure of the resulting socio-occupational categories becomes as follows: each category consists of 'hard-core cases', 'assimilated cases', and 'included borderline cases'.

Table 18.1 Classification of socio-occupational categories; links between different levels of aggregation

Most aggregated level (eight items, including six for the economically active)	Standard publication level (24 items, including 19 for the economically active)	Detailed level (42 items, including 32 for the economically active)
1. Farmers	10. Farmers	11. Small farmers 12. Medium farmers 13. Large farmers
2. Craftsmen, tradesmen and general managers	21. Craftsmen 22. Tradesmen and related workers 23. Managers of business with ten or more employees	21. Craftsmen 22. Tradesmen and related workers 23. Managers of businesses with ten or more employees
3. Senior civil servants, senior managerial staff and higher intellectual professions	31. Liberal professions 32. Senior civil servants, higher intellectual and artistic professions 36. Senior administrative managerial and technical staff, industry and commerce	31. Liberal professions 33. Senior civil servants 34. Higher intellectual professions including university teachers 35. Information workers, creative artists and performing artists 37. Senior administrative and managerial staff, industry and commerce 38. Engineers and senior technical staff, industry and commerce
4. Middle-level professions	41. Middle-level professions in education, health, civil service and related 46. Middle-level administrative and managerial staff, industry and commerce 47. Technicians 48. Production supervisors and General foremen	42. Teachers and related workers 43. Middle-level health and social welfare workers 44. Ministers of religion and members of religious orders 45. Middle-level civil servants 46. Middle-level administrative and managerial staff, industry and commerce 47. Technicians 48. Production supervisors and general foremen

Category		
5. Clerical and service staff	51. Civil servants, clerical staff 54. Clerical workers, industry and commerce 55. Sales staff 56. Domestic and other service workers	52. Clerical-level civil servants 53. Police and armed forces 54. Clerical workers, industry and commerce 55. Sales staff 56. Domestic and other service workers
6. Manual workers	61. Skilled workers 66. Unskilled workers 69. Agricultural workers	62. Skilled industrial workers 63. Skilled artisanal workers 64. Drivers 65. Skilled freight handlers, warehousemen and transport equipment operators 67. Unskilled industrial workers 68. Unskilled artisanal workers 69. Agricultural workers
7. Retired persons	71. Retired farmers 72. Retired craftsmen, tradesmen and general managers 73. Retired senior managerial staff and members of middle-level professions 76. Retired clerical service and manual workers	71. Retired farmers 72. Retired craftsmen, tradesmen and general managers 74. Retired senior managerial staff 75. Retired members of middle-level professions 77. Retired clerical and service staff 78. Retired manual workers
8. Other persons without occupational activities	81. Unemployed who have never worked 82. Various persons not gainfully employed (excluding retired persons)	81. Unemployed who have never worked 83. National servicemen 84. Pupils and students 85. Various persons, aged under 60* 86. Various persons, aged 60 and over*

* not gainfully employed, excluding the retired.

However, all headings of the cases within each category are listed; in other words, the context of each category is defined in an enumerative way.

As has been already stated, the PCS was not constructed by the systematic application of intersecting criteria. Consequently, it cannot be presented in the form of a table on which there are cross-references between columns and rows. On the basis of the above-described principles, the PCS was built as a pyramid whose different layers interlock.

The basic layer consists of 489 *occupational groups*. These groups were aggregated to 42, 24 and 8 *socio-occupational categories* of which 32, 19 and 6 respectively represent the economically active population. Information obtained by INSEE through different surveys will always be coded at the aggregate level of 42 (32), but the results of these surveys will be published at the aggregate levels of 24 (19) and 8 (6). The top level of aggregation is meant for small sample-surveys and international statistical comparisons. The link between different layers of the PCS pyramid is ensured by a four-digit coding system. Each *occupation* carries a four-digit code of which the first two digits refer primarily to the relevant socio-occupational category, while the last two digits describe occupation. At the most aggregated level that of 8 (6) categories, only the first digit of the four-digit code was used. Names of all occupations, together with corresponding codes, are listed in the INSEE publication *PCS – Index alphabétique*. This publication contains some 7,000–8,000 different occupational titles.

As can be seen from Table 18.1, the PCS at its most aggregate level consists of the following eight (six) major categories:

1. farmers;
2. craftsmen, tradesmen and general managers;
3. senior civil service, senior managerial staff and higher intellectual professions;
4. middle-level professions;
5. clerical and service staff;
6. manual workers;
7. retired persons;
8. other persons without occupational activities.

The content of different categories shown in the table, as well as the criteria used for drawing boundaries between categories are, of course, most evident at the least aggregated level – that of 42 (32) categories.

At that level of aggregation an analysis of the table shows that *self-employed* are mainly classified in categories 11, 12, 13, 21, 22, 23 and 31 (small, medium and large farmers; craftsmen; tradesmen and related workers; managers of business with ten or more employees; liberal professions) while the *salary* and *wage earners* are distributed among the remaining categories used for the economically active population. It is interesting that the category of craftsmen includes self-employed butchers, pork-butchers (*charcutiers*), bakers, self-employed pastry cooks (*pâtissiers*), dry-cleaners, etc., on the grounds that in their cases the production (*artisanal*) side of the business is more important than the commercial. It is also evident that the size of the enterprises and farms was taken into consideration for further breakdown of the self-employed, and that salary earners were first divided according to whether they were civil servants, i.e. employed in central and local government, or worked in industrial and commercial firms and enterprises.

Subsequent divisions of *salary* and *wage earners* point clearly to the *vertical hierarchical structure* which exists in the PCS.

Civil servants are found in categories 33, 45 and 52 – senior civil servants, middle-level civil servants and clerical-level civil servants.

Managerial and administrative staff in firms and enterprises are found in categories 37, 46 and 54: senior administrative and managerial staff; middle-level administrative and managerial staff; and clerical workers.

Salaried engineers and senior technical staff are grouped in category 38, technicians in 47, while production supervisors and general foremen are in 48.

However, from Table 18.1 it is not apparent to what extent existing grading systems, either that of the civil service or those of the collective agreements, were used as one of the criteria according to which *salary* and *wage earners* were grouped into different categories.

Other sources like the INSEE publication, *Guide to the socio-occupational categories*, show that out of 32 categories of the economically active population, 18 or 58 per cent, mention either civil service grades or collective agreements grading systems as one of the rules, i.e. criteria, on the basis of which the category in question was delimited. For instance, among civil servants, persons in grade A were grouped in category 33 and those in grade B in 45, while those in grades C and D went to category 52. Similarly those in category 37 were *cadres* and those in categories 54 and 55 were clerical workers and shop assistants 'in the sense of collective agreements'. Delimitation between skilled and unskilled manual workers (categories 62, 63, 67 and 68), creation of the technicians category (47), and of the production supervisors and foremen category (48), was also done according to the division contained in these agreements. It should be noted that in the PCS apprentices are considered as unskilled manual workers.

Conclusion

Although the main aim of this paper has been to describe the conceptual and structural characteristics of the PCS, rather than to analyse its relative merits and shortcomings, the following brief evaluation may be offered by way of conclusion. The PCS succeeds in combining an occupational classification with the main dimensions of a status-in-employment classification and with a number of features from socio-economic classifications. It is a classification whose structure takes into account the empirical statistical evidence of the French socio-economic scene and combines it with the selective application of a number of general criteria. It is thus very much a reflection of French society and therefore, cannot necessarily be regarded as a model tailored to the needs of other countries. Nevertheless, some of the distinctions made by the PCS, such as those between self-employed and wage and salary earners, or between industrial and artisanal workers, or between the civil service and the staff of various industrial and commercial firms and enterprises, should be of considerable interest and relevance for a number of countries.

Bibliography

Boltanski, L., 'Les systèmes de représentation d'un groupe social: les cadres', *Revue française de sociologie*, vol. XX, no. 4 (1979).

Boltanski, L., *Les cadres – la formation d'un groupe social* (Paris, Les Editions de Minuit, 1982).

Bourdieu, P. and Boltanski, L., 'Le titre et le poste: rapports entre le système de production et le système de reproduction', *Actes de la recherche en science sociale* no. 2 (1975).

Desrosières, A., 'Eléments pour l'histoire des nomenclatures socioprofessionnelles', in *Pour une histoire de la statistique* (Paris, INSEE, 1977), Vol. 1.

Desrosières, A., 'La nouvelle nomenclature des professions et catégories socioprofessionelles', *Données sociales* (Paris, INSEE, 1984).

Desrosières, A. and Thévenot, L., 'Les mots et les chiffres: les nomenclatures socioprofessionnelles', *Economie et statistique*, no. 110 (1979).

Desrosières, A., Goy, A. and Thévenot, L., 'L'identité sociale dans le travail statistique, la nouvelle nomenclature des professions et catégories socioprofessionelles', *Economie et statistique*, no. 152 (1983).

Girard, J.P., 'Les agriculteurs', *Données sociales* (Paris, INSEE, 1984).

Gollac, M., 'Nomenclature des professions et catégories socioprofessionnelles – PCS: édition de nouveaux guides d'utilisation', *Courrier des statistiques*, no 29 (1984)

Gollac, M., and Seys, B., 'Les professions et catégories socioprofessionnelles: premiers croquis', *Economie et statistique*, nos 171–2 (1984).

Gollac, M., and Seys, B., '1954–1982: Les bouleversements du paysage social', *Economic et statistique*, nos 171–2 (1984).

Goy, A., 'La nouvelle nomenclature des professions et des catégories socioprofessionnelles', *Courrier des statistiques*, no 22, (1982).

INSEE, *Guide des catégories socioprofessionnelles (Nomenclature PCS)* (Paris, 1983).

INSEE, *Index alphabétique pour le chiffrement des catégories socioprofessionnelles (Nomenclature PCS)* (Paris, 1983).

INSEE, *Nomenclature des professions et catégories socioprofessionnelles (PCS), index alphabétique* (Paris, 1983).

INSEE, *Nomenclature des professions et catégories socioprofessionnelles (PCS), index analytique*, (Paris, 1983).

Seys, B., 'Première édition de la nomenclature des professions et catégories socioprofessionnelles – PCS', *Courrier des statistiques* no. 26 (1983).

Seys, B., 'De l'ancien code à la nouvelle nomenclature des catégories socioprofessionnelles', *Economie et statistique*, nos 171–2 (1984).

Simula, P., 'La nouvelle nomenclature des professions', *Formation et emploi*, no. 2 (1983).

Thévenot, L., 'L'économie du codage social', *Critiques de l'économie politique*, no 23–4 (1983).

Thévenot, L., 'Des cadres moyens aux professions intermédiaires', *Données sociales*, (Paris, INSEE, 1984).

19 Coding of occupation and industry – some experiences from Statistics Sweden

L. Lyberg

The coding operation and the characteristics of the control problem

Consider a collective of objects ('elements') of some kind and a set of mutually disjointed categories. Each element belongs to one and only one of these categories. Coding denotes the act of assigning the elements into these categories.

In practice the coding is based upon access to verbal information about the elements of the population or sample under study. This information is usually obtained on schedules in the data-collection operation and is entered either by the respondents themselves or by interviewers or enumerators. Unlike certain other kinds of information, numerical data on household expenditures, for instance, verbal information cannot be processed immediately into statistical tables. It must first be coded into different categories where each category is labelled with, for instance, a number. These numbers are called code numbers and the key to these code numbers is called the code. (Naturally, numerical data also may be subject to coding; thus in a census of businesses the objects enumerated can be assigned to categories defined with respect to, for example, total turnover.)

The coding operation has three components:

(1) Each element in, for instance, a population is to be coded with respect to a specific variable by means of verbal descriptions.
(2) There exists a code for this variable, i.e. a set of code numbers in which each code number denotes a specific category of the variable under study.
(3) There is a coding function relating (1) and (2), i.e. a set of coding

instructions relating verbal descriptions with code numbers.

Coding is a major operation in such statistical studies as census of population, censuses of business and labour force surveys. Example of variables are occupation and industry.

The problems with coding are of different kinds. As with most other survey operations, coding is susceptible to errors. The errors occur because the coding function is not always properly applied and because either the coding function itself or the code is improper. In fact, in some statistical studies coding is the most error-prone operation next to data collection. For some variables error frequencies at the 10% level are not unusual. Another problem is that coding is difficult to control. Accurate coding requires a lot of judgement on the part of the coder, and it can be extremely hard to decide upon the correct code number. Even experienced coders display a great deal of variation in their coding. Thus there are problems in finding efficient designs for controlling the coding operation. A third problem is that many coding operations are difficult to administer. Coding is generally time-consuming and costly: for instance, in the 1970 Swedish Census of Population carrying out the coding took more than 300 man-years. In many countries coders in large-scale operations must be hired on a temporary basis, and the consequences for maintaining good quality are obvious. There are even reasons to believe that in the future it might be difficult to obtain even temporary coders for this kind of relatively monotonous work. So there is certainly room for new ideas on the effectiveness of the coding operation.

Coding can be carried out manually outside an agency, manually within an agency, or automatically by a computer. Manual coding outside an agency is more common than one might think. In the continuous Swedish Labour Force Survey the coding of occupation is done by interviewers. In the 1975 Swedish Census of Population local authorities coded some of the census variables in order to make it possible to produce some employment statistics without the usual time-lag. A third example is when the respondents themselves code different variables. At one extreme we have the case when respondents receive a copy of the code and are asked to use it for coding purposes. At the other extreme we have the case called 'self-coding' where the respondent is presented with a number of fixed alternatives and asked to choose one of them.

Coding outside an agency shifts the burden of coding. Generally the procedure generates low coding costs for the agency but the control of the agency over the coding is reduced as well. The literature on evaluation of this kind of decentralised coding is not very extensive.

Manual coding inside an agency (centralised coding) is very common. At Statistics Sweden such coding is used in over 100 surveys each year. However, in many of these cases, the coding operation is small and presents no serious problems. In other and more interesting cases, we have large-scale coding on a continuous basis. Examples are the censuses, in which Statistics Sweden during the last decades has hired around 300 coders on a temporary basis for each census. The coding operation is complex and many variables must be coded for each element. Such operations put tremendous pressures on the central staff and the organisation. Examples of such operations are continuous surveys where variables such as occupation, industry, education and employment status are coded – the Labour Force Survey (both centralised and decentralised coding), different pupil surveys, income distribution surveys, etc. The coding in these surveys is done by a regular coding staff.

Large-scale coding is costly and time-consuming and computer coding could be an attractive alternative. Automated coding is used as a complement to manual coding: manual coders take care of cases rejected by the computer. The methods for automated coding have been used experimentally for some years. Quite recently it was applied for the first time in production, in the 1978 Household Expenditure Survey where the variable 'goods' was coded by computer. An immediate successor was the Swedish Authors' Fund where authors and book titles were coded.

These different types of coding operations generate specific problems. In a decentralised coding situation there are problems involved in supervising and controlling the operation. In a centralised situation one often faces complex coding and has to make compromises between quality and cost. In computerised coding one must administer parallel manual systems and be very alert with respect to the performance of the computer programs.

Thus the main dimensions of the coding operations are manual versus computerised; and centralised versus decentralised. In practice, combinations of these dimensions may be used.

Coding errors

The meaning of 'coding error'

In this paper it is assumed that a true code number exists for each element with respect to the variable under study. A coding error occurs if an element is assigned to a code number other than the true one. This seemingly simple definition needs some further elaboration. Three different aspects will be considered.

First, it is often difficult to decide upon a true code number. The basic assumption is that every element belongs to one and only one category. In practice there are difficult situations where a specific description is such that it can be assigned different code numbers depending on interpretation.

Second, even if the description is detailed problems might arise in assigning true code numbers. Who are the experts to decide them? Studies show that the variation between 'experts' can be considerable and as a consequence true code numbers often have to be defined operationally – for instance, three or more experts may code the same element, with a code number being assigned by means of a majority decision.

Third, consider the following example. A dentist fills out a mail questionnaire. One of the questions is 'What is your occupation?' For some reason or other the dentist answers 'brain surgeon'. Thus the information available to the coder is 'brain surgeon'; if the code number of 'brain surgeon' is, say, 411 and the coder assigns 411 then the coding is correct. If any other code number is assigned, including the one for dentist, a coding error has occurred. Thus we say that the coding operation starts with the available element description, whether or not it is proper, and ends with the assignment of a code number. This limitation is practical from the standpoint of control. The obvious response error in the example must be dealt with by other means.

When the code has two or more digits, the notion of a coding error must take this fact into account. Assume, for example, that six coders code a specific element with respect to the variable industry using a 6-digit code. The outcome may be as follows:

True code number		3 6 9 9 2 2
Coder	1	3 6 9 9 2 1
	2	3 6 9 9 1 1
	3	3 6 9 1 1 0
	4	3 6 2 0 9 0
	5	3 5 5 1 1 0
	6	2 1 0 0 0 0

According to the definition of 'coding error' all six code numbers assigned are wrong since none of them coincides with the true one. However, the errors are of different kinds. The first code number, 3 6 9 9 2 1, differs from the true one with respect to the last digit. The second coder has been able to code correctly down to the fourth level. The third, fourth and fifth coders have been able to code correctly down to the third, second and first level, respectively. The sixth coder has not been able to assign the first digit correctly, and as a result the element has been coded to the main group 'mining' instead of 'manufacture'. The point is that as soon as an error occurs on a specific level all subsequent levels are erroneously coded as well. Furthermore, as a consequence of the way an x-digit code is constructed, an error in the first position is more serious than an error in the second position which, in turn, is more serious than an error in the third, etc. For instance, an error in the sixth position only does not affect the quality of a presentation of results on the fifth level, but an error in the first position affects the presentation of results on any level.

The error rate is the number of incorrectly coded elements divided by the total number of elements coded. The error rate can be calculated for a specific material, for a specific time period, for individual coders and for different levels of the code.

Error rates are *gross* errors. Normally the results of the coding operation are displayed in statistical tables. The coding errors which remain in the table are *net* errors and can sometimes be much less than the gross errors, since the errors tend to some extent to cancel out.

The magnitude of the coding error

A Labour Force Survey example

An early study in Sweden concerning coding errors treated the coding variability for the variables occupation and industry. It was found that coding errors seriously affected the estimation of parameters for gross changes, i.e. the flow between different categories. Some main results were that only 40 per cent of the changes in major (one-digit) occupation categories were real; the rest were coding errors (the corresponding figure for industry was 46 per cent); and that only 30 per cent of the changes in two-digit occupation categories were real (The corresponding figure for industry was 34 per cent). Obviously, publishing such estimates would indeed create an exaggerated picture of the mobility of the labour market. In fact, for some categories these coding errors lead to an overestimation of 100–200 per cent.

The 1965 Swedish Census of Population

In 1967 an evaluation study of coding errors in the 1965 Swedish Census of Population was conducted (see Dalenius and Lyberg, n.d.). From a population of census material comprising about 70 per cent of the 1965 population a two-stage sample of verified census schedules was selected. The population was partitioned into four strata and four subsamples were obtained. The evaluation study was confined to industry among other variables. The code used for industry was a three-digit code.

Since we were dealing with four subsamples we obtained four different estimates of error rates. These are given in Table 19.1. The four strata reflected the organisation of the census operations. Thus subsample 1 consisted of large city schedules subjected to total verification; subsample 2 consisted of large city schedules subjected to sample verification; subsample 3 consisted of totally verified schedules from other areas; and subsample 4 consisted of sample verified schedules from these other areas. Most of the total verification was done for still inexperienced production coders; this explains the differences in error rates between total and sampling verification.

Table 19.1   Estimates of error rates (%) in production coding of industry in the 1965 Swedish Census of Population

Subsample	Error rate
1	14.5
2	8.2
3	14.5
4	8.7

In Lyberg (n.d.) studies concerning within-coder replication in the evaluation of the 1965 Swedish Census are presented. Each of the three coders X, Y and Z in the experiment made one original coding (trial 1). After three weeks the material was coded once again by the same coders (trial 2). These independent trials gave the estimates shown in Table 19.2 of the within-coder variability $P = m/n$, where n is the total number of coded elements for the specific variable and m is the number of elements differently coded when comparing the two trials. Industry variability ranges from 1.8 per cent to 7.4 per cent; this illuminates the difficulty of coding more complex variables.

Table 19.2 Estimates of within-coder variability, P (%), in the 1965 Swedish Census of Population.

Variable	P for coder			Subsample
	X	Y	Z	
Industry	7.4	5.7	4.5	1
	6.5	5.2	3.2	2
	6.7	1.8	1.8	3
	5.8	5.3	2.9	4

When we are dealing with variables such as occupation and industry we must use hundreds of categories. The codes must therefore be multi-digit and they are built upon the principle of Chinese boxes, i.e. the first digit in the code associates the elements with a major group, the second digit in the code associates the element with a subgroup, and so on. Statistical tables often present only the major group data. Data for subgroups and minor groups, i.e. those represented by the last digits in the code, are available on request for special purposes. The conclusion must be that errors in major group coding are more serious than errors in the last digits. In addition, an error in a major group automatically results in errors in subgroups and decimals. For most purposes errors in, say, the third or fourth digit (or sometimes the fifth or sixth) are of little vital importance. A self-evident question arises: are most of the errors in occupation coding, for instance, concentrated in the last digits? If so, an estimated total error rate of, say, 12 per cent is very misleading.

In the evaluation of the 1965 Swedish Census the error distribution for the three-digit variable industry was studied. The three digits represent a major group, a subgroup, and a minor group within the subgroup (decimal). The error distribution is displayed in Tables 19.3 and 19.4. The results are given separately for the four different subsamples and for the regular coder and the verifier.

Table 19.3 Error distribution for industry coding in the 1965 Swedish Census of Population, regular coder.

Sample	Major group	Subgroup	Decimal	Total number of errors
1	41	17	22	80
2	22	8	7	37
3	37	17	20	74
4	28	8	16	52
Unweighted total	128	50	65	243

Table 19.4 Error distribution for industry coding in the 1965 Swedish Census of Population, verifier.

Sample	Major group	Subgroup	Decimal	Total number of errors
1	28	9	16	53
2	18	7	8	33
3	27	10	15	52
4	23	4	15	42
Unweighted total	96	30	54	180

The 1970 Swedish Census of Population

In the 1970 Swedish Census of Population the number of variables to be coded increased over that in 1965. For evaluation purposes a sample was drawn from the population of census schedules. A pool of expert coders was used to generate a set of 'true' evaluation code numbers for each schedule in this sample. These code numbers were compared with the production code numbers after verification, and this led to estimates of error rates for the different variables on economic activity. Estimates of error rates for industry and occupation are given in Table 19.5. The table shows that these variables are difficult to code.

Table 19.5 Estimated error rates in coding economic activity in the 1970 Swedish Census of Population.

Variable	Code	Error rate, total population (%)
Occupation	3-digit	13.5
Industry	4-digit	9.9

In the evaluation of the 1970 Census coding the experiments for investigating the within-coder variability were repeated. This time five expert coders were used. The results are given in Table 19.6. The estimates are based on sample sizes ranging from 300 to 1000; this range reflects the fact that the economic variables are coded only for economically active persons. There were also some differences in expert coder workload. As Table 19.6 shows, the within-coder variability is considerable. This is disturbing when we remember that these coders were used as producers of 'true' code numbers to evaluate the coding operation.

Table 19.6 Estimates of within-coder variability (%) in the 1970 Swedish Census of Population.

Variable	Expert coders				
	A	B	C	D	E
Occupation	8.0	10.6	10.9	9.2	7.1
Industry	3.7	8.8	11.6	6.9	5.4

Table 19.7 Absolute between-coder variability distributed over coding combinations and variables in a 1970 Swedish Census study.

Variable Coding combination	5–0	4–1	3–2	3–1–1	2–2–1	2–1–1–1	1–1–1–1–1	Number of elements
Occupation	146	35	12	5	3	3	0	204
Industry	157	31	10	3	1	2	0	204

The between-coder variability can be obtained as a byproduct of a verification process. If more than two coders are involved P, as defined above, could be replaced by

$$P' = 1 - \frac{m'}{n}$$

where m' is the number of elements for which all coders involved agreed upon a specific code number. The use of P' is deceptive, however, since it depends on the number of coders involved. In some experiments during the evaluation of the coding in the 1965 Swedish census P' took values from 13.0 to 14.1 per cent for the three independent coders coding industry.

During the evaluation of the 1970 Census coding we used five coders in a between-coder-variability study. These five coders independently coded 482 individuals. When using five coders the following combinations might occur:

5–0, 4–1, 3–2, 3–1–1,
2–2–1, 2–1–1–1,
1–1–1–1–1,

where 2–2–1, for instance, means that two coders have agreed upon a specific code number, two others have agreed upon another specific code number and the fifth has assigned a third code number. The results are shown in Table 19.7. The between-coder variability is apparent. Let us define our P' as

$$P' = \left(1 - \frac{N_{5-0}}{N}\right) 100$$

where N_{5-0} is the number of cases for which all five coders agreed upon a specific code number and N is the total number of elements. The two different values of P' are presented in Table 19.8. These P'-values are not very informative, since a 100 per cent variability can be expected if the number of coders is permitted to increase without restriction. Furthermore, these simple P- and P'-indexes can only be used for each variable separately. A P-value for variable X can seldom be compared to a P-value for variable Y since the index is biased: P obviously tends to increase with the number of possible categories. Thus we cannot compare P-values to say that the coding of industry is better than that of occupation.

Table 19.8 Estimated between-coder variability (%) per variable in a 1970 Swedish Census study.

Variable	$\hat{P}'$
Occupation	28.4
Industry	23.0

The experiment with error distribution was repeated during the evaluation of the 1970 Swedish Census coding. This time occupation (a three-digit code) was also investigated, and by this time the industry variable had become four-digit, the first two digits representing the major group and the last two the subgroup. The results are given in Tables 19.9 and 19.10. The results here are given for different subsamples after verification.

Table 19.9   Error distribution for occupation coding in the 1970 Swedish Census of Population, after verification.

Sample	Major group	Subgroup	Decimal	Total number of errors
1	67	36	56	159
2	84	39	52	175
3	68	13	35	116
Unweighted total	219	88	143	450

Table 19.10   Error distribution for industry coding in the 1970 Swedish Census of Population, after verification.

Sample	Major group	Subgroup	Total number of errors
1	77	22	99
2	88	35	123
3	56	18	74
Unweighted total	221	75	296

The 1975 Swedish Census of Population

The number of variables was smaller in the 1975 Census of Population than in the 1970 Census. Evaluation studies show that the error rates also were smaller in this census than in the 1970 Census. As for industry and occupation estimated error rates are given in Table 19.11. The results given in this table differ strikingly from those obtained in the 1970 evaluation study. The error rates have dropped for both variables. The occupation error rate of almost 8 per cent is still very serious, but compared to the 13.5 percent rate in 1970 it is a good result. Even better is the estimate for industry.

Table 19.11   Estimated error rates in coding economic activity in the 1975 Swedish Census of Population.

Variable	Code	Error rate, total population (%)
Occupation	3-digit	7.8
Industry	4-digit	3.5

The error distribution experiments gave the results shown in Tables 19.12 and 19.13. The tables show a pattern which is quite clear: serious errors are most frequent. This might seem remarkable at first glance since intuitively it does not appear to be so difficult to choose between, say, ten major occupation groups. One would expect that this would be carried out correctly and that then some difficulties might perhaps appear in the details of the code. On the contrary, things seem to work the other way: provided the major group is identified correctly it is relatively easy to code the details. This indicates that we have problems with the code dictionary and that the dividing-lines between major categories may be diffuse.

Table 19.12 Error distribution for occupation coding in the 1975 Swedish Census of Population, after verification.

Major group	Subgroup	Decimal	Total number of errors
138	68	116	322

Table 19.13 Error distribution for industry coding in the 1975 Swedish Census of Population, after verification.

Major group	Subgroup	Total number of errors
83	61	144

In Lyberg (1977b) and in Andersson (1977) the distribution of the major group code numbers for occupation in the evaluation studies were compared with the distribution of code numbers in the 1970 and 1975 Censuses. It was found that the marginal distributions were rather similar; this illustrates the fact that gross errors cancel out to some extent in statistical tables.

Some other studies of error rates at Statistics Sweden

Most of the coding studies at Statistics Sweden have been carried out within the Censuses. This is natural since the coding is a very extensive operation in a census. During recent years interest in coding errors has grown and as a result some evaluation studies have been carried out in other surveys as well. Here some estimates of coding errors from such studies are given.

In Olofsson (1976) an industry error rate of 5.7 per cent is noted in the 1974 Labour Force Survey. Occupation in the same survey had an error rate of 6.2 per cent. In Harvig (1973) an 11 per cent error rate in occupation coding is estimated for coding data for university graduates.

A note on the experience of the US Bureau of the Census

At the US Bureau of the Census, interest in coding problems has existed for many years. As early as the 1950 Censuses of Population and Housing an extensive quality control programme was part of the coding operation.

In US Bureau of the Census (1974) the extensive coding evaluation program for the 1970 Census of Population is described. The estimate of the error rate for industry coding in that census was 9.1 per cent and for occupation 13.3 per cent. These results coincide almost exactly with those obtained in the Swedish 1970 Census. In a pre-test for the 1980 Census, experienced Current Population Survey coders had an estimated error rate of 6.9 per cent when coding industry and an estimated error rate of 8.1 per cent when coding occupation. The latter experiment is described in US Bureau of the Census (1977).

Control of coding operations

The need for control

We have noted that error frequencies can be substantial, i.e. gross errors can be large. Such errors may or may not have a significant impact on survey results (for instance, estimates in statistical tables). The general experience seems to be that coding errors do not affect tables of overall statistics very much, since gross errors have a tendency to cancel out and become rather small net errors.

Statistical tables on overall statistics are seldom, however, the single and final output from surveys. Statistics in breakdowns may be seriously in error even if overall statistics are not. Besides, most surveys are multi-purpose and coded materials are often saved for future known or unknown analyses. It is common that coded material with large gross errors is presented as a frequency distribution, say N_1, N_2, ... , N_k for k categories, where the net effects of coding errors are small. After some time it is decided that a new survey or a special analysis should be carried out for individuals belonging to one or a few specific categories. Now, the gross errors may become serious as discussed above.

Other difficult situations occur when the material is used in cross-classification or in prediction.

These problems make it imperative in most statistical series that coding control be part of the overall programme for producing the statistics. However, knowledge of the error rate is not enough if we want to be farsighted. We need to know about the error structure, the reliability of the coding process, different types of errors, the seriousness of different errors and the effects of errors, in order to take suitable corrective measures with respect to the code or the coder.

It should be pointed out, though, that the control called for must be designed so as to take into account the fact that there are also other sources of errors. What is called for is a rational balance of various control efforts, as discussed in Dalenius (1974).

Schemes for statistical quality control

Manual coding can be characterised as an endless sequence of operations, and it thus seems rather well suited for the application of statistical quality control schemes as originally developed for industrial applications. More specifically, control of coding could be based on various quality control sampling plans. However, coding differs somewhat from, say, car manufacturing. Often there is a problem in finding the true code number; this forms a sharp contrast to the situation where the diameter of a screw nut is to be checked. As a consequence, errors of the first kind (altering a correct code) and second kind (failing to alter an incorrect code) are usually much more common in administrative applications than in other quality control areas. Furthermore, it is often impractical or even impossible to establish risk functions for producers and consumers, since coding is only one part of the statistical production process. Nevertheless statistical quality control has been used for several decades as a means for keeping the desired quality level of coding.

A sampling inspection plan can assure quality for any prespecified level. The literature discussing such plans is extensive; an early example is Dodge and Romig (1944).

The statistical quality control of coding aims at controlling the code numbers assigned (a control oriented towards the user of data) and at controlling the coder (a control oriented towards the producer of data). The major instruments available are acceptance sampling, process control, and combined procedures which utilise both acceptance sampling and process control. Applications of these techniques may be found in Fasteau *et al.* (1964); Minton (1969; 1970) and US Bureau of the Census (1965).

Specific coding control schemes

There are certain control schemes designed specifically for coding. These schemes are applicable in three different areas: training of coders; dependent and independent verification; and evaluation.

Training of coders

The training and education of coders is indeed valuable since the error rate often decreases with time. If it is possible to 'cut' error rates at the beginning of a coding process one will probably end up with a higher average outgoing quality. The literature on the training and education of clerks is not very extensive. However, the subject is discussed in Minton (1969) and in Dalenius and Frank (1968).

Verification

There are two main schemes for verification of coding, i.e. for deciding whether or not a code number is correctly assigned: dependent and independent verification. Independent verification the verifier has access to the code number assigned by the production coder. In independent verification the verifier has no such access and the decision on outgoing code number must be based on a set of rules such as majority or modal rules. Within these major schemes several realistic sub-schemes can be defined. Dependent and independent verification is dealt with in Lyberg (n.d.; 1969) and Minton (1969).

Let us start with a definition of dependent verification. An element is coded by production coder A. The code number is then reviewed by verifier B. B inspects the code number assigned by A and decides if it is correct or not. If it is considered correct it remains unchanged; otherwise B changes the code number. With this type of verification experience tells us that the verifier has a tendency to let erroneous code numbers remain unchanged: his judgement is influenced by (*depends* on) the code number assigned by A. Various studies show that the proportion of incorrect code numbers which remain unchanged can be substantial. At Statistics Sweden we often use 50 per cent as a rule of thumb.

Independent verification is defined as follows. An element is production-coded by a coder A. The code number is denoted x_1. The element is also coded by N other coders, where $N \geqslant 1$. Their code numbers are denoted $x_2, x_3, \ldots , x_{n+1}$. These code numbers are matched and a decision rule defines the outgoing code number. This definition gives rise to at least two questions. How do we create a situation in which each coder works independently of the other coders? What decision rules are possible?

The first question is a matter of administrative resources. One option is to code directly on the schedule and then mask the code numbers after each coding. This is a rather clumsy procedure, however, and is seldom used. Another option is to copy the schedules to be verified. This procedure is costly, of course, but it has been used in some studies. A third alternative is to code on special forms. This is the best alternative so far, and could be very smooth in a computerised environment, where the matching is done by a computer program.

There are various possible decision rules. One rather natural one is the majority rule: if a majority of the $N+1$ coders involved agrees upon a specific code number, then this code number is the outgoing one. (If a majority is not reached, then special measures are taken.) One early example of this rule is the use of the three-way independent verification system in the coding process of the 1960 US Censuses of Population and Housing. With three coders involved in each decision we have three possible outcomes, which can be denoted 3–0, 2–1 and 1–1–1; a majority is reached in all cases except the last.

A very natural way to improve efficiency is to use a sequential procedure. In the three-way system this means that we start with two coders. After the matching of their code numbers, it is decided whether a third coder is needed or not. Obviously if the outcome of the first matching is 2–0, then the code number of the third coder is completely unnecessary to reach a majority. His contribution could only lead to either 3–0 or 2–1, and we have probably wasted some money. However, if the outcome is 1–1 the third coder must enter the scene and his contribution leads to a majority

2–1 case or a 1–1–1 case. This sequential system, sometimes called the two-way independent system, was used in the 1970 US and 1970 Swedish Censuses of Population and Housing.

Evaluation

Evaluation of coding results provides a basis for the allocation of quality control efforts. We have already given examples of results from different evaluation studies. The results of such studies give suggestions concerning the size and emphasis of the necessary quality control programme.

Evaluation studies assume the existence of 'true' code numbers, which are usually those generated by more skilled coders or expert coders. By comparing these true code numbers with those assigned by the production coders an estimate of the gross error rate for the production coding can be obtained.

It is obvious that many of the coding errors do not depend on the ability of coders: the codes and the coding manuals may be insufficient and thus cause great variability in the coding process. Improvements of these tools therefore seems an urgent task.

Automated coding as a control technique

Manual coding is error-prone, and within- and between-coder variabilities are common. An evaluation of manual coding from the viewpoint of control reveals that the error-detection process is complicated by the difficulty of defining the true code numbers and by difficulties of supervising the coding staff. There are problems in implementing the coding instructions together with all the changes and code supplements which always show up with probability one in coding operations of at least moderate size. Furthermore, variabilities exist at all levels and all times in the process. For instance, a single coder has a tendency to look upon the same coding problem differently at different times. Two or more different coders have an even stronger tendency to look at the same coding problem differently at the same time. Different teams have a tendency to look at the coding problems from different points of view. This pattern applies to experienced coders, too.

Generally, manual coding and the necessary control efforts consume lots of time and money. This fact, and the fact that the process generates many errors, call for some new solution. A possible alternative is to let a computer take over the process, at least to a large extent.

Computerised or automated coding can be carried out in the following way. The code is stored in the computer. (This code is usually referred to as a 'dictionary'.) The (verbal) information to be coded is input into the computer, which is programmed to 'match' the input with the dictionary. For those cases with a 'match', the corresponding code number is assigned. Other cases are referred to manual coding.

The variability in manual coding is not present in computerised coding (except, naturally, for those elements which are referred to manual coding). However, the method presents new problems.

Verification schemes

Dependent verification

In 1967 a study, presented in Lyberg (n.d.), was conducted in order to illuminate, in a concrete fashion, the performance of the dependent verification used in the 1965 Swedish Census of Population. A general evaluation of the coding was obtained as a by-product.

In our Swedish study verified schedules from the 1965 Census material were sampled from four strata covering about 70 per cent of the population. The stratification was based on geographic area and on whether the schedules were verified totally or on a sampling basis. The study was confined to the industry variable, among others.

The samples were coded by a team of three experimental coders who were considered especially skilled. Each coder coded independently of the others and then the code numbers were matched. Three cases were possible. First, all three coders could agree; we call that case 3–0. Second, two could agree but not the third; we call that case 2–1. Finally, we have the case when no two coders agree; we call that case 1–1–1. In the first and second cases, clearly, we were able to define a majority code number, which was used as an evaluation code number. In the 1–1–1 cases we let an expert decide the evaluation code number. After that the evaluation code number was compared both to the unverified production code number (*P*) and to the dependent verification code number (*V*). Tables 19.14 and 19.15 show the results for industry for one of the subsamples. This is a difficult variable for the coders: they agreed in only 475 of the 553 cases (86 per cent). The error rate in production coding, estimated by (48 + 8 + 24)/548, is a striking 14.6 per cent. The 80 cases within the triangle in Table 19.14 were reduced to 53 by means of the verification system. This time the system took care of only 34 per cent of the errors. A summary of the error reduction rates for all subsamples in the study is given in Table 19.16.

Table 19.14   A comparison between the majority code number and the production code number (*P*) (number of cases).

Experimental coder combinations	*P* agrees with ... experimental coders					
	3	2	1	0	Expert cases	Total
3 – 0	427	–	–	48	–	475
2 – 1	–	41	24	8	–	73
1 – 1 – 1	–	–	–	–	5	5
						553

Table 19.15   A comparison between the majority code number and the dependent verification code number (*V*) (number of cases).

Experimental coder combinations	*V* agrees with ... experimental coders					
	3	2	1	0	Expert cases	Total
3 – 0	451	–	–	24	–	475
2 – 1	–	44	23	6	–	73
1 – 1 – 1	–	–	–	–	5	5
						553

Table 19.16   Estimates of error reduction rates (%) when using dependent verification (rounded figures). (Absolute error rate before verification in parentheses.)

Subsample	Industry
1	34(80)
2	11(37)
3	30(74)
4	19(52)

As pointed out in Linebarger *et al.* (1976), dependent verification does have certain advantages. The operation is quick, fairly non-disruptive to handle, requires little work if handled clerically, and is rather inexpensive. The serious disadvantages are to be found in the quality dimension. And if the disadvantages of a verification system are found in the quality dimension we are in big trouble.

Independent verification

In Dalenius and Frank (1968) and in Lyberg (1969) several alternative schemes for independent verification are discussed. The schemes differ in complexity, cost and probability characteristics. Here we give two examples of such schemes.

In both schemes the coding team consists of three production coders, C_1, C_2 and C_3, chosen at random and a referee, A. The code numbers assigned by these coders are denoted c_1, c_2, c_3, and a respectively. z is the outgoing code number of the scheme.

The coding decision rule for the first scheme, which we described earlier as three-way independent verification, is shown in Figure 19.1. An improved version of this, with the same probability characteristics but more efficient, is shown in Figure 19.2.

Independent verification is a more reliable process than dependent verification: it generally allows more accurate estimation of errors and the coding results are more credible. However, the advantages of dependent verification, listed in Linebarger *et al.* (1976), simultaneously constitute the drawbacks of independent verification.

The basic idea in all independent schemes is that the outgoing code number is very likely to be the correct one. Thus very seldom will a

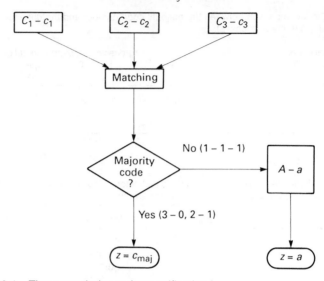

Figure 19.1   Three-way independent verification.

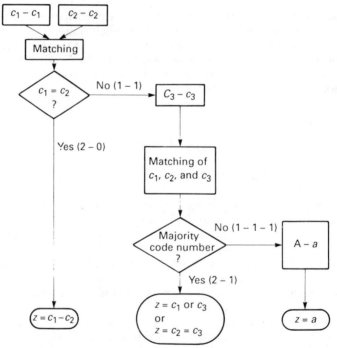

Figure 19.2   Two-way independent verification.

minority coder be unjustly charged with an error. However, it is important that the coders whose code numbers are compared be of approximately equal ability. In Harris (1974) it is pointed out that two 'poor' coders could overrule a 'good' coder simply because the former have not read the instructions properly.

In Boston (1977a) some doubts are thrown on the basic idea of independent verification. An expert evaluation of cases of coding agreement shows that the error rate in occupation coding cannot be neglected: a series of tests showed that the majority code number was incorrect in 0.7 to 1.8 per cent of the cases. However, everything depends on what is meant by 'highly likely to be correct'.

Despite what has been said about error rates in agreement cases, independent verification is the best system we have today in terms of quality. However, the administrative apparatus required and the costs can be large.

Decentralised coding

Centralised coding is a very expensive operation. In the 1970 Swedish Census of Population, for example, the cost exceeded 5 million kronor (about 1.2 million). It is therefore natural to look for alternatives which may significantly reduce costs. We will consider here the use of decentralised coding. More specifically, we will consider two types of such coding: first, where the respondents themselves are requested to tick a box or (more interesting from our viewpoint) to code by means of a dictionary; and second, where interviewers are instructed to code certain variables by means of a dictionary. It is clear that decentralised coding is in conflict with other important goals such as decreased respondent burden and low error rates due to non-response.

The error problem in decentralised coding differs in no substantial way from that in centralised coding. However, the possibilities for detecting and correcting the errors are more limited in the former case.

Respondent coding

In Jabine and Tepping (1973) the possibility of using decentralised coding of occupation and industry is discussed. Sometimes one might consider using a schedule that requires the respondent to self-code his occupation and industry major group. Jabine and Tepping also suggest mixed centralised-decentralised strategies in situations where data for both large and small areas are collected. Thus a self-coding check-box procedure can be used in large samples drawn in order to provide small-area major-group data, while a centralised procedure can be used for detailed data for large areas. In this latter case a rather small sample could be sufficient.

In Winch *et al.* (1969) it is shown that when untrained college students coded their fathers' occupations little quality was lost but the savings in costs were considerable.

In Eckhardt and Wenger (1975) the households of a number of low-performing students at grade levels 1–3 and 7–9 were surveyed. The resulting sample was much more heterogeneous with respect to race, education and income than in the Winch *et al.* study. The respondents were asked to self-code occupation, among other things. A high correlation between expert coding and the self-coding procedure was found.

Also, in Taubman (1973) some evidence is given which favours decentralised coding on major group occupation coding, at least when the respondent population consists of highly educated people.

In Bauman and Chase (1974) a study of married females is described in which interviewers coded occupation. The main conclusion from the study is that for the entire sample central coders were more successful than interviews when coding occupation.

We know of one decentralised system, used by the Swedish army. In that system all males liable to military service are required to self-code their occupation and education in order to make it easier for the authorities to put them into proper positions. The system is updated by mail surveys in which each respondent receives extensive lists of code numbers for the two variables. The codes are represented by alphabetic registers and the respondents are supposed to find their proper categories and write down the appropriate code numbers on the schedule. This is exactly the kind of system we should like to know something about. Unfortunately the data are used without any controls whatsoever.

Interviewer coding

Another possibility is to ask the interviewers to code in connection with the interview. This method has been used in the Swedish Labor Force Survey for many years for coding occupation. Error rates are moderate but we do not know how well either the respondents themselves or a central coding staff would perform on the same survey.

Automated coding: the challenge

As illustrated, manual coding has various drawbacks. In particular, it is time-consuming, costly, error-prone and boring. To cope with these drawbacks, one must inevitably focus on the very basis of manual coding and consider the possibilities offered by access to a computer of developing a basically new approach. This idea is, of course, not in principle new: for instance, at the US Bureau of the Census geographic coding has been conducted by means of computers since 1963. What is new is the suggestion in that agency that the computer be used extensively in the coding of such complex variables as occupation and industry. This suggestion may be viewed as a natural extension of earlier uses of computers in the editing operations.

During the last decade we have conducted a series of experiments in Statistics Sweden in order to find out whether or not it is possible to automate the coding process. We distinguish four operations: construction of a computer-stored dictionary; entering element descriptions into the computer; matching and coding; and evaluation. We will describe them briefly in turn.

Construction of a computer-stored dictionary

In automated coding a dictionary stored in the computer takes the place of the coding instructions used in manual coding. Obviously the construction of such a dictionary is a very important task. The construction work could be carried out manually but, when dealing with multi-digit variables, using the computer seems to be a better alternative. The resulting dictionary should consist of a number of verbal descriptions with associated code numbers. The descriptions could be a sample from the population to be coded or a sample from an earlier survey of the same kind. Of course an important problem is the size of the sample underlying the dictionary construction. Whether the dictionary is constructed manually or by computer the code numbers appearing in it should be those assigned by the best of the available coders with previous special independent verification procedures.

Entering element descriptions into the computer

One possible method of entering descriptions into the computer is to punch the descriptions in a more or less free format on cards or magnetic tape. However, this method has some serious drawbacks: first, it consumes a lot of 'space'; and second, the errors involved in large-scale keypunching of alphabetic information are relatively unknown. Moreover, such keypunching is rather costly. There are reasons to believe that at present the entering of verbal descriptions to the computer is the most important practical problem in designing systems for automated coding.

Matching and coding

Each element description now put into the computer is compared with the list of occupation descriptions in the dictionary. If an element description agrees with an occupation description (is a 'match'), it is assigned the corresponding code number, otherwise it is referred to manual coding.

In an automated coding system we will obtain exact matching for only a fraction of all elements. A primary task in developing such a system is to design criteria for the degree of similarity between input words and dictionary words necessary for them to be considered to match.

Evaluation

The system must include continuous evaluation studies. Such studies aim at controlling the quality of computerised coding; improving the dictionary; and controlling the cost.

Some experiments

Non-Swedish illustrations

At the US Bureau of the Census the main interest in developing automated coding, at least for the time being, concerns the occupation and industry variables. The different algorithms developed and tested so far are documented in O'Reagan (n.d.; 1967) and in Lakatos (1977a; 1977b). These papers give many experimental results. The most up-to-date results concern an evaluation study carried out in 1976. The test material was a sample of 127,000 coded records, one-fifth of which were used as a test file and the rest for dictionary construction. The test material had been verified by a two-way independent system with dependent adjudication for differences.

For industry coding the best coding degree obtained was 71.5 per cent, with an 87.6 per cent agreement with manual coding. The speed rate was 2,100 records processed per minute. The corresponding rates for occupation were 64.8, 83.5 and 1500, respectively.

Automated coding of occupation is used in the Central Bureau of Statistics in Denmark (see Danmarks Statistik, 1976). This system performs extremely well because *the system itself decides the code*; i.e. during the dictionary construction process the decision on how the code should be built is based on the empirical pattern of descriptions. With this technique many problems vanish.

Automated coding of occupation is also being considered in the United Kingdom. In Boston (1977b; 1978) some preliminary calculations are made on the characteristics of such a system.

There also exist plans for computerisation of job-matching operations in the US Federal-State Employment Service system in the 1980s. There already exists a Handbook of Occupational Keywords published in US Department of Labor (1978) which reflects three years of pilot studies in automated job-matching.

Swedish illustrations: industry

The very first experiment with automated coding (see Lyberg, 1972; 1974a; 1977a, 1977b) concerned the industry variable. This experiment gave the following results. Out of 419 input verbal descriptions 213 were coded (51 per cent). Of these, 170 or (80%) were correctly coded when compared to verified manual census coding.

Automated coding of industry has also been carried out in an experiment with data from the Labour Force Survey (LFS). We used a PLEX[1] dictionary containing 531 descriptions and a SLEX[2] dictionary containing 400 descriptions. A total of 712 verbal descriptions of industry were entered into the computer. The computer was able to code 65 per cent of them, but of these only 69% were 'correctly' coded (in agreement with the LFS manually assigned code numbers). This result was worse than those of the previous census experiments. However, the reason is obvious; in the LFS the interviewers collecting the data strive for detailed descriptions, and as a consequence the descriptions are sometimes composed of one or two whole sentences. In the censuses the respondents themselves fill in the answers and this usually results in short descriptions. The experiment showed that out of the 315 coded descriptions only 50 per cent were coded by means of PLEX. Usually a large majority is coded by that dictionary, but this time many SLEX words fitted the long input descriptions. For census data we have also tested a computerised dictionary based on 6,000 descriptions in the basic file. This time the descriptions came from the 1970 Census; the computer coded 61 per cent, and 83% of these were correctly coded. The main experiment's are summarised in Table 19.17.

Table 19.17   Automated coding of Swedish industry.

Experiment	Type of dictionary	Survey	Coding degree (%)	Quality (% agreement)
1	Manual	1965 Census	51	80
2	Manual	Labour Force Survey 1974	65	69
3	Computerised	1970 Census	61	83

Perhaps one can accept the low coding degree, but the errors are too frequent. However, we have not been working with this variable very long. In fact, almost all the 'trial and error' work, in our opinion the very essence in developing methods for automated coding, is still waiting to be done for the industry variable.

Swedish illustrations: occupation

When we first started to deal with the occupation variable we had the results from the first industry experiments at hand. Thus we were convinced that the size of the dictionary must be quite large to start with. The basic file consisted of 14,000 verbal descriptions from census material which were coded using an independent verification scheme. The final dictionary, constructed manually, consisted of 900 descriptions. This first dictionary was a type of PLEX dictionary, but the different matching methods (scanning, rank correlation coefficient) could be used if necessary. The first experiment, which was carried out with an independent set of 3,800 occupation descriptions from the 1965 census, gave some encouraging results: the coding degree was 62 per cent and 95% of these were 'correctly' coded. This was considered to be very satisfactory. Later on several trials were carried out and we introduced both PLEX and SLEX. With PLEX and SLEX together we sometimes obtained coding degrees around 80 per cent and qualities around 90%.

We also tested our program for computerised dictionary construction on census descriptions. An experiment with this resulted in a coding degree of 69 per cent; 87 per cent of these were correctly coded. This dictionary is still 'untouched by human hands' but is obviously good raw material for further work.

Furthermore, we have constructed a dictionary for LFS occupations. When coding occupations in LFS we do not use the same dictionary as in census coding (as we do when coding industry). We were merely curious to investigate how well the census dictionary would work in LFS coding, and thus the census three-digit code numbers were simply translated into LFS two-digit code numbers. This was done manually and resulted in a PLEX with 1,131 descriptions and a SLEX with 393 descriptions.

Thus, 711 independent descriptions were entered into the computer. Of these 81 per cent were coded and 81 per cent were in accordance with the LFS coding. This result is worse than those obtained in the census coding experiments. The reason is obvious. A direct translation is not to be recommended due to the different data collection methods: occupation in censuses and occupation in the LFS are not really the same variable. A special LFS dictionary should be constructed by means of a basic material consisting of LFS descriptions.

During 1978 a new set of experiments on LFS material was conducted. This time the computerised construction program was used on a basic file consisting of 6,000 descriptions. From these descriptions the program created a PLEX containing 1,637 descriptions and a SLEX containing 1,230 discriminating words. Three sets of independent new records were coded by means of PLEX or a combination of PLEX and SLEX. Between each run certain changes were made in the PLEX dictionary. In a fourth run a greatly extended dictionary was used.

First run. One thousand and two verbal descriptions were coded. The coding degree was 84.3 per cent. Of these 84.6 per cent were in agreement with the manual code number assigned in the LFS. The dictionary was PLEX and SLEX. When only PLEX was used the coding degree decreased to 69 per cent while the agreement rate increased to 92.2 per cent. Obviously SLEX was not very accurate.

Second run. Prior to the second run some minor changes were made in PLEX: 22 descriptions were removed and 162 were added. Then a new set of 1,000 records was coded by the modified PLEX. The resulting coding degree was 69.1 per cent, with an agreement rate of 93.3 per cent. The cost of coding 1,000 occupations was 18 kronor (approximately $4).

Third run. Prior to the third run some further minor changes were made in PLEX: 19 descriptions were removed and 145 were added. Again only PLEX was used for coding 989 new records. The resulting coding degree was 69.2 per cent, with an agreement rate of 91.8 per cent. An evaluation of the disagreements revealed that the absolute automated coding error rate was 4.7 per cent, which we think is a good result.

Fourth run. The minor modifications of PLEX had no effect on the coding degree. However, the manual coders had an alphabetic list of approximately 11,000 occupations at their disposal. This list, provided by Statistics Sweden, is not based on knowledge of empirical response patterns. We were anxious to know what would happen if that list, already available on tape, was used as a PLEX. We reran the materials used in the first and second runs and obtained the coding degrees 40.2 per cent and 36.0 per cent respectively. When we merged the alphabetic list with our computerised constructed PLEX the coding degree increased to 75.8 per cent and 74.2 per cent, respectively, and the agreement rates increased to 93.0 per cent and 93.8 per cent respectively. The cost of coding 1,000 descriptions by means of this large dictionary was 127 kronor (approximately $30). The main experiments are summarised in Table 19.18.

Table 19.18   Automated coding of Swedish occupation.

Experiment	Type of dictionary	Survey	Coding degree (%)	Quality or agreement rate (%)
1	Manual	1965 Census	62	95
2	Manual	1970 Census	66	92
3	Manual	1970 Census	74	84
4	Manual	1970 Census	80	90
5	Manual	Labour Force 1974	81	81
6	Computerised (PLEX + SLEX)	1970 Census	69	87
7	Computerised (PLEX + SLEX)	Labour Force 1976	84	85
8	Computerised (PLEX)	Labour Force 1976	69	93
9	Computerised (PLEX)	Labour Force 1976	69	92
10	Computerised and manual combined	Labour Force 1976	74–76	93–94

We think that it is possible to code occupation in our surveys by means of the program package together with some manual efforts in the dictionary construction phase. However, for an automated system to be considered, the cost situation must be carefully evaluated.

Our experiments with occupation coding are described in, for example, Lyberg (1972; 1974a; 1977a; 1977b, 1979).

Epilogue

The background: increasing use of administrative records and development of computers

The future of coding control, like that of other fields, is hard to predict. However, we know a few things for sure. We know that administrative records will be increasingly used for statistical purposes.

An efficient link between administrative records and statistics production implies the necessity of uniform coding. Uniform coding means uniform codes, i.e. for the variable under study a specific verbal description should be assigned the same code number irrespective of the system. This is not always the case even within statistics production. Uniform coding is the necessary basis for effective coding control and is therefore one of the most urgent tasks.

Coding within administrative systems is, of course, very sensitive to errors since each error can have important effects on the individuals for whom the system is designed. The coding control must therefore be tighter than in statistical systems, where the errors sometimes tend to cancel out. However, special care must be taken in using administrative systems in statistics production. Suppose that data in an administrative system are used to construct sampling frames for statistics production. Each individual error might constitute a serious flaw. Thus, it seems obvious that one can expect in the future new intensive use of efficient control methods such as independent verification.

The development of computers has been important over the years. We have seen, for instance, that the replacement of manual matching of code numbers by computer matching facilitates things a great deal. Recent studies show that data processing can be made more efficient by letting a single clerk carry out several processing tasks more or less simultaneously. For instance, in Rustemayer (1977) it is shown how interviewing can be computer-assisted by means of a system in which telephone interviewing is carried out at a computer terminal. Little imagination is needed to see that such a procedure can be extended to such operations as editing, coding and punching as well. Concentration of several operations, including coding, in a centralised facility makes things a lot easier. Coding instructions can be displayed, and quick changes in codes and instructions entered, on terminals. Verification and feedback can be conducted more easily in a computerised environment. Coding in such an environment should be a cheaper and more effective operation.

The future of automated coding

Obviously the success of automated coding is a function of language complexity. It seems that the Swedish language is more forgiving than English in this respect. Our experiments have shown that automated coding might be a possible option when designing the coding operation.

Our experiments with industry and occupation show that occupation is much easier to code than industry. It may well be possible to use automated coding in the Labour Force Survey. Currently we are very close to the payoff point in that survey. Automated coding of census occupations is also possible and is used in the 1980 Swedish Census of Population. Our experiments with industry have been very limited since this variable is semantically much more complex than occupation. (Curiously, overseas it is the other way around.) Our strategy has been to put the easier variables to test first, and then, if possible, proceed to the more difficult ones.

Notes

1. PLEX is a dictionary containing whole words or sentences.
2. SLEX is a dictionary containing parts of words (discriminating word strings).

References

Andersson, R. (1977) 'Kodningskvaliteten i FoB 75 – ekonomisk aktivitet', memo, Statistics Sweden.

Bauman, K. E. and Chase, C. L. (1974) 'Interviewers as Coders of Occupation', *Public Opinion Quarterly*, Spring, pp. 107–12.

Boston, G. F. P. (1977a) 'Quality Control of Occupation Coding', unpublished draft, Office of Population Censuses and Surveys, London.

Boston, G. F. P. (1977b) 'Machine Coding of Occupation', unpublished memo, Office of Population Censuses and Surveys, London.

Boston, G. F. P. (1978) 'Computer Coding of Occupations', paper MG 67, Office of Population Censuses and Surveys, London.

Dalenius, T. (1974) 'Ends and Means of Total Survey Design', research project Fel i Undersökningar, Stockholms universitet, Statistiska Institutionen.

Dalenius, T. and Frank, O. (1968) 'Control of Classification', *Review of the International Statistical Institute*, vol. 36, no. 6, pp. 279–95.

Dalenius, T. and Lyberg, L. (n.d.) 'An Experimental Comparison of Dependent and Independent Verification of Coding', memo from Tore Dalenius to Leon Pritzker.

Danmarks Statistik (1976) 'Erhvervsstatus – og stillingskodesystemet', Memo, Danmarks Statistik.

Dodge, H. F. and Romig, H. G. (1944) *Sampling Inspection Tables*. Wiley.

Eckhardt, K. W. and Wenger, D. E. (1975): 'Respondent Coding of Occupation', *Public Opinion Quarterly*, Summer, pp. 246–54.

Fasteau, H. H., Ingram, J. J. and Minton, G. (1964) 'Control of Quality of Coding in the 1960 Censuses', *Journal of the American Statistical Association*, vol. 59, no. 305, pp. 120–32.

Harris, K. (1974) 'Analysis of the Independent Three-Way Verification System in Mortality Medical Coding', Memo, US Department of Health, Education and Welfare.

Harvig, H. (1973) 'Kontrollkodningsexperiment på blanketter för inskrivnings-uppgifter till högre studier', memo, Statistics Sweden.

Jabine, T. B. and Tepping, B. J. (1973) 'Controlling the Quality of Occupation and Industry Data', invited paper presented at the International statistical institute meeting, Austria.

Lakatos, E. (1977a) 'Automated I & O Coding', memo, US Bureau of the Census.

Lakatos, E. (1977b) 'Computerized Coding of Free Verbal Responses', memo, US Bureau of the Census.

Linebarger, J. S., Jablin, C. and Davie, W. C. (1976) 'Dependent versus Independent Verification', memo, US Bureau of the Census.

Lyberg, L. (n.d.) 'Beroende och oberoende kontroll av kodning' report no. 4, research project fel i Undersökningar, Stockholms universitet.

Lyberg, L. (1969) 'On the Formation of Coding Teams in the Case of Independent Verification Under Cost Considerations', report no. 18, research project fel i Undersökningar, Stockholms universitet.

Lyberg, L. (1972) 'A Note on Automatic Coding', *Statistik Tidskrift*, no. 2, pp. 137–42.

Lyberg, L. (1974a) 'Automatic Classification of Industry and Occupation – Some Experiments', memo, Statistics Sweden.

Lyberg, L. (1974b) 'Kodningskvaliteten i FoB 70 – ekonomisk aktivitet', Memo, Statistics Sweden.

Lyberg, L. (1977a) 'Coding of Verbal Information', *Proceedings of the Social Statistics Section, American Statistical Association*, Part I, pp. 354–9.

Lyberg, L. (1977b) 'Coding of Verbal Information', memo, Statistics Sweden.

Lyberg, L. (1979) 'Några experiment med automatisk kodning i AKU', memo, Statistics Sweden.

Lyberg, L. (1981) 'Control of the Coding Operation in Statistical Investigations – Some Contributions', PhD thesis, Statistics Sweden, Urval no. 13.

Minton, G. (1969) 'Inspection and Correction Error in Data Processing', *Journal of the American Statistical Association*, vol. 64, pp. 1256–75.

Minton, G. (1970) 'Comments on Quality Control and Research in Data Processing Programs', paper presented at the American Society for Quality Control, 12–13 March, Arlington, Virginia.

Olofsson, A. (1976) 'Kvalitetskontroll av näringsgrenskodningen i AKU hösten – 74', memo, Statistics Sweden.

O'Reagan, R. T. (n.d.) 'Computer-Assigned Codes from Verbal Descriptions', Memo, US Bureau of the Census.

O'Reagan, R. T. (1967) 'Project to Study Potential for SIC Coding of Establishments on the Computer', memo, US Bureau of the Census.

Rustemeyer, A. (1977) 'Toward Development of a Computer-Assisted Telephone Interviewing System', memo, US Bureau of the Census.

Taubman, P. (1973) 'Occupational Coding', *Annals of Economic and Social Measurement*, pp. 71–87.

US Bureau of the Census (1965) *United States Censuses of Population and Housing, 1960: Quality Control of Preparatory Operations, Microfilming, and Coding*. Washington, DC.

US Bureau of the Census (1974) *Coding Performance in the 1970 Census. Evaluation and Research Program PHC(E)–8*. US Government Printing Office, Washington, DC.

US Bureau of the Census (1977) '1976 Census of Camden, New Jersey', Memo.

US Department of Labor (1978) *Handbook of Occupational Keywords*, 2nd edn.

Winch, R.F., Mueller, S.A. and Godiksen, L. (1969) 'The Reliability of Respondent-Coded Occupational Prestige', *American Sociological Review*, vol. 34, no. 2, pp. 244–51.

Part Five: Labour Cost, Earnings and Productivity

20 Labour cost: an international comparison of concepts

K. Taswell

The International Labour Office published for the first time in the 1983 edition of the *Year Book of Labour Statistics* a chapter presenting national series of statistics of labour cost in manufacturing industries.[1] This was in response to the increasing demand for information on labour cost registered from a large number of users. Wage payment systems have broadened considerably over the years by the introduction, liberalisation and expansion of social security and other benefits and expenditures, and in many countries the cost of these already accounts for a substantial part of the income of employees and of the costs to employers for employing labour. The aim of this paper is to provide information on the national concepts and definitions behind the series published in the *Year Book*, in order to permit a greater understanding of the figures.

International standards

Labour cost statistics, in the proper sense of the term, are a relatively recent concern of international organisations. The subject of international differences in wages and labour cost were discussed at the First European Regional Conference of the ILO in 1955, which invited the ILO to expand its inquiries and studies relating to the economic and social aspects of resources allocated to social security and other social advantages for workers in order to obtain an objective and complete international comparison. As a result, the ILO undertook statistical inquiries into wages and related elements of labour cost in selected branches of European industry.[2]

Following this, the Governing Body of the International Labour Office, at its 157th Session in 1963, noted that 'one of the most critical aspects of the cost of production is the element of wages and other labour cost, while the identification and measurement of indirect labour costs is a difficult task even under the most favourable conditions', and authorised the convening of a Meeting of Experts 'to identify and describe the several components of wages and labour cost and to advise the Office in the preparation of proposals for international standards for statistics on the subject, with particular reference to definitions, methodology and classifications and tabulation of the data'.[3] The recommendations of the Meeting of Experts on Statistics of Wages and Labour Cost (Geneva, 1964) formed the basis for the consideration of labour cost by the Eleventh International Conference of Labour Statisticians (Geneva, 1966), which adopted a resolution concerning statistics of labour cost. In this resolution, 'labour cost' is defined as follows: 'For purposes of labour cost statistics, labour cost is the cost incurred by the employer in the employment of labour. The statistical concept of labour cost comprises remuneration for work performed, payments in respect of time paid for but not worked, bonuses and gratuities, the cost of food, drink and other payments in kind, the cost of workers' housing borne by employers, employers' social security expenditures, the cost to the employer of vocational training, welfare services and miscellaneous items, such as transport of workers, work clothes and recruitment, together with taxes regarded as labour costs.'[4]

In addition to defining the concept of labour cost, the resolution also recommended an International Standard Classification of Labour Cost (ISCLC), which is presented in full in Table 20.1.

Table 20.1   International Standard Classification of Labour Cost (ISCLS)

I. Direct wages and salaries:
(1) straight-time pay of time-rated workers;*
(2) incentive pay of time-rated workers;
(3) earnings of piece-workers (excluding overtime premiums);*
(4) premium pay for overtime, late shift and holiday work.

II. Remuneration for time not worked:
(1) annual vacation, other paid leave, including long-service leave;
(2) public holidays and other recognised holidays;
(3) other time off granted with pay (e.g. birth or death of family members, marriage of employees, functions of titular office, union activities);
(4) severance and termination pay where not regarded as social security expenditure.**

III. Bonuses and gratuities:
(1) year-end and seasonal bonuses;
(2) profit-sharing bonus;
(3) additional payments in respect of vacation, supplementary to normal vacation pay and other bonuses and gratuities.

IV. Food, drink, fuel and other payments in kind:

V. Cost of workers' housing borne by employers:
(1) cost for establishment-owned dwellings;†
(2) cost for dwellings not establishment-owned (allowances, grants, etc.);
(3) other housing costs.

VI. Employers' social security expenditure:
(1) statutory social security contributions (for schemes covering: old-age, invalidity and survivors: sickness, maternity; employment injury; unemployment; and family allowances);
(2) collectively agreed, contractual and non-obligatory contributions to private social security schemes and insurances (for schemes covering: old age, invalidity and survivors; sickness, maternity; employment injury; unemployment; and family allowances);
(3) *(a)* Direct payments to employees in respect of absence from work due to sickness, maternity or employment injury, to compensate for loss of earnings;
    (b) other direct payments to employees regarded as social security benefits;
(4) cost of medical care and health services;†
(5) severance and termination pay where regarded as social security expenditure.

VII. Cost of vocational training:†
(Including also fees and other payments for services of outside instructors, training institutions, teaching material, reimbursements of school fees to workers, etc.)

VIII. Cost of welfare services:
(1) cost of canteens and other food services;†
(2) cost of education, cultural, recreational and related facilities and services;†
(3) grants to credit unions and cost of related services for employees.

IX. Labour cost not elsewhere classified:
(Such as costs of transport of workers to and from work undertaken by employer† (including also reimbursement of fare, etc.), cost of work clothes, cost of recruitment and other labour costs.)

X. Taxes regarded as labour cost.
(For instance, taxes on employment or payrolls. Such taxes should be included on a net basis, i.e. after deduction of allowances or rebates made by the State.)

---

* Including also responsibility premiums, dirt, danger and discomfort allowances, cash indemnities for meals, sandwiches, etc., payments under guaranteed wage systems, cost of living allowances and other regular allowances which are regarded as direct wages or salaries.
** Otherwise these should be classified under VI (5).
† Other than wages and salaries for personnel in the provision of the service, e.g. the depreciation on buildings and equipment, interest, repairs and maintenance and other cost, *less* grants-in-aid, tax rebates, etc. received from public authorities and receipts from workers. Capital investment made during the year is to be excluded.

At the same time, the need for a coherent framework for recording and presenting the main flows relating to production, consumption, accumulation and external trade was recognised, and as a result, the United Nations, in 1953, published a System of National Accounts (SNA). The main aim was to provide a uniform basis for reporting national income statistics, including as one element the concept of compensation of employees. This system was revised in 1968, to take account of development and experience in this area, and the concept of *compensation of employees* was defined as follows: 'The compensation of employees comprises all payments by producers of wages and salaries to their employees, in kind as well as in cash, and of contributions in respect of their employees to social security and to private pension, casualty insurance, life insurance schemes.'[5]

It can be seen, therefore, that labour cost and compensation of employees as defined in the international recommendations are closely related concepts, with many common elements. The major part of labour cost comprises compensation of employees, with the remainder consisting of employers' expenditure on vocational training, on welfare services (such as canteens, educational, cultural and recreational facilities and services, grants to credit unions, etc.) on recruitment and other miscellaneous items (such as work, etc.) and taxes regarded as labour cost. Figure 20.1 demonstrates the relationship between these two concepts.

The major difference between the two concepts lies in their objectives. Labour cost is intended to represent the cost to the employer of employing labour, not the benefits received by employees in compensation for their labour, although, in fact, many of the costs are also of direct or indirect benefit to employees. It is for this reason that items such as vocational training costs, recruitment costs, and employment and payroll taxes are included in the international recommendation. Compensation of employees, on the other hand, is intended to represent the benefits accruing to employees, either directly or indirectly, as compensation for their labour, and therefore elements of labour cost which are not of direct benefit to employees are excluded.

National concepts and definitions

The national concepts used in the statistical series presented in the new chapter of the 1983 *Year Book of Labour Statistics* are divided more or less equally between labour cost and compensation of employees. In general, the national definitions follow the international recommendations fairly closely, with the variations usually resulting from the differences in national practices with regard to the financing of social security, vocational training, other welfare costs, and the treatment of taxes and subsidies. A summary of the major characteristics of the national definitions, as compared to the ISCLC, is presented in Table 20.2.

As a rule, the state, as well as employers and employees, contribute towards the financing of social security schemes, although the levels of participation of each may vary considerably between countries, and even between the different types of scheme, particularly those which are not legally required. Furthermore, the types of social security scheme existing in different countries can vary considerably.[6] Similarly, vocational training is financed in a variety of ways: in some cases, the major burden falls on the employer, while in others the state contributes heavily, in the form of subsidies paid to employers, or by financing grants to trainees or by directly providing training in state-financed institutions. In addition, taxes are levied in certain countries, either on employment or on payrolls, and in others subsidies are paid by the state to employers, principally to encourage employment in specific regions or industries, or the employment of certain types of workers, particularly young workers. There may also be variations in practices relating to the provision of time paid for but not worked, in the form of paid vacations and other types of paid leave, such as maternity or sick leave. All these, and other factors, have a bearing on what is considered to be a cost to the employer, and therefore the definition of labour cost used in different countries.

Table 20.2 Composition of national concepts of labour cost

Components of labour cost according to ISCLS	Austria	Bangladesh	Belgium	Colombia	Cyprus	Denmark	Fiji	Finland	France	Germany (Fed. Rep. of)	Hong Kong	India	Indonesia	Ireland	Israel	Italy	Japan	Kenya	Luxembourg	Madagascar	Mauritius	Mexico	Netherlands	Norway	Panama	Philippines	Singapore	Sweden	United Kingdom	United States	Zimbabwe
I Direct wages and salaries:																															
(1) Straight-time pay	X		X	X	X	X	X	X	X	X	X	X		X	X		X	X	X	X	X	X	X	X	X	X	X	X	X	X	X
(2) Incentive pay	X		X	X	X	X	X	X	X	X	X	X		X	X		X		X		X	X	X	X	X	X		X	X	X	
(3) Earnings of piece-workers	X		X	X	X	X	X	X	X	X	X	X		X	X		X		X		X	X	X	X	X	X		X	X	X	
(4) Premium pay for overtime, etc.	X		X	X	X	X	X	X	X	X	X	X		X	X		X		X		X	X	X	X	X	X		X	X	X	
II Remuneration for time not worked:																															
(1) Annual vacation, other paid leave		X							X	X	X							X		X	X	X	X	X	X	X	X				X
(2) Public holidays, etc.	X		X	X	X	X		X	X	X	X	X		X	X		X		X		X	X	X	X	X	X		X	X	X	
(3) Other time off granted with pay	X		X	X	X	X	X		X	X	X	X		X	X		X		X		X	X	X	X	X	X		X	X	X	
(4) Severance and termination pay	X	X	X		X			X	X	X	X	X		X	X		X		X		X	X	X		X	X		X	X	X	
III Bonuses and gratuities:																															
(1) Year-end seasonal bonuses	X	X				X	X	X	X	X	X	X		X	X		X	X	X	X	X	X	X	X	X	X	X		X		X
(2) Profit-sharing bonus	X	X	X	X	X				X	X	X	X		X	X		X		X			X		X	X	X		X	X	X	
(3) Addition payments for vacations	X				X	X		X	X	X	X	X					X		X		X	X	X		X	X		X	X	X	

Table 20.2 Composition of national concepts of labour cost

Components of labour cost according to ISCLS	Austria	Bangladesh	Belgium	Colombia	Cyprus	Denmark	Fiji	Finland	France	Germany (Fed. Rep. of)	Hong Kong	India	Indonesia	Ireland	Israel	Italy	Japan	Kenya	Luxembourg	Madagascar	Mauritius	Mexico	Netherlands	Norway	Panama	Philippines	Singapore	Sweden	United Kingdom	United States	Zimbabwe
IV Food, drink, fuel and other payments in kind	X		X	X	X	X	X	X	X	X	X	X		X	X		X	X	X	X	X	X	X	X	X	X	X	X	X		X
V Cost of workers' housing borne by employers: (1) for establishment-owned dwellings	X		X					X	X	X		X		X	X		X	X	X			X	X				X	X			
(2) for dwellings not establishment-owned	X		X					X	X	X	X	X		X	X		X		X		X	X	X	X				X	X		
(3) other housing costs	X		X					X	X	X	X	X		X	X		X		X		X	X	X					X	X		
VI Employers' social security expenditure: (1) Statutory social security contributions	X		X	X	X	X	X	X	X	X	X	X		X	X		X	X	X	X	X	X	X	X	X	X	X	X	X	X	X
(2) Collectively agreed, etc., contributions to private social security schemes and insurances	X		X	X				X	X	X	X	X		X	X		X	X	X	X	X	X	X	X	X	X	X	X	X	X	X
(3) (a) Direct payments to employees as compensation for loss of earnings	X		X	X		X		X	X	X	X	X		X	X		X	X	X	X		X	X	X	X		X	X	X	X	
(b) Other direct payments to employees	X							X	X	X	X	X		X	X		X		X			X	X	X	X		X	X	X	X	
(4) Cost of medical care and	X		X					X	X	X	X	X		X	X		X	X	X		X	X	X	X	X		X	X	X	X	

Country

Components of labour cost according to ISCLS	Austria	Bangladesh	Belgium	Colombia	Cyprus	Denmark	Fiji	Finland	France	Germany (Fed. Rep. of)	Hong Kong	India	Indonesia	Ireland	Israel	Italy	Japan	Kenya	Luxembourg	Madagascar	Mauritius	Mexico	Netherlands	Norway	Panama	Philippines	Singapore	Sweden	United Kingdom	United States	Zimbabwe
health services	X		X						X	X	X	X		X			X		X			X	X		X		X		X		
(5) Severance and termination pay	X											X													X					X	
VII Cost of vocational training	X		X			X			X	X				X			X		X				X		X				X		
VIII Cost of welfare services:																															
(1) Canteens and other food services	X		X						X	X	X	X		X	X		X		X		X		X						X		
(2) Cost of educational, etc., facilities	X		X						X	X		X		X	X		X		X				X							X	
(3) Grants to credit unions	X		X						X	X					X		X		X				X						X		
IX Other labour cost:																															
(1) Workers' transport	X		X	X		X			X	X	X			X			X		X				X				X	X	X		
(2) Work clothing	X		X	X		X			X	X				X	X		X		X		X		X					X	X		
(3) Recruitment			X			X			X	X				X			X		X									X	X		
(4) Other			X							X					X				X				X								
Taxes regarded as labour cost	X								X	X															X						

X = included

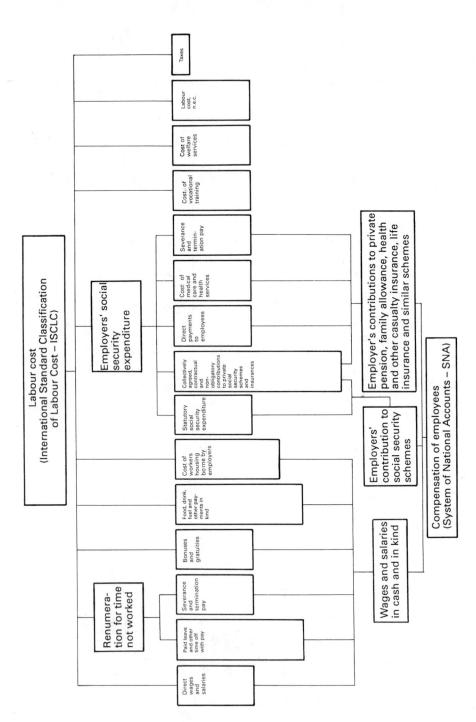

Figure 20.1 Relationship between labour cost and compensation of

The sources of national series of labour cost and compensation of employees also affect the definitions used. The principal sources comprise establishment surveys – either special-purpose labour-cost surveys or industrial censuses or surveys – although in a few countries labour cost is estimated by national statistical offices.

Labour cost surveys are usually sample surveys of establishments above a given size, which are generally conducted at intervals of three or more years. As a rule, the principal objective of these surveys is the compilation of detailed data on labour cost and its components, together with information on the corresponding employment, which usually covers all paid employees. These surveys are sometimes also used for collecting supplementary information on establishment practices and policies which have a bearing on labour cost (such as paid vacations, paid leave, etc.). Information on compensation of employees, however, is usually compiled through industrial censuses or surveys, covering all or samples of establishments above a given size, and conducted, in general, each year. The emphasis of such surveys is on the compilation of data on gross and net inputs and outputs, value added, stocks, inventories, assets, capital formation, etc. Compensation of employees is thus only one of a series of measures compiled, for which only aggregate estimates are generally required. It is therefore often limited to those elements which are readily available from establishment payrolls and other accounts. The official estimates of labour cost calculated in a few countries are usually made on the basis of data from a number of sources, such as current surveys of earnings, and administrative records of organisations responsible for social security schemes and insurances or for taxation, employers' organisations, etc. These estimates are therefore generally restricted to the wage-related elements of labour cost. Brief descriptions of the national sources used for the compilation of the series presented in the new chapter of the *Year Book* are provided in Appendix 20. This appendix also lists relevant national publications.

The following section comprises brief accounts of the different national definitions of labour cost or compensation of employees used in the series published in the 1983 *Year Book of Labour Statistics*.

Austria: Concept used–labour cost

(Source: labour cost survey)

Wages and salaries for work performed, including basic wages and salaries for normal hours and overtime hours worked, and premium pay relating to these hours.

Payments for time not worked.

Bonuses and gratuities: for Christmas, year-end, vacation and other bonuses.

Termination and severance pay.

Sickness and maternity benefit in compensation for loss of earnings.

Housing allowance.

Employers' statutory social security expenditure: employers' contributions to social insurance and other statutory social security payments.

Collectively agreed, contractual or voluntary social welfare expenditure: cash allowances for current employees (child and family allowances, housing allowances, sickness allowance, etc.); cash allowances for former employees; contributions to funds; payments in kind (food, drink, fuel, clothing, etc.); cost of employees' housing; cost of welfare services and facilities for staff (medical services, canteens and similar services, works' laundry and detergents; work clothing and protective clothing; recreation and leisure facilities; day nurseries; compensation for travel expenses to workplace).

Bangladesh: Concept used—compensation of employees
(Source: industrial census)

Belgium: Concept used—labour cost
(Source: labour cost survey)

Direct wages and salaries, regular bonuses and gratuities: wages and salaries paid for hours actually worked, including payments relating to overtime, night work, or work on Sundays and public holidays; cost-of-living or dearness allowances; bonuses and gratuities paid regularly each pay period (such as production or productivity bonuses; premiums for duties, responsibilities, regularity, hard work, seniority, dangerous, dirty or unpleasant work, shift work; allowances paid for work at a place other than the normal place of work; allowances for snacks, etc.; compensatory wages or salaries for reduced working hours).

Other bonuses and gratuities not paid regularly each pay period: bonuses for Christmas, end of year, thirteenth month, etc.; production or productivity bonuses not paid each pay period: supplementary vacation allowances and holiday bonuses; net amounts paid by the employer to holiday funds.

Remuneration for days not worked: all paid vacation and paid leave, as well as payments for leave not taken, including supplementary leave for mothers and seniority leave; public holidays and other days not worked but paid for (including the day of an industrial accident, the birth of a child, death of a spouse or close relative, marriage of employee, unpaid honorary duties, family council, army medical board, home removal at employer's request, marriage of family member, various ceremonies, absence for civic duties, absence for union duties, etc.); indemnities for lay-off or in lieu of notice.

Employers' social security costs:

Statutory costs: employers' contributions for social security; other legally required contributions for accidents at work, paid either directly to employees or through private organisations; guaranteed payment of wages and salaries in case of accident or illness; other legally required costs.

Contractual, collectively agreed or voluntary costs: contributions to complementary schemes run by the employer or the industry; complementary pension schemes; guaranteed wages or salaries in case of accident or injury; family allowances.

Payments in kind: cost to employer of products provided free to employees or sold to them at less than cost price: food and drink, coal, gas, electricity, oil, heating, footwear, clothing (except canteens and work clothing); and housing paid for by the employer (housing owned by the establishment, including hostels for single employees).

Other expenditure for social welfare: expenditure by the employer on purchase, maintenance and distribution of work clothing and protective clothing; subsidies for services such as medical services, canteens, holiday camps and centres. Christmas trees, leisure facilities, libraries, etc.; grants for studies; subsidies for cultural activities; contributions to union funds; recruitment costs (transport expenses to interviews and cost of installation, etc.); expenditure for training activities of a purely social or cultural nature; transport costs for workers between home and normal place of work.

Cost of vocational training: wages and salaries paid to apprentices and trainees; costs for theoretical and practical courses for employees; fees for outside instructors; expenditure on materials, fuel, tools and maintenance of building and machines used exclusively for vocational training; contributions or subsidies paid by employer to institutions providing vocational training; special taxes for vocational training. *Less*: value of output produced by persons receiving training and sold to clients or staff; subsidies, etc., received by employer from the state for vocational training.

Taxes: taxes based on employment or payrolls.

Subsidies: subsidies relating directly to labour cost, such as subsidies received from the state for the engagement of young trainees.

Colombia: Concept used–compensation of employees
(Source: industrial survey)

Wages and salaries: remuneration received by workers in cash or in kind, regularly or as deferred payments, for services provided to the industrial establishment, including paid vacations, transport allowances, pay for overtime and public holidays, and other payments covered in the *Código Sustantivo del Trabajo* (Labour code).

Social security payments: obligatory or voluntary payments made by employers on behalf of their employees.

Cyprus: Concept used–compensation of employees
(Source: industrial survey)

Wages and salaries: direct wages and salaries, overtime earnings, bonuses, value of receipts in kind, cost of living allowances, payments for leave days and dismissal compensations.

Employers' contributions: contributions to various funds, including social insurance, medical, redudancy, annual leave with pay, pension, provident and other funds for their employees.

Denmark: Concept used–labour cost
(Source: labour cost survey)

Direct wages and salaries (as in ISCLC).

Remuneration for time not worked: annual vacation, other paid leave, including long-service leave; public holidays and other recognised holidays.

Bonuses and gratuities: additional payments in respect of vacation, supplementary to normal vacation pay and other bonuses and gratuities.

Food, drink, fuel and other payments in kind.

Employers' social security expenditure: statutory social security expenditure and collectively agreed, contractual and non-obligatory contributions to private social security schemes and insurances.

Cost of vocational training (as in ISCLC).

Labour cost not elsewhere classified.

Fiji: Concept used–compensation of employees
(Source: industrial census)

Income of employees from the provision of their labour, i.e. the sum of wages and salaries (in cash and in kind) and contributions by employers in respect of their employees to social security schemes, private pension arrangements, health insurance and other similar schemes.

Finland: Concept used–compensation of employees
(Source: industrial survey)

Direct wages and salaries (as in ISCLC).

Remuneration for time not worked (as in ISCLC).

Bonuses and gratuities (as in ISCLC).

Food, drink, fuel and other payments in kind (as in ISCLC).

Cost of workers' housing borne by employers (as in ISCLC).

Employers' social security expenditure: statutory social security contributions; direct payments to employees in respect of absence from work due to sickness, maternity or employment injury, to compensate for loss of earnings and other direct payment to employees regarded as social security benefits.

France: Concept used–labour cost
(Source: labour cost survey)

Direct wages and salaries (as in ISCLC).

Remuneration for time not worked (as in ISCLC).

Bonuses and gratuities (as in ISCLC).

Food, drink, fuel and other payments in kind (as in ISCLC).

Cost of workers' housing borne by employers (as in ISCLC).

Employers' social security expenditure: statutory social security contributions; collectively agreed, contractual and non-obligatory contributions to private social security schemes and insurances; direct payments to employees in respect of absence from work due to sickness, maternity or employment injury, to compensate for loss of earnings and other direct payment to employees regarded as social security benefits.

Cost of vocational training (as in ISCLC).

Cost of welfare services: cost of canteens and similar food services; cost of educational, cultural and recreational facilities and services, including costs of holiday camps and centres, Christmas trees, etc.

Other labour cost not elsewhere classified: cost of work clothing, cost of workers' transport between home and normal place of work.

Less: subsidies received by employers aimed at reducing labour cost in order to encourage employment.

Federal Republic of Germany: Concept used–labour cost
(Source: labour cost survey)
Direct wages and salaries (as in ISCLC).
Remuneration for time not worked (as in ISCLC).
Bonuses and gratuities (as in ISCLC).
Food, drink, fuel and other payments in kind (as in ISCLC).
Cost of workers' housing borne by employers (as in ISCLC).
Employers' expenditure on social security (as in ISCLC).
Cost of vocational training (as in ISCLC).
Cost of welfare services (as in ISCLC).
Other labour costs not elsewhere classified.
Taxes regarded as labour cost.

Hong Kong: Concept used–compensation of employees
(Source: industrial survey)
Wages and salaries: basic wages and salaries, including commission paid to sales staff; premium pay for overtime, late shift or night shift and holiday work; bonuses and gratuities (such as year-end or seasonal bonuses, profit-sharing bonus, good attendance bonus, production or efficiency bonus, long-service and retirement gratuities), severance and termination pay, cash allowances (such as cost of living, food, accommodation and transport allowances, etc.)
Payments in kind: net cost to the employer in providing housing, food, drink, fuel and other goods and services to employees free of charge or at markedly reduced prices (such as cost incurred in providing free or subsidised meals, including the cost of maintaining canteens, free or subsidised accommodation and free transport, etc.)
Employers' social security expenditure and cost of welfare services: contributions to provident funds and retirement funds, and other schemes covering old-age, invalidity and survivors, sickness and maternity and workmen's compensation due to employment injury or diseases: direct payments other than paid sick leave and maternity leave to employees, in respect of absences from work due to sickness, maternity or employment injury or diseases, to compensate for loss of earnings; cost of medical care and health services; cost of education, cultural, recreational and related facilities and services; educational grants to children of employees; grants to credit unions and related services to employees.

India: Concept used–labour cost
(Source: industrial survey)
Wages and salaries: basic wages and salaries; overtime payments; paid vacation and holidays; dearness, compensatory house rent and other allowances paid regularly; regularly paid bonuses such as production bonuses, good attendance bonuses, incentive bonuses, etc.
Bonuses: profit-sharing, festival and year-end and other bonuses and *ex gratia* payments made at less frequent intervals.
Benefits in kind: includes the imputed value of individual and group benefits such as concessions in respect of supplies, food, beverages, tobacco

and clothing (except uniforms), transport, accommodation, electricity, water, sanitary services, schools, reading rooms, adult education centres, hospitals, canteens, etc.

Social security charges: contributions to provident funds, pension, gratuity, etc., and expenses incurred in the form of employers' contributions to the Employees' State Insurance, compensation for work injuries and occupational diseases, maternity benefits, retrenchment and lay-off compensation, etc., whether statutorily required or not.

Indonesia: Concept used—employment cost
(Source: industrial survey)

Ireland: Concept used—labour cost
(Source: labour cost survey)

Total wages and salaries paid to employees: all wage and salary payments, overtime, shift allowances, holiday pay and bonuses, etc.; sick pay (paid by employer) and redundancy payments (lump sum less rebates) and payments of wages and other liabilities to employees in lieu of notice.

Employers' contributions to social security:

Statutory contributions by employers: cost to employer of social insurance stamps and contributions with respect to pay-related benefits.

Voluntary contributions or benefits: employers' contributions to superannuation funds and payments of life assurance premiums by employers on behalf of employees; amount of pensions paid directly by employers to past employees and their dependants; payments of insurance premiums by employers on behalf of employees for sickness or injury (additional to statutory requirements); other non-statutory payments of a social security nature (such as family allowances, payments related to birth of a child, etc., excluding payments in kind).

Payments in kind and costs associated with providing accommodation for employees: costs of accommodation owned by the firm or not owned by the firm, and reduced-interest housing loans, goods and services supplied either free of charge or at a reduced rate.

Other social expenditure: all other labour costs or costs of a social nature such as canteens, medical services, provision of recreational facilities, cost of protective clothing (including laundry costs), cost of providing scholarships (other than for job-related training), library facilities, cost involved in providing reduced-interest car loans, cost to firm of private use of company cars.

Vocational training: wages and salaries of apprentices and associated social security expenditure of employers; ANCO levies less rebates; cost relating to courses arranged for trainees including payments made to lecturers hired externally; fees for training courses; incidental expenses; scholarships.

Israel: Concept used—labour cost
(Source: industrial survey)

Wages and salaries: all payments on which income tax is due appearing on payrolls, including basic wages and salaries; cost of living, professional, seniority and family allowances (excluding employees' children's allowance) and bus fares; premiums, bonuses and payments for overtime, absence (leave, sickness, festivals, etc.), convalescence, professional literature and thirteenth month's salary; maintenance of vehicle, telephone, clothing, lodging (on which income tax is due) and payments in kind (such as meals, presents, housing, etc.).

Other labour expenses: expenses connected with engaging employees, which do not appear on payrolls, such as national insurance and other funds; Mivtahim (pension fund administered by the central trade union organisation, the Histadrut); army reserve, pension and severance pay, and pensions paid by employers; payments for transport of workers to work; upkeep of restaurants, etc.

Italy: Concept used–labour cost
(Source: labour cost survey)

Japan: Concept used–labour cost
(Source: labour cost survey)
Cash payroll:
Money earned, comprising contractual cash earnings: earnings paid on the basis of method and conditions previously determined by the labour contracts, collective agreements or wage regulations of establishments.

Special cash payments: amounts paid to employees for extraordinary or emergency cases without any previous agreement, contract or rule, including retroactive payments, including also summer and year-end bonuses, marriage allowances and other allowances for unforeseen events.

Payments in kind: employers' shares in estimated value of meals supplied.

Severance pay: payments made from employers or trustees to employees when the employment relationship is nullified as a result of voluntary resignation, fixed-age retirement, discharge or death.

Cost of legal welfare contributions: contributions for health insurance, welfare pension, labour insurance or employment insurance and workmen's accident compensation, employment benefit for handicapped and other obligatory compensation cost.

Cost of non-legal welfare expenses: cost of company housing; cost of medical and health services; cost of canteens and other food services; cost of cultural, sporting and recreational facilities; contributions to private insurance plans; cost of supplementary workmen's accidental compensation; cost of solatium for congratulations and condolences; other costs.

Cost of recruitment.
Cost of education and training.
Other labour cost.

Kenya: Concept used–labour cost
(Source: industrial survey)
Labour costs including: salaries and wages paid in cash, including bonuses, all non-cash benefits, such as rations, housing, clothing, and employers'

National Social Security contributions, medical benefits, etc.

Luxembourg: Concept used–labour cost
(Source: labour cost survey)

Direct remuneration: wages and salaries paid for hours actually worked, including payments for overtime, night work, work on Sundays and public holidays, cost of living allowances, regular bonuses and gratuities.

Other bonuses and gratuities not paid regularly: end-of-year and Christmas bonuses, thirteenth month, vacation bonuses, productivity and profit-sharing bonuses.

Remuneration for days not worked: payments for paid leave, including supplementary leave for mothers and for long service, as well as allowances for leave not taken; public holidays and other days paid for but not worked; severance and termination pay.

Employers' social security and family allowance expenditure:

Legally required expenditure: guaranteed wages and salaries in case of sickness, contributions of employers towards occupational and other insurance, contributions towards funds providing family allowances, and others.

Contractual, collectively agreed or voluntary payments: contributions to complementary schemes covering sickness, maternity, invalidity, occupational illnesses and industrial accidents, employers' contributions to life assurance schemes and pension funds, etc.; payments made to workers to compensate for loss of earnings due to illness or accident, amounts paid directly by employers to employees as family supplements.

Payments in kind: products provided free of charge or at less than cost price, in the form of coal, coke, gas, electricity, drinks, food, footwear, clothing, etc., as well as allowances provided directly to employees for these items; housing provided free of charge, housing allowances and non-reimbursable or interest-free loans to employees for housing.

Other welfare expenditure: expenditures for medical services, canteens, holidays camps and centres, Christmas trees, leisure activities, libraries etc.; education grants; subsidies of a cultural nature; value of work clothing; various contributions to union funds or for union activities; cost of workers' transport between home and normal place of work, including company cars; cost of recruitment.

Vocational training costs: wages and salaries of apprentices and trainees; employers' contributions for their social security; course expenditure; fees paid to outside instructors; running costs; payments to outside organisations providing training; special taxes for vocational training; and grants for vocational training.

Subsidies relating directly to labour cost in general, in particular subsidies relating to *Notstandarbeiten* (relief work).

Madagascar: Concept used–personnel costs
(Source: industrial census)

Total payments made by the employer on behalf of his workers including allowances, bonuses and gratuities, paid leave, social costs, etc., and payments in kind.

Mauritius: Concept used–compensation of employees
(Source: industrial survey)
Direct wages and salaries (as in ISCLC).
Remuneration for time not worked (as in ISCLC).
Bonuses and gratuities: year-end and seasonal bonuses.
Food, drink, fuel and other payments in kind (as in ISCLC).
Cost of workers' housing borne by employers: housing allowances, etc. and other housing costs.
Employers' statutory social security contributions, direct payments to employees regarded as social security benefits, and casualty insurance.
Cost of canteens and other food services, work and clothes.

Mexico: Concept used–compensation of employees
(Source: industrial survey)
Wages and salaries: cash payments to employees as remuneration for work performed, including payments for overtime; bonuses, vacation and temporary lay-offs; commissions received by employees, except by sales staff paid by commission only.
Social security costs: payments made by the employer to employees in addition to wages and salaries, in the form of allowances, services or in kind, including medical services, medicines, food, housing, insurance, work clothing, removal expenses, other social services, end-of-year bonuses, employers' contributions to social security, to INFONAVIT (Institute of the National Fund for Workers' Housing), payments for redundancy and indemnities for occupational risks, etc.
Profit-sharing bonuses.

Netherlands: Concept used–labour cost
(Source: labour cost survey)
Direct wages and salaries (as in ISCLC).
Remuneration for time not worked (as in ISCLC).
Bonuses and gratuities (as in ISCLC, but excluding profit-sharing bonus).
Food, drink, fuel and other payments in kind (as in ISCLC).
Cost of workers' housing borne by employers (as in ISCLC).
Employers' social security expenditure (as in ISCLC).
Cost of vocational training (as in ISCLC).
Other labour cost: cost of transport between home and workplace, cost of work clothing, others.

Norway: Concept used–compensation of employees
(Source: industrial census)
Direct wages and salaries: pay for normal time worked, premium pay for overtime, premium pay for shift work, incentive and other regular bonuses, including commissions earned by salesmen and representatives, cost of living allowances.
Remuneration for time not worked: annual leave, vacation, etc.; public holidays, other time off with pay, military leave.
Bonuses and gratuities.

Food, drink, fuel and other payments in kind.
House rent allowances.
Employers' social security expenditure: social expenses levied by law; employers' contributions to private pension, family allowance, health and casualty insurance, life insurance, etc.; family allowances paid directly to employees.

Panama: Concept used–compensation of employees
(Source: industrial survey)
Direct wages and salaries (as in ISCLC).
Remuneration for time not worked (as in ISCLC).
Bonuses and gratuities (as in ISCLC).
Food, drink, fuel and other payments in kind (as in ISCLC).
Employers' social security expenditure (as in ISCLC.)
Cost of vocational training (as in ISCLC).
Taxes regarded as labour cost.

Philippines: Concept used–compensation of employees
(Source: industrial survey)
Direct wages and salaries (as in ISCLC).
Remuneration for time not worked (as in ISCLC).
Bonuses and gratuities (as in ISCLC).
Food, drink, fuel and other payments in kind (as in ISCLC).
Employers' statutory social security contributions.

Singapore: Concept used–remuneration of employees
(Source: industrial census)
Wages and salaries including bonuses, contributions to the Central Provident Fund, pension and other funds, and the value of other benefits provided such as food, lodging, transport and medical care.

Sweden: Concept used–labour cost
(Source: official estimates)
Direct wages: pay for hours worked, supplements for shift work, and inconvenient or staggered hours, overtime supplement and pay, compensation for down time and for on-duty time.
Remuneration for time not worked: holiday pay and compensation, vacation pay and compensation and vacation funds, compensation over and above social insurance benefits for pregnancy and confinement, compensation for military service and other service in the national defence, compensation for training, lay-off compensation, stand-by compensation, and other compensation.
Payments in kind, gratuities and other industrial benefits: compensation to members of joint employer-employee councils, safety officers, compensation for suggestions and inventions, other cash payments (allowances for housing costs, meal costs, travel to and from work, work clothing, bonuses); free or subsidised housing, meals, travel to and from work, work clothing, free car, etc.

Collective fees, pension costs: Employers' social expenditure: statutory social security contributions, etc., for national supplementary pension scheme, national basic pension scheme, health insurance, national scheme for part-time pensions, occupational injuries, unemployment; cost of negotiated pension benefits, insurances, etc.

Other collective premiums: health insurance, group life insurance, severance/compensation payments, security insurance, etc.

Other statutory employer levies for adult education, labour market training, community child care.

United Kingdom: Concept used–labour cost
(Source: labour cost survey)

Wages and salaries: gross total amounts paid to employees, pay supplements, pay for overtime, night work and weekend work; payments under bonus, productivity and other incentive schemes; commissions and gratuities; payments for annual, public and customary holidays; payments for sickness, injury and maternity absence; payments in lieu of notice; other payments for time not worked (including guaranteed payments, payments for attending training courses); and miscellaneous additional allowances (such as cost-of-living allowances).

Employers' National Insurance Contributions.

Redundancy payments and rebates.

Voluntary social welfare expenditure: contributions to funds which provide pensions, superannuations and other retirement benefits and death benefits for employees and to funds which provide for widows, orphans, and other dependants of employees, including insurance premiums for providing free or subsidised life insurance for employees; amounts set aside by way of insurance premiums or payments to special sickness funds to provide benefits to employees while absent from work on account of sickness or maternity, industrial injury or diseases caused by work; amounts paid directly to employees, their dependants or other beneficiaries in respect of retirement, sickness, accident or death, including *ex gratia* and goodwill payments and marriage gratuities, awards for long service, etc.; other voluntary payments (to funds or schemes which provide medical benefits, family allowances or educational allowances for employees and their children).

Benefits in kind: cost to the employer of goods provided free or below cost price to employees, dependants or former employees, such as food, drink, fuel, etc., and luncheon vouchers.

Housing expenditures: for accommodation owned by employers and assistance to employees with rent and interest forgone or housing loans at reduced rates.

Subsidised services to employees: cost of canteens, staff restaurants, etc.; cost of first-aid rooms, rest rooms, other medical, dental and health services provided by the employer; cost of sports grounds, pavilions, club houses, reading rooms and other educational services; cost of staff magazines; cost of provision of works bus, assistance with fares, repayment of normal daily travelling expenses, company cars; cost to employer of uniforms, overalls, protective clothing and footwear.

Vocational training; cost of courses, fees paid to instructors, running costs, etc.; amount of levy actually paid or to be paid to industrial training boards; grants received or due from industrial training boards.

Government subsidies: amounts received under special employment measures, such as Temporary Employment Subsidy (and supplement). Youth Employment Subsidy and other special employment measures in operation.

United States: Concept used–compensation of employees
(Source: official estimates)
Direct wages and salaries (as in ISCLC).
Remuneration for time not worked (as in ISCLC).
Bonuses and gratuities (as in ISCLC).
Employers' social security expenditure (as in ISCLC, but excluding medical care and health services).

Zimbabwe: Concept used–compensation of employees
(Source: industrial census)
Wages and salaries, including all salaries and other emoluments paid by the employer, such as income in kind at cost to the employer, and sums contributed by the employer to pension, medical aid and similar schemes, commissions paid to regular employees.

Notes

1. See ILO, *Year Book of Labour Statistics, 1983*, Chapter VI, (Geneva, 1983). International series of labour cost statistics, using different definitions, are also compiled by a number of other organisations, among which are the following:
   (*a*) Organisation for Economic Co-operation and Development (OECD) (publication: *Main Economic Indicators*; monthly).
   (*b*) Statistisches Bundesamt, Wiesbaden (publication: *Statistik des Auslandes*, Reihe 4.1: Arbeitnehmerverdienste im Ausland, annual).
   (*c*) Swedish Employers' Confederation (SAF) (publication: *Wages and Total Labour Costs for Workers*, International Survey; annual).
   (*d*) United States Department of Labor, Bureau of Labor Statistics (not published, annual).
2. See ILO, *Labour Costs in European Industry*, Studies and Reports, new series, no. 52 (Geneva, 1959).
3. See ILO, 'Report of the Meeting of Experts on Statistics of Wages and Labour Costs' (Geneva, 1964; doc. MELC/D.2/1964, mimeo).
4. For the full text of the resolution, see ILO, *International Recommendations on Labour Statistics* (Geneva, 1976). See also ILO, 'Statistics of Labour Cost', Eleventh International Conference of Labour Statisticians, Report II (Geneva, 1966, mimeo).
5. For further details, see United Nations, *A System of National Accounts*, Studies in methods, series F, no. 2, rev. 3 (New York, 1968).
6. For further information concerning national social security schemes, see ILO, *The Cost of Social Security*, International Inquiry (Geneva, annual).

Appendix 20 Characteristics of sources of labour cost statistics published in 1983 edition of *Year Book of Labour Statistics*

Country: 1. Title of source 2. Organisation responsible	Coverage of survey: 1. Industrial 2. Geographic 3. Establishment or enterprise 4. Employee	Periodicity of survey	Sampling: 1. Sampling design 2. Sampling frame 3. Sampling unit 4. Sample size	Method of data collection	Reference period for collection of data on labour cost	Estimation procedures	Time unit according to which data are published	Principal publication in which statistics appear
1	2	3	4	5	6	7	8	9
AUSTRIA 1. Erhebung der Lohnnebenkosten (Survey of wage costs) 2. Bundeskammer der Gewerblichen Wirtschaft, Abteilung für Statistik und Dokumentation	1. Manufacturing: mining and quarrying; petroleum; gas and heating supply 2. Whole country 3. 4. All paid employees	3-yearly, since 1960		Questionnaire survey	Calendar year		For wage earners: per hour worked For salaried employees: per month	*Die Arbeitskosten in der Industrie Österreichs,* Bundeswirtschaftskammer. Abteilung für Statistik und Dokumentation
BANGLADESH 1. Annual census of manufacturing industries 2. Bangladesh Bureau of Statistics	1. Manufacturing 2. Whole country 3. Establishments with 10 or more workers 4. All paid employees	Annual			Fiscal year: 1 July to 30 June		Per year	*Statistical Yearbook of Bangladesh,* Statistics Division. Ministry of Planning
BELGIUM 1. Enquête sur le coût de la main-d'oeuvre dans l'industrie; 2. Institut National de Statistique	1. Mining and quarrying; manufacturing; electricity, gas and water; construction, wholesale and retail trade; banking and insurance 2. Whole country 3. Establishments employing 10 or more employees	3-yearly, since 1966	1. Single stage sampling; establishments classified according to industry group and size 2. Social insurance register of establishments, and survey of industries 3. Establishment	Questionnaire survey	Calendar year	Labour cost series are updated twice a year between survey years, using current earnings statistics and an estimate of trends in other wage cost elements	Per hour worked	*Labour Costs,* Statistical Office of the European Communities

Country: 1. Title of source 2. Organisation responsible	Coverage of survey: 1. Industrial 2. Geographic 3. Establishment or enterprise 4. Employee	Periodicity of survey	Sampling: 1. Sample design 2. Sampling frame 3. Sampling unit 4. Sample size	Method of data collection	Reference period for collection of data on labour cost	Estimation procedures	Time unit according to which data are published	Principal publication in which statistics appear
1	2	3	4	5	6	7	8	9
BELGIUM	4. Persons employed in the establishments under contract, including those working part-time; excluding home-workers		4. 27% of establishments and 69% of employees covered in 1975					
COLOMBIA 1. Encuesta anual manufacturera 2. Departamento Administrativo Nacional de Estadística (DANE)	1. Manufacturing 2. Whole country 3. Establishments with 10 or more persons employed 4. Persons on establishment payrolls during week including 15 November or nearest period; excluding homeworkers; including apprentices	Annual, since 1966					Per year	*Boletín mensual de estadística* (La industria Manufacturera) Departamento Administrativo Nacional de Estadística (DANE)
CYPRUS 1. Industrial Production Survey 2. Statistics and Research Department, Ministry of Finance	1. Mining and quarrying; manufacturing; electricity, gas and water 2. Up to 1974: whole country; 1974 onwards: government-controlled areas	Annual, since 1962	1. Single stage sampling, establishments classified according to industry group and size class 2. Registration of establishments 3. Establishment 4. 14% of all	Questionnaire survey	Calendar year		Per year	*Industrial Production Survey* Statistics and Research Department, Ministry of Finance

Title / Agency	Frequency	Scope (1–4)	Method of collection	Reference period	Remarks	Unit	Publication / Source
(continued)		establishments covered in 1977 only 3. All sizes of enterprise 4. Employees, including apprentices			Labour cost series are updated twice a year between survey years using current earnings and statistics and an estimate of trends in other wage cost elements	Per hour worked	*Labour Costs* Statistical Office of the European Communities
DENMARK 1. Lønomkostninger industri og byggeri (Labour cost in industry and construction) 2. Danmarks Statistik	3-yearly since 1975; first survey 1973	1. Mining and quarrying; manufacturing; electricity, gas and water; construction; wholesale and retail trade; banking and insurance 2. Whole country 3. Establishments with 10 or more employees 4. Persons employed in the establishment under contract, including part-time workers; excluding home-workers	1. Single stage sampling, establishments classified according to industry group and size class 2. 3. Establishment 4. 1973: 524,000 employees	Questionnaire survey	Calendar year			
FIJI 1. Census of Industrial Production 2. Bureau of Statistics	Annual, since 1971	1. Mining and quarrying; manufacturing; electricity, gas and water (private sector, and public sector for electricity, gas and water) 2. Whole territory 3. All sizes 4. Paid employees	1. Census 2. List of establishments maintained by Bureau of Statistics, updated by reference to telephone directory, Ministry of Commerce and industry, and Fiji National Provident Fund records 3. Establishment 4. 1978: 86% of establishments covered; 97% of employment	Mailed questionnaire survey, with personal visits by field workers when assistance required to complete forms	Calendar year or accounting year which covered the major portion of the calendar year	Rate-up factors used for grossing up data for non-respondents	Per year	*Census of Industrial Production* Bureau of Statistics

Country: 1. Title of source 2. Organisation responsible	Coverage of survey: 1. Industrial 2. Geographic 3. Establishment or enterprise 4. Employee	Periodicity of survey	Sampling: 1. Sample design 2. Sampling frame 3. Sampling unit 4. Sample size	Method of data collection	Reference period for collection of data on labour cost	Estimation procedures	Time unit according to which data are published	Principal publication in which statistics appear
1	2	3	4	5	6	7	8	9
FINLAND 1. Industrial Statistics Inquiry 2. Tilastokeskus Statistikcentralen (Central Statistical Office)	1. Mining and quarrying; manufacturing; electricity, gas and water 2. Whole country 3. Establishments employing 5 persons or more on average, including working proprietors 4. All paid employees	Annual since 1971	1. 2. 3. Establishment 4. 1978: 42% of manufacturing establishments; 97% of all manufacturing employment	Questionnaire survey	Calendar year		Per hour	*Teollisuustilasto* (Industrial Statistics) Tilastokeskus Statistikcentralen (Central Statistical Office)
FRANCE 1. Enquête sur le coût de la main-d'oeuvre dans l'industrie, le bâtiment et les travaux publics 2. Institut National de la Statistique et des Études Économiques (INSEE)	1. Mining and quarrying; manufacturing; electricity, gas and water; construction; wholesale and retail trade; banking and insurance 2. Whole country 3. Establishments with 10 or more employees 4. Persons employed in the establishment under contract, including part-time workers; excluding home-workers	3-yearly, since 1966	1. Single stage sampling, establishments classified according to industry group, size class and region 2. INSEE Register of establishments 3. Establishment 4. 1975: 18% of establishments covered	Questionnaire survey	Calendar year	Labour cost statistics are updated twice a year, between survey years, using current earnings statistics and an estimate of trends in other wage cost elements	Per hour worked	*Economie et statistique* Institut National de la Statistique et des Études Économiques (INSEE)
GERMANY (FED. REP. OF) 1. Erhebung über die Arbeitskosten, produzierendes	1. Mining and quarrying; manufacturing;	3-yearly, since 1966	1. Single stage sampling, enterprises	Questionnaire survey	Calendar year or financial year	Labour cost statistics are updated twice a year, between survey	Per hour worked	*Labour costs* Statistical Office of the European

Survey / Organization	Coverage	Method	Reference period	Survey method	Per	Publication
2. Gewerbe / Statistisches Bundesamt	electricity, gas and water; construction; wholesale and retail trade; banking and insurance 2. Whole country 3. Enterprises with 10 or more employees 4. Persons employed in the establishment, including part-time workers; excluding homeworkers	classified according to industry group and size class 2. Census of places of work 3. Enterprise 4. 1975: 11% of enterprises covered			years, using current earnings statistics and an estimate of trends in other wage elements	Communities
HONG KONG 1. Survey of Industrial Production 2. Census and Statistics Department	1. Mining and quarrying; manufacturing; electricity, gas and water (including government industrial undertakings) 2. Whole territory 3. All sizes of establishments 4. Paid employees	1. Single stage sampling, establishments classified according to industry group and size class 2. Register of Manufacturing Establishments, maintained by the Census and Statistics Department 3. Establishment 4. 1978: 37.5% of establishments covered	Calendar year, or financial year ending between 31 December and 31 March	Mailed questionnaire survey, with field officers providing assistance	Per year	Hong Kong Monthly Digest of Statistics Census and Statistics Department
INDIA 1. Annual Survey of Industries 2. Labour Bureau, Ministry of Labour	1. Manufacturing; electricity supply covered under the 'Factories Act' 2. Whole country 3. Establishments with 10 or more workers on any day during the preceding 12 months, or with 20 or more workers, where the manufacturing	1. Probability sample 2. List of factories furnished by the Chief Inspector of Factories 3. Factory 4.	Accounting year ending between 1 April and 31 March	Questionnaire survey	Per man-day worked	Labour Statistics under the Annual Survey of Industries Labour Bureau, Ministry of Labour

(Annual — frequency, India)

Country: 1. Title of source 2. Organisation responsible	Coverage of survey: 1. Industrial 2. Geographic 3. Establishment or enterprise 4. Employee	Periodicity of survey	Sampling: 1. Sample design 2. Sampling frame 3. Sampling unit 4. Sample size	Method of data collection	Reference period for collection of data on labour cost	Estimation procedures	Time unit according to which data are published	Principal publication in which statistics appear
1	2	3	4	5	6	7	8	9
INDIA	process is not carried on with the aid of power 4. All employees engaged in work connected directly or indirectly with the manufacturing process, excluding sales, publicity or transport staff							
INDONESIA 1. Annual Industrial Survey 2. Central Bureau of Statistics	1. Manufacturing 2. Whole country 3. Establishments with 20 or more persons engaged 4. Employees	Annual	1. Complete enumeration 2. 3. Establishment 4.	For regions where establishments are concentrated; field interviews; for other regions; mailed questionnaires	Financial year ending in March		Per year	*Statistical Yearbook of Indonesia* Central Bureau of Statistics
IRELAND 1. Labour costs survey – industrial establishments 2. Central Statistical Office	1. Mining and quarrying; manufacturing; electricity, gas and water; construction; wholesale and retail trade; banking and insurance 2. Whole country 3. Establishments with 10 or more employees 4. Employees paid a definite wage or salary, or with a contract of employment, excluding outside piece-workers	3-yearly since 1975	1. Single stage sampling, establishments classified according to industry group and size class 2. 3. Establishment 4.	Mailed questionnaire survey	Calendar year or closest accounting year	Labour cost series are updated twice a year between survey years, using current earnings statistics and an estimate of trends in other wage cost elements	Per hour worked	*Labour Costs* Statistical Office of the European Communities

ISRAEL

1. Industry and Crafts Survey	
2. Central Bureau of Statistics	

Coverage:
1. Mining and quarrying; manufacturing
2. Whole country
3. All establishments with 5 employed persons or more on average
4. All workers appearing on payrolls for employees and members of co-operative societies

Frequency: Quarterly (with reference to four representative months each year)

Method/Unit:
1. Sample survey
2.
3. Establishment
4.

Reference period: Budget year

Pay period: Per day

Publication: *Statistical Abstract of Israel*, Central Bureau of Statistics

ITALY

1. Indagine sul costo della manodopera nell'industria, nel commercio, nelle branche e nelle assicurazioni	
2. Ministero del Lavoro e della Previdenza Sociale	

Coverage:
1. Mining and quarrying; manufacturing; electricity gas and water; construction; wholesale and retail trade; banking and insurance
2. Whole country
3. Establishments 10 or more employees
4. Persons employed in the establishment under contract

Frequency: 3-yearly since 1966

Method/Unit:
1. Census
2.
3. Establishment
4. 1975: 45,000 establishments

Survey method: Mailed questionnaire survey

Reference period: Calendar year

Labour cost series are updated twice a year for years between surveys, using current earnings statistics and estimates of trends in other wage cost elements

Pay period: Per hour worked

Publication: *Labour costs*, Statistical Office of the European Communities

JAPAN

1. Survey on the system of welfare facilities for employees	
2. Labour Standards Administration	

Coverage:
1. Mining; manufacturing; electricity, gas and water; construction; wholesale and retail trade; transport and communication; finance and insurance; real estate; services

Frequency: Annual

Method/Unit:
1.
2.
3. Establishment
4.

Survey method: Field interviews by members of staff of each prefectural Labour Standards Bureau, Labour Standards Inspections offices and enumerators

Reference period: Calendar Year

Pay period: Per month

Publication: *Year Book of Labour Statistics*, Statistics and Information Department, Minister's Secretariat, Ministry of Labour

Country: 1. Title of source 2. Organisation responsible	Coverage of survey: 1. Industrial 2. Geographic 3. Establishment or enterprise 4. Employee	Periodicity of survey	Sampling: 1. Sample design 2. Sampling frame 3. Sampling unit 4. Sample size	Method of data collection	Reference period for collection of data on labour cost	Estimation procedures	Time unit according to which data are published	Principal publication in which statistics appear
1	2	3	4	5	6	7	8	9
JAPAN	2. Whole country 3. Private sector establishments or enterprises with 30 or more regular employees 4. Employees employed indefinitely or under a contract for a period of one month, in general							
KENYA 1. Survey of industrial production 2. Central Bureau of Statistics	1. Mining and quarrying; manufacturing and repairs; building and construction 2. Whole country 3. Firms with 50 or more persons employed 4. Persons engaged	Annual since 1963	1. Complete enumeration 2. 3. Firm 4.	Mailed questionnaire survey	Calendar year or accounting year ending between 1 April and 31 March		Per year	*Statistical Abstract* Central Bureau of Statistics
LUXEMBOURG 1. Enquête sur les salaires (coût de la main-d'oeuvre dans l'industrie) 2. Service Central de la Statistique et des Études Économiques	1. Mining and quarrying; manufacturing; electricity, gas and water; construction; wholesale and retail trade; banking and insurance 2. Whole country 3. Establishments with 10 or more employees	3-yearly since 1966	1. Census 2. 3. Establishment 4. 1975: 350 establishments	Questionnaire survey	Calendar year	Labour cost series are updated twice a year for years between surveys; using current earnings statistics and estimates of trends in other wage cost elements	Per hour worked	*Labour Costs* Statistical Office of the European Communities

	Periodicity	Scope	Method	Reference period	Notes	Measurement	Publication
MADAGASCAR 1. Recensement industriel 2. Institut National de la Statistique et de la Recherche Économique	Annual	1. Mining and quarrying; manufacturing; electricity and water 2. Whole country 3. In general, establishments employing at least 5 persons 4. Paid employees	1. Complete enumeration 2. List of establishments maintained by the Institut National de la Statistique et de la Recherche Économique 3. Establishment 4.	Calendar year or accounting year		Per hour worked	*Recensement Industriel* Institut National de la Statistique et de la Recherche Économique
MAURITIUS 1. Census of industrial production 2. Central Statistical Office	Annual	1. Mining and quarrying; manufacturing electricity 2. Whole territory 3. Establishments with 10 or more employees, excluding government and semi-government establishments 4. Paid employees	1. Complete enumeration 2. 3. Establishment 4.	Calendar year, in general		Per year	*The Census of Industrial Production* Central Statistical Office
MEXICO 1. Annual industrial survey 2. Secretaria de Programación y Presupuesto. Coordinación General de los Servicios Nacionales de Estadística, Geografía e informática	Annual	1. Selected manufacturing industries (varies from year to year) 2. Whole country 3. 4. Paid employees	1. Single stage sampling; establishments classified according to industry group and size class 2. Central Bureau of Statistics Register of Establishments	Per year			*Estadística industrial Anual* Secretaria de Programación y Presupuesto, Coordinación General de Estadística, Geografía e Informática
NETHERLANDS 1. Loonkostenonderzoek nijverheid, handel, banken en verzekeringsmaatschappijen 2. Centraal Bureau voor de Statistiek	3-yearly since 1966	1. Mining and quarrying; manufacturing; electricity, gas and water; construction; wholesale and retail trades; banking and insurance	Questionnaire survey	Calendar year or nearest financial year	Labour cost series are updated twice a year between survey years, using current earnings statistics and estimated trends in other wage cost elements	Per hour worked	*Sociale maandstatistiek* Centraal Bureau voor de Statistiek

Country: 1. Title of source 2. Organisation responsible	Coverage of survey: 1. Industrial 2. Geographic 3. Establishment or enterprise 4. Employee	Periodicity of survey	Sampling: 1. Sample design 2. Sampling frame 3. Sampling unit 4. Sample size	Method of data collection	Reference period for collection of data on labour cost	Estimation procedures	Time unit according to which data are published	Principal publication in which statistics appear
1	2	3	4	5	6	7	8	9
NETHERLANDS	2. Whole country 3. *Bedrijven* with 10 or more employees 4. Persons employed in *bedrijf* under contract, including part-time workers, excluding home-workers		3. *Bedrijf* 4. 1975: 27% of *bedrijven* and 69% of employees					
NORWAY 1. Annual industrial statistics inquiry 2. Statistisk Sentralbyrå	1. Mining and quarrying; manufacturing 2. Whole country 3. Establishments with 5 persons or more engaged on average each year 4. All persons working in the establishment, excluding homeworkers and persons on military leave	Annual, since 1961	1. Complete enumeration 2. Central Bureau of Statistics Register of Establishments and Enterprises, updated from Census of Entrepreneurs liable to Value Added Tax 3. Establishments 4.		Calendar year		Per year	*Industristatistikk* (Industrial Statistics) Statistisk Sentralbyrå
PANAMA 1. Encuesta de la Industria Manufacturera 2. Dirección de Estadística y Censo	1. Manufacturing 2. Whole country 3. Establishments with 5 or more persons engaged 4. Employees receiving regular wages and salaries or commissions, excluding home-workers	Annual		Field interviews by enumerators	Calendar year		Per year	*Estadística Panameña: Situación Económica Industria (Encuesta)* Dirección de Estadística y Censo

Survey / Organisation	Coverage	Periodicity	Method / Sampling	Reference period	Per unit	Publication
PHILIPPINES 1. Annual Survey of Manufactures 2. National Census and Statistics Office	1. Manufacturing 2. Whole country 3. Establishments with average total employment of 5 or more workers 4. Paid employees	Annual since 1956	1. Sample survey of establishments with 5-19 workers, complete enumeration of those with 20 or more workers 2. 3. Establishment 4.	Calendar year	Per year	*Annual Survey of Manufactures* National Census and Statistics Office
SINGAPORE 1. Census of industrial production 2. Department of Statistics	1. Granite quarrying; manufacturing; electricity and gas 2. Whole country 3. Establishments with 10 or more workers engaged 4. Paid employees	Annual, since 1959	1. Complete enumeration 2. 3. Establishment 4. 3,391 establishments (out of 3,753) in 1981 — Mailed questionnaire survey, with follow-up where necessary by telephone, personal visit or correspondence	Calendar year or financial year ending on or before 31 March	Per year	*Report on the Census of Industrial Production* Department of Statistics
SWEDEN 1. Labour cost index for workers in mining and manufacturing 2. Statistika Centralbyrån	1. Mining and quarrying; manufacturing 2. Whole country 3. 4. Wage earners	Quarterly			Labour cost series are estimated using current earnings statistics and an estimate of trends in other wage cost elements — Per hour	*Statistika Meddelanden* Statistika Centralbyrån
UNITED KINGDOM 1. Survey of labour costs 2. Department of Employment	1. Mining and quarrying; manufacturing; electricity, gas and water; construction; wholesale and retail trades; banking and insurance 2. Great Britain 3. Establishments with 10 or more employees 4. Full-time and part-time employees on payroll, excluding home-workers	3-yearly since 1975 (1st survey in 1973)	1. Single stage sample; establishments classified according to industry group and size class 2. Register of enterprises 3. Establishment 4. — Mailed questionnaire survey	Calendar year or accounting year ending between 6 April and 5 April	Labour cost series are updated once a year for years between surveys, using current earnings statistics and an estimate of trends in other wage cost elements — Per hour worked	*Employment Gazette* Department of Employment

Country: 1. Title of source 2. Organisation responsible	Coverage of survey: 1. Industrial 2. Geographic 3. Establishment or enterprise 4. Employee	Periodicity of survey	Sampling: 1. Sample design 2. Sampling frame 3. Sampling unit 4. Sample size	Method of data collection	Reference period for collection of data on labour cost	Estimation procedures	Time unit according to which data are published	Principal publication in which statistics appear
1	2	3	4	5	6	7	8	9
UNITED STATES 1. Hourly compensation costs 2. Bureau of Labor Statistics, US Department of Labor	1. Manufacturing 2. Whole country 3. 4. Production and related workers	Annual estimations				Compensation is estimated by adjusting average hourly earnings series for items of direct pay not included in earnings and for employer expenditures for social security, contractual and private insurance programmes and other labour taxes	Per hour paid for	Not published
ZIMBABWE 1. Census of production 2. Central Statistical Office	1. Mining; manufacturing; electricity and water supply; construction 2. Whole country 3. Establishments with gross output of $2,000 or more 4. All persons on payrolls, whether full-time or part-time	Annual, since 1966	1. Complete enumeration 2. 3. Establishment 4.	Mailed questionnaire survey, with assistance when required from field staff	12 months, generally ending on 31 March		Per year	*The Census of Industrial Production* Central Statistical Office

21 Labour productivity

R. Turvey

Introduction

In June 1985, the International Labour Conference approved Labour-Statistics Convention no. 160 and Recommendation no. 170, these jointly updating Convention no. 63, concerning statistics of wages and hours of work (1938). The new Convention does not mention productivity statistics, but paragraph 15 of the Recommendation states that: 'Statistics of productivity should be progressively developed and compiled covering important branches of economic activity.'

There are no formal recommendations on this subject, nor will any be developed in the next few years. Hence this paper has been written to provide a brief survey of concepts, definitions and methodologies in this field and to furnish a short account of the productivity statistics published in a selected number of countries.

Labour productivity measurement requires the measurement of both output and labour input.[1] If this is done for the economy as a whole, it falls within the sphere of national income accounting rather than labour statistics. If, at the other extreme, it is done for inter-firm comparisons, it requires data which are confidential and, in any case, belongs to management consultancy rather than to labour statistics.[2] Here we shall consider productivity measurement between these two extremes, that is to say for branches, sectors or industries.

Labour productivity thus conceived is not the same as efficiency or effectiveness, though, when properly understood, it can help to judge these things, provided that other information is brought into the picture. There are two reasons why it is different from efficiency or effectiveness. The first (which multi-factor productivity measures seek to allow for) is that most production uses other resources besides labour. The second is that labour productivity is a matter of the amount of output, not of its usefulness. Thus if an unchanged labour force produces more than previously but nobody wants its output, labour productivity has risen but economic efficiency has not.

Both the measurement of labour input and the measurement of output for branches, sectors or industries are extremely large topics, encompassing a major part of labour statistics and a major part of economic statistics, respectively. This report cannot possibly survey the whole of these two topics; instead it concentrates on the more limited set of problems involved in relating the two of them in order to measure labour productivity.[3]

Labour productivity has not figured in the work of the Bureau of Statistics for a long time. However, in 1969 the ILO published (in French as well as English) a book entitled *Measuring Labour Productivity*. This reviewed methods of calculation, provided a comparative analysis of national labour productivity statistics, examined problems of international comparability and, in the appendices, gave an account of national statistical series concerned with labour productivity.

On the methodological front, there have been two major developments since the 1969 publication, but neither is relevant in the present context. One is in the field of multi-factor productivity indices and the econometric estimation of production functions. These relate output to an estimate of the capital stock (and sometimes other inputs, too) as well as to labour. Since they require reliable estimates of capital stocks, they have been estimated only in very few countries, at least as regards branch or sectoral calculations. Calculations at the GNP level for the economy as a whole are more common, especially in academic research, but fall outside labour statistics. The other is the International Comparison Project,[4] which makes international comparisons of GDP in a way which is independent of exchange rates. The components of the calculation are expenditure categories (e.g. consumer purchase of durable goods), not output categories as is necessary for productivity statistics for branches or sectors.

Relevant methodological development has thus been limited. In any case, it is not methodological problems which constrain the computation of productivity statistics. Today, as in 1969, it is the nature, availability and comparability of output data and of labour input data that primarily determine what can be calculated and published. Hence this paper relates primarily to data problems, though it first catalogues the main alternative methods, which remain what they were in the 1960s.

Alternative measures of labour productivity

The chief ways in which productivity can be measured are shown in Figure 21.1. Since it shows 11 methods for output and 4 for labour input, it can be seen that there are 44 possible major productivity measures. In practice, the choice of measure that is made depends upon what data are available much more than upon grounds of principle, where the answer selected would depend upon the question that is asked. However data quality as well as data availability should be considered in determining which productivity measure is used and how it is calculated. The sensible choice

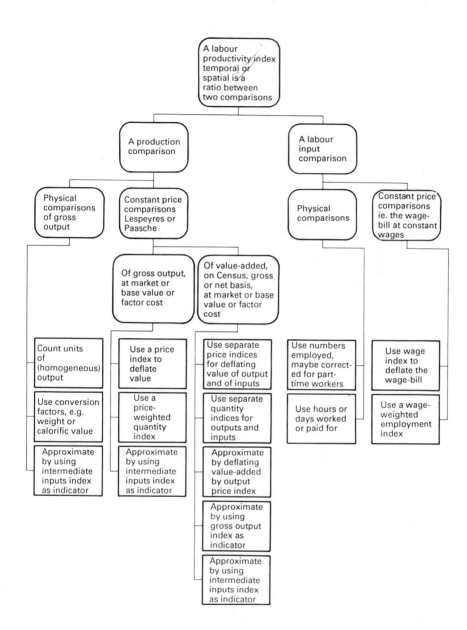

Figure 21.1 Measurement of productivity may vary not only between countries or data sources but even, for a given set of data sources, between industries.

Combining sub-indices: Composition effects

When production and labour input in each of a group of industries are measured in the same way and when production is additive, as with value-added, then, since labour input is additive, an aggregate productivity index for the whole group can be calculated. But this will reflect both changes in productivity in the component industries and changes in the relative importance of the industries composing the group, i.e. 'composition effects'. To exclude these, one can take a weighted mean of the productivity indices for each of the industries. The weights can be production or labour inputs. In the first case, the overall index compares what current total production would be if labour input of each industry had remained at the base-period level, with total base-period production. In the second case, the overall index compares what current total labour input would be if productivity in each industry had remained at the base period level, with total base-period labour input.

While these procedures are possible for separate industries, each with its own productivity index, they are not usually possible when calculating the separate productivity index for each industry, since this would require a breakdown of labour input according to the products produced. Thus composition effects are usually unavoidable at the level of the single industry.

Some problems of productivity measurement

Double deflation

By 'double deflation' is meant the calculation of a time series of value-added at constant prices as the difference between gross output at constant prices and the value of intermediate inputs at constant prices. (Sometimes the latter may cover only intermediate inputs of goods, neglecting intermediate inputs of services.) If depreciation at constant prices is also deducted the result is 'net' value-added, but the phrase 'net output' is also used to mean gross output net of intermediate inputs, i.e. value-added.

The literature devotes considerable attention to the theoretical possibility that double deflation can produce a negative figure for value-added, but this does not seem to arise in practice. The practical problems of double deflation arise from data quality issues, in a way that can be briefly explained as follows. If L is the ratio of gross output to value-added, a value-added-output index, V, is a weighted sum of a gross output index, O, whose weight, L, exceeds unity and an input index I with a correspondingly negative weight of $-(L-1)$, i.e. $V = OL - (L-1)I$. It follows that the difference between V and O is equal to $(L-1)(O-I)$. This difference is likely to be larger, the larger is L, i.e. the smaller is the share of value-added in gross output.

The variance in the index of value-added at constant prices is the sum of

L^2 times the variance of the output index O and $(L - 1)^2$ times the variance of the input index I.[5] It follows that using the output index alone or the input index alone as an indicator of value-added at constant prices may be preferable to double deflation. Alternatively, gross output productivity may be explicitly chosen instead of value-added productivity in order to have a reliable measure.

Imputation and surrogate measures

Outputs measured by input

When outputs cannot be measured, either because there are no physical data or because no price index for deflating the value of output is available, statisticans frequently resort to using some input measure as a surrogate for output. For non-market production, this is frequently done by using labour input as the surrogate, which by definition gives the result, useless in the present context, that productivity growth is zero. Occasionally the assumption that productivity grows at a certain assumed annual rate is applied. Anyone wishing to calculate productivity indices obviously has to beware of such cases.

Alternatively, the input of one or more intermediate goods may be used. For example, construction output may be proxied by the amount of bricks and cement used. If there is reason to believe that this is a good index of output, then productivity can be calculated.

Finally, there is the device of deflating the value of output by an earnings index in the case of labour-intensive market services for which no price index exists. Since the earnings index is the ratio of an index of the wage-bill to one of employment, and since the index of deflated output is divided by an employment index to obtain the productivity index, the employment index occurs in both numerator and denominator. So this procedure yields a productivity index which is the ratio of a value of output index to the wage-bill index. It will rise not only because of higher productivity but also because of any increase in the price/wage ratio.

Imputing hours of non-manual or salaried workers

Most establishment surveys which obtain data about either hours worked or hours paid do so only for manual workers or only for wage-earners. No establishment surveys obtain such data in respect of self-employed and unpaid family workers. Hence productivity measures which relate to output per hour for all workers require a good deal of imputation of hours for those workers not covered by the surveys. The most usual device is to assume that the number of hours per head for the non-measured group is the same as the corresponding number of hours for the measured group. Alternatively, some data may be obtainable from household surveys, though this involves a number of problems in ensuring that hours reported in such surveys correspond to data reported by employing establishments. In either case, error is possible.

Special problems of gross output indices

Changes in the extent of vertical integration can create problems in the interpretation of productivity indices which reflect gross output. If, for example, certain services which an enterprise performed for itself are now contracted out, with a reduction in the labour force, productivity will appear to have risen. But even when there are insufficient data to calculate a value-added measure of productivity, it may be possible to detect changes in integration or specialisation, either by examining figures for the cost of intermediate inputs as a percentage of the value of gross output or by direct information obtained from enterprises. Where there appear to be large changes, it is best to conclude that reliable productivity indices cannot be calculated, unless the industry definition can be adjusted to internalise such organisational changes.

Services

General poor coverage of market services

Output measurement difficulties Where sales or expenditure data and a price index are both available, as in retailing, output estimates can be reasonably well based. But for financial and business services, one or other of these conditions is not met and other output indicators are difficult to obtain. Quality adjustments for services are also more difficult than for goods.[6]

Employment measurement difficulties Full-time employees can be usually counted because of the administrative needs of tax and social security administration, but the existence of part-time workers and the self-employed is more difficult to ascertain or check. In many countries, much of the recent expansion in employment in the service trades has consisted of part-time workers. If, as often is the case, hours of work cannot be estimated, some correction should be made to employment figures in order to allow for the shorter hours of work of the part-timers. Counting two part-timers as one full-time equivalent is better than making no adjustment, though data for some sectors or for particular years may allow estimation of a better correction factor than this.

Finally, there is a most important point which applies as much to the measurement of output as to that of labour input. This is the fact that in many service industries small firms predominate, with new ones appearing frequently and old ones disappearing. This makes it extremely difficult to construct and maintain a good register of such firms. Hence their output and employment alike are poorly measured.

Poor coverage of non-market output

Productivity is easy to measure when outputs are easy to measure and to aggregate. One of the factors ensuring this is that outputs are sold and have market values. Changes in them can then be measured either by deflating current value by a price index or by revaluing current output at base-period prices. Where there is no market, such measures are not possible. In most countries' national accounts, the output of public sector services is measured in terms of the value of the inputs used to produce them, so that zero productivity growth is implicitly assumed. Yet it is just where there is absence of a market and where there is no check exercised by competition upon inefficiency that productivity and other measures would be particularly useful. Thus the computation of productivity statistics for those operations of government which are common to the market and to the planned economies is a matter of world-wide interest.

One general point worth noting is that it is easier, or at any rate less difficult, to measure final government outputs than to measure intermediate ones. Thus schools' output of graduates and dropouts is easier to measure than an educational administration's output of personnel management. A partial remedy is to calculate a sectoral productivity for teachers, other school staff and administrators added together. However, this leaves open the problem of measuring the performance of groups more narrowly defined.

A recent publication relating to the United Kingdom[7] provides a conveniently up-to-date survey of the problem in one country by way of example. It makes it clear that labour productivity is not necessarily the only or even the most useful performance indicator. Thus government departments with large executive functions have many offices which can be said to have a caseload of people or paperwork to deal with and where valid output measures may be 'payments made' or 'documents dispatched'. Output per worker, if the output is not too heterogeneous, can be calculated, and unit costs, average time taken, accuracy and customer satisfaction are also useful measures of performance.

This conclusion is no doubt valid in most countries. But the case studies presented for the UK suggest that although there is an internationally common need for such indicators, there may be considerable difficulties in the way of any attempt to establish any internationally common methodologies of a general statistical sort, and even greater problems in making international comparisons. The studies show that the development of the indicators used required a detailed study of the operations in question. In other words, the construction of indicators for, say, British or French hospitals demands detailed practical understanding of the functioning of the hospitals in question. Comparisons between hospitals in the two countries would require this kind of detailed understanding of both. Specialists who have the requisite competence would have to be consulted, and the way they made the comparison might be inapplicable to, say, a comparison of productivity in Indian and Thai hospitals.[8]

Thus, despite the obvious interest of such work, it has to be recognised that, with limited resources, any studies conducted by the ILO would have to be limited, at least initially, to only one or two types of government activity in a limited group of countries. However successful the results, it might turn out that they could not be generalised to provide methodological recommendations of the type formulated by the International Conference of

Labour Statisticians.

Consistency between Labour and output measures

Care has to be taken that the two sets of data are consistent with one another in a number of respects. Problems are least likely to arise when they both come from a single source. Frequently, however, calculations of productivity divide an output index, which may be a value series deflated by a price index (or two of them in the case of double deflation), by a labour input index, which may be constructed by multiplying total employment by average hours. Thus quite a number of sources may be used. The simplicity of the operation of dividing the one index by the other makes it easy to overlook the need to examine their consistency. The following headings, which are not exhaustive, point to some of the possible problems of inconsistency.

The composition of labour input

There is an obvious asymmetry between measuring output at constant prices or combining physical output measures by using value weights, on the one hand, and counting labour input in the physical terms of heads or hours, on the other. However, this is what is done in all the productivity indices published by governments which are reviewed later on in this paper. It can be said to assume that all labour is equally productive, or at least that the relative proportions of different types of labour input do not change much. The obvious remedy is to treat input and output symmetrically.

If output is measured by deflating the value of output at current prices, then symmetry would involve measuring labour input as labour cost or total compensation deflated by a labour cost or compensation index to obtain what may be called 'the wage bill at constant wages'. This is a much less familiar concept than the value of output at constant prices, but would entail analogous problems of imputation and index computation.[9]

There is also the possibility of measuring output as a value-weighted sum of physical output indices. The symmetric procedure with respect to labour input is to measure it as a value-weighted sum. An approach much favoured by some US researchers is to break down the number of workers or, preferably, the number of hours paid or worked, by variables which are considered casually relevant to productivity, such as years of education and length of work experience, and to weight each unit of type of labour thus distinguished by the estimated base-period wage or earnings returns to these variables. The estimates endeavour to adjust for other factors which affect earnings and thus pose econometric problems and require extensive data. The approach is founded upon the economic theory of human capital. An alternative and more pragmatic approach is to compute a value-weighted summation over those groupings of workers defined with respect to occupation (and maybe other variables) for which mean earnings in the base period are available, thus estimating the wage bill at constant wages.

Both approaches have been criticised on the grounds that wages or labour cost as observed on the labour market may constitute a poor measure of relative productivity. The critics overlook the fact that exactly the same problems exist in measuring output in constant price terms; the only difference is that people are used to the latter. In both cases, the point is not that prices/wages provide perfect weights, it is simply that they are better than assuming that equal weights of output are of equivalent value and that all workers are equally productive!

Scope, classification and coverage

It is well known that data on employment classified by industry obtained from household labour force surveys can differ from employment data obtained from establishment surveys. Less obviously, different establishment surveys of the same industry may not cover exactly the same group of establishments, especially when they are based on different establishment registers. Hence the industrial coverage used for output may not match that used for labour input.

Absences reflected in output but not employment data

Some measures of employment count workers who are locked out or on strike as employed. Strikes will then lower the index of productivity. Similar problems may arise with respect to absence from work caused by illness or bad weather.

Timing and reference period

Employment and hours data may be obtained for a point of time or for a period shorter than that for which production and sales data are obtained. What is more, the length of this latter period may be variable, as when the number of working days varies from month to month.

Variation in the number of working days can be dealt with by simple adjustments, but the main problem remains – that employment and/or hours as measured for a single week may diverge from their average values over the period for which output is ascertained. There is a similar problem when the prices obtained for constructing a deflator relate to only part of the period covered by the value that is deflated. Thus extra care is needed in times of rapid change.

An example of one way in which the problems of strikes and of differences in reference periods can be dealt with is provided by Statistics Canada, where annual output data and monthly labour input data relating to a reference period of one week in the month are combined to compute annual productivity indices.[10]

Monthly data from the Labour Force Survey refer only to the survey week. The survey week can be taken as representative of other weeks in the month except for the non-random events of holidays and strikes. The procedure is first to adjust the survey weeks for the effects of strikes and holidays falling in that week.

This yields a nominal value of the hours worked in that week if there were no strikes or holidays. The survey generates the data necessary to make these corrections. Corresponding nominal values for non-survey weeks are estimated by interpolation. These nominal values for each week of the year are then adjusted by the known impact of strikes and/or holidays on that week. The necessary data on strikes are tabulated by Labour Canada. Only the paid workers series is adjusted for strikes. The holiday adjustment is based on statutory holidays and studies of employment practices in industries. Average annual hours worked per week is calculated as the average of the weekly values adjusted for strikes and holidays. The number of hours worked per year is simply the weekly average multiplied by the number of weeks in the year. The number of weeks in the year is not taken as constant, but reflects the vagaries of the calendar. A calendar year encompasses 52 complete weeks plus one, or in leap years, two extra days. If these extra day(s) fall on a normal day of rest, the year is considered to have 52 weeks even. If not, the number of weeks is greater. There can be a slight variation in the year-to-year change in hours worked on this account.

Industry versus commodity classification

When output data relate to commodities X and Y, rather than to industries X and Y, the following problem may arise. Establishments are normally classified to industries according to the most important commodity or commodities which they produce. But the establishments composing the X industry may also produce some Y, and the establishments composing the Y industry, and other industries, too, may also produce some X. Hence relating the total production of X to the labour input of industry X may include some production not produced by the labour force of X and some labour not engaged in the production of X. This may happen when the production and employment data come from different sources. If this can be avoided, it should be possible to relate the whole output of industry X to its labour input, including non-X production in its production measure. Sometimes, however, such correction may not be feasible, in which case it is necessary to judge whether the resulting distortion is big enough to invalidate the productivity computation. When the share of non-X output is fairly constant, the distortion may be small.

Statistics available in selected countries

United States

US government productivity statistics fall into four groups. The first three are the responsibility of the Bureau of Labor Statistics, the fourth is the province of the Department of Agriculture. There is a continuing effort to extend coverage and to improve methods, so that some published descriptions may be out of date.[11]

Major sectors

Quarterly productivity indices for 'Business', 'Non-farm business' and 'Non-financial corporations', and for 'Manufacturing' (and, within it, for 'Durable' and 'Non-durable goods') are published, together with related indices for output, hours, compensation per hour and unit labour costs.[12] The business sector accounts for some 78 per cent of GNP. The main exclusions are government output and the outputs of non-profit organisations, which are measured in terms of labour inputs, and the imputed value of the services of owner-occupied dwellings, an output for which a corresponding measure of labour input is not feasible. The productivity indices related to value-added, i.e. contribution to Gross National Product, per hour.

The double deflation method is used for as many of the component outputs as possible, e.g. in farming and manufacturing. For construction, mining and some service industries, net output in a base year is extrapolated by using indices of gross output, while for a few services it is necessary to extrapolate it by using a measure of inputs at constant prices, mainly labour inputs. The price indices used for deflation come from components of the Consumer Price Index and the Producer Price Index. There are hundreds of component gross output series, most of them, in the case of goods, relating to shipments which are corrected for stock changes. Even where double deflation is possible, the number of intermediate input series is smaller than the number of output series.

The labour input measures are based mainly on Current Population Survey and establishment survey data. For sectors where the weekly hours of work of supervisory employees are not surveyed, they are assumed to equal those of non-supervisory employees. The weekly hours are multiplied by 52, the data relating to hours paid.

Multi-factor productivity measures are also produced for the same sector.[13]

Industries

Annual indices of gross output per employee and per employee-hour, in most cases for production workers and non-production workers separately, as well as for all employees, are published for about 150 industries.[14] Unpublished indices are calculated at a lower level of aggregation for a much larger number of industries and work has been undertaken on selected service industries.

Physical quantity data are used for most manufacturing and mining industries, especially for quinquennial bench-mark estimates for years when detailed census data are available. Otherwise, deflated sales or shipment data are used. The detailed data are combined using unit-value weights up to the level of aggregation where unit employee-hour weights can be applied. These labour weights are used to the maximum possible extent in order to exclude composition effects.

The employee-hours measure relates in some cases to hours paid and in other cases to hours worked. For trade and service industries, the hours of self-employed and unpaid family workers are included.

Government

There is a very extensive programme of work on government productivity. Annual indices of output per employee year are developed annually for various functional levels within federal,[15] state and local government. Indices for individual agencies are not published, but are sent to them for their own use. The list of output measures is enormous; they include such diverse items as studies completed, trade marks disposed, weather observations made, persons interviewed, square feet cleaned. Labour input weights are used for combining the measures. For the federal government, some two-thirds of employees are covered.

Agriculture

The US Department of Agriculture publishes labour productivity (and multi-factor) productivity data for agriculture.

USSR

For manufacturing industry, output is the value of final output for sale valued at the prices set on 1 January 1982. Labour input is the average number of production staff over the period. It is calculated using daily employment data. Hence the productivity measure is gross output at constant prices per work day. Since 1987, net production (output minus material outlays) rather than gross has been increasingly used in calculating productivity at the enterprise level. For building and repair work, the volume of work carried out by building organisations is calculated at estimated project prices.

Productivity in agriculture, aggregatively and for crop and stock farming, is calculated as gross agricultural yield (harvest plus change in the value of standing crops) at constant 1983 prices per average annual agricultural worker and per hour worked.

In addition, physical productivity measures are calculated in many fields, for example: coal output per miner, cubic metres of timber and logs sold per worker, thousands of tonne kilometres per railway worker, etc.

Federal Republic of Germany

The Federal Statistical Office is the main publisher of productivity statistics in the Federal Republic of Germany (FRG). One set forms part of the System of National Accounts[16] where annual data on value-added at constant prices are available for 57 industries and data on employment for 47, so that 47 productivity series can be calculated. (The 1985 revision will have raised the number of industries with employment data to 56.) The intermediate inputs deducted from gross output are: semi-manufactures, auxiliary materials, raw materials, fuels and other energy inputs, repairs, transport costs, postage, attorney's and other fees, and rental payments. Persons employed include self-employed and unpaid family workers; no adjustment is made for part-time work. Base years have been 1960, 1970, 1976 and 1980, and chained series are calculated. Thus when 1976 superseded 1970, the figures up through 1967 at 1970 prices were multiplied by the ratio of the 1968 figures at 1976 prices to their values at 1970 prices. With the change to 1980, 1980 prices will be applied to the data from 1975 onwards, earlier figures being rebased and chained.

The other set of FRG productivity figures is based on data from establishment survey data relating to mining and manufacturing plants with 20 or more employees.[17] Monthly indices are published for mining and four divisions within manufacturing. They relate to net output per person employed, per hour worked, per production worker and per production worker-hour worked. Corresponding annual figures are published for all 29 two-digit industries in mining and manufacturing and for 37 selected four-digit industries. The concept of net output is almost identical with that of value-added in the national accounts, but these indices in fact are calculated using gross output indices from 356 product groups combined with base year net output weights. As with the national accounts, base years have been 1970, 1976, and 1980.

United Kingdom

Annual and (seasonally adjusted) quarterly productivity indices are published in the *Monthly Digest of Statistics* for the whole economy, for what are called 'total production industries', namely energy and water supply, manufacturing and construction, for manufacturing and for construction separately and for seven subgroups constituting manufacturing. Figures for a more detailed breakdown are not published but may be made available. In addition, a monthly index is published for manufacturing alone. These indices are all derived by dividing gross output indices by estimates of the employed labour force, no adjustment being made for changes in hours worked except, with regard to full-time workers only, in one quarterly series of output per hour in manufacturing which is additional to those just listed. Finally, the Ministry of Agriculture, Fisheries and Food publishes an annual index of gross agricultural product at constant prices per whole-time man equivalent.

The production indices for the 'Production industries' are made up of 329 component series. Four per cent are based on gross output, 37 per cent on final production (adjusted for changes in the amount of work in progress) and 59 per cent on sales. The latter have to be adjusted for changes in stocks and work in progress. Current value data are deflated to 1980 values using the appropriate producer prices indices and the series are combined into aggregates using 1980 Census of Production value-added weights. Where the basic data used refer to months, adjustment is made for the number of working days in the month in order to ensure comparability between months.

Bench-mark data for employees in employment are derived from the latest Census of Employment (based on a different register than that used for Censuses of Production) while bench-mark estimates for the self-employed are based on the latest Population Census and on the Labour Force Survey. Sample surveys of employers and the Labour Force Survey are used to carry forward the bench-mark estimates.

Canada

As part of its system of national accounts, Statistics Canada produces annual figures of output per person and output per man-hour (and of unit labour cost) for agriculture, manufacturing industry, other commercial goods producing industries (forestry, fishing, mining, construction, electricity and gas), and commercial service producing industries.[18] Non-commercial industries, public administration and defence are the main industries not covered. The output data are the estimates of GDP by industry at constant prices. They are thus value-added estimates.

Persons employed include paid and own-account workers, working employers and unpaid family workers. Man-hours worked exclude holidays, illness, etc., referring to man-hours spent at the place of work. Both Labour Force Survey and establishment survey data are used in the estimates.

Scandinavia

There are remarkably few statistics of labour productivity published by government statistical offices in Scandinavia. The only regular series, published with a two-year time-lag, appears to be annual indices at the four-digit level for Swedish manufacturing. Yet the Scandinavian countries have excellent statistics; Norway, Sweden and Finland produce fairly detailed figures of output or value-added at current prices per person engaged or hour worked in industry. These are extensively used in economic modelling, along with production functions, which means that there is no call for explicit productivity indices.

In Sweden, an Expert Group on public sector economics set up by the Ministry of Finance has recently published a pilot study on public sector productivity.[19] It provides independent output measures and hence productivity indices for various subsectors of the public sector in a national accounting framework.

China

Figures of gross output per person at constant prices have been published for the years from 1952.[20] They relate to state-owned units and are provided for 16 industries. Figures at 1980 prices for 1985 are also provided for a finer breakdown of industries. Similar data are separately shown for collectively owned units in townships.

These productivity series, expressed as yuan per person per year, are given both at 1980 prices for the whole period and, in another table, at 1952, 1957, 1970 and 1980 prices for sub-periods, with one-year overlaps. It is to be noted that, within each sub-period, the ratio of productivity at the constant prices used for that sub-period to productivity at 1980 prices is the same for each year to three decimal places. Had each year's output been independently revalued both at the prices used for that sub-period and at 1980 prices, this constancy would have occurred only in the absence of relative price changes. Thus the relationship between the two sets of series is not entirely clear.

Two tables of monthly productivity data are regularly published.[21] One provides figures of labour productivity (in yuan) per employed person in state owned industries which have independent accounting, distinguishing light and heavy industry. The other, which expresses productivity in physical terms, gives data for four industries: coal (stoping, tons per worker; tunnelling, metres per worker); metallurgy (iron-smelting, open-hearth steel and electric steel, all tons, per person); textiles (cotton yarn, workers per ton; cotton cloth, workers per 10,000 metres); and papermaking (tons per person). No description of sources and methods is currently available.

Special problems of cross-country comparisons

Comparing levels

There is a useful survey and extensive bibliography concerning international productivity comparisons by Irving Kravis.[22] Some methodological aspects of such comparisons are discussed in more detail in a study prepared for the Economic Commission for Europe by J. Kux.[23] Despite the time which has passed since then, there is, as already noted, little to add. So in view of the availability of these two excellent studies, the present discussion is limited to a brief description of some of the ways in which comparisons between countries at a point in time are more difficult to make than comparisons within a single country over a period of time.

A major difference is that whereas there is normally continuity in the definitions, classifications and collection methods used within a country, there may be considerable differences in them between countries. Within a country, there are problems of consistency between one temporal output and one temporal labour input index. Internationally, the problems of consistency in scope and coverage between two measures of output and two measures of labour input are much more difficult.[24] Enormous care is therefore necessary to secure comparability, and in many cases the data have to be adjusted to allow for differences. Obviously no complete list of all such problems can be given, but just two examples may usefully be given to illustrate them. One comes from a Czech–French comparison, where two offsetting differences for which it was not possible to adjust were assumed to cancel out. The first was that women on maternity leave were included in the French but not in the Czech labour input data; the second was that the French data included only those part-time workers who worked at least 20 hours a week, while the Czech data included all part-time workers, converted to a full-time basis. The other example comes from an Austrian–Hungarian comparison, where the Hungarian coverage of the sub-branches of the manufacture of scientific instruments had to be narrowed to match Austrian practice.

Next, there is the point that the composition of output, the quality of products and the division of labour can differ considerably between countries. Hence both physical output comparisons, output value comparisons and the price comparisons necessary for deflation of these output values are rendered difficult. Three examples will suffice. The output of aluminous earth is part of the production of non-ferrous basic metal industries in Hungary; there is no such output in Austria. The standard size of bricks and other clay products differs between countries, impeding comparisons both of physical outputs and of prices. Textile finishing may be subcontracted in one country and integrated with spinning and weaving in another.

For these two sets of reasons, the methods of productivity comparison used have to be chosen in the light of the particular data availability and the particular circumstances of each case, so that even within a single investigation, different methods may be used for different branches of industry or between different pairs of countries for the same branch. Because double deflation is particularly demanding, it has rarely been used. Discussion of the theoretical aspects of the different methods is of little relevance to the work that has been done. Furthermore, these international comparisons of productivity levels require an enormous amount of work. Those undertaken collaboratively by national statistical offices have involved contributions by several people from each country and have necessitated a number of visits between them.[25] Similarly, a study of six aggregative sectors (with a more detailed breakdown within manufacturing) in three countries necessitated a fairly large team effort.[26]

Comparing changes

Comparing changes in productivity between countries raises the same problems, though it is easier to overlook them and in a sense they matter less. The analyst making such comparisons by relating the movement of one country's productivity index to those of other countries should always enquire whether the definitions of output and labour input are comparable. Comparison using data obtained from all firms in one country and only from large firms in the other will not do. Again, a comparison of growth in productivity per employee with growth in productivity per hour can be acceptable only if hours worked per head have been changing in neither country.

An example of careful comparison is provided by the work of the US Bureau of Labor Statistics in producing annual series of output per employee-hour (along with hourly compensation and unit labour costs) for manufacturing in eleven industrial countries and for the iron and steel industry in five countries.[27]

Notes

1. When data on labour cost (or the part of it consisting of labour compensation), which are comparable with the labour input figures, are available, a unit labour cost index as well as a productivity index can be calculated. It shows changes in the ratio of the labour cost (or compensation) index to the output index. This comes to the same thing as change in the ratio of the index of labour cost (or compensation) to the productivity index. This paper does not examine unit labour cost indices, but the work could be extended to include these statistics.

2. See Joseph Prokopenko, *Productivity Management: A Practical Handbook* (ILO, Geneva 1987).

3. The measurement of output in constant price terms is the subject of the excellent *Manual on National Accounts at Constant Prices* (United Nations Statistical Papers M.64, New York, 1979) for which T. P. Hill was mainly responsible. See also his OECD publication cited in note 5.

4. For a useful summary, see Irving B. Kravis, 'Comparative studies of national incomes and prices', *Journal of Economic Literature*, vol. XXII, March 1984, pp. 1–39.

5. For more details on the subject of this paragraph, see T. P. Hill, *The Measurement of Real Product* (OECD Economic Studies series, 1971), pp. 19ff.

6. A useful survey of methods used to estimate real value added for market services in the national accounts of a number of countries is contained in an annex to *Measurement of Value Added at Constant Prices in Service Activities* (OECD, 1987).

7. Sue Lewis (ed.), *Output and Performance Measurement in Central Government: Progress in Departments*, (Treasury Working Paper no. 38 (London, 1986).

8. For a discussion of the problem in the case of US hospitals, see Sharon de Sha, 'Measuring outputs in hospitals' in *Measurement and Interpretation of Productivity* (National Academy of Sciences, Washington, DC, 1979).

9. See R. Turvey, 'What kinds of earnings indices are useful?' in this volume.

10. See *Aggregate Productivity Measures* (Statistics Canada, 1982), p. 39.

11. To some extent this is true of the Rees Report, which contained a number of recommendations which have subsequently been implemented. None the less it remains a useful and detailed source of information on US productivity statistics. See *Measurement and Interpretation of Productivity*.

12. The indices appear in *Monthly Labor Review* and in *Employment and Earnings*, both published monthly by the US Department of Labor, Bureau of Labor Statistics.

13. An excellent description of US productivity statistics is provided in Jerome A. Mark, 'From labor to multifactor productivity', paper prepared for the International Productivity Symposium 2, Munich, October 1986.

14. They appear in an annual bulletin, *Productivity Measures for Selected Industries*, published by the US Department of Labor, Bureau of Labor Statistics.

15. They form the subject of an annual article in *Monthly Labor Review*.

16. The central publication of the Federal Statistical Office on national accounts is *Fachserie 18: Volkswirtschaftliche Gesamtrechnungen, Reihe 1: Konten und Standardtabellen*.

17. Published by the Federal Statistical Office in *Fachserie 4: Produzierendes Gewerbe*,

Reihe 2.1: Indizes der Produktion und der Arbeitsproduktivität, Produktion ausgewälter Erzeugnisse im Produzierenden Gewerbe.

18. A general description and back data are to be found in *Aggregate Productivity Measures.*

19. *Offentliga Tjänster – sökarljus mot produktivitet och användare* (Finans-Departementet, Stockholm Ds Fi 1986:13).

20. They appear in *Labour and Wage Statistics of China* published by the State Statistical Bureau, People's Republic of China (in Chinese).

21. They appear in *Monthly Bulletin of Statistics – China* published by the State Statistical Bureau, People's Republic of China (in Chinese).

22. I. Kravis, 'A survey of international comparisons of productivity', (*Economic Journal*, Vol.86 no. 341, March 1976, pp. 1–44.

23. J. Kux, *Methodological problems of international comparison of levels of labour productivity in industry*, Conference of European Statisticians Statistical Standards and Studies no. 21 (UN, New York, 1971).

24. For instance, in an effort to obtain production statistics which are comparable, and thus additive, between its member countries, the Statistical Office of the European Communities notes that 'The main obstacles are caused above all by the extreme diversity of methodologies on which production statistics in the individual member states are based: each country has its own product classification, its own nomenclatures, a different level of breakdown by product group, different survey periodicity, different units, etc' (*Industrial Production: Methodology*, EUROSTAT Theme 4, Series 4 (Luxembourg, 1987).

25. One of the few recent examples is *Productivity Comparison in Food, Metallurgy and Engineering Industries between Austria and Hungary*, published jointly by the central statistical offices of Austria and Hungary, 1980.

26. A. D. Smith, D. M. W. N. Hitchens and S. W. Davies, *International Industrial Productivity*, National Institute of Economic and Social Research Occasional Papers XXXIV (Cambridge University Press, 1982)

27. See the occasional articles in *Monthly Labor Review*. The OECD has produced annual productivity series for the nine ISIC two-digit groups of manufacturing for 14 countries by dividing the number of wage and salary earners employed (from OECD labour force statistics) into GDP at constant prices (from OECD National Accounts). Tables are given in *Productivity in Industry: Prospects and Policies* (OECD, Paris, 1986). There are some discontinuities in some of the labour force series and some are annual averages while others relate to a single month. Part-time workers are not distinguished.

22 Establishment surveys of hours and earnings

R. Turvey

This paper is based on a survey of the questionnaire forms used in establishment-based surveys of hours and earnings in a large number of countries. It describes the items of information about numbers employed, hours and earnings that are requested, but does not attempt to provide a country by country account of which information is obtained in each survey.

It is not the purpose of this paper to prescribe what statistics should be collected. The Convention and Recommendation concerning labour statistics,[1] the Resolutions of the International Conference of Labour Statisticians[2] and the manual *An Integrated System of Wages Statistics*[3] already do this. In fact, most of the surveys examined conform to these. None the less, the scope for variation is considerable. The producers of earnings and hours statistics may therefore find it useful to see what other countries do, and the users of these statistics need to know what are the variations that can impede comparability. Hence this paper has the purely descriptive aim of showing how much the nature and range of data collected differs between countries and how many are the sources of possible non-comparability; it does not attempt to draw any conclusions.

Besides hours and earnings, the questionnaires used in these surveys also obtain background information identifying and describing each establishment, but this is not reviewed here. Nor are surveys which are primarily production censuses or labour cost surveys or which serve to track earnings and employment for aggregative economic statistics rather than to provide data on earnings per person or per hour.[4] Surveys which ascertain rates of pay rather than earnings are mentioned only in passing.

Apart from differences in the degree of detail demanded in different questionnaires, there are variations because some countries include certain groups of employees or particular components of pay or hours which other countries exclude. Three especially important examples of variations are the treatment of employees who did not work throughout the reference period, the treatment of payment in kind and the treatment of irregular or annual bonuses and other extra payments. Furthermore, when wage earners are distinguished from salary earners, the dividing line between the two kinds of employee varies somewhat between countries.

The paper does not describe the coverage and scope of surveys, being limited to descriptions of what employment, hours and earnings information participating establishments are asked to provide and of definitions or instructions furnished to the respondents. These descriptions are presented as follows: Paragraphs in small print reproduce or summarise particular examples; Items separated by slashes are alternatives; Items separated by commas are not; Paragraphs in italics reproduce relevant definitions from the recommendations of the International Conference of Labour Statisticians.

Survey contents

Surveys may differ in form rather than in substance because of definitional relationships. Where $A + B = C$, *or* $A/B = C$, the questionnaire may either ask the respondent to provide all three, or it may ask for only two. For example, total hours and their overtime component may be obtained or, alternatively, normal hours and overtime hours. Or again, total and female employment may be obtained, leaving male employment to be calculated by the statistical office.

In many surveys, a short form requiring the respondent to provide less detail is sent to employers in small enterprises.

Different versions of a questionnaire may be used for different industries even though the data required are similar. Thus they may differ in respect of the instructions provided, for example in a list of occupational codes. Another example is that payment in kind may be asked for only in industries such as hotels and agriculture, where meals and/or lodging are frequently provided by the employer.

The response burden of filling in a questionnaire depends upon its frequency as well as upon its complexity. The latter is not just a function of the number of figures demanded, since some figures may be readily and directly available in employer records and accounts, while others may have to be calculated. Thus a request for numbers employed in each of, say, six earnings brackets will require the respondent to check through the earnings of each employee individually in order to make the counts. Again, the provision of separate data for full- and part-time employees may impose a considerable task upon the respondent. If the nature of payroll records differs between countries, the same form can be easy to complete in some countries and difficult in others.

Leaving this aside, the apparent complexity of the survey forms differs enormously between surveys. Some ask for only a dozen or so figures or codes; others ask for many times as many.

Surveys which obtain aggregate data

Wages and salaries in the same questionnaire

Some surveys use a single form to cover both wage and salary earners, distinguishing them according to the length of the pay period or by applying a status, occupation or skill-level classification. Since the categories applied and data obtained can be described as if these surveys used forms consisting of two parts, or two forms, they are mostly covered in the following descriptions of separate forms for wage earners and salary earners.

Wage earners

Categories distinguished Separate data are obtained for one or more groups defined by one or by the intersections of two or more of the following classifications.

Age
  Adults and juniors, with an age limit of 18, 19 or 21 are often distinguished, more detailed age breakdowns being rare.
Sex
  Male/Female.
Nationality
  National/Foreign.
  Citizen/Non-citizen.
Full-/Part-time
  Part-time may be broken down into number of hours per week categories.
Pay system
  Even where only one pay system applies to all the employees in an establishment within the scope of the survey (e.g. all production workers) the frequency of pay has to be ascertained so that the statistical office can adjust all data to a common period.
  Frequency of pay: Weekly/Every 2 weeks/Semi-monthly/Monthly/Every 4 weeks/Other.
  Time-rated/Piece-rated/Commission remunerated. (Alternatively, gross earnings of each type may be separately ascertained, without distinguishing such groups.)
  Day work/Two-shift work/Intermittent three-shift work/Continual three-shift work/Underground work. (Alternatively, premiums may be ascertained as one separate component of gross earnings, without distinguishing such groups.)
  Whether or not shiftwork and, if so, whether two or three shifts.
  Separate data for workers provided with board and lodging.
Collective agreement
  Name and date of collective agreement (when all workers constituting an aggregate are covered by one agreement).

Status, occupation or skill-level

The classifications of this kind that are used for categorising wage earners reflect national institutions and labour market organisation, thus varying very considerably between countries or, within a country, between industries. The enquiry may be limited to one category, e.g. covering only manual workers.

> Regular/Temporary (or casual).
> Permanent/Temporary.
> Foremen/Other adult workers/Apprentices and all workers under 18.

In countries with a widespread training system, for example with apprenticeships and/or trade qualifications, workers can readily be allocated to categories using national classifications. These obviously vary in detail between countries.

> Skilled or Qualified/Semi-skilled or Semi-qualified/Unskilled or Non-qualified/ Apprentices/Other.
> Carpenters/Joiners/Painters/Semi-qualified/Non-qualified/Apprentices. (This is an example of industry specific categories, with different survey forms being used for different industries.)

Otherwise, broad occupational groupings may be used.

> Industrial workers/Clerical & other office etc. staff (industry only).
> Production workers, defined as non-supervisory workers in such occupations as fabricating, storage, receiving, warehousing, shipping, trucking, packing, handling, maintenance, product development, record keeping related to production, processing, assembling, janitorial and repair. Supervisors whose supervisory functions are only incidental to their regular work are also included.

Data obtained for each category. The data requested may be limited to full-time workers who worked for the whole of the reference period. In one case this is defined as excluding both workers who received no pay for more than three working days during the reference month and workers on paid leave (whose hours cannot therefore be recorded.)

Other surveys, which obtain numbers employed and gross cash remuneration, ask both for data for all workers and in addition, for full-time or regular employees only. In the latter case, a breakdown of the number of non-regular workers is obtained:

> Part-time
> Seasonal
> Occasional
> Laid-off
> Those for whom absence entailed pay deductions.

The number of workers and gross earnings are universally obtained. Additionally, all or some of the following are obtained in most cases:

> Total hours and/or days worked and/or paid.
> Work schedule or normal hours.
> Overtime included in total hours.
> Overtime earnings included in gross earnings.
> Other allowances included in gross pay (e.g. productivity bonuses and other allowances paid each pay period, end of year and similar bonuses).

One particularly complex questionnaire requests:

Hourly rate for time work and quarterly total earnings for piece-work excluding overtime and shift work allowances, hours worked on time-work and on piece-work quarterly, overtime included in total quarterly hours, allowances for overtime excluding base pay, payment for public holidays, other allowances. (The hourly rate for workers paid a fixed weekly or monthly wage is to be calculated by the respondent by dividing quarterly pay by 13 times the standard work week. This rate for these workers is to be used in calculating the time-related part of any earnings for piece-work and payment for public holidays.)

Another, where the same form is used for all employees, requests:

Normal working hours per day, standard working days per month, basic pay – weighted average, maximum and minimum, cost of living allowance, meal benefits, commission and tips, days paid and amount of good attendance bonus, night shift allowance per shift and per pay period, Year-end bonus in terms of pay period & amount in cash, other bonuses & allowances.

Another asks for only days worked and total pay for temporary and daily workers, but obtains a wide range of data for regular workers.

The existence of special groups may influence the nature of the data requested:

Days paid and gross earnings – obtained separately for temporary workers.

Commissions – obtained for sales staff.

Normal weekly hours, overtime hours, hours absent not paid, base wage for normal hours including regular primes, total pay for overtime – obtained separately for monthly paid workers.

Salary earners

Separate data are obtained for one or more groups defined by one or by the intersections of two or more of the following classifications.

Categories distinguished Most of the categories distinguished are the same as for wage earners, so need not be repeated.

Pay system

Normally, salary earners are assumed to be monthly paid, though employees paid wholly or partly on commission may be distinguished.

Status, occupation or skill-level

As with wage earners, national institutions and the characteristics of the labour market determine the groupings that are can be distinguished in each country. The last three breakdowns below provide examples of the use of national qualification categorisations.

Permanent/Temporary.

Working proprietors, family workers, employees subdivided into: administrators, technicians and workers.

Sales, accounting, clerical and administrative staff/Technical staff and master craftsmen: each subdivided into a number of level of qualification groups.

Directeurs, gérants, fondés de pouvoir/Two qualification staff levels (each subdivided into specified occupations or, more broadly, into *Employés de commerce/Employés techniques/Vendeurs dans les magasins)/Aides employés/* Employees under 19 excluding apprentices/Apprentices/Commercial travellers and representatives.

Professional engineer, class I engineer, class II engineer, master craftsman, class I craftsman, class II craftsman, assistant craftsman, other officially authorised engineer, unlicensed skilled worker, apprentice, simple worker.

Data obtained for each category The number of employees and gross earnings are ascertained in all cases. In addition data may be sought on:

Overtime pay included in total earnings.

Hours in standard work week (normal hours and days) or the work schedule.

Overtime hours paid.

Total hours worked or paid (when different from normal hours plus overtime).

Hours absent and not paid.

though actual hours data are much less often sought than for wage earners, hours not being recorded for many salary earners.

Surveys which obtain individual data

Data may be required only for those employees who were paid for the whole of the pay period, though the more detailed questionnaires obtain the information necessary to distinguish such workers.

Wage and salary earners together

Where the data required for wage and salary earners are identical or nearly so, a single form rather than a two-part form or separate forms may be used. A question about the length of the pay period is then included unless monthly earnings are requested for all employees. Two particular examples follow; otherwise the range of information obtained is covered in the descriptions below for wage earners and salary earners separately.

One such survey asks for the weekly equivalent of salaries, allowing no entry for the hours of managers etc. The characteristics, hours and earnings ascertained are: Male/Female; Adult/Junior; Permanent/Casual; Full-/Part-time; Managerial etc./Supervisory etc./Apprentice/All other; Title and main tasks of occupation; Weekly standard hours; Ordinary and overtime weekly hours paid for; award pay and allowances; other time pay; piece-work pay; overtime pay; other pay; pay in advance.

Another such survey (for wholesaling and retailing) ascertains: Male/Female, Full/Part-time, normal weekly hours excluding meal breaks, gross salary per month or week, regular allowances per month including payment in kind, bonuses and gratuities during previous year, overtime payment during previous year, date of appointment if after beginning of previous year.

Wage earners

Characteristics ascertained for each person.

Age

Adults and juniors, with an age limit of 18, 19 or 21 are often distinguished.

Year of birth or an estimate if not available.
Date of birth.

Sex

Male/Female.

Marital status

Single/Married.

Nationality

National/Foreign.

Education

No school/Primary/Secondary/Technical/Higher.
Elementary and less/Middle school/High school/Junior college/College or higher.
Highest academic qualification, if any, and any vocational certificates.

Years of service

Years in occupation, years in present job.
Career below 1yr/1–2/3–4/5–9/10 or more years.
Years of work experience relevant for present job, years with present employer.

Full/Part-time

Pay system

Time rate/Piece-work. (Alternatively, separate figures may be requested for time-work and piece-work earnings.)

Collective agreement, Arbitration award etc.

The information required may be limited to an arrangement covering the employee. Alternatively it may be more widely defined, extending to an arrangement affecting the pay and conditions of employment directly or indirectly.

Listing for coding supplied.
Name and date of collective agreement.

Status, occupation or skill-level

Permanent/Casual/Temporary.
Family worker/Newly recruited/Working and attending school/All other.
Precise specification of occupation, or job title and description of main tasks (to be coded by the statistical office).
Job title, occupational code (according to a list provided or universally used).
Production worker/Non-production worker.

Earnings affected by absence

Yes/No for absence due to sickness, holiday or other absence, short-time working or employment lasting only part of period. Ignore absences which did not affect earnings because of guaranteed payments.

Earnings and hours data obtained for each person. Where weekly earnings are demanded for all wage earners, one week's proportion of payments made other than on a weekly basis may be requested. Where quarterly data are demanded, hours and earnings have to be summed over a succession of pay periods. Practically all surveys obtain

Total gross earnings and total hours paid, and overtime pay or premium and overtime hours.

Alternatively or additionally to the former,

Normal (agreed) wage and hours or, where normal hours cannot be stated, whether full- or part-time

may be obtained, in some cases the total of pay and hours being calculated by the statistical office by adding overtime pay and hours to normal pay and hours. A breakdown is frequently obtained between

Earnings and hours for piece-work and time-work

Other items sometimes included are

Bonuses for the week

$1/52$ of annual bonuses and allowances or an appropriate fraction of incentive payments made for periods longer than the pay period.

$1/x$ of bonuses, premiums, commissions, etc., payable every x months and paid in the last x months (in data for one month obtained in an annual survey).

Shift allowances, Sunday work supplements or supplements for inconveniently timed work.

Pay for public holidays.

Payment in kind.

Whether earnings for pay period were affected by absence.

Adult/Other rates.

Employer's contributions to pension and insurance schemes (a question unnecessary with uniform national schemes).

Whether or not the employer pays a cost of living allowance and, if so, its percentage of basic pay.

Salary earners

Characteristics ascertained for each person. Many of these are the same as for wage earners, so most of the above examples for the latter serve also for salary earners and are not repeated here.

Education.

In some cases, more detail may be asked for than in the case of wage earners.

Two or three-digit code for level and specialism, and year of final examination.

Year of appointment.

Status, occupation or skill level

Executive/Family worker/Newly recruited/Working and attending school/All other.

Coding of position related to collective agreement and coding of occupation according to standard classification or list provided; enter job title if not in that list. (The form and its list may be different for different industries.)

Occupational title and two-digit occupational code.

Coding both of nature of activity and skill level in two-dimensional code according to table provided.

Earnings and hours data obtained for each person. Where weekly earnings are demanded for all employees, one week's proportion of payments made other than on a weekly basis may be requested. Most surveys ask for:

Normal hours of work or, where this cannot be answered,whether full- or part-time.

Agreed (normal) gross monthly salary or total monthly earnings.

Premium (pay for overtime or gross overtime earnings.

Regular monthly bonuses, commissions, etc.

Shift allowances for Sunday work and similar allowances.

Other data gathered may include

Value of remuneration in kind, possibly assessed by applying tables used by tax authorities.

Adult/Other rates.

Whether earnings for pay period were affected by absence.

The treatment of irregular bonuses etc. varies considerably

Bonuses and extra month's salary paid in last accounting year.

Variable allowances earned in last 12 months.

$1/_{12}$ (or overage monthly amount) of annual bonuses and allowances.

Appropriate fraction of incentive, etc., payments for longer period than one month.

Occupational wage surveys

These require the employer to provide aggregate data for the employees in each of a number of specified occupations.

USA: The occupational wage surveys relate to rates of pay rather than to earnings. For each wage or salary rate within each specified occupation, the employer returns: sex, method of pay (incentive or hourly, weekly, monthly etc.), number of workers, standard weekly hours, salary or rate of pay excluding overtime.

Sweden: Pay for a specified quarter (or as close to the latter as possible).

Survey reference periods

Some surveys ask that data for the preceding period be supplied when the establishment was closed for the specified period.

Some questionnaires ask for one week's earnings for all employees, including those with longer pay periods, or for one month's, including those with shorter pay periods.

For individual data.

Pay period ending in specified week; specify its length.

Specify first day and last day.

Earnings for a specified month or specified week.

For aggregate data

Some questionnaires obtain data for the last pay period before a given date separately for employee groups defined in terms of their pay periods.

Number employed during the month.

Number employed and hours worked in the week ending on a specified date/last complete week of the month, and earnings for the pay period covering that week.

Number employed on last day of pay period.

Number employed on last day of month or a day as near as possible.

Number employed as recorded in the register for the month.

Specify a reference date for number employed and give earnings for the calendar month including that date.

Earnings for a specified month or specified week.

Provide data for the last pay period ending on or before a specified date. If a fire or industrial dispute seriously curtailed operations, provide data for the previous normal pay period and explain in a note. If the normal pay period is not a week, provide one week's proportion.

Provide data for the pay period which includes the 12th of the month. When the period is Mon.-Fri. and this is Sat. report for the week of the 6th through 12th; when it is a Sunday, report for the week of the 12th through 18th.

For hourly paid workers, state the pay period (week, fortnight, four weeks or month) and provide numbers, hours and pay for that period. If there are different pay periods for different workers, report them separately or convert to common pay period. For monthly paid workers, include pay and extra hours only of those employed throughout the month.

If the pay period is less than a month or four weeks, provide data summed over more than one successive pay period to cover at least four weeks. In case of strike or lockout, provide data for the last unaffected pay period(s).

If the pay period includes public holidays, paid leave or compensatory days off, then the corresponding hours should be omitted from total hours if the corresponding pay is omitted from earnings; alternatively, both should be included in the respective totals.

Number employed at the end of last month, accessions and separations during the month, number employed at the end of the month (hours and days worked and earnings being ascertained for the whole month).

Definitions provided to respondents

The following paragraphs relate to instructions and notes for guidance provided to survey respondents, not to definitions attached to descriptions or tabulations of surveys. The latter may be more formal and complete, while the former may simply specify some of the inclusions and exclusions which are not likely to be obvious to respondents. Thus if all employers in a country regard overtime pay as additional pay at premium rates for hours paid for in excess of normal hours, there is no need to take up space on the form by providing this definition. Similarly, if everyone can distinguish, say, manual from non-manual workers, no definition is necessary. Hence many of the statements reproduced below are clarifications rather than proper definitions.

Definitions which relate to specific national circumstances and institutions are not included in this survey.

Numbers employed

General definitions are rare and are qualified by inclusions and exclusions

All persons in a dependent position who are obliged to participate in a pension scheme.

Persons who worked full- or part-time or received pay for any part of the pay period.

Specific inclusions are rare

Part-time employees and employees on leave or out sick (with or without pay).

Salaried officials of corporations, executives and their staff, persons on paid vacation, sick leave or other paid leave and trainees.

Employees who commenced or finished work during the reference period and employees on paid or pre-paid leave or on workers' compensation who continue to be paid.

Exclusions differ considerably between different surveys

Owners, proprietors, partners.

The chairman and chief executive, senior executives and directors.

Employees whose regular monthly earnings exceed 12,000 DM.

Part-time employees.

Family workers with no employment contract.

Trainees and voluntary workers.

Employees in probationary employment.

Apprentices and youths engaged in the framework of social measures designed to absorb unemployment.

Home-workers.

Self-employed persons such as subcontractors, consultants, owner/drivers and persons paid solely by commission without a driver.

People paid on commission.

Employees who, on account of illness, recruitment or termination of employment, were not paid for the whole of the reference period.

Persons on strike or leave without pay the entire period.

Employees who for other reasons were not paid for over three days of the reference period.

Employees on reduced earnings because they receive a pension.

Partially handicapped persons who are specially paid.

Conscripts, retired persons, persons on indefinite leave.

Distinction between wage and salary earners

These are distinctions between groups for which partly different data are obtained. In some cases, data are obtained only for wage earners for whom the term 'workers' is often used. Monthly payment constitutes the distinction in many cases; a related distinction is between employees belonging to a wage earners' and a salary earners' pension scheme. It should be noted that, in some countries, clerical and sales staff are paid monthly and included among salary earners while, in others, some employees regarded as wage earners are paid monthly.

Alternatives to the binary wage-earner/salary-earner distinction are:

Production workers/All other.

Managerial/Non-managerial.

Employees paid by the hour/Salaried employees/Other (commission agents, piece-workers, etc.).

Salaried employees (including business apprentices and foremen)/Workers (including trade apprentices)/Home-workers.

Production workers/Administrative, technical and sales workers.

Status, occupation or skill level

Workers

Categorisation often uses a specific institutional national classification. One example of a categorisation which is not, is as follows:

Casual – Casual workers are those the terms of whose engagements provide for payment at the end of each day and who are not engaged for a period longer than 30 days.

Skilled, Qualified – Have served an apprenticeship, practice the trade learned or a similar activity, and by reason of their knowledge and vocational capacity are given tasks which are particularly difficult, involving varied responsibilities or fields.

Semi-skilled, Semi-qualified – Can only perform their job after a period of instruction of several months in general and are given tasks – mostly specific to the industry – which are regularly repeated, are less difficult and involve less responsibility.

Unskilled, Unqualified – Require no specific vocational training or only brief initiation and work on auxiliary tasks.

Salary earners

Categorisation often uses a specific institutional national classification. One example of a categorisation which is not, is as follows:

Top management – Chiefs and leaders with administrative responsibility for larger units who direct the work with the help of subordinates or who have specialist functions.

Staff with independent professional responsibilities – Chiefs and supervisors who independently lead smaller, or part of larger units, with the help of subordinates *or* who independently deal with or execute complex tasks. The work demands thorough knowledge of routines followed.

Professional staff – Act as foremen in relation to subordinate assistants or are at the same level as such persons. The work follows general instructions and requires good knowledge of the routines followed and the ability to make independent judgements.

Staff with routine work – Detailed instructions are followed; some knowledge of routines followed is necessary.

Part-time

Employees regularly working less than 30 hours per week.

Employees who work fewer hours than is normal for the establishment or division within it.

Employed on average less than 38 hours a week or 165 hours a month, but not including workers on short-time.

Employees who work half-days or only some days per pay period or only one week per month.

Include only those part-time employees who are permanent employees; thus a person hired for three months part-time is separately counted as a casual worker.

Hours

Normal hours

Normal hours of work are the hours of work fixed by or in pursuance of laws or regulations, collective agreements or arbitral awards. Where not fixed by or in pursuance of laws or regulations, collecive agreements or arbitral awards, normal hours of work should be taken as meaning the number of hours per day or week in excess of which any time worked is remunerated at overtime rates or forms an exception to the rules or custom of the establishment relating to the classes of workers concerned.[5]

Leave out main meal breaks, include all guaranteed hours even if they were not worked in the reference period, leave out all overtime hours even if these are worked regularly or are part of the contract.

Where monthly data are requested: monthly normal hours may be defined at 4.33 times normal weekly hours.

For monthly paid employees, should include paid public holiday hours.

Do not specify for a week that includes a public holiday.

Established by national regulations or normally practised by most full-time workers.

Hours worked

Statistics of hours worked should include: (a) hours actually worked during normal periods of work; (b) time worked in addition to hours worked during normal periods of work, and generally paid at higher rates than normal rates (overtime); (c) time spent at the place of work on work such as the preparation of the workplace, repairs and maintenance, preparation and cleaning of tools, and the preparation of receipts, time sheets and reports; (d) time spent at the place of work waiting or standing by for such reasons as lack of supply of work, breakdown of machinery, or accidents, or time spent at the place of work during which no work is done but for which payment is made under a guaranteed employment contract; (e) time corresponding to short periods of rest at the workplace, including tea and coffee breaks.

Statistics of hours actually worked should exclude: (a) hours paid for but not worked, such as paid annual leave, paid public holidays, paid sick leave; (b) meal breaks; (c) time spent on travel from home to work and vice versa.[6]

Time actually worked (includimg time during which piece-work has been done) on day or shift work in ordinary time or overtime, and also walking time, waiting time and paid travel time, but not travel time separately compensated, nor time when mixed performance pay is applied.

Hours worked on regular shift and overtime, excluding vacation, sick and other leave.

Hours worked in the establishment, including overtime and small breaks, but excluding: hours paid but not worked, travelling time (unless considered part of work), paid holidays and lunch breaks etc.

Piece-work time worked is time for which earnings in some way depend upon performance on day or shift work in ordinary time or overtime, including time when some mixed form of performance pay is applied.

Hours paid

Because of the wide differences among countries with respect to wage payments and other periods when no work is performed, it does not seem feasible at this time to adopt international definitions of hours paid for. Many countries will find, however, that statistics of hours paid for, while not suitable as a substitute for hours actually worked, can be useful for internal purposes and that they will commonly be readily available from payrolls and other records.[7]

Often defined by starting with actual hours worked, specified in one survey as

> Usually the time spent at the workplace after clocking in or, for monthly paid workers, normal hours.
>
> One country specifies 173 or 174 hours per month as the hours of monthly-paid wage earners.

Inclusions and additions specified may be

> Paid overtime hours.
>
> Paid leave granted for reasons particular to the establishment such as staff meetings, excursions organised by the firm.
>
> Illness, accidents and military service when the worker receives a full wage, less hours lost that are not paid.
>
> Hours paid for standby or reporting time.
>
> Hours not worked but for which pay was received directly from the firm such as public holidays, vacations, paid rest periods during work, sick leave and other paid leave, e.g. permitted absence for family events.

Exclusions sometimes listed are

> Hours worked which are compensated as time off.
>
> Breaks such as lunch breaks ruled by general agreement.
>
> Fictitious hours used for calculating pay supplements for hazard, etc.

Overtime

Most definitions are variations upon the following:

> Hours in excess of agreed, standard, normal or award hours of work.

Additional clarifications may be:

> Exclude hours compensated as time off.
>
> Include all extra hours, whether or not an overtime premium is paid.
>
> Include Saturday, Sunday and holiday hours only if overtime premiums were paid, not hours for which shift differential, hazard, incentive or other similar types of premiums were paid.
>
> Should be the number of hours worked, not any greater number of hours attributed for the purpose of calculating overtime payments.

Earnings

Total

The concept of earnings, as applied in wage statistics, relates to remuneration in cash and in kind paid to employees, as a rule at regular intervals, for time worked or work done together with remuneration for time not worked, such as for annual vacation, other paid leave or holidays. Earnings exclude employers' contributions in respect of their employees paid to social security and pension schemes and also the benefits received by employees under these schemes. Earnings also exclude severance and termination pay.

Statistics of earnings should relate to employees' gross remuneration, i.e. the total before any deductions are made by the employer in respect of taxes, contributions of employees to social security and pension schemes, life insurance premiums, union dues and other obligations of employees.

Earnings should include: direct wages and salaries, remuneration for time not worked (excluding severance and termination pay), bonuses and gratuities and housing and family allowances paid by the employer directly to his employee.

(a) Direct wages and salaries for time worked, or work done, cover: (i) straight time pay of time-rated workers, (ii) incentive pay of time-rated workers, (iii) premium pay for overtime, shift, night and holiday work, (iv) commissions paid to sales and other personnel. Included are: premiums for seniority and special skills, geographical zone differentials, responsibility premiums, dirt, danger and discomfort allowances, payments under guaranteed wage systems, cost-of-living allowances and other regular allowances.

(b) Remuneration for time not worked comprises direct payments to employees in respect of public holidays, annual vacations and other time off with pay granted by the employer.

(c) Bonuses and gratuities cover seasonal and end-of-year bonuses, additional payments in respect of vacation period (supplementary to normal pay) and profit-sharing bonuses. Statistics of earnings should distinguish cash earnings from payments in kind.[8]

Earnings are variously described as:

Gross pay before tax and social security deductions.

All remuneration received by an employee before deduction of tax and employee social security, etc, contributions.

Gross amount before deduction of tax etc. payable to employees for a pay period.

All remuneration received for work done during the pay period such as regular pay, piecework remuneration and allowances paid each pay period.

Pay before deductions for tax, union dues and social security.

Payments regularly made in each pay period, excluding payments made at longer intervals.

Agreed wage or salary including any cost of living allowance and any family allowance, plus a specified list of other inclusions.

The inclusions and exclusions specified may be limited to those where doubt may arise, rather than complete lists. Thus an item which is explicitly included or excluded in one country may be implicitly included or excluded in another. Common inclusions are:

Payment for overtime, shiftwork, night or Sunday work.

Allowances for dirty or dangerous work.

Sick pay.

Public holiday and paid leave.

Less common inclusions are:

Payments made by the employer on behalf of the employee by mutual agreement and deducted from pay.

Reimbursement of travel-to-work expenses.

Reimbursement of travel-to-work expenses if they are taxed.

Commissions and retainers.

Salary payments to directors.

Cost-of-living allowances, family and education allowances.

Other bonuses, paid vacations not taken, incentive payments.

Pay for thirteenth month.

Vacation bonuses.

Extra payment for extra responsibilities.

End of service gratuities, retirement and severance allowances.

Advance and retrospective payments (arrears for previous periods).
Amount paid to employees on workers' compensation which are not covered by insurance.

The last three of these are probably examples of components which must be reported, so that, though included in total gross pay, they can be excluded from the tabulations. Thus they are inclusions that serve as an alternative device for exclusion!

Common exclusions are:
Pay relating to other pay periods – back pay or pay advances.
Reimbursement of expenses.

Less common exclusions are:
Redundancy payments and (if not taxed) severance pay.
Lump-sum payments.
Provision of working clothes.
Payment for leave not taken.
Winter and bad weather pay in the construction industry.
State-financed supplementation of employees on short time.
Directors' fees.
Payments to proprietors/partners of unincorporated businesses.
Per diem allowances.

The treatment of payments in kind varies considerably.
Excluded, or excluded except for agriculture and catering workers.
Included, sometimes at value to the recipient or at standard rates used by the social security system or by the tax authorities.
Include only the (tax value of) meals and/or lodging provided, but not occasional meals.

The treatment of bonuses, commissions, profit-sharing payments and a thirteenth-month salary or similar occasional premium also varies considerably
Include the appropriately allocated fraction of bonuses or similar payments not made in this pay period, e.g. dividing the last such payments (or the next, if known) by the number of pay periods they cover.
Include bonuses and commissions.
Include regular bonuses (bonuses related to the reference period) and exclude irregular bonuses or, more precisely, exclude bonuses, profit-sharing payments, etc., not included in each month's pay.

Note that in some cases, bonuses, thirteenth-month salary or similar which are excluded from monthly or quarterly survey may be captured in an annual survey covering the whole year.

Components of earnings

Regular pay includes basic pay before deductions, commissions, overtime, etc., allowances, cash allowances, e.g. for transport and regular bonuses; irregular pay includes irregular bonuses and gratuities such as year-end or seasonal or profit-sharing bonuses, together with severance and terminal pay.
Bonuses and allowances for the week or month include rent, shift, noise and family allowances, commissions, gifts, the value of benefits in kind, etc.

Reimbursements of travelling, subsistence, etc., expenses should be excluded. Portion of annual bonuses and allowances is $1/52$ of the 53rd and 54th weeks, etc., or $1/12$ of the 13th and 14th month salaries, etc.

Time rate earnings include compensation for absence of piecework, journey and walking time, foreman's supplement, hazard and shiftwork allowances. Piece rate earnings include the whole earnings of workers on performance-related pay, including any fixed-time wage component.

Explanations of changes

Space for explanations or a checklist of factors responsible for changes since the previous round of the survey is often incorporated in the questionnaires. An example of an explanation given on one questionnaire is:

Part-time male employment is 50% higher than normal because of new contracts. As these employees are paid less than our more experienced full-time male staff, average weekly earnings have declined.

Factors to be found in checklists are, for pay:
New collective agreement or general wage change.
Pay increase/decrease.
Overtime increase/decrease.
Short-time increase/decrease.
Scheduled work-week increase/decrease.
Vacation pay increase/decrease.
Commissions increase/decrease.
Piece-work earnings increase/decrease.
Cost-of-living allowances increase/decrease.
Bonuses increase/decrease.
Short-time working for economic reasons.
Short-time working for technical reasons.
Prepayment of leave (if not excluded from gross pay).

Factors to be found in checklists are, for employment (and sometimes pay, too):
Orders increase/decrease.
Recruitment.
Redundancies and dismissals.
Strikes.
Casual workers stood down (if they were included).
Seasonal operations increase/decrease.
Temporary or permanent shutdown.
Transfer between establishments of the same enterprise.
Retirement.
Work accidents.
Interruption to production.
Financial problems.
Resignation.
End of contract.

Notes

1. Reprinted in the ILO *Bulletin of Labour Statistics*, 1985–3.
2. See *Current International Recommendations on Labour Statistics* ILO, 1988, for the relevant resolutions.
3. ILO, 1979.
4. Here are two examples: One survey obtains total employees by sex and, for both together, regular payroll and irregular payroll (bonuses, etc.). Another obtains gross wages & salaries; severance, termination and redundancy payments; directors' fees; number of male/female full-time/part-time employees.
5. Tenth International Conference of Labour Statisticians: Resolution concerning statistics of hours of work, 1962.
6. Ibid.
7. Ibid.
8. Twelfth International Conference of Labour Statisticians Resolution concerning an integrated system of wage statistics, 1973.

23 What kinds of earnings indices are useful?

R. Turvey

Introduction

The argument of this paper is that earnings and labour cost indices ought to be more like price indices and that, in some contexts, just as material and service inputs are measured at constant prices, so should labour inputs be measured at constant wages. As regards the first point, two indices which do resemble price indices in that they relate to a given 'basket' of labour, are described in some detail.

The central argument can be illustrated by using French data for 1962 and 1975 obtained from the *déclarations annuelles de salaire* made by employers. They cover the private and semi-public sectors and relate to full-time employees classified by socio-professional group. The breakdown used distinguishes 12 such groups, including *cadres administratifs supérieurs, techniciens, employés, ouvriers qualifiés*, etc.

Total earnings in 1975 were 472, with 1962 as 100. This can be decomposed into an average earnings index of 342.6 and an index of numbers employed of 137.8. One reason for the rise in average earnings, however, was a shift in the composition of the labour force in question towards the higher qualified groups. This means that the index of 137.8 understates the increase in labour input by omitting the quality improvement.

These effects can be removed by decomposing the rise in total earnings differently into a Laspeyres quantity index of 149 and a Paasche earnings index of 316.7. Alternatively, the figure of 472 can also be decomposed into a Paasche quantity index of 148.4 and a Laspeyres earnings index of 318.1. Because the relative earnings of the 12 socio-professional groups changed but little, these two decompositions are almost the same. But they both differ very considerably from the earlier figures, demonstrating the quantitative importance of the point made.

Since the data exclude part-time employees, no productivity index can be calculated but it is apparent that output per capita rose considerably faster than the ratio of output to the wage bill at constant wages.

Earnings and price indices

In the present context it is not necessary to distinguish earnings, total compensation and labour cost since the argument applies equally to all three. Thus it suffices to speak of 'earnings'. Wage rates are another matter, however. There is one very important difference between a wage rate index and a price index. It arises because the earnings of many workers, and hence earnings indices, are a function of more than one wage rate, e.g. of a regular time rate, overtime rate, piece rate, bonus, etc.

But wage rate indices relate to only one single standard rate for each group of workers. There is no comparable distinction between two sorts of price index because for most consumer purchases 'the' price equals the amount paid. Hence this paper concentrates on earnings indices rather than wage rate indices.

The big difference between earnings and prices is that while it is customary and useful to use the concept of average earnings in, say, manufacturing industry, it is unusual to speak of unit value in manufacturing. A 'worker' seems to be a useful unit, whereas an 'item of manufacturing output' is not. Hence while the manufacturing wage bill can be multiplicatively decomposed into (number of workers) × (average earnings), no such decomposition is useful for manufacturing output. In terms of indices, therefore, there is a multiplicative relationship between the index of average earnings and an index of numbers employed, while on the output side the multiplicative relationship is between the price index and output at constant prices – provided that one is Laspeyres and the other is Paasche.

Since workers are people, and since people are important, humanly, socially, politically and morally, a measure of numbers employed is an important and useful statistic. Nevertheless, and this is the point to be made, workers are not homogeneous or of equal value in an economic context. A teenage shop assistant does not contribute as much to economic output as a skilled mechanic or an accountant. The relative earnings in these occupations are a better guide to their economic importance than the assumption that they all have the same economic importance. Similarly, the economic importance of a brick and of a tractor is reflected, albeit imperfectly, in their prices much better than if we assume them to be equal. Thus just as the value of output at constant prices is a good measure of output, so the wage bill at constant earnings is a good measure of labour input. In an economic context, it is a better measure than the number of workers.

What is suggested, then, is that just as price indices measure the cost of given baskets of goods rather than being simple unit values, so should earnings indices measure the cost of given baskets of labour.[1] However these should supplement, not replace, average earnings figures since these, unlike unit values, are meaningful for aggregates. Furthermore, just as price indices are, in practice, used as deflators for the components of an output or expenditure value in order to estimate its constant-price equivalent, so should earnings indices be used to deflate the components of the wage bill in order to estimate its constant-wage equivalent.[2] In an economic context, the evolution of the wage bill at constant wages is a better guide to the evolution of labour input than is the evolution of the number of workers. In fact this concept is already used in constructing constant-price national product data for those outputs, particularly governmental, which are measured as inputs.

The importance of occupation or level of qualification

Just as the basket of goods which is valued in constructing a price index should contain a representative collection of the goods that are bought, so should an earnings index reflect the cost of employing a representative collection of employees. In principle this means that the specification of the employees for whom earnings are measured should be in terms of all those variables which account for earnings differences. These include industry, occupation, level of skill or qualification, experience, location, age and sex.

Earnings specifications appear to be more difficult to formulate than pricing specifications. Apart from this, collecting earnings observations may be more difficult than collecting price observations. Hence what can be done in practice will fall short of the ideal. But at present most published earnings indices fall too short of it and need some improvement. They are usually no more than calculations of average earnings using base-year weights of numbers employed by industry. Any breakdown is limited to sex, to full- and part-time and to manual and non-manual employees or some similar binary distinction. In view of the importance of occupation and/or level or skill or qualification as a factor in the determination of earnings, this is inadequate.

In some countries an occupational classification can be used; in others a classification by level of qualification or skill is used as in the case of the French statistics cited at the beginning of this article. The point is that to use either or both of these in the calculation of earnings and labour cost indices would constitute a vast improvement. Thus suppose that occupational data are available. A rise in the wage bill over a period, as already noted, can be multiplicatively decomposed into the rise in numbers employed and the rise in earnings per person. The latter will exceed the rise in the usual kind of earnings index to the extent that there has been a shift of employment towards industries with higher earnings. The rise in the usual kind of earnings index in its turn will exceed the rise in the cost of earnings of a representative set of jobs to the extent that there has been a shift of employment towards occupations with higher earnings. Thus, in these circumstances, the usual kind of earnings index will be too low from one point of view and too high from another.

But now suppose instead that the earnings index used both industry and occupational weights. The rise in this index would reflect only a rise in the cost and income of a specified set of jobs. Deflation of the wage and salary bill by this index would provide a quantity variable which reflected not only changes in total numbers employed but also shifts in the composition of employment from lower- to higher-paid jobs. The earnings index and the quantity variable would now become comparable with price indices and with constant-price national accounting magnitudes.

It may be asked whether occupational weights alone would not be sufficient. Two reasons suggest that they may not be. One is that occupations with the same name may in fact differ somewhat between industries. The other is that even apart from this there is an apparent tendency for earnings to reflect industry as well as occupation, a phenomenon comparable (in the present context) to the fact that the retail price of consumer goods may vary according to the type of retail outlet.

Some problems

It is unfortunately the case that calculation of such an earnings index will run into difficulties on account of new occupations and new industries. But new jobs only create the same difficulties for an earnings index as new products create for a price index. The same is true in a national accounting context with respect to imputation. If imputed rents are included in consumer expenditure, the national accounting consumption deflator must include them, while the inclusion of the self-employed among numbers employed requires their imputed wages to be included in the wage bill. Thus the need to approach earnings indices in the same way as price indices unfortunately extends to the difficulties of the latter as well as to their advantages.

Clearly, there are many detailed and difficult problems to tackle in the construction of useful earnings indices. But the first step is to agree on broad principles. One major principle has been suggested here, namely that the earnings and their weights should relate to a set of workers defined by occupation and/or level of qualification and not just by industry.

Two indices which follow this principle will now be described, one from the United States and one from the Federal Republic of Germany.

The US Employment Cost Index

In the United States the Bureau of Labor Statistics has published an Employment Cost Index since 1976. This measures employer expenditures per hour worked for obligations incurred in employing labour in a set of specified occupations in a sample of establishments. The index is published quarterly. Until March 1980 the index only included the cost of straight time wages. In March 1980 a measure of the change in total compensation was also published.[3]

The base period weights are employment in 1970 in 62 industries cross-classified by 441 occupations. A finer job classification would be desirable but is not possible because of the need to use the 1970 census occupation classification in order to obtain the weights. The 1980 census will be used to revise the weights.

For salaried employees average or normal hours are used in the calculation. Where these are not available, it is assumed that hours are the same as for other employees in the same establishment whose hours are known. The hours are hours worked, not hours paid for.

The earnings component consists of straight time hourly earnings. These exclude premium payments for overtime, holiday work, etc., and also exclude payments in kind and tips but include production bonuses, commissions and cost of living allowances. The data collected are wage and salary rates for the occupation, not the wage bill divided by total hours.

To obtain total compensation, costs incurred by employers for 23 specified employee benefits such as premium pay, pay for leave and expenditures for retirement and insurance programmes are also included. Base period expenditures per hour worked were collected for each benefit and updated by obtaining information on changes in those expenditure rates. Where data on benefits are not obtainable separately for each occupation, overall levels in the establishment are used for inputing benefit expenditure to each occupation. There is a detailed manual which describes the benefits studied and identifies the changes in each which are relevant to updating.

Where both part-time and full-time or both time-rate and piece-rate workers are found in an establishment within an occupation, only the larger group is included. When the index was initiated, each reporting establishment was visited in order to agree necessary details with the respondent. These included determining which jobs and workers match the occupations as defined for the survey. The precise way in which the data were to be reported was also agreed.

Twenty-three occupations were selected from 441 defined occupations on the basis of employment in 1970 for each of 62 industries. The occupations selected differed between industries. A sample of establishments was selected for each industry on the basis of establishment employment. The total sample for all industries was 10,000 establishments. The employment for each selected establishment for each selected occupation was collected. From these data, establishments and occupations were jointly selected. The final sample was 2,200 establishments with an average of about five occupations assigned to each establishment.

The Federal Republic of Germany wage and salary earnings indices

Three sets of indices are calculated. Two relate to gross weekly and gross hourly earnings of wage earners in industry. The third relates to the gross monthly earnings of salary-earners in industry, trade (*Gross-und Einzelhandel*) and finance (*Kreditinstitute und Versicherungsgewerbe*). They are published both as aggregates and broken down by sex, branch of economic activity and qualification (*Leistungsgruppe*).[4]

The data are obtained quarterly from a sample of establishments generally employing more than ten people. For sampling the establishments are stratified by location (i.e. by *Land*), economic activity and size. Generally 13 per cent of the establishments with ten and more people employed are included. The persons included in the survey are limited to full-time workers (*Arbeiter*) and full-time employees (*Angestellte*), excluding those who did not receive full pay for the reference period because, for example, of sickness, absence, recruiting or dismissal within the month. Further exclusions are top management executives, apprentices and trainees, working proprietors and persons receiving reduced pay because they are in receipt of benefits from the national social insurance system.

Each establishment reports total weekly hours paid for, earnings and employment of wage earners for each of three qualification groups by sex; total monthly earnings and employment of salary earners for each of four qualification groups[5] by sex.

Earnings include all gross amounts currently paid by the company to the worker/employee. Excluded are annual (e.g. Christmas, holiday) and irregular bonuses which would give an incorrect picture of the earnings situation of the month when they are paid to the employees. Furthermore, earnings which refer to work done outside the reference period (e.g. back payments) are excluded, as are reimbursements of expenses incurred by employees in carrying out company business.

The calculated means of earnings, wage earners' hours paid for, etc., are divided by their corresponding means for 1970 to obtain relatives (*Messzahlen*). Altogether 1,321 earnings and hours relatives are calculated for wage earners and 1,364 earnings relatives are calculated for salary earners.

The weights used for combining these relatives are the products of the earnings in the four quarters of 1970 and the numbers in each cell. The latter were obtained from the survey of the structure of earnings carried out in 1966. The survey carried out in 1972 showed such small differences that no updating was necessary. The indices are expressed with 1976 = 100.

The classification of employees into qualification groups has been carried out with great care in order to achieve comparability between industries. The work involved detailed study of all collective agreements (*Kollektivverträge, Firmentarifverträge, Betriebsvereinbarungen*) in order to assess the training and experience required for different jobs. For wage earners, three groups were formed, roughly consisting of skilled, trained and unskilled workers. For salary earners, where job activities are more differentiated, five groups were distinguished. The work was done in consultation with employers' associations and trade unions.

Establishments receiving the questionnaire are given instructions as to the allocation of their employees between qualification groups according to the way they are described in the relevant collective agreement. (The employer performs the allocation only in the very rare cases where no collective agreement exists.) These instructions have been formulated centrally in order to achieve a uniform application of the entire system of collective bargaining and detailed study of all collective agreements.

Notes

1. The ideas of this paper, though (to the author) extremely obvious, do not seem to have been put forward much. An honourable exception is Sir Roy Allen. See his *Index Numbers in Theory and Practice* (Macmillan, 1975), section 6.8. The ILO manual, *An Integrated System of Wages Statistics*, prepared by K. Bashir with the assistance of K. Hempstead, firmly commends the use of occupational as well as industrial weights.
2. The plural is used here because although, in principle, deflation should be done with one Paasche index, it is in practice done by disaggregating to the maximum extent possible and then deflating each component by the corresponding Laspeyres index, Paasche indices not being available.
3. For a more recent description see *BLS Handbook of Methods* (US Department of Labor, Bureau of Labor Statistics, Bulletin 2285).
4. For a more detailed description, see *Wirtschaft und Statistik*, 7/1972, 10/1973, 12/1979 and 8/1985.
5. Five qualification groups are distinguished altogether. However top management executives, who belong to *Leistungsgruppe* I, are not included in the current statistics on earnings but only in the survey of the structure of earnings (hitherto conducted every sixth year).

24 Net earnings statistics

R. Turvey

Statistics of (wage and salary) earnings can be obtained from household surveys, but in the majority of countries they are more often obtained from statistical surveys of employers. Some of these surveys obtain data about individual employees, but more usual are surveys which only provide averages and aggregates for whole groups of workers.

Whatever their source, there are two complications which affect the use of time series of earnings data. The first is that labour cost, which is what concerns the employer, exceeds earnings, while the amount of their earnings which employees can spend, which is what concerns them and their families, generally falls short of earnings because of tax and social security contributions. Hence earnings data need to be supplemented by data on labour cost (which is not discussed further here) and on net earnings. Furthermore, it is the purchasing power of net earnings which matters to their recipients, so that for comparisons through time, net earnings need to be deflated by an appropriate consumer price index, yielding 'real net earnings'. The second, which applies equally to labour cost, to gross earnings and to net earnings (though only the last of these is examined here) is that there are several different ways of defining and measuring changes through time which need to be very carefully distinguished.

Thus the subject of this paper is the problem of defining and measuring changes through time in the nominal and the real net earnings of employees. It is limited to households whose only or dominant source of income is from wages or salaries, possibly supplemented by universally available social security cash benefits. It is thus concerned only with their spendable cash flow from wages and salaries and certain cash benefits.

No attempt is made to cover the related subjects of measuring household welfare or the distribution of disposable income among all households. Furthermore, even within its narrower framework, the paper leaves out some of the fringe benefits whose value cannot be ascertained as a component of earnings for practical reasons. Stock options, the provision of a car for private use and collective membership of private health insurance are examples.

A general framework

In setting up a general framework for defining and measuring changes in net earnings, we must first confront the two complications mentioned above. The first of these is simple to understand, though complicated to deal with: income tax, and in some cases, social security contributions, which are both to be deducted from gross earnings to obtain net earnings, and social security benefits (notably family allowances) which, in some cases, are to be added and do not depend simply upon an individual employee's earnings. They partly depend upon the circumstances of the household of which he or she is a member. Whether the household contains more than one earner and the number and ages of children are normally very important factors in determining tax payments and social security benefits.

Earnings data can be obtained from households or from employers, though it may be necessary to combine data from both sources to obtain net earnings. Household data on the amount of wage or salary received may be less reliable than data provided by employers and classification by industry of employment in household surveys is usually less detailed and less reliable than the classification in employer surveys.

The second complication is that the average net earnings of a group of employees can change through time for a whole variety of reasons, including:

(a) More or less overtime, layoffs, strikes, unemployment, absence from work.
(b) Changes in the composition of a group, i.e. changes in characteristics which are not used to define it but which do affect earnings, tax etc. Thus if the group is defined in employer terms, e.g. as full-time male manual workers in a particular manufacturing plant, the proportion of higher-paid workers or of workers paid by results may change, and, if the data cover both men and women, the proportion of women may alter. Alternatively, if the group is defined in household terms, e.g. as urban wage-earning couples with two children, there may be occupational and industrial changes in the composition of the group.
(c) Systematic changes in the characteristics of a group which is defined as a cohort, i.e. the same band of people continuing in the same jobs or with the same employers, for whom data are obtained on successive occasions. In particular, they and their children grow older, which may give them seniority pay increments and affect their tax position and perhaps their entitlement to family allowances.
(d) Changes in rates of pay and in the rates and allowances of the tax and social security system.

The relevance of these various sources of change will depend upon the context. If interest centres upon changes in the standard of living of a cohort of households of a certain type, their job changes, illnesses, unemployment and ageing should all be taken into account. But if the aim is to compare the standard of living of a group of full-time employees this year with that of the comparable group last year, then illnesses, unemployment and ageing should not be taken into account, but differences in the occupational and industrial composition of the group probably should be. In either case, any changes in free services provided by the state would have to be included in a complete analysis of living standards.

Labour market analysis

No attempt is made here to set out all the possible kinds of inquiry that can be made and to specify for each of them what should be included and what are the 'other things' that should be held constant so that the answer is matched to the purposes of the question. Instead, consider only seven particular questions which may be asked in economic analysis of the labour market. All relate to net earnings. They are set out below in increasing order of precision, with a numbering system which will be explained later.

(7) How have average net earnings differed between periods for employees of a specified type?

(3) How have average net earnings differed between periods for households of a specified type?

(5) How have average net earnings differed between periods for households of a specified type whose members have jobs of a specified type?

(4) How have average net earnings evolved between periods for a cohort of households?

(6) How have average net earnings evolved between periods for a cohort of employees of a specified type whose households are of a specified type?

(2) How would net earnings have evolved between periods for unchanged groups of employees in continuous unchanged employment of a specified type whose households had not changed in any way?

Here are examples to display the difference between these seven more clearly:

(7) What are the differences over time in the average net take-home pay of adult unskilled males in the steel industry?

(3) What are the differences over time between the average net earnings of households with one adult full-time male wage earner in manufacturing, a wife with a part-time job in retailing and one child of school age?

(5) What are the differences over time between the average net earnings of households with one adult full-time male lathe operator in the aircraft industry, a wife with no job and two children of school age?

(4) What has happened to the average net earnings of the one-child

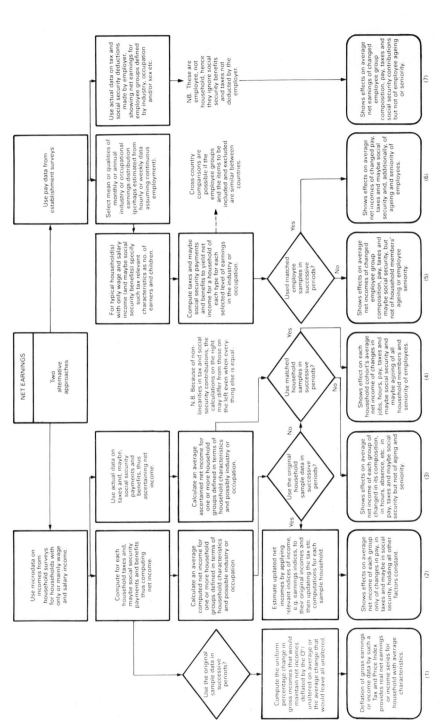

Figure 24.1 Approaches to defining net earnings.

households where the husband and wife both worked and the child was aged 11 in the base year?

(6) What has happened to the average net earnings of the one-child households where the husband has continued in the same job in insurance as a clerk, the wife has continued work in a job yielding a wage equal to 80 per cent of that of her husband and the child was aged 11 in the base year?

(2) What would have happened to the average net earnings of the one-child households where the husband remained continuously in identical work as a bank clerk without either promotion or gaining any seniority, the wife continued work in a job yielding a wage equal to 80 per cent of that of her husband and the child remained 11 years old?

Only the last of these holds 'everything equal' except for wages, tax and social security rules and rates. The last but one allows in addition for the effect of seniority payments, which can be very important in some countries and occupations, and for any effect upon tax allowances or family benefits of the fact that children grow older as time passes. Both assume continuous employment, no absences from work of any kind and no changes in overtime.

Figure 24.1 sets out the relationships between the different possible approaches and the kind of answers they provide. The left-hand side shows the use of data relating to (a sample of) individual households. The data may include tax and social security schedules and rules to the earnings data and the characteristics of the household. In either case, a possible difficulty is that respondents will not always be able to provide good figures for gross earnings.

The right-hand side of the diagram shows the use of earnings data obtained from employers. Either a number of standard households are specified, with all the characteristics necessary to apply the tax and social security schedules and rules, or net earnings are ascertained directly from the employers. In the latter case, the tax deducted by the employer may depend upon the circumstances of the household to which the employee belongs as reflected in the particular tax schedules and rules which the employer is instructed to apply by the tax authorities. Hence the reasons why the net earnings of successive unmatched samples of employees can differ include differences in any of those of their household circumstances which affect the application of tax and social security schedules and rules.

One difference between the approaches which involve computation of tax and social security results from the non-linearity of the relevant schedules: the amounts payable on an average income will differ from the average of the amounts payable by each of the households entering into the average.

Another difference results from what is held constant in matched samples of households in household surveys and matched samples of employees in employer surveys. In both cases, the employees get older and more senior, but in the household sample some of them may change jobs. Also, the children will get older in the first case, whereas their age is specified for each standard household. Finally, the employer earnings data may be estimated as annual or monthly earnings of employees with no absences or changes in overtime, whereas these may be manifested in the household survey data.

All this explains why the six boxes (2) through (7) at the bottom of Figure 24.1 correspond to different questions, and justifies their numbering. Box (1) shows a different approach. While an index of real disposable income of the type shown in box (2) measures the change in real disposable income, a tax and price index measures what change in gross nominal income would have maintained real disposable income unchanged (i.e. an index which combines the consumer price index with an index of tax payments, using weights reflecting net income and tax payments in the base period). If marginal tax rates are constant over the relevant range, the index of real disposable income equals an index of gross nominal income deflated by the tax and price index.

Practical complications

The availability and reliability of data are obviously the major problem, particularly when household survey data are used. But apart from this there are certain issues which are likely to be relevant in most countries.

One set of problems arises when some taxes and some social security benefits depend upon such factors as the size and terms of mortgages, rents paid, the health status of elderly relatives, and so on. It is tempting and, in the context of economic analysis, it may well be appropriate, to ignore such matters, including only those taxes, social security contributions and benefits which depend upon income and upon the composition of the household.

Another set of problems arises when taxes are a function of annual income but the reference period for income in household surveys or for earnings in employer surveys is shorter. The easiest case arises with annual calculations for standard households using estimates of what annual earnings would be with continuous employment in the same jobs throughout the year. Even here, however, annual or semi-annual bonus payments to employees create a problem.

Then there is a choice to be made about what to include in earnings. The bonus payments just mentioned deserve inclusion, but what, for example, about reimbursement of travel to work expenses or pay during maternity leave, and employer contributions to voluntary insurance schemes? Again, data availability will determine what is possible, but limitation of the analysis to just the main components of pay may be the best choice.

Complications can also arise with respect to social security contributions. If some employees pay them while other workers contribute instead to private insurance schemes, then perhaps both or neither should be included.

Some examples.[1]

OECD

An international collaborative study covering a number of countries and a number of years[2] gathers together national estimates of the net earnings of a single person and of a one-earner couple with two children, including family allowances; in both cases with earnings equal to the average earnings of production workers (of both sexes) in manufacturing. The presentation is extremely detailed. These estimates correspond to box (5) of Figure 24.1

EUROSTAT

In a release also covering a number of countries and a number of years,[3] where the calculations were provided by national statistical offices, the Statistical Office of the European Communities provides data, but only in index number form. These estimates correspond to box (5) of Figure 24.1 They show gross and net earnings, both nominal and deflated, with the percentage breakdown between gross wage, tax, social security contribution and family allowance, for a single male manual worker with an average male manufacturing wage, with 80 per cent of it and with 120 per cent of it; a single female manual worker with an average female manufacturing wage; a married couple with both an average male and an average female manufacturing wage, with two children; a married couple with only an average male manufacturing wage, with two children. The exposition is much less detailed than that provided in the OECD document, since, on the insistence of one or two countries, the absolute figures and hence the calculations are regarded as confidential. It is understood, however, that considerable effort was put into ensuring that each country took into account a comparable set of items to be included in the calculations.

Canada

Statistics Canada does not calculate any net earnings series, but it does provide micro data which could be used for this purpose. Its Social Policy Simulation Database and Model, to be released commercially, could be used to construct indices of types (1) and (2) disaggregated in a variety of ways.

Federal Republic of Germany

Data of type (5) are obtained at longer intervals through the salary and wage structure survey, which relates to a 10 per cent sample of employees in establishments with ten or more employees. There was a survey in 1978 and the next survey will be taken in 1990.[4] The data gathered are to include the tax group of each employee, so that some of the proposed tabulations will show gross and net annual earnings of wage earners and of salary earners broken down by alternatively by industry, size of enterprise, seniority, age, educational level or other variables.

Finland

Since 1977 the Central Statistical Office has compiled annual income distribution statistics, combining data obtained from a household survey and data from administrative registers relating to taxation and social security. Households whose head is classified as a wage or salary earner are distinguished from other households. The tabulations show 'primary income' (wages and salaries plus entrepreneurial income), 'factor income' (which in addition includes capital income) and, adding transfers received and substracting transfers paid, 'available income'. (For all wage and salary earner households together, the total amount of entrepreneurial and capital income amounted to less than 7 per cent of available income in 1984.) The tabulations provide breakdowns by area, household size, educational level and occupational group and industry of the employee head of household.[5] They correspond to box (3) of Figure 24.1.

Israel

The annual income survey (a sub-sample of the labour force survey), which is limited to urban households, collects information on the incomes of individual wage-earners, households whose heads are not working and households whose heads are employees. Since 1979, data on income tax and national insurance contributions have been computed and a number of tables relate to annual net income of households,[6] which corresponds to box (3) of Figure 24.1.

Japan

The reports on the annual Family Income and Expenditure Survey[7] provide data, which correspond to box (3) of Figure 24.1 on disposable income separately for workers' households, namely households whose heads are employees. (Well over 90 per cent of their incomes consist of wages and salaries.) Various breakdowns are provided, including one by one-digit industry of employment of the head of household. There is also a survey of wages and salaries of private enterprises, conducted by the National Tax Administration Agency which provides annual net earnings data, corresponding to box (7) of Figure 24.1, relating to employees subject to withholding taxes. The occupational classification of each employee is ascertained.

Netherlands

In 1983 the Netherlands Central Bureau of Statistics conducted a pilot study, using sample income and tax data from files of the fiscal authorities.[8] The study distinguished a 'static' measure of real income changes, corresponding to box (2) of Figure 24.1, and a 'dynamic' measure based on longitudinal data, corresponding to box (4). The matching was of individuals and a correction for changes in household size was made by applying an equivalence factor. Percentage real income changes in the periods 1977–9 and 1979–81, both static and dynamic, are provided for certain income quartiles, certain types of household in the first year and the socio-economic category of the main earner in the first year. Two bar charts show the much greater spread between the first and third quartiles of dynamic percentage real income changes than that for the static changes.

The Central Bureau of Statistics conducts an annual earnings survey which provides data for a sample of individual employees in a sample of establishments. The tabulations include distributions and means of the gross and net annual earnings of full-time employees by industry and by sex and age. The net earnings figures correspond to box (5) of Figure 24.1, though it seems that the taxes and social security contributions are obtained in the survey rather than computed.[9]

New Zealand

Since 1982, the New Zealand Department of Statistics has published quarterly series of real disposable income for the average full-time wage and salary earner, for the quintiles of the distribution and for the average of all households where the principal income earner is a full-time wage and salary earner. Base period household survey data on household characteristics and incomes are used, with the various income components extrapolated to later periods using appropriate indicators.[10]

The indices thus correspond to box (2) of Figure 24.1. However, the average weekly earnings in each of ten industry groups are the indicators used for wages and salaries. Thus any compositional shifts within each of these ten earnings groups will affect the index.

Norway

Annual income surveys since 1984, based on tax returns from a sample of personal taxpayers, provide average gross and net income figures for employee households classified by the number of adults and children. (Employee households are defined as those where over 50 per cent of income comes from wages and salaries.[11]) These data correspond to box (3) of Figure 24.1

Switzerland

The Swiss Office Fédéral de l'Industrie, des Arts et Métiers et du Travail publishes[12] two annual series of net earnings for normal working hours, an index for each and a deflation of each index to provide an index of real annual net earnings. The two gross earnings series used related to wage earners and to salaried employees and apply fixed industry weights. The federal, cantonal and communal income taxes applicable to employees earning these national averages are calculated for a married employee with no children in ten major towns and a 1941-population-weighted average used. Some allowance is made for the fact that taxes are paid at least a year after the income is earned, though the details are unclear.

The series extend back to 1939, with some chaining. They correspond to box (5) of Figure 24.1, though the fixed industry weighting cuts out some of the changes in employee group composition.

United Kingdom

The Central Statistical Office of the UK publishes a monthly tax and price index which can be used with an appropriate earnings series as in box (1) of Figure 24.1 to produce a real net earnings index.[13]

Annual estimates entitled 'The effects of taxes and benefits on household income' based on the annual Family Expenditure Survey are published.[14] These provide estimates of income (including imputed rents for households provided with rent-free accommodation) plus cash benefits less income tax and employees' social security contributions. They thus correspond to box (3) of Figure 24.1. Estimates are given for quintile groups of 'non-retired' households ranked by original income and for such households with one, two and three or more economically active persons. The definition of these households is rather wider than wage and salary earners, and wage and salary income is not shown separately. It is interesting to note that the estimates also go beyond net income as here understood, in that imputations for indirect taxes paid and for the value of state-provided education and health services, etc., are also made. The latter imputation amounts to as much as 15 per cent of disposable income for non-retired households, reinforcing the point that the concepts appropriate for examining the standard of living are different from net income as dealt with in this paper.

Annual figures showing the percentage of income paid in income tax and social security contributions by a single person and by a one-earner married couple, where income equals the average, half the average and twice the average earnings of full-time adult male manual employees are calculated by the tax authorities.[15] These correspond to box (5) of Figure 24.1

United States

A statistical series on the real spendable earnings of workers with three dependants, which again corresponds to box (5) of Figure 24.1, was abandoned in 1982, but deserves mention as illustrating some of the problems described in the framework part of this paper. From 1964 onwards, it had been based on the average weekly earnings for all production and non-supervisory workers in all private non-farm establishments, applying information about federal income tax and social security rates.

The main problem with this[16] was that there was a big shift in the composition of the labour force, with women and younger workers, often part-time, constituting an increasing proportion of the total and lowering the average. In addition, state and local income taxes were ignored.

The Bureau of the Census publishes an annual bulletin[17] containing extensive tables corresponding to box (3) of Figure 24.1. These show aggregate and mean income per household and per household member, by levels of income before tax and income after income, property and social security taxes, for different racial groups, regions, householder age groups, type and size of household. The data come from the Current Population Survey, supplemented by the use of data from other sources for capital gains and property taxes.

An experimental Tax and Price Index covering the years 1967–85 has been calculated.[18]

Notes

1. A more detailed description of some of the examples briefly described here has been provided in an unpublished working paper by my colleagues, 'Net earnings – A working paper' K. Taswell & M. Copin.
2. *The tax/benefit position of production workers 1984-1987* (Paris, 1988). The text is in English and French.
3. 'Gains nets des ouvriers de l'industrie dans la Communauté' in *Statistiques Rapides: Population et conditions sociales*, (Luxembourg, 1987)
4. *Gehalt und Lohnstrukturerhebung 1990*, draft tabulation plan.
5. See *Income Distribution Statistics 1984* (Official Statistics of Finland XLI:7, Helsinki, 1987).
6. See *Surveys of Income: 1984* (Special series no. 779, Central Bureau of Statistics, Jerusalem, 1986).
7. *Annual report on the Family Income and Expenditure Survey* (Statistics Bureau, Management and Co-ordination Agency, Tokyo).
8. Wouter J. Keller *et al.*, 'Real income changes of households in the Netherlands, 1977-83' *Proceedings of the 45th session of the International Statistical Institute*, Amsterdam, 1985.
9. Three CBS series on net earnings are described in 'Netto lonen, 1977-1984', *Supplement bij de sociaal-economische maandstatistiek* (1986, no. 7). The results of the annual survey, including the net earnings tables described above are published in *Sociaal-economische maandstatistiek*.
10. See 'Real disposable income measures and related series' (Appendix III to *Monthly Abstract of Statistics*, August 1983) and the 'Introduction' to *Wages and Earnings*, 1984-85.
11. See *Wages, Salaries and Income 1984* in English and Norwegian (Norges Offisielle Statistikk B 741, Oslo 1988).
12. See *La Vie économique* (Berne, monthly).
13. A full description is provided in 'The tax and price index – sources and methods', *Economic Trends*, no. 310, August 1979., J. A. Kay and C. N. Morris, 'The gross earnings deflator', *The Economic Journal* (June 1984) sets out an alternative method of calculation which, the authors claim, is methodologically superior in its treatment of the problem of deriving a monthly index when the tax system has an annual basis and in the tax model used.

14. In *Economic Trends*, e.g. no. 405 (July 1987), providing the results for 1985.
15. They are to be found in the chapter on income and wealth in *Social Trends*.
16. Paul O. Flaim, 'The spendable earnings series: Has it outlived its usefulness?', *Monthly Labour Review*, January 1982.
17. *Household After-Tax Income* (US Department of Commerce, Bureau of the Census, Current Population Reports, Special Studies). The methodology of the estimates is described in detail in an appendix.
18. See Robert Gillingham and John S. Greenlees, 'The impact of direct taxes on the cost of living', *Journal of Political Economy*, 95:4, August 1987.

25 Statistics of paid vacations[1]

R. Turvey

Introduction

Paid vacations and holidays are of great importance. First, from the social point of view they are an important positive element in the working conditions of employees. An increase in their length has certainly been an important component of the rise in the standard of living, even though comprehensive statistics are extremely rare. Secondly, from the economic point of view, including the analysis of productivity, data concerning holidays and vacations are one necessary component in any calculation of total annual hours worked. (Sick leave, strikes, bad weather and absenteeism are other components which are necessary for such a calculation.) Until such calculation can be made, labour input into the productive process can only be measured in terms of numbers employed, so that what is really a flow is measured as a stock. Furthermore, paid holidays and vacations enter into labour costs so that statistics of them add to the usefulness of labour cost statistics.

International comparisons of holidays and paid vacations could be made both in a social and in an economic context. For most purposes, national and international, it would probably suffice to know the average number of days of paid holiday and vacation per person per year for broad sectors of the economy.

Excluding paid sickness, maternity, parental, study or training and emergency leave, e.g. for funerals, two broad groups should be distinguished:

(1) *Public holidays* are non-working days recognised by the community at large. They can be taken to include days that are normally working days but which are taken in lieu of public holidays that fall on non-working days.
(2) *Vacations* or annual holidays. These are non-working periods whose timing and duration are a matter for employer and employees and are sometimes the subject of legislation regarding minimum duration and qualifying conditions.

The distinction is not completely clear in some countries. Not only may public holidays differ between regions or religious groups within a country, but certain days may be treated as public holidays by some but not all employers, e.g. the days between Christmas and the New Year. In other countries it is possible to specify a certain number of days as constituting public holidays which are very widely observed. Most people either do not work on these days or receive alternative days off or some extra compensation if they do.

Whether or not public holidays are uniform within a country, they are readily ascertainable. Hence the main problem relates to statistics of paid vacations and it is principally with these that this paper deals. It should be noted, however, that statistics on the total of all kinds of paid leave might provide a better basis for international comparisons.

Entitlement versus actual days taken

Paid vacation entitlement may differ from the number of days actually taken because entitlement may be carried over from one period to another, or people may receive pay in lieu of entitlement when they leave a job, or some people may even take less than their entitlement without recompense or carry forward, a phenomenon that does not arise in industries where establishments close down for a vacation period. The situation may be further complicated by people who work at a second job during their paid vacation from their main job.

Entitlement is easier to ascertain than the number of days actually taken. This is because it can be measured at a point of time. Ascertaining the number of days actually taken requires either recall by a person being questioned or access to employee records relating to a period of time. The use of such records creates problems where accounting procedures are not standardised and employees have worked for more than one employer during the period. Note that in many cases entitlement is a function of the length of service of the employee, so that length of service needs to be taken account of in recording entitlement.

Entitlement may be of interest both as a rough proxy for the amount of leave actually taken and for its own sake as one component of working conditions.

Methods of obtaining data

Data on vacations with pay can be obtained from three main sources. The first of these can provide entitlement but not days actually taken, while the others could provide either or both:

1. *Legislation, etc.*
   The analysis of collective agreements, arbitration awards and legislation. These may enable classification by occupation and/or

industry but the number of people covered may not be available.

2. *Employers*

(a) Questionnaires directed to employers requesting information about a sample of individual employees.

(b) Questionnaires directed to employers relating to all employees or to groups of employees.

3. *Households*

(a) Regular labour force surveys.

(b) Other household surveys.

Examples of each of these will now be described. Note that many countries have no vacation statistics at all, however.

Collective agreements, etc.

Analyses of minimum entitlements by industry are provided in Canada, the Federal Republic of Germany, Kenya, the Philippines, the United Kingdom, the United States and Switzerland. The coverage of recorded collective agreements or awards varies widely. In Australia, for example, a large proportion of employees are covered by recorded wage awards and collective agreements. The numbers involved can be estimated from the sample survey of weekly earnings, in which the award or agreement relevant to the employees in the sample is ascertained.

Employers

Individual questionnaires

The United Kingdom annual *New Earnings Survey* obtains data from employers about a 1 per cent sample of employees. In 1970, 1974 and 1981 questions were included on the paid holiday entitlement of full-time workers.

Group questionnaires

In the EEC labour cost surveys, each establishment included is asked for data on the cost of vacation pay and, in some of the surveys, for data on days of vacation or hours paid for but not worked due to paid vacation.

In the United States, area wage surveys obtain data on annual paid vacations and paid vacation entitlements 'provisions' by length of service groups for full-time workers. These are weighted and projected to obtain regional and national estimates. Similar data are obtained in industry wage surveys and detailed information is also collected about vacation plans in the Level of Benefits Survey used for considering civil service salary determination.

In France the Minister of Labour carries out a six-monthly survey on activity and employment conditions of the labour force in all large and a fraction of small establishments. In 1970, 1976 and 1981 questions were included on paid vacations. In 1976 the number of working days granted as paid annual vacations was asked separately for wage earners and for other employees.

In Italy an annual survey is conducted among establishments with more than 500 employees to collect statistics of absences by causes, which include vacations and festivals.

In Japan the annual General Survey on Wages and Working Hours Systems, which covers 6,000 enterprises, irregularly obtains information on special summer vacations and paid annual vacations.

In Canada the Annual Survey of Wages and Working Conditions, for office and non-office (and, in a few industries, for other) employees, asks about normal practice regarding the number of public holidays observed by the employees and the number of years service required to qualify for paid vacations by weekly earners and asks the number of days of public holiday observed by the majority of the employees and expenditure for vacations with pay or the total number of hours or days of vacation with pay.

In the Federal Republic of Germany 1972 Survey of the Wage and Salary Structure, data were obtained on paid vacation entitlements of full-time employees.

The socialist countries of Europe have fairly detailed reporting by all enterprises as part of the statistics on working time balances. Thus in Poland there is annual and quarterly reporting on time used by all enterprises in the material production sphere excluding agriculture. In the German Democratic Republic all institutions and enterprises prepare data on a monthly, quarterly or annual basis on actual days of vacation taken. Every four to five years, the duration of vacations and changes therein are calculated for all working people. In Hungary there is similar detailed reporting of paid vacations taken. In view of the stability of the data, collection is to take place only every two years but coverage will be extended. In 1978 the CMEA adopted new standards for the compilation of these statistics.

An example of the collection of entitlement data is provided by a Puerto Rican survey of vacation and sickness leave regulations in industry undertaken in 1976.

Households

Labour force surveys

Labour force surveys, which normally relate to a reference period of one week, often distinguish paid vacation as one reason for absence from work during part or whole of the reference period. The Federal Republic of Germany micro-census and the labour force surveys of Israel, Finland, Sweden and Canada offer examples. Such surveys provide little information about the total annual length of vacations, though it might be possible to devise some rough estimates if the surveys are carried out over all the weeks of the year as in the case of Israel.

Other household surveys

A number of countries, including Denmark, the Federal Republic of Germany, the Netherlands, Norway, Spain, Sweden and the United States, have at one time or another carried out sample household surveys relating to vacations or vacation trips and travel. These have not all provided data of the sort discussed here since that was not their primary purpose, but such data obviously can be obtained as part of a household survey. Thus the 1978 Finnish Living Condition Survey of 3,000 people included a question on the length of paid vacations, as did a 1978 Austrian micro-census survey. A vacation survey carried out in Spain in 1973 provided some data on length of vacations according to occupational groups.

In Australia special purpose surveys on leave-taking by wage and salary earners employed at the time of the survey were carried out in 1974 and 1979. Information was asked for on the number of days' leave (converted later into weeks according to a standard table) taken within each month of a 12-month period and covered 'long-service' leave as well as annual vacations. The Australian Bureau of Statistics tested the questionnaires prior to the survey and concluded that satisfactory data could be obtained for a year by the recall method. The United States experience in this regard is that there is a good deal of telescoping of the period of leave taken obtained by the recall method.

Conclusions

Some preliminary generalisations emerge from the information used in making this survey of the statistical problem. It is clear that good standardised statistics of paid vacations taken are obtained in socialist countries, and that vacation statistics are extremely rare in developing countries, being confined to the modern sector where they do exist. In most developed countries vacation statistics are also not systematic. For these countries and for the modern sector or developing countries it appears that:

(1) In some countries there are regional or local variations in public holidays.
(2) Some employers give extra days of paid holiday before or after public holidays; these extra days are not part of the annual paid vacation entitlement by qualifying condition, e.g. length of service.
(3) The analysis of collective agreements, arbitration awards or legislation yields information only about minimum paid vacation entitlements by qualifying conditions, e.g. length of service.
(4) Household surveys alone can provide data about actual days or weeks of paid vacation taken over a whole year for people who have had more than one job during the year and for the self-employed. However the recall problem would appear to arise, although the Australian special survey of leave-taking has been successful.

(5) Establishment data are easier to obtain if: they relate to entitlement rather than to actual vacation taken; they are confined to full-time employees; and they relate either to a specified person or persons or to what is most usual or normal for an easily delimited group of employees.

(6) Entitlement is of interest both for its own sake and as approximating leave actually taken. However it is relevant only to employees.

(7) Entitlement is frequently a function of length of service, so questionnaires relating to entitlement have either to relate to specified persons or to entitlement by length of service.

(8) Since vacation entitlements do not change frequently it is not essential to obtain data annually but it would be very useful to obtain data every few years.

Note

1. The paper was presented to the 13th International Conference of Labour Statisticians (Report VI) and has been revised by Mr A. C. Basu to take account of points made during the discussion of it.

Part Six: Other topics

26 The measurement of inequality of basic needs attributes

F. Mehran[1]

Introduction

Although considerable and varied efforts have been made, particularly in the last decade, to develop methodologies for the measurement and analysis of the inequality of income and related concepts, less attention has been devoted to developing similar methodologies for measuring inequalities of other attributes, such as access to education, medical care or other components of the basic needs of individuals or households. In much the same way that the knowledge of the average income of a population does not necessarily provide information on its distribution among the members of the population, the knowledge of the value of a basic needs indicator, say, the percentage of literates in the population, does not generally provide information on its distribution. Clearly, not everyone has equal protection against natural elements or access to basic infrastructures and services. For example, the population of some favoured regions may have greater housing facilities than have others. Some ethnical communities may have easier access to schooling than others. Some occupational groups may face more hazards than other groups.

The purpose of this paper is to suggest a method for measuring and analysing such inequalities. The measurement of inequality involves two elements: a grouping of the population by regions, ethnics, socio-economic groups, or other similar groupings; and a dichotomous basic needs attribute such as literacy, employment, access to medical facilities, etc.[2] The idea, then, is to measure the regional, ethnical, or socio-economic inequality of literacy, employment or access to medical facilities. For this purpose, an index widely used for measuring income inequality, the Gini index, is adapted and modified for use for the measurement of inequality of basic needs attributes. The reason why modification is necessary is that, while income is a continuous and numerical variable, most basic needs

401

attributes are discrete and categorical variables. For example, literacy is a dichotomous variable taking the two values literate or illiterate. It does not, therefore, lend itself to the same type of arithmetic as performed with the variable income which may take a whole range of numeric values. The modification is described in the next section; the resulting method of measuring inequality is then illustrated with numerical applications to the geographical distributions of certain durable goods and housing facilities in the United Kingdom and Trinidad and Tobago, and the ethnical distribution of schooling in Sri Lanka.

Measuring inequality of dichotomous attributes

Consider a population of 100 households of which none has electricity: 40 households live in the capital city, 10 in large towns, 20 in small towns, and the remaining 30 in rural areas. Suppose there is enough budget to provide electricity to 50 households. Four alternative plans are being considered. The distribution of provision of electricity under the four different plans is shown below. Other things being equal, the question is which of these plans would provide a more equal distribution of electricity among the households in the different regions. In more general terms, what is the ranking of the plans in terms of inequality in provision of electricity?

It can be readily observed that plan 2 gives the most unequal distribution as it assigns all the electricity discriminately to the households in the capital and large towns. Plan 1, on the other hand, allocates the electricity to the four regions in proportion to their population. In this sense then plan 1 may be said to be the most equal distribution. Plans 3 and 4 are in between the two extreme distributions of plan 1 and plan 2. It is not readily apparent which of the two is more equitable than the other.

	Rural areas	Small towns	Large towns	Capital city	Total
Number of households in population	30	20	10	40	100
Number of households with electricity					
under plan 1	15	10	5	20	50
under plan 2	0	0	10	40	50
under plan 3	10	10	5	25	50
under plan 4	15	0	5	30	50

To formulate the problem in general terms, let A denote a dichotomous attribute like access to electricity and let $X(A)$ be the corresponding variable which takes the value 1 if a particular household has A and 0 otherwise. Suppose there are n households in the population which is divided into k groups, e.g. geographical regions, with n_1 households in group 1, n_2 households in group 2, and so on. Of course, $n_1 + n_2 + \ldots + n_k = n$. Denoting by x_{ij} of the value of the variable $X(A)$ for households i in group j, we have $\sum_{i-1}^{n_j} x_{ij} = m_j, j = 1, 2, \ldots, k$, where m_j is the number of households in group j with electricity. If m is the total number of households with electricity in the population, then $mt_1 + mt_2 + \ldots + m_k = m$.

In measuring the extent of inequality in the distribution of A among the groups, the main quantities to compare are the proportions of households with A in the k groups. These proportions are denoted by $p_j = m_j/n_j, j = 1, 2, \ldots, k$. If all the p_js are equal to each other, then there is perfect equality in the distribution of A. This means that the mechanism which allocates the attribute of A gives equal chance to each household irrespective of the group to which it belongs. Stated differently, because $m_j/m = n_j/n, j = 1, 2, \ldots, k$, we say that there is perfect equality if attribute A is allocated among the k groups in proportion to the number of households lacking A in each group.

Similarly, we say there is extreme inequality if some p_js are equal to 1 and all others are equal to 0, i.e. the mechanism which distributes A systematically discriminates in favour of some groups and against all the other groups. If a household lacking A belongs to a favoured group, it has 100 per cent chance of receiving A, while households in other groups have no chance to receive A.

In general, the ps are not all equal and differ from 0 and 1. The problem then is to obtain a measure of inequality among the p_js.

By analogy with the measurement of income inequality let us consider the Gini's relative mean difference as a basis for the measurement of inequality among the p_js.[3] This gives

$$G(A) = \frac{1}{2p_{ij}} \Sigma\ y_i\ y_j\ (p_i - p_j) \tag{26.1}$$

where $y_i = n_i/n$ is the fraction of number of households in group i and $p =$

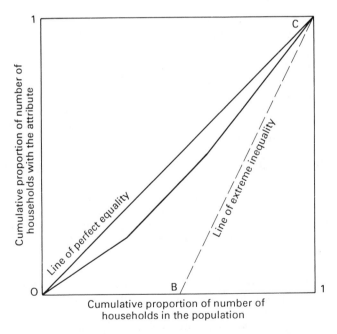

Figure 26.1 Lorenz curve for attribute data

m/n is the fraction of number of households with A in the whole population, $p = y_1 p_1 + \ldots + y_k p_k$. Straightforward manipulations show that G has a geometric interpretation in terms of the Lorenz curve. The Lorenz curve for an attribute is obtained by ranking the groups in ascending order of p_j and by plotting the cumulative fraction of households with A against the cumulative fraction of households in the population. Figure 26.1 shows the Lorenz curve for the distribution of provision of electricity under plan 3 of the simple example cited earlier. The coefficient G is equal to twice the area between the Lorenz curve and the diagonal line of perfect equality.

Although this definition of G appears simple and attractive, it has a problem. The problem is that in the case of extreme inequality with attribute data, when some of the p_js are equal to 1 and the others equal to 0, G is not equal to 1 as it would have been in the case of income data. Contrary to income data, dichotomous attribute data are not cumulative, in the sense that a household with attribute A, say, cannot be still given more A, so to speak. Therefore, extreme inequality is not achieved when one household has all the As while the others have none.

In order to account for this fact, the Gini index for attribute data should be redefined as the area between the Lorenz curve and the line of perfect equality divided by the maximum possible area, which is not the area of the triangle OCD in the figure, but the area of triangle OCB. The triangle OCB is obtained by allocating A to all households in some groups and nothing to others. This gives the value $(1-p)$ as the co-ordinate of the point B in the horizontal axis. The definition of the modified G is then

$$G(A) = \frac{1}{2p(1-p)} \sum_{ij}^{k} y_i y_j (p_i - p_j) \tag{26.2}$$

In terms of the frequency distributions m_j and n_j, $G(A)$ may be expressed as follows

$$G(A) = \frac{1}{2m(n-m)} \sum_{ij}^{k} (n_i m_j - n_j m_i) \tag{26.3}$$

where, it is recalled, $m = m_1 + \ldots + m_k$ and $n = n_1 + \ldots + n_k$.

The modified Gini index for attribute data has various statistical properties. It has a unit range, $0 \leq G(A) \leq 1$, and attains in principle the upper as well as the lower limits. $G(A) = 0$ represents perfect equality, which holds when $p_j = p$, for all i, and $G(A) = 1$ represents extreme inequality, which holds when $p_j = 1$ for some js and $p_j = 0$ for the remaining js.

Returning to the electricity example, note that the values of the modified Gini index for the four alternative plans are $G(A_1) = 0$, $G(A_2) = 1$, $G(A_3) = 0.26$ and $G(A_4) = 0.32$, respectively. Thus gives the result that the most equitable plan is plan 1, followed by plan 3, plan 4 and plan 2, which is the most inequitable plan possible. It should be mentioned that, in this example, the corresponding Lorenz curves, when drawn on the same diagram, do not intersect (except, of course, at the two extreme points through which all Lorenz curves pass). When Lorenz curves intersect, arguments may be advanced on the ambiguity of inequality comparisons similar to those developed regarding income inequality comparisons.[4]

The modified Gini index is symmetric in the sense that its value is unchanged when the attribute is replaced by its complement. Mathematically, we have $G(A) = G(\bar{A})$, where $\bar{A}$ represents the complement of A. Thus, according to the Gini index, the extent of inequality in the distribution of, say, literacy is the same as that of illiteracy.

The modified Gini index as defined by Equation (26.2) is similar to the dissimilarity index introduced in sociological literature for measuring segregation,[5] and comparable to the localisation coefficient commonly used by human geographers to measure the extent of inequality of the geographical distribution of characteristics.[6] The modified Gini index may also be viewed as an alternative to the entropy measure[7] and the measures of association for cross-classification data.[8]

A limitation of the modified Gini index shared also with other measures of inequality is the sensitivity of the index to the manner in which the groups are formed. Thus, a particular grouping of the population may give a highly unequal distribution of the attribute, while a different grouping may give a much more equal distribution. Thus, the application of the method described here should be limited to situations where there are natural groupings of the population, e.g. geographical groupings or ethnical groupings. The method is not suitable for use when the population is grouped according to income groups.

In addition to the above statistical properties, the modified Gini index has some economic properties. It satisfies an equivalent of the Pigou–Dalton transfer principle for attributes. According to the Pigou–Dalton principle, any transfer of income from a richer to a poorer person, everything else remaining the same including the rank of the population in the distribution, should decrease the inequality in the distribution of income. In terms of attributes, it may be restated as follows: any transfer of the attribute from a more favoured group to a less favoured group, everything else remaining the same, should decrease the inequality in the distribution of the attribute among the groups. Consider again plan 3 in the electricity example. Suppose we alter plan 3 by transferring one unit from the more favoured capital city to the less favoured rural areas to obtain the following distribution of provision of electricity: 11, 10, 5 and 24, among the 4 regions, rural areas, small towns, large towns and capital city respectively. The value of the modified Gini index of the resulting distribution is 0.208 which in comparison with the value of the modified Gini index of the original distribution 0.260, indicates a decrease in inequality as one would require on the basis of the transfer principle.

The transfer principle, however, is not a natural principle to stipulate in the case of dichotomous attributes. The underlying idea of the transfer principle, which is the notion of income redistribution through taxes, has no equivalent meaning with attributes. Moreover, with regard to some attributes, the very notion of transfer is without meaning. For example, if the attribute is literacy, one cannot meaningfully consider taking literacy from one person who has it and transferring it to someone who lacks it. A more natural consideration than transfer in the case of attributes is the notion of allocation. Governments allocate funds to various regions, communities or groups to increase literacy, employment, access to

education or health facilities or other attributes. The allocation is implicitly
or explicitly based on some allocation formula which in turn is essentially
stated in terms of the distribution of some characteristics of the population.[9]
An allocation principle that one may stipulate is as follows: inequality
should decrease if a specified desirable attribute is allocated among groups
of population according to the number of persons that lack the attribute in
the group. For example, suppose ten jobs are to be created in a country
with the following employment distribution among three regions of the
country:

	Region 1	Region 2	Region 3
Labour force	20	30	20
Employed	16	24	10

If the ten jobs are distributed in proportion of the number of unemployed,
the resulting distribution of the employed persons would be:

Employed	18	27	15

It can be easily verified that the modified Gini index shows a decrease of
inequality and, therefore, satisfies the allocation principle. In fact, it can be
shown that the Gini index satisfies the allocation principle in more general
settings.

Numerical applications

In this section numerical applications are presented on the measurement
of geographical inequalities of certain housing facilities and durable goods
in Trinidad and Tobago and the United Kingdom, and the ethnical
inequality of schooling in Sri Lanka.

Inequality of distribution of certain housing facilities in Trinidad and Tobago

Given in Table 26.1 are data on the distribution of sampled households by
administrative area of Trinidad and Tobago and selected types of facilities
owned or available for use. The data are extracted from the results of the
1971–2 household budgetary survey of Trinidad and Tobago. Although
the principal objective of the survey was the measurement of income,
expenditures and consumption patterns of households, general data on
socio-economic characteristics and living conditions of the households were
also collected. The results of this survey and the subsequent similar survey
in 1975–6 provide an important source of information for studying the
level and inequalities of living conditions in Trinidad and Tobago. Here,

we confine the study to the measurement of geographical inequalities and trends in living accommodation as measured by access to pipe-borne water, electricity and telephone.

Table 26.1 Geographical distribution of households with certain facilities, Trinidad and Tobago, 1971–2

Area	No. of hlds in sample	No. of households in sample with:		
		Pipe-borne water	Electricity	Telephone
Port of Spain	288	251	258	96
San Fernando	96	90	88	26
St George	984	587	807	160
Caroni	288	118	174	6
Nariva/Mayaro	96	24	30	2
St Andrew/St David	136	42	59	5
Victoria	472	191	297	27
St Patrick	312	135	185	29
Tobago	88	39	56	5
Trinidad and Tobago	2,760	1,463	1,951	345

Note: The data in Report no. 1 are given in terms of percentages. They have been converted into absolute figures using the information on the sample design and responses given in Report no. 2, Table 3, column 4. Columns may not sum due to conversion and rounding errors.
Source: Household Budgetary Survey 1971/72, Report no. 1 (Port of Spain Central Statistical Office, 1973), p. 5.

The ratio of the number of households with pipe-borne water to the number of households in the total sample in each of the nine administrative areas gives the values of p and p_i. Accordingly, 53 per cent of the sample households had access to pipe-borne water in 1971–2, but in six of the administrative areas the percentage of households with pipe-borne water was lower than the overall average percentage while the other areas had higher than average. Ranked in ascending order of p_i, the administrative areas are Nariva/Mayaro, St Andrew/St David, Victoria, Caroni, St Patrick, Tobago, St George, Port of Spain and San Fernando. The value of the percentages did of course change in 1975–6, as did the ranking of the administrative areas except for the last three areas.[10] Assuming that these changes of levels and ranks are significant and not due essentially to sampling variations, Equation (26.3) is applied to compute the modified Gini index for both the 1971–2 and 1975–6 data. The results are shown in Table 26.2, where the results of similar computations for electricity and telephone are also shown.

Table 26.2 Percentage level and geographical inequality of distribution of certain facilities, Trinidad and Tobago

Year	Pipe-borne water		Electricity		Telephone	
	p	G	p	G	p	G
1971–2	53.0	0.345	70.7	0.374	12.5	0.429
1975–7	58.6	0.316	77.0	0.331	11.5	0.378

Source: Household Budgetary Surveys.

It can be observed that geographical inequality has decreased for all three types of facility from 1971–2 to 1975–6. It can also be observed that, according to the Gini index, the telephone is more unequally distributed than electricity and electricity is more unequally distributed than pipe-borne water. This result is the same for 1971–2 as well as 1975–6. It should also be noted that scarce facilities are not necessarily the most unequally distributed. Although pipe-borne water is more scarce than electricity, it is more equally distributed.

Regional inequality of distribution of certain durable goods in the United Kingdom

A similar analysis has been performed on the geographical distribution of certain durable goods in the United Kingdom. The data, obtained from the annual *Family Expenditure Survey*, consist of the distribution of the number of households with central heating, refrigerator, and telephone by 11 regions of the UK in each of the two-year periods 1975–6, 1976–7, and 1977–8. On the basis of these data, the modified Gini index of regional inequalities of the three attributes are computed and the results shown in Table 26.3. The resulting values indicate that there is no unique direction in the movement of the trend of regional inequality of these durable goods. The inequality of the distribution of refrigerators has decreased during the period, while that of telephones has increased. The trend in the inequality of central heating has been mixed: it initially decreased and then increased.

Table 26.3 Percentage level and geographical inequality of distribution of certain durable goods, United Kingdom

Year	Central heating		Refrigerator		Telephone	
	p	G	p	G	p	G
1975–6	46.9	0.115	86.7	0.264	52.3	0.140
1976–7	48.9	0.112	89.0	0.263	54.7	0.194
1977–8	52.3	0.121	90.7	0.236	59.4	0.195

Source: Family Expenditure Survey (London, HMSO), 1976, p.127; 1977, p.131; 1978, p.119.

Comparing the results for telephones in the UK with those of Trinidad and Tobago, it can be noted that inequality is greater in Trinidad and Tobago than in the UK. To what extent this result is due to the scarcity factor cannot be readily ascertained. There is also an influencing factor due to the different number of groups: nine in the Trinidad and Tobago data and 11 in the United Kingdom data.

Ethnical inequality in schooling in Sri Lanka

The final numerical application deals with the inequality in schooling. The distributions of sample population with and without schooling for six ethnical communities in Sri Lanka are considered for 1953, 1963 and 1973.

The data are obtained from the decennial household survey on consumer finances, which is primarily directed to obtaining information on personal income, consumption and saving, but also includes enquiries on demographic and employment characteristics of the households as well as details regarding the nature of dwellings.

The results of the computations of the modified Gini index for the ethnical inequality of schooling and no schooling are shown in Table 26.4. Three remarks may be made. First, note that the inequality index for schooling is the same as the inequality index for no schooling. This is because of the symmetry property of the Gini index mentioned earlier. Second, note that the ethnical inequality has been decreasing steadily during the period 1953–73. Third, although there is a wide gap with respect to schooling between Indian Tamils and the other communities, because the number of Indian Tamils is small in comparison with the other communities, the gap is not reflected in the Gini index of inequality which shows mild overall inequality. This last point indicates that, in the analysis of inequality, one should not restrict the examination to the value of an overall index. The data on individual groups should be examined and compared, for example, by computing the p_is.

Table 26.4 Percentage level of and ethnical inequality in schooling, Sri Lanka

Year	Schooling		No schooling	
	p	G	p	G
1953	58.4	0.190	41.6	0.190
1963	63.4	0.176	36.6	0.176
1973	67.8	0.164	32.2	0.164

Sources: Survey of Ceylon's Consumer Finances, 1953 (Colombo, 1954, Table 6); *Survey of Ceylon's Consumer Finances, 1963* (Colombo, 1964, p. 8, Part 1); *Survey of Sri Lanka's Consumer Finances 1973*, Part II Colombo, Central Bank of Sri Lanka, 1974, p. 8).

Concluding remarks

The discussion in this paper is only intended to suggest a potential topic for methodological inquiry. Its aim is limited: to obtain recognition that a coherent set of statistical tools is needed to measure and analyse the distributional aspects of non-monetary as well as monetary components of living standards. The particular methodology proposed here for the measurement of inequality of dichotomous attributes is merely illustrative and is not meant to be binding. It is used as a vehicle for the exploration of the various issues one may encounter when dealing with non-monetary attributes.

Notes

1. The author is grateful to Peter Richards, Employment and Development Department, ILO, for helpful discussion and comments on an earlier version of this paper.
2. G. P. Ghai, A. R. Khan, E. L. H. Lee and T. Althan, *The basic-needs approach to development – Some issues regarding concepts and methodology* (Geneva, ILO, 1977).
3. For a description of the Gini index of incomes inequality and related statistics see e.g. N. C. Kakwani, *Income inequality and poverty* (New York, Oxford University Press, 1980).
4. A. B. Atkinson. 'On the measurement of inequality', *Journal of Economic Theory*, vol. 2, 1970, pp. 244–63.
5. O. D. Duncan and B. Duncan, 'A methodological analysis of segregation indexes', *American Sociological Review*, vol. 20, 1975, pp. 210–17.
6. D. M. Smith, *Human geography: A welfare approach* (Edward Arnold, 1977, p. 134). For other measures of geographical inequalities, see M. Chisholm and J. Oeppen, *The changing pattern of employment, regional specialisation and industrial localisation in Britain* (London, Croom Helm, 1973).
7. H. Theil, *Statistical decomposition analysis* (Amsterdam, North-Holland, 1972, p. 65).
8. The series of articles by L. A. Goodman and W. H. Kruskal in *Journal of the American Statistical Association*, 1954, 1959, 1963, and 1972. Specially relevant here is the 1959 article.
9. In the United States, for example, considerable attention is devoted to allocation techniques. See *Report on statistics for allocation of funds*, Statistical Working Paper 1 (Office of Federal Statistical Policy and Standards, Washington, DC, 1978).
10. *Household Budgetary Survey 1975/76*, Report no. 1 (Port of Spain, Central Statistical Office, 1977), p. 9.

27 Statistics on employees in the service sector, particularly the public sector

Some experiences with employment statistics from an administrative information system in Norway

J. Stokkan

Introduction

The development of a statistical system for employees in Norway has demonstrated some general problems in producing statistics from an employer-based reporting system, especially in classifying the employees by industry and by region. In this paper experiences from this work will be discussed and illustrated by examples, particularly from the service and the public sector.

The employee statistics are based on an administrative information system – which will in future be the main source of employment statistics in Norway – giving detailed breakdowns by demographic variables, industry and region. The statistics will eventually be produced monthly. The information system was set up in 1978, but the system for continuous updating of the relevant register has not yet managed to yield a quality of data sufficient for statistical purposes. There are still some problems to be overcome in the reporting system before it is possible to publish statistics on a regular basis.

The reporting unit in the system is the employer, which may correspond either to the establishment or to the enterprise. For most analytical and planning purposes, variables referring to the establishment, i.e. the physical place of work, are required from the statistics. The problems encountered in tackling these problems, which are general in employer/enterprise-based statistics, are reviewed below. Our experience seems to indicate that these problems are especially pronounced in parts of the service sector, and in particular in large, functionally or regionally, diversified public agencies.

The administrative basis for the statistics on employees

The administrative basis for the statistics is a register of employees which is linked to a register of employers (employee/employer registers). These are used for administrative purposes by several public authorities. The main administrative users are the National Insurance Institution and the tax authorities. The registers are updated by the local insurance offices and centrally co-ordinated copies of the local registers are created weekly for administrative and statistical purposes.

The updating of the register of employers is based on reports to the local insurance authority. The register of employers is linked to the register of enterprises and establishments in the Central Bureau of Statistics in order to obtain information on the industry and the institutional sector of the employers from that of the relevant enterprises and establishments.

The updating of the register on employees is based on reports from the employer that are supplied whenever a person starts or leaves employment. Such a report must be made within eight days after the start or termination of employment. All residents in Norway have a personal identification number which is used in all administrative contexts – and thus also in the register of employees. Figure 27.1 on the following page describes the linkages between the various registers involved.

There is a legal obligation, but no automatic incentive, for the employer to report the start or the termination of an employment, but a system of controls and sanctions (fines) has been established in order to avoid non-reporting. The administration of the control procedure is mainly the responsibility of the local insurance authorities, but the central authorities have also established control routines.

The main type of control is the control for duplicates. A person may have only one main employer but several secondary employers. The rules for identifying the main employer are based on the expected weekly hours of work and the date of starting work.

The statistical product

All employees who are expected to work for at least one week and for at least four hours during the week must be reported to the register of employees. People absent from work (because of illness, vacation, etc.), but who have not left their employment, will still be registered as employees.

The linkage between the register of employees and the register of employers gives information on the location (municipality) of the workplace. The linkage between the register of employers and the register of enterprises and establishments gives the industry. By linking the register of employees to the Central Population Register it will be possible to get

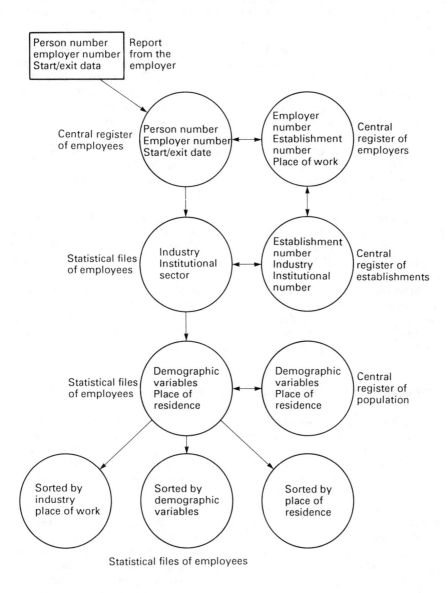

Figure 27.1 Linkages between registers for the production of employee statistics

age, sex, marital status, citizenship and location (municipality) of residence.

The registers will be used to produce the following types of statistics regularly:

(*a*) Working tables for the Central Bureau of Statistics (CBS) which describe in detail the working and quality of the reporting system. These will be used to monitor the quality of the statistical data to be published, and used as a tool when it becomes necessary to check strange developments in the statistics prepared for publication.

(*b*) Monthly data on employees, covering age, sex, industry and place of work.

(*c*) Quarterly data on employees, similar to the monthly series, with additional specification of marital status and citizenship.

(*d*) Yearly data on employees, on place of residence, turnover, size of firms, etc., are added to the quarterly data.

In addition to the statistics produced regularly, the registers will make possible the analysis of a large number of important questions relating to the working of the labour market. It will also be possible to link the observations for individual employees and/or firms over time and with other data.

These plans for the regular statistical programmes have not yet been implemented, as the administrative information systems do not yet provide data of the necessary quality. The most important problems are obtaining estimates of short-term (monthly) changes fast enough and securing reliable estimates of the distribution by place of work.

Classification by industry and region

The classification by industry and by place of work is based first on the link between the employee and the employer and second on the link between the employer and the establishment in the register of enterprises and establishments maintained by the CBS (see Figure 27.1). This is the method for linking each employer with the correct information about his industry and region (place of work).

Two important requirements must be fulfilled if we are to obtain the correct linkage between the employee and the establishment (place of work). First, the employer must subdivide the enterprise into the appropriate establishments (according to the establishment definition based on ISIC) to get a correct subdivision by industry and by region. Second, the employer must connect each employee to the right establishment when reporting the start and termination of employment.

Experience so far has demonstrated that many employers have not subdivided their enterprises according to the instructions. For example, some employers use a sub-division which follows their administrative organisation and in some cases does not coincide with the definition of 'establishment'.

This demonstrates a conflict between the convenience of employers, who wish to use their established administrative routines in reporting about their employees – even though this may in fact be cumbersome – and the statistical and administrative requirement for the definitions of the system to be followed. The result is incorrect classification of employees, by industry and/or region. We believe that this is a common problem in all statistical systems when the employer is responsible for the statistical information, i.e. in all establishment-based employment statistics. It seems to be especially pronounced among public employers (state agencies and local authorities).

Classification by region (place of work)

An establishment is in principle defined as 'a functional unit which is engaged predominantly in activities within a specific activity group' at a single physical location. With some exceptions, for the building industry and construction and transport, activities engaged in by an enterprise in different municipalities are always considered to be locally distinct and are therefore treated as relating to separate establishments.

It is the enterprise (the legal entity) which has the responsibility of reporting to the employee/employer registers. In some cases the actual reporting is done by the local administration. However, in other cases the reports are sent by the central office in the enterprise. This is the case especially when the enterprise consists of a large head office with a number of regional offices – each with only a few persons employed, for example the distribution system of the oil companies, and the local offices of the insurance companies. This is a very common pattern in the public sector, where we often find agencies with only a few employees situated in each municipality. The responsibilities of the employer are often delegated to an intermediate regional level and sometimes even combined for several government agencies (which may belong to different industries). It has consequently been difficult to establish the regional dimension of the register system for the public sector. This is partly because the identification of local establishments has not been as well developed in the register of establishments for the public sector as in the private sector. Thus the administration of the enterprise is not accustomed to deal with such requirements, partly because of the combination of widely regionally dispersed employees and a centralised personnel administration.

An example will illustrate the situation of many agencies. The following table compares the number of employees of the Norwegian Meteorological Institute in different municipalities according to a wage register system of the central government employees and the employee/employer register. (The wage register system has a different reporting system which ensures relatively reliable information about workplaces but which is deficient in other respects.)

Place of employment: municipalities	Employees according to wage register (Nov. 1980)	Employees according to employee/employer register (Nov. 1980)
Oslo	189	489
Bergen	0	0
Tromsø	45	27
21 different municipalities	253	0
Total	487	516

We find that 300 persons too many were reported to the employee/ employer register as employed in Oslo and correspondingly 253 employees were not registered in the employee/employer register in the 21 municipalities of their actual employment.

The consequences of these biases are that too many employees are registered as working in Oslo and in the administrative centres of the counties and too few employees are registered as working in other municipalities. Special institutions with a special pattern of location can give other distortions in the employment picture given by the administrative, employer-based records.

Classification by industry

The definition of an establishment requires that an enterprise which is engaged in a number of different activities within a local area shall be subdivided into separate establishments in the register of establishments and the register of employers. In practice, some operational rules of thumb are followed. Even so, employers often do not have personnel records for these units and it has proved difficult to persuade employers to give information in such cases. This problem is most pronounced in the public sector, especially in local (municipal) administrations.

The municipalities in Norway vary greatly as regards the size of their population, and the magnitude of their local authority activities, so the same pattern of subdivisions cannot be applied to all municipal employers. However, to provide a reliable basis for the industry classification, the municipal employees within each municipality ought to be allocated to 20–50 different establishments depending upon the population size. An examination of the situation in one local administration area or 'county' showed that nearly half of the municipalities had been divided into less than ten establishments. Twenty per cent of the municipalities had not established a special unit for education. The same case applies to establishments belonging to other industries, for example health services and social welfare services. Statistics by industry will therefore show too many employees in local government administration and too few in, for instance, education. This will be the case for the statistics for both the whole country and for many municipalities. Regional comparisons are thus made impossible.

The following table compares data from the employee/employer register and the labour force sample survey. Although the definitions are not directly comparable, the distortion between the industries is clearly illustrated.

Industry	Statistics of employees from the employee/employer register (no. of employees)	Labour force sample survey (no. of employees)
91 Public administration and defence	145,000	106,000
93 Social and related community services	311,000	377,000

The system used to specify the public sector

When formulating plans for the new statistics on employees, we wished to meet the demand for statistics of the public sector as such. We have noticed a great interest in statistics identifying the public sector from the side of the public planning institutions, the national accounts and others. The classification by industry is not satisfactory for this purpose, because many industry sectors include both private and public activities. A system has been established for classifying all employers by institutional sector, but some work remains to be done before the system is fully implemented.

The system utilises an institutional code already used in the financial statistics, and for that purpose embodied in the register of enterprises and establishments.

The institutional sector codes refer to the following:

(*a*) National government (state) and social security administration.
(*b*) Local (municipal) administration.
(*c*) State banks, central government enterprises (for example Norway's State Railways, Norway's State Telephone Company).
(*d*) Bank of Norway.
(*e*) Autonomous state enterprises.
(*f*) Private sector.

The time dimension

Whenever a person starts or leaves employment data on this will be entered on the register on employees. An exception occurs when a person moves from one establishment to another within the same enterprise. This information will be updated only once a year and the register contains only the most recent situation.

The registers thus allow an analysis of the labour market history of employees. The registers give data showing for which periods employees have worked with different employers.

On the other hand, the employees can be aggregated according to the employers they work for, giving, for each employer, the number of employees at work at any time, how long they stayed, etc. This shows when a firm started as an employer, when it stopped as an employer and how the number of employees varies with time. There can, however, be a problem in following a firm when it splits into other firms, is taken over by a larger firm or even changes owner. When an establishment number is assigned to an establishment this number is stable over time.

The present situation and problems to be solved

The registers were originally intended to be operational from 1 July 1978. However, the system for the continuous updating of the registers proved to be inadequate on a number of important points. Some of the problems have been solved, but detailed controls of the registers, monitoring of the reporting system, and trial production of statistics have demonstrated that there still remain a number of difficult questions which must be solved before we can publish official statistics on a regular basis. These are as follows:

(a) The special reporting systems established for people working in the merchant marine and in the offshore oil industries do not yet work satisfactorily.

(b) A number of large and important employers, especially in the public sector, have not subdivided their enterprises into the required local and/or functional units (establishments). Detailed statistics by industry or place of work (municipality) are therefore not yet possible.

(c) Not all instances of start and termination of employment are reported, and there is strong suspicion that job-leavers in particular are significantly underreported.

(d) The reports from employers are much too late in arriving, thus making statistics impossible.

Work is continuing to improve the system on all these points. The improvements presently being carried out and planned for the future cover both legal changes which will make the controls and sanctions work more efficiently, and adjustments in the local administrative procedures both for the purposes of the registers and their use in the everyday tasks of the local insurance offices.

In 1982 the CBS started a limited distribution of a quarterly report with some data from the register system. It has not yet been decided when official statistics will be published on a regular basis. This report both describes the working of the administrative information system (time-lags, results of control procedures, etc.) and presents a selection of statistics on employees. We feel that these statistics, although flawed, will provide useful background information for many purposes.

Conclusions

Based on Norwegian experiences it seems that although the problems related to obtaining satisfactory employment statistics from the service sectors – and in particular the public sector – are no different in principle from those of other sectors, there may be some difference in the importance of these problems between the various sectors, as follows:

(a) The problem of defining the geographical 'place of work' of an employee is found more often in some service sectors – for example in transportation, wholesale trade, business and technical consultancy, repair work – than in other sectors. However, this is also a major problem for the construction and building industries.

(b) The administrations of the employers in the service sector in general, and the public sector in particular, seem less willing or able to tackle the practical administrative problems in identifying the separate functional units and different regional units of a large organisation. Correspondingly there also seem to be more difficult problems in allocating the new employees to the correct sub-unit (establishment) in the multi-establishment enterprises.

(c) A disproportionate number of the 'difficult' organisations, i.e. the employers who do not comply with the reporting requirements of the combined administrative/statistical information system, are to be found in the public sector.

We believe that these problems are common to all employer-based reporting systems. This means that detailed and extensive quality controls are necessary for statistics where good 'place-of-work'-related variables are required from such systems. Important examples of such statistics are: statistics on the industry distribution of employees; statistics on the geographic distribution of the place of work of employees; and statistics on the geographic pattern of work-related travelling (commuting).

28 National computer networking of employment statistics; the British example

A. R. Townsend, M. J. Blakemore and R. Nelson

Introduction

The ability to collect statistics is not always matched by an ability to retrieve and analyse them. This may be the case even within a country with a centralised and computerised statistical service and standard definitions of variables and geographical areas.

Recall, however, the computer seat-reservation systems now used by national airlines or railway systems. Both in some industrialised countries and in some developing economies it is normal practice for travel-office staff to use a visual display unit (VDU) to check the up-to-date pattern of unreserved seats by means of a telecommunications link to a national computer. This computer can be simultaneously accessed by travel-office staff in many different towns throughout the country.

Modern telecommunications can do a similar job for labour market analysts and policy-makers spread over many different towns in a given country. It would be possible to use a computer system to match job-seekers and job vacancies with each other in the same town or different towns. Here, we will confine ourselves to the supply of information, the retrieval, display, analysis and mapping of labour-market data, particularly of unpublished analyses for individual labour-market areas. The emphasis of the system which we will describe is on access by ordinary office staff to data which they may select for standard or non-standard aggregations of variables and/or areas, according to regional or local needs and circumstances.

This article describes the National Online Manpower Information System (NOMIS), which has been developed since 1978 by the British government's Manpower Services Commission (MSC). The system is maintained at the computer of the University of Durham, in the North of England, and can be accessed at any one moment by up to 25 simultaneous users. At the date of writing there were 90 such users in different towns in England, Scotland and Wales, including the headquarters of the Manpower Services Commission in the northern city of Sheffield, and ten Regional Manpower Intelligence Units in principal towns. Users also included the House of Commons, local authorities, educational and research institutions, and commercial users.

The collection of data and definition of variables remain the responsibility of the Department of Employment, which publishes the results of the monthly measurement of unemployment and vacancies in press notices and, along with many other variables, in the long-established *Employment Gazette*. NOMIS provides for the storage and organised retrieval of 750 million items of data from 1971 to the latest month. It covers data for unemployment, vacancies, employment, population, population projections and (prospectively) migration at a wide variety of spatial scales. The key feature of its operation is to store data at the basic level at which it was collected, the 'building brick', and to provide rapid aggregation of these 'bricks' according to users' needs.

Statisticians internationally will probably be interested in the concepts which underpin NOMIS. We are well aware that it is not a system which can be transferred directly to another country's data. However, the logic and technical procedures are transferable, and advice can be provided to other governments on the design and implementation of a national system for their own country. International statisticians who are interested in British data at any geographical level are invited to become users of NOMIS through the international public computer networks.

History and objectives

The British National Online Manpower Information System was started at first as a research project to assist the extraction of large amounts of manpower data at the level of local labour markets. Following the success of a pilot project for the northern region of England in 1978 to 1980, the system was expanded to cover the whole of Great Britain (i.e. England, Scotland and Wales) and to cover a greater range of data types. It is important to stress that development has taken place in response to the practical requests of existing and potential users as well as the professional skills of geographers and computing staff of the Universities of Durham and Newcastle-upon-Tyne, all of whom have been represented on the national steering committee of the system.

The aim of the system is to provide and further develop a permanent 'online' manpower information system, allowing instant access to current and historical data on employment, unemployment, job vacancies and the Census of Population. The system is 'interactive'; that is, it permits users who have no computer-programming experience to extract, sort, sift and analyse data according to their local or national requirements. At an individual VDU the user can select different data types and analyse changes over time, variations between areas, or combinations of both, for a range of variables. The data can be selected for a given range of classifications of occupations, industries or areas, or 'user-defined' combinations.

The system has been costed and approved by central Treasury authorities for the ten years 1986–96 on the basis of full operation since 1982. The practical results include rapid or extensive analyses of labour market data for ministers of different government departments, Members of Parliament, senior officials, local authorities, development agencies and research institutions. The system has been found to allow more cost-effective use of staff in regional offices. Particularly, it enables users to provide a more comprehensive service than would otherwise be possible. It provides much better facilities of analysis for MSC staff engaged in monitoring employment trends in local, regional and national labour markets. These assist in the preparation and monitoring of MSC plans for training and 'special employment measures' (or 'job creation' programmes). In turn they contribute to improved analysis of 'assisted areas' under British regional policy, which are eligible for benefits from the European Regional Development Fund.

Technical management of NOMIS

The system is housed entirely at the University of Durham's Computer Centre on an AMDAHL V8 computer, using the Michigan Terminal System (MTS) as the operating system. Full-time staff of the system have been employed in the Department of Geography since 1980, where the Systems Manager is Mr Nelson and the Systems Programmer is Dr L. G. O'Brien. The database is regularly updated and information is mounted usually within 24 hours of the receipt of tapes of raw uncompressed data from the Department of Employment.

Given the large number of local geographical areas included on these national tapes, a key problem for such a system is that of the 'compaction' of geographical data sets. At times in the past it has seemed that the availability of a certain large amount of storage has encouraged computer users to avoid the question of storage compression. It would seem that compaction of geographical data sets is only likely to take place as the result of two pressures. First is the case where the data sets exceed the capacity provided even by modern disk technology. The second is where the real money is being paid in 'disk charges'. In either of these cases data compression, while involving extra processing costs, is likely to result in an overall decrease in real cost. Both pressures exist on NOMIS. The dominant use of NOMIS is during normal office hours, when the largest number of users are using the system, at the same time as researchers in Regional Manpower Intelligence Units, or the House of Commons Library. Most want fast and effective response. Two major areas of development make NOMIS usable during such a pressured time period. The first is a tightly written 'source code' which aims to minimise the amount of 'memory' used by any one user. Thus each user's time on the main computer is kept as low as possible, and, while this is not discussed further here, it does allow a larger number of NOMIS users to be 'signed on' simultaneously without seriously impairing the overall performance of the main university computer.

The second major area is the efficient use of data compaction. All the data sets have to be geographically available in a wide range of aggregations and temporarily available as extensive time series. Of fundamental importance here is the ability to utilise highly efficient methods of data compaction (Blakemore and Nelson, 1985). Given the work pattern of most users, the majority of usage is between 9.30 a.m. and 5 p.m., although the system is available at all times, subject to computer maintenance schedules. The competition from other university computer users, combined with the mandate to provide interactive access to all data sets, has meant a careful consideration of data compaction. Mr Nelson utilises a variant of 'coded delta technique' with remarkable results. At the first level a set of non-negative value is scanned to see how many zero elements can be compressed. This reduces a set

123 000 10050 0 33 34 0 0 0 9

to

123-3 10050-1 33 34-39.

The second stage examines the set to find the highest value and uses 'assembler coding' to compress the numbers further from 32-bit sequences into either 12, 16 and 24 bits, or keeps them as 32 bits. This latter stage has proved crucial in keeping down the size of the database which comprises in excess of 750 million data items.

Stored uncompacted, the current data matrix would occupy some 2,500 megabytes of storage, but is compacted to 600 megabytes. In disk charges alone, at commercial rates, this would save £1.25 million a year! The efficiency of compactions is such that it is quicker to read the compacted disk file and unpack it in memory than it is to store it uncompacted and read it back. Blakemore and Nelson (1985) also give the example of the biggest single file, the ward-level 1981 Census of Population (some 60 million raw data items) which is compacted to 30.52 per cent of the original yet takes only 26 per cent more processor time to reconstitute entirely when compared with the time to read an expensively stored uncompacted version. Translated into commercial cost this is only £30 for processing the whole census.

Data provided

The general British system of providing labour market information is distinctive and has several implications for NOMIS. The most striking feature is the reliance on direct information from employers for employment data, and from the administration of unemployment benefit (financial payments) for data on unemployment. There is increasing use of sample household ('labour force') surveys, but so far this has been used in a supplementary role at local level and cannot compare with the 100 per cent coverage of 'employees in employment' intended in the Census of Employment or the full enumeration of claimants of unemployment benefit.

These records, together with data on notified vacancies and placings, provide the main data of NOMIS. The data tapes as received are already in the form of aggregated statistics which exclude the identification of individual employers or workpeople. This means that the NOMIS system does not include confidential data on individual people or firms, and it is this in turn which facilitates its extension to non-government users (subject to special procedures where a figure for employment in a local industry may include only a very small number of employers).

Since 1982, the computerisation of payments of unemployment benefit has also facilitated the introduction of 'labour force flow statistics' (see Chapter 14) in providing for given periods the number of workpeople entering or completing a spell of time in which they receive unemployment benefit. These spells can readily be analysed on NOMIS in terms of duration, and attributed to different age and sex groups.

Including also full details of the Census of Population, 1981, there are thus four basic sets of information: employment, unemployment, vacancy and population data. Details for each are determined by what is collected in the first place, what is useful to know and what can practicably be stored on a single computer system:

Employees in employment: aggregate data for local areas by
   Males/females: full-time/part-time and the
   UK Standard Industrial Classification, 1968 – June 1971–78, Sept. 1981; 1980 – Sept. 1981, 1984
   Unemployment: totals for local areas by
   Males/females: school leavers: principal age/duration categories – monthly, Oct. 1982 onwards
     'Flow and stock counts' of the unemployed – monthly, Oct. 1982 onwards
     Detailed age and duration bands – quarterly, Apr. 1983 onwards
   Vacancies and placings
   Industrial analysis of vacancies
     unfilled and placings – quarterly, May 1984 onwards
   Monthly vacancies and placings – Sept. 1985 onwards
   Population
   All tables of the standard GB Small Area Statistics (1981 Census) – Apr. 1981
   Population projections for one-year age groups – June 1981–2001

The addition of other data sets is kept continuously under review. Prospective additions at the time of writing include the analysis of vacancy durations, and of migration between local authorities. The most comprehensive coverage remains that of unemployment data; with the exception of seasonal adjustments it now includes *at local level*, and aggregates thereof, all unemployment data regularly published at national or other levels in the *Employment Gazette*. Full variants are retained back to 1978 (but not listed above) of the previous count of unemployed registrants, with a summary series of data back to June 1972.

Geographical detail within Great Britain

In the past, the British pattern of local authority boundaries (used by the Census of Population) had proved too archaic for regular labour market analysis, and Department of Employment statistics were based on separate Employment Exchange, now Job Centre, boundaries. The reform of local government boundaries in 1974 (England and Wales) and Scotland (1975) provided a more coherent pattern of 459 local authority districts, to which employment and unemployment statistics have been related since 1984. For dates before 1984, NOMIS continues to carry remnants of the previous dual system, and had to adopt a system of 852 'amalgamated office areas' to deal with the opening and closure of Job Centres, which are still the basis of vacancy statistics.

The basic 'building brick' of the present system comprises approximately 10,000 'wards', which are constituent areas of districts. Employers' and employees' addresses are allocated to wards by reference to the six-digit 'postcode' areas used in the census or in dispatching benefit cheques to the unemployed.

The NOMIS computer programs will aggregate unemployment and population data for individual wards to produce data for several boundary systems which cover Great Britain:

(a) 459 local authority districts, 95 local education authority areas, 64 counties and 11 regions;
(b) 653 parliamentary constituencies;
(c) 322 travel-to-work areas;
(d) MSC administrative regions (various).

The 322 travel-to-work areas were defined by the Department of Employment on the basis of detailed computer analysis of journeys between wards, as reported in the 1981 Census of Population. They are the smallest areas for which unemployment percentage rates may be quoted, and provide the fullest version on NOMIS of the Census of Employment at the four-digit level of the UK Standard Industrial Classification, 1980.

The extraction and analysis of statistics

The user requires no experience of computer programming to access NOMIS data on a VDU. Each user is supplied with a 14-page introductory guide (which includes worked examples), a 143-page reference manual, and a 142-page directory of geographical and other classifications. Different categories of data share as far as possible the same set of computer commands, concerning the date(s) required; the sex(es) for which data are required; the part(s) of the relevant industrial or occupational classification which are required; and the geographical area(s). These areas can be any subset of the aggregations already defined. Users can define their own specialised area definitions, and can adduce other aggregations for purposes of comparison. The online help system has a search facility which details which units of a certain type are contained within a particular region. For ward-level data a search technique exists to list wards within any standard geographical area.

Even the simplest analytical procedures have been found to be of great benefit to the average users. In most data sets it is possible to include percentages in the rows or columns of a table, and unemployment for travel-to-work areas can be expressed as a percentage rate. The values or percentages of a table can be used to re-sort and rank the order of entries. A common requirement is to express the change occurring between the beginning and end of a given time-period. The last two points are illustrated in Table 28.1. In the year ending February 1986, Great Britain was still sustaining gently rising unemployment; it was little known how much geographical variation in the trend occurred in this period, but the leading five areas of increase are shown in Table 28.1. The data show that the worst areas of deterioration lay in 'peripheral' regions. The worst three areas of proportionate change were all connected with coalmining. However, values of chi-squared show that the most significant change in the whole country lay in South Yorkshire, concurrently with industrial problems in heavy industry (notably coal).

Table 28.1 Leading areas of Great Britain for increased unemployment, year ending February 1986 (counties of England and Wales, regions of Scotland)

Area	Unemployed (claimants of benefit)				
	February 1985	February 1986	Change		
			Nos.	%	Chi-squared
Fife	20.625	22,683	+ 2,058	+ 10.0	138.5
South Yorkshire	96,474	105,832	+ 9,358	+ 9.7	604.9
Northumberland	15,403	16,659	+ 1,256	+ 8.2	62.8
Somerset	17,413	18,478	+ 1,065	+ 6.1	33.2
Cornwall	27,052	28,609	+ 1,557	+ 5.8	43.4
Great Britain	3,200,719	3,255,589	+ 54,870	+ 1.7	0.0

Table 28.2 Shift-share analysis of employees in employment, counties of Tyne and Wear and Durham, 1971–81 (thousands)

	Total employment		Change 1971–81		National component	Structural component		Differential component	
	1971	1981	Nos.	%		Nos.	%	Nos.	%
Primary industries	52.1	29.3	− 22.8	− 43.7	− 1.3	− 7.4	− 14.1	− 14.1	− 27.1
Manufacturing	259.5	186.4	− 73.1	− 28.2	− 6.5	− 56.6	− 21.8	− 10.0	− 3.8
Construction	46.4	38.3	− 8.2	− 17.6	− 1.2	− 2.6	− 5.6	− 4.4	− 9.5
Services	353.2	383.6	+ 30.4	+ 8.6	− 8.9	+ 56.4	+ 16.0	− 17.1	− 4.9
Unclassified	0	0.7	+ 0.7	+ 0.0	0	0	+ 2.5	+ 0.7	+ 0.0
Total	711.2	638.3	− 72.9	− 10.3	− 17.9	− 10.1	− 1.4	− 44.9	− 6.3

There are specialised output structures, for instance to calculate the median duration of unemployment or the likelihood of becoming or remaining unemployed. Chi-squared techniques are available to distinguish significant from other changes (as used in Townsend, 1986). The system readily provides for the use of 'location quotients', which are related to 'shift-share analysis'. Table 28.2 employs a special aggregation of two counties in the analysis of employment change over a decade; for reasons of space the shift-share analysis is provided at the level of five sectors only of the economy, although this exercise could have been undertaken just as readily at the level of 159 industrial categories. The table shows how a 10 per cent decline in total employment can, for the major part, be attributed to its structural dependence on manufacturing industry. In terms of a 'differential shift' the dominant elements of change lay in the primary and service sectors.

The NOMIS system provides one of the most efficient ways of accessing the Census of Population, 1981; the user may express the relationship between any pair of variables (which may themselves sum different items of the original tabulation) as a ratio.

Mapping of data

Virtually all data on the system can, when converted into ratios, be mapped, using five or more shades of black and white or of three colours. The basis of mapping lies in the storage of 'digitised' map files based on the whole country's wards. From these it is possible to build to any of the spatial hierarchies which use wards as their building block (parliamentary constituencies, regions, counties, travel-to-work areas, etc.), and to extract subsets of the country for specific regional or local mapping in the GIMMS mapping system, which provides high-quality cartographic results which are posted to the user. The use of automatic charts and graphs is being planned, but is not implemented as yet.

Retrieving results

Output is usually obtained immediately as hard copy on a printer attached to the VDU, but there are options to transfer data in tabular form to a micro-computer or another computer for further manipulation or local printing; or direct the output to the Durham University high-quality printer for posting on, usually within 48 hours.

Communications with the system are mainly by the use of public telephone lines, although there is limited use of non-public systems. A wide variety of terminals can be used with the Durham Computer System, using a unique identifier and password.

Costs

Costs to a user organisation comprise those of equipment; communications costs; computer usage of the Durham University computer; a small surcharge to cover costs of data collection (as required by government policy since January 1985); and costs of a user's manual, newsletters and help and assistance (these latter charges are varied according to the level of support required by different kinds of user). For further details readers are invited to write to:

Mr. Norman Davis,
Chief Statistician,
Manpower Services Commission,
Moorfoot,
Sheffield S1 4PQ
(for intending users)

Mr. Michael Blakemore,
NOMIS,
Department of Geography,
Science Site,
University of Durham,
Durham DH1 3LE
(for technical advice)

Conclusion

The Manpower Services Commission funds the NOMIS System through a current budget of £580,000 for the three years 1986–9, including a full allowance for their own expected usage. In addition the system greatly simplifies for them the transmission of data to local authorities, universities, polytechnics and research institutes, which can find what data and analyses they want on a 'self-service' basis. Since the system was advertised to such users in April 1986 there has been a large increase in the number of local authority users. One interesting response was that the prime value of the system to them (given that they can also purchase output or tapes for their own areas) lay in its analytical facilities, and the ability to make comparisons between their own area and other parts of the country.

Of course, any improvement in the availability of labour market information is only partial, and is in itself no substitute for improved policies. The NOMIS System has not of itself generated the collection of new data which constitute fresh variables. However, the great improvements now made in access to complex data sets are almost the same thing. With proper attention to staff training NOMIS has greatly speeded up the analysis of data and thereby produced many refinements in its regular use. These benefits have been particularly apparent in regional offices of the Manpower Services Commission.

References

Blakemore, M., and Nelson, R. (1985) 'Data compaction in NOMIS: A geographic information system for the management of employment, unemployment and population data', *University Computing*, vol. 7, no. 3, pp. 144-7.

Townsend, A. R. (1986) 'The location of employment growth after 1978: The surprising significance of dispersed centres' *Environment and Planning A*, vol. 18, pp. 529–45.

Acknowledgements

The present NOMIS System has been developed at the University of Durham, Department of Geography, since 1981, designed and programmed by Robert Nelson. This followed an initial contract in 1978 between the Manpower Services Commission (MSC) and the Universities of Durham and Newcastle-upon-Tyne, this project being led by Professors David Rhind and John Goddard. It has achieved operational status since 1982, and the present contract, due to run until 1991, involves Robert Nelson as Systems Manager, Larry O'Brien as Systems Programmer, Peter Dodds as Mapping Supervisor, and overall direction by Alan Townsend and Michael Blakemore.

29 The redesign of a major establishment survey in the United States

T. J. Plewes

Introduction

In view of the pressing need to widen the availability of statistics on the economic situation of workers, the attention of the international statistical community has, until the recent past, correctly been focused on means of designing and implementing surveys to provide information where none existed. Indeed, the development of data gathering operations from the beginning has been the signal challenge to the international statistical community over the past several decades. It is a complex undertaking which brings to bear skills in all aspects of statistical operations, from basic survey design through to the analysis and publication of results.

The comparative success of these past efforts to initiate and then maintain labour statistics programmes, however, now confronts the international statistical community with a new set of challenges. That is, as the survey operations mature and become interwoven into the national and international information fabric, statistical agencies are increasingly being called upon to review and evaluate the survey operations to determine the quality and upgrade the relevance of the results. Frequently, this evaluation process leads to the conclusion that a midstream redesign of the survey operation is necessary to update both the statistical and analytical foundations of the information.

The recent experience in the United States, where this process is taking place with regard to several major survey operations, leads to the observation that survey redesign incorporates many of the same challenges to the statistical agency that design from the beginning encompasses. In many ways, redesign is a more complex administrative undertaking, for redesign differs from initial design in several critical respects.

First, there is a need to overcome that natural inertia that becomes embedded into any ongoing survey operation. Once the intensive effort and considerable resources have been expended on developing a survey and once the information from that survey becomes generally accepted, the natural tendency is to continue past practices. Survey operations become institutionalised over time and tend to take on, literally, a life of their own.

Second, resources for a redesign, both in terms of technical skills of the persons who must be involved and of financial resources, are often quite difficult to obtain. It may be difficult to 'sell' the need for a redesign, since one must walk the tightrope of defending the adequacy of the current programme, on the one hand, while demonstrating its inadequacies, on the other. Moreover, redesign resources must, in most cases, be added to the resources devoted to the ongoing programme. In order to continue to meet the current demands for information, a redesign operation often must go on concurrently with the production of information under the old system.

Third, in the redesign process, there may be a conflict between the desirability of undertaking those activities which would improve the statistical and conceptual basis of the data and the need to maintain a consistency in the time series. Frequently, the end result of an improvement would be to create a discontinuity in the time series at the point at which the data under the new system are released. This unfavourable impact can be mitigated somewhat if it is possible to provide an overlap of information on both the old and new basis for a period, but that overlap requires duplicative collection and tabulation and further places a burden on technical skills and financial resources.

For some, it may be a wonder, then, that statistical surveys, once initiated, are ever reviewed and modernised. Eventually, however, statistical redesign programmes become inevitable, and programmes are under way in a number of countries, relating to redesign of a wide variety of statistics. Clearly, the need for modernisation of the surveys has been viewed as of sufficient importance to overcome the natural inertia, the resource constraints, and the dangers to the time series.

The purpose of this paper is to consider the process of redesign of one survey – the establishment-based monthly survey of employment, hours and earnings – in one country, the United States. Though the redesign process has not been completed, sufficient lessons have been learned to enable a review of the process of redesign and to identify the central focus of the effort. And though this particular survey has characteristics unique to its own history of development and to the US statistical system, the process of redesign of this survey undoubtedly contains some elements of commonality with other surveys and other nations.

Description of the current survey

In approaching a redesign, it is critically important to understand the strengths and weaknesses of the current survey. In a redesign, this is the starting place.

In the United States the establishment survey of employment, hours and earnings is one of a family of surveys, censuses, and administrative records sources which provides key economic intelligence on the status of the workforce as input to economic decision-making by government, industry, labour organisations, and the public. In both scope and coverage, this survey operation has few rivals, being one of the largest collections of data in the field of economic statistics.

Scope and coverage

Each month the Bureau of Labor Statistics (BLS) and co-operating statistical agencies in each of the 50 states, the District of Columbia, Puerto Rico and the Virgin Islands collect, tabulate and publish data on employment, hours and earnings from a sample of establishments representing all non-agricultural industries and government. The sample is impressively large, with an active sample of nearly 190,000 reporting units representing the approximately 4.5 million employers in the United States economy. Because the sample is designed to cover, with certainty, the largest employing units, the sample returns reflect coverage of a rather high proportion of the universe – about 35 per cent of total non-agricultural employment. The extent of that coverage varies by industry and size of firm, creating coverage problems which affect the quality of the data; more will be made of this point later in this paper.

Due to the size and pervasiveness of the survey, data are published in extensive detail. Over 2,600 separate series on employment hours and earnings by industry are available and tracked at the national level, while some 8,700 series covering 3,400 industry groupings are published in the aggregate for the states, territories and 200 substate areas.

A number of data types are available. These series types range from total employment, production and non-supervisory worker employment and female employment to average weekly and hourly earnings, average weekly hours and average overtime hours (for manufacturing only). For many of the data series seasonally adjusted data are published.

Timing

Employment hours and earnings are measured for the pay period including the 12th of the month, which is standard for all federal agencies collecting employment data on an establishment basis. They are among the most timely of economic statistics with initial monthly estimates published in a press release just three weeks after the reference period. The press release contains preliminary national estimates of non-agricultural employment, weekly hours, and gross average weekly and hourly earnings in the preceding month, for major industry categories, with considerable seasonally adjusted detail. The press release also includes a brief analysis of current trends in employment hours and earnings, pointing up current developments as compared with those for the previous month and the same month in the preceding year.

Multiple closings

The timeliness of release of survey results is both a virtue and drawback of the employment, hours and earnings survey programme. While these data add an important current dimension to understanding the economic situation – in that they provide rich supplementation to the data collected and released simultaneously from the labour force survey of households and they constitute several important leading and coincident indicators of the cyclical behaviour of the economy – the initial survey results are based on a preliminary sample take. At the time of issuance of the initial estimates (first closing) about 40–50 per cent of the sample reporters have submitted usable reports; a month later, at second closing, this percentage jumps to 80 per cent; and at third closing, two months after the reference period, 95 per cent of reports are incorporated in the estimates. Hence, the practice of the Bureau of Labor Statistics is to issue two sets of preliminary estimates, with final estimates for the reference period published two months later. Since it is the initial estimate, based on the least adequate sample reporting, that is the most closely watched and weighed in economic decision-making, attention must be paid to making this estimate as good as possible. The measure of success in this endeavour is the amount of revision in the estimate with the additional sample that comes with subsequent closings and, once yearly, as the sample-based estimates are bench-marked to the universe.

Concepts

The basic concepts which underscore the survey have remained consistent for some 35 years.

An establishment is defined as an economic unit which produces goods or services, such as a factory, mine, office, or store. It is generally at a single physical location and it is engaged predominantly in one type of economic activity. Where a single physical location encompasses two or more distinct and separate activities these are treated as separate establishments, provided that separate payroll records are available and certain other criteria are met.

Employed persons include both permanent and temporary employees and those who are working either full- or part-time. Workers on an establishment payroll who are on paid sick leave (when pay is received directly from the employer), on paid holiday or paid vacation, or who work during only a part of the specified pay period are counted as employed. Persons on the payroll of more than one establishment during the pay period are counted in each establishment which reports them, whether the duplication is due to turnover or dual jobholding. Persons are considered employed if they receive pay for any part of the specified pay period, but are not considered employed if they received no pay at all for the pay period. Thus, persons not on pay status as a result of an industrial dispute, for example, are excluded from the employment count. Since proprietors, the self-employed, and unpaid family workers do not have the status of 'paid employees', they are not included. Domestic workers in households are excluded from the data for non-agricultural establishments. Government employment statistics refer to civilian employees only, and employment on farms is not covered.

The figure which includes all persons who meet these specifications is designated 'all employees'. Major categories of employment are differentiated from this overall total, primarily to ensure the expeditious collection of current statistics on hours and earnings; these groups of employees are designated production workers, construction workers, or non-supervisory workers, depending upon the industry.

For example, in manufacturing ·and mining industries, data on employment, hours, and payrolls are collected for production workers. This group, in general, covers those employees, up through the level of working supervisors, who are engaged directly in the manufacture of the product of the establishment. Among the exclusions from this category are persons in executive and managerial positions, and persons engaged in activities such as accounting, sales, advertising, routine office work, professional and technical functions, and force account construction.

Collection

The primary collection of the current sample is conducted by the state agencies which have co-operative agreements with the BLS. The agencies mail schedules to a sample of establishments in the states each month. A 'shuttle' schedule is used (BLS Form 790 series), that is, one which is submitted each month in the calendar year by the respondent, edited by the state agency, and returned to the respondent for use again the following month. The state agency uses the current month's information provided on the forms to develop state and area estimates of employment, hours and earnings, and simultaneously forwards the latest month's data, by telecommunication linkages or in machine-readable form, to the Washington, DC, office of the Bureau of Labor Statistics, where they are used independently to prepare estimates at the national level.

The shuttle schedule has been used in this programme since 1930. The report forms are not exactly alike for every industry, but most of them request data on total employment, number of women employees, number of production workers (in manufacturing and mining), construction workers (in contract construction industries), or non-supervisory workers (in other non-manufacturing industries), and, for these workers, data on payroll, paid hours, and, for manufacturing, overtime hours. The schedule contains detailed instructions and definitions of the data items to be reported by the respondent.

The characteristics of the shuttle schedule are particularly important in maintaining continuity and consistency in reporting from month to month. The design exhibits automatically to the respondent the trend of the reported data during the year covered by the schedule, and therefore, the relationship of the current figure to the data for the previous month. The schedule also has operational advantages; for example, accuracy and economy are obtained by entering identifying codes and the address of the respondent only once a year. But use of the shuttle schedule also has a statistical disadvantage in that display of previous responses may bias the reporting by establishments.

All schedules are carefully edited by the state agencies each month to make sure that the data are correctly reported and that they are consistent within themselves, with the data reported by the establishment in earlier months, and with those reported by other establishments in their industry. This editing process is carried out in accordance with a detailed manual of instructions prepared by the Bureau of Labor Statistics. When the reports are sent to Washington, they are screened by use of a computer to detect processing errors and reporting errors which may have escaped the states' editing.

Sampling

The state agencies that are responsible for collecting data are also responsible for implementing the sample design, drawn from the universe of establishments which is stratified by industry, and, within each industry, by size of establishment in terms of employment. The primary sample 'frame' of the universe is the listing of establishments covered under state unemployment insurance laws (now numbering over 4,500,000 estab- lishments), supplemented by locally developed employer name and address files for industries and size classes not covered under state unemployment insurance laws.

Sample-derived estimates, by nature, differ a certain amount from the data that would be derived from a complete census or universe count of all establishments. To remove the effects of these small sampling errors from the estimates, as well as to reflect changes in the industrial classification of firms and the formation of new establishments, the Bureau annually 'bench-marks' the survey data against the latest available census of universe information. The source of the census – or bench-mark review – is the periodic tabulation of employment data by industry and size of establishment compiled by state agencies from reports of establishments covered by state unemployment insurance laws (the ES-202 programme). In the course of the annual bench-mark adjustment, the sample-based total employment estimates are revised by tapering the differences between the census and the sample. Coincident with this adjustment, estimates of employment of women, production worker hours and earnings, and the seasonally adjusted series are revised, because they are derived from or weighted by the total employment estimates. The employment estimates on a monthly basis are prepared for over 900 estimating cells or groups of establishments in an industry defined by a three- or four-digit Standard Industrial Classification (SIC) code and by size and regional strata by industry. The estimates for these estimating cells are then aggregated to provide estimates for higher-order industrial groupings. Three basic steps are followed in the computation of estimates for each cell. A total employment figure (bench-mark) for the estimating cell, as of March of each year, is obtained in the annual bench-mark process described below. For each cell, the ratio of employment in one month to that in the preceding month (i.e. a link relative) is computed for sample establishments reporting in both months. Beginning with the bench-mark month, the estimates for each month are obtained by multiplying the estimate for the previous month by the link relative for the current month.

During the year, the sample-based estimates are adjusted on a monthly basis to correct for historical downward bias in the employment estimates caused by the late introduction of new firms into the sample by use of a bias adjustment factor, computed coincidently with the annual benchmark view.[1]

Uses of the data

One important initial stage in any redesign is an assessment of the uses made of the data. An understanding of all key data uses is critical to assuring that the basis of support of the survey operation is continued, that improvements made in the name of statistical enhancement do not eliminate a current or potential usefulness of the data, and to the extent possible, that the redesigned survey will better serve data users. In the final analysis, the data users define the need for the survey, the scope of the operation and statistical reliability standards to which the survey should be targeted.

Over the years the survey of employment, hours and earnings has enjoyed a growing range of uses by virtue of its character, consistency and accessibility. The primary function of the survey remains to provide basic, current economic intelligence on the industrial composition and trends in employment, hours and earnings. In and of themselves, the data have a utility and an economic role in the nation's information base. But the secondary uses which have emerged over the years constitute the source of the most intensive demand and, hence, the greatest challenge in the redesign process.

Within the Bureau, for example, the data have the following major uses:

(1) *In productivity measurement.* Monthly total hours by industry detail and production worker employment data are key inputs to productivity measurement and the quarterly productivity estimates. The annual employment and hours data for detailed industries are used for developing labour inputs for measure of output for employee hour.
(2) *In occupational employment projections.* National employment data by industry detail are projected forward and occupational staffing patterns of the industries are applied to those projected industry levels to produce projected occupational patterns.
(3) *In economic growth studies.* A key input into the BLS economic growth mode is annual employment data by detailed industry.
(4) *In development of subnational unemployment statistics.* The monthly employment data are used both by the BLS and the state agencies as

the source of employment data for those subnational areas for which the household survey fails to provide reliable estimates. Currently the unemployment rates for 40 states and about 200 areas are computed using these survey results as a key input.

(5) *In occupational health and safety statistics.* Detailed annual industry employment levels are used for computing total injury rates, with actual injury experience based on an annual survey and administrative records.

Other federal agencies also use these data extensively:

(1) *In developing economic indicators.* The Bureau of Economic Analysis of the Department of Commerce uses a number of the aggregates series as key economic indicators. For example, average weekly hours for manufacturing is a leading economic indicator in the BEA composite index of leading economic indicators. Average weekly overtime hours in manufacturing is also a leading indicator; while total non-agricultural employment, employee hours and employment in goods-producing industries are coincident indicators.

(2) *In industrial production indexes.* The Federal Reserve Board uses monthly industry hours in computing the Industrial Production Index.

(3) *In personal income and gross national product estimation.* The BEA uses the monthly employment and earnings series as key inputs into estimating the wage component of these economic measures.

(4) *In management of trade policy.* Detailed industry employment trends are used to determine job loss associated with increased imports from foreign countries.

(5) *In escalation of long-term government contracts.* Earnings in shipyards are used by the Navy and US Coast Guard to escalate the labour components of long-term shipbuilding contracts; similar uses are made of earnings data for aircraft, vehicles, electronics and turbines by other federal agencies which negotiate long-term contracts with suppliers.

In addition to these critical, continuing governmental uses of the data, the private and public sectors also rely on the survey results for:

- marketing studies;
- economic research and planning;
- government funding and policy analysis,
- regional analysis;
- industry studies;
- plant location planning;
- wage negotiations;
- adjustment of labour costs in escalation of long-term contracts.

This wide range of uses serves, of course, to provide the basic justification for the expense of data collection. In terms of considering a redesign, however, the multiplicity of users serves to increase the complexity of the undertaking. For the data-producing agency, each use becomes a data requirement, and each data requirement must be considered in the redesign process. It is truly a two-edged sword. A long list of data requirements provides the basis for securing resources to improve the data but delimits the range of options that the statistician has in seeking to streamline and modernise the statistical operation.

The need for a redesign

In approaching the significant undertaking that survey redesign represents, a useful rule of thumb must be to avoid spending scarce resources on fixing those aspects of the programme that are not truly in need of repair. How does the statistician identify, then, these aspects of the operation that are in need of repair and sort them into some priority order? The simple answer is that users will invariably provide input on aspects of the survey that are in need of improvement, whether invited or not.

In the United States the programme has benefited from a series of internal and external evaluations over the years. Each of these reviews has identified programme shortfalls, and some have recommended revisions in the programme. We are confronted with an accumulation of evidence that the programme is in need of repair and modernisation.

In 1962 the President's Committee to Appraise Employment and Unemployment Statistics, known as the Gordon Committee, recommended the development of probability sampling, improvements in methods of estimation, measures to expand coverage and speed up the reporting, as well as improvements in bench-marking and quality control.[2] Over the 18-year period since this comprehensive study was completed, a number of the recommendations, especially those pertaining to coverage, timeliness and techniques for bench-marking and estimation have been implemented. Still, the sample was never put on a true probability basis, nor were the recommended quality control procedures put in place. One result is that the Bureau has serious questions about the adequacy of the data but does not have a capacity for identification of error (in the usual sense that those familiar with probability sampling techniques would feel comfortable) on an ongoing basis. On the bottom line, the survey is still not what might be termed a 'statistical' survey, with fairly sophisticated procedures for computation of the validity of the estimates that are available, for example, in the Current Population Survey.

The need for an integrated, ongoing review capacity for the survey was again addressed in the early 1970s by a task force, composed of representatives of the Bureau, other federal government and co-operating state agencies. The task force examined programme content, data sources, bench-mark estimates, sample selection, schedule design and data processing and estimation. In addition to emphasising the need for integration of systems of statistics covering the nation, states and local areas and the desirability of federal/state co-operative programmes, the task force recommended continuing reviews of: the bench-mark adjustments and their frequency; sample adjustment procedures; a regular response analysis programme; upgrading the SIC coding; and the greater use of personal visits and/or telephone contacts with respondents.[3]

More recently, an intense internal review of procedures in the co-operating state agencies in 1978, conducted by BLS staff, provided a snapshot of state programme operations. The final report of this review indicated the need for improving and standardising the state agencies' approach to sample design and solicitation, bench-marking, estimating, publications and automation. The report indicated the need for additional research, continuing review and validation, training, and the upgrading of automation capacity.

Data users have also weighed in with their reviews and have suggested programme and conceptual improvements. One such group, the Advisory Committee on Gross National Product Data Improvement (1977), also known as the Creamer Committee, recommended improvements in the employment, hours and earnings data that are used as input into the gross national product accounts.[4] The Creamer Committee recommended expanding the scope of the survey to obtain hours and earnings data for supervisory workers, and 'a broadly based research and development programme to strengthen the sampling, estimating, and reporting aspects of the monthly payroll survey'. Among the specific areas for strengthening were: the response rates for the sampled firms and the procedures for introducing new firms into the sample; collection of total wage payments for the calendar month; the need for a periodic drawing of a complete new sample and implementing a full probability sample; ways of improving processing of the data; the state and local government component of the estimates; and seasonal adjustment procedures.

Another user-oriented group, the Panel to Review Productivity Statistics of the National Academy of Sciences, has recommended the collection of hours-worked data to improve estimates of industrial productivity.[5]

The most recent comprehensive review of the establishment survey of employment, hours and earnings was conducted by the National Commission on Employment and Unemployment Statistics (the Levitan Commission). The Commission's final report, issued in September 1979, assessed the adequacy of the 790 programme (a data collection programme of US Bureau of Labor Statistics (BLS) which uses questionnaire form BLS-790), and made recommendations to upgrade the scope and coverage, as well as methodology, of the survey.[6] The Commission recommended increasing the sample size to provide better estimates for underrepresented industries; expanding the geographical coverage to permit aggregate employment estimates for all Standard Metropolitan Statistical Areas (SMSAs) and balances of states; research into improving sample design; better current documentation of the survey; initiation of a quality control programme; strengthening the hours and earnings estimates; and testing the feasibility and cost-effectiveness of data for non-production workers, full- and part-time work, and hours worked. The Commission held that the BLS should devote substantial resources to the enhancement of the programme, and stressed the urgent need to upgrade the design and implementation of the programme, and to document what is being done. The Commission recommended that 'efforts in this direction begin at once'.

Approach to the redesign

In statistical programmes, as in other fields, good execution is preceded by good planning. Good planning of sample survey programmes, perhaps more than is the case in other fields, requires a close and constant interaction between user and survey sampler. As Professor Leslie Kish points out in his text on survey design, the dialogue is necessary because survey objectives and sample design are a two-way process. While objectives should determine design, problems of sample design often influence and change the objectives.

As the survey design proceeds, this dialogue increases in intensity. The BLS found that it was useful, at the beginning, to establish certain terms of reference for this dialogue (in planning terms, a work breakdown structure). This dialogue now takes place in terms of the overall conceptual basis and scope of the survey, and, more specifically, in terms of the major statistical methodology functions – sample design, data collection and estimation – and in terms of the programme-related support functions – computer systems, procedures, training, and publication and analysis of the data. Within this framework, the BLS developed a programme of research, testing, evaluation and development to lead to improvements in the methodological basis of the survey. The principal statistical methodology issues pertain to the design and implementation of the sample, and the procedures which translate the raw sample into estimates.

Sample design

The fundamental issue that was addressed in considering the design of the survey sample was, quite simply, in defining the statistical character of the present sample design. The programme objectives of the present sample design are fairly straightforward: to provide for the preparation of reliable monthly estimates of employment, hours of work, and weekly and hourly earnings which can be published promptly and regularly; through a single general system, to yield considerable industry detail for metropolitan areas, states, and the nation; be appropriate for the existing framework of operating procedures, administrative practices, resource availability, and other institutional characteristics of the programme; and, because this is a federal/state co-operative programme, to provide a technical framework which meets the objectives of the national programme and within which state and area sample designs can be determined. (In practice, this latter objective is usually attained as a fallout of the national design. Since estimates for states and areas are generally not prepared at the same level of detail as the national estimates, the national design usually provides a sufficient basis for the subnational estimates, with some minor supplementation.)

The current sample design in large measure meets these programme objectives. But there is a higher-order statistical objective of producing reliable estimates, and how well the survey meets that objective has never been adequately assessed. Although the current sample design is sound, there are problems in implementation. The options are to improve implementation or to develop a new sample design which may be more easily implemented.

In developing the sample design, the universe of establishments is first stratified by industry and within each industry by size of establishment in terms of employment, using six standard size classes. Within each industry, an optimum allocation design is obtained by sampling with probability proportionate to the average size of establishment within each of the strata. Within each stratum, the sample members are selected at random.

In effect, there is not one sample, but a combination of samples with a varying degree of coverage from industry to industry. Within the industry samples, large establishments (those with 250 or more employees) tend to fall into sample with certainty.

While the selection of sample units is guided by common-sense rules aimed at good representation of the various industries and types of establishment, it is not made under the same well-defined rules that underpin the household survey and that would permit the calculation of the amount of variation to be expected as a result of the sampling process. Over the years, the procedures have been criticised for not being grounded in classical inference theory. Some have suggested implementation of a full-scale probability design.

Is the US establishment survey of employment, hours and earnings susceptible to a standard probability sample structure? The character of the survey suggests that it would be difficult to implement an optimal probability design where control of the selection process is decentralised. The survey is voluntary, and will probably remain so, and is conducted in an exceedingly tight time frame. The problem of non-response is a real one and is likely to continue, even if efforts to reduce it below current levels are successful. A standard probability design does not handle non-response very well, though some encouraging work in the area of adjusting for non-response is now under way.[7] The Levitan Commission considered endorsing a random probability design, but stopped short of making that recommendation, finding that:

1. A radical change in the design would be expensive and disruptive. Many establishments have procedures within the firms to complete the forms efficiently on a regular basis and furnish the data month after month, year after year. It would be foolish, as well as costly, to reject reports from good reporters in favour of an attempt to bring on other establishments which happen to be selected in a probability design scheme.
2. Many reports not needed for the national estimates are needed for estimates at the state and local level. This gives a useful purpose to oversampling, which has no convenient place in probability sampling schemes.
3. Although probability sampling would provide ongoing estimates of error, whether the estimates would be improved is open to question. The bench-mark revisions, for most industries, are within acceptable

ranges, suggesting that even in the absence of standard errors in the light of potential biases, the results are fairly reliable.[8]

Still, the current design is not satisfactory, from a statistical point of view. In the review and revision process, alternatives that build on the present strengths of the survey without radically changing its character are being explored. One such promising option is represented in recent model-based developments in finite population sampling theory.[9] Early in the redesign effort, the Bureau is investigating possible advantages of incorporating prediction theory as well as probability techniques to produce an improved strategy for redesign.

All of this suggests that, with respect to the employment estimates, a radical change in sample design may not be propitious. However, as more uses are made of the earnings data, changes in the sample design, in types of data collected and in estimation procedures may need to be introduced.

Estimation

The sample selection and estimation processes are inexorably joined in the survey design. Any changes in the design of the sample must filter through into changes in the estimation process. Thus, if for example a model-dependent sample design is selected, a model-dependent estimation procedure should follow. These issues are being jointly considered in our revision work.

The need for modernising the current estimating procedure is widely recognised, despite the fact that the values generated from the estimators are in reasonably close agreement with the bench-mark values. It is useful to turn the survey on its head and look at it as an annual series of measures provided by the bench-mark data source (ES-202 universe counts) and an ongoing system of estimates derived from payroll data, obtained on the shuttle schedules, permit extrapolation of the series from the most recent bench-mark datum. The continuity of employer reporting on the shuttle schedule form permits derivation of estimates for the more than 900 estimating cells by use of the link relative technique.

By approaching the problem in this way, it is possible to identify the characteristics of the estimator that require some attention. For example, due primarily to inadequate coverage of small firms, and underrepresentation of new firm births, it has been necessary to introduce a bias adjustment factor on the current month's estimates which essentially moves forward the discrepancy between the estimated values for small size classes (hence, certain industries which have a predominance of such firms) and the bench-mark values. Thus, a fairly large component of the month-to-month charge is generated not by the sample derived estimates, but by imposition of bias adjustment factors. This creates a potential source of error, especially around cyclical turning points when the smaller firms go out of business more quickly in a downturn and form more quickly in an upturn.

Data collection

The ultimate limit of a survey operation is that data to be collected must be readily accessible to the responding unit. Since the source of information for the employment, hours and earnings survey are the payroll records of establishments, early in the redesign process the Bureau analysed employer records and record-keeping practices in a sample of establishments.

In 1981 the BLS conducted an extensive survey of the records and record-keeping practices of employers who co-operate in the employment, hours and earnings survey programme. This was the first such review since 1956. As might be expected, with changes in tax laws and a shift to more intensive automation of payrolls, record-keeping practices have changed substantially in the interim.

Some highlights of the survey in regard to record-keeping practices were that:

1. About two-thirds of US employers now use a computerised process for maintaining and computing payrolls. Despite the growth of service bureaux which provide outside accounting services for establishments, most private sector firms perform this function within the firm. Only 10 per cent of employers use an outside accounting service, and only a few of those have the summary schedules prepared by the contractor.
2. While, at present, hours and earnings are collected only for production and non-supervisory workers, the survey found that in about half of the establishments, this created a hardship in that a separate record-keeping system was required to capture this information. In those firms, it would be easier to provide payroll and hours figures for *all* workers. All employee reporting is certainly preferable to reporting for the subset, thus this finding opens the possibility of expanding coverage as had never before been considered possible.
3. The survey found that many employers maintain current records of other data types of interest. Nearly nine out of ten firms maintain records of overtime pay and hours, and many others maintain separate records of overtime pay. The possibility of additional information on employer practices was opened by the finding that many employers keep records on pay and work practices such as bonuses, rest and wash-up time, and other paid time. Over half of employers maintain records on hours worked in addition to, or in place of, hours paid.

As a general conclusion, employers have little difficulty in completing the monthly questionnaire and can do so expeditiously. The average firm spends 10–20 minutes per month, primarily because their payroll summaries have been so developed over the years to provide the data in an easily accessible form. Moreover, the findings that many employers now maintain such previously unreportable items as hours worked and payrolls for all employees indicate that additional items of interest may be collected.

Summary and conclusions

A statistical agency that embarks on a programme to redesign an ongoing, well-established survey is hoisting its sails in relatively uncharted waters. Certainly, those standards which define good statistical practice in the design of a survey from the beginning provide a set of principles to be considered. But the complexity of the undertaking is increased by the need to overcome the natural inertia that comes from operating a programme in the same mode over time, by constraints on resources accompanying the need to continue to produce data while seeking to improve the operation, and by the requirements to ensure the continuity of the basic time series for comparative purposes.

None the less, survey operations have matured in many nations to the point where a basic reconsideration and modernisation is necessary. In the United States this realisation came about through a number of outside reviews of the data over a period of years.

Although the redesign of the employment, hours and earnings survey in the United States is still under way, some important lessons have been learned:

1. The uses of the data constitute basic requirements, and those requirements define the redesign effort. Particularly in the case of a multi-use survey, it is necessary to establish a dialogue with many users and do so in a framework in which design decisions can be made.
2. Today, there are a number of options for survey design and management that simply did not exist when the surveys were originally designed. The possibilities for sample design have expanded from a strict reliance on probability design to consideration of the new ideas represented by model-based, or mixed design systems. The availability of computers opens new vistas, and allows the designer to think beyond past computer approaches which have, for the most part, been directed at automating past manual procedures.
3. Perhaps of most personal importance to the labour statistician, a redesign is stimulating. It forces a rethinking of past practices, allows the testing of innovative ideas, and, at least in the experience of the United States, creates an atmosphere in which even the current operations are enhanced in the process.

Notes

1. Lillian Madow, 'An error profile: Employment as measured by the current employment statistics program' in *Proceedings of the social statistics sections* (American Statistical Association, Washington, DC, 1977, pp. 33–44); Bureau of Labor Statistics), *Handbook of methods* (Government Printing Office, Washington, DC, 1978), Ch. 3.
2. President's Committee to Appraise Employment and Unemployment Statistics, *Measuring employment and unemployment* (Government Printing Office, Washington, DC, 1962).

3. Bureau of Labor Statistics, '*Report of task force on establishment employment and related statistics*', Feb. 1971, unpublished.
4. US Department of Commerce, Office of Federal Statistical Policy and Standards, Advisory Committee on Gross National Product Data Improvement, *Gross national product data improvement project report* (Government Printing Office, Washington, DC, 1977).
5. National Research Council, *Measurement and interpretation of productivity* (National Academy of Sciences, Washington, DC, 1979).
6. National Commission on Employment and Unemployment Statistics, *Counting the labor force* (Government Printing Office, Washington, DC, 1979).
7. National Research Council, *Symposium on incomplete data: Preliminary proceedings* (Social Security Administration, Washington, DC, 1979).
8. National Commission on Employment and Unemployment Statistics, *Counting the labour force*, p. 158.
9. Morris, H. Hansen, William G. Madow and Benjamin J. Tepping, 'On inference and estimation from sample surveys' in *Proceedings of the Survey Methods Section* (American Statistical Association, Washington, DC, 1978); and Richard M. Royali and William G. Cumberland, 'An empirical study of the ratio estimator and estimations of its variance', *Journal of the American Statistical Association* (76, pp. 66–68).

This book is a selection of Jacques Drèze's work over the last ten years on the topics of lasting unemployment, stagflation and unused capacity. At the theoretical level, the author has contributed to the formulation and analysis of general equilibrium models which allow for price rigidities and excess supply and lend themselves to econometric implementation, thus helping to pull together separate branches of economics. The book also contains papers focussing on policy analysis at a Belgian and European level. This collection thus represents an attempt to integrate micro- and macroeconomics, and to use theory for empirical and policy purposes.

Underemployment equilibria

Underemployment Equilibria

Essays in Theory, Econometrics and Policy

JACQUES H. DRÈZE

The right of the
University of Cambridge
to print and sell
all manner of books
was granted by
Henry VIII in 1534.
The University has printed
and published continuously
since 1584.

CAMBRIDGE UNIVERSITY PRESS

Cambridge
New York   Port Chester
Melbourne   Sydney

Published by the Press Syndicate of the University of Cambridge
The Pitt Building, Trumpington Street, Cambridge CB2 1RP
40 West Street, New York, NY 10011–4211, USA
10 Stamford Road, Oakleigh, Melbourne 3166, Australia

© Cambridge University Press 1991

First published 1991

Printed in Great Britain at Cambridge University Press

British Library cataloguing in publication data
Drèze, Jacques H. 1929–
    Underemployment equilibria: essays in theory,
    econometrics and policy.
    1. Economics, Theories
    I. Title
    330.1

Library of Congress cataloguing in publication data
Drèze, Jacques H.
    Underemployment equilibria: essays in theory, econometrics, and
    policy/Jacques H. Drèze.
        p.   cm.
    Includes index.
    ISBN 0 521 39318 3
    1. Underemployment – Mathematical models. 2. Equilibria (Economics) –
    Mathematical models. 3. Prices – Mathematical models. I. Title.
    HD5707.5.D74   1991
    331.13 – dc20   90-1848   CIP

ISBN 0 521 39318 3 hardback

To my students

Contents

Preface

Economics is an endless challenge. It is intellectually demanding, and practically important. The intellectual challenge can only be met through basic research – the patient construction of knowledge, which has advanced dramatically over the past decades, yet remains grossly inadequate today. The practical challenge calls for making the best possible use of whatever knowledge we have, in order to assess or suggest policies. That practical challenge also leads economists, occasionally, to redefine research priorities, in an attempt at understanding better the policy issues of the day. But even then, the long-run goal of constructing economic knowledge creeps under the surface, ready to take precedence again.

Except for Chapter 2, which was written in 1972 and published in 1975, all the essays collected in this volume have appeared over the decade 1979–89. They are representative of my attempt, starting in 1978, at understanding better the nature of, and likely remedies to, the macroeconomic problems of Europe – in particular persistent unemploy- ment.

The quest for a better understanding was definitely practical, as it became increasingly clear that the recession born in 1974–75 would not be short lived; but it was also intellectual, as the reading of Malinvaud's *Theory of Unemployment Reconsidered* (1977) had revealed to me how a new synthesis of microeconomic and macroeconomic thinking could be sought.

With welcome support form the *Fonds National de la Recherche Scientifique*, I took sabbatical leave during academic year 1978–79 and set to work – knowing well that 'learning-by-doing' was the only realistic way. I was fortunate on several counts: first, in renewing my fruitful association with Franco Modigliani, as evidenced by Chapter 14; next in entertaining constructive contacts with a generation of creative French theorists, like Jean-Pascal Bénassy, Jean-Michel Grandmont, Guy Laroque and Yves Younès; then, in being surrounded by imaginative graduate students, like Henri Sneessens, Jean Dermine or Jean-Paul Lambert; and more recently, in participating in such collective activities as the European Unemployment Program or the Macroeconomic Policy Group (about which more below).

Altogether, it was an exciting decade, in spite of the intellectual frustrations awaiting a microtheorist trying to learn macroeconomics, and of the practical frustrations linked to the elusiveness of the policy issues. Of course, my initial goal of understanding the nature of the day's macroeconomic problems could only be fulfilled to a limited extent; and the long-run goal of expressing the little I have learned in a form contributing to the construction of economic knowledge remains to be fulfilled. The desire to communicate with others towards further advancement of these two goals prompted the decision to publish this collection of essays, which makes available in one place the scatter of minor findings which have fed my broader reflexions.

The title of this volume is borrowed from that of my Presidential Address to the European Economic Association in 1986. The address itself is reproduced as Chapter 1[1] and provides an overview of the book's contents. I do accordingly urge readers to use that chapter for orientation purposes. The remaining parts of the book are largely self-contained.

A special comment should be made about Chapter 2, and its fate. As said above, that paper was written in 1972, and according to footnote 1, 'was motivated by research in progress on the rational aspects of wage rigidities and unemployment compensation, viewed as a form of income insurance for which market opportunities offer no substitute' (p. 34). I was at the time concerned with risk-sharing and second-best efficiency in an incomplete markets set-up.[2] I realised that price flexibility, geared to continuous clearing of spot markets, could be less efficient than suitable forms of price stability, commonly labelled 'price rigidities'. In order to investigate that issue formally, I needed to specify how trade would take place at non-clearing prices. Chapter 2 contains such a specification, and thus serves as foundation for many other chapters.

[1] With a couple of editorial notes (Ed. note) updating the references.
[2] See Drèze (1974 b); the theoretical work on incomplete markets has recently become more formal – see Duffie et al. (1988) – but the same issues remain in the foreground.

In writing that paper, with realistic applications in mind, I endeavoured to establish, for simple types of price rigidity (inequality constraints on nominal or real prices), the consistency of suitable forms of quantity determination (rationing of supply under downward price rigidity, of demand under upward rigidity). It came as a surprise to me that more macroeconomically oriented colleagues concentrated their attention on the special case of fixed prices – so that their work was labelled 'fixed-price equilibrium macroeconomics', and was eventually discounted on grounds of insufficient rationale for the fixed-price assumption. I still feel that income insurance, in a dynamic incomplete markets set-up, is a convincing rationale for downward wage rigidities. I realise now, in the light of Chapters 12 and 13, that the issues are more complex than I had thought at first. In particular, they involve time, uncertainty and successive (overlapping) generations of workers in an essential way.

Hopefully, readers of Parts V, VI and VII will convince themselves that I regard prices and wages as economic variables, the determination of which needs to be explained – though not invariably in terms of spot-markets clearing. Other parts, especially III and IV, contain papers based on a fixed-price model, because they deal with technically difficult issues, that could not be handled at once in a more general setting. Thus, as noted on p. 95, 'when individual money prices are only subject to inequality constraints ..., the set of feasible allocations is not convex' and this introduces a major additional complication. Thus, the characterisation of Shapley-value allocations in large markets is obtained in Chapter 6 for fixed-price economies at considerable technical difficulty; extending that analysis to economies with limited price flexibility – hence with a non-convex feasible set – raises another layer of technical complications. For the purpose of understanding the phenomenon of stagflation, fixed-price models are easily disqualified. But for the long-run objective of constructing economic knowledge, the analysis of general equilibrium models with fixed prices *was* a necessary intermediate step; the stability analysis of Chapter 10, which could not dispense from a specification of quantities traded at non-clearing prices, bears witness to the usefulness of that intermediate step, also for students of inflation ...

Although most of the theoretical chapters (2–13) rely on a microeconomic approach, the motivation and the applications are of a macroeconomic nature.

The last fifteen years have been a period of intense activity in macroeconomics. In the words of Blanchard and Fischer (1989, pp. 26–7), 'the field is now too large and fragmented' for a unified presentation; 'the Keynesian framework ... is in theoretical crisis, searching for micro-foundations; no new theory has emerged to dominate the field, and the time is one of explorations in several directions ...'. I quite agree; and I cannot claim more, for the work presented or referred to here, than a place among these directed explorations.

Yet, even when research explores alternative directions, the mind attempts to bring the separate contributions together, to envision how they might fit into a unified broader picture. There remains a long way, from the first glimpses of consistency among separately developed theories, to their formal integration. But the intuition of the unified theory is already valuable.

General equilibrium theory has for a number of years provided a unified framework for microeconomics. The more recent developments of a 'non-Walrasian' general equilibrium theory,[3] as exemplified in Parts II–V of this volume, holds the promise of providing a framework sufficiently broad and versatile to encompass a good deal of macroeconomics as well. I claim in Chapter 1 that general equilibrium theory, suitably developed in that broader perspective, 'covers macroeconomics automatically, sparing us the need to need to develop two separate fields' (p. 7). Hence the reference to 'general equilibrium macroeconomics'. One clearcut illustration (multiplier analysis) is offered in Chapter 8. Other chapters, like 4 or 10, deal with microfoundations rather than with 'macroeconomic implications of microeconomics'; but the potential overall consistency is clearly discernible.

The major limitation of the models in Parts II–V is that they do not come explicitly to grips with uncertainly and incomplete markets – hence with information, expectations and dynamics. Yet the need to do so is omnipresent, and sometimes recognised explicitly (for instance in Chapters 10, 16 or 18). The difficulties, and promise, are illustrated in Part VI, devoted to the central theme of wage flexibility.

The next step is to search for the macroeconomic implications of non-Walrasian *temporary* general equilibrium theory, a framework designed to deal explicitly with uncertainty, expectations and so on in an incomplete markets setting.[4] That step is suggested by the work collected here. It is

---

[3] The term 'non-Walrasian' is non-appealing to me, in particular because it seems to exclude the Walrasian special case; in chapter 1, I refer to 'general equilibrium with rationing', but I have learned from readers that these words prompt an unduly narrow interpretation.

[4] See Grandmont (1977, 1988) for a survey and selected readings.

also suggested, I think, by many alternative explorations (dealing, for instance, with rational expectations, bubbles, real business cycles ...). Thus Blanchard and Fischer (1989, p. 29) note that 'modern approaches can be defined as the study of dynamic general equilibrium under uncertainty, with incomplete (and possibly imperfect) markets'. Again, I agree. Because macroeconomics has not reached a standstill, the task of retrieving major results as implications of a suitably extended general equilibrium theory is an endless challenge, and will never be complete. In my opinion, the most appealing avenue for basic research at this time remains, in spite of the formal difficulty, temporary-general-equilibrium macroeconomics. I hope that others may share that view, so that good company be enjoyed down that avenue.

The subtitle of Chapter 1 (*From* theory *to* econometrics and policy) claims more than the subtitle of the Book (Essays *in* theory, econometrics and policy). One must choose style for a Presidential Address, and I thought that the occasion (the launching of the European Economic Association) called for punch. Yet, between the theory of Parts II–VI, the econometrics of Part VII and the policy assessments or recommendations of Part VIII, the links remain somewhat informal. It is, of course, an ultimate ambition of economists to develop theoretical models that are susceptible of precise empirical implementation leading to specific and quantified policy recommendations. Most of the time, that ambition seems just as remote as the ambition to fit most current research orientations into a single unified framework ... In the present case, the ambition seems no more remote than with other approaches to macroeconomics.

The logical filiation goes from non-Walrasian general equilibrium theory to the macroeconomic models with quantity rationing of Barro–Grossman (1971, 1976) and Malinvaud (1977), then to the econometric work outlined in Section 4 of Chapter 1 and culminating in Chapters 15 and 16. These two chapters stand a long way from naive fixed-price models. They present a sparse econometric specification that was found flexible enough to fit consistently the data for ten countries both over a period of fast balanced growth (until 1974) and over a period of slow growth with unemployment. But the precision of the estimations is not uniformly impressive, and the specifications could be improved in several directions. I hope that the work will continue.

That cooperative venture by researchers in ten countries, known as the European Unemployment Program, seems to have made quite efficient use of sparse means. It is a sign of hope that a 'Stimulation Program for Economic Science' (SPES) has recently been set up by the EEC to promote international research cooperation.

The two papers selected for the 'Policy' Part VIII were written for the Macroeconomic Policy Group, a revolving group of five economists advising the Directorate for Economic and Monetary Affairs at the Commission of the European Communities, with the logistic intermediation of the Center for European Policy Studies (CEPS) in Brussels. The theoretical sections of Chapter 17 are closely related to Chapters 12 and 13 in Part VI. (Actually, Chapter 13 was developed from a blueprint initially published as an appendix to Chapter 17 – not reproduced here.) Chapter 18 is a group report; it is interesting that so much agreement could be reached among economists with so diverse backgrounds and theoretical frameworks. That paper addresses itself to contemporaneous issues, and should accordingly become outdated fast. It seemed nevertheless worthy of inclusion, both because it contributes to the picture of economic thinking in Europe over the past decade, and because it stresses some points of lasting interest – like the link between openness and fiscal policy effectiveness (Section 5).

Both the econometrics and the policy studies feed back into the theoretical research, because they suggest specifications that can be retained, or raise problems that can be studied, in further theoretical work. For instance, as noted in Chapter 10, the empirical record suggests concentrating attention on excess supply equilibria. It also suggests that European economies are characterised by multiplicity of stable, or nearly stable, equilibria – a characteristic that students of general equilibrium theory can easily accept ...

The work brought together in this volume has a distinctly European flavour. During the past fifteen years, the research interests and methodology of macroeconomists in Western Europe, and in North America, drew further apart than had been the case in earlier years. Although that trend seemed unfortunate at the time, it may have been a manifestation of the emergence of independent macroeconomic research in Europe – a phenomenon less visible in earlier years. I guess that the gap was also deepened by the importance attached to policy issues on both sides. As the long-run objectives of basic research regain prevalence, we may expect that the more significant advances on both sides will be recognised by all concerned, and that the gap will be filled progressively. In particular, recognition of a unifying framework should improve communication.

At the time of resigning from my teaching position at Université Catholique de Louvain, I take pleasure in dedicating this volume to my students. I wish thereby to thank them for all that I have learned from them, for the continued inspiration and motivation which they have provided. I also wish to encourage them, and their contemporaries, to meet the endless challenge of economics. I hope that we may still meet for a while along the avenues of research.

Similarly, I wish to thank my co-authors for their intellectual contributions as well as for the fun of working together. And I hope that we may continue to cooperate in research.

All the work underlying this volume was carried out at the Center for Operations Research and Econometrics (CORE), Université Catholique de Louvain, in close cooperation with the Department of Economics there. I am grateful to my colleagues and to the staff of CORE for the generous provision of intellectual stimulation, logistic assistance and warm friendship. My special gratitude goes to Ginette Vincent, who not only processed all the papers when initially written, but also prepared this manuscript for the printer, and merged all the references into a single combined list[5] while I was sailing around ...

Archipelago de Cabo Verde, November 1989

---

[5] In the combined list of references, discussion papers that are quoted at a later date in print are not listed separately, and all references are to the published version. But no systematic effort is made to trace discussion papers through publication generally.

Acknowledgements

The author would like to thank the publishers of the following articles for their kind permission to reprint them in this book.

Chapter 1: 'Underemployment equilibria: from theory to econometrics and policy', *European Economic Review*, 31, 1987 (North-Holland).

Chapter 2: 'Existence of an exchange equilibrium under price rigidities', *International Economic Review*, 16, 1975 (University of Pennsylvania).

Chapter 3: 'On supply-constrained equilibria', *Journal of Economic Theory*, 33, 1984 (Academic Press).

Chapter 4: 'Competitive equilibria with quantity-taking producers and increasing returns to scale', *Journal of Mathematical Economics*, 17, 1988 (North-Holland).

Chapter 5: 'Optimality properties of rationing schemes', *Journal of Economic Theory*, 23, 1980 (Academic Press).

Chapter 6: 'Values of markets with satiation or fixed prices', *Econometrica*, 54, 1986 (Tieto Ltd).

Chapter 7: 'Public goods with exclusion', *Journal of Public Economics*, 13, 1980 (North-Holland).

Chapter 8: 'Second-best analysis with markets in disequilibrium: public sector pricing in a Keynesian regime', in *The Performance of Public Enterprises: Concepts and Measurement* (edited by M. Marchand, P. Pestieau and H. Tulkens), North-Holland, 1984.

Chapter 9: 'Demand estimation, risk aversion and sticky prices', *Economic Letters*, 4, 1979 (North-Holland).

Chapter 11: 'The role of securities and labour contracts in the optimal allocation of risk-bearing', in *Risk, Information and Insurance: Essays in Memory of Karl Borch* (edited by H. Loubergé), Kluwer, 1989.

Chapter 12: 'Wages, employment and the equity-efficiency trade-off', *Recherches Economiques de Louvain*, 55, 1989 (Université Catholique de Louvain).
Chapter 13: 'Labour management, contracts and capital markets: some macroeconomic aspects, and conclusions', in *Labour Management, Contracts and Capital Markets*, Basil Blackwell, 1989.
Chapter 14: 'The trade-off between real wages and employment in an open economy (Belgium)', *European Economic Review*, 15, 1981 (North-Holland).
Chapter 15: 'A discussion of Belgian unemployment, combining traditional concepts and disequilibrium econometrics', *Economica*, 53, 1986 (London School of Economics and Political Science).
Chapter 16: 'Europe's unemployment problem: introduction and synthesis', in *Europe's Unemployment Problem* (edited by J.H. Drèze, C.R. Bean, J.P. Lambert, F. Mehta and H.R. Sneessens), M.I.T. Press, 1991.
Chapter 18: 'The two-handed growth strategy for Europe: autonomy through flexible cooperation', *Recherches Economiques de Louvain*, 54, 1988 (Université Catholique de Louvain).

Overview

1 Underemployment equilibria
From theory to econometrics and policy*

1. Introduction

Over the years, I have had a number of interesting dreams. But I had not dreamt that I would stand in front of such a large and distinguished audience to address the first Congress of the European Economic Association.

Unbeknown to them, students often figure in my dreams. (On one occasion, I dreamt that I had fallen asleep while lecturing – and woke up in a nightmare, to realise that I was indeed standing in front of my undergraduate statistics class...) Recurrently, I dream about students at the University of Nirvanah, taking up different subjects – like microtheory, macrotheory, welfare economics, business cycles and economic policy – all taught within the same methodological framework and fitting nicely together, like the pieces of a jig-saw puzzle, to form a coherent picture. I wish to share with you today some glimpses of that dream, and my hope that it may come true.

My topic is 'underemployment equilibria', meaning situations where substantial unemployment, as defined in statistical practice, persists with no clear tendency to disappear. 'Equilibrium' is thus defined by absence of movement, not by conformity to some concept.

Today, most European countries are in a situation of underemployment equilibrium; this is a *fact*, a distressing fact (see table 1.1). Unemployment rates among the young are alarmingly high (see table 1.1). The social cost of letting one out of three or four young adults out of work for a prolonged period is hard to assess. To economists of my

* *European Economic Review*, 31 (1987), 9–34. Presidential Address to the First Congress of the European Economic Association,Vienna, August 1986.

Table 1.1   *Unemployment rates*

	Total %		Young (< 25 years of age) %		Long term (> 1 year) % of total	
	1978	1985	1979	1983	1979	1983
Belgium	8.1	14.8	14.0	30.0	38.1	49.9
Denmark	7.1	9.9	14.7	27.9	6.8	5.6
West Germany	3.8	8.3	4.5	13.3	22.2	29.9
France	5.2	12.6	17.5	21.7	19.4	24.4
Italy	7.1	12.9	26.2	35.7	35.0	40.2
Netherlands	5.4	14.8	11.5	31.0	28.9	49.4
United Kingdom	5.3	11.7	10.5	25.9	30.4	41.5
EC 10	5.5	11.5	13.5	24.5	28.4	38.8

Source: European Economy 22, November 1984, p. 16 (Table 8).

generation, it is a disappointing fact. We had indeed been trained to believe that severe unemployment, of the kind experienced in the thirties, would not occur again: Keynesian economics had supplied the explanation and identified remedies, built-in stabilisers (in particular, social security transfers and unemployment benefits) had rendered our economies immune to demand deficiencies, the experience of the thirties had revealed what policy blunders should be avoided. As we all know, these hopes were vain. Underemployment equilibrium is with us again, we do not know for how long.

Explanations which are held useful today differ from those available fifteen years ago. At that time, the only relevant theoretical framework was that of Keynesian macroeconomics, pointing to the demand side as both the culprit and potential saviour. Today, many agree that underemployment equilibria in our open economies exhibit a mixture of Keynesian and classical features, which bring both demand and supply considerations to bear on explanation and remedy alike. The broader theoretical outlook has resulted from important contributions, inspired by the seminal work of Clower (1965, 1967) and Barro and Grossman (1971, 1976) in the U.S., but developed by European economists in the past fifteen years. The distinctly European flavour of these contributions, for which many speakers at this Congress deserve credit, makes them a natural theme for my Address. Given the scope of these contributions, I shall concentrate on those with which I have been associated in one way or another, in particular through the work of my students. This easy option is not meant to belittle the numerous contributions not cited.

2. Theory of unemployment reconsidered: An orientation ToUR

2.1.

To orient ourselves, I will first remind you of the basic message conveyed by the best known among these contributions, namely Malinvaud's *Theory of Unemployment Reconsidered*. That message is easily captured at the level of a single firm, producing a single output y by means of given facilities and a quantity of labour l. The technology and size of the facilities define a production function relating output to labour input: $y = y(l)$. If the output price p and the wage cost w are given, and if we disregard inventories, there will under standard assumptions exist profit-maximising levels of output and employment, that I shall refer to as notional levels and denote by y^* and l^* respectively; they satisfy $y^* = y(l^*)$ and, assuming differentiability, $y'(l^*) = w/\tilde{p}$, where $\tilde{p} = p$ for a competitive firm, $\tilde{p} = p(1 + \eta_{p \cdot q})$ for a monopolistic firm.

Actual levels of output and employment will correspond to these in a static equilibrium where prices, quantities and production facilities are mutually adjusted. But when we study the impact of short-run fluctuations, like shifts in input prices or aggregate demand, we must consider two additional conditions, namely (i) that output y can be sold, at the going price – which may not be the case if supply and demand have shifted away from the positions to which price and capacity were adjusted; and (ii) that the supply of labour l^S to the firm is at least as high as l^*. Otherwise, the firm will be *constrained* on either the goods market or the labour market, and its actual output will fall down to either the level corresponding to demand, y^D, or the level corresponding to full use of available labour, $y(l^S)$, whichever is smaller. That is

$$y = \min(y^*, y^D, y(l^S)). \tag{1}$$

Writing $l(y)$ for the inverse production function, we obtain similarly

$$l = l(y) = \min(l^*, l(y^D), l^S). \tag{2}$$

These two relations embody the common sense observation that goods will only be produced if that is profitable and if the goods can be sold. Similarly, workers will only be employed if there exist suitable places of work, if there is a demand for what they produce, and if they offer their labour.

That straightforward reasoning can be reproduced at the aggregate, macroeconomic level, with the help of fig. 1.1. The aggregate production function of the economy is drawn there as $Y = Y(L)$, displaying the

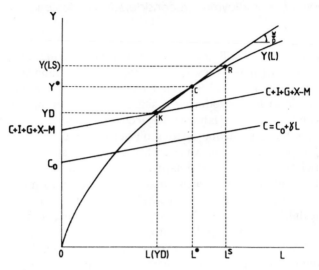

Figure 1.1

neoclassical features of smoothly diminishing returns. Aggregate labour supply is *LS*. Aggregate demand is now partly endogenous and defined as the sum of consumption *C*, which I have for simplicity drawn as increasing linearly with employment; and other components treated provisionally as exogenous, namely investment *I*, government expenditures *G* and the trade balance $X - M$. Aggregate demand is $YD = C + I + G + X - M$.

To complete the picture, there remains to locate the point (Y^*, L^*) corresponding to the notional output supply and labour demand. It is defined implicitly by the condition $Y'(L^*) = w/\tilde{p}$ (marginal revenue product of labour equals real wage) and is found at the point *C*.

We now have three interesting points on the production function, namely the point *K*, where $Y = YD$; the point *C*, where $Y = Y^*$; and the point *R*, where $Y = Y(LS)$. If the economy could be treated as a single firm producing a single commodity by means of a single type of labour, then one could conclude from the reasoning at the firm level that

$$Y = \min(Y^*, YD, Y(LS)). \tag{3}$$

The main modification is that now $YD = YD(Y)$.

Fig. 1.1 is drawn with $YD(Y) < Y^* < Y(LS)$, leading to the Keynesian solution $Y = YD$. But that is only one among several possible orderings, and the three points K (for Keynesian), C (for classical) and R (for repressed inflation) define solutions associated with alternative data. (Thus, increasing G would eventually lead to $YD > Y(LS)$, and lowering $w/\tilde{p}$ would similarly lead to $Y^* > Y(LS)$, in my figure.)

2.2.

In comparison with the Keynesian multiplier, fig. 1.1 contains two important innovations.

First, it brings in the supply side explicitly and from the start – a step postponed to ch. 21 in Keynes (1936). Macroeconomics thus becomes intrinsically two-sided, and a proper framework is at hand to study the balance of supply-side policies and effective demand policies, or to meet such concerns of policy-makers as the limitations placed on fiscal expansion by latent inflationary pressures and capacity constraints. *The substantive theme of this address is that supply and demand both matter, today.*

A second innovation relates to the multiplicity of solutions, at the aggregate level (K, C, R) or at the firm level. The different solutions carry different policy implications. Also, in an economy with many firms, making up diverse industries or service sectors, there is no reason to expect that all firms will be simultaneously in similar situations. Casual observation suggests that European steel producers satisfy demand with excess capacities, whilst producers of equipment goods quote long delivery lags.

Thus aggregation over firms means aggregation over non-homogeneous units, some of which realise their notional trade offers, whilst others cannot – just as in the case of households. This consideration has important implications for econometric work – to be mentioned later. It may also be related to the methodological comment by Malinvaud (p. 4 of ToUR) that progress in macroeconomics had been held back by 'the lack of a general equilibrium framework concerning an economy with rationing'. Indeed, general equilibrium is the limiting framework where each firm and each household appears as a separate entity. Recognising microeconomic heterogeneity is thus a definite step towards what I shall call 'General Equilibrium Macroeconomics' – or GEM for short. *The methodological theme of this address is that general equilibrium with rationing covers macroeconomics automatically, sparing us the need to develop two separate fields.*

Of course, macroeconomics had been a general equilibrium venture all along, and Keynes belongs right next to Walras as a founder of that approach. But Walrasian and Keynesian economics had for many years developed along parallel, disjoint paths – an unfortunate development, reflecting the segmentation of our profession, and making life difficult for our students. Keynes was obviously right in attempting to develop a theoretical framework in which the undisputed fact of persistent unemployment could be fitted. It was up to microeconomists to extend their own models accordingly. It is surprising that it took them so long to do so. It is also surprising that, once that step was taken, in particular by Yves Younès (1975) and Jean-Pascal Bénassy (1975), the integration with Keynesian macroeconomics came so easily, as illustrated by ToUR or more systematically by Bénassy's treatment in *The Economics of Market Disequilibrium* (1982). I hope to convince you that both general equilibrium and macroeconomics benefit from the integration.

2.3.

Before turning to that task, I must first consider in what sense the alternative solutions to the firm's problem define 'equilibria', i.e. situations which do not call for any adjustments in *quantities*, *prices* or *production capacities*.

To begin with the goods market, if $y^* = y^D$, the firm realises its desired production plan, and the market for its output clears, so there is no natural inducement to a change and equilibrium prevails. If $y^* < y^D$, unsatisfied demand invites buyers to bid up the price, or the firm to raise price so as to boost profits. Such a situation is not an equilibrium. It should only be observed temporarily, pending an increase in price and/or an expansion of production capacities. And indeed we do not observe prolonged rationing of demand. Yet, elimination of excess demand need not result in higher employment, if it is achieved through a price increase and additional imports. Such cases of stagflation are particularly likely if the excess demand initially resulted from a supply shock rather than from a demand shock.

The third possibility, $y^* > y^D$, is more interesting. Could it happen that a firm's notional supply exceeds its sales, without this creating a tendency for the price to fall, or for the production capacities to be reduced? The answer is: yes – if the firm is operating under increasing returns to scale! For in that case the firm would prefer to sell more at the same price, but it would not supply the same output at a lower price, nor could it reduce costs by producing the same output from smaller facilities. And such conditions may have a competitive flavour, with price equal to average cost (plus markup), as in 'contestable markets' – see, e.g. Baumol, Panzar and Willig (1982); or they may have a monopolistic flavour, with marginal revenue equal to (non-increasing) marginal cost.

To my eyes, increasing returns are the rule rather than the exception – a conclusion already drawn 25 years ago from a study of the qualitative attributes of Belgium's exports and imports (Drèze (1960)). Increasing returns arise whenever the technology entails economies of mass production (through assembly lines, high-speed machine tools, etc. . . .); whenever commodities (like clothing and durables, but also bread or processed foods) are produced or procured in batches subject to set up costs; they result from the overhead costs of opening up and maintaining facilities, from the economies of bulk transportation, from the law of large numbers in storing spare parts, etc. . . . . These are all circumstances where equilibrium – either competitive or monopolistic – is consistent with excess supply.

By contrast, under diminishing returns, excess supply would induce the firm to reduce price, or capacity, or both. If it reduced capacity, the Keynesian unemployment would eventually become classical.

Turning to the labour market, I would again suggest that excess demand – $y(l^S) < y^*$ – is not a candidate for lasting equilibrium, as firms will then outbid each other to attract additional labour, will train less skilled workers internally or will substitute capital for labour. But excess supply of labour, i.e. unemployment, is a widespread phenomenon. It does not lead to significant adjustments in labour supply. I shall return later to reasons why it does not lead to wage cuts.

2.4.

The foregoing should help dispel two misconceptions. First, excess supply, but not excess demand, is consistent with equilibrium. In particular, 'classical unemployment', i.e. a situation where employment is determined by the notional labour demand of firms rather than by the effective demand for output, need not carry any connotation of demand rationing, if prices are flexible upwards and imported substitutes are available. It is a characterisation of the unemployment which arises when weaving mills or shipyards close down, under the competition of lower cost producers in Newly Industrialised Countries. It is a reminder of the simple fact that employment requires places of work, hence an appropriate capital stock created and maintained by appropriate investment. In the *Price Theory* textbook of my entertaining teacher George Stigler (1942), there was a student problem reading as follows: 'With a Cobb–Douglas production function, one could grow the world's output of corn from a flower pot. Comment.' I may have commented at the time that the world's labour supply would not suffice. I appreciate better today the simple wisdom of the question. Employment definitely requires work places – which flower pots do not provide.

Second, equilibrium of the firm concerns not only quantities but also prices and capital investments. Thus, GEM is not restricted to fix-price models. On the contrary, the more flexible framework should open new avenues for the study of price dynamics – as illustrated below (Section 3.2).

I thus hope to share with you my conviction that GEM provides a theoretical framework sufficiently broad and general to be used effectively by most of us, with contributions from many sides fitting together naturally. I shall consider first the contributions of general equilibrium theory.

3.   General equilibrium with rationing

The general equilibrium model of Walras, Arrow and Debreu has contributed much elegance and clarity to economics. But its program remains unfinished, and some extensions – in particular to increasing returns, price dynamics and uncertainty – involve rationing in a natural way. (The term 'rationing' is here understood broadly, and covers in particular situations of 'voluntary' or 'efficient' excess supply of goods, as well as situations of unemployment.)

3.1.

Starting with increasing returns, it stands to reason that firms operating with declining average costs will typically wish to sell more at the same price, precluding existence of competitive equilibria where firms maximise profits at given prices. But competitive equilibria can also be characterised by an alternative set of properties, namely (i) that firms minimise their production costs, (ii) that they supply their output voluntarily (meaning that profits could not be increased by reducing sales), and (iii) that lower output prices would not sustain the same supply. Under diminishing returns, the second condition says that output prices should cover marginal costs, and the third says that output prices should not exceed marginal costs – hence the equality of output prices and marginal costs, characteristic of competitive equilibria. Under increasing returns, or more generally under U-shaped average costs, the second condition says the output prices should cover both average and marginal costs. That is still a reasonable condition. And the third condition says that output prices should not exceed the *maximum* of average and marginal cost, in the absence of monopolistic exploitation.

The alternative characterisation can be applied under increasing as well as constant or diminishing returns. Pierre Dehez and I (1988a) show that equilibria so defined exist, at the general equilibrium level, under minimal assumptions. For the firms with convex production possibilities, they correspond to competitive profit maximisation at given prices. For the firms with increasing returns, they correspond to profit maximisation at given prices *subject to a sales constraint* (thus allowing for excess supply); and the sales constraint is only binding when downward price rigidity sets in, because lower prices would not cover overhead costs. Rationing thus comes in naturally when we extend general equilibrium theory to the realistic case of increasing returns. (I may mention in passing that rationing comes in equally naturally when we introduce public goods with exclusion – see Drèze (1980b).)

3.2.

It also stands to reason that interesting price dynamics should allow trades to occur during the process of price adjustment. To assume that prices adjust continuously and instantaneously to clear all markets is not only unrealistic; it is very restrictive. Allowing for price rigidities yields a more flexible framework to study price dynamics. But when trades occur at non-market-clearing prices, some form of temporary rationing is unavoidable. Concepts of general equilibrium with rationing are thus indispensable to study price adjustments.

The idea that quantities adjust faster than prices, along such a process, has been stressed by Keynes and some of his commentators, in particular Leijonhufvud (1968). That idea finds its natural expression in the require-ment that all advantageous trades compatible with given prices take place, before prices adjust. That requirement in turn finds expression in the condition that only one side of a given market, the short side, should be subject to quantity rationing. The theory of general equilibrium with rationing has established the feasibility of that condition: Given an arbitrary set of prices, all markets can be made to clear through voluntary trading by imposing quantity constraints on the short side only, and no constraints on the numeraire (money). That result is robust relative to the precise definition of rationing equilibria; see Bénassy (1975, 1982), Drèze (1975), Younès (1975), Malinvaud and Younès (1977a, b).

That existence result does not specify how the appropriate levels of one-sided rationing constraints emerge. And it does not bring in the spontaneous price increases which, we observe, eliminate excess demands. For a framework (introduced by Morishima (1976) in his 'Bastard Keynesian Theory') where production is described by a capacitated activity analysis model and where prices of final goods are derived from input prices through a markup formula, I have studied (Drèze (1983)) a simple tâtonnement process defined on the prices of inputs (including rents on installed capacities) and the quantities of these inputs which the owners can sell or use. The nominal prices of inputs are downward rigid and adjusted upward in case of excess demands. No price adjustments take place so long as desirable adjustments in the rationing constraints exist – thereby expressing the Keynes–Leijonhufvud idea. (The order in which the allowed adjustments take place is otherwise unrestricted.) Under natural assumptions, such a process converges to an equilibrium with constraints on the supply of inputs only (with unemployment and excess capacities). If arbitrarily small discrepancies between effective supplies and demands are tolerated, a strong finite convergence result is obtained. (I need not assume any substitutability, but well that no input is inferior, in the sense of being used less when aggregate demand expands. A nontâtonnement version is under study.)* That work corroborates the otherwise unfilled promise that adjustment processes in prices and quantity constraints would be more naturally stable than price tâtonnements. (It was inspired by a pioneering contribution of van der Laan (1980), later extended by Kurz (1982), Dehez and Drèze (1984) and van der Laan (1984) again.)

3.3.

Uncertainty and incomplete markets suggest another link between rationing equilibria and price dynamics.

There are, in my opinion, two main sources of persistent downward rigidities of prices and wages.

A first source is the non-competitive behaviour of firms and labour unions attempting to maximise revenues against demands perceived as inelastic. It is always difficult to estimate demand elasticities – and it is

* (Ed. Note) See Chapter 10 below.

not clear whether, and how, elasticity estimates should be revised when demand shifts. Under constant marginal costs or reservation wages, monopolistic prices and wages fail to respond to downward shifts.

This is illustrated in fig. 1.2, borrowed from Sneessens (1987). The figure is drawn for a canonical example. The technology entails a fixed cost and constant variable (marginal) costs C, up to a rigid capacity y^*. A constant elasticity demand function is subject to multiplicative shocks, which leave the monopoly price unchanged at $\tilde{p} = C.(1 + \eta_{p\cdot q})^{-1}$ so long as demand at that price does not exceed capacity. For demand realisations like D or D' inducing output levels inferior to capacity, there is *excess supply* with *downward price rigidity*.[1]

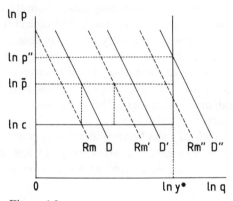

Figure 1.2

In a world of uncertainty and incomplete insurance markets, a second source of rigidities lies in the advantages of maintaining a degree of price stability across uncertain contingencies, as a risk-sharing and information generating device. There are many situations where continuous market-clearing through prices would make economic life as hectic as a rodeo.

The clearest illustration of this point comes from wages; the application to commodity prices is less transparent – see, however, the classic treatise by Okun (1981). In capitalist economies, one may expect wage-earners to be more risk-averse than asset-holders, because the latter can diversify risks through the stock market, whereas the former cannot. There is thus scope for mutually advantageous risk-sharing. But there is no organised

---

[1] The figure is drawn in logs to obtain linear relationships; from the demand function $q = Ap^{-\alpha}$, we obtain $\ln p = (1/\alpha)\ln A - (1/\alpha)\ln q$, $\ln Rm = \ln(dpq/dq) = (1/\alpha)\ln A + \ln(\alpha - 1)/\alpha - 1/\alpha \ln q = \ln p + \ln(\alpha - 1)/\alpha$.

insurance against deficient labour incomes, other than downwards wage rigidity and unemployment benefits. In such a world, efficiency consider-ations call for linking wages to national income and wealth; they do *not* call for letting wages fluctuate to clear labour markets continuously.* The argument to that effect, initially discovered in implicit contracts theory,[2] extends to the markets for new hirings as well, when labour demand is relatively inelastic; see Drèze (1986b, section 4 and appendix).† In this context, inelastic demand does not mean scope for monopolistic exploitation, but rather limited output losses under non-market clearing prices.

Typically, the two sources of rigidity are intertwined, and it is difficult to separate the inefficient use of *ex post* monopoly power from the efficient provision of *ex ante* income insurance. Expectations and time consistency raise additional difficulties. The wage elasticity of labour demand is low in the short run, substantial in the long run.[3] Wage rigidities that make sense in the face of a short-lived recession may become severely harmful in the face of a prolonged depression. The proper response may be both difficult to diagnose, and inconsistent with the expectations rationally held prior to a genuine surprise.

These considerations, to which I shall return in drawing policy conclu-sions, help us understand the existence and asymmetry of wage rigidities, as well as the difficulty of reaching agreement on wage policies.

3.4.

By way of conclusion to this section and of transition to the next one, let me move to a domain where general equilibrium theory has been put to practical uses, namely second-best analysis. In the methodology of the second-best, as pioneered by Ramsey (1927) and Boiteux (1956) and developed for instance by Diamond and Mirrlees (1971) or Guesnerie (1980), one uses the abstract general equilibrium model to trace out the implications of specific policies, like indirect taxes or public utility rates, under conditions where the realisation of a Pareto optimum as a competitive equilibrium is not feasible (for instance because overhead

---

* (Ed. Note) See Chapter 11.
[2] See in particular Azariadis (1975), Baily (1974), the informal exposition by Drèze (1979a) or the survey by Rosen (1985).
† (Ed. Note) See also Chapters 12 and 13.
[3] See e.g. Drèze and Modigliani (1981).

government expenditures must be covered by indirect taxes; or because the public utility operates with increasing returns, under a budget constraint ruling out marginal cost pricing). Traditionally, the competitive equilibrium framework has been used, whereas Keynesian macroeconomics was the dominant approach to fiscal policy. Why use two mutually inconsistent frameworks to study respectively the desired level of tax revenue and the desired structure of tax rates? There is no logical justification for such schizophrenia... .

I have found the study of public sector pricing in a Keynesian regime particularly instructive. The program was to retrace the steps of Boiteux who, assuming all private agents to be in competitive equilibrium, discovered the well-known 'inverse elasticity rule' for public utility pricing. Assume instead, as a simple alternative, that the private agents are in Keynesian equilibrium, with unemployment, excess supply of commodities and sticky prices. The public utility pricing rule is then derived from a cost–benefit calculation, where the relevant costs and benefits come from the effects of price changes on the rate of inflation, the rate of unemployment and profits; these total effects are computed through a matrix multiplier operating on direct effects. In other words, the general equilibrium methodology leads naturally to evaluate costs and benefits by means of the 'comparative statics' approach of macroeconomics, taking all multiplier effects into account (Drèze (1984b), section 3.3). Furthermore, the trade-off between inflation, unemployment and profits is derived from primitive welfare weights assigned to individuals. There is no need to specify a global trade-off directly. These features reveal the intimate consistency between general equilibrium with rationing and standard macroeconomics. They suggest that the macroeconomic implications of microeconomics may be a more fruitful research topic than the microeconomic foundations of macroeconomics... .

I will consider next how that program can be realised at the empirical, econometric level.

4. General equilibrium macroeconomics and econometrics

4.1.

The step from the detailed general equilibrium model, with many goods and many agents, to an operational macroeconomic model, has been taken boldly by some European econometricians. The path which they were to follow had been prepared by two significant sets of contributions, one empirical and one theoretical.

On the empirical side, the simple aggregate model of ToUR had been estimated as such for several European countries, with an employment relation derived from the min-condition:

$$L_t = \min [L_t^*, L(YD_t), LS_t], \tag{4}$$

up to disturbance terms and lagged adjustments.

The seminal contributions seem to have come from Benelux, with the work of Kooiman and Kloek (1985) for the Netherlands and of Sneessens (1981) for Belgium; see also Artus et al. (1984) and the Quandt Bibliography (1986).

These pioneering efforts demonstrated the workability of the approach. But they met with the objection that a model whereby the whole economy switches, between one year and the next, from a regime of Keynesian employment to a regime of classical unemployment or repressed inflation is too crude. It would be more realistic, and more germane to GEM, to view the national economy as a patchwork of individual markets for goods and for types of labour, some of which may be characterised by excess demand while others experience excess supply. Over time, the *proportion* of markets in the different regimes changes; for instance, a fall in aggregate demand is accompanied by an increase in the proportion of markets for individual goods or labour services where excess supply prevails.

A *description* of the state of the national economy should thus be given in terms of *regime proportions* for individual markets rather than in terms of a single regime prevailing at the aggregate level.

That pertinent observation was given content in theoretical papers by Muellbauer (1978) and Malinvaud (1980, 1982a), which inspired empirical econometric work, starting again with the Netherlands – Kooiman (1984) – and Belgium – Lambert (1988).

4.2.

The approach taken by these authors consists in postulating a *statistical distribution* of supplies and demands on micromarkets for goods and types of labour. The means of the distribution are related to the standard definitions of aggregate supply and demand for the national economy. The deviations from the mean reflect the idiosyncrasies of individual markets.

The authors mentioned above, and several others – Gourieroux *et al.* (1984), Martin (1986) – make a specific assumption about the form of the statistical distribution. The lognormal distribution, or a close substitute, is theoretically appealing and analytically tractable, especially when a convenient structure is imposed on covariances. It has led to the following approximate expression:

$$Y_t = [(Y_t^*)^{-\rho} + (YD_t)^{-\rho} + (Y(LS_t))^{-\rho}]^{-1/\rho}, \tag{5}$$

which 'explains' actual aggregate output Y_t in terms of the three standard quantities: notional supply Y_t^* (usually called potential output), final demand YD_t (usually called Keynesian demand) and full employment output $Y(LS_t)$. The parameter ρ, derived from the covariance matrix of deviations from the means, is a measure of the 'mismatch' between supply and demand across micromarkets – that is, of the extent to which firms supply iron rods while consumers buy Japanese video sets to watch the Mundial. For finite ρ,

$$Y_t < \min(Y_t^*, YD_t, Y(LS_t)). \tag{6}$$

When ρ tends to infinity, the mismatch disappears and the min is attained in the limit.

The proportions of micromarkets in the different regimes – say, π_K, π_C and π_R with $\pi_K + \pi_C + \pi_R = 1$ – are related as follows to the arguments of the output equation in the lognormal case:

$$\pi_{Kt} = \left(\frac{YD_t}{Y_t}\right)^{-\rho} = \eta_{Y_t.YD_t}, \quad \pi_{Ct} = \left(\frac{Y_t^*}{Y_t}\right)^{-\rho} = \eta_{Y_t.Y_t^*},$$

$$\pi_{Rt} = \left(\frac{Y(LS_t)}{Y_t}\right)^{-\rho} = \eta_{Y_t.Y(LS_t)}. \tag{7}$$

In models of the manufacturing sector, like those of Kooiman and Lambert, these proportions are measured directly from business survey data, at a substantial gain in estimation efficiency.

It follows in particular from (5) and (7) that

$$\dot{Y}_t = \pi_{Ct}\dot{Y}_t^* + \pi_{Kt}\dot{Y}D_t + \pi_{Rt}\dot{Y}(LS_t), \tag{8}$$

a simple relationship between the rate of growth of actual output and the rates of growth of its determinants, weighted by the regime proportions describing the state of the economy.

All these expressions have natural counterparts for employment with

$$L_t = [(L_t^*)^{-\rho} + (L(YD_t))^{-\rho} + (LS_t)^{-\rho}]^{-1/\rho}. \tag{9}$$

An illustrative implication would be

$$\eta_{L_t . w_t} = \pi_{Ct} . \eta_{L\hat{t} . w_t} + \pi_{Kt} . \eta_{L(YD_t) . w_t} + \pi_{Rt} . \eta_{LS_t . w_t}. \tag{10}$$

Let us look at an empirical application. fig. 1.3, reproduced from Sneessens and Drèze (1986a), presents empirical estimates of the four variables in (9) for the Belgian economy over the period 1955–82. We observe balanced growth during the sixties and early seventies, when potential employment L^*, Keynesian labour demand $L(YD)$ and labour supply LS followed the same trend. The Keynesian series displays less regularity, reflecting the greater short-run volatility of demand in comparison to capital and labour supply. Over that period, actual employment follows a parallel path, yet at a slightly lower level, with a growing structural mismatch between the supplies and demands for specific goods and labour services. A sharp break occurs in 1975, from which date onward the three basic series diverge. Labour supply continues to grow on the same trend. Potential employment (notional labour demand) stagnates from 1975 to 1980 and thereafter begins to fall, a tendency which extends to the present. Keynesian labour demand falls abruptly in 1975 and again in 1981. At the end of the period, actual employment is close to the level induced by final demand, with a large number of unemployed, of which less than half could be put back to work under a reflation of aggregate demand. This is due to the insufficient capital formation over the past decade, compounded by accelerated scrapping, due in particular to bankruptcies. The picture reveals the complex nature of our current predicament, where insufficient demand appears as the immediate constraint on employment, but where insufficient productive capacities lurk in the background as another potential constraint standing in the way of a return to full employment.

4.3.

At the risk of losing readers in a technical maze, I have summarised in the appendix the structure of a 'streamlined' GEM econometric model.[4]

---

[4] Taking the liberty to quote myself from the pages of the respectable *Economic Journal*: 'Models basically play the same role in economics as in fashion: they provide an articulated frame on which to show off your material to advantage...; a useful role, but fraught with the dangers that the designer may get carried away by his personal inclination for the model, while the customers may forget that the model is more streamlined than reality' (Drèze (1985a, p. 3)).

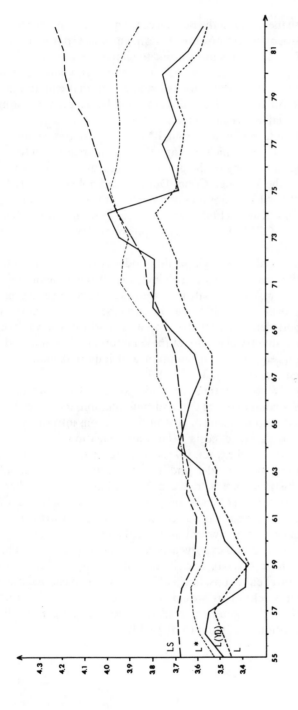

Figure 1.3. Labour supply (*LS*), potential employment (*L**), Keynesian labour demand (*L(YD)*) and actual employment (*L*) (millions of man years).

Source: Sneessens and Dréze (1986a)

It corresponds to the model of the Belgian economy estimated by Sneessens and Drèze (1986a, b), where however investment and exports are treated as exogenous. Lag structures are left out to simplify exposition.

The output equation appears as (A.7), next to the standard accounting identity (A.6). The specific difficulty associated with that equation is that YD_t, Y_t^* and $Y(LS_t)$ are *not observed*. They must be replaced by estimates in terms of observables, as suggested by (A.8).

On the supply side, potential output Y_t^* is estimated from an aggregate production function, into which the capital stock and relative factor prices are plugged. Our modelling of the production function in (A.1) and (A.2) is quite simple – the Leontief–Cobb–Douglas technology already found in Sneessens (1981). More ambitious approaches are possible, as illustrated by Kooiman and Kloek (1985) for instance. I would hope that the new challenges of GEModelling may inspire new developments on the production front(ier).

On the demand side, the logic of the model is that $Y_t < YD_t$. In the case of the small open economy of Belgium, we felt safe in assuming that consumer demand was always satisfied, with excesses relative to domestic supply spilling over into additional imports beyond the 'normal' or 'structural' import demand MD. To simplify exposition I have assumed in the appendix a unitary elasticity of these imports to final demand, and solved for YD in eq. (A.5). Consumption and import demands receive traditional specifications in (A.3) and (A.4).

The price and wage equations are quite simple. The price equation (A.10) combines a component of demand-pull inflation, introduced by the ratio YD_t/Y_t, and a component of cost-push inflation, introduced by the first differences of average costs. The wage equation (A.11) is more problematic, as one could expect. It lacks the theoretical underpinning of a theoretical bargaining model and relates instead wages to labour productivity. This is at best a 'reduced form' representation, where the twin causation from technological progress to wage demands and from wage concessions to labour saving technologies is left unstructured. We naturally introduce unemployment as an explanatory variable.

Although investment and exports are treated as exogenous variables in Sneessens and Drèze (1986a), one should, and easily could, introduce additional structural equations, like (A.12) and (A.13), to endogenise them (and the capital stock). This would lead to a system of 7 structural equations for the endogenous observed variables C_t, I_t, X_t, Y_t, L_t, P_t and W_t – namely equations (A.3) and (A.8)–(A.13).

4.4.

An attempt at estimating such a model in several European countries is under way, coordinated by Richard Layard and myself, and sponsored by the Commission of the European Economic Community.* We are in acute need of imaginative empirical work along such lines. Europe suffers from its segmentation in national economies. Models of individual countries are not directly comparable, and of limited interest to foreigners. This holds back the accumulation of empirical knowledge, in comparison with the U.S. where the large army of applied economists and econometricians works with the same data set. Let me mention in passing the instructive experiment under way at the Commission of the European Communities, where André Dramais (1986) has estimated a macroeconometric model directly on aggregate data for the community as a whole.[5] The same specification will be estimated on country data, and the simulations of the aggregate model will be compared with the simulations of the linked country models. Clearly, if we could work with aggregate European data, empirical research would leap forward. More realistically, we should aim at making a data base covering at least the four major European countries widely available for systematic replications of empirical studies. And we should watch closely the experience of the Macromodelling Bureau at the University of Warwick, which documents and makes accessible to outside users a set of British models. A similar initiative at the European level would make sense, and might be worth promoting by the European Economic Association.

Returning to the model of the appendix, let me mention briefly a few problems. The approach of aggregating over microunits by means of a statistical distribution is not entirely new. It has been used by Houthakker (1955) and his followers to construct aggregate production functions. Imaginative related work by Hildenbrand (1981, 1983) on both production and consumption should also be mentioned. In the present context, that approach smooths out the min condition, thereby reducing considerably the computational efforts. There are several important open issues. One of them relates to the robustness of the aggregate specifications *vis-à-vis* the choice of distributional form (lognormal, logistic, Weilbull, . . .). Another relates to the restrictive assumptions on covariances, leading in the model presented here to a single mismatch parameter ρ. One would like at least to distinguish the mismatch on labour markets from the mismatch on

[5] Interestingly, the employment function in that model uses the min specification (4).
* (Ed. Note) See Chapter 16.

goods markets. (My suspicion is that the latter is much more important than the former.) Another still relates to the statistical flexibility of the approach for dynamic specifications – a point (over)emphasised by Hendry (1982) – for full information estimation or for Bayesian analysis. And the 'small economy' assumption will need to be relaxed when we move from Belgium or the Netherlands to more significant areas.

Two more fundamental issues should be mentioned. They concern respectively aggregation and integration. There is no doubt that aggregation of microrelationships by means of statistical distributions entails a substantial loss of potential information. We know a lot about the tensions or latitudes on individual markets, and would prefer to use that information. A simple meaningful step would call for separating the manufacturing sector from the services and the public sector. (One advantage of that step comes from the availability of business survey data for manufacturing firms.)

The integration issue is altogether different – although related as well to efficient use of information. The model of the appendix uses explicitly the aggregation over micromarkets to derive the aggregate output and employment expressions. But several other equations are specified in a more or less *ad hoc* – though plausible – way. Such is the case in particular for the price and wage equations, and for the investment equation (to be added). And the concept of 'micromarket' itself remains ambiguous. The logic of General Equilibrium Macroeconomics would call for aggregating relationships describing the behaviour of individual agents – an 'integrated' behaviour which, in the case of firms, bears simultaneously on output, employment, prices and investment. That idea is partly, but imperfectly, reflected in the presence of the variable YD_t/Y_t in the price equation, or the variables YD_t/Y_t and Y_t^*/Y_t in the proposed investment equation. A more satisfactory approach would call for deriving the demand-pull term of the price equation directly from the aggregation of 'excess demand' terms of the micromarkets – thereby probably bringing in the parameter ρ; and similarly for the investment equation. There should result a more efficient integration of the information contained in the output, employment, price and investment data. That approach remains to be worked out. A preliminary exploration is found in Sneessens (1987).

4.5.

On the positive side, the model outlined in the appendix has a number of interesting implications for macroeconomic theory.

This may be illustrated with reference to the short-run multiplier of autonomous expenditure. From (5), with $YD = CD(Y) + I + G + X - MD(Y)$, we obtain easily

$$\frac{dY}{dG} = \frac{1}{\left(\dfrac{YD}{Y}\right)^{\rho+1} + \dfrac{\partial MD}{\partial Y} - \dfrac{\partial CD}{\partial Y}} < \frac{1}{1 + \dfrac{\partial MD}{\partial Y} - \dfrac{\partial CD}{\partial Y}}$$

$$\simeq \frac{1}{\dfrac{1}{\pi_K} + \dfrac{\partial MD}{\partial Y} - \dfrac{\partial CD}{\partial Y}}. \tag{11}$$

This formula calls for two comments. First, the multiplier is reduced – in comparison with the standard Keynesian formula – because the response of actual output to demand is dampened by the extent of classical unemployment and repressed inflation in the economy.

Second, even if the marginal propensities to import and to consume were estimated as constants, the multiplier would not be constant; it would vary over time with the proportion of Keynesian unemployment in the economy – being an increasing function of that proportion.

Another interesting application concerns the inflation–unemployment trade-off, for which bringing in the supply-side also makes a difference. Much use is made, in some macroeconomic literature, of the concept of 'non-accelerating-inflation rate of unemployment', or NAIRU. But NAIRU also stands for 'Not Always Instructive Rate of Unemployment'. If the aggregate economy were predominantly in a classical regime, the NAIRU as usually defined would be a 'Now Altogether Irrelevant Rate of Unemployment', because the main source of price inflation would originate in the pressure of excess demand.

The kind of Phillips curve associated with our model is more general. The relationship between unemployment and wage or price inflation is twofold. On the one hand, there is the causation from the rate of unemployment to wages: the higher unemployment, the slower the rate of increase of wages – hence of prices, through cost-push inflation. On the other hand, there is the demand-pull inflation, associated with high levels of demand, hence with low levels of unemployment. Here the causation is from excess demand to high inflation and low unemployment. Empirically, the two relationships are entangled. The natural identifying variable is the degree of capacity utilisation, Y^*/Y or DUC, and the reduced form equation, which endogenises shifts in the Phillips curve, is

$$d \ln P = -\alpha \ln [1 - DUC^\rho - (1 - UR)^\rho] - \beta UR. \tag{12}$$

All these points may have been known to enlightened macrotheorists for some time. But GEM provides a rigorous framework within which the needed qualifications and extensions to Keynesian economics fit naturally – and emerge from microeconomic reasoning.

5. Policy conclusions and agenda

5.1.

I may not have convinced you that macroeconomics should best be taught within a 'General Equilibrium Theory' course, as I do in Louvain-la-Neuve. And the unity of the theoretical framework may stand out more clearly in my own mind, where it has been at work for ten years, than I could express in one hour today. But hopefully you may share my conviction that macroeconomic thinking and teaching requires due attention to the supply side, and to the constraints placed on output and employment by productive capacities and the number of work places.

If the estimates obtained for Belgium and reproduced in fig. 1.3 are at all typical, or if the estimates obtained by Dramais (1986) for the Common Market as a whole are correct, we must conclude: on the one hand, that an insufficient level of effective demand is the main factor holding back employment in Europe today; but on the other hand, that only part of our shocking level of unemployment could be eliminated by a demand revival, due to capital shortages and structural mismatches.

We thus need two-handed policies,[6]* where the demand side and the supply side both receive due attention. There is little point in arguing about which side is the more important – in the same way that there is little point in debating whether the ham or the cheese is more essential to the preparation of a ham and cheese sandwich. For the purpose of defining an appropriate mix of demand-side and supply-side policies, econometric work of the kind outlined here seems definitely helpful. An immediate usefulness emerges at the diagnostic level, to evaluate the strength of inflationary demand tensions and the threats of classical unemployment, The relevant quantities are not observable, so that we need imaginative use of all available information (including business surveys, I would say). I see here a major role for GEM econometrics, in addition to the usual role of providing the quantitative orders of magnitude without which policy recommendations remain platonic.

---

[6] 'A two-handed approach', in the words of Blanchard et al. (1985).
* (Ed. Note) See Chapter 18.

In these conclusions, the supply side is not done full justice, because no reference is made to the relevance of supply factors in the determination of effective demand. Given the magnitude of imports and exports in relation to GDP for Europe as a whole, competitiveness vis-à-vis the rest of the world plays an important role in the determination of final demand for domestic output. It also plays an important role as a determinant of investment. My conclusions point to an investment boom as being particularly welcome – if only we knew how to engineer it. Demand expectations put on investment the same lid that effective demand puts on output – pointing again to the need of a two-handed approach. Work on investment, to fit it properly in the theoretical framework of General Equilibrium Macroeconomics, and to fit appropriate econometric relationships, continues to deserve a high priority on the research agenda. Our policy needs point in the same direction as more theoretical considerations. As for stimulating desirable capital widening investment without at the same time stimulating undesirable capital deepening, I am afraid that the dilemma is genuine. In sectors open to international competition, the more capital intensive technologies seem to offer the better long-run prospects to European producers. And recent technological advances offer prospects for capital–labour substitution in services that seem difficult to counteract. Overall stimulation of demand and investment are thus likely to offer the better chances for employment recovery.

5.2.

An important area of uncertainty concerns incomes policies – a prudish name for wage moderation. In this respect as well, we need to keep an eye on both the demand side and the supply side. There is no doubt that aggregate consumption remains a prime determinant of effective demand, for Europe as a whole. And I have not seen any evidence yet pointing to a spending propensity higher for profits than for wages. At the same time, spending on investment is more desirable today than spending on imported consumables. And I am convinced that the short-run elasticity of employment with respect to real wages is small, whereas the long-run elasticity is substantially negative, so that the issue of time horizon mentioned in Section 3.3 is essential.

The GEM framework and the econometric work reviewed here suggest two propositions. If it is indeed the case that only half of our unemployment could be eliminated by demand reflation, with capital widening investments indispensable for attacking the other half, then: (i) a fairly long time is bound to be needed before Europe attains again a reasonable degree of full employment – so that a middle to long-term time horizon is definitely relevant; (ii) although indispensable in the long run, wage restraint could not be fully effective in the short run, due to the insufficient number of working places resulting from the low investment levels of the past decade.

Many of us feel that real wages rose abnormally in the mid seventies, when Europe was struck by the conjunction of worsening terms of trade, increased competition from the NIC's and a slower growth of world imports. We struggle today with the consequences of that mistake, in which all participants to the wage bargaining process share responsibility. It is not a pleasant struggle. If my two propositions are correct, we must combine structural measures that prevent the repetition of such a mistake with short-term remedial measures that alleviate the burden of unemployment, especially unemployment of the young – and, I shall argue in a moment, of the less skilled. The relevant structural measures are those which will keep our real wages on a suitable path, whether the recovery unfolds or whether the recession continues.

A genuine hazard of the present situation still lies with the temptation of beggar-thy-neighbour policies of intra-European competition through exchange rates *and wage levels*. We need instead concerted reflation with stable real wages that can be maintained in the longer run in the face of a long-awaited recovery. In some countries, a more realistic pattern of indexation, combining in suitable proportions nominal GDP with consumer prices, belongs in such a policy. The temporary disappearance of inflation offers an exceptional opportunity for negotiating such a structural change, which strikes me as more promising and less fraught with deflationary hazards than nominal wage cuts of uncertain longer-run consequences. Expectations of stable wage developments are also more relevant to hiring decision than short-lived concessions. Additional structural measures aimed at greater efficiency of our productive sphere and of our market mechanisms, measures promoting investment and reducing mismatches, would thereby gain in overall effectiveness.

As someone whose value judgements entail special concern for the less privileged members of our societies, I wish at the same time to see an improvement in the employment prospects of the less skilled fringe of our labour force. That is a difficult project, because persistent unemployment invariably results in a high concentration of the unemployment in the less skilled group. Remedial measures should include special employment programs, which seem to entail lower net costs per job than most alternatives. Our experience with work-sharing is by and large sobering, except for early retirement schemes; but there remains scope for more part-time work – see Drèze (1986b). Given the low levels of disposable income associated with unskilled work, I would favour a restructuring of wage costs through exemption of social security contributions on the part of earnings corresponding to minimum wages, and a funding of the corresponding social security expenditures (which reflect citizen's rights rather than worker's rights) through general taxation.[7]

5.3

All the issues touched so briefly in my conclusions, from two-handed policies through investment stimulation to incomes policies and social security financing, deserve further analysis. I have tried to convince you that General Equilibrium Macroeconomics provide an appropriate theoretical framework for such analysis, including the indispensable econometric verifications and quantifications. Our mastery of that framework is still fragmentary, but avenues of research are open, and I hope that many of you will explore them. That hope seems justified, in view of the liveliness and inventiveness of European economists, as witnessed by the program of this Congress. The developments reviewed this morning, which reflect European efforts of the past fifteen years, provide another testimony. Contributions, to which time did not allow me to devote proper attention, have come from Scandinavia and the Mediterranean as well as from continental Europe and the British Isles. And the proposed framework is apt to promote intellectual exchanges between East and West. The quantity and quality of the European research efforts in economics are undeniable. There remains scope for increasing the effectiveness of these efforts, through more intimate cooperation between specialists of different fields, of different countries, of different ages, of different ways of life. It is the aim of the European Economic Association to promote such cooperation. I wish you much success in realising that aim, and making my dream come true.

---

[7] That suggestion, and its ethical basis, are presented in Drèze (1985b).

Appendix. Streamlined GEM econometric model

(A.1) Notional output (supply) Y_t^*, unobserved, is equal to the capital stock K_t times the desired output/capital ratio B_t, estimated as a function of the relative prices of labour W_t and of capital V_t, shifted by technological progress.

$$Y_t^* = K_t \cdot e^{a_0 + a_1 t} \left(\frac{W_t}{V_t}\right)^{-a_2} := K_t \cdot B_t\left(\frac{W_t}{V_t}\right).$$

(A.2) Full employment output $Y(LS_t)$, unobserved, is equal to the labour force LS_t times the desired output/labour ratio A_t

$$Y(LS_t) = LS_t \cdot e^{a_3 + a_1 t} \left(\frac{W_t}{V_t}\right)^{1 - a_2} := LS_t \cdot A_t\left(\frac{W_t}{V_t}\right).$$

(A.3) Consumption demand CD_t is equal to actual consumption C_t and is a function of labour incomes $W_t L_t$, transfers, gross profits $P_t Y_t - W_t L_t \ldots$; $UR = (LS - L)/LS$ is the unemployment rate

$$CD_t = C(W_t L_t, LS_t - L_t, P_t Y_t = W_t L_t, \ldots) = C(Y_t, UR_t, \ldots).$$

(A.4) Import demand MD_t, unobserved, is a proportion μ_t of final demand YD_t, where μ_t depends upon import prices PM_t (exogenous), domestic prices $P_t, \ldots$

$$MD_t = YD_t \cdot \mu(PM_t, P_t, \ldots).$$

(A.5) $$YD_t := CD_t + I_t + G_t + X_t - MD_t = \frac{C_t + I_t + G_t + X_t}{1 + \mu(PM_t, P_t, \ldots)}.$$

(A.6) $$Y_t := C_t + I_t + G_t + X_t - M_t$$

(A.7) $$= \{(YD_t)^{-\rho} + (Y_t^*)^{-\rho} + [Y(LS_t)]^{-\rho}\}^{-1/\rho}$$

(A.8) $$= \left\{ \left[\frac{C_t + I_t + G_t + X_t}{1 + \mu(PM_t, P_t, \ldots)}\right]^{-\rho} + \left[K_t \cdot e^{a_0 + a_1 t}\left(\frac{W_t}{V_t}\right)^{-a_2}\right]^{-\rho} \right.$$
$$\left. + \left[LS_t \cdot e^{a_3 + a_1 t}\left(\frac{W_t}{V_t}\right)^{1 - a_2}\right]^{-\rho} \right\}^{-1/\rho}.$$

(A.9) $$L_t = \{[L(YD_t)]^{-\rho} + (L_t^*)^{-\rho} + (LS_t)^{-\rho}\}^{-1/\rho} = A_t^{-1} Y_t.$$

(A.10) Price inflation reflects demand pull YD_t/Y_t and cost-push, where average production cost is equal to $A^{-1}W + B^{-1}V$

$$\Delta \ln P_t = \Delta \ln P\left(\ln \frac{YD_t}{Y_t}, \Delta \ln [A_t^{-1} W_t + B_t^{-1} V_t] \right).$$

(A.11) Wage inflation reflects price indexation, changes in labour productivity A and the rate of unemployment

$$\Delta \ln W_t = \Delta \ln W(\Delta \ln P_t, \Delta \ln A_t, UR_t).$$

(A.12) An investment equation, to be added, should combine the effects of potential demand and excess capacities with those of factor prices and profitability

$$I_t = I\left(\frac{YD_t}{Y_t}, \frac{Y_t^*}{Y_t}, \frac{W_t}{V_t}, \frac{A_t^{-1} W_t + B_t^{-1} V_t}{P_t}, \ldots \right).$$

The capital stock becomes then endogenous.

(A.13) An exports equation, to be added, should combine the effects of world demand, export prices,..., with those of excess demand and excess capacities

$$X_t = X\left(\frac{YD_t}{Y_t}, \frac{Y_t^*}{Y_t}, \ldots \right).$$

Eq. (A.5) is to be modified when (A.12) and (A.13) are added.

II Equilibria with price rigidities

2 Existence of an exchange equilibrium under price rigidities*

1. Introduction and contents

In this paper, we study an exchange economy where allocation of resources is guided by a price mechanism, but prices are subject to inequality constraints. An equilibrium is obtained by introducing quantity constraints on the net trades of those commodities for which the price constraints are binding. The set of admissible quantity constraints is defined in a way which avoids trivial equilibria.

Two kinds of price rigidities are considered in turn, namely constraints on nominal prices in an economy with a numeraire (Sections 4 and 5) and constraints on relative or real prices in an economy without a numeraire (Section 6). The two kinds are then considered simultaneously (Section 7). In each case, we find that inequality constraints on net trades may be substituted for price adjustments, one-to-one, as devices to equate supply and demand. (Clearly, this is a statement about feasibility, not about efficiency.)

Some background remarks on price rigidities and quantity rationing (Section 2) precede the description of the model (Section 3). The results are so organized that the basic technique of proof is introduced first on a simple problem (constraints on all nominal prices); the technique is then extended in two directions (constraints on some but not all nominal prices, constraints on all real prices); these extensions are combined in a final theorem, of which the first three are special cases (constraints on some nominal and/or some real prices).

International Economic Review, 16, 2 (1975), 301–320. I wish to thank Gérard Debreu, Jean Jaskold Gabzewicz, Jean-Michel Grandmont, Birgit Grodal, Werner Hildenbrand and Karl Vind for interesting discussions and helpful suggestions; I am particularly grateful to Pierre Dehez and Dieter Sondermann who discovered mistakes in earlier versions of this paper; responsibility for remaining errors is mine.

2. Price rigidities and quantity rationing

The phenomenon of price rigidity, i.e. the persistence of prices at which supply and demand are not equal, is frequently observed, and plays an important role in some macro-economic models. Downward wage rigidity in the presence of underemployment, with or without minimum wage laws, is the foremost example.[1] Rent controls, price controls aimed at curbing inflationary pressures, usury laws, price uniformity over time or space, provide other examples.

In most cases, price rigidities may be described as inequality constraints on individual prices – either absolute or relative.[2] Absolute limits are usually expressed in monetary units. The first model considered in this paper uses a 'numeraire' commodity, always desired, whose price is set equal to 1. The other prices are constrained by absolute limits. This asymmetrical treatment is natural, when money is used as a numeraire. In a model without money, this asymmetry is no longer natural, but then price rigidities are more naturally expressed in relative, or 'real' terms. Such rigidities take the form of price limits tied to certain index numbers. In existing price-guided economies, both types of rigidities are observed simultaneously. That case is also considered below.

The imbalance between supply and demand, which may result from price rigidities, is typically absorbed by some kind of quantity rationing. The 'kind' varies from market to market. It may consist in inequality constraints on consumption (for instance, housing consumption) or on net trades (for instance, labour supply). Constraints on net trades may be absolute (i.e., an upper limit on individual demands, as under point rationing) or relative (i.e. the same fraction of all individual demands is satisfied, as under many bond issues). The rationing may also be random (as in the case of overloaded telephone exchanges) or involve priorities (e.g. workers are laid off in order of increasing seniority).

In this paper, only the simplest form of quantity rationing will be considered, namely *absolute constraints on net trades*. The reasoning applies, with minimal modifications, to absolute constraints on consumption. Other schemes (proportional or random rationing, priorities, ...) would require independent study.

---

[1] The present note was motivated by research in progress on the rational aspects of wage rigidities and unemployment compensation, viewed as a form of income insurance for which market opportunities offer no substitute.

[2] Price uniformity over time or space takes the different form of equality constraints among several prices.

In order to avoid trivial equilibria (e.g. all net trades constrained to vanish), two conditions are imposed: (i) rationing may affect either supply or demand, but it may not affect simultaneously both supply and demand; (ii) upward (downward) price rigidity must be binding if there is quantity rationing of demand (supply). The existence theorems below confirm the intuitive expectation that this simple form of rationing adequately absorbs the excess demands that may result from price rigidities.

The extension of the theorems to economies with production presents no new difficulties. However, absolute limits on individual net trades seem more natural in the case of consumers, than in the case of firms of arbitrary sizes. Absolute limits that vary from individual to individual, according to fixed quotas, could easily be accommodated.

The converse problem, namely existence of an equilibrium under quantity rationing of either consumptions or net trades (by means of absolute constraints), is covered by the standard theory. Indeed, the constraints may be included in the definition of the consumption sets (or the production sets), so long as convexity of these sets is preserved.[3]

3. The model and a lemma

Consider an exchange economy with n commodities indexed $j = 1, 2, \cdots n$ and N consumers indexed $i = 1 \cdots N$.

Consumer i is defined by $(X^i, \succcurlyeq_i, w^i)$. $x \geq y$ means $x_j \geq y_j \forall j$ and $x \neq y$; $x > y$ means $x_j > y_j \forall j$.

Throughout this paper, we shall make the following assumptions:

ASSUMPTION 1. The consumption set $X^i \subset R^n_+$, with elements x^i, is closed, convex and satisfies: $x \in X^i$ implies $\{x\} + R^n_+ \subset X_i$.

ASSUMPTION 2. The preference ordering $\succcurlyeq_i$ on X^i is complete, continuous and convex; $x \geq y$ implies $x \succcurlyeq_i y$; there is an index set $I \subset \{1, 2, \ldots n\}$ such that $x \geq y$ and $x_j > y_j \forall j \in I$ imply $x \succ_i y$.

ASSUMPTION 3. The initial resources w^i belong to the interior of X^i.

The index set I in Assumption 2 will consist of that commodity (numeraire) or those commodities (base of an index number) in terms of whose price the constraints are expressed. Clearly, it would be meaningless to use a worthless commodity as numeraire... .

---

[3] This would not be the case if the consumer had the choice of 'consuming' either nothing, or else a minimum quantity, of some good.

Define $w = \sum_i w^i$, the total resources of the economy; and $z^i = x^i - w^i$, the net trade of consumer i.

A *price system* p is a vector of R^n. The price constraints will require that p should belong to some set

$$P = \{p \in R^n_+ \mid f(p) = 1, \bar{p} \geq p \geq \underline{p}\}.$$

Alternative definitions of the normalization rule $f(p)$ and of the bounds $(\bar{p}, \underline{p})$ will be considered below. In some cases (when the bounds are tied to index numbers), $\bar{p} = \bar{p}(p)$.

A *rationing scheme* is a pair of vectors $(L, l) \in R^n \times R^n$, with $L \geq 0 \geq l$.

Given a price vector p and a rationing scheme (L, l), the budget set of consumer i is defined by

$$\gamma^i(p, L, l) = \{x \in X^i \mid p(x - w^i) \leq 0, L \geq x - w^i \geq l\}.$$

$w^i \in X^i$ implies $\gamma^i(p, L, l) \neq \phi$ for all admissible p and (L, l).

An *exchange economy with price rigidities* is here defined as

$$\mathscr{E} = \{(X^i, \succcurlyeq_i, w^i), P\}.$$

An *equilibrium under price rigidities and rationing*, or 'equilibrium for $\mathscr{E}$', is here defined as an N-tuple of consumption vectors $\{x^i\}$, a price system $p \in P$ and a rationing scheme (L, l) such that

(i)   for all i, x^i is a maximal element for $\succcurlyeq_i$ of $\gamma^i(p, L, l)$;

(ii) $\sum_i(x^i - w^i) = 0$;

(iii) $\forall j, L_j = x^i_j - w^i_j$ for some i implies $x^h_j - w^h_j > l_j \forall h$

        $l_j = x^i_j - w^i_j$ for some i implies $x^h_j - w^h_j < L_j \forall h$;

(iv) $\forall j, \bar{p}_j > p_j$ implies $L_j > x^i_j - w^i_j \forall i$

        $p_j > \underline{p}_j$ implies $l_j < x^i_j - w^i_j \forall i$.

Condition (ii) is stated in equality form because quantity rationing may be used to eliminate excess supply. Condition (iii) states that rationing may affect either supply or demand, but may not affect simultaneously both supply and demand. Condition (iv) states that no quantity rationing is allowed unless price rigidities are binding.

The continuity properties of the budget set correspondence γ^i, from $R^n_+ \times R^n_+ \times R^n_-$ to X^i, play an important role in the technical derivations below. In the usual model, where

$$P = R^n_+, \quad L = +\infty, \quad l = -\infty,$$

$\gamma^i(p)$ is continuous, under Assumptions 1 and 3, at every $p \geq 0$;[4] that is, whenever γ^i owns some $\bar{x}$ such that $p(\bar{x} - w^i) < 0$. A similar result holds in the present model; however, the existence of the required $\bar{x}$ depends not only on $p \geq 0$ but also on $l \leq 0$, $p \cdot l < 0$.

LEMMA. *The correspondence* $\gamma^i(p, L, l)$ *from* $R^n_+ \times R^n_+ \times R^n_-$ *to* X^i *is continuous at every point* (p^0, L^0, l^0) *where for some* $j, p^0_j > 0$ *and* $l^0_j < 0$.

PROOF. Define

$$\alpha^i(p) = \{x \mid x \in R^n, p(x - w^i) \leq 0\}$$

$$\beta^i(L, l) = \{x \mid x \in X^i, L \geq x - w^i \geq l\}.$$

$\alpha^i(p)$ and $\beta^i(L, l)$ are convex; α^i is continuous at every $p \geq 0$; we first prove that β^i is continuous as well.

$$\beta^i(L, l) = \beta^i(L) \cap \beta^i(l),$$

where

$$\beta^i(L) = \{x \mid x \in X^i, L \geq x - w^i\}$$

$$\beta^i(l) = \{x \mid x \in X^i, x - w^i \geq l\}.$$

Because $w^i \in \text{int } X^i$, $\beta^i(L)$ and $\beta^i(l)$ have non-empty interiors for all

$$(L, l) \in R^n_+ \times R^n_-$$

and are continuous. $\beta^i(L, l)$ is upper hemicontinuous, as an intersection of continuous correspondence.

To prove lower hemicontinuity, let

$$(L^s, l^s) \to (L^0, l^0)$$

and let

$$x^0 \in \beta^i(L^0, l^0).$$

Define

$$J_1 = \{j \mid j = 1 \cdots n, L^0_j = 0 = l^0_j\},$$

$$J_2 = \{j \mid j = 1 \cdots n, L^0_j > l^0_j\};$$

---

[4] See e.g. Debreu (1959) (proposition (i) of 4.8.).

by appropriate reindexing, let

$$J_1 = \{1 \cdots m\},$$
$$J_2 = \{m + 1, \cdots n\}$$

and write

$$L^0 = (L_1^0, L_2^0), \; l^0 = (l_1^0, l_2^0), \; x^0 = (x_1^0, x_2^0), \; w^i = (w_1^i, w_2^i)$$

with

$$L_1^0 = l_1^0 = x_1^0 = 0 \text{ and } L_2^0 \geq x_2^0 \geq l_2^0.$$

The set

$$\{x_2 \,|\, (0, x_2) \in X^i, L_2^0 \geq x_2 - w_2^i\} \cap \{x_2 \,|\, (0, x_2) \in X^i, x_2 - w_2^i \geq l_2^0\}$$

in R^{n-m} has a nonempty interior; therefore, there exists a sequence

$$x^s = (0, x_2^s), \; x^s \to x^0, \; x^s \in \beta^i(L^s, l^s) \,\forall\, s.$$

Accordingly, β^i is continuous for all

$$(L, l) \in R_+^n \times R_-^n.$$

Now, γ^i is upper hemicontinuous, as an intersection of continuous correspondences.

To prove lower hemicontinuity, let

$$(p^s, L^s, l^s) \to (p^0, L^0, l^0), \qquad\qquad p_j^0 > 0, \; l_j^0 < 0,$$

and let

$$x^0 \in \gamma^i(p^0, L^0, l^0).$$

Because β^i is continuous, there exists a sequence $\{\hat{x}^s\}$,

$$\hat{x}^s \in \beta^i(p^s, L^s, l^s), \qquad\qquad \hat{x}^s \to x^0.$$

If

$$x^0 \in \text{int } \gamma^i(p^0, L^0, l^0),$$

there exists s' such that

$$\hat{x}^s \in \alpha^i(p^s, L^s, l^s)$$

for all $s \geq s'$; indeed,

$$p^0(x^0 - w^i) < 0$$

implies

$$p^s(\hat{x}^s - w^i) < 0, \qquad\qquad s \geq s'.$$

Let then

$$p^0(x^0 - w^i) = 0.$$

There exists

$$\bar{x} \in \alpha^i(p^0), \qquad\qquad \bar{x}_j < w^i_j, \; \bar{x}_k = w^i_k, \; k \neq j,$$

with

$$\bar{x} \in \beta^i(L^0, l^0), \; p^s(\bar{x} - w^i) < 0, \qquad\qquad s \geq s'.$$

Define $\{x^s\}$ by:

$$\left.\begin{array}{l} p^s(x^s - w^i) = 0 \\ x^s = \lambda^s \hat{x}^s + (1 - \lambda^s)\bar{x} \end{array}\right\} \quad \text{for all } s \text{ such that } \hat{x}^s \notin \alpha^i(p^s)$$

$$x^s = \hat{x}^s \qquad\qquad \text{otherwise.}$$

x^s exists and is unique.

$$x^s \in \gamma^i(p^s, L^s, l^s).$$

Also, $x^s \to x^0$; indeed, when $p^s \to p^0$,

$$p^s(\hat{x}^s - w^i) \to p^0(x^0 - w^i) = 0$$

but

$$p^s(\bar{x} - w^i) \to p^0(\bar{x} - w^i) < 0,$$

so that $p^s(x^s - w^i) = 0$ implies that $\lambda^s \to 1$, $x^s \to x^0$. The sequence x^s has all the required properties to complete the proof of lower hemicontinuity.
$$\text{QED}$$

4. Limited flexibility of all nominal prices

In this section, we prove the existence of an equilibrium when there exists a numeraire (money) and prices are subject to constraints in terms of that numeraire. It simplifies exposition to assume the existence of an upper limit on every price. Proceeding under that assumption, we introduce a technique of proof that will be used again in later sections. The assumption that every price is bounded upward is relaxed in Section 5.

THEOREM 1. *Let*

$$\mathscr{E} = \{(X^i, \succcurlyeq_i, w^i), P\}$$

satisfy Assumptions 1, 2 with index set $I = \{1\}$, and 3; let

$$P = \{p \in R^n \mid p_1 = 1, +\infty > \bar{p} \geq p \geq \underline{p} \geq 0\};$$

there exists an equilibrium for $\mathscr{E}$.

The proof of the theorem rests upon a definition and a remark.
Consider the pair of vectors $(M, m) \in R^n \times R^n$ defined by

$$M_j = \bar{p}_j + w_j, m_j = \underline{p}_j - w_j, \qquad\qquad j = 1 \cdots n,$$

and the compact, convex set

$$Q = \{q \in R^n \mid M \geq q \geq m\}.$$

DEFINITION. For every $q \in Q$ define the price system $p(q)$ and the
rationing scheme $(L(q), l(q))$ by:

$$(D) \begin{cases} p_j(q) = \min\left[\bar{p}_j, \max(q_j, \underline{p}_j)\right] = \max(\underline{p}_j, \min(q_j, \bar{p}_j)), \\ L_j(q) = M_j - \max(\bar{p}_j, q_j), \\ l_j(q) = m_j - \min(\underline{p}_j, q_j), \qquad\qquad j = 1 \cdots n. \end{cases}$$

This definition is illustrated in figure 2.1, which is drawn for a case

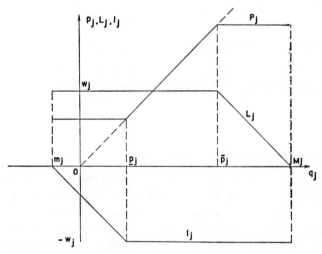

Figure 2.1

where $\bar{p}_j > w_j > \underline{p}_j > 0$. The figure reveals that, given $(w_j, \bar{p}_j, \underline{p}_j)$, there exists a one-to-one relation between q_j and the triplet (p_j, L_j, l_j).

Obviously, for all

$$q \in Q, \bar{p} \geq p(q) \geq \underline{p}, w \geq L(q) \geq 0, 0 \geq l(q) \geq -w;$$

and (p, L, l) is a continuous vector-valued function of q, $\forall q \in Q$.

Remark. Let $x^i \in \gamma^i(q)$; it then follows from (D) that

$$(q + x^i - w^i) = \text{def}(q + z^i) \in Q.$$

Indeed:

$$q + z^i \leq q + L(q) = q + M - \max(\bar{p}, q) \leq M$$

$$q + z^i \geq q + l(q) = q + m - \min(q, \underline{p}) \geq m.$$

PROOF OF THEOREM 1. The proof will establish the existence of an equilibrium for $\mathcal{E}$ with $p = p(q)$, $L = L(q)$, $l = l(q)$, for some $q \in Q$ with $q_1 = 1$. Let

$$Q_1 = \{q \in Q \mid q_1 = 1\}, \, _1q = (q_2 \cdots q_n),$$

$$Q' = \{_1q \in R^{n-1} \mid (1, \, _1q) \in Q_1 \subset Q\}.$$

Let $\xi^i(q)$ be the subset of $\gamma^i(q)$ consisting of those elements which are maximal for $\succcurlyeq_i$. When $q_1 = 1$, $l_1(q) < 0$ and $p_1 = 1$. Therefore (lemma in Section 3), γ^i is continuous at $[p(q), L(q), l(q)]$, ξ^i is upper hemicontinuous there, and the correspondence $\xi^i(q)$, from Q_1 to X^i, is upper hemicontinuous on Q_1. Because commodity 1 is always desired, $p(q)(x^i - w^i) = 0$ for all $x^i \in \xi^i(b)$. Because $\gamma^i(q)$ is compact and $\succcurlyeq_i$ is continuous and convex, $\xi^i(q)$ is nonempty and convex.

Define

$$\zeta(q) = \{z \mid z \in R^n, z + w \in \sum_i \xi^i(q)\},$$

the aggregate excess demand correspondence (from Q_1 to R^n).

Let $_1z = \text{def}(z_2 \cdots z_n)$ and define a correspondence μ from Q' to Q' by:

$$\mu(_1q) = \{_1q' \in R^{n-1} \mid \, _1q' = \, _1q + \frac{_1z}{N}, z \in \zeta(q)\}.$$

$\mu(_1q)$ is convex, because $\zeta(q)$ is convex. μ is upper hemicontinuous, because ζ is upper hemicontinuous, $\mu(_1q) \subset Q'$, because $_1q + \, _1z^i \in Q'$ for all $x^i \in \gamma^i(q)$ by the remark above, and Q' is convex. Also, Q' is nonempty and compact.

All the conditions of Kakutani's theorem are satisfied, and μ has a fixed point $_1q^*$. There exist $q^* \in Q_1$ and $z^* \in \zeta(q^*)$ with $_1z^* = 0$. Because $p(q)z^i = 0$ for all $z^i \in \zeta^i(q)$, $_1z^* = 0$ implies $z^* = 0$. There exist $\{x^{*i}\}$, $p^* = p(q^*)$, $L^* = L(q^*)$, $l^* = l(q^*)$, such that conditions (i) and (ii) in the definition of an equilibrium for $\mathscr{E}$ are satisfied. We now verify that conditions (iii) and (iv) are satisfied as well.

To begin with (iv), $\bar{p}_j > p_j$ implies

$$L_j = M_j - \bar{p}_j = w_j$$

and

$$w_j - z_j^i = w_j - x_j^i + w_j^i = \sum_h x_j^h - x_j^i + w_j^i > \sum_h x_j^h - x_j^i \geq 0.$$

Hence $\bar{p}_j > p_j$ implies

$$L_j - z_j^i > 0 \,\forall\, i,$$

and $L_j - z_j^i = 0$ for some i implies $p_j = \bar{p}_j$. The reasoning for $p_j > \underline{p}_j$ is similar.

To prove (iii), note first that $L_1 > x_1^i - w_1^i > l_1$. For some j, $2 \leq j \leq n$, let $p_j = \bar{p}_j$; then

$$l_j = m_j - \underline{p}_j = -w_j$$

and

$$z_j^i + w_j = x_j^i + w_j - w_j^i > 0$$

because $x_j^i \geq 0$ and $\sum_{h \neq i} w_j^h > 0$. Hence, if $L_j - z_j^i = 0$ for some i, then $p_j = \bar{p}_j$ by the proof of (iv) and $z_j^h - l_j > 0 \,\forall\, h$. The reasoning for $p_j = \underline{p}_j$ is similar.   QED

5. Limited flexibility of some nominal prices

To relax the assumption that P is compact is a straightforward technical task. In view of Assumption (2), we may assume without loss of generality that $p \geq 0$. Let us now allow $\bar{p}_j = +\infty$ for some, possibly all $j = 2 \cdots n$. (In particular, when $\bar{p}_j = +\infty$ and $\underline{p}_j = 0$, $j = 2 \cdots n$, we have a traditional exchange economy without price rigidities.)

THEOREM 2. *Let*

$$\mathscr{E} = \{(X^i, \succcurlyeq_i, w^i), P\}$$

satisfy Assumptions 1, 2 with index set $I = \{1\}$, and 3; let

$$P = \{p \in R^n \mid p_1 = 1, \ +\infty \geq \bar{p} \geq p \geq \underline{p} \geq 0\};$$

there exists an equilibrium for $\mathscr{E}$.

PROOF. Consider a sequence of economies

$$\mathscr{E}^k = \{(X^i, \succsim_i. w^i), p^k\},$$

where

$$P^k = \{p \in R^n \mid p_1 = 1, \ +\infty > \bar{p}^k \geq p \geq \underline{p}\}$$

with $\bar{p}^k_j = \bar{p}_j$ whenever

$$\bar{p}_j < +\infty, \ \bar{p}^k_j \to +\infty$$

otherwise. For every $k = 1, 2, \cdots$, there exists an equilibrium for $\mathscr{E}^k$, say $\{(x^i)^k, p^k, L^k, l^k\}$, with

$$p^k \in P^k \quad \text{and} \quad w \geq L^k \geq 0 \geq l^k \geq -w.$$

For all i, the sequences $(x^i)^k$ are bounded and there exists a converging subsequence, say

$$(x^i)^k \to \hat{x}^i, \quad i = 1 \cdots N, \ L^k \to \hat{L}, \ l^k \to \hat{l}.$$

To show that the sequence p^k is bounded, assume on the contrary that

$$\|p^k\| \to +\infty.$$

Let

$$\Pi^k = \text{def} \frac{p^k}{\|p^k\|}; \quad \|\Pi^k\| = 1$$

and there exists a converging subsequence, say $\Pi^k \to \hat{\Pi}$, with $\|\hat{\Pi}\| = 1$, $\hat{\Pi}_1 = 0$ and $\hat{\Pi}_j > 0$ for some j. For that j, $p^k_j \to +\infty$ and there exists k' such that

$$p^k_j > \underline{p}_j, \ l^k_j = -w_j < 0, \ \forall k \geq k';$$

hence, $\hat{l}_j < 0$, γ^i is continuous at $(\hat{\Pi}, \hat{L}, l)$, ξ^i (compact-valued, since $M \geq L \geq 0 \geq l \geq m$) is upper hemicontinuous and closed there, and $\hat{x}^i \in \xi^i(\hat{\Pi}, \hat{L}, \hat{l})$. But this contradicts Assumption 2 with $I = \{1\}$, since $\hat{\Pi}_1 = 0$. Therefore, p^k is bounded and there exists a subsequence with

$$\{(x^i)^k, p^k, L^k, l^k\} \to \{(\hat{x}^i), \hat{p}, \hat{L}, \hat{l}\},$$

an equilibrium for $\mathscr{E}$. Indeed,

$$\hat{x}^i \in \xi^i(\hat{p}, \hat{L}, \hat{l}) \subset X^i, \hat{p} \in P,$$

and conditions (ii)–(iv) in the definition of an equilibrium are satisfied for all k. The verification that these conditions also hold in the limit is straightforward.   QED

COROLLARY. *Under the assumptions of Theorem 2, let* $\{(\hat{x}^i), \hat{p}, L, \hat{l}\}$ *be an equilibrium for $\mathscr{E}$; for all j such that*

$$\bar{p}_j = +\infty, \ L_j > \hat{x}^i_j - w^i_j, \qquad\qquad i = 1 \cdots N.$$

PROOF. Follows from condition (iv) and $+\infty > \hat{p}$.   QED

6. Limited flexibility of some or all real prices

We will now consider rigidities of real prices, instead of nominal prices. To that effect, let Π be a price index defined by

$$\Pi = \sum_{i=1}^{n} \alpha_i p_i,$$

and consider constraints of the type

$$\bar{k}_j \Pi \geq p_j \geq \underline{k}_j \Pi.$$

To simplify exposition, we assume in this section that $\alpha_i > 0$ for *all* $i = 1 \cdots n$. The more general case is treated in Section 7.

Because the physical units in which we measure quantities of the commodities are arbitrary, we may multiply these units by α_i, $i = 1 \cdots n$. The individual prices being similarly multiplied by α_i, the price index becomes

$$\Pi = \sum_{i=1}^{n} p_i.$$

It is now convenient to normalize prices on the unit simplex by setting

$$\Pi = \sum_{i=1}^{n} p_i = 1.$$

The constraints then become

$$\bar{p}_j = \bar{k}_j \Pi \geq p_j \geq \underline{k}_j \Pi = \underline{p}_j, \qquad\qquad j = 1 \cdots n.$$

With this normalization, it suffices to assume weak monotonicity of preferences: $x > y$ implies $x \succ_i y$. That is, the index set I in Assumption 2 is the full set $\{1, 2, \cdots n\}$. Under monotonicity of preferences, there is no loss of generality in assuming

$$1 = \sum_{i=1}^{n} p_i \geq p_j \geq 0, \qquad\qquad j = 1 \cdots n.$$

Let ι denote the n-vector $\{1, 1, \cdots 1\}$.

THEOREM 3. *Let*

$$\mathscr{E} = \{(X^i, \succcurlyeq_i, w^i), P\}$$

satisfy Assumptions 1, 2 with index set $I = \{1, 2, \cdots n\}$*, and 3; let*

$$P = \{p \in R^n \mid \sum_{i=1}^{n} p_i = 1, \iota \geq \bar{p} \geq p \geq \underline{p} \geq 0\}$$

with

$$\sum_{i=1}^{n} \bar{p}_i \geq 1 > \sum_{i=1}^{n} \underline{p}_i;$$

there exists an equilibrium for $\mathscr{E}$*.*

PROOF. Let again

$$Q = \{q \in R^n \mid \bar{p} + w = M \geq q \geq m = \underline{p} - w\}$$

and let $p(q)$, $L(q)$, $l(q)$ be defined as per (D) in Section 4 above. $\sum_{i=1}^{n} p_i(q)$ is a monotonic non-decreasing function of q. Because

$$\sum_{i=1}^{n} \bar{p}_i \geq 1 > \sum_{i=1}^{n} \underline{p}_i,$$

there exists q such that

$$\sum_{i=1}^{n} p_i(q) \geq (\leq) 1.$$

For arbitrary $q \in Q$, define

$$q'_j(q) = \min(M_j, \max(q_j + \alpha, m_j)), \qquad\qquad j = 1 \cdots n,$$

α such that

$$\sum_{i=1}^{n} p_i(q') = 1.$$

$q'(q)$ is an always defined, single-valued, continuous function from Q to Q. Let then

$$p'(q) = p(q'(q)),$$
$$L'(q) = L(q'(q)),$$

$$l'(q) = l(q'(q)),$$

$$\gamma'^i(q) = \gamma^i(q'(q)),$$

and

$$\xi'^i(q) = \xi^i(q'(q)).$$

Because

$$\sum_{i=1}^{n} p_i'(q) \equiv 1 > \sum_{i=1}^{n} \underline{p_i},$$

there exists for every $q \in Q$ some j such that

$$p_j'(q) > \underline{p_j} \geq 0, l_j'(q) < 0.$$

Accordingly (lemma above), $\gamma'^i(q)$ is continuous at

$$(p'(q), L'(q), l'(q)) \; \forall \, q \in Q,$$

and $\xi^i(q)$ is upper hemicontinuous (as well as nonempty and convex).
   Let

$$\zeta'(q) = \{z \in R^n \,|\, z + w \in \sum_{i=1}^{n} \xi'^i(q)\}$$

and define a correspondence μ' from Q to Q by:

$$\mu'(q) = \{q'' \,|\, q'' = q' + \frac{z}{N}, z \in \zeta'(q)\}.$$

$\mu'(q) \subset Q$ because $q' + z^i \in Q$ for all $x^i \in \gamma^i(q') = \gamma'^i(q)$ and Q is convex. $\mu'(q)$ is convex, because $\zeta'(q)$ is convex. μ' is upper hemicontinuous, because q' is continuous, ζ' is upper hemicontinuous and Q is compact. All the conditions of Kakutani's theorem are satisfied, and μ' has a fixed point

$$q^* = q'(q^*) + \frac{z^*}{N}, \qquad\qquad z^* \in \zeta'(q^*),$$

where

$$q_j'(q^*) = \min(M_j, \max(q_j^* + \alpha^*, m_j))$$

and $p'(q^*) \cdot z^* \leq 0$. If $\alpha^* < 0$, then

$$\forall j \frac{z_j^*}{N} = \min(q_j^* - m_j, -\alpha^*) \geq 0, \, p_j'(q^*)z_j^* \geq 0;$$

hence

$$p'(q^*) \cdot z^* \leq 0 \text{ implies } p'_j(q^*)z^*_j = 0.$$

There exists j such that $p'_j(q^*) > p_j \geq 0$ and $l'_j(q^*) < 0$, so that $q^*_j + \alpha^* > m_j$, $z^*_j > 0$. This contradicts $p'_j(q^*)z^*_j = 0$, therefore $\alpha^* \geq 0$. If $\alpha^* = 0$, then $q'(q^*) = q^*$ and $z^* = 0$. If $\alpha^* > 0$, then

$$\forall j \frac{z^*_j}{N} = \max(q^*_j - M_j, -\alpha^*) \leq 0, \, p'_j(q^*)z^*_j \leq 0.$$

Let

$$J_1 = \text{def} \{j \mid j = 1 \cdots n, \, z^*_j = 0\},$$

$$J_2 = \text{def} \{j \mid j = 1 \cdots n, \, z^*_j < 0\}.$$

We know that there exist

$$x^i \in \xi'^i(q^*), \qquad\qquad\qquad i = 1 \cdots N,$$

such that

$$z^* = \sum_{i=1}^n (x^i - w^i) \leq 0.$$

In view of Assumption 2, there must exist

$$y^i \in \xi'^i(q^*), \qquad\qquad\qquad i = 1 \cdots N,$$

with

$$y^i_j = x^i_j \, \forall j \in J_1, \, y^i_j \geq x^i_j \, \forall j \in J_2$$

and

$$\sum_{i=1}^n (y^i - w^i) = 0.$$

We may thus conclude that $\alpha^* \geq 0$ implies $0 \in \zeta'(q^*)$.
    Accordingly, there exist $\{x^{*i}\}$,

$$p^* = p'(q^*) = p(q'(q^*)),$$

$$L^* = L'(q^*) = L(q'(q^*)),$$

$$l^* = l'(q^*) = l(q'(q^*)),$$

$x^{*i} \in X^i$, $p^* \in P$, such that conditions (i) and (ii) in the definition of an equilibrium for $\mathcal{E}$ are satisfied. To verify that conditions (iii) and (iv) are satisfied as well, note that $p(q')$, $L(q')$, $l(q')$ satisfy definition (D), so that the reasoning in the proof of Theorem 1 applies again without modification.

QED

7. Limited flexibility of some nominal and some real prices

We will now finally consider simultaneously rigidities of some real prices and of some nominal prices – still restricting attention, for each commodity, to either type of rigidity but not both. At the same time, we will generalize the assumption of Theorem 3 to the effect that all commodities enter with positive weight in the definition of the relevant price index. Theorem 4 below includes as special cases Theorems 1, 2 and 3 above. The technique of proof combines the reasoning in these three simpler cases.

The basic structure of the model in this section is as follows. There are n commodities, indexed $j = 1 \cdots n$. Commodity 1, with price $p_1 = 1$, is an always desired numeraire. Commodities 2, 3, $\cdots m \leq n$ are subject to price constraints in terms of the numeraire:

$$\bar{p}_j \geq p_j \geq \underline{p}_j, \qquad\qquad\qquad j = 2 \cdots m.$$

We admit $\bar{p}_j = +\infty$ for some (all) j. There exists a price index

$$\Pi = \sum_{j \in J} \alpha_j p_j, \qquad\qquad\qquad J \subset \{1, 2, \cdots n\},$$

where J is an arbitrary (nonempty) index set. Commodities $m + 1 \cdots n$ are subject to price constraints in terms of the index

$$\Pi : \bar{k}_j \Pi \geq p_j \geq \underline{k}_j \Pi, \qquad\qquad\qquad j = m + 1 \cdots n.$$

The following monotonicity assumptions on preferences are made:

ASSUMPTION 4. $x \geq y$ and $x_1 > y_1 \Rightarrow x \succ_i y$.

ASSUMPTION 5. $x \geq y$ and $x_j > y_j$ for some $j \in J \Rightarrow x \succ_i y$.

That is, we assume Assumption 2 with $I = \{1\}$ *and* with $I = \{j\}$ for each j in J.

Assumptions 4 and 5 will guarantee that no constraints are expressed with reference to a worthless numeraire or commodity basket, and specifically that $+\infty > \Pi > 0$ in equilibrium.

Technically, it will prove more convenient to normalize prices by the rule

$$\sum_{j \in J} p_j = 1 = \Pi$$

(under rescaling by α_j of the physical units and prices of commodity j, $\forall\, j \in J$) and to define the admissible set P as follows (where $\bar{p}_j \equiv \bar{k}_j$, $\underline{p}_j \equiv \underline{k}_j$, $j = m + 1 \cdots n$):

$$P = \{p \in R^n \mid \sum_{j \in J} p_j = 1, p_1 \geq 0, \bar{p}_j p_1 \geq p_j \geq \underline{p}_j p_1, \quad j = 2 \cdots m,$$

$$\bar{p}_j \geq p_j \geq \underline{p}_j, \quad j = m + 1 \cdots n\}.$$

$P \neq \phi$ whenever

$$\sum_{\substack{j \in J \\ j > m}} \bar{p}_j \geq 1 > \sum_{\substack{j \in J \\ j > m}} \underline{p}_j.$$

Given some $p^0 \in P$ with $p_1^0 > 0$, there exists $p^* = p^0/p_1^0$ with

$$p_1^* = 1, \bar{p}_j \geq p_j^* \geq \underline{p}_j, \qquad\qquad j = 2 \cdots m,$$

$$\bar{p}_j \sum_{j \in J} p_j^* = \bar{k}_j \Pi^* \geq p_j^* \geq \underline{k}_j \Pi^* = \underline{p}_j \sum_{j \in J} p_j^*, \qquad j = m + 1 \cdots n.$$

THEOREM 4. Let

$$\mathscr{E} = \{(X^i, \succcurlyeq_i, w^i), P\}$$

satisfy Assumptions 1, 2 with $I = \{1\}$ *and* with $I = \{j\}\ \forall\, j \in J \subset \{1, 2, \cdots n\}$, and 3; let

$$P = \{p \in R^n \mid \sum_{j \in J} p_j = 1, p_1 \geq 0, \bar{p}_j p_1 \geq p_j \geq \underline{p}_j p_1, \qquad j = 2 \cdots m,$$

$$\bar{p}_j \geq p_j \geq \underline{p}_j, \quad j = m + 1 \cdots n\}$$

with

$$\sum_{\substack{j \in J \\ j > m}} \bar{p}_j \geq 1 > \sum_{\substack{j \in J \\ j > m}} \underline{p}_j;$$

there exists an equilibrium for $\mathscr{E}$, with $p_1 > 0$.[5]

PROOF. Let

$$\mathscr{E}^k = \{(X^i, \succcurlyeq_i w^i), P^k\}$$

---

[5] For $j = 2 \cdots m$, condition (iv) in the definition of an equilibrium for $\mathscr{E}$ should obviously be read as:

$$\bar{p}_j p_1 > p_j \text{ implies } L_j > x_j^i - w_j^i \forall i$$
$$p_j > \underline{p}_j p_1 \text{ implies } l_j < x_j^i - w_j^i \forall i.$$

where

$$P^k = \{p \in P \mid \bar{p}_1^k \geq p_1 \geq \underline{p}_1 = 0, \bar{p}_j^k p_1 \geq p_j \geq \underline{p}_j p_1, \qquad j = 2 \cdots m,$$
$$\bar{p}_j^k \geq p_j \geq \underline{p}_j, \quad j = m + 1 \cdots n\},$$

with $\bar{p}_1^k < \infty, \bar{p}_j^k = \bar{p}_j$ whenever $\bar{p}_j < \infty, \bar{p}_j^k \to +\infty$ otherwise. $P \neq \phi$ implies $P^k \neq \phi$, for $\bar{p}_j^k$ large enough. We first prove the existence of an equilibrium for $\mathscr{E}^k$. In this part of the proof, the superscript k is omitted, for notational convenience.

Define

$$M_j = w_j + \bar{p}_j, m_j = \underline{p}_j - w_j, \qquad\qquad j = 1, m + 1 \cdots n;$$
$$M_j(q_1) = w_j + \bar{p}_j w_1 + \bar{p}_j \min(\bar{p}_1, q_1),$$

$$m_j(q_1) = \underline{p}_j \max(\underline{p}_1, q_1) - w_j - \underline{p}_j(w_1 + \bar{p}_1), \qquad j = 2 \cdots m;$$
$$Q = \{q \in R^n \mid M \geq q \geq m\},$$

a convex, compact set

The convexity of Q is illustrated in figure 2.2 for the subspace (q_1, q_2).

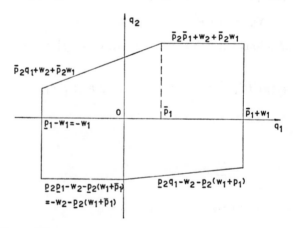

Figure 2.2

For every $q \in Q$, define:

$$\text{(D)} \begin{cases} p_j(q) = \min(\bar{p}_j, \max(q_j, \underline{p}_j)) \\ L_j(q) = M_j - \max(\bar{p}_j, q_j) \\ l_j(q) = m_j - \min(q_j, \underline{p}_j) \end{cases} \qquad j = 1, m + 1 \cdots n$$

$$(D') \begin{cases} p_j(q) = \min\left(\bar{p}_j p_1(q), \max\{q_j, \underline{p}_j p_1(q)\}\right) \\ L_j(q) = M_j(q_1) - \max\{\bar{p}_j p_1(q), q_j\} \\ l_j(q) = m_j(q_1) - \min\{q_j, \underline{p}_j p_1(q)\} \end{cases} \qquad j = 2\cdots m.$$

We remark the following implications of this definition:

(i) $\forall q \in Q, p(q) \in P$

(ii) $\forall q \in Q, w + w_1 \bar{p} \geq L(q) \geq 0$

$$0 \geq l(q) \geq -w - (w_1 + \bar{p}_1)\underline{p}.$$

These inequalities are obviously enough for $j = 1, m+1 \cdots n$.
For $j = 2 \cdots m$, they may be verified as follows:

$$\begin{aligned} L_j(q) &= M_j(q_1) - \max\left(\bar{p}_j p_1(q), q_j\right) \\ &= M_j(q_1) - \max\left(\bar{p}_j \min\{\bar{p}_1, \max(q_1, \underline{p}_1)\}, q_j\right) \\ &\leq M_j(q_1) - \max\left(\bar{p}_j \min(\bar{p}_1, q_1), q_j\right) \\ &= w_j + \bar{p}_j w_1 + \bar{p}_j \min(\bar{p}_1, q_1) - \max\left(\bar{p}_j \min(\bar{p}_1 q_1), q_j\right) \\ &\leq w_j + \bar{p}_j w_1. \end{aligned}$$

$$\begin{aligned} L_j(q) &= M_j(q_1) - \max\left(\bar{p}_j p_1(q), q_j\right) \\ &= \min\left(M_j(q_1) - q_j, M_j(q_1) - \bar{p}_j p_1(q)\right) \\ &\geq \min\left(M_j(q_1) - \max_Q q_j, M_j(q_1) - \bar{p}_j p_1(q)\right) = 0 \end{aligned}$$

$$\begin{aligned} l_j(q) &= m_j(q_1) - \min\left(q_j, \underline{p}_j p_1(q)\right) \\ &= m_j(q_1) - \min\left(q_j, \underline{p}_j \min\{\bar{p}_1, \max(q_1, \underline{p}_1)\}\right) \\ &\geq m_j(q_1) - \min\left(q_j, \underline{p}_j \max(q_1, \underline{p}_1)\right) \\ &= \underline{p}_j \max(\underline{p}_1, q_1) - w_j - \underline{p}_j(w_1 + \bar{p}_1) - \min\left(q_j, \underline{p}_j \max(\underline{p}_1, q_1)\right) \\ &\geq -w_j - \underline{p}_j(w_1 + \bar{p}_1). \end{aligned}$$

$$\begin{aligned} l_j(q) &= m_j(q_1) - \min\left(q_j, \underline{p}_j p_1(q)\right) \\ &= \max\left(m_j(q_1) - q_j, m_j(q_1) - \underline{p}_j p_1(q)\right) \\ &\leq \max\left(m_j(q_1) - \min_Q q_j, m_j(q_1) - \underline{p}_j p_1(q)\right) = 0 \end{aligned}$$

(iii)   Accordingly, the budget set correspondence

$$\begin{aligned} \gamma^i(q) &= \gamma^i(p(q), L(q), l(q)) \\ &= \{x \mid x \in X^i, p(q)(x - w^i) \leq 0, L(q) \geq x - w^i \geq l(q)\} \end{aligned}$$

is compact-valued; *a fortiori*, $\xi^i(q) \subset \gamma^i(q)$ is compact-valued.

(iv)   for all $x^i \in \gamma^i(q)$,

$$M_j \geq q_j + L_j(q) \geq q_j + z^i_j \geq q_j + l_j(q) \geq m_j, \qquad\qquad j = 1 \cdots n.$$

(v) $\sum_{j \in J} p_j(q)$ is a monotonic, non-decreasing function of q.

Define

$$q'_j(q) = \text{Max}\,[M_j(q'_1), \min\{q_j + \alpha, m_j(q'_1)\}], \qquad\qquad j = 1 \cdots n,$$

α such that $\sum_{j \in J} p_j(q') = 1$. [Of course,

$$M_j(q'_1) = M_j, m_j(q'_1) = m_j, j = 1, m + 1 \cdots n.]$$

$q'(q)$ is an always defined, single-valued, continuous function from Q to Q.
Define

$$p'(q) = p(q'(q)),$$
$$L'(q) = L(q'(q)),$$
$$l'(q) = l(q'(q)),$$
$$\gamma'^i(q) = \gamma^i(q'(q)),$$
$$\xi'^i(q) = \xi^i(q'(q)), \qquad\qquad i = 1 \cdots N.$$

There exists $j \in \{1 \cdots n\}$ such that $p'_j(q) > 0$ and $l'_j(q) < 0$. Indeed, if $p'_1(q) > 0$, then $l'_1(q) < 0$ and the result obtains with $j = 1$. If $p'_1(q) = 0$, then

$$\sum_{j \in J} p'_j(q) = 1 > \sum_{\substack{j \in J \\ J < m}} p_j$$

implies

$$p'_j(q) > \underline{p}_j(q) \geqq 0$$

for some $i \in J, j > m$, or

$$p'_j(q) > \underline{p}_j p'_1(q) = 0$$

for some $j \in J, m \geq j > 1$.[6] In either case, $l'_j(q) < 0$ for that same j, as desired. Consequently (lemma above), $\gamma'^i(q)$ is continuous at $p'(q)$, $L'(q)$, $l'(q)$ and $\xi'^i(q)$ is upper hemicontinuous (as well as nonempty and convex).

We may now repeat the reasoning in the proof of Theorem 3. Letting

$$\zeta'(q) = \{z \in R^n \,|\, z + w \in \sum_{i=1}^{N} \xi'^i(q)\},$$

[6] Actually, when $\bar{p}^*_j < \infty$, $p = 0$ implies $p_j = 0 \,\forall j = 2 \cdots m$; the more general statement in the text avoids the use of $\bar{p}^*_j < \infty$ in preparation for the last part of the proof.

we define

$$\mu'(q) = \{q'' \mid q'' = q' + \frac{z}{N}, z \in \zeta'(q)\}.$$

$\mu'(q)$ has a fixed point

$$q^* = q'(q^*) + \frac{z^*}{N},$$

$$z^* \in \zeta'(q^*),$$

$$q'_j(q^*) = \min(M_j, \max(q^*_j + \alpha^*, m_j))$$

where

$$M_j = M_j(q'_1(q^*)),$$
$$m_j = m_j(q'_1(q^*)), \qquad\qquad j = 2 \cdots m,$$

and

$$p'(q^*)z^* \leq 0.$$

One verifies that $\alpha^* \geq 0$, and $\alpha^* \geq 0$ implies $0 \in \zeta'(q^*)$. There exist $\{x^{*i}\}$, $p^* = p'(q^*)$, $L^* = L'(q^*)$, $l^* = l'(q^*)$ defining an equilibrium for $\mathscr{E}^k$.

We may now repeat the reasoning in the proof of Theorem 2. That is, we consider a sequence of economies

$$\mathscr{E}^k = \{(X^i, \succcurlyeq_i, w^i), P^k\}$$

with $\bar{p}^k_1 \to \infty$, $\bar{p}^k_j \to \infty$, whenever $\bar{p}_j = +\infty$. For every $k = 1, 2, \cdots$, there exists an equilibrium for $\mathscr{E}^k$, say $\{(x^i)^k, p^k, L^k, l^k\}$, with $p^k \in P^k$ and

$$w + w_1 \bar{p}^k \geq L^k \geq 0 \geq l^k \geq -w - (w_1 + \bar{p}^k_1)\underline{p} - \text{see remark (ii) } supra.$$

At an equilibrium for $\mathscr{E}^k$, we may replace L^k by

$$\underline{L}^k = \min\{w, L^k\},$$

and we may replace l_k by

$$\bar{l}^k = \max\{l_k, -w\},$$

without affecting the allocation or its equilibrium property. Thus, $\{(x^i)^k, p^k, \underline{L}^k, \bar{l}^k\}$ is an equilibrium for $\mathscr{E}^k$, with

$$w \geq \underline{L}^k \geq 0 \geq \bar{l}^k \geq -w,$$

and there exists a subsequence with $(x^i)^k \to \hat{x}^i$, $\underline{L}^k \to \hat{L}$, $\bar{l}^k \to \hat{l}$. To show that the sequence p^k is bounded, assume on the contrary that $\| p^k \| \to \infty$ and define

$$\Pi^k = \frac{p^k}{\| p^k \|};$$

$$\Pi^k \to \hat{\Pi} \quad \text{with} \quad \| \hat{\Pi} \| = 1,$$

$$\sum_{j \in J} \hat{\Pi}_j = 0$$

and $\hat{\Pi}_j > 0$ for some $j \notin J$. The fact that $\hat{x}^i \in \xi^i(\hat{\Pi}, \hat{L}, \hat{l})$ contradicts Assumption 2 with $I = \{ j \} \; \forall j \in J$, since $\sum_{j \in J} \hat{\Pi}_j = 0$. Hence, p^k is bounded and there exists a subsequence with

$$\{ (x^i)^k, p^k, \underline{L}^k, \bar{l}^k \} \to \{ (\hat{x}^i), \hat{p}, \hat{L}, \hat{l} \}.$$

Furthermore, $\hat{x}^i \in \xi^i(\hat{p}, \hat{L}, \hat{l})$ implies $\hat{p}_1 > 0$ in view of Assumption 2 with $I = \{ 1 \}$. Finally, we note that

$$\hat{x}^i \in \xi^i(\hat{p}, \hat{L}, \hat{l}) \subset X^i,$$

$\hat{p} \in P$ and conditions (ii)–(iv) in the definition of an equilibrium are satisfied for all k. They also hold in the limit, and $\{ (\hat{x}^i), \hat{p}, \hat{L}, \hat{l} \}$ defines an equilibrium for $\mathscr{E}$, with $\hat{p}_1 > 0$.   QED

8. Concluding remarks

The lengthy proof of Theorem 4 suggests that a more powerful technique might be required to handle more complicated cases – for instance, cases where constraints on different prices are tied to different index numbers.

One might also wish to consider at once the more general case, where the set of admissible prices P is an arbitrary (convex) set in R^n. The difficulty with this more general approach is that one would loose the one-to-one correspondence between price rigidities and quantity rationing.

Before exploring these formal generalisations, it might be wise to gain further insight in the meaningfulness and implications of the equilibrium concept used in this paper. Such insight will hopefully be gained through detailed analysis of specific models (for instance, models of temporary equilibrium with downwards rigidities of real wages, or with money and price controls aimed at curbing inflation).[7]

---

[7] Instances of such analysis may already be found in unpublished papers of Jean-Pascal Bénassy (1975, 1982).

One normative implication of the equilibrium concept used here is immediate. Let $(\{\bar{x}^i\}, \bar{p}, \bar{L}, \bar{l})$ be an equilibrium for the economy

$$\mathscr{E} = \{(X^i, \succcurlyeq_i, w^i), P\}.$$

Consider then the economy defined by the same agents *and the constraints on net trades*

$$\bar{L} \geq x^i - w^i \geq \bar{l}.$$

The allocation $\{\bar{x}^i\}$ is Pareto efficient for the economy, and sustained by the price system $\bar{p}$.[8]

The relative efficiency of alternative rationing schemes (absolute, relative, random, ...) designed to cope with the same rigidities is another open question – a much more difficult question, however.

---

[8] *Proof.* Replace X^i by $\{x \mid x \in X^i, \bar{L} + w^i \geq x \geq \bar{l} + w^i\} = \bar{X}^i$; $(\{\bar{x}^i\}, \bar{p})$ defines a competitive equilibrium for the economy $\{(\bar{X}^i, \succcurlyeq_i, w^i), R^n_+\}$.

3 On supply-constrained equilibria*

1. Introduction

1.1.

In the microeconomic literature on equilibrium under price rigidities and quantity rationing, starting with the work of Bénassy (1975), Drèze (1975) and Younès (1975), it has been customary to impose as part of the definition of equilibrium that a given numeraire commodity should not be rationed. This practice has two distinct motivations. On the one hand, it guarantees that at least one commodity is not rationed, thereby ruling out the trivial equilibrium enforced by rationing to zero the supply of all commodities or, alternatively, their demand.[1] On the other hand, this practice provides a more realistic treatment of money as a numeraire, since quantity constraints on *net* trades of money are very rarely observed. This second motivation, unlike the first, requires that the never-constrained commodity be chosen *a priori*.

For the remaining commodities, rationing may affect either supply or demand but not both sides of a same market simultaneously. This requirement of 'orderly rationing' (Hahn, 1978) seems generally accepted, at least to study systematic imbalance as distinct from frictional imbalance.[2] It

* *Journal of Economic Theory*, 33 (1984), 172–182. With Pierre Dehez. Support from the Projet d'Action Concertée financed by the Belgian government (Contract 80/85–12) is gratefully acknowledged. The authors wish to thank T. Andersen, P. Champsaur and a referee for interesting comments.

[1] If in addition, the unrationed numeraire always has a positive price, then consumers' constrained demands are upper hemi-continuous in prices and quantity constraints whenever initial endowment of the numeraire is positive (see Drèze (1975), p. 304).

[2] Although this point has not been investigated systematically, it would seem possible to relax the usual requirement, allowing instead for a limited amount of frictional rationing on the short side of a market; see also Henin (1980).

is supported by casual observations as well as theoretical arguments; see Malinvaud and Younès (1977b) and Grandmont *et al.* (1978). For a commodity with a predetermined price, the rationing may affect either side of the market. For a commodity with downward (resp. upward) price rigidity, rationing is limited to supply (resp. demand). When the price of a given commodity is constrained to lie in a given interval, possibly consisting of a single point, it is not possible to rule out *a priori* that a given side of the market be constrained.

This feature has sometimes been regarded as unsatisfactory, on grounds of realism again. For experience suggests that certain types of market imbalances are more common than others. Broadly speaking, there seems to be a tacit concensus that rationing of supply occurs more frequently than rationing of demand, outside exceptional situations (like wartime rationing or accidental power shortages). This view has been defended explicitly by two authors, van der Laan (1980) and Kurz (1982), whose seminal work on supply-constrained equilibria has inspired the present contribution.

Thus, van der Laan (1980, p. 63) writes:

> In our opinion constraints on the supply side can often more easily be realized than constraints on the demand side, for in most cases the number of sellers is less than the number of buyers. On the labor market, the reverse is true, but a restriction on the number of working hours is easily implemented.

Accordingly, van der Laan introduces a concept of equilibrium where demand is never rationed (even when prices are upward rigid) and supply is rationed only if prices are downward rigid. Under assumptions similar to those of Drèze (1975), he proves existence of an exchange equilibrium where *not all* net supplies are constrained to zero. He thereupon proves the existence of an equilibrium, where the net supply of some commodity is not rationed.[3] But it is not possible to choose a priori the commodity whose supply is not rationed.

Kurz introduces a different equilibrium concept where supply rationing takes the form of 'unemployment probabilities' and demand is never rationed. His motivation is similar and is stated as follows (1982, p. 102):

> Since in practice it is difficult to implement rationing of demand it appears to us as a very satisfactory result that the markets of an economy with distorted price structure can be cleared with a supplementary mechanism of endogenous

---

[3] This result can be found in another paper by van der Laan (1982). In his first paper (1980), he proves the existence of an equilibrium where the supply constraint is positive for at least one commodity.

probabilities of resource unemployment which are uniformly perceived... This conclusion is reinforced by the fact that demand rationings rarely occur in market economies while resource unemployments are very common.

For a pure exchange economy where price rigidities take the form of '*linkages*', i.e. functional relations between the prices of different commodities, he shows that: '*Markets can be made to clear with unemployment only and with one of the commodities being fully employed*' (p. 107, his italics). Suppliers of the fully employed commodity are not rationed but again it is not possible to choose *a priori* the commodity which is to remain unconstrained

1.2.

The present paper has the modest goal of providing sufficient conditions for the existence of an equilibrium with price rigidities and quantity rationing, where:

(i)   demand is never rationed;

(ii)   net trades of an *a priori* chosen always desired numeraire (hereafter called 'money') are never rationed;

(iii)   supply is rationed only when *real* prices are downward rigid, real prices being defined by money prices deflated by some given price index.

The justification for stating (iii) in terms of real prices is twofold. This is the appropriate formulation when rigidities affect real prices (e.g. downward rigidity of real wages). It is equivalent to rigidity of money prices when the relevant price index is itself constrained (e.g. money prices historically non-decreasing).

A set of sufficient conditions appears in the statement of the existence theorem. The simplest case where they are satisfied is that of an economy where the relative prices of all commodities other than the numeraire are fixed (i.e. real prices are fixed) and the general level of money prices is flexible upwards.[4] More generally, our theorem allows for a partition of the set of commodities other than the numeraire into two groups; namely, a first group used to define the price index, with real prices fixed and money prices flexible upwards, and a second group of commodities whose real prices are subject to arbitrary upper and lower bounds.

---

[4] A symmetrical result for demand-constrained equilibria would require the general level of money prices to be flexible downwards, with weak desirability for commodities.

When the real prices of the commodities used to define the price index (hereafter called 'index commodities') are not all fixed but some are constrained by upper and lower bounds, it still follows from our theorem that an equilibrium exists if property (iii) is relaxed to allow supply constraints for all commodities used to define the price index. We show that this relaxation is consistent with the definition of equilibrium proposed by Chetty and Nayak (1978) for a similar situation.[5] And we show by means of an example that this relaxation is unavoidable.

1.3.

We deal with a private ownership production economy. The model and the basic assumptions are introduced in Section 2. The concept of supply-constrained equilibrium is defined in Section 3. The statement and proof of the existence theorem are given in Section 4. In Section 5, we discuss the possibility of extending our result. A speculative concluding remark is offered in Section 6.

2. The model

Let us consider a private ownership economy with m consumers, n producers and $l + 1$ commodities, indexed respectively $i = 1 \ldots m$, $j = 1 \ldots n$ and $h = 0, 1 \cdots l$. Commodity $h = 0$ is used as numeraire and its price is set equal to one. For convenience, we call it '*money*' and refer to the other commodities as '*real*' commodities.

A price system is a vector $p \in R_+^{l+1}$ with $p_0 = 1$. Rationing of the agents takes the form of absolute constraints on individual net supplies. A rationing scheme is a set of $m + n$ constraints[6] $(l_1 \cdots l_m, s_1 \cdots s_n)$, where $l_i, s_j \in R_+^{l+1}$.

Consumer i is characterized by a consumption set $X_i \subset R^{l+1}$ on which his preferences are defined, a vector $\omega_i \in R_+^{l+1}$ of initial resources and a vector of shares $\theta_i \in R_+^n$, with $\sum_i \theta_{ij} = 1, j = 1 \cdots n$. The following assumptions hold for all consumers:

A.1. X_i is a non-empty closed and convex subset of R_+^{l+1};

A.2. $\succsim_i$ is a complete, continuous and convex preorder on X_i;

[5] The authors prove the existence of an exchange equilibrium when prices are constrained to belong to a convex polyhedron or to a (strictly) convex set.
[6] The rationing constraints are therefore allowed to vary from one agent to another (although, in the existence proof, we restrict ourselves to a uniform rationing scheme). But each agent's constraint must be independent of his actions.

A.3.   money is desirable, i.e. $x_i \in X_i$, $x_i' \in R_+^{l+1}$, $x_{ih}' = x_{ih}$ for all $h \neq 0$ and $x_{i0}' > x_{i0}$ imply $x_i' \in X_i$ and $x_i' \succ_i x_i$;

A.4. $\omega_i \in \text{int } X_i$.

Producer j is characterised by a production set $Y_j \subset R^{l+1}$ and the following assumptions hold for all producers:

A.5. Y_j is a non-empty, closed and convex subset of R^{l+1};

A.6. $0 \in Y_j$.

Furthermore, the following assumptions[7] hold for the total production set $Y = \sum Y_j$:

A.7. Y is a closed subset of R^{l+1};

A.8. $Y \cap (-Y) \subset \{0\}$;

A.9. $R_-^{l+1} \subset Y$.

A price index is defined as a function $f: R_+^{l+1} \to R_+$; for a given price system p, $f(p)$ represents the general price level. The following assumptions hold for the price index:

A.10.   the function f is homogeneous of degree one;

A.11.   there exists a non-empty subset $I \subset \{1 \cdots l\}$ such that $f(p) = f((p_h)_{h \in I})$ for all $p \in R_+^{l+1}$.

The set of admissible price systems is defined by

$$P = \{p \in R_+^{l+1} \mid p_0 = 1, \underline{p}_h \leqslant \frac{p_h}{f(p)} \leqslant \bar{p}_h (h = 1 \cdots l), f(p) \geqslant b\}$$

where the constraints $(\underline{p}_h, \bar{p}_h)_{h=1}^l$ and b satisfy the following assumptions:

A.12. $0 \leqslant \underline{p}_h \leqslant \bar{p}_h < +\infty$, $\bar{p}_h > 0$ for all $h = 1 \cdots l$ and $b > 0$;

A.13. $f((\underline{p}_h)_{h \in I}) \leqslant 1 \leqslant f((\bar{p}_h)_{h \in I})$.

These assumptions ensure that P is a non-empty set.

---

[7] For a discussion of these assumptions, see Debreu (1959). Notice that these assumptions ensure that $Y \cap R_+^{l+1} = \{0\}$ and $(Y + R_-^{l+1}) \subset Y$. As in Debreu, the assumptions of closedness and convexity made on the *individual* production sets could have been made on the *total* production set instead. In the process of proving the existence of an equilibrium, the individual production sets would then have to be replaced by their closed convex hull.

3. Supply-constrained equilibrium

A *supply-constrained equilibrium* is defined by a set of consumption plans $(x_1^* \cdots x_m^*)$, a set of production plans $(y_1^* \cdots y_n^*)$, a price system $p \in P$ and a rationing scheme $(l_1 \cdots l_m, s_1 \cdots s_n)$ satisfying the following conditions:

E.1. $\sum x_i^* = \sum \omega_i + \sum y_j^*$;

E.2. for all i, x_i^* is $\succsim_i$-maximal on the budget set

$$\{x_i \in X_i \,|\, p(x_i - \omega_i) \leqslant \sum_j \theta_{ij} p y_j^*, \omega_i - x_i \leqslant l_i\};$$

E.3. for all j, y_j^* maximizes $p y_j$ on the set $\{y_j \in Y_j \,|\, y_j \leqslant s_j\}$;

E.4. $l_{ih} = s_{jh} = +\infty$ for all i and all j whenever $h = 0$, or h is such that $\underline{p}_h = 0$ or $\underline{p}_h < p_h / f(p)$.

Condition E.1 is consistent with the assumption A.9 of free disposal. Condition E.4 excludes the rationing of money and of the commodities for which either the real price is downward flexible or the lower bound on the real price is not binding.

4. Existence of a supply-constrained equilibrium

We prove the existence of a supply-constrained equilibrium when *the real prices of the index commodities are fixed* using a technique introduced by van der Laan (1980).

THEOREM. *Under the assumptions A.1 to A.13, there exists a supply-constrained equilibrium if $\underline{p}_h = \bar{p}_h$ for all $h \in I$.*

PROOF. Let us define $\underline{p}_0 = 0$ and $\bar{p}_0 = 1/b$. For our convenience, we shall work with the following admissible price set:

$$P' = \{p \in R_+^{l+1} \,|\, \underline{p} \leqslant p \leqslant \bar{p}, f(p) = 1\}.$$

This set is 'equivalent' to P given that the agents' behaviour is invariant under any proportional change in the price system. Indeed, on the one hand, $p \in P'$, $p_0 > 0$, implies $(1/p_0) p \in P$ and, on the other hand, $p \in P$ implies $(1/f(p)) p \in P'$.

We will actually prove the existence of an equilibrium where supply is *uniformly* rationed, i.e. $l_i = s_j = s$ for all i and all j.

Let us define $\omega = \sum \omega_i$ and $M = \{h \,|\, p_h = 0\}$. Thus $0 \in M$; furthermore, the assumptions of the theorem require that $f(\underline{p}) = f(\bar{p}) = 1$ and $I \subset M^c$, $M^c = \{0, 1 \cdots l\} \backslash M$.

Following Debreu (1959, p. 76), we define the set $A \subset R^{(l+1)(m+n)}$ of attainable states by $(x_1 \cdots x_m, y_1 \cdots y_n) \in A$ if and only if $x_i \in X_i$ for all $i = 1 \cdots m$, $y_j \in Y_j$ for all $j = 1 \cdots n$ and $\sum x_i = \omega + \sum y_j$. We then define the set $\hat{X}_i$ of attainable consumption plans for consumer i, i.e., the projection of A on X_i. Similarly, we define the set $\hat{Y}_j$ of attainable production plans for producer j.

The assumptions on the consumption sets and on the production sets ensure that A is a compact set (Debreu (1959, p. 77)). Let K be a closed cube of R^{l+1} with centre 0 and containing *in its interior* the $\hat{X}_i$'s and the $\hat{Y}_j$'s. Let $2a$ be the length of one of its sides. We then define $\bar{X}_i = X_i \cap K$ $(i = 1 \cdots m)$ and $\bar{Y}_j = Y_j \cap K$ $(j = 1 \cdots n)$. These sets are compact. By construction, $x_i \in \bar{X}_i$ for all i, with $x_{i0} = a$ for some i, and $y_i \in \bar{Y}_j$ for all j imply $\sum x_{i0} > \omega_0 + \sum y_{j0}$. This property is used later to prove (i) and (iii).

The set of admissible rationing constraints is defined by

$$S = \{s \in R_+^{l+1} \mid s_h = a \text{ for all } h \in M, 0 \leqslant s_h \leqslant a \text{ for all } h \in M^c\}.$$

Following van der Laan (1980, p. 66) we consider the set

$$Q = \{q \in R_+^{l+1} \mid \lambda_h \bar{p}_h \leqslant q_h \leqslant \bar{p}_h, y_h \geqslant 0 \ (h = 0, 1 \cdots l), \sum_{h=0}^{l} \lambda_h = 1\}$$

on which we define the functions $p(\cdot)$ and $s(\cdot)$ by

$$p_h(q) = \max(\underline{p}_h, q_h) \qquad (h = 0, 1 \cdots l)$$

and

$$s_h(q) = a \qquad (h \in M)$$
$$= \min(1, q_h/\underline{p}_h) a \qquad (h \in M^c).$$

These functions are continuous on Q and satisfy $p(q) \in P'$ and $s(q) \in S$ for all $q \in Q$. Indeed, $h \in I$ implies $p_h(q) = \bar{p}_h$ by hypothesis; hence $f(p(q)) = f(\bar{p}) = 1$. Furthermore, $p(q) s(q) > 0$ for all $q \in Q$. Indeed, $0 \notin Q$, i.e. for all $q \in Q$, there exists h such that $q_h > 0$. Either $h \in M$, in which case $p_h(q) = q_h > 0$ and $s_h(q) = a > 0$ or $h \in M^c$, in which case $p_h(q) \geqslant \underline{p}_h > 0$ and $s_h(q) > 0$.

We define successively the set $\eta_j(q)$ of production plans which maximize $p(q) y_j$ on the set $\{y_j \in \bar{Y}_j \mid y_j \leqslant s(q)\}$, the corresponding level of profit $\pi_j(q)$ and the set $\xi_i(q)$ of consumption plans which are $\succsim_i$-maximal on the set

$$\gamma_i(q) = \{x_i \in X_i \mid p(q)(x_i - \omega_i) \leqslant \sum_j \theta_{ij} \pi_j(q), \omega_i - x_i \leqslant s(q)\}.$$

The assumptions A.5 and A.6 on Y_j ensure that the correspondence defined on R_+^{l+1} by $\{y_j \in \bar{Y}_j \mid y_j \leqslant s\}$ is continuous.[8] By continuity of the function $s(\cdot)$, the correspondence defined on Q by $\{y_j \in \bar{Y}_j \mid y_j \leqslant s(q)\}$ is itself continuous. Thus, the correspondence η_j is u.h.c. on Q and the function π_j is continuous on Q. Furthermore, $\eta_j(q)$ is non-empty and convex for all $q \in Q$.

The correspondence defined by $\{x_i \in X_i \mid p(x_i - \omega_i) \leqslant r, \omega_i - x_i \leqslant s\}$ is continuous in (p, r, s) whenever $p \cdot s > 0$ and $r \geqslant 0$; see Drèze (1975, p. 304). Therefore, by continuity of the functions $p(\cdot)$, $s(\cdot)$ and $\pi_j(\cdot)$, the correspondence γ_i is itself continuous on Q. Thus, the correspondence ξ_i is u.h.c. on Q. Furthermore, $\xi_i(q)$ is non-empty and convex for all $q \in Q$.

Let us now consider the correspondence μ defined on $Z = \Pi \bar{X}_i \times \Pi \bar{Y}_j$ by

$$\mu(x_1 \cdots x_m, y_1 \cdots y_n)$$
$$= \{q' \in Q \mid q' \text{ maximizes } q(\textstyle\sum x_i - \omega - \sum y_j) \text{ on } Q\}.$$

Consider finally the correspondence $\varphi = \mu \times \Pi \xi_i \times \Pi \eta_i$ from $Z \times Q$ into itself. It is u.h.c. and non-empty and convex-valued. Furthermore, the set $Z \times Q$ is non-empty, convex and compact. Thus, by Kakutani's theorem, the correspondence φ has a fixed point. Let us denote by $(x_1^* \cdots x_m^*, y_1 \cdots y_n, q^*)$ such a fixed point, i.e. $x_i^* \in \xi_i(q^*)$ for all $i = 1 \cdots m$, $y_j \in \eta_j(q^*)$ for all $j = 1 \cdots n$, $q^* \in Q$ and $q^*z \geqslant qz$ for all $q \in Q$, where $z = \sum x_i^* - \omega - \sum y_j$.

(i) $q_0^* > 0$. Assume on the contrary that $q_0^* = 0$. Then $p_0(q^*) = 0$ and therefore, by A.3, $x_{i0}^* = a$ for all i. As we have seen before, this implies $z_0 > 0$, and hence $q_0^* = \bar{p}_0 > 0$ by definition of μ, a contradiction.

This ensures that the price system $p^* = (1/q_0^*)p(q^*)$ is well defined and belongs to P. Summing over all budget constraints, we get $p^*z \leqslant 0$. Let us define $s^* = s(q^*)$.

(ii) $z \leqslant 0$. Assume on the contrary that $z_k > 0$ for some k. Then $q_k^* = \bar{p}_k$, implying $p_k^* > 0$. Hence, $p^*z \leqslant 0$ requires the existence of some $h \neq k$ such that $p_h^* > 0$ and $z_h < 0$. By definition of Q, the intersection of this set with $\{q \in R_+^{l+1} \mid q_k = \bar{p}_k\}$ contains the point where $q_h = 0$ for all $h \neq k$. Therefore $z_h < 0$ implies $q_h^* = 0$. If $h \in M$, we have $p_h^* = 0$, a contradiction to $p_h^* > 0$; if $h \notin M$, we have $s_h^* = 0$, a contradiction to $z_h < 0$.

---

[8] If $Y_j = \{0\}$, it is trivial; if not, Proposition 2 (p. 23) and Problem 6 (p. 35) in Hildenbrand (1974) can be used to prove continuity, taking the assumptions A.5 and A.6 into account.

(iii) $p^*z = 0$.   Assume on the contrary that $p^*z < 0$. There must exist a consumer, say, i, whose budget constraint is not binding. By A.3, this is possible only if $x^*_{i0} = a$. But $z_0 \leqslant 0$ which implies $x^*_{i0} < a$, a contradiction.

Together (ii) and (iii) imply $p^*_h z_h = 0$ for all h. Hence, by A.9, there exists $(y^*_1 \cdots y^*_n)$ such that $\sum y^*_j = z + \sum y_j$ and $y^*_j \in \eta_j(q^*)$ for all j. Condition E.1 is therefore fulfilled.

Using a standard argument, one shows that the x^*_i's and the y^*_j's actually satisfy the conditions E.2 and E.3 (see Debreu (1959, p. 87)).

On the one hand, $y^*_{jh} < a$ for all j and all h; on the other hand, by A.4, $\omega_{ih} < a$ for all i and h, implying $\omega_{ih} - x^*_{ih} < a$ for all i and all h. Condition E.4 is then automatically satisfied given the definition of the functions $p(\cdot)$ and $s(\cdot)$. Indeed if $h \in M$, $s^*_h = a$; if $h \notin M$, $p^*_h > \bar{p}_h f(p)$ is equivalent to $q^*_h > p_h$, implying $s^*_h = a$.   QED

It is to be noticed that the equilibrium defined in the above proof satisfies the following additional condition:

E.5. $s_h = 0$ for all $h \notin M$ and $p_h = 0$ for all $h \in M$, $h \neq 0$, implies $f(p) = b$.

Indeed, $s^*_h = 0$ for all $h \notin M$ and $p_h = 0$ for all $h \in M$, $h \neq 0$, is equivalent to $q^*_h = 0$ for all $h \neq 0$ which implies $q^*_0 = \bar{p}_0$, i.e., $p_0(q^*) = \bar{p}_0$ and $f(p^*) = b$.

Let us consider the case where $p_h > 0$ for all $h \neq 0$, i.e., $M = \{0\}$. In that case, condition E.5 rules out the situation where no supply of real commodities is allowed while the general price level is not at its lower bound. It therefore allows for the case where the lower bound imposed on the general price level is so high that it is necessary to constrain to zero the net supply of all real commodities. But it excludes the case where an equilibrium would be obtained by constraining to zero all net supplies while increasing sufficiently the general price level. This argument shows that if the preferences of at least one consumer are monotone on a subset of real commodities, then $s^*_h > 0$ for some $h \neq 0$, whenever b is sufficiently small. In other words, complete flexibility of the general price level ensures existence of an equilibrium where the supply of at least one real commodity is allowed.[9]

---

[9] One would have preferred $s_h = +\infty$ for some $h \neq 0$. This has been proved (under different assumptions) by van der Laan in a recent paper (1984) using the technique of simplicial approximation.

5. Extension of the existence theorem: a counterexample

For our convenience, we still work with price systems in the equivalent set P'.

5.1.

When the prices of the index commodities are not all fixed but some are allowed to vary between given bounds,[10] it may be necessary to constrain the supply of some index commodity, the price of which exceeds its lower bound. Indeed, a price index function is typically monotone increasing. Accordingly, lowering the price of that commodity would require raising the price of some other index commodity k in order to keep $f(p)$ equal to one; and raising some other price may bring about the very situation one is trying to avoid, namely, the necessity to constrain the supply of commodity k, the price of which now exceeds its lower bound.

The following example illustrates this point. It concerns a pure exchange economy with four commodities. Let $f(p) = p_2 + p_3$, the set P' being given by

$$P' = \{p \in R_+^4 \mid 0 \leqslant p_0 \leqslant 1; 0 \leqslant p_1 \leqslant 0.3; 0.4 \leqslant p_2, p_3 \leqslant 1;$$
$$p_2 + p_3 = 1\}.$$

There is a single consumer with initial endowment $(1, 1, 1, 1)$ and preferences represented by the utility function $x_0 x_1 x_2 x_3$.

A supply-constrained equilibrium must have net trades equal to zero, no constraints on demands and no constraint on commodity 0. Under the assumed preferences, this means $s_h = 0$ whenever $p_h > p_k$ for some $k \neq h$; for otherwise, the consumer will wish to sell commodity h to buy commodity k. And P' imposes that $p_2, p_3 > p_1$. Hence $s_2 = s_3 = 0$. But P' also imposes that $p_2 + p_3 = 1 > \underline{p}_2 + \underline{p}_3$. Hence, either $p_2 > \underline{p}_2$ with $s_2 = 0$, or $p_3 > \underline{p}_3$ with $s_3 = 0$, or both.[11]

5.2.

The equilibrium concept introduced by Chetty and Nayak (1978) for the case where P is a convex polyhedron or a strictly convex set stipulates:

---

[10] In such a case, the index set I contains at least two commodities and there exist h and k in I, $h \neq k$, such that $p_h < \bar{p}_h$ and $p_k < \bar{p}_k$.

[11] Situation of this kind could be avoided if no upper bound on prices were ever effective, in which case existence of a supply-constrained equilibrium would immediately follow from the results in Drèze (1975).

'If a selling restriction is binding for some agent, for some commodity, one cannot decrease the price of the concerned commodity *keeping the price of all other commodities fixed*' (p. 4, our italics). For any commodity $h \in I$, the condition $f(p) = 1$ has precisely that connotation. Hence, the equilibrium concept of Chetty and Nayak authorizes supply constraints on all the index commodities. Therefore, if one allows every index commodity to be supply-constrained, existence follows from our theorem since we have proved existence for *every* admissible $(p_h)_{h \in I}$.

6. Concluding remark

Altogether, the situations covered by our existence theorem are of some speculative interest. If real prices are subject to exogenous constraints (as they would, for instance, under mark-up pricing, at least in the short run), and if prices do not adjust immediately downwards to eliminate excess supply but do adjust upwards to eliminate excess demand, then a supply-constrained equilibrium as defined here would have some claim to realism *in the short run*. Also, it would be partially self-fulfilling because a built-in bias toward increases in the general price level strengthens reluctance to lower money prices in response to excess supply: better to let the price level rise and keep your money prices unchanged, thereby saving the costs of two successive price changes.[12]

---

[12] The convergence toward a supply-constrained equilibrium along an adjustment process of that general type is being investigated and will be the subject of another paper.

4 Competitive equilibria with quantity-taking producers and increasing returns to scale*

1. Introduction

In the competitive model, where production sets are convex, firms are assumed to maximise profit at given prices. In the non-convex case, this assumption is known to be inadequate. Profit maximisation may lead to unbounded outputs and, more generally, the supply correspondence which assigns profit-maximising production plans to prices may be neither convex valued nor upper hemicontinuous. Beyond these problems, even in the convex case, this behaviour often lacks in realism: many producers announce prices and satisfy the demand which materialises at these prices,[1] instead of choosing optimal quantities in reaction to prices (formed on commodity exchange for instance).

In the present paper, we introduce axiomatically a concept of equilibrium, which combines the following two properties: (i) producers announce prices for their outputs and satisfy the demand which materialises at these prices and (ii) these output prices are 'competitive'. We first prove that under the assumption of convexity, these equilibria coincide with the usual competitive equilibria, thus deserving the label of the 'competitive equilibria with price-taking agents'. In the general case, allowing for non-convex

*Journal of Mathematical Economics, 17 (1988), 209–30. With Pierre Dehez. This is a revised version of a paper which has appeared as CORE Discussion paper 8623 and EUI Working paper 86/243. The initial motivation for this work came from a remark by Jean Dermine. Early progress owes much to discussions with Bernard Cornet and Jean-Philippe Vial. At a later stage, important technical arguments and continued interest came from Bernard Cornet. We express our thanks to them, to Martin Hellwig and referees who read the manuscript carefully, as well as to colleagues or seminar participants who over the years provided an inspiring mixture of criticisms and encouragements.

[1] Under convexity, when supply is defined by a correspondence rather than by a function, meeting demand naturally determines output levels.

technologies, we then prove the existence of competitive equilibria with quantity-taking producers where conditions (i) and (ii) are satisfied for each producer.

Condition (i) is a condition of *voluntary trading* on prices and quantities: the output must be such that, at the given prices, it is not more profitable for the producers to produce less. Thus, at an equilibrium, producers maximise profit subject to a sales constraint.[2] The competitive property for output prices referred to in condition (ii) is a condition of minimality. For a convex production set with a smooth boundary, output prices coincide with marginal costs if and only if they satisfy voluntary trading and are the lowest prices which satisfy that condition: output prices could not be lowered without violating voluntary trading. We also show that minimality of output prices is the only complement to voluntary trading which retrieves competitive prices in the convex case. Applied to the general case, this definition is analogous to that of '*supply price*' introduced by Marshall: '...the price, the expectation of which will *just* suffice to maintain the existing aggregate amount of production...' (Marshall (1920, p. 343, our emphasis)), and used by Pigou (1928) and by Keynes (1936, p. 24).

To formalise these conditions, we shall in this introduction consider a single producer with a technology described by a production set Y, a closed subset of $\mathbb{R}^l$ containing the origin and satisfying free disposal and absence of free production. To simplify further our presentation, we shall consider the case where inputs are distinguished from outputs and the associated cost function is differentiable, so that marginal costs are well defined. Production plans are then decomposed as $y = (a, b)$, where $a \leqq 0$ denotes the vector of inputs and b the vector of outputs.[3] Price systems are decomposed accordingly as $p = (p_a, p_b)$ and the cost function is defined by

$$c(b, p_a) = \min_{(a,b)\in Y} (-p_a \cdot a).$$

A price system $p = (p_a, p_b)$ and a production plan $\bar{y} = (\bar{a}, \bar{b})$ satisfy the condition of voluntary trading if the following inequalities are satisfied:

$$p_a \cdot \bar{a} + p_b \cdot \bar{b} \geqq p_a \cdot a + p_b \cdot b \quad \text{for all} \quad (a, b) \in Y, b \leqq \bar{b}. \tag{*}$$

---

[2] This is to be contrasted with the work of Scarf (1986) who considers an economy with a production sector described by an aggregate production set displaying a form of increasing returns. At an equilibrium, profits are zero but maximum subject to an input constraint. For a detailed comparison, see our paper on distributive production sets (Dehez and Drèze, 1988b).

[3] For vector inequalities, we adopt the following sequence of symbols: $\geqq$, $>$, $\gg$.

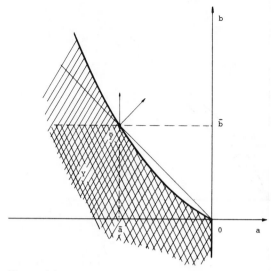

Figure 4.1

This condition says that at prices p, no smaller output yields higher profits, although the producer may be eager to sell more at these prices (as would be the case under diminishing marginal costs, a situation illustrated in fig. 4.1). Voluntary trading clearly implies that production costs are minimised. Furthermore, because inactivity is feasible, voluntary trading implies non-negative profits.

The condition (*) can equivalently be written as $p_b \in \psi(\bar{b}, p_a)$, where ψ is the correspondence defined by

$$\psi(\bar{b}, p_a) = \{p_b \geq 0 \,|\, p_b \cdot \bar{b} - c(\bar{b}, p_a) \geq p_b \cdot b - c(b, p_a), \,\forall\, b \leq \bar{b}\}.$$

In fig. 4.2, $\psi(\bar{b}, p_a)$ is the set of all prices p_b greater than or equal to average cost at $\bar{b}$, given p_a. More generally, it may happen that all prices satisfying voluntary trading exceed average cost and therefore entail positive profits, as in fig. 4.3.

To understand the content of condition (ii), it is useful to refer to the convex case first in which voluntary trading alone allows for output prices which exceed competitive levels by an arbitrary margin. Indeed, if marginal costs are well defined at $\bar{b}$, hence equal to the gradient vector $V_b c(\bar{b}, p_a)$, we have

$$\psi(\bar{b}, p_a) = \{p_b \,|\, p_b \geq V_b c(\bar{b}, p_a)\},$$

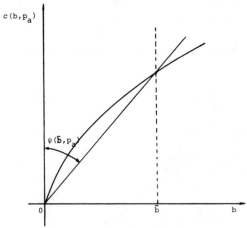

Figure 4.2

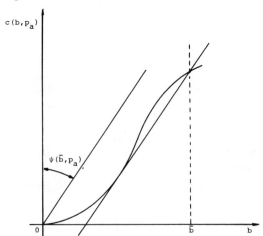

Figure 4.3

as illustrated in fig. 4.4. Competitive prices are then extracted from that set by the straightforward condition that output prices should be minimal in that set. This additional condition can be written as $p_b \in \psi^*(\bar{b}, p_a)$, where ψ^* is the correspondence defined by

$$\psi^*(\bar{b}, p_a) = \{p_b \in \psi(\bar{b}, p_a) \mid \nexists\, p'_b \in \psi(\bar{b}, p_a), p'_b < p_b\}.$$

In the differentiable and convex case, we then have $\psi^*(\bar{b}, p_a) = \nabla_b c(\bar{b}, p_a)$. Consequently, competitive outputs are characterized indifferently by the

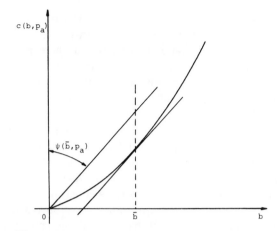

Figure 4.4

property that profit is maximised at given prices or by the property that output prices satisfy voluntary trading and are minimal.

Let us now review the economic arguments which suggest that 'minimal output prices under voluntary trading' is a competitive-like property, in the light of the arguments put forward to justify the concept of competitive equilibrium in the convex case. We shall treat positive and normative aspects separately.

From a positive viewpoint, competitive equilibria have predictive appeal in a convex economy at two distinct logical levels. In the case of a constant returns technology freely accessible to all, a deep argument says that profits will be eliminated by entry of new producers or by spontaneous coalition formation. As shown in a companion paper (Dehez and Drèze (1988b)), the argument of elimination of profit by the entry of new producers carries over to the case of increasing returns for a particular class of technologies, called *output-distributive*, which thus appear as non-convex counterparts to convex cones.

When some (convex) producers use non-reproducible resources to which potential contestants do not have access and to which a rent accrues in the form of profits, this argument no longer applies. In such situations, where returns are strictly diminishing, a competitive equilibrium will emerge only if producers follow certain rules of behaviour, like profit maximisation at given prices; or if the economic organisation privileges competitive outcomes, for instance through auction markets; or if a substitute to free entry exists, for instance through close substitutes.

Beyond the special case of output-distributive production sets, not treated here explicitly, the positive appeal (if any...) of our equilibrium concept is of this second kind. It will emerge, for instance, if producers quote prices, meet whatever demand materialises at these prices, and revise output prices downward when demand falls short of supply, whenever these lower prices remain compatible with voluntary trading. Alternatively, if markets are organised by auctioneers or regulators who adjust prices in the direction of excess supply subject to the downward rigidities induced by voluntary trading, then an equilibrium will be characterised by minimal output prices under voluntary trading. The example of fig. 4.1 should convince anyone that excess supply at given prices is a natural byproduct of increasing returns. Once that conclusion is accepted, it seems natural to require that sales constraints only set in when prices become downward rigid,[4] and prices have no reason to be downward rigid if they are not minimal, barring monopolistic elements. Of course, increasing returns provide a natural invitation to model monopolistic competition along the lines suggested by Negishi (1961); like a number of others, we are currently investigating that possibility.

Short of being able to model the tâtonnement process leading to a competitive equilibrium with quantity-taking producers,[5] we prove existence of an equilibrium by a fixed point argument involving a correspondence under which:

– market prices respond to excess demand,
– consumers announce their (excess) demands given market prices and given incomes which incorporate the profits computed at market prices,
– for given production plans, producers announce prices such that output prices are minimal subject to voluntary trading at the given input prices,
– *producers revise their production plans in the direction of discrepancies between market prices and the prices which they announce.*

From a normative viewpoint, competitive equilibria have the compelling appeal of Pareto optimality. Our equilibria formalise the natural tendency of regulators to impose minimal output prices, a tendency presumably based on the idea that lower prices compatible with voluntary trading (hence covering marginal costs) are better from a welfare point of view.[6]

[4] This corresponds to the concept of equilibrium with price rigidities and quantity rationing introduced by Drèze (1975).

[5] See, however, Drèze (1990) for an example of a process which leads to a supply-constrained equilibrium as defined in Dehez and Drèze (1984).

[6] Regulation often takes the related, yet distinct, form of imposing 'competitive' (i.e. minimal subject to voluntary trading) rates of return on investment. However, we shall show that imposing minimum profit under voluntary trading is not competitive in the sense that this condition, when added to voluntary trading, does not necessarily reproduce marginal costs in the convex case.

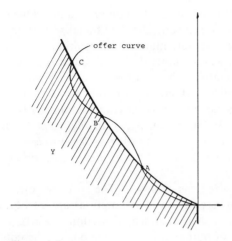

Figure 4.5

However, in the example of fig. 4.5, our definition of equilibrium admits three equilibria, labelled *A*, *B* and *C* respectively, where *C* Pareto dominates *B* which Pareto dominates *A*. We are unwilling to introduce further conditions which would privilege the global optimum *C*, because they would require more sophisticated information.[7] Furthermore, simple examples, like the one illustrated in fig. 4.6, show that second-best Pareto

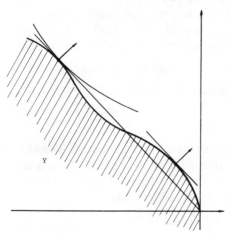

Figure 4.6

[7] Note that, in the absence of convexity, marginal cost pricing is necessary, but not sufficient, for Pareto efficiency (see Guesnerie, 1975b).

optimality may require the violation of voluntary trading. Our equilibria may thus be viewed as *third-best*, the additional constraint beyond voluntary trading being that only minimal information be used, namely prices and quantities. However, our work is best viewed as complementary to that inspired by normative considerations, like marginal cost pricing equilibria; see the important literature on this subject, starting with Guesnerie (1975b), in particular the recent contributions by Brown et al. (1986) and Dierker et al. (1985), and the papers in *Journal of Mathematical Economics*, 17 (1988). Our emphasis instead is on *decentralisation* through simple signals and incentive compatible mechanisms, i.e. on *equilibrium analysis*.

The paper is organized as follows. The private ownership is described in Section 2 where the basic assumptions are introduced. The behaviour of producers is then analysed in Section 3 where voluntary trading and minimality of output prices are combined. The equilibrium concept is then defined and existence is proved in Section 4.

2. Description of the economy

The model we shall consider is the private ownership economy as described in Debreu's *Theory of Value* (1959). There are l commodities, n producers and m consumers. Producer j is characterised by a production set Y_j. Consumer i is characterised by a consumption set X_i, a preference relation $\succeq_i$, an initial endowment ω_i and shares in profits $(\theta_{i1}, \ldots, \theta_{in})$. By definition, the latter satisfy $0 \leqq \theta_{ij} \leqq 1$ for all i and j, and $\sum_i \theta_{ij} = 1$ for all j. We make the following assumptions on consumer's characteristics:

C.1. X_i is a closed subset of $\mathbb{R}^l$, convex and bounded below.

C.2. $\succeq_i$ is a complete, continuous, convex[8] and non-satiated preordering of X_i.

C.3. There exists $\hat{x}_i \in X_i$ such that $\hat{x}_i \ll \omega_i$.

These are the assumptions used in *Theory of Value*. Although they could be weakened through more specific assumptions on preferences and endowments, our focus is here on the production side. We make the following assumptions on the production sets:

P.1. For all j, Y_j is a closed subset of $\mathbb{R}^l$.

P.2. For all j, $Y_j + \mathbb{R}^l_- \subset Y_j$.

P.3. For all j, $Y_j \cap \mathbb{R}^l_+ = \{0\}$.

[8] By *convex*, we mean: $x \succ \bar{x}$ implies $\lambda x + (1 - \lambda)\bar{x} \succ \bar{x}$ for all λ, $0 < \lambda < 1$.

These are again usual assumptions, except that the aggregate production set $\sum Y_j$ is not assumed to be convex. Furthermore, *free disposal* (P.2) and *absence of free production* (P.3) are assumed to hold at the individual level. Note that P.3 implies that *inactivity is feasible*: $0 \in Y_j$ for all j. The set of feasible allocations, $A = \{(x_1, \ldots, x_m, \ y_1, \ldots, y_n) \in \Pi X_i \times \Pi Y_j \mid \sum x_i \leqq \sum \omega_i + \sum y_j\}$ is non-empty as a consequence of the assumptions C.3 and P.3. The following assumption[9] is introduced in addition to C.1 to ensure that A is a bounded set in $\mathbb{R}^{l(m+n)}$:

> *P.4.* For all $z \in \mathbb{R}^l$, the set $\{(y_1, \ldots, y_n) \in \Pi Y_j \mid \sum y_j \geqq z\}$ is bounded in $\mathbb{R}^{ln}$.

Altogether, our assumptions ensure the existence of a competitive equilibrium in the case where the aggregate production set is convex [see Debreu (1959)].

The behaviour of the consumers is the usual one: they take the prices and profits as given when choosing the consumption plans which are best with respect to their preferences in their budget sets. As stressed in the introduction, the behaviour of the producers differs from the usual one; it is the object of the next section.

3. Behaviour of the producers

In this section, we shall be concerned with a given producer characterised by a production set Y which satisfies P.1 and P.2. It is therefore a closed and comprehensive[10] set, and consequently its boundary coincides with the set of weakly efficient production plans:

$$\partial Y = \{y^* \in Y \mid \not\exists\, y \in Y, y \gg y^*\}.$$

In the standard competitive model, the production sets are convex and the behaviour of producers is summarized by their supply correspondences which define profit-maximising production plans at given prices. Here instead, we proceed along the lines initiated by Dierker *et al.* (1985) who use the concept of 'pricing rule' defining 'acceptable' prices associated with production plans. More precisely, a pricing rule is a correspondence $\phi \colon \partial Y \to \mathbb{R}^l_+$, and a price system $\bar{p} \in \mathbb{R}^l_+$ and a production plan $\bar{y} \in \partial Y$ are said to be 'in equilibrium' (from the point of view of the producer) if and only if $\bar{p} \in \phi(\bar{y})$. When Y is convex, profit maximisation is obtained when

---

[9] This assumption has been preferred to the usual assumptions on the asymptotic cone of the aggregate production set because it is less restrictive.

[10] A set X is *comprehensive* if it satisfies free disposal: $X + \mathbb{R}^l_- \subset X$.

the pricing rule is the normal cone, i.e. $\phi(\bar{y}) = \mathbb{N}_Y(\bar{y})$.[11] Indeed, in that case, the condition $\bar{p} \in \phi(\bar{y})$ reads $\bar{p} \cdot \bar{y} \geqq \bar{p} \cdot y$ for all $y \in Y$.

To prove existence of an equilibrium for given pricing rules, one assumes that the latter are correspondences which, when intersected with the unit simplex, are upper hemicontinuous with non-empty, compact and convex values.

The subject of the present section is precisely to construct a pricing rule ϕ which embodies the idea of voluntary trading and minimality of output prices, while satisfying these requirements. That pricing rule is obtained after a sequence of intermediate definitions – ψ, ψ^* and ψ^{**} – which generalise the reasoning made in the introduction. As we proceed, we shall use systematically the convex case as a benchmark.

To formalise voluntary trading, we define the set of price systems which are compatible with it:[12]

$$\psi(\bar{y}) = \{ p \in \mathbb{R}^l_+ \mid p \cdot \bar{y} \geqq p \cdot y \text{ for all } y \in Y, y \leqq \bar{y}^+ \}. \tag{1}$$

Thus, at any price $p \in \psi(\bar{y})$, it is profitable for the producer to meet the demand as given by $\bar{y}^+$, instead of producing less.

REMARK 1.   The set $\psi(\bar{y})$ can equivalently be defined as the normal cone to the convex set co $\{ y \in Y \mid y \leqq \bar{y}^+ \}$ at $\bar{y}$.[13]

REMARK 2.   If $\bar{y} \in \partial Y \cap \mathbb{R}^l_-$, then $\psi(\bar{y})$ coincides with the normal cone of $\mathbb{R}^l_-$ at $\bar{y}$ which is given by $\{ p \in \mathbb{R}^l_+ \mid p \cdot \bar{y} = 0 \}$. Furthermore, $\psi(0) = \mathbb{R}^l_+$.

The following Lemma establishes the basic properties of the associated correspondence ψ:

LEMMA 1   *If Y satisfies P.1 to P.3, the correspondence $\psi: \partial Y \rightarrow \mathbb{R}^l_+$ is closed[14] and its values are non-degenerate,[15] closed and convex cones with vertex zero.*

(The proofs of the lemmata are given in the appendix.)

---

[11] Formally, the *normal cone* to a convex set X at a point $\bar{x} \in X$ is defined by $\mathbb{N}_X(\bar{x}) = \{ p \in \mathbb{R}^l \mid p \cdot \bar{x} \geqq p \cdot x$ for all $x \in X \}$; for more details on the concepts of convex analysis, see Rockafellar (1970).

[12] For any vector $x \in \mathbb{R}^l$, x^+ denotes the vector with coordinates $\max(0, x_h)$.

[13] Here, co denotes the convex hull and $\overline{co}$ will denote its closure.

[14] As pointed out to us by Bernard Cornet, closedness of the correspondence ψ follows also from the continuity of the correspondence $\mu(\bar{y}) = \{ y \in Y \mid y \leqq \bar{y}^+ \}$. It is interesting to note that this correspondence is lower hemicontinuous while the isoquant correspondence does not generally have this property. See Hildenbrand (1974) for the definitions of the various concepts of continuity of correspondence.

[15] A closed cone is *non-degenerate* if it differs from its vertex.

As we do not want to make an *a priori* distinction between inputs and outputs, we must identify the inputs and outputs for every production plan. The *set of inputs* at $\bar{y} \in Y$ is the subset of $\{1, \ldots, l\}$ defined by

$$I(\bar{y}) = \{h \mid \bar{y}_h < 0 \quad \text{or} \quad y_h \leqq 0 \text{ for all } y \in Y\}.$$

It is the index set of the commodities which are either effectively used as inputs at $\bar{y}$ or never appear as outputs. It therefore includes the commodities which are not related to the production process. Its complement in $\{1, \ldots, l\}$, $I^c(\bar{y})$, defines the set of outputs, effective and potential, at $\bar{y}$: Commodity h is an output at $\bar{y}$ if $\bar{y}_h \geqq 0$ and $y_h > 0$ for some $y \in Y$.

REMARK 3. Under P.3, the set $I(\bar{y})$ is non-empty except possibly at $\bar{y} = 0$.

The following lemma provides a simple characterisation of $\psi(\bar{y})$ in the convex case:

LEMMA 2. *Let Y be a convex set satisfying P.1 to P.3. Then, for all $\bar{y} \in \partial Y$,*

$$\psi(\bar{y}) = \mathbb{N}_Y(\bar{y}) + C(\bar{y}), \tag{2}$$

where $C(\bar{y}) = \{p \in \mathbb{R}^l_+ \mid p_h = 0 \text{ for all } h \in I(\bar{y})\}$.

As an immediate consequence of Lemma 2, the normal cone, $\mathbb{N}_Y(\bar{y})$ is seen to be a subset of $\psi(\bar{y})$ in the convex case. Furthermore, the lemma indicates that to retrieve competitive prices from voluntary trading in the convex case, one should lower the output prices. We then approach the general case by considering first the set of prices whose output components are minimal subject to voluntary trading:

$$\psi^*(\bar{y}) = \{p \in \psi(\bar{y}) \mid \not\exists p \in \psi(\bar{y}), p < \bar{p}, p_h = \bar{p}_h \forall h \in I(\bar{y})\}. \tag{3}$$

This is a cone with vertex zero which is generally not convex when several outputs are involved, and which is possibly degenerate. The conditions under which it is degenerate are given in the following lemma:

LEMMA 3. *Let Y satisfy P.1 to P.3. Then, $\psi^*(\bar{y}) = \{0\}$ if and only if $p \in \psi(\bar{y})$ implies $p_h = 0$ for all $h \in I(\bar{y})$.*

In words, $\psi^*(\bar{y})$ is degenerate *if and only if* voluntary trading imposes zero input prices.

REMARK 4. If $\bar{y} \neq 0$ and $\psi^*(\bar{y}) = \{0\}$ then $\bar{y} \notin \mathbb{R}^l_-$ and all inputs must be in use at $\bar{y}$, i.e. $\bar{y}_h < 0$ for all $h \in I(\bar{y})$.

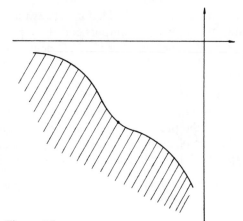

Figure 4.7

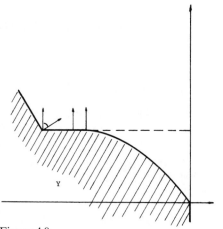

Figure 4.8

Such a situation may occur at points where isoquants are not convex or at inefficient boundary points. This condition follows from the fact that production costs are minimised under voluntary trading. Such a situation may also occur at efficient points where the normal cone – *generalised*[16] in the sense of Clarke – contains non-zero elements with zero coordinates for all inputs. These cases are illustrated in figs. 4.7 and 4.8. It should be noticed that $\psi^*(\bar{y}) = \{0\}$ may occur in the convex case as well.

[16] Clarke (1975) has proposed the definition of a generalised normal cone for the boundary of closed sets, which coincides with the standard normal cone in the convex case and is always different from $\{0\}$ (see also Clarke (1983) and Rockafellar (1979)).

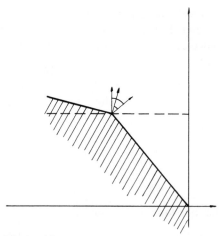

Figure 4.9

From Lemma 2, we can immediately conclude that, in the convex case, the following sequence of inclusions holds for all $\bar{y} \in \partial Y$:

$$\psi^*(\bar{y}) \subset \mathbb{N}_Y(\bar{y}) \subset \psi(\bar{y}), \tag{4}$$

and, as a corollary, we get the following result:

LEMMA 4.   *Let Y be a convex set satisfying P.1 to P.3, and consider a point $\bar{y} \in \partial Y$ at which $\psi^*(\bar{y}) \neq \{0\}$ and $\mathbb{N}_Y(\bar{y})$ is a half-line. Then, $\psi^*(\bar{y}) \equiv \mathbb{N}_Y(\bar{y})$.*

Hence, when Y is convex and has a 'smooth' boundary, minimality of output prices subject to voluntary trading is equivalent to profit maximization, except in the extreme situation where all inputs are in use and voluntary trading imposes zero input prices.

As can be seen from the proof of Lemma 2, $C(\bar{y})$ in (2) is the smallest set which, when added to the normal cone, yields $\psi(\bar{y})$. Therefore, minimizing the prices of all outputs, potential and effective, is the only way to retrieve competitive prices from voluntary trading in the convex and smooth case. At points where the boundary is not smooth, $\mathbb{N}_Y(\bar{y})$ is typically larger than $\psi^*(\bar{y})$, as shown in fig. 4.9.

To study the general case, we shall distinguish three possibilities:

Case 1. $\psi^*(\bar{y}) \neq \{0\}$,

Case 2. $\psi^*(\bar{y}) = \{0\}$ and $\psi(\bar{y}) \cap \mathbb{N}_Y(\bar{y}) \neq \{0\}$,

Case 3. $\psi^*(\bar{y}) = \{0\}$ and $\psi(\bar{y}) \cap \mathbb{N}_Y(\bar{y}) = \{0\}$.

While the second case may arise with convex production sets, the third does not. Indeed, from Lemma 2, $\psi(\bar{y}) \cap \mathbb{N}_Y(\bar{y}) = \mathbb{N}_Y(\bar{y})$ for all $\bar{y} \in \partial Y$, where $\mathbb{N}_Y(\bar{y}) \neq \{0\}$. We conjecture that actually the third case does not arise if isoquants are convex:

CONJECTURE   Assume that the set $\{y \in Y \mid y^+ = \bar{y}^+\}$ is convex. Then, if $\psi^*(\bar{y}) = \{0\}$, there exists $p \in \mathbb{N}_Y(\bar{y})$, $p \neq 0$, such that $p_h = 0$ for all $h \in I(\bar{y})$.

Let us consider the correspondence $\psi^{**} \colon \partial Y \to \mathbb{R}_+^l$ defined by

$$
\begin{aligned}
\psi^{**}(\bar{y}) &= \psi^*(\bar{y}) && \text{in Case 1,} \\
&= \psi(\bar{y}) \cap \mathbb{N}_Y(\bar{y}) && \text{in Case 2,} \\
&= \psi(\bar{y}) && \text{in Case 3.}
\end{aligned}
\tag{5}
$$

Then Lemma 5 suggests the following definition for our pricing rule:

$$
\phi(\bar{y}) = \overline{\text{co}} \{ p \in \mathbb{R}_+^l \mid \exists (p^v, y^v) \to (p, \bar{y}), y^v \in \partial Y, p^v \in \psi^{**}(y^v) \forall v \}
\tag{6}
$$

where ψ^{**} is defined in (5). By construction, $\phi(\bar{y})$ is a non-degenerate closed convex cone with vertex zero. However, because the convex hull of a closed correspondence is not necessarily a closed correspondence, we must prove the following:

LEMMA 5.   *The correspondence $\phi \colon \partial Y \to \mathbb{R}_+^l$ is closed.*

Hence ϕ is the smallest closed and convex-valued correspondence containing ψ^{**}, and it satisfies the technical requirements necessary to qualify as a pricing rule: when intersected with the unit simplex, it defines a correspondence $\bar{\phi} \colon \partial Y \to S$ which has non-empty, convex and compact values and is upper hemicontinuous.

As an immediate consequence of the fact that ψ is a closed correspondence with convex values, the following result holds:

LEMMA 6.   *For all $\bar{y} \in \partial Y$, $\phi(\bar{y}) \subset \psi(\bar{y})$.*

Hence, prices in $\phi(\bar{y})$ are compatible with voluntary trading. Therefore, production costs are minimized and, if $0 \in Y$, profit is non-negative.

THEOREM 1.   *Let Y be a set satisfying P.1 to P.3. If Y is convex, then $\phi(\bar{y}) \equiv N_Y(\bar{y})$ for all $\bar{y} \in \partial Y$.*

PROOF.   Because Y is convex, Case 3 does not arise and, by Lemma 2, we have:

$$
\begin{aligned}
\psi^{**}(\bar{y}) &= \psi^*(\bar{y}) && \text{in Case 1,} \\
&= \mathbb{N}_Y(\bar{y}) && \text{in Case 2.}
\end{aligned}
$$

Hence, $\psi^{**}(\bar{y}) \subset \mathbb{N}_Y(\bar{y})$ for all $\bar{y} \in \partial Y$. Because the normal cone defines a closed correspondence with convex values [see Rockafellar (1970)], we have

$$\overline{\mathrm{co}} \left\{ p \in \mathbb{R}^l_+ \mid \exists (p^v, y^v) \to (p, \bar{y}), y^v \in \partial Y, p^v \in \psi^{**}(y^v) \,\forall\, v \right\} \subset \mathbb{N}_Y(\bar{y}).$$

The converse inclusion follows from a result which has been communicated to us by Bernard Cornet, according to which *the boundary of a convex set is almost everywhere 'smooth'*:

LEMMA 7.   *Let* Y *be a non-empty, closed, convex and comprehensive subset of* $\mathbb{R}^l$, $Y \neq \mathbb{R}^l$. *Then there exists a dense subset* $E \subset \partial Y$ *such that the normal cone is a half-line at every point in* E *and can be defined for all* $\bar{y} \in \partial Y$ *as*

$$\mathbb{N}_Y(\bar{y}) = \overline{\mathrm{co}} \left\{ p \in \mathbb{R}^l_+ \mid \exists (p^v, y^v) \to (p, \bar{y}), y^v \in E, p^v \in \mathbb{N}_Y(y^v) \,\forall\, v \right\}.$$

Then, by Lemma 4, $\psi^{**}(\bar{y}) = \mathbb{N}_Y(\bar{y})$ for all $\bar{y} \in E$, and

$$\overline{\mathrm{co}} \left\{ p \in \mathbb{R}^l_+ \mid \exists (p^v, y^v) \to (p, \bar{y}), y^v \in E, p^v \in \psi^{**}(y^v) \,\forall\, v \right\} \equiv \mathbb{N}_Y(\bar{y}).$$

The desired inclusion then follows when the sequences are taken in $\partial Y \backslash E$ as well.

REMARK 5.   Under our definition of inputs, choosing output prices which minimise profits under voluntary trading does generally not select a subset of $\psi^*(\bar{y})$: $\hat{\psi}(\bar{y}) \not\subset \psi^*(\bar{y})$ for all $\bar{y} \in \partial Y$, where

$$\hat{\psi}(\bar{y}) = \left\{ \bar{p} \in \psi(\bar{y}) \mid \nexists\, p \in \psi(\bar{y}), p \cdot \bar{y} < \bar{p} \cdot \bar{y}, p_h = \bar{p}_h \,\forall\, h \in I(\bar{y}) \right\}.$$

This inclusion would hold if an alternative definition of output had been adopted, restricting attention to effectively produced commodities. But in that case, one would loose the equivalence result in the convex case as the latter requires the minimisation of the prices of potential outputs as well.

REMARK 6.   The pricing rule ϕ defined in (6) does not yield minimal output prices, properly speaking, outside of Case 1. Continuity of the voluntary trading correspondence defined in the introduction has been established for the case of a continuously differentiable cost function. In that case, minimal output prices can be obtained by minimising a convex norm, yielding a closed correspondence, and existence of an equilibrium at which output prices are minimal could then be proved. Moreover, proving that the correspondence ψ is lower hemicontinuous when the boundary of Y is 'smooth' (in the sense that the cone of Clarke is a half-line everywhere except possibly at the origin) remains an open problem.

4. The equilibrium concept

In this section, we shall formally define what we mean by a 'competitive equilibrium with quantity-taking producers' and prove its existence under the assumptions listed in section 2.

A competitive equilibrium with quantity-taking producers is defined by a price system $\bar{p} \neq 0$, a list of production plans $(\bar{y}_1, \ldots, \bar{y}_n)$ and a list of consumption plans $(\bar{x}_1, \ldots, \bar{x}_m)$ satisfying the following properties:

E.1.   It is a feasible allocation, up to free disposal:

$\sum \bar{x}_i \leqq \sum \bar{y}_j + \sum \omega_i,$ with equality for the commodities whose price is positive.

E.2.   It is a best choice for the consumers given the prices and profits:

For all i, $\bar{x}_i$ is $\succeq_i$-maximal in

$$\{x_i \in X_i \mid \bar{p} \cdot x_i \leqq \bar{p} \cdot \omega_i + \sum_j \theta_{ij} \bar{p} \cdot \bar{y}_j\}.$$

E.3.   It is a best choice for the producers given the prices and demand levels:

For all j, $\bar{p} \cdot \bar{y}_j \geqq \bar{p} \cdot y_j$ for all $y_j \in Y_j, y_j \leqq \bar{y}_j^+$.

E.4.   For every producer, output prices are minimal under voluntary trading:

For all j, $\bar{y}_j \in \partial Y_j$ and $\bar{p} \in \phi_j(\bar{y}_j)$.

The first two conditions are standard.[17] The third condition imposes voluntary trading: at the going prices, every producer chooses to satisfy the demand fully. As a consequence, production costs are minimised at $\bar{p}$ and $\bar{y}_j \in \partial Y_j$ for all j. In terms of the correspondence defined in (1), this condition simply reads: $\bar{p} \in \psi_j(\bar{y}_j)$ for all j. The pricing rule ϕ_j which appears in E.4 is as defined in (6) and prices are therefore convex combinations of limits of prices whose output components are minimal. By Lemma 6, condition E.4 actually embodies E.3.

THEOREM 2.   *Under the assumptions C.1 to C.3 and P.1 to P.4, an equilibrium exists.*

This theorem follows from the general existence theorem in Bonnisseau and Cornet (1988) which covers pricing rules with bounded losses. Our

---

[17] If there was a producer with a convex production set satisfying free disposal, condition E.1 could be written with equality.

special case, where profits are non-negative by construction, permits, however, a comparatively simple proof which is given in the appendix.[18]

REMARK 7. It is well known that the condition $\sum \bar{y}_j \in \partial \sum Y_j$ cannot be expected to hold when non-convexities prevail in production; see, for instance, Beato and Mas-Colell (1985). Accordingly, our equilibrium is in general not production efficient in the aggregate.

REMARK 8. Following Theorem 1, at an equilibrium, convex producers actually maximise their profit at given prices. As a consequence, for a convex economy, our equilibrium concept coincides with the standard notion of competitive equilibrium.

REMARK 9. Our definition allows for a trivial existence proof when $\phi_j(0) = \mathbb{R}^l_+$ for all non-convex producers, a case where they all face set-up costs. The proof would consist in constraining the non-convex producers to inactivity and in noting the existence of a competitive equilibrium in the resulting convex economy.

Appendix

PROOF OF LEMMA 1

For any given $\bar{y} \in \partial Y$, $\psi(\bar{y})$ is clearly a convex cone with vertex zero. The assumptions P.1 to P.3 ensure that $\bar{y}$ belongs to the boundary of the convex set $co\{y \in Y \mid y \leqq \bar{y}^+\}$. Because $\psi(\bar{y})$ is equivalently defined as the normal cone to that set at $\bar{y}$ (cf. Remark 1), it is non-degenerate. To prove closedness, let us fix some $\bar{y} \in \partial Y$ and consider a sequence (p^v, y^v) converging to $(\bar{p}, \bar{y})$ such that $y^v \in \partial Y$ and $p^v \in \psi(y^v)$ for all v. Assume that $\bar{p} \notin \psi(\bar{y})$, i.e. $\bar{p} \cdot \hat{y} > \bar{p} \cdot \bar{y}$ for some $\hat{y} \in Y$, $\hat{y} \leqq \bar{y}^+$. For v large enough, (p^v, y^v) is close to $(\bar{p}, \bar{y})$ and we then have successively: $\bar{p} \cdot \hat{y} > \bar{p} \cdot y^v$ and $p^v \cdot \hat{y} > p^v \cdot y^v$. If $\hat{y} \leqq (y^v)^+$, the last inequality would contradict $p^v \in \psi(y^v)$. If not, let us consider the sequence $(\hat{y}^v)$ defined by $\hat{y}^v_h = y^v_h$ if h satisfies $\hat{y}_h > \max(0, y^v_h)$, and by $\hat{y}^v_h = \hat{y}_h$ if h satisfies $\hat{y}_h \leqq \max(0, y^v_h)$. By construction, $\hat{y}^v \leqq \hat{y}$. Therefore $\hat{y}^v \in Y$ because Y is comprehensive. Also by construction, $\hat{y}^v \leqq (y^v)^+$. Furthermore, if h satisfies $\hat{y}_h > \max(0, y^v_h)$, we have $\hat{y}^v_h = y^v_h < \hat{y}_h \leqq \bar{y}_h$. Hence, for v large enough, $\hat{y}^v$ is arbitrarily close to $\hat{y}$ and we have: $p^v \cdot \hat{y}^v > p^v \cdot y^v$, contradicting $p^v \in \psi(y^v)$.

[18] The proof supplied in the appendix is inspired by the existence proof in Vohra (1988). Our proof can be viewed as the proof of existence of an equilibrium for pricing rules entailing no loss (like, for instance, average cost pricing) and could be generalised to pricing rules depending on all production and consumption plans and on 'market' prices. We are grateful to the Editors for publishing this proof, thereby making our paper self-contained.

PROOF OF LEMMA 2

When Y is convex, $\psi(\bar{y})$ is the normal cone to the intersection of Y with the set $\{y \in \mathbb{R}^l \,|\, y \leq \bar{y}^+\}$. Following Rockafellar (1970, p. 233), $\psi(\bar{y})$ can then be written as $\psi(\bar{y}) = \mathbb{N}_Y(\bar{y}) + \{p \in \mathbb{R}^l_+ \,|\, p_h = 0$ for all h such that $y_h < 0\}$, where the last term is the normal cone to $\{y \in \mathbb{R}^l \,|\, y \leq \bar{y}^+\}$ at $\bar{y}$. Let us now fix some $\bar{p} \in \mathbb{N}_Y(\bar{y})$ and assume that for some h, $\bar{y}_h = 0$ and $y_h \leq 0$ for all $y \in Y$. Then the vector p obtained from $\bar{p}$ by adding a positive quantity δ to its hth coordinate is again an element of $\mathbb{N}_Y(\bar{y})$. Indeed, we then have $p \cdot \bar{y} = \bar{p} \cdot \bar{y} \geq \bar{p} \cdot y$ for all $y \in Y$ and $\bar{p} \cdot y \geq \bar{p} \cdot y + \delta y_h = p \cdot y$ for all $y \in Y$. Hence, $p \in \mathbb{N}_Y(\bar{y})$.

PROOF OF LEMMA 3

It is immediate that $\psi^*(\bar{y}) = \{0\}$ can occur only if for all $p \in \psi(\bar{y})$, $p_h = 0$ for all $h \in I(\bar{y})$. To prove the converse, let us fix some $\bar{y} \in \partial Y$ and assume that this condition holds. Then, the vectors in $\psi(\bar{y})$ have arbitrary coordinates in $\mathbb{R}_+$ for the non-negative outputs, and $\psi^*(\bar{y}) = \{0\}$ follows.

PROOF OF LEMMA 4

$\psi^*(\bar{y})$ is a cone contained in $\mathbb{N}_Y(\bar{y})$. Hence, if $\psi^*(\bar{y})$ is non-degenerate and $\mathbb{N}_Y(\bar{y})$ is a half-line, the equality follows.

PROOF OF LEMMA 5

Let S be the unit simplex of $\mathbb{R}^l_+$. The correspondence γ defined on ∂Y by $\gamma(\bar{y}) = \mathrm{co}\,(S \cap \{p \in \mathbb{R}^l_+ \,|\, \exists\,(p^v . y^v) \to (p, \bar{y}),\ y^v \in \partial Y,\ p^v \in \phi^{**}(y^v)\,\forall\,v\})$ is upper hemicontinuous (see Hildenbrand (1974, pp. 23 and 26)). We first show that, for any non-degenerate cone of $\mathbb{R}^l_+$ with vertex zero, $\mathrm{co}\,C \equiv \mathrm{cone}\ (\mathrm{co}\,(C \cap S))$, where the right-hand side is the cone with vertex zero generated by $\mathrm{co}\,(C \cap S)$. Because $C \cap S \subset C$, a first inclusion follows. To establish the converse inclusion, let us take some $\bar{p} \in \mathrm{co}\,C$, $\bar{p} \neq 0$. Then, there exists (p^i, λ^i) such that $\bar{p} = \sum_i \lambda^i p^i$, $\sum_i \lambda^i = 1$, $p^i \in C$ and $\lambda^i \geq 0$ for all i. The p^i's can be taken all different from zero and we define the vectors $q^i = (1/\sum_h p^i_h) p^i$; $q^i \in S$ by construction and $q^i \in C$ because C is a cone. Hence, $q^i \in C \cap S$ for all i. We then define $\beta = 1/(\sum_i \lambda^i \sum_h p^i_h)$ and $\mu^i = (\lambda^i/\beta) \sum_h p^i_h$. By construction, $\beta \sum_i \mu^i q^i = \sum_i \lambda^i p^i = \bar{p}$, $\sum_i \mu^i = 1$ and $\mu^i \geq 0$ for all i and $\beta > 0$. Hence, $\bar{p} \in \mathrm{cone}\,(\mathrm{co}\,(C \cap S))$ and $\phi(\bar{y}) = \mathrm{cone}\ (\gamma(\bar{y}))$. Let us now consider a sequence $(p^v, y^v) \to (\bar{p}, \bar{y})$ such that $p^v \in \phi(y^v)$ for all v. Then there exist sequences (λ^v) and (q^v) such that $p^v = \lambda^v q^v$ and

$q^v \in \gamma(y^v)$ for all v. Because $\gamma(\bar{y}) \subset S$, we have $\lambda^v = \sum p_h^v \to \sum \bar{p}_h = \bar{\lambda}$. Because γ is upper hemicontinuous, there exists a subsequence (q^v) converging to some $\bar{q}$, such that $\bar{q} \in \gamma(\bar{y})$ [see Hildenbrand (1974, p. 24)]. Hence, $\lambda\bar{q} = \bar{p}$ and $\bar{p} \in \phi(\bar{y})$.

PROOF OF LEMMA 6

Let $\bar{p} \in \{p \in \mathbb{R}_+^l \mid \exists (p^v, y^v) \to (p, \bar{y}), \, y^v \in \partial Y, \, p^v \in \psi^{**}(y^v) \forall v\}$ for some $\bar{y} \in \partial Y$, $\bar{p} \neq 0$. Using the inclusion $\psi^*(\bar{y}) \subset \psi(\bar{y})$ and applying the definition, $(\bar{p}, \bar{y}) = \lim (p^v, y^v)$ with $p^v \in \psi(y^v)$ for all v. Because ψ is a closed correspondence, $\bar{p} \in \psi(\bar{y})$, and because it has convex values, the result follows.

PROOF OF LEMMA 7 (Cornet)

Let us consider $e^\perp = \{y \in \mathbb{R}^l \mid e \cdot y = 0\}$, the space orthogonal to e, the vector of $\mathbb{R}^l$ with all coordinates equal to 1. From Lemma 5.1 in Bonnisseau and Cornet (1988), we know that there exists a continuous function λ: $e^\perp \to \mathbb{R}$ such that for all $s \in e^\perp$, $\lambda(s)$ is the unique real number satisfying $(s - \lambda(s)e) \in \partial Y$. Moreover, the mapping Λ defined by $\Lambda(s) = s - \lambda(s)e$ is a homeomorphism from $e^\perp$ onto ∂Y. Consequently, the boundary of Y can be written as $\partial Y = \{y \in \mathbb{R}^l \mid y = s - \lambda(s)e, \, s \in e^\perp\}$ and, because Y is comprehensive, we also have $Y = \{y \in \mathbb{R}^l \mid y = s - \lambda e, \, \lambda \geq \lambda(s), \, s \in e^\perp\}$. Hence, Y coincides with $a(\text{epi } \lambda)$ where epi λ denotes the epigraph of λ and $a: e^\perp \times \mathbb{R} \to \mathbb{R}^l$ is the linear isomorphism defined by $a(s, \lambda) = s - \lambda e$. Hence, Y being a convex set, epi λ is itself convex, implying that λ is a convex function.

Let $\partial \lambda$ denote the subdifferential of λ. As an intermediary result, we shall prove that $\mathbb{N}_Y(s - \lambda(s)e) \cap S = \partial\lambda(s) + \{(1/l)e\}$ for all $s \in e^\perp$. Let us define $\bar{y} = \bar{s} - \lambda(\bar{s})e$, for some $\bar{s} \in e^\perp$. Then, $\bar{y} \in \partial Y$. We first fix some $\bar{p} \in \mathbb{N}_Y(\bar{y})$. Then $\bar{p} = \bar{q} + (1/l)e$, where $\bar{q} \in \text{proj}_{e^\perp} \bar{p}$. Since $\bar{p} \in S$, we have $\bar{q} \in e^\perp$. Applying the definition of the normal cone, we get $\bar{p} \cdot \bar{y} = \bar{p} \cdot (\bar{s} - \lambda(\bar{s})e) \geq \bar{p} \cdot (s - \lambda(s)e)$ for all $s \in e^\perp$. Then, by definition of $e^\perp$, $\bar{q} \cdot \bar{s} - \lambda(\bar{s})e \geq \bar{q} \cdot s - \lambda(s)e$ for all $s \in e^\perp$, i.e. $\bar{q} \in \partial\lambda(\bar{s})$. Conversely, let us fix some $\bar{p} \in \bar{q} + (1/l)e$, with $\bar{q} \in \partial\lambda(\bar{s})$. Applying the definition of the subdifferential, we get $\bar{p} \cdot \bar{y} = \bar{q} \cdot \bar{s} - \lambda(\bar{s})e \geq \bar{q} \cdot s - \lambda(s)e \geq \bar{q} \cdot s \cdot - \lambda e$ for all $\lambda \geq \lambda(s)$ and $s \in e^\perp$. Hence, $\bar{p} \cdot \bar{y} \geq \bar{p} \cdot y$ for all $y \in Y$, i.e. $\bar{p} \in \mathbb{N}_Y(\bar{y})$.

Let D denote the set of points in $e^\perp$ where λ is differentiable. By Rockafellar (1970, Theorems 25.1, 25.5 and 25.6), we have $\partial\lambda(s) = \{\nabla\lambda(s)\}$ for all $s \in D$, D is a dense subset of $e^\perp$ and $\partial\lambda(s) = \overline{\text{co}}\{q \in e^\perp \mid \exists (s^v) \to s, \, s^v \in D \forall v, \, q = \lim \nabla\lambda(s^v)\}$ for all $s \in e^\perp$. Let us finally define

$E = \{y \in \mathbb{R}^l \,|\, y = s - \lambda(s), \; s \in D\}$. Because Λ is a homeomorphism, E is a dense subset of ∂Y. Furthermore, using our intermediary result, $\mathbb{N}_Y(y)$ is a half-line for all $y \in E$, and we have $\mathbb{N}_Y(y) \cap S = \overline{co}\{p \in S \,|\, \exists (p^v, y^v) \to (p, y), y^v \in E, p^v \in \mathbb{N}_Y(y^v) \cap S \; \forall v\}$. Because $\mathbb{N}_Y$ defines a closed correspondence, the conclusion of the lemma then follows.

PROOF OF THEOREM 2

Because the set of feasible allocations is non-empty and bounded, the attainable consumption and production sets, defined as the projections on A of X_i and Y_j respectively, are bounded. Therefore, there exists a closed cube K in $\mathbb{R}^l$ with length k, centered at the origin and containing in its interior the attainable consumption and production sets [see Debreu (1959, p. 85)]. We define $\bar{X}_i = X_i \cap K$ and $\bar{Y}_j = \{y' \in Y'_j \,|\, \nexists\, y \in Y_j, \, y \geq y'$, with strict inequality if $y'_h > 0\}$, where $Y'_j = \partial(Y_j + \{ke\}) \cap \mathbb{R}^l_+$ and $e = (1, \ldots, 1) \in \mathbb{R}^l_+$. Let f_j denote the projection of points in $\mathbb{R}^l_+ \setminus \{0\}$ on the unit simplex $S = \{x \in \mathbb{R}^l_+ \,|\, \sum x_h = 1\}$. It is well known that under P.1 to P.4, as a function from $\bar{Y}_j$ into S, f_j defines a homeomorphism which satisfies

(a) $f_j(y_j) \gg 0$ if and only if $y_j \gg 0$.

(See for instance Brown *et al.* (1986).) Let us then define the function g_j on S by $g_j(s) = f_j^{-1}(s) - ke$. The assumption P.2 ensures that $g_j(s) \in \partial Y_j$ for all $s \in S$.

The *demand correspondence* of consumer i, $\xi_i: S^{n+1} \to \bar{X}_i$, is defined by $\xi_i(p, s_1, \ldots, s_n)$, the set of $\succeq_i$-maximisers on $\{x \in \bar{X}_i \,|\, p \cdot x \leq p \cdot \omega_i + \sum_j \theta_{ij} p \cdot g_j(s_j)\}$ if the right-hand side of the budget constraint exceeds $\min p \cdot \bar{X}_i$, and by arg min $p \cdot \bar{X}_i$ if not. This (quasi) demand correspondence is upper hemicontinuous and has non-empty, compact and convex values [see Debreu (1962, p. 261)].

The *supply correspondence* of producer j is a function $\beta_j: S^3 \to S$ defined by

$$\beta_j(p, q_j, s_j) = \frac{1}{\lambda_j(\cdot)} F_j(\cdot)$$

where $F_{jh}(\cdot) = \max(0, s_{jh} + p_h - q_{jh})$ and $\lambda_j(\cdot) = \sum_h F_{jh}(\cdot)$. Clearly, $\lambda_j(\cdot) \geq 1$ on S^3, ensuring the continuity of β_j. Here p denotes 'market prices' as opposed to the q_j which denote 'producer prices'.

Market prices are determined through the standard 'market' correspondence $\mu: \Pi \bar{X}_i \times S^n \to S$ defined by $\mu(x_1, \ldots, x_m, s_1, \ldots, s_n) = $ arg

$\max_{p \in S} p \cdot (\sum x_i - \sum \omega_i - \sum g_j(s_j))$. The continuity of the g_j's ensures that this correspondence is upper hemicontinuous with non-empty, convex and compact values.

The prices of producer j are determined through the correspondence $\bar{\phi}_j: S \to S$ defined by $\bar{\phi}_j(s_j) = \phi_j(g_j(s_j)) \cap S$. Because the correspondences ϕ_j are closed (by Lemma 5) with values which are non-degenerate convex cones with vertex zero, and the g_j's are continuous functions, the correspondences $\bar{\phi}_j$ are upper hemicontinuous with non-empty, convex and compact values [see Hildenbrand (1974, p. 23)].

We are now in a position to construct a correspondence Φ from $S^{2n+1} \times \Pi X_i$ into itself whose fixed points are equilibria:

$$\Phi(p, q_1, \ldots, q_n, s_1, \ldots, s_n, x_1, \ldots, x_m)$$
$$= \mu(\cdot) \times \Pi \beta_j(\cdot) \times \Pi \bar{\phi}_j(\cdot) \times \Pi \xi_i(\cdot).$$

By Kakutani's theorem, Φ has a fixed point $(\bar{p}, \bar{q}_1, \ldots, \bar{q}_n, \bar{s}_1, \ldots, \bar{s}_n, \bar{x}_1, \ldots, \bar{x}_m)$ and we define $\bar{y}_j = g_j(\bar{s}_j)$ and $\bar{z} = \sum \bar{x}_i - \sum \bar{y}_j - \sum \omega_i$. Then $\bar{y}_j \in \partial Y_j$ for all j and the following conditions are satisfied:

(b) $\bar{s}_j = \beta_j(\bar{p}, \bar{q}_j, \bar{s}_j)$.

(c) $\bar{x}_i \in \xi_i(\bar{p}, \bar{s}_1, \ldots, \bar{s}_n)$ for all i.

(d) $p \cdot \bar{z} \leq \bar{p} \cdot \bar{z}$ for all $p \in S$.

(e) $\bar{q}_j \in \phi_j(\bar{y}_j) \cap S$ for all j.

Let us define $\bar{\lambda}_j = \lambda_j(\bar{p}, \bar{q}_j, \bar{s}_j)$. Then, (b) implies

(f) $\bar{\lambda}_j \bar{s}_{jh} \geq \bar{s}_{jh} + \bar{p}_h - \bar{q}_{jh}$,

with equality whenever $\bar{s}_{jh} > 0$. Multiplying both sides of (1) by $\bar{s}_{jh}$ and summing over all h, we get $(\bar{\lambda}_j - 1)\bar{s}_j \cdot \bar{s}_j = (\bar{p} - \bar{q}_j) \cdot \bar{s}_j$ where $\bar{\lambda}_j \geq 1$ and $\bar{s}_j \cdot \bar{s}_j \geq 1/l$. We therefore have the following set of inequalities:

(g) $(\bar{p} - \bar{q}_j) \cdot \bar{s}_j \geq 0$ for all j.

By definition of f_j, there exists $\bar{\mu}_j \succ 0$ such that $\bar{s}_j = \bar{\mu}_j(\bar{y}_j + ke)$. Using the fact that $(\bar{p} - \bar{q}_j) \cdot e = 0$, we then have $(\bar{p} - \bar{q}_j) \cdot \bar{s}_j = \bar{\mu}_j(\bar{p} - \bar{q}_j) \cdot \bar{y}_j$ which, combined with (g), gives

(h) $\bar{p} \cdot \bar{y}_j \geq \bar{q}_j \cdot \bar{y}_j$ for all j.

By (e) $\bar{q}_j \cdot \bar{y}_j \geq 0$ and therefore $\bar{p} \cdot \bar{y}_j \geq 0$ for all j and C.3 ensures that for all i, $\bar{p} \cdot \omega_i + \sum_j \theta_{ij} \bar{p} \cdot \bar{y}_j > \min p \cdot \bar{X}_i$. Combined with (c), this implies that the budget constraints apply. Summing over all budget constraints, we get $\bar{p} \cdot \bar{z} \leq 0$ which, combined with (d), gives $\bar{z} \leq 0$. The fixed point therefore defines an attainable state and consequently $f_j^{-1}(\bar{s}_j) \gg 0$ for all j. Hence, by (a), $\bar{s}_j \gg 0$ for all j; and by (f), $\bar{\lambda}_j = 1$ and $\bar{q}_j = \bar{p}$ for all j. Conditions E.3 and E.4 are therefore established. Condition E.2 follows from (c) by a standard argument (see Debreu (1959, p. 87)). On the other hand, C.2. implies local non-satiation. As a consequence, the budget constraints hold with equality, and condition E.1 follows from $\bar{p} \cdot \bar{z} = 0$.

III Efficiency of constrained equilibria

5 Optimality properties of rationing schemes*

1. Introduction and summary

1.1.

General equilibrium theory has recently been enlarged with a formal analysis of equilibrium under price rigidities and quantity rationing – see, e.g., the survey paper by Grandmont (1977). Although the relevant concepts are at least as old as Keynes' 'General Theory', the formal analysis within the general equilibrium methodology is still young. So far, theorists have devoted much of their attention to very simple models, starting with a pure exchange economy. On the price side, they have privileged the case of fixed prices, and to a lesser extent the case of prices subject to inequality constraints, defined independently for each commodity. On the quantity side, they have privileged the case of inequality constraints on net trades defined independently for each commodity; this case is sometimes described as 'market-by-market rationing'. An always desired numeraire with unit price is never rationed, however.

Under standard assumptions (initial resources interior to a convex consumption set; complete, continuous, convex preferences), there exist equilibria where for each commodity either supply or demand is rationed, or neither, but not both simultaneously; and where supply (resp. demand) is rationed only in case of downward (resp. upward) price rigidity.[1] Here

*Journal of Economic Theory, 23, 2 (1980), 131–49. With Heinz Müller. The authors are grateful to Pierre Dehez for many helpful comments.

[1] This last feature is somewhat surprising, considering the possibility of excess demand for a Giffen good – a point that has been discussed orally, but not in the literature, to the best of our knowledge. The problems connected with Giffen goods are clearly recognized in the literature on the stability of tâtonnement processes—see, e.g. Arrow and Hahn (1971, p. 300).

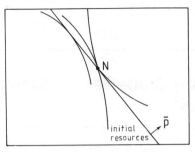

Figure 5.1. Examples of efficient non-Walrasian equilibrium

'equilibrium' means that each consumer attains a best point, for his preferences, over the intersection of his budget set with the quantity constraints.

The efficiency of such equilibria may be considered at three levels, namely (i) relative to the set of all physically feasible allocations; (ii) relative to the set of physically feasible allocations for which the net trades of all consumers have zero value at an admissible price vector; (iii) relative to the set of allocations sustained as equilibria by an admissible price vector and by admissible quantity constraints. Allocations that are efficient at the first level are called 'unconstrained Pareto optima'; allocations that are efficient at the second or third level are 'constrained Pareto optima'.

Clearly, efficiency at one level implies efficiency at the next level, and inefficiency at one level implies inefficiency at the previous level, but not conversely.

Walrasian equilibria are always efficient at the first level. Non-Walrasian equilibria may be efficient at that level. An example is given in the Edgeworth box of fig. 5.1 (for the fixed prices $\bar{p}$, at the point N, where the preferred sets of the two consumers can be separated). But this is the exception rather than the rule.[2] The inefficiency at the first level of non-Walrasian equilibria is due to the constraint that all net trades must have zero value at prices belonging to a predetermined set.[3]

[2] It cannot happen under convex smooth preferences. Indeed, in that case, a non-Walrasian equilibrium (as defined above in the text) which is also an unconstrained Pareto optimum must involve 'forced trading' and therefore cannot be sustained by market-by-market rationing. Here 'forced trading' means that a proportional reduction of the net trades on all commodities would be preferred; feasible sets that are convex and contain the initial endowment rule out forced trading in equilibrium. See also Theorem 3 in Madden (1978).

[3] A recent paper by Balasko (1978) shows that, under an asumption of smooth preferences, there always exists an unconstrained Pareto optimum, where all net trades have zero value at arbitrary predetermined prices. But that particular Pareto optimum is usually not an equilibrium. It may also fail to be individually rational, as can easily be verified in an Edgeworth box.

Non-Walrasian equilibria may, or again may not, be efficient at the second level. The relative inefficiency is now due to the constraint that quantity rationing must operate 'market-by-market'. In contrast, efficiency may require, say, that some individuals *increase their trading on the short side of one market in exchange for less rationing on the long side of another market*. In other words, efficiency may require some form of interdependent rationing. Examples are given in Younès (1975) or Böhm and Müller (1977).

The inefficiency of non-Walrasian equilibria at the third level is at the heart of Keynesian theory. It is often referred to as 'spillover effects' – see Bénassy (1975). Given a non-Walrasian equilibrium, a Pareto improvement could result if *the quantity constraints on several markets were relaxed simultaneously*; see, for instance, the example in Grandmont (1978).

1.2.

It is not generally possible to achieve efficiency at the first level without restoring price flexibility. But efficiency at the second level can be achieved through more sophisticated rationing schemes. For a fixed-price vector, the characterisation of allocations that are efficient at the second level (Section 4) is an immediate application of standard optimality theory – as presented for instance in Chapter 6 of Debreu's *Theory of Value* (1959).

Indeed, when the numeraire has a price of unity and is always desired but never rationed, the quantity of numeraire consumed by an individual subject to a budget constraint and an arbitrary rationing scheme is always equal to his initial endowment minus the value of his net trades on other commodities. Using this identity to eliminate the numeraire and the budget constraints, one may define a new exchange economy on the remaining goods. The initial endowments for these goods are unchanged. The consumption sets and preferences among these goods are derived from those of the original economy by associating with each consumption vector the corresponding consumption of numeraire (as defined above), and then referring to the original consumption set and preferences. The new exchange economy satisfies (in the reduced commodity space) the same standard assumptions as the original economy (initial resources interior to a convex consumption set; complete, continuous, convex preferences). Accordingly, one may apply to the new economy the second theorem of welfare economics: *An optimum is an equilibrium relative to a price system* – see Debreu (1959, Sect. 6.4).

The interpretation in a fixed-price exchange economy is the following:

With every allocation that is efficient at the second level, one can associate a vector of *coupon prices* for commodities other than the numeraire; the (relatively) efficient allocation assigns to every individual a consumption preferred by him to any other element of his budget set with smaller coupon value.

Going back to our remark about the inefficiency of 'market-by-market' rationing, we note that coupon prices express the trade-offs that characterise, explicitly or implicitly, any form of interdependent rationing. Efficiency requires identical trade-offs (marginal rates of substitution among commodities other than the numeraire) for all individuals.

The name 'coupon prices' evokes the coupon rationing schemes sometimes implemented to cope with scarcities. It should prevent confusion with the fixed prices in terms of the numeraire, to which we shall refer as 'money prices'. We call '*coupons equilibrium*' an allocation sustained by coupon prices, in the above sense (Definition 1).

The coupon values of the net trades at such an equilibrium sum up to zero (for market clearing), but are of arbitrary sign for a given consumer. A coupons equilibrium may thus fail to be individually rational, and may involve 'forced trading.'

The same remark applies to unconstrained Pareto optima – but not to competitive equilibria, which involve individual net trades of zero value; and competitive equilibria exist, under standard assumptions. An example (Appendix 5.1) shows that coupons equilibria where all net trades have a coupon value of zero may fail to exist. On the other hand, there always exist coupons equilibria where each consumer realizes the net trade which he prefers among those in his budget set whose coupon value *does not exceed* a given, nonnegative constant (the same for all individuals). We reserve the name '*uniform coupons equilibrium*' for those allocations, and we call '*coupons endowment*' the upper-limit set on the coupon value of individual net trades. It is positive when some individuals attain the best point of their budget set through a net trade of negative coupon value; it is zero otherwise.

Uniform coupons equilibria may be regarded as counterparts of competitive equilibria. The existence theorem is proved by similar techniques. The implied net trades are always 'fair' (remark at the end of Section 4). Also (Section 3), there always exist uniform coupons equilibria with coupon prices that are *positive* in case of *upward* price rigidity, *negative* in case of *downward* price rigidity, and zero otherwise.[4] A

---

[4] An example (Appendix 5.2) shows, unfortunately, that this particular set of coupons equilibria may fail to contain any allocation which is Pareto optimal relative to the set of admissible prices.

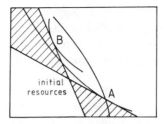

Figure 5.2.   Example of Pareto-inefficient coupons equilibrium

companion paper by Aumann and Drèze (1986) relates uniform coupons equilibria to Shapley value allocations in large economies.

The characterisation of allocations that are efficient at the second level as coupons equilibria has three immediate extensions, namely:

(i)   an allocation which is efficient relative to an arbitrary *set of admissible prices* must *a fortiori* be efficient relative to the particular prices at which its net trades have zero value,[5] hence it must be a coupons equilibrium;

(ii)   every coupons equilibrium is efficient relative to all the other allocations compatible with the *same* money prices (Proposition 1);

(iii)   a coupons equilibrium at which no pair of consumers could profitably exchange coupons against the numeraire is an unconstrained Pareto optimum (Section 5).

1.3.

This discussion reveals that optimality of rationing schemes does not raise new problems when prices are fixed. When individual money prices are only subject to inequality constraints, much deeper issues arise. First, the set of feasible allocations is not convex, as the Edgeworth box of fig. 5.2 illustrates. (When prices p are restricted to the interval $\bar{p} \geqslant p \geqslant \underline{p}$, the set of feasible allocations is the shaded 'bow-tie' area.) Second, a coupons equilibrium may fail to be efficient relative to the set of feasible allocations. Indeed, there may exist, *at different prices* (belonging to the admissible set), another coupons equilibrium which is Pareto superior, i.e., better from the viewpoint of all consumers (compare points A and B in fig. 5.2).

---

[5] Such prices exist, by the definition of 'efficiency at the second level'.

The present paper addresses itself (Section 6) to the following question. Suppose that an allocation x is efficient relative to a given vector of money prices p. It is then a coupons equilibrium, say with coupon prices a. Consider an alternative price system $\hat{p} \neq p$. We would like to know whether or not there exists an allocation compatible with $\hat{p}$ which is preferred by all consumers to the given allocation x. In the affirmative, one could conclude that the allocation x is inefficient with respect to any set of admissible prices containing $\hat{p}$; under a slight misuse of terminology, one could also say that '$\hat{p}$ is Pareto superior to p'. The question studied here is: Do the coupon prices a contain any information about the set of prices $\hat{p}$ (possibly empty) which are Pareto superior to p?

One could have hoped that positive (respectively negative) coupon prices provide an unambiguous signal that higher (respectively lower) prices could sustain Pareto superior allocations. This is unfortunately not true.[6] However, a necessary condition for the prices $\hat{p}$ to be Pareto superior to p can be stated as follows. We still consider the allocation x, efficient relative to the prices p. We ask each consumer what minimal coupons endowment would be required in order for him to attain, at the alternative money prices $\hat{p}$ and *at the prevailing coupon prices a*, a consumption at least as good as his consumption under the allocation x. The sum over all consumers of the required endowments must be *negative* in order for $\hat{p}$ to be Pareto superior to p (Proposition 3). Unfortunately, this necessary condition is not sufficient. Also, in order to verify that a given allocation x, compatible with prices p, is Pareto optimal relative to some set of admissible prices P, one should verify that the necessary condition is violated for *every* $\hat{p}$ in P.

Sufficient conditions of constructive interest can be defined, for $\hat{p}$ in a neighbourhood of p. We ask each consumer how much numeraire he would be just willing to forego in order to increase his coupons endowment by one (infinitesimal) unit; that is, we elicit the (marginal) money value of coupons to consumers. If that value is the same for all consumers, we already know that the prevailing allocation is an unconstrained Pareto optimum, so that no $\hat{p}$ Pareto superior to p exists. If that value is zero for some consumers, any (respectively some) $\hat{p}$ close to p at which the prevailing net trades of all these consumers have negative (respectively nonpositive) money values is Pareto superior to p. If that value is positive for all consumers, call its reciprocal the coupon value of money, and calculate the vector of covariances (over the consumers) of net trades with

---

[6] See also footnotes 2, 4.

the coupon value of money. Infinitesimal price changes with signs *opposite* to those of the respective covariances define a Pareto superior price vector. These sufficient conditions are not necessary, however.

In view of the nonconvexity of the set of allocations that are feasible relative to a convex set of admissible prices (fig. 5.2), it seems unlikely that these results could be strengthened substantially.

2. The model

An exchange economy with price rigidity $\mathscr{E}$ is defined by:

$M = \{0 \dots m\}$ the set of commodities:

$\Delta = \{p \in R_+^{m+1} \mid p_0 = 1, -\infty < \underline{p}_h \leqslant p_h \leqslant \bar{p}_h < \infty, h = 1 \dots m\}$ the set of admissible prices:

$N = \{1 \dots n\}$ the set of consumers, where each consumer i is characterized by his consumption set, $X^i \subseteq R_+^{m+1}$, his initial endowment, $w^i \in R_+^{m+1}$ and his preferences.

For the optimality analysis of Sections 4–6, we make the standard assumption that i's preferences are defined by a complete preordering $\succcurlyeq_i$ on X^i. For the existence theorem in Section 3, we allow more generality. Let $S = \{a \in R^{m+1} \mid a_0 = 0\}$ and $c^i \in R$ define, respectively, the set of coupon prices and the coupons endowment of consumer i; for $p \in \Delta$, $a \in S$, $c^i \in R$, the budget set of consumer i is

$$B^i(p, a, c^i) = \{w^i + z^i \in X^i \mid pz^i = 0, az^i \leqslant c^i\}. \tag{1}$$

The preferences of consumer i are given by the correspondence $D^i : X \times \Delta \times S \times R^n \to R^{m+1}$, where $X = \Pi_{i \in N} X^i$. Thus, $D^i(x, p, a, (c^j)_{j \in N}) \cap X^i$ is the set of all $\bar{x}^i \in X^i$ which consumer i prefers to x^i, when all other individuals $h \neq i$ consume x^h, the price system is p, the vector of coupon prices is a and the vector of coupons endowments is $(c^j)_{j \in N}$.[7] The set of feasible net trades relative to Δ is defined for later reference by

$$Z(\Delta) := \left\{ (z^1 \dots z^n) \in R^{n(m+1)} \left| \begin{array}{l} w^i + z^i \in X^i \, \forall i \in N, \sum_{i \in N} z^i = 0, \\[2mm] \exists \, p \in \Delta \text{ s.t. } \forall i \in N, pz^i = 0 \end{array} \right. \right\}. \tag{2}$$

We shall also need

$$Z^i(p) := \{z^i \mid pz^i = 0, w^i + z^i \in X^i\}; \quad Y^i = X^i - \{w^i\}. \tag{3}$$

---

[7] This allows for noncomplete and nontransitive preferences.

DEFINITION 1.   For the economy $\mathscr{E}$ a *coupons equilibrium* is a list of net trades $(z^i)_{i \in N}$, coupons endowments $(c^i)_{i \in N}$, a price $p \in \Delta$, and a coupon price $a \in S$ such that

$$\sum_{i \in N} z^i = 0 \tag{4}$$

$$w^i + z^i \in B^i(p, a, c^i) \quad \text{and}$$
$$D^i(w + z, p, a, (c^j)_{j \in N}) \cap B^i(p, a, c^i) = \phi \; \forall \, i \in N. \tag{5}$$

A coupons equilibrium $\{(z^i, c^i)_{i \in N}, p, a\}$ is called *uniform* if $c^i = c \; \forall \, i \in N$.

Note.   Equations (4) and (5) imply $\sum_{i \in N} c^i \geqslant 0$.

In the sequel, we shall have occasion to use the following assumptions, for all $i \in N$:[8]

A.1 X^i is a closed convex subset of R^{m+1} with $X^i \supseteq X^i + R_+^{m+1}$.

A.2 $w^i \in \text{Int} \, X^i$.

A.3 D^i has a relative open graph, is convex valued and is irreflexive, i.e., $x^i \notin D^i(x, p, a, (c^j)_{j \in N})$.

A.3' $\succcurlyeq_i$ is continuous; if $x^1, x^2 \in X^i$, and $t \in (0, 1)$ then $x^2 \succ_i x^1 \Rightarrow tx^2 + (1 - t)x^1 \succ_i x^1$.

A.3'' $\succcurlyeq_i$ is representable by a strictly quasi-concave, twice continuously differentiable utility function

$$u^i \colon Y^i \to R \quad \text{with} \quad \frac{\partial u^i}{\partial z_0} > 0 \; \forall \, z \in Y^i.$$

A.4   Strict desirability for commodity 0.

3. Existence of coupons equilibria

THEOREM.   *For every economy $\mathscr{E}$ which satisfies A.1, A.2, A.3, and A.4 there exists a uniform coupons equilibrium $\{(z^i, c)_{i \in N}, p, a\}$ such that for $h = 1 \dots m$,*

$$a_h > 0 \Rightarrow p_h = \bar{p}_h$$
$$a_h < 0 \Rightarrow p_h = \underline{p}_h. \tag{6}$$

---

[8] For the preference relation on net trades and on consumption bundles the same symbol $\succcurlyeq_i$ is used. No confusion should arise. Of course, $z^1 \succcurlyeq_i z^2$ iff $w^i + z^1 \succcurlyeq_i w^i + z^2$.

Under the additional assumption that Δ contains no Walrasian equilibrium price, there exists a uniform coupons equilibrium satisfying (6) with $a \neq 0$.

REMARK: An example in Appendix 5.1 shows that a coupons equilibrium with $c^i = 0$ $\forall i \in N$ may fail to exist. On the other hand, if $x \in X$ satisfies $\sum_i z^i = 0$ and for some $p \in \Delta$, $pz^i = 0$ $\forall i \in N$, there always exists a coupons equilibrium $\{(\hat{z}^i, c^i)_{i \in N}, p, a\}$ such that $x^i \in B^i(p, a, c^i) \forall i \in N$. More specifically, define continuous functions $t^i: \Delta \to R^{m+1}, i \in N$ s.t.

$$pt^i(p) = 0 \,\forall i \in N$$
$$\sum_{i \in N} t^i(p) = 0, \tag{7}$$

and replace A.2 by

A.2′ $w^i + t^i(p) \in \text{int } X^i \, \forall \, i \in N, \forall \, p \in \Delta$.

Then under A.1, A.2′, A.3′, and A.4 there exist a coupons equilibrium $\{(z^i, c^i)_{i \in N}, p, a\}$ and a nonnegative number k such that $c^i = at^i(p) + k$.

The functions t^i are introduced to determine the distribution of coupons. $t^i(p)$ is always a feasible net trade for consumer $i \in N$. Therefore, we have in equilibrium $w^i + z^i \succcurlyeq_i w^i + t^i(p)$ $\forall i \in N$. For the special case $t^i(p) \equiv 0$ $\forall i \in N$ a uniform coupons equilibrium is obtained.

Note that A.2′ is a generalization of A.2.

PROOF OF THE THEOREM. First we convert $\mathscr{E}$ into an abstract economy Γ with $n + 2$ players (see Greenberg and Müller (1979); Shafer and Sonnenschein (1975)). After defining the abstract economy Γ, we show (Lemma 1) that it has an equilibrium. Next, we show (Lemma 2) that an equilibrium for Γ defines a coupons equilibrium for $\mathscr{E}$, which satisfies (6). Finally, we prove the last statement in the theorem.

Since $\mathscr{E}$ is an exchange economy, by using standard techniques one can replace $X^i i \in N$ by the compact sets.

$$\hat{X}^i : X^i \cap [-\alpha, \alpha]^{m+1}, \qquad i \in N, \alpha \text{ sufficiently large.}$$

Let $\Gamma = (\hat{X}^i, \mathscr{A}^i, \hat{D}^i)_{i=1}^{n+2}$ be the abstract economy defined by:[9]

$\hat{X}^i i \in N$, the consumption sets;

$\hat{X}^{n+1} := \Delta;$

$\hat{X}^{n+2} := \hat{S} := \{(e, f) \mid e \in R_+^{m+1}, f \in R_-^{m+1}, e_0 = f_0 = 0, \|(e, f)\| \leqslant 1\};$

---

[9] For $b \in R^l$, $\| b \| = \sum_{h=1}^l |b_h|$. The definition of $\mathscr{A}^i, i \in N$, follows Bergström (1976).

$$\mathscr{A}^i(p,e,f) := \{x^i \in \hat{X}^i \mid p(x^i - w^i) \leqslant 0, (e+f)(x^i - w^i)$$
$$\leqslant 1 - \|e+f\|\} i \in N;$$
$$\mathscr{A}^i = \hat{X}^i, \ i = n+1, n+2;$$
$$\hat{D}^i(p,x,e,f) = D^i(x,p,e+f,(1 - \|e+f\|)_{j\in N}), i \in N;$$
$$\hat{D}^{n+1}(p,x,e,f) := \{\hat{p} \in \Delta \mid \hat{p}z > pz\}, \ z := \sum_{i\in N}(x^i - w^i);$$
$$\hat{D}^{n+2}(p,x,e,f) := \{(\hat{e},\hat{f}) \in \hat{S} \mid \hat{e}(z+p-\bar{p}) + \hat{f}(z+p-\underline{p})$$
$$> e(z+p-\bar{p}) + f(z+p-\underline{p})\}.$$

LEMMA 1. Γ *has an equilibrium* $(x,p,e,f) \in \hat{X} := \prod_{i=1}^{n+2} \hat{X}^i$, *i.e.,*

$$(x,p,e,f) \in \prod_{i=1}^{n+2} \mathscr{A}^i(p,e,f) \tag{8}$$

and

$$\mathscr{A}^i(p,e,f) \cap \hat{D}^i(x,p,e,f) = \phi, \qquad i = 1 \ldots n+2. \tag{9}$$

Proof.   1. $\mathscr{A}^i(p,e,f)$ is continuous.

a.   Upper-hemicontinuity follows from A.2.

b.   We want to show that $\mathscr{A}^i$ is lower hemicontinuous at (p^0,e^0,f^0) if $p^0 \in \Delta$, $(e^0,f^0) \in \hat{S}$.

b.1   If $\|e^0 + f^0\| < 1$ the lower-hemicontinuity of $\mathscr{A}^i$ is obtained by a standard argument from A.2.

b.2   If $\|e^0 + f^0\| = 1$ then (i) $w^i \in \mathscr{A}^i(p^0,e^0,f^0)$; (ii) from $w^i \in \text{Int } X^i$ and the linear independence of p^0 and $e^0 + f^0$ $(e_0^0 + f_0^0 = 0, p_0^0 = 1)$, one concludes: $\exists \hat{x}^i \in \text{Int } \mathscr{A}^i(p^0,e^0,f^0)$.

Again lower-hemicontinuity follows from a standard argument.

2.   For $i = 1 \ldots n+2$, $\hat{X}^i$ is a nonempty compact and convex subset of R^{m+1}.

3.   For $i = 1 \ldots n+2$, $\mathscr{A}^i(p,e,f)$ is nonempty, compact, and convex if $p \in \Delta, (e,f) \in \hat{S}$.

Therefore by the theorem in Shafer and Sonnenschein (1975), Γ has an equilibrium (x,p,e,f).   QED

LEMMA 2. $\{(z^i,c)_{i\in N}, p, e+f\}$ *with* $c := 1 - \|e+f\|$, $z^i := x^i - w^i$, *is a coupons equilibrium for* $\mathscr{E}$, *which satisfies* (6).

PROOF. Denote

$$\bar{R} := \{ j \in M \setminus \{0\} \mid z_j = \max_{h \in M \setminus \{0\}} |z_h| \},$$

$$\underline{R} := \{ j \in M \setminus \{0\} \mid -z_j = \max_{h \in M \setminus \{0\}} |z_h| \}.$$

Assume $\max_{h \in M \setminus \{0\}} |z_h| > 0$. Then, using (9) for $i = n + 1$, $j \in \bar{R} \Rightarrow p_j = \bar{p}_j, j \in \underline{R} \Rightarrow p_j = \underline{p}_j$.

For $h \in M \setminus \{0\}, p_h - \bar{p}_h \leqslant 0$ and $p_h - \underline{p}_h \geqslant 0$; hence, using (9) for $i = n + 2$, we have $\sum_{j \in \bar{R} \cup \underline{R}} (e_j + |f_j|) = 1$, and $\|e + f\| = 1$. Also, $(e + f)z = \sum_{j \in \bar{R} \cup \underline{R}} (e_j + f_j)z_j = \max_{h \in M \setminus \{0\}} |z_h| > 0$.

This leads to a contradiction with $(e + f)(x^i - w^i) \leqslant 0$. Hence $z_h = 0 \, \forall h \in M \setminus \{0\}$ and $z_0 = 0$ by Walras law and A.1, A.4. Therefore, we have $pz^i = 0 \, \forall i \in N$.

Obviously $\{(z^i, c)_{i \in N}, p, e + f\}$ with $c = 1 - \|e + f\|$ satisfies (4) and (5) in the definition of a coupons equilibrium. Equation (6) follows from (9) with $i = n + 2$. QED

Turning to the last statement in the theorem, assume $a = e + f = 0$. Then $\mathscr{A}^i(p, e, f) = \{ x^i \in \hat{X}^i \mid p(x^i - w^i) \leqslant 0 \} \, \forall i \in N$. Therefore p is a Walrasian equilibrium price contrary to assumption and the theorem is proved. QED

4. Coupons equilibria and optimality

DEFINITION 2. $(z^1 \dots z^n) \in Z(\Delta)$ is a constrained Pareto optimum if there exists no $(\hat{z}^1 \dots \hat{z}^n) \in Z(\Delta)$ such that

$$\hat{z}^i \succcurlyeq_i z^i \qquad \forall i \in N$$

$$\hat{z}^j \succ_j z^j \qquad \text{for some } j \in N.$$

It is a weak constrained Pareto optimum if there exists no $(\hat{z}^1 \dots \hat{z}^n) \in Z(\Delta)$ such that $\hat{z}^i \succ_i z^i \, \forall i \in N$.

PROPOSITION 1.[10] *Assume*[11]

1. X^i *is convex for all* $i \in N$;

2. *the preferences* $\succcurlyeq_i$ *are strictly convex* $(i \in N)$, *i.e., if* $y \succcurlyeq_i x$ *then* $\lambda x + (1 - \lambda)y \succ_i x \, \forall \lambda \in (0, 1)$.

[10] This proposition already appears in Hahn (1978) for the case where $c_i = 0 \, \forall i \in N$; the example in Appendix A shows that coupons equilibria may fail to exist, in that case.

[11] Without any assumption we obtain weak constrained Pareto optimality of coupons equilibria if $\Delta = \{p\}$.

Then every coupons equilibrium with prices p is a Pareto optimum relative to $\Delta = \{p\}$.

PROOF.   Let $\{(z^i, c^i)_{i \in N}, p, a\}$ be a coupons equilibrium. Assume there exists $(\hat{z}^1 \ldots \hat{z}^n) \in Z(p)$ with $\hat{z}^i \succcurlyeq_i z^i \, \forall i \in N$ and $\hat{z}^j \succ_j z^j$ for some $j \in N$. Then $a\hat{z}^i \geqslant az^i \, \forall i \in N$ and $a\hat{z}^j > c^j \geqslant az^j$. Hence $\sum_{i \in N} a\hat{z}^i > 0$. But this contradicts $\sum_{i \in N} \hat{z}^i = 0$.   QED

The example in Appendix 5.1 shows that this result cannot be extended to the general case (where Δ is not a singleton).

On the other hand, a constrained Pareto optimum can be represented as a coupons equilibrium. By reformulating a theorem in Debreu (1959) one obtains

PROPOSITION 2.   *Assume A.1 and A.3'. If $(z^{*i})_{i \in N}$ is Pareto optimal relative to $\Delta = \{p\}$, where some $z^{*j}(j \in N)$ is not a satiation point in $Z^j(p)$,[12] there exist a coupons price $a \in S, a \neq 0$, and real numbers $(c^i)_{i \in N}$ such that*

1. $\sum_{i \in N} c^i = 0, az^{*i} = c^i$;

2. $c^i = \min \{az^i \mid z^i \in Z^i(p), z^i \succcurlyeq_i z^{*i}\} \, i \in N$.

Remarks.   1.   If there exists $z^i \in Z^i(p)$ with $az^i < c^i$ then A.3' and 2 imply $z^{*i} \succcurlyeq_i z^i \, \forall \, z^i \in \{z^i \in Z^i(p) \mid az^i \leqslant c^i\}$. See Debreu (1959, pp. 68–69).

2.   The example in Appendix C shows that one cannot impose (6) if Δ is not a singleton.

PROOF OF PROPOSITION 2. $(z^{*i})_{i \in N}$ is Pareto optimal on $Z(\{p\})$. Replacing X^i by $Z^i(p)$, the assumptions in the theorem on pp. 95–96 of Debreu (1959) are verified and there exists $\hat{a} \in R^{m+1} \backslash \{0\}$ and $c^i \in R\,(i \in N)$ satisfying 1 and 2. But $\hat{a}_0 \neq 0$ is not ruled out. However, one can choose $\hat{a}$ s.t. $p\hat{a} = 0$. This implies that $\hat{a}$ and p are linearly independent. Therefore one checks easily that $a = \hat{a} - \hat{a}_0 \, p \neq 0$ is the coupons price we are looking for.   QED

REMARKS.   1. Δ is of the form $\{p \in R_+^{m+1} \mid p_0 = 1, \; \underline{p}_h \leqslant p_h \leqslant \bar{p}_h, \; h = 1 \ldots m\}$ and $a_o = 0$ is imposed in the definition of a coupons equilibrium. Therefore, commodity 0 has some properties which are typical of money. Usually the positive value of money is guaranteed by a price dependent expected utility index and special assumptions. Pareto optimality should then be redefined in that broader context. This remark does not apply to the case where Δ is a singleton.

---

[12]If z^{*i} is a satiation point for all $i \in N$, then $(z^{*i})_{i \in N}$ can be represented as a coupons equilibrium with $a = 0, c^i = 0$ for all i.

2. Referring to the paper by Schmeidler and Vind (1972) on 'Fair Net Trades', we note that, when $X^i = R_+^{m+1}$, then:

(i) the net trades implied by a *uniform* coupons equilibrium are fair, but not necessarily strongly fair;

(ii) the net trades implied by a coupons equilibrium are not necessarily fair.

5. Trading of coupons against the numeraire

When coupons may be traded like commodities, the budget set for consumer $i \in N$ is given by

$$pz^i - \mu r^i \leqslant 0, \quad z^i \in Y^i \tag{10}$$

$$az^i + r^i \leqslant c^i, \tag{11}$$

where $\mu \in R_+$ is the price of coupons in units of the numeraire and $r^i \in R$ is the number of coupons sold by i. Equations (10) and (11) can be reduced to

$$(p + \mu a)z^i \leqslant \mu c^i, \quad z^i \in Y^i$$

and we are in the Walrasian framework with prices $(p + \mu a)$ and lump-sum transfers $(\mu c^i)_{i \in N}, \mu \sum_{i \in N} c^i = 0$.

6. Coupons equilibria and Pareto improving price changes

We mentioned already that in general a coupons equilibrium is not Pareto optimal relative to Δ, if Δ is not a singleton. This section consists of two propositions. Starting from a coupons equilibrium $\{(z^i, c^i)_{i \in N}, p, a\}$ the first proposition gives a necessary condition for the existence of a Pareto-superior allocation at prices $\hat{p} \in \Delta$. The second proposition provides us with conditions which are sufficient to find a Pareto-superior coupons equilibrium in the neighbourhood of the first equilibrium.

If $a = 0$, then the coupons equilibrium $\{(z^i, c^i)_{i \in N}, p, a\}$ is a Walrasian equilibrium and therefore is Pareto optimal. Therefore, we shall assume $a \neq 0$.

PROPOSITION 3. *Assume A.1, A.2 and A.3'.*

Let $((z^i, c^i)_{i \in N}, p, a)$ *be a coupons equilibrium, with* $a \neq 0$ *and* $\forall i \in N$
$c^i = \min\{a\hat{z}^i \mid \hat{z}^i \in Z^i(p), \hat{z}^i \succcurlyeq_i z^i\}$.

If there exists $\hat{p}$ *and* $(\hat{z}^1 \ldots \hat{z}^n) \in Z(\{\hat{p}\})$ *with* $\hat{z}^i \succ_i z^i \forall i \in N$, *then*

(I)   *there exist* $(\hat{c}^i)_{i\in N}$ *and* $(\tilde{x}^i)_{i\in N}$, $\tilde{x}^i \in B^i(\hat{p}, a, \hat{c}^i)$ *such that* $\sum_i \hat{c}^i < 0$ *and* $\tilde{x}^i \succ_i w^i + z^i \, \forall \, i \in N$.[13]

PROOF.   Using A.1, A.2, and A.3', there exists λ in $(0,1)$ such that $\forall \, i \in N, \bar{z}^i := \lambda \hat{z}^i$ belongs to the relative interior of $Z^i(\hat{p})$ with $\bar{z}^i \succ_i z^i$. Let $\bar{c}^i := a\bar{z}^i$, $\sum_{i\in N} \bar{z}^i = 0$ implies $\sum_{i\in N} \bar{c}^i = 0$. Let $c^{*i} := \mathrm{Min}\,\{a\hat{z}^i \mid \hat{z}^i \in Z^i(\hat{p}), \hat{z}^i \succcurlyeq_i z^i\}$. Then $c^{*i} < \bar{c}^i$; indeed, $a_0 = 0$, $a \neq 0$, and $\hat{p}_0 = 1$ implies that a and $\hat{p}$ are linearly independent; A.3' and $\bar{z}^i \in$ rel. int. $Z^i(\hat{p})$ imply the inequality. Consequently, $\sum_i c^{*i} < \sum_i \bar{c}^i = 0$ and because of A.3', (I) is satisfied by taking, say

$$\hat{c}^i = \frac{\bar{c}^i + c^{*i}}{2}, \quad \forall \, i \in N. \hspace{3cm} \text{QED}$$

Our last proposition uses the following definition. The marginal value of coupons in terms of the numeraire, abbreviated as *'money value of coupons'*, is defined for individual i at a best point $w^i + z^i$ of the budget set $B^i(p, a, c^i)$, as the following limit $\bar{\mu}^i$, when it exists and is unique:

$$\bar{\mu}^i = \lim_{\Delta c^i \to 0} \left\{ \min \frac{\Delta \, w_0^i}{\Delta \, c^i} \,\middle|\, \exists \hat{z}^i, p\hat{z}^i = -\Delta \, w_0^i, a\hat{z}^i = c^i + \Delta \, c^i, \hat{z}^i \succcurlyeq_i z^i \right\}.$$

$$(12)$$

PROPOSITION 4.   *Assume A.1 and A.3''.*
Let $((z^i, c^i)_{i\in N}, p, a)$. $a \neq 0$, *be a coupons equilibrium with* $\forall \, i \in N \, z^i \in \mathrm{int}\, Y^i$. *Then* $\bar{\mu}^i$, *the money value of coupons to* i, *is well defined. Let* $I = \{i \in N \mid \bar{\mu}^i = 0\}$.
If either
   (i) $I = \phi$ *and* $\exists l \in \{1 \dots m\}$ *such that* $\sum_{i\in N} z_l^i / \bar{\mu}^i \neq 0$, *or*
   (ii) $I \neq \phi$, $I \neq N$ *and* $Q = \{q \in R^m \mid \sum_{l=1}^m q_l z_l^i \leqslant 0 \, \forall \, i \in I\} \neq \{0\}$, *then*
there exists a coupons equilibrium $((\hat{z}^i, \hat{c}^i)_{i\in N}, \hat{p}, \hat{a})$, *with* $\hat{p}$ *in a neighborhood of* p *and with* $\hat{z}^i \succcurlyeq_i z^i \, \forall \, i \in N, \hat{z}^h \succ_h z^h$ *some* $h \in N$.

PROOF.   1.   Under the assumptions of the proposition, $\forall \, i \in n, z^i$ is the unique optimal solution of the problem $\max U^i(z)$ subject to $z \in Y^i$, $pz = 0$, $az - c^i \leqslant 0$. By part (iii) of the 'Kuhn–Tucker stationary-point necessary optimality theorem' in Mangasarian (1969, p. 173), there exist $v^i \in R$, $\mu^i \in R_+$ such that $\mathrm{grad}\, U^i(z) - v^i p - \mu^i a = 0$. Furthermore A.3'' implies $v^i > 0$. The ratio μ^i / v^i is unique and equal to the limit in (12).

---

[13]See also the interpretation on p. 96. One checks easily that condition (I) is not sufficient.

2. The notation $p = (1, \bar{p})$, $a = (0, \bar{a})$, $z = (z_0, \bar{z})$ is used. First we are looking for Δp, $(\Delta z^i)_{i \in N}$ s.t.

$$z^i + \Delta z^i \in Y^i, \quad (p + \Delta p)(z^i + \Delta z^i) = 0, \quad \sum_{i \in N} \Delta z^i = 0 \tag{13}$$

and

$$U^i(z^i + \Delta z^i) \geqslant U^i(z^i) \quad \text{for all } i \in N$$
$$U^h(z^h + \Delta z^h) > U^h(z^h) \quad \text{for some } h \in N.$$

From (13), one obtains

$$\Delta z_0^i + \bar{p}\,\Delta \bar{z}^i + \bar{z}^i\,\Delta \bar{p} + \Delta \bar{p}\,\Delta \bar{z}^i = 0. \tag{14}$$

On the other hand,

$$U^i(z^i + \Delta z^i) - U^i(z^i)$$

$$= \Delta z^i \cdot \operatorname{grad} U^i(z^i) + R^i(\Delta z^i) \tag{15}$$

$$= \Delta z^i \cdot (v^i p + \mu^i a) + R^i(\Delta z^i) \quad by \ 1 \tag{16}$$

$$= v^i\,\Delta z_0^i + v^i\,\Delta \bar{z}^i \cdot \bar{p} + \mu^i\,\Delta \bar{z}^i \cdot \bar{a} + R^i(\Delta z^i). \tag{17}$$

In order to obtain

$$U^i(z^i + \Delta z^i) - U^i(z^i) > 0 \tag{18}$$

we need by (14), (17)

$$\mu^i\,\Delta \bar{z}^i \cdot \bar{a} - v^i\,\Delta \bar{p} \cdot \bar{z}^i + R^i(\Delta z^i) - v^i\,\Delta \bar{p} \cdot \Delta \bar{z}^i > 0. \tag{19}$$

3. If $\bar{\mu}^i > 0 \,\forall\, i \in N$ take

$$k, l \in \{1 \dots m\} \quad \text{s.t.} \quad \frac{1}{n} \sum_{i \in N} \frac{z_l^i}{\bar{\mu}^i} := \operatorname{cov}\left(z_l^i, \frac{1}{\bar{\mu}^i}\right) \neq 0, a_k \neq 0$$

and define

$$\Delta p_h = -\varepsilon \operatorname{cov}(z_l^i, 1/\bar{\mu}^i) \quad \text{if } h = l$$
$$= 0 \qquad\qquad\qquad \text{if } h \neq l$$

$$\Delta z_h^i = -\frac{\varepsilon z_l^i \operatorname{cov}(z_l^i, 1/\bar{\mu}^i)}{a_k \bar{\mu}^i} + \frac{\varepsilon\,[\operatorname{cov}(z_l^i, 1/\bar{\mu}^i)]^2}{a_k} \quad \text{if } h = k,$$

$$= 0 \qquad\qquad\qquad\qquad\qquad\qquad \text{if } h \neq k, h \in \{1 \dots m\}.$$

106   *Efficiency of constrained equilibria*

For $\varepsilon > 0$ small enough, (19) is satisfied since

$$\mu^i a_k \frac{-\varepsilon z_l^i \operatorname{cov}(z_l^i, 1/\bar{\mu}^i)}{a_k \bar{\mu}^i} + \mu^i \varepsilon \left[\operatorname{cov}\left(z_l^i, \frac{1}{\bar{\mu}^i}\right) \right]^2 > -\varepsilon v^i z_l^i \operatorname{cov}\left(z_l^i, \frac{1}{\bar{\mu}^i}\right) + o(\varepsilon)$$

and (14), (18) are satisfied, too, by a proper choice of Δz_0^i.
Also for ε small enough, $z^i + \Delta z^i \in \operatorname{int} Y^i, i \in N$.

4. If $\bar{\mu}^i = 0$ for some but not all $i \in N$, then we distinguish two cases, namely:
(1) $\hat{Q} := \{q \in Q \mid q\bar{z}^i < 0 \text{ for some } i \in I\} \neq \phi$
(2) $\hat{Q} = \phi$.

4.1.   If $\hat{Q} \neq \phi$ take $q \in \hat{Q}$ and $j \in I$ s.t. $q\bar{z}^j < 0$. Choose, $\forall i \in N \backslash I, y^i$ such that $\bar{\mu}^i \bar{y}^i \cdot \bar{a} > q\bar{z}^i$.
Then there exists $\varepsilon > 0$ s.t.

$$\bar{\mu}^i \Delta \bar{z}^i \cdot \bar{a} > \Delta \bar{p} \cdot \bar{z}^i - \frac{1}{v^i} R^i(\Delta z^i) + \Delta \bar{p} \cdot \Delta \bar{z}^i \, \forall i \in N \backslash I$$

$$\text{with } \Delta \bar{z}^i = \varepsilon \bar{y}^i, \Delta \bar{p} = \varepsilon q$$

and

$$0 > \Delta \bar{p} \cdot \bar{z}^j - \frac{1}{v^j} R^j(\Delta z^j) + \Delta \bar{p} \cdot \Delta \bar{z}^j \text{ with } \Delta \bar{z}^j = - \sum_{i \in N \backslash I} \Delta \bar{z}^i.$$

In addition we define $\Delta z^i = 0 \, \forall i \in I \backslash \{j\}$.
For ε small enough, $z^i + \Delta z^i \in \operatorname{int} Y^i$ and $z^i + \Delta z^i \succcurlyeq_i z^i \forall i \in N$, $z^h + \Delta z^h \succ_h z^h$ for some $h \in N$.

4.2.   If $\hat{Q} = \phi$ then define

$$P := \{q \in R^m \mid q\bar{z}^i = 0 \, \forall i \in I\} \neq \{0\}; \quad P \text{ is a linear subspace.}$$

We shall look for $\Delta \bar{p} \in P$ such that

$$0 \geqslant -\frac{1}{v^i} R^i(\Delta z^i) + \Delta \bar{p} \cdot \Delta \bar{z}^i \, \forall i \in I \tag{20}$$

$$\bar{a} \cdot \Delta \bar{z}^j > \Delta \bar{p} \cdot \left(\frac{1}{\bar{\mu}^j} \bar{z}^j \right) - \frac{1}{\mu^j} R^j (\Delta z^j) + \frac{1}{\bar{\mu}^j} \Delta \bar{p} \cdot \Delta \bar{z}^j \, \forall \, j \in N \backslash I. \tag{21}$$

A necessary condition for (21) is

$$\bar{a} \cdot \left(\sum_{j \in N \backslash I} \Delta \bar{z}^j \right) > \Delta \bar{p} \cdot \left(\sum_{j \in N \backslash I} \frac{1}{\bar{\mu}^j} \bar{z}^j \right)$$

$$- \sum_{j \in N \backslash I} \frac{1}{\mu^j} R^j (\Delta z^j) + \Delta \bar{p} \cdot \left(\sum_{j \in N \backslash I} \frac{1}{\bar{\mu}^j} \Delta \bar{z}^j \right).$$

(a) If there exists $q \in P$ s.t. $q \cdot (\sum_{j \in N \backslash I} \bar{z}^j / \bar{\mu}^j) < 0$, then by choosing $\Delta \bar{z}^i = 0 \, \forall \, i \in I$, $\Delta p = \varepsilon q$ with $\varepsilon > 0$, (20) is fulfilled. Furthermore, choose $y \in R^m$ s.t. $\bar{a} \cdot y > 0$. Then there exist $\alpha_j \in R, j \in N \backslash I$, with $\sum_{j \in N \backslash I} \alpha_j = 0$ s.t. (21) holds for $\Delta \bar{z}^j := \alpha_j \varepsilon y$, $\varepsilon > 0$ small enough.

(b) Finally, let

$$q \left(\sum_{j \in N \backslash I} \frac{1}{\bar{\mu}^j} \bar{z}^j \right) = 0 \, \forall \, q \in P. \tag{22}$$

Since there exist $y \in R^m$ and $q \in P$ with $\bar{a} y > 0, q y > 0$, we can, in view of A.3″, find $M > 0$ and $\bar{\varepsilon} > 0$ s.t. (20) holds $\forall \, i \in I$ when $\Delta \bar{p} := M \varepsilon q$, $\Delta \bar{z}^i := - (\varepsilon / \# I) y$ and $0 < \varepsilon \leqslant \bar{\varepsilon}$.

Furthermore by (22), there exist $\alpha^j \in R \, (j \in N \backslash I)$ with $\sum_{j \in N \backslash I} \alpha^j = 1$, and $\bar{\varepsilon} > 0$ s.t. (21) holds $\forall \, j \in N \backslash I$ at $\Delta \bar{p} = M \varepsilon q$, when $\Delta z^j := \alpha^j \varepsilon y$ and $0 < \varepsilon \leqslant \bar{\varepsilon}$.

Under either (a) or (b) for ε small enough, $z^i + \Delta z^i \in \text{int } Y^i$ and $z^i + \Delta z^i \succcurlyeq_i z^i \, \forall \, i \in N$, $z^h + \Delta z^h \succ_h z^h$ some $h \in N$.

5. With $\Delta p, (\Delta z^i)_{i \in N}$ introduced in 3 or 4, as the case may be, we define an economy $\hat{\mathcal{E}}$ for which $\hat{A} := \{ p + \Delta p \} = \{ \hat{p} \}$, and the other elements are as before; and we define $t^i(\hat{p}) = z^i + \Delta z^i, i \in N$. By the theorem and remark of Section 3, there exists a coupons equilibrium $((\hat{z}^i, \hat{c}^i)_{i \in N}, \hat{p}, \hat{a})$, where $\hat{c}^i = \hat{a} t^i(\hat{p}) + \hat{k} \geqslant 0$ and $\hat{z}^i \succcurlyeq_i z^i + \Delta z^i \, \forall \, i \in N$. By construction, $z^i + \Delta z^i \succcurlyeq_i z^i \, \forall \, i \in N$ and $z^h + \Delta^h \succ_h z^h$ some $h \in N$.   QED

Appendix 5.1

The first example shows that, for the coupons endowment $c^i = 0 \, \forall \, i \in N$, coupons equilibria may fail to exist.

EXAMPLE. $N = \{i, j\}, M = \{0, 1\}$.

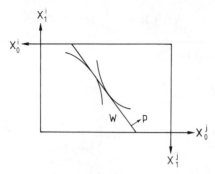

Figure 5.3.   Example of an economy for which no coupons
equilibrium exists when $c^i = 0 \,\forall\, i$

Obviously for the coupons endowments $c^i = c^j = 0$ (i.e., coupons endowments corresponding to zero net trades) no coupons equilibrium exists. The nonexistence of equilibria in the example is related to satiation. If one consumer wants to throw away some of his coupons the market clearing condition $\sum_{i \in N} z^i = 0$ can no longer be satisfied. This leads to nonexistence.

Appendix 5.2

The next example shows that the set of uniform coupons equilibria satisfying condition (6) may fail to contain any constrained Pareto optimum.

EXAMPLE.

$$N = \{i, j\}, \quad M = \{0, 1, 2\}, \quad X^i = X^j = R_+^3, \quad w^i = (6, 5, 4),$$

$$w^j = (6, 1, 1)$$

$$\Delta = \{(1, \bar{p}) \,|\, 0 \leqslant \bar{p} \leqslant (2, 3)\}.$$

The preferences are given by

$$U^i(x_0, x_1, x_2) = x_0 + 10x_1 + 5x_2$$

$$U^j(x_0, x_1, x_2) = x_0 + 10x_1 + 10x_2.$$

Only $p = (1, 2, 3)$ can be an equilibrium price. Otherwise there would be excess supply for good 0. By condition (6), a uniform coupons equilibrium then entails $a_1 > 0, a_2 > 0$. Figure 5.4 is drawn on that basis, in the space

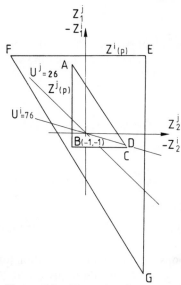

Figure 5.4. Example of an economy for which the uniform coupons equilibria are Pareto inefficient

of net trades for goods 1 and 2. The set $Z^j(p)$ is the triangle ABC. The set $Z^i(p)$ is the bigger triangle EFG with vertices parallel to those of ABC. The indifference curves of i and j are straight lines, parallel, respectively, to the line $U^i = 76$ or $8z_1 + 2z_2 = 0$ and to the line $U^j = 26$ or $8z_1 + 7z_2 = 0$. When $c^i = c^j = 0$ and $a_1/a_2 = 4$, individual i is indifferent among all the net trades z^i with $z_1^i = -(1/4)z_2^i$; whereas the best point of $B^j(p, a, c^j)$ takes z^j to D on the boundary of $Z^j(p)$, with coordinates $z_1 = -3/5, z_2 = 12/5$. Accordingly, the prices $(1, 2, 3)$; the coupon prices $(0, .8, .2)$; the coupons endowments $(0, 0)$; and the net trades $z^i = (6, 3/5, -12/5), z^j = (-6, -3/5, 12/5)$ define a uniform coupons equilibrium with utility levels $U^i = 76$, $U^j = 38$.

When $c^i \geqslant 0$ and $a_1/a_2 \neq 4$, the best point of $B^i(p, a, c^i)$ takes z_i to the boundary of $Z^i(p)$, so that $-z^i$ lies outside of $Z^j(p)$ and no coupons equilibrium exists. Furthermore one verifies easily that there are no uniform coupons equilibria with $c^i = c^j > 0$. We have thus exhibited the only uniform coupons equilibrium satisfying (6). Its inefficiency is revealed by considering the price vector $\hat{p} = (1, 1/2, 2) \in \Delta$ and the net trades $\hat{z}^i = (5.5, 1, -3)$, $\hat{z}^j = (-5.5, -1, 3)$ which entail the utility levels $U^i = 76.5$, $U^j = 40.5$.

Appendix 5.3

From Proposition 2 we know that a constrained Pareto optimum can be represented as a coupons equilibrium. The last example shows, however, that condition (6) cannot be imposed.

EXAMPLE.

$$N = \{i, j, k\}, \quad M = \{0, 1\}, \quad X^i = X^j = X^k = R_+^2,$$

$$w^i = (0, 4), \quad w^j = (2, 0), \quad w^k = (5, 1)$$

$$\Delta = \{(1, p_1) \mid 0.5 \leqslant p_1 \leqslant 2\}$$

$$U^h(x_0, x_1) = x_0 x_1 \quad h = i, j, k.$$

Obviously $(z^i, z^j, z^k) = ((2, -2), (-1, 1), (-1, 1))$ is a constrained Pareto optimum $(p = (1, 1))$.

It can be represented as a coupons equilibrium but condition (6) cannot be imposed. This can be seen easily. $p_1 = 1$ would imply $a = 0$. But then consumer k would choose $\hat{z}^k = (-2, 2)$.

6 Values of markets with satiation or fixed prices*

1. Introduction

Pure exchange economies, or *markets*, in which the preferences satisfy conditions of monotonicity and nonsatiation have been studied thoroughly in the past. In this paper we investigate the opposite situation: the utility functions need not be monotonic, and do have absolute maxima. The resulting theory has significant new qualitative features.

This study is not motivated by an abstract desire to remove as many assumptions as possible. It originated in the analysis of *fixed price* economies, which have been used extensively in the past decade[1] to model market failures such as unemployment. In such economies, all trade is restricted to take place at exogenously fixed prices $\bar{p}$. In effect, this limits each trader t to his *fixed price hyperplane*, i.e. the set of all bundles x in his original consumption set for which $\bar{p} \cdot x = \bar{p} \cdot e(t)$, where $e(t)$ is t's endowment; under the usual assumptions, t's utility has an absolute maximum on this set, and is not monotonic there.[2]

* *Econometrica*, 54, 6 (1986), 1271–1318. With Robert Aumann. Sections 7, 8, 9, 12, 13 and appendices A, B, C and D are not reproduced here. The work of R. J. Aumann was supported by CORE at Université Catholique de Louvain, by the Institute for Advanced Studies at the Hebrew University of Jerusalem, and by the Institute for Mathematical Studies in the Social Sciences (Economics) at Stanford University under a grant from the U.S. National Science Foundation. This work is part of the Projet d'Action Concertée on 'Applications of Economic Decision Theory' sponsored by the Belgian Government under Contract No. 80/85-12. We are grateful to Jean-François Mertens for carefully reading the manuscript and suggesting significant improvements.

[1] See, e.g., the survey by Drazen (1980).

[2] Indeed, monontonicity is meaningless in this context, since there is no natural partial order on the fixed price hyperplane.

In general, price rigidities prevent a market from 'clearing' (i.e., supply from matching demand); various quantity constraints or rationing schemes have been proposed to bring the situation back into equilibrium. In the more traditional markets, without fixed prices, there is a close relationship between competitive equilibria and game theoretic concepts such as the core[3] and the Shapley value;[4] thus one may expect game theory also to be helpful in suggesting equilibria for fixed price economies. It turns out that the core is not well suited to this purpose (see Section 8). But we shall find that the Shapley value allocations in fixed price economies correspond to a natural extension of competitive equilibria, closely related to the concept of coupons equilibria defined by Drèze and Müller (1980).

To describe our results, let us return to the more general context of markets with satiation. The reason that competitive equilibria may fail to exist in such markets is that no matter what the prices[5] are, the satiation points of some traders may be in the interiors of their budget sets.[6] Thus some traders will be using less than the maximum budget available to them, creating a total budget excess. This suggests a revision of the equilibrium concept that allows the budget excess to be divided among all the traders, say as *dividends*: Each trader's budget is then the sum of his dividend and the market value of his endowment at the market prices. A given system of dividends and prices is in equilibrium if it generates equal supply and demand.

This in itself is not satisfactory because it is too broad: Drèze and Müller showed that the fundamental proposition of welfare economics continues to apply here, i.e., that *every* Pareto optimal allocation is generated by some system of dividends and prices. However, the Shapley value yields much more specific information. Our main result says that when there are many individually insignificant agents, every Shapley value allocation is generated by a system of dividends and prices in which all dividends are nonnegative and depend only on the net trade sets[7] of the agents, not on their utilities. Thus the income allocated to each agent – over and above the market value of his endowment – depends only on his trading *opportunities*; on what he is *able* to offer, not on what he wants

---

[3] Cf., e.g., Hildenbrand (1982).

[4] Cf., e.g., Aumann (1975) or Hart (1977b).

[5] We are here discussing endogenous market prices q, which should not be confused with the exogenous prices $\bar{p}$ in fixed price economies. See Section 7.

[6] See Section 3 for an example.

[7] The net trade set of agent t is $C(t) - e(t)$, where $C(t)$ is his consumption set, and $e(t)$ his endowment.

to offer. Moreover, the dependence is monotonic; the larger the net trade set, the higher the dividend.

Two brief illustrations may clarify this point. When a bond issue is over-subscribed, bonds are normally rationed to the subscribers in proportion to the amount requested. Under complete information, this procedure has no equilibrium; the subscribers will always request more than they really want, this will be taken into account by the other subscribers, and so on. But in the rationing scheme implied by the Shapley value, the maximum that a subscriber may buy is based not on what he requests, which is subject to manipulation, but on what he *could* buy; on his net worth, say.

The second illustration deals with unemployment in a fixed wage context. Various rationing schemes that involve cutting down on working hours have been proposed. In the scheme suggested by the Shapley value, the maximum work week for any particular worker would depend on how much time he has. Thus a youngster who must by law attend school, or a kidney patient undergoing time-consuming dialysis, would be assigned a quota smaller than the average, *even though he might be able to fill the average quota.*

Economic models have two basic components, the objective and the subjective. The first consists of the physical opportunities or *abilities* of the agents: resources, technologies, constraints on consumption, and so on. The second consists of the utilities or *preferences*. In a market, the objective component is completely described by the net trade sets of the agents. Outcomes of economic models usually depend on both components, often quite intricately.

Competitive equilibria 'decouple' the two components. Each agent optimizes over an endogenous choice set, his budget set; in equilibrium, the choices mesh, they 'clear' the market. The optimisation, of course, is subjective; it depends on the agent's preferences. But the choice set itself does not; it depends only on his net trade set, i.e., on purely objective factors. Our result implies that the dividend equilibria to which the Shapley value leads also decouple in this way.

On a more technical level, our analysis has several unusual features. Though we are dealing with a large number of individually insignificant agents, we do not model it with a nonatomic continuum; rather, we use a finite-type asymptotic model of the Debreu and Scarf (1963) genre. Asymptotic and continuous results may differ in various ways,[8] but

---

[8] E.g. in ease and transparency of the formulation, in the generality of the results, in methods of proof, and in the discussion of errors and rates of convergence. Compare Aumann and Shapley (1974, Section 34, 208–210).

usually, the results are qualitatively similar. Here they are not. The continuum is too rough a tool; it obliterates the fine structure of the problem, and so leads to inconclusive results. The matter will be discussed further in Section 8.2.

Another unusual feature, related to the first, is the critical importance of small coalitions. The Shapley value of a player is the expectation of his 'contribution to Society' when the players are ordered at random; the probability that he is second or third in the order is small, and is usually ignored. Here, we are led to equations in which the first-order terms cancel, and the second-order terms, which take events of small probability into account, become decisive. When there is an excess supply of labour, the length of the work week allocated to a given worker depends on his expected contribution when he arrives on the scene; unless he is very early, this is negligible.

The plan of the paper is as follows. In Sections 2–5, we present the model and state our main result. Since the proof of that result is quite complex, we do not reproduce it here, but refer readers to the original article in *Econometrica*, 54, 6 (1986), 1282–92 and 1305–10. Section 7 contains the application to fixed prices, and Section 8 is devoted to a discussion of some alternative approaches. Finally, Section 9 summarises some additional results of a more quantitative nature and discusses open problems. For a formal statement, proofs and illustration of the additional results, readers are again referred to the original article in *Econometrica*, 54, 6 (1986), 1299–1304 and 1311–17.[9]

2. Markets with satiation

A (finite) *market with satiation* is defined by:

(2.1)   a finite set T (the *trader space*);

(2.2)   a positive integer d (the number of *commodities*);

(2.3)   for each trader, t, a compact convex subset X_t of R^d, whose interior is nonempty and contains the origin 0 (t's *net trade set*); and

(2.4)   for each trader t, a concave continuous function u_t on X_t (t's *utility function*).

Because X_t is compact, the continuous functions u_t must attain its maximum; denote by B_t the set of all points in X_t at which the maximum is attained (the *satiation* or *bliss* set of trader t), and note that it is compact and convex. To avoid trivialities, assume $0 \notin B_t$, i.e., the initial bundle never satiates.

[9] Sections 7, 8, 9 here correspond to sections 10, 11 and 14 respectively in the original article.

A few matters of terminology and notation: the inner product of two vectors q and x is denoted $q \cdot x$; 'w.r.t.' means 'with respect to' and 'w.l.o.g.' means 'without loss of generality'; R^k, R^k_+, and R^k_{++} denote, respectively, Euclidean k-space, its (closed) nonnegative orthant, and its (open) strictly positive orthant; int and bd denote 'interior' and 'boundary' respectively.

3. Dividend equilibria

An *allocation* in a market with satiation is a vector $x = (x_t)_{t \in T}$, where x_t is a feasible net trade for trader t (i.e., $x_t \in X_t$), and $\sum_{t \in T} x_t = 0$. A *price vector* is any member of R^d other than 0; since utilities need not be monotonic, one cannot confine oneself to nonnegative prices. The classical notion of *competitive equilibrium* is defined for markets with satiation just as it is for ordinary markets: it consists of a price vector q and an allocation x such that for all t, x_t maximizes u_t over the *budget set* $\{x \in X_t : q \cdot x \leqslant 0\}$.

Competitive equilibria do not in general exist in markets with satiation. Consider, for example,[10] a market with two agents, 1 and 2, and one commodity; suppose that the satiation points are on opposite sides of the origin, e.g., $u_1(x) = -(x-1)^2$, $u_2(x) = -(x+2)^2$. W.l.o.g. the price vector is ± 1; in either case one agent receives 0 and the other his satiation point, and these do not sum to 0.

The example is not due to any pathologies associated with the low dimension.[11] Consider a market with two commodities and three agents having the same net trade set, and with indifference maps as illustrated in figure 6.1. No matter what the price vector is, the satiation point of at least one trader must be in the interior of the budget set,[12] so that his utility will be maximised there over the budget set; whereas the utilities of the remaining agents will be maximised on the budget line. The resulting three points cannot sum to 0.

What is happening is that at least one trader creates a surplus by refusing to make use of his entire budget; but the definition of competitive equilibrium does not permit the other agents to use this surplus, so an imbalance results.[13]

---

[10] This example appears in Drèze and Müller (1980).

[11] Such as the disconnectedness of the set of price vectors.

[12] This holds as long as 0 is in the interior of the convex hull of the three satiation points.

[13] If free disposal were permitted, the example would go away; but this is not a reasonable assumption in the absence of monotonicity. Moreover, 'disposal' is not really possible in the fixed-price application (Section 7).

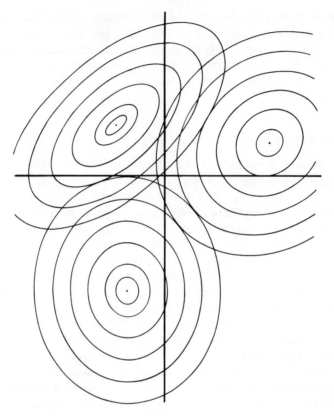

Figure 6.1

To overcome this problem, define a *dividend* to be a vector $c = (c_t)_{t \in T}$ whose components c_t are real numbers. A *dividend equilibrium* consists of a price vector q, a dividend c, and an allocation x, such that for all t, x_t maximizes u_t over the *dividend budget set*

$$\{x \in X_t: q \cdot x \leqslant c_t\}.$$

A dividend may be thought of as a cash allowance added to the budget of each trader; its function is to distribute among the unsatiated agents the surplus created by the failure of the satiated agents to use their entire budget.

A dividend c is *nonnegative* if all the c_t are nonnegative; *monotonic in the net trade sets*, if $X_t \supset X_s$ implies $c_t \geqslant c_s$. Occasionally, the word dividend will also be used for a component c_t of c.

4. Value allocations

A *comparison vector* on the trader space T is a vector $\lambda = (\lambda_t)_{t \in T}$, where each λ_t is a positive real number. For each comparison vector λ and coalition[14] S, define

$$v_\lambda(S) := \max \{ \sum_{t \in S} \lambda_t u_t(x_t) : \sum_{t \in S} x_t = 0 \text{ and } x_t \in X_t \text{ for all } t \text{ in } S \}. \quad (4.1)$$

In words, $v_\lambda(S)$ is the maximum total utility that S can get for itself by redistributing its endowment among its members, when the utilities u_t are weighted by the λ_t. A *value allocation* (in a given market with satiation) is an allocation x for which there exists a comparison vector λ such that for all traders t,

$$(\phi v_\lambda)(t) = \lambda_t u_t(x_t), \quad (4.2)$$

where ϕv_λ denotes the Shapley value of the game v_λ; we say that λ and x are *associated* with each other. (Recall that

$$(\phi v_\lambda)(t) = E(v_\lambda(S \cup t) - v_\lambda(S)), \quad (4.3)$$

where E denotes 'expectation', and S is the set of traders preceding t in a random order on all traders.[15])

At a value allocation, the weighted utility each player receives is equal to his Shapley value in the game v_λ. In other words, if transfers of utility are permitted with exchange rates λ_t, then the Shapley value of the resulting game is achieved, *without transfers of utility*, at the allocation x. Compare Shapley (1969) and Aumann (1975).

5. The main theorem

Let M^1 be a market with satiation; denote the traders by $1, \ldots, k$, the utility functions by $u_1, \ldots, u_k$, the net trade sets by $X_1, \ldots, X_k$, and the satiation sets by $B_1, \ldots, B_k$. The *n-fold replication* M^n of M^1 is the market with satiation in which there are nk traders, n of each of the k 'types' in M^1; i.e. the trader space T^n in M^n is the union of k disjoint sets $T_1^n, \ldots, T_k^n$ (the *types*), such that $u_t = u_i$ and $X_t = X_i$ whenever $t \in T_i^n$. We assume as follows:

---

[14] A *coalition* is a subset of T.
[15] Shapley's definition (1953) of ϕ is in terms of a set of axioms, from which (4.3) is derived. See Roth (1977) for an interesting discussion of Shapley's axioms.

ELBOW ROOM ASSUMPTION: *For each* $J \subset \{1, \ldots, k\}$,

$$0 \notin \mathrm{bd}\left[\sum_{i \in J} B_i + \sum_{i \notin J} X_i \right]. \tag{5.1}$$

In words, for any coalition J in M^1, if it is at all possible simultaneously to satiate all agents in J, then this can also be done 'with room to spare', i.e. when all other agents are restricted to the interiors of their net trade sets.[16]

This assumption holds generically in a certain very natural sense. The left side of (5.1) represents the total endowment of the market, whereas its right side is the boundary of a convex set in R^d, hence at most $(d - 1)$-dimensional. Since there are only finitely many J, the assumption holds for all but a $(d - 1)$-dimensional set of total endowments. A formal genericity statement can be made in terms of translates of the X_i; translating the net trade set is equivalent to varying the endowment. For details, see Section 8.3.

Note also that since the J's are sets of types, the number of conditions (5.1) is fixed at 2^k, and does not vary with n.

Call an allocation $\hat{x}$ in M^n *equal treatment* if it assigns the same net trade to traders of the same type. Such an allocation $\hat{x}$ defines a k-tuple x of net trades, one for each type; x is an allocation in M^1, which is said to *correspond* to $\hat{x}$.

MAIN THEOREM: *For each n, let x^n be an allocation in the unreplicated market M^1, corresponding to an equal treatment value allocation in the n-fold replication M^n. Let x^∞ be a limit point[17] of $\{x^n\}$. Then there is a nonnegative dividend c that is monotonic in the net trade sets, and a price vector q, such that (q, c, x^∞) is a dividend equilibrium in M^1.*

From the monotonicity it follows that the dividends are determined by the net trade sets, i.e., $X_i = X_j$ implies $c_i = c_j$. Thus, the theorem says that all value allocations in large markets with satiation approximate dividend equilibrium allocations, where the dividends depend only on the net trade sets, and monotonically so.[18] In particular, call a dividend

---

[16] See Section 7 for an interpretation in the fixed price case.

[17] Limit of a subsequence.

[18] Of course, the dividends are endogenously determined by all the data of the market, including all the utilities. Yet, in any given market, traders with the same net trade set have the same dividend.

equilibrium (q, c, x) *uniform*[19] if all the c_t are the same. Then we have the following:

COROLLARY 5.3: *Under the conditions of the theorem, assume that all traders have the same net trade set. Then* (q, c, x^∞) *is a uniform dividend equilibrium.*

The following existence result, for which (5.1) is not needed, gives substance to the main theorem:

PROPOSITION 5.4: *For every* n*, there is an equal treatment value allocation in the n-fold replication* M^n.

Further results will be stated in Section 9.

6. An informal demonstration of the main theorem

Let $\lambda^n = (\lambda^n_1, \ldots, \lambda^n_k)$ be a comparison vector associated[20] with x^n. Normalize λ^n so that the sum of its coordinates is 1. For simplicity,[21] assume for each i that x^n_i and λ^n_i converge as $n \to \infty$; that each of the x^n_i as well as their limit x^∞_i is interior to the net trade set X_i; and that the utility function u_i is strictly convex and continuously differentiable on X_i.

In the classical context of monotonicity and nonsatiation, λ_i tends to a positive limit for all types i (Champsaur, 1975). But as we shall see below, in our context some of the λ^n_i may tend to 0. This is the crucial difference between the two contexts, and it is this that leads to the positive dividends.

The situation may in fact be quite complicated; there may be differences in order of magnitude even between those λ^n_i that tend to 0. In this section, though, we will assume for simplicity that those λ^n_i that do tend to 0 all have the same order of magnitude.[22] If there are such types, they are called *lightweight*, the others heavyweight.[23]

By definition, the allocation x^n is optimal[24] for the all-trader set T^n. This implies that all the (weighted) utility gradients $\lambda^n_i u'_i(x^n_i)$ are equal;

[19] This concept is due to Drèze and Müller (1980), who showed, using fixed point methods, that uniform dividend equilibria always exist. They worked in a fixed price context, using 'uniform coupons equilibrium' for what we call 'uniform dividend equilibrium'.

[20] More precisely λ^n is a k-dimensional vector corresponding to an nk-dimensional equal treatment comparison vector $\hat{\lambda}^n$ associated with the equal treatment allocation $\hat{x}^n$ corresponding to x^n. There must always be such a $\hat{\lambda}^n$.

[21] Use of the phrase 'for simplicity' means that the restriction involved is for purposes of the informal demonstration in this section only, and is not needed for the rigorous treatment in the omitted sections.

[22] More precisely, $\lim_{n \to \infty} \lambda^n_i / \lambda^n_j$ exists and is positive whenever both λ^n_i and λ^n_j tend to 0.

[23] The formal definition of 'lightweight' is slightly different, but yields the same result.

[24] An allocation is called *optimal* for a coalition S if it achieves the maximum total utility for S when the utilities u_i are multiplied by the weights λ^n_i.

otherwise transfers could lead to gains in total utility. Denote the common value of all these gradients by q^n; thus

$$\lambda_i^n u_i'(x_i^n) = \lambda_j^n u_j'(x_j^n) = q^n \tag{6.1}$$

for all i and j. If we let $n \to \infty$ and set $\lambda_i^\infty := \lim_{n \to \infty} \lambda_i^n$, $q^\infty := \lim_{n \to \infty} q^n$, we get

$$\lambda_i^\infty u_i'(x_i^\infty) = \lambda_j^\infty u_j'(x_j^\infty) = q^\infty. \tag{6.2}$$

Our demonstration is based on (4.3), which says that the Shapley value of a given trader t is his expected contribution to a randomly chosen coalition; more precisely, to the coalition S of traders before t in a randomly chosen order on all traders.

If S is large, it is very likely to be a good sample of all the traders, i.e. to have approximately equal numbers of traders of each type. The allocation that is optimal for S is then approximately the same as the allocation x^n that is optimal for the all-trader coalition T^n.

Adding t to S will not change this optimal allocation by much; each trader will be allocated approximately the same net trade as before. In particular, if t is of type i, he will be allocated approximately x_i^n. Since all the net trades must sum to 0, the net trade of t must somehow be divided among all the traders, with each trader subtracting a small part of x_i^n from his net trade. Since all the utility gradients are q^n, the utility of each trader is decreased by q^n times that small part. Altogether, this causes a change in total utility of $-q^n \cdot x_i^n$. To this must be added the utility $\lambda_i^n u_i(x_i^n)$ that t himself now enjoys. Thus t's contribution to S (the worth of $S \cup t$ less the worth of S) is given approximately by

$$\Delta := \lambda_i^n u_i(x_i^n) - q^n \cdot x_i^n. \tag{6.3}$$

All this is valid only when S is reasonably large. Otherwise – e.g. when S has no more than a fixed finite number of traders (such as one or a hundred or a thousand) – the reasoning breaks down. Denote by P^n the probability that S is 'small', so that t's contribution is not measured by Δ. This event is perhaps not very well defined, but in this section we are making no attempt at precision. It is in any case clear that $P^n \to 0$ as $n \to \infty$, and that the order of P^n is at least $1/n$ (obtained already when S has only one trader).

Letting δ denote the conditional expectation of t's contribution given that S is small,[25] we conclude that

---

[25] Both Δ and δ depend on n; we suppress the corresponding superscript to keep our notation as uncluttered as possible.

$$(\phi v_*^n)((t) \approx (1 - P^n)\Delta + P^n\delta. \tag{6.4}$$

Note that we are ignoring the probability that S is large but nevertheless not a good sample of the entire population; this probability is very small indeed, much smaller than P^n, and in fact has no influence on the value. Note that δ is uniformly bounded; this follows, e.g., from the continuous differentiability of the utilities u_i on the compact sets X_i.

The definition (4.2) of the value stipulates that

$$(\phi v_*^n)(t) = \lambda_i^n u_i(x_i^n).$$

Together with (6.4) and the definition of Δ, this yields

$$q^n \cdot x_i^n \approx \varepsilon^n(\delta - \lambda_i^n u_i(x_i^n)), \tag{6.5}$$

where $\varepsilon^n := P^n/(1 - P^n) \to 0$.

The case in which none of the λ_i^n tend to 0 is the simplest, and we dispose of it first. With strict convexity, the elbow room assumption (5.1) rules out the possibility of simultaneously satiating all traders, a situation that is in any case rather uninteresting. Hence $u_i'(x_i^\infty) \neq 0$ for at least one i; and since $\lambda_i^\infty > 0$ for all i, it follows from (6.2) that x^∞ satiates no one, that $q^\infty \neq 0$, and that for all i, the gradient of u_i at x_i^∞ is in the direction of q^∞. Letting $n \to \infty$ in (6.5), we obtain $q^\infty \cdot x_i^\infty = 0$; hence the net trade x_i^∞ maximises u_i over the budget set $\{x \in X_i : q \cdot x \leqslant 0\}$. Thus x^∞ is an ordinary competitive allocation, and hence trivially part of a dividend equilibrium that satisfies the appropriate conditions.

Up to now the analysis has been as in the classical context of monotonicity and nonsatiation, where limits of value allocations are always competitive (Champsaur, 1975). But as we saw in Section 3, in our context there are situations in which competitive allocations need not even exist. By the above analysis, then, there must be some lightweights; of course there must also be heavyweights, since the sum of the k weights λ_i^n is normalised to be 1. This is the case of central interest in this paper, to which we now turn.

If we take i lightweight in (6.2), we find $q^\infty = 0$; hence $u_j'(x_j^\infty) = 0$ for heavyweight j, and hence x^∞ satiates all heavyweights. Suppose now that t is a lightweight trader of type i. Since $q^\infty = 0$, letting $n \to \infty$ in (6.5) as before would simply yield $0 = 0$. For something more informative, we must look at the fine structure, at the second order effects. This is done by dividing (6.5) by $\|q^n\|$ which, like q^n, tends to 0 as $n \to \infty$.

Assume for simplicity that $q^n/\|q_n\|$ actually tends to a limit q; note that $\|q\| = 1$. We shall see below that t's expected contribution δ to small coalitions is of larger order of magnitude than the term $\lambda_i^n u_i(x_i^n)$ on the right side of (6.5). Hence dividing (6.5) by $\|q^n\|$ and letting $n \to \infty$, we find

$$q \cdot x_i = \lim_{n \to \infty} (\varepsilon^n / \|q^n\|) \delta =: c_i; \tag{6.6}$$

the limit exists on the right because it exists on the left.

By definition, q^n is proportional to the unweighted utility gradient $u_i'(x_i^n)$; therefore its direction $q^n / \|q^n\|$ is equal to the direction of $u_i'(x_i^n)$. Letting $n \to \infty$, we deduce that q is the direction of $u_i'(x_i^\infty)$ whenever x_i^∞ does not satiate t. In that case, therefore, (6.6) says that x_i^∞ maximises t's utility over the dividend budget set defined by prices q and dividend c_i. Of course, when x_i^∞ *does* satiate t, his utility is maximised globally, and *a fortiori* over his dividend budget set.

For lightweight i, it remains therefore only to show that c_i depends monotonically on the net trade set X_i, and in particular is independent of the utility u_i. To see this, let us examine the contribution of t when joining a fixed small coalition S. This may be divided into three components:

(i) t's own utility after joining;

(ii) the change in the total utility of the lightweight traders in S due to t's joining; and

(iii) the change in the total utility of the heavyweight traders in S due to t's joining.

In the first two of these three components, the utilities have weights tending to 0; in the third they do not. Thus for large n, the contribution of t to himself and to other lightweights is negligible; the importance of his contribution to S comes from what he can do to improve the lot of the heavyweights in S. Therefore he should distribute his resources so as to maximise the heavyweights' gain in utility, paying no attention to his own. His ability to do this is limited only by his net trade set, and has nothing to do with his utility. Moreover, the larger his net trade set, the more he can do, and this yields the monotonicity.

The reasoning works only when S is a fixed coalition of relatively small size. In that case the heavyweights in S cannot, in general, be simultaneously satiated; since S is small, they will then be a significant distance from satiation.[26] When t joins, he brings in resources (not utility!) that could

---

[26] In principle, the equality of marginal utilities expressed by (6.1) should still hold when x_i^n and x_j^n are replaced by y_i^n and y_j^n, where y^n is optimal for an arbitrary (fixed) S. In fact, when S is small and n large, y_i^n is very likely to be on the boundary of X_i, so that we have a corner situation, in which marginal utilities need not be equal. We therefore cannot deduce that y_j^n is close to satiation for heavyweight j, and indeed it will usually not be.

be used significantly to improve the lot of at least one heavyweight trader, perhaps even to bring that one all the way to satiation; that would be a good deal more worthwhile than using the resources for himself or for other lightweight traders, whose utilities have weights tending to 0. A more even handed distribution of the resources among the heavyweights would yield still more, but giving it all to one gives us a lower bound on t's contribution, and indicates that it is of larger order than λ_i^n.

If, however, S is large, it is probably a good sample of all agents, and then all types j will be close to x_j^∞; in particular, the heavyweights will already be satiated, even before t joins. Thus by joining, t cannot improve the heavyweights by much. The upshot is that no matter how t uses his resources – whether for himself, for his lightweight colleagues, or for the heavyweights – the increment in total utility will be the same; in the first two cases the utilities are weighted by small weights of the order λ_i^n, and in the last, the increase in the utility u_j is small.

We come finally to the case in which the type i of the additional trader t is heavyweight. In calculating the contribution δ to small coalitions, the significant components are now (i) and (iii), rather than just (iii); component (ii) remains negligible. Note, though, that on the right side of (6.5) we now have not δ, but something close to $\delta - \lambda_i^\infty u_i(x_i^\infty)$. Since $\lambda_i^\infty u_i(x_i^\infty)$ is the absolute maximum that t can get, component (i) of δ is certainly at least cancelled out, and very likely more than cancelled out. Thus what is left is at most component (iii). The rest of the argument is as before, with (6.6) modified to read:[27]

$$q \cdot x_i^\infty \leqslant \lim_{n \to \infty} (\varepsilon^n / \|q^n\|)[\text{component (iii) of } \delta] =: c_i. \qquad (6.7)$$

Since i is heavyweight, x_i^∞ satiates; hence we must only show that it satisfies the budget inequality, which (6.7) indeed shows.

We end with a word of caution. The argument in this section is meant only to be indicative, and cannot easily be made rigorous. The difficulties we encounter in the rigorous treatment are intrinsic; they are not due to the generality of the treatment. Assuming differentiability, strict concavity, and so on enabled a simplified presentation in this section, but it would not help appreciably in the formal treatment.

---

[27] For technical reasons, the definition of the dividend c_i for heavyweight types i that we use in the formal proof is a little different from (6.7). Since x_i^∞ is generally in the interior of the dividend budget set when i is heavyweight, there is sometimes a little leeway in defining the dividend. Of course, if $X_i = X_j$ for some lightweight j, then we must have $c_i = c_j$, so the leeway disappears.

7. Fixed price markets

A (finite) fixed price market is defined by:

(7.1) a finite set T (the *trader space*);

(7.2) an integer $d + 1$ that is at least 2 (the *number of commodities*);

(7.3) for each trader t, a point e_t in R_{++}^{d+1} (t's *endowment*);

(7.4) for each trader t, a concave continuous function u_t^* on R_+^{d+1} (t's *utility function*); and

(7.5) a point $\bar{p}$ in R_{++}^{d+1} (the *fixed price vector*).

A fixed price market is just like an ordinary market (without satiation), except that all trade is constrained to take place at the exogenously given prices $\bar{p}$. In effect, this means that each trader t can only consume bundles in his *fixed price hyperplane*

$$H_t := \{y \in R_+^{d+1} : \bar{p} \cdot y = \bar{p} \cdot e_t\}.$$

The utility u_t^* is defined on the entire orthant R_+^{d+1} only for convenience; all that is actually used is its restriction to H_t.

An *allocation* in a fixed price market is a vector $y = (y_t)_{t \in T}$, where $y_t \in H_t$ for each t (trading takes place at prices $\bar{p}$ and all consumptions are nonnegative), and $\sum_{t \in T} y_t = \sum_{t \in T} e_t$ (trading does not affect the total quantity of each good). A *coupons price vector* is a member q^* of R^{d+1} not proportional to $\bar{p}$ (i.e., unequal to $\alpha \bar{p}$ for any real α). A *coupons endowment* for agent t is a real number c_t. A *coupons equilibrium* consists of a coupons price vector q^*, a vector $c = (c_t)_{t \in T}$ of coupons endowments, and an allocation y, such that for all traders t, y_t maximises u_t^* over the *coupons budget set*

$$\{y \in R_+^{d+1} : \bar{p} \cdot y = \bar{p} \cdot e_t \text{ and } q^* \cdot y \leqslant q^* \cdot e_t + c_t\}.$$

The notion of coupons equilibrium is due to Drèze and Müller (1980). If the traders maximise their utilities subject only to the fixed prices $\bar{p}$, then in general the market will not clear. To obtain market clearing, one introduces an auxiliary currency, *in addition* to the ordinary currency in which the fixed prices $\bar{p}$ are stated. This auxiliary currency may be thought of as rationing 'coupons'; each transfer of commodities must be paid for both in ordinary money, at prices $\bar{p}$, and in coupons, at prices q^*. Coupons may not be exchanged for ordinary money.

The coupons endowments c_t are called *monotonic in the commodity endowments* if $e_t \geqslant e_s$ (coordinatewise) implies $c_t \geqslant c_s$; and *uniform* if all the c_t are the same.

In a $(d + 1)$-commodity fixed price market M^*, the spaces $H_t - e_t =: X_t$ of net trades are compact convex subsets of the d-dimensional subspace Q of R^{m+1} that is orthogonal to $\bar{p}$; M^* may be viewed as a d-commodity market M with satiation. If (q, c, x) is a dividend equilibrium in this market, then q is a linear functional on Q, and x is in Q^k; extending q in an arbitrary way to a linear functional q^* on all of R^{d+1} yields a coupons equilibrium $(q^*, c, x + e)$ in M^*, where e is the initial allocation in M^*. In brief, dividend equilibria in M correspond naturally to coupons equilibria in M^* (cf. Drèze and Müller, 1980, p. 133). Hence our main theorem implies that in fixed price markets with k types, limiting value allocations are associated with coupons equilibria enjoying the appropriate monotonicity properties.

Clearly, monotonicity in the net trade sets is equivalent to monotonicity in the endowments:

$$X_t \supset X_s \text{ if and only if } e_t \geqslant e_s \text{ (coordinatewise).} \tag{7.6}$$

Thus, *all value allocations in large fixed price markets approximate coupons equilibrium allocations, where the coupons endowments depend only on the commodity endowments, and monotonically so.* In particular, if all commodity endowments are the same, we are led to uniform coupons equilibria.

Note that in the context of fixed prices, the elbow room assumption is satisfied if there is no set J of types whose aggregate demand for some good h precisely exhausts the total supply of that good.[28]

So much for the technical treatment. We end this section with some remarks of a more conceptual nature, which relate this work to other work on fixed prices.

As mentioned in the introduction, our interest in markets with satiation arose from the desire to discover what kind of allocations the Shapley value would generate, in markets with fixed prices. The study of these markets in economic theory has been mostly oriented towards equilibria with one-sided, market-by-market rationing. The specific features of the equilibrium concept are either imposed directly, as in Drèze (1975), or derived from more basic assumptions (no involuntary trading, efficient recourse to a set of admissible trades,...), as in Malinvaud and Younès (1977a). By contrast, the analysis presented here imposes no conditions on the problem or its solution, beyond the constraint that all trading should take place at exogenously given prices.[29] Rather, we apply a general

---

[28] That is, $\sum_{i \in J} y_i^h = \sum e_i^h$, where y_i maximizes u_i^* over H_i.

[29] This is not the place to discuss the rationale for studying markets with fixed prices.

solution concept (the Shapley value) to the problem. The equilibrium concept (coupons equilibrium) and its specific features (nonnegative coupons endowments monotonically geared to initial resources) are an output of the analysis, not an input.

Whatever further properties Shapley value allocations may be found to possess, these properties will also emerge from the problem formulation, kept here to essentials. By this we mean in particular keeping out of the problem formulation elements like 'market-by-market rationing', which make the solution set depend upon inessentials like the definition of commodities.[30]

To clarify this point, note that the formal description of a market specifies for each trader a set (the consumption set), a real function on it (the utility function), and a point in it (the endowment). The set must also be endowed with an additive structure (to enable us to describe transfers between traders). Nothing more is required to describe a market from the economic viewpoint; the above structure completely specifies the opportunities as well as the incentives.

This suggests that one might want an economic 'solution' (such as an equilibrium concept) to depend only on this structure, to be invariant under 'inessential' changes, changes in the specification of the situation that leave this basic structure invariant. Familiar examples of such 'inessential' changes are changing the units of the commodities, or using different commodities that are utility substitutes, or permuting the commodities. But the principle of invariance under inessential changes applies equally well in less familiar cases, e.g. for rotations or other affine transformations.[31]

The Walras equilibrium is invariant in this sense; so are the kinds of dividend equilibrium and coupons equilibrium defined in this paper.[32] But the 'market-by-market' rationing equilibria mentioned above are not; they depend on identifying specific 'commodities', which are not present in the opportunities or the incentives.

All this is reflected in the game-theoretic treatment. Game theory gets at the essence; it separates the intrinsic from the conventional. Thus it is

---

[30] Indeed, in applied work, identifying specific 'commodities' is often quite difficult.

[31] For example, suppose that each of two mutual funds is composed of stock in the same two companies, but in different proportions. Suppose that the companies themselves are not public, but that the funds are; in essence, therefore, one can buy into the companies in any proportion between those offered by the two funds. Then it should make no difference whether the 'commodities' are defined to be company stock or fund stock.

[32] The monotonicity conditions for coupons equilibria ostensibly involves the commodities, but (7.6) shows that it is merely a restatement of an 'invariant' condition.

not surprising that the game-theoretic analysis leads to a 'commodity-free' solution.

When institutional aspects (like market-by-market rationing) are deemed important, they should perhaps be introduced exogenously into the problem formulation. This brings us to the basic methodological dichotomy, whether economic theory should be concerned with 'explaining' the genesis of institutions, or with 'predicting' their consequences. In the end, each of these activities has its own validity.

8. Alternative approaches

8.1. The core

The core of a market is the set of all allocations that cannot be improved upon by any coalition S. 'Improved upon' has two possible meanings:

(a) Some members of S are better off and none worse off.

(b) All members of S are better off.

In classical markets these two meanings lead to the same core, but here they do not. Neither core is very interesting; the first is too small, the second is too large.

Let M^1 be a market with satiation, M^n its n-fold replication. For simplicity we assume that the utilities are strictly convex and that not all traders can be simultaneously satiated; the elbow room assumption (5.1) is, however, unnecessary here.

Under (a), the Debreu-Scarf Theorem (1963) applies; the proof goes through without difficulty. Specifically, the a-core of M^n enjoys the equal treatment property. Hence it may be represented by a set C_a^n of allocations in the unreplicated market M^1. Then $C_a^{n+1} \subset C_a^n$, and the limiting a-core, $C_a^\infty := \cap_{n=1}^\infty C_a^n$, coincides with the set of competitive allocations.

As we saw in Section 3, markets with satiation often have no competitive allocations; the limiting a-core is then empty. This is what we meant by 'too small'.

Under (b), the core M^n may be very large, and does not even enjoy the equal treatment property. If we nevertheless confine ourselves to equal treatment allocations, we are, as above, led to a set C_b^n of allocations in M^1, where again $C_b^{n+1} \subset C_b^n$. We are interested in $C_b^\infty := \cap_{n=1}^\infty C_b^n$.

For each allocation x in M^1, let $G_i(x) := \{x \in X_i : u_i(x) > u_i(x_i)\}$ be the set of net trades preferred by i to x. Then C_b^∞ consists precisely of those allocations x for which 0 is not in the convex hull of the union of the preferred sets $G_i(x)$; since the preferred set is empty for satiated traders, we may take the union over unsatiated i only. For example, any dividend equilibrium allocation with nonnegative dividends is in the limiting b-core, even if the dividends are not in any sense monotonic; they may even be different for identical[33] types. Any individually rational allocation x at which only one type is unsatiated will also be in the limiting b-core. What is happening is that the satiated traders are useless as partners in an improving scheme; the unsatiated must fend for themselves, and they may well lack the resources for this. This makes the b-core very large.

We note for the record that the limiting value allocations are in the limiting b-core; but in general they constitute only a small subset. This fits in well with our experience in other market contexts with cores. For example, in large transferable utility markets with nondifferentiable utilities the core may be quite big, but if it has a centre of symmetry, then the value is that centre of symmetry (Hart, 1977a). More generally (asymmetric core, nontransferable utility), the value allocations in a large nondifferentiable market often constitute a small 'central' subset of a relatively big core (Hart, 1977b, 1980; Mertens, 1988; Tauman, 1981).

8.2.   The continuum approach

There is no difficulty in defining nonatomic markets with satiation. One simply replaces the trader space T by a nonatomic measure space $(T, \mathscr{C}, \mu)$ with $\mu(T) = 1$, and requires that the net trade sets X_t and the utility functions u_t be measurable in an appropriate sense, and the u_t uniformly bounded. An *allocation* is now a measurable function x from T to R^d with $x(t) \in X_t$ for all t and $\int_T x = 0$. As before, we assume that no allocation satiates all traders, but do not require anything like the 'elbow room' assumption (5.1). The definition of competitive equilibrium remains literally unchanged.

A *generalized comparison function* is an integrable function from T to R^1_+ with a positive integral; if it is to R^1_{++}, it is a *comparison function*. A *coalition* is a measurable subset of T (i.e. a member of $\mathscr{C}$). Given a generalized comparison function λ, define a nonatomic game v_λ by

$$v_\lambda(S) := \max\left(\int_S \lambda(t)u_t(x(t))\mu(dt) : \int_S x = 0 \quad \text{and } x(t) \in X_t \text{ for all } t \in S\right)$$

---

[33] Having the same utilities and net trade sets. Confining ourselves to equal treatment allocations in M^n does not mean that identical types get the same net trade; it only means that in M^n, different replicas of the same trader in M^1 get the same net trade.

for each coalition S. A (*generalised*) *value allocation* is an allocation x for which there exists a (generalised) comparison function λ such that

$$(\phi v_\lambda)(dt) = \lambda(t)u_t(x(t))\mu(dt) \tag{8.1}$$

for all 'infinitesimal' agents dt, where ϕ is an appropriate[34] value operator. (A more formal statement of (8.1) is that $(\phi v_\lambda)(S) = \int_S \lambda(t)u_t(x(t))\mu(dt)$ for all coalitions S.)

So much for the definitions. Unfortunately, the results are rather disappointing. All we can say is:

(8.2)   *Every value allocation is competitive.*

(8.3)   *An allocation is a generalised value allocation if and only if it is competitive or satiates some agents.*

We have already noted that markets with satiation often have no competitive equilibria; in that case there are *no* value allocations in the continuum approach. The *generalised* value allocations, on the other hand, constitute a very large set even then, consisting of all allocations satiating at least one agent. There is no restriction at all on what nonsatiated agents get; they may even be assigned individually irrational net trades.

To demonstrate these results, assume for simplicity that the u_t are continuously differentiable and strictly convex, and that the allocations in question are interior (i.e., $x(t) \in \text{int } X_t$ for all t). Let x be a generalised value allocation. As at (6.1), there is a vector q such that

$$\lambda(t)u_t'(x(t)) = q, \tag{8.4}$$

for all t. Moreover, the value $(\phi v_\lambda)(dt)$ is the average contribution of dt to a coalition S. In the continuum case, 'almost all' coalitions are large; hence as at (6.3),

$$(\phi v_\lambda)(dt) = \lambda(t)u_t(x(t))\mu(dt) = q \cdot x(t)\mu(dt),$$

and together with (8.1), we obtain that for all t,

$$q \cdot x(t) = 0. \tag{8.5}$$

If x is a value allocation, i.e., $\lambda(t) > 0$ for all t, then $u_t'(x(t))$ is either equal to 0 for all t or is unequal to 0 for all t. If it is equal to 0 for all t, then all traders are simultaneously satiated, which we have ruled out. Hence

---

[34] See, e.g., Kannai (1966), Aumann and Shapley (1974), Hart (1980), Mertens (1980, 1988), or Neyman and Tauman (1979). What is needed here is a value with the 'diagonal' property.

it is unequal to 0 for all t, whence $q \neq 0$; together, (8.4) and (8.5) then assert precisely that (q, x) is a competitive equilibrium, whence x is a competitive allocation.

If x is not a value allocation, i.e., $\lambda(t) = 0$ for some t, then $q = 0$. Hence for those t for which $\lambda(t) \neq 0$, we must have $u'_t(x(t)) = 0$, and hence these t are satiated. Conversely, if x is any allocation that satiates some traders, let λ be a generalised comparison function that assigns weight 0 to all traders unsatiated at x. The value $(\phi v_\lambda)(dt)$ is the average contribution of dt to a diagonal[35] coalition θT, where θ ranges from 0 to 1. The case $\theta = 0$ has no effect on the average and may be ignored. As soon as $\theta > 0$, there are enough unsatiated traders in θT to supply all the resources desired by the satiated traders in θT. Thus dt contributes nothing if he is unsatiated, and only his own utility $\lambda(t)u_t(x(t))\mu(dt)$ if he is satiated, which means that (8.1) is satisfied. Thus any such x is a generalised value allocation.

The reader will have realised that what prevents the continuum approach from achieving a more satisfactory result is that 'small' coalitions play no role. Coalitions either have positive measure, in which case they behave like 'large' coalitions, or have measure 0, in which case they are ignored. The crucial coalitions in the limit approach[36] (the one used in this paper) are those whose size is positive but of smaller order of magnitude than that of the all-trader set; the continuum approach is not equipped to take account of such coalitions.

8.3. The elbow room assumption in a model with explicit endowments

To show that (5.1) holds generically, we must reformulate the definition of a market with satiation so that the endowments appear explicitly. Accordingly, define a *market with satiation and explicit endowments* to consist of a finite set T (the *trader space*), a positive integer d (the number of *commodities*), and for each trader t,

a compact convex subset X_t^0 of R^d (t's *consumption set*);

a concave continuous function u_t^0 on X_t^0 (t's *utility function*); and

a point e_t in the interior of X_t^0 (t's *endowment*).

To regain from this a market with satiation as in Section 2, simply define

[35] See Aumann and Shapley (1974, Chapter III).

[36] Of course, the value operator ϕ may itself be defined by a limit approach, even when it is applied to nonatonic games. Nevertheless, the kind of second-order effect that is crucial in the proof of the main theorem does not obtain then.

$X_t := X_t^0 - e_t$ (algebraic subtraction!) and $u_t(x) := u_t^0(x + e_t)$. The remainder of the treatment is then exactly as before.

In this formulation, the elbow room assumption is equivalent to the following: for each $J \subset \{1, \ldots, k\}$,

$$\sum_{i=1}^k e_i \notin \text{bd}\left[\sum_{i \in J} B_i^0 + \sum_{i \notin J} X_i^0\right], \tag{8.6}$$

where e_i is the endowment of a type i trader, and B_i^0 is the set of points in X_i^0 at which u_i^0 is maximised. Note that for each J, the right side of (8.6) represents the boundary of a compact convex set in R^d that is independent of the endowments; such sets are closed and of measure 0. The left side is simply the total endowment. Since there are only finitely many different possible choices of J, it follows that the elbow room assumption holds for all total endowment vectors except for a closed set of measure 0 in R^d; hence also for all k-tuples $(e_1, \ldots, e_k)$ of endowments except for a closed set of measure 0 in R^{dk}.

Conceptually, the situation here is perhaps a little different from that of other generic theorems in the literature. The exceptional set is entirely explicit and has transparent geometric and economic meanings; in any given market one can, so to speak, 'see at a glance' whether or not the elbow room assumption is satisfied.

9. Further results and open problems

The main theorem (Section 5) shows that the dividends depend only on the net trade sets, and monotonically so. In fact, we know much more about them both qualitatively and quantitatively.

The competitive case is from our point of view less interesting, and it is convenient to exclude it. A summary of additional results is then as follows.

The dividends c_i are all strictly positive (rather than just nonnegative); in addition to monotonicity, they satisfy a concavity condition; and there is an 'explicit' formula for them. The order of magnitude of the weights λ_i^n of each lightweight type i is exactly $1/n$. Lightweight types whose utilities are differentiable, and whose maxima are interior, are unsatiated; hence if all utilities are differentiable and all maxima interior, then the heavyweights are precisely the satiated types, the lightweights precisely the unsatiated. In the case of one commodity ($d = 1$), all traders on the 'short' side are satiated.

All these results are stated formally and proved in Section 12 and Appendix C of the original *Econometrica* paper; some illustrations are also given in Section 13 there.

Foremost among the open problems is that of the converse. To what extent are the necessary conditions that we have found for limiting value allocations also sufficient? In the case of ordinary markets, without satiation, this is related to smoothness: see Mas-Colell (1977) and Hart (1977b). It is quite likely that smoothness is relevant here too.

Another interesting task is to dispense with the finite type assumption. As we have seen, one cannot simply use a continuum; what is called for is a limiting approach, in which the limit is a continuum of different types. There is a large literature on this type of model in connection with the core equivalence principle; cf. Hildenbrand's book (1974) and survey article (1982). Another approach that could conceivably be helpful for this purpose is that of nonstandard analysis (cf. Brown and Robinson, 1972).

One might also like to explore the consequences of dispensing with the equal treatment restriction, the elbow room assumption, or the assumption that 0 is in the interior of each net trade set.

Perhaps most interesting at this stage would be to derive additional qualitative properties of the solution in particular contexts. In the case $d = 1$ (one commodity), for example, what happens to the dividends when the capacity of the long side is much larger than the supply of the short side? When they are almost equal? Can this kind of result, once obtained, be generalised to $d > 1$? The 'explicit formula' gives us a powerful tool for investigating these and other questions arising in particular contexts.

IV Public goods and the public sector

7 Public goods with exclusion*

1. Introduction

Equilibrium concepts for public goods discussed in the literature rely upon 'individualised prices', i.e. upon unlimited price discrimination between consumers. Such is the case, notably, for Lindahl equilibria, pseudo-equilibria and subscription equilibria; see, for example, Malinvaud (1972). In practice, however, price discrimination is either nonexistent or limited to a few broad categories of consumers. There are many good reasons for this practice, in particular: the lack of incentives for correct revelation of the preferences to which 'individualised prices' are related; the costs of administering and policing tariffs, of collecting and processing the necessary information, etc.; and the political and ethical constraints imposed on public services or licensed private monopolies, on grounds of equal treatment for instance.

Concepts of equilibrium with price rigidities and quantity constraints recently introduced for private goods (see, for example, Bénassy (1975), Drèze (1975) or the survey article by Grandmont (1977)) are susceptible of application to public goods. This idea underlies some work of de Carvalho (1979) on tâtonnement processes for public goods of the type defined by Malinvaud (1971) and Drèze and de la Vallée Poussin (1971). de Carvalho introduces (chapter 5) the additional constraint that individual contributions towards financing the public goods must be kept equal over predetermined groups of consumers. The properties of the constrained

*Journal of Public Economics, 13 (1980), 5-24. Helpful comments by Peter Hammond, Claude Henry, Guy Laroque, Maurice Marchand, Jean-Philippe Vial and Claus Weddepohl are gratefully acknowledged. Part of the work on this manuscript was done during visits to the University of Essex, and to the Institute for Mathematical Studies in Social Sciences at Stanford University under support from National Science Foundation Grant SOC 75-21820-A01.

135

processes are analysed, with the help of an appropriate concept of second-best Pareto optimality.

The present paper investigates a parallel application for public goods with exclusion. Public goods with exclusion are public goods (physical feasibility requires only that no single individual should consume more than total output), the consumption of which by individuals can be controlled, measured and subjected to payment or other contractual limitations. A nearly perfect example is provided by cable television with coin-operated unscramblers or with meters. Public facilities with controlled access and excess capacity (trains, parks, theatres, etc.) also provide good examples. Some information services (weather reports, credit rating, etc.) or intellectual services (computer programs, copyrights, musical authorship, etc.) fall in the same category. The services of fire or police departments provide another extreme example.[1]

The simple idea underlying the present paper is that public goods with exclusion are typically made available at fixed prices *up to the total quantity produced.* Individual consumers may thus buy at given prices an amount of their choice, not exceeding total output.[2] This may be contrasted with the concept of Lindahl equilibrium, where each consumer buys the total output at a price of his own.

The theory of demand under quantity rationing (see, for example, Tobin (1952)) provides an adequate tool to develop the demand side of our model. We find it convenient to work with demand *functions*; accordingly, we assume that preferences are strictly convex. Constrained demand functions then define the single most preferred element from those in the budget set which satisfy the quantity constraints. We assume that constrained demand functions are Lipschitz continuous (differentiability would not be a reasonable requirement, in the presence of quantity constraints). (A few details are given in Section 3 below.)

On the supply side, we assume that each public good is produced by a single firm. This seems empirically realistic, and saves us the trouble of specifying how individual purchases are distributed among producers. And we consider alternative institutional arrangements.

---

[1] In some of these examples, congestion phenomena occur, and the quality of the public goods varies with the number of users – a feature analysed in Lévy-Lambert (1968). The model and results presented here apply to the variable quality case as well, even though that case is not treated explicitly.

[2] More generally, a limited amount of price discrimination could be introduced, either between consumers or according to quantities purchased. The model and results presented here lend themselves to natural extensions in these directions.

Thus, an individual producer could be a public monopoly, aiming at welfare maximisation, with or without a budget constraint (as in Boiteux (1956)); it could be a profit-maximising private monopoly; or it could be a licensed private monopoly, pursuing profit maximisation within statutory regulations. Two types of regulations will be considered here, namely price regulation (the prices of public goods are set by the regulatory agency, the quantities are set for profit maximisation at these fixed prices); and quantity regulation (the quantities of public goods are set by the regulatory agency, the prices are set for profit maximisation at these quantities). The not uncommon practice of price regulation for licensed private monopolies (railroads, urban transportation companies, cable television networks, etc.) lends particular relevance to that arrangement, which is singled out for the existence theorem in Section 4 below.

Our equilibrium concept thus combines consumer equilibrium, under given prices and quantity constraints, with producer equilibrium of one type or another. When producer behaviour reflects welfare maximisation (either constrained or unconstrained), equilibrium is defined by the Pareto principle, and the existence of equilibrium is not an issue if the set of feasible allocations is compact. In the case of private monopolies, one must first define precisely what is meant by 'profit maximisation'. After introducing the model in Section 2, we define our concept of profit maximisation in Section 3. It assumes that producers of public goods know the constrained demand functions for their output. (In particular, they know the marginal revenue associated with an increase in output.) We argue that such an assumption is needed to avoid trivial solutions. Unfortunately, the resulting profit function generally is not concave.

A *market equilibrium* is characterised by physical feasibility, consumer equilibrium and profit maximisation. The existence of a market equilibrium is proved in section 4 for the special case where each producer of public goods supplies a single commodity, at a regulated price. It is shown in section 5 that output of public goods at a market equilibrium is then generically *less* than required for second-best Pareto efficiency (given the prices).

In general, market equilibria may fail to exist, owing to nonconcavity of the profit functions. The profit-maximisation problem may then be difficult to solve, and a 'bounded rationality' approach may be more realistic. As a first step in that direction, we define a *market stationary point* by the properties of physical feasibility, consumer equilibrium, and stationarity of the profit functions. The existence of a market stationary point, under price regulation, is proved in Section 4. The technique of proof is readily adapted to other cases as well, under appropriate assumptions. But we emphasise that stationary points of the profit functions need not be local maxima.

An important issue raised, but not treated, in Section 4, concerns the properties of the correspondence relating market stationary points to the prices of public goods, under price regulation. Treating that issue properly would require mathematical developments lying beyond the scope of the present paper.

Finally, some efficiency issues are discussed in Section 5. It is first recalled that a welfare-maximising public utility, capable of financing its deficit by lump-sum taxes, should set the public good prices at a level sufficiently low that each consumer demands the entire output. This is neither surprising nor very interesting. Attention is therefore focussed on situations where a budget constraint is imposed on the producer. Four sets of first-order conditions are then contrasted, namely those of the public monopoly and of the private monopoly successively unregulated, price regulated and quantity regulated. Although a general case can be made in favour of the public monopoly and against the unregulated private monopoly, it is not possible to rank the intermediate alternatives of price versus quantity regulation. A rigorous comparison of these alternatives would also require further progress with the unanswered question raised at the end of Section 4.

Because the present paper is meant to be suggestive rather than exhaustive, the choice of assumptions is dictated by convenience rather than generality.

2. The model

We consider an economy with:

n private goods, indexed $j = 1 \ldots n$, with $N = \{1 \ldots n\}$;

m public goods, indexed $i = 1 \ldots m$, with $M = \{1 \ldots m\}$;

l consumers, indexed $h = 1 \ldots l$, with $L = \{1 \ldots l\}$;

k producers of private goods or private producers, indexed $g = 1 \ldots k$, with $K = \{1 \ldots k\}$;

f producers of public goods or public producers, indexed $e = 1 \ldots f$, with $F = \{1 \ldots f\}$.

The set M is *partitioned* into subsets $M^1 \ldots M^e \ldots M^f$, with cardinality $m^1 \ldots m^e \ldots m^f$. For $i \in M^e$ and $i' \in M^{e'}, i < i'$ implies $e \leqq e'$; and $e < e'$ implies $i < i'$. (That is, the public producers specialise in disjoint sets of goods; and the indices of public producers are monotonic nondecreasing in the indices of goods.) If ζ is a vector of R^m, we denote by ζ^e the subvector with indices in M^e; and by $^e\zeta$ its complement, with indices in $M \backslash M^e$.

For the private goods, we denote by:[3]

$p \in \Delta \subset R^n_+$ their prices; $\Delta = \{p \in R^n_+ \mid \sum_j p_j = 1\}$;

$x^h \in X^h \subset R^n$ the consumption of consumer h; X^h is closed, convex and bounded below;

$w^h \in \text{int } X^h$ the initial resources of consumer h;

$y^g \in Y^g \subset R^n$ the production of private producer g; Y^g is closed and convex;

$Y^g \cap R^n_+ = \{0\}; (\sum_g Y^g) \cap - (\sum_g Y^g) = \{0\}$;

$y^e \in R^n_-$ the imputs of public producer e.

For the public goods, we denote by:

$q \in R^m_+$ their prices; $q = (q^1 \ldots q^e \ldots q^f)$;

$z^h \in R^m_+$ the consumption of consumer h; $z^h = (z^{h1} \ldots z^{he} \ldots z^{hf})$;

$Q \in R^m_+$ their production; $Q = (Q^1 \ldots Q^e \ldots Q^f)$.

The public producer e chooses a production plan (y^e, Q^e) $\in Y^e \subset R^n_- \times R^{m^e}_+$; Y^e is closed, convex, and $R^n_- \times \{0\} \subset Y^e$. Furthermore, it is assumed that for every y^e, the section of Y^e in R^m_+, i.e. the set $\{Q^e \mid (y^e, Q^e) \in Y^e\}$, is bounded; it will be denoted $S_{y^e}(Y^e)$. This condition is automatically satisfied when the asymptotic cone of Y^e does not contain any nonnegative element other than zero.

Physical feasibility requires:

$$\sum_h (x^h - w^h) \leq \sum_g y^g + \sum_e y^e; \qquad (1)$$

$$z^h \leq Q, \text{ for all } h \in L. \qquad (2)$$

A feasible allocation, a, is an $(l + k + f)$-tuple of vectors

$$(x^h, z^h) \in X^h \times R^m_+, \; h = 1 \ldots l,$$

$$y^g \in Y^g, \; g = 1 \ldots k,$$

$$(y^e, Q^e) \in Y^e, \; e = 1 \ldots f,$$

satisfying (1) and (2). The set of feasible allocations is A.

LEMMA. A is bounded.

[3] $\leq$ means $\leq$ coordinate-wise; $<$ means $\leq$ and $\neq$; $R^n_+ = \{x \in R^n \mid x \geq 0\}$; $R^n_- = \{x \in R^n \mid x \leq 0\}$.

PROOF. In so far as private goods are concerned, see proposition (2) on p. 77 of Debreu (1959). This also implies that $\sum_e y^e$ is bounded, hence that $y^e \leq 0$ is bounded for each e. The lemma then follows from our assumption that $S_{y^e}(Y^e)$ is bounded for every y^e.   QED

The profits of private producers, $v^g = py^g$, belong to the consumers according to the ownership fractions $\theta_{hg} \geq 0$, $\sum_h \theta_{hg} = 1$.

The profits of the public producers are defined by

$$v^e = py^e + q^e \sum_h \min(z^{he}, Q^e),\tag{3}$$

an expression that simplifies somewhat when (2) is taken into account, and that is discussed extensively in section 3 below.

These profits belong to the consumers according to the ownership fractions $\theta_{he} \geq 0$, $\sum_h \theta_{he} = 1$.

A budgeted allocation consists of a feasible allocation a and price vectors $(p, q) \in \Delta \times R_+^m$ such that, for all h, the budget constraint

$$p(x^h - w^h) + qz^h \leq \sum_g \theta_{hg}v^g + \sum_e \theta_{he}v^e = {}_{\text{def}} r^h\tag{4}$$

is satisfied. Define $r = (r^1 \ldots r^h \ldots r^l) \in R_+^l$.

For each $h \in L$, there exists a preference ordering $\succsim_h$ defined on $X^h \times R_+^m$; $\succsim_h$ is complete, continuous and strictly convex; $(x, z) \geq (x', z')$ implies $(x, z) \succsim_h (x', z')$; $x > x'$ implies $(x, z) \succ_h (x', z)$.

Natural conditions for $(a, p, q) \in A \times \Delta \times R_+^m$ to define a *market equilibrium* include:

$\forall h \in L$, (x^h, z^h) is the best element[4] for $\succsim_h$ over the set of vectors satisfying (2) and (4);   (5)

$\forall g \in K$, y^g maximizes v^g on Y^g.   (6)

To these conditions must be added a specification of the behaviour of the public producers. In the case of a public monopoly aiming at welfare maximisation, this specification will involve the standard concept of Pareto optimality.

In the case of a private monopoly aiming at profit maximisation, it would seem natural to impose

(q^e, y^e, Q^e) maximise v^e on Y^e,   (7)

---

[4] In view of our assumption of strict convexity of preferences, that element is unique, and we work with demand *functions*.

subject possibly to $q^e = \bar{q}^e$ under price regulation or to $Q^e = \bar{Q}^e$ under quantity regulation. We now turn to a discussion of condition (7).

3. Behaviour of the public producers

3.1.

Whereas conditions (5) and (6) are standard and well understood, conditions (7) raise some difficulties. Going back to expression (3), we see that the profits v^e of public producer e depend upon p, y^e, q^e, the demand levels z^{he}, and Q^e. We must now specify which among these variables enter as decision variables, as functions of the decision variables, and as parameters, in the maximisation problem.

The list of decision variables will depend upon the institutional arrangements. Under price regulation, the decision variables will be y^e and Q^e, with $q^e = \bar{q}^e$ entering as a parameter. Under quantity regulation, the decision variables will be y^e and q^e, with $Q^e = \bar{Q}^e$ entering as a parameter. In the absence of regulation, the decision variables will be y^e, q^e and Q^e.

Let us consider first, and in some detail, the case of a price-regulated public producer who maximises profits with respect to y^e and Q^e. Three different specifications of the maximisation problem are possible.

(i)   First, one could treat p and z^{he}, $h \in L$, as parameters. Then, condition (7) becomes: (y^e, Q^e) maximise $\bar{p} y^e + \bar{q}^e \sum_h \min(\bar{z}^{he}, Q^e)$ on Y^e (where all parameters are identified by overbars). The drawback of this approach is that (5) and (7) will hold trivially with $z^{he} = Q^e = 0$ and $y^e = 0;$[5] our economy then reduces to a standard private goods economy, with well-known properties.

(ii)   Going to the other extreme, one could treat p and $z^{he}, h \in L$, as jointly determined endogenous variables, the levels of which would depend upon y^e and Q^e. Under this approach the public producer would be assumed capable of tracing the influence of his decisions (y^e, Q^e), not only on the demands for public goods z^{he} through the constraints (2), but also on the prices of private goods p (both directly via y^e and indirectly via the influence of Q^e on the private demands x^{he}) and on the other determinants of z^{he} (namely p, r^h and $^e Q$, all of which are jointly determined in equilibrium). This approach is technically difficult, because the market

---

[5] Indeed, if $\bar{z}^{he} = 0$, then $\min(\bar{z}^{he}, Q^e)$ is equal to zero identically in Q^e; hence $v^e = p y^e \leq 0$ is maximal at $y^e = 0$, $Q^e = 0$; but when $Q^e = 0$, then $z^{he} = 0$ by (2); accordingly, the trivial solution $z^{he} = Q^e = 0$ satisfies simultaneously (5) and (7).

clearing prices p need not be unique; it is quite unrealistic because it endows the public producer with too much information and computing abilities; and it is not in the spirit of competitive analysis, which aims at modelling price-taking behaviour.

(iii) More realistically, one should treat p, r and $^e Q$ as parameters, and assume that the public producer recognises only the *direct* influence of his output decisions Q^e on the demand levels $z^{he}(Q^e; \bar{p}, \bar{q}, \bar{r}^h, {}^e \bar{Q})$. This middle course seems natural and still consistent with the spirit of competitive analysis. Indeed, we noted under (i) that it would be illogical for the public producer to assume that an increase in his output would leave sales unchanged. It would be equally unsatisfactory for him to assume that the additional output would be bought by *all* consumers, including those currently buying quantities $z_i^h < Q_i$. Barring these two extremes leads to recognise the direct influence of Q^e on $z^{he}(Q^e; \bar{p}, \bar{q}, \bar{r}^h, {}^e \bar{Q})$, neither more nor less.[6]

3.2.

Under this third approach, retained here, the next issue to be settled is *how* the public producer perceives the influence of Q^e on z^{he}, $h \in L$. One possibility would be to use the concept of *effective demand* as defined by Clower (1965) or Bénassy (1975). Let $\zeta_i^h = z_i^h(Q_1 \ldots Q_{i-1}, + \infty, Q_{i+1} \ldots Q_m;$ $p, q, r^h)$, $\zeta^h = (\zeta_1^h \ldots \zeta_m^h) = (\zeta^{h1} \ldots \zeta^{he} \ldots \zeta^{hf})$; one could then rewrite (7) as follows:

$$(y^e, Q^e) \text{ maximise } \bar{p} \, y^e + \bar{q}^e \sum_h \min(\bar{\zeta}^{he}, Q^e) \text{ on } Y^e. \tag{8}$$

This formulation is adequate when $m^e = 1$ (each public producer supplies a single good), but not when $m^e = 1$, *because it implies that the public producer ignores the relationships of substitution or complementarity among the public goods which he supplies.*

Indeed, if goods i and $i + 1$ in M^e are strongly complementary, with $z_i^h = Q_i$ and $z_{i+1}^h = Q_{i+1}$, it could be that simultaneous increases of Q_i and Q_{i+1} by δ bring about increases in both z_i^h and z_{i+1}^h by δ; whereas $\zeta_i^h < z_i^h + \delta$, and $\zeta_{i+1}^h < z_{i+1}^h + \delta$, owing to the limited appeal of increasing the consumption of either good when its complement remains constrained.[7]

---

[6] As a technical side remark, we note that the public producer could indifferently recognise, or ignore as we assume here, the influence of his own profits v^e on individual incomes r^h. At a point where the profit function is stationary, the two formulations are identical to the first order.

[7] More frequent service on a local bus route may fail to stimulate demand if the connecting railroad service is not improved simultaneously...

Conversely, if the two goods are close substitutes, it could be that simultaneous increases of Q_i and Q_{i+1} by δ bring about smaller increases in z_i^h and z_{i+1}^h than suggested by ζ^h.[8]

When simultaneous modifications of several quantities are contemplated, the relevant concept is the vector-valued *constrained demand function* $z^{he}(Q^e; p, q, r^h, {}^eQ)$ defined by (5) for alternative values of Q^e. We shall assume here that, with the aid of his econometric and marketing consultants, the public producer knows the aggregate demand functions

$$z^e(Q^e; \bar{p}, \bar{q}, \bar{r}, {}^e\bar{Q}) = \sum_h z^{he}(Q^e; \bar{p}, \bar{q}, \bar{r}^h, {}^e\bar{Q}).$$

Since these functions satisfy (2), we may now rewrite (7) as

$$(y^e, Q^e) \text{ maximize } \bar{p}\, y^e + \bar{q}^e \sum_h z^{he}(Q^e; \bar{p}, \bar{q}, \bar{r}^h, {}^e\bar{Q})$$

$$= {}_{def} v^e(y^e, Q^e; \bar{p}, \bar{q}, \bar{r}, {}^e\bar{Q}), \text{ on } Y^e. \tag{9}$$

We shall then say that a budgeted allocation (a, p, q) is a *market equilibrium, under price regulation,* if it satisfies (5), (6) and (9). We prove in Section 4, the existence of such a market equilibrium, with arbitrary q, for the special case where M^e is a singleton for all e in F. And we show in Section 5 that output of public goods, at such an equilibrium, is generically less than required for second-best Pareto efficiency, given q.

3.3.

The optimization problem faced by public producer e, namely (9), is in general neither differentiable nor concave. Indeed, conditions (2) imply that demand functions cannot be everywhere differentiable. And the constrained demand functions $z^{he}(Q^e; \cdot)$ need not be concave, as an example in the appendix illustrates.

The fact that problem (9) is not concave has two important implications.

First, a market equilibrium may fail to exist. An example in the appendix illustrates the point. In that example, public goods are demanded by a single consumer, and are therefore not different from private goods. The existence problem lies with the behaviour of the public producer, who takes into account the influence of his output decisions on demand levels. Similar

---

[8] The prospective audiences for additional coverage by a TV network of domestic soccer games and foreign soccer games cannot be evaluated independently...

problems are encountered in general equilibrium models with imperfect competition – see, for example, Arrow and Hahn (1971, ch. 6.4). Still, it should be noted that lack of existence follows here from the absence of market-clearing prices *for the private goods*, owing to a discontinuity in the behaviour (here the demand for inputs) of the public producers. In most practical situations this problem should be of secondary importance, given sufficiently well-behaved markets for private goods. The purpose of the example in the appendix is thus to orient, not to discourage, the search for reasonable assumptions implying the existence of market equilibria, under price regulation.

The fact that problem (9) is not concave has another implication, namely that public producer *e* may find it difficult to solve that problem. Operational sufficient conditions for a maximum are not available, except in special cases; and the development of algorithms for nondifferentiable, nonconvex optimisation is still in an early stage – see, for example, Mifflin (1976). It may seem unnatural to impose on the behaviour of public producers a requirement (ability to solve problem (9)) that could be very hard to meet. Some kind of 'bounded rationality' approach may seem more natural.

As a modest step in that direction, we note that *necessary conditions* for a solution of problem (9) are available, provided only the relevant functions be Lipschitz – see Clarke (1975, 1976). These necessary conditions define stationary points of the optimization problem. To impose that these conditions be satisfied is to impose a minimal requirement upon the behaviour of public producers. We shall verify that this requirement is consistent with general equilibrium. But we recognise that this is only a first step towards a satisfactory 'bounded rationality' approach, because public producers may typically do better than simply finding a stationary point of their profit function; they may for instance be able to find a local maximum, in which case continuity problems arise once again.

Sufficient conditions for preferences to yield Lipschitz demand functions satisfying (2) can be defined. Because these conditions are somewhat technical and may not have received a definitive formulation, we shall not reproduce them here. Instead, we shall stipulate directly in the statement of our existence theorem below that individual demand functions are locally Lipschitz. We note from Cornet and Laroque (1980) that assumptions under which unconstrained demand functions are differentiable imply that constrained demand functions satisfying (2) are Lipschitz. And we note for further reference that Lipschitz functions are almost everywhere differentiable. At points where they are not differentiable one can, following Clarke (1975, 1976), define generalised gradients.

DEFINITIONS.

(i)   The demand functions $z^h(p, q, r^h, Q)$, which associate with every point $(p, q, r^h, Q) \in \varDelta \times R_+^{2m+1}$ the best element for $\succ_h$ over (2) and (4), are Lipschitz if, for every compact set B in $\varDelta \times R_+^{2m+1}$, there is a constant k_B^h such that, for all (p, q, r^h, Q) and $(\hat{p}, \hat{q}, \hat{r}^h, \hat{Q})$ in B,

$$\| z^h(p, q, r^h, Q) - z^h(\hat{p}, \hat{q}, \hat{r}^h, \hat{Q}) \| \leq k_B^h \| (p, q, r^h, Q) - (\hat{p}, \hat{q}, \hat{r}^h, \hat{Q}) \|,$$

where $\| \cdot \|$ denotes the Euclidean norm.

(ii)   The generalized gradient of the Lipschitz function $f: R^n \to R$ at x, denoted $\partial f(x)$, is the convex hull of all points ζ of the form $\zeta = \lim_{s \to \infty} \nabla f(x_s)$, where $\{x_s\}$ is a sequence converging to x such that f is differentiable at each x_s and where $\nabla f(x)$ is the gradient (vector of partial derivatives) of f at x_s.

(iii)   For $C \in R^n$ convex, the normal cone to C at $x \in C$ is

$$N_C(x) = \{w \in R^n : (x' - x)w \leq 0, \quad \forall x' \in C\}.$$

First-order necessary conditions for problem (9) can be defined by means of theorem 1 in Clarke (1976), if the decision variables are restricted to a compact convex set. For convenience, we eliminate y^e from problem (9), and solve the problem in Q^e over an arbitrary compact convex set – to be defined in section 4. To that end, define:

$$\gamma^e(p, Q^e) = \min \{ -py^e \,|\, (y^e, Q^e) \in Y^e) \}$$

$$= \min \{ -py^e \,|\, y^e \in S_{Q^e}(Y^e) \}; \tag{10}$$

$$v^e(Q^e; \bar{p}, \bar{q}, \bar{r}, {}^e\bar{Q}) = \bar{q}^e \sum_h z^{he}(Q^e; \bar{p}, \bar{q}, \bar{r}^h, {}^e\bar{Q})$$

$$- \gamma^e(Q^e; \bar{p}), Q^e \in \mathrm{Pr}_{M^e}(Y^e), \quad e = 1 \ldots f. \tag{11}$$

When Y^e is convex, then γ^e is a convex function of Q^e for given p, hence a Lipschitz function of Q^e – see theorem 10.4 in Rockafellar (1970).

PROPOSITION.

If Q^{e*} maximises the Lipschitz function $v^e(Q^e; \cdot)$ over the compact convex set $Z^e \subset R_+^{m^e}$, then

$$0 \in -\partial v^e(Q^{e*}; \bar{p}, \bar{q}, \bar{r}, {}^e\bar{Q}) + N_{Z^e}(Q^{e*})$$

$$\subset -\bar{q}^e \sum_h \partial z^{he}(Q^{e*}; \bar{p}, \bar{q}, \bar{r}^h, {}^e\bar{Q}) + \partial \gamma^e(Q^{e*}; \bar{p}) + N_{Z^e}(Q^{e*}). \tag{12}$$

[The inclusion follows from proposition 8 in Clarke (1976).]

We shall then say that a budgeted allocation (a, p, q) is *a market stationary point, under price regulation,* if it satisfies conditions (5), (6) and (12). We prove in section 4 the existence of market stationary points, under price regulation, with the mild assumption that demand functions are Lipschitz. The terms 'stationary point' reflect the property that conditions (12) are not *sufficient* for (y^{e*}, Q^{e*}) to define a maximum for problem (9), not even locally.

3.4.

Applying a similar reasoning to the quantity-regulated public producer would lead us to reformulate (7) as

$$(y^e, q^e) \text{ maximise } \bar{p} y^e + q^e \sum_h z^{he}(q^e; \bar{Q}, \bar{p}, {}^e\bar{q}, \bar{r}^h)$$

$$= {}_{\text{def}} v^e(y^e, q^e; \bar{Q}, \bar{p}, {}^e\bar{q}, \bar{r}) \text{ subject to } (y^e, \bar{Q}^e) \in Y^e, \tag{13}$$

for which a necessary first-order condition is

$$0 \in - \partial v^e(y^{e*}, q^{e*}; \bar{p}, {}^e\bar{q}, \bar{r}, \bar{Q}) + N_{Z^e}(y^{e*}, q^{e*}). \tag{14}$$

Finally, for the unregulated public producer, (7) would become

$$(y^e, Q^e, q^e) \text{ maximise } p y^e + q^e \sum_h z^{he}(q^e, Q^e; {}^e\bar{Q}, \bar{p}, {}^e\bar{q}, \bar{r}^h)$$

$$= {}_{\text{def}} v^e(q^e, y^e, Q^e; {}^e\bar{Q}, \bar{p}, {}^e\bar{q}, \bar{r}) \text{ subject to } (y^e, Q^e) \in Y^e, \tag{15}$$

with first-order condition

$$0 \in - \partial v^e(q^{e*}, y^{e*}, Q^{e*}; \bar{p}, {}^e\bar{q}, \bar{r}, {}^e\bar{Q}) + N_{Z^e}(q^{e*}, y^{e*}, Q^{e*}). \tag{16}$$

In both cases Z^e is an arbitrary convex set in the relevant space; and the argument for recognising the influence of q^e on z^{he} is that we want to avoid the trivial solutions $q_i = +\infty$, which could obtain if z_i^h were treated as a parameter.

4. Existence of market stationary points or equilibria, under price regulation

THEOREM. *For the economy described in section 2, if the demand functions are Lipschitz, then given any* $q \in R_+^m$:

(i)   *there exists* $a \in A$ *and* $p \in \Delta$ *such that* (a, p, q) *is a market stationary point, under price regulation; and*

(ii)   *when each public producer supplies a single public good, every market stationary point is a market equilibrium, under price regulation.*

PROOF

(i) The proof is an application of Kakutani's theorem.

In view of the lemma in Section 2 we may, for α and α' in R_+ sufficiently large, replace the consumption set $X^h \times R^m_+$ by the compact set $\hat{X}^h = (X^h \cap [-\alpha,\alpha]^n) \times [0,\alpha]^m, \forall h \in L$; replace the production set Y^g by the compact set $\hat{Y}^g = Y^g \cap [-\alpha,\alpha]^n, \forall g \in K$; and replace the production set Y^e by the compact set $\hat{Y}^e = Y^e \cap ([-\alpha',0]^n \times [0,\alpha]^{m^e}), \forall e \in F$.

Let $Z^e = _{\text{def}} [0,\alpha]^{m^e}$, and let $\text{Pr}_{M^e}(\hat{Y}^e)$ denote the projection of Y^e on $R^{m^e}_+$, i.e. the set $\{Q^e \mid \exists \, y^e \text{ s.t. } (y^e, Q^e) \in \hat{Y}^e\}$. If $\text{Pr}_{M^e}(\hat{Y}^e) \neq Z^e$, then using the assumptions that $\hat{Y}^e$ is closed and that the demand functions are Lipschitz, we can extend $\hat{Y}^e$ *to a larger set* $\tilde{Y}^e$ with $\text{Pr}_{M^e}(\tilde{Y}^e) = Z^e$, in such a way that the sets of solutions to (12) on Z^e are thereby unaffected, for given $q \in R^m_+$, identically in $p \in \Delta, r \in R^l_+$ and $Q \in [0,\alpha]^m$.

To that end let $\tilde{Q}^e(Q^e)$ be the unique element in the closed convex set $\text{Pr}_{M^e}(\hat{Y}^e)$ such that

$$\| \tilde{Q}^e(Q^e) - Q^e \| \leq \| \hat{Q}^e - Q^e \|, \text{ for all } \hat{Q}^e \in \text{Pr}_{M^e}(\hat{Y}^e).$$

We may then define, for all e in F:

$$\tilde{Y}^e = \hat{Y}^e \cup \{ (y^e, Q^e) \in R^n_- \times Z^e \mid y^e \in S_{\tilde{Q}^e(Q^e)}(\hat{Y}^e)$$

$$- \{ T \| \tilde{Q}^e(Q^e) - Q^e \| i^n \} \}, \tag{17}$$

where $i^n = (1 \ldots 1) \in R^n$ and T is a suitable constant.[9]

Then, for $p \in \Delta$,

$$\tilde{\gamma}^e(Q^e; p) = _{\text{def}} \min \{ -py^e \mid (y^e, Q^e) \in \tilde{Y}^e \}$$

$$= \gamma^e(\tilde{Q}^e(Q^e); p) + T \cdot \| \tilde{Q}^e(Q^e) - Q^e \|, Q^e \in Z^e;$$

$$\tilde{v}^e(Q^e; p, q, r, {}^eQ) = _{\text{def}} q^e \sum_h z^{he}(Q^e; p, q, r^h, {}^eQ) - \tilde{\gamma}^e(Q^e; p). \tag{18}$$

That is, we have extended $\hat{Y}^e$ in such a way that the (hypothetical) cost of an unfeasible output Q^e increases, at an arbitrarily large but finite rate T, with the distance of Q^e from the set of feasible outputs $\text{Pr}_{M^e}(\hat{Y}^e)$. By the Lipschitz property, T may be chosen such that $\partial \tilde{v}^e(Q^e; p, q, r, {}^eQ) < 0$ for

---

[9] The constant T implicitly defines α' and must be chosen so as to preserve convexity of the function $\tilde{\gamma}^e(Q^e; p)$ in (18).

all $Q^e \in Z^e \backslash \mathrm{Pr}_{M^e}(\hat{Y}^e)$, identically in $p \in \Delta, r \in R^l_+$ and $Q \in [0, \alpha]^m$. This construction has the further property that

$$\partial \bar{\gamma}^e(Q^e; p) + N_{Z^e}(Q^e) \subset \partial \gamma^e(Q^e; p)$$

$$+ N_{\mathrm{Pr}_{M^e}(Y^e)}(Q^e) \forall Q^e \in \mathrm{Pr}_{M^e}(Y^e). \tag{19}$$

(See proposition 11 in Clarke (1976).) It follows that the sets of solutions to (12) are unaffected by our extension.

We shall accordingly proceed on the assumption that $\mathrm{Pr}_{M^e}(\hat{Y}^e) = Z^e$.

In order to apply Kakutani's theorem, we define functions x^h, z^h and correspondences $\eta^g, \eta^e, \phi^e, \psi$ as follows:

Let $B = {}_{\mathrm{def}}(\Pi_h \hat{X}^h) \times (\Pi_g \hat{Y}^g) \times (\Pi_e \hat{Y}^e) \times \Delta$, a compact set with elements b, b', etc.

For each h, let $\beta^h(b)$ be the subset of $\hat{X}^h$ satisfying (2) and (4), and let $(x^h(b), z^h(b))$ be the best point in $\beta^h(b)$ for $\succ_h$; β^h is a continuous correspondence (see the lemma in Drèze (1975)); $(x^h(b), z^h(b))$ are continuous vector-valued functions.

For each g, let

$$\eta^g(b) = \eta^g(p) = \{y^g \in \hat{Y}^g \mid py^g \geqq py \forall y \in \hat{Y}^g\}.$$

For each e, let

$$\eta^e(b) = \eta^e(p, Q^e) = \{y^e \in S_{Q^e}(\hat{Y}^e) \mid -py^e = \gamma^e(p, Q^e)\},$$

$$\phi^e(b) = \{Q^e \in R^{m^e}_+ \mid \exists \chi^e \in \partial v^e(Q^e; p, q, r, {}^eQ),$$

$$Q_i = \max[0, \min(Q_i + \chi_i, \alpha)], \forall i \in M^e\}.$$

Let

$$\psi(b) = \left\{ p \in \Delta \mid (p - p') \left(\sum_h x^h - \sum_h w^h - \sum_g y^g - \sum_e y^e \right) \geqq 0 \forall p' \in \Delta \right\};$$

the correspondences η^g, η^e, ϕ^e and ψ are nonempty, compact-valued, convex-valued and upper hemicontinuous (for ϕ^e, see propositions 1 and 7 in Clarke (1976)).

All the conditions of Kakutani's theorem being verified, the correspondence from B to B defined by $(x^h, z^h, \eta^g, \eta^e, \phi^e, \psi)$ has a fixed point – say b^*. That b^* is a market stationary point is verified as follows.

For the private goods, standard arguments imply that $p^*_j > 0 \forall j \in N$. Therefore, $b^* = (a^*, p^*)$ with $a^* \in A, p^* \in \mathrm{int}\, \Delta$. This implies $Q^*_i < \alpha \forall i \in M$.

Consider the vector ϕ^{e*}. By definition, there exists $\chi^{e*} \in \partial v^e(Q^{e*} \mid p^*, q, r^*, {}^eQ^*)$ such that $\forall i \in M^e$, either $\chi^*_i = 0$, or $Q^*_i = 0$

with $\chi_i^* \leq 0$. In both cases, $0 \in -\partial v^e(Q^{e*} \mid p^*, q, r^*, {}^eQ^*) + N_{Z^e}(Q^{e*})$, with $Q_i^* < \alpha \, \forall \, i \in M^e$, and (12) is satisfied.

(ii) There remains to show that, when M^e is a singleton, then any (y^{e*}, Q^{e*}) satisfying (12) at (p^*, q, r^*, Q^*) also solve (9) there. To that end, we remark that $v^e(Q^e; p^*, q, r^*, {}^eQ^*)$ is a concave function of $Q^e \in R_+$. Indeed, each demand function $z^{he}(Q^e; p^*, q, r^{h*}, {}^eQ^*)$ is of the form $z^{he} = \min(\zeta^{he}, Q^e)$, and $\gamma^e(Q^e; p^*)$ is a convex function of Q^e.[10]   QED

REMARK

In order to prove (i), it is not necessary to assume that Y^e is convex; it would suffice to assume that $\mathrm{Pr}_{M^e}(Y^e)$ is convex; that, for every Q^e in $\mathrm{Pr}_{M^e}(Y^e)$, the section of Y^e in R^n_-, $S_{Q^e}(Y^e)$, is convex; and that $\gamma^e(Q; \cdot)$ is Lipschitz. These assumptions are still restrictive, but they are definitely less restrictive than the convexity of Y^e. In particular, they allow for production by means of a single process with fixed relative coefficients and increasing returns to scale; but not for a mixture of several such processes.

Similar techniques could be used to prove the existence of market stationary points under quantity-regulation, or in the absence of regulation. Additional precautions are needed, however, to rule out situations where arbitrarily small quantities would be sold at arbitrarily large prices.

The interpretation of the conditions (12) defining the supply of public goods under price regulation is straightforward. If the individual demand functions z^h and the cost function γ^e are differentiable at b^* (implying $Q_i > 0, \forall \, i \in M^e$), then (12) reduces to

$$q^e \sum_h \frac{\partial z^{he}}{\partial Q_i} = \frac{\partial \gamma^e}{\partial Q_i}, \quad \forall \, i \in M^e. \tag{20}$$

These conditions assert that the marginal cost of each public good is equal to the marginal revenue associated with its production. At a point of differentiability, either $z_i^h < Q_i$, in which case $\partial z^{he}/\partial Q_i = 0$; or $z_i^h = Q_i$, in which case $\partial z_i^h/\partial Q_i = 1$ and $\partial z_j^h/\partial Q_i$ is arbitrary as to sign (being equal to zero when $z_j^h = Q_j$). Total differentiation of (20) could then yield the partial derivatives of the supply of public goods with respect to their own prices, to the prices of private goods and to the individual incomes. More generally, however, one must recognise the possibility that demand or cost functions may fail to be differentiable. The equality (20) among partial

[10] Of course, a simple existence proof can be presented directly for this special case.

derivatives is then replaced by an inclusion relation among generalised gradients. Although the interpretation is basically unchanged, total differentiation is no longer well defined, and another approach should (and undoubtedly could) be devised to study the dependence of public good supply on their own prices and on other parameters.

5.　Some efficiency considerations

Leaving aside questions of incentives and of technological efficiency, the best institutional arrangements for the provision of public goods with exclusion is a public monopoly operating without a budget constraint and financing its deficit by means of lump-sum taxes. Such a monopoly may indeed choose public good prices low enough to generate from each consumer a demand equal to the entire supply – for instance zero price. A Pareto optimum may then be achieved, but the 'exclusion' feature is lost. In order to obtain more relevant and more interesting results, one must introduce a budget constraint and resort to a second-best optimum. The presence of a budget constraint is probably the main reason why a public agency would price public goods in the first place.

The rules of behaviour of a public monopoly aiming at welfare maximisation under a budget constraint will depend upon the degree of sophistication with which the welfare objective is pursued. In a refined analysis, where the effects of the supply and pricing of public goods on private goods prices and consumer incomes are taken into account, rather complex – and unrealistic – rules of behaviour emerge. When these indirect effects are ignored, the rules of behavior are easier to understand and less unrealistic.[11] A simple formulation of the second-best Pareto-optimisation problem for producer e[12] is the following:

$$\max_{q^e, Q^e} \sum_h \lambda^h U^h(x^h, z^h) \text{ subject to } q^e \sum_h z^{he}(q^e, Q^e; p, {}^eq, r^h, {}^eQ)$$

$$- \gamma^e(Q^e; p) \geqq t^e, \tag{21}$$

where

U^h　　is a utility function representing the preferences of consumer h,
λ^h　　is a weight assigned to consumer h, to be eliminated from the efficiency conditions,

[11] Similar comments were made in section 3 regarding the degree of sophistication with which the profit-maximisation objective is pursued.

[12] The additional complexities of a simultaneous analysis for several public producers are illustrated in Boiteux (1956).

(x^h, z^h) are functions of (p, q, Q, r^h), and
t^e is a preassigned budget.

The prices p of private goods, the incomes r^h, and the prices and quantities of the remaining public goods $({}^e q, {}^e Q)$ are treated as parameters.

For ease of interpretation, first-order conditions will be stated at a point of differentiability; under the further assumption that the public monopoly accepts the prevailing income distribution and does not itself attempt to correct it, the weights λ^h may be eliminated, and the first-order efficiency conditions may be written as follows:

$$\sum_h [(1 - v^e) \pi^{he} + v^e q^e] \frac{\partial z^{he}}{\partial Q^e} = \frac{\partial \gamma^e}{\partial Q^e}, \tag{22}$$

$$\sum_h \left(v^e z^{he} + q^e \frac{\partial z^{he}}{\partial q^e} \right) = 0, \tag{23}$$

where v^e is a parameter set at the smallest value in $(0, 1)$ such that the budget constraint is satisfied, and where π^h is the vector of marginal rates of substitution between public goods and income, measuring the marginal willingness to pay for public goods, of consumer h. Of course, $\pi^h \geqq q ; \pi_i^h = q_i$ whenever $z_i^h < Q_i$; and $z_i^h = Q_i$ whenever $\pi_i^h > q_i, i = 1 \ldots m$.

The interpretation of conditions (22) and (23) is quite straightforward. If the budget constraint were not binding (t^e large negative), then $v^e = 0$ and a first-best solution in (22)–(23) is given by $z^{he} = Q^e, \forall h$,

$$\frac{\partial \gamma^e}{\partial Q^e} = \sum_h \pi^{he} \frac{\partial z^{he}}{\partial Q^e} = \sum_h \pi^{he}.$$

Every consumer buys the whole supply of public goods; and each public good is produced in such a quantity that its marginal cost is equal to the sum over all consumers of their marginal willingness to pay for it (i.e. the so-called 'Lindahl–Samuelson' conditions are satisfied).

At the other extreme, if the public monopoly could only meet its budget constraint by maximising profits, then $v^e = 1$ and the solution to (22)–(23) is the same as that which would prevail under an unregulated private monopoly: Prices of public goods are set at such levels that marginal revenue is equal to zero; and quantities of public goods are such that marginal revenue (measured in terms of q^e, not of π^{he}) is equal to marginal cost.

Between these two extremes we find intermediate solutions. Thus, in (23) with $1 > v^e > 0$, marginal revenues are set equal to zero after 'inflating' the price elasticities by a factor $1/v^e$; in (22), marginal revenues and marginal willingnesses to pay are combined (in the proportions v^e and $1 - v^e$, respectively).

The information required to implement these conditions is substantial, but not unreasonable. It combines the information needed for welfare maximization, namely the vectors π^{he}; and the information needed for profit maximization, namely the demand derivatives $\{\partial z^{he}/\partial Q^e, \partial z^{he}/\partial q^e\}$. In addition, the parameter v^e must be evaluated somehow – probably by trial and error. The general picture is reminiscent of that obtained for telephone services, where the quality of service obeys a 'public good' condition like (22) whereas tariffs geared to a budget constraint obey conditions like (23) – see, for example, Marchand (1973) or Deschamps (1976). The telephone industry also offers a good illustration of the difficulties associated with implementation of these formulae.

In the case of regulated private monopolies, price regulation would lead to quantities set according to formula (22) with $v^e = 1$, i.e. according to formula (20); and quantity regulation would lead to prices set according to formula (23) with $v^e = 1$.

In the special case where each public producer supplies a single commodity, under price regulation, we may conclude from (20) and (22) that output of each public good is generically less than the output required for Pareto efficiency, at the given prices q. This is so because

$$\frac{\partial z_i^h}{\partial Q_i} \geq 0 \text{ and } \pi_i^h \geq q_i,$$

as remarked earlier. Consequently,

$$\frac{\partial \gamma^e}{\partial Q_i} = q_i \sum_h \frac{\partial z_i^h}{\partial Q_i} \leq \sum_h [(1 - v^e) \pi^{he} + v^e q^e] \frac{\partial z^{he}}{\partial Q^e}, \quad (24)$$

identically in $v^e < 1$, with equality obtaining only in the limiting case where $\pi_i^h = q_i$ for all h such that $\partial z_i^h/\partial Q_i = 1 > 0$. The willingness of consumers to pay for an additional unit of public good generically exceeds the marginal cost of that unit. Output geared to equality of marginal cost and marginal revenue is inefficient by default, never by excess.

An interesting question concerns the regulation mechanism. Thus, under price regulation, what levels should be chosen for the public good prices q^e, given that quantities will be determined by formula (20)? Two remarks are in order here. *First*, a satisfactory answer to that question requires knowledge of the way in which the supply of public goods Q^e will react to the prices q^e. This is the question raised – but not answered – at the end of Section 4. *Second*, a realistic view of the problem must again reckon with a budget constraint, that is with the possibility that a private producer would discontinue its operation (set $Q^e = 0$) if it could not obtain a satisfactory profit level at the imposed prices q^e.

If the regulatory agency ignores the influence of public good prices on the supply of public goods, but recognizes that prices must be high enough to guarantee a given level of profits to the private monopoly, then prices will be set according to formula (23), with v^e taking the smallest value in $(0, 1)$ such that the required profit level is attained, when quantities are determined by (20), i.e. by (22) with $v^e = 1$.

Similarly, an agency setting quantities would apply formula (22), and the private monopoly would set prices according to formula (23) with $v^e = 1$. Although these solutions are not 'optimal', they would seem to provide reasonable, realistic goals. Note that under price regulation the only information required consists in the price elasticities of demand, and the parameter v^e. Under quantity regulation, the required information bears on willingness to pay for public goods, on quantity elasticities of demand, and on v^e. (The need to collect information about willingness to pay for public goods may be regarded as a drawback of quantity regulation.)

From the foregoing discussions it seems safe to conclude that a public monopoly could be more efficient than a regulated private monopoly, and a regulated private monopoly could be more efficient than an unregulated private monopoly. The reasoning is simply that under the more efficient arrangement it is possible to bring about exactly the same solution as under the less efficient one, but it is also possible to do better. This conclusion is hardly surprising. More interesting would be a comparison of the efficiency levels achievable under price regulation and quantity regulation, respectively. Such a comparison is of a global, not of a local nature and therefore difficult to make. Even locally (say for small departures from either the public monopoly solution or the unregulated private monopoly solution), the comparison is difficult because it involves the response of public good supply to a change in their prices, under price regulation; or the response of public good prices to a change in their quantities, under quantity regulation. We must again conclude to the need of further research on these topics.

Appendix

A.1. Example of preferences yielding nonconcave constrained demand functions

There is a single private good, with price $p = 1$. There are two public goods, with prices $q_1 = 1$ and $q_2 = \frac{1}{2}$. The preferences of consumer h (superscript omitted) are representable by the strictly quasiconcave utility function

$$u = \tfrac{1}{2}x + \min\{\sqrt{z_1} + \sqrt{z_2}, \tfrac{1}{3}(\sqrt{z_1} + \sqrt{z_2} + 2)\}. \qquad (A.1)$$

Maximising u subject to

$$x + z_1 + \tfrac{1}{2}z_2 \leqq r, z_1 \leqq Q_1, z_2 \leqq Q_2, \qquad (A.2)$$

yields the solutions given in table A.1 for alternative values of Q_1 and Q_2.

Table A.1

$Q = (Q_1, Q_2)$	$z = (z_1, z_2)$	$qz = z_1 + (z_2/2)$
$(1, 0)$	$(1, 0)$	1
$(0, 1)$	$(0, 1)$	$\frac{1}{2}$
$(\frac{1}{2}, \frac{1}{2})$	$(\frac{1}{9}, \frac{4}{9})$	$\frac{1}{3}$

A.2. Example of an economy for which a market equilibrium may fail to exist

In order to simplify exposition and aid intuition, we use utility functions which are not *strictly* quasiconcave and increasing. There is no difficulty in extending the example to strictly convex and monotone preferences.

There are two private goods, with prices $p_1 \geqq 0$ and $p_2 = 1 - p_1 \geqq 0$. There are two public goods, with prices $q_1 = 1$ and $q_2 = \frac{1}{2}$. There are two consumers, g and h. Their preferences are representable by the concave utility functions:

$$u^h = \tfrac{1}{2}\min(x_1^h, x_2^h) + \min\{\sqrt{z_1^h} + \sqrt{z_2^h}, \tfrac{1}{3}(\sqrt{z_1^h} + \sqrt{z_2^h} + 2)\},$$

$$u^g = \min(x_1^g + 4x_2^g, 4x_1^g + x_2^g). \qquad (A.3)$$

The initial resources are defined by $w_1^h = w_2^h = w_1^g = w_2^g = 2$.

There are no private producers. There is a single public producer (superscript omitted) with production set

$$Y = \{y, Q \mid y_1 + Q_1 \leqq 0, y_2 + Q_2 \leqq 0\}. \qquad (A.4)$$

The profits of the public producer belong to consumer h (i.e. $\theta_h = 1, \theta_g = 0$). The preferences of consumer h and the production technology imply that profits are maximised at the point $Q = (1,0) = -y$ when $p_1 \leq \frac{3}{4}$; at the point $Q' = (0,1) = -y'$ when $p_1 \geq \frac{3}{4}$. The preferences of consumer h also imply $x_1^h = x_2^h$ identically in p. Under these conditions, and given the levels of initial resources, physical feasibility requires $x_1^g = x_2^g - 1$ if $p_1 \leq \frac{3}{4}$ and $x_1^g = x_2^g + 1$ when $p_1 \geq \frac{3}{4}$. But equilibrium of consumer g requires $p_1 = \frac{4}{5}$ when $x_1^g = x_2^g - 1 > 0$ and $p_1 = \frac{1}{5}$ when $x_1^g = x_2^g + 1 > 1$. Accordingly, no market equilibrium exists at the assumed prices q.

In this particular example, market equilibria will exist at other prices q – like $q_1 = q_2 = 1$. Trivial equilibria will always exist at $q = 0$, $Q = 0$. We have not attempted to construct an example where only trivial equilibria exist.

8 Second-best analysis with markets in disequilibrium: public sector pricing in a Keynesian regime*

1. Introduction

In second-best models, attention is typically focussed on a particular source of departure from economic efficiency (like taxes, a budget constraint, monopoly power, an externality, incomplete markets ...).[1] The analysis aims at defining optimal policies to cope with this source of inefficiency. It is usually assumed that the economy is otherwise competitive. This makes the problem well defined, and amenable to analysis with the powerful tools of microeconomics and general equilibrium theory. In some cases, this assumption is justified. In other cases, it is clearly inappropriate, as when imperfect competition or quantity rationing (especially of labour supply) prevail. The practical problems of defining second-best public policies in an environment where prices do not reflect economic scarcities are particularly challenging in Western Europe today.[2]

* In *The Performance of Public Enterprises: Concepts and Measurements*, M. Marchand, P. Pestieau and H. Tulkens, eds. (North-Holland, 1984); and in *European Economic Review*, 29, 3, pp. 263–301. This is a revised version of a paper prepared for the Symposium on 'Price and Quantity Controls' held in New Delhi, February 1981, on the occasion of the Golden Jubilee of the Indian Statistical Institute and presented at the Conference on the Concept and the Measurement of the Performance of Public Enterprises held at Université de Liège in September 1982. I have benefited from constructive suggestions by Paul Champsaur, V. K. Chetty, Jean P. Drèze, Maurice Marchand, Knud Munk, Pierre Pestieau and Henry Tulkens; and I am particularly indebted to Christophe Chamley and Roger Guesnerie for pointing out deficiencies in the earlier version and suggesting improvements. Responsibility for remaining errors is entirely mine. This work is part of Projet d'Action Concertée on 'Applications of Economic Decisions Theory' sponsored by the Belgian Government under contract no 80/85–12.

[1] See e.g. Guesnerie (1975a) for a survey and references.
[2] See Dermine and Drèze (1981) for an example.

To some extent, macroeconomic theory is concerned with welfare-improving public policies in non-competitive environments. And recent contributions have developed some links between macroeconomics and general equilibrium theory.[3] These developments are conducive to sharper statements of welfare objectives in macroeconomic analysis.

A beginning has also been made at extending the traditional second-best methodology to more general assumptions about the regime prevailing in the rest of the economy; see Bronsard and Wagneur (1982), Jean P. Drèze (1982), Picard (1982) or Roberts (1982).[4] Obviously, concepts are now available tò pose well-defined problems, tools and techniques are available to analyse them.

The present paper studies a simple and well-known problem, namely second-best pricing by a public sector operating under a binding budget constraint;[5] the private sector is not assumed to be in competitive equilibrium, but rather in a regime of Keynesian underemployment (excess supply of labour and of commodities, quantity rationing). The purpose of the paper is twofold. First, I wished to investigate the possibility of defining operational policies, and the nature of economic information required to implement them. (Operational implementation has been of less concern in the references given above.) Second, I wished to investigate whether and how elements of both microeconomic and macroeconomic reasoning fitted into the definition of such policies.

For the simple problem under discussion, these two questions were answered unequivocally. Operational rules can be defined, both for second-best policies and locally for welfare-improving policies. In special cases, they are even relatively simple. In general, they tend to be complex, but not more complex than similar rules in otherwise competitive environments. The informational requirements are different, however. On the one hand, welfare analysis involves reservation prices, which differ from market prices when there is quantity rationing. Reservation prices are not directly observable from market data. On the other hand, the welfare implications of price adjustments cannot be retrieved from supply and demand functions alone. Multiplier effects through aggregate income and employment must be assessed as well. General equilibrium macro-economic model building appears indispensable for second-best analysis.

---

[3] See e.g. Malinvaud (1977) or the survey paper by Drazen (1980).

[4] A complementary problem has also been treated recently by Guesnerie and Roberts (1984), namely the role of quantity constraints as instruments towards achieving second-best optimality; an example of this role is found in Section 3 below.

[5] See Boiteux (1956), Drèze (1964), pp. 27–34, or Drèze and Marchand (1976) for the neoclassical treatment of the problem.

This brings me to the second question. It was revealing for me to discover progressively how these macroeconomic multiplier effects emerged naturally from the general equilibrium analysis of the reactions by individual agents. There was no need to introduce elements of macroeconomic reasoning specifically, as they were definitely present to start with. In this context, the quest for microeconomic foundations of macroeconomics is replaced by the discovery of macroeconomic implications of microeconomics!

These answers to my two queries seemed sufficiently instructive to justify presentation of a very simple analysis. The model and main result are contained in Section 3, methodological conclusions are given in Section 5. These two sections are self-contained, and form the core of the paper. Section 2 restates the neo-classical analysis of Boiteux [1956]. Additional results and elements of comparison are presented in Section 4.

2. The Boiteux model

2.1.

Boiteux (1956) considers the problem of optimal pricing policies for a public firm, or public sector, operating under a budget constraint.[6] In order to facilitate comparisons with the next section, I specialise his model to the case of a single type of labour. There are l physical commodities, indexed $i = 1, \ldots, l$ with prices $p = (p_1, \ldots, p_l)$. The price of labour is w, and serves as a numeraire (w is fixed).

There are m households, indexed $h = 1, \ldots, m$. Household h consumes a vector x^h in R^l and supplies a quantity of labour l^h in R_+. Its preferences are represented by the strongly quasi-concave, twice continuously differentiable utility function $U^h(x^h, l^h)$. The budget constraint of household h is

$$px^h \leqslant r^h + wl^h, \tag{2.1}$$

where r^h is an 'income' resulting from transfers and shares in private profits. It is convenient to represent household preferences by means of the indirect utility function $V^h(p, w, r^h)$, written simply as $V^h(p, r^h)$ under

---

[6] The motivation for the work of Boiteux came from the problem of defining pricing policies in a nationalised firm, the French railroads, operating under increasing returns to scale. A first-best optimum, with prices equal to marginal costs, would result in a budget deficit, to be covered by taxes. The budget constraint is supposed to provide incentives for cost minimisation. See Drèze [1964], pp. 27–8, for a brief review of the issues and a few references. The same analysis applies when the budget constraint arises from the need to finance the production of public goods; see Drèze and Marchand (1976).

fixed w, and defined by

$$V^h(p, r^h) = \max_{x^h, l^h} [U^h(x^h, l^h) \mid px^h = r^h + wl^h].$$ (2.2)

In (2.2), the budget constraint is written as an equality, reflecting a monotonicity assumption. The indirect utility function is then endowed with the useful property

$$\frac{\partial V^h}{\partial p} \bigg/ \frac{\partial V^h}{\partial r^h} = -x^h = \frac{\partial r^h}{\partial p} \bigg|_{V^h}.$$ (2.3)

See Roy (1942) or Phlips (1974) for details.

The commodity demand and labour supply functions implied by (2.2) are denoted $x^h(p, r^h)$, $l^h(p, r^h)$ respectively, and assumed differentiable for convenience.[7]

There are n private firms, indexed $j = 1, \ldots, n$. Firm j produces a vector of commodities y^j in R^l, using a quantity of labour l^j in R_+. Its technology is defined by a strongly convex production set $Y^j \subset R^l \times R_+$, containing the origin. The efficient boundary of that set is implicitly defined by a differentiable, convex function expressing the minimal labour requirement l^j as a function of the output vector y^j, namely $l^j(y^j)$. The profits of firm j are

$$\Pi^j = py^j - wl^j(y^j).$$ (2.4)

Profit maximisation at given prices defines the supply functions $y^j(p)$ and the labour demand function $l^j(y^j(p)) = l^j(p)$. They are assumed differentiable[7] and satisfy

$$p\frac{\partial y^j}{\partial p} - w\frac{\partial l^j}{\partial p} = 0.$$ (2.5)

The public sector produces a vector of commodities z in R^l, using a quantity of labour l^z in R_+. No convexity assumption is made on the production set of the public sector. The efficient boundary of that set is implicitly defined by the differentiable function $l^z(z)$ defining the minimal labour requirement l^z as a function of the output vector z.

The public sector is subject to the budget constraint

$$\Phi =_{\text{def}} pz - wl^z(z) \geqslant b,$$ (2.6)

where b is some given number.

---

[7] See the comments on this assumption in Section 4.3.

The model is closed by imposing the market clearing conditions

$$\sum_h x^h(p, r^h) - \sum_j y^j(p) - z \leqslant 0 \tag{2.7}$$

$$\sum_h l^h(p, r^h) - \sum_j l^j(p) - l^z(z) = 0 \tag{2.8}$$

and by relating the household incomes to profits in the private firms and the public sector. Note that conditions (2.7)–(2.8) imply by aggregation

$$\sum_h r^h - \sum_j (py^j - wl^j) - (pz - wl^z) \leqslant 0. \tag{2.9}$$

In a private ownership economy, business profits are redistributed to households according to given ownership fractions $\theta^{hj} \geqslant 0$, $h = 1, \ldots, m$, $j = 1, \ldots, n$, satisfying $\sum_h \theta^{hj} = 1$ for all j. It is natural to specify similarly that the public budget (positive or negative) is shared among households according to given fractions β^h, $\sum_h \beta^h = 1$. One may think of β^h as defining the marginal share of household h in the public budget; indeed, it would make no difference to the analysis if the contribution of household h were defined as $b_0^h + \beta^h(pz - wl^z - b_0)$ where $b_0 = \sum_h b_0^h$ is some arbitrary number.

On this basis, r^h is defined by

$$r^h = \sum_j \theta^{hj}[py^j(p) - wl^j(p)] + \beta^h[pz - wl^z(z)], \quad h = 1, \ldots, m. \tag{2.10}$$

Adding the conditions (2.10) over h yields (2.9). Also when the conditions (2.7) hold with equality, then (2.7) and (2.10) together imply (2.8) – as could be expected from Walras' law.

The problem of defining a Pareto-optimal public policy may then be stated as

(P1) $\max_{p,z} \sum_h \lambda^h V^h(p, r^h)$ subject to (2.6), (2.7) and (2.10)

where the non-negative vector $\lambda = (\lambda^1, \ldots, \lambda^m)$ reflects distributive goals (together with some chosen representation of household preferences in the functions V^h).

2.2

First-order necessary conditions for problem (P1) are summarized in the following:

PROPOSITION 1

At an interior solution of Problem (P1), there exists a multiplier $\rho \geqslant 0$, such that

$$\sum_h \lambda^h \frac{\partial V^h}{\partial r^h}\left[x^h - \sum_j \theta^{hj}\frac{d\Pi^j}{dp} - \beta^h\frac{d\Phi}{dp}\right] = \rho\frac{d\Phi}{dp}, \tag{2.11}$$

where $\dfrac{d\Pi^j}{dp} = y^j$ *and*

$$\frac{d\Phi}{dp} = \frac{z + \left(p - w\frac{\partial l^z}{\partial z}\right)\left[\sum_h\left(\frac{\partial x^h}{\partial p} + \frac{\partial x^h}{\partial r^h}\sum_j \theta^{hj}y^j\right) - \sum_j \frac{\partial y^j}{\partial p}\right]}{1 - \left(p - w\frac{\partial l^z}{\partial z}\right)\sum_h \beta^h\frac{\partial x^h}{\partial r^h}}; \tag{2.12}$$

if $\Phi > b$ *at the solution, then* $\rho = 0$.

PROOF

Substituting from (2.10) for r^h in the maximand, the Lagrangean of problem (P1) is

$$\Lambda = \sum_h \lambda^h V^h(p, \sum_j \theta^{hj}(py^j(p) - wl^j(p)) + \beta^h(pz - wl^z(z)))$$

$$- \mu(\sum_h x^h(p, \sum_j \theta^{hj}(py^j(p) - wl^j(p)) + \beta^h(pz - wl^z(z))) - \sum_j(y^j(p)) - z)$$

$$- \rho(b - pz - wl^z(z)). \tag{2.13}$$

The first-order conditions are – using (2.3) and (2.5) –

$$\frac{\partial \Lambda}{\partial p} = \sum_h \lambda^h \frac{\partial V^h}{\partial r^h}(-x^h + \sum_j \theta^{hj}y^j + \beta^h z)$$

$$- \mu\left[\sum_h\left(\frac{\partial x^h}{\partial p} + \frac{\partial x^h}{\partial r^h}(\sum_j \theta^{hj}y^j + \beta^h z)\right) - \sum_j \frac{\partial y^j}{\partial p}\right] + \rho z = 0; \tag{2.14}$$

$$\frac{\partial \Lambda}{\partial z} = \sum_h \lambda^h \frac{\partial V^h}{\partial r^h}\beta^h\left(p - w\frac{\partial l^z}{\partial z}\right)$$

$$+ \mu\left[1 - \sum_h \frac{\partial x^h}{\partial r^h}\beta^h\left(p - w\frac{\partial l^z}{\partial z}\right)\right] + \rho\left(p - w\frac{\partial l^z}{\partial z}\right) = 0. \tag{2.15}$$

Conditions (2.15) can be solved explicitly for

$$
\mu = -\frac{\left[\sum_h \lambda^h \dfrac{\partial V^h}{\partial r^h}\beta^h + \rho\right]\left(p - w\dfrac{\partial l^z}{\partial z}\right)}{1 - \left(p - w\dfrac{\partial l^z}{\partial z}\right)\sum_h \beta^h \dfrac{\partial x^h}{\partial r^h}}.
\tag{2.16}
$$

Substituting from (2.16) into (2.14) and collecting terms yields

$$
\sum_h \lambda^h \frac{\partial V^h}{\partial r^h}(x^h - \sum_j \theta^{hj}y^j) = z\left[\rho + \sum_h \beta^h\left(\lambda^h \frac{\partial V^h}{\partial r^h} - \mu\frac{\partial x^h}{\partial r^h}\right)\right]
$$

$$
- \mu\left[\sum_h\left(\frac{\partial x^h}{\partial p} + \frac{\partial x^h}{\partial r^h}\sum_j \theta^{hj}y^j\right) - \sum_j \frac{\partial y^j}{\partial p}\right]
$$

$$
= \frac{\left[\sum_h \lambda^h \dfrac{\partial V^h}{\partial r^h}\beta^h + \rho\right]\left[z + \left(p - w\dfrac{\partial l^z}{\partial z}\right)\left(\sum_h \dfrac{\partial x^h}{\partial p} + \sum_h \dfrac{\partial x^h}{\partial r^h}\sum_j \theta^{hj}y^j - \sum_j \dfrac{\partial y^j}{\partial p}\right)\right]}{1 - \left(p - w\dfrac{\partial l^z}{\partial z}\right)\sum_h \beta^h \dfrac{\partial x^h}{\partial r^h}},
\tag{2.17}
$$

which is the same as (2.11)–(2.12). That $\rho = 0$ when $\Phi > b$ at the solution reflects complementary slackness.   QED

When the budget constraint of the public sector is not binding ($\rho = 0$), the left-hand side of (2.11) should be equal to zero. These conditions then state that the net effect on the real income of households of a small change in p should vanish, when real incomes are weighted by the terms $\lambda^h \partial V^h/\partial r^h$ reflecting distributive goals. Indeed, a change in p affects the real income of household h directly through the price level – a unit increase in p_i being equivalent to a loss of nominal income in the amount x_i^h – and indirectly through the 'property and transfer income' $\sum_j \theta^{hj}\Pi^j + \beta^h\Phi$. The effects of a change in p on Π^j and on Φ are asymmetrical, because $p - w\,\partial l^j/\partial y^j = 0$ for all j. It is noteworthy that the effect of a change in p on Φ in (2.12) is a 'final' effect, taking into account the income effects through the Π^j's (in the numerator) and the multiplier effect through Φ itself (via the denominator).[8]

When $\rho = 0$, conditions (2.11) depart from marginal cost pricing on distributive grounds alone. Indeed, if the weights $\lambda^h \partial V^h / \partial r^h$ were equal, reflecting a form of endorsement of the resulting income distribution,[9] then (2.11) would reduce to

$$\sum_h x^h - \sum_j y^j - \frac{d\Phi}{dp} = z - \frac{d\Phi}{dp} = 0. \tag{2.18}$$

Setting $p = w \, \partial l^z / \partial z$ in (2.12) would entail $d\Phi/dp = z$, satisfying (2.18).

When the budget constraint of the public sector is binding ($\rho > 0$), conditions (2.11) assert that the (marginal) costs to households of an increase in p (as measured by the left-hand side) should be proportional to the (marginal) benefits to the public sector, $d\Phi/dp$; the factor of proportionality (ρ) being adjusted so as to satisfy the constraint.[10]

2.3.

When lump-sum transfers of income among households are introduced as a policy option in problem (P1), first-order conditions are simplified on two grounds. First, distributive goals are pursued through transfers, so that first-order conditions are freed from that aspect. Second, the transfers implicitly redistribute all business profits as well as the public budget. As a consequence, the income effects associated with private

---

[8] This multiplier effect is not mentioned in the literature, because conditions (2.11) may be stated alternatively as

$$\sum_h \lambda^h \frac{\partial V^h}{\partial r^h} \left(x^h - \sum_j \theta^{hj} \frac{d\Pi^j}{dp} \right) = \hat{\rho} \frac{d\Phi}{dp}$$

with

$$\hat{\rho} = \left(\sum_h \lambda^h \frac{\partial V^h}{\partial r^h} \beta^h + \rho \right) \bigg/ \left[1 - \left(p - w \frac{\partial l^z}{\partial z} \right) \sum_h \beta^h \frac{\partial x^h}{\partial r^h} \right].$$

When interest is centred on situations where the budget constraint is binding, it suffices to find $\hat{\rho}$ such that $\Phi = b$.

[9] The endorsement consists in not favouring further transfers of consumption, under unchanged production levels; as distinct from transfers of disposable incomes, which would affect demand, hence production and prices.

[10] It is readily verified that formula (2.11) is the same as formula (5.21) in Drèze and Marchand (1976), where the Boiteux results using lump-sum transfers are also recorded. The cost-benefit interpretation of second-best results is stressed and discussed in Jean P. Drèze (1982).

profits and the multiplier effects associated with the public budget no longer appear in the first-order conditions, but the price derivatives $\partial x^h/\partial p$ are replaced by the *compensated* price derivatives $\partial x^h/\partial p + x^h\, \partial x^h/\partial r^h =_{\text{def}} \partial \hat{x}^h/\partial p$.

Denoting the transfers by t^h, $h = 1,\ldots,m$, the new problem is:

(P2) $\displaystyle \max_{p,z,t^h} \sum_h \lambda^h V^h(p, r^h + t^h)$

subject to (2.6), (2.7), (2.10) and

$$\sum_h t^h = 0 \qquad (\tau). \tag{2.19}$$

Proposition 2

At an interior solution of problem (P2), *there exists a multiplier* $\hat{\rho} \geqslant 0$ *such that*

$$x - \frac{d\Pi}{dp} - \frac{d\hat{\Phi}}{dp} = \hat{\rho}\frac{d\hat{\Phi}}{dp}, \tag{2.20}$$

where $\dfrac{d\hat{\Phi}}{dp} = z + \left(p - w\dfrac{\partial l^z}{\partial z}\right)\dfrac{\partial \hat{z}}{\partial p}$; *if* $\Phi > b$ *at the solution, then* $\hat{\rho} = 0$.

Proof

The first-order conditions (2.14)–(2.15) of problem (P1) are not modified by the addition of constraints (2.19). The first-order condition for t^h is

$$\frac{\partial \Lambda}{\partial t^h} = \lambda^h \frac{\partial V^h}{\partial r^h} - \mu \frac{\partial x^h}{\partial r^h} - \tau = 0. \tag{2.21}$$

(Note that $\tau > 0$ by monotonicity of preferences.)

Substituting from (2.21) into (2.15), then into (2.14), yields

$$\frac{\partial \Lambda}{\partial z} = (\tau + \rho)\left(p - w\frac{\partial l^z}{\partial z}\right) + \mu = 0, \quad \mu = -(\tau + \rho)\left(p - w\frac{\partial l^z}{\partial z}\right); \tag{2.22}$$

$$\frac{\partial \Lambda}{\partial p} = -\sum_h \lambda^h \frac{\partial V^h}{\partial r^h} x^h + \tau x - \mu\left(\sum_h \frac{\partial x^h}{\partial p} - \sum_j \frac{\partial y^j}{\partial p}\right) + \rho z = 0$$

$$= -\left(\tau x + \mu \sum_h \frac{\partial x^h}{\partial r^h} x^h\right) + \tau x - \mu\left(\sum_h \frac{\partial x^h}{\partial p} - \sum_j \frac{\partial y^j}{\partial p}\right) + \rho z$$

$$= (\tau + \rho)\left(p - w\frac{\partial l^z}{\partial z}\right)\left[\sum_h\left(\frac{\partial x^h}{\partial p} + x^h\frac{\partial x^h}{\partial r^h}\right) - \sum_j \frac{\partial y^j}{\partial p}\right] + \rho z = 0.$$
(2.23)

Noting that $x - \dfrac{d\Pi}{dp} = x - y = z$, this last condition is equivalent to

(2.20) with $\hat{\rho} = \rho/\tau$, under the obvious definition of $\partial \hat{z}/\partial p$. That $\rho = 0$ when $\Phi > b$ at the solution reflects complementary slackness.   QED

An alternative statement of conditions (2.20), after cancelling z between $x - d\Pi/dp$ and $d\hat{\Phi}/dp$, is

$$-\left(p - w\frac{\partial l^z}{\partial z}\right)\frac{\partial \hat{z}}{\partial p} = \hat{\rho}\frac{d\hat{\Phi}}{dp}.$$
(2.20′)

The left-hand side of (2.20′) measures the *cost* to households of a *compensated* change in p, account being taken of the fact that the compensation (x) is paid out of private profits $(d\Pi/dp)$ and the part of the public budget reflecting the direct effect of the price change (z). That cost is then simply minus the change in Φ net of the direct effect of the price change, i.e. *the cost is minus the change in household incomes net of the compensation.* This seems to provide a slightly contrived, but still natural, interpretation of proposition 2 in cost-benefit terms.

2.4.

More recently, welfare economists have become interested in the related problem of defining, for an arbitrary initial position satisfying all the constraints, *directions of policy adjustments*, along which infinitesimal moves are *welfare improving*, see in particular Guesnerie (1977) and Guesnerie and Tirole (1981), where this problem is labelled 'the reform problem'.

In the case of problem (P1) the reform problem is easily stated: find dp such that

$$\Phi + \frac{d\Phi}{dp}dp \geqslant b,$$
(2.24)

$$\sum_h \lambda^h \frac{\partial V^h}{\partial r^h}\left(x^h - \sum_j \theta^{hj}y^j - \beta^h \frac{d\Phi}{dp}\right)dp < 0. \tag{2.25}$$

Condition (2.24) corresponds to budgetary feasibility and condition (2.25) to welfare improvement. Technological feasibility is not an issue here, because the marginal cost of the change in z associated with dp is included in the term $(d\Phi/dp)dp$.

If $\Phi > b$ at the initial position, then condition (2.24) is redundant. For each $i = 1,\ldots,l$, considered separately, one may ascertain the sign of

$$\sum_h \lambda^h \frac{\partial V^h}{\partial r^h}\left(x_i^h - \sum_j \theta^{hj}y_i^j - \beta \frac{d\Phi}{dp_i}\right) = {}_{\text{def}} -\frac{d\Lambda}{dp_i}. \tag{2.26}$$

If these terms are equal to zero for all i, the initial position is an optimum. Otherwise, directions of welfare improvement are readily identified (choose dp_i with a sign opposite to that of $-d\Lambda/dp_i$).

If $\Phi = b$ at the initial position, then attention is restricted to adjustments dp such that $(d\Phi/dp)dp \geqslant 0$. Directions of welfare improvement are again readily identified, unless the terms (2.26) were collinear with $d\Phi/dp$, in which case the initial position is an optimum.

A direction of welfare improvement is naturally interpreted as a direction along which the cost to households of price inflation $x^h\,dp$ is more than offset by the income effect $(\sum_j \theta^{hj}y^j + \beta^h\,d\Phi/dp)\,dp$, on the (weighted) average; i.e. the change in income is more than sufficient to permit an unchanged consumption, at the new prices.

When $\Phi = b$ and $(d\Phi/dp)dp = 0$ along a direction of welfare improvement, then the cost to households of price inflation should be more than offset by the income effect through private profits. If distributional aspects were neglected, the condition for welfare improvement would reduce to

$$(\sum_h x^h - \sum_j y^j)dp = z\,dp < 0. \tag{2.27}$$

Since $d\Phi/dp \propto z + (p - w\,\partial l^z/\partial z)\,dz/dp$, the conditions $(d\Phi/dp)dp = 0$ *and* $z\,dp < 0$ together imply

$$\left(p - w\frac{\partial l^z}{\partial z}\right)\frac{dz}{dp}\,dp > 0, \tag{2.28}$$

which says that the market value of the induced change in public production exceeds its marginal cost. This interpretation is also applicable to (2.20′).

3. A simple Keynesian model

3.1.

For ease of exposition, I consider a very simple Keynesian model, where:

(i) the private and public sectors supply disjoint sets of consumption goods, using a single type of labour as their only variable primary input;

(ii) labour and privately produced goods are traded at given fixed prices, and excess supply prevails on these markets;

(iii) the numeraire, in terms of which prices are defined, is a non-produced, always desired, never rationed commodity (a 'money'). The extension to other regime specifications is briefly discussed in Section 4.3. In Section 3.1, I introduce the notation, and discuss the assumptions on market clearing, consumer decisions and the budget constraint. In Section 3.2, I discuss existence of Keynesian equilibria and I give a simple example. Second-best pricing rules without lump-sum transfers of income are derived in Section 3.3. Local welfare improvements are discussed in Section 3.4.

There are $1 + l + k + 1$ commodities. The first commodity is the non-produced numeraire, with price $p_0 \equiv 1$. The next l commodities are supplied by the private sector. Their prices $p_y = (p_{y1}, \ldots, p_{yl})$ are exogenously given and fixed. The next k commodities are supplied by the public sector, which sets their prices $p_z = (p_{z1}, \ldots, p_{zk})$. The last commodity is homogeneous labour. The wage rate w is exogenously given and fixed. I also write $p = (1, p_y, p_z, w)$ for the price system.

Household h consumes a quantity m^h of the numeraire commodity, a vector of privately produced commodities y^h in R^l_+ and a vector of publicly produced commodities z^h in R^k_+; it supplies a quantity of labour l^h in R_+. I also write $x^h = (m^h, y^h, z^h, -l^h)$ for the consumption (and labour supply) of household h. The preferences of household h are represented by the twice continuously differentiable utility function $U^h(x^h)$, monotonic and strongly quasi-concave in m^h, y^h and z^h. The budget constraint of household h is

$$px^h = m^h + p_y y^h + p_z z^h - wl^h \leqslant r^h. \tag{3.1}$$

The corresponding indirect utility function is $V^h(p, r^h)$.

The private sector is treated as an aggregate, in order to avoid the complication of specifying how the aggregate supply constraint is projected on individual firms. The private sector supplies a demand-determined vector of goods y in R^l_+, using a technology-determined quantity of labour l^y in R_+, where

$$y = \sum_h y^h, \quad l^y = l^y(y). \tag{3.2}$$

The function l^y is convex and twice continuously differentiable. Private profits are

$$\Pi = p_y y - w l^y. \tag{3.3}$$

The vector of marginal costs is denoted $m_y = w \dfrac{\partial l^y}{\partial y}$. The assumption of excess supply is equivalent to

$$p_y - m_y(y) \geqslant 0. \tag{3.4}$$

This assumption is understood as holding: (i) at an arbitrary starting point, where one seeks to define directions of welfare improvement; or (ii) at a second-best optimum, which one seeks to characterise. Of course, one would also like to treat a deeper question, namely: given an arbitrary starting point where excess supply prevails, and given optimal feasible policies, will the resulting second-best optimum still be characterised by excess supply (of labour and privately produced commodities)? That deeper question, treated in Guesnerie (1981), is not taken up here – except for the peripheral comments in Sections 3.2 and 4.3.[11]

The public sector supplies a vector of goods z in R^k_+, using a technology-determined quantity of labour l^z in R_+, where

$$z = \sum_h z^h, \quad l^z = l^z(z). \tag{3.5}$$

The function l^z is twice continuously differentiable. No convexity assumption is made. The vector of marginal costs is denoted $m_z = w \, \partial l^z / \partial z$. The public sector is subject to the budget constraint

$$\Phi = p_z z - w l^z \geqslant b, \tag{3.6}$$

where Φ denotes net public revenue.

[11] Under a constant returns technology, (3.4) holds globally whenever it holds locally. But constant returns is a long-run phenomenon, whereas rigid prices are a short-run phenomenon.

Aggregate labour demand L is defined by

$$L = l^y(y) + l^z(z). \tag{3.7}$$

The supply of labour by household h is subject to the quantity constraint

$$l^h \leqslant \bar{l}^h(L). \tag{3.8}$$

This constraint is understood to reflect both (i) underemployment arising from imbalance between labour demand and labour supply; and (ii) institutional rigidities preventing an employed person from choosing freely the number of hours worked.

Household h maximises $U^h(x^h)$ subject to (3.1) and (3.8). It simplifies exposition drastically, at very little cost in realism, if we assume that the constraint (3.8) is strictly binding for all h.[12] In particular, this preserves the differentiability of individual demand functions, thereby avoiding the need to use the heavier formalism of generalised gradients. The more general case is reviewed in Section 4.3.

The approach taken here consists in assuming that the individual constraints $\bar{l}^h(L)$ are adjusted in a continuously differentiable way, with

$$\sum_h l^h = \sum_h \bar{l}^h(L) = L, \quad \sum_h \frac{\partial l^h}{\partial L} = \sum_h \frac{\partial \bar{l}^h}{\partial L} = 1. \tag{3.9}$$

No precise specification of the individual constraints is introduced, and the individual decision x^h is written directly as a function of aggregate employment L:

$$x^h = x^h(p, r^h, L). \tag{3.10}$$

The function x^h consists of a constrained labour supply $l^h = \bar{l}^h(L)$, inelastic to (p, r^h), and a consumption demand $m^h(p, r^h; \bar{l}^h)$, $y^h(p, r^h; \bar{l}^h)$, $z^h(p, r^h; \bar{l}^h)$ endowed with standard properties. Indeed, consumption demand maximises U^h subject to (3.1), with l^h fixed. In particular, it satisfies

$$\frac{\partial m^h}{\partial r^h} + p_y \frac{\partial y^h}{\partial r^h} + p_z \frac{\partial z^h}{\partial r^h} = 1;$$

$$\frac{\partial m^h}{\partial p_z} + p_y \frac{\partial y^h}{\partial p_z} + p_z \frac{\partial z^h}{\partial p_z} + z^h = 0. \tag{3.11}$$

---

[12] Strictly, in the sense that

$$l^h = \bar{l}^h \quad \text{and} \quad \frac{\partial l^h}{\partial \bar{l}^h} = 1, \quad \frac{\partial l^h}{\partial p} = 0, \quad \frac{\partial l^h}{\partial r^h} = 0.$$

Also, m^h, y^h and z^h are differentiable with respect to $l^h = \bar{l}^h(L)$, hence with respect to L, with

$$\frac{\partial m^h}{\partial L} + p_y \frac{\partial y^h}{\partial L} + p_z \frac{\partial z^h}{\partial L} = w \frac{\partial l^h}{\partial L}. \tag{3.12}$$

The assumption of excess supply of labour is conveniently stated, if one defines

$$\frac{\partial U^h}{\partial r^h} = \frac{\partial U^h}{\partial x^h} \frac{\partial x^h}{\partial r^h} \geq 0, \quad w_R^h = -\frac{\partial U^h}{\partial l^h} \bigg/ \frac{\partial U^h}{\partial r^h}. \tag{3.13}$$

Thus, w_R^h is the 'reservation wage' of household h. Since no assumption is made about the sign of $\partial U^h/\partial l^h$, the sign of w_R^h is also indeterminate. This allows for the possibility that an unemployed person would prefer to work, even at no gain in disposable income. Excess supply of labour means

$$w \geq w_R^h. \tag{3.14}$$

A *compensated* change in the constraint $\bar{l}^h$ is a change $d\bar{l}^h$ accompanied by an income transfer $(w_R^h - w)d\bar{l}^h$, resulting in an unchanged utility level. Using the symbol $\hat{x}^h$ for compensated demand functions, I define[13]

$$\frac{\partial \hat{m}^h}{\partial L} = \frac{\partial m^h}{\partial \bar{l}^h} \frac{\partial \bar{l}^h}{\partial L} + (w_R^h - w)\frac{\partial \bar{l}^h}{\partial L}\frac{\partial m^h}{\partial r^h} = \underset{\text{def}}{=} \frac{\partial m^h}{\partial L} + (w_R^h - w)\frac{\partial \bar{l}^h}{\partial L}\frac{\partial m^h}{\partial r^h};$$

$$\frac{\partial \hat{y}^h}{\partial L} = \frac{\partial y^h}{\partial L} + (w_R^h - w)\frac{\partial \bar{l}^h}{\partial L}\frac{\partial y^h}{\partial r^h}, \quad \frac{\partial \hat{z}^h}{\partial L} = \frac{\partial z^h}{\partial L} + (w_R^h - w)\frac{\partial \bar{l}^h}{\partial L}\frac{\partial z^h}{\partial r^h};$$

$$\frac{\partial \hat{y}}{\partial L} = \sum_h \frac{\partial \hat{y}^h}{\partial L}, \quad \frac{\partial \hat{z}}{\partial L} = \sum_h \frac{\partial \hat{z}^h}{\partial L}. \tag{3.15}$$

Finally, I define

$$\bar{w}_R = \sum_h w_R^h \frac{\partial \bar{l}^h}{\partial L}, \tag{3.16}$$

[13] If preferences were additive between l^h on the one hand, (m^h, y^h, z^h) on the other hand, then

$$\frac{\partial \hat{m}^h}{\partial L} = w_R^h \frac{\partial \bar{l}^h}{\partial L}\frac{\partial m^h}{\partial r^h}, \quad \frac{\partial \hat{y}^h}{\partial L} = w_R^h \frac{\partial \bar{l}^h}{\partial L}\frac{\partial y^h}{\partial r^h}, \quad \frac{\partial \hat{z}^h}{\partial L} = w_R^h \frac{\partial \bar{l}^h}{\partial L}\frac{\partial z^h}{\partial r^h} \quad \text{and}$$

$$\frac{\partial \hat{m}^h}{\partial L} + p_y \frac{\partial \hat{y}^h}{\partial L} + p_z \frac{\partial \hat{z}^h}{\partial L} = w_R^h \frac{\partial \bar{l}^h}{\partial L}.$$

the aggregate, or average 'reservation wage'; it reflects both the individual reservation wages and the projection on individual households of the changes in overall employment.

The indirect utility function should now be written as $V^h(p, r^h, \bar{l}^h(L))$ $=_{\text{def}} V^h(p, r^h, L)$, with

$$\frac{\partial V^h}{\partial L} = \frac{\partial U^h}{\partial l^h}\frac{\partial \bar{l}^h}{\partial L} + w\frac{\partial V^h}{\partial r^h}\frac{\partial \bar{l}^h}{\partial L} = (w - w^h_R)\frac{\partial V^h}{\partial r^h}\frac{\partial \bar{l}^h}{\partial L}. \tag{3.17}$$

As for r^h, it is here defined as

$$r^h = m^h_0 + \theta^h \Pi + \beta^h \Phi, \tag{3.18}$$

where $m^h_0 > 0$ is the initial holding of the numeraire commodity.

3.2.

For a given wage w, vector of private sector prices p_y, and rationing scheme $\bar{l}(L)$ satisfying (3.9), a *Keynesian equilibrium* for the economy just described is defined by a vector of public sector prices p_z and an m-tuple of consumption vectors $x^h = (m^h, y^h, z^h, l^h)$ such that, if we define r^h as in (3.18) and Π, Φ and L as in (3.3), (3.6) and (3.7):

$$\Pi = p_y\sum_h y^h - wl^y(\sum_h y^h) \tag{3.3'}$$

$$\Phi = p_z\sum_h z^h - wl^z(\sum_h z^h) \tag{3.6'}$$

$$L = l^y(\sum_h y^h) + l^z(\sum_h z^h) \tag{3.7'}$$

then

(i) $x^h = x^h(p, r^h, L) = x^h(p, m^h_0 + \theta^h \Pi + \beta^h \Phi, L)$ with $l^h = \bar{l}^h(L)$;

(ii) $\sum_h m^h = \sum_h m^h_0$ and $\sum_h l^h = L$;

(iii)   the inequality constraints (3.4), (3.6) and (3.14) are satisfied:

$$p_y - w\frac{\partial l^y}{\partial y} \geqslant 0, \quad \Phi \geqslant b \quad \text{and, for all } h, \quad w - w^h_R \geqslant 0.$$

It may be noted that condition (ii) is implied by the other conditions, since (3.9) implies $\sum_h l^h = L$ and (3.18) then implies

$$\sum_h m^h + p_y \sum_h y^h + p_z \sum_h z^h - w \sum_h l^h = \sum_h m^h + \Pi + \Phi$$

$$= \sum_h r^h = \sum_h m_0^h + \Pi + \Phi. \qquad (3.19)$$

Does such an equilibrium exist? This question is of course far from trivial. Even in the absence of a public sector, it is a difficult question, to which a partial answer only can be given. The partial answer comes from the theory of 'supply-constrained equilibria', as developed initially by van der Laan (1980) and extended more recently by van der Laan (1982, 1984), Kurz (1982) and Dehez and Drèze (1984).

A 'supply-constrained equilibrium' is an equilibrium with quantity rationing of supply only. For the private sector of the economy described in Section 3.1, a supply-constrained equilibrium is almost the same as a Keynesian equilibrium. The main difference is that, under the original definition by van der Laan (1980), supply of the numeraire commodity 0 could be rationed (in which case $p_{yj} = m_{yj}$ for some produced commodity j). Under this proviso, and under the additional assumption that each household initially holds a strictly positive quantity of every commodity, van der Laan (1980) proves the existence of a supply-constrained equilibrium for any given (fixed) price vector.[14] Without additional assumptions,[15] Dehez and Drèze (1984) prove that, for an arbitrary fixed vector of relative prices p_y/w, and for an arbitrary positive lower bound w_0 on w, there exists a supply-constrained equilibrium with $w \geqslant w_0$ and no rationing of the numeraire – i.e. there exists a Keynesian equilibrium with $w \geqslant w_0$.

Both of these results can be extended to the economy with a public sector described in Section 3.1, under the additional assumptions that $l(z)$

---

[14] The analysis of van der Laan (1980) is confined to a pure exchange economy, but the extension to production raises no difficulty, as can be inferred from the treatment in Dehez and Drèze (1984). Also, the theorem in van der Laan (1980) asserts only that supply of some commodity is not constrained to zero; that supply of some commodity is actually unconstrained was established later by van der Laan (1982).

[15] Although Dehez and Drèze assume strictly positive initial holdings of all commodities, that assumption is used only to guarantee the continuity of demand functions, which results here from positive holdings of the numeraire ($m_0^h > 0$) and positive prices p_y.

is convex and $b = 0$.[16] The result of van der Laan will then imply existence of a supply-constrained equilibrium, for given p_y and w, at *all* prices p_z of the public sector. The result of Dehez and Drèze on the other hand will imply that, for an arbitrary fixed vector of relative prices p_y/w and p_z/w, and an arbitrary $w_0 > 0$, there exists a Keynesian equilibrium with $w \geqslant w_0$.

These extensions remain incompletely satisfactory, however. Using van der Laan's approach, one needs to assume strictly positive initial holdings of all commodities, and it could be that households are rationed in their supplies of some commodity other than labour – contrary to the spirit of a Keynesian equilibrium. Using the approach of Dehez and Drèze, one cannot conclude that there exists a Keynesian equilibrium at *all* prices p_z of the public sector, for some *fixed* $w \geqslant w_0$.

It seems likely that further research will overcome these shortcomings. In the meantime, some comfort is derived from the observation that a Keynesian equilibrium exists, at some w, for the private sector of the economy described in Section 3.1.[17] If the public sector forms a 'small' part of the economy, the presumption that a Keynesian equilibrium will also exist at all prices p_z is not unreasonable.

Finally, it should be noted that a supply-constrained equilibrium could possibly be competitive – with either Walrasian or non-Walrasian prices.

Being unable to present satisfactory existence results at this stage, I shall motivate the sequel by giving a very simple example, where an equilibrium with involuntary unemployment exists, at *all* admissible public sector prices.

Consider an economy with a single household, a numeraire, one good produced by the public sector and labour. Household preferences are

---

[16] The extension consists in treating the public sector as a firm which maximises $p_z z$ subject to the constraints $z \in Z$, $p_z z - w l^z(z) \geqslant b$ and $z \leqslant \sum_h z^h(.)$. Convexity of Z is required for the continuity (with respect to $\sum_h z^h$) of the constraint set. It is not surprising that reliance on a standard existence proof requires convexity of the production set. For a new approach to the existence problem, see Dierker, Guesnerie and Neuefeind (1985). The condition $b = 0$ guarantees that a feasible z exists (which might fail to be the case when $b > 0$); for the approach followed by Dehez and Drèze it implies that the constraint set depends only on p_z/w and is independent of w. Although the assumption that Z is convex runs against the initial motivation of the problem, the presence of excess supply in the private sector introduces other distortions under which second-best pricing by the public sector still poses an interesting problem, even under convexity – as the example below clearly reveals.

[17] That is also the reason for introducing explicitly a numeraire, which is never rationed, and of which households hold positive endowments. (That it is not produced is unimportant, since it would not be produced anyhow at high values of w.) I am grateful to Christophe Chamley for pointing out the shortcomings of my earlier formulation, where I had neglected that precaution.

represented by the utility function

$$U = m + 2z^{1/2} - \frac{l^2}{2}. \tag{3.20}$$

Given the price vector $p = (1, p_z, w)$, the endowment m_0 and the income r, the unconstrained demand and supply functions are given by

$$l = w, \quad z = \frac{1}{p_z^2}, \quad m = m_0 + w^2 + r - \frac{1}{p_z}, \tag{3.21}$$

for all parameter values at which non-negativity constraints are not binding. Then,

$$V(p, r) = m_0 + r + \frac{w^2}{2} + \frac{1}{p_z}. \tag{3.22}$$

The production set of the public sector is defined by

$$l^z(z) = z. \tag{3.23}$$

Substituting for l from (3.23) into (3.20), a first-best optimum is obtained by solving

$$\max_z m_0 + 2z^{1/2} - \frac{z^2}{2}, \quad z = 1. \tag{3.24}$$

Suppose now that the wage level is set at $w = 2$. If no budget constraint is imposed on the public sector, then

$$\Phi = p_z z - w l^z(z) = (p_z - 2)z. \tag{3.25}$$

The first best can still be achieved at $z = 1$ by setting $p_z = 1$ and letting the household choose z and l, subject to $l \leq \bar{l} = 1$ and $r = \Phi = -1$; the solution is $z = 1/p_z^2 = 1$, $l = \bar{l} = 1$, $m = m_0 + wl + r - p_z z = m_0 + 2 - 1 - 1 = m_0$. This is an instance of a Walrasian allocation sustained by non-Walrasian prices and a quantity constraint.

Suppose next that $w = 2$ and $b = 0$, so that the public sector must satisfy the constraint

$$\Phi = p_z z - w l^z(z) = (p_z - 2)z \geq 0, p_z \geq 2. \tag{3.26}$$

Recognising that $p_z \geq 2$ implies $z = 1/p_z^2 \leq 1/4$, it follows that the labour supply will be constrained by $l \leq \bar{l} = 1/p_z^2$, so that a second-best optimum is obtained by solving

$$\max_{z \leq 1/4} m_0 + 2z^{1/2} - \frac{z^2}{2}, \quad z = \frac{1}{4}. \tag{3.27}$$

This allocation is achieved by setting $p_z = 2$, and letting the household choose z and l, subject to $l \leqslant \bar{l} = 1/4$, $r = \Phi = 0$; the solution is $z = 1/p_z^2 = 1/4$, $l = \bar{l} = 1/4$, $m = m_0 + wl + r - p_z z = m_0 + 1/2 + 0 - 1/2 = m_0$.

3.3.

The problem of second-best public sector pricing in the Keynesian environment of Section 3.1 is[18]:

(P3) $$\max_{p_z, \Pi, \Phi, L} \sum_h \lambda^h V^h[p, m_0^h + \theta^h \Pi + \beta^h \Phi, L] = \sum_h \lambda^h V^h[p, \Pi, \Phi, L]$$

subject to

$$\Pi - p_y \sum_h y^h(p, \Pi, \Phi, L) + wl^y(\sum_h y^h(p, \Pi, \Phi, L)) = 0 \quad (\pi) \quad (3.3)$$

$$\Phi - p_z \sum_h z^h(p, \Pi, \Phi, L) + wl^z(\sum_h z^h(p, \Pi, \Phi, L)) = 0 \quad (\phi) \quad (3.6)$$

$$L - l^y(\sum_h y^h(p, \Pi, \Phi, L)) - l^z(\sum_h z^h(p, \Pi, \Phi, L)) = 0 \quad (\nu) \quad (3.7)$$

$$b - \Phi \leqslant 0 \quad (\rho). \quad (3.6')$$

Proposition 3

At an interior solution of problem (P3), there exists a multiplier $\rho \geqslant 0$, such that

$$\sum_h \lambda^h \frac{\partial V^h}{\partial r^h} \left[z^h - \theta^h \frac{d\Pi}{dp_z} - \beta^h \frac{d\Phi}{dp_z} - (w - w_R^h) \frac{\partial \bar{l}^h}{\partial L} \frac{dL}{dp_z} \right] = \rho \frac{d\Phi}{dp_z},$$

(3.28)

where

$$\begin{bmatrix} \dfrac{d\Pi}{dp_z} \\[2ex] \dfrac{d\Phi}{dp_z} \\[2ex] \dfrac{dL}{dp_z} \end{bmatrix} = (I - M)^{-1} \begin{bmatrix} (p_y - m_y)\dfrac{\partial y}{\partial p_z} \\[2ex] z + (p_z - m_z)\dfrac{\partial z}{\partial p_z} \\[2ex] \dfrac{\partial l^y}{\partial y}\dfrac{\partial y}{\partial p_z} + \dfrac{\partial l^z}{\partial z}\dfrac{\partial z}{\partial p_z} \end{bmatrix}, \quad (3.29)$$

[18] The formulation of the problem with Π, Φ and L as arguments, but subject to equality constraints, is a matter of technical convenience.

$$M = \begin{bmatrix} (p_y - m_y)\sum_h \dfrac{\partial y^h}{\partial r^h}\theta^h & (p_y - m_y)\sum_h \dfrac{\partial y^h}{\partial r^h}\beta^h & (p_y - m_y)\sum_h \dfrac{\partial y^h}{\partial \bar{l}^h}\dfrac{\partial \bar{l}^h}{\partial L} \\[2ex] (p_z - m_z)\sum_h \dfrac{\partial z^h}{\partial r^h}\theta^h & (p_z - m_z)\sum_h \dfrac{\partial z^h}{\partial r^h}\beta^h & (p_z - m_z)\sum_h \dfrac{\partial z^h}{\partial \bar{l}^h}\dfrac{\partial \bar{l}^h}{\partial L} \\[2ex] \dfrac{\partial l^y}{\partial y}\sum_h \dfrac{\partial y^h}{\partial r^h}\theta^h & \dfrac{\partial l^y}{\partial y}\sum_h \dfrac{\partial y^h}{\partial r^h}\beta^h & \dfrac{\partial l^y}{\partial y}\sum_h \dfrac{\partial y^h}{\partial \bar{l}^h}\dfrac{\partial \bar{l}^h}{\partial L} \\[2ex] + \dfrac{\partial l^z}{\partial z}\sum_h \dfrac{\partial z^h}{\partial r^h}\theta^h & + \dfrac{\partial l^z}{\partial z}\sum_h \dfrac{\partial z^h}{\partial r^h}\beta^h & + \dfrac{\partial l^z}{\partial z}\sum_h \dfrac{\partial z^h}{\partial \bar{l}^h}\dfrac{\partial \bar{l}^h}{\partial L} \end{bmatrix}$$

if $\Phi > b$ at the solution, then $\rho = 0$.

PROOF

The proof consists in differentiating the Lagrangean Λ of problem (P3) and eliminating unknowns by substitution.

$$\frac{\partial \Lambda}{\partial \Pi} = \sum_h \lambda^h \frac{\partial V^h}{\partial r^h}\theta^h - \pi\left[1 - \left(p_y - w\frac{\partial l^y}{\partial y}\right)\sum_h \frac{\partial y^h}{\partial r^h}\theta^h\right]$$

$$+ \phi\left(p_z - w\frac{\partial l^z}{\partial z}\right)\sum_h \frac{\partial z^h}{\partial r^h}\theta^h$$

$$+ v\left(\frac{\partial l^y}{\partial y}\sum_h \frac{\partial y^h}{\partial r^h}\theta^h + \frac{\partial l^z}{\partial z}\sum_h \frac{\partial z^h}{\partial r^h}\theta^h\right) = 0. \qquad (3.30)$$

$$\frac{\partial \Lambda}{\partial \Phi} = \sum_h \lambda^h \frac{\partial V^h}{\partial r^h}\beta^h + \pi\left(p_y - w\frac{\partial l^y}{\partial y}\right)\sum_h \frac{\partial y^h}{\partial r^h}\beta^h$$

$$- \phi\left[1 - \left(p_z - w\frac{\partial l^z}{\partial z}\right)\sum_h \frac{\partial z^h}{\partial r^h}\beta^h\right]$$

$$+ v\left(\frac{\partial l^y}{\partial y}\sum_h \frac{\partial y^h}{\partial r^h}\beta^h + \frac{\partial l^z}{\partial z}\sum_h \frac{\partial z^h}{\partial r^h}\beta^h\right) + \rho = 0. \qquad (3.31)$$

$$\frac{\partial \Lambda}{\partial L} = \sum_h \lambda^h \frac{\partial V^h}{\partial L} + \pi\left(p_y - w\frac{\partial l^y}{\partial y}\right)\sum_h \frac{\partial y^h}{\partial L} + \phi\left(p_z - w\frac{\partial l^z}{\partial z}\right)\sum_h \frac{\partial z^h}{\partial L}$$

$$- v\left(1 - \frac{\partial l^y}{\partial y}\sum_h \frac{\partial y^h}{\partial L} - \frac{\partial l^z}{\partial z}\sum_h \frac{\partial z^h}{\partial L}\right) = 0. \qquad (3.32)$$

$$(I - M') \begin{bmatrix} \pi \\ \phi \\ \nu \end{bmatrix} = \begin{bmatrix} \sum_h \lambda^h \dfrac{\partial V^h}{\partial r^h} \theta^h \\[2ex] \sum_h \lambda^h \dfrac{\partial V^h}{\partial r^h} \beta^h + \rho \\[2ex] \sum_h \lambda^h \dfrac{\partial V^h}{\partial L} \end{bmatrix} = \begin{bmatrix} \sum_h \lambda^h \dfrac{\partial V^h}{\partial r^h} \theta^h \\[2ex] \sum_h \lambda^h \dfrac{\partial V^h}{\partial r^h} \beta^h + \rho \\[2ex] \sum_h \lambda^h \dfrac{\partial V^h}{\partial r^h} (w - w_R^h) \dfrac{\partial \bar{l}^h}{\partial L} \end{bmatrix}.$$

$$(3.33)$$

$$(\pi, \phi, \nu) = \left(\sum_h \lambda^h \frac{\partial V^h}{\partial r^h} \theta^h, \sum_h \lambda^h \frac{\partial V^h}{\partial r^h} \beta^h + \rho, \right.$$

$$\left. \sum_h \lambda^h \frac{\partial V^h}{\partial r^h} (w - w_R^h) \frac{\partial \bar{l}^h}{\partial L} \right) . (I - M)^{-1}. \tag{3.34}$$

$$\frac{\partial \Lambda}{\partial p_z} = \sum_h \lambda^h \frac{\partial V^h}{\partial p_z} + \pi \left(p_y - w \frac{\partial l^y}{\partial y} \right) \sum_h \frac{\partial y^h}{\partial p_z} \tag{3.35}$$

$$+ \phi \left[z + \left(p_z - w \frac{\partial l^z}{\partial z} \right) \sum_h \frac{\partial z^h}{\partial p_z} \right]$$

$$+ \nu \left(\frac{\partial l^y}{\partial y} \sum_h \frac{\partial y^h}{\partial p_z} + \frac{\partial l^z}{\partial z} \sum_h \frac{\partial z^h}{\partial p_z} \right) = 0$$

$$= -\sum_h \lambda^h \frac{\partial V^h}{\partial r^h} z^h + (\pi, \phi, \nu) \begin{bmatrix} (p_y - m_y) \dfrac{\partial y}{\partial p_z} \\[2ex] z + (p_z - m_z) \dfrac{\partial z}{\partial p_z} \\[2ex] \dfrac{\partial l^y}{\partial y} \dfrac{\partial y}{\partial p_z} + \dfrac{\partial l^z}{\partial z} \dfrac{\partial z}{\partial p_z} \end{bmatrix}$$

$$= -\sum_h \lambda^h \frac{\partial V^h}{\partial r^h} z^h + \begin{bmatrix} \sum_h \lambda^h \dfrac{\partial V^h}{\partial r^h} \theta^h \\[2ex] \sum_h \lambda^h \dfrac{\partial V^h}{\partial r^h} \beta^h + \rho \\[2ex] \sum_h \lambda^h \dfrac{\partial V^h}{\partial r^h} (w - w_R^h) \dfrac{\partial \bar{l}^h}{\partial L} \end{bmatrix} . (I - M)^{-1} \begin{bmatrix} (p_y - m_y) \dfrac{\partial y}{\partial p_z} \\[2ex] z + (p_z - m_z) \dfrac{\partial z}{\partial p_z} \\[2ex] \dfrac{\partial l^y}{\partial y} \dfrac{\partial y}{\partial p_z} + \dfrac{\partial l^z}{\partial z} \dfrac{\partial z}{\partial p_z} \end{bmatrix}$$

$$
= -\sum_{h} \lambda^h \frac{\partial V^h}{\partial r^h} z^h + \left(\sum_{h} \lambda^h \frac{\partial V^h}{\partial r^h} \theta^h, \sum_{h} \lambda^h \frac{\partial V^h}{\partial r^h} \beta^h + \rho, \sum_{h} \lambda^h \frac{\partial V^h}{\partial r^h} (w - w_R^h) \frac{\partial \bar{l}^h}{\partial L} \right) \begin{bmatrix} \dfrac{d\Pi}{dp_z} \\[2mm] \dfrac{d\Phi}{dp_z} \\[2mm] \dfrac{dL}{dp_z} \end{bmatrix},
$$

which is the same as (3.28).

The justification for the notation $(d\Pi/dp_z, d\Phi/dp_z, dL/dp_z)$ is provided by differentiating totally the system (3.3), (3.6), (3.7):

$$
(I - M) \begin{bmatrix} d\Pi \\[2mm] d\Phi \\[2mm] dL \end{bmatrix} - \begin{bmatrix} (p_y - m_y)\dfrac{\partial y}{\partial p_z} \\[2mm] z + (p_z - m_z)\dfrac{\partial z}{\partial p_z} \\[2mm] \dfrac{\partial l^y}{\partial y}\dfrac{\partial y}{\partial p_z} + \dfrac{\partial l^z}{\partial z}\dfrac{\partial z}{\partial p_z} \end{bmatrix} dp_z = 0, \quad (3.36)
$$

which yields (3.29). That $\rho = 0$ when $\Phi > b$ at the solution reflects complementary slackness.   QED

Let us first interpret formula (3.28) in cost-benefit terms and compare it with formula (2.11). The marginal revenue to the public sector of, say, increasing p_z still appears on the right-hand side. The difference lies in the formulae for evaluating appropriately that marginal revenue, (3.29) instead of (2.12). The left-hand side of (3.28) still measures the total marginal cost to consumers of an increase in p_z. That cost now consists of four components, reflecting the four capacities in which a household is affected by adjustments in public sector prices; namely, qua consumer (z^h), qua asset holder $(\theta^h d\Pi/dp_z)$, qua taxpayer $(\beta^h d\Phi/dp_z)$ and qua constrained supplier of labour $((w - w_R^h)\,(\partial \bar{l}^h/\partial L)(dL/dp_z))$. The first three terms appeared already in (2.11); the only difference concerns again the evaluation of $d\Pi/dp_z$ and of $d\Phi/dp_z$, which is discussed below. The fourth term on the right-hand side of (3.28) is more novel; it evaluates the welfare implications of a change in aggregate employment. If increasing p_z leads to less employment $(dL/dp_z < 0)$, some households see their labour supply further constrained $((\partial \bar{l}^h/\partial L)(dL/dp_z) < 0)$, at a loss of welfare (per unit of labour time) equal to the difference between the forgone market wage w and the reservation wage w_R^h. This kind of effect had no place in (2.11), since in the Boiteux framework market wage and reservation wage are equal, for each household. Here is thus a term whose *raison d'être* lies in the presence of market disequilibrium. Note that quantitative evaluation of this term raises a new problem, to the extent that w_R^h is not directly observable, or measurable from market data.

In order to understand formula (3.29), a word of comment on the nature of 'multiplier effects' in problem (P3) is in order. When public sector prices p_z are adjusted, household demands react, due to the price derivatives $\partial y/\partial p_z$, $\partial z/\partial p_z$. This primary reaction entails adjustments in employment given by

$$\frac{\partial L}{\partial p_z} dp_z = \left(\frac{\partial l^y}{\partial y} \frac{\partial y}{\partial p_z} + \frac{\partial l^z}{\partial z} \frac{\partial z}{\partial p_z} \right) dp_z$$

and in private profits given by

$$\frac{\partial \Pi}{\partial p_z} dp_z = (p_y - m_y) \frac{\partial y}{\partial p_z} dp_z;$$

as for the public budget, it is adjusted by

$$\frac{\partial \Phi}{\partial p_z} dp_z = \left[z + (p_z - m_z) \frac{\partial z}{\partial p_z} \right] dp_z.$$

These adjustments in employment, profits and the public budget affect households via the employment constraints $\bar{l}^h(L)$ and the incomes $\theta^h \Pi + \beta^h \Phi$; this induces further reactions of demand, due to the derivatives $\partial x^h/\partial L$ and $\partial x^h/\partial r^h$. The matrix M describes the direct impact on Π (first row), Φ (second row) and L (third row) of unitary adjustments in Π (first column), Φ (second column) and L (third column) respectively. Multiplying M into the vector of adjustments

$$\left(\frac{\partial \Pi}{\partial p_z} dp_z, \frac{\partial \Phi}{\partial p_z} dp_z, \frac{\partial L}{\partial p_z} dp_z \right)'$$

defines the next round of adjustments in Π, Φ, and L; multiplying M into this second round defines the third round; and so on. The familiar matrix-multiplier process operates, and the final outcome is

$$
\begin{bmatrix}
\dfrac{d\Pi}{dp_z} \\[2ex]
\dfrac{d\Phi}{dp_z} \\[2ex]
\dfrac{dL}{dp_z}
\end{bmatrix}
= (I + M + M^2 + M^3 + \ldots)
\begin{bmatrix}
(p_y - m_y)\dfrac{\partial y}{\partial p_z} \\[2ex]
z + (p_z - m_z)\dfrac{\partial z}{\partial p_z} \\[2ex]
\dfrac{\partial l^y}{\partial y}\dfrac{\partial y}{\partial p_z} + \dfrac{\partial l^z}{\partial z}\dfrac{\partial z}{\partial p_z}
\end{bmatrix}
$$

$$
= (I - M)^{-1}
\begin{bmatrix}
(p_y - m_y)\dfrac{\partial y}{\partial p_z} \\[2ex]
z + (p_z - m_z)\dfrac{\partial z}{\partial p_z} \\[2ex]
\dfrac{\partial l^y}{\partial y}\dfrac{\partial y}{\partial p_z} + \dfrac{\partial l^z}{\partial z}\dfrac{\partial z}{\partial p_z}
\end{bmatrix}.
\tag{3.37}
$$

Thus, *conditions (3.28) reduce to a cost-benefit analysis of adjustments in public sector prices, where costs and benefits are evaluated by means of the 'comparative statics' approach of macroeconomics, taking all multiplier effects into account.* This is the Keynesian counterpart to the cost-benefit analysis appropriate for (2.11), where price effects had the leading role. Although the computations underlying (3.28) look much more forbidding than those underlying (2.11), the added complexity is to a large extent apparent rather than real, as I will show in Section 4.2 below. A basic principle is common to both results, namely the 'comparative statics' evaluation of the relevant costs and benefits. How the comparative statics analysis should be conducted is dictated by the assumptions made about market clearing in the private sector – either through price flexibility or through quantity rationing (in the short run).

3.4.

The result stated in proposition 3 is directly applicable to the 'reform problem' of Section 2.4.

Starting from a situation where the budget constraint is not binding ($\Phi > b$), the reform problem is: find dp_z such that

$$
\sum_h \lambda^h \frac{\partial V^h}{\partial r^h}\left[z^h - \theta^h \frac{d\Pi}{dp_z} - \beta^h \frac{d\Phi}{dp_z} - (w - w_R^h)\frac{\partial \bar{l}^h}{\partial L}\frac{dL}{dp_z}\right] dp_z < 0.
\tag{3.38}
$$

Starting instead from a situation where $\Phi = b$, and $\rho > 0$, the reform problem becomes: find dp_z such that[19]

$$\frac{d\Phi}{dp_z}dp_z = 0, \sum_h \lambda^h \frac{\partial V^h}{\partial r^h}\left[z^h - \theta^h \frac{d\Pi}{dp_z} - (w - w_R^h)\frac{\partial \bar{l}^h}{\partial L}\frac{dL}{dp_z}\right]dp_z < 0.$$

(3.39)

These conditions are easily checked, provided one can estimate the final impact of dp_z on Π, Φ and L; and provided the coefficients of these impact terms be somehow available. To gain insight, consider the special case where the distributive weights $\lambda^h \frac{\partial V^h}{\partial r^h}$ are taken equal for all h. Then, (3.39) reduces to

$$\frac{d\Phi}{dp_z}dp_z = 0, \left[z - \frac{d\Pi}{dp_z} - (w - \bar{w}_R)\frac{dL}{dp_z}\right]dp_z < 0.$$

(3.40)

The welfare-improvement condition for price increases is that the cost of inflation, zdp_z, be more than offset by the gains associated with private profits, $d\Pi$, and employment, $(w - \bar{w}_R)dL$. It is interesting to bring out how these three aspects are combined in (3.40). In the present model, aggregate value added is equal to $p_y y + p_z z$. Dividing through by that quantity, we may rewrite the welfare-improvement condition as

$$\frac{zdp_z}{p_y y + p_z z} - \frac{\Pi}{p_y y + p_z z}\frac{d\Pi}{\Pi} - \frac{wL}{p_y y + p_z z}\frac{w - \bar{w}_R}{w}\frac{dL}{L} < 0. \quad (3.41)$$

The first term is a rate of inflation (relative increase in the cost of an unchanged aggregate consumption); the second term weighs the rate of increase in profits $d\Pi/\Pi$, by the share of profits in value added; the third terms weighs the rate of increase in employment, dL/L, by the share of wages in value added *times* one minus the ratio of the reservation wage to the nominal wage. Even if the reservation wage were zero, and if private profits were unaffected by a change in p_z, then one percentage point of inflation would still carry more weight than an increase in employment by one percentage point – unless value added consisted of wages alone. A negative reservation wage (which is not to be ruled out) is needed before employment carries more weight than inflation. This somewhat

---

[19] The condition $d\Phi/dp_z = 0$ is imposed to keep the public budget unchanged; $d\Phi/dp_z > 0$ would be acceptable, but would modify the condition for welfare improvement.

counterintuitive conclusion rests on the special assumptions that distributive aspects may be ignored, and that nominal wage rates remain constant. Clearly, more realistic assumptions would be required to reach substantive conclusions, in particular about the welfare cost of inflation; but the methodological path is clearly delineated.

More generally, the welfare-improvement condition in (3.39) could be approached by treating the problem of income redistribution at the functional rather than at the personal level. Defining

$$\lambda_{zi} = \sum_h \lambda^h \frac{\partial U^h}{\partial r^h} z_i^h / z_i, \quad \lambda_\Pi = \sum_h \lambda^h \frac{\partial U^h}{\partial r^h} \theta^h,$$

$$\lambda_w = \sum_h \lambda^h \frac{\partial U^h}{\partial r^h} \frac{\partial l^h}{\partial L}, \quad \bar{w}_R = \sum_h \lambda^h \frac{\partial U^h}{\partial r^h} w_R^h \frac{\partial l^h}{\partial L} / \lambda_w, \tag{3.42}$$

one would express (3.39) as

$$\frac{d\Phi}{dp_z} dp_z = 0, \quad \left[\lambda_z z - \lambda_\Pi \frac{d\Pi}{dp_z} - \lambda_w (w - \bar{w}_R) \frac{dL}{dp_z} \right] dp_z < 0. \tag{3.43}$$

This condition could be verified, once the relative weights λ_z / λ_w (consumers versus workers) and λ_z / λ_Π (consumers versus business shareholders) are evaluated. A further simplification would result if λ_z were not evaluated for each commodity separately, as suggested by (3.42), but only for a few groups of commodities. A broad value judgement of that kind seems inherent in any realistic policy analysis.

4. Some comparisons and extensions

Proposition 3 states the main result on which the methodological comments of Section 5 are based. These comments do not rely significantly on the contents of the present section, which may thus be skipped without loss of continuity.

The comparisons bear successively on the simple Keynesian model with lump-sum transfers of income (Section 4.1) and on a neoclassical analogue to this model (Section 4.2). Some extensions are taken up in Section 4.3.

4.1.

When lump-sum transfers of income among households are introduced as a policy option in problem (P3), simplifications comparable to those mentioned in Section 2.3 for problem (P1) are achieved: The first-order conditions are freed from distributive aspects; income multipliers no longer appear in the first-order conditions, but derivatives of the demand functions are *compensated* derivatives. This remark applies both to price derivatives $(\partial y^h/\partial p_z, \partial z^h/\partial p_z)$ and to derivatives with respect to the employment constraint $(\partial y^h/\partial L, \partial z^h/\partial L)$, for which the relevant expressions were given in (3.15). Note that these expressions involve the reservation wages w_R^h, which are not directly observable. For this reason, the result given below in proposition 4 has less operational usefulness than its counterpart in proposition 2, which involves only the familiar compensated price derivatives. One may think about proposition 4 as giving the second-best pricing rule for an economy with exact price indexation of *individual* incomes and with 100% unemployment insurance (that is, with unemployment compensations offsetting exactly the *individual* utility losses due to unemployment).

An employment multiplier still appears in proposition 4, in spite of the unemployment compensation, because the employment constraint is an argument of the compensated demand functions. If that were not the case,[20] then the employment multiplier could be eliminated from the formulae in proposition 4, as revealed by the alternative formulation (4.4').

There are two equally natural ways of introducing lump-sum transfers (of the numeraire) into problem (P3). The first consists in treating the initial holdings m_0^h as policy variables, subject to a constraint on their sum:

$$\sum_h m_0^h \leqslant m_0 \qquad\qquad (\mu). \qquad (4.1)$$

One then solves problem (P4) with these additional variables. This is equivalent to the procedure followed in proposition 2. Alternatively, one can treat the incomes r^h as policy variables, subject to a single constraint on their sum, i.e.

(P4) $\displaystyle\max_{p_z, r^h, L} \sum_h \lambda^h V^h(p, r^h, L)$

subject to (3.7) and

---

[20] In terms of footnote 13 above, additive preferences between labour and physical commodities lead to derivatives of the compensated demand functions with respect to the employment constraint equal to the income effects of the reservation wages; these derivatives would vanish if in addition reservation wages were equal to zero.

$$\sum_h r^h - p_y \sum_h y^h(p, r^h, L)$$

$$+ wl^y(\sum_h y^h(p, r^h, L)) - p_z \sum_h z^h(p, r^h, L)$$

$$+ wl^z(\sum_h z^h(p, r^h, L)) \leqslant 0 \qquad\qquad (\sigma) \quad (4.2)$$

$$b - p_z \sum_h z^h(p, r^h, L) + wl^z(\sum_h z^h(p, r^h, L)) \leqslant 0 \qquad\qquad (\rho). \quad (4.3)$$

PROPOSITION 4

At an interior solution of problem (P4), there exists a multiplier $\hat{\rho} \geqslant 0$ such that

$$z - (p_y - m_y)\left(\frac{\partial \hat{y}}{\partial p_z} + \frac{\partial \hat{y}}{\partial L}\frac{d\hat{L}}{dp_z}\right) - \left[z + (p_z - m_z)\left(\frac{\partial \hat{z}}{\partial p_z} + \frac{\partial \hat{z}}{\partial L}\frac{d\hat{L}}{dp_z}\right)\right]$$

$$- (w - \bar{w}_R)\frac{d\hat{L}}{dp_z} = \hat{\rho}\left[z + (p_z - m_z)\left(\frac{\partial \hat{z}}{\partial p_z} + \frac{\partial \hat{z}}{\partial L}\frac{d\hat{L}}{dp_z}\right)\right] \qquad (4.4)$$

where $(\hat{y}, \hat{z})$ denote compensated demand functions and

$$\frac{d\hat{L}}{dp_z} = \left(\frac{\partial l^y}{\partial y}\frac{\partial \hat{y}}{\partial p_z} + \frac{\partial l^z}{\partial z}\frac{\partial \hat{z}}{\partial p_z}\right)\left(1 - \frac{\partial l^y}{\partial y}\frac{\partial \hat{y}}{\partial L} - \frac{\partial l^z}{\partial z}\frac{\partial \hat{z}}{\partial L}\right)^{-1}; \qquad (4.5)$$

if $\Phi > b$ at the solution, then $\hat{\rho} = 0$.

PROOF

Instead of solving problem (P4) directly, I solve problem (P3) with m_0^h a policy variable, subject to constraints (4.1). (The interested reader may verify that the direct solution is indeed given by (4.4)–(4.5).) The first-order conditions (3.30)–(3.32), (3.35) of problem (P3) are not modified by the addition of constraint (4.1). The first-order condition for m_0^h is

$$\frac{\partial \Lambda}{\partial m_0^h} = \lambda^h \frac{\partial V^h}{\partial r^h} + \pi\left(p_y - w\frac{\partial l^y}{\partial y}\right)\frac{\partial y^h}{\partial r^h} + \phi\left(p_z - w\frac{\partial l^z}{\partial z}\right)\frac{\partial z^h}{\partial r^h}$$

$$+ v\left(\frac{\partial l^y}{\partial y}\frac{\partial y^h}{\partial r^h} + \frac{\partial l^z}{\partial z}\frac{\partial z^h}{\partial r^h}\right) - \mu = 0. \qquad (4.6)$$

Combining this new condition successively with (3.30), (3.31) and (3.32), we obtain – using (3.15) and (3.18) –

$$\frac{\partial A}{\partial \Pi} - \sum_h \frac{\partial A}{\partial m_0^h} \theta^h = -\pi + \mu = 0; \tag{4.7}$$

$$\frac{\partial A}{\partial \Phi} - \sum_h \frac{\partial A}{\partial m_0^h} \beta^h = -\phi + \rho + \mu = 0; \tag{4.8}$$

$$\frac{\partial A}{\partial L} - \sum_h \frac{\partial A}{\partial m_0^h}(w - w_R^h)\frac{\partial \bar{l}^h}{\partial L} = \pi\left(p_y - w\frac{\partial l^y}{\partial y}\right)\sum_h \frac{\partial \hat{y}^h}{\partial L}$$

$$+ \phi\left(p_z - w\frac{\partial l^z}{\partial z}\right)\sum_h \frac{\partial \hat{z}^h}{\partial L} - v\left[1 - \frac{\partial l^y}{\partial y}\sum_h \frac{\partial \hat{y}^h}{\partial L} - \frac{\partial l^z}{\partial z}\sum_h \frac{\partial \hat{z}^h}{\partial L}\right]$$

$$+ \mu(w - \bar{w}_R) = 0. \tag{4.9}$$

Substituting from (4.7)–(4.8) into (4.9) and solving for v/μ yields:

$$\frac{v}{\mu} = \left[\left(p_y - w\frac{\partial l^y}{\partial y}\right)\frac{\partial \hat{y}}{\partial L} + \left(1 + \frac{\rho}{\mu}\right)\left(p_z - w\frac{\partial l^z}{\partial z}\right)\frac{\partial \hat{z}}{\partial L} + (w - \bar{w}_R)\right]$$

$$\left(1 - \frac{\partial l^y}{\partial y}\frac{\partial \hat{y}}{\partial L} - \frac{\partial l^z}{\partial z}\frac{\partial \hat{z}}{\partial z}\right)^{-1}. \tag{4.10}$$

(Note that $\mu > 0$ by desirability of the numeraire commodity.)

Combining finally (4.6) with (3.35), we obtain

$$\frac{\partial A}{\partial p_z} + \sum_h \frac{\partial A}{\partial m_0^h} z^h = \pi\left(p_y - w\frac{\partial l^y}{\partial y}\right)\sum_h \frac{\partial \hat{y}^h}{\partial p_z}$$

$$+ \phi\left[z + \left(p_z - w\frac{\partial l^z}{\partial z}\right)\sum_h \frac{\partial \hat{z}^h}{\partial p_z}\right]$$

$$+ v\left(\frac{\partial l^y}{\partial y}\sum_h \frac{\partial \hat{y}^h}{\partial p_z} + \frac{\partial l^z}{\partial z}\sum_h \frac{\partial \hat{z}^h}{\partial p_z}\right) - \mu z = 0. \tag{4.11}$$

Defining $d\hat{L}/dp_z$ as per (4.5), and substituting from (4.7), (4.8) and (4.10) into (4.11) yields

$$\left(p_y - w\frac{\partial l^y}{\partial y}\right)\left(\frac{\partial \hat{y}}{\partial p_z} + \frac{\partial \hat{y}}{\partial L}\frac{\partial \hat{L}}{dp_z}\right)$$

$$+ \left(1 + \frac{\rho}{\mu}\right)\left[z + \left(p_z - w\frac{\partial l^z}{\partial z}\right)\left(\frac{\partial \hat{z}}{\partial p_z} + \frac{\partial \hat{z}}{\partial L}\frac{\partial \hat{L}}{dp_z}\right)\right]$$

$$+ (w - \bar{w}_R)\frac{d\hat{L}}{dp_z} - z = 0. \tag{4.12}$$

which is the same as (4.4), with $\hat{\rho} = \rho/\mu$. That $\hat{\rho} = 0$ when $\Phi > b$ at the solution reflects complementary slackness.   QED

An alternative statement of conditions (4.4), after cancelling the compensation terms, is

$$-\left(p_y - \bar{w}_R\frac{\partial l^y}{\partial y}\right)\left(\frac{\partial \hat{y}}{\partial p_z} + \frac{\partial \hat{y}}{\partial L}\frac{d\hat{L}}{dp_z}\right)$$

$$+ \left(p_z - \bar{w}_R\frac{\partial l^z}{\partial z}\right)\left(\frac{\partial \hat{z}}{\partial p_z} + \frac{\partial \hat{z}}{\partial L}\frac{d\hat{L}}{dp_z}\right)$$

$$= \hat{\rho}\left[z + \left(p_z - w\frac{\partial l^z}{\partial z}\right)\left(\frac{\partial \hat{z}}{\partial p_z} + \frac{\partial \hat{z}}{\partial L}\frac{d\hat{L}}{dp_z}\right)\right]. \tag{4.4'}$$

PROOF OF FORMULA (4.4')

Remembering that $m_y = w\,\partial l^y/\partial y, m_z = w\,dl^z/\partial z$, we collect and rearrange the terms involving w in (4.4), obtaining

$$w\left[\frac{\partial l^y}{\partial y}\frac{\partial \hat{y}}{\partial p_z} + \frac{\partial l^z}{\partial z}\frac{\partial \hat{z}}{\partial p_z} + \left(\frac{\partial l^y}{\partial y}\frac{\partial \hat{y}}{\partial L} + \frac{\partial l^z}{\partial z}\frac{\partial \hat{z}}{\partial L} - 1\right)\frac{d\hat{L}}{dp_z}\right]$$

which is equal to zero in view of (4.5). Collecting similarly the terms involving $\bar{w}_R$ in (4.4'), we obtain

$$\bar{w}_R\left[\frac{\partial l^y}{\partial y}\frac{\partial \hat{y}}{\partial p_z} + \frac{\partial l^z}{\partial z}\frac{\partial \hat{z}}{\partial p_z} + \left(\frac{\partial l^y}{\partial y}\frac{\partial \hat{y}}{\partial L} + \frac{\partial l^z}{\partial z}\frac{\partial \hat{z}}{\partial L}\right)\frac{d\hat{L}}{dp_z}\right]$$

which is equal to $\bar{w}_R\,d\hat{L}/dp_z$, as required by (4.4).   QED

The interpretation of (4.4') is similar to that of (2.20'). The left-hand side measures the cost to households of a change in p_z, under exact compensation for both the price effects (z) and the employment effects ($\bar{w}_R - w$)$d\hat{L}/dp_z$; that cost is equal to minus the change in household incomes net of the compensation; this corresponds to the change in private profits and the public budget, computed at the reservation wage and net of the direct effect of price changes (z). (The right-hand side still measures the 'monetary' benefit to the public sector of the price change, i.e. its contribution towards meeting the budget constraint.)

Formula (4.4') is directly applicable to the reform problem. Starting from a situation where $\Phi = b$ and imposing $d\Phi = (d\phi/dp_z)dp_z = 0$, we obtain:

PROPOSITION 5

Under suitable lump-sum transfers of income among households and 100% unemployment compensation, compensated price adjustments that leave unchanged the public budget are welfare improving if and only if they lead to adjustments in private and public productions whose market value exceeds their marginal cost evaluated at the reservation wage.

In proposition 5, reservation wages correspond to a 'shadow price for labour', in terms of which definite conclusions are reached. This is in contrast to proposition 3, where altogether different computations are required.

4.2.

Lest the reader be misled about the relative complexity of welfare pricing rules in Keynesian and neoclassical models, I sketch the counterpart to proposition 3, under the assumption that the wage rate w and the private sector prices p_y adjust to clear markets competitively. It will be seen that the first-order conditions, albeit different, are just as complex as in proposition 3.

In comparison with the model of Section 2, the different feature is that w and p_y are no longer policy instruments, but adjust to clear markets. The problem of second-best public sector pricing now becomes:

$$x^h = x^h(p, r^h), \quad l^y = l^y(p), \quad y = y(p). \tag{4.13}$$

In comparison with the model of Section 2, the different feature is that w and p_y are no longer policy instruments, but adjust to clear markets. The problem of second-best public sector pricing now becomes:

(P6) $\qquad \max_{p,\Phi} \sum_h \lambda^h V^h(p, m_0^h + \theta^h(p_y y(p) - wl^y(p)) + \beta^h\Phi)$

subject to

$$Y(p, \Phi) = {}_{\text{def}} \sum_h y^h(p, m_0^h + \theta^h(p_y y(p) - wl^y(p))) + \beta^h \Phi)$$

$$- y(p) = 0 \qquad\qquad (\eta) \quad (4.14)$$

$$L(p, \Phi) = {}_{\text{def}} \sum_h l^h(p, m_0^h + \theta^h(p_y y(p) - wl^y(p))) + \beta^h \Phi)$$

$$- l^y(p) - l^z \left(\sum_h z^h(p, m_0^h + \theta^h(p_y y(p) - wl^y(p))) \right.$$

$$\left. + \beta^h \Phi) \right) = 0 \qquad\qquad (\nu) \quad (4.15)$$

$$\Phi - p_z \sum_h z^h(p, m_0^h + \theta^h(p_y y(p) - wl^y(p))) + \beta^h \Phi)$$

$$+ wl^z (\sum_h z^h(p, m_0^h + \theta^h(p_y y(p) - wl^y(p))) + \beta^h \Phi)) = 0 \,(\phi) \quad (3.6)$$

$$b - \Phi \leqslant 0 \qquad\qquad (\rho). \quad (3.6')$$

PROPOSITION 6

At an interior solution of problem (P6) *there exists a multiplier* $\rho \geqslant 0$ *such that*

$$\sum_h \lambda^h \frac{\partial V^h}{\partial r^h} \left[z^h + y^h \frac{dp_y}{dp_z} - l^h \frac{dw}{dp_z} - \theta^h \frac{d\Pi}{dp_z} - \beta^h \frac{d\Phi}{dp_z} \right] = \rho \frac{d\Phi}{dp_z} \quad (4.16)$$

where

$$\frac{d\Pi}{dp_z} = y \frac{dp_y}{dp_z} - l^y \frac{dw}{dp_z}$$

and

$$\begin{bmatrix} \dfrac{dp_y}{dp_z} \\[2ex] \dfrac{dw}{dp_z} \\[2ex] \dfrac{d\Phi}{dp_z} \end{bmatrix} = D^{-1} \begin{bmatrix} -\dfrac{\partial Y}{\partial p_z} \\[2ex] -\dfrac{\partial L}{\partial p_z} \\[2ex] z + (p_z - m_z)\dfrac{\partial z}{\partial p_z} \end{bmatrix}, \qquad (4.17)$$

$$D = \begin{bmatrix} \dfrac{\partial Y}{\partial p_y} & \dfrac{\partial Y}{\partial w} & \dfrac{\partial Y}{\partial \Phi} \\[2ex] \dfrac{\partial L}{\partial p_y} & \dfrac{\partial L}{\partial w} & \dfrac{\partial L}{\partial \Phi} \\[2ex] -(p_z - m_z)\left(\dfrac{\partial z}{\partial p_y} + \dfrac{\partial z}{\partial \Pi}\dfrac{\partial \Pi}{\partial p_y}\right) & -(p_z - m_z)\left(\dfrac{\partial z}{\partial w} + \dfrac{\partial z}{\partial \Pi}\dfrac{\partial \Pi}{\partial w}\right) & 1 - (p_z - m_z)\dfrac{\partial z}{\partial \Phi} \end{bmatrix};$$

if $\Phi > b$ at the solution, then $\rho = 0$.[21]

PROOF

As before, we differentiate the Lagrangean Λ of problem (P6) and eliminate unknowns by substitution.

$$\frac{\partial \Lambda}{\partial p_y} = \sum_h \lambda^h \left(\frac{\partial V^h}{\partial p_y} + \frac{\partial V^h}{\partial r^h}\theta^h y\right) - \eta\left(\sum_h \frac{\partial y^h}{\partial p_y} + \sum_h \frac{\partial y^h}{\partial r^h}\theta^h y - \frac{\partial y}{\partial p_y}\right)$$

$$- \nu\left[\sum_h \frac{\partial l^h}{\partial p_y} + \sum_h \frac{\partial l^h}{\partial r^h}\theta^h y - \frac{\partial l^y}{\partial p_y} - \frac{\partial l^z}{\partial z}\left(\sum_h \frac{\partial z^h}{\partial p_y} + \sum_h \frac{\partial z^h}{\partial r^h}\theta^h y\right)\right]$$

$$+ \phi\left(p_z - w\frac{\partial l^z}{\partial z}\right)\left(\sum_h \frac{\partial z^h}{\partial p_y} + \sum_h \frac{\partial z^h}{\partial r^h}\theta^h y\right) = 0. \tag{4.18}$$

$$\frac{\partial \Lambda}{\partial w} = \sum_h \lambda^h \left(\frac{\partial V^h}{\partial w} - \frac{\partial V^h}{\partial r^h}\theta^h l^y\right) - \eta\left(\sum_h \frac{\partial y^h}{\partial w} - \sum_h \frac{\partial y^h}{\partial r^h}\theta^h l^y - \frac{\partial y}{\partial w}\right)$$

$$- \nu\left[\sum_h \frac{\partial l^h}{\partial w} - \sum_h \frac{\partial l^h}{\partial r^h}\theta^h l^y - \frac{\partial l^y}{\partial w} - \frac{\partial l^z}{\partial z}\left(\sum_h \frac{\partial z^h}{\partial w} - \sum_h \frac{\partial z^h}{\partial r^h}\theta^h l^y\right)\right]$$

$$+ \phi\left(p_z - w\frac{\partial l^z}{\partial z}\right)\left(\sum_h \frac{\partial z^h}{\partial w} - \sum_h \frac{\partial z^h}{\partial r^h}\theta^h l^y\right) = 0. \tag{4.19}$$

$$\frac{\partial \Lambda}{\partial \Phi} = \sum_h \lambda^h \frac{\partial V^h}{\partial r^h}\beta^h - \eta\sum_h \frac{\partial y^h}{\partial r^h}\beta^h - \nu\left(\sum_h \frac{\partial l^h}{\partial r^h}\beta^h - \frac{\partial l^z}{\partial z}\sum_h \frac{\partial z^h}{\partial r^h}\beta^h\right)$$

$$- \phi\left[1 - \left(p_z - w\frac{\partial l^z}{\partial z}\right)\sum_h \frac{\partial z^h}{\partial r^h}\beta^h\right] + \rho = 0. \tag{4.20}$$

---

[21] These conditions could undoubtedly be reconciled explicitly with (2.11), by introducing in the statement of problem (P1) the condition that z^h is equal to zero for a subset of commodities.

Adopting a more concise notation, we may solve these equations for (η, v, ϕ):

$$
D' \begin{bmatrix} \eta \\ v \\ \phi \end{bmatrix} = \begin{bmatrix} \dfrac{\partial Y}{\partial p_y} & \dfrac{\partial L}{\partial p_y} & -(p_z - m_z)\left(\dfrac{\partial z}{\partial p_y} + \dfrac{\partial z}{\partial \Pi}\dfrac{\partial \Pi}{\partial p_y}\right) \\[3ex] \dfrac{\partial Y}{\partial w} & \dfrac{\partial L}{\partial w} & -(p_z - m_z)\left(\dfrac{\partial z}{\partial w} + \dfrac{\partial z}{\partial \Pi}\dfrac{\partial \Pi}{\partial w}\right) \\[3ex] \dfrac{\partial Y}{\partial \Phi} & \dfrac{\partial L}{\partial \Phi} & 1-(p_z - m_z)\dfrac{\partial z}{\partial \Phi} \end{bmatrix} \begin{bmatrix} \eta \\ v \\ \phi \end{bmatrix}
$$

$$
= \begin{bmatrix} \displaystyle\sum_h \lambda^h \dfrac{\partial V^h}{\partial r^h}(-y^h + \theta^h y) \\[3ex] \displaystyle\sum_h \lambda^h \dfrac{\partial V^h}{\partial r^h}(l^h - \theta^h l^y) \\[3ex] \displaystyle\sum_h \lambda^h \dfrac{\partial V^h}{\partial r^h}\beta^h + \rho \end{bmatrix}. \tag{4.21}
$$

$$
(\eta, v, \phi) = \left(\sum_h \lambda^h \frac{\partial V^h}{\partial r^h}(-y^h + \theta^h y), \ \sum_h \lambda^h \frac{\partial V^h}{\partial r^h}(l^h - \theta^h l^y),\right.
$$

$$
\left. \sum_h \lambda^h \frac{\partial V^h}{\partial r^h}\beta^h + \rho\right). D^{-1}. \tag{4.22}
$$

$$
\frac{\partial \Lambda}{\partial p_z} = \sum_h \lambda^h \frac{\partial V^h}{\partial p_z} - \eta \sum_h \frac{\partial y^h}{\partial p_z} - v\left(\sum_h \frac{\partial l^h}{\partial p_z} - \frac{\partial l^z}{\partial z}\sum_h \frac{\partial z^h}{\partial p_z}\right)
$$

$$
+ \phi\left[z + \left(p_z - w\frac{\partial l^z}{\partial z}\right)\sum_h \frac{\partial z^h}{\partial p_z}\right] = 0
$$

$$
= -\sum_h \lambda^h \frac{\partial V^h}{\partial r^h}z^h + (\eta, v, \phi)\begin{bmatrix} -\dfrac{\partial Y}{\partial p_z} \\[3ex] -\dfrac{\partial L}{\partial p_z} \\[3ex] z + (p_z - m_z)\dfrac{\partial z}{\partial p_z} \end{bmatrix} \tag{4.23}
$$

$$= -\sum_h \lambda^h \frac{\partial V^h}{\partial r^h} z^h + \begin{bmatrix} \sum_h \lambda^h \frac{\partial V^h}{\partial r^h}(-y^h + \theta^h y) \\ \sum_h \lambda^h \frac{\partial V^h}{\partial r^h}(l^h - \theta^h l^y) \\ \sum_h \lambda^h \frac{\partial V^h}{\partial r^h} \beta^h + \rho \end{bmatrix}' \quad D^{-1} \begin{bmatrix} -\dfrac{\partial Y}{\partial p_z} \\ -\dfrac{\partial L}{\partial p_z} \\ z + (p_z - m_z)\dfrac{\partial z}{\partial p_z} \end{bmatrix}$$

$$= -\sum_h \lambda^h \frac{\partial V^h}{\partial r^h} z^h$$

$$+ \left(\sum_h \lambda^h \frac{\partial V^h}{\partial r^h}(-y^h + \theta^h y), \sum_h \lambda^h \frac{\partial V^h}{\partial r_h}(l^h - \theta^h l^y), \sum_h \lambda^h \frac{\partial V^h}{\partial r^h} \beta^h + \rho \right) \begin{bmatrix} \dfrac{dp_y}{dp_z} \\ \dfrac{dw}{dp_z} \\ \dfrac{d\Phi}{dp_z} \end{bmatrix} = 0,$$

which is the same as (4.16).

The justification for the notation $(dp_y/dp_z, dw/dp_z, d\Phi/dp_z)$ is provided by differentiating totally the system (4.14), (4.15), (3.6):

$$D \begin{bmatrix} dp_y \\ dw \\ d\Phi \end{bmatrix} + \begin{bmatrix} \dfrac{\partial Y}{\partial p_z} \\ \dfrac{\partial L}{\partial p_z} \\ -z - (p_z - m_z)\dfrac{\partial z}{\partial p_z} \end{bmatrix} dp_z = 0, \qquad (4.24)$$

which yields (4.17). That $\rho = 0$ when $\Phi > b$ at the solution reflects complementary slackness.   QED

It is an easy exercise to combine the approaches of propositions 3 and 6 to cover the case where markets for privately produced commodities clear through price adjustments whereas the labour market 'clears' through quantity rationing (involuntary unemployment) at a fixed nominal wage w.

The main modification to problem (P6) consists of reintroducing L as an argument of V^h, y^h and z^h while replacing (4.15) by (3.7) with $l^y = l^y(p_y)$. This leads to the problem:

(P7) $\max\limits_{p, \Phi, L} \sum\limits_h \lambda^h V^h(p, m_0^h + \theta^h(p_y y(p_y) - wl^y(p_y)) + \beta^h \Phi, L)$

subject to:

$$Y(p, \Phi, L) = {}_{\text{def}} \sum_h y^h(p, m_0^h + \theta^h(p_y y(p_y)$$

$$- wl^y(p_y)) + \beta^h \Phi, L) - y(p_y) = 0 \qquad (\eta) \quad (4.14')$$

$$L - l^y(p_y) - l^z(\sum_h z^h(p, m_0^h + \theta^h(p_y y(p_y) - wl^y(p_y))$$

$$+ \beta^h \Phi, L)) = 0 \qquad (\nu) \quad (4.15')$$

$$\Phi - p_z \sum_h z^h(p, m_0^h + \theta^h(p_y y(p_y) - wl^y(p_y)) + \beta^h \Phi, L)$$

$$+ wl^z(\sum_h z^h(p, m_0^h + \theta^h(p_y y(p_y) - wl^y(p_y)) + \beta^h \Phi, L))$$

$$= 0 \qquad (\phi) \quad (3.6)$$

$$b - \Phi \leqslant 0 \qquad (\rho). \quad (3.6')$$

PROPOSITION 7

At an interior solution of problem (P7), *there exists a multiplier* $\rho \geqslant 0$ *such that*

$$\sum_h \lambda^h \frac{\partial V^h}{\partial r^h} \left[z^h + y^h \frac{dp_y}{dp_z} - \theta^h \frac{d\Pi}{dp_z} - \beta^h \frac{d\Phi}{dp_z} - (w - w_R^h) \frac{\partial \bar{l}^h}{\partial L} \frac{dL}{dp_z} \right] = \rho \frac{d\Phi}{dp}$$

$$(4.25)$$

where

$$\frac{d\Pi}{dp_z} = y \frac{dp_y}{dp_z}$$

and

$$
\begin{bmatrix} \dfrac{dp_y}{dp_z} \\[2ex] \dfrac{d\Phi}{dp_z} \\[2ex] \dfrac{dL}{dp_z} \end{bmatrix} = Q^{-1} \begin{bmatrix} -\dfrac{\partial Y}{\partial p_z} \\[2ex] z + (p_z - m_z)\dfrac{\partial z}{\partial p_z} \\[2ex] \dfrac{\partial l^z}{\partial z}\dfrac{\partial z}{\partial p_z} \end{bmatrix}, \tag{4.26}
$$

$$
Q = \begin{bmatrix} \dfrac{\partial Y}{\partial p_y} & \dfrac{\partial Y}{\partial \Phi} & \dfrac{\partial Y}{\partial L} \\[3ex] -\dfrac{\partial l^y}{\partial p_y} - \dfrac{\partial l^z}{\partial z}\left(\dfrac{\partial z}{\partial p_y} + \dfrac{\partial z}{\partial \Pi}y\right) & -\dfrac{\partial l^z}{\partial z}\dfrac{\partial z}{\partial \Phi} & 1 - \dfrac{\partial l^z}{\partial z}\dfrac{\partial z}{\partial L} \\[3ex] -(p_z - m_z)\left(\dfrac{\partial z}{\partial p_y} + \dfrac{\partial z}{\partial \Pi}y\right) & 1 - (p_z - m_z)\dfrac{\partial z}{\partial \Phi} & -(p_z - m_z)\dfrac{\partial z}{\partial L} \end{bmatrix};
$$

if $\Phi > b$ at the solution, then $\rho = 0$.

The proof follows the same lines as that of proposition 6 and is left to the reader. The interpretation of proposition 7 is analogous to that of proposition 3.

4.3.

I conclude this section with three remarks about extensions of the results recorded here.

First, the analytics of the present paper lack in either rigour or realism, where differentiability is concerned. As is well known, the conditions required to obtain differentiability of household demand functions at all prices and incomes are severe and unrealistic;[22] they imply strictly positive consumption of *all* commodities at *all* prices and incomes. And in the present context, the differentiability problem is compounded by the presence of quantity rationing, as recognised in Section 3.1.

The appropriate remedy to this deficiency will be to free the analysis of differentiability assumptions, relying instead upon the property of Lipschitz continuity. Under assumptions much more reasonable than those required for differentiability of ordinary demand functions, constrained

[22] See, e.g. Debreu (1972).

demand functions are Lipschitz continuous in prices, income and quantity constraints.[23] I thus feel confident that a rigorous extension to the more realistic non-differentiable case is possible, and will be forthcoming as soon as the required mathematical talent is mobilised.

Second, the Keynesian model introduced in Section 3 is very simple, and calls in particular for a generalisation to several types of labour, and arbitrary sets of inputs in private and public production. I have attempted that extension and found that it lay beyond the scope (and length!) of the present paper. Yet, a neat characterisation (in cost-benefit terms) of second-best input decisions in the public sector will have its place on the record.

Third, the kind of analysis presented here for a Keynesian environment can be replicated for alternative regimes, and it would seem natural to work out general formulae allowing for some markets to be in excess demand, others in excess supply and others still in equilibrium.[24] These formulae will combine elements of the multiplier analysis in Section 3.3 and the price adjustments analysis in Section 4.2. No logical difficulties are involved in the study of local welfare improvements. For second-best optimality, *a priori* identification of the regime that will prevail on each market at the solution is problematic, from a theoretical as well as an empirical viewpoint. One must go back to a more basic approach, like that of Guesnerie (1981) to study this problem in theory and discover the associated empirical requirements (like measures of excess supplies and demands...). This difficulty does not arise in the reform problem, however.

5. Methodological conclusions

Although the model used in this paper is very simple and special, the answers which it has provided to the questions raised in the introduction seem endowed with broader methodological validity. Here are the main conclusions which I have drawn for myself.

(i) It is possible to exhibit operational solutions to second-best or reform problems in non-competitive environments; where the term 'operational' refers to solutions involving well-defined quantities, directly amenable to empirical evaluation, as distinct from quantities defined only conceptually, in terms of other quantities themselves defined only

[23] See Cornet and Laroque (1980).
[24] The general formulae obtained by Bronsard and Wagneur (1982), Jean P. Drèze (1982), Picard (1982), ... provide the starting point for this extension.

conceptually ... The methodology of general equilibrium with quantity rationing has been found adequate to our task. Hopefully, further extensions of general equilibrium theory (imperfect competition, increasing returns to scale...) will eventually enlarge our research potential in directions of greater realism. For the kind of problems studied here, the main difficulties do not seem to lie with the theoretical definition of solutions, but rather with their empirical implementation.

(ii) In situations involving quantity rationing, second-best or welfare-improving policies will typically depend upon quantities which, though amenable to empirical evaluation, are not directly observable and cannot be inferred from currently available economic data. In our example, reservation wages and marginal costs in supply constrained private firms were found relevant. In general, reservation prices for commodities subject to quantity constraints will be relevant. These vary from one agent to the next, and are not revealed through their choices. Special programs of data collection (like sample surveys) will be needed in order to evaluate these quantities.

(iii) The information needed to implement second-best or welfare-improving policies will typically be the kind of information which macroeconometric models seek to summarize. In our example, traditional quantities like price and income elasticities of demand need to be supplemented with such quantities as elasticities of employment with respect to output, separate demand estimates for employed and unemployed consumers, or for wage earners and property holders... To a particular second-best problem will correspond particular information needs, which the agency faced with the problem[25] cannot be expected to meet by itself. Some coordination of econometric investigations, or access to general information services, will typically be called for. If the demand for econometric information of the kind needed in my example develops, it may exert an influence on the design of econometric models, in order to make them fully consistent with the theoretical framework used to define second-best or welfare-improving policies.

(iv) Precision of the econometric estimates used for implementing second-best policies is apt to be limited. Special attention should be given to the compounding of errors in formulae – like (3.29) – involving non-linear functions of many estimated coefficients.

(v) The theoretical framework of general equilibrium analysis, based upon choices of individual economic agents, is adequate to study second-

[25] Like the French railroads, in the instance which motivated Boiteux.

best policy problems; there is no need to appeal specifically to macro-economic reasoning. The link with macroeconomic thinking comes from reconciling concepts which are new to microeconomics with those traditionally used in macroeconomics; and from reconciling the quantities defined by aggregation over individuals or commodities[26] with the quantities entering traditional macroeconomic models. To repeat a concise introductory statement, the rediscovery of the macroeconomic implications of microeconomics may well be a more fruitful research agenda than the exhibition of the microeconomic foundations of macroeconomics.

(vi) No comments of a substantive nature about the contents of propositions 3–5 will be offered here. The main point about the contents of my results is that welfare implications of public policies are ultimately derived from their impact on the welfare of individual agents, in their quadruple capacity as consumers, asset-holders, taxpayers and suppliers of labour. General equilibrium analysis is the natural tool to bring out the exact nature of these individual impacts. If the example discussed here is not misleading, the same approach will eventually be reconciled with macroeconomic policy models involving global objectives like increased employment with a more stable price level. There is of course a long way to go, before a satisfactory second-best analysis of models with dynamics and money is available. An immediate goal may be to explore more realistic and more general models than my simple Keynesian example, allowing for aggregation of markets in different regimes. A canonical formulation of such models, difficult as it may still seem, would justify a systematic search for substantive characterisation of second-best and welfare-improving policies.

---

[26] As in the calculations involving profits.

V Price adjustments

9 Demand estimation, risk aversion and sticky prices*

1. Introduction and summary

The purpose of this chapter is to point out that uncertainty about the price elasticity of demand has an effect comparable to that of a kink in the demand curve, for a risk-averse firm; the kink being located at the prevailing price and quantity. The reason for this effect, namely estimation uncertainty, is entirely distinct from the standard reason invoked in the literature on kinky demand curves, since Sweezy (1939), namely asymmetrical reactions of competitors. Thus symmetrical, but imperfectly known reactions would produce asymmetrical effects. And asymmetrical, but imperfectly known, reactions would produce doubly asymmetrical effects – the asymmetry generated by uncertainty being compounded with that generated by the reactions themselves.

The effect of uncertainty in the context considered here is analogous to the effect of uncertainty about rates of return on savings decisions by consumers. Variance of rates of return affects these decisions in the same way as *adverse* changes in expected returns – see Drèze and Modigliani (1972) or Sandmo (1974). Thus, uncertainty about rates of return has an effect comparable to that of a kink in the budget line constraining present and future consumption; the kink being located at the endowment point. (The reason for that kink is again distinct from the standard reason, namely a difference between lending and borrowing rates; both asymmetries must again be compounded.)

We first illustrate our point for the special case of a linear demand curve, a linear cost curve, and a 'truncated minimax' decision criterion – see Van Moeseke (1965) for a discussion of that criterion, which calls for maximising expected value minus a multiple of standard deviation. In

*Economics Letters, 4 (1979), 1–6; © North-Holland Publishing Co.

that special case, the effect of uncertainty about the price elasticities of demand is precisely equivalent to that of a kink in the demand curve. We then extend our argument to local analysis of a general situation.

Whether firms are risk averse or not is a sometimes debated issue, which is not taken up here. The author's current views on that issue are summarised by Drèze (1979a).

A number of possible extensions (uncertainty about the level of demand at the prevailing price, uncertainty about costs, price decisions aimed at gathering information about the demand elasticity, costs associated with price changes, multiperiod problems ...) seem to raise unrewarding analytical difficulties and are therefore left as exercises for the readers!

2. A special case

We consider first the linear demand and cost functions

$$q = a - bp, \tag{2.1}$$

$$C(q) = cq + d, \tag{2.2}$$

where q denotes quantity, p denotes price, and (a, b, c, d) are positive scalars. Starting from a point (q_0, p_0) on the demand function, we may express profits Π as a function of price,

$$\Pi(p) = pq - C(q) = (p - c)[q_0 + b(p_0 - p)] - [C(q_0) - cq_0]$$
$$= \Pi(p_0) + (p - p_0)[q_0 - b(p - c)]. \tag{2.3}$$

If b is unknown, but estimated by means of a probability density, then $\Pi(p)$ is a random variable with moments

$$E[\Pi(p)] = (p - c)[q_0 + E(b)(p_0 - p)] - [C(q_0) - cq_0], \tag{2.4}$$

$$V[\Pi(p)] = V(b)(p - c)^2(p_0 - p)^2, \tag{2.5}$$

and standard deviation

$$\sigma[\Pi(p)] = \sigma(b)(p - c)|p_0 - p|, \tag{2.6}$$

over the relevant range where $p > c$.

The 'truncated minimax' criterion calls for maximising the linear homogeneous function of Π,

$$E[\Pi(p)] - \alpha\sigma[\Pi(p)]$$
$$= (p - c)[q_0 + E(b)(p_0 - p) - \alpha\sigma(b)|p_0 - p|] - [C(q_0) - cq_0]$$

$$= (p - c)\left[q_0 + \left\{ E(b) + \alpha\sigma(b)\frac{|p_0 - p|}{p - p_0} \right\}(p_0 - p) \right]$$

$$- [C(q_0) - cq_0]$$

$$= (p - c)[q_0 + \beta(p)\cdot(p_0 - p)] - [C(q_0) - cq_0]$$

$$= \Pi(p_0) + (p - p_0)[q_0 - \beta(p)\cdot(p - c)], \tag{2.7}$$

where

$$\beta(p) = E(b) + \alpha\sigma(b)\cdot s(p - p_0),$$

$$s(x) = \text{sign of } x = 1 \quad \text{if } x > 0$$
$$= -1 \quad \text{if } x < 0$$
$$= 0 \quad \text{if } x = 0.$$

We thus verify that, in this special case, uncertainty about b is equivalent to an *adverse* change in $E(b)$; indeed, the term in $\sigma(b)$ works like an increase in the response of demand to price increases, and a decrease in the response of demand to price decreases, i.e. it is equivalent to a kink in the demand function at (q_0, p_0), see figure 9.1.

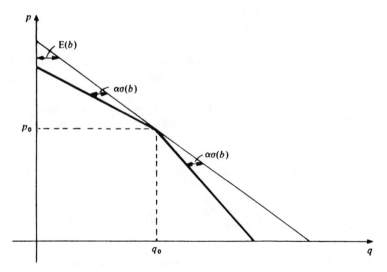

Figure 9.1

3. The general case (local analysis)

For a local analysis of the general case, we write

$$\Pi(p) = p \cdot q(p) - C(q), \tag{3.1}$$

with

$$q(p_0) = q_0, \quad \left.\frac{dq}{dp}\right|_{p_0} = -b, \quad \left.\frac{dC}{dq}\right|_{q_0} = c,$$

and expand the utility function of the firm, $u[\Pi(p)]$, in a Taylor series around $u[\Pi(p_0)]$,

$$u[\Pi(p)] \simeq u[\Pi(p_0)] + (p - p_0)\frac{du}{d\Pi}\frac{d\Pi}{dp}\bigg|_{p_0}$$

$$+ \frac{(p - p_0)^2}{2}\left[\frac{d^2u}{d\Pi^2}\left(\frac{d\Pi}{dp}\right)^2\bigg|_{p_0} + \frac{du}{d\Pi}\frac{d^2\Pi}{dp^2}\bigg|_{p_0}\right]$$

$$\simeq u[\Pi(p_0)] + \frac{du}{d\Pi}\bigg|_{p_0}\{(p - p_0)[q_0 - b(p_0 - c)]$$

$$- (p - p_0)^2 b\}$$

$$+ \frac{d^2u}{d\Pi^2}\bigg|_{p_0}\frac{(p - p_0)^2}{2}[q_0 - b(p_0 - c)]^2. \tag{3.2}$$

Expression (3.2) is meant to hold for p close to p_0. Accordingly, the fourth-order terms $(p - p_0)^2(d^2q/dp^2)$ and $(p - p_0)^2(d^2c/dq^2)$ have been dropped.

Uncertainty about the demand elasticity means uncertainty about b in (3.2). The expected utility associated with a given p is then

$$Eu[\Pi(p)] \simeq u[\Pi(p_0)] + \frac{du}{d\Pi}\bigg|_{p_0}(p - p_0)[q_0 - E(b)(p - c)]$$

$$+ \frac{d^2u}{d\Pi^2}\bigg|_{p_0}\frac{(p - p_0)^2}{2}E[q_0 - b(p_0 - c)]^2. \tag{3.3}$$

Let $\phi[\Pi(p_0)] = \phi_0$ denote the absolute risk-aversion function of the firm evaluated at $\Pi(p_0)$, i.e.

$$\phi_0 = -\left.\frac{d^2u}{d\Pi^2}\right|_{\Pi(p_0)} \bigg/ \left.\frac{du}{d\Pi}\right|_{\Pi(p_0)} \geq 0. \tag{3.4}$$

Under risk aversion, $\phi_0 > 0$, under risk neutrality, $\phi_0 = 0$, see Pratt (1964) or Arrow (1965). We may then rewrite (3.3) as

$$\frac{Eu[\Pi(p)] - u[\Pi(p_0)]}{du/d\Pi|_{\Pi(p_0)}} \simeq (p - p_0)[q_0 - E(b)(p - c)]$$

$$- \frac{\phi_0}{2}(p - p_0)^2 E[q_0 - b(p_0 - c)]^2, \tag{3.5}$$

or equivalently as

$$\frac{Eu[\Pi(p)] - u[\Pi(p_0)]}{du/d\Pi|_{\Pi(p_0)}} \simeq (p - p_0)\Bigg\{q_0 - (p - c)\Bigg[E(b)$$

$$+ \frac{\phi_0}{2}\frac{p - p_0}{p - c}\{(p_0 - c)^2 V(b)$$

$$+ [q_0 - E(b)(p_0 - c)]^2\}\Bigg]\Bigg\}$$

$$= (p - p_0)\{q_0 - (p - c)\beta(p)\}, \tag{3.6}$$

where $\beta(p) \gtreqless E(b)$ as $p \gtreqless p_0$, when $\phi_0 > 0$.

The expression for $\beta(p)$ plays the same role in (3.6) as in (2.7). In both cases, the sign of $\beta(p) - E(b)$ is the sign of $(p - p_0)$. Unfortunately, the expression for $\beta(p)$ is much more complicated in (3.6) than in (2.7). (This is of course the reason for considering the special case first.) In (2.7), the difference $\beta(p) - E(b)$ is equal to a constant times the sign of the difference $p - p_0$; in (3.6), the difference $\beta(p) - E(b)$ is a non-linear function of $(p - p_0)$. In other words, the 'certainty equivalent' demand derivative $\beta(p)$ is not constant over half lines but moves away from $E(b)$ in a non-linear way as p moves away from p_0; see Figure 9.2.[1]

If changes in p (away from p_0) must take place in multiples of a certain 'unit' δ, this non-linearity implies that $\beta(p_0 + \delta) - \beta(p_0) \neq \beta(p_0) - \beta(p_0 - \delta)$; finite differences will be evaluated as if the 'certainty equivalent' demand function had a kink at (p_0, q_0).

Maximisation of the left-hand side of (3.5) or (3.6) with respect to p is

[1] It is readily verified that $\beta(p)$ is a concave function of $p - p_0$. A few printing errors have been corrected in this section.

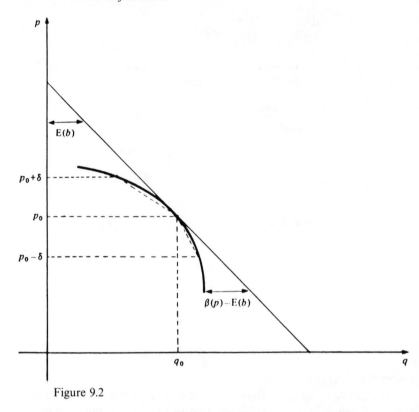

Figure 9.2

equivalent to maximisation of expected utility. A risk-neutral firm would simply maximise the first term on the right-hand side. This would also maximise $(p - p_0)[q_0 - E(b)(p - c)] - (\phi_0/2)(p - p_0)^2 [q_0 - E(b)(p - c)]^2$, over the range where the quadratic approximation is valid. The remaining term,[2] $- (\phi_0/2)(p - p_0)^2(p_0 - c)^2 V(b)$, is maximal at $p = p_0$ and therefore pulls the optimal p towards p_0 in the case of a risk-averse firm. (This justifies the reference to sticky prices in the title of this note.)

---

[2] Omitting third and higher powers of $(p - p_0)$.

10 Stability of a Keynesian adjustment process*

1. Introduction

1.1. Outline

In this paper, I study the stability of an adjustment process on prices and quantities that converges in finitely many steps to an equilibrium admitting excess supply of (some) factors of production. The finite convergence results from the fact that the leading adjustments are finite, and the equilibrium concept allows for ε-discrepancies between transacted *input* levels and those required by technology. The excess supply of factors of production at the equilibrium is associated with downward rigidities of nominal factor prices. Such an equilibrium is a special case of the so-called 'supply-constrained equilibria' studied by Dehez and Drèze (1984), following a seminal contribution of van der Laan (1980). These rigidities are best understood as reflecting non-competitive supply behaviour by owners of the production factors. (Here, the supply of factors by individual households is modelled as totally inelastic to prices, whose downward rigidity may be viewed as a form of collective income protection.)

The modelling of the economy embodies a distinction between primary inputs and other commodities. The leading adjustments concern the prices and quantities of primary inputs; quantity adjustments reflect the profit seeking decisions of producers (firms) and price increases take place under the pressure of excess demand. Thus, the quantity adjustments are decentralised firm by firm, and the price adjustments are decentralised market by market.

* In *Equilibrium Theory and Applications*, W. Barnett, B. Cornet, C. d'Aspremont, J. Jaskold-Gabsewicz and A. Mas-Colell, eds., Cambridge University Press, Cambridge, forthcoming. Helpful suggestions from Paul Champsaur, Pierre Dehez, Henry Tulkens and Gerd Weinrich are gratefully acknowledged.

A tâtonnement process is studied first, to clear the ground on a simpler case. My main interest, however, goes to a non-tâtonnement process, with production and consumption activities carried out in continuous time out of equilibrium. Feasibility of these activities is ensured by inventories, and it is shown that bounded inventory levels are sufficient for feasibility.

To establish finite convergence of a simple decentralised non-tâtonnement adjustment process, with ongoing production and consumption, is a major step towards realism. The equilibrium concept also has claims to realism. The empirical record clearly supports the view that non-storable factors of production, in particular labour and the services of capital, are not fully used all the time; see figure 10.1 for European data, 1973–89. It thus seems meaningful to study the stability properties of equilibria with that property. (The ε-feature I regard as entirely innocuous; some might claim that it adds to realism; to me, it is a convenience – neither more nor less.)

Of course, a price has to be paid for these results, in the form of assumptions. These come at three distinct levels.

(i) Most basic are the behavioural assumptions about consumers and producers. Consumers are, as usual, price takers and preference maximisers. They hold endowments of the primary factors of production and supply these inelastically – an assumption that is not quite realistic for (female) labour services, but could be relaxed. Producers are modelled implicitly as setting prices of commodities through a mark-up on production costs (where the mark-up rates may reflect perceived demand elasticities or fixed costs); their demand for factors is derived from their input needs to meet the demand for commodities at these prices. As suggested in Section 1.2, these behavioural assumptions seem consistent with empirical findings. I regard them as specific, but not particularly restrictive.

(ii) A major difficulty arising in non-tâtonnement processes with ongoing production and consumption concerns the modelling of expectations and intertemporal optimisation under uncertainty. That difficulty is completely eschewed here, to concentrate on stability. Both firms and consumers are assumed to hold static point expectations, that is to anticipate that prices and quantity constraints observed today will continue to prevail forever after. That assumption is very crude, and motivated exclusively by the understandable desire to split difficulties. It is accompanied by an assumption of stationary preferences for consumers and by an equally crude assumption about inventory decisions by firms. I regard these (standard) assumptions as very strong, but provisional.

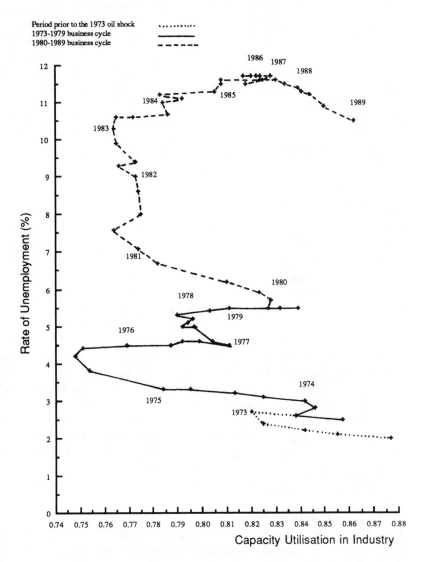

Figure 10.1 Rate of unemployment and capacity utilisation in industry in the European Community. Quarterly observations are shown, with the years marked against the first quarter. *Source: European Economy*

(iii) At a third level, I will introduce two assumptions – one on technology and the other on consumer preferences – which are clearly restrictive, but are needed for my stability proofs. The assumption on technology is absence of joint production and constant returns. This permits choosing input coefficients on the basis of input prices alone, without reference to output levels. It would complicate matters to dispense with that simplifying assumption. The assumption on consumer preferences is absence of inferior goods – an assumption that is clearly unrealistic,[1] but which plays for quantity adjustments a role similar to that played by gross substituability (not assumed here) for price adjustments. I do not know to what extent these two assumptions, which permit a reasonably straightforward derivation of strong results, could be generalised. Here lies a natural topic for further research.

1.2. Origins and organisation

The intellectual origins of this paper are twofold. On the one hand, there was a theoretical inspiration, arising from my work with Pierre Dehez on supply-constrained equilibria. This led me in 1983 to study the stability of a tâtonnement process, for an economy with a Leontief technology (no joint production, constant returns and fixed coefficients); see Drèze (1983). The motivation was to obtain a supply-constrained equilibrium as the outcome of a decentralised adjustment process on prices and quantity constraints, without assuming outright such properties as 'orderly' (one-sided) rationing. As a by-product, I wanted to investigate the presumptions that constrained demands could guide an adjustment process just as effectively as notional demands, whereas quantity constraints could make a useful contribution to stability. Both presumptions were verified on a simple but suggestive example, borrowed without modifications from Chapter 7 of Morishima's book *The Economic Theory of Modern Society* (1976). That paper, which forms the core of Sections 2 and 3 below, was never published, because I wanted to extend my analysis to non-tâtonnement; my intellectual wanderings in real time kept postponing the task.

The second source of inspiration was empirical. In the years 1984–89, I was involved in the European Unemployment Program (EUP), a (successful) joint effort by researchers in ten countries to analyse the determination of aggregate output and employment by means of a small

---

[1] See however Section 8.5.

macroeconometric model, the specification of which would be the same in each country but flexible enough to encompass equilibrium as well as disequilibrium situations; see Drèze *et al.* (1991). That methodology led to the verification of a number of empirical regularities, in which I recognised interesting similitudes with the structure of Morishima's model. These regularities include econometric results compatible with the following specifications: (i) pricing at average cost plus a mark-up; (ii) no rationing of final demand; (iii) downwards rigidity of nominal wages; (iv) persistent unemployment; (v) CES-Leontief technology with constant returns; see Drèze and Bean (1990).

These findings provided the motivation to extend my earlier analysis in two directions, namely: a more general technology encompassing the CES-Leontief specification (general convex production sets, subject only to the twin restrictions of constant returns and absence of joint production); and non-tâtonnement. These extensions are included in the present paper. In the process of carrying out the extensions, I also realised that my 1983 stability proof could be simplified significantly.

The paper is divided in two parts. Part I presents the tâtonnement process corresponding to Morishima's model (Sections 2 and 3), with a simple illustration for the Barro and Grossman (1971)–Malinvaud (1977) Macroeconomic Model (Section 4) and the extension to variable input coefficients (Section 5). Part II presents the extension to non-tâtonnement (Sections 6 and 7). Some comments and concluding remarks are offered in Section 8.

PART I: TÂTONNEMENT

2. The economy and the process

2.1. The economy

The tâtonnement process studied in Part I may be viewed as a formalisation of the system described in Chapter 7 of Morishima's book *The Economic Theory of Modern Society* (1976), and summarised as follows by the author:

The Keynesian system we have described above has the following system of transmission between its parts. First, suppose that prices of factors of production are given arbitrarily or historically. The prices of products are determined so that they satisfy the equation: prices = costs + normal profits. Now all prices are given, and therefore the income of workers and capitalists per unit of product is determined, and we can determine the remaining unknowns, l individual outputs, by the equations of the theory of effective demand ... since we take the gross investment in capital goods as given. Outputs thus determined decide the demand for labour and the services of capital goods. When these demands do not exceed the existing quantities of capital goods and the supplies of various kinds of labour corresponding to given prices and wages, then there is no excess demand for producer goods. Therefore ... prices are stationary because of the downward rigidity of wages and the prices of capital services, and we have an underemployment equilibrium accompanied by idle capital or unemployment.

In contrast to this, if excess demand exists for capital services or for labour, the prices of producer goods will change ... . The change spreads in turn to product prices, the outputs of each good and the excess demands for producer goods, and then back once again to the point of departure, namely the prices of producer goods. The process of price adjustment is repeated until full-employment equilibrium or underemployment equilibrium is eventually established.

The structure of the economy is summarised in the upper half of table 10.1 (p. 213).

There are $1 + m + n$ commodities. Commodity 0 is 'money', commodities $1 \ldots m$ are inputs, commodities $m + 1 \ldots m + n$ are consumer goods. The price of money is equal to 1. The prices of inputs are denoted $p \in R^m$, the prices of outputs are denoted $q \in R^n$.

An $m \times n$ technology matrix A describes the net input requirements for producing consumer goods. Thus, A_{kj} is the quantity of input k consumed per unit of consumer good j. It is a net quantity, in the sense that intermediate commodities are not recognised explicitly but instead are represented by their own input requirements. This assumes that the economy is 'productive' (no A_{kj} is infinite). Inputs are of three types: labour services, natural resources (land, minerals, ...) and 'machines'. The availability of inputs is fixed in the short run and is the only limiting factor in the production of consumer goods.[2]

There are N consumers indexed $i = 1 \ldots N$. Consumer i initially holds a positive quantity of money m_0^i and a non-negative vector of input

---

[2] It is suggestive, although not necessary, to think about each consumer good as being produced on a specific 'machine', the capacity of which sets an upper limit to the production of that good. In this interpretation, a 'machine' is typically a shop or plant (e.g. a weaving plant with many looms, rather than a single loom). All the facilities which permit production of a given consumer good with the same unit requirements in labour and natural resources may thus be lumped into a single 'machine'. When the input requirements differ, variable coefficients and diminishing returns fit into the linear technology – but at the cost of handling perfect substitutes in consumption, hence demand correspondences.

endowments $z^i \in R^m$. Typically, each consumer will supply one type of labour services, up to a maximal amount corresponding to his or her endowment. Ownership of natural resources and 'machines' is shared among consumers, possibly reflecting their fixed ownership fractions in firms controlling these inputs.

The (nominal) prices of inputs are initially set at given levels $p(0)$ and are eventually adjusted *upwards* along the process in response to excess demand; they are never adjusted downwards. At these prices, consumers supply their total endowments z^i. Excess supply of an input is accompanied by quantity rationing. I denote by $\zeta_k^i(t)$ the upper bound on the net sales of input k by consumer i at stage t of the process. By construction, $z_k^i \geq \zeta_k^i(t) \geq 0$. (Under an alternative interpretation, the ζ^i's denote input levels for which household i has contracted with the production sector.) I also define the *effective aggregate supply* of inputs by

$$z_k^S(t) = \sum_i \zeta_k^i(t). \tag{2.1}$$

The corresponding vectors are

$$\zeta^i(t) = (\zeta_1^i(t) \dots \zeta_m^i(t))', \; z^S(t) = (z_1^S(t) \dots z_m^S(t))'. \tag{2.2}$$

The prices of consumer goods are derived from the prices of inputs through the mark-up formula

$$q'(t) = p'(t)A\mathcal{M}, \tag{2.3}$$

where $\mathcal{M}$ is an $n \times n$ diagonal matrix such that $\mathcal{M}_{jj} - 1 \geq 0$ is the mark-up factor for commodity j, $j = 1 \dots n$.

Under the price formula (2.3), consumer goods are supplied inelastically to meet consumer demand. That is, output of consumer goods is determined by effective demand, say $y(t)$, generating a factor demand

$$z^D(t) = Ay(t). \tag{2.4}$$

Comparison of the demand $z_k^D(t)$ and the supply $z_k^S(t)$ for factor k leads to the adjustments in price $p_k(t)$ and quantity constraints $\zeta_k^i(t)$ described below.

The effective demands of consumer goods depend upon their prices $q(t)$ and upon the consumer incomes $r^i(t)$, defined by

$$r^i(t) = m_0^i + \sum_k p_k(t)\zeta_k^i(t) = m_0^i + p'(t)\zeta^i(t). \tag{2.5}$$

In this formulation consumers collect income only for the quantities of factors which they can sell, at a given stage of the process. They do not, *along the process*, collect their shares of current profits arising from the mark-up factor. This formulation is somewhat hybrid; greater realism would suggest distribution of profits with explicit lags. The chosen simplification seems unimportant, for my purposes here.

Assuming strictly convex preferences for money and consumer goods, I shall use the demand *functions*

$$y_0^i(q(t), r^i(t)) \in R, \, y^i(q(t), r^i(t)) \in R^n.$$

Thus, demand for consumer goods depends upon input prices and quantity constraints only through the incomes $r^i(t)$. (A more general formulation is used in Part II.)

Two assumptions about individual demand functions will be used below, namely:

ASSUMPTION NI

For all i, for all q, r^i and $\hat{r}^i \geq r^i$, $y^i(q, \hat{r}^i) \geq y^i(q, r^i)$.

ASSUMPTION MPC

For each i, there exists $\gamma^i > 0$ (independent of q and r^i) such that, for all q, r^i and $\hat{r}^i \leq r^i$, $y_0^i(q, \hat{r}^i) \geq y_0^i(q, r^i) + \gamma^i(\hat{r}^i - r^i)$.

Assumption NI (Non Inferiority) rules out inferior goods, which is very unfortunate, since there is nothing pathological about such goods (see however Section 8.5). Assumption MPC (Marginal Propensity to Consume) states that the marginal propensity to spend is bounded away from unity.

The description of the economy is now complete, and may be summarised as follows (see also table 10.1):

(i) Given a vector of input prices $p(t)$ and a matrix of quantity constraints $[\zeta_k^i(t)]$, individual incomes are defined by

$$r^i(t) = m_0^i + \sum_k p_k(t)\zeta_k^i(t) = m_0^i + p'(t)\zeta^i(t) \tag{2.5}$$

and prices for consumer goods are defined by:

$$q(t) = p'(t)A\mathcal{M}; \tag{2.3}$$

(ii) Demand for consumer goods is defined by:

$$y(t) = \sum_i y^i(t) = \sum_i y^i(q(t), r^i(t)); \tag{2.6}$$

Table 10.1

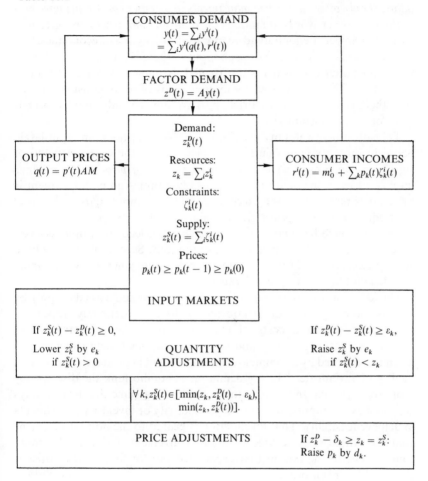

that demand implies a demand for inputs

$$z^D(t) = Ay(t). \tag{2.4}$$

2.2. The process

Upon comparing the demand vector for inputs $z^D(t)$ with the supply vector $z^S(t) = \Sigma_i\zeta^i(t)$, adjustments in prices and quantity constraints can be defined. I shall consider a *hierarchical process*, under which *prices are adjusted only after all justified adjustments in quantity constraints have been realised*; in other words, quantities move faster than prices, in agreement with the Clower–Leijonhufvud reappraisal of Keynesian economics.[3]

The process is *discrete*. For each input k, there is a quantity unit e_k, of which all initial endowments are treated as integer multiples. Quantity constraints $\zeta_k^i(t)$ are adjusted by discrete steps of fixed, constant size e_k. And there is a price unit d_k. Prices $p_k(t)$ are similarly adjusted by discrete steps of fixed, constant size d_k.

The adjustment rules involve *thresholds*. No adjustment in input levels, hence in quantity constraints, takes place unless the excess demand or supply for an input, $|z_k^D(t) - z_k^S(t)|$, reaches some *a priori* given minimal level ε_k (at least one quantity unit, possibly more). And no adjustment in price takes place unless the excess *demand* for an input, $z_k^D(t) - z_k^S(t)$, is at least equal to some *a priori* given minimal level δ_k ($\geq \varepsilon_k$).

This approach has two consequences. First, it leads to a finite convergence theorem, under rather weak assumptions. Second, it leads only to an *approximate equilibrium*, where a small discrepancy between supply and demand (at most δ_k) is tolerated.

The idea that prices are not adjusted unless demand exceeds supply by at least some given (but arbitrarily small) δ_k is definitely appealing, considering the fixed costs of changing prices. An arbitrarily small discrepancy between supply and demand of an *input* seems tolerable, as it can be absorbed by a commensurate adjustment in productivity, product quality or inventories.[4] In my definition of equilibrium, the discrepancy is of arbitrary sign. In the adjustment process, I assume that firms always get rid of excess inputs, and rely on productivity or inventory adjustments to achieve feasibility. That formulation is geared to the non-tâtonnement analysis, where it is technically more convenient and logically more congruent with the notion that excess demand for final commodities is absorbed by inventories.

---

[3] 'In the Keynesian macro-system the Marshallian ranking of price– and quantity–adjustment speeds is reversed: in the shortest period flow quantities are freely variable, but one or more prices are given, and the admissible range of variation for the rest of the prices is thereby limited': Leijonhufvud (1968), p. 52.

[4] Note that, if profits are defined as $\pi = q'y - p'\sum_i \zeta^i$, so that any discrepancy between supply and demand of inputs is absorbed by the production sector, then automatically $\sum_i y_0^i + \pi = \sum_i m_0^i$ in equilibrium. Indeed, $\sum_i y_0^i + \pi = \sum_i (r^i - q'y^i) + \pi = \sum_i (m_0^i + p'\zeta^i) - q'y + q'y - p'\sum_i \zeta^i = \sum_i m_0^i$, which corresponds to Walras law in this model.

DEFINITION

An *ε-equilibrium with excess supply* consists of a vector of input prices $p \in R^m$, a matrix of quantity constraints $[\zeta_k^i] \in R^{Nm}$, a vector of inputs $z^D \in R^m$, a vector of outputs $y \in R^n$, a vector of prices $q \in R^n$ with $q' = p'A\mathcal{M}$ and an N-tuple of vectors $(y_0^i, y^i) \in R \times R^n$ such that:

(i) (z^D, y) maximises $q'y - p'z^D$ subject to $z^D \geq Ay$, $y \leq \sum_i y^i$;

(ii) (y_0^i, y^i) maximises i's preferences, subject to $y_0^i + q'y^i \leq m_0^i + p'\zeta^i$;

(iii) $[0] \leq [\zeta_k^i] \leq [z_k^i]$, $\sum_i y^i \leq y$;

(iv) for all $k = 1 \ldots m$, $|z_k^D - \sum_i \zeta_k^i| \leq \varepsilon$.

DESCRIPTION OF THE PROCESS P

The process is defined in terms of the sequence $(p(t), [\zeta_k^i(t)])$, $t = 0, 1, 2 \ldots$. The other parameters are at all stages defined through (2.3)–(2.6).

(*P i*) *Initiation.* Initial input prices $p(0)$ are historically given, with $p_k(0) > 0$ for all k.

Initial quantity constraints are historically set at $\zeta_k^i(0)$, an integer multiple of e_k, with $z_k^i \geq \zeta_k^i(0) \geq 0$ for all i and k.

(*P ii*) *General Step – Adjustment of a Quantity Constraint.* At stage t, a single quantity constraint is adjusted, provided there exists an input k for which such an adjustment is justified. (The order in which markets are visited is immaterial.)

Two situations are distinguished:

(a) $z_k^S(t) - z_k^D(t) > 0$.

Then necessarily $z_k^S(t) > 0$, and there exists i such that $\zeta_k^i(t) > 0$. For some (any) such i, set

$$\zeta_k^i(t + 1) = \zeta_k^i(t) - e_k. \tag{2.7}$$

(That is, the constraint on net sales of input k by consumer i is lowered by one unit e_k. Because $\zeta_k^i(t)$ results from the operation of the process, starting from an integer multiple of e_k, $\zeta_k^i(t) > 0$ implies $\zeta_k^i(t + 1) \geq 0$.)

(b) $z_k^D(t) - z_k^S(t) \geq \varepsilon_k$ with $z_k^S(t) < z_k$.

Then necessarily there exists i such that $\zeta_k^i(t) < z_k^i$. For some (any) such i, set

$$\zeta_k^i(t + 1) = \zeta_k^i(t) + e_k. \tag{2.8}$$

(That is, the constraint on net sales of input k by consumer i is raised by one unit e_k. Because both $\zeta_k^i(t)$ and z_k^i are integer multiples of e_k, $\zeta_k^i(t) < z_k^i$ implies $\zeta_k^i(t + 1) \leq z_k^i$.)

(*P iii*) *General Step – Adjustment of a Price.* If, at stage t, no adjustment of quantity constraints is justified, then it must be the case, that for all k,

$$z_k^S(t) \in [\min(z_k, z_k^D(t) - \varepsilon_k), \min(z_k, z_k^D(t))], z_k^S(t) \leq z_k^D(t). \tag{2.9}$$

If there exists k such that $z_k^D(t) - \delta_k \geq z_k^S(t) = z_k$, set

$$p_k(t + 1) = p_k(t) + d_k. \tag{2.10}$$

(That is, if input k is in excess demand by at least δ_k, with no binding constraints on net sales, the price of that input is raised by a fixed amount d_k.)

(*P iv*) *Termination.* If, for all k, (2.9) holds with $z_k^D(t) < z_k + \delta_k$, the process terminates.

A state of the economy where the process terminates is an ε–*equilibrium with excess supply*, where

$$\varepsilon \leq \max_k \delta_k, \tag{2.11}$$

an arbitrarily small quantity.

Indeed, conditions (i)–(iii) in the above definition are always satisfied along process P. Conditions (iv) are satisfied when the process terminates, since (2.9) implies $z_k^S(t) - z_k^D(t) \leq 0$ and (P iv) implies $z_k^S(t) - z_k^D(t) > -\delta_k$, so that $|z_k^D(t) - z_k^S(t)| \leq \delta_k$ as desired.

3. Stability

The proof of the stability theorem below rests upon the following lemma, which establishes that *all prices are bounded along the process* P.

LEMMA I

Under process P, for all k, for all t,

$$p_k(t) \leq \max\left(\frac{\sum_i m_0^i}{\delta_k} + d_k, p_k(0)\right) \overset{\text{def}}{=} \bar{p}_k.$$

PROOF

From the definition of the process, $p_k(t + 1) = p_k(t)$ unless

$$z_l^D(t) - z_l^S(t) \geq 0 \text{ for all } l, z_k^D(t) - z_k^S(t) \geq \delta_k. \tag{3.1}$$

Moreover,

$$\sum_l p_l(t) z_l^D(t) = \sum_l p_l(t) \sum_{j=1}^n A_{lj} y_j(t) \qquad \text{by (2.4)}$$

$$= \sum_{j=1}^n \frac{1}{\mu_{jj}} q_j(t) y_j(t) \leq \sum_{j=1}^n q_j(t) y_j(t) \qquad \text{by (2.3)}$$

$$= \sum_i (r^i(t) - y_0^i(t)) \qquad \text{by (2.6)}$$

$$= \sum_i \left[\sum_l p_l(t) \zeta_l^i(t) + m_0^i - y_0^i(t) \right] \qquad \text{by (2.5)}$$

$$= \sum_l p_l(t) z_l^S(t) + \sum_i (m_0^i - y_0^i(t)).$$

Thus

$$\sum_{\substack{l=1 \\ l \neq k}}^m p_l(t)[z_l^D(t) - z_l^S(t)] + p_k(t)[z_k^D(t) - z_k^S(t)] \leq \sum_i (m_0^i - y_0^i(t)).$$

If $p_k(t + 1) > p_k(t)$, then

$$\delta_k p_k(t) \leq p_k(t)[z_k^D(t) - z_k^S(t)] \leq \sum_i (m_0^i - y_0^i(t))$$

$$- \sum_{\substack{l=1 \\ l \neq k}}^m p_l(t)[z_l^D(t) - z_l^S(t)]$$

$$\leq \sum_i m_0^i,$$

where the last inequalities follow from (3.1), and $y_0^i(t) \geq 0$. Thus, $p_k(t + 1)$ will not rise above $p_k(t)$ unless $p_k(t) \leq \sum_i m_0^i/\delta_k$, which proves the lemma.

QED

The logic of the above proof is straightforward. If the demand for input k exceeds its supply by the finite amount δ_k, *and no input is in excess supply*, then even with zero mark-up the value of aggregate demand must exceed the revenue from the sale of factors by at least $\delta_k p_k(t)$; that discrepancy must be financed from initial money holdings, so that $\delta_k p_k(t) \leq \sum_i m_0^i(t)$.

The lemma has a very important implication, namely that *only a finite bounded number of price adjustments can occur under process* P. Indeed, each such adjustment calls for increasing some price p_k by the constant finite amount d_k, and each p_k has a finite upper bound $\bar{p}_k$. In order to establish finite convergence of the process, it will thus suffice to establish that only a finite, *uniformly* bounded number of quantity adjustments can take place between two price adjustments. The overall process will thus consist of a bounded number of uniformly bounded numbers of steps, i.e. of a bounded number of steps.

THEOREM I

Under assumptions NI and MPC, provided for all $k = 1 \ldots m$, e_k is small enough ($e_k \leq \frac{1}{2}\varepsilon_k$), the process P is stable, and converges in a bounded number of steps to an ε-equilibrium with excess supply.

PROOF

We only need to prove that at most a finite uniformly bounded number of quantity adjustments can take place between two price adjustments. Let p denote the price vector resulting from either initiation or some price adjustment, and let $t + 1$ denote a general quantity adjustment step. The process P is best viewed, over the set of quantity adjustment steps between two successive price adjustments, as associating with $(p, [\zeta_k^i(t)])$ $\in R^m \times R^{Nm}$ the set of solutions $(p, [\zeta_k^i(t + 1)]) \in R^m \times R^{Nm}$ compatible with the description of the process. This is a finite set, with elements generated by alternative choices of k or i, where alternative choices exist. Hence, it is closed, and compact because the solutions are bounded: $z_k^i \geq \zeta_k^i(t) \geq 0$ for all i, k and t. The proof is a simplified version of the proof of theorem 6.2, pp. 290–291 in Champsaur, Drèze and Henry (1977), using the Lyapunov function

$$L(t) = \sum_{l=1}^{m} p_l \max \left[z_l^D(t) - \varepsilon_l - z_l^S(t), z_l^S(t) - z_l^D(t) \right]$$

$$\leq \sum_{l=1}^{m} p_l \max \left[z_l^D(t), z_l^S(t) \right]. \tag{3.2}$$

That function is uniformly bounded above, because p_l is bounded (by $\bar{p}_l$ in the lemma), $z_l^S(t) \leq \sum_i z_l^i$ and $p_l z_l^D(t) \leq \sum_j p_j z_j^D(t) \leq \sum_j p_j \sum_i z_j^i + \sum_i m_0^i$ as verified in the proof of the lemma. Also, $L(t) \geq -\sum_{l=1}^{m} p_l \varepsilon_l \geq -\sum_{l=1}^{m} \bar{p}_l \varepsilon_l$. Thus, $L(t)$ is uniformly bounded, both above and below. The proof consists in showing that there exists a positive constant $c = \min_{k=1\ldots m} c_k$, *bounded away from zero*, such that $L(t) - L(t+1) \geq c$, unless no further quantity adjustment is possible at $(t+1)$. The two possibilities corresponding to (P ii) (a) and (P ii) (b) are considered successively.

Case (P ii) (a)

In this case, for all $l = 1 \ldots m$, $p_l(t+1) = p_l(t) = p_l$, so that $q(t+1) = q(t)$ as well. Also, for all $h = 1 \ldots N$, $h \neq i$, $\zeta^h(t+1) = \zeta^h(t)$, so that $r^h(t+1) = r^h(t)$ and $y^h(t+1) = y^h(q(t), r^h(t)) = y^h(t)$. For all $l = 1 \ldots m$, $l \neq k$, $\zeta_l^i(t+1) = \zeta_l^i(t)$, so that $z_l^S(t+1) = z_l^S(t)$. On the other hand $\zeta_k^i(t+1) = \zeta_k^i(t) - e_k$, so that $z_k^S(t+1) = z_k^S(t) - e_k$. Finally, $r^i(t+1) = r^i(t) + p_k \left[\zeta_k^i(t+1) - \zeta_k^i(t) \right] = r^i(t) - e_k p_k < r^i(t)$. In view of assumption NI, $y^i(t+1) = y^i(q(t), r^i(t+1)) \leq y^i(q(t), r^i(t)) = y^i(t)$, so that $y(t+1) \leq y(t)$ and $z^D(t+1) \leq z^D(t)$.

For all $l = 1 \ldots m$, $l \neq k$,

$$\max \left[z_l^D(t+1) - \varepsilon_l - z_l^S(t+1), \ z_l^S(t+1) - z_l^D(t+1) \right]$$
$$= \max \left[z_l^D(t+1) - \varepsilon_l - z_l^S(t), \ z_l^S(t) - z_l^D(t+1) \right]$$
$$\leq z_l^D(t) - z_l^D(t+1)$$
$$\quad + \max \left[z_l^D(t) - \varepsilon_l - z_l^S(t), \ z_l^S(t) - z_l^D(t) \right].$$

Also, $z_k^D(t+1) \leq z_k^D(t) < z_k^S(t) = z_k^S(t+1) + e_k$, and for e_k small enough $(e_k \leq \frac{1}{2}\varepsilon_k)$,

$$z_k^D(t+1) - \varepsilon_k - z_k^S(t+1) = z_k^D(t+1) - \varepsilon_k - z_k^S(t) + e_k$$
$$\leq z_k^D(t+1) - e_k - z_k^S(t) \leq z_k^D(t) - e_k - z_k^S(t) < -e_k$$

$$< z_k^S(t) - e_k - z_k^D(t)$$
$$= z_k^S(t + 1) - z_k^D(t) \le z_k^S(t + 1) - z_k^D(t + 1),$$

so that

$$\max \left[z_k^D(t + 1) - \varepsilon_k - z_k^S(t + 1), z_k^S(t + 1) - z_k^D(t + 1) \right]$$
$$= z_k^S(t + 1) - z_k^D(t + 1)$$
$$= z_k^S(t) - z_k^D(t) - e_k + z_k^D(t) - z_k^D(t + 1)$$
$$= \max \left[z_k^D(t) - \varepsilon_k - z_k^S(t), z_k^S(t) - z_k^D(t) \right]$$
$$+ z_k^D(t) - z_k^D(t + 1) - e_k.$$

Consequently,

$$L(t + 1) - L(t) \le \sum_{l=1}^{m} p_l[z_l^D(t) - z_l^D(t + 1)] - e_k p_k.$$

Furthermore,

$$z_l^D(t) - z_l^D(t + 1) = \sum_{j=1}^{n} A_{lj}[y_j^i(t) - y_j^i(t + 1)]$$

and $\displaystyle \sum_{l=1}^{m} p_l A_{lj} = \frac{1}{\mu_{jj}} q_j$,

so that

$$\sum_{l=1}^{m} p_l[z_l^D(t) - z_l^D(t + 1)] = \sum_{j} \frac{1}{\mu_{jj}} q_j(t)[y_j^i(t) - y_j^i(t + 1)]$$
$$\le \sum_{j} q_j(t)[y_j^i(t) - y_j^i(t + 1)]$$
$$= [r^i(t) - y_0^i(t) - r^i(t + 1) + y_0^i(t + 1)]$$
$$= [e_k p_k + y_0^i(t + 1) - y_0^i(t)] \le e_k p_k(1 - \gamma^i),$$

where the last inequality follows from assumption MPC. Hence,

$$L(t + 1) - L(t) \le e_k p_k(1 - \gamma^i - 1) \le - e_k p_k \gamma^i \le - c_k < 0,$$

where the existence of $c_k > 0$ follows from $p_k \ge p_k(0) > 0$.

Case (P ii) (b)

This case is entirely symmetrical to the previous one, and the same reasoning applies, with $\zeta_k^i(t + 1) = \zeta_k^i(t) + e_k$, $r^i(t + 1) = r^i(t) + e_k p_k$ and $z^D(t + 1) \ge z^D(t)$.

For all $l = 1 \ldots m$, $l \neq k$, we have $z_l^S(t + 1) = z_l^S(t)$ and

$$\max \left[z_l^D(t + 1) - \varepsilon_l - z_l^S(t + 1), \ z_l^S(t + 1) - z_l^D(t + 1) \right]$$
$$\leq \max \left[z_l^D(t + 1) - \varepsilon_l - z_l^S(t), \ z_l^S(t) - z_l^D(t) \right]$$
$$\leq z_l^D(t + 1) - z_l^D(t) + \max \left[z_l^D - \varepsilon_l - z_l^S(t), \ z_l^S(t) - z_l^D(t) \right].$$

Also, for $e_k \leq \dfrac{\varepsilon_k}{2}$,

$$z_k^D(t + 1) - \varepsilon_k - z_k^S(t + 1) \geq z_k^D(t) - \varepsilon_k - z_k^S(t) - e_k \geq -e_k$$
$$\geq e_k - \varepsilon_k \geq z_k^S(t) + e_k - z_k^D(t) \geq z_k^S(t + 1) - z_k^D(t + 1),$$

so that

$$\max \left[z_k^D(t + 1) - \varepsilon_k - z_k^S(t + 1), \ z_k^S(t + 1) - z_k^D(t + 1) \right]$$
$$= z_k^D(t + 1) - \varepsilon_k - z_k^S(t + 1)$$
$$= z_k^D(t + 1) - z_k^D(t) - e_k + z_k^D(t) - \varepsilon_k - z_k^S(t)$$
$$= z_k^D(t + 1) - z_k^D(t) - e_k + \max \left[z_k^D(t) - \varepsilon_k - z_k^S(t), \ z_k^S(t) - z_k^D(t) \right].$$

By the reasoning of the previous case,

$$\sum_{l=1}^{m} p_l [z_l^D(t + 1) - z_l^D(t)] \leq r^i(t + 1) - y_0^i(t + 1) - r^i(t) + y_0^i(t)$$

$$\leq e_k p_k (1 - \gamma^i),$$
$$L(t + 1) - L(t) \leq -e_k p_k \gamma^i \leq -c_k < 0.$$

Combining the two cases, and writing c for $\min_k c_k$, we have shown that $L(t + 1) - L(t) \leq -c < 0$ unless (2.9) holds and no further quantity adjustment is possible. Since $L(t)$ is uniformly bounded above and below for all t, only a finite number of successive quantity adjustments is possible. The condition $e_k p_k(t) \gamma^i \geq c_k > 0$ may be imposed in the form $e_k p_k(t) \gamma^i \geq e_k p_k(0) \gamma^i \geq c_k > 0$, so that c_k is independent of the stage of the process, and the number of successive quantity adjustments is uniformly bounded, as desired.　　　　　　　　　　　　　　　　　　　QED

The logic of the second part of the proof is again straightforward. Each quantity adjustment on z_k^S reduces the absolute money value of excess demand for input k by $e_k p_k(t)$ at unchanged demand for commodities, and affects only the disposable income of a single consumer by that same amount. By MPC, the money value of effective demand for commodities will adjust by at most $(1 - \gamma^i) e_k p_k(t)$, leaving a positively bounded margin of $e_k p_k(t) \gamma^i \geq c$ by which the absolute money value of excess demand for inputs must fall.

4. Illustration

The so-called 'three goods economy' dear to macro-theorists has money, a single input labour ($m = 1$), and a single produced commodity ($n = 1$). In the specification of Malinvaud (1977), the N consumers are identical. At a given money wage $p(t)$ and commodity price $q(t) = p(t) a \mu$, the economy is conveniently described by figure 10.2. The horizontal axis corresponds to labour, the vertical axis to the commodity. The ray OA describes the Leontief technology. Let each household supply a single unit of labour – the e_k of Section 2 being here renormalised to unity; hence, its labour supply constraint (ζ_k^i) can take two values: 0 or 1. To these two values correspond the incomes $r^i = m_0^i$ and $r^i = m_0^i + p(t)$, respectively, with associated demand levels $y^i(m_0^i, q(t))$ and $y^i(m_0^i + p(t), q(t))$. Aggregate demand is thus a linear function of employment, for which the relevant measure during the tâtonnement is $z^S(t) = \sum_i \zeta^i(t)$; namely:

$$y(t) = z^S(t) y^i(m_0^i + p(t), q(t)) + [N - z^S(t)] y^i(m_0^i, q(t)). \tag{4.1}$$

That linear function, defined over the domain $[0, N]$, is plotted in figure 10.2. If the upper end of that line segment (point B) belonged to the line OA, reflecting equality of supply and demand for the commodity at full employment of labour, one could conclude that $(p(t), q(t))$ are competitive prices. In figure 10.2a, point B lies below the line OA, whereas in figure 10.2b, point B lies above the line OA.

To start with figure 10.2a, let $t = 0$ and $\sum_i \zeta^i(0) = z^S(0)$ be a relatively small number, as drawn. One can then read from the graph $z^D(0) \gg z^S(0)$, which calls for a quantity adjustment step (P ii) (b), i.e. for a unit increase in employment: $z^S(1) = z^S(0) + 1$. This reasoning will continue to hold so long as $z^D(t) - z^S(t) > \varepsilon$; it will cease to hold when $y(t)$ is close enough to the point K so that an ε-equilibrium with excess supply has been reached.

The same reasoning applies with a starting point $z^S(0)$ relatively large (close to N), the only difference being that the quantity adjustment steps are of the type (P ii) (a). Thus, in the case of figure 10.2a, process P converges through a sequence of quantity adjustments to the vicinity of a Keynesian equilibrium (point K) at the original wage and price ($p(0), q(0)$).

Turning to figure 10.2b, we note that $z^D(0) \gg z^S(0)$ for all $z^S(0) \in [0, N]$. This leads to a sequence of quantity adjustment steps (P ii) (b) until eventually $z^S(t) = N = z \ll z^D(t)$. Because $z^S(t) = z$, no further quantity adjustment is possible, and the process triggers a price adjustment (P iii): the excess demand for labour leads to a nominal wage increase, so that $p(t + 1) = p(t) + d \ (= p(0) + d)$. The commodity price q is immediately

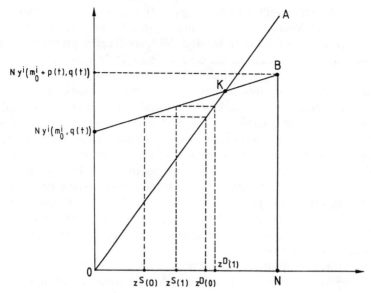

Figure 10.2a

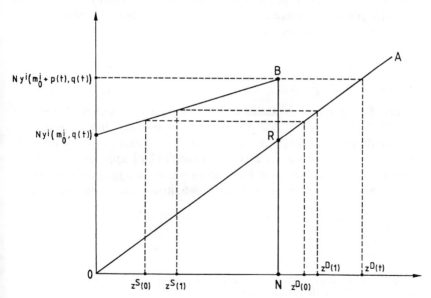

Figure 10.2b

raised from $q(t) = q(0) = p(0)a\mu$ to $q(t + 1) = p(t + 1)a\mu$ – leading to the new demand level $y(t + 1) = Ny^i(m_0^i + p(t + 1), q(t + 1))$. If $y(t + 1) \gg \overline{NR} = N/a$, i.e. if commodity demand still exceeds appreciably full employment output, we remain in the case of figure 10.2b and a further wage-price increase is triggered by the process. The reasoning in the proof of lemma I shows that this cannot happen infinitely many times, so that eventually point B falls back to the vicinity of line OA (at R) and an allocation close to a competitive equilibrium is attained. That reasoning says that, when prices cover wage costs, wage income can at best purchase produced output; thus, excess demand is financed entirely by initial money holdings, and must become negligible as the price level keeps rising. (That compelling argument does not assert that excess demand falls *monotonically* – only that it falls *eventually*.) Thus, in the case of figure 10.2b, process P converges, through a sequence of quantity adjustments followed by a sequence of wage-price increases, to the vicinity of a competitive equilibrium.

A further complication arises when existing equipment permits employing only $M < N$ workers. In order to fit that complication into process P, one must treat equipment as another input, with a price (rent) that will rise under the pressure of excess demand, eventually bringing the economy to the vicinity of a point with a clearing commodity market and unemployment – at the original wage and at a commodity price inflated by the rent on capital equipment.[5] Details are left to the reader.

5. Variable coefficients

The description of the technology in the model of Sections 2–3 is very specific. The *a priori* distinction between primary inputs and final commodities is perhaps acceptable at the economy-wide level. But the Leontief technology is extreme. The standard approach in general equilibrium economics would introduce a convex aggregate production set Y, then rewrite condition (i) in the definition of an ε-equilibrium as

$$(z^D, y) \text{ maximises } q'y - p'z^D \text{ subject to } (z^D, y) \in Y, y \leq \sum_i y^i. \qquad \text{(i*)}$$

---

[5] In the standard terminology of equilibria with quantity rationing, the process terminates at the intersection of the Keynesian and classical regimes – as suggested in Keynes' *General Theory*.

The Leontief specification says that '$(z^D, y) \in Y$ if and only if $z^D \geq Ay$', where A is a given matrix.

There is no difficulty in extending the definition of process P to a general specification of the technology. For instance, one could define $z^D(t)$ at each step through cost minimisation at given input prices and output levels:

$$(z^D, y) \text{ minimises } p'(t)z^D(t) \text{ subject to } (z^D(t), y(t)) \in Y. \qquad (5.1)$$

It would be interesting to know whether the extended process converges. My conjecture is that it would – possibly under some mild conditions; but the technique of proof would be more complicated. Short of having investigated the matter, I can at least give an example of a variable coefficients technology under which the extended process has the same properties as the original process – namely a convex technology with constant returns and no joint production.

In that case, the aggregate production set Y is the sum of n distinct production sets Y^j, one for each commodity $j = 1 \dots n$, and Y^i is a convex cone with vertex zero (constant returns), such that, for all $(z^D, y) \in Y^j$, $y_l = 0$, $l = 1 \dots n$, $l \neq j$ (no joint production). The important implication of such a technology, for my purposes, is that *technological choices are fully determined by input prices and do not depend upon output levels.* If either cuts of Y^j in z^D-space for given y_j are strictly convex, or an appropriate selection is made when (5.1) has multiple solutions,[6] then *we are back to the Leontief technology so long as input prices do not change.*

For process P, this means that we can work with the Leontief specification along sequences of quantity adjustment steps (P ii), and update the input-output matrix at (within) price adjustment steps (P iii) only. Consequently, the proof of theorem I remains valid without modification. This establishes the following:

COROLLARY

If the Leontief technology of Section 2 is extended to a general convex technology with constant returns and no joint production, theorem I still holds, wording unchanged.

Some econometricians – including Sneessens and Drèze (1986a) or Drèze and Bean (1991) – would argue that technical coefficients are revised infrequently anyhow; accordingly a more realistic extension of process P

---

[6]For instance, minimise $|z^D(t) - z^D(t-1)|$.

would retain the hierarchical structure, and introduce revisions of technical coefficients only when the process terminates. This would lead to consider a sequence of processes, each of which converges in finitely many steps, with technical coefficients for the *v*-th process minimising cost for the input prices and output levels at the termination of process $v - 1$. I would again conjecture that convergence of such a sequence would follow from mild conditions.

PART II: NON-TÂTONNEMENT

6. A non-tâtonnement process

6.1. Principles

It is not difficult to suggest a guiding principle towards one extension of theorem I to a non-tâtonnement process, with production and consumption activities carried out in continuous time out of equilibrium. Suppose that firms hold inventories of consumer goods, out of which consumer demand can be satisfied *temporarily* when it exceeds production. Such an assumption is not as general as one would like, because it rules out non-storable commodities, like electricity, opera seats or labour services (which are occasionally subject to demand rationing). This is an exploratory paper, and storable commodities will do. If consumer demand is never rationed, and the production sector is still treated as an aggregate, then activities 'out of equilibrium' differ from activities 'at equilibrium' (of the process) in a single respect, namely that the quantities of inputs stipulated by the process may differ from those needed to satisfy demand. That households may experience excess supply of inputs, along the process, is not a novel feature, since that possibility is already accepted at equilibrium. But firms realise their input demands at equilibrium, whereas that may not be possible out of equilibrium. Still, excess demand for some inputs should not prevent firms from making use of whatever production possibilities they have, in order to satisfy at least partially the demand for their outputs, while drawing *temporarily* on inventories for the balance. And hoarding some inputs *temporarily* is common place, when firms adjust progressively to a demand shortfall or are prevented from using some input k because the complementary input l is in short supply. Modelling production activities out of equilibrium is a natural task, as those who have worked on dynamic planning of production, inventories and workforce know.

A key word in my tale so far is 'temporarily'. Clearly, inventory depletion cannot go on forever, nor will firms hoard factors of production forever. Regarding the first point, adjustment in either production levels or prices (to choke off demand) should be fast enough that the drain on inventories comes to a halt before the warehouse, or the shelves, are empty.[7] A reasonable assignment for non-tâtonnement stability analysis is thus to investigate *sufficient conditions* on the adjustment process under which *a form of equilibrium is reached, in real time, before reasonable levels of initial inventories are depleted.* This is where the finite convergence property established in theorem I pays off! If that property can be extended to a non-tâtonnement framework, with production and consumption activities out of equilibrium, then it will suffice to show that the amount of inventory depletion between two steps of the process is uniformly bounded; one will then conclude that bounded initial inventories are sufficient to guarantee feasibility of the non-tâtonnement process. That is precisely the approach followed here, and the nature of the result established by theorem II.

The second point, namely that hoarding of factors of production should also be temporary, has two aspects. One aspect concerns the optimising behaviour of firms with respect to hiring and firing of inputs given their anticipations regarding input prices and product demand. This is a topic in the difficult area of stochastic optimisation. Another aspect concerns the drain on liquidities associated with temporary hoarding of factors of production. Bankruptcies present genuine modelling difficulties. Again, these can be avoided if initial cash holdings plus proceeds from the sale of inventories suffice to finance factor hoardings out of equilibrium.

In this paper, stochastic optimisation will be bypassed altogether, through assumptions on (static and deterministic) expectations. And the idea that quantities move faster than prices will be carried to the extreme, so that disequilibrium during the real time devoted to quantity adjustments (hiring and firing of primary factors of production) will not have destabilising consequences. (This is explained in Section 6.5.) Under these conditions, the key to the stability analysis will still be provided by a lemma establishing that input prices are bounded above, so that finitely many upward price adjustments need be considered.

6.2.   Time

In reality, firms make decisions about prices and input levels at arbitrary

[7]This property is *assumed*, not demonstrated, in the imaginative, and rather unique, analysis of non-tâtonnement stability by Fisher (1983).

points in time, whereas production and consumption activities are carried out as continuous flows. I will model the non-tâtonnement counterpart of the adjustment process introduced in Part I in terms of *rates of flow per unit of calendar time* of input uses, incomes, consumption and production; and in terms of *steps of the process*, i.e., adjustments of prices or input flows, occurring at *finitely spaced points of calendar time*. It is natural to think of these steps as taking place in quick succession, and to ignore the variations of the rates of flow (of consumption or production) inside the short intervals separating two steps. Accordingly, *the points in calendar time corresponding to the steps of the process are also the decision points for the agents.* Stock variables – like money or inventories – are then easily updated (integrals of flows are obtained as the product of a constant rate of flow by the length of a time span).

The basic notation for Part II consists in using the integers $\ldots t, t + 1,$ $\ldots$ to number the steps of the process; and in using the symbol $\tau(t)$ to denote the span of calendar time separating steps t and $t + 1$, with the natural normalisation $\tau(t) \leq 1$. Furthermore, the symbols z, ζ, y used with appropriate indices in Part I to denote the supply and demand of inputs or commodities, retain the same definition; they are now interpreted as rates of flow per unit of calendar time. Production and consumption decisions concern these rates of flow. Equilibrium requires equality (up to ε, in so far as inputs are concerned) of the demand *rates* and supply *rates*.

6.3. Consumer demand

In so far as consumers are concerned, I shall now use *stationary demand functions* with three arguments: $m^i(t)$, $p'(t)\zeta^i(t)$ and $q(t)$. Thus, the income $r^i(t) = m_0^i + p'(t)\zeta^i(t)$ of (2.5) is split into two components: a stock of money balances $m^i(t)$ and a flow of income from the sale of inputs $p'(t)\zeta^i(t)$. The reason for separating out these two components is of course that the intertemporal budget constraint recognises the repetitive nature of the income flow associated with the input sales. I shall assume that the endowments of inputs are perpetual flows at the constant rates $[z_k^i]$, and that consumers hold *static point expectations* about p, q and ζ^i.[8] Thus, after observing $p(t)$, $q(t)$, $\zeta^i(t)$, household i expects $p(t') = p(t)$, $q(t') = q(t)$ and $\zeta^i(t') = \zeta^i(t)$ for all $t' > t$; and it solves the problem of optimally

---

[8] If consumers are infinitely lived and have stationary additive consumption tastes (so that past consumption is irrelevant to current decisions), the stationarity of demand should follow; I have not investigated that question in detail.

allocating its resources – consisting of the stock $m^i(t)$ and the perpetual constant flow $p'(t)\zeta^i(t)$ – to consumption over time. The solution of that problem is an infinite sequence of flows of consumption per unit of calendar time, the first component of which, to be denoted $y^i(t)$, is implemented. Because $\tau(t) \leq 1$, a new step of the process will take place before the unit of calendar time covered by $y^i(t)$ is exhausted; at that point, the household will observe $p(t + 1)$, $q(t + 1)$, $\zeta^i(t + 1)$ and choose $y^i(t + 1)$ in the same way. The stationarity of the demand functions says that, if $m^i(t + 1) = m^i(t)$, $p'(t + 1)\zeta^i(t + 1) = p'(t)\zeta^i(t)$ and $q(t + 1) = q(t)$, then $y^i(t + 1) = y^i(t)$.

Money balances are defined recursively by

$$m^i(t + 1) = m^i(t) + \tau(t)[p'(t)\zeta^i(t) - q'(t)y^i(t)] \geq 0. \tag{6.1}$$

That is, money balances are updated by the flow of receipts minus expenditures since the previous step and they are not allowed to become negative. With static expectations and stationary demand functions, households typically plan to deplete gradually their money balances; in that case $m^i(t + 1) < m^i(t)$ and, when $p'(t + 1)\zeta^i(t + 1) = p'(t)\zeta^i(t)$ and $q'(t + 1) = q'(t)$, then $y^i(t + 1) < y^i(t)$.

At the date of step t of the process, the rate of consumption flow per unit of calendar time chosen by household i is thus

$$y^i(t) = y^i(m^i(t), p'(t)\zeta^i(t), q(t)) \in R^n. \tag{6.2}$$

It satisfies suitable extensions of assumptions NI and MPC, namely:

ASSUMPTION NI′

For all i, for all q, m^i, $p'\zeta^i$ and $\hat{m}^i \geq m^i$, $\hat{p}'\hat{\zeta}^i \geq p'\zeta^i$, $y^i(\hat{m}^i, \hat{p}'\hat{\zeta}^i, q) \geq y^i(m^i, p'\zeta^i, q)$.

ASSUMPTION MPC′

For each i, there exist $\beta^i > 0$ and $\gamma^i > 0$ (independent of q, m^i and $p'\zeta^i$) such that, for all q, m^i, $p'\zeta^i$ and $\hat{m}^i \geq m^i$, $\hat{p}'\hat{\zeta}^i \geq p'\zeta^i$, $\hat{p}'\hat{\zeta}^i - q' y^i(\hat{m}^i, \hat{p}'\hat{\zeta}^i, q) \geq p'\zeta^i - q'y^i(m, p'\zeta^i, q) + \gamma^i(\hat{m}^i - m^i) + \beta^i(\hat{p}'\hat{\zeta} - p'\zeta^i)$.

6.4. Production and factor demand

In the non-tâtonnement process, it is suggestive to think about the ζ's as *levels of contracts between consumers and producers*. This is most transparent for labour services: $\zeta_k^i(t)$ measures the flow of labour service k for which household i is engaged in a labour contract at the date of step t. To say that $\zeta_k^i(t + 1) = \zeta^i(t) + (-)e_k$, is to say that employment of household i goes up (down) by e_k, i.e. by one elementary unit of labour type k. Similarly, if good k is a plot of land owned by household i, then $\zeta_k^i \leq z_k^i$ is the acreage rented out at the date of step t. In a more contrived way perhaps, if good k is an oil refinery belonging to a firm in which household i holds a fraction z_k^i of the shares, and if the refinery operates at 60% of capacity, earning an imputed rent equal to 60% of p_k, then $\zeta_k^i = .6\,z_k^i$ is the *share* of the rent accruing to household i.

The behaviour of producers (or 'implicit firms') at the date of step t will then be defined by the solution of the following problem, where $\hat{y}(t)$ denotes the flow of production at that date:

$$\max_{y(t)} q'(t)\hat{y}(t) \text{ subject to } \hat{y}(t) \leq y(t) = \sum_i y^i(t)$$

$$A\hat{y}(t) \leq \sum_i \zeta^i(t) \tag{6.3}$$

where $q'(t) = p'(t)A\mathcal{M}$ as per (2.3). This formulation reflects revenue maximising production decisions under two constraints: production should not exceed demand $y(t)$; production cannot use more inputs than currently under contract. (Treating the cost of inputs as given by the extant contracts, revenue maximisation is equivalent to profit maximisation.)

The first constraint is introduced as a shortcut, to eschew the more complex issue of inventory accumulation, that should be faced in a further elaboration of the model introduced here. (It is indeed inelegant to assume that firms withdraw from inventories to fill the gap between sales and production, but never replenish inventories during the time span covered by the adjustment process; the saving grace is of course the finiteness of that time span, established in theorem II below.) The second constraint is transparent. Note however the implicit efficiency in the use of inputs. Because production is here modelled in aggregate terms, it will not be the case that some inputs are idle in one firm whilst another firm has to forego profitable production due to lack of the same inputs. There would be no difficulty whatever, and some gain of realism, in treating subsets of commodities as the outputs of different firms, say $f = 1\ldots F$, and denoting by $\zeta_{kf}^i(t)$ the amount of input k sold by household i to firm f at t.

As another related shortcut, I shall assume that firms hire (fire) inputs when the quantity contracted is inferior (superior) to the level *needed to meet final effective demand* $y(t)$. In that way, step (P ii) of process P is kept unchanged. This formulation remains somewhat unsatisfactory, because it implies for instance that an airline will react to an increase in demand by hiring pilots and stewards, even though its planes are used to capacity. Under a more realistic formulation, these quantity adjustments should depend upon information regarding the *potential* availability of *all* inputs, $\sum_i (z^i - \zeta^i)$. (Thus, the airline might hire personnel if it knows that there exist idle planes for sale or hire.) It should be possible to develop such an approach.

I shall introduce a simplification that reduces drastically the extent to which firms keep under contract (and remunerate) idle inputs. The simplification consists in carrying to the limit the idea (introduced in Section 2.2) that quantity adjustments are faster than price adjustments. A natural way to implement that idea consists in imposing that the span of calendar time separating a quantity adjustment from the previous step is much shorter than the corresponding span separating a price adjustment from the previous step. Since the latter time span is finite, the limit of 'much shorter' is zero, and I shall assume that *stocks do not change* (the integral of the flows vanishes) *between a quantity adjustment and the previous step of the process.* That is, I will suppress the calendar time required to make quantity adjustments; only between successive price adjustments will there elapse sufficient time to justify updating stocks. (Boundedness of all rates of flow is not an issue.)

An important implication of this specification is that, provided the finite convergence properties are preserved, conditions (2.9) will hold all the time, except for a set of measure zero (the finite set of time spans, themselves each of measure zero, preceding quantity adjustments). Accordingly, the quantities of inputs hired by firms will never exceed those needed to satisfy commodity demand, except over a set of measure zero in calendar time. This does not mean that firms never retain idle inputs. But the reason for idleness will then be always the same (except again over the null set just defined), namely that *other* inputs are not currently available. Inputs in excess of the requirements associated with commodity demand are assumed to be 'fired' instantaneously. (Similarly, inputs corresponding to these requirements are 'hired' instantaneously, *if available* in idle supply.) This is a major simplification, which could eventually be relaxed in an attempt at greater realism.

Under that specification, the receipts of firms from the sale of commodities always cover their outlays for payment of inputs, when $\mathcal{M} - I \geq [0]$. This is because the quantities of inputs contracted do not exceed the requirements corresponding to the sales: given that output prices cover (possibly with a margin) input costs, sales receipts cover outlays for inputs. It does not follow that the margin exceeds the value of inventory depletion; only that net cash flows are non-negative, outside of the null set. Liquidity is thus never an issue for the firms (for the production sector). Moreover, *the stock of money held by households is non-increasing over calendar time.* Indeed, net cash flows of households and producers sum to zero and the set of measure zero in calendar time does not affect moneys stocks.

7. Stability

7.1. Formal definitions

Putting together the elements introduced in Section 6, we may describe the state of the economy at the time of step t by the triple $(p(t), \zeta^i(t), m^i(t))_{i=1\ldots N}$. From these variables, we may compute successively

(i) output prices $q(t)$, via (2.3)
(ii) demand for consumer goods, via (6.2)
(iii) demand for inputs, via (2.4).

The evolution of the economy is governed by the process P', defined in terms of the sequences $(p(t), \zeta^i(t), m^i(t), \tau(t))$, $t = 0, 1, 2, \ldots$ and of the conditions (2.3), (2.4), (6.1) and (6.2).

DESCRIPTION OF PROCESS P

    (P'i) Initiation.   Initial input prices $p(0) > 0$, quantity constraints $[\zeta^i_k(0)]$, $[z^i_k] \geq [\zeta^i_k(0)] \geq [0]$, and money stocks $m^i(0) > 0$ are historically given.

    (P' ii) General Step – Adjustment of a Quantity Constraint.   Such a step is carried out if there exists k such that either

$$z^S_k(t) - z^D_k(t) > 0 \tag{7.1}$$

or

$$z^D_k(t) - z^S_k(t) \geq \varepsilon_k \text{ with } z^S_k(t) < z_k. \tag{7.2}$$

Let then $p(t + 1) = p(t)$, $\tau(t) = 0$, and $m^i(t + 1) = m^i(t)$ for all i. Two situations are distinguished.

(a) If some (any) k is such that (7.1) holds, then necessarily $z_k^S(t) > 0$ and there exists i such that $\zeta_k^i(t) > 0$. For some (any) such i, set

$$\zeta_k^i(t + 1) = \zeta_k^i(t) - e_k. \tag{2.7}$$

Then,

$$y^i(t + 1) = y^i(m^i(t), p'(t)\zeta^i(t) - p_k(t)e_k, q(t))$$

and, for all $h \neq i$,

$$y^h(t + 1) = y^h(t) = y^h(m^i(t), p'(t)\zeta^h(t), q(t)).$$

(b) If some (any) k is such that (7.2) holds, then necessarily there exists i such that $\zeta_k^i(t) < z_k^i$. For some (any) such i, set

$$\zeta_k^i(t + 1) = \zeta_k^i(t) + e_k. \tag{2.8}$$

Then,

$$y^i(t + 1) = y^i(m^i(t), p'(t)\zeta^i(t) + p_k(t)e_k, q(t))$$

and for all $h \neq i$,

$$y^h(t + 1) = y^h(t) = y^h(m^h(t), p'(t)\zeta^h(t), q(t)).$$

(P' *iii*) *General Step – Adjustment of a Price.* Such a step is carried out if there exists no k for which either (7.1) or (7.2) holds. It must then be the case that, for all k,

$$z_k^S(t) \in [\min(z_k, z_k^D(t) - \varepsilon_k), \min(z_k, z_k^D(t)], \quad z_k^S(t) \leq z_k^D(t). \tag{2.9}$$

If there exists k such that $z_k^D(t) - \delta_k \geq z_k^S(t) = z_k$, set

$$p_k(t + 1) = p_k(t) + d_k; \tag{7.3}$$

for all $j \neq k$, set $p_j(t + 1) = p_j(t)$; and set $[\zeta^i(t + 1)] = [\zeta^i(t)]$. Also, for some $1 \geq \tau(t) > 0$, let

$$m^i(t + 1) = m^i(t) + \tau(t)[p'(t)\zeta^i(t) - q'(t)y^i(t)] \tag{6.1}$$

$$y^i(t + 1) = y^i(m^i(t + 1), p'(t)\zeta^i(t) + d_k\zeta_k^i(t), q(t + 1)) \tag{6.2}$$

where $q_j(t + 1) = q_j(t) + A_{kj}d_k$.

(P' *iv*) *Termination.* If for all k, (2.9) holds with $z_k^D(t) < z_k + \delta_k$, the process terminates.

DEFINITION

An *ε-equilibrium with excess supply* consists of a state (p, ζ^i, m^i), a vector of inputs $z^D \in R^m$, a vector of outputs $\hat{y} \in R^n$, a vector of prices $q \in R^n$, with $q' = p'A\mathcal{M}$, and an N-tuple of vectors $y^i \in R^n$ such that

(i) $(z^D, \hat{y})$ maximises $q'\hat{y} - p'z^D$ subject to $z^D \geq A\hat{y}$, $\hat{y} \leq \sum_i y^i$;

(ii) $y^i = y^i(m^i, p'\zeta^i, q)$

(iii) $0 \leq \zeta_i \leq z_i$, $\sum_i y_i \leq \hat{y}$;

(iv) for all $k = 1 \ldots m$, $|z_k^D - \sum_i \zeta_k^{ri}| \leq \varepsilon$.

As before, a state of the economy where the process terminates defines an ε-equilibrium with excess supply, where ε satisfies (2.11). The equilibrium is defined by the terminal values of (p, ζ^i, m^i) together with $\hat{y} = \sum_i y^i$ $z^D = A\hat{y}$, $q' = p'A\mathcal{M}$ and $y^i = y^i(m^i, p'\zeta^{i\prime}, q)$. These values satisfy conditions (i)–(iii) in the definition. (2.9) and (P′ iv) still imply that condition (iv) holds as well.

7.2.   Theorem

The proof of stability theorem II below rests upon the analogue of lemma I, proved here in two easy steps.

LEMMA II

Under process P′, for all $t = 0, 1, 2 \ldots, \sum_i m^i(t + 1) \leq \sum_i m^i(t) \leq \sum_i m^i(0)$.

PROOF

From the definition of the process, $\tau(t) = 0$ unless $z_l^S(t) \leq z_l^D(t)$ for all l. Thus, $\tau(t) > 0$ implies

$$p'(t)z^S(t) \leq p'(t)z^D(t) = p'(t)Ay(t)$$
$$\leq p'(t)A\mathcal{M}y(t) = q'(t)y(t). \tag{7.4}$$

Consequently, for all t:

$$\tau(t)[p'(t)z^S(t) - q'(t)y(t)] \leq 0. \tag{7.5}$$

Aggregating (6.1) over i, then using (7.5):

$$\sum_i m^i(t + 1) = \sum_i m^i(t) + \tau(t)[p'(t)z^S(t) - q'(t)y(t)]$$

$$\leq \sum_i m^i(t), \tag{7.6}$$

which proves the lemma. QED

LEMMA III

Under process P', for all k, for all t,

$$p_k(t) \leq \max\left(\frac{\sum_i m^i(0)}{\delta_k} + d_k, p_k(0)\right) \overset{\text{def}}{=} \bar{p}_k.$$

PROOF

From the definition of the process, $p_k(t + 1) = p_k(t)$ unless $z_l^S(t) \leq z_l^D(t)$ for all l; and $p'(t)z^D(t) \leq q'(t)y(t)$ by (7.4). The condition that $m^i(t + 1) \geq 0$ for all $\tau(t) \in [0, 1]$ implies – see (6.1) with $\tau(t) = 1$ – that:

$$q'(t)y^i(t) \leq m^i(t) + p'(t)\zeta^i(t). \tag{7.7}$$

Summing over i, and using (7.4), then lemma II:

$$p'(t)z^D(t) \leq \sum_i m^i(t) + p'(t)z^S(t)$$

$$\leq \sum_i m^i(0) + p'(t)z^S(t). \tag{7.8}$$

Proceeding as in the proof of lemma I,

$$\delta_k p_k(t) \leq p_k(t)[z_k^D(t) - z_k^S(t)]$$

$$\leq \sum_i m^i(0) - \sum_{l \neq k} p_l(t)[z_l^D(t) - z_l^S(t)] \leq \sum_i m^i(0)$$

and the proof of the lemma follows. QED

THEOREM II

Under assumptions NI' and MPC', provided for all $k = 1 \ldots m$, e_k is small enough ($e_k \leq \varepsilon_k/2$) and provided initial inventories are high enough (meaning

*at least equal to a finite lower bound related to the data of the economy),
the process P' is feasible, is stable and converges in a bounded number of
steps to an ε-equilibrium with excess supply.*

PROOF

The proof is entirely parallel to that of theorem I.

It follows from lemma III that the number of price adjustments is
bounded. Let *their* number be $T \leq \bar{T}$ and number them $\theta = 1 \dots T$. Also,
because the quantity adjustments are treated as instantaneous, the
aggregate withdrawals from inventories are given by:

$$\sum_{\theta=1}^{T} \tau(\theta)\left[y(\theta) - \hat{y}(\theta)\right] \leq \sum_{\theta=1}^{T} \left[y(\theta) - \hat{y}(\theta)\right] \leq \sum_{\theta=1}^{T} y(\theta). \tag{7.9}$$

For each θ, $y(\theta)$ is a uniformly bounded quantity, because

$$q'(\theta)y(\theta) \leq \sum_{i} m^i(\theta) + p'(\theta)z^S(\theta)$$

$$\leq \sum_{i} m^i(0) + \bar{p}'z \tag{7.10}$$

and $q'(\theta)$ is bounded below by $q'(0) = p'(0)A\mathcal{M} > 0$. This establishes the
boundedness of the initial inventory levels that are required in order for
process P' to be feasible at all steps (without any need for quantity
rationing of consumer demand).

To complete the proof, there remains only to verify that the number of
quantity adjustment steps (P' ii) between any pair of price adjustment
steps (P' iii) is uniformly bounded. The reasoning used in the proof of
theorem I to establish that property is readily extended to the present
case. Indeed, if t denotes a price adjustment step and $p(t + v) = p(t)$, $v > 0$,
then $t + v$ is a general quantity adjustment step, and $\tau(t + v) = 0$. For all
$v > 1$, it follows that $m^i(t + v) = m^i(t + v - 1)$. We may accordingly use
that property in the proof (adding the single step corresponding to $v = 1$
does not affect the boundedness property). We may then repeat the
reasoning in the proof of theorem I, substituting $m^i(t + 1)$ for $m^i(0)$ and
$p'(t)\zeta^i(t + v)$ for $r^i(t)$. In the discussion of case (P ii)(a), the equality
$r^i(t + 1) = r^i(t) - e_k p_k$ is then replaced by

$$p'(t)\zeta^i(t + v + 1) = p'(t)\zeta^i(t + v) - e_k p_k; \tag{7.11}$$

and assumption NI' implies $y^i(t + v + 1) \leq y^i(t + v)$. The discussion of
that case then proceeds without modification, until assumption MPC is

used. That specific step is now replaced by:

$$\sum_l p_l[z_l^D(t + v) - z_l^D(t + v + 1)]$$

$$\leq \sum_j q_j(t)[y_j^i(t + v) - y_j^i(t + v + 1)]$$

$$\leq e_k p_k(1 - \beta^i) \qquad (7.12)$$

where the last inequality follows directly from MPC' and (7.11). Similar remarks apply to the discussion of case (P ii)(b), and the proof of theorem II is complete.   QED

8. Comments and conclusions

8.1. Summary

In the broadest outline, this paper gives content to a very simple idea: if nominal prices are downwards rigid, and if they are prevented by some nominal rigidity from rising indefinitely, then price dynamics are apt to converge. A realistic feature of this paper, inspired by the work of Morishima (1976), is to trace back all downwards price rigidities to primary factors of production. As for the upper bound on inflation, it comes from the combination of a nonvanishing demand for, and an exogenous stock of, nominal balances. These two aspects deserve some discussion, provided in Sections 8.2 and 8.3.

The downwards price rigidities impose an equilibrium concept allowing for excess supply. Some claim to the realism of such a concept was made in the introduction. At any rate, it is a necessary corollary to price rigidities. Still, I discuss in Section 8.4 the two main avenues towards a competitive equilibrium, namely price flexibility and fiscal expansion.

These specifications contribute some novel features to stability analysis. They have enabled me to prove stability of a tâtonnement process from the minimal assumption of non-inferiority (further discussed in Section 8.5); then to define a rather realistic non-tâtonnement process, and to prove its feasibility and stability under a reasonable condition on inventory holdings.

The non-tâtonnement process allows for production and consumption activities out of equilibrium. But I do not take here the crucial step of modelling explicitly the uncertainty surrounding future prices and quantity constraints, then the stochastic optimisation problems faced by consumers and producers. That step deserves priority on the research agenda. It is related to the issue of money demand, taken up in Section 8.2.

The specific formulation of the processes P and P', the assumptions and methods of proof used in this paper are quite crude. No doubt, the presentation could be improved substantially through further technical work. One comment in that direction is offered in Section 8.6.

8.2. Temporary equilibrium and money demand

The uncertainty about future prices (and quantity constraints) is modelled explicitly in the theory of temporary equilibrium – see Grandmont (1974, 1977) – where much attention has been given to the conditions (on expectations) under which inflation remains bounded. Clearly, that is the proper way to study price dynamics; but it is a hard way.

The notion that money supply has something to do with inflation is familiar to many. But it needs to be spelled out in microeconomic models of price making, of which one example is offered here.

The assumption MPC, putting a floor to money demand, is rather crude and should be generalised, both by deriving money demand explicitly from consumer behaviour, and by including assets and their prices (e.g. interest rate) in the analysis.

An intriguing question is whether the supply of money, or direct controls on the prices of primary inputs, are the only conceivable instruments to check inflation in models of the type studied here (in models with downward price rigidities and mark-up pricing).

8.3. Downward price rigidities

Why some prices remain downwards rigid in the face of excess supply is an intriguing question, revived in particular by the persistence of European unemployment.

In the case of labour services, the protection by trade unions of workers' incomes is undoubtedly an important element of the answer. The extent to which that protection should be regarded as inefficient use of monopoly power, or as a second-best efficient arrangement in the absence of contingent or forward markets for jobs, remains to be ascertained; see Drèze (1989b), Gollier (1988), and Drèze and Gollier (1989) for a theoretical second-best analysis.

The issue concerns other inputs as well, in particular plant and equipment. When excess capacity prevails, the prices of commodities (e.g. automobiles) are not automatically geared to short-run marginal cost. This is probably a mixture once again of monopolistic profit maximisation and of second-best efficient arrangements under incomplete markets. Price fluctuations are costly for consumers, and are apt to generate erratic patterns of intertemporal substitution, compounding the difficulty of investment decisions under incomplete markets. Our understanding of these issues is still limited: the combination of non convex technology, monopolistic competition and incomplete markets remains forbidding ...

One clearcut difference between labour on the one hand and plant or equipment on the other is the ease with which excess physical capacities can be eliminated through scrapping and postponement of investment; whereas excess demand for physical capacities can be eliminated through investment. There lies probably the reason for the differences in the evolution of unemployment and excess capacities in Figure 10.1.

In the model presented here, physical capacities are treated as primary inputs. It would be natural to put an upper bound on their real prices, reflecting the cost of additional investment; and to introduce a scrapping or investment postponement feature, to eliminate progressively the excess capacities. The model would gain in realism, probably at little technical complication. And the role of wages in explaining downwards price rigidities would stand out all the more sharply.

8.4. Towards competitive equilibria

The quantity adjustment steps of processes P or P′ bring about 'orderly' (one-sided) rationing; the price adjustment steps eliminate all forms of excess demand. What sort of additional steps could eliminate the excess supplies?

Price flexibility is a first answer – even though I have just argued that some form of downwards rigidity makes sense. Since the process is governed by input prices, it seems plausible that an assumption of gross substitutability for inputs would pave the way to convergence of a process with flexible prices towards competitive equilibria. And most econometricians would find the substitutability assumption for inputs quite acceptable. Eventually this issue should be investigated.

It is appropriate to remind ourselves, at this point, that Keynes regarded wage flexibility as the hard way, and thought that demand stimulation through monetary policy provided an easier way. (On pp. 267–9 of *The General Theory*, he argues that 'it can only be a foolish ... an unjust ... an inexperienced person who would prefer a flexible wage policy to a flexible money policy'.) The model of the present paper lends itself to study the effect of increasing the money balances of the households –

which amounts to a fiscal expansion through income transfers, with accommodating money supply.

It is easy to construct examples where no finite amount of fiscal expansion will eliminate excess supplies altogether. (Thus, if two inputs are always used in the ratio one to two, but are supplied inelastically in the ratio one to one, so that the competitive price of the first is zero; then a competitive equilibrium could only be obtained in the limit, with *infinite* fiscal expansion *cum* inflation.)[9] But it is also easy to think about assumptions under which fiscal policy would be effective. (Some degree of input substitutability would help ...) A serious attack on these problems again requires explicit treatment of the uncertainties associated with fiscal policy (whether it will ultimately be financed by taxes or monetised, for instance). So I must refer back to Section 8.2 ...

8.5.   The non-inferiority assumption

Of all the undesirable assumptions used in this paper, none is more *blatantly* unrealistic than absence of inferior goods (NI). That assumption is used only once, in the proof of theorem I, to show that lower (higher) household incomes lead to lower (higher) demand for *all primary inputs*. In that sense, the relevant assumption is one of 'non-inferior factors' – and is perhaps less blatantly unrealistic ... Still, if potatoes are an inferior good, and a plot of land is good only for growing potatoes, we have an instance of 'inferior factor'. I have accordingly used assumption NI, because I could not think of any other primitive assumption ruling out inferior factors.

It is plausible that further research may permit weakening even the 'non-inferior factors' assumptions; perhaps I have convinced myself too quickly that it was a natural requirement for the problem at hand ... Otherwise, it would be a matter of empirical research to discover how significant the problem is.[10]

8.6.   Farewell

As intimated above, I regard the basic idea of this paper as sound and useful, but the formulation as technically crude. In particular, the technical

[9] More technically: at full use of the second input, fiscal expansion would create excess demand, hence an increase in the price of that input, passed into output prices; but the price of the first input (in excess supply) remains fixed, so that its relative (real) price tends to zero as fiscal expansion keeps feeding inflation.

[10] The more relevant empirical question is probably whether some broad types of labour (like unskilled physical labour) are inferior factors.

formulation is more extreme than common sense and casual empiricism would suggest. Thus, not all output prices are set by producers as a mark-up on costs; not all primary inputs have downwards rigid prices; increases in input prices are apt to be passed into output prices only if they are viewed as permanent; and so on. I can only hope that the crude formulation does not obliterate the useful ideas.

Among the improvements that seem easiest to achieve, I should mention first explicit disaggregation of production into the activities of a number of producers, each endowed with its own production set, hiring its own factors, setting its own prices and possibly distributing its profits. Readers are invited to interpret the paper as if that improvement had already been achieved – it would have, had more time been available ...

Also, suppressing altogether the calendar time needed for quantity adjustments, or the redistribution of profits during the time span covered by the process, are convenient simplifications that do not seem essential.

The lasting usefulness of the contribution attempted in this paper is apt to stand or fall on the realism of widespread downwards factor price rigidities and widespread mark-up pricing of produced commodities. And the major challenge to all *students* of price dynamics remains that of *modelling* non-deterministic expectations and stochastic sequential decision-making by consumers and firms.

VI Wage policies

11 The role of securities and labour contracts in the optimal allocation of risk-bearing*

1. In memoriam

1.1.

The economics of uncertainty should some day inspire students of economic thought. Developments over the past few decades provide a vivid illustration of the interplay between abstract theorising and applied interests. In any account of these developments, the specific early contribution of Karl Borch (1960) is bound to stand out. The circumstances are noteworthy. In 1959, Karl Borch (then forty years old) came to Bergen from a succession of jobs for international organisations. He writes:[1] 'When in 1959 I got a research post which gave me almost complete freedom, as long as my work was relevant to insurance, I naturally set out to develop an economic theory of insurance.' That he should *within a year*[2] have made a decisive step in that direction is amazing.

The nature of the step is also noteworthy. Borch knew the recent theoretical papers of Allais (1953) and especially of Arrow (1953). He understood perfectly their significance as well as their limitations, at a time when very few economists had taken notice. As he explained more explicitly in 1962,[3] he attributed that lack of recognition to the fact that these 'relatively simple models appear too remote from any really

* In *Risk, Information and Insurance: Essays in the Memory of Karl Borch*, H. Loubergé, ed., Kluwer Academic Publishers, Boston, 1989.
[1] See Blaug (1986), p. 103.
[2] The chronology is a bit uncertain, since the publication in *Skandinavisk Aktuarietidskrift*, 1960, pp. 163–84, mentions 'Received January 1961'.
[3] Borch (1962), p. 425.

interesting practical economic situation'. 'However, the model they consider gives a fairly accurate description of a *reinsurance market*.' The contribution of Karl Borch in 1960 was to give empirical content to the abstract model of general equilibrium with markets for contingent claims. In this way, he brought economic theory to bear on insurance problems, thereby opening up that field considerably; and he brought the experience of reinsurance contracts to bear on the interpretation of economic theory, thereby enlivening considerably the interest for that theory. In his subsequent publications, Karl Borch often related advanced theoretical results to casual observations – sometimes in a genuinely entertaining manner, which transmits to younger generations a glimpse of the wit and personal charm of our late friend.[4]

1.2.

Several papers by Karl Borch follow a simple lucid pattern: after a brief problem-oriented introduction, the first-order conditions for efficient risk-sharing are recalled, then applied to the problem at hand; the paper ends with a discussion of applicability and confrontation with stylised facts. And the author prefers a succession of light touches, in numbered subsections, to formal theorems and lengthy discussions.

Borch helped establish, and travelled repeatedly, the bridge linking the theory of (re)insurance markets and the 'Capital Asset Pricing Model', developed by his student Jan Mossin (1966) among others. Although Borch was keenly conscious of the restrictive nature of the assumptions underlying the CAPM,[5] he often used that model as an illustration, stressing that 'the applications of CAPM have led to deeper insight into the functioning of financial markets'.[6] The purpose of this paper is to introduce labour incomes in an asset pricing model, and to show that the assumptions underlying CAPM lead to a simple operational characterisation of Pareto-efficient risk-sharing through capital markets *and labour contracts*. The characterisation of efficient labour contracts takes the form of a simple wage indexation scheme, to which Karl Borch might have recognised the merit of bringing abstract theory to bear on an interesting practical economic situation. The integrated treatment of capital markets and labour contracts bears some analogy to the integrated treatment of

[4] See e.g. Borch (1976).
[5] See e.g. Borch (1968a).
[6] Quoted from Borch (1985).

insurance markets and capital markets. It also has some implications for private insurance and reinsurance contracts.

2. Efficient and linear-sharing rules

2.1.

A simple form of risk-sharing problem arises when n agents, indexed $i = 1 \ldots n$ and endowed with (differentiable, concave monotone increasing) cardinal utility functions for wealth $u^i(y^i)$, have to share an aggregate wealth level Y, which depends upon exogenous circumstances. Let there be S alternative 'states' indexed $s = 1 \ldots S$, with associated aggregate wealth levels Y_s. Feasible sharing arrangements must satisfy

$$\sum_i y_s^i = Y_s, s = 1 \ldots S, \tag{1}$$

where y_s^i is the wealth of agent i in state s. Write $y^i = (y_1^i \ldots y_s^i)$, an S-vector; $y_s = (y_s^1, \ldots y_s^n)$, an n-vector; $y = (y^1 \ldots y^n)$, an nS-vector and assume that the n agents agree about the probabilities $\phi_1 \ldots \phi_s$ of the S states. A Pareto-efficient sharing arrangement y is defined by the property that there exists no $\hat{y}$ satisfying (1) with $E_s u^i(\hat{y}_s^i) = \sum_s \phi_s u^i(\hat{y}_s^i) \geq \sum_s \phi_s u^i(y_s^i) = E_s u^i(y_s^i)$ for all i, $\sum_i E_s u^i(\hat{y}_s^i) > \sum_i E_s u^i(y_s^i)$. As shown by Borch (1960), if y is Pareto efficient, then there exist n positive constants k_1, $k_2 \ldots k_n$, normalised by $k_1 = 1$, such that

$$\frac{du^1}{dy_s^1} = k_i \frac{du^i}{dy_s^i}, \quad s = 1 \ldots S, \quad i = 2 \ldots n. \tag{2}$$

There also exist S non-negative prices for contingent claims $q_1 \ldots q_S$, normalised by $\sum_s q_s = 1$, such that

$$\frac{q_s}{q_1} = \frac{\phi_s}{\phi_1} \frac{\dfrac{du^i}{dy_s^i}}{\dfrac{du^i}{dy_1^i}}, \quad s = 2 \ldots S, \quad i = 1 \ldots n. \tag{3}$$

The constants k_i may reflect the initial wealth endowments of agents reaching an efficient sharing arrangement through trade in contingent claims; or they may reflect the bargaining strengths of agents reaching that arrangement through cooperative negociations; or they may reflect the distributive ethics of a central authority responsible for implementing the arrangement; or again they may remain undetermined and be used for analytical convenience alone. In every case, it is true that y solves problem (P 1):

$$\max_{y} \sum_{i} k_i E_s u^i(y_s^i) \tag{P1}$$

subject to (1).

It follows from (2) and our assumptions that

$$\frac{dy_s^i}{dY_s} > 0, \quad i = 1 \ldots n, \quad s = 1 \ldots S. \tag{4}$$

More specifically, define the absolute risk tolerance of agent i, T_A^i by[7]

$$T_A^i(y_s^i) = -\frac{\dfrac{du^i}{dy_s^i}}{\dfrac{d^2u^i}{d(y_s^i)^2}}; \tag{5}$$

and define similarly the aggregate relative risk tolerance of the group of agents, T_A, by

$$T_A(y_s) = \sum_i T_A^i(y_s^i) = -\sum_i \frac{\dfrac{du^i}{dy_s^i}}{\dfrac{d^2u^i}{d(y_s^i)^2}}. \tag{6}$$

Then, as shown in Borch (1960, p. 169)

$$\frac{dy_s^i}{dY_s} = \frac{T_A^i(y_s^i)}{T_A(y_s)}. \tag{7}$$

Defining similarly the relative risk tolerances T_R^i, T_R by

$$T_R^i(y_s^i) = \frac{T_A^i(y^i)}{y_s^i}, \quad T_R(y_s) = \sum_i \frac{y_s^i}{Y_s} T_R^i(y_s^i) = \frac{1}{Y_s} T_A(y_s), \tag{8}$$

we may write

$$\frac{Y_s}{y_s^i} \frac{dy_s^i}{dY_s} = \eta_{y_s^i Y_s} = \frac{T_R^i(y_s^i)}{T_R(y_s)}. \tag{9}$$

---

[7] T_A^i is the reciprocal of the absolute risk aversion introduced by Arrow (1965) and Pratt (1964).

2.2.

For application purposes, it is of interest to consider the special case of *linear sharing rules* where dy_s^i/dY_s is a constant, say β_i, independent of s. In such cases,

$$y_s^i = \alpha_i + \beta_i Y_s, \quad s = 1\ldots S; \quad \sum_i \alpha_i = 0, \quad \sum_i \beta_i = 1. \tag{10}$$

It is readily verified, and shown for instance in Borch (1968b, p. 253) or Wilson (1968), that Pareto-efficient sharing rules are linear if and only if all agents have utility functions belonging to one and the same of the following classes (up to monotone linear transformations):[8]

$$u^i(y_s^i) = |c_i|^\gamma - |c_i - y_s^i|^\gamma, \quad \gamma > 1, c_i \ge y_s^i \ge 0, \quad \text{or}$$
$$\gamma < 0, y_s^i \ge 0 \ge c_i; \tag{11}$$

$$u^i(y_s^i) = (y_s^i - c_i)^\gamma, \quad \gamma < 1, \quad y_s^i \ge 0 \ge c_i; \tag{12}$$

$$u^i(y_s^i) = \log(y_s^i - c_i), \quad y_s^i \ge 0 \ge c_i; \tag{13}$$

$$u^i(y_s^i) = 1 - e^{-\gamma_i(y_s^i - c_i)}$$

or equivalently

$$u^i(y_s^i) = 1 - e^{-\gamma_i y_s^i}, \quad \gamma_i > 0, \quad y_s^i \ge 0. \tag{14}$$

The values of β_i in (10) and of the expressions for T_A^i corresponding to (11)–(14) are given by:

$$\beta^i = k_i^{\frac{1}{1-\gamma}} / \sum_j k_j^{\frac{1}{1-\gamma}}, \quad T_A^i(y_s^i) = \frac{|y_s^i - c_i|}{|\gamma - 1|} \quad \text{under (11)–(13)} \tag{15}$$

$$\beta_i = \gamma_i^{-1} / \sum_j \gamma_j^{-1}, \quad T_A^i(y_s^i) = \gamma_i^{-1} \quad \text{under (14).} \tag{16}$$

The linearity of the sharing rules follows from the linearity of the absolute risk tolerance – a property usually referred to as 'hyperbolic absolute risk aversion' (HARA).

---

[8] (13) is a special case of (12) with $\gamma = 0$; c_i is introduced in (14) for the sake of symmetry but plays no role there.

3. Capital asset pricing

3.1.

The special case of (11) corresponding to $\gamma = 2$ (quadratic utility) leads to a particularly elegant treatment of portfolio choices and capital asset pricing. The simplest model involves m assets indexed $j = 1 \ldots m$ with (non-negative) random payoffs π_s^j, so that $Y_s = \sum_j \pi_s^j$. The n agents are initially endowed with shares $\bar{\theta}_{ij} \geq 0$, $\sum_i \bar{\theta}_{ij} = 1$ for all j, of the m assets. The assets are traded on a stock exchange at prices $p_j, j = 1 \ldots m$, leading to terminal shares $\theta_{ij} \geq 0$, $\sum_i \theta_{ij} = 1$ for all j. In addition, the agents may stipulate deterministic side-payments a_i, $\sum_i a_i = 0$. Accordingly, the budget constraints and terminal wealths of the agents are

$$\sum_j p_j \theta_{ij} + a_i = \sum_j p_j \bar{\theta}_{ij} \tag{17}$$

$$y_s^i = a_i + \sum_j \theta_{ij} \pi_s^j, \quad i = 1 \ldots n, \quad s = 1 \ldots S. \tag{18}$$

From section 2, it follows that efficient portfolios will satisfy (10) with $\alpha_i = a_i$, $\beta_i = \theta_{ij} \equiv \theta_i$ (identically in j), $\sum_i \theta_i = 1$, so that

$$y_s^i = a_i + \theta_i \sum_j \pi_s^j, \quad i = 1 \ldots n, \quad s = 1 \ldots S. \tag{19}$$

The CAPM theory consists in showing that competitive clearing of the markets for assets (of the stock market) leads to asset prices at which all individuals (maximising expected utility subject to (17) with given p_j's) choose to hold fully diversified portfolios ($\theta_{ij} \equiv \theta_i$), with

$$\theta_i = \frac{T_A^i(\bar{Y})}{T_A(\bar{Y})}, \quad i = 1 \ldots n; \tag{20}$$

$$p_j = E\pi^j - \frac{1}{T_A(\bar{Y})} \text{cov}(\pi^j, Y), \quad j = 1 \ldots m. \tag{21}$$

In expression (21), the market price of asset j is obtained as equal to its expected payoff minus a risk premium, computed as the product of that asset's contribution to the variance of the aggregate payoff $Y = \sum_j \pi^j$ times a market price of risk (per unit of variance), namely $1/T_A(\bar{Y})$.

3.2.

An important byproduct of the CAPM is the existence of an S-vector q of prices for contingent claims, with[9]

$$q_s = \phi_s \left[1 - \frac{1}{T_A(\bar{Y})}(Y_s - \bar{Y}) \right], s = 1 \ldots S, \sum_s q_s = 1; \tag{22}$$

$$p_j = \sum_s q_s \pi_s^j, \quad j = 1 \ldots m. \tag{23}$$

If the payoffs π_s^j to the different assets result from some parallel choice, say from a set $\Pi^j \subset R^S$ of feasible payoffs, then efficient choices should satisfy

$$\sum_s q_s \pi_s^j \geq \sum_s q_s \hat{\pi}_s^j \,\forall\, (\hat{\pi}_1^j \ldots \hat{\pi}_S^j) \in \Pi^j, \quad j = 1 \ldots m. \tag{24}$$

Conditions (24) give operational content to the familiar notion that (production) choices by firms maximise their market value. In general, that decision criterion is ill-defined; see, e.g. Drèze (1974b, section 6.3). It takes a specific framework, like that of CAPM, to make it operational.

I also note for further reference that the CAPM formulas remain valid if the agents hold in addition state-dependent endowments so long as the endowment vectors lie in the span of the $m + 1$ vectors $(\iota, \pi^1 \ldots \pi^m)$ where $\iota = (1 \ldots 1)'$ and $\pi^j = (\pi_1^j \ldots \pi_S^j)$; see Geanakopolos in Duffie *et al.* (1988).

3.3.

Under the formulation of the CAPM outlined here, it is not imposed that $y_s^i \geq 0$ for all i and s. These natural non-negativity constraints complicate the presentation considerably, and are often ignored in analytical work. A possible justification for that practice goes as follows.

Under (11) with $\gamma = 2$, $T_A^i(\bar{Y}) = c_i - \bar{y}^i$ and $T_A(\bar{Y}) = \sum_i c_i - \bar{Y} := C - \bar{Y}$. Inserting these expressions in (20) and noting from (19) that $\bar{y}^i = a_i + \theta_i \bar{Y}$, we may relate a_i to θ_i as follows:

$$\theta_i = \frac{c_i - a_i - \theta_i \bar{Y}}{C - \bar{Y}}, a_i = c_i - \theta_i C. \tag{25}$$

---

[9] See e.g. Drèze (1982, formula (2.21)).

Write v_i for $\sum_i \bar{\theta}_{ij} p_j$ and define $V = \sum_i v_i = \sum_j p_j$. It also follows from (21) and (8) that

$$V = \bar{Y} - \frac{\sigma_Y^2}{T_A(\bar{Y})} = \bar{Y} - \frac{\sigma^2 Y}{\bar{Y} T_R(\bar{Y})} = \bar{Y}\left(1 - \frac{\sigma_Y^2}{\bar{Y}^2 T_R(\bar{Y})}\right). \tag{26}$$

The budget equation (17), with $\theta_{ij} = \theta_i$ for all j, becomes in that notation

$$\theta_i V + c_i - \theta_i C = v_i, \quad \theta_i = \frac{c_i - v_i}{C - V}. \tag{27}$$

Using (25) and (27), the non-negativity condition on y_s^i takes the form

$$y_s^i = a_i + \theta_i Y_s = c_i - \theta_i C + \theta_i Y_s = c_i - \theta_i(C - Y_s)$$

$$= c_i - (C - Y_s)\frac{c_i - v_i}{C - V} = v_i - (c_i - v_i)\frac{V - Y_s}{C - V} \geq 0; \tag{28}$$

$$\frac{v_i}{V}\frac{C - V}{c_i - v_i} = \frac{T_R(V)}{T_R^i(v_i)} \geq \frac{V - Y_s}{V} = 1 - \frac{Y_s}{\bar{Y}\left(1 - \frac{\sigma_Y^2}{\bar{Y}^2 T_R(\bar{Y})}\right)}, \tag{29}$$

where use has been made of the definition (8) to obtain a relationship among dimensionless ratios. In order for the inequality (29) to hold for all i and s, it must be the case that

$$\frac{\sum_i \frac{v_i}{V} T_R^i(v_i)}{\max_i T_R^i(v_i)} \geq 1 - \frac{\min_s Y_s}{\bar{Y}\left(1 - \frac{\sigma_Y^2}{\bar{Y}^2 T_R(\bar{Y})}\right)} = \frac{\sum_j p_j - \min_s Y_s}{\sum_j p_j}. \tag{30}$$

In words: the maximal (over states) relative loss on the market portfolio should not exceed the ratio of the average to the maximal (over agents) relative risk–tolerance index (evaluated at the initial wealth).

In an economy with many heterogeneous agents and many states, condition (30) is unlikely to be verified. On the other hand, in applications where Y_s stands for national income, the quantity

$$\frac{\bar{Y} - \min_s Y_s}{\bar{Y}} \geq 1 - \frac{Y_s}{\bar{Y}\left(1 - \frac{\sigma_Y^2}{\bar{Y}^2 T_R(\bar{Y})}\right)}$$

is apt to be quite small in the short run – like 3 or 4 per cent – and condition

(30) is quite likely to be fulfilled. Also, in an economy with many agents, it will be of limited relevance to the equilibrium and efficiency of asset markets that a few agents are prevented by non-negativity constraints from holding a portfolio satisfying the tangential first-order conditions. I shall accordingly follow in the sequel the standard practice of ignoring the non-negativity constraints on y_s^i. And I shall similarly ignore the conditions $c_i \geq y_s^i$ which define the range over which representation of preferences by a quadratic utility is meaningful.

4. A model of asset pricing and labour contracts

4.1.

The CAPM has provided a useful framework to analyse a number of problems related to financial markets. From a practical viewpoint, that model has helped private investors or investment services understand and implement better the principles of asset diversification; it has also supplied financial intermediaries with a theoretical underpinning for their autonomous discovery of the merits of mutual funds. Yet, for most families, human wealth is the major component of total wealth, and uncertainties about labour income are of greater concern than uncertainties about portfolio returns.

Taking labour incomes into account raises two questions about the CAPM, a positive one and a normative one. From a positive viewpoint, is the model still valid when the endowment of agents includes uncertain labour incomes? That question has been taken up by Mayers (1973) and his followers – in particular Fama and Schwert (1977) at the empirical level.[10]

The normative issue is broader. In capitalist economies, tradeable assets are typically shares of stock in business firms that engage in the production of goods and services; labour incomes consist mostly of wages and salaries paid out by these firms. Profits are equal to value added minus wages, and constitute the basic element of the payoffs which enter as elementary data in the CAPM. The question of efficient risk-sharing should accordingly be raised simultaneously for the division of value added between profits and wages, for the portfolio choices of agents earning wages as well as returns on their portfolios, and for the resulting capital market equilibria.

---

[10] Of related interest is the so-called 'consumption-based CAPM' of Breeden (1979), Cornell (1981) and Grossman-Shiller (1982).

4.2.

In a simple model, each asset j corresponds to a business firm employing, in state s, a (homogeneous) labour force l_s^j to produce an output $f_s^j(l_s^j)$. The state-dependent production function f_s^j is assumed differentiable monotone concave. If the total wage bill paid by firm j in state s is denoted t_s^j then profits π_s^j are given by

$$\pi_s^j = f_s^j(l_s^j) - t_s^j. \tag{31}$$

The theory of implicit (labour) contracts, as initially developed by Azariadis (1975), Baily (1974) and Gordon (1974) – see Rosen (1985) or Hart and Holmström (1987) for recent surveys – has been concerned with a characterisation of efficient production as well as risk-sharing between firms and employees, through *ex ante* agreements regarding t_s^j and l_s^j.

The *ex ante* aspect is important. It means that employees are hired, and contractual agreements are reached, prior to observing the true state. This feature is essential to permit risk-sharing, i.e. transfers of income across states. Typically, these transfers take the form of wages above the marginal product of labour in some states, below it in other states.

Up to incentive compatibility and institutional feasibility, efficient contracts are characterised by two sets of conditions:

(i) l_s^j should be such that the marginal value product of labour, df_s^j/dl_s^j, is equal to the reservation wage of employees;

(ii) t_s^j, the wage bill of the firm in state s, should be such that the division of income between capital and labour corresponds to efficient risk-sharing.

In order to give empirical content to these conditions, it is typically assumed that the reservation wages and utility functions of all employees are identical, and that the firm has well-defined risk preferences, represented by some 'utility function of the firm'.

Under the assumptions of the CAPM, suitably extended, sharper conclusions are possible.

4.3.

An important practical issue raised by labour contracts is the extent to which labour times and wages are allowed to vary (across individuals and across states). Clearly, the answer to that question varies from firm to firm, depending upon technological and economic constraints. Thus, team work requires close coordination of individual labour times; some processes admit more readily part-time work than others; and so on. A simple formulation allows labour times to vary across individuals (thus allowing part-time work) while requiring that variations across states be in the same proportions for all members of a given firm. I shall retain that formulation. And I shall follow the standard practice in the theory of implicit contracts of imposing that, for all s, $l_s^j \le l^j$, where l^j is the quantity of labour (the number of full-time equivalent workers) covered by the contract.

On the other hand, I shall not at this stage impose specific restrictions on the individual wages beyond the natural requirement that wage costs per unit of labour to the firm be the same for all its employees. As we shall see, it is easy to express that requirement in operational terms, under the CAPM framework.

To formalise these ideas, let there be n agents (households) $i = 1 \ldots n$, each supplying inelastically a quantity of labour $\bar{l}^i$ and owning initially a fraction $\bar{\theta}_{ij} \ge 0$ of the capital of firm j, with $\sum_i \bar{\theta}_{ij} = 1$ for each j.

Let each agent i supply a fraction $\zeta_{ij} \ge 0$ of the labour inputs of firm j, with $\sum_j \zeta_{ij} l^j \le \bar{l}^i$ and $\sum_i \zeta_{ij} = 1$ in equilibrium. Write w_s^{ij} for the wage rate paid by firm j to agent i in state s. Then, the wage bill t_s^j and the profits π_s^j are defined by

$$t_s^j = l_s^j \sum_i \zeta_{ij} w_s^{ij}, \quad \pi_s^j = f_s^j(l_s^j) - l_s^j \sum_i \zeta_{ij} w_s^{ij}. \tag{32}$$

To simplify exposition, I shall *not* impose the limited liability conditions $\pi_s^j \ge 0$.

Wages and dividends (profit shares) are paid out *after* observing the state. Shares of stock are traded, at prices p_j, *before* observing the state. If terminal holdings of agent i are denoted θ_{ij}, then the budget constraints of the agents are still given by (17), but their terminal wealths are now given by

$$y_s^i = a_i + \sum_j \theta_{ij} \pi_s^j + \sum_j \zeta_{ij} l_s^j w_s^{ij}, \quad i = 1 \ldots n, \quad s = 1 \ldots S. \tag{33}$$

4.4.

The decisions of the firms concern the employment levels l_s^j and the wage rates w_s^{ij}. In a world of uncertainty, it is not easy to specify decision criteria for business firms when markets are incomplete; see Drèze (1982, 1985a, 1989a). However, it was noted above that there exists under the CAPM a vector q of prices for contingent claims such that $p_j = \sum_s q_s \pi_s^j$; see (23). In that case, the criterion of *maximising the market value of the firm* becomes unambiguous. It is then consistent with market-value maximisation for the firm to contract with agent i for a positive fraction ζ_{ij} of the firm's employment if and only if

$$\zeta_{ij} \sum_s q_s \left(\frac{df_s^j}{dl_s^j} - w_s^{ij} \right) = 0, \quad i = 1 \ldots n, \quad j = 1 \ldots m. \tag{34}$$

Conditions (34) are a specific illustration of the general conditions (24) characterising market-value maximisation. They also imply that wage costs per unit of labour be the same for all the employees of a given firm.

Conditions (34) are of course predicated upon the existence (and observability) of a vector q of prices for contingent claims, which is verified in the CAPM and will need to be established for the generalised framework under discussion.

4.5.

To close the model, there remains only to consider the joint decisions of the agents (households) about labour supply to firms and portfolios of assets.

The decision problem of a representative agent is:

$$\max_{a_i, \theta_{ij}, \zeta_{ij}} \sum_s \phi_s u^i (a_i + \sum_j \theta_{ij} \pi_s^j + \sum_j \zeta_{ij} l_s^j w_s^{ij}) \tag{P2}$$

subject to (17) and $\sum_j \zeta_{ij} l_s^j \leq \bar{l}^i$, $s = 1 \ldots S$.

The first-order conditions for a solution of problem (P2) are

$$\theta_{ij} \sum_s \phi_s \frac{du^i}{dy_s^i} (\pi_s^j - p_j) = 0, \quad a_i = \sum_j p_j(\bar{\theta}_{ij} - \theta_{ij}), \tag{35}$$

$$\zeta_{ij} \left[\sum_s \phi_s \frac{du^i}{dy_s^i} l_s^j w_s^{ij} - \lambda^i \right] = 0, \exists s: \sum_j \zeta_{ij} l_s^j = \bar{l}^i \tag{36}$$

where $\lambda^i \geq 0$ is the dual variable associated with the constraint $\sum_j \zeta_{ij} l_s^j \leq \bar{l}^i$.

4.6.

In short, a *feasible arrangement* for the economy consists of m employment vectors $l^j = (l^j_1 \ldots l^j_S)$ in R^S_+ and n decision vectors $d^i = (a_i, \theta_{i1} \ldots \theta_{im}, \zeta_{i1} \ldots \zeta_{im})$ in $R \times R^{2m}_+$, satisfying $\sum_i a_i = 0$, $\sum_i \theta_{ij} = \sum_i \zeta_{ij} = 1$ for all $j = 1 \ldots m$ and $\sum_j \zeta_{ij} l^j_s \le \bar{l}^i$ for all $i = 1 \ldots n$, $s = 1 \ldots S$. Denote a feasible arrangement by $z \in Z$.

A feasible arrangement does not specify the terminal wealth levels of the agents, until the personalised wages w^{ij}_s are also specified. Let then a *feasible allocation* for the economy be defined by a feasible arrangement z and an m-tuple W of matrices of personalised wages $W^j = [w^{ij}_s]$ in R^{nS}_+, $j = 1 \ldots m$. The associated terminal wealth levels are then defined by (33), with π^j_s as defined in (32).

A feasible allocation (z, W) is *Pareto efficient* if there exists no alternative feasible allocation $(\hat{z}, \hat{W})$ such that the alternative wealth vectors

$$\hat{y}^i = (\hat{y}^i_1 \ldots \hat{y}^i_S), \hat{y}^i_s = \hat{a}_i + \sum_j \hat{\theta}_{ij} \hat{\pi}^j_s + \sum_j \hat{\zeta}_{ij} \hat{l}^j_s \hat{w}^{ij}_s,$$

$$i = 1 \ldots n, \quad s = 1 \ldots S,$$

satisfy

$$E_s u^i(\hat{y}^i_s) = \sum_s \phi_s u^i(\hat{y}^i_s) \ge \sum_s \phi_s u^i(y^i_s) = E_s u^i(y^i_s),$$

$$\sum_i E_s u^i(\hat{y}^i_s) > \sum_i E_s u^i(y^i_s). \tag{37}$$

A feasible allocation (z, W) is *decentralised* by the asset prices p in R^m_+ and the prices for contingent claims q in R^S_+ if it satisfies (17), (34), (35) and (36).

5. Efficiency and equilibrium

5.1.

Let the preferences of the n agents be represented by the quadratic utility functions

$$u^i(y^i_s) = c^2_i - (c_i - y^i_s)^2, \quad E_s u^i(y^i_s) = \sum_s \phi_s u^i(y^i_s), \quad i = 1 \ldots n. \tag{38}$$

Then, necessary and sufficient conditions for the Pareto efficiency of a feasible allocation (z, W), at which $c_i > y_s^i > 0$ for all i and s, and $\sum_s \dfrac{df_s^j}{dl_s^j} > 0$ for all j, are

(i) for each j, let $l^j = \max_t l_t^j$; then, for each s, $(l^j - l_s^j)\dfrac{df_s^j}{dl_s^j} = 0$; and $\sum_j l^j = \sum_i \bar{l}^i$;

(ii) there exists a vector q in R_+^S of prices for contingent claims and a risk premium R such that, for each $j, k = 1 \ldots m$,

$$l^j l^k \sum_s q_s \left[\frac{df_s^j}{dl_s^j} - \frac{df_s^k}{dl_s^k} \right] = 0; \tag{39}$$

for each $i = 1 \ldots n$, for each $s = 1 \ldots S$:

$$q_s = \phi_s \frac{c_i - y_s^i}{c_i - E_s y_s^i} \tag{40a}$$

$$= \phi_s \left[1 - R \left\{ \sum_j f_s^j(l_s^j) - E_s \sum_j f_s^j(l_s^j) \right\} \right] := \phi_s[1 - R(Y_s - \bar{Y})]; \tag{40b}$$

(iii) for each i, there exists a pair (α_i, β_i) in $R \times R_+$ such that, for all $s = 1 \ldots S$,

$$y_s^i = \alpha_i + \beta_i \sum_j f_s^j(l_s^j), \quad \alpha_i = c_i - \beta_i \sum_h c_h, \quad \beta_i = \frac{c_i - E_s y_s^i}{\sum_h c_h - E_s \sum_h y_s^h}.$$

Properties (i) and (ii) characterise efficient employment levels, property (iii) efficient risk-sharing. The remainder of section 5.1 is devoted to establish these properties.

Let $(k_1 \ldots k_n)$ be a vector of positive constants, and consider the problem

$$\max_{l^j, l_s^j, y_s^i, \zeta_{ij}} \Lambda = \sum_i k_i E_s u^i(y_s^i)$$

subject to

$$\sum_i y_s^i \le \sum_j f_s^j(l_s^j) \quad s = 1\ldots S$$

$$l_s^j \le l^j \quad s = 1\ldots S, \quad j = 1\ldots m \tag{P3}$$

$$\sum_j \zeta_{ij} l^j \le \bar{l}^i \quad i = 1\ldots n$$

$$1 \le \sum_i \zeta_{ij} \quad j = 1\ldots m.$$

It follows from $du^i/dy_s^i > 0$, $df_s^j/dl_s^j \ge 0$ and $\sum_s df_s^j/dl_s^j > 0$ that all constraints may be imposed with equality, establishing (i). The problem is then reduced to:

$$\max_{l^j, y_s^i} \Lambda = \sum_i k_i E_s u^i(y_s^i) \tag{P4}$$

subject to

$$\sum_i y_s^i = \sum_j f_s^j(l^j) \quad s = 1\ldots S \quad (\mu_s)$$

$$\sum_j l^j = \sum_i \bar{l}^i \tag{v}$$

where (μ_s, v) denote the Lagrange multipliers associated with the constraints.

The first-order conditions for problem (P4) are

$$\frac{\partial \Lambda}{\partial y_s^i} = k_i \phi_s \frac{du^i}{dy_s^i} - \mu_s = k_i \phi_s(c_i - y_s^i) - \mu_s = 0, \tag{41}$$

$$\frac{\partial \Lambda}{\partial l^j} = \sum_s \mu_s \frac{df_s^j}{dl^j} - v = 0. \tag{42}$$

Because problem (P4) calls for maximising a concave function over a convex set, the first-order conditions are both necessary and sufficient. Defining $q_s := \mu_s/\sum_t \mu_t > 0$, (39) follows from (42) and (40a) follows from (41). To verify (40b) write (40a) as $q_s = \phi_s[1 - y_s^i - E_s y_s^i/c_i - E_s y_s^i]$ and sum over i both the numerator and denominator of the fraction. Letting $R := [\sum_t c_i - \sum_t E_s y_s^i]^{-1}$ and using $Y_s = \sum_i y_s^i = \sum_j f_s^j(l^j)$, the equality in (40b) follows, and (ii) is verified.

In order to verify (iii), let $Y_s = \sum_i y_s^i = \sum_i c_i - \dfrac{\mu_s}{\phi_s}\sum_i \dfrac{1}{k_i}$ from (41). Hence,

$$\frac{\mu_s}{\phi_s} = \frac{\sum\limits_i c_i - Y_s}{\sum\limits_i \dfrac{l}{k_i}} \quad \text{and}$$

$$y_s^i = c_i - \frac{1}{k_i}\frac{\sum\limits_h c_h - Y_s}{\sum\limits_h \dfrac{1}{k_h}} = \alpha_i + \beta_i Y_s$$

with

$$\beta_i = \frac{\dfrac{1}{k_i}}{\sum\limits_h \dfrac{1}{k_h}} = \frac{c_i - y_s^i}{\sum\limits_h c_h - Y_s}, \quad \alpha_i = c_i - \beta_i \sum_h c_h$$

as desired. This completes the proof.

To reconcile property (iii) with (22), one simply notes that

$$T_A(\bar{Y}) = \sum_i T_A^i(\bar{Y}) = \sum_i [c_i - E_s y_s^i], \tag{43}$$

so that β_i in property (iii) is indeed equal to $\dfrac{T_A^i(\bar{Y})}{T_A(\bar{Y})}$.

5.2.

The characterisation of Pareto efficiency in section 5.1 is helpful to define personalised wages which, together with competitive asset markets and with employment levels that maximise market value, sustain a Pareto-efficient allocation as a decentralised equilibrium. From property (iii), we learn that linear sharing rules remain optimal, in the extended setting with endogenous output and employment levels.[11] Two conclusions follow immediately. First, for an agent supplying no labour and interested in portfolio returns alone, a diversified portfolio ($\theta_{ij} = \theta_i$ for all j) remains optimal if and only if aggregate profits $\sum_j \pi_s^j$ are linearly related to aggregate wealth (output) $\sum_j f_s^j(l^j)$. Aggregate profits are equal to aggregate

---

[11] For examples of related situations where the linearity of optimal rules is violated, see Drèze (1989b) or Drèze and Gollier (1989).

output minus the aggregate wage bill. Accordingly, aggregate profits are linearly related to aggregate output if and only if wages are linearly related to aggregate output. Second, for an agent supplying labour but owning no assets, Pareto efficiency requires that wage income be linearly related to aggregate output. These two conclusions thus converge to suggest that wages should be linearly related to aggregate output. In particular, this confirms that adjusting wages to the marginal product of labour in each state is not consistent with efficient risk-sharing, outside of the special case where the marginal product of labour is linearly related to its average product. In general, *ex post* competitive clearing of the labour market is *ex ante* inefficient! A simple approach to efficiency would consist in setting a fixed wage $\bar{w}$, independent of the state, and relying entirely on the stock market to generate efficient risk-sharing (through diversified portfolios). This, however, would typically require that wage earners not endowed with initial assets borrow in order to hold risky assets. In practice, such borrowing is impractical, costly and subject to moral hazard. A natural alternative is to specify personalised wages consisting of a fixed part and a part indexed on aggregate wealth, with individual wage earners free to choose the respective magnitudes of the constant and variable parts of their wages. If these two parts satisfy (34), the allocation will be decentralised under the criterion of market value maximisation; it will then automatically satisfy (i) and (ii) of section 5.1.

To implement these ideas, consider a fixed wage $\bar{w}$, an indexed wage $w_s = \delta Y_s$ and personalised wages $w_s^{ij} = \eta_i \bar{w} + (1 - \eta_i)w_s$, $i = 1 \dots n$, $j = 1 \dots m, s = 1 \dots S$. The following definition embodies a natural concept of decentralised equilibrium.

An *equilibrium with flexible wage indexation* consists of a feasible arrangement $z \in Z$, a vector of asset prices $p \in R_+^m$, a fixed wage $\bar{w}$ and an indexed wage $w_s = \delta Y_s = \delta \sum_j f_s^j(l^j)$, $s = 1 \dots S$, n individual indexing weights $\eta_i \in [0, 1]$, and a risk premium R such that:

(a) for each agent $i = 1 \dots n$, the portfolio $(\theta_{ij})_{j = 1 \dots m}$ and the indexing weight η_i solve

$$\max_{\theta_{ij}, \eta_i} \sum_s \phi_s u^i(y_s^i)$$

where $\qquad\qquad\qquad\qquad\qquad\qquad\qquad\qquad\qquad$ (P5)

$$y_s^i = \bar{l}^i[\eta_i \bar{w} + (1 - \eta_i)\delta Y_s] + \sum_j p_j(\bar{\theta}_{ij} - \theta_{ij}) + \sum_j \theta_{ij}\pi_s^j$$

(b) for each firm $j = 1 \dots m$, the employment level l^j solves

$$\max_{l_j} \sum_s \phi_s[1 - R(Y_s - \bar{Y})][f_s^j(l^j) - \bar{w}l^j]$$

$$= \sum_s \phi_s[1 - R(Y_s - \bar{Y})][f_s^j(l^j) - w_s l_j]$$

$$= \sum_s \phi_s[1 - R(Y_s - \bar{Y})]\pi_s^j;$$

(c) $\sum_i \theta_{ij} = 1, \quad \sum_i \bar{l}^i = \sum_j l^j.$

5.3.

When the preferences of the n agents are represented by the quadratic utility functions (38), then

(i) There exists an equilibrium with flexible wage indexation, where $\theta_{ij} = \theta_i, \quad j = 1\ldots m, \quad i = 1\ldots n, \quad R^{-1} = T_A(\bar{Y}) = \sum_i T_A^i(\bar{Y})$ and $\bar{w} = \delta(\bar{Y} - R\sigma_Y^2).$

(ii) Every equilibrium with flexible wage indexation is Pareto efficient.

The remainder of this section is devoted to a proof of these two propositions, starting with (i).

The simplest approach to prove existence is to introduce explicitly the prices for contingent claims q_s and to consider the production economy with a single type of labour and S contingent commodities, of respective prices $(\bar{w}, q_1 \ldots q_s)$. The initial ownership fractions $\bar{\theta}_{ij}$ are treated as fixed, and the individual budget constraints are replaced by

$$\sum_s q_s y_s^i - \bar{w}\bar{l}^i - \sum_j \bar{\theta}_{ij} \sum_s q_s[f_s^j(l^j) - \bar{w}l^j] \le 0. \tag{44}$$

The resulting economy is a particular case of that considered in chapter 7 of *Theory of Value* (Debreu, 1959), so that there exists a competitive equilibrium where for each j

$$\sum_s q_s \frac{df_s^j}{dl^j} - \bar{w} = 0 \tag{45}$$

(profit maximisation) and for each i

$$\frac{q_s}{\sum_t q_t} = \frac{\phi_s \dfrac{du^i}{dy_s^i}}{\sum_t \phi_t \dfrac{du^i}{dy_t^i}} = \phi_s \frac{c_i - y_s^i}{c_i - \sum_t \phi_t y_t^i} \tag{46}$$

(expected utility maximisation). Because that competitive equilibrium is Pareto efficient, it must have the properties listed in section 5.1. Thus, there exists for each i a pair (α_i, β_i) as defined in property (iii) there; and there exists a risk premium $R = 1/T_A(\bar{Y})$ such that, for each $s, q_s = \phi_s[1 - R(Y_s - \bar{Y})]$. At the competitive equilibrium, l^j maximises

$$\sum_s q_s[f_s^j(l_s) - \bar{w}l^j] = \sum_s \phi_s[1 - R(Y_s - \bar{Y})][f_s^j(l^j) - \bar{w}l^j],$$

as required.

In order to implement the competitive equilibrium as an equilibrium with flexible wage indexation, we need to define the share prices p and the flexible wage parameter δ; and we need to specify for each individual i the 'market' portfolio $\theta_{ij} = \theta_i$, $j = 1 \ldots m$, the lump-sum transfer a_i and the indexing weight η_i. The portfolio and indexing weight must satisfy $1 \geq \theta_{ij} \geq 0$, $1 \geq \eta_i \geq 0$, $i = 1 \ldots n$ and $\sum_i \theta_{ij} = 1$, $j = 1 \ldots m$.

I first choose δ such that $\sum_s q_s w_s = \delta \sum_s q_s Y_s = \bar{w}$; i.e.

$$\delta = \frac{\bar{w}}{[\bar{Y} - R\sigma_Y^2]}, \tag{47}$$

as required. Defining next as usual $p_j = \sum_s q_s \pi_s^j$, we verify at once

$$p_j = \sum_s q_s[f_s^j(l^j) - \bar{w}l^j] = \sum_s q_s[f_s^j(l^j) - \delta Y_s l^j]. \tag{48}$$

If each agent i earns a labour income equal to $\bar{l}^i[\eta_i \bar{w} + (1 - \eta_i)\delta Y_s]$, then we may define the aggregate wage bill as

$$\sum_i \bar{l}^i[\eta_i \bar{w} + (1 - \eta_i)\delta Y_s] = \bar{w}\sum_i \bar{l}^i \eta_i + \delta \left[\sum_i \bar{l}^i(1 - \eta_i) \right] Y_s$$

$$:= F + DY_s \tag{49}$$

thereby defining the fixed component F and the variable (indexed) component DY_s of the aggregate wage bill. (That $1 \geq D \geq 0$ is verified below.) It then follows that, for each s

$$\sum_j \pi_s^j = \sum_j f_s^j(l^j) - \sum_i \bar{l}^i[\eta_i \bar{w} + (1 - \eta_i)\delta Y_s]$$

$$= Y_s(1 - D) - F. \tag{50}$$

A portfolio consisting of a constant share $\theta_{ij} = \theta_i$ of all firms will then yield $\theta_i \sum_j \pi_s^j = \theta_i[Y_s(1 - D) - F]$ in state s. Under such a portfolio, the expression for y_s^i in (a) of the definition becomes

$$y_s^i = \bar{l}^i \eta_i \bar{w} + \sum_j p_j(\bar{\theta}_{ij} - \theta_i) - \theta_i F$$

$$+ \bar{l}^i(1 - \eta_i)\delta Y_s + \theta_i(1 - D)Y_s \tag{51}$$

which is of the form $y_s^i = \alpha_i + \beta_i Y_s$ with

$$\alpha_i = \bar{l}^i \eta_i \bar{w} + \sum_j p_j(\bar{\theta}_{ij} - \theta_i) - \theta_i F,$$

$$\beta_i = \bar{l}^i(1 - \eta_i)\delta + \theta_i(1 - D). \tag{52}$$

A solution to (52) with $1 \geq \eta_i \geq 0$ and $1 \geq \theta_i \geq 0$ is obtained as follows. For any D, $1 \geq D \geq 0$, start with $\theta_i = \beta_i$ and $\bar{l}^i(1 - \eta_i)\delta = \beta_i D$. Then, $\delta \sum_i \bar{l}^i(1 - \eta_i) = D$ and for each i, $\beta_i = \beta_i D + \beta_i(1 - D)$, $\theta_i \in [0, 1]$ and $1 - \eta_i > 0$. Also, $\beta_i - \bar{l}^i(1 - \eta_i)\delta \geq 0$, since $\beta_i \geq 0$ and $1 - D \geq 0$. If it were the case that $\eta_i < 0$, then set $\hat{\eta}_i = 0$, $\hat{\theta}_i(1 - \hat{D}) = \beta_i - \bar{l}^i\delta \geq \beta_i\hat{D}$, where $\hat{D} = \delta \sum_i \bar{l}^i(1 - \hat{\eta}_i)$. It is still true that $\beta_h - \bar{l}^h(1 - \hat{\eta}_h)\delta \geq 0$ for all h; hence, $1 > D \geq \hat{D} \geq 0$ and $1 \geq \hat{\theta}_i \geq 0$ since

$$\hat{\theta}_i = \frac{\beta_i - \bar{l}^i(1 - \hat{\eta}_i)\delta}{\sum_h \beta_h - \delta \sum_h \bar{l}_h(1 - \hat{\eta}_h)} \leq 1.$$

In this way we construct a solution with $1 \geq \eta_i \geq 0$ and $1 \geq \theta_i \geq 0$ for all i, $1 \geq D \geq 0$ as desired. It is fully defined by $1 - \eta_i = \min(\beta_i D / \bar{l}^i \delta, 1)$ and $\theta_i = [\beta_i - \bar{l}^i(1 - \eta_i)\delta]/(1 - D)$.

To verify that the solution just defined solves problem (P 5) in condition (a) of the definition, write the first-order conditions, which are necessary and sufficient since the maximand is concave and the feasible set convex:

$$\frac{\partial E_s u^i(y_s^i)}{\partial \theta_{ij}} = E_s \frac{du^i}{dy_s^i}(\pi_s^j - p_j) = 0 = \sum_s \phi_s(c^i - y_s^i)(\pi_s^j - p_j) \tag{53}$$

$$\frac{\partial E_s u^i(y_s^i)}{\partial \eta_i} = \bar{l}^i E_s \frac{du^i}{dy_s^i}(\bar{w} - \delta Y_s) = 0$$

$$= \sum_s \phi_s(c_i - y_s^i)(\bar{w} - \delta Y_s). \tag{54}$$

Using the definition of y_s^i, and writing Θ_i for the vector $(\theta_{i1} \ldots \theta_{im})'$, conditions (53)–(54) may be written in an obvious matrix notation as

$$
(c_i - \bar{y}_i) \begin{pmatrix} \bar{\pi} - p \\ \bar{Y} - \dfrac{\bar{w}}{\delta} \end{pmatrix} + \begin{bmatrix} \sum_{\pi Y} & \sum_{\pi\pi} \\ \sum_{YY} & \sum_{Y\pi} \end{bmatrix} \begin{pmatrix} \bar{l}^i(1 - \eta_i)\delta \\ \Theta_i \end{pmatrix} = 0.
\tag{55}
$$

Summing these conditions over i, using the definition of D and $\sum_i \theta_{ij} = 1$,

$$
\sum_i (c_i - \bar{y}_i) \begin{pmatrix} \bar{\pi} - p \\ \bar{Y} - \dfrac{\bar{w}}{\delta} \end{pmatrix} + \begin{bmatrix} \sum_{\pi Y} & \sum_{\pi\pi} \\ \sum_{YY} & \sum_{Y\pi} \end{bmatrix} \begin{pmatrix} D \\ l \end{pmatrix} = 0.
\tag{56}
$$

Inserting (56) into (55),

$$
\begin{bmatrix} \sum_{\pi Y} & \sum_{\pi\pi} \\ \sum_{YY} & \sum_{Y\pi} \end{bmatrix} \left[\frac{c_i - \bar{y}_i}{\sum_h c_h - \bar{Y}} \begin{pmatrix} D \\ l \end{pmatrix} - \begin{pmatrix} \bar{l}^i(1 - \eta_i)\delta \\ \Theta_i \end{pmatrix} \right] = 0
\tag{57}
$$

which always admit the solution $\bar{l}^i(1 - \eta_i)\delta = \beta_i D$, $\Theta_i = \beta_i l$, where $\beta_i = (c_i - \bar{y}_i)/(\sum_h c_h - \bar{Y}) = T_A^i(\bar{Y})/T_A(\bar{Y})$. Since furthermore y^i is constant over all pairs $(\hat{\eta}_i, \hat{\theta}_i)$ such that $\beta_i = \bar{l}^i(1 - \hat{\eta}_i)\delta + \hat{\theta}_i(1 - D)$, the modifications introduced in the previous paragraph do not violate the first-order conditions (57). This completes the proof of proposition (i).

To show next that an equilibrium with flexible wage indexation is Pareto efficient, one notes from (56) that, in equilibrium, $p = \bar{\pi} - R \sum_{\pi Y}$, $\bar{w} = \delta[\bar{Y} - R\sigma_Y^2]$, where $R^{-1} = \sum_i c_i - \bar{Y}$. (Indeed, $\sum_{\pi Y} D + \sum_{\pi\pi} l = \sum_{\pi Y}$ and $\sum_{YY} D + \sum_{Y\pi} l = \sum_{YY} = \sigma_Y^2$.) Therefore, maximisation of market value by firms is equivalent to maximisation of profits $\sum_s q_s \pi_s^j$ at prices $q_s = \phi_s[1 - R(Y_s - \bar{Y})]$. And one notes from (57) that $y_s^i = \alpha_i + \beta_i Y_s$, with $\beta_i = \bar{l}^i(1 - \eta_i)\delta + \theta_i(1 - D) = T_A^i(\bar{Y})/T_A(\bar{Y})$. The verification of the conditions listed at the beginning of section 5.1 is then immediate.

6. Concluding comments

6.1.

The results presented in section 5 may be summarised as follows. I have studied an economy consisting of a given set of firms, which hire labour to produce a state-dependent output, and whose shares are traded on a stock market. Efficient risk-sharing among all the agents in the economy calls for individual incomes related to aggregate output (or wealth). In the simple special case of quadratic utilities, efficiency requires that individual incomes be linearly related to aggregate wealth, i.e. consist of a fixed part and a variable part, proportional to aggregate wealth.The variable part should distribute the random fluctuations of aggregate wealth over individuals in proportion to their risk tolerances – independently of the extent to which the individual incomes come from wages or from profit shares.

If wages were fixed (state independent), an efficient allocation of risk would require that workers buy shares of stock on credit, using their wage earnings as collateral. Such arrangements are impractical, costly and subject to moral hazard. If wages were set after observing the state and equal to the marginal value product of labour, an efficient allocation of risks would require that workers insure their wage uncertainty, either by selling short a portfolio perfectly positively correlated with their wages or by buying on credit a portfolio perfectly negatively correlated with their wages. Such portfolios may not exist; at best, the arrangements are impractical, costly and subject to moral hazard.

Flexible wage indexation is a more practical alternative. It calls for setting wages that consist of two parts, namely a fixed part (indexed on consumer prices, in practice) and a variable part, indexed on aggregate output (wealth). Each individual chooses freely the relative importance of the two parts of his or her wage income, as well as the composition of his or her portfolio. Efficient risk-sharing emerges naturally, without recourse to short sales or credit. The only requirement is that the risk premium by which the expected value of a variable wage exceeds the fixed wage should be consistent with the risk premium by which the expected value of a firm's profits differs from the market price of its shares. That is, a single price of risk determines simultaneously the trade-off between the fixed and variable wage, and the prices of shares on the stock market. And the efficient allocation is sustained as a decentralised equilibrium.

Although the results were established for quadratic utilities, they can be extended to the 'hyperbolic absolute risk aversion' class at a small technical cost. The implicit property on which the results rest is the extended validity of the CAPM to situations where the endowments (here, the labour incomes) of the agents lie in the span of the vectors of returns to the marketed assets – see Geanakoplos in Duffie *et al.* (1988). The fact that all firms have the same shareholders leads them to offer the same labour contracts – see Drèze (1989a).

6.2.

The nature of the result should be properly understood. It applies to the compensation of *workers under contract*, not directly to the wages of new entrants to the labour market in state *s*. The presentation is timeless, but it should be remembered that two 'dates' are involved: an initial date, at which firms hire employees, the labour market clears, and asset markets clear; and a future date, at which production materialises, wages and dividends are paid out. The 'state' is unknown at the initial date, but will be known at the future date.

The market clearing fixed wage at the initial date is $\bar{w}$. But labour contracts offer the prospect of stipulating state-dependent wages that bring about efficient risk-sharing between firms and their employees. The results of section 5 give a simple operational content to the abstract model of labour contracts. But it should be understood that the *level* of all wages is determined by the condition of market clearing at the initial date – that is, by the condition $\sum_i \bar{l}^i = \sum_j l^j$, which determines $\bar{w}$ and affects w_s which is proportional to $\bar{w}$ (as well as to Y_s) according to formula (47). Should the labour market reopen at the future date in state *s*, with new entrants to the labour market, then a new market clearing wage for new contracts, $\bar{w}_s$, will prevail. Since $\bar{w}_s$ will be determined by the supply and demand for new contracts, whereas w_s is predetermined as part of the initial contracts, one should not expect that $\bar{w}_s = w_s$ identically in *s*. Wage differentiation between successive cohorts of workers will generally be required for efficiency. That topic goes beyond the scope of the present paper. It is treated in Drèze and Gollier (1989).

6.3.

In the model of section 5, firms hire labour at the initial date, and are constrained not to use additional labour in any state. Because the opportunity cost of labour is equal to zero in every state, no layoffs ever occur. This feature calls for two remarks.

First, when the labour market clears, the weighted expected marginal product of labour (adjusted for risk), $\sum_s q_s \, df^j_s/dl^j$, is the same in all firms and equal to the fixed wage. It may still be the case that the marginal product of labour differs across firms in specific states. In such states, a more efficient use of labour could be achieved if some labour were transferred from the low productivity to the high productivity firms. Such arrangements are sometimes observed (for instance, fishermen may find casual employment on shore on days of sea storm or boat maintenance), but they are the exception rather than the rule. A smooth organisation of such arrangements would require *ex ante* evaluation of the marginal product of labour in every state. That kind of contingent information is typically unavailable.

Second, under a more general specification, where labour supply would reflect the disutility or opportunity cost of labour, it may no longer be efficient to set $l^j_s = l^j$ for all s. In particular, under a high opportunity cost of labour (due for instance to generous unemployment benefits), it would be natural to set $l^j_s < l^j$ in those states s where the marginal product of labour is low ('bad' states). In order for the analysis to go through, it would then be required that (cardinal) individual preferences for leisure and wealth be representable by separable functions:

$$U^i(l^i, y^i) = v^i(l^i) + u^i(y^i), \quad i = 1 \ldots n. \tag{58}$$

That assumption, under which risk tolerance remains independent of leisure time or work effort, is rather restrictive when U^i is defined up to an affine transformation.

6.4.

The superiority of flexible wage indexation over fixed wages comes from the reduction in the risk premium $R = 1/T_A(\bar{Y}) = 1/\sum_i T^i_A(\bar{y}^i)$. Consider an economy with two types of agents, n_1 asset owners with $\sum_{i=1}^{n_1} \theta_{ij} = 1$ for all j and n_2 workers with no endowment of initial assets. The firms could hire the available labour at a fixed wage $\bar{w}_1$ such that

$$\bar{w}_1 = \sum_s \frac{df^j_s}{dl^j} \phi_s [1 - R_1(Y_s - \bar{Y})] \tag{59}$$

where R_1 is the risk premium incorporated in the asset prices and verifying $R_1^{-1} = \sum_{i=1}^{n_1} T_A^i(\bar{y}^i)$. The risk premium R_1 exceeds the risk premium R of section 5, which verifies instead $R^{-1} = \sum_{i=1}^{n_1+n_2} T_A^i(\bar{y}^i)$. In order to assess the reduction in the risk premium, it is useful to write it in terms of the relative risk tolerances defined in (8):

$$R^{-1} = \sum_{i=1}^{n_1+n_2} \frac{T_A^i(\bar{y}^i)}{\bar{y}^i} \cdot \bar{y}^i = \bar{Y} \sum_{i=1}^{n_1+n_2} \frac{\bar{y}^i}{\bar{Y}} T_R^i(\bar{y}^i) = \bar{Y} T_R(\bar{Y}) \tag{60}$$

$$R_1^{-1} = \sum_{i=1}^{n_1} \frac{T_A^i(\bar{y}^i)}{\bar{y}^i} \cdot \bar{y}^i = \bar{Y}_1 \sum_{i=1}^{n_1} \frac{\bar{y}^i}{\bar{Y}_1} T_R^i(\bar{y}^i)$$

$$= \bar{Y}_1 T_R(\bar{Y}_1), \quad \bar{Y}_1 = \sum_{i=1}^{n_1} \bar{y}^i. \tag{61}$$

If it were the case that the average relative risk tolerance for all the agents, $T_R(\bar{Y})$, is equal to the average risk tolerance for the asset owners, $T_R(\bar{Y}_1)$; then it would follow from (60)–(61) that

$$\frac{R_1}{R} = \frac{\bar{Y}}{\bar{Y}_1} \tag{62}$$

where $\bar{Y}/\bar{Y}_1$ is the ratio of total wealth to non-human wealth (of national income to capital income). That ratio should be approximately equal to the reciprocal of the capital share in income and wealth (one minus the labour share), hence it should fall in the range from 3 to 4. The reduction in the risk premium resulting from flexible wage indexation versus fixed wages would be dramatic. The calculation is probably an overestimation, to the extent that the average risk tolerance of asset owners may exceed that of wage earners. Unfortunately, the logical arguments to that effect are ambiguous, and the empirical evidence is very limited.

It should be noted that the reduction in the risk premium benefits the wage earners, because

$$\bar{w} = \sum_s \phi_s \frac{df_s^j}{dl^j} - R \sum_s \phi_s \frac{df_s^j}{dl^j}(Y_s - \bar{Y}) > \bar{w}_1$$

$$= \sum_s \phi_s \frac{df_s^j}{dl^j} - R_1 \sum_s \phi_s \frac{df_s^j}{dl_s^j}(Y_s - \bar{Y}). \tag{63}$$

6.5.

The main difficulty in applying a flexible indexation scheme lies with the measurement of the 'aggregate wealth' variable Y_s. That difficulty has a logical side and a practical side.

The logical issue concerns the wealth *concept*. A static (timeless) framework was used here for simplicity of exposition. In reality, one would need to choose between a flow concept like national income, justified for instance by the argument that wealth is the present value of income; or a stock concept combining asset values and some evaluation of human wealth. The former approach is definitely the more practical. Although the period over which the flow should be measured is arbitrary, the year seems inescapable ... Another issue concerns the geographical area over which the aggregate income flow should be measured. A national measure again seems inescapable. Yet, capital markets are linked internationally. To the extent that national incomes are imperfectly correlated across countries, the international linkage should reduce the national risk premia.

The practical issue concerns the speed and objectivity with which national income is measured. Up-to-date information about labour incomes and wage costs is part of our system, and is forthcoming when wages are geared to a monthly index of consumer prices. National income is measured less frequently, less accurately and with longer delay.

6.6.

From the standpoint of individual firms, the proposed indexation scheme should be a matter of indifference, so long as they accept the market risk-premium as a guideline and attempt to maximise market value. That principle does not apply to small firms which are not traded on a stock exchange. Thus, a private entrepreneur who owns an independent firm typically invests in that firm most of his (her) wealth, instead of holding a diversified portfolio. The relevant risk premium for that firm should then reflect the owner's risk tolerance rather than the market price of risk. Being unable to shed risks on the market, that entrepreneur could benefit from sharing risks with his (her) employees, through profit-sharing at the firm level. In a small firm, productivity may also be enhanced by the incentive effects of profit-sharing.

On the other hand, many contracts, like house rental or life insurance, could embody partial indexation on national income as a further step towards more efficient risk-sharing at the economy-wide level.

12 Wages, employment and the equity–efficiency trade-off*

1. Introduction

In a decentralised market economy, prices play two roles: an *economic* role, as prices guide production and consumption decisions; and a *financial* role, as prices determine the receipts of the seller and the expenditure (hence the real income) of the buyer.[1] The first role is geared to *efficiency* of resource allocation; the second is related to *equity* of the personal distribution of real incomes...

The dual role of prices is obvious in the case of *wages*. In a market economy, the level and hierarchy of wages guide the labour demand by firms; and wages determine the real incomes of workers.[2] An economically efficient use of human labour, free of involuntary unemployment as well as unfilled job offers, may lead to an 'inequitable' income distribution. (The meaning of 'inequitable' is explained below.) This may be linked to the functional distribution between capital and labour, or to the wage disparities by skills. In this paper, I use a streamlined model, with identical workers and a single wage rate; but I consider the spread between wages and unemployment benefits.

The second theorem of welfare economics[3] *suggests* a general solution to the potential conflict between efficiency and equity. Under the conditions

* Expository Paper written for the session on 'Equity–Efficiency Trade-Off' at the 9th Meeting of French-Speaking Belgian Economists, Liège, November 1988 and published in *Recherches Economiques de Louvain*, 55, 1, 1–31; translated from the French by the author.
[1] Cf. Lévy-Lambert (1969) for a systematic discussion of that theme.
[2] The same duality remains present in a labour-managed economy: see Drèze (1984a, 1989a).
[3] See e.g. Koopmans (1957).

of the theorem, every Pareto-efficient allocation of resources[4] corresponds to competitive clearing of all markets, under an appropriate redistribution of wealth (i.e. under a proper set of individualised lump-sum taxes and transfers). Economic policy thus boils down to two specific tasks: bring about competitive clearing of all markets, and implement the lump-sum transfers suggested by equity considerations.

Without reviewing here the conditions of the theorem,[5] I will mention the two main difficulties surrounding its applicability.

(i) The argument rests on existence of a complete set of markets, and does not apply to an economy with incomplete markets. In a temporal economy with uncertain future, this calls for existence of an insurance market for each good at each date conditionally on each possible 'state' of the economic environment (as defined by demography, natural resources, technology, tastes, institutions ...). In real economies, markets are incomplete – due to many reasons, one of which is close to my subject matter. *In a temporal economy, some agents concerned with markets at future dates are unable to trade today.* This applies in particular to labour markets. Each year, a new generation of young workers enters the labour market. The future generations (whose members are in school today) do not sell their labour services forward and contingently (on graduation, on the state of the economy ...). To that extent, markets are incomplete, and the second welfare theorem is not applicable. In particular, it is not demonstrated, and *it is in general not the case, that sequential competitive clearing of labour markets is Pareto efficient.* (In other words, the alleged efficiency of fully flexible wages is not to be taken for granted; I show in Section 3 that full flexibility can be inefficient.)

The nature of the inefficiency is the following. Economic fluctuations may cause substantial wages fluctuations (due to inelastic labour supply), hence substantial uncertainty of workers' incomes. It is inefficient to let workers bear that uncertainty, which could be shared better. (As shown in Section 3, a suitable degree of wage rigidity, combined with unemployment benefits, provides income insurance and is more efficient than full wage flexibility.)

(ii) The argument of the second welfare theorem also rests on the possibility of implementing lump-sum transfers among households, at

[4] I.e., such that no household could be made better off without some other household being made worse off.

[5] The most restrictive assumption concerns convexity of production sets. That assumption is definitely unrealistic, but unfortunately essential for decentralisation of efficient decisions through prices. See Dehez and Drèze (1988a) for a concept of decentralised *equilibrium* with increasing returns to scale.

no real cost. This has two aspects. First, individualised transfers, or discriminatory taxes, must be ethically acceptable. (Which house of representatives would vote a special tax on eyesight accuracy or knowledge of foreign languages, on grounds of measured correlation with high productivity?) Second, the transfers and taxes must be 'neutral' (non-distorting); for instance, they should not affect labour supply, entrepreneurship, savings, investment, consumer or technological choices, a.s.o.

In reality, taxes and transfers are always based on simple, objective characteristics, that keep discrimination to a minimum; and they always entail some loss of efficiency, due to administrative costs, incentive effects and distortions. That real cost must be taken into account. *It is sometimes less inefficient to tamper with prices, in order to modify directly the income distribution, than to correct that distribution through taxes and transfers.* Wages are a good example. To modify the distribution of income between property owners and workers, wage setting and income taxes provide alternative instruments, whose real costs should be contrasted.

In this paper, I use a very simple model to characterise the efficiency–equity trade-off, when wage setting is used to correct the income distribution (Section 2) or improve risk-sharing (Section 3), in a market economy where firms hire and fire labour so as to maximise market value. Some implications and extensions are mentioned briefly at the end (Section 4).

2. Wages, transfers and distortions

2.1.

In this section, I bring out the role of wages and unemployment benefits to correct the income distribution, when taxes are distorting and thus entail a real cost.

The simplest relevant model involves n identical workers, who either work (sell one unit of labour) for a wage w, or do not work and collect unemployment benefits t. (Working time is not a variable here.) Moreover, workers may have to pay a lump-sum tax $a < 0$ or may receive a lump-sum transfer $a > 0$ (sometimes called 'universal grant' or 'negative income tax', but here specific to workers). The income of a worker is thus $w + a \geq 0$ if employed, $t + a \geq 0$ if unemployed. I write m for the monetary equivalent of the utility or disutility of work, here assumed for convenience invariant with income. The utility of a worker is therefore $u(w - m + a)$ if employed, $u(t + a)$ if unemployed. The function u is concave (diminishing marginal utility) and differentiable, with $u' > 0$, $u'' < 0$. Its (cardinal) interpretation is discussed below.

Workers are employed in the production sector, here treated as an aggregate; value added is defined through a concave production function (diminishing returns) $f(l)$, where l denotes employment, determined by the first-order condition for profit maximisation $f'(l) = w$ (the marginal value product of labour is equal to the wage rate). I write $l(w)$ for 'l such that $f'(l) = w$'.[6] A wage cost w thus implies gross profits in the amount $f(l(w)) - wl(w)$.

Profits are distributed to shareholders, a group distinct from the workers. (Shareholders' preferences are taken into account in Section 3, but play no role in Section 2.) Profits are subject to a lump-sum tax $T < 0$ or subsidy $T > 0$.[7]

Budgetary equilibrium requires that taxes, transfers and unemployment benefits sum to zero, i.e. $T + na + (n - l)t = 0$. I wish to take into account the real cost of (distorting) taxes. In order to study the choice between wages and transfers, without being specific about the nature of tax distortions, I will impute a real cost $d \geq 0$ to each dollar of tax or subsidy on profits. The total real cost of taxation is thus $d|T| = d|na + (n - l)t| \geq 0$. The *net* profits associated with wages w, benefits t and transfers a are thus defined by

$$\Pi(w, t, a) = f(l(w)) - wl(w) - [na + (n - l(w))t]$$
$$- d|na + (n - l(w))t|. \tag{1}$$

When $t = 0$, the competitive wage w^* is equal to the maximum of $f'(n)$ and m. When $f'(n) \geq m$, then $w^* = f'(n)$ and $l(w^*) = n$. When $f'(n) < m$, then $w^* = m$ and $l(w^*) < n$. Unemployment $n - l(w^*)$ is 'voluntary' since $u(w - m + a) = u(a) = u(t + a)$. The two cases are illustrated in figure 12.1, with the marginal value product of labour given respectively by curve $\bar{f}'(l)$ and by curve $\hat{f}'(l)$.

More generally, when $t > 0$, wages must be such that $w - m \geq t$, because otherwise the labour supply would vanish.

2.2.

Competitive wages might induce a distribution of income among workers and shareholders which the government wishes to correct, which amounts

---

[6] Technically, labour demand is defined by the inverse function $l(w) = (f')^{-1}(w)$.
[7] That convenient formulation is realistic when profits are taxed at a flat rate, independent of personal income. (Such is by and large the case in Belgium.)

to say that the income distribution is judged 'inequitable'. Thus, if $w^* = m$ and $a = 0$, the government would typically wish to raise the income of workers. More generally, $w^* > m$ may be judged intolerably low, or high, relatively to profits (to shareholders' income).

In such a model, the government has the choice of two instruments to correct the income distribution, a or t. (At full employment, or when $t = 0$, nobody collects benefits and the only instrument available to *reduce* workers' income is a.)

Assume that the government wishes to raise workers' income, starting from a situation where $w - m + a = t + a$ (unemployment nonexistent or voluntary). *The best instrument is that which permits a given increment of workers' income at the least cost in terms of net profits.* ('Best' means here 'second-best'; the income distribution condition and the real cost of transfers rule out the 'first-best'.)

The choice of the better instrument is given by the solution of the following problem:

PROBLEM P.1

$\max\limits_{w,a,t} \Pi(w, t, a)$ subject to

$$u(w - m + a) = u(t + a) \geq u(b),$$
$$0 \leq t \leq w - m, \, l(w) \leq n, f'(l) = w.$$

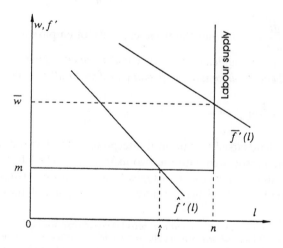

Figure 12.1

From the definition (1), when $na + (n - l)t \geq 0$, we may compute:

$$\frac{d\Pi(w, t, a)}{da} = \frac{\partial\Pi(w, t, a)}{\partial a} = -(1 + d)n; \tag{2}$$

$$\frac{d\Pi(w, t, a)}{dt} = \frac{\partial\Pi(w, t, a)}{\partial t} + \frac{\partial\Pi(w, t, a)}{\partial w}\frac{dw}{dt}$$

$$= \frac{\partial\Pi(w, t, a)}{\partial t} + \frac{\partial\Pi(w, t, a)}{\partial w}$$

$$= -(1 + d)(n - l) + f' \cdot \frac{dl}{dw} - w\frac{dl}{dw}$$

$$- l + (1 + d)t\frac{dl}{dw}$$

$$= -(1 + d)(n - l) - l + (1 + d)t\frac{dl}{dw}; \tag{3}$$

$$\frac{d\Pi(w, t, a)}{dt} - \frac{d\Pi(w, t, a)}{da} = ld + (1 + d)t\frac{dl}{dw}$$

$$= (1 + d)l\left[\frac{d}{1 + d} + \frac{t}{l}\frac{dl}{dw}\right]$$

$$= (1 + d)l\left[\frac{d}{1 + d} + \frac{t}{w}\eta_{lw}\right] \tag{4}$$

where $\eta_{lw} = \dfrac{w}{l}\dfrac{dl}{dw} < 0$ denotes the wage elasticity of employment.

The necessary and sufficient condition under which higher wages and unemployment benefits dominate lump-sum transfers to all workers[8] *is*

$$\frac{d}{1 + d} \geq \frac{t}{w}|\eta_{lw}| = \frac{w - m}{w}|\eta_{lw}| = \frac{w - m}{l}\left|\frac{dl}{dw}\right|. \tag{5}$$

Condition (5) lends itself to a natural interpretation in terms of the real costs (distortions) associated with the two instruments. The left-hand side measures the real cost per dollar of taxes levied on profits. (Indeed, the cost is d for one dollar of net revenue, i.e. for $1 + d$ dollars of gross

[8] If the lump-sum transfers were granted to a broader group than workers alone, the real cost of transfers would increase proportionately, and the relative efficiency of wages to raise workers' income would be enhanced. This remark applies in particular to 'universal grants' available to all.

revenue.) The right-hand side measures the real cost per dollar of incremental wage bill. (A unit increase of w increases the wage bill by l and reduces employment by $dl/dw < 0$, at a loss of output $f' \, dl/dw = w \, dl/dw$; but the employment change contributes directly $-m \, dl/dw$ to the real income of workers; the real cost is thus $(w - m) \, dl/dw$ per unit increase of w or $(w - m)/l \cdot (dl/dw)$ per dollar of wage bill.) Thus condition (5) reads: *wages are a more efficient instrument of income redistribution than lump-sum transfers when wages induce less costly distortions than taxes, dollar for dollar.*

Looking at the limiting cases $d = 0$ and $t \, dl/dw = 0$, one concludes from (5) that either instrument might qualify: *when taxes are non-distorting* $(d = 0)$, lump-sum transfers are a more efficient instrument of income redistribution than wages; on the other hand, *when wages cover exactly the real opportunity cost of work* $(w - m = 0)$, *or when the wage elasticity of employment is non-negative, then wages are a more efficient instrument of income redistribution than lump-sum transfers financed by non-neutral taxes.*

The use of both instruments is balanced, and problem P.1 is solved, when (5) holds as equality, i.e. when

$$
\frac{w - m}{w} = \frac{\dfrac{d}{1 + d}}{|\eta_{lw}|}. \tag{6}
$$

Readers familiar with second-best tax theory will interpret (6) as a 'Boiteux–Ramsey rule' or 'inverse elasticity rule' for the relative spread between the market price (w) and the social cost (m) of a factor of production. (The same readers will interpret (5) in terms of 'direction of improvement' for the 'reform' problem.)

I will discuss in Section 2.4 the measurement of the parameters (m, d, η) of (5)–(6), and the practical circumstances under which condition (5) is apt to hold.

2.3.

I turn now to a more sophisticated point. *When condition* (5) *holds at less than full employment* $(n > l)$, *raising wages at unchanged unemployment benefits is less distortionary, per dollar of labour income, than raising simultaneously wages and benefits.* That conclusion follows directly from the fact that unemployment benefits are financed by taxes which entail more distortions than wage increases, when (5) holds. Yet the proposed policy would induce *involuntary* unemployment, because it would eventually result in $w - m > t$, i.e. a real income disparity between employed and unemployed workers. Is that a desirable component of income redistribution policies?

We encounter here the difficult choice between *ex post* and *ex ante* policies. To clarify the nature of that choice, it helps to reason with fixed transfers, and to investigate whether it would be desirable to simultaneously reduce benefits and raise wages. Could one in this way reduce the deadweight loss of distortions, at unchanged expected utility for a worker? If so, one could also raise net profits at unchanged workers' (expected) utility, *a Pareto improvement.*

Since all workers are identical, it is natural to stipulate that they are hired randomly, so that each individual worker is employed with probability l/n, unemployed with probability $(n - l)/n$. A worker's expected utility is then computed as

$$Eu = \frac{l}{n}u(w - m + a) + \frac{n - l}{n}u(t + a).\tag{7}$$

When $w - m = t$, unemployment is voluntary and $Eu(w - m + a) = u(t + a)$. On the other hand, under involuntary unemployment $(w - m > t)$, expected utility is a weighted average of the two different levels $u(w - m + a)$ and $u(t + a)$. Formula (7) then takes on its full meaning, based on the axiomatic decision theory underpinning the definition of cardinal, or von Neumann-Morgenstern utility.[9] The interpretation, also illustrated in figure 12.2, goes as follows: the uncertain prospect promising the net incomes $w - m + a$ and $t + a$ with respective probabilities l/n and $(n - l)/n$ is indifferent to the sure income y, such that

$$u(y) = \frac{l}{n}u(w - m + a) + \frac{n - l}{n}u(t + a) = Eu.\tag{8}$$

The utility function u is calibrated on the basis of such indifference

---

[9] For an elementary presentation of that theory, see Drèze (1974a).

relations. Decision theory tells us that such a calibration is always possible, provided preferences are 'consistent', according to the axioms.

We are here faced with the question: precisely what are we trying to achieve through income redistribution? If we wish to correct the income distribution on behalf of workers, in order to raise their real income to b, should we impose the twin conditions

$$u(w - m + a) \geq u(b), \quad u(t + a) \geq b; \tag{9}$$

or should we impose the single condition

$$Eu = \frac{l(w)}{n} u(w - m + a) + \frac{n - l(w)}{n} u(t + a) \geq u(b)? \tag{10}$$

The first formulation (9) implies directly the solution $w - m + a = t + a = b$; unemployment is voluntary, with benefits dictated by income distribution targets. When inequality (5) holds, the second formulation (10) leads to a different solution, with $w - m + a > t + a$ and $Eu = u(b)$. That solution is inegalitarian *ex post*, but egalitarian *ex ante* (before it is known who is hired and who remains unemployed), in terms of expected utility. It preserves equal chances for all workers, and grants to them acceptable income 'expectations' – but at the cost of an *ex post* disparity between the real incomes of employed and unemployed workers. That solution is less attractive in terms of *equity*, but with undeniable merits in terms of *efficiency*.

In order to understand the nature of the trade-off, it is helpful to look at the properties of the solution induced by the *ex ante* criterion when (5) holds. At given transfers $\bar{a}$, the first-order condition for efficient values of w and t corresponds to maximisation of $\Pi(w, t; \bar{a})$ *under the constraint* (10); i.e. it corresponds to a solution of the following problem:

PROBLEM P.2

$$\max_{w,t} \Pi(w, t; \bar{a}) \text{ subject to}$$

$$\frac{l(w)}{n} u(w - m + \bar{a}) + \frac{n - l(w)}{n} u(t + \bar{a}) \geq u(b),$$

$$0 \leq t \leq w - m, \quad l(w) \leq n, \quad f'(l) = w.$$

In order to solve that problem, one may differentiate condition (10), to compute by how much unemployment benefits could be cut, at unchanged expected utility, when wages are raised:

$$\frac{dt}{dw}\bigg|_{Eu} = -\frac{\dfrac{\partial Eu}{\partial w}}{\dfrac{\partial Eu}{\partial t}}$$

$$= -\frac{lu'(w - m + \bar{a}) + [u(w - m + \bar{a}) - u(t + \bar{a})]\dfrac{dl}{dw}}{(n - l)u'(t + \bar{a})}. \qquad (11)$$

Using (1), one obtains the first-order condition:

$$0 = \frac{d\Pi(w, t; \bar{a})}{dw} = \frac{\partial \Pi(w, t; \bar{a})}{\partial w} + \frac{\partial \Pi(w, t; \bar{a})}{\partial t}\frac{dt}{dw}\bigg|_{Eu}$$

$$= -l + (1 + d)t\frac{dl}{dw} \qquad (12)$$

$$+ \frac{(1 + d)}{u'(t + \bar{a})}\left\{lu'(w - m + \bar{a}) + \frac{dl}{dw}[u(w - m + \bar{a}) - u(t + \bar{a})]\right\}$$

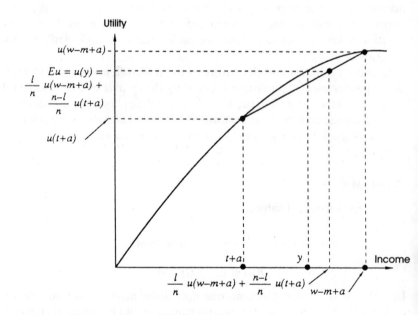

Figure 12.2

In order to interpret that condition, it is helpful to use the linear approximation:

$$u(w - m + \bar{a}) \approx u(t + \bar{a}) + (w - m - t)u'(t + \bar{a}). \qquad (13)$$

Inserting (13) into (12), we obtain the equality

$$\frac{u'(w - m + \bar{a})}{u'(t + \bar{a})} = \frac{1}{1 + d} - \frac{w - m}{l}\frac{dl}{dw}. \qquad (14)$$

In order to translate that condition on marginal utilities into a condition on real income disparities, one may use a further linear approximation:

$$u'(w - m + \bar{a}) \approx u'(t + \bar{a}) + (w - m - t)u''(t + \bar{a})$$

$$= u'(t + \bar{a})\left[1 + (w - m - t)\frac{u''(t + \bar{a})}{u'(t + \bar{a})}\right]$$

$$= u'(t + \bar{a})\left[1 - \frac{w - m - t}{t + \bar{a}}\left\{-(t + \bar{a})\frac{u''(t + \bar{a})}{u'(t + \bar{a})}\right\}\right]$$

$$= u'(t + \bar{a})\left[1 - \frac{w - m - t}{t + \bar{a}}R_R(t + \bar{a})\right] \qquad (15)$$

where $R_R(t + \bar{a}) = -(t + \bar{a})\dfrac{u''(t + \bar{a})}{u'(t + \bar{a})} > 0$ denotes the Arrow (1965) and Pratt (1964) relative risk-aversion measure. That quantity corresponds to a risk premium per unit of coefficient of variation (variance/expectation). It comes into the picture here, because our distributive target is the expected utility of an uncertain prospect between $w - m + \bar{a}$ and $t + \bar{a}$. The curvature of utility over that interval, as measured by R_R, defines the spread between the slopes (marginal utilities) at $w - m + \bar{a}$ and $t + \bar{a}$, respectively. Although marginal utilities are not identified, R_R is a pure number, and can be estimated from choices among uncertain prospects.

Combining (14) and (15), we can solve for the relative spread between $w - m + \bar{a}$ and $t + \bar{a}$:

$$\frac{(w - m + \bar{a}) - (t + \bar{a})}{t + \bar{a}} = \frac{\dfrac{d}{1 + d} - \dfrac{w - m}{l}\left|\dfrac{dl}{dw}\right|}{R_R(t + \bar{a})}. \qquad (16)$$

The ex ante criterion recommends a relative spread between the real incomes of employed and unemployed workers equal to the ratio between the efficiency gain due to the use of wages rather than tax-financed benefits (numerator), on the one hand, and the cost of income disparity as measured by R_R, on the other hand. That ratio is thus a cost (denominator) – benefit (numerator) ratio. Accepting the *ex ante* criterion amounts to accepting a trade-off between equity and efficiency; in contrast, the *ex post* criterion imposes an egalitarian norm (for employed and unemployed workers) as an absolute equity requirement, without regard for its efficiency cost.

2.4.

It will be seen in Section 3 that the *ex ante* criterion is the only meaningful one, when one considers prospectively the situation that will prevail *in the future*. Section 2.3 was meant to introduce the *ex ante* criterion in a simpler context, to bring out its logic. The idea of an equity-efficiency trade-off just outlined strikes me as reasonable, and congruent with the general methodology of the second-best.

The *ex ante* criterion is used by several authors to model union behaviour, in the framework of the so-called 'union wage model'. That model[10] rests precisely on the assumption that unions attempt to set wages so as to maximise expected utility, namely (10), taking into account the wage elasticity of labour demand. The repeated use of a model does not make it realistic, but suggests at least that it is not meaningless.

In order to bring out explicitly the circumstances under which condition (5) is apt to hold, one should spell out the nature of tax-induced distortions. Such a task lies outside the scope of the present paper, and I will limit myself to one remark. At the time of writing (1988), the Belgian Government, keen on reducing the public deficit, has been known to reduce the number of public servants, in particular teachers or social workers, at a significant welfare loss per frank ultimately saved. That loss is comparable to a distortion cost of taxation, since it defines the 'opportunity cost' of public expenditures. The magnitude of that loss is probably such that we cannot dismiss the possibility of more severe distortions for transfers than for wages.[11]

Yet, I must admit that such formulae as (6) or (16) are not easily implemented, due to our econometric uncertainties. The real cost of tax distortions d, the real opportunity cost of labour m, the wage elasticity of

---

[10] See Oswald (1985) or Pencavel (1985) for a survey presentation. McDonald and Solow (1981), who use that model for purposes different from mine, quote Cartter (1959) among their forerunners.

[11] With reference to 'universal grants' or negative income taxes, one must remember that the number of beneficiaries exceeds the number of wage earners.

labour demand η_{lw} or the relative risk aversion of workers R_R are unknown parameters, estimated with sizeable standard errors. The need to take into account our econometric uncertainty is another reason to work with an *ex ante* criterion. When the effects of economic policies are uncertain, it is impossible to optimise *ex post*. Even if one adopts a *strategy* under which policies are revised after observing their effects, the time series of consequences is stochastic, and calls for *ex ante* assessment of costs and benefits. One convenient byproduct of decision theory is that it provides a justification and method for compounding econometric uncertainties with real uncertainties.

There is also scope for disagreement regarding the estimation of the relevant parameters. What model specification should we adopt, to estimate the wage elasticity of employment? Are the effects symmetrical for positive and negative shocks? Should we use estimates of a short-run, or a long-run elasticity? (The orders of magnitudes differ by a factor of 1 to 5 or more ... .)[12] We know even less about risk aversion, and the underlying decision theory is not unanimously accepted.[13] Much remains to be done, if we want to tackle rigorously even the simplest problems of income policies. It is not surprising that a pragmatic approach remains prevalent ...

3. Wages, profits and risk-sharing

3.1.

I now wish to consider prospectively, from an *ex ante* viewpoint, the pros and cons of wage flexibility. I shall again use the simplest relevant model.

In Section 2, labour demand was deduced from the production function $f(l)$, and the first-order condition $f'(l) = w$. But labour demand *tomorrow* is not known exactly today. It will depend upon economic conditions, unknown today, described tomorrow by any one of S mutually exclusive 'states', indexed $s = 1 \ldots S$, with probabilities $\phi_s > 0$. I now write $f_s(l_s)$ for the production function and $f'_s(l_s) = w_s$ for the first-order condition fixing employment l_s in state s. The other variables of the model will be indexed similarly.

According to that formulation, tomorrow's employment will be determined, in each state s, by the equality of labour's marginal value

---

[12] See Drèze and Modigliani (1981).
[13] See Drèze (1974a) and Machina (1987) for contrasting viewpoints.

product and wage cost. That is, employment will be determined *ex post*, conditionally on the state of the economy, by profit maximisation. But the economist investigates *ex ante* (today) the Pareto efficiency of the wage formation mechanism.

The *ex ante* efficiency analysis runs per force in terms of expected utilities – a natural approach, if one relies upon decision theory to represent preferences among uncertain prospects. In so far as workers are concerned, that representation has already been introduced in Section 2. For a worker seeking employment tomorrow, the hiring probability will be $l_s(w_s)/n$ if state s occurs.[14] Expected utility *conditionally on s* is

$$E(u \mid s) = \frac{l_s(w_s)}{n} u(w_s - m + a_s) + \frac{n - l_s(w_s)}{n} u(t_s + a_s). \tag{17}$$

Unconditional expected utility is then given today by

$$Eu = \sum_s \phi_s \left\{ \frac{l_s(w_s)}{n} u(w_s - m + a_s) + \frac{n - l_s(w_s)}{n} u(t + a_s) \right\}, \tag{18}$$

where Eu is a function of the vectors $(w_s, a_s, t_s)_{s=1...S}$. As noted above, one convenient byproduct of decision theory is the compounding of uncertainties through probabilities. An *ex ante* incomes policy is then formulated simply by

$$Eu \geq u(b). \tag{19}$$

The profits side is less transparent. In the deterministic framework of Section 2, Pareto efficiency could be achieved by maximising profits Π under a constraint on workers' utility like (9) or (10). In a prospective framework with uncertainty, profits will depend upon the state that occurs. There is a *vector* of profits $(\Pi_1 ... \Pi_s ... \Pi_S)$; *ex ante* efficiency analysis must reckon with uncertainty, and *perform with profits some form of expected utility calculations*.

Net profits of business firms are typically distributed to shareholders according to their ownership fractions – say $\theta_i \geq 0$, $\sum_i \theta_i = 1$. There exist alternative interpretations of the expected utility of profits calculation

$$EV = \sum_s \phi_s V(\Pi_s). \tag{20}$$

[14] I could have written n_s for the sake of generality – but that would make little difference.

One could interpret V as the outcome of a linear aggregation of shareholders' utilities

$$V(\Pi_s) = \sum_i \lambda_i u_i(\theta_i \Pi_s), \lambda_i > 0. \tag{21}$$

Harsanyi (1955) has proposed axiomatic foundations for that approach. One could interpret V as the outcome of aggregation by the stock market of the risk preferences of investors holding equilibrium portfolios. The 'Capital Asset Pricing Model' (CAPM) provides a justification of that approach,[15] see e.g., Mossin (1977). Finally, one could interpret V as a direct representation of social preferences for private profits (taking into account, inter alia, the influence of profits on investment ...). A more detailed discussion of these alternative approaches lies beyond the scope of this paper; it can be found in Drèze (1987a) for instance.

I will thus introduce a function $V(\Pi)$, $V' > 0$, $V'' < 0$, characterised in particular by the relative risk-aversion measure $R_R(\Pi) = -\Pi V''(\Pi)/V'(\Pi)$. (In the CAPM framework, $R_R(\Pi)$ can be computed from asset prices.) One can then formulate as follows the problem of finding an *ex ante* efficient policy regarding wages, unemployment benefits and transfers $(w_s, t_s, a_s)_{s=1\ldots S}$:

PROBLEM P.3

$$\max_{(w_s, a_s, t_s)_{s=1\ldots S}} \sum_s \phi_s V(f_s(l_s(w_s))) - w_s l_s(w_s) - [na_s + (n - l_s(w_s))t_s]$$

$$- d |na_s + (n - l_s(w_s))t_s|$$

subject to $Eu \geq u(b)$.

3.2.

Problem P.3 is technically more complex than those of Section 2. It is closely related to problems analysed in Drèze (1986b, 1989a), Gollier (1988) and Drèze and Gollier (1989). A slight modification (simplification) reduces problem P.3 to a case treated in these references. The modification calls for imposing $a_s \leq 0$ (wages can be taxed, but not directly subsidised)

---

[15] Because all individual investors hold market portfolios, under the CAPM assumptions, the aggregation of all business firms into a single productive sector is warranted.

and $d = 0$ (there exist neutral taxes). Using the results of Section 2, one can see how that modification affects the solution. The condition $a_s \leq 0$ imposes wages and benefits as the single instrument for boosting workers' incomes. (Yet, $a_s < 0$ allows transfers from wages towards profits.) The condition $d = 0$ implies that unemployment is always voluntary, at a solution (at a second-best optimum). These remarks will help us reconsider the solution of P.3, after looking at the solution of the simplified version.

The simplified problem is as follows:

PROBLEM P.4

$$\max_{(w_s,a_s,t_s)_{s=1\ldots S}} \sum_s \phi_s V(f_s(l_s(w_s)) - w_s l_s(w_s) - [na_s + (n - l_s(w_s))t_s])$$

subject to

$$\sum_s \phi_s \left\{ \frac{l_s(w_s)}{n} u(w_s - m + a_s) + \frac{n - l_s(w_s)}{n} u(t_s + a_s) \right\} \geq u(b),$$

$$a_s \leq 0, \quad 0 \leq t_s \leq w_s - m, \quad l_s(w_s) \leq n,$$

$l_s(w_s)$ such that $f_s'(l_s) = w_s$.

Using Lagrange multipliers, problem P.4 may also be written as

$$\max_{(w_s,a_s,t_s)_{s=1\ldots S}} \sum_s \phi_s V(f_s(l_s(w_s)) - w_s l_s(w_s) - [na_s + (n - l_s(w_s))t_s])$$

$$+ \lambda \left\{ \sum_s \phi_s \left[\frac{l_s(w_s)}{n} u(w_s - m + a_s) \right. \right.$$

$$\left. \left. + \frac{n - l_s(w_s)}{n} u(t_s + a_s) \right] - u(b) \right\}, \tag{22}$$

subject to

$$a_s \leq 0, \quad 0 \leq t_s \leq w_s - m, \quad l_s(w_s) \leq n, \quad f_s'(l_s) = w_s.$$

In that formulation, $\lambda \geq 0$ is an undetermined multiplier, such that $\lambda[Eu - u(b)] = 0$ and $\lambda > 0$ when the condition $Eu \geq u(b)$ is binding. I shall restrict my attention to the case where $\lambda > 0$, which holds whenever $b > 0$.

In order to characterise the solutions to problem P.4, I write w_s^* for the competitive wages, defined as explained in Section 2.1 by

$$w_s^* = \max(f_s'(n), m). \tag{23}$$

PROPOSITION 1 (Drèze–Gollier)

For all $b > 0$, a solution to problem P.4 is characterised by the existence of a multiplier $\lambda > 0$ and, for each $s = 1 \ldots S$, by $w_s \geq w_s^*$, $t_s = w_s - m$, and one of the following conditions:[16]

(i) $l_s(w_s) = n$, $w_s = w_s^*$, $a_s < 0$ and $\lambda u'(w_s - m + a_s) = V'(\Pi_s)$

(full employment with taxes on wages);

(ii) $l_s(w_s) = n$, $w_s = w_s^*$, $a_s = 0$ and

$$\left(1 - \frac{w_s - m}{n} \frac{dl_s}{dw_s}\right) V'(\Pi_s) > \lambda u'(w_s - m) > V'(\Pi_s)$$

(full employment, no taxes);

(iii) $l_s(w_s) < n$, $w_s > w_s^*$, $a_s = 0$ and

$$\lambda u'(t_s) = \lambda u'(w_s - m) = V'(\Pi_s) \cdot \left[1 - \frac{w_s - m}{n} \frac{dl_s}{dw_s}\right]$$

(voluntary unemployment with unemployment benefits financed by a tax on profits).

That proposition is straightforward, yet complex … Here is an attempt at intuitive unravelling.

A pure risk-sharing problem calls for allocating efficiently among several agents a state-dependent aggregate income – say Y_s, $s = 1 \ldots S$. Let there be n identical agents, with utility functions u, each receiving the same amounts y_s; and one agent with utility function V, receiving $Y_s - ny_s$. It is well known, from the work of Borch (1960), Arrow (1965) or Wilson (1968), that efficient risk-sharing is characterised by existence of a parameter $\lambda > 0$ such that the following conditions hold:

$$\lambda u'(y_s) = V'(Y_s - ny_s), \qquad \frac{u'(y_s)}{u'(y_t)} = \frac{V'(Y_s - ny_s)}{V'(Y_t - ny_t)}, \qquad s, t = 1 \ldots S. \qquad (24)$$

These conditions impose that all agents have identical marginal rates of substitution (between income in state s and income in state t). Accordingly, if aggregate income $Y_s = f_s(l_s)$ were given independently of the policy

---

[16] These three conditions are mutually exclusive and collectively exhaustive.

(w_s, a_s, t_s), then *ex ante* efficiency would be attained in problem P.4 when

$$\lambda u'(w_s - m + a_s) = \lambda u'(t_s + a_s) = V'(\Pi_s), s = 1\ldots S, \qquad (25)$$

with parameter λ chosen so that $Eu = u(b)$. If the transfer variables a_s were free (unconstrained and non-distorting), one could set them at levels (positive or negative) such that conditions (25) hold. Setting simultaneously $w_s = w_s^*$, aggregate real income would be maximal in each state.

In problem P.4, the transfers a_s are constrained ($a_s \leq 0$). Accordingly, conditions (25) can only be implemented in those states where competitive wages are high enough that implementation requires $a_s < 0$. These states correspond to case (i) of proposition 1; in these states, the solution is that of a pure risk-sharing problem.

On the other hand, in states where condition (25) would require positive transfers $a_s > 0$, it cannot be implemented in that way. Correcting the income distribution in favour of workers requires raising wages. But raising wages above their competitive level entails a distortion, the real cost of which per dollar of wages is equal to $(w - m) dl/dw < 0$ – i.e. the net marginal product times the fall in employment, as explained in Section 2.3. In our model, where benefits are adjusted to keep unemployment voluntary, a wage increase goes to n workers, so that the real cost of the distortion per dollar of foregone profits is equal to $(w - m)/n \cdot dl/dw$.

The first-order condition for efficient risk-sharing *when aggregate income is influenced by the allocation parameter* y[17] becomes

$$\lambda u'(y) = V'(Y - ny) \cdot \left(1 - \frac{1}{n}\frac{dY}{dy}\right); \qquad (26)$$

see e.g. Holmström (1979). Applied to problem P.4, that condition takes the form

$$\lambda u'(w_s - m + a_s) = \lambda u'(t_s + a_s) = V'(\Pi_s) \cdot \left(1 - \frac{w_s - m}{n}\frac{dl_s}{dw_s}\right), \qquad (27)$$

which is precisely the characterisation of case (iii) in proposition 1.

---

[17] The first-order condition for $\max_y V(Y(y) - ny) + \lambda n u(y)$ is indeed $V' \cdot \left(\frac{dY}{dy} - n\right)$ $+ \lambda n u' = 0; \lambda u' = V' \cdot \left(1 - \frac{1}{n}\frac{dY}{dy}\right).$

Thus, cases (i) and (iii) correspond to risk-sharing: pure in case (i), modified by a distortion cost in case (iii). As for (ii), it brings about a smooth transition between (i) and (iii). That case occurs when competitive wages fall below the level corresponding to the desired distribution of income – but not enough to warrant the distortion cost $(w - m) \, dl/dw$ associated with a wage increase. It is more efficient to accept the competitive income distribution *in those states* – while lowering wage taxes in other states, so as to keep a worker's expected utility at the required level $u(b)$. The undetermined multiplier λ, associated with the constraint $Eu \geq u(b)$, sees to that.

Combining the three cases, proposition 1 can be summarised as stating that wages w_s are equal to the minimum of two quantities: competitive wages and risk-sharing wages, where the latter are defined with due allowance for the distortion cost of underemployment. Risk-sharing between workers and shareholders calls for taxing wages when they are too high, for taxing profits to finance unemployment benefits when competitive wages are too low. 'Too high' and 'too low' should here be understood 'relatively to the requirements of efficient risk-sharing, given the average level of workers' income (b) suggested by incomes policy'. That is, once b is chosen, the risk aversion of the two groups (workers and shareholders) decides when wages should be taxed and when they should be kept above the competitive level.

3.3.

After presenting in Section 3.2 the basic features of an *ex ante* efficient wage policy, corresponding to a given distributive target, I can now bring out more directly the potential contribution of wage rigidities to economic efficiency.

In an economy where efficient risk-sharing between shareholders and workers is not implemented through state-dependent taxes and transfers, it is generally not efficient to let wages fluctuate to clear the labour market in each state; a more efficient policy generally calls for limited wage flexibility, ruling out excessive increases as well as excessive reductions, even though in unfavourable states that policy entails some unemployment, kept voluntary through adequate benefits; that conclusion rests on efficiency arguments, and is free of distributive arguments.

The conclusion follows directly from proposition 1. Indeed, with w_s^*

denoting competitive wages, one may define b^* implicitly by

$$u(b^*) = Eu(w_s^*, a_s = 0, t_s = 0)$$

$$= \sum_s \phi_s \left\{ \frac{l_s(w_s^*)}{n} u(w_s^* - m) + \frac{n - l_s(w_s^*)}{n} u(0) \right\}. \tag{28}$$

That is, b^* is the sure net income regarded by a worker equivalent (utilitywise) to the random prospect defined by competitive wages and no transfers. One may then solve problem P.4 for $b = b^*$, i.e. subject to $Eu \geq u(b^*)$. The solution is characterised by proposition 1. In general, the solution will not allow $w_s = w_s^*$ for all $s = 1 \ldots S$; in general, the solution will involve case (iii), where $w_s > w_s^*$ – and that solution Pareto-dominates competitive market clearing ($w_s^* = w_s$ for all s). That solution leads to a higher expected utility, or present market value, for profits, at unchanged expected utility for workers.)

It is easy to give a *sufficient* condition under which case (iii) appears non-trivially in the solution of problem P.4; namely that there should exist two states s and t such that

$$\frac{u'(w_t^* - m)}{u'(w_s^* - m)} > \frac{V'(\Pi_t)}{V'(\Pi_s)} \left(1 - \frac{w_t^* - m}{n} \frac{dl_t}{dw_t} \right). \tag{29}$$

(The proof is given in the Appendix.) Because the marginal rates of substitution $\dfrac{u'(w_t^* - m)}{u'(w_s^* - m)}$ and $\dfrac{V'(\Pi_t)}{V'(\Pi_s)}$ are not directly observable (in the absence of insurance markets specific to states s and t), it is helpful to use the linear approximation (15) and to rewrite (29) in the alternative form (derived in the Appendix)

$$\left[1 + \frac{w_s^* - w_t^*}{w_s^* - m} R_R(w_s^* - m) \right]$$

$$> \left[1 + \frac{\Pi_s - \Pi_t}{\Pi_s} R_R(\Pi_s) \right] \left(1 - \frac{w_t^* - m}{n} \frac{dl_t}{dw_t} \right). \tag{30}$$

That condition holds when state s entails high competitive wages, which are taxed at the solution to P.4 – case (i) – whereas state t entails low competitive wages, which are raised at the solution – case (iii).

In condition (30), the terms $(w_s^* - w_t^*)/(w_s^* - m)$ and $(\Pi_s - \Pi_t)/\Pi_s$ measure the relative spread of wages, and of profits, between states s and t. The parameters $R_R(w_s^* - m)$ and $R_R(\Pi_s)$ translate these relative spreads into risk premia (uncertainty costs) or 'income disparity penalties'. According to condition (30), *it is efficient to intervene on the labour market and to organise risk-sharing between wages and profits, whenever the disparity penalty for wages exceeds the disparity penalty for profits by a factor high enough to cover the distortion costs caused by a wage increase* (in state *t*). That condition is the more likely to hold, the more (1) wages disparities (between states) are high, relative to profits disparities; (2) the risk aversion of workers is high, relative to that of shareholders; (3) the wage elasticity of employment is low (in absolute value). When condition (30) holds, competitive wage flexibility is Pareto-dominated by limited flexibility (with upward as well as downward rigidity).

3.4.

In concluding this section, I wish to return briefly to problem P.3, which differs from P.4 in that it allows for wage subsidies ($a_s > 0$) and takes into account the distortion cost of taxes ($d > 0$). (This section is more technical and may be skipped at no breach of continuity.)

With a_s unrestricted as to sign, but $d = 0$, the solution to the (modified) problem P.4 would generalise case (i) of proposition 1 and satisfy

(i′) $w_s = w_s^*, \lambda u'(w_s - m + a_s) = V'(\Pi_s)$

(competitive wages, efficient risk-sharing through either wages taxes or transfers to workers). Cases (ii) and (iii) would drop out, and so would Section 3.3. Condition (i′) includes (25) and solves a pure risk-sharing problem.

As soon as one brings in a distortion cost of taxation, that appealing simplicity evaporates. Instead of seeing the three cases of proposition 1 boil down to the single case (i′), we must now distinguish *five* cases, and their respective properties become more intricate as well! The five cases emerge from combining the three-way partition ($a_s < 0$, $a_s = 0$, $a_s > 0$) with the two-way partition ($w_s = w_s^*, w_s > w_s^*$). One of the six possibilities, namely ($a_s < 0, w_s > w_s^*$) drops out, because it would be inefficient.[18] The whole difficulty arises from the distortion cost d.

---

[18] The three cases of proposition 1 similarly emerged from combining the two-way partition ($a_s < 0, a_s = 0$) with ($w_s = w_s^*, w_s > w_s^*$), and ignoring the inefficient pair ($a_s < 0, w_s > w_s^*$).

PROPOSITION 2

For all $b > 0$, a solution to problem P.3 is characterised by the existence of a multiplier $\lambda > 0$ and, for each $s = 1\ldots S$, by one of the following conditions:

(i) $l_s(w_s) = n$, $w_s = w_s^*$, $a_s < 0$ and $\lambda u'(w_s - m + a_s) = V'(\Pi_s)(1 - d)$
(full employment with taxes on wages);

(ii) $l_s(w_s) = n$, $w_s = w_s^*$, $a_s = 0$ and

$$\min\left\{1 + d, 1 - (1 + d)\frac{w_s^* - m}{w_s^*}\eta_{l_sw_s}\right\}V'(\Pi_s)$$

$$\geq \lambda u'(w_s - m) \geq V'(\Pi_s)(1 - d)$$
(full employment, no taxes);

(iii) $l_s(w_s) = n$, $w_s = w_s^*$, $a_s > 0$ and

$$\left[1 - (1 + d)\frac{w_s - m}{w_s}\eta_{l_sw_s}\right]V'(\Pi_s) > \lambda u'(w_s - m + a_s)$$

$$= V'(\Pi_s)(1 + d)$$

(full employment and transfers to all workers financed by a tax on profits);

(iv) $l_s(w_s) < n$, $w_s > w_s^*$, $a_s = 0$,

$$\frac{w_s - m - t_s}{t_s} = \frac{\dfrac{d}{1 + d} - \dfrac{w_s - m}{l_s}\left|\dfrac{dl_s}{dw_s}\right|}{R_R(t_s)} = \frac{\dfrac{d}{1 + d} + \dfrac{w_s - m}{w_s}\eta_{l_sw_s}}{R_R(t_s)} \text{ and}$$

$$V'(\Pi_s)(1 + d) > \lambda u'(w_s - m) = V'(\Pi_s)\left[1 - (1 + d)\frac{w_s - m}{w_s}\eta_{l_sw_s}\right]$$

(involuntary unemployment with benefits financed by a tax on profits);

(v) $l_s(w_s) < n$, $w_s > w_s^*$, $a_s > 0$, $w_s - m = t_s$ and

$$\lambda u'(w_s - m + a_s) = \lambda u'(t_s + a_s)$$

$$= V'(\Pi_s)(1 + d)$$

$$= V'(\Pi_s)\left[1 - (1 + d)\frac{w_s - m}{w_s}\eta_{l_sw_s}\right]$$

(voluntary unemployment with unemployment benefits and transfers to all workers financed by a tax on profits).

That proposition is rather complex, so I will save the proof and full discussion for a separate occasion, and provide only a general guideline. Case (i) of proposition 2 differs from case (i) of proposition 1 by the cost of taxation; therefore, taxes on wages are lower, in order to save on that cost; the ratio of the marginal utility of wages to that of profits is reduced by a factor $1 - d$. Case (ii) admits the same interpretation here as under proposition 1, but holds under wider conditions (the case for no taxation is strengthened by the distortion cost). The distinction between case (iii) and case (iv) corresponds to the selection of the less costly (distortionwise) instrument to boost workers' incomes – either transfers, in case (iii), or wages and unemployment benefits, in case (iv). Eventually, both instruments are used simultaneously, in case (v), at rates that equate their respective efficiencies at the margin, as per equation (6) above.

The arguments adduced in Section 3.3 to the effect that limited wage flexibility (with upward as well as downward rigidities) typically Pareto-dominates competitive flexibility remain valid in this broader framework; that conclusion also remains free of distributive arguments.

4. Conclusion

4.1.

The model of Sections 2 and 3 is in many respects too crude; yet, its analysis has carried us through increasingly sophisticated arguments, culminating with proposition 2. It is not easy to relate the formal analysis to our daily experience: real world problems are more complex, yet receive less sophisticated solutions ...

Among the more important aspects of reality which are ignored here, I would stress worker heterogeneity. One major source of heterogeneity concerns workers under contract versus job seekers. In the prospective analysis, that distinction is crucial. Indeed, long-term labour contracts permit relaxing the condition equating labour's marginal value product to wage cost: that condition only needs to hold *in expectation*, i.e. *ex ante* – instead of *ex post*, i.e. state by state. The theory of (implicit) labour contracts[19] has spelled out the main characteristics of efficient contracts. Gollier (1988) has analysed a model with overlapping generations of workers. He obtains simultaneous first-order efficiency conditions for the wages and transfers applicable to future generations, and for the wages

---

[19] Cf. Rosen (1985) for a survey.

stipulated in today's contracts. One important conclusion of his analysis concerns wage discrimination between generations. Efficiency arguments go against the equity principle 'equal pay for equal work' – but to an extent limited by conditions analogous to (16) above, defining second-best efficient income disparities (here, between employed and unemployed workers).

Another important source of heterogeneity relates to the individual circumstances of workers and firms. I have focussed here exclusively on macroeconomic aspects of the labour market, on the general level of wages and on national income. There also exist individual risks, which are by and large uncorrelated with aggregate risks. The implications of that distinction have been investigated more carefully for capital markets than for wages and social security. Important issues remain open in this area and should challenge imaginative young researchers.

4.2.

The subject matter of this paper is the equity–efficiency trade-off for wages and employment. I hope to have illustrated the relevance as well as the difficulty of the subject. When taxes and transfers do not bring about the desired income distribution, wages provide another instrument worthy of attention. But non-competitive wages always entail a deadweight efficiency loss, that should be weighed against the equity gain on the one hand, against the real costs of alternative policies on the other hand. The complexity of the trade-off also means that formal analysis can suggest ways to improve upon established practice.

In practice, taxes and transfers do not bring about an equitable distribution of income – between capital and labour, between employed and unemployed workers, or between workers of different skills. These shortcomings reflect both a lack of consensus about goals and the distortion costs of taxation. It should not surprise us that labour unions try to influence wage formation, in order to boost the incomes of members.

That activity is justified, but its efficiency cost cannot be ignored. One conclusion is that union militancy is the less necessary, the more effective are general incomes policies. This conclusion is sometimes applied to corporatist countries, like Austria or Sweden, about which it is claimed that wages and fiscal policy are negotiated jointly.[20] The present paper

[20] See e.g. Rowthorn and Glyn (1987).

stresses the complementarity of wages and transfers to implement an income policy responsive to both equity and efficiency considerations.

We are used to hybrid systems, where wages are kept up by unemployment benefits, and these are viewed as instruments of income policy, alongside other social security transfers. The system has grown through time in a haphazard way, and its overall consistency is open to question. One weakness of the system concerns sensitivity to economic fluctuations, in particular to external shocks. Section 3 is addressed to that topic, at a high level of abstraction. The message is that full flexibility of wages is inefficient, but also that full rigidity of real wages (100% indexation of nominal wages on consumer prices) is inefficient. I have presented elsewhere[21] the risk-sharing arguments suggesting to index wages partly on consumer prices and partly on nominal national income. Our understanding of these issues is still fragmentary. Policy recommendations should be voiced with restraint, but research conclusions should be analysed carefully.[22]

Appendix: Derivations of relationships (29) and (30)

Case (iii) of proposition 1 arises whenever problem P.4 does not admit any solution with $w_s = w_s^*$ for all s; that is whenever it is more efficient to set $w_t = w_t^* + \delta > w_t^*$ for at least one state t – while compensating the drain on profits Π_t by a wage tax $a_s < 0$ and a transfer towards profits $-na_s > 0$ in some state $s \neq t$. The compensation is possible, at unchanged expected utility (or market value) of profits, provided

$$dEV(\Pi) = \phi_s V'(\Pi_s)\,d\Pi_s + \phi_t V'(\Pi_t)\,d\Pi_t = 0, \tag{31}$$

with

$$d\Pi_s = -na_s \text{ and } d\Pi_t = \left[-n + (w_t^* - m)\frac{dl_t}{dw_t} \right]\delta$$

---

[21] See Drèze (1989a), chapters 3 and 5; chapter 5 is reproduced here as chapter 13; see also chapter 11 above.

[22] One policy recommendation that strikes me as well-documented concerns the funding of social security. At times of persistent unemployment, it is desirable to reduce wage costs. This calls for lowering labour taxes and seeking other means of funding social security. That recommendation is consistent with the logic of state dependent transfers as investigated in Section 3.

as can be seen from equation (3) when $l_t = n$, $d = 0$ and $t_t = w_t^* - m$. Substituting in (31) and solving for a_s yields

$$-a_s = \delta\left(1 - \frac{w_t^* - m}{n}\frac{dl_t}{dw_t}\right)\frac{\phi_t V'(\Pi_t)}{\phi_s V'(\Pi_s)}. \tag{32}$$

In order for that modification to increase the expected utility of a worker, it is necessary and sufficient that

$$
\begin{aligned}
dEu &= \phi_s u'(w_s^* - m)a_s + \phi_t u'(w_t^* - m)\,\delta \\
&= -\phi_s u'(w_s^* - m)\,\delta\left(1 - \frac{w_t^* - m}{n}\frac{dl_t}{dw_t}\right)\frac{\phi_t V'(\Pi_t)}{\phi_s V'(\Pi_s)} \\
&\quad + \phi_t u'(w_t^* - m)\delta \\
&= \delta\phi_t u'(w_s^* - m)\left\{\frac{u'(w_t^* - m)}{u'(w_s^* - m)}\right. \\
&\quad \left. - \frac{V'(\Pi_t)}{V'(\Pi_s)}\left(1 - \frac{w_t^* - m}{n}\frac{dl_t}{dw_t}\right)\right\} > 0. \tag{33}
\end{aligned}
$$

Because $\delta\phi_t u'(w_s^* - m) > 0$, condition (33) is indeed equivalent to (29).

Using the linear approximation (15), we may write

$$u'(w_t^* - m) \approx u'(w_s^* - m) + (w_t^* - w_s^*)u''(w_s^* - m), \tag{34}$$

$$\frac{u'(w_t^* - m)}{u'(w_s^* - m)} \approx \left[1 + \frac{w_s^* - w_t^*}{w_s^* - m} R_R(w_s^* - m)\right]. \tag{35}$$

Inserting (35) into (29), yields (30).

13 Labour management, contracts and capital markets: some macroeconomic aspects, and conclusions*

1. Provisional conclusions

So far, I have considered the relationship between labour and capital at the *firm* level, while taking into account some implications of market clearing. Two main conclusions stand out. In a world of complete markets with labour mobility, no specific gains should be expected, in equilibrium, from action by labour at the firm level: labour-management equilibria correspond to competitive (wage) equilibria. In a more realistic world of uncertainty with incomplete markets, efficient risk-sharing between capital owners (holding diversified portfolios) and workers (unable to protect their human capital through diversification) is not organised by the market and requires instead sophisticated *contractual* arrangements.

In the capitalist system, labour contracts (explicit or implicit) are the institutional support of such arrangements. Under labour management, equity contracts would be needed to the same end, but do not seem to be in systematic use, either in Yugoslavia or in capitalist countries.

Uncertainty is the standard instance of incomplete markets, but it is by no means the only one. In so far as labour services are concerned, working schedules and working conditions are other significant instances.[1] As indicated already in chapter 1, these are in the nature of public goods – on a par with the investment decisions considered in chapters 2–4. These

---

* Chap. 5 and Appendix 5 in *Labour Management, Contracts and Capital Markets*, Basil Blackwell, Oxford, 1989. All references to earlier chapters, sections or equations are references to that book.
[1] The formal analogy between uncertainty and quality choices as instances of incomplete markets is brought out in Drèze and Hagen (1978).

decisions do not seem to be fully guided by market-clearing prices, and require some form of collective decision-making at the firm level.

In so far as working conditions are concerned, labour management seems to be a natural answer. Experience suggests that partnerships are most common in situations where working conditions are an important parameter, and capital requirements are low. In so far as uncertainty is concerned, capital markets are the natural answer, because they allow for efficient risk-sharing through portfolio diversification. The standard argument, to the effect that workers are unable to bear themselves the risks of capital-intensive ventures, is a valid one. But it does not preclude equity financing of labour-managed firms. To explain why that form of organisation is seldom practised, I think that one must invoke the relative difficulty of stipulating and monitoring efficient equity contracts, for labour-managed firms, in a world of uncertainty and incomplete markets. In comparison, efficient labour contracts are easier to draw. Also, the more developed are capital markets, the easier it becomes to write down efficient labour contracts.[2] In the interesting case where all firm-specific risks are diversified away through capital markets, efficient labour contracts would simply link labour incomes to national income, to a first approximation. Drawing instead an efficient equity contract would be a very difficult task, and monitoring the contract would either be very cumbersome or be equivalent to restoring indirectly a 'capital hires labour' situation.

Efficient labour contracts transfer to workers the benefits of efficient risk-sharing on capital markets. It was noted in chapter 3 that prevailing labour contracts seem to be less than fully efficient in that respect. That remark suggests scope for improvement, about which more later; it also casts additional doubts on the practical feasibility of implementing efficient equity contracts.

These considerations go a long way towards explaining why labour management remains exceptional in industrial societies, in spite of its moral appeal and of the fact (theoretically documented in chapter 1) that it could easily coexist with salaried employment. But the analysis at the firm level must still be extended on two counts, of a more macroeconomic nature.

---

[2] That point is distinct from the point illustrated in Section 4.2, to the effect that more developed capital markets may lead to better terms for labour contracts.

2. A static macroeconomic aspect

2.1. Labour's comparative advantage

It was noted in chapter 3 that efficient capital markets would, as a first approximation (at the level of approximation embodied in the capital asset pricing model), result in individual portfolios combining a safe asset with identical tiny shares of all firms. As a consequence, all firms would have the same shareholders, or at any rate shareholders with similar preferences. If risk preferences of workers in different firms were also similar, it would then follow that, to a first approximation, efficient labour contracts imply labour incomes that are perfectly correlated across firms. In other words, a single labour contract drawn for the whole economy would come close to achieving overall efficiency; negotiations over the terms of labour contracts could become centralised at the economy-wide level, at a substantial saving of time and effort in conducting the negotiations. The counterpart for that property, in so far as the equity contracts of labour-managed firms are concerned, is that efficient contracts could be based on a stipulation of labour incomes geared to a national formula, with the rest of value added going to capital. These equity contracts would thus be indistinguishable from labour contracts.

Of course, the statements just made only hold as a first approximation. Actual capital markets do not exactly operate as predicted by the CAPM. Not all firms are financed through shares traded on the stock exchange. Individual firms, including those quoted on the stock exchange, are controlled by managers and directors, whose decisions need not fully reflect shareholder preferences. Fear of bankruptcy, which typically generates significant transaction costs, leads to aversion *vis-à-vis* individual (diversifiable) risks and to greater risk aversion at the firm level than at the market level. As noted earlier, the employees of individual firms may be particularly concerned with specific risks (because their human capital is specialised). Employees of different firms may also display different degrees of risk aversion, due for instance to self-selection or to demographic characteristics.[3] But all this being said, it remains true that negotiating the terms of labour contracts at the economy-wide level is apt to capture most of the benefits associated with efficient risk-sharing, and to avoid most of the transaction costs associated with decentralised negotiations at the firm level.

---

[3] It is explained in Drèze and Modigliani (1972) that risk aversion is apt to increase with age.

The significance of that remark is enhanced by the fact that, to a large extent, labour organisations derive their strength from their ability to operate across firms, at the level of a craft, of an industrial sector or even of the whole economy. At these levels, labour unions are in a much better position to exert an influence on the terms of the labour contracts of capitalist firms than on the terms of the equity contracts of labour-managed firms. Evidently, it is within closer reach of union power to push wages up than to pull the cost of capital down! The intersectoral and international mobility of financial capital is a source of immunity from organised influences, especially by labour. The threat of strike by the employees of a capitalist firm is apt to be more effective than the threat by members of a labour-managed firm to dispense with an equity issue! Monitoring labour markets is a much more natural target for a union than monitoring capital markets. And yet, the latter target would have to receive priority in the labour-managed economy. It is thus understandable that unions devote little energy to the promotion of labour management.

2.2. Second-best heuristics

It was noted in Section 3.4 that efficient labour contracts should result in a degree of stability of workers' incomes comparable with the stability of returns to a diversified portfolio. And yet, for blue-collar workers subject to temporary or part-time layoffs, the contracts tend to stipulate instead some degree of stability for hourly wages (either nominal or real). It has been part of the strategies of organised labour to strive for income protection at a national level, through unemployment benefits, rather than at the firm level. I can see three reasons for this.

The first reason, just mentioned, is that labour organisations can often operate more effectively at that level, with greater strength and smaller transaction costs. The second reason is that not all firms are financed through equity floated on the stock market. For the smaller, more closely held firms, a national scheme of unemployment compensation is a form of risk-sharing between all members of the firm (owners and employees) and the rest of the economy. The third reason is that firms face risks of bankruptcy, so that protection of the workers is more effective when based on national schemes than when based at the firm level.

The combination of efficient economy-wide labour contracts and unemployment insurance strikes me, in the end, as a reasonable first step towards efficient risk-sharing, in the presence of uncertainty, incomplete markets and transaction costs. The last element, which is central to the explanation of market incompleteness, cannot be ignored when considering labour contracts. It would be fallacious to assume without justification that a difficulty standing in the way of market organisation disappears altogether at the firm level.

Two complementary features were mentioned, which seem worth adding to that combination. In the smaller firms, not quoted on the stock exchange or otherwise included in the risk pool of capital markets, some participation of labour in the firm-specific risks makes sense; it should be accompanied with participation in managerial decisions. Limiting forms of participation include the bond-financed labour-managed firm, the partnership or the family enterprise. They flourish in the less capital-intensive sectors of our economies. In the larger firms, financed through the stock exchange and using contract labour, one would hope that the internal organisation makes room for labour-managed or participatory decisions about working conditions.

2.3.   *A digression on working time*

It is interesting to speculate, as a brief digression, about the extent to which the argument of collective pressure applies to working conditions as well as to income formation. The issue of working time is an intriguing case in point. Is the secular reduction in working time[4] a by-product of labour-market equilibrium, reflecting the equality of the reservation wage for hours and the marginal value product of labour according to equations (1.36) or (3.18); or is it an (explicit or implicit) component of union strategies to boost hourly wages? If the latter motivation were absent, and unions were eager to promote the welfare of their members (an acceptable hypothesis, in the small world where I live), then we should witness more union support for flexibility of individual working times.

3.   A dynamic macroeconomic aspect

3.1.   *New entrants to the labour market*

One important dimension of efficient risk-sharing between capital and labour is missing from my presentation so far. It concerns new entrants into the labour market. Bringing in that dimension explains why concern

---

[4] The combination of shorter weekly hours, longer vacations and shorter careers has nearly halved lifetime working time over the past century; see for example Armstrong (1984) or Maddison (1982).

by labour organisations about the outcome of collective wage negotiations and the organisation of economy-wide unemployment insurance is well placed. It provides a suggestive explanation of downward wage rigidity and unemployment, flowing from microeconomic considerations.

In the general equilibrium analysis of chapters 3 and 4, I focussed on efficient risk-sharing through two-period labour contracts, assuming that the markets for such labour contracts cleared in the initial period. Spot markets for labour in the second period were not needed. In reality, however, a new generation of school leavers enters the market for labour contracts each year, whereas older workers go into retirement. In the streamlined models with only two explicit periods, the present and the future, there is a specific need to consider spot markets in the second period, if one wishes to include in the analysis these future entrants into the labour market. These spot markets stand in fact for markets for new labour contracts in the future.

That extension introduces an important feature, which does not seem to have received in the theoretical literature the attention which it deserves. Future entrants into the labour market are not present when multiperiod contracts are drawn, and the markets for such contracts clear, in an initial period. In other words, whereas long-term labour contracts are commonplace, we do not observe *forward labour contracts*, binding today a firm and a prospective worker on the terms of an employment relationship taking effect in the future. Consequently, future entrants into the labour market are left to bear fully the risks associated with labour-market conditions at their time of entry. They do not participate in the risk-sharing between capital and labour embodied in the extant long-term contracts.

To be more specific, think about an economy operating under conditions of technological uncertainty. Labour productivity tomorrow will depend upon the state of the environment, so that market-clearing wage levels will also depend upon that state. Labour contracts drawn today, and capital markets, organise risk-sharing among property owners and workers. If the technological developments are particularly adverse to labour (if they result in a very low marginal value product of labour at full employment), contract wages will be kept above the marginal product, in exchange for slightly lower wages today or in other states. But the future entrants, who are not covered by the terms of a forward contract, are not insured against that contingency. When contracting tomorrow, they will have to accept wages reflecting the marginal product of their labour in the state that obtains. Because market-clearing wages are apt to vary widely, and most prospective workers have no assets, that degree of income uncertainty is costly to bear, and should be alleviated through some mutually advantageous insurance supplied by property owners and workers under contract.

The absence of forward labour contracts means that such insurance is not organised at the microeconomic level of individual firms and individual workers. The difficulty of matching on a forward basis the future supply and demand of labour services at the firm level, and the even greater difficulty of organising such matching on a contingent basis,[5] explain fully why each generation of new entrants has to look for jobs when the time comes. And there is no natural motivation for individual firms (whether capitalist or labour managed) to offer insurance against wage fluctuations to the anonymous set of prospective job seekers. By its very nature, that problem must be faced at the macroeconomic level. This is another interesting instance where microeconomic reasoning leads spontaneously to macroeconomic considerations – a situation for which I have an intimate liking.[6]

At the macroeconomic level, income insurance for new job seekers could be organised in either of two ways: namely general income maintenance programmes, or downward wage rigidity coupled with unemployment insurance. Both systems entail some costs. A general income maintenance programme, financed by taxes levied on property owners and employed workers, is costly on account of the distortive incidence of the taxes. Being a general programme, it has more beneficiaries than unemployment insurance; hence it typically calls for more tax revenue, creating more inefficiency on that score. On the other hand, downward wage rigidity results in wasteful underutilisation of labour. The two sources of inefficiency must be compared, to decide which programme (or combination of programmes) is least inefficient. Also, the amounts of insurance supplied to the newcomers will have to take these costs into account.

From the viewpoint of labour, a general income maintenance programme is less attractive, because its benefits are widely distributed. Also, it is not within the power of labour to organize such a programme. But labour organisations have indeed turned their efforts towards implement-

---

[5] With how many firms would students need to contract on a contingent basis to be sure of having a job at the end of their studies? With how many students would a firm need to contract in order to cover contingent needs a few years hence?

[6] See for example Drèze (1987b, p. 20) or Drèze (1984b, pp. 282–3).

ing downward wage rigidity coupled with unemployment insurance.[7] By its very nature, downward wage rigidity is a macroeconomic phenomenon; as a form of income insurance for newcomers, it is meaningless at the firm level.

3.2. Ex-ante *efficient downward wage rigidity*

What can be said about *efficient* provision of income insurance on behalf of newcomers through downward wage rigidity and unemployment benefits? A simple model, based on Drèze (1986b), Gollier (1988) and joint work in progress by the two of us, is presented in appendix to help investigate that novel question.

That model is meant to exhibit the simplest possible structure within which the issue can be discussed. It is accordingly an aggregate model, with a single good and a single aggregate production function whose shifts introduce 'technological uncertainty'. For simplicity, employment is the only argument of the production function. Investment and demand aspects are provisionally ignored, to concentrate on the insurance problem.

There are two generations of workers: an older generation, whose members are covered by labour contracts, the terms of which are state dependent, but set before observing the state; and a younger generation, whose members are hired after observing the state. For simplicity, I assume that all the older workers are employed under all states, and earn the state-dependent wages w_{0s}. The wages $w_s \leq w_{0s}$ of the younger workers are also state dependent and set *ex ante*, but their employment level is determined *ex post* by equality between the wage and the marginal value product of labour (equal to the marginal physical product, upon normalising to unity the price of the good in every state). Unemployed younger workers receive unemployment benefits $t_s \leq w_s$. (The conditions $t_s \leq w_s \leq w_{0s}$ are introduced for incentive compatibility.)

The wages w_{0s} and w_s are net of taxes and all workers have identical preferences, represented by the twice continuously differentiable utility function $u(w)$. These workers supply inelastically one unit of labour. There are L_0 older workers and L younger workers. The unemployment benefits are subtracted from the gross profits to define the property income

$$\pi_s = f_s(L_0 + L_s) - w_{0s}L_0 - w_sL_s - t_s(L - L_s) \tag{1}$$

---

[7] Historically, unemployment insurance did not cover new entrants into the labour force until quite recently, and still does not cover them at all in many countries; see Emerson (1988).

where $L_s \leqslant L$, the employment of younger workers, is such that

$$f'_s(L_0 + L_s) = w_s. \tag{2}$$

The preferences of property owners are represented by the utility function $V(\pi)$, best understood as reflecting portfolio choices, consistent for instance with the Capital Asset Pricing Model.

Using an undetermined parameter λ to represent the distributive choices between workers and property owners, the problem of defining *ex ante* Pareto-efficient wages and unemployment benefits becomes

$$\max_{w_{0s}, w_s, t_s} \lambda E_s V[f_s(L_0 + L_s) - w_{0s}L_0 - w_s L_s - t_s(L - L_s)]$$

$$+ E_s[L_0 u(w_{0s}) + L_s u(w_s) + (L - L_s)u(t_s)]$$

subject to $f'_s(L_0 + L_s) = w_s, L_s \leqslant L, w_{0s} \geqslant w_s \geqslant t_s. \tag{3}$

The solution to this problem is best understood by looking successively at its implications for the older and for the younger generation.

For older workers under contract, efficient risk-sharing with property owners requires

$$u'(w_{0s}) = \lambda V'(\pi_s). \tag{4}$$

That is also the condition obtained in equation (3.16) as a characterization of an efficient contract at the firm level. (The simplification here comes from identical workers and anonymous shareholders.) Condition (4) prevails here, as long as $f'_s(L_0 + L) \leqslant w_{0s}$; that is, as long as it implies wages w_{0s} at least as high as the market-clearing wages for the younger generation. Otherwise (in very good states), the pressure of labour demand leads to wages higher than required by risk-sharing considerations, and determined by the conditions

$$f'_s(L_0 + L) = w_{0s} \qquad u'(w_{0s}) < \lambda V'(\pi_s). \tag{5}$$

In short, the wages of older workers correspond to the maximum of a risk-sharing wage and a market-clearing wage.

Turning to the younger generation, the solution assigns to them market-clearing wages, as long as these do not fall too much below the contractual wages. There is a maximal degree of intergenerational wage discrimination, endogenously determined, at which downward wage rigidity and unemployment set in. That solution has several interesting features:

(i) Some degree of downward wage rigidity, leading to unemployment at positive wages (in bad states), is warranted on efficiency grounds.

(ii) The wages of newcomers are lower than those of workers under contract (wage discrimination by hiring date), unless there is full employment at wages higher than warranted by risk-sharing considerations for workers under contract; the degree of discrimination depends upon the wage elasticity of labour demand and upon the risk aversion of workers.

(iii) Unemployment benefits are equal to minimum wages, so that all unemployment is voluntary *ex post* from the individual viewpoint.

Some of these features reflect the specificity of the model. The more important point for my present purposes is the first, which validates the practice of downward wage rigidity as a 'second-best efficient' risk-sharing device. That conclusion seems quite robust, in models where future generations are not otherwise insured against fluctuations in market-clearing wages. It also validates the concern of labour unions about the strength of their bargaining position in collective wage settlements. The rest of the analysis does, however, confirm that prevailing wage determination schemes are not second-best efficient – a point to which I shall return later.

Looking at the first conclusion from another angle, one could say that economy-wide wage policies form an essential part of efficient risk-sharing between property owners and workers, when the interests of future generations of workers are taken into account. (When the third conclusion holds, wages and unemployment benefits are perfect substitutes as policy instruments.)

3.3. Wage discrimination by hiring date

It is interesting that I can write down explicitly, in this simple model, the conditions under which downward wage rigidity and unemployment set in. Assuming that contractual wages automatically satisfy condition (4), and market-clearing wages condition (2), one first observes from (ii) that wage discrimination by hiring date sets in as soon as market-clearing wages fall short of contractual wages. The reason for the discrimination is simply that wages of workers under contract can be kept above the market-clearing level without adverse implications for the employment of these workers (labour hoarding), whereas wages of new workers could not exceed the market-clearing level without generating unemployment. That unemployment would be wasteful, because the marginal product of labour is higher than the disutility of work (assumed non-existent in the appendix, but easily introduced into the model, as verified in Gollier, 1988). When market-clearing wages are close to the contractual wages reflecting efficient risk-sharing between workers and property owners, the inefficiency associated with unemployment would outweigh the gain in risk-sharing efficiency associated with higher wages for newcomers. These two considerations exactly outweigh each other, in the simple model under review, when

$$u'(w_s) = u'(w_{0s})(1 - \eta_{L_s w_s}) > u'(w_{0s}) \tag{6}$$

where $\eta_{L_s w_s}$ is the elasticity of new hirings with respect to the hiring wages.

The logic behind that condition can be explained as follows. Using (4), (2) and the definition of the elasticity, (6) is equivalent, at $L_s = L$, to

$$Lu'(w_s) = \lambda V'(\pi_s)\left[L - f'_s(L_0 + L)\frac{\mathrm{d}L_s}{\mathrm{d}w_s}\right]. \tag{7}$$

In (7), the left-hand side measures the utility gains to younger workers of receiving higher wages (higher by one unit). The right-hand side measures the utility loss to property owners of paying these higher wages to younger workers (alone). That utility loss comes from lower profits, due first to the extra unit of wages going to L workers, and next to the loss of output from lower employment; that loss of output is measured by the marginal product of labour times the change in labour demand. (Thus the elasticity comes into the formula to account for the waste associated with unemployment, not to account for any form of monopolistic behaviour.)

Condition (6) is stated in terms of the marginal utilities of workers under contract and of newcomers. Assuming identical preferences for both groups, and expanding marginal utilities in a Taylor series through quadratic terms, one can approximate (6) by the more operational condition

$$w_s = w_{0s}\left[1 + \frac{\eta_{L_s w_s}}{R_R(w_{0s})}\right], \qquad \frac{w_{0s} - w_s}{w_{0s}} = \frac{|\eta_{L_s w_s}|}{R_R(w_{0s})}, \tag{8}$$

where $R_R(w_{0s})$ is the Arrow–Pratt measure of relative risk aversion for the workers, evaluated at the contractual wage.

It conforms to intuition that the loss associated with inefficient risk-sharing is a function of the degree of risk aversion of the workers. In the operational formula (8), the maximal relative wage discrimination by hiring date is directly proportional to the wage elasticity of labour demand by firms and inversely proportional to the risk aversion of workers. When that maximal discrimination separates contractual wages from market clearing wages, downward wage rigidity sets in to prevent further discrimination. The formula which applies from there on is a slight generalisation of (6), namely

$$u'(w_s) = u'(w_{0s})\left(1 - \frac{L_s}{L}\eta_{L_s w_s}\right) = u'(w_{0s})\left(1 - w_s\frac{dL_s}{dw_s}\right). \tag{9}$$

It is interesting to speculate about the order of magnitude of the implied discrimination. To that effect, I note first that η_s, the wage elasticity of new hirings, is related to the wage elasticity of employment by the formula

$$\eta_s = \frac{w_s L_s'}{L_s} = \frac{w_s L_s'}{L_0 + L_s}\frac{L_0 + L_s}{L_s}.$$

That is, η_s is equal to the wage elasticity of employment times the ratio of total employment to new hirings. This is a fortunate feature, because it dispenses with the need to decide whether we should use a short- or a long-run elasticity number. As is well known, the orders or magnitude of the short-run and long-run elasticities of employment are quite different. According to Drèze and Modigliani (1981), for instance, the long-run elasticity could easily be 6 to 10 times as high as the short-run elasticity. But the ratio of total employment to new hirings is also very different in the two cases. According again to Belgian data, it is close to 6 on a yearly basis, whereas it should tend to 1 in the long run. Thus we may for practical purposes use the long-run wage elasticity of employment as an estimate of 'the' wage elasticity of new hirings. Unity is then a reasonable order of magnitude, even if the precision of our estimates leaves much to be desired. Hoping that L_s/L is reasonably close to unity as well, we would then conclude that the margin of wage discrimination is of the same order of magnitude as the reciprocal of the Arrow–Pratt relative risk-aversion measure for workers. Here again, we face an estimation problem. Casual appraisal of insurance deductibles suggests a margin of discrimination of the order of 20 per cent (a relative risk-aversion measure of the order of 5),[8] say plus or minus 5 per cent.

Could one translate conditions (4)–(8) into operational guidelines? Attempting to do so rigorously leads to complicated formulas of doubtful applicability. There is, however, one approximation conducive to major technical as well as logical simplification, which seems commensurate with the precision of available econometric estimates of the relevant parameters

---

[8] See Drèze (1981). It would of course be improper to use here a relative risk-aversion measure based on portfolio choices of asset owners.

(namely the wage elasticity of employment and the relative risk-aversion measure). The approximation consists in treating the factor of proportionality between $u'(w_s)$ and $u'(w_{0s})$ in (9) as a constant – say $1/\mu$.[9] The solution is then entirely characterised by

$$u'(w_{0s}) = \lambda V'(\pi_s) = \mu u'(w_s) \tag{10}$$

whenever there is less than full employment. Equation (10) is of the same form as (3.21); it is simply a characterisation of efficient risk-sharing between the three groups of agents: workers under contract, property owners and new entrants to the labour market. Implementing the solution is now a matter of achieving efficient risk-sharing through the labour contracts, linking the wage of new hires (and/or the unemployment benefits) to the contractual wages by means of formula (8), and hopefully letting demand pressure reduce the extent of discrimination at full employment. The resulting heuristic guidelines are basically the following.

Let the wages of workers under contract be determined by a simple economy-wide convention (like indexation in part on consumer prices and in part on nominal national income), giving content to the conditions (4) – or (3.16) – which characterise efficient risk-sharing between workers under contract and property owners. As long as market-clearing wages for all workers (those under contract and the new entrants) are equal to or higher than these contractual wages, the pressure of labour demand will result in full employment at these higher wages. When the market-clearing wages fall below the contractual level, wage discrimination between the workers under contract and the new workers sets in, with the new workers earning market-clearing wages, while the workers under contract continue to earn their (higher) contractual wages. That situation is allowed to prevail as long as the relative discrimination remains moderate – say not exceeding 20 per cent or so. When that level of discrimination is reached, downward wage rigidity for the new workers sets in, and there results some (inefficient) unemployment, with unemployment benefits high enough to make the unemployment voluntary. The wages of the new workers, and the unemployment benefits, are then tied to the contractual wages, to which they remain proportional (though at the lower level corresponding to the maximal tolerated discrimination).

These guidelines are presented here as 'heuristic', first because they are derived within a very incomplete model, and second because they

[9] Those rigorous formulas which I could obtain suggest that the approximation introduces a bias in the elasticity of wages to national income (thus not in the wage level itself) which is definitely upward, but moderate (say of the order of 5 per cent).

correspond to approximate and not to exact formulas. They should thus be regarded as *indicative* of the general nature of desirable policies, with no weight being attached to specific details.

Much simplicity of exposition is gained from assuming that prevailing long-term contracts are efficient, and from tailoring the wages of new workers to these contractual wages. The guidelines could thus be called 'operational'. This should not be allowed to conceal the need for characterising efficient contracts as part of the policy. The simple index-ation scheme proposed for illustration is indicative of desirable properties. Why it is not encountered in practice remains to be properly understood. That fact in itself is a ground for caution. Neither should one underestimate the practical difficulty of giving empirical content to the theoretical concept of market-clearing wages, a difficulty already mentioned in section 1.5. Several recent contributions to the theory of employment address that topic from different angles, like job search, efficiency wages, intertemporal labour-leisure substitution, insider-outsider differentials, and so on.[10] A common theme of these contributions is that the concept of market-clearing wages is by no means straightforward.

3.4. Complications

The analysis sketched here ignores several complications, among which the following three seem to be particularly significant.

First, the model of the appendix is a model of pure technological uncertainty, which ignores altogether demand and investment. Demand matters whenever observed unemployment has a Keynesian dimension, with output determined at least in part by aggregate demand, at a level where the marginal value product of labour exceeds the wages of marginal workers. It is then important to take into account the marginal propensities to spend wage income and property income respectively. And investment matters because the production possibilities (hence the marginal product of labour) are influenced by investments, as well as by the state of the environment. Once these considerations are introduced, the repercussions of the wage formation (and in particular of the downward wage rigidities) on employment become much more complex, and can only be spelled out in the framework of a complete macroeconomic model.[11] Such a task lies

---

[10] See Lindbeck and Snower (1985) for a recent survey.

[11] Of course, empirical estimates of the wage elasticity of employment hope to incorporate these repercussions. To that extent, they are implicitly incorporated here as well.

beyond the scope of this book. It is, of course, of paramount importance for policy choices.

Second, the present discussion is based entirely on a two-period model, that is on a simple dichotomy between the present and the future. In reality, history unfolds progressively: every day is part of the previous day's future, and is in turn endowed with its own future. The risk-sharing considerations introduced here must be embedded in a dynamic picture, with a view to characterise optimal paths.[12] The dynamics of intergenerational wage discrimination are an intriguing subject.

Third, the model of the appendix is an aggregate model, which ignores the diversity among firms, skills or sectors. In reality, one typically observes more diversity; some firms or sectors operate at full capacity and hire additional labour, while others experience excess capacities and hoard labour; and there are shortages of specialised skills in the midst of serious unemployment. That diversity is another source of complication, which restricts the immediate relevance of the aggregate guidelines drawn above.

3.5. Inegalitarian cooperatives

It is of some interest to relate, by way of a brief digression, conclusion (ii) (following (5)) regarding wage discrimination by hiring date, to a similar conclusion reached by Meade (1982) in his discussion of the promotion of employment in labour-managed cooperatives. Recognizing that labour-managed firms would not be inclined to take on new members, when the value added per member exceeds the reservation wage of outsiders, Meade advocates the principle of 'inegalitarian cooperatives', who take on new members at a lower share in value added than existing members, or possibly even at a market wage with employee status. This corresponds to the practice, witnessed in some Israeli kibbutzim and some Western cooperatives, of hiring salaried workers at wages inferior to the earnings of members. A macroeconomic justification for that practice is provided by the second conclusion just recalled. The fuller analysis here reveals under what conditions that practice is justified, and defines an upper bound on the degree of income discrimination warranted by efficiency considerations.

---

[12] See Gollier (1988, chapter 2) for a multiperiod extension of the model in the appendix.

4. Overall conclusion

Putting together the conclusions collected in earlier sections of this chapter, I feel confident in formulating an overall conclusion.

In economies operating with uncertainty and incomplete insurance markets, it is natural to find capital hiring labour, because efficient labour contracts in capitalist firms are easier to draw and monitor than efficient equity contracts for labour-managed firms. That form of organisation meets the preference of capitalists for vesting managerial authority with representatives of capital. It also meets the preference of labour organisations for acting on labour markets rather than on capital markets. It lends itself more naturally to economies of transaction costs through centralised negotiations over contracts (sectoral or economy-wide wage settlements). Finally, it lends itself naturally to the inclusion of future generations of workers in the risk-sharing arrangements between capital and labour, through downward wage rigidity and unemployment insurance.

It seems doubtful that labour contracts prevailing in capitalist economies correspond closely to efficient risk-sharing, because they fail to link labour incomes to aggregate wealth. (Constant real wages provide too much insurance, constant nominal wages potentially too little.) Improvements are possible, but may not be easy to implement. My main suggestion would be to index wages partly on consumer prices and partly on nominal national income. Smaller firms with closely held equity could be labour managed, if working conditions call for frequent and subtle adjustments, or could practise profit-sharing and participatory decision-making. The main challenge of the day, however, lies with improving the efficiency of collective wage bargaining.

Appendix

In order to investigate some of the issues raised in this chapter, I use a variant of the highly streamlined model introduced in the appendix of Drèze (1986b) and extended in Gollier (1988).

The physical model is one where aggregate production *tomorrow* is constrained by a state-dependent neoclassical production function relating output Y_s to labour input L_s in every state s:

$$Y_s = f_s(L_s) \quad f_s'(L_s) > 0 \quad f_s''(L_s) < 0 \quad s = 1, \ldots, S. \tag{A.1}$$

Thus the stock of capital available for use tomorrow is taken as given (predetermined), and is therefore not mentioned explicitly. The labour input is split between L_0 workers under contract (insiders), who are assumed to be employed in all states, and $L_s \leqslant L$ workers of a new generation, who are assumed to supply inelastically one unit of labour each. (L is the size of the new generation.) Thus the utility of leisure is ignored (for instance, on the grounds that it is offset by the positive value of having a job; more realistic specifications are possible, but introduce unnecessary complications). The wage paid to workers under contract is w_{0s}, that specified in a new contract is w_s, and the cardinal (von Neumann-Morgenstern) utility function for income of a worker (of either generation) is denoted $u(y)$; it is assumed to be strictly concave (risk aversion) and twice continuously differentiable:

$$u = u(y) \qquad u'(y) > 0 \qquad u''(y) < 0. \tag{A.2}$$

Output price is normalised to unity in every state. Hence profits associated with the employment of newcomers are simply (subsuming L_0 under f_s)

$$\hat{\pi}_s = f_s(L_s) - w_{0s}L_0 - w_sL_s \qquad s = 1,\ldots,S. \tag{A.3}$$

I assume that firms maximise these profits *ex post* in every state, by choosing L_s while taking wages as given. This calls for equating the wage rate to the marginal (value) product of labour:

$$f'_s(L_s) = w_s \qquad s = 1,\ldots,S. \tag{A.4}$$

I shall denote by $L_s(w_s)$ the labour demand function implicitly defined by (A.4). It satisfies

$$L'_s(w_s) = \frac{1}{f''_s(L_s)} < 0 \qquad \eta_{L_sw_s} := \eta_s = \frac{w_sL'_s}{L_s} = \frac{f'_s(L_s)}{L_sf''_s(L_s)} < 0 \tag{A.5}$$

where η_s denotes the wage elasticity of *new hirings* (*not* of total employment).

I assume that profit earners hold market portfolios, and that their preferences can be represented by an aggregate utility function V, with argument profits minus taxes. The latter are simply a lump-sum tax on profits, used to finance a scheme of unemployment benefits, in an amount t_s per unemployed person. The after-tax profits are thus $\hat{\pi}_s - t_s(L - L_s) = \mathrm{def}\,\pi_s$.

The characterization of *ex ante* Pareto-efficient transfer-and-wage policies is obtained from the first-order conditions for maximising a weighted sum of expected utilities, namely that of profit earners (a function of their net profits) with weight λ and that of workers with weight unity, where the expected utility of a worker is computed with probabilities of employment and unemployment equal to L_s/L and $(L - L_s)/L$ respectively. The weight λ reflects distributive ethics.

It is assumed that all agents agree about the probabilities of the states, $\phi_s > 0$, $s = 1, \ldots, S$. Expectations in terms of these probabilities are denoted E_s. Finally, it is assumed that $u'(y) \to +\infty$ as $y \to 0$, so that the conditions $(L - L_s)t_s \geq 0$ are never binding (for t_s); and that $f_s'(L_s)$ is high enough so that the conditions $L_s \geq 0$ are never binding.

These specifications lead to the following problem:

$$\max_{w_{0s}, w_s, t_s} \Lambda = \lambda E_s V[f_s(L_s) - w_{0s}L_0 - w_s L_s - t_s(L - L_s)]$$

$$+ E_s \left\{ L_0 u(w_{0s}) + L \left[\frac{L_s}{L} u(w_s) + \frac{L - L_s}{L} u(t_s) \right] \right\} \quad \text{(A.6)}$$

subject to (A.4) and to

$$\begin{aligned} w_{0s} &\geq w_s & (\rho_s) \\ w_s &\geq t_s & (\mu_s) \\ L &\geq L_s & (v_s) \end{aligned}$$

where ρ_s, μ_s and v_s are Lagrange multipliers.

The condition $w_s \geq t_s$ is introduced to guarantee that workers will accept employment at the wage w_s. (The implicit rate of income taxation should not exceed 100 per cent.) The condition $w_{0s} \geq w_s$ is a standard requirement (of incentive compatibility).

The first-order necessary conditions for this problem are:

$$\frac{\partial \Lambda}{\partial w_{0s}} = -\lambda \phi_s V'(\pi_s) L_0 + \phi_s u'(w_{0s}) L_0 + \rho_s = 0 \quad \text{(A.7)}$$

$$\frac{\partial \Lambda}{\partial w_s} = -\lambda \phi_s V'(\pi_s)[L_s - t_s L_s'(w_s)] + \phi_s[L_s u'(w_s)$$

$$+ L_s'(w_s)\{u(w_s) - u(t_s)\}] + \mu_s - v_s L'(w_s) - \rho_s = 0 \quad \text{(A.8)}$$

$$\frac{\partial \Lambda}{\partial t_s} = -\lambda \phi_s V'(\pi_s)(L - L_s) + \phi_s u'(t_s)(L - L_s) - \mu_s = 0. \quad \text{(A.9)}$$

In order to analyse these conditions, I first show that (i) $L = L_s$ implies $\mu_s = 0$, and (ii) $L > L_s$ implies $\mu_s > 0$. I will next show that (iii) $\mu_s > 0$ implies $w_{0s} > w_s$ and $\rho_s = 0$.

Property (i) follows immediately from (A.9).

To establish property (ii), I note that $L > L_s$ with $\mu_s = 0$ would imply through (A.9) that $u'(t_s) = \lambda V'(\pi_s)$. Also, $L > L_s$ implies $v_s = 0$. Using these two properties, (A.8) could be solved for

$$\frac{\rho_s}{\phi_s} = u'(t_s)t_sL_s'(w_s) + L_s[u'(w_s) - u'(t_s)]$$

$$+ L_s'(w_s)[u(w_s) - u(t_s)] < 0, \tag{A.10}$$

contradicting $\rho_s \geq 0$; where the negative sign in (A.10) follows from $L_s' < 0$ and $w_s \geq t_s$. Hence $L > L_s$ implies $\mu_s > 0$.

To establish property (iii), I note that $\mu_s > 0$ and $w_{0s} = w_s$ would imply $w_{0s} = w_s = t_s$ with $L > L_s$. It would then follow from (A.7) that $\lambda V'(\pi_s) - u'(t_s) = \rho_s/\phi_sL_0 \geq 0$, and from (A.9) that $\lambda V'(\pi_s) - u'(t_s) = -\mu_s/\phi_s(L - L_s) < 0$, a contradiction. Hence $\mu_s > 0$ implies $w_{0s} > w_s$ and $\rho_s = 0$.

Using these properties, and noting that t_s is irrelevant when $L = L_s$, we may confine the analysis to three cases:

(a) $L = L_s$ with $w_{0s} = w_s$
(b) $L = L_s$ with $w_{0s} > w_s$
(c) $L > L_s$ with $w_{0s} > w_s = t_s$.

The relevant characteristics for these three cases go as follows.

First, $L = L_s$ means that $w_s = f_s'(L) := w_s^*$, where w_s^* denotes the market-clearing wage; and $L > L_s$ means that $w_s > w_s^*$.

Second, when $w_{0s} > w_s$ so that $\rho_s = 0$, it follows from (A.7) that

$$u'(w_{0s}) = \lambda V'(\pi_s), \tag{A.11}$$

namely the condition for optimal sharing (of income and risks) between workers under contract and property owners. On the other hand, when $\rho_s > 0$, then $u'(w_{0s}) = \lambda V'(\pi_s) - (\rho_s/\phi_sL_0) < \lambda V'(\pi_s)$, and wages exceed the level desired on distributive grounds.

Third, when $L > L_s$ so that $\mu_s > 0$, $\rho_s = v_s = 0$, and $w_{0s} > w_s = t_s > w_s^*$, then (A.7)–(A.9) imply

$$u'(w_s) = u'(t_s) = \lambda V'(\pi_s)\left[1 - \frac{w_s}{L}L_s'(w_s)\right]$$

$$= \lambda V'(\pi_s)\left(1 - \frac{L_s}{L}\eta_s\right)$$

$$= u'(w_{0s})\left(1 - \frac{L_s}{L}\eta_s\right). \tag{A.12}$$

Condition (A.12) implies that unemployment sets in when $u'(w_s^*) = u'(w_{0s})(1 - \eta_s)$, that is when the market-clearing wage w_s^* carries a marginal utility exceeding that of the contractual wage w_{0s} by a percentage equal to $-100\,\eta_s$ (per cent).

One way to interpret (A.12) is as follows: raising $w_s(=t_s)$ yields additional utility to workers, evaluated as $Lu'(w_s)$; the cost to property owners is the higher level of payments to labour – either as wages or as unemployment benefits financed by the tax – plus the loss of output due to the reduced employment, a loss measured by $f'_s(L_s)\,L'_s(w_s) = w_s L'_s(w_s) = L_s\eta_s$. Hence the first-order condition:

$$Lu'(w_s) = \lambda V'(\pi_s)[L - w_s L'_s(w_s)]. \tag{A.12'}$$

To sum up, a solution to problem (A.6), defining *ex ante efficient* wage and unemployment benefits, can take either one of three forms, depending upon the position of the technological frontier $f_s(L_s)$ and hence upon the level of the full employment wages:

(a) $w_s = w_s^* = w_{0s}$ $u'(w_{0s}) \leqslant \lambda V'(\pi_s).$

There is full employment, wages of the two generations of workers are both equal to the marginal value product of labour, and (possibly) higher than the level corresponding to optimal risk-sharing between workers under contract and property owners.

(b) $w_s = w_s^* < w_{0s}$ $u'(w_{0s}) = \lambda V'(\pi_s)$ $u'(w_s) \leqslant u'(w_{0s})(1 - \eta_s).$

There is full employment, but the wages of the two generations of workers are different (though not too different), those of the workers under contract being higher than the marginal value product of labour thanks to the income insurance supplied by property owners (against lower wages in the earlier periods).

(c) $w_{0s} > w_s = t_s > w_s^*$ $L_s < L$

$$u'(w_s) = u'(w_{0s})\left(1 - \frac{L_s}{L}\eta_s\right) = \lambda V'(\pi_s)\left(1 - \frac{L_s}{L}\eta_s\right).$$

There is less than full employment, the wages of the two generations are different, with those of the older generation exceeding the marginal value product of labour, those of the younger generation equal to that marginal product and equal to the level of the unemployment benefits; thus all the unemployment is voluntary.

These conclusions may also be put in more sanguine terms as follows: all unemployment is voluntary and necessarily accompanied by wage discrimination between the two generations.

The fact that unemployment is voluntary is a consequence of allowing $t_s = w_s$. If one imposed instead, for incentive reasons, that $t_s \leqslant \alpha w_s$, $\alpha < 1$, then unemployment would be voluntary *ex ante* for workers as a group, but involuntary *ex post* for unemployed individuals.

The practical implications of conditions (A.12) are most conveniently explored by means of the linear approximation

$$u'(w_s) = u'(w_{0s}) + (w_s - w_{0s})u''(w_{0s})$$

$$= u'(w_{0s}) \left\{ 1 + (w_{0s} - w_s) \left[-\frac{u''(w_{0s})}{u'(w_{0s})} \right] \right\}$$

$$= u'(w_{0s})[1 + (w_{0s} - w_s)R_A(w_{0s})]$$

$$= u'(w_{0s}) \left[1 + \frac{w_{0s} - w_s}{w_{0s}} R_R(w_{0s}) \right] \qquad (A.13)$$

where $R_A(w_{0s})$ and $R_R(w_{0s})$ are respectively the absolute and relative risk-aversion measures of Arrow (1965) and Pratt (1964) evaluated at w_{0s}. Inserting (A.13) into (A.12) yields

$$\frac{w_{0s} - w_s}{w_{0s}} = \frac{-(L_s/L)\eta_s}{R_R(w_{0s})} \geqslant 0 \qquad w_s = w_{0s} \left[1 + \frac{(L_s/L)\eta_s}{R_R(w_{0s})} \right]. \qquad (A.14)$$

Thus the margin of relative discrimination $(w_{0s} - w_s)/w_{0s}$ is inversely proportional to the relative risk aversion of the workers, and directly proportional to the absolute value of the wage elasticity of new hirings. These two properties are intuitively natural.

VII Econometrics

14 The trade-off between real wages and employment in an open economy (Belgium)*

1. Introduction and preview

1.1. Theoretical background

The purpose of this paper is twofold. First, we discuss the nature and quantitative order of magnitude of the trade-off between real wages and employment in the small open economy Belgium. Second, we draw policy conclusions from our positive analysis, and compare income policies with alternative approaches to employment stimulation (including shorter working hours and currency depreciation).

Although our analysis is very coarse and recognises sizeable uncertainties, we hope to contribute a coherent view to the debate about the nature and likely remedies of the current state of underemployment in Belgium. Opinions differ about the respective roles of effective demand versus cost and production structures in explaining that situation.[1] The unions' demand of a shorter working week without pay cut is strongly opposed by employers on grounds of international competitiveness.

Indecisiveness is sustained by the lack of a generally accepted theoretical framework bringing both Keynesian and neo-classical reasoning to bear on the problems of an open economy. Available econometric models suffer from similar limitations.[2]

* *European Economic Review*, 15, 1–40, 1981. With Franco Modigliani. The authors thank Luc Bauwens, Gonzague d'Alcantara and Jean Dermine who collected or supplied material for the empirical analysis; Hans Tompa who skilfully carried out the computations; Jean Waelbroeck and an anonymous referee who commented on the manuscript; and numerous colleagues who participated in stimulating seminar discussions at Louvain-la-Neuve.

[1] Cf., for instance, Bleeckx et al. (1978, p. 3.39 ff) versus Eyskens (1978, pp. 13–14).
[2] Our survey has covered the models ANELISE – cf. Adams et al. (1973), Blomme (1978), BREUGHEL – cf. Berckmans and Thys-Clément (1977), COMET – cf. Barten et al. (1976), DESMOS – cf. Waelbroeck and Dramais (1974), LINK – cf. Basevi (1973), and RENA – cf. Thys-Clément et al. (1973).

321

Our own thinking has been influenced by two recent analytical contributions which have stressed the significance of the trade-off between real wages and employment:

(i) Malinvaud's *Theory of Unemployment Reconsidered* (1977) brings out the possibility that demand stimulation policies may be ineffective in reducing unemployment, if supply is unresponsive to aggregate demand at the going wages and prices – a situation referred to by Malinvaud as 'classical unemployment'.

(ii) In a paper initially published in Italian, Modigliani and Padoa-Schioppa (1977, 1978) have argued that, in an open economy, external balance implies a constraining relationship between the levels of real wages and employment.[3]

Malinvaud's analysis is presented for a closed economy.[4] International trade has important implications for the evaluation of the wages–employment trade-off, a point brought out by the Modigliani–Padoa-Schioppa approach. Their argument is essentially dynamic, including a mechanism of price adjustments in an open economy with fully indexed wages. We shall restate their argument in elementary comparative statics terms, and extend it to a more explicit treatment of the influence of real wages on employment through capacity adjustments. The main contribution of the present paper consists however in our attempt at quantitative evaluation of the trade-off between real wages and employment. Our empirical conclusions have shaped significantly our views on policy.

1.2. Factual background

Wages and salaries in Belgium are almost fully indexed. Real wages have risen by some 50% between 1970 and 1976, as compared with some 30% in other EEC countries. Their absolute level is reported to be among the highest in the world.[5] Unemployment currently stands at an alarming

---

[3] These two lines of analysis have come into contact at the IEA Conference on 'Unemployment in Western Countries Today' held in Strasbourg, September 1978. See the discussion by Modigliani of Malinvaud's paper *Macroeconomic Rationing of Employment*, (1980).

[4] Dixit (1978) extends Malinvaud's model to an open economy, along lines that are different from those followed here. Indeed, Dixit assumes that the country under study faces a perfectly elastic demand for its exports; whereas we assume that it faces a perfectly elastic supply for its imports. See Section 2.2 below.

[5] See Nyssens and Wittman (1976).

level, well above the EEC average, under due allowance for heterogeneity of definitions.[6]

The interplay of effective demand and international competitiveness in accounting for the decline of employment in Belgium is clearly illustrated by the steel, textile and clothing industries. From September 1976 through December 1977, employment of wage earners in these three industries alone fell by 29,365 persons, or 51% of the total decline experienced in manufacturing. In steel, where wages represent 50% of production costs, Belgium exports 70% of its output – but the share of Japan in world exports to countries outside the EEC and Comecon had reached 45% by 1976 (coming from 15% in 1962), whereas the share of EEC exporters had fallen to 15% (coming from 35% in 1962). Over the same period, the low-wage producers from Eastern Europe and Asia had increased their share in world exports of textiles and clothing respectively by 10 and 20 percentage points. In all three cases, the new international distribution of employment had particularly severe implications for Belgium, resulting in accelerated scrapping of capacity. The names of firms closed down, or transferred to low-wage areas, are locally familiar.

Further evidence of capacity scrapping is implied by the figures on Government disbursement of severance pay to workers dismissed by bankrupt firms with at least 10 employees (and not rehired). In 1975, 1976 and 1977, respectively 21,123, 32,262 and 24,739 persons received such payments. (These numbers correspond to 13%, 14% and 10%, respectively, of the total unemployment figures in the same year.)

Over the past decade, the volume of gross capital formation in Belgian manufacturing has been stagnant (hence falling markedly in relation to output), whereas the capital–labour ratio was undoubtedly rising.[7] Both accelerated scrapping and incomplete replacement of capacity have reduced the demand for labour.

Turning to international relations, we note that Belgium has over the years maintained its balance of trade very close to equilibrium – closer, in fact, than most countries (see fig. 14.1). Since 1970, the Belgian franc has appreciated steadily relative to all currencies except the Swiss franc, the yen, the mark and the guilder – staying fairly close to these last two currencies. The rate of inflation had been brought back to less than 4% by 1978.

[6] The unemployment rate in Belgium may be evaluated at some 8 to 11% (of the total labour force), depending upon the treatment of workers temporarily employed under special government programs.

[7] The Dutch estimates by den Hartog and Tjan (1976) and the unpublished Belgian estimates by d'Alcantara (1979) and by Vandoorne and Meeusen (1978) concur in suggesting that this ratio increases at a rate of some 5% per year.

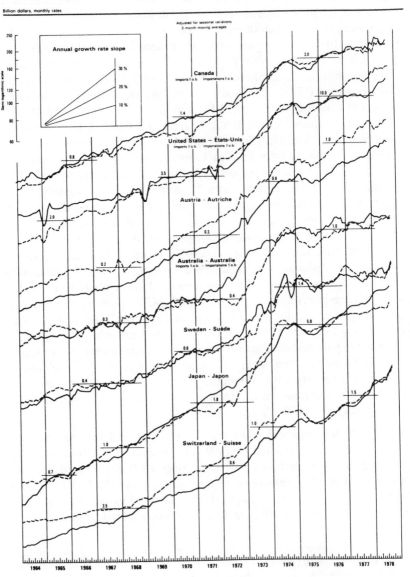

Fig. 14.1.   Organization for economic cooperation and development statistics of foreign trade, December 1978.

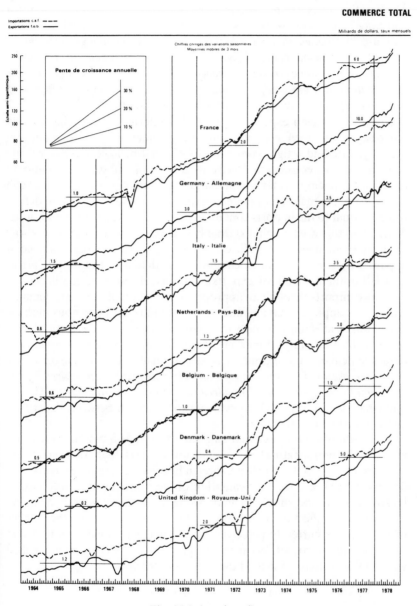

Fig. 14.1. (continued).

1.3. General approach

Against this background, we propose to study the trade-off between real wages and employment as follows. First, following Modigliani–Padoa-Schioppa, *we shall treat external balance as a binding constraint on demand management policies.*[8] Second, *we shall endeavour to assess the influence of real wages on output, hence employment, both through the rate' of utilization of a given capacity and through the creation or scrapping of that capacity.* These two points are now explained briefly.

Given the Belgian experience, we find it relevant to consider initially the case of an open economy operating under a fixed (or managed) exchange rate and a tight constraint of external balance. (Exchange rate adjustments are considered briefly in Section 4.) If such an economy experiences unemployment, stimulation of domestic demand through policy measures that do not increase exports will create an external deficit, roughly equal to the imports content (direct and indirect) of the additional demand. In this way, a tight external balance constraint stands in the way of demand management policies. Similarly, if the external balance is impaired by some exogenous circumstances (like a rise in import prices or a fall in the demand for exports), one way of restoring equilibrium is to reduce imports through an appropriate reduction of domestic demand. Another example of such a circumstance would be an exogenous increase in real wages, affecting adversely the competitiveness of domestic producers on the export and import markets. If external balance implies equality of domestic demand and output, at least marginally, then *the impact of the wage increase on domestic output* (hence employment) *is measured by the reduction in domestic demand required to restore external balance.* This, in a nutshell, is our approach to evaluate the trade-off between real wages and employment in Belgium.

The assumption that external balance operates as a binding constraint is probably more natural in a long-run analysis than in a short-run analysis. Indeed, in the short run, foreign borrowing may cover temporary deficits. To that extent, our evaluation of the short-run trade-off may be biased upwards and should be understood as an upper bound – a feature that would not affect our conclusions. Moreover, it seems that the balance of payments is currently perceived by the Belgian monetary authorities as a binding constraint, because an appreciable current account deficit would make it hard to defend the desired exchange rate.

[8] Other previous work in the same spirit includes Oates (1966), McKinnon (1969) and Steinherr (1975).

The assumption that external balance operates as a binding constraint on demand management policies frees us from the necessity of considering these policies explicitly (or evaluating multiplier effects, and so on), at least in a first approximation where the influence of the *composition* of domestic demand on imports is ignored. For estimation purposes, the analytical burden is shifted towards estimation of the impact on external balance of domestic costs and domestic demand.

How to estimate that impact raises the second point mentioned above. The standard link between wage costs and the balance of trade goes through the behaviour of domestic producers who react to cost increases by raising their prices and/or reducing their supply (for instance by adjusting sales promotion expenditures to the new margin between price and costs). In the open economy, both measures result in a transfer of market shares from domestic toward foreign producers, and this affects the balance of trade adversely. (Price increases for exports have a positive effect, which must be subtracted.)

But it makes a difference whether a firm experiencing a rise in wage costs merely accepts some loss of sales and/or of profits, or closes down a plant altogether. The difference is twofold. In the first case, but not in the second, the reduction in employment (i) is apt to be less than proportional to the reduction in output, at least initially, and (ii) is reversible under a more favourable turn of events. Thus, capacity scrapping implies a permanent reduction in the potential demand for labour, thereby contributing an element of 'structural' or 'classical' unemployment. But *it also implies a permanent deterioration of the balance of trade* (through loss of exports or imports substitution) which, under a tight external balance constraint, requires a compensating reduction in domestic demand. The final impact on output (hence employment) is again measured by the reduction in domestic demand required to restore external balance.

We shall accordingly endeavour to evaluate separately the influence on exports and imports of domestic costs at unchanged capacity levels, and of capacity levels themselves. And we shall endeavour to evaluate the influence of real wages not only on operating costs but also on capacity levels through scrapping and investment.

1.4. Summary

Quantitative evaluation of these influences is subject to much imprecision. We have combined two approaches, both with a Bayesian inspiration, to evaluate the international trade elasticities.

First, we have collected the estimates from published econometric models of the Belgian economy, as listed in footnote 2. These estimates do not always agree, but are not too widely different either. We have averaged point estimates across models and attached to these averages subjective standard errors, reflecting the dispersion of estimates.

Second, d'Alcantara and Associates (1979) have kindly made available to us the progress report describing the international trade sector of the new model SERENA currently being estimated on behalf of the Belgian Planning Office. The specification of exports and imports functions for manufactured goods corresponds very closely to our needs. And Bauwens (1979) has conducted a Bayesian analysis of the export equations in that model. We have accordingly used as an alternative the posterior densities corresponding to the SERENA equations, with some corrections to unreasonably low standard errors.

The influence of wage costs on capacity is more difficult to quantify. Our evaluation is based on the work of den Hartog and Tjan (1976) and Kuipers and Bosch (1976), who have estimated a clay–clay vintage model for The Netherlands.[9] Simulation of that model provides an evaluation that we have treated as unbiased, but to which we have attached a substantial standard error

Making generous use of normal approximations, we obtain through a mixture of analytical and numerical integration marginal densities for the trade-off between real wages and employment in Belgium. They are reproduced as figs. 14.2–14.6 below. The variances of these densities measure the imprecision of our knowledge.

The conclusions from our empirical investigation are first that estimates of the trade-off between real wages and employment in Belgium are subject to considerable imprecision; second that the short-run elasticity of employment with respect to real wages keeping capacity constant is probably quite small (like -0.2), and definitely less than unity in absolute value; third that the corresponding medium-run elasticity taking into account capacity adjustments is probably sizeable (like -2), and definitely larger than unity in absolute value; and fourth that exchange rate adjustments might not make too much difference, in either the short or the medium run.

Turning to a discussion of policy, we shall argue that these conclusions give support to a policy of constant real labour incomes, of comprehensive efforts to redistribute work through shorter working hours or related schemes, and of selective efforts to slow down capacity scrapping.

Section 2 contains a theoretical derivation of our formulae for evaluating

[9] The research in progress by Vandoorne and Meeusen (1978) came to our attention after most of our work was completed.

the trade-off between real wages and employment in Belgium. Section 3 contains our attempt at empirical evaluation, summarized in figs. 14.2–14.6. Exchange rate adjustments are discussed in Section 4. Policy implications and recommendations are presented in Section 5 which is largely self-contained.

2. The trade-off under a fixed exchange rate and a tight external balance constraint

2.1. *Notation and definitions*

We use the following notation:

P_e = level of world prices (expressed in 'dollars'),
P = level of domestic prices (in domestic currency),
P_x = level of export prices (in domestic currency),
P_m = level of import prices (in domestic currency),
W = level of domestic wages (in domestic currency), a component of
C = level of domestic factor prices or costs (in domestic currency),
e = exchange rate (domestic price of 'dollars'),
L = employment (number of employed persons),
X = volume of exports,
M = volume of imports,
E = volume of aggregate world demand,
G = volume of aggregate domestic government expenditures,
H = volume of aggregate domestic private demand (consumption plus investment),
Y = volume of domestic output,
$\bar{Y}$ = volume of capacity output (defined below).

The level of import prices is immediately equated to the exogenous level of world prices, reflecting our assumption of a perfectly elastic supply of imports to the small country Belgium: $P_m/e = P_e$.[10]

Capacity output is here identified, for conceptual clarity, with notional supply. It is the volume of output that domestic producers would choose to supply, for profit maximisation, at the prevailing prices and wages, under unlimited output demand and factor supply. In the short run, $\bar{Y}$ is constrained by the existing plants and equipment; it may also be influenced by extant labour contracts (if firms would rather produce than fire workers; but would not hire new workers, even to replace voluntary leaves). In the

[10] See footnote 4. In the SERENA model, the elasticity of import prices with respect to world prices – a weighted average of the export prices of Belgium's trade partners – is estimated at 0.98 for industrial goods, which account for 80% of imports.

longer run, $\bar{Y}$ is affected by depreciation or scrapping of existing equipment and by new investment, in a manner that will be discussed further below.

In the short run, we ignore inventory adjustments and relate domestic output to final demand through an accounting identity (which also satisfies a definitional inequality),

$$Y = G + H + X - M \leqq \bar{Y}. \tag{1}$$

This formulation is used, instead of the now standard min condition,[11] because: (i) we concentrate on situations of underemployment, and ignore constraints imposed by labour supply, (ii) in the open economy, excess demand for output is absorbed by imports, (iii) formulation (1) is consistent with excess supply, absorbed by reduced output ($Y < \bar{Y}$).

2.2. The determinants of exports and imports

The trade balance, in dollars, is defined by

$$B_e = \frac{P_x}{e} X - \frac{P_m}{e} M = \frac{P_x}{e} X - P_e M. \tag{2}$$

For the purposes of this paper, what matters is not the determination of the absolute value of exports and imports, but mostly their dependence on domestic costs (wages), both directly and through capacity adjustments. The significance of capacity is obvious enough. When a plant located in Belgium is closed down and new facilities are built abroad, the exported share of that plant's output drops out of Belgian exports, and the complementary share sold domestically may reappear (at least partly) under Belgian imports. The influence of costs is also well known, but less transparent, because it may exert itself through quantity adjustments, or through prices adjustments, or through a mixture of both.

To illustrate this point with an exports-tale, one may describe two hypothetical polar cases.[12] In the first case, domestic producers accept international prices 'passively', but react to price and cost conditions by adjusting their supply (possibly by adjusting their sales promotion efforts). The volume of exports then corresponds to the volume of supply at world prices P_e, given a supply curve shaped by domestic costs C and capacity $\bar{Y}$. In the second case, the domestic producers set their own export prices,

---

[11] Actual output is the minimum of notional supply, effective demand or full employment output; se Malinvaud (1977, 1980).
[12] These two cases are also distinguished under a different approach by Ginsburgh and Zang (1978).

then meet 'passively' the demand resulting from these prices (and from their sales promotion effort). The volume of exports then corresponds to world demand at export prices P_x/e, given a demand curve shaped by world demand E and world prices P_e (the prices charged by competitors). Furthermore, export prices will depend upon domestic costs C and capacity $\bar{Y}$ as well as upon the parameters of the world's demand function. (These export prices should in principle bring about equality of marginal costs and marginal revenues.)

If we could disaggregate exports by commodities i, and if we knew the set of indices I corresponding to the first case, then we could write (using lower case letters for microeconomic variables, using superscripts to denote supply S or demand D, and doing all our accounting in 'dollars')

$$\frac{P_{x_i}}{e} = P_{e_i}, \qquad x_i = x_i^S\left(\frac{P_{x_i}}{e}, \frac{C}{e}, \bar{y}_i\right) \quad \text{for} \quad i \in I,$$

$$\frac{P_{x_i}}{e} = \frac{P_{x_i}}{e}\left(\frac{C}{e}, \bar{y}_i, E, \ldots\right), \quad x_i = x_i^D\left(\frac{P_{x_i}}{e}, E, P_{e_i}\right) \quad \text{for} \quad i \notin I.$$

Aggregating over commodities within the set I and within its complement, $\bar{I}$, we could write

$$\frac{P_x}{e} = P_e, \qquad X = X^S\left(\frac{P_x}{e} = P_e, \frac{C}{e}, \bar{Y}\right) \quad \text{for } I,$$

$$\frac{P_x}{e} = \frac{P_x}{e}\left(\frac{C}{e}, \bar{Y}, E, \ldots\right), \quad X = X^D\left(\frac{P_x}{e}, E, P_e\right) \qquad \text{for } \bar{I}.$$

Short of having all the relevant microeconomic information, we could still pool the arguments of both price equations, and then of both quantity equations, into single aggregate relationships of the form

$$\frac{P_x}{e} = \frac{P_x}{e}\left(P_e, \frac{C}{e}, \bar{Y}, E, \ldots\right), \qquad X = X\left(P_e, \frac{P_x}{e}, \frac{C}{e}, E, \bar{Y}\right). \tag{3}$$

The burden of the analysis is then shifted to the empirical level, at which one would hope to capture the relevant influence of each variable, through appropriate functional specifications and estimation procedures.

This tale is meant as an illustration and heuristic rationale for our approach, which is dictated by the availability of empirical evidence. It consists indeed in basing our empirical evaluation on eqs. (3).

However, due to meagreness of the data base, we neglect the influence of $\bar{Y}$, E and other variables on P_x/e, which is estimated as a function of

P_e and C/e alone. That being the case, it simplifies notations and derivations to substitute in (3) for P_x/e in the quantity equation from the price equation, thereby obtaining the simpler specification,[13]

$$\frac{P_x}{e} = \frac{P_x}{e}\left(P_e, \frac{C}{e}\right), \qquad X = X\left(P_e, \frac{C}{e}, E, \bar{Y}\right). \tag{4}$$

Turning to the imports side, we could tell a similar story (somewhat less convincingly, perhaps). But it would have the disadvantage of forcing us into specification and estimation of an equation defining the domestic price level P. This complication seems largely unnecessary, because empirical analyses of the dependence of Belgian imports on domestic prices or on domestic costs give similar results. Accordingly, theoretically justified distinctions would have no empirical counterpart. We shall proceed directly to a quantity equation similar to that in (4), with either C/e or P/e as second argument.

To complete the specification, we must still define aggregate domestic demand. In principle, that variable is best represented through its individual *gross* components: G, H (possibly divided into consumption and investment), and X (on account of the share of imports in intermediate deliveries to export industries).[14] Because we neglect the possible influence of the *composition* of final demand, we retain only $G + H$ and X. And because the Belgian balance of trade is so close to equilibrium, we use (1) and replace $G + H$ by the single variable Y, to simplify notation and derivations. Accordingly, our import equation is simply

$$M = M\left(P_e, \frac{C}{e}, Y, X, \bar{Y}\right) \quad \text{or} \quad M = M\left(P_e, \frac{P}{e}, Y, X, \bar{Y}\right). \tag{5}$$

2.3.   The elasticity of employment with respect to real wages

Substituting from (4) and (5) into (2), we obtain the external balance constraint in a form suitable for our purposes,

$$B_e = \left(\frac{P_x}{e}\left(P_e, \frac{C}{e}\right)\right)X\left(P_e, \frac{C}{e}, E, \bar{Y}\right) - P_e M\left(P_e, \frac{C}{e}, Y, X, \bar{Y}\right) \geq \bar{B}_e,$$

$$\tag{6}$$

[13] In empirical evaluation, we shall have to remember that X depends upon C/e and P_e both directly and through P_x/e.

[14] In the import equations of SERENA, these components are weighted by import shares and aggregated into a single variable.

where $\bar{B}_e$ is some preassigned number of 'dollars' (close to zero in the Belgian historical experience). Total differentiation of (6) enables us to estimate the adjustment in domestic demand dY that should accompany an exogenous change in some other variable $d\theta$, if B_e is to *remain equal* to $\bar{B}_e$,

$$0 = dB_e = \frac{\partial B_e}{\partial \theta} d\theta + \frac{\partial B_e}{\partial Y} dY = \frac{\partial B_e}{\partial \theta} d\theta - P_e \frac{\partial M}{\partial Y} dY, \tag{7}$$

$$\frac{dY}{d\theta}\bigg|_{B_e} = \frac{\partial B_e}{\partial \theta} \bigg/ P_e \frac{\partial M}{\partial Y}. \tag{8}$$

In order to estimate the trade-off between real wages and output, then employment, under the assumptions of this section, there remains only to apply formula (8), with $\theta = W/P$ (*real* wages), then translate output changes into employment changes.

For clarity of exposition, we first keep $\bar{Y}$ fixed, and look at a change in nominal wages; thus,

$$
\begin{aligned}
\frac{dY}{dW}\bigg|_{B_e,\bar{Y}} &= \left[\frac{X}{e} \frac{\partial P_x}{\partial(C/e)} \frac{\partial(C/e)}{\partial W} + \left(\frac{P_x}{e} - P_e \frac{\partial M}{\partial X} \right) \frac{\partial X}{\partial(C/e)} \frac{\partial(C/e)}{\partial W} \right. \\
&\quad \left. - P_e \frac{\partial M}{\partial(C/e)} \frac{\partial(C/e)}{\partial W} \right] \bigg/ P_e \frac{\partial M}{\partial Y} \\
&= \left[\frac{X}{e} \frac{\partial P_x}{\partial C} \frac{\partial C}{\partial W} + \left(\frac{P_x}{e} - P_e \frac{\partial M}{\partial X} \right) \frac{\partial X}{\partial C} \frac{\partial C}{\partial W} \right. \\
&\quad \left. - P_e \frac{\partial M}{\partial C} \frac{\partial C}{\partial W} \right] \bigg/ P_e \frac{\partial M}{\partial Y}.
\end{aligned}
\tag{9}
$$

In elasticity terms (denoting all elasticities by η),

$$\eta_{YW}|_{B_e,\bar{Y}} = \left[\frac{XP_x}{MeP_e} \eta_{P_xC} + \left(\frac{XP_x}{MeP_e} - \eta_{MX} \right) \eta_{XC} - \eta_{MC} \right] \eta_{CW}/\eta_{MY}. \tag{10}$$

Under balance of trade equilibrium, $X(P_x/e) = MP_e$, so that

$$\eta_{YW}|_{B_e=0,\bar{Y}} = [\eta_{P_xC} + (1 - \eta_{MX})\eta_{XC} - \eta_{MC}]\eta_{CW}/\eta_{MY}, \tag{11}$$

$$
\begin{aligned}
\eta_{LW}|_{B_e=0,\bar{Y}} &= \eta_{LY} \cdot \eta_{YW}|_{B_e=0,\bar{Y}} \\
&= [\eta_{P_xC} + (1 - \eta_{MX})\eta_{XC} - \eta_{MC}]\eta_{CW}\eta_{LY}/\eta_{MY}.
\end{aligned}
\tag{12}
$$

Going on to real wages, we note that

$$\eta_{Y \cdot W/P} = \eta_{YW} \eta_{W \cdot W/P} = \eta_{YW}/\eta_{W/P \cdot W} = \eta_{YW}/(1 - \eta_{PW}), \qquad (13)$$

so that

$$\eta_{L \cdot W/P}|_{B_e = 0, \bar{Y}} = [\eta_{P_x C} + (1 - \eta_{MX})\eta_{XC} - \eta_{MC}]\eta_{CW}\eta_{LY}/\eta_{MY}(1 - \eta_{PW}). \qquad (14)$$

We shall use eq. (14) to estimate the short-run elasticity of employment with respect to real wages, keeping capacity constant. The interpretation of this formula is easier if one starts with (11). In the numerator of (11), we find the percentage impact of a rise in wages on export prices, exports and imports, hence on the balance of trade. (The impact on imports is adjusted for the import content of exports, through the term η_{MX}.) Dividing by the income elasticity of imports gives us the percentage reduction of domestic demand needed to restore external balance. Multiplying by the elasticity of employment with respect to output, η_{LY}, yields the corresponding percentage adjustment in employment (12). Finally, a mechanical formula enables us to go from nominal wages to real wages (14).

In order to take the influence of capacity into account, we extend (9)–(14) into

$$\left. \frac{dY}{dW} \right|_{B_e} = \left[\left(\frac{X}{e} \frac{\partial P_x}{\partial C} + \frac{P_x}{e} \frac{\partial X}{\partial C} - P_e \frac{\partial M}{\partial X} \frac{\partial X}{\partial C} - P_e \frac{\partial M}{\partial C} \right) \frac{\partial C}{\partial W} \right. $$
$$\left. + \left(\frac{P_x}{e} \frac{\partial X}{\partial \bar{Y}} - P_e \frac{\partial M}{\partial X} \frac{\partial X}{\partial \bar{Y}} - P_e \frac{\partial M}{\partial \bar{Y}} \right) \frac{\partial \bar{Y}}{\partial W} \right] \bigg/ P_e \frac{\partial M}{\partial Y}, \qquad (15)$$

$$\eta_{L(W/P)}|_{B_e = 0} = [(\eta_{P_x C} + \eta_{XC} - \eta_{MX}\eta_{XC} - \eta_{MC})\eta_{CW}$$
$$+ (\eta_{X\bar{Y}} - \eta_{MX}\eta_{X\bar{Y}} - \eta_{M\bar{Y}})\eta_{\bar{Y}W}]\eta_{LY}/\eta_{MY}(1 - \eta_{PW}). \qquad (16)$$

We shall use eq. (16) to estimate the medium-run elasticity of employment with respect to real wages, taking capacity adjustments into account.

The distinction between short and medium run is particularly relevant for the estimation of η_{LY} – a point elaborated below. Capacity adjustments through scrapping require little time and could thus take place in the short run. Being irreversible, however, they are decided on the basis of medium-run considerations. And capacity adjustments through new investment take time.

In concluding this section, we wish to remind the reader of three approximations embodied in our formulae, namely: $\eta_{P_x\bar{Y}} = 0$, $\eta_{P_m W} = 0$ and $\eta_{P_m\bar{Y}} = 0$. In other empirical contexts, the corresponding terms should be reintroduced in formulae (14) and (16).

3. Empirical Evaluation

3.1. Organization

As announced in the introduction, our empirical analysis combines three sources of information:

(i) the published models of the Belgian economy – ANELISE, BREUGHEL, COMET, DESMOS, LINK and RENA,
(ii) the international trade sector of the new model SERENA,
(iii) the simulation of the Dutch clay–clay vintage model, on which our estimation of $\eta_{\bar{Y}W}$ is based.

We first introduce our methodology by discussing the evaluation of $\eta_{Y(W/P)}|_{B_e=0,\bar{Y}}$ as defined through (11) and (13).

3.2. Import and export elasticities

Most of the models referred to above contain estimates of the elasticities of export prices with respect to wages, of the volume of exports with respect to export prices, and of imports with respect to domestic prices and domestic demand. In order to use these estimates, we write

$$\eta_{Y(W/P)}|_{B_e=0,\bar{Y}} = [\eta_{P_x W} + (1 - \eta_{MX})\eta_{XW} - \eta_{MW}]/\eta_{MY}(1 - \eta_{PW}),$$

$$\eta_{XW} = \eta_{XP_x} \cdot \eta_{P_x W}, \quad \eta_{MW} = \eta_{MP} \cdot \eta_{PW}, \tag{13'}$$

$$\eta_{Y(W/P)}|_{B_e=0,\bar{Y}} = [\eta_{P_x W} + (1 - \eta_{MX})\eta_{XP_x}\eta_{P_x W}$$
$$- \eta_{MP}\eta_{PW}]/\eta_{MY}(1 - \eta_{PW})$$

$$=_{\text{def}} \frac{\eta_{\Xi W} - \eta_{MP}\eta_{PW}}{\eta_{MY}(1 - \eta_{PW})},$$

$$\eta_{\Xi W} =_{\text{def}} \eta_{P_x W} + (1 - \eta_{MX})\eta_{XP_x}\eta_{P_x W}. \tag{13''}$$

In formula (13″), $\eta_{Y\cdot(W/P)}$ is expressed as a function of 4 elasticities, namely $\eta_{\Xi W}$ (as just defined), η_{MP}, η_{PW} and η_{MY}. In table 14.1, we present

Table 14.1

	$\eta_{P_xW} \times \eta_{XP_x} = \eta_{XW}$			$\eta_{\Xi W}$[a]	$\eta_{MP} \times \eta_{PW} = \eta_{MW}$			η_{MY}	$\eta_{Y(W/P)}\big|_{B_e=0.\bar{Y}}$	η_{LY}
	η_{P_xW}	η_{XP_x}	η_{XW}		η_{MP}	η_{PW}	η_{MW}			
(1) ANELISE[b]					0.38			1.35		0.5 (0.9)[c]
(2) BREUGHEL	0.44	−0.5	−0.22	+0.31	0.36	0.56	0.20	1.67	+0.15	0.23
(3) COMET	0	−0.6	0	0	0.17	0.33	0.056	1.42	−0.06	0.3
(4) DESMOS	0.45	−1.6	−0.72	+0.02	0.32	0.3	0.10	1.26	−0.09	0.3 (0.88)[c]
(5) LINK	0.23	−2.6	−0.6	−0.13						
(6) RENA	0.58 or 0.14	−2.7	−1.57	−0.36	0.44	0.2	0.09	1.95	−0.29 or −0.08	
(7) AVERAGE	0.30	−1.6	−0.30 / −0.57	0.004 / −0.04	0.33	0.35	0.11	1.55	−0.07[d] or −0.15[e]	
(8) σ (subjective) Range				0.20	0.15	0.20 / ≦0.85		0.25		
(9) SERENA	0.08		−0.64	−0.30			0.19	1.53 (1.24)[c]	−0.48	
(10) σ (adjusted)[f]				0.20			0.18	0.25		

[a] Always computed with $\eta_{MX} = 0.4$.
[b] Exports are exogenous in ANELISE.
[c] Long-term elasticities.
[d] Average of computed values in the same column.
[e] Computed from average values in the same row.
[f] Covariance $(\eta_{MW}, \eta_{MY}) = 0.00875$.

the point estimates for each of these elasticities, or its components, as reported in the various econometric models for Belgium. Subjective probability densities for $\eta_{\equiv W}$, η_{MP}, η_{PW} and η_{MY} are specified by means of independent normal densities, centred at the average values of these point estimates [line (7)], with standard deviations subjectively assessed so as to reflect (conservatively) the dispersion of the point estimates [line (8)]. The density for η_{PW} is truncated at 0.85 to avoid dividing by arbitrarily small numbers in (13″).[15]

From the four normal densities so defined one can compute a marginal density for $\eta_{Y(W/P)}$.[16] It is exhibited as fig. 14.2. The density is unimodal and moderately skewed, with a mean of -0.2, a median of -0.15, a mode of -0.12, and a standard deviation of 0.32 roughly equal to the interquartile range. The probability of a positive elasticity, corresponding to situations where the positive term $\eta_{P_x W}$ dominates the negative terms, is close to 0.25, which seems excessive.

Line (9) of table 14.1 gives the point estimates obtained for the manufacturing sector in the SERENA model. The import and export equations of that model, which correspond closely to the specification of Section 2.2, are reproduced in the appendix. The estimation is based on (annual) data for the period 1966–1976, which we regard as more directly relevant than earlier years. These points estimates are not very different from the *average* values coming from the other models. The major discrepancy concerns $\eta_{P_x W}$, and should be investigated further.[17]

A systematic Bayesian analysis of the SERENA equations for export prices and export quantities has been carried out by Bauwens (1979). His analysis includes the case of non-informative priors, which we have retained throughout. He has kindly extended his computations, to obtain the marginal posterior density for $\eta_{\equiv W}$; results and analytical details are given in the appendix. On the import side, a posterior joint density for η_{MW} and η_{MY} is easily obtained. Using again normal approximations and combining these two densities with that defined above for η_{PW}, we have computed the marginal posterior density for $\eta_{Y(W/P)}$. It is exhibited as fig. 14.3. It is again unimodal and moderately skewed, with a mean of -0.6,

---

[15] A similar precaution for η_{MY} was not necessary, because that variable is integrated out analytically, and zero is more than 6 standard deviations away from the mean.

[16] We thank Hans Tompa for carrying out these computations, using the bivariate numerical integration routines developed by him under the auspices of the Programme National d'Impulsion à la Recherche en Informatique of the Belgian Government.

[17] The model SERENA estimates $\eta_{P_x C}$ as ~ 0.22, leading to $\eta_{P_x W} = \eta_{P_x C} \eta_{CW} \sim 0.08$ when $\eta_{CW} \sim \frac{1}{3}$. Replacing C by W in appendix eq. (A.5) yields the direct estimate $\eta_{P_x W} \sim 0.15$, which we suspect to be biased upwards by the fact that W then serves in part as a proxy for other components of C.

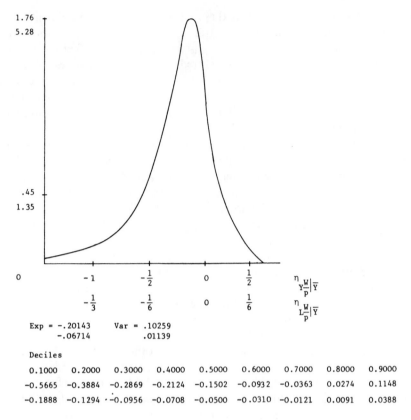

Fig. 14.2.   Short-run estimates from macromodels.

a median of -0.5, a mode of -0.36, and a standard deviation of 0.44 roughly equal to the interquartile range. The probability of a positive elasticity is now much smaller – some 7%.

To the extent that the densities in figs. 14.2 and 14.3 are derived from the same data base, it would be improper to use one of them to revise the other through Bayes theorem. But it would be legitimate to average them, with weights reflecting the subjective probabilities assigned to the alternative specifications underlying the two approaches. Because both densities ultimately lead to the same substantive conclusions, we do not pursue the matter further.

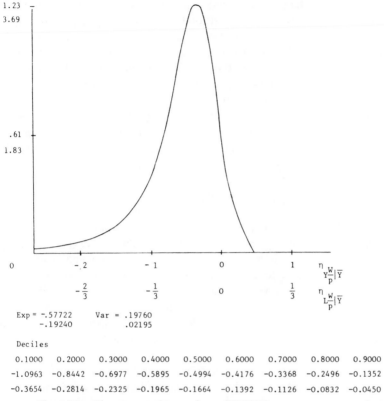

Fig. 14.3.   Short-run estimates from SERENA.

3.3.   Output elasticity of employment

As for η_{LY}, which is almost the same concept as in Okun's Law, we must distinguish carefully between the short-run elasticity and the medium-run elasticity. The models do likewise, suggesting short-run elasticities of 0.3 as in COMET and DESMOS[18] but long-run elasticities of 0.9 as in ANELISE and DESMOS. The main reason for the distinction is of course that labour is a semi-fixed factor in the short run but not in the medium or long run.

[18] The short-run estimate of η_{LY} is 0.23 in BREUGHEL and 0.5 in ANELISE. Okun's estimate is 0.33 for the U.S., where employment is less stable than in Europe, but where participation rates are also less stable, and included in Okun's estimate.

Given the high probability that $\eta_{Y(W/P)}$ is small, it did not seem important to refine the analysis of the transition from $\eta_{Y(W/P)}$ to $\eta_{L(W/P)} = \eta_{Y(W/P)} \cdot \eta_{LY}$. In principle, one should multiply $\eta_{Y(W/P)}$ by a random variable, centred around 0.3 for the short-run analysis and endowed with a suitable distribution. We have omitted that refinement and supplied an alternative scale in figs. 14.2 and 14.3; the conditional density of $\eta_{L(W/P)}$, given that $\eta_{LY} = 0.3$, is simply the density of $\eta_{Y(W/P)}$, rescaled by a factor of 0.3. The substantive conclusions to which both figures lead are the same; namely that $\eta_{L(W/P)}|_{B_e = 0, \bar{Y}}$ is small in absolute value, the order of magnitude being -0.1 to -0.2, and is contained in the interval $(-0.5, 0)$ with a probability close to 0.9.

3.4. Capacity adjustments

Turning to the role of capacity adjustments, we shall retain the SERENA point estimates of $\eta_{X\bar{Y}} = 0.77$ and $\eta_{M\bar{Y}} = 0.29$, whereby $(1 - \eta_{MX})\eta_{X\bar{Y}} - \eta_{M\bar{Y}} = 0.75$. Although capacity variables (usually a degree of utilisation) play little role in the foreign trade equations of other models, a coefficient close to unity also appears in the DESMOS model, and corresponds well to what we want to capture. The more elusive coefficient is of course $\eta_{\bar{Y}W}$. On *a priori* grounds, one would expect that elasticity to be sizeable, reflecting the spatial relocation of capacity induced by comparisons of labour costs in Belgium with those prevailing: In low-wage areas of Asia, North Africa etc., where multinational as well as domestic firms invest; in other EEC countries, where real wages have increased more slowly than in Belgium over the past decade; in industrialised countries like the U.S. or the U.K., whose competitiveness has improved through real currency depreciation.

An empirical basis appropriate for quantifying this phenomenon is obviously lacking. We do feel, however, that an *indication* about the value of $\eta_{\bar{Y}W}$ is given by the simulation results for the Dutch clay–clay vintage model, as reported by Kuipers and Bosch (1976). The model, based on earlier work of Solow (1962) or Phelps (1963), is described as follows by den Hartog and Tjan (1976, p. 37):

Equipment is classified into vintages according to the year of installation. With respect to the relation between installed equipment, production and labour for each vintage the following assumptions hold:

—Production capacity is determined by installed equipment. Capital productivity – that is, the inverse of the capital-output ratio – is equal for all vintages of equipment and, in addition, remains constant in the course of time.

—Labour requirements per unit of equipment decrease with a constant relative rate the younger a vintage of equipment is; labour requirements, however, become fixed at the moment of installation of new equipment.

The workings of the model are described as follows by the same authors (*ibid*, p. 40):

... if the revenue of a vintage covers its wage sum... this vintage will be kept in operation. If this revenue is lower the vintage will be scrapped ... . Thus, if real labour costs either fall or remain constant this brings about a lengthening of economic life span of the oldest vintage. If the rate of increase of real labour costs, however, equals the rate of labour saving technical progress then the economic life span remains constant. A faster rate of increase causes a shortening of the economic life span of the oldest vintage in operation.

Using this model, and empirical estimates of its parameters for the Netherlands (including a rate of labour saving technical progress close to 5%), Kuipers and Bosch (1976) have simulated labour demand six years ahead under alternative assumptions about the rate of investment and the rate of increase of real wages. The differences in employment associated with differences in the level of real wages imply elasticities ranging from -1.4 in the first year to nearly -2 in the last year.[19]

These elasticities reflect accelerated scrapping of existing equipment becoming unprofitable at the higher real wages. They do not include any influence of real wages on new investment. On this score, they provide a lower bound to the elasticity of employment with respect to real wages through capacity adjustments. On the other hand, the clay–clay approach exaggerates the elasticity of capacity with respect to real wages. Some *ex post* substitution of capital for labour would slow down the scrapping process. These two sources of bias go in opposite directions, and we use the median figure of -1.7 in the case of Belgium. We realise that estimation and simulation of a similar model with Belgian data could give different results. But we are unable to guess in what direction the difference would go, and can only account for that by assigning to this estimate a substantial standard error.

---

[19] See the figures in table 14.2. With an initial employment level of 3,863,000 persons, a decrease of 55,000 jobs amounts to 1.42% of the total labour force.

Table 14.2[a]

Year	i = 6%				i = 5%				i = 4%			
	ω = 6%	ω = 5%	ω = 4%	ω = 3%	ω = 6%	ω = 5%	ω = 4%	ω = 3%	ω = 6%	ω = 5%	ω = 4%	ω = 3%
Predictions of capacity demand for labour in the period 1975–1980 in thousands of man-years												
1974	3863[b]	3863[b]	3863[b]	3863[b]	3863[b]	3863[b]	3863[b]	3863[b]	3863[b]	3863[b]	3863[b]	3863[b]
1975	3879	3934	3989	4045	3876	3931	3986	4042	3873	3928	3983	4039
1976	3816	3927	4036	4146	3807	3918	4027	4136	3798	3909	4017	4127
1977	3742	3919	4086	4252	3723	3900	4067	4233	3705	3882	4049	4215
1978	3669	3903	4136	4362	3638	3872	4105	4331	3607	3841	4073	4300
1979	3566	3881	4180	4468	3518	3834	4132	4420	3472	3788	4086	4374
1980	3448	3854	4227	4576	3381	3787	4161	4509	3317	3722	4096	4444
Predictions of structural unemployment in the period 1975–1980 in thousands of man-years												
1974	246[b]	246[b]	246[b]	246[b]	246[b]	246[b]	246[b]	246[b]	246[b]	246[b]	246[b]	246[b]
1975	229	174	119	63	232	177	122	66	235	181	125	69
1976	292	181	72	−38	301	190	81	−28	311	199	91	−19
1977	366	189	22	−144	385	207	41	−125	407	226	59	−107
1978	439	205	−28	−256	470	237	3	−223	501	267	34	−192
1979	542	227	−72	−360	590	274	−25	−312	636	320	21	−266
1980	660	254	−119	−468	727	321	−53	−401	792	386	11	−337

[a] i = rate of growth of investment; ω = rate of growth of real wages.
[b] Actual figures.
Source: Kuipers and Bosch (1976, p. 78, tables 4.1 and 4.2).

We have evaluated (16) as

$$\eta_{L(W/P)}|_{B_e=0} = \frac{\eta_{\Xi W} - \eta_{MP}\eta_{PW}}{\eta_{MY}(1 - \eta_{PW})}\eta_{LY}$$

$$+ \frac{\eta_{X\bar{Y}}(1 - \eta_{MX}) - \eta_{M\bar{Y}}}{\eta_{MY}}\eta_{L\bar{Y}}\eta_{\bar{Y}(W/P)}$$

$$=_{\text{def}} \frac{\eta_{\Xi W} - \eta_{MP}\eta_{PW}}{\eta_{MY}(1 - \eta_{PW})}(0.9) + \frac{0.75\eta_{L\bar{Y}}\eta_{\bar{Y}(W/P)}}{\eta_{MY}}$$

$$= \eta_{Y(W/P)}|_{B_e=0,\bar{Y}}(0.9) + \frac{\eta_{L\bar{Y}}\eta_{\bar{Y}(W/P)}}{\eta_{MY}}(0.75), \qquad (16')$$

with the first term as already discussed in section 3.2 and with a normal density for $\eta_{L\bar{Y}}\eta_{\bar{Y}(W/P)}$ centred at -1.7 with a standard error of 0.7. The resulting densities for $\eta_{L(W/P)}|_{B_e=0}$ are given in fig. 14.4, using the information from published econometric models; and in fig. 14.5, using the information from SERENA.

These two densities are similar in shape – being both unimodal and moderately skewed – but their moments are not equal. On the basis of the published models, we have in fig. 14.4 an expected value of -1.12 and a standard deviation of 0.53. On the basis of SERENA, we have in fig. 14.5 an expected value of -1.82 and a standard deviation of 0.8. The difference in expectations is due in part to different densities for $\eta_{Y(W/P)}|_{\bar{Y}}$, as already revealed by figs. 14.2 and 14.3, and in part to different densities for η_{MY} in the denominators. The expectation of η_{MY} is 1.55 in the case of fig. 14.4, but 1.24 in the case of fig. 14.5. We regard the latter figure as more reasonable.[20]

For this reason, and because we regard the export equations in SERENA as more satisfactory on theoretical grounds (specification) as well as empirical grounds (sample period and estimation method), we do not average the densities in figs. 14.4 and 14.5. We use instead the density of fig. 14.5 to estimate the medium-run elasticity of employment with respect to real wages. That density implies an elasticity greater than unity (in absolute value) with probability 0.87.[21]

---

[20] Import equations estimated for EEC countries with annual data for the period 1953–1976 yield estimates of η_{MY} ranging from -1.33 to -1.81, with very small standard errors; and estimates for $\eta_{M(W/P)}$ and $\eta_{M\bar{Y}}$ which are generally insignificant or unreasonable. But income elasticities probably reflect the positive trend in the share of international trade in economic activities. Conditionally on estimates of η_{MY} adjusted downwards by 0.3 or so, the estimates of the other coefficients become much more reasonable. A value of η_{MY} close to unity would make sense in the case of Belgium.

[21] The corresponding probability in fig. 14.4 is 0.57. If the expectation of η_{MY} were lowered from 1.55 to 1.24, that probability would become 0.7.

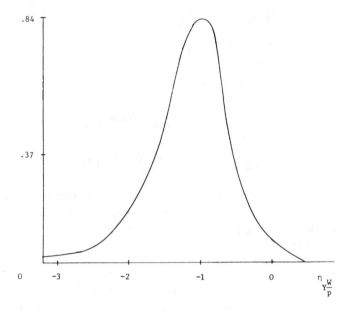

Exp = -1.1230   Var = .27454

Deciles
0.1000   0.2000   0.3000   0.4000   0.5000   0.6000   0.7000   0.8000   0.9000
-1.7834 -1.5150 -1.3411 -1.2015 -1.0775 -0.9587 -0.8361 -0.6973 -0.5106

Fig. 14.4.   Medium-run estimates from macro-models.

The results of our empirical analysis, crude as it may be, are summarised in fig. 14.6, which reproduces the densities of figs. 14.3 and 14.5 drawn to the same scale. This figure is the starting point for our policy discussion in Section 5. In order to avoid giving a spurious impression of accuracy, we do refer in Section 5 to a short-run elasticity like -0.2 and to a medium-run elasticity like -2. The reader is referred to fig. 14.6 for drawing his own sharper conclusions.

4.   Exchange rate adjustments

4.1.   Formula

Without attempting to treat the subject as extensively as it deserves, we may apply the methodology of Section 2 to evaluate the effects on

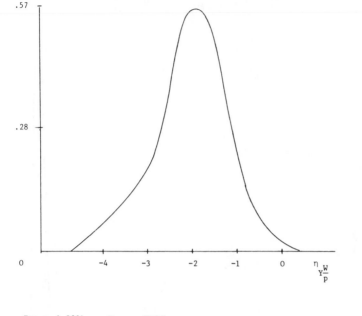

Exp = -1.8221   Var = .63052

Deciles

0.1000	0.2000	0.3000	0.4000	0.5000	0.6000	0.7000	0.8000	0.9000
-2.8210	-2.3968	-2.1270	-1.9152	-1.7298	-1.5547	-1.3769	-1.1793	-0.9202

Fig. 14.5.   Medium-run estimates from SERENA.

employment of exchange rate adjustments. We shall go quickly through the derivation, introduce some estimates borrowed from two recent Belgian studies, and conclude with a few comments.

We use formula (8) with $\theta = e$. In order to capitalize on our work in section 3 and because the published studies deal with η_{Ce} and η_{Pe}, but not directly with η_{P_xe}, we shall work through η_{XC} and η_{MP}. To that end, we note from eq. (4) that $\eta_{P_xe} = 1 + \eta_{P_xC}(-1 + \eta_{Ce})$, and use the following relationships:

$$\frac{\partial X}{\partial e} = \frac{\partial X}{\partial C}\left(\frac{\partial C}{\partial e} - \frac{C}{e}\right), \qquad \frac{\partial M}{\partial e} = \frac{\partial M}{\partial P}\left(\frac{\partial P}{\partial e} - \frac{P}{e}\right). \tag{17}$$

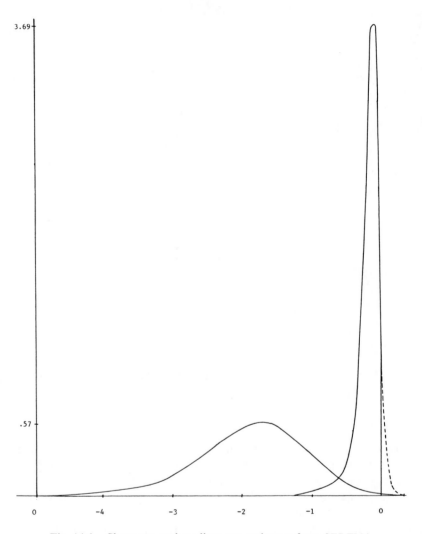

Fig. 14.6. Short-run and medium-run estimates from SERENA.

Consequently,

$$
\frac{\partial B_e}{\partial e} = -\frac{P_x X}{e^2} + \frac{X}{e}\frac{\partial P_x}{\partial e} + \left(\frac{P_x}{e} - P_e\frac{\partial M}{\partial X}\right)\frac{\partial X}{\partial C}
$$

$$
\times \left(-\frac{C}{e} + \frac{\partial C}{\partial e}\right) - P_e\frac{\partial M}{\partial P}\left(-\frac{P}{e} + \frac{\partial P}{\partial e}\right)
$$

$$
= \frac{XP_x}{e^2}[-1 + \eta_{P_x e} + \eta_{XC}(-1 + \eta_{Ce})]
$$

$$
-\frac{P_e M}{e}[\eta_{MP}(-1 + \eta_{Pe}) + \eta_{MX}\eta_{XC}(-1 + \eta_{Ce})]
$$

$$
= \frac{XP_x}{e^2}(\eta_{P_x C} + \eta_{XC})(-1 + \eta_{Ce})
$$

$$
-\frac{PeM}{e}[\eta_{MP}(-1 + \eta_{Pe}) + \eta_{MX}\eta_{XC}(-1 + \eta_{Ce})], \tag{18}
$$

$$
\eta_{Ye|B_e} = \left[\frac{XP_x}{MeP_e}(\eta_{P_x C} + \eta_{XC})(-1 + \eta_{Ce})\right.
$$

$$
\left. - \eta_{MP}(-1 + \eta_{Pe}) - \eta_{MX}\eta_{XC}(-1 + \eta_{Ce})\right]\bigg/\eta_{MY}, \tag{19}
$$

$$
\eta_{Le|B_e=0} = [(\eta_{P_x C} + \eta_{XC} - \eta_{MX}\eta_{XC})(-1 + \eta_{Ce})
$$

$$
- \eta_{MP}(-1 + \eta_{Pe})]\eta_{LY}/\eta_{MY}. \tag{20}
$$

4.2. Numerical evaluation

In a recent publication, the Banque Nationale de Belgique (1978) has used input–output matrices to study the impact of a devaluation on domestic prices P and on costs in export industries C. Both short-run (1 year) and medium-run (3 years) elasticities are reported, first under the assumption that wages only are indexed, next under the assumption that all costs are indexed (remain constant in real terms). The results are summarised in table 14.3, rows 1 and 2. It would seem most natural to assume that non-wage costs do not adjust in the short run, but do so in the medium run. The first and fourth columns of table 14.3 would thus seem most significant. Still, we do the computation for each column, using the figures collected in section 3, with η_{LY} equal to 0.3 in the '1 year' calculations and to 0.9 in the '3 years' calculations.

Table 14.3

	Banque Nationale de Belgique				De Grauwe–Holvoet	
	Only wages indexed		All costs indexed			
	1 year	3 years	1 year	3 years		
η_{Pe}	0.52	0.56	0.74	1.11	0.64	
η_{Ce}	0.64	0.66	0.73	0.88	0.80	
η_{LY}	0.3	0.9	0.3	0.9	0.3	0.9
$\eta_{Le}\vert_{B_e=0}$[a]	0.12	0.33	0.08	0.03	0.08	0.24

[a]Computed by (20′).

In an independent publication, De Grauwe and Holvoet (1978), using the so-called Scandinavian model, estimate η_{Pe} and η_{Ce} for EEC-countries. Their results appear in column 5, for the case where wages are indexed. It is assumed that export prices in 'dollars' do not change and that cost increases in the sheltered sector are passed on to domestic prices. Using the point estimates from SERENA, our evaluation of (20) is

$$\eta_{Le}\vert_{B_e=0} \simeq [-0.92(-1 + \eta_{Ce}) - 0.56(-1 + \eta_{Pe})]\frac{\eta_{LY}}{1.53}. \qquad (20')$$

The results are given in row 4 of table 14.3.

4.3. Comments

The figures in the first two rows of table 14.3 are not all equally plausible, and some of them are difficult to fit into a consistent overall picture. We do not mean to endorse them uniformly. But they cover a broad range of hypotheses, and the calculations uniformly suggest a rather limited impact of a devaluation on employment.

With Belgian exporters behaving largely as price-takers, a devaluation would hardly stimulate employment in the short run, where the elasticity of employment to output is low. With Belgian wages fully indexed, a devaluation would not stimulate employment appreciably in the long run, where domestic prices and costs progressively adjust and restore the previous conditions of international competitiveness.

Of course, a short-run elasticity of employment with respect to the exchange rate equal to 0.12 is not really negligible, and some might suggest that a 30% devaluation would be justified if it did result in a 4% increase in employment. But there is room for argument here. Important elements are neglected – like the elusive effects of a devaluation on the non-trade items in the balance of payments or on capacity adjustments; and the distributive aspects of a sharp rise in prices cannot be ignored.

The purpose of the exercise in this section is not to claim that the present exchange rate, or exchange rate policy, of Belgium are optimal. It is rather to suggest that the analysis of Sections 2 and 3, under a fixed (managed) exchange rate, is not grossly misleading, in the short run as well as in the long run.

5. Policy Implications

5.1. Summary of findings

As announced in Section 1.4, 'the conclusions from our empirical investigation are first that estimates of the trade-off between real wages and employment in Belgium are subject to considerable imprecision; second that the short-run elasticity of employment with respect to real wages keeping capacity constant is probably quite small (like -0.2), and definitely less than unity in absolute value; third that the corresponding medium-run elasticity taking into account capacity adjustments is probably sizeable (like -2), and definitely larger than unity in absolute value; and fourth that exchange rate adjustments might not make too much difference, in either the short or the medium run'. Also, it is worth emphasising that the capacity adjustments affecting employment take the form of accelerated scrapping. The simulations by Kuipers and Bosch reveal that the effects of new investment are less sizeable, in addition to being less immediate; of course, given enough time, they become dominant.

These findings are not surprising, considering on the one hand that labour has become a semi-fixed factor of production; on the other hand that an international redistribution of employment is under way. For policy purposes, our results provide, in spite of their imprecision, unequivocal answers to several questions of immediate interest to decision-makers, including labour unions.

The short-run inelasticity means that general wage policies (for instance general rebates on employer contributions to social security) are unlikely to provide an effective stimulus to employment in the short run. Measures aimed at an immediate impact must be sought in different directions – like selective wage policies or work-sharing schemes, about which more below. But the medium-run elasticity means that such measures should be designed in a way that carefully avoids increases in wage costs – for otherwise the medium-run effects could become adverse. Instead, measures promoting simultaneously work sharing and wage restraint over time could provide a much needed stimulus to employment in the short as well as the medium run.

5.2. Wages and union policies

Looking at these problems from the viewpoint of labour unions, the question of central interest is whether the elasticity of employment with respect to real wages is greater or smaller than unity, in absolute value. This question is of central interest because total real labour income is equal to $(W/P)L$, and

$$\frac{\mathrm{d}(W/P)L}{\mathrm{d}(W/P)} = L + \frac{W}{P}\frac{\mathrm{d}L}{\mathrm{d}(W/P)} = L(1 + \eta_{L(W/P)}). \tag{21}$$

So long as $\eta_{L(W/P)} > -1$ *(or* $|\eta_{L(W/P)}| < 1$), *the unions have an obvious motivation to press for higher real wages, even in full awareness of a negative impact on employment. The motivation is particularly strong if the reduction in employment is distributed more or less evenly through a reduction of working hours* instead of being concentrated on a smaller number of totally unemployed workers; for in this way there are no victims, and everybody enjoys additional leisure. Our findings accordingly suggest that *the unions' demand of a shorter working week without pay cut is entirely rational on short-run considerations.* Long-run considerations tell a different story, however, in which the numerical magnitude of the wage elasticity of employment plays a role.

Indeed, pursuing our line of analysis one step further, we may bring out the first-order condition for an *optimal real wage and working week, taking the utility of leisure into account.* Using the symbol L to denote total labour demand in man hours and N to denote the working population, here assumed given, we write $h = L/N$ for the amount of labour (hours) performed by one worker and $r = (W/P)(L/N)$ for the corresponding real labour income. Conceptually, the choice of a working week is a collective choice, to which public-goods theory is applicable – see Weddepohl (1979). It is still of some interest to consider the solution that would emerge, taking $\eta_{L(W/P)}$ into account, if all workers had the same utility function $u(r, h)$ with arguments real income r and hours worked h. In that case,[22]

$$u(r, h) = u\left(\frac{W}{P}\frac{L}{N}, \frac{L}{N}\right), \quad \frac{du}{d(W/P)} = \frac{\partial u}{\partial r} \cdot \left(\frac{L}{N} + \frac{W}{PN}\frac{\partial L}{\partial(W/P)}\right) + \frac{\partial u}{\partial h}\left(\frac{1}{N}\frac{\partial L}{\partial(W/P)}\right),$$
(22)

$$\frac{du}{d(W/P)} \lessgtr 0 \quad \text{as} \quad -\frac{\partial u/\partial h}{\partial u/\partial r} = \frac{dr}{dh}\bigg|_u \lessgtr \frac{W}{P}(1 + \eta_{(W/P)\cdot L}).$$
(23)

This is of course a familiar monopolistic solution[23] which requires $|\eta_{L(W/P)}| > 1$ at an optimum. If $\eta_{L(W/P)}|_{B_e} \simeq -2$, then (23) requires $dr/dh|_u \simeq \frac{1}{2}(W/P)$; and if $\eta_{L(W/P)} \simeq -1.5$, then (23) requires $dr/dh|_u \simeq \frac{1}{3}(W/P)$; that is, a real wage equal respectively to two or three times the marginal rate of substitution between leisure and income.

It is thus conceivable for labour to choose deliberately a combination of relatively high real wages and relatively low (but equally distributed) employment, at a solution of (23). For moderate values of $\eta_{L(W/P)}$, such a solution makes sense.[24] But its monopolistic nature also implies that each *individual* would prefer to work more hours at the going wage rate, to

---

[22] Formula (23) remains valid if one takes into account unemployment in an attempt to define a real wage, a working week *and an implied unemployment rate* which are *simultaneously optimal* from labour's viewpoint. If unemployment compensation is equal to U and treated as exogenously given, then a worker's utility is equal to $u((W/P)h, h)$ if employed but to $u(U, 0)$ if unemployed. The number of employed workers is $(1/h) L(W/P)$, not necessarily equal to the working population N. The implied unemployment rate is then $[1 - (1/Nh)L(W/P)]$. The expected utility of an 'anonymous' worker is given by

$$Eu = \frac{1}{Nh}L\left(\frac{W}{P}\right) \cdot u\left(\frac{W}{P}h, h\right) + \left[1 - \frac{1}{Nh}L\left(\frac{W}{P}\right)\right] \cdot u(U, 0).$$
(22')

Maximising this expression with respect to *both* W/P and h leads to first-order conditions which still imply

$$\frac{dr}{dh}\bigg|_u = \frac{W}{P}(1 + \eta_{(W/P)\cdot L})$$

at an interior solution. Whether or not unemployment compensation should be taken as given in this analysis raises further issues, that lie beyond the scope of the present paper. For a microeconomic analysis of a related issue, see Baily (1974) and the survey in Dreze (1979a).

[23] The 'public goods' aspect calls for replacing the marginal rate of substitution in (23) by an average over all workers, in the general case.

[24] As an empirical proposition, it seems more likely that union leaders underestimate the longer run elasticity of employment with respect to real wages. The imprecision of the long-run estimate may also play a role here – although expected utility theory provides a justification for using the expected value of $L(W/P)$ in (22'), hence the expected value of $\eta_{L(W/P)}$ in (23).

work overtime, to engage in moonlighting, etc. The difficulties of policing a monopolistic solution, which is rational for a syndicate but not for its individual members, are well known and confirmed by casual empiricism in our context.

5.3. Distributive aspects

When labour unions set wages at a level implying monopolistic advantages, who is the monopolist exploiting? Our approach provides a suitable vehicle for analytical discussion of that issue, but a limited basis for empirical purposes. (There comes indeed a point where there is no satisfactory substitute for numerical simulation of a complete model.)

Starting from eqs. (13)–(14) we may note the following:

(i) Labour can enforce arbitrary levels of *real* wages only to the extent that $\eta_{PW} < 1$. As η_{PW} tends to 1, the adjustments in output implied by changes in real wages tend to infinity. A feature of the Belgian economy is that η_{PW} is relatively small – like one third. This reflects the large ratio of imports to GNP (0.55 in 1976). In less open economies, η_{PW} is closer to one. If all firms were setting prices in a fixed proportion to costs (proportional mark-up), then η_{PW} would differ from unity only to the extent that the prices of imported or non-produced goods (land a.s.o.) are inelastic to domestic wages and prices.

(ii) An increase in wages has both real effects and distributive effects; the real effects recognized here concern output, and labour inputs; a wage increase brings about a reduction of output, which is a real social loss; this loss is partly offset by a reduction in labour inputs, which is a gain to the extent that it means additional desired leisure shared by all, but could be a real loss if it meant involuntary unemployment for some with unchanged hours for the others.

(iii) When $|\eta_{L(W/P)}| < 1$, an increase in real wages entails an increase in real labour income. The real income to other sectors must then fall by the sum of the loss of output and the gain to labour. How this fall is distributed over the other sectors depends upon the extent to which firms transfer the burden to buyers of goods and services, through price increases. When $\eta_{PW} < 1$, the transfer is incomplete and the fall in profits absorbs part of labour's gain in addition to the loss of output.

(iv) To whom is part of the burden transferred through higher prices? Clearly not back to labour, since wages are by assumption fully indexed. Rather, to earners of relatively fixed incomes (mostly from property or self-employment), and to the rest of the world (in the form of improved terms of trade). In the case of Belgium, the part of the burden shifted to the rest of the world is small.

(v) When $|\eta_{L(W/P)}| > 1$, an increase in real wages entails a fall in real labour income, which absorbs part of the loss of output. The real income to other sectors must then fall by the difference between the loss of output and the loss to labour. (The rest of the reasoning is unchanged.)

Empirical assessment of these real and distributive effects requires a more elaborate model of price and income formation than has been introduced here. Still, for illustrative purposes, we have computed a crude estimate, on the following premises for the short run:

$$\eta_{PW} = 0.33, \qquad \eta_{Y(W/P)} = -0.6, \qquad \eta_{L(W/P)} = -0.2, \qquad \eta_{P_xW} = 0.2,$$

and

$$X/Y = M/Y = 0.5, \qquad WL/PY = 0.75.$$

A 10% autonomous increase in real wages, $\Delta(W/P) = 10\% \, (W/P)$, would then have the following implications, when evaluated marginally.[25]

Increase in
  nominal wages:

$$\frac{1}{W}\Delta W = \frac{10\%}{1 - \eta_{PW}} = 15\%,$$

  prices:

$$\frac{1}{P}\Delta P = \eta_{PW} \times 15\% = 5\%,$$

  export prices:

$$\frac{1}{P_x}\Delta P_x = \eta_{P_xW} \times 15\% = 3\%,$$

  import prices:

$$\frac{1}{P_m}\Delta P_m = 0,$$

price of domestic product sold domestically:

$$\frac{1}{P_h}\Delta P_h = \left(\frac{1}{P}\Delta P - \frac{M}{Y}\frac{1}{P_m}\Delta P_m\right) \bigg/ \left(1 - \frac{M}{Y}\right) = \frac{5\%}{0.5} = 10\%,$$

[25] That is, the calculations hold strictly for arbitrarily small wage increases; they are presented in terms of a finite change for case of interpretation.

price of value added:

$$\frac{1}{P_Y} P_Y = \frac{X}{Y} \frac{1}{P_x} \Delta P_x + \left(1 - \frac{X}{Y}\right) \frac{1}{P_h} \Delta P_h$$
$$= 0.5 \times 3\% + 0.5 \times 10\% = 6.5\%.$$

Change in
output:

$$\frac{1}{Y} \Delta Y = \eta_{Y(W/P)} \times 10\% = -6\%,$$

employment:

$$\frac{1}{L} \Delta L = \eta_{L(W/P)} \times 10\% = -2\%,$$

nominal domestic income:

$$\frac{1}{P_Y Y} \Delta P_Y Y = \frac{1}{P_Y} \Delta P_y + \frac{1}{Y} \Delta Y = 6.5\% - 6\% = +0.5\%,$$

real domestic income:

$$\frac{P}{P_Y Y} \Delta \frac{P_Y Y}{P} = \frac{1}{P_Y Y} \Delta P_Y Y - \frac{1}{P} \Delta P = 0.5\% - 5\% = -4.5\%.$$

Net income effects (expressed in percentage of national income before the wage increase) *on*

domestic labour income:

$$\frac{1}{Y} \Delta L \frac{W}{P} = \frac{L(W/P)}{Y} \left(\frac{1}{L} \Delta L + \frac{P}{W} \Delta \frac{W}{P}\right) = +6\%,$$

domestic non-labour income:

$$\frac{1}{Y} \left(\Delta \frac{P_Y Y - LW}{P}\right) = -4.5\% - 6\% = -10.5\%,$$

rest of the world:

$$\frac{1}{Y} \left(\Delta Y - \Delta \frac{P_Y Y}{P}\right) = -6\% + 4.5\% = -1.5\%.$$

In the longer run, assuming $\eta_{Y(W/P)} = \eta_{L(W/P)} = -2$, these implications become

$$\frac{1}{Y}\Delta Y = \frac{1}{L}\Delta L = -20\%,$$

$$\frac{1}{P_Y Y}\Delta P_Y Y = 6.5\% - 20\% = -13.5\%,$$

$$\frac{P}{P_Y Y}\Delta\frac{P_Y Y}{P} = -13.5\% - 5\% = -18.5\%,$$

$$\frac{1}{Y}\Delta L\frac{W}{P} = 0.75(-20\% + 10\%) = -7.5\%,$$

$$\frac{1}{Y}\Delta\frac{P_Y Y - LW}{P} = -18.5\% + 7.5\% = -11\%,$$

$$\frac{1}{Y}\left(\Delta Y - \Delta\frac{P_Y Y}{P}\right) = -20\% + 18.5\% = -1.5\%.$$

The overall picture is thus the following. In both the short and the long run, a wage increase causes a fall in output and real income, of which only a minor part is shifted to the rest of the world (through export prices). In the short run, labour gains, thanks to higher real wages and inelastic employment. Domestic non-labour incomes fall by the *sum* of the loss in real national income and the gain to labour; this sum is roughly equal to 1.75 times labour's gain.

In the longer run, the losses to non-labour income and to the rest of the world are unchanged. But the larger fall in real income is absorbed by labour, whose real income falls markedly. Yet, to the extent that the decline in employment reflects additional leisure, the utility level of workers falls less sharply than their measured real income, and may even rise somewhat.[26]

5.4. Work-sharing through shorter hours

The foregoing discussion brings out the relevance of our empirical findings for the current debate about work-sharing through shorter hours. *First*, it is not surprising that labour unions should press for shorter

---

[26] In our illustrative calculations, workers' utility would rise if $dr/dh|_u = \frac{1}{2}(W, P)$, but not if $dr/dh|_u = \frac{1}{3}(W/P)$.

hours, as part of a strategy designed to maximize workers' welfare at non-competitive wages. For a given level of aggregate labour input, less unemployment through shorter hours entails definite distributive advantages.

This distributive proposition has fairly general validity. If the conditions of world demand and of domestic supply at the prevailing wages entail less than full employment, work-sharing through shorter hours deserves serious consideration. Indeed, we have seen that the scope for demand management is limited by the external balance constraint, whereas wage cuts would have little short-run impact.

Second, it is understandable that unions should press for shorter hours at unchanged take-home pay. Indeed, if the wage rate exceeds the marginal rate of substitution between income and leisure, shorter hours at unchanged hourly wages entail a loss of utility for employed workers – whereas shorter hours at unchanged take-home pay entail a definite gain of utility.

Third, it is not surprising to find employers strongly opposed to shorter hours at unchanged take-home pay, since this entails a commensurate increase in hourly wage costs. Wage increases lead to a substantial fall in domestic non-labour incomes (including profits) in the short run as well as in the longer run.

Fourth, shorter hours at unchanged take-home pay could have a positive impact on employment in the short run, but would have a negative longer run impact, unless accompanied by some form of cost absorption. Indeed, if employment were determined simply as $N = (1/h)L(W/P)$, and take-home pay were given as $\bar{r} = (W/P)h$, then

$$N = \frac{1}{h}L\left(\frac{\bar{r}}{h}\right),$$

$$\frac{dN}{dh} = \frac{-L}{h^2} + \frac{1}{h}\frac{dL}{d(W/P)}\left(\frac{-\bar{r}}{h^2}\right)$$

$$= \frac{-L}{h^2}\left(1 + \frac{\bar{r}}{Lh}\frac{dL}{d(W/P)}\right) = \frac{-L}{h^2}(1 + \eta_{L(W/P)}), \tag{24}$$

$$\eta_{Nh} = -(1 + \eta_{L(W/P)}) \gtreqless 0 \quad \text{as} \quad |\eta_{L(W/P)}| \gtreqless 1. \tag{25}$$

Thus, $\eta_{Nh} < 0$ in the short run but $\eta_{Nh} > 0$ in the medium or long run, if our empirical analysis is correct.[27]

[27] Remember that shorter hours amount to reducing h; the effect on N has a sign opposite to that of η_{Nh}.

Actually, the impact of shorter hours on employment is apt to be still more unfavourable, to the extent that employment is not simply determined as $(1/h)L(W/P)$. Thus shorter hours could be absorbed without new hirings by those firms which currently hoard labour. And a gradual reduction in hours per week would in many cases accelerate capital–labour substitution instead of stimulating employment. Empirical evidence bearing on this issue is deceptively meagre, and further research is needed. But the qualitative conclusions are not apt to change. In the short run, $\eta_{L(W/P)}$ is sufficiently small, so that η_{Nh} would remain negative even if new hirings amount only to one third or even less of the reduction in labour inputs through shorter hours. In the longer run, our conclusion would be strengthened.

In summary, then, shorter hours make sense, if and only if they permit some form of cost absorption, like productivity gains, wage restraint or selective subsidies.

Productivity gains are possible when shorter hours for individual workers permit a more intensive use of capital through additional shifts. The clearest example consists in operating a plant 6 days per week instead of 5, with individuals working 4 days per week instead of 5; the number of employees can then be increased by 50% without additional investment.[28] This means a reduction in the capital–output ratio and a substitution of labour for capital. But the substitution is realised either through increased output (if there is a commensurate demand), or through concentration of production in the more efficient plants (which are apt to be the less labour intensive), or through postponement of new investments. These conditions are restrictive, and we do not know how frequently they would be satisfied.

Wage restraint may take the form of constant take-home pay (in real terms) and more leisure, as a substitute for rising take-home pay. If the shorter work schedule can be made attractive to workers, such restraint is more likely to be accepted. But it is still unlikely to emerge spontaneously, so long as the wage rate exceeds the marginal rate of substitution between income and leisure. And the cost savings arising from a break in the trend of real wages accrue only progressively over time; whereas the effectiveness of some schemes may require that major reductions in individual working hours (like 10%) be implemented at once.

Therefore, selective subsidies covering part of the incremental costs associated with shorter hours at constant take-home pay might be needed to anticipate future cost savings and to provide adequate motivation for

[28]Further examples are given in Drèze (1979c).

the needed reorganisations. Such subsidies should naturally be linked to new hirings and conditioned to wage restraint. They should be temporary, and leave incentives for productivity gains. They could hopefully be recovered over time through the savings resulting for the treasury from a higher level of employment.[29]

5.5. Capacity adjustments and selective wage subsidies

The observation that capacity adjustments affect employment first and foremost through accelerated scrapping has policy implications too.

Faced with the prospect of capacity scrapping, union leaders frequently urge for (and elicit) public support of marginally unprofitable activities (for instance through rebates on employers' contributions to social security), on the grounds of a smaller final cost to the treasury.[30] This argument is correct on short-run considerations: In situations of unemployment, the private and social costs of labour differ, and corrective measures should be attempted. In the long run, this practice carries the dangers of reducing labour mobility, and of being anticipated by employers and unions, who could regard public support as a substitute for productive efficiency and wage restraint. Also, it should be judged against the alternative of investment subsidies, which have less impact on employment in the short run, but hold more long-run promise.

Appendix: Foreign trade equations from SERENA

The foreign trade sector consists of three structural equations explaining M_t, P_{xt} and X_t respectively. This system is treated as block-recursive between M_t (first block) and P_{xt}, X_t (second block). The estimates pertain to the manufacturing sector, which accounts for 80% of Belgium's foreign trade.

---

[29] A comprehensive program, calling for shorter hours, wage restraint, new hirings and rebates on employers' contributions to social security, was proposed by the Belgian Government in the Spring of 1979, as a basis for nationwide collective bargaining. The program received cautious support from some unions but was rejected by other unions and by the employers' organisations. Eventually, a more limited program, including selective subsidies to new hirings under work-sharing schemes, was started in the fall of 1979.

[30] Such is the case, at times of severe unemployment, when the required support is less than unemployment compensation plus total contributions to social security plus income taxes – or approximately U.S.$10,000 per wage-earner per year in Belgium today.

(i) Imports of manufactured goods

$$\ln M_t = \delta_0 + \delta_1 \ln Y_t^0 + \delta_2 \ln \frac{P_{et}}{C_t} + \delta_3 \ln \frac{\overline{Y}_t}{Y_t} + v_t, \tag{A.1}$$

where Y_t^0 is a weighted average of government expenditures on goods and services, consumption, investment, intermediate deliveries and inventory variations.

Estimation by ordinary least squares from annual data, 1966–1976, yields

$$\ln M_t = -0.45 + 1.24 \ln Y_t^0 - 0.56 \ln \frac{P_{et}}{C_t} - 0.29 \ln \frac{\overline{Y}_t}{Y_t}. \tag{A.2}$$
$$\quad\ (0.11)\ \ (0.07) \qquad\quad (0.19) \qquad\quad (0.14)$$

The elasticity of imports with respect to domestic demand has been estimated by $\delta_1 - \delta_3 = 1.53$ in the short run ($\overline{Y}$ given) and by $\delta_1 = 1.24$ in the longer run ($\overline{Y}/Y$ given). As indicated in the text, the variance and covariances from (A.2) have been multiplied by four for the purpose of evaluating the posterior density of η_{YW} in figs. 14.3 and 14.5.

(ii) Exports of manufactured goods

$$\ln P_{xt} = (1 - \alpha)\ln P_{et} + \alpha \ln C_t + u_{1t}, \tag{A.3}$$

$$\ln X_t = \beta_0 + \beta_1 \Delta \ln E_t$$
$$\quad + \alpha \left[\eta_1 \ln E_t + \eta_2 \ln \frac{P_{xt}}{P_{et}} + \eta_3 \ln \frac{P_{xt-1}}{P_{et-1}} \right]$$
$$\quad + (1 - \alpha) \left[\ln \overline{Y}_t + \gamma \ln \frac{P_{xt-1}}{C_{t-1}} \right] + u_{2t} \tag{A.4}$$
$$\equiv \beta_0 + \beta_1 \Delta \ln E_t + \beta_2 \ln E_t + \beta_3 \ln \frac{P_{xt}}{P_{et}} + \beta_4 \ln \frac{P_{xt-1}}{P_{et-1}}$$
$$\quad + (1 - \alpha)\ln \overline{Y}_t + \beta_5 \ln \frac{P_{xt-1}}{C_{t-1}} + u_{2t}.$$

Full information maximum likelihood estimation of this simultaneous system of 2 equations from annual data, 1966–1976, yields

$$\ln P_{xt} = 0.77 \ln P_{et} + 0.22 \ln C_t, \tag{A.5}$$
$$\qquad\ (0.09)$$

$$\ln X_t = -1.6 + 0.7\,\Delta \ln E_t + 0.64 \ln E_t - 3.01 \ln \frac{P_{xt}}{P_{et}}$$

$$\ \ (0.18)\quad\ \ (0.16)\qquad\ (0.07)\qquad (0.44)$$

$$\ \ [0.22]\quad\ \ [0.29]\qquad\ [0.11]\qquad [2.71]$$

$$-2.12 \ln \frac{P_{xt-1}}{P_{et-1}} + 0.77 \ln \bar{Y}_t + 1.03 \ln \frac{P_{xt-1}}{C_{t-1}}. \tag{A.6}$$

$$(0.60)\qquad\qquad (0.10)\qquad\ \ (0.42)$$

$$[1.13]\qquad\qquad\qquad\quad\ \ [0.80]$$

The numbers in parentheses are *asymptotic* standard errors, which are definitely unreliable in our small sample case. The numbers in square brackets are posterior standard deviations computed by Bauwens (1979), conditionally on α, in his Bayesian analysis with a non-informative prior. These exact finite sample results confirm the strong downward bias of the asymptotic formulae.

The coefficients of the export equations are related to $\eta_{\Xi W}$ of formula (13″) by

$$\eta_{\Xi W} = \tfrac{1}{3}\{\alpha + 0.6[\alpha(\beta_3 + \beta_4) - (1 - \alpha)\beta_5]\}, \tag{A.7}$$

when $\eta_{CW} = \tfrac{1}{3}$.

Proceeding from a non-informative prior density, the posterior joint density for the coefficients α and $\beta = (\beta_0, \beta_1, \dots, \beta_5)$, evaluated marginally with respect to the covariance matrix of the disturbances, may be written as

$$f(\beta|\alpha, \text{data}) \cdot f(\alpha|\text{data}), \tag{A.8}$$

with $f(\beta|\alpha, \text{data})$ taking the form of a multivariate t density with expectation $\bar{\beta}_\alpha$, covariance matrix V_α and $\nu = 11$ degrees of freedom[31] – say $f_t(\beta|\bar{\beta}_\alpha, V_\alpha, \nu)$. We may write from (A.7)

$$\eta_{\Xi W} = \alpha/3 + C'_\alpha\beta, \qquad C'_\alpha = (0,\, 0,\, 0,\, 0.2\alpha,\, 0.2\alpha,\, -0.2(1 - \alpha)), \tag{A.7'}$$

so that

$$f(\eta_{\Xi W}|\alpha, \text{data}) = f_t(\eta_{\Xi W}|\alpha/3 + C'_\alpha\bar{\beta}_\alpha, C'_\alpha V_\alpha C_\alpha, \nu). \tag{A.8}$$

---

[31] There is some arbitrariness in the choice of the 'degress of freedom' parameter in the (non-informative) prior density. We have experimented with alternative values. They only affect the posterior variances, which are inflated anyhow, as indicated below.

Integrating (A.8) with respect to the posterior density $f(\alpha|\text{data})$ by numerical methods yields the density in fig. 14.7, with expected value -0.31 and standard deviation 0.11. This density has been approximated by the normal density with that same mean and twice that standard deviation for the purpose of evaluating the posterior density of η_{YW} in figs. 14.3 and 14.5.

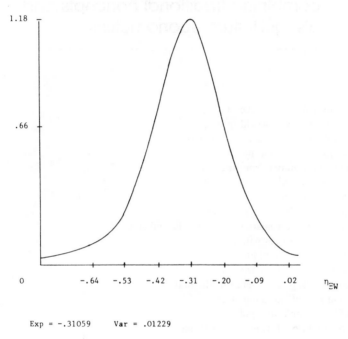

Exp = −.31059   Var = .01229

Fig. 14.7.   Estimate of $\eta_{\Xi W}$ from SERENA.

15 A discussion of Belgian unemployment, combining traditional concepts and disequilibrium econometrics*

The sorest ill that Heaven hath
Sent on this lower world in wrath—
Unemployment (to call it by its name)
Waged war on economics,
Sparing no country from the plague.
They died not all, but all were sick.
No jobs were left;
So hope and therefore joy were dead.
Richard the Lion-hearted council held and said:
'Let us all turn eyes within
And ferret out the hidden sin.'
Himself let no one spare nor flatter,
But make clean conscience in the matter.
'I Yield myself', concluded he;
'And yet I think, in equity,
Each should confess his sins with me.'
Belgians, confessing in their turn,
Thus spoke in tones of deep concern:
'We have little to say
That you do not know anyway.
Without claiming to be exhaustive
We put a few facts in perspective.
Then turn to summarising

* *Economica*, 53 (1986), S89–S119. With Henri Sneessens. We wish to acknowledge gratefully the collaboration of Robert Leroy and Serge Wibaut in collecting and organising data, of Fati Mehta in estimating the model of Section 4, and of Yves Leruth in preparing auxiliary computations. Responsibility for all the views expressed or omitted here is our own. We also acknowledge the financial support of the Belgian Government under Projet d'Action Concertée, no. 80/85-12.

Scanty results on manufacturing.
Next we illustrate a methodology
That was pioneered in our country.
By way of conclusions
We share our interrogations.'

1. Factual perspectives

With a GDP of less than $100 billion and exports of more than $60 billion, Belgium comes perhaps closer than any other country to being a 'small open economy'. Consequently, trends in world trade and export performance have a major impact on domestic activity, whereas the impact of domestic fiscal policy is damped by import leakages. Table 15.1 presents a few figures confirming these observations.

The rise in Belgian unemployment since 1974 has been appalling. Figure 15.1 compares the unemployment rate in Belgium with that of the European Community (EC9) since 1960. It displays clearly the sharper take-off of Belgian unemployment since 1974.

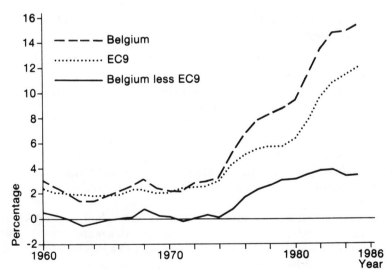

Fig. 15.1.   Unemployment rate, Belgium, 1960–84.

Table 15.1. *GDP, Belgium 1975–83, at 1980 prices*

	% of GDP, 1975	% change, 1975–80	% change, 1980–83	% change, 1975–83	% of GDP, 1983
Private consumption	63	17	−1	16	63
Public consumption	18	18	0	18	18
Gross fixed investment	22	9	−22	−15	16
Exports	47	48	7	58	63
Imports	48	50	−3	45	60
GDP	100	15	0	15	100
Public deficit	6	67	32	119	14

Source: OECD National Accounts (1984).

Additional facts about employment and unemployment over the period 1974–83 are collected in table 15.2. The salient features are as follows.

1. Male employment has gone down by 10 per cent while female employment has gone up by 3 per cent; the sharper increase in female unemployment is thus due to the increase in active population.
2. The increase in female employment is equal to the number of women in special employment programmes; otherwise, there are offsetting movements in public employment (+ 69,200) and private employment (− 71,000) of women.
3. The decline in private employment (15.3 per cent altogether) is concentrated (up to 88 per cent) in manufacturing, where the decline is staggering: 29.8 per cent!

The evolution of total employment (private and public) in five sectors is given in figure 15.2.

Another useful piece of information concerns hours worked and the evolution of labour inputs in man-hours. In the manufacturing sector, average hours went down by 11 per cent in 10 years (1973–83), so that labour inputs went down by 37.3 per cent.[1] Taking into account a 15 per cent increase in value added at constant prices, the apparent increase in gross hourly productivity is nearly 85 per cent. In services, average hours went down by 9 per cent and gross hourly productivity went up by 27 per cent.

That enormous apparent increase in gross hourly productivity in manufacturing accounts for much of the differential rise in Belgian unemployment; it is one of the main facts to be explained if anything is to be learned from the rise in Belgian unemployment.

[1] Indeed, 70.2 × 0.89 = 62.5. The figures in this paragraph come from Sonnet (1985).

Table 15.2. *Belgian population and employment, by sex and status, 1974–83*

	Men			Women			Total		
	1974 ('000)	1974–83 ('000)	(%)	1974 ('000)	1974–83 ('000)	(%)	1974 ('000)	1974–83 ('000)	(%)
(1) Population of working age (men: 15–64, women: 15–59)	3103.1	+225.9	+7.3	2827.6	+199.8	+7.3	5930.7	+425.7	+7.2
(2) Active population	2625.1	−45.9	−1.8	1354.2	+279.9	+20.7	3979.3	+233.0	+5.9
(3) Participation rates	84.6		−7.1	47.9		+6.1	67.1		−0.8
(4) Early retirements	0	+99.8		0	+26.4		0	+126.2	
(5) Unemployment	45.7	+207.1		51.2	+241.1		96.9	+448.2	
(6) Unemployment rates	1.7		+8.1	3.8		+14.1	2.4		+10.5
(7) Total employment	2579.4	−253.0	−9.8	1302.9	+38.9	+3.0	3882.3	−214.1	−5.5
(8) *of which:* special programmes	7.6	+35.4		1.4	+40.5		9.0	+75.9	
(9) Public servants	537.4	+57.9	+10.8	262.0	+109.7	+41.9	799.4	+167.6	+21.0
(10) Self-employed	405.8	−9.1	−2.2	228.5	+1.5	+0.7	634.3	−7.6	−1.2
(11) Wage-earners	1636.0	−301.6	−18.4	812.5	72.5	−8.9	2448.5	−374.1	−15.3
(12) *of which:* manufacturing	805.2	−213.7	−26.5	295.9	−114.8	−38.8	1101.1	−328.5	−29.8

Source: Official statistics and calculations at ECOS and IRES, Université Catholique de Louvain.

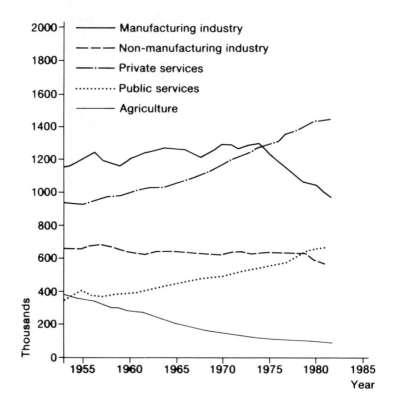

Fig. 15.2.   Belgian employment in five sectors, 1953–81.

A broader picture of the Belgian economy is given by figure 15.3, which presents time-series for the income share of labour, unemployment, budget deficits and balance of payments deficits. The striking (though not unexpected) aspect of these series is the concomitant break in trends in the early 1970s. At that time Belgium underwent a deep and swift transformation: the country, previously one of relatively stable prices and labour share, with low unemployment and low deficits, thereafter came to be characterized by significant inflation, including real wage inflation, high unemployment and sizeable deficits.

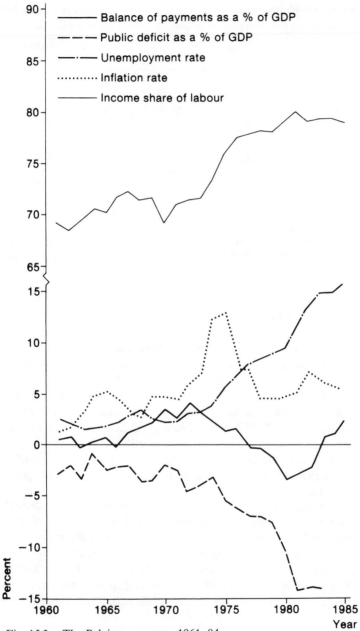

Fig. 15.3. The Belgian economy, 1961–84.

Table 15.3. *Growth rates of real wages and income shares of labour, 1971–80*

	Growth of real compensation per employee, total economy, 1971–80		Adjusted share of labour income total economy		
	Ave. rate	Cumulative percentage	1971	1980	1980–71
Belgium	∕ 4.6	57	70.9	79	8.1
Japan	4.2	51	73.4	80.6	7.2
France	4.1	49	70.9	75.7	4.8
Italy	3.4	40	80.7	81.7	1
EC9	**3.2**	**37**	**74.6**	**76.3**	**1.7**
W. Germany	3.1	36	73.2	73	−0.2
Netherlands	2.8	32	74.2	73.9	−0.3
UK	2.3	26	73.2	75.4	2.2
Denmark	1.4	15	79.4	79.4	0
USA	1.0	11	74.1	74.1	0

Source: European Economy (1984, Tables 23 and 24). The deflator of compensation per employee is the consumer price index.

The percentage change in real wages for the period 1971–80 amounts to 57 per cent for Belgium as against 37 per cent for the rest of the European Community (EC9). The third and fourth columns of table 15.3 give the income share of labour in 1971 and 1980. The picture emerging from the table is by no means clear-cut. There is a mild suggestion that real wages rose more rapidly in countries where the income share of labour was initially lower, and typically rose quickly enough there to bring about, by 1980, a labour share exceeding the average (with Italy and Denmark the more obvious exceptions). The more solid fact, in so far as Belgium is concerned, is the exceptionally high rate of increase of real wages in the 1970s – a fact that one would like to explain, and the consequences of which one would like to evaluate.

A similar picture of rapid transition from balanced growth to pronounced disequilibrium is conveyed by figure 15.4. This figure, which is discussed at greater length in Section 4, presents estimates of labour supply (*LS*), 'potential employment' (*LP* – defined as the employment corresponding to the desired utilization of productive capacities) and 'Keynesian labour demand' (*LK* – defined as the employment needed to meet effective demand for domestic output). Three distinct time periods stand out clearly on that figure: 1955–62, 1963–74 and 1975 onward. In the first subperiod, structural unemployment was progressively eliminated

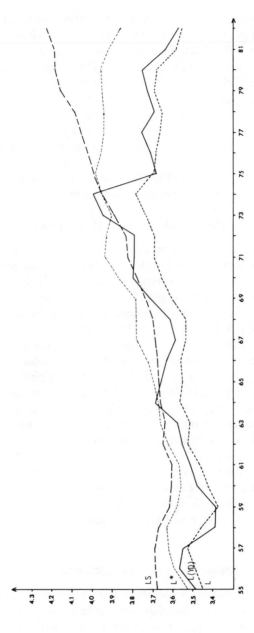

Fig. 15.4. Labour supply (*LS*), potential employment (*LP*), Keynesian labour demand (*LK*) and actual employment (*LT*), Belgium, 1955–82.

by industrialisation in Flanders – see Leroy (1962). The development of new industrial activities there had by 1963 led to a situation of near equilibrium ($LS \simeq LP \simeq LK$). That situation prevailed until 1974. The 'golden sixties' give an almost perfect picture of balanced growth: the three series move on parallel trends, with cyclical fluctuations superimposed on the demand series (LK). Since 1975, however, the three series diverge markedly: labour supply keeps growing (owing to the growth of female population and participation rates); potential employment stagnates until 1979 and then falls off (owing to the decline in investment), and Keynesian labour demand declines sharply in 1975 and again in 1981 (owing to insufficient effective demand). The behaviour of LP and LK is also influenced by labour-saving investment and technological progress (see below).

On the policy side, three points seem worth mentioning.

1. Ever since unemployment became a major issue in the mid-1970s, Belgium has actively developed a number of special programmes: early retirement, apprenticeships for the young, the fully subsidised hiring of unemployed persons in non-profit organisations, etc. Without these programmes, the unemployment rate would be another 5 percentage points higher (table 15.2, rows (4), (5) and (8)).

2. Until 1981, Belgium tried to maintain the stability of its exchange rate *vis-à-vis* the German mark and Dutch guilder; by 1981 a substantial current deficit had developed. In February 1982 the Belgian franc devalued by 8 per cent. This measure was accompanied by an incomes policy which has been continued until now. Whereas almost all wages and salaries had previously been fully indexed, the government has imposed real wage reductions of some 2 to 3 per cent per year since then.

3. Business investments have for many years benefited from interest rate subsidies. Over the past three years, tax advantages have been granted to individuals investing in stocks and to individuals or institutions subscribing new equity issues.

2.   Some tightrope exercises over manufacturing

In this section, we report briefly on three empirical studies of the Belgian manufacturing sector, which hopefully bear some relevance to the decline of employment there. Our reports are brief because these studies proceed from a very thin data base; their results are suggestive, but not conducive to precise quantitative conclusions. Accordingly, we simply quote a few relevant results, with a minimum of explanations.

d'Alcantara (1983) has estimated a seven-sector model of the Belgian economy, with a putty–clay vintage production model for each sector. There are four inputs (capital, labour, energy and materials). The model is estimated from 14 annual observations (1963–76). As of 1977, the estimated output elasticity of manufacturing labour demand was 2.5 times higher when computed for scrapping old equipment than when computed for new investment. In other words, when replacing old equipment by new at unchanged capacity, three out of every five workers concerned could be dispensed with. The loss of some 150,000 jobs in manufacturing from 1973 to 1977 is explained by d'Alcantara as the net outcome of 'destroying' 340,000 jobs by scrapping old equipment, while 'creating' 190,000 jobs through new investment (of which some 135,000 correspond to modernisation and some 55,000 correspond only to capacity expansion).

Lambert (1988) has estimated a streamlined model of the Belgian manufacturing sector, defined by aggregation of micro-markets in disequilibrium. On specific micro-markets, transactions correspond to the minimum of supply and demand. Assuming lognormality of the distribution over micro-markets of the ratio of supply to demand, one obtains an approximate expression for aggregate transactions as a *CES* function of aggregate supply and aggregate demand. The exponent of the *CES* function can be estimated from business survey data, namely from the proportion of firms reporting excess supply of goods and or excess demand for labour.

The model is estimated from 18 annual observations (1963–80). The estimation results permit a decomposition of the observed decline in manufacturing employment from 1974 to 1980 (namely, 23.5 per cent) into four components: the change in frictional unemployment (negligible), the change in demand (accounting for 4.5 out of 23.5 per cent), the change in the stock of capital (negligible), and the substitution of capital for labour induced by relative prices (accounting for 19 out of 23.5 per cent).

A related approach is followed by Gérard and Vanden Berghe (1984) in their analysis of manufacturing investment. These authors recognise that at any point in time some firms operate on competitive product markets and gear investment to a desired capital stock reflecting relative prices, whereas other firms operate on imperfectly competitive product markets and gear investment to a desired capital stock reflecting effective demand. An aggregation procedure comparable to that of Lambert (1988) leads again to an approximate expression for the desired stock of capital as a *CES* function of two expressions, one of which involves relative prices and the other effective demand. Estimates of the parameters of that expression imply estimates of the elasticity of desired capital with respect to relative prices (here, the ratio of the cost of capital to the price of output) and with respect to effective demand (here, actual output). These two elasticities vary over time. The former is positively related to the proportion of firms constrained by sales expectations; the latter, negatively related. Estimates derived from annual observations for the period 1956–82 (without reliance on business survey data) suggest a rapidly growing influence of effective demand on investment after 1974. Tentative as it may still be, that finding is worth keeping in mind when speculating about the determinants of investment.

When considering the share of exports in the final demand for Belgian manufactures, it is also important to treat exports endogenously, and to investigate the influence on exports of domestic costs and production capacities. Bauwens and d'Alcantara (1983) have estimated a two-equation model (price and quantities) for Belgian exports of manufactures. Their results are consistent with an elasticity of export quantities with respect to domestic production capacities equal to unity and suggest an elasticity of the value of exports with respect to domestic wages of the order of −0.3. As for export prices, they seem to be determined largely by world prices (elasticity 0.8) and less so by domestic costs (elasticity 0.2).

Before drawing a tentative conclusion from the material collected in this section, we wish to introduce an additional bit of evidence. It concerns the number of (blue- and white-collar) workers laid off as a result of their employers' bankruptcy. The exact coverage of the statistic is not entirely clear; bankruptcies involving less than 20 employees are not included, and there may be other omissions. On the other hand, some of the bankrupt firms continued under new ownership (typically with a much smaller workforce). Be that as it may, it is striking to find an annual average (1976–83) of at least 30,000 workers laid off because of bankruptcy. It was noted in table 15.2 that, over the period 1974–83, an average of 37,400 jobs a year were destroyed in the private sector. The rate of attrition suggested by bankruptcies is thus not far from the actual overall rate!

We conclude that all the findings reported in this section are consistent with, and give empirical content to, the frequently heard diagnostic that the Belgian manufacturing sector was choked by the *combination* of domestic labour costs growing faster than those of competitors and effective demand slackening off in a context of world recession. That *combination* was particularly damaging for two reasons. First, high costs and low output resulted in a severe loss of profitability, leading some firms to scrap capacity and lay off workers, while other firms simply went bankrupt. Second, slack demand at the world level prevented Belgian producers from passing on wage costs into prices and enabled foreign competitors to take over the market share thus abandoned. (From 1975 to 1979, wholesale prices of manufactures showed no trend, whereas retail and service prices went up 40 per cent.)

If one adds the observation that those firms that survived could do so only thanks to major gains in productivity, one has come a long way towards explaining the exceptional increase in apparent gross labour productivity of Belgian manufacturing industries. It would be hazardous to attempt to impute the overall increase back to individual causes, as there was much interaction. But it seems clear that wage behaviour has played a significant role; without that additional complication, the impact of the recession on manufacturing employment (down by 29.8 per cent from 1974 to 1983) would have been less severe. The differential rise of unemployment in Belgium relative to EC9 since 1974 corresponds to some 10 per cent of the employment in manufacturing; with a differential rise in real wages of some 20 percentage points in Belgium relative to EC9 over the period 1971–80, a moderate wage elasticity of employment of −0.5 would account for the differential rise in unemployment.

3. A macroeconomic rationing model

This section is devoted to the presentation and estimation of a two-market macroeconomic rationing (or disequilibrium) model of the Belgian economy. The background is thus a Barro–Grossman–Benassy–Malinvaud model, i.e. a situation in which price and wage adjustments are not sufficient to clear the goods and labour markets at each moment of time, so that employment can be, broadly speaking, determined by a sales constraint (Keynesian unemployment), by a capacity constraint (classical unemployment), or by a labour supply constraint (repressed inflation and underconsumption).[2] The model that will be developed rests on previous work on Belgian data by Sneessens (1981, 1983) and Lambert (1988). The

---

[2] For the sake of simplicity, we shall not make explicit the distinction between the repressed inflation and underconsumption regimes, although this distinction will be taken into account in estimation via the labour hoarding phenomenon.

first subsection below will be devoted to the discussion of production constraints. These are the cornerstone of the model, around which the rest is organised. The first part of the model describes the determination of production and employment, given the production constraints just mentioned. The second part describes the formation of prices and wages. Prices are represented by a mark-up on costs, plus a positive demand pressure effect. Wages are determined by productivity gains plus a negative unemployment effect. These specifications are rather crude, and we do not claim that they reflect a fully satisfactory theory of price and wage formation. Rather, they reflect minimal influences taken into account in most empirical studies. The simplicity of these specifications is convenient to bring out the properties of the whole model, which are considered in the second subsection below. We pay special attention to the inflation-unemployment trade-off and to the meaning of the non-inflationary rate of unemployment (*NIRU*) in a quantity rationing model. Empirical results are presented in Section 4.

Production constraints

Traditional macroeconomic models typically contain production relationships appearing indirectly in the form of factor demand functions. In a rationing context, production constraints will furthermore be used to determine the highest production level at which firms can reasonably aim, given the availability of production factors (capital and labour) and the prevailing production technology. The determination of these upper bounds on production is crucial for the distinction between the three regimes alluded to above, namely Keynesian unemployment, classical unemployment and repressed inflation. These upper bounds can be modelled in several ways. We shall use an extended version of the Leontief–Cobb–Douglas model already used in Sneessens (1981).

Optimal factor proportions (or technical coefficients) are chosen so as to minimise production costs. Let us assume that changing these technical coefficients is costly. When these costs are high, transitory stimuli (such as a sales constraint) will not induce a firm to modify its production technique. Consequently, labour and capital appear as complementary inputs in the short run although they are substitutes in the longer run. This seems realistic enough.

If long-run cost considerations only are taken into account and temporary disturbances such as sales constraints are neglected, a Cobb–

Douglas production function is readily shown to imply a capital–labour ratio that remains proportional to relative labour costs:

$$\ln\frac{K}{L} = C_0 + \Theta(\Lambda)\ln\frac{W}{V} \tag{1}$$

where W and V stand for labour and capital usage costs, respectively, and Λ is the lag operator. The lag polynomial function $\Theta(\Lambda)$ represents the slow adjustment of the capital–labour ratio to relative cost changes. By substitution into the Cobb–Douglas function itself, one can derive expressions for the output–labour and output–capital ratios:

$$\ln\frac{Y}{L} = C_1 + a_1(t) + (1 - a_2)\Theta(\Lambda)\ln\frac{W}{V}$$
$$\ln\frac{Y}{K} = C_2 + a_1(t) - a_2\Theta(\Lambda)\ln\frac{W}{V} \tag{2}$$

where $a_1(t)$ allows for exogenous technical progress and a_2 is the coefficient of labour in the Cobb–Douglas function. Constant returns to scale are implicitly assumed. Equation (2) can be written more compactly as

$$\frac{Y}{L} = A\left(t, \frac{W}{V}\right)$$
$$\frac{Y}{K} = B\left(t, \frac{W}{V}\right). \tag{3}$$

In the very short run, the technical coefficients A and B are fairly rigid, as in a Leontief production model. The limits imposed on production by the availability of production factors are $A \times LS$ and $B \times KA$, where LS and KA stand for the supply of labour and the available capital stock, respectively. *Repressed inflation* occurs when the labour constraint is operative, *classical unemployment* when the capital constraint is operative. *Keynesian unemployment* occurs when the demand for goods remains below these two upper bounds, so that the production level is determined by the demand for goods.

When production capacities are fully utilised, the production level is $YP \equiv B \times KA$. The corresponding 'potential' employment level is $LP = A^{-1} \times YP = A^{-1} \times B \times KA$. After substitution for A and B and first-differencing, one obtains

$$\Delta\ln LP = -\Theta(\Lambda)(\Delta\ln W - \Delta\ln V) + \Delta\ln KA. \tag{4}$$

The rate of growth of potential employment is equal to minus the rate of growth of relative labour costs plus the investment rate ($\Delta \ln KA \simeq I/KA$). Notice that the lag polynomial $\Theta(\Lambda)$ implies that the effects of a wage change will be slow to appear, while the effects of changes in the investment rate are more immediate. Figure 15.5 reproduces the evolution of the two series $\Theta(\Lambda)$ ($\Delta \ln W - \Delta \ln V$) and $\Delta \ln KA$ from 1955 to 1982. The values of the lag polynomial are those obtained by ML estimation (see Section 4). The potential employment level declines whenever the investment rate falls below the rate of growth of relative labour costs, that is, whenever the rate of growth of the economy does not induce the creation of enough new jobs to replace those lost by productivity gains. This situation has been observed in every year since 1975, except for 1979. The investment slack has become especially important in 1981–82. It is responsible for the fall in the potential employment level indicated in figure 15.4.

Potential employment is not a constraint that can be relaxed overnight through wage adjustments. Technical adjustment costs imply that changes in relative factor costs are only progressively translated into capital–labour substitution. It is even likely that the adjustment to a wage fall is slower than the adjustment to a rise, because there is little incentive to get rid of capital-intensive equipment once it has been paid for. More precisely, wage moderation in the short run is likely to have a larger impact on the demand for goods than on supply and potential employment. This point has already been stressed forcefully by Malinvaud (1982b).

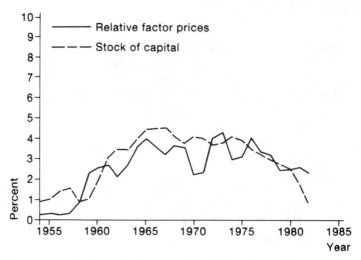

Fig. 15.5.   Rates of change in the stock of capital and relative factor prices.

Properties of the model

Our definition in the previous section of the Keynesian, classical and inflation regimes applies to individual firms only. What we observe at the aggregate level is a time-varying mixture of the three regimes. This point has been illustrated by Muellbauer (1978) and Malinvaud (1980). It is taken into account by aggregating explicitly over 'micro-markets', as in Lambert (1988). For expository reasons, we first consider an homogeneous economy and analyse each polar case separately; that is, we proceed as though all firms were always at the same time in the same regime. The consequences of aggregation and of structural imbalances are then reintroduced.

Specification details will not be given until Section 4. Moreover, because investment is kept exogenous, we take as given throughout this subsection the technical coefficients A and B. This places us in a short-run perspective.

Keynesian unemployment. The relevant set of equations is reproduced in table 14.1. Suffixes D and S denote demanded and supplied quantities respectively; suffix T denotes transacted quantities. Total final demand FD is defined as private consumption plus an exogenous component that includes public expenditures, investment and exports. Private consumption demand is determined by total disposable income DI. The demand for imports MD is the usual function of total final demand and relative prices. The difference between FD and MD defines the demand for domestic goods YD which, together with other variables such as the previous employment level (not shown), determines the demand for labour. As we are by assumption in a situation of generalised excess supply, transactions on both the goods and the labour markets are determined by the demand side. The wage equation simply says that the expected real wage rate is proportional to the expected productivity of labour. With an elasticity of real wage demands to productivity gains equal to one (as assumed), the proportionality factor is merely the share of total value added claimed by labour. That share is here inversely related to the unemployment rate. The last equation defines the price of value-added by a mark-up on expected average production costs APC. Coefficient π_0 represents the share of total value-added that firms claim over and above interest and depreciation. It is equal to the mark-up rate. It corresponds to pure profits and/or to a margin for incomplete utilisation of factors (labour hoarding, excess capacity).

Table 15.4. *Determination of macroeconomic aggregates in a pure Keynesian regime* ($YD < YP$, $LD < LS$)

Demand for goods:	$\begin{cases} FD = CD(DI) + EXO \\ MD = MD(FD, PF, PM) \\ YD = FD - MD \end{cases}$	
Demand for labour:	$LD = L(YD)$	
Transacted quantities:	$\begin{cases} CT = CD,\ MT = MD,\ YT = YD \\ LT = LD \end{cases}$	
Wages and prices:	$\begin{cases} W = \omega_0 (LD/LS)^{\omega_1} A^e P^e \\ P = e^{\pi_0} APC^e \\ \text{where } APC = A^{-1}W + B^{-1}V \end{cases}$	$\begin{array}{l} \omega_0, \omega_1 \geqslant 0 \\ \pi_0 \geqslant 0 \end{array}$

The basic properties of the real part of the model are well known. For given wages and prices, the levels of output and employment are determined by final demand. To increase employment, one must increase either the exogenous component of final demand or consumption demand. Under reasonable assumptions, higher real wages imply more consumption demand.

The price equation in table 15.4 embodies an assumption of downward price rigidity: the excess supply of goods does not lead to price decreases. Consequently, prices are entirely determined by costs and the only form of inflation is 'cost-push'. Aside from exogenous shocks, a systematic inflationary bias may or may not be present, depending upon the presence or absence of excessive income claims relative to value added. This is most easily seen by looking at a stationary perfect foresight equilibrium.

With correct expectations, the price equation can indeed be rewritten (using the approximation $e^{-\pi_0} \simeq 1 - \pi_0$) as

$$1 = \pi_0 + A^{-1}\frac{W}{P} + B^{-1}\frac{V}{P},$$

that is, total value added is divided into three parts: mark-up π_0, labour income $A^{-1}(W/P)$, and capital income $B^{-1}(V/P)$. Let us assume a fixed capital share κ_0, as if capital usage costs were perfectly indexed on the price of value added. The share of total value-added left for labour is then simply

$$A^{-1}\frac{W}{P} = 1 - \pi_0 - \kappa_0. \tag{5}$$

The desired labour share is in turn obtained from the wage equation as[3]

$$A^{-1}\frac{W}{P} = \omega_0 - \omega_1 UR. \tag{6}$$

Coefficient ω_0 thus represents the share of total value added that would be claimed by workers in a zero unemployment economy.

The income claims represented by equations (5)–(6) include a single *endogenous* influence, namely, that of unemployment on wages. Accordingly, any inflationary bias arising from conflicting income claims can be corrected only through unemployment, a crude specification made popular by the discussion of 'non-inflationary rates of unemployment' (*NIRU*). The *NIRU* is in our case the unemployment rate that reconciles (5) and (6):

$$NIRU = \frac{1}{\omega_1}(\pi_0 + \kappa_0 + \omega_0 - 1) \underset{\text{def}}{=} \frac{1}{\omega_1}DG \tag{7}$$

where *DG* stands for 'distributive gap', i.e. the relative excess of income claims over value added. The *NIRU* is proportional to the 'distributive gap', with a factor of proportionality equal to the reciprocal of the elasticity of wages with respect to unemployment. In other words, a Keynesian equilibrium with stationarity of both prices and quantities implies an employment level $LS(1 - NIRU)$ uniquely determined by the sum of income claims $(\pi_0 + \kappa_0 + \omega_0)$ and the elasticity ω_1. With $\omega_1 \simeq 0.4$ (see empirical results, Section 4), a discrepancy of four percentage points would imply a *NIRU* of 10 per cent! Notice, though, that the *NIRU* should be lowered by the extent to which firms lower $(\pi_0 + \kappa_0)$ when demand is slack. This is not modelled here. Finally, an oil shock with full indexation of wages on consumer prices is in this setting equivalent to an increase in ω_0, hence in the *NIRU*.

Needless to say, a perfect-foresight stationary Keynesian equilibrium can exist if and only if the *NIRU* defined in (7) is feasible, i.e. if it is non-negative *and* larger than the rate of unemployment that would prevail if all production capacities, were utilised. Otherwise, the economy would end up in either repressed inflation or classical unemployment.

Classical unemployment. The relevant equations are reproduced in table 15.5.

---

[3] We use the approximations $\omega_0(LD/LS)^{\omega_1} \simeq e^{\omega_0-1}e^{-\omega_1 UR} \simeq \omega_0 - \omega_1 UR$.

Table 15.5. *Determination of macroeconomic aggregates in a pure classical unemployment regime*
$(LD < LS, YD > YS)$

Demand for goods:	Same as in table 15.4
Demand for labour:	$LD = L(YP) = L'(KA)$
Transacted quantities:	$\begin{cases} LT = LD \\ YT = Y(KA) \\ MT = MD + M(YD/YT) \\ CT = CD \end{cases}$
Wages and prices:	$\begin{cases} W = \omega_0(LD/LS)^{\omega_1}A^eP^e \\ P = e^{\pi_0}(YD/YT)^{\pi_1}APC^e \\ \text{where } APC = A^{-1}W + B^{-1}V \end{cases}$

The goods demand equations remain unchanged. Labour demand and employment are now determined by the availability of capital rather than the demand for goods. The availability of capital determines production, which falls short of the demand for goods.[4] Total imports are therefore the sum of 'structural' imports MD plus a positive component representing the spillover from the domestic goods market $(M(YD/YT) \geqslant 0)$. Despite the shortage of domestic goods, we still assume that the demand for consumption goods is not rationed $(CT = CD)$. Implicitly, this means that the shortage of production capacities is fully compensated by a combination of increased imports, higher factor utilisation rates (overtime working, for example) and inventory decumulation, although the latter effects are not explicitly modelled here. (Pure rationing could also appear in the form of delivery lags; it seemed wiser not to overemphasise their role in an annual macro-model.)

The wage equation remains unchanged. The price equation includes a positive effect of demand pressure on the mark-up rate. This asymmetric treatment of excess demand versus excess supply amounts to assuming that prices are more flexible upwards than downwards.

Again, the properties of the real part of the model are well known. Output and employment are determined by production capacities – which in turn depend upon available physical capital and real wages. Demand management does not affect output and employment except via investment. Real wages affect employment via capital–labour substitution and investment levels.

[4] Notice however that, because of employment adjustment costs, the observed employment and production levels may also be influenced by past employment and production levels; i.e. LT and YT do not necessarily coincide exactly in the short run with the potential levels of LP and YP defined earlier.

Demand pressures affect prices, which are assumed flexible upwards. Accordingly, there are now two sources of inflation: cost-push and demand-pull. With excess demand for output, demand-pull introduces a systematic inflationary bias. Price stability accordingly requires an offsetting trend in costs. The rate of classical unemployment introduces a downward bias in wages, to be considered jointly with the income claims.

In this framework, the NIRU is a meaningless concept, but one can define a 'non-inflationary rate of excess demand', or *NIRED*, to express conveniently the single endogenous influence on prices and wages.

The properties of the perfect-foresight stationary classical unemployment equilibrium are derived in exactly the same fashion as for the Keynesian regime. In this case, however, the unemployment rate is fully determined by production capacities. At given technical coefficients, this unemployment rate measures the 'capital gap' (CG), i.e. the shortage of production capacities relatively to the capacity required to eliminate unemployment:

$$CG = \frac{LS - L(YP)}{LS} = 1 - \frac{L(YP)}{LS}.$$

From the price and wage equations we obtain, respectively,

$$A^{-1}\frac{W}{P} = 1 - \pi_0 - \pi_1 \ln\frac{YD}{YT} - \kappa_0 \tag{8}$$

and

$$A^{-1}\frac{W}{P} = \omega_0 - \omega_1 CG. \tag{9}$$

Combining these two results and solving for the rate of excess demand, $RED = (YD - YT)/YT \simeq \ln YD/YT$, yields the 'non-inflationary rate of excess demand':

$$NIRED = \frac{1}{\pi_1}(\omega_1 CG - DG). \tag{10}$$

It is a positive function of the capital gap (owing to the negative effect of CG on wage claims) and a negative function of the distributive gap $DG = (\pi_0 + \kappa_0 + \omega_0 - 1)$. Inflation will develop if and only if $RED > NIRED$. This can be avoided by adequate demand management policies. The *RED* thus becomes the relevant policy indicator in the classical regime, a role played by UR in a Keynesian regime.

The stationary classical unemployment equilibrium described by (10) will of course obtain if and only if $NIRED \geqslant 0$ and $CG \geqslant 0$. Given (7), the first condition can also be recast as $CG \geqslant NIRU$. There is otherwise no stationary classical unemployment equilibrium.

Repressed inflation. The relevant equations are similar to those of the classical regime, except for the production and employment levels, which are now constrained by the availability of labour rather than capital ($LT = LS$, $YT = Y(LS)$). Demand pressures are now positive on both the goods and the labour markets.

A stationary 'repressed inflation' equilibrium[5] will not exist unless the distributive gap DG and the capital gap CG are both negative. The first condition would imply weak income claims ($\omega_0 + \pi_0 + \kappa_0 < 1$); the second would imply a potential employment level larger than the supply of labour. If these two conditions are not satisfied, price adjustment will progressively lead to either Keynesian or classical unemployment, depending on the values of DG and CG.

Aggregation. We now abandon the fiction of an homogeneous economy in favour of an explicit aggregation over micro-markets. This procedure calls for specifying a joint frequency distribution over the demand for goods, the supply of labour and the availability of production capacities. Simple assumptions (see Lambert, 1988) lead to an employment equation where the aggregate employment level is a CES function of the aggregate concepts $L(YD)$, $L(YP)$ and LS used so far. This CES function thus replaces the usual 'min' condition. More formally, we have

$$LT = \{L(YD)^{-\rho} + L(YP)^{-\rho} + LS^{-\rho}\}^{-1/\rho}, \quad \rho \geqslant 0 \qquad (11)$$

where ρ is linked to the correlations between the values across micro-markets of the demand for goods, the availability of production capacities and the supply of labour. The lower the value of ρ, the lower the correlation between these values and thus the more important the mismatch between the distribution of these three quantities across micro-markets. Note that this simple formulation makes impossible the distinction between labour mismatch and capacity mismatch. Such a distinction would require the use of a different exponent for each aggregate variable appearing in (11).

---

[5] The now well-established terminology 'repressed inflation' may seem inappropriate in our case, as all three regimes can actually witness inflation or deflation, depending on the values of the parameters and of starting conditions. We use it only to mean 'generalised excess demand'.

We define as the 'structural unemployment rate at equilibrium' ($SURE$) the unemployment rate that would be observed in a situation of macroeconomic equilibrium, i.e. for $L(YD) = L(YP) = LS$. Given (11), one obtains

$$SURE = \frac{LS - LT}{LS} = 1 - 3^{-1/\rho}. \tag{12}$$

It is a negative function of ρ. For $\rho \to \infty$, $SURE \to 0$, structural imbalances disappear, and equation (11) boils down to the usual min condition.

An immediate implication of (11) is that the elasticities of employment with respect to $L(YD)$, $L(YP)$ and LS are all less than unity and correspond to the proportions of firms or micro-markets in each regime (denoted ϕ_K, ϕ_C and ϕ_I, respectively):

$$\eta_{LT \cdot L(YD)} = \left\{ \frac{LT}{L(YD)} \right\}^{\rho} = \phi_K \tag{13}$$

$$\eta_{LT \cdot L(YP)} = \left\{ \frac{LT}{L(YP)} \right\}^{\rho} = \phi_C$$

$$\eta_{LT \cdot LS} = \left(\frac{LT}{LS} \right)^{\rho} = \phi_I.$$

The elasticities of aggregate employment to the wage rate or to the demand for domestic goods will thus be a weighted average of the elasticities in each pure regime, with weights ϕ_K, ϕ_C and ϕ_I, respectively. With respect to the wage rate, we have

$$\eta_{LT \cdot w} = \phi_K \eta_{L(YD) \cdot w} + \phi_C \eta_{L(YP) \cdot w} + \phi_I \eta_{LS \cdot w}. \tag{14}$$
$$+ \qquad\qquad - \qquad\qquad ?$$

As for the demand for domestic goods, we may reasonably assume that it has no short-term effect on production capacities or on labour supply. The elasticity of aggregate employment to YD is then simply

$$\eta_{LT \cdot YD} = \phi_K \eta_{L(YD) \cdot YD}. \tag{15}$$

Because all three regimes are simultaneously present, inflationary pressures are again a mixture of cost-push and demand-pull, as in the classical unemployment regime. The endogenous influences on wages and prices are now twofold, namely, unemployment UR (which moderates wages) and demand pressures RED. They operate against the background of income claims DG and classical unemployment CG. Price stability again requires that demand-pull inflationary pressures be exactly offset by cost-push deflationary pressures. The stationary equilibrium relationship between the rates of unemployment and excess demand is given by the wage and price equations. With perfect foresight we obtain – say from (10), written in terms of observed rates,

$$UR = \frac{1}{\omega_1}(DG + \pi_1\, RED).$$ (16)

To determine the $NIRU$ and the $NIRED$, we need a second relationship between these two variables. It is given by the employment equation (11). The latter can be rewritten as

$$1 = \left\{\frac{L(YD)}{LT}\right\}^{-\rho} + \left\{\frac{L(YP)}{LS}\frac{LS}{LT}\right\}^{-\rho} + \left(\frac{LS}{LT}\right)^{-\rho}$$

$$= (1 + RED)^{-\rho} + (1 - CG)^{-\rho}(1 - UR)^{\rho} + (1 - UR)^{\rho}$$

where we use the definitions

$$CG = \frac{LS - L(YP)}{LS} \quad \text{and} \quad RED = \frac{YD - YT}{YT} = \frac{L(YD) - LT}{LT}$$

(with given technical coefficients and no labour hoarding). Simply rearranging the terms leads to

$$(1 - UR)^{\rho} = \frac{1 - (1 + RED)^{-\rho}}{1 + (1 - CG)^{-\rho}}.$$ (17)

Equations (16) and (17) are reproduced in figure 15.6. The positively sloped linear function PP' is (16), the negatively sloped nonlinear function LL' is (17). The effects of changes in the parameters DG, CG and ρ are indicated by dashed curves. When ρ decreases and goes to zero (growing mismatch), the negatively sloped curve becomes steeper and steeper; in the limit ($\rho = 0$), it becomes vertical at $UR = 1$. At the other end, when ρ goes to infinity, the curvature of the function increases until it becomes a right angle with vertex at CG on the horizontal axis. The employment equation (11) then boils down to the 'min' condition used in the previous subsections. The intersection of the functions depicted in figure 15.6 determines the stationary equilibrium of the economy. The $NIRU$ is seen to be a positive function of the capital gap CG, of the distributive gap DG and of the degree of mismatch ($1/\rho$). The $NIRED$ is positively affected by the capital gap and the degree of mismatch, negatively affected by the distributive gap. This is summarised in table 15.6.

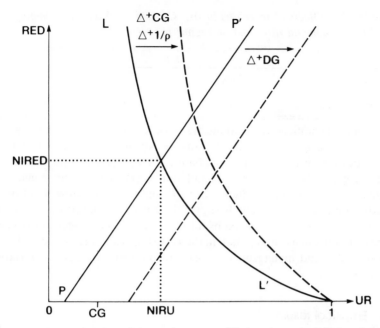

Fig. 15.6. Determination of the stationary equilibrium (equations (16) and (17)).

The table also indicates the effects of DG, CG and $1/\rho$ on the proportion of firms in each regime. The signs of these effects follow from the definitions of ϕ_K, ϕ_C and ϕ_I given in (13):

$$\phi_K = \left\{\frac{L(YD)}{LT}\right\}^{-1/\rho} = (1 + RED)^{-\rho}$$

$$\phi_C = \left\{\frac{L(YP)}{LT}\right\}^{-1/\rho} = (1 - UR)(1 - CG)^{-\rho}$$

$$\phi_I = \left\{\frac{LS}{LT}\right\}^{-1/\rho} = (1 - UR)^{-\rho}$$

with $\phi_K + \phi_C + \phi_I = 1$.

The LL' and PP' curves depicted in figure 15.6 only describe stationary equilibrium conditions. In the very short run, the economy can be off these two curves and in either one of the four regions they delineate. The slow adjustment of labour to its equilibrium value (the so-called labour

Table 15.6. *Effects of increases in DG, CG and* $(1/\rho)$ *on the unemployment and excess demand rates and on regime proportions*

	UR	RED	ϕ_K	ϕ_C	ϕ_I
Distributive gap (DG)	+	−	+	−	−
Capital gap (CG)	+	+	−	+	−
Mismatch $(1/\rho)$	+	+	0	0	0

hoarding phenomenon) is responsible for deviations from LL'; the sluggishness of wage and price expectations or adjustments is responsible for deviations from PP'. The rate of change of employment is positive above LL', negative below; the rate of inflation is positive (or more generally larger than its expected value) above PP' and negative below. Traditional fix-price models completely disregard the PP' curve and proceed as if any point on LL' could be reached by adequate demand management policies. This amounts to assuming that, in the very short run, wage-price stickiness enables demand management policies to produce any desired deviation from PP'.

4. Empirical results

We have six equations to estimate: the two technical relationships (2), the consumption function, the import and employment equations, the wage and price equations. Ideally, one would like to estimate all these equations jointly by *FIML*, in order to take account in an efficient way of simultaneity and of the many cross-equation restrictions. Because of the strong nonlinearities involved and of the danger of not being able to control effectively an iterative optimization procedure involving all the parameters at once, we used instead a sequential block-by-block limited information procedure. This means (1) joint *ML* estimation of the two technical relationships; (2) OLS estimation of the consumption function; (3) joint *ML* estimation of the import and employment equations (this joint estimation is motivated by the presence in both equations of the unobserved variable YD, the demand for domestic goods defined as (observed) total final demand minus (unobserved) structural imports – see p. 377 above); (4) instrumental variable estimation of the wage and price equations.

This sequential estimation procedure implies that the values of the technical coefficients A and B used in estimating the employment and the price equations are those obtained in step (1) from the estimation of the technical relationships. Similarly, the values of the excess demand indicator

$\ln YD/YT^* \simeq RED$ used in estimating the price equation are the values previously derived from the estimation of the import and employment equations. The results of this sequential estimation procedure are reproduced in table 15.7. We first discuss each equation separately; these comments are numbered (1)–(16), and those that are specific to our approach are italicised. We then turn to the implied values of the *NIRU* and *NIRED*.

Table 15.7. *Estimated equations*
(Standard errors in parentheses; estimated variables denoted ˜)

(1) $\quad \ln \dfrac{YT}{LT} = 2.58 + 0.022t - 0.013t' + 0.55 \dfrac{0.27}{1 - 0.73\Lambda} \ln \dfrac{W}{PI} + 0.06 \ln DUL$

$\qquad$ (0.27) (0.002) (0.001) (0.05) $\qquad\qquad\qquad$ (0.04)

$\qquad$ s.e.e. $= 0.0075 \qquad DW = 2.00 \qquad$ sample $= 1954$–82

---

(2) $\quad \ln \dfrac{YT}{KA} = 1.55 + 0.022t - 0.013t' - 0.45 \dfrac{0.27}{1 - 0.73\Lambda} \ln \dfrac{W}{PI} + 0.25 \ln DUC$

$\qquad$ (0.27) (0.002) (0.001) (0.05) $\qquad\qquad\qquad$ (0.06)

$\qquad$ s.e.e. $= 0.0149 \qquad DW = 2.00 \qquad$ sample $= 1964$–82

Notes to equations (1) *and* (2): Correlation between the residuals of equations (1) and (2): 0.71

$\qquad t' = 0$ before 1974 ($t = 22$), $t' = t - 22$ afterwards

---

(3) $\quad \Delta \ln CT = 0.28 + 0.22UR - 0.76\Delta UR + 0.013\Delta \ln PC$

$\qquad\qquad$ (0.15) (0.17) $\quad$ (0.30) $\qquad$ (0.10)

$\qquad\qquad + 0.46\Delta \ln DI + 0.42 \quad \ln DI_{-1} - 0.47 \ln CT_{-1}$

$\qquad\qquad$ (0.14) $\qquad\qquad$ (0.13) $\qquad\qquad$ (0.15)

$\qquad$ s.e.e. $= 0.0087 \qquad DW = 2.00 \qquad$ sample $= 1954$–82

---

(4) $\quad \ln MT = -2.08 + 1.14 \ln FD - 0.28 \ln PM^* + 0.69 \ln PF^* + 1.79 \ln \dfrac{\tilde{YD}}{YT^*}$

$\qquad$ (0.0008)(0.00004) $\quad$ (0.01) $\qquad\qquad$ (0.0002) $\qquad$ (0.24)

$\qquad$ s.e.e. $= 0.0173 \qquad DW = 2.13 \qquad$ sample $= 1955$–82

where $\ln PM^* \equiv (0.70 + 0.20\,\Lambda + 0.10\,\Lambda^2) \ln PM$
$\qquad \ln PF^* \equiv (0.15 + 0.25\,\Lambda + 0.60\,\Lambda^2) \ln PF$

---

(5) $\quad LT = \{L(YD)^{-\rho} + L(YP)^{-\rho} + LS^{-\rho}\}^{-1/\rho}$

$\qquad \ln L(YD) \equiv 0.014 + 0.73\{-\ln \tilde{A} + (0.96 \ln YD + 0.04 \ln \tilde{YP})\} + 0.27 LT_{-1}$

$\qquad\qquad$ (0.004) (0.01) $\qquad\qquad$ (0.05) $\qquad$ (0.05) $\qquad\qquad$ (0.01)

$\qquad \ln L(YP) \equiv 0.023 + 0.73(-\ln \tilde{A} + \ln \tilde{YP}) + 0.27 \ln LT_{-1}$

$\qquad\qquad$ (0.000) (0.01) $\qquad\qquad\qquad$ (0.01)

$\qquad LS \equiv LT + U$

$\qquad \rho \equiv (0.0065 + 0.0012t)^{-1}$

$\qquad\qquad$ (0.001) (0.000005)

$\qquad$ s.e.e. $= 0.004 \qquad DW = 2.28 \qquad$ sample $= 1955$–82

Table 15.7 (*cont.*)

(6) $\Delta \ln W = 1.31 \,\Delta \ln P - 0.004 - 0.11 \, UR$
                (0.22)   (0.13) (0.50)

$$+ 0.55 \,\Delta \ln \frac{YT}{LT} + 0.04 \left\{ \ln \left(\frac{YT}{LT} \right)_{-1} - \ln \left(\frac{W}{P} \right)_{-1} \right\}$$
                (0.30)   (0.27)

            s.e.e. = 0.0126 $DW = 1.70$ sample = 1956–82

(6') $\Delta \ln WN = 0.91 \,\Delta \ln PC - 0.092 - 0.43 \, UR$
                (0.17)   (0.095) (0.15)

$$+ 0.48 \,\Delta \ln \frac{YT}{LT} + 0.17 \left\{ \ln \left(\frac{Y\,T}{L\,T} \right)_{-1} - \ln \left(\frac{WN}{PC} \right)_{-1} \right\}$$
                (0.25)   (0.15)

            s.e.e. = 0.0166 $DW = 2.01$ sample = 1956–82

Instruments: $t, t', DUL, DUC, \ln \left(\dfrac{\widetilde{YD}}{YT^*} \right)_{-1}, \Delta \ln \left(\dfrac{YT}{LT} \right)_{-1}, \left(\dfrac{0.27}{1 - 0.73\Lambda} \ln \dfrac{W}{PI} \right)_{-1}$

(7) $\Delta \ln P = 0.038 + 1.04 \ln \left(\dfrac{\widetilde{YD}}{YT^*} \right)_{-1} - 0.54 \,\Delta \ln \left(\dfrac{\widetilde{YD}}{YT^*} \right)$
                (0.064) (0.50)   (0.33)

$$+ 0.63 \,\Delta \ln APC - 0.27 \,\Delta^2 \ln APC + 0.41(\ln APC_{-1} - \ln P_{-1})$$
                (0.17)   (0.16)   (0.28)

            s.e.e. = 0.010 $DW = 1.70$ sample = 1956–82
        $APC \equiv (\tilde{A}^{-1} W + \tilde{B}^{-1} 0.20 \, PI)$
                (0.06)

Instruments: $t, t', DUL, DUC, \ln \left(\dfrac{\widetilde{YD}}{YT^*} \right)_{-1}, \ln \left(\dfrac{YT}{LT} \right)_{-1}, \left(\dfrac{0.27}{1 - 0.73\Lambda} \ln \dfrac{W}{PI} \right)_{-1}, \Delta \ln P_{-1}$

Technical coefficients (equations (1) and (2))

1. The *observed* productivities of labour and capital are not in general equal to the *technical* productivities. This discrepancy is taken into account by using two indicators of factor utilization, DUL and DUC. The former is based on partial unemployment figures, the latter on business surveys in the manufacturing sector. The values of the coefficients of these variables should not be given too much economic significance, except to note that a coefficient of DUC smaller than unity may indicate that the fluctuations in the rate of capital utilisation as reported by firms in the manufacturing sector overestimate the fluctuations at the aggregate level.

2. The coefficients of the trend variables t and t' indicate that the rate

of exogenous technical progress has decreased from 2.2 per cent before 1974 to 0.9 per cent afterwards.

3. The values of the relative factor costs lag polynomial function were generated recursively, according to

$$\left\{\Theta(\Lambda)\ln\frac{W}{V}\right\}_t \equiv \frac{1-\theta}{1-\theta\Lambda}\ln\left(\frac{W}{V}\right)_t$$

$$\equiv (1-\theta)\ln\left(\frac{W}{V}\right)_t + \theta\left\{\Theta(\Lambda)\ln\frac{W}{V}\right\}_{t-1}.$$

The starting value $\{\Theta(\Lambda)\ln W/V\}_{t=0}$ was set at 5.45, close to the 1953 value of $\ln W/V$. This restriction was not rejected by a LR test. A value of θ equal to 0.73 means that only 27 per cent of the change in the optimal technical coefficients A and B implied by a change in relative factor costs is realized within a year.

4. In all this, we assumed the capital usage cost V to be proportional to the price of investment goods PI, which amounts to assuming, *inter alia*, a constant long-term real interest rate. More elaborate specifications, based on the observed nominal interest rate minus a weighted average of current and past inflation rates, proved unsuccessful.

Consumption function (equation (3))

5. We postulate a constant elasticity of private consumption CT to household disposable income DI. The static specification is written as

$$CT = e^{c_0 + c_1 UR}(DI^e)^{c_2} \tag{18}$$

where DI^e stands for expected disposable income and coefficient c_1 allows for an effect of unemployment on consumption. The dynamic specification is in the form of an error correction mechanism. Simple rearrangements of (18) lead to

$$\Delta\ln CT = c_1 UR + c_2\Delta\ln DI^e + (c_0 + c_2\ln DI_{-1} - \ln CT_{-1}). \tag{19}$$

In words a change in CT may result from an abnormal unemployment rate, from an expected change in disposable income, or from a previous discrepancy between desired and realized values. Let us now assume that only a fraction $\delta_2 \geqslant 1$ of such a discrepancy is corrected in the subsequent period. Let us furthermore define $\Delta\ln DI^e$ as $(\delta_0\Delta\ln DI + \delta_1\Delta\ln DI_{-1})$ and generalise $c_1 UR$ to $(c_{10}UR + c_{11}UR_{-1})$. Equation (19) then becomes

$$\Delta \ln CT = c_0 \delta_2 + (c_{10} + c_{11})UR - c_{11}\Delta UR$$
$$+ c_2(\delta_0 + \delta_1)\Delta \ln DI - c_1 \delta_1 \Delta^2 \ln DI$$
$$+ \delta_2(c_2 \ln DI_{-1} - \ln CT_{-1}). \tag{20}$$

6. With δ_1 set equal to zero, OLS estimation of (20) yields an elasticity of aggregate consumption to disposable income of $c_2 = 0.90$ in the long run and $\delta_0 c_2 = 0.46$ in the short run. The interpretation of the unemployment rate effect is unclear; the effect appears strongly negative in the short run, but positive in the long run. When added as an explanatory variable, the inflation rate appears insignificant.

Imports (equation (4))

7. The structural demand for imports MD (excluding energy, which is left exogenous) is specified as a log-linear function of total final demand (less public consumption and energy imports) FD, import prices PM and domestic prices PF. That is,

$$\ln \widetilde{MD} \underset{\text{def}}{=} -2.08 + 1.14 \ln FD - 0.28 \ln PM^* + 0.69 \ln PF^*.$$

8. *As there are always some domestic 'micro-markets' in excess demand, observed imports will always be larger than or equal to the structural demand MD. The discrepancy between the two is a function of the importance of domestic production shortages, measured by $\ln YD/YT^* \simeq RED \geqslant 0$, where YT^* is the production level that could be reached with currently available inputs and a normal input utilisation rate, after correction for the hoarding of labour.*

9. The dynamics of the price effects turned out to be poorly defined. The weights given to past and current values were fixed at what seemed to be reasonable values in view of the unconstrained estimation results. These restrictions decrease the log-likelihood from 175 to 171 but leave the other parameter estimates basically unchanged. The elasticity of imports to final demand prices is (in absolute value) about twice their elasticity to import price themselves. The bundles of goods involved are perhaps different; or changes in PM may have repercussions on PF, so that their impact is split among the two variables.

10. *The elasticity of imports to total final demand is not very far from unity and substantially below that obtained with traditional methods, i.e. when demand pressure effects are not modelled explicitly but are simply replaced by a term (most often insignificant) involving the degree of capacity utilisation. The demand pressure coefficient is here significant and implies*

that a 1 percentage point increase in the excess demand for domestic goods increases imports by 1.79 per cent. With imports representing about 50 per cent of GDP in the 1970s, about 90 per cent of any excess demand for goods is immediately compensated by additional imports.

Figure 15.7 reproduces the ratio of total imports to structural imports (MT/MD) and of domestic demand to normal domestic supply – given available inputs – (YD/YT*) from 1955 to 1982. These two demand pressure indicators are always larger than one, thereby indicating that there always subsists a certain proportion of firms in the classical and inflation regimes which are constrained by capacity and labour shortages respectively rather than sales. That proportion, however, becomes especially weak in 1958 and after 1980, when the proportion of firms in the Keynesian regime becomes more important (77 per cent in 1982).

Employment equation (equation (5))

11. The employment equation has the form suggested in (11). Variable $\tilde{A}$ is the technical productivity of labour as estimated from equation (1). That is,

$$\ln \tilde{A} \underset{\text{def}}{=} 2.58 + 0.022t - 0.013t' + 0.55\Theta(\Lambda)\ln\frac{W}{V}.$$

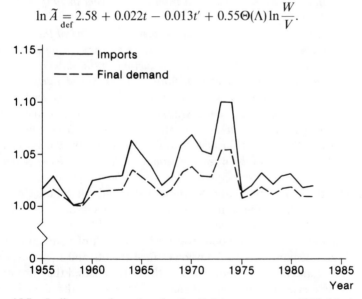

Fig. 15.7. Indicators of tension in the Belgian economy, 1955–82: imports (MT/MD) and final demand (YD/YT*).

The potential and past employment levels appearing in the Keynesian labour demand function $L(YD)$ represent the effects of adjustment costs and the ensuing hoarding of labour during recessions. The interpretation of LT_{-1} in $L(YP)$ is similar. *The short-run elasticity of the Keynesian demand for labour $L(YD)$ to demand for domestic goods is estimated at*

$$\frac{\partial \ln L(YD)}{\partial \ln YD} = (0.96)(0.73) = 0.70.$$

The short-run elasticity of actual employment can be substantially lower and depends on the proportion of firms in the Keynesian regime ϕ_K:

$$\frac{\partial \ln LT}{\partial \ln YD} = \phi_K \frac{\partial \ln L(YD)}{\partial \ln YD}.$$

A typical value of ϕ_K is 0.55, which would imply a short-run elasticity equal to 0.39.

12. *The mismatch parameter ρ is represented as an inverse linear function of time. The values of ρ_0 and ρ_1 indicate a regular and significant increase in structural imbalances. As a consequence, the structural unemployment rate at equilibrium (SURE) has risen from 1.39 per cent in 1955 to 4.5 per cent in 1982.*

13. *The values of the Keynesian labour demand LK and of the potential employment level LP are reproduced in figure 15.4. They are obtained from $L(YD)$ and $L(YP)$, respectively, after deduction of the labour hoarding effect (no lagged employment effect). Both series remained fairly close to the supply of labour LS throughout the 1960s and early 1970s. In 1975 the Keynesian demand for labour collapsed; it has never recovered since. After 1975, the decline in the investment rate (see figure 15.5) caused the stagnation, and then the decline of potential employment. In 1982 the capital gap (i.e. the discrepancy between the supply of labour and the potential employment level in percentage points) reached about 9 per cent.*

14. The dramatic fall in the Keynesian demand for labour in 1975 resulted mainly from the collapse of the demand for domestic goods, enhanced by the effects of productivity gains (see table 15.8). The change in the demand for domestic goods was itself the result of a similar change in total final demand arising from lower investments and lower exports. By 1976 investments and exports had both recovered, and they produced a strong increase of total final demand. The rise in the demand for domestic goods turned out to be much weaker, however, while the demand for imports rose strongly, with 40 per cent of the increase owing to a

Table 15.8. *Analysis of the changes in the Keynesian demand for labour and its determinants after 1975*
(Percentage points)

	1975	1976	1981	1982
Growth in Keynesian demand for labour	−8.0	+0.7	−3.0	−1.8
of which: wages	−2.8	−3.3	−2.4	−2.2
demand for domestic goods	−5.2	+4.0	−0.6	+0.4
Growth in final demand	−4.4	+7.3	−1.3	+1.2
of which: consumption	+1.2	+4.9	−0.1	+1.3
government spending	+4.8	+3.9	+1.2	−1.5
investment:				
fixed capital	−2.1	+2.8	−16.4	−0.8
total investment	−14.1	+7.1	−17.0	−1.5
exports	−9.4	+11.8	+3.3	+3.4
Growth in imports demand	−2.8	+15.4	−1.1	+3.2
of which: final demand	−7.0	+9.3	−1.9	+1.9
prices	+4.2	+6.1	+0.8	+1.3

significant loss of competitiveness. The years 1981–82 witnessed again an important decrease in investment. This time, however, exports remained steady and there was no additional loss of competitiveness.

Wage equation (equations (6)–(6'))

15. The dynamic structure of the wage equation is similar to that of the consumption function (see above). The wage equation can be written in terms of either labour costs or net labour income per employee. In the former case, the dependent variable is defined as the wage cost per employee, including employers' social security contributions, and the relevant price index is the price of value added. In the latter case, the dependent variable is the net wage rate, after deduction for direct taxes and employees' social security contributions, and the relevant price index is the price of consumption goods. In both cases the observed productivity of labour proved to have a larger explanatory power than the technical concept derived from equation (1). The sign of the unemployment rate coefficient is negative, as expected, albeit not significantly different from zero in the labour cost formulation. In the latter case, also, the coefficient of the inflation rate at 1.31 is larger than (although not significantly different from) unity. This is the sort of result one would expect in the face of an oil shock with wage demands indexed on the price of consumption goods rather than the price of value added. From the

estimates of equation (6) and (6′), one can retrieve the values of ω_0 and ω_1 mentioned in tables 15.4 and 15.5. One obtains from (6) $\hat{\omega}_0 = 0.90$, $\hat{\omega}_1 = 0.1$ and from equation (6′) $\hat{\omega}_0 = 0.58$, $\hat{\omega}_1 = 0.43$. One must be aware, however, of the extremely poor precision of these estimates. Further work is obviously needed on this point.

Price equation (equation (7))

16. The dynamic structure is again similar to that of the consumption function. The specification imposes that, in the long run, cost increases are fully passed on to prices. This restriction is not rejected by the data. When freely estimated, the long-run elasticity of prices to average production costs turns out to be 0.97 and not significantly different from unity. The capital usage cost is approximated by a constant α times the price index of investment goods, *PI*. This amounts to assuming that the sum of the depreciation and real interest rates (corrected for taxation) remains constant at α. The latter is estimated at 0.20. It follows that $\hat{\kappa}_0 \simeq \hat{\alpha}(KA/YP) \simeq 0.4$. One notices the strong and significant demand pressure effect, implying that the mark-up on costs increases by one percentage point for every 1 per cent increase in excess demand. The constant term and the error correction coefficient imply a normal mark-up rate equal to $\hat{\pi}_0 = 0.038/0.4 = 9.5$ per cent, which seems quite reasonable (but again is subject to a high standard error).

Estimates of the NIRU and NIRED

The 1973, 1975 and 1982 estimated values of the *NIRU* and the *NIRED* are reproduced in table 15.9. Each of these three years corresponds to a turning point in the economic developments between 1970 and 1985. 1973 is the last year with rapid growth and one-digit inflation; 1975 coincides with the trough of the recession consecutive to the first oil shock; 1982, the last year covered by our data, is also the starting point of a strict incomes policy.

The values of the capital gap *CG* and of the mismatch parameter ρ used to compute the *NIRU* and the *NIRED* and reported in table 15.9 are those obtained from the estimation of the econometric model. This is *not* the case however for the values of the distributive gap *DG*. The extremely poor precision of the parameter estimates underlying *DG* (especially ω_0 and κ_0), and the crude specification whereby ω_0 and π_0 are constant through time, call for the use of extraneous information. It

Table 15.9. *Estimates of the non-inflationary unemployment rate (NIRU) and non-inflationary rate of excess demand (NIRED)*

	Distributive gap, DG (%)	Capital gap, CG (%)	Mismatch ρ	Equilibrium structural unemployment rate, SURE (%)	Non-inflationary unemployment rate, NIRU (%)	Non-inflationary rate of excess demand, NIRED (%)	Unemployment rate, UR (%)	Rate of excess demand, RED (%)
1973	0.00	−0.41	31.8	3.4	4.5	1.9	3.8	5.6
1975	4.00	0.30	29.6	3.6	10.1	0.3	7.5	0.8
Variant	0.00	0.30	29.6	3.6	5.0	2.1		
1982	0.00	8.77	23.8	4.5	10.8	4.5	16.0	1.0
Variant 1	0.00	0.00	23.8	4.5	6.1	2.5		
Variant 2	4.00	8.77	23.8	4.5	13.4	1.7		

seemed reasonable to us to assume a widening of the distributive gap from 0 per cent in 1973 to 4 per cent in 1975, as a result of the first oil shock. The distributive gap may have been reduced towards zero again in 1982 as a result of the strict incomes policy.

From table 15.9, we draw the following conclusions.

1. The estimated decline in ρ (an inverse function of time, as an approximation) entails a growing mismatch (whether due to the labour market or to the production facilities and product mix), and hence a steadily growing 'structural unemployment rate at equilibrium' (*SURE*).

2. The assumption made about the distributive gap is very important: the difference in the estimated value of the *NIRU* is 5.1 per cent in 1975 and 2.6 per cent in 1982. If $DG = 4$ per cent is indeed more plausible for 1975 and $DG = 0$ is more plausible for 1982, one would estimate that the *NIRU* has not changed much between 1975 and 1982, remaining at the embarrassing level of 10–11 per cent.

3. The factors behind the *NIRU* in 1974–75 and in 1982 are quite different. The main difference comes from the 'capital gap' – the insufficient number of working posts – which accounts for 4.7 percentage points in the 1982 estimate of the *NIRU* ($10.8 - 6.1 = 4.7$). The observed level of unemployment for 1982 could be decomposed as follows:

	(%)
Total unemployment	16.0
due to: the capital gap	4.7
structural mismatch	4.5
need to offset potential demand pressures	1.6
insufficient demand	5.2

An important conclusion is that *stronger demand could reduce unemployment* (in 1982) *by 5 per cent without inflationary pressure*, so long as the 'distributive gap' *DG* remains close to zero. Another important conclusion is that *creation of additional capacity* (*to eliminate the capital gap*) *and better adjustment of supply to demand* (*to eliminate structural mismatch*) *would be needed to reduce unemployment* (*and the NIRU*) *below 11 per cent*.

The results of table 15.9 are portrayed in figure 15.8. The figure reproduces the positions in 1973, 1975 and 1982 of the two curves *LL'* and *PP'*, the intersection of which determines the *NIRU* and the *NIRED*. The 1982 curves are represented by continuous lines. The points E_{73}, E_{75}

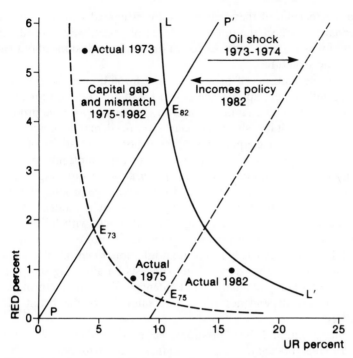

Fig. 15.8.   Actual and non-inflationary values of *UR* and *RED* in Belgium,
1973, 1975 and 1982.

and E_{82} describe the values of the *NIRU* and the *NIRED* in 1973, 1975
and 1982, respectively.

5.   Concluding remarks

We embarked on this confession with the modest aims of (1) seeking an
explanation for the differential rate of growth of Belgian real wages in the
1970s; (2) seeking an explanation for the dramatic decline in employment
and increase in gross apparent labour productivity of the Belgian
manufacturing sector over the past decade; and (3) summarising what we
had learned from the estimation of quantity rationing models.

   On the first point, we note that our price and wage equations, crude
as their specification may be, track the sample data quite accurately
without revealing residual anomalies in the 1970s. At the same time,

several coefficients of these equations are estimated with low precision. The equations reflect the interdependence of prices, wages, productivity and employment; caution is needed in drawing conclusions about causal or dynamic structures.

Are the mechanisms of price and wage formation in Belgium apt to create an inflationary spiral? The *estimation* of our equation for the price of value added yields a unitary long-run elasticity to average production costs, and a unitary short-run elasticity to demand pressures. The *estimation* of our wage equation suggest a short-run elasticity of nominal wage costs to prices (of either value added or consumption) close to, and possibly exceeding, unity. Also, the *specification* of our wage equation imposes a unitary long-run elasticity to gross average productivity, which itself is positively related to real wages. In such a model, exogenous inflationary pressures through wages (an oil shock, with full indexation of wages on consumption prices) or prices (a temporarily excessive level of final demand) may easily result in an inflationary spiral. The record of the 1970s confirms that danger, and suggests an alarming sensitivity of the Belgian economy to inflationary tendencies. The manufacturing sector, with its heavy dependence on export sales, bears the brunt of that sensitivity.

On the second and third questions, we reach parallel conclusions: *it is difficult to separate out the respective influences of factor prices (real wages) and effective demand in accounting for the inadequate performance of Belgian employment since 1974. The only safe conclusion is that both aspects matter.*

Looking at history through the filter of quantity rationing models, we feel that the concepts of 'potential employment' and 'Keynesian labour demand' provide a convincing (to us) interpretation, which is still grossly incomplete. These concepts are helpful to portray the supply side and demand side of the economy. It seems definitely useful to evaluate by how much output and employment could be boosted without either additional investment or the high rates of capacity utilisation suspected of 'rekindling inflation'. Expressing these evaluations in terms of 'non-inflationary rates' of unemployment and excess demand is also helpful. As a corollary, one evaluates how many new working posts should be made available (through investment, additional shifts or work-sharing, in order of decreasing contributions to potential output) along the road to full employment to bridge the 'capital gap'. Hopefully, this combination of traditional and disequilibrium concepts may help bridge an 'intellectual gap' as well.

At the same time, one must be careful not to interpret the spread between labour supply (or potential employment) and Keynesian labour demand as being 'due' to insufficient demand. In a country that exports more than one-third of its value added and competes with imports for another third, excess supply may simply reflect excessive, though non-increasing, costs – either marginal (quantity-setting firms) or average (price-setting firms). Thus, *a part of what is commonly labelled 'Keynesian unemployment' may well be the consequence of a real-wage problem.* And that part could be significant in Belgium.

Similarly, one must be careful not to interpret the spread between labour supply and potential employment as being 'due' to factor prices (real wages). When potential employment corresponds to full use of given facilities, and varies over time through scrapping and/or new investments, *one must reckon with the decisive influence of demand expectations on scrapping and investment decisions.* Then, *a part of what is commonly labelled 'classical unemployment' may well be the consequence of an effective demand problem* – and that part could be significant in Belgium.

We must accordingly conclude that an analysis of the employment problem which does not treat exports and investment endogenously is grossly inadequate. If, as suggested by Bauwens and d'Alcantara (1983), the elasticity of exports with respect to domestic production capacity is three times as high as the elasticity with respect to domestic wages, then a better understanding of the investment process deserves first priority on the research agenda. Given the complexity of the problem, it would seem imperative to rely on more disaggregated data, using all available sources of information.

There is an additional reason why such a research strategy commends itself. A number of authors have stressed the growing extent to which labour is now regarded as fixed factor – a remark that is particularly applicable to Europe, and even more so to Belgium. New hirings and new fixed investments are then best viewed as a joint decision, and should be analysed as such – even though the choice of techniques (factor proportions) deserves separate attention.

There is an element of paradox here, since the model of Section 4 suggests instead a quite rapid adjustment of employment to desired levels, as if labour were in fact a variable factor. However, the 'investment' aspect of hiring decisions is much less significant in periods of growth (1963–74) than in periods of stagnation, or high uncertainty about future growth rates (today). Again, that aspect may affect less significantly layoffs (as in the period 1975–83) than new hirings (today?).

Needless to say, the care needed to interpret the result of our disequilibrium econometrics is equally appropriate when interpreting traditional concepts, like the *NIRU* (see in particular our comments about table 15.9).

A related question left unanswered in this confession came up in the first part of Section 3: Is the elasticity of employment with respect to real wages the same in case of wage increases and wage decreases? Or could it be that the relationship of employment to real wages is 'kinky', in a small open economy like Belgium, with a higher elasticity of employment to wage increases than to wage cuts? What prompts us to repeat this interrogation is the feeling that employment in the Belgian manufacturing sector is unlikely to grow, in response to the incomes policy of the 1980s, at a rate comparable to that at which it fell in response (partially at least) to the differential growth of real wages in the 1970s.

There is again an element of paradox here, since contractual and legal measures have attempted to protect labour from easy dismissals. These measures have clearly been of limited effectiveness in the manufacturing sector. One type of situation when they are bound to be ineffective is of course bankruptcy – a phenomenon of quantitative significance, as revealed above, but seldom modelled explicitly in econom(etr)ics. A realistic model of investment decisions should thus treat scrapping and new investment separately, and should consider financial constraints explicitly. A combination of traditional and disequilibrium concepts is also appropriate in that area.

16 Europe's unemployment problem: introduction and synthesis*

1. General presentation

The economic record of Europe over the past thirty years is divided into two contrasting subperiods: a period of fast balanced growth until 1974, a period of slow growth with unemployment since then. The contrast between the two subperiods, and the contrast vis-à-vis the US which has followed throughout a path of relatively slow but sustained growth, are brought out in table 16.1, which gives average growth rates for major macroeconomic variables over the two subperiods. The developments in Europe during the second subperiod are illustrated by figure 16.1, which traces unemployment against excess capacity in manufacturing since 1975. The gradual rise of unemployment and the cyclical behaviour of capacity utilisation are clearly visible.

The originality of the European Unemployment Programme (EUP) consists in presenting the results obtained from estimating the same model (broadly speaking) in ten countries (the US, the eight major EEC countries and Austria)[1] for periods from the late fifties or early sixties to the mid eighties.[2] Thus, the model specification had to be flexible enough to cover

* Chap. 1 in *Europe's Unemployment Problem*, J. H. Drèze, C. R. Bean, J. P. Lambert, F. Mehta and H. Sneessens, eds., MIT Press, Cambridge, Mass., 1991. The authors have benefited from the invaluable assistance of Fatemeh Mehta, who has in particular prepared all the tables and figures. Her work was supported by contract II/09602 of DG II at the Commission of the European Communities. We have also benefited from comments and suggestions from Torben Andersen, Michael Burda, Wolfgang Franz, Jean-Paul Lambert, Guy Laroque, Fiorella Padoa-Schioppa and Henri Sneessens. Our main debt naturally goes to the 24 authors of the ten country papers collected in this book.
[1] A related study for Switzerland (Stalder, 1989) also exists.
[2] See Appendix 16.2 for a list of papers and authors.

Table 16.1. *Macroeconomic indicators, Europe/US*

	Average Real Growth Rates	Europe	US
GDP (table 10)	61–74	4.6	3.6
	75–88	2.1	3.2
Employment (table 2)	61–74	0.3	1.9
	75–88	0.1	1.9
Private Consumption (table 17)	61–74	4.8	3.8
	75–88	2.4	3.2
Public Consumption (table 19)	61–74	3.6	3.1
	75–88	2.3	3.2
Investment (table 21)	61–74	5.0	3.8
	75–88	1.2	3.2
Real Wages (table 29)	61–74	4.6	1.8
	75–88	1.6	0.9
Labour Productivity	61–74	4.3	1.7
	75–88	2.0	1.3
Unemployment Rate (table 3)	1960	2.5	5.5
	1974	2.6	5.6
	1988	11.3	5.5

Source: Statistical Annex, European Economy, No. 38, November 1988, Commission of the European Community.

the diversity of experiences in the different countries, and for each country in the two subperiods. When the research project was initiated in 1986, it was by no means obvious that such an attempt would succeed. The idea came out of the Conference on *The Rise of Unemployment*, held at Chelwood Gate, Sussex, in May 1985, with Proceedings published in *Economica*, Supplement, 1986.[3] At that conference, much was learned from comparing the unemployment experience in a dozen countries.[4] But the reasons for the differences and similarities were difficult to identify, because different authors had adopted different analytical frameworks. It was difficult to separate out real differences from differences of approach. The authors therefore decided to adopt a common framework, combining the best elements from the different papers, and to estimate a set of country models using the same broad specification.

It may be said at the outset that the project has met with at least one measure of success; namely, that the common specification has indeed proven flexible enough to describe the main developments in the different

[3] Also available as a book edited by C. Bean, R. Layard and S. Nickell and published by Basil Blackwell.
[4] The same as here, plus Australia and Japan.

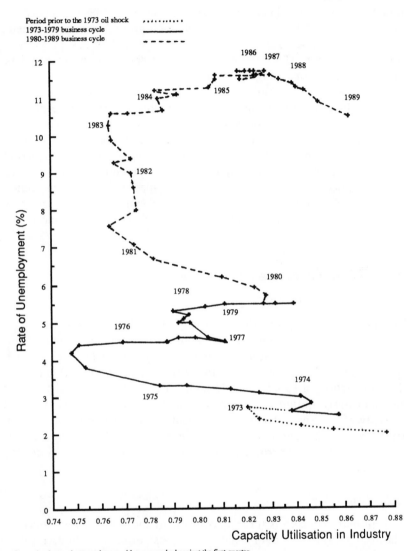

Quarterly observations are shown, with years marked against the first quarter.
Source: European Commission, DG2, 1989.

Figure 16.1   Rate of unemployment and capacity utilisation in industry in the European Community. Quarterly observations are shown, with the years marked against the first quarter. *Source: European Economy.*

countries over the different subperiods. Our model has provided a framework within which the advocates of the different analytical approaches could identify more precisely their grounds for disagreement, and evaluate these against empirical findings; and it has provided a framework within which the experience of different countries could be interpreted more (meaning)fully than before.

This paper is an overall report about empirical results, stressing the aspects where a comparison of national findings is instructive and the aspects which are more specific to our model. These empirical results are discussed under two headings: prices, wages and productivity (Section 4); then output, employment and demand (Section 5). In order to permit interpretation of the empirical findings, a brief presentation of the model is given in Section 2, followed by a more detailed presentation in Section 3. A concise, non-technical summary of the main findings is given in Section 6 (to which hurried readers may turn), leading to some policy conclusions.

2.   Overview and microeconomic foundations

2.1.   Broad structure

The model describes the short-run evolution of an open economy in terms of two aggregate domestic commodities: a physical good and labour. The broad structure is outlined in figure 16.2. The model defines for each period (year)[5] the supply and demand of the physical good and of labour. The interaction of supply and demand on the two markets determines simultaneously output and employment and hence also the rates of capacity utilisation and of unemployment.[6] These two variables in turn trigger price and wage adjustments. The evolution of prices and quantities feeds back into the determinants of supply and demand, thereby closing the model.

2.2.   Employment

Our primary concern is (un)employment. At the heart of the model lies the recognition that for a filled job to exist three conditions must be satisfied. First, that there exists a worker in the right place and with the right skills for the job. Second, that there is the capital available to employ the worker. Third, that there is a demand for the worker's output.

[5] Only the French model is estimated from quarterly data.
[6] This joint determination is explained below.

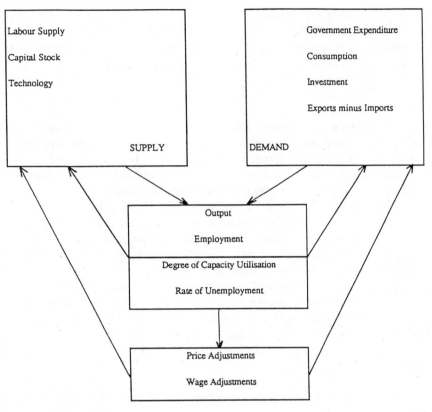

Figure 16.2

The first of these requires little explanation. However, the second and third do require an explanation of the underlying model of production technology and firm behaviour. Within the neoclassical paradigm of perfect competition, with smooth production functions, firms will always vary the capital/labour proportions when relative prices provide incentives to do so, and firms can in principle sell as much as they wish at the prevailing price.

That paradigm seems inconsistent with the results of business surveys. These regularly show a small proportion of firms claiming that capacity is a constraint and a significant proportion claiming to experience demand constraints. Instead, the managers of a neoclassical firm should always claim that capacity is a constraint if they operate with an upward sloping short-run marginal cost curve; and they should never refer to a demand constraint if they face a perfectly elastic demand curve. This suggests replacing the assumption of short-run substitutability between capital and labour by an assumption of limited *ex post* factor substitutability, leading to well-defined concepts of 'capacity output' and 'capacity employment' in the short run. It also suggests replacing the assumption of 'profit maximisation at given prices' by the assumption that firms announce selling prices and then meet demand. Price setting is the natural formulation under imperfect competition, in which case price is set so as to equate (expected) marginal revenue and (expected) marginal cost. It remains valid in the limiting case of perfect competition where marginal revenue is equal to price, so that price is set equal to (expected) marginal cost.[7]

Our setting is thus one where firms set output prices and choose input levels, given their observations or expectations regarding demand conditions and input prices. At any point in time, firms inherit a given capital stock as a result of past investment decisions. If *ex post* factor substitution possibilities are limited (in particular, take time), there is at that point an upper bound to employment dictated by the available number of job slots (capacity employment – *LC*) and an associated upper bound on the level of output (capacity output – *YC*) determined by the level of capital and the embodied technical coefficients.

However, employment may fall short of capacity employment because the firm cannot hire as many workers as it would like. In that case employment will be equal to the available workforce (labour supply – *LS*) and the output level will be determined accordingly (full employment output – *YS*).

Employment may also fall short of capacity employment and labour supply because at the prevailing output price there is insufficient demand forthcoming. In that case output will be determined by effective demand (demand-determined output – *YD*) and the employment level will be determined accordingly (demand-determined employment – *LD*).

These three employment concepts (and their output counterparts) correspond to the three prerequisites for the existence of a filled job, that were outlined at the start of this section. In a given plant or shop *i*, actual

---

[7] For a rigorous definition of competitive equilibria with price setting firms, see Dehez and Drèze (1988a). That paper extends the concept of competitive equilibrium to the case of fixed costs and increasing returns to scale. A further extension to imperfect competition is in preparation.

employment L_i and output Y_i will correspond to the minimum of these three conceptual levels:

$$L_i = \min(LC_i, LD_i, LS_i) \tag{1}$$

$$Y_i = \min(YC_i, YD_i, YS_i). \tag{2}$$

A word of caution about these relationships is needed. They are introduced here to describe some of the constraints (physical and economic) under which firms operate. The formulation is quite general, and compatible in principle with an equilibrium interpretation as well as a disequilibrium interpretation. For instance, when capacity exceeds demand, it could still be the case that demand is precisely at the level for which the chosen price is optimal, whereas the excess capacity is consistent with minimisation of the total cost of producing that output from indivisible equipment. But it could also be the case that excess capacity is due to a depressed demand level, and will be eliminated (through layoffs or scrapping) if demand expectations do not recover soon enough.

Still relationships (1)–(2) are not the end of the story, because one needs to explain (i) the decisions of the firms about the level of capital, the embodied technical coefficients and the output price; (ii) the clearing of output markets; (iii) the aggregation of firm level variables into macro-economic variables; and (iv) the determination of input prices and 'demand' for output. We take up these four items in sequence.

2.3. The rest of the model

(i) Firms treat factor prices as given when making their pricing and investment decisions. Profit maximisation dictates that prices are set as a mark-up over short-run marginal cost. The markup reflects either the elasticity of demand for output on imperfectly competitive markets, or the margin needed to cover fixed costs at normal rates of capacity utilisation, or both. Short-run marginal cost depends on wages and the level of productivity embodied in the technology, at least when capacity and labour supply constraints do not bite.

However, it is costly to continuously adjust prices, which consequently have to be posted in advance on the basis of demand expectations, If there is a chance that demand will be so high that capacity or labour supply constraints bite, then the firm may wish to increase its mark-up to choke off some or all of the excess demand. Alternatively, it may prefer to maintain a reputation for 'fair' pricing, while running down inventories (generally ignored here)[8] and possibly building up back orders. Which combination of these two policies prevails is an important empirical question; the specification of the price equations needs to be flexible enough to admit either answer.[9]

The embodied technical coefficients and the rate of capital accumulation will depend upon (expected) factor prices. Because the level of demand fluctuates over time, the expected level of utilisation of new machines or facilities matters: having capital lying idle some of the time increases the effective cost of that capital and reduces the profitability of investment. Finally, the investment rate will obviously depend on the gap between the desired stock of capital and existing capital. For these two reasons, investment should be positively related to the degree of capacity utilisation.

(ii) Having set prices, on the basis of their demand expectations, firms which are not constrained by capacity or labour supply will *always* be willing to meet the level of demand forthcoming at the posted price, because that price necessarily exceeds marginal cost. There is no rationing of demand when supply bottlenecks do not operate. On the other hand, supply bottlenecks may lead to excess demand for output, which individual firms may not wish to choke off through price increases. In such cases, the demand for the products of other firms producing close substitutes will increase accordingly. Some of these will be foreign firms, so the level of imports may increase.[10] If some domestic suppliers choose to divert output from the foreign to the domestic market, exports will fall, thereby adding to the deterioration of the trade balance. The upshot is that demand pressures will be associated with a combination of price increases and trade spillovers. These demand pressures will also be accompanied by undesirably high degrees of capacity utilisation, spurring investment. The model assumes that these mechanisms are sufficiently powerful that no quantity rationing of domestic demand is ever observed (in aggregate annual data).

(iii) The aggregation of the employment and output decisions of firms into the corresponding macroeconomic variables recognises the heterogeneity of the situations faced by individual firms. Because there are many products, there will exist simultaneously cases where product

[8] The German model does, however, contain an inventories equation.

[9] As explained in Section 4.1, the combined evidence from the 10 countries supports the reputation argument.

[10] This is best understood as reflecting the activity of (wholesale) traders who chase supplies wherever they can be found, either domestically or abroad, when not available from the usual sources.

demand exceeds capacity output, and cases where it falls short of capacity. Similarly, because there are many skills, there will simultaneously exist job vacancies and unemployed workers. Aggregating equations (2), for instance, yields

$$Y = \Sigma_i Y_i = \Sigma_i \min (YC_i, YD_i, YS_i)$$
$$\leqslant \min (\Sigma_i YC_i, \Sigma_i YD_i, \Sigma_i YS_i)$$
$$= \min (YC, YD, YS). \tag{3}$$

With many firms, skills and products, the min conditions are smoothed by aggregation. A simple functional relationship among the aggregate variables – used in most of the papers – can be derived from plausible (lognormality) assumptions about the distribution across firms of the relative magnitudes of the three proximate determinants of output, viz:

$$Y = [YC^{-\rho} + YD^{-\rho} + YS^{-\rho}]^{-\frac{1}{\rho}}. \tag{4}$$

This relationship, and in particular the parameter ρ (>0), is discussed in section 3.3 below.

The corresponding employment relationship is

$$L = [LC^{-\rho} + LD^{-\rho} + LS^{-\rho}]^{-\frac{1}{\rho}}. \tag{5}$$

(iv) Turning to input prices and output demands, the model is fairly standard. For simplicity, the papers generally do not model the financial sector of the economy, instead treating interest rates as exogenous. To the extent that (real) interest rates are determined in global rather than national capital markets, this is a justifiable assumption.

Wages however clearly do not need to be endogenised. In general these will respond to tightness of the labour market, as well as to productivity growth. In addition, there are a number of variables, such as terms of trade movements, changes in taxes and changes in benefit levels that may affect wage settlements. Through the tightness of the labour market, unemployment affects wages; that is the only relationship where unemployment appears explicitly.

Aggregate demand is the sum of: consumption, mostly related to disposable income; investment, whose determinants were mentioned above; government expenditures (exogenous) and export demand minus import demand, both of which are related to the relevant measure of final expenditure (at the world level for exports, the domestic level for imports) and to international competitiveness (world prices relative to domestic prices). Through the trade equations, domestic prices and hence domestic costs (in particular wages) affect aggregate demand, output and employment.

3. The model in detail

A more detailed presentation of the model is conveniently organised around the four blocks of figure 16.2 as spelled out in figure 16.3, namely: supply; demand; output and employment; prices and wages.

3.1. Technology and supply

Labour supply *LS* is typically exogenous.[11] Capacity output *YC* is equal to the stock of capital *K* times the output/capital ratio at full utilisation of capital. The stock of capital is that inherited from the past. The output/capital ratio B, and the associated output/labour ratio *A*, are assumed to reflect cost minimisation subject to a linearly homogeneous constant elasticity of substitution production function.[12] These ratios are assumed fixed in the short run (over the year), because adjustments in factor proportions take time. This *ex post* Leontief technology is somewhat more extreme than we would like but provides a convenient organising benchmark.

The estimated productivity equations allow for technical progress through time trends and use a distributed lag $\Theta(\Lambda)$ on relative factor prices $\dfrac{W}{Q}$ (where *W* denotes wages and *Q* the appropriate user cost of capital). That distributed lag captures both the sluggishness of the adjustment in technical coefficients due to the putty-clay nature of the technology *and* the process by which expectations of future factor prices are formed. The resulting equations for *technical* productivities take the form

$$\left(\frac{Y}{K}\right)_{tech} = B_t = B\left(t, \Theta(\Lambda)\frac{W}{Q}\right) \tag{6}$$

$$\left(\frac{Y}{L}\right)_{tech} = A_t = A\left(t, \Theta(\Lambda)\frac{W}{Q}\right) \tag{7}$$

[11] The French, Dutch and British papers contain labour supply equations.
[12] In the Austrian, Belgian, Danish and US papers, the Cobb–Douglas specification is not rejected by the data. The estimated elasticity of substitution is 0.94 in Italy, but much lower in France (0.5) and Germany (0.3).

and are estimated in a log-linear specification. To these technical coefficients correspond the concepts of capacity output $YC = BK$, full employment output $YS = ALS$ and capacity employment $LC = YC/A$.

Capacity output and capacity employment are latent variables, not directly observed. In principle, *measured* average productivities Y/K and Y/L are related to the technical productivities B, A by identities defining the degree of utilisation of the factors of production, DUC and DUL respectively: $DUC = Y/BK$, $DUL = Y/AL$. These two definitions are not quite symmetrical, however. K defines at the same time the aggregate capital stock available to the economy, and the sum of the capital stocks installed in the firms. *Ex post*, that capital may not be fully utilised, because there is insufficient labour to man the machines or (more likely) there is insufficient demand for the output. An empirical measure of DUC is available from business surveys of the manufacturing sector, where firms are asked to report their estimates of $Y/YC = Y/BK$. Such measures are used in most papers. In order to allow for data inadequacies, the estimated equations do not impose that measured capital productivity be equal to B times DUC, but rather to B times DUC^β, where β is a freely estimated elasticity.[13]

The story for labour utilisation is slightly different, because the aggregate labour force available to the economy is not equal to the sum of the labour forces employed in the firms. Hence, DUL is not a measure of unemployment. If labour were a fully variable factor, employment in the firm would be adjusted continuously to production needs, and measured labour productivity would be equal to technical productivity, independently of the ratio of actual employment to capacity employment. But labour is not a fully variable factor in the short run. There are two aspects to this: heads and hours. A straightforward story, quite appropriate for blue collar workers, would say that actual hours correspond closely to production needs, and are reconciled with employment (heads) through departures of actual hours per head from standard hours: overtime, when there are too few heads; part-time unemployment or temporary layoffs, when there are too many heads. Under that story, the number of heads would be explained through, say, a partial adjustment mechanism on the gap between desired and past employment; whereas productivity per head

---

[13] The coefficients β reported in table 16.7 range from 0.3 to 0.7, up to an Italian outlier (0.13).

would be equal to technical productivity times the degree of utilisation of labour, measured by the ratio of actual hours per head to standard hours per head.[14] In many countries, there exist some data on the ratio of actual to standard hours per head (typically, for blue collar workers in manufacturing). These data are used in most papers, again with a freely estimated elasticity parameter α to allow for data inadequacies.[15] That story carries over to white collar workers, with the proviso that their actual hours are typically kept equal to standard hours, with the intensity of work taking up the slack. It is of course rather heroic to assume that the ratio of actual to standard hours per head for blue collar workers in manufacturing alone correctly measures the degree of utilisation of employed labour in the whole economy.

The general form of the estimated equations appears in figure 16.3. The log-linear counterpart appears in the text, with the same numbering, and with lower case letters denoting logarithms. For the productivity equations, we have:

$$y_t - k_t = \beta_0 + \beta_1 t + \beta_2 \Theta(\Lambda)(w - q) + \beta_3 \, duc \tag{8}$$

$$y_t - l_t = \alpha_0 + \alpha_1 t + \alpha_2 \Theta(\Lambda)(w - q) + \alpha_3 \, dul. \tag{9}$$

To go from these to estimates of YC and $\underline{LC}$, one simply sets the DUC and DUL variables at their upper limits $\overline{DUC}$ and $\overline{DUL}$ – either unity or the highest level attained over the sample period. This yields

$$yc = y + \beta_3(\overline{duc} - duc); lc = l + \beta_3(\overline{duc} - duc) - \alpha_3(\overline{dul} - dul). \tag{10}$$

3.2. Demand

The demand side of the model is relatively conventional, except for the introduction of capacity utilisation terms into the trade equations to take account of the supply bottlenecks discussed above.

Government expenditure is treated as exogenous. The consumption function typically uses disposable income of households as the main

---

[14] By the same argument, the DUL variable could meaningfully be introduced in the capital productivity equation. Rien n'est parfait, dit le renard.

[15] The coefficients α reported in table 16.7 range from 0.4 to 1, up to a Belgian (0.05) and an Italian (1.9) ouliers.

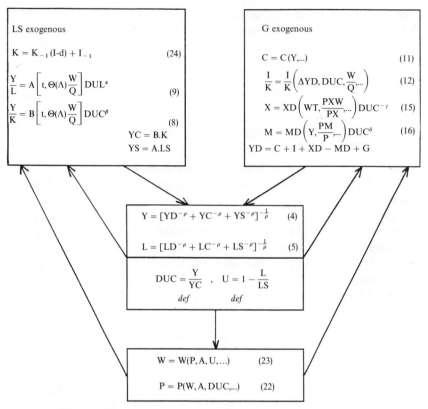

Figure 16.3

explanatory variable.[16] As indicated in Section 5.6 below, it might have been desirable to introduce wage income, transfers and property income as separate arguments – but the merits of that more ambitious specification are not unanimously recognised. As explained in Section 5.3 below, the treatment of investment differs somewhat from country to country. The dependent variable is typically the accumulation rate I/K, but several alternatives come up. Many papers find that the degree of capacity utilisation serves as a useful proxy for expected future capacity utilisation, and possibly also for future profitability.

In line with the general principles outlined above, the models assume that domestic final demand is never rationed. Aggregate demand YD is

[16] A couple of papers treat consumption as exogenous.

the sum of consumption C, investment I, government expenditure G, and export demand XD minus import demand MD. A stylised specification goes as follows:

$$c = \gamma_0 + \gamma_1 y + \cdots \tag{11}$$

$$i - k = \delta_0 + \delta_1 \Delta yd + \delta_2(yd - yc) + \cdots \tag{12}$$

$$xd = \varepsilon_0 + \varepsilon_1 wt + \varepsilon_2(pw - px)\ldots \tag{13}$$

$$md = \eta_0 + \eta_1 yd + \eta_2(p - pm)\ldots \tag{14}$$

where WT denotes world trade with price index PW, whereas PX, PM and P denote export prices, import prices and the value-added deflator respectively.

As explained above, the excess of YD over Y is absorbed by inventories (not modelled) or spills over into the trade balance. Accordingly, realised imports and exports are allowed to deviate from the levels specified in (13)–(14) to an extent that depends upon the degree of capacity utilisation. It is convenient to express that last variable relative to a minimal level $\underline{DUC}$ at which no spillover would occur.[17] This leads to the following specification:

$$x = \varepsilon_0 + \varepsilon_1 wt + \varepsilon_2(pw - px) - \varepsilon_3(duc - \underline{duc}) \tag{15}$$

$$m = \eta_0 + \eta_1 yd + \eta_2(p - pm) + \eta_3(duc - \underline{duc}). \tag{16}$$

As will be seen in Section 5.1, the empirical analysis mostly yields significant parameter values for ε_3 and especially for η_3.

Using (15) and (16), we can express YD as

$$YD = Y + (XD - X) - (MD - M)$$

a relationship that could also be approximated by[18]

$$yd = y + \left(\frac{X}{Y}\varepsilon_3 + \frac{M}{Y}\eta_3\right)(duc - \underline{duc}). \tag{17}$$

---

[17] The introduction of $\underline{DUC}$ is motivated by the desire to obtain a convenient expression for YD (see footnote 18). This amounts simply to redefining the constants ε_0 and η_0. In practice, $\underline{DUC}$ is measured as the lowest value of DUC observed over the sample period.

[18] The approximation comes from

$$YD = Y + X\left[\left(\frac{DUC}{\underline{DUC}}\right)^{\varepsilon_3} - 1\right] - M\left[\left(\frac{DUC}{\underline{DUC}}\right)^{-\eta_3} - 1\right]$$

$$= Y\left\{1 + \frac{X}{Y}\frac{DUC^{\varepsilon_3} - \underline{DUC}^{\varepsilon_3}}{\underline{DUC}^{\varepsilon_3}} + \frac{M}{Y}\frac{DUC^{\eta_3} - \underline{DUC}^{\eta_3}}{DUC^{\eta_3}}\right\}.$$

3.3. Output and employment

The definition of output and employment through aggregation over firms was introduced in (iii) of Section 2.3. Ignoring for the moment the labour supply bottlenecks, one may concentrate attention on the firm level capacity output YC_i and demand-determined output YD_i. Assuming the ratio of these two quantities to be (approximately) lognormally distributed over the set of firms, one obtains by aggregation a simple CES-type relationship between actual output (sales) Y, capacity YC and demand YD, namely

$$Y = (YC^{-\rho} + YD^{-\rho})^{-\frac{1}{\rho}}, \tag{18}$$

where the parameter $\rho > 0$ is related to the variance of the ratio of demand to capacity across firms; see Lambert (1988). That relationship is illustrated in figure 16.4, which shows how the 'CES-bow' replaces the 'min-boomerang' through aggregation. In that figure, b denotes unfilled orders and c denotes unused capacity. At the price which would equate aggregate supply and aggregate demand, b and c would be equal. In terms of equation (18), when $YC = YD$, then $Y = YC \cdot 2^{-\frac{1}{\rho}}$ and $(YC - Y)/YC = 1 - 2^{-\frac{1}{\rho}}$ measures the 'structural underutilisation rate of capacity at equilibrium' (SURE), in the terminology of Sneessens and Drèze (1986a).[19] As ρ tends to infinity, the CES-bow of figure 16.4 tends to the min-boomerang, and SURE goes to zero. As ρ decreases, SURE increases (tending to 1, or 100%, as ρ tends to zero), reflecting a growing 'mismatch' between capacity (supply) and demand at the firm level.

The *demand for labour* by firms is derived from their manpower needs to produce output – say $L(Y) = Y/A$, satisfying

$$L(Y) = \frac{Y}{A} = \left[\left(\frac{YC}{A} \right)^{-\rho} + \left(\frac{YD}{A} \right)^{-\rho} \right]^{-\frac{1}{\rho}}$$

$$= (LC^{-\rho} + LD^{-\rho})^{-\frac{1}{\rho}}. \tag{19}$$

Abstracting from short-term dynamics, actual *employment* will be the minimum of labour demand and labour supply, with the latter operating

---

[19] Referring to the labour market, these authors define SURE as the 'Structural Unemployment Rate at Equilibrium'.

as a binding constraint when the required skills are not available locally. Aggregating again over firms under a lognormality assumption, we obtain another CES-type relationship between aggregate employment L, aggregate labour demand $L(Y)$ and aggregate labour supply LS, say with parameter ρ':

$$L = (L(Y)^{-\rho'} + LS^{-\rho'})^{\frac{-1}{\rho'}}. \tag{20}$$

Inserting (19) into (20), we obtain the general 'nested CES' relationship

$$L = [(LC^{-\rho} + LD^{-\rho})^{\frac{\rho'}{\rho}} + LS^{-\rho'}]^{-\frac{1}{\rho'}} \tag{21}$$

which allows for different degrees of 'mismatch' on the goods markets and on the labour markets. That general formulation is used in the French model and is discussed further in Section 4.3 below. The other country models introduce the assumption that $\rho = \rho'$, so that (21) simplifies to (5). The output and employment determination is then given by (4)–(5).

3.4. Prices and wages

At the level of the firm, demand is uncertain and prices have to be set before the uncertainty is resolved. The technological assumptions imply

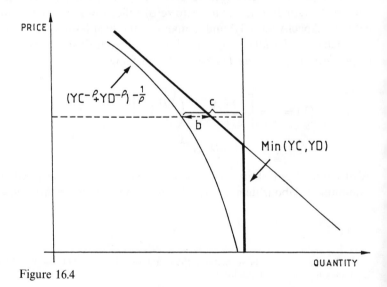

Figure 16.4

that the firm's short-run marginal cost curve is backward *L*-shaped as in figure 16.5. In the absence of capacity or labour supply constraints, therefore, imperfect competition theory suggests that the (value-added) price *P* will be a mark-up over (constant) unit labour costs *W/A*, where the mark-up depends upon the price elasticity of demand. Alternatively, as for instance in the contestable markets literature (e.g. Baumol *et al.*, 1982), competitive forces may keep the price in line with unit (average) production cost at a 'normal' degree of capacity utilisation *DUC**, i.e. *W/A + Q/B DUC**. In either case, the level of output and employment will then be determined by the level of demand *YD*.

As explained in Section 2.3 (i), the pricing relationship should also include a term in the expected level of (*YD/Y*), to pick up any spillover of supply bottlenecks onto pricing behaviour. However, since *YD* is a latent variable which can only be constructed from within the model itself,

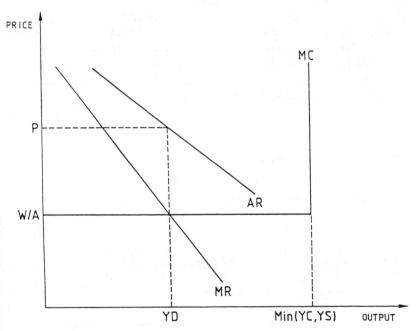

Figure 16.5

most papers pursue a short-cut by using the observed degree of capacity utilisation DUC as a proxy. Thus, the price equation becomes

$$p = \zeta_0 + \zeta_1(w - a) + \zeta_2(q - b) + \zeta_3 duc - \zeta_4(w - w^e), \tag{22}$$

where the nominal wage surprise $w - w^e$ is included to allow for the possibility that prices may have to be fixed before wage levels are agreed.[20] Several papers impose $\zeta_1 = 1$, $\zeta_2 = 0$ (mark up over unit labour costs), whereas others estimate $\zeta_1 < 1$ (close to the wage share in value added, in agreement with a unit elasticity of prices with respect to average cost at normal capacity).

Finally, we need to consider how wages are determined. Suppressing inessential dynamics, an eclectic specification of the real (product) wage equation might take the form

$$w - p = \xi_0 + \xi_1 a + \xi_2(l - ls) - \xi_3(p - p^e) + \xi_4 z \tag{23}$$

where $(p - p^e)$, usually proxied by $\Delta^2 p$, is the price surprise reflecting the fact that some wages are set before prices are known, and Z is a vector of shift variables such as the terms of trade, tax rates, benefit levels, the share of long-term unemployed, measures of union power and the like. This equation is open to a variety of interpretations depending on the variables that are included in Z (see Layard and Nickell, 1985). The fact that over long periods unemployment is generally untrended suggests that ξ_1 should be unity, in which case the equation basically relates the wage shares W/PA to the unemployment rate.[21] This equation is discussed at greater length in Section 4.2 below.

3.5.   *Structural and reduced forms*

Equations (4), (5), (8), (9), (11), (12), (15), (16), (22) and (23) form a system of ten equations in the ten endogenous variables, Y, L, DUC, DUL, C, I,

---

[20] In the papers, this is usually proxied by $\Delta^2 w$, the change in wage inflation.

[21] Simultaneously setting $\xi_1 = 1$ in the wage equation, and $\zeta_1 = 1$, $\zeta_2 = 0$ in the price equation, leads to

$$p - w + a = \zeta_0 + \zeta_3 duc - \zeta_4(w - w^e) \tag{22'}$$

$$w - p - a = \xi_0 + \xi_2(l - ls) - \xi_3(p - p^e) + \xi_4 z. \tag{23'}$$

The issue of identification of these two equations should then receive more attention than it has typically been given in this work.

X, M, P and W. (See also figure 16.3.) The system is completed by the identity

$$K_{t+1} = (1 - d)K_t + \dot{I}_t \qquad (24)$$

where d is the scrapping rate.

This common structure forms the basis of the ten country papers. The exact specification of each equation was chosen by the country authors to reflect national idiosyncracies. Although the resulting diversity of precise specifications sometimes restricts comparability of results, it turns out to be quite instructive. In particular, the commonality of freely adopted specifications sometimes conveys a significant message, as we shall see.

In principle, the ten equations form a simultaneous system and should be estimated as such. Experimentation with estimation methods performed on the Belgian model has revealed that simultaneous FIML estimation of the ten equations yielded parameter values very close to those obtained by a block recursive method, but at a considerably heavier computational cost. Accordingly, the simpler method was adopted for the other countries.[22] That procedure led to repeated use of an instrumental variables representation for some of the endogenous variables.

In practice, all the equations except (4)–(5) are specified as log-linear. The simultaneous system is non-linear. When formulated in terms of growth rates, however, the system is nearly linear, up to some parameters computed for each observation from the level values of the variables. That property is useful for short term analysis, as illustrated in Section 5.

Whether it be expressed in levels or in growth rates, the ten-equation model is fairly complex, and its qualitative properties may not be immediately obvious; see, however, Sneessens and Drèze (1986a, Section 3) for a discussion of some basic properties.

It is common practice in macroeconomics to seek a condensed representation through a few reduced form relationships, preferably suited for graphical analysis in two dimensions. Given our primary concern with (un)employment, we could try to derive two reduced form relationships describing the labour market, in terms of which the determination and comparative statics of the real wage and (un)employment could then be discussed.

Our reduced form analysis of the labour market is based on two blocks

---

[22] There is one exception: the Italian model was estimated by FIML.

of 4 structural equations each. Treating DUC and DUL as 'state' or 'shift' variables, the productivity equations (8)–(9) and the price-wage equations (22)–(23) can be solved for the four variables A, B, P, W as functions of U and additional shift variables (including Q). We shall deal with these four equations in Section 4. Logically, they could be summarised in a single relationship, say between U and W/P, to be labelled 'wage-price-productivity' equation. (Clearly, the coefficient of unemployment in the wage equation plays the same important role here as in other work.) Such a relationship could be interpreted as giving the unemployment rate which brings about consistency between the wage formation (23), the price formation (22) and the labour productivity (9) – after using (8) to eliminate B from (22). That reduction is illustrated formally in Appendix 16.1 and for a particular specification in Section 4.5. Shifting the 'wage-price-productivity' schedule inwards is a major goal of so-called supply-side policies.

Turn next to the demand block. Treating DUC and K_{-1} as 'state' or 'shift' variables, the four equations (11), (12), (15) and (16) can be solved for the four endogenous variables C, I, XD and MD – hence for YD – as functions of P and of exogenous shift variables like G, WT, PW, PM, ... The role of P comes via the price terms PW/PX and PM/P appearing in the trade equations. For the purposes of the present exercise, it is more convenient to relate trade competitiveness directly to real wages W/P.[23] The reduced equation summarising the demand side would thus relate YD and W/P through competitiveness.

The transition from aggregate demand to (un)employment consists of two steps. One of these relates output to aggregate demand by means of (4), which brings in capacity output YC and full employment output YS – as well as the important parameter ρ capturing microeconomic mismatch between supply and demand. The other relates output and employment through the technical labour productivity $Y/L = A$, itself related to real wages. The net effect of these two steps, detailed in Section 5, is to combine the competitiveness effect with the effects of real wages on factor

---

[23] The standard argument to the effect that rises in real wages impair competitiveness rests on the same relation. Explicit modelling of the links from W/P to PW/PX and PM/P would add to be the complexity of the model ...

substitution, which go in the same direction.[24] This produces a reduced form 'labour demand' equation, whereby employment is negatively related (unemployment is positively related) to real wages; the main shift factors come from exogenous demand (G and WT), from exogenous competitiveness (PW and PM) and from the inherited capital K_{-1}.[25]

Combining this 'labour demand' equation with the previously derived 'wage-price-productivity' equation yields the reduced form description of the labour market. Major departures from previous studies reside in the greater attention paid (i) to technical productivities and factor substitution; (ii) to the possible mismatch of supply and demand; and (iii) to the role of the capital stock in defining the supply potential of the economy.

Some macroeconomic authors (including Blanchard in Drèze *et al.* 1991, Ch. 2) use a particular specification of the price and wage equations, which can then be solved uniquely for the real wage and (un)employment; the reduced form demand equation is then solved for the nominal price level.

At the other end of the spectrum, the first generation of disequilibrium models treated wages and prices as exogenous, then concentrated upon the interplay of effective demand with capacity in the relationships (4)–(5) determining output and employment. Again, this is a particular specification.

These two extremes may be viewed as focussing respectively on the 'wage–price' equation[26] and on the 'labour demand' equation of a labour market reduced form. The present model is more general, because it specifies explicitly and quite generally the structural relationships lying behind each of these two equations. The price paid for increased realism is increased complexity.

4. Prices, wages and productivity

4.1. Prices

A first important empirical regularity of the empirical results is the lack of a significant influence of demand pressure on prices. Table 16.2

Table 16.2. *Elasticities of prices (GDP deflator)*

(Upper rows = short run, lower rows = long run)

Variable	Austria	Belgium	Britain	Denmark	France	Germany	Italy	Netherlands	Spain	U.S.
Demand pressure (DUC)	0.225	0.188[1]	−0.054[3]	no price equation estimated		0.155	0.720		−0.270	−0.001
		0.003	−0.084			0.277	0.970		−0.443	−0.005
Cost push (Wages)	0.510	0.749[2]	0.880		0.490	0.477	0.740	0.163	1	1.361
	1	1	1			0.855	1	0.403	1	1

[1] The demand pressure variable is YD/Y, with YD estimated within the model.
[2] The cost variable is average production cost, estimated within the model.
[3] Numerical value not comparable with those for other countries.

reproduces the point estimates of the elasticities of prices (the deflator of GDP) with respect to the degree of capacity utilisation, used as a measure of demand relative to capacity output, and with respect to wages. Nine equations were estimated. In two countries (France, Netherlands), no significant influence of capacity utilisation on prices could be measured. In three countries (Spain, UK, US), a significant but small *negative* elasticity was estimated.[27] In three countries (Austria, Belgium, Germany) a significant but small *positive* elasticity was estimated. In Italy, the estimated elasticity is positive and quite high (0.72) – but it is partly offset by a negative elasticity with respect to the degree of utilisation of labour (measured by the ratio of actual to normal working hours). The prevailing picture is thus one of negligible measured influence of demand pressure on prices. In that light, the reference to high rates of capacity utilisation as a warning that demand stimulation would be inflationary is questionable.

The absence of a significant influence of demand pressure on prices is all the more instructive, because authors sought for such an influence, and tried alternative measures of demand pressure. One must hasten to add that the elasticity of prices with respect to wage costs is substantial everywhere[28] – ranging between 0.5 and 1 in the short run, and typically set equal to 1 (after suitable testing) in the long run. In that light, the more relevant question is whether demand stimulation is likely to generate upward pressure on wages, which would then promptly be transmitted to prices. We return to price-wage dynamics below (Section 4.5).

4.2. Wages

The empirical results concerning wage equations are summarised in table 16.3, which gives the elasticity of real product wages with respect to average labour productivity and the derivatives of the rate of growth of real wages with respect to the unemployment rate (measured in percentage points). In every single European country, measured productivity gains seem to be passed on quite rapidly into wages, with short-run elasticities ranging from 0.4 to 0.8 and with a long-run elasticity close to unity. Similarly, the dampening effect of unemployment on real wage growth is present everywhere, with sensible orders of magnitude, but the coefficients

---

[27] A negative influence could reflect increasing returns to scale or procyclical movements in perceived demand elasticities.

[28] Except in the Netherlands, where the dependent variable is the price deflator of output and where the equation is estimated for the period 1971–1987; higher elasticities are obtained there when the dependent variable is consumer prices instead of output prices.

Table 16.3. *Wages*

(Upper rows = short run, lower rows = long run)

Variable	Austria	Belgium	Britain	Denmark	France	Germany	Italy	Netherlands	Spain	U.S.
Productivity (elasticity)	0.412	0.882	0.100	0.360	0.420	0.660	0.710	0.562	0.830	0.0017[2]
	1.060	0.821	1			1	1	0.839		0.017
Unemploy. (semi-elasticity)	−0.025	−0.004[3]	−0.011[4]	−0.012[3]	−0.003	−0.004	−0.014		−0.011	−0.002[3]
	−0.028	−0.007	−0.110	−0.055		−0.004	−0.020			−0.013
Vac. rate			0.011[1]					0.025		
			0.110					0.093		

[1] Vacancy rate is estimated from the percentage of firms reporting an excess demand for labour in business surveys.
[2] Productivity is proxied by a time trend; the coefficient, 0.0017, may be compared with the estimated trend coefficient of 0.0023 in the labour productivity equation, suggesting an elasticity of real wages to labour productivity close to 0.8.
[3] Unemployment variable appears with a lag of one period.
[4] The explanatory variable is (U *Effective* − V). The nature of this variable means the numerical value of the semi-elasticity is not comparable with those for other countries.

are not precisely estimated. In the US, measured productivity did not enter significantly, and was replaced by a time trend.

The specification of the wage equations turns out to be quite interesting, and deserves some discussion. We first note that all equations, except the French one based on quarterly data, fit quite well, with estimated standard errors ranging from 0.5% to 1%. This may be compared with the results presented at the first Chelwood Gate Conference, where the standard errors of wage equations ranged between 1.5% and 2%.[29]

These wage equations, which are listed in table 16.4, display two notable features. First, with the exception of France, they all embody an error correction mechanism which relates the *level* of real wages to the *level* of unemployment in the long run. This is in marked contrast to the orthodox 'Phillips curve' relationship (of which the French equation is an example) which links the unemployment rate to the *rate of change* of real wages. This level specification originates in the classic paper of Sargan (1964).

The second notable feature is that, with the exception of the Danish, French and American wage equations, the error correction mechanisms imply that in the long run, it is essentially the share of wages in GNP (rather than the real wage itself) that is related to the unemployment rate. This would seem to correspond to the notion that wage formation in Europe today is dominated by unions who are heavily concerned over distributional fairness, in contrast to the United States.[30] As we shall see below in Section 4.5, this has important implications for the susceptibility of the European economies to inflationary shocks.

Finally there is the issue of the responsiveness of wage demands to unemployment. There are two dimensions to this: the overall size of the effect; and the speed with which it operates. Measuring the overall size by the long-run semi-elasticities of the real wage to the unemployment rate (given in table 16.3), we see that they range from 0.4% in Germany to 2.8% in Austria.[31] In *all* countries this sensitivity of real wages to

---

[29] See Bean *et al.* (1987) or *Economica*, Supplement 1986. As a further reference, we note that average standard errors of the wage equations estimated by Grubb *et al.* (1983) for 19 OECD countries on annual data 1957–1980 with the parsimonious specification $\Delta w = \alpha \Delta p + (1 - \alpha)\Delta w_{-1} - \gamma u + \delta t + \text{constant}$ was 2.35%.

[30] Hellwig and Neumann (1987) describe as follows the negotiating stand of West German trade unions: 'As political organisations, they are very much concerned with the "fairness" of the distribution of income. In principle, they want to raise or at least maintain the share of wages in GNP.'

[31] The semi-elasticity for Denmark is even larger at 5.5% but as noted in the Danish paper, this equation is less than satisfactory in a number of respects, despite its low standard error, suggesting that it should be treated as an anomalous outlier.

Table 16.4. *Survey of wage equations*

Austria

$$\Delta \ln\left[\frac{WH}{P}\right] = -0.4\left[ln\left(\frac{WH.L}{P.Y}\right)_{-1} + 0.025U^{-1} - 0.55\ln TAX2_{-1} + \text{const.}\right]$$
$$- 0.65\Delta^2 \ln P - 0.025\Delta U + 0.5\Delta \ln TAX2 - 1.2\Delta \ln TAX3 + \text{const.}$$

Belgium

$$\Delta \ln\left[\frac{WN}{PC}\right] = -0.5\left[ln\left(\frac{WN.L}{PC.Y}\right)_{-1} + 0.01U_{-1} + \text{const.}\right] + 0.88\Delta \ln\left(\frac{Y}{L}\right) + \text{const.}$$

Denmark

$$\Delta \ln\left[\frac{W}{PC}\right] = -0.21\left[ln\left(\frac{W}{PC}\right)_{-1} + 0.055U_{-1} + 0.3HOURS_{-1} + \text{const.}\right] + 0.36\Delta \ln A - 0.76\Delta \ln\left(\frac{PC}{P}\right) + \text{const.}$$

France

$$\Delta \ln\left[\frac{W}{P}\right] = 0.4\Delta \ln\left(\frac{Y}{L}\right) - 0.6\Delta \ln\left(\frac{PC}{P}\right) - 0.08U + \text{dummies} + \text{const.}$$

Germany

$$\Delta \ln\left[\frac{W}{P}\right] = -0.17\left[\ln\left(\frac{W.L}{P.Y}\right)_{-1} + 0.004U_{-1} + \text{const.}\right]$$
$$- 0.004\Delta U + 0.66\Delta \ln A + 0.18\Delta \ln\left(\frac{W}{WN}\right) + 0.04\Delta \ln\left(\frac{PM}{P}\right) + 0.27\Delta \ln\left(\frac{W}{P}\right)_{-1} + \text{dummies.}$$

Italy

$$\Delta \ln\left[\frac{W}{P}\right] = -0.71\left[ln\left(\frac{W.L}{P.Y}\right)_{-1} + 0.02U + 0.01\ln DUC - 0.9\ln TAX4 + \text{const.}\right] + 0.2\Delta \ln\left(\frac{PM}{P}\right)$$

Netherlands

$$\Delta \ln\left[\frac{W}{PC}\right] = -0.34\left[\ln\left(\frac{W}{PC}\right)\right]_{-1} - 0.8\ln\left(\frac{Y}{L}\right)_{-1} - 0.1V_{-1} - TAX2_{-1} - 0.64TAX1_{-1} + \text{const.}\right]$$

$$+ 0.56\Delta\ln A + \Delta TAX2 + 0.4\Delta TAX1 + 0.025\Delta V + \text{const.}$$

Spain

$$\ln\left[\frac{W}{P(1 + TAX3)}\right] = 0.16\ln\left(\frac{Y}{L}\right) - 0.01U - 0.27\Delta^2\ln P + 0.8[\text{mismatch} + \text{replacement ratio} + \text{import wedge}] + \text{dummies} + \text{const.}$$

U.K.

$$\Delta\ln\left[\frac{W}{P}\right] = -0.1\left[\ln\left(\frac{W}{P}\right)_{-1} - \ln\left(\frac{YC}{LC}\right) + 0.11(U_{Effective} - V) + 0.65\ln(\text{Repl. Ratio})\right] - 0.1\Delta^2\ln P$$

US

$$\Delta\ln\left[\frac{W}{P}\right] = -0.1\left[\ln\left(\frac{W}{P}\right)_{-1} - 0.2t + 0.013U_{-1} + 0.45\,\text{Wedge}_{-1} + \text{const.}\right] - 0.001\Delta U - 0.06\Delta\text{DEMOG} - 0.32\Delta^2\ln P + \text{const.}$$

TAX1: labour taxes paid by employees
TAX2: labour taxes paid by employers
TAX3: indirect taxes
TAX4: income taxes
WH: hourly wage cost
WN: take-home wage
W: wage cost
PC: consumer prices

unemployment is too low to ensure that unemployment is substantially self-correcting in the face of adverse shocks (see Section 4.5).

As far as the speed of the effect of unemployment on real wages goes, that too varies across countries. For instance in Austria and Germany lags in the response of wages to unemployment are very short[32] – virtually all of the effect comes through in the first year – while for most of the other countries the effect of unemployment on real wages is quite drawn out. Some of these differences whether short or long run, will be attributable to differences in choice of specification and sampling error, but some also no doubt reflect real institutional differences.[33]

4.3. Shifts of the U–V curve

There is another striking empirical regularity in the results. It is most conveniently described as additional evidence corroborating outward shifts in the so-called Beveridge, or U–V curve. The estimated employment equations, neglecting partial adjustment terms, are of the form

$$L_t = [LD_t^{-\rho_t} + LC_t^{-\rho_t} + LS_t^{-\rho_t}]^{\frac{-1}{\rho_t}}, \tag{25}$$

with $\dfrac{1}{\rho_t} = a + bt, b > 0$, representing a growing 'mismatch' of supplies and demands at the microeconomic level. Table 16.5 reproduces the values of a and b for the different countries, as well as the implied estimates of the 'structural unemployment rate at equilibrium' (SURE) for 1960 and 1986. The rise over time in 'mismatch' is clear everywhere.

The specification of the French employment equation is slightly different, namely

$$L_t = [(LD_t^{-\rho_1} + LC_t^{-\rho_1})^{\frac{\rho_{2t}}{\rho_1}} + LS_t^{-\rho_{2t}}]^{\frac{-1}{\rho_{2t}}}, \tag{26}$$

with $\dfrac{1}{\rho_{2t}} = a + bt, t > 0$ but ρ_1 constant (not a function of t).[34] Let us denote by ELD_t the 'effective labour demand' at t, namely

$$ELD_t = (LD_t^{-\rho_1} + LC_t^{-\rho_1})^{\frac{-1}{\rho_1}}, \tag{27}$$

[32] In these countries, the coefficients of U_{-1} in the error correction term, and of ΔU, are *equal*. Accordingly, a rise in unemployment leads to a lower permanent level of real wages but then calls for no further adjustment (brings no further pressure to bear on real wages).

[33] The earlier Chelwood Gate volume included a discussion of these issues. We do not address them further here.

[34] The French entry in table 16.5 concerns $1/\rho_{2t}$.

Table 16.5. *Mismatch (1/RHO)*

Variable	Austria	Belgium	Britain	Denmark	France	Germany	Italy	Netherlands	Spain	U.S.
Constant	0.004 0.03 (69-72) 0.01 (73 onwards)	0.0292	found as a solution	-0.008	-0.009	0.016	0.014	0.02	0.008	0.035
Trend	0.008 (1966-1968) -0.004 (1969-1972) 0.004 (1981-1986)	0.0005		0.003	0.0028	0.001	0.003	0.000005	0.00098	0.0005
SURE 1960	0.004[1]	0.035		0.017	0.0[1]	0.019	0.029	0.022	0.009	0.041
1986	0.036	0.047		0.071[2]	0.033	0.046	0.090[2]	0.022	0.035	0.053

[1] This value is for 1966
[2] This value is for 1984

Table 16.6. *Mismatch*

Variable	Austria	Belgium	Britain	Denmark	France	Germany	Italy	Netherlands	Spain	U.S.
1/RHO2										
Constant		0.199			-0.009		0.024		-0.036	
Trend		0.0018			0.0028		0.003		0.0056	
1/RHO1										
Constant		0.099			0.01		0.01		0.023	

a CES-combination of the notional labour demand LC_t and the labour requirement corresponding to output demand LD_t. We may then rewrite (26) successively as

$$L_t = (ELD_t^{-\rho_{2t}} + LS_t^{-\rho_{2t}})^{\frac{-1}{\rho_{2t}}}, \tag{28}$$

$$1 = \left[\left(\frac{ELD_t}{L_t}\right)^{-\rho_{2t}} + \left(\frac{LS_t}{L_t}\right)^{-\rho_{2t}}\right]^{\frac{-1}{\rho_{2t}}} \tag{29}$$

$$1 = (1 + V_t)^{-\rho_{2t}} + (1 + U_t)^{-\rho_{2t}}. \tag{30}$$

Equation (30) defines a relationship between the unemployment rate U_t and the vacancies rate V_t which, *for a fixed value of* ρ_{2t}, is simply a Beveridge curve. The location of the curve is determined by ρ_{2t} because, when $U_t = V_t$ (along the diagonal), then $U_t = V_t = 2^{-\rho_{2t}} - 1 > 0$.

To say that ρ_{2t} *is a function of t is to say that the Beveridge curve* (30) *is shifting over time. When* $1/\rho_{2t}$ *increases with t the Beveridge curve is shifting outwards*, as revealed by the intersection of the curve with the diagonal.

The French estimates thus suggest that the degree of matching between supply and demand for goods has remained constant over time, whereas the Beveridge curve has shifted outwards, revealing a growing mismatch between the supply and demand for labour services at the microeconomic level.

It would be interesting to verify whether the French finding applies to other countries as well. A prima facie confirmation of that hypothesis is found in the British, Dutch and Spanish papers, which introduce and estimate a concept of 'effective labour supply'. In the UK, the corresponding 'effective unemployment rate' is hardly trended, suggesting that the rise in measured unemployment since 1975 reflects the growing mismatch, alluded to in the previous paragraph. In the Netherlands, the trend factor in ρ_t is considerably reduced when labour supply is replaced by effective labour supply. In Spain, where an equation explaining ρ_t is estimated, the retained specification changes, and the trend term drops out.

To investigate the matter further, we have used the estimated levels of LD_t, LC_t and LS_t in the Belgian, Italian and Spanish models to test the specification (26) – namely, a constant value of ρ_1 and a trended value for $1/\rho_{2t}$. The results are reported in table 16.6. In the case of Belgium and Spain, the French specification is unambiguously accepted. In the case of Italy, the hypothesis that $1/\rho_{1t}$ is constant is accepted at the 1%, but rejected at the 5% level, against the hypothesis that $1/\rho_{1t}$ is trended. But the trend in $1/\rho_{2t}$ is unambiguously significant under both specifications. The estimated models are thus consistent with outward shifts in the Beveridge curve.

4.4. Productivity

Much effort was directed, in the EUP, at estimating the 'technical' productivity of labour and capital, i.e. productivity at 'normal' or 'full' rates of utilisation of labour and capital. To that end, measures of utilisation rates – DUL and DUC respectively – were introduced in the (productivity) equations used to estimate simultaneously the production function and the first-order condition on desired factor proportions. Both variables proved significant in most cases – particularly the DUC variable (with t-ratios ranging from four to twelve in seven countries). The parameter estimates in the productivity equations are given in table 16.7.

A natural benchmark is the identity relating the rates of growth of output Y, employment L and labour productivity A:

$$\dot{l} = \dot{y} - \dot{a}. \tag{31}$$

Figures 16.6a and 16.6b give plots of the time-series (1960–1986) for the observed values of $\dot{l}$, $\dot{y}$ and the estimated values of $\dot{a}$ at normal rates of factor utilisation. Except for equation residuals and variations in utilisation rates, these three series satisfy equation (31).[35] Also plotted are the growth rates of labour supply, $\dot{l}s$; the vertical difference $\dot{l}s - \dot{l}$ measures the increase in unemployment, and can be cumulated over time to trace the unemployment rate.

The global picture for the seven European countries is one of stationary employment ($\dot{l} \approx 0$ *on average*), with a trend decrease in output growth offset by a trend decrease in productivity growth. By contrast, the US series display no trend in output growth, but portray the so-called 'employment miracle': employment growth is positive throughout – up to short lived recessions – and oscillates around the labour supply series. Labour productivity growth (at normal utilisation rates) was positive in the sixties, but almost came to a halt in 1970.

From the productivity equations, one can obtain a decomposition of labour productivity gains into that part reflecting pure technical progress

---

[35] Two countries (France and the Netherlands) are missing, due to data constraints at the time of writing.

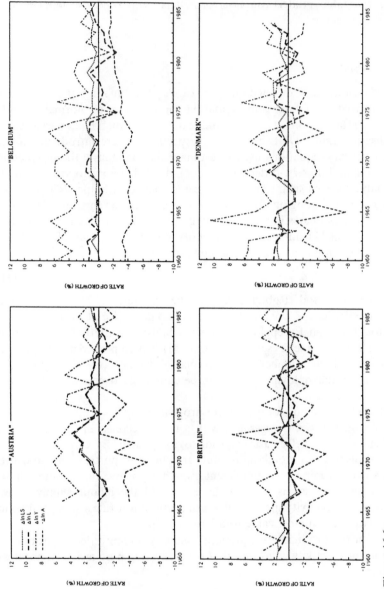

Figure 16.6a

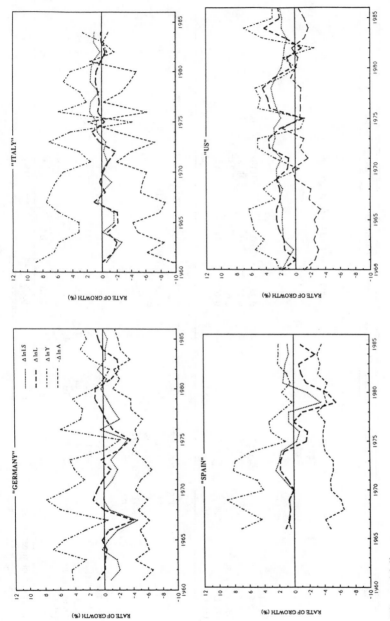

Figure 16.6b

Table 16.7. *Technical coefficients*

Variable	Austria	Belgium	Britain	Denmark	France	Germany	Italy	Netherlands	Spain	U.S.
Labour productivity										
Trend	1966–1972 0.025; 1973–1977 0.007; 1978–1986 0.011	1954–1973 0.02; 1974–1985 0.007			0.004	$0.007t(7 - 0.1t)$	0.009		1978–1985 0.01	1952–1973 0.02; 1974–1986 0.016
Rel. prices										
SR elasticity	0.1	0.17	0.19	0.46	0.24	0.13	0.18	0.05	0.11	0.02
LR elasticity	0.26	0.59	0.83	0.88	0.48	0.3	0.58	0.18	0.51	0.15
Mean lag in yrs	1.5	2.57	3.37	1.53	1.6	1.35	3.23	2.51	3.55	6.67
DUL										
DUC	0.8	0.05	5.13	0.63	0.46	1.06	1.87	0.81	0.15	0.59
Capital productivity										
Trend	1966–1972 0.049; 1973–1977 0.041; 1978–1986 0.006	1954–1973 0.02; 1974–1985 0.007				$-0.003 - 0.007t(1 + 0.01t)$	0.014	CONSTANT	1978–1985 0.01	1952–1973 0.004; 1974–1986 0.001
Rel. prices										
SR elasticity	−0.3	−0.11	−0.1	−0.15	0.24	0.13	−0.27		−0.11	0.01
LR elasticity	−0.74	−0.41	−0.44	−0.37	0.48	0.3	−0.36		−0.49	0.07
Mean lag in yrs	1.5	2.57	3.37	2.4	1.6	1.35	4.1		3.55	5.33
DUL							0.35			
DUC			6.12		0.56	0.53	0.13		0.5	0.43
Elasticity of substitution	0.65	0.27	1.27	0.75	0.48	0.3	0.94		1	

and that part reflecting choices of factor proportions induced by changes in relative prices. A common feature of most models is the measurement of the user cost of capital through a price index for investment goods. (Only in the UK and US could an effect from interest rates be detected.) The productivity equations embody distributed lags on relative factor prices – both to model price expectations, and to reflect adjustment lags in technological choices. Mean lags of three years are typical.

The contribution of factor prices to labour productivity is negligible in the US. In Europe, where real wages as well as productivity grew faster than in the US, there is a distinct influence of relative factor prices on technical labour productivity. That influence hovered around 2% to 2.5% per year until the late seventies, then started declining towards levels of 0.5% to 1% around 1986.

Crude as these estimates may be, they have the merit of quantifying a phenomenon about which qualitative evidence seems undisputed, namely that substitution of capital for labour has been an important phenomenon in Europe over the past 30 years, including the period of high unemployment. Whereas productivity growth is the engine of progress under full employment, the substitution of capital for labour is wasteful when there is unemployment.

4.5. The wage–price–productivity spiral

The role of relative prices in guiding choices of factor proportions may be linked to the specification of the price and wage equations. To illustrate the phenomenon of induced substitution, we introduce a streamlined example, broadly consistent with the findings reported in this section.[36] With a constant real interest rate, and with prices of investment goods moving closely with output prices, one may approximate relative factor prices by real product wages. Neglecting dynamics and cyclical fluctuations, a streamlined labour productivity equation then reads as follows:

$$a = y - l = \alpha_1 t + \alpha_2(w - p) + \text{constant},\tag{32}$$

$$\dot{a} = \alpha_1 + \alpha_2(\dot{w} - \dot{p}),\tag{33}$$

where in the constant returns Cobb–Douglas case, α_2 is the capital elasticity of output.

If the error correction term in the wage equation may be written in terms of the labour share, a streamlined version of that equation is:

$$\dot{w} = \dot{p} + \dot{a} + z_1,\tag{34}$$

[36] See Appendix 16.1 for a more general specification.

where z_1 denotes additional influences on wages, in particular unemployment. Under the assumption made about the cost of capital, prices are a markup on wage costs, up to additional factors z_2:

$$\dot{p} = \gamma(\dot{w} - \dot{a}) + z_2. \tag{35}$$

The solution to equations (33)–(35) is:

$$\dot{a} = \frac{\alpha_1 + \alpha_2 z_1}{1 - \alpha_2} \tag{36}$$

$$\dot{w} = \frac{\alpha_1}{1 - \alpha_2} + \frac{z_1}{1 - \alpha_2} \frac{1 - \gamma\alpha_2}{1 - \gamma} + \frac{z_2}{1 - \gamma} \tag{37}$$

$$\dot{p} = \frac{z_1\gamma}{1 - \gamma} + \frac{z_2}{1 - \gamma} \tag{38}$$

$$\dot{w} - \dot{p} = \frac{\alpha_1 + z_1}{1 - \alpha_2}. \tag{39}$$

The rate of growth of labour productivity can thus be decomposed into an exogenous part corresponding to pure technological progress α_1 and an endogenous part induced by relative prices, $\alpha^2(\dot{w} - \dot{p}) = \frac{\alpha_2(\alpha_1 + z_1)}{(1 - \alpha_2)}$ or roughly $\frac{\alpha_1 + z_1}{2}$.

In terms of equation (36) the downward pressure exerted by unemployment on wages (through z_1), will not reverse the capital/labour substitution ($\dot{a} < 0$) unless it reduces real wages at a rate at least equal to $\frac{\alpha_1}{\alpha_2}$, or roughly $3\alpha_1$. Thus, with a typical value of α_1 like 0.02, and a rise in unemployment of one percentage point per year, the coefficient of U (or ΔU) in the wage equation should be as large as -0.06 in order for the downward pressure on wages to bring capital/labour substitution to a halt (after a mean lag of some three years ...). In no single country do we find a coefficient that large. Clearly, the mechanism through which unemployment could be self-correcting is weak. We should not be surprised that unemployment has been persistent, in Europe.

We also note from equation (38), and from the elasticities in table 16.3, that shocks affecting price (z_2) or wage (z_1) inflation are multiplied respectively by a factor of 3 or so $\left(\frac{1}{1 - \gamma}\right)$ and 2 or so $\left(\frac{\gamma}{1 - \gamma}\right)$ – revealing a high sensitivity to inflationary shocks. The sensitivity to wage shocks is less pronounced in the US where measured productivity gains do not seem to be incorporated into wages.[37]

A more refined analysis should consider explicitly the 'wedges' between consumption wages and product wages (including in particular labour taxes, which have increased everywhere), or between the value-added deflator and import prices (as influenced also by exchange rates), as well as between the prices of investment goods and those of consumer goods. In economies as exposed to inflationary spirals as suggested by equations (36)–(38), exogenous shocks affecting these wedges can have serious real consequences.

5. Output, employment and demand

5.1. Trade spillovers

Before reviewing the determination of output and employment in the EUP models, we wish to handle a simple question related to the comment made in Section 4.1 about the price equations. If prices do not react to demand pressure, how does one explain that quantity rationing of demand is hardly ever observed? In the EUP models, it is assumed that demand pressure spills over into foreign trade – either in the form of more imports, or in the form of less exports; see equations (15)–(16). To the extent that domestic producers may be reluctant to give up foreign markets, the penetration of which is a costly investment, the impact of capacity utilisation should be weaker for exports than for imports. (In particular, if export markets receive priority in case of excess demand for domestic output, the size of the import spillover is thereby increased.)

The estimated elasticities from the trade equations are reproduced in table 16.8. Except for a couple of perverse signs in the export equations, suggesting that export *demand* (as distinct from supply) may have failed to be identified, the results are quite straightforward. The spillover terms in the import equations are all significant and quite sizeable. As expected, the quantitative order of magnitude is lower in the export equations.[38]

---

[37] In the US wage equation, $\dot{a}$ is replaced by a trend. Equation (38) then takes the form

$$\dot{p} = \frac{\gamma z_1 (1 - \alpha_2)}{1 - \gamma} + \frac{z_2}{1 - \gamma}.$$

[38] In addition to the reason mentioned above, this may also reflect a simultaneity bias, since exports require use of capacity – a bias that might also affect the DUC coefficient in the import equation. An interesting alternative hypothesis was mentioned to us by Michael Burda, namely that import spillovers concern investment goods, acquired in order to restore capacity margins. That hypothesis, verified by Burda on US data, is fully consistent with our discussion of investment behaviour in Section 5.3 below.

Table 16.8. *Trade elasticities*

(Upper rows = short run, lower rows = long run)

Variable	Austria	Belgium	Britain	Denmark	France	Germany	Italy	Netherlands	Spain	U.S.
Elasticities of imports										
Final demand	1.72	1.25	No separate equations	1.22	1.7	1.98	1	1.22	1.43	0.22
	1			1.19			1	1.52		2.03
Rel. prices	−0.81	−0.63		−0.23	−0.56	−0.74	−0.61	−0.18	−0.29	−0.22
	−1.65			−0.6		−1.47	−3.81	−0.37		−0.11
Spillover	0.62	1.89		0.49		1.46	0.88	0.62	1.15	1.37
	0.62					1.46	2.12	1.31		1.37
Elasticities of exports										
World trade	1.1	1.04	for exports and imports	2.47	1.33 + 0.006t	0.76	0.28	0.99	1.86	1.64
	1			2.12		1.15	1	1.06		1.01
Rel. prices	−0.47	0.13		0.11	−0.74	−0.33	−0.14	−0.65	−1.01	−0.79
	−0.49			0.14		−0.5	−0.5	−1.98		−1.58
Spillover	0.01	−1.77				−0.21	0.62	−0.27	−0.76	−0.35
	0.01					−0.21	−2.07	−0.83		−0.35
Sum of price elasticities										
	1.28				1.3	1.07	0.75	0.83	1.3	1.01
	2.14					1.97	4.31	2.35		1.7
Sum of spillover elasticities										
	−0.62	−3.66		−0.49		−1.67	−4.19	−0.89	−1.91	−1.72
	−0.62					−1.67		−2.14		−1.72

Adding together the import and export elasticities and looking at the median (over the nine countries) of the sums, we obtain for relative prices the values 1 in the short run, 1.5 in the long run; and for capacity utilisation 1 in the short run and 2 in the long run (with no clear relationship to import shares).

These results call for further analysis. We know that rates of capacity utilisation are positively correlated across countries, and that some 70% of the trade of the ten countries in our sample is internal to the group. It would be more satisfactory to take these two facts into account and explain trade flows (and spillovers) through the rates of capacity utilisation at the two ends of the flow.

Returning to the issue of demand pressure, and the lack of justification for the inflationary fears grounded in high rates of capacity utilisation, it must now be recognised that domestic stimulation of demand in a country experiencing demand pressure is likely to generate import spillovers and hence a further deterioration of the trade balance. Since European governments are typically allergic to current account deficits, we find here an alternative explanation for the oft heard reference to capacity utilisation as a ground for cautious fiscal policies.

5.2. *Proximate determinants of growth*

The models estimated under the EUP lead to a natural decomposition of the growth rate of output into three proximate components, corresponding respectively to the growth rates of output demand, of capacity output and of full employment output. The decomposition follows directly from the relationship defining output

$$Y = (YD^{-\rho} + YC^{-\rho} + YS^{-\rho})^{\frac{-1}{\rho}}, \tag{4}$$

$$\dot{y} = \eta_{Y \cdot YD}\dot{y}d + \eta_{Y \cdot YC}\dot{y}c + \eta_{Y \cdot YS}\dot{y}s \tag{40}$$

where $\eta_{Y/YD}$ denotes the elasticity of Y with respect to $YD\left(= \dfrac{Y^\rho}{YD^\rho}\right)$, and so on. These elasticities satisfy

$$\eta_{Y \cdot YD} + \eta_{Y \cdot YC} + \eta_{Y \cdot YS} \equiv 1. \tag{41}$$

This identity has theoretical foundations in the model of aggregation underlying (4). It leads to an interpretation of the three elasticities as the proportions π_D, π_C and π_S of micromarkets where domestic output is

440 *Econometrics*

Table 16.9. *Regime proportions*

Year	Austria		Belgium		Britain		Denmark		Germany
	π_D	π_C	π_D	π_C	π_D	π_C	π_D	π_C	π_D
1965			0.36	0.26	0.40	0.15	0.13	0.65	0.23
1966	0.65	0.23	0.37	0.24	0.50	0.10	0.22	0.35	0.27
1967	0.69	0.09	0.54	0.16	0.72	0.08	0.34	0.18	0.54
1968	0.46	0.21	0.50	0.19	0.53	0.15	0.40	0.30	0.56
1969	0.29	0.36	0.35	0.28	0.46	0.20	0.13	0.60	0.22
1970	0.24	0.52	0.34	0.26	0.50	0.19	0.15	0.69	0.03
1971	0.28	0.42	0.43	0.20	0.71	0.14	0.28	0.46	0.09
1972	0.28	0.53	0.41	0.22	0.73	0.13	0.22	0.54	0.23
1973	0.37	0.16	0.29	0.34	0.33	0.22	0.16	0.76	0.24
1974	0.24	0.11	0.33	0.34	0.37	0.15	0.34	0.45	0.33
1975	0.88	0.01	0.67	0.17	0.75	0.07	0.88	0.03	0.73
1976	0.91	0.01	0.65	0.23	0.75	0.10	0.58	0.32	0.81
1977	0.87	0.01	0.69	0.22	0.66	0.11	0.61	0.32	0.60
1978	0.87	0.01	0.78	0.17	0.67	0.10	0.66	0.29	0.56
1979	0.73	0.04	0.71	0.24	0.65	0.12	0.30	0.63	0.47
1980	0.77	0.04	0.70	0.24	0.86	0.05	0.37	0.53	0.39
1981	0.79	0.08	0.83	0.14	0.91	0.05	0.63	0.28	0.52
1982	0.86	0.03	0.81	0.17	0.92	0.04	0.64	0.26	0.74
1983	0.86	0.03	0.79	0.20	0.86	0.09	0.52	0.34	0.84
1984	0.74	0.06	0.71	0.28	0.78	0.13	0.38	0.44	0.74
1985	0.60	0.19	0.72	0.27	0.71	0.15			0.53
1986	0.58	0.21	0.82	0.17	0.75	0.13			0.40

determined by demand, by capacity and by availability of labour respectively (see Lambert, 1988). In that notation, we may rewrite (40) as

$$\dot{y} = \pi_D \dot{y}d + \pi_C \dot{y}c + \pi_S \dot{y}s, \tag{42}$$

a linear relationship among growth rates.

Table 16.9 gives the time series of (π_D, π_C, π_S) for various countries. The main message is again the contrast between the European and US patterns. *In Europe the proportion of micromarkets where output is demand-determined grew markedly from 1975 and especially 1981 onwards. In the US, there is little trend in the proportions; π_D moves procyclically, and π_C countercyclically.*

An alternative presentation of that message is offered by figures 16.7a and 16.7b, which display the series $\pi_D \dot{y}d$, $\pi_C \dot{y}c$ and $\pi_S \dot{y}s$ – i.e. the decomposition of output growth into its three proximate determinants.

A remarkable feature of figure 16.7 is the negligible contribution of capacity and labour supply growth to output growth in the eighties, for most European countries and particularly so for Austria, Belgium,

Table 16.9. (continued) *Regime proportions*

Germany	Italy		Netherlands		Spain		U.S.		Year
π_C	π_D	π_C	π_D	π_C	π_D	π_C	π_D	π_C	
0.44	0.28	0.15	0.25	0.29			0.25	0.49	1965
0.37	0.23	0.14	0.32	0.24	0.22	0.20	0.16	0.58	1966
0.18	0.42	0.18	0.55	0.08	0.49	0.06	0.12	0.61	1967
0.17	0.46	0.16	0.54	0.08	0.36	0.15	0.21	0.50	1968
0.42	0.45	0.27	0.36	0.24	0.16	0.23	0.19	0.49	1969
0.79	0.39	0.27	0.25	0.41	0.18	0.14	0.19	0.49	1970
0.69	0.58	0.27	0.36	0.31	0.31	0.25	0.41	0.33	1971
0.33	0.45	0.19	0.61	0.16	0.06	0.66	0.44	0.31	1972
0.36	0.20	0.25	0.48	0.29	0.02	0.76	0.31	0.42	1973
0.34	0.21	0.31	0.66	0.15	0.13	0.63	0.20	0.54	1974
0.13	0.61	0.26	0.79	0.13	0.53	0.27	0.31	0.45	1975
0.10	0.51	0.22	0.78	0.13	0.48	0.31	0.59	0.25	1976
0.22	0.48	0.19	0.76	0.13	0.37	0.46	0.45	0.34	1977
0.25	0.40	0.21	0.66	0.22	0.50	0.43	0.36	0.42	1978
0.31	0.35	0.20	0.41	0.48	0.66	0.30	0.28	0.49	1979
0.38	0.24	0.20	0.43	0.50	0.83	0.15	0.25	0.53	1980
0.29	0.44	0.19	0.64	0.34	0.80	0.19	0.40	0.40	1981
0.16	0.58	0.19	0.85	0.14	0.70	0.29	0.41	0.39	1982
0.12	0.73	0.19	0.83	0.16	0.70	0.30	0.65	0.24	1983
0.20	0.60	0.20	0.65	0.34	0.78	0.22	0.53	0.30	1984
0.36			0.42	0.56	0.81	0.19	0.37	0.40	1985
0.47			0.32	0.65			0.38	0.39	1986

Germany and the UK. The proximate importance of demand for output growth since the second oil shock is thus clearly confirmed – in contrast again to the US, where capacity and labour supply availability retain significance.

Since demand for domestic output is the sum of consumption, investment, government expenditure and the trade balance, it is instructive to decompose in turn the rate of growth of *YD* into these four components:

$$\dot{y}d = S_C\dot{c} + S_I\dot{i} + S_G\dot{g} + (S_X\dot{x} - S_M\dot{m}), \tag{43}$$

where S_C is the ratio of consumption to *YD*, and similarly for the other shares. That decomposition is presented in figures 16.8a and 16.8b. In comparison to European countries, one may note for the US: (i) the relatively limited amplitude of the foreign trade component in that relatively closed economy; (ii) the positive contribution of government expenditure ever since the mid-seventies and especially in the eighties; (iii) the sustained contribution of consumption, especially again in the eighties. In Europe, the amplitude of the foreign trade component is much

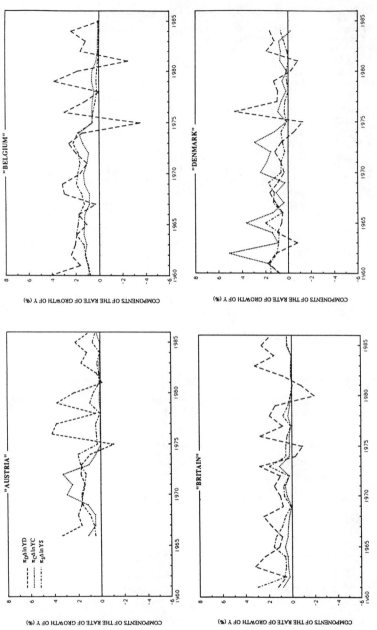

Figure 16.7a

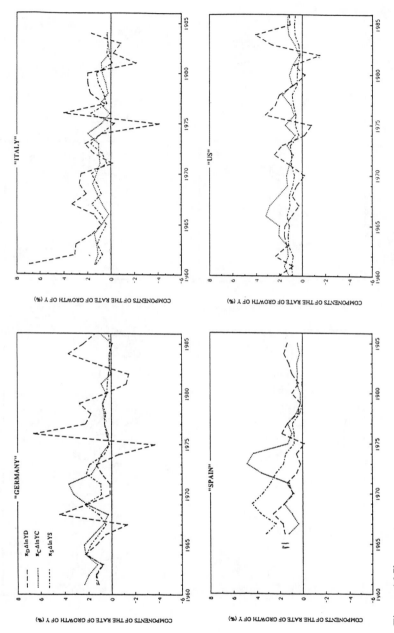

Figure 16.7b

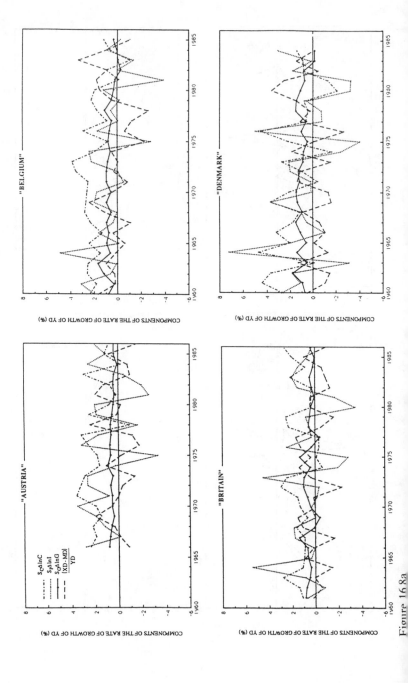

Figure 16.8a

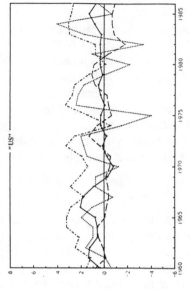

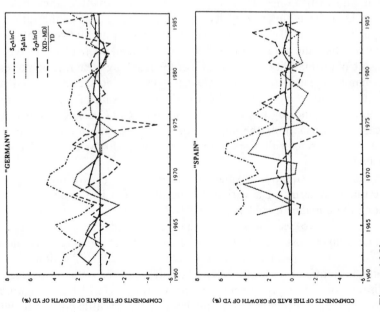

Figure 16.8b

more pronounced, especially in the smaller countries like Austria, Belgium and Denmark.

Another striking feature, shared by Europe and the US, is the amplitude of the *contributions to GDP growth* coming from investment. This is somewhat surprising, because investment amounts to less than 20% of *GDP*; yet, it repeatedly contributes plus or minus four percentage points to *GDP* growth, because it is much more volatile than the other components. In particular, the sharp declines of aggregate demand in 1975 and 1981 (see figure 16.7) are largely due to the collapse of investment in those years. We report accordingly on investment equations, before turning to impact multipliers in Section 5.4.

5.3. Investment

The first impression made by the nine investment equations of the EUP models (investment is exogenous in the French model) is one of disconcerting diversity. The six different dependent variables, the broad array of explanatory variables and specifications, span the corresponding variety of investment theories! Upon closer examination, one notes that four equations are quite similar after all, namely the Austrian, German, Italian and British ones. These express the rate of growth of the stock of capital as a linear function of its own lagged value and of the ratio of output demand to full capacity output – with possibly one or two additional variables, like the rate of growth of output demand (Austria, Italy), a measure of profitability (Austria, UK) or the real long-term rate of interest (Germany). Typical coefficients are near 0.8 for the lagged dependent variable, 0.1 for the log of YD/YC or 0.25 for the sum of the coefficients of $\log YD/YC$ and $\log YD/YD_{-1}$. Noting that $\Delta \ln K \simeq I/K$ minus (rate of capital depreciation), the implied long-run elasticity of the net capital accumulation rate with respect to DUC is not too far from unity – a sensible property.

Another four equations explain the level, or the growth rate, of gross investment in terms of a variety of specifications. The main regularity among these is the significance of a DUC variable.

Going back to Section 4.1, note that, in a world where prices are set as a markup on costs with little sensitivity to demand pressures, 'profitability' is mostly dependent upon the rate of capacity utilisation; hence capital accumulation should depend heavily upon the *expected* degree of utilisation of additional capacity. The currently observed DUC is a natural proxy for that expected DUC – if only because there is little point in *adding* to capacity when unused capacity is currently available.

5.4. Output dynamics

When looking at the evolution of demand components, one must remember first that most of them are endogenous, being simultaneously determined with output; and second that relative prices affect at least the trade component. A partial endogenisation of demand growth is obtained from a stripped version of the demand block consisting of equations (11), (13) and (14). Treating provisionally investment and government expenditure as exogenous, one may rewrite these three equations in growth rates form, then substitute them in (43) and (42), obtaining finally:

$$\dot{y} = \frac{\pi_D}{1 + S_M \eta_{M \cdot YD} - \pi_D S_C \eta_{CY}} \cdot \{ S_i \dot{i} + S_G \dot{g} + S_X \eta_{X \cdot WT} \dot{w} t$$

$$+ S_X \eta_X \cdot \tfrac{PW}{PX} (\dot{p}w - \dot{p}x) - S_M \eta_M \cdot \tfrac{PM}{P} (\dot{p}m - \dot{p}) \}$$

$$+ \frac{1 + S_M \eta_{M \cdot YD}}{1 + S_M \eta_{M \cdot YD} - \pi_D S_C \eta_{C \cdot Y}} \{ \pi_C \dot{y}c + \pi_S \dot{y}s \}, \qquad (44)$$

where $\dot{y}c = \dot{k} + \dot{b}$ and $\dot{y}s = \dot{I}s + \dot{a}$.

Although that expression may appear forbidding, its interpretation is in fact quite straightforward. A synthetic formulation would be:

$\dot{y} = \pi_D \times$ open economy multiplier

$\times$ [contribution from growth rates of investment

and exogenous demand components

$+$ contributions from price effects of trade component]

$+$ contributions from $\dot{y}c$ and $\dot{y}s$. (45)

As is well known, the impact of demand shocks in such models is dampened by the factor π_D, because output adjusts only when it is demand-determined. For the same reason, the multiplier is reduced, because the propensity to consume (in the denominator) generates output only in the proportion π_D. Knowledge of the proportions (π_D, π_C, π_S) of table 16.9 is thus important for policy evaluation.

Remembering that $\dot{b}$ and $\dot{a}$ are functions of $(\dot{w} - \dot{p}i)$, one message of equation (44) is that three relative prices play a role in the short-run dynamics of output and employment, namely $(\dot{p}w - \dot{p}x)$, $(\dot{p}m - \dot{p})$ and $(\dot{w} - \dot{p}i)$. It was already mentioned in Section 3.4 that relative-price 'wedges' could affect the price–wage spiral. We note here that the same wedges also affect directly output and employment dynamics in a manner worthy of further investigation.

Equation (44) also reveals the complexity of the growth process, whereby output growth is related to other physical growth rates (capital, government demand, world trade), to labour supply and productivity growth, and to changes in relative prices. The balanced growth of the sixties and early seventies was characterised in Europe by stable labour supply and relative prices, high productivity growth and parallel growth of output, capital, government demand and trade – see table 16.1.[39] Once the pattern is broken – due to shocks in relative prices and exogenous demand components – it is natural that time be required to regain the balance. It is conceivable, but by no means certain, that we are now approaching again a path of balanced growth – although not necessarily at the same rate.

5.5. Employment dynamics

In view of the interest attached to a 'reduced form' labour demand equation, as explained in Section 3.5, it is suggestive to examine more closely the counterpart of (42) for employment, namely

$$\dot{l} = \pi_D \dot{l} d + \pi_C \dot{l} c + \pi_S \dot{l} s$$
$$= \pi_D(\dot{y}d - \dot{a}) + \pi_C(\dot{k} + \dot{b} - \dot{a}) + \pi_S \dot{l} s. \tag{46}$$

Using (8)–(9) and (43), we can use this equation to bring out the structure of the short-run elasticity of employment with respect to real wages in the reduced form labour demand equation, namely:

$$\eta_{L \cdot \frac{W}{P}} = \frac{\partial \dot{l}}{\partial(\dot{w} - \dot{p})} = \pi_D\left(\frac{\partial \dot{y}d}{\partial(\dot{w} - \dot{p})} - \frac{\partial \dot{a}}{\partial(\dot{w} - \dot{p})}\right) + \pi_C \frac{\partial(\dot{b} - \dot{a})}{\partial(\dot{w} - \dot{p})}$$

$$= -(\pi_D + \pi_C)\frac{\partial \dot{a}}{\partial(\dot{w} - \dot{p})} + \pi_D \frac{\partial \dot{y}d}{\partial(\dot{w} - \dot{p})} + \pi_C \frac{\partial \dot{b}}{\partial(\dot{w} - \dot{p})}. \tag{47}$$

The first term in (47) captures the impact of real wages on labour productivity; i.e., the impact of the capital/labour substitution induced by relative prices. In the notation of equations (9) and (33), it is equal to $-(\pi_D + \pi_C)\alpha_2 \simeq -\alpha_2$.

The third term in (47) captures the impact of real wages on capital productivity; i.e., the impact of the capital deepening induced by relative prices. In the notation of equation (8), it is equal to $-\pi_C\beta_2 \simeq -\pi_C(1 - \alpha_2)$;

---

[39]The US example is there to remind us that a different growth pattern is possible.

that approximation is exact under a Cobb–Douglas production function. The relevance of that term is open to question, however, to the extent that factor proportions *on existing capital* may prove difficult to adjust *ex post*. The putty–clay models rule out that possibility. We assume that such adjustments take time, thus adopting an intermediate position between the more extreme putty–clay or putty–putty views.

The middle term in (47) captures the impact of real wages on aggregate demand, which is transmitted to employment in a proportion π_D. In the EUP specification of the demand block, that impact comes from the trade equations. Taking multiplier effects into account, but still treating investment, public expenditure and world trade as exogenous, one obtains:

$$\frac{\partial \dot{y}d}{\partial(\dot{w} - \dot{p})} = \frac{S_X \eta_X \cdot \frac{W}{P} - S_M \eta_M \cdot \frac{W}{P}}{1 + S_M \eta_{M \cdot YD} - \pi_D S_C \eta_{CY}}$$

$$\simeq S_M \cdot \eta_{(X-M)} \cdot \frac{W}{P} \cdot \mathscr{M}_D \tag{48}$$

where we have written $\mathscr{M}_D$ for the demand multiplier and assumed (near) equilibrium of the trade balance.

In summary, under these assumptions

$$\eta_L \cdot \frac{W}{P} \simeq -\alpha_2 - \pi_C(1 - \alpha_2) - \pi_D S_M |\eta_{(X-M)} \cdot \frac{W}{P}| \mathscr{M}_D. \tag{49}$$

The three distinct components of this formula have their place in the discussion to follow.

5.6. Wages and demand

We may now take up the difficult, but essential, question of the interplay of wages and demand. We should first of all note that the EUP models embody rather crude consumption functions (or no consumption function at all, in Austria, Denmark, Italy and the US). Thus, *the role of wages in sustaining consumer demand is not captured*. According to some, little loss of information is involved, because they regard the hypothesis of a higher propensity to consume out of wage income than out of gross profits as unsubstantiated (presumably, due to the chain from profits to asset prices to wealth to consumption). Even so, there would remain scope for *unemployment* to depress consumption through a 'permanent income' effect. These issues will not be settled by the work under review. (Still, we note that the well-behaved German consumption function implies a fall in consumer demand of 0.25% for a 1% decrease in employment, at unchanged disposable income).

The direct channel through which wages influence final demand in equations (44) and (49) comes from the price elasticities of foreign trade. It is important, in that connection, to draw a distinction between a wage shock in a single country and a wage shock affecting simultaneously several (most) European countries. In the former case, the wage shock being quickly transmitted to prices, and the sum of the price elasticities being of the order of one in the short run and higher in the long run, the impact on final demand is quite sizeable, and roughly proportional to the country's degree of openness, as measured by $S_M \simeq S_X$. In the latter case, the elasticity of prices to wage costs being of comparable magnitude in the different countries, and some 60% of the trade being intra-European, the relative prices would be much less affected, and the influence on final demand would be significantly dampened, both for individual countries and for Europe as a whole (whose degree of openness is roughly comparable to that of the US).

The difficult question concerns the interaction between wage formation and fiscal stance: Have European Governments adjusted their fiscal stance in response to wage shocks? (The adjustment could be contractionary, to fight inflation or to avoid current account disequilibria; but it could also be expansionary to prevent a rise in unemployment, resulting from the loss of competitiveness and from the induced capital–labour substitution.)

The econometric work within the EUP is not instructive in this respect, because government spending is exogenous in all models. But the papers contain a number of interesting anecdotes. These include such classics as the German fiscal contraction following the 'locomotive experiment' of the late seventies. They also include the temporarily successful Austrian and Danish attempts to counter the first oil shock through expansionary fiscal policies – and the reversal to budget consolidation as the public debt built up.

Beyond these individual anecdotes, there is a common experience. Temporary demand stimulation through fiscal policy exerts only temporary effects, in these models. That is, a temporary stimulus does not by itself raise the level of output permanently. It could in principle happen that growing public expenditures become self-financing as the growth rates of other components of final demand match that of government spending. But that would fail to happen if investment and exports lag behind. The fiscal deficit then results in a growing public debt and current account deficit, eventually inducing a reversal of policies. A wise use of the fiscal instrument rests on a comparative assessment of the state of the economy today, and tomorrow at the time of the policy reversal required to reimburse the debt. The chain of events which led European governments to tighten fiscal policy in the wake of the second oil shock was most unfortunate. That episode contains a lesson for the future.

The temporary nature of fiscal stimuli is confirmed by the simulations carried out with some of the EUP models.

5.7. A synthesis

Bringing together the contents of Sections 4 and 5 regarding the influence of wages on employment, we note that the models under review embody two explicit channels and one implicit channel through which that influence exerts itself. The two explicit channels are (i) the demand side, through the foreign trade elasticities – a channel of greater significance in case of single country wage movements than in case of parallel wage movements in several countries; (ii) the supply side, through capital-labour substitution – a channel that is equally significant in the single country case as in the multi-country case.[40] The implicit channel concerns fiscal policy reactions to wage shocks.

It is interesting to speculate briefly about the relative importance of the two explicit channels. From formulae (36)–(38) and (49), and from the figures in tables 16.3 and 16.8, one would guess that the two channels are of comparable importance in the case of single-country shocks – the exact answer being related to that country's degree of openness. In the case of European-wide shocks, the capital-labour substitution channel is probably the dominant one. As noted above, capital-labour substitution induced by the incorporation of productivity gains into wages are wasteful when the economy operates under inefficient unemployment.

One message from the work under review is that wage moderation has to fight the tide, in the supply channel as well as in the demand channel, if it is to pave the way for a reduction in unemployment. As noted in Section 4.5, real wage adjustments will not increase the employment content of growth unless they amount to something like three times the rate of autonomous technological progress; the tide is thus quite strong along the supply channel. In the demand channel, the growth rates of capital, government demand and world trade define another tide. When these rates fall below the growth rate of labour productivity, the effects of wage adjustments on the trade balance again need to overcome that

---

[40] To this should be added all the general equilibrium interactions, like the investment accelerator, whereby the supply side reacts to demand conditions, and so on.

adverse tide before they result in employment growth. Lags in the reaction of wages to unemployment, then in the reactions of prices and factor proportions to wages, slow down the adjustment process. It is always difficult to fight the tide with insufficient boat speed ...

6. Summary and conclusions

6.1. Summary

The broad empirical regularities of the EUP may be summarised as follows.

1. The measured influence of demand pressure on prices is negligible, but the elasticity of prices with respect to wage costs is substantial, ranging from minimal values of 0.5 in the short run to 1 in the long run.

2. Real wages incorporate measured productivity gains quite rapidly in Europe, with short-run elasticities ranging from 0.4 to 0.8 and long-run elasticities close to 1. Measured productivity does not enter significantly in the US wage equation.

3. The level of unemployment typically enters the wage equations through an error correction term, relating the share of wages in value added to the level of unemployment. The estimated coefficients imply a reduction in the wage share, per percentage point of unemployment, ranging from 0.4% in the high unemployment countries to 2.5% in Austria – revealing the weak self- correcting mechanism for unemployment in the former group. That specification is consistent with the view that European labour unions are much concerned with the fairness of the distribution of income.

4. The $U-V$ (Beveridge) curve has shifted outwards, in all countries (including the US).

5. The incorporation of measured productivity gains into real wages induces capital-labour substitution, which is wasteful in economies operating under inefficient unemployment. Employment growth in Europe was curtailed by factor substitution at an average rate of some 2% per year until the late seventies, and 1% per year more recently. If that substitution had stopped when it became wasteful, the rise of unemployment in Europe could have been avoided.

6. Shocks on prices are multiplied by a factor of 2 to 4, and shocks on wages by a factor of 1 to 3, through the wage-price-productivity spiral. The European economies are thus inflation-prone.

7. Demand pressures, which as suggested under point 1 are not choked

off through price increases, spill over into imports, and to a lesser extent exports, thereby deteriorating the trade balance. That robust country-level finding remains to be analysed in a multi-country setting.

8. The main and nearly unique proximate determinant of output growth in the eighties in Europe has been effective demand. The growth of demand is linked to the growth of its exogenous components, namely government expenditures and world trade. It is also linked to the relative growth rates of domestic and foreign prices, through the price elasticities of exports and imports. This last channel is much less significant for Europe as a whole than for individual countries.

9. The degree of capacity utilisation is a significant determinant of investment. (In line with the suggestion under point 1 that prices are geared to costs but not to demand pressures, the profitability of investment should depend largely upon utilisation rates.)

10. Besides affecting employment through their influence on the foreign trade component of demand, wages also affect employment through capital-labour substitution, as noted under point 5. For Europe as a whole, that second channel is probably more significant than the first.

11. Temporary demand stimulation through fiscal policy exerts only temporary effects, in within-sample-period simulations of the EUP models. And the papers contain anecdotes about policy reversals induced by cumulated deficits.

6.2. Conclusions

The empirical findings suggest explaining the contrast between the US 'employment miracle' and the European persistent unemployment in terms of two proximate causes: (i) the wage formation process differs as between the two zones, in particular regarding the incorporation of measured productivity gains into real wages; (ii) whereas the proportion of firms where output and employment are demand determined grew markedly in all European countries in the late seventies and mostly remained high, that proportion is not trended in the US – presumably due to a combination of relative closedness, sustained consumption and lasting deficits.

The European wage-formation process makes non-declining employment dependent upon sustained output growth. In small open economies, this in turn requires parallel growth in exports – as determined by world demand and competitiveness. When some of these elements are missing, fiscal policy alone is not a very effective instrument.

These conclusions must be taken with a ... pound of salt! After due

454   *Econometrics*

pruning, it will probably remain inescapable that the elimination of European unemployment is a very difficult challenge. The work reviewed here suggests strongly that the mechanism through which unemployment could be self-correcting is weak and slow, in Europe. A gradual elimination will tautologically call for a prolonged period during which output grows faster than productivity – a situation not witnessed over the past 30 or 40 years. Because growth of real wages induces gains in measured productivity through capital-labour substitution, the goal will be easier to reach if medium-run expected wage growth is strictly contained. We do not know whether, and how, that condition could be met. Under that condition, the fear that faster output growth would rekindle inflation is probably misplaced – but a temporary deterioration in current accounts would need to be faced. And the expansion would require cooperation among several European countries, if national current account problems are to remain manageable. On the other hand, if demand stimulation through fiscal policy has only temporary effects, the accumulation of public deficits is unlikely to be tolerated.

We do not wish to eschew these dilemmas by resorting to fine tuning. Still the following remarks appear timely:

(a) Public deficits are more tolerable, from an intertemporal perspective, if they correspond to productive investments.

(b) Labour taxes have an obvious role to play in containing, or reversing, the growth of labour costs and medium-run expectations about them; one advantage of tax adjustments is that they are not apt to be perceived as transitory; granted that many among the currently unemployed are at best candidates for low-paid jobs, a reduction in labour taxes should be targeted towards the low end of the wage scale (for example by exempting minimum wages from social security contributions).

(c) In order to alleviate labour market tensions, it is important to increase the supply of those specific skills which are in excess demand; both training opportunities and wage differentials have a role to play here. There is also scope for initiatives to make wage differentials more acceptable, and to limit their unnecessary spreading to other skills. Still, it must be recognised that the required skills will not be supplied by the long-term unemployed; for these, special programs remain needed.

From a longer-run perspective, there is ground to be concerned about the vulnerability of Europe to inflation as well to output and employment fluctuations. The division into relatively open national economies compounds these problems, by creating complex interdependencies between countries. This also leads to a need for international cooperation in demand management, public investment, etc. The proces of wage formation has almost certainly been destabilising in the seventies, and the experience could be repeated. The goal of distributional equity needs to be implemented more efficiently. We need an operational way of separating out technical progress from measured productivity gains associated with capital deepening induced by wage increases. The incorporation into real wages of productivity gains following from capital deepening is entirely desirable when an economy is at full employment, but the resulting substitution of capital for labour becomes wasteful in the presence of unemployment.

Appendix 16.1

Consider the linearly homogeneous constant elasticity of substitution technology

$$Y^{1-\frac{1}{\sigma}} = [\Theta(t)L]^{1-\frac{1}{\sigma}} + [\Phi(t)K]^{1-\frac{1}{\sigma}} \tag{A.1}$$

where $\Theta(t)$, $\Phi(t)$ reflect labour-augmenting and capital-augmenting technical progress respectively. Cost minimisation gives equilibrium factor proportions, $\left(\dfrac{K}{L}\right)^*$, as

$$\left(\frac{K}{L}\right)^* = \left(\frac{\Theta}{\Phi}\right)^{1-\sigma}\left(\frac{W}{Q}\right)^{\sigma} \tag{A.2}$$

where Q is the appropriate user cost of capital. Also,

$$\left(\frac{Y}{L}\right)^* = \Theta\left[1 + \left(\frac{\Theta Q}{\Phi W}\right)^{1-\sigma}\right]^{\frac{\sigma}{\sigma-1}}. \tag{A.3}$$

If prices P are set as a mark-up on average cost, then

$$P = \mu \cdot \frac{WL + QK}{Y} = \mu\frac{WL}{Y}\left(1 + \frac{Q}{W}\frac{K}{L}\right). \tag{A.4}$$

Using (A.2) and (A.3),

$$\frac{WL}{PY} = \mu^{-1}\left[1 + \left(\frac{\Theta Q}{\Phi W}\right)^{1-\sigma}\right]^{-1} \tag{A.5}$$

$$\frac{W}{P} = \mu^{-1}\Theta\left[1 + \left(\frac{\Theta Q}{\Phi W}\right)^{1-\sigma}\right]^{\frac{1}{\sigma-1}}$$

(A.6)

$$\frac{WL}{PY} = \mu^{-\sigma}\Theta^{\sigma-1}\left(\frac{W}{P}\right)^{1-\sigma}.$$

(A.7)

Equation (A.7) combines the production function and the price equation to yield a (long-run) equilibrium relationship between the wage share and the real (product) wage.[1] It implies that the wage share will be constant if the mark-up rate μ is constant and real wages grow at the same rate as the labour-augmenting technical progress Θ.

Let the wage equation yield a long-run relationship between the wage share and the unemployment rate, say

$$\ln\frac{WL}{PY} = \omega_0 - \omega_1 U.$$

(A.8)

Using (A.7), that relationship may indifferently be expressed in terms of the real wage, namely

$$\ln\frac{W}{P} = \ln\Theta + \frac{\sigma}{1-\sigma}\ln\mu + \frac{\omega_0}{1-\sigma} - \frac{\omega_1}{1-\sigma}U$$
$$= \ln\Theta + \omega_0' - \omega_1'U.$$

(A.9)

(A.9) is the reduced 'wage-setting' equation implied by the production and wage-price block of the model, under the assumptions of this appendix. It can be combined with a reduced 'labour demand' equation to determine equilibrium in the labour market and to investigate its comparative statics properties.

Note that under (A.7) two alternative specifications of the error-correction term in the wage equation, using respectively the wage share and the real wage, are not identified.

---

[1] Two special cases where the relationship is degenerate are:
(i) $\sigma = 1$ (Cobb–Douglas production function), in which case the wage share is uniquely determined by the technology and the mark-up factor;
(ii) $Q \propto P$, say $Q = RP$ (cost of capital proportional to the price of value added), in which case the real wage is given by (A.6) and the wage share is determined by the technology, the mark-up factor and R.

Appendix 16.2

Table of Contents of *Europe's Unemployment Problem*, J. H. Drèze, C. R. Bean, J. P. Lambert, F. Mehta and H. Sneessens, eds., MIT Press, Cambridge, Mass., 1991.

List of symbols

Lower case letters denote logarithms; dots denote time derivatives.

A	Technical (or full capacity) output/labour ratio
B	Technical (or full capacity) output/capital ratio
C	Consumption (real)
DUC	Degree of capacity utilisation
DUL	Degree of labour utilisation by firms (ratio of actual to normal hours)
FD	Final demand $(C + I + G + XD)$ (real)
G	Government expenditures (real)
GDP	Gross domestic product (real)
I	Investment (real)
K	Capital stock
L	Employment (actual) in persons
LC	Full capacity employment
LD	Employment at demand-determined output
LS	Labour supply
M	Imports (actual, real)
MD	Import demand (real)
P	Price deflator of GDP
PI	Price index of investment goods
PM	Price index of imports
PW	Price index of world imports
PX	Price index of exports
Q	User cost of capital
$S_C, S_G, S_I, \ldots$	Shares of $C, G, I, \ldots$ in YD
U	Unemployment rate
V	Vacancies rate
W	Wage rate, nominal
WT	World imports (real)
X	Exports (actual, real)
XD	Export Demand (real)
Y	Gross domestic product, output (real)
YC	Capacity output
YD	Demand-determined output
YS	Full-employment output

VIII Policy

17 Work-sharing: some theory and recent European experience*

1. Introduction

As soon as it became clear that the current recession in Europe was likely to be severe and protracted, commentators and politicians became attracted to the possibility of *redistributing work amongst people so as to reduce involuntary unemployment*, i.e. *work-sharing*. This was not a new development. Similar concern had arisen in the thirties, leading to the dramatic and unsuccessful attempt by the Front Populaire to introduce a 40 hour week in France (see for instance *Economie Européenne*, 1980 or Fontaine, 1984, for a summary account of that earlier development, and Carré *et al.*, 1972, for a survey of French experience). In recent years, a number of policy measures designed to promote work-sharing have been implemented in European countries, and several reports have attempted to assess their impact (Van Den Bergh and Wittelsburger, 1981; Hart, 1984; or Commissariat Général du Plan, 1985). The overall impression conveyed by these reports is one of limited effectiveness in reducing unemployment – at least if one goes by hard evidence – while it is sometimes even asserted that these measures are misdirected and bound to be self-defeating (see Layard *et al.*, 1984). Yet, with youth unemployment rates reaching 25% or more in several European countries, and no major improvement in sight, it is understandable that the motivation to bring about some degree of work-sharing should persist.

* *Economic Policy*, 1, 3 (1986), 562–619; Post-scriptum, Discussion and Appendix (pp. 599–617) not reproduced here. This is a much revised and extended version of a paper (Drèze, 1986a) initially commissioned by the Macroeconomic Policy Group of the Center for European Policy Studies (CEPS) under contract with the Directorate-General for Economic and Financial Affairs (DG II) of the Commission of the European Communities, whose financial support is gratefully acknowledged. The assistance of Yves Leruth in collecting data is also gratefully acknowledged. Hopefully, the revisions will dispel the erroneous impression of early readers that I regard implicit contract theory as an explanation of involuntary unemployment (which it is not) and as the only explanation of relevance to work-sharing. Comments and suggestions by Charles Wyplosz, members of staff of DG II, referees and members of the *Economic Policy* Panel are gratefully acknowledged.

461

The present paper is not meant to replicate the existing collective reports, but rather to appraise recent European experience and the prospects for work-sharing in the light of the modern microeconomic analysis of labour contracts. This calls for some theoretical considerations (Section 2) before turning to the evidence (Section 4), and I must beg readers to endure the detour. A brief summary of the arguments may serve the dual purpose of providing patient readers with markers, and less patient or less interested readers with an excuse for jumping to the conclusions, or even discarding the paper altogether! It may also help those familiar with my earlier work in this area to assess quickly how my thinking has evolved (see Drèze and Modigliani, 1981; Drèze, 1979c, 1980a).

To begin with (Section 2.1), I shall argue that most people attach a positive value to having a 'regular' job, as opposed to a 'casual' job, or no job at all. There are substantial variations across individuals, and over time for a given individual, in the value of a job and in the supply of hours. From the viewpoint of employers, 'regular' jobs are typically the preferred form of employment, but the provision of such jobs usually entails incurring fixed hiring costs (of screening, training and long-term commitments). In addition there must be a current and continuing need for the additional employee. Accordingly, the supply of regular jobs is inelastic to their short-run cost. Next (Section 2.2), I shall argue that short-run disequilibria on the market for regular jobs can occur, can sometimes become sizeable and are subject to self-aggravating tendencies. In such situations (well illustrated by present circumstances), the elimination of disequilibrium can be very slow. It would be both undesirable and unrealistic to rely on wage flexibility alone to clear the labour market in the short run. The theory of 'implicit labour contracts' predicts that the wages of employees in regular jobs remain downward rigid in periods of slack demand for labour while adjustments take place in the form of partial unemployment or temporary layoffs. These combine labour hoarding by firms with some degree of work-sharing among employees under contract. New entrants to the labour market are not party to these arrangements. There is no market mechanism whereby work could be redistributed efficiently between workers under contract (insiders) and newcomers (outsiders). Instead, as insiders attempt to shelter their wages from competition by outsiders, and the latter seek income insurance or exert market power, a degree of wage rigidity spreads to the new contracts as well. Also the fixed costs of new hirings, coupled with rigidities in the organisation of work, stand in the way of work-sharing among newcomers in the form of part-time employment. An inefficient allocation of regular jobs results, from which many newcomers – in particular the young – are left out. Special measures are needed to correct this inefficiency (Section 2.3), based on three considerations (Section 2.4). First, there are externalities, the most obvious of them being unemployment compensation, which is a cost to society but not to individual agents. Second, there are complex legal provisions, which may or may not facilitate work-sharing. Third, there are many 'public good' aspects to the organisation of working time, providing scope for leadership through public policy.

After a brief interlude (Section 3), which offers a normative alternative to Section 2, I turn to the record in Section 4. Selected fragments of evidence from various sources are organized under three headings:

(i) *Trading jobs*, i.e. replacing a worker under contract by a newcomer (Section 4.1). There is scope for such replacements to the extent that the value of a job varies widely over individuals. The most obvious measure calls for early (voluntary) retirement with mandatory replacement; measures of that kind have been introduced in several countries, pulling large numbers of workers out of the labour force. Although hard figures on new hirings are scanty, those which exist reveal a large measure of success when, but only when, replacement is mandatory.

(ii) *Sharing jobs* can take two forms (Section 4.2). First, a worker under contract is replaced by a newcomer on a part-time basis (typically half-time); while such measures have been introduced in some countries, with negligible effects, surveys suggest substantial potential interest in progressive retirement schemes. Second, newcomers are hired on a part-time basis, so that a single working post is filled by more than one person. This is in principle easier, since no worker under contract is involved. Measures facilitating part-time employment have been taken in some countries, and hiring of public servants on an 80% basis has been introduced in the Benelux countries. There is no indication of growth in part-time work by men; for women growth is concentrated in those countries which have lagged behind in this respect, and reflects a trend towards greater accommodation of worker preferences rather than a cyclical pattern. One specific difficulty seems to arise from rigidities in the organization of working schedules which stand in the way of part-time early retirement and of part-time contracts on a 75% or 80% basis. This is the area where innovative measures, difficult as they may be, seem to offer the greatest challenge.

(iii) *Trading hours for jobs*, i.e. reducing weekly (or annual) working time for workers under contract in order to create new jobs (Section 4.3). This is the most controversial measure and also a difficult one, because large numbers of workers under contract are involved, and because the measure interferes with the organization of work. Firms engaged in labour hoarding will not hire additional employees in response to reductions in hours, whereas expanding firms will resist such reductions; the short-run elasticity of employment with respect to hours worked is probably very small, and we know very little about the long-run elasticity. There is no clear evidence of promising prospects along this line, apart from isolated situations (like continuous operation with multiple shifts).

In conclusion, both short-run and long-run policy prospects are evaluated (Section 5). As the paper covers a broad range of issues, I deal with some of them very briefly. In particular, aspects well covered in accessible documents (like implicit contract theory) will be treated summarily (Chapters 2 and 3 of Okun, 1981, provide an excellent background reference for the whole paper). And I shall refrain from any peripheral developments. This is not a paper on employment policies in general, but specifically on work-sharing. Thus, the issues of the trade-off between work-sharing and other measures, or between employment and other objectives (like price stability), are not taken up. This does not belittle their significance. Promoting overall employment through an adequate combination of supply-side and demand-management measures remains the first priority.

2. Theory

2.1. Regular jobs

2.1.1. Regular and casual jobs. The distinction between the total number of hours worked and the number of persons employed is now part of any serious discussion of labour use and employment (OECD, 1983, 1985). It has also found its way progressively into econometric practice (see Fair, 1969, for an early account). The relevance of the distinction is brought out by the figures on hours worked per person in tables 17.1 and 17.2, which reveal a steady decline, both in the long run and in the recent past.

Another useful distinction concerns 'regular' jobs and 'casual' jobs, as already developed in some detail by Hicks in *The Theory of Wages* (1932). A 'regular' job is an employment relationship that is expected by both parties to have some stability and to last as long as circumstances will permit, with neither party forcing termination whimsically. Stability may be guaranteed through an explicit contract. Due, however, to the difficulty of covering enough relevant contingencies in formal terms, the typical contract will be largely implicit and rely on accepted norms of behaviour to which both parties are expected to conform. 'Regular' jobs should be distinguished from 'casual' jobs, which carry no expectation of stability and require the performance of a specific task over a specific, typically short, time span for a given wage. Neither party commits itself, even implicitly, to continue the relationship.

Table 17.1. *Life hours of work in the United Kingdom*

Year	1891	1911	1931	1951	1971	1981
Men	153	146	126	118	100	88
Women	51	46	41	40	40	40
All Workers	102	96	83	79	69	64

Source: Armstrong, P. J. (1984). 'Technical Change and Reductions in Life Hours of Work', The Technical Change Centre, London.

Table 17.2. *Annual hours worked per person, 1890–1979*

	1890	1913	1929	1950	1970	1979
Austria	2,760	2,580	2,281	1,976	1,848	1,660
Belgium	2,789	2,605	2,272	2,283	1,986	1,747
Canada	2,789	2,605	2,399	1,967	1,805	1,730
France	2,770	2,588	2,297	1,989	1,888	1,727
Germany	2.765	2,584	2,284	2,316	1,907	1,719
Italy	2,714	2,536	2,228	1,997	1,768	—
Japan	2,770	2,588	2,364	2,272	2,252	2,129
Sweden	2,770	2,588	2,283	1,951	1,660	1,451
UK	2,807	2,624	2,286	1,958	1,735	1,617
US	2,789	2,605	2,342	1,867	1,707	1,607
Median	2,770	2,588	2,285	1,982	1,825	1,690

Source: Maddison, A. (1982). *Phases of Capitalist Development*, Oxford University Press, Oxford.

There are many cogent reasons why regular jobs are a superior form of employment, from the viewpoint of firms and workers alike. First, most jobs are performed better with the benefit of experience, including some experience that is specific to the workplace itself; when the job involves teamwork, experience is frequently a team attribute, and needs to be rebuilt whenever a member of the team is replaced. Second, most firms are complex organisations, where individual workers interact with many other members of the firm (supervisors, personnel department, mainten-ance or inventory services, etc.); such relationships are facilitated by repeated contact. Third, the employer–employee relationship is itself complex, involving a measure of trust and mutual understanding which can only be developed gradually. Fourth, a longer-run employment contract provides opportunities not present in short-lived contracts; thus, rewarding realised performance *ex post*, averaging between good and bad years, or between periods of pressure and slack, is possible with regular jobs, but not with casual jobs.

2.1.2. The viewpoint of workers. The workplace provides one among many examples of areas of life where regular relationships, developed over time on a continuing basis, are essential to the pursuit of human goals. The foremost examples are of course the family and friendship. Medical care, education, community relationships, trade, services, leisure activities, and so on, provide additional examples. An important indirect benefit from a regular job lies in the prospects which it affords for founding a family, buying a house, and establishing consumption patterns. In modern economies, fringe benefits and social security benefits are more extensive for holders of regular jobs, thereby increasing their attractiveness as they form a growing part of overall compensation. It is thus safe to assume that *most individuals attach a positive value to having a regular job*. Within the context of such jobs, they supply hours (and effort) in accordance with the traditional assumption that the marginal disutility of work (relative to leisure) increases with working time, resulting in an upward sloping supply curve for hours. (This eminently sensible view is not incorporated in standard textbook treatments of labour supply, because it is technically unwieldy; it is however incorporated indirectly in the models of 'learning by doing' and 'embodied human capital' or in the models of employment over time under uncertainty.)

For a proper appraisal of work-sharing measures, the significance of regular jobs is twofold. First the distribution of an aggregate number of hours over individual jobs matters, to an extent imperfectly captured by the supply of hours. A distribution over more jobs carries the advantage of shorter hours and more leisure for all concerned; in addition, it carries the advantage of endowing more individuals with regular jobs that are valued positively. Second, the value attached to a regular job varies considerably, both across individuals, and for given individuals over time. That different individuals may attach a different weight to the stability of employment is an immediate corollary of the diversity of tastes. At given wage rates, different individuals would prefer to supply a different quantity of hours. Yet it is a commonplace observation that most regular jobs specify a standard working week, imposed on whole sets of employees, with little room for individual variation. Also, these standard working times vary little from firm to firm. Hopefully, standard working times reflect the preferences of the 'median worker', being too long for half the labour force and too short for the other half. When faced with the choice of either working the standard time, or not at all, each worker takes an all-or-nothing decision. The net value of the job will, other things equal, be higher the closer standard working time comes to an individual's preferences. In particular, those who would prefer appreciably shorter hours will benefit less from holding the job. It would seem plausible that older workers fall into that category and hence place a lower net value on regular jobs. (There are two additional reasons why the value to any individual of having a regular job is bound to decline as the age of retirement draws near. On the one hand, the period over which a stable relationship is anticipated becomes shorter, and hence less significant. On the other hand, the link with other durable patterns of behaviour – family, house, and so on – becomes less important, as these are well established already.) The significance of individual variations on the value of regular jobs is of course that they offer prospects for gains through redistribution – a point that is central to some work-sharing measures, and is taken up in Section 4.1 below.

2.1.3. The viewpoint of firms. First, *the provision of a regular job requires an initial investment on the part of the firm* – which 'toll', discussed at length by Okun (1981, chapters 2, 3) turns labour into a 'semi-fixed factor' (Oi, 1962). Obviously, the benefits of experience acquired on the job, of integration in a work team and in the firm's organization, of mutual trust or of averaging rewards over time and across states, will accrue only progressively after a period of initiation. There will often be a period of training, during which a worker's productivity may be insufficient to cover his or her wage. Furthermore, because workers are heterogeneous, firms will attempt to identify the more promising candidates through screening. Also, to the extent that the firm is offering some degree of income and employment stability, it is undertaking a commitment which may prove costly under adverse circumstances. The present value of whatever costs or risk premium may be associated with that commitment is another component of the fixed cost of a new hiring. An implication of this initial investment is the typical preference of firms for hiring employees on a full-time rather than a part-time basis. By typical, I mean here that special advantages linked to part-time work must be present in order for that form of employment to be offered (the foremost example comes from peak loads within the week, as in retailing, where part-time work is indeed widespread). Otherwise the initial investment is basically the same whether a person works full time or part time. Consequently full-time work is altogether cheaper, and part-time work is typically confined to casual jobs, failing other inducements.

Second, *'regular' jobs are not created at will, they must correspond to some real employment prospect in the firm*. At the start, this requires a place of work, demand for the output, and relative prices at which the additional job is profitable. In addition, the firm must anticipate that the additional employee will remain wanted with sufficient probability for a sufficient time. Adverse anticipations or considerable uncertainty about technological developments, demand or relative prices, would destroy the prospect of potential employment. The disconcerting fact is that so many conditions must be fulfilled *simultaneously* for a regular job to be forthcoming whereas failure of any *one* condition is enough to annihilate the prospect.

An implication is that the supply of regular jobs is bound to be highly inelastic to their short-run cost. Specifically, temporary wage cuts or employment subsidies will not be very effective in increasing the supply of regular jobs: the other elements must be there (places of work and demand for output) and the relevant cost consideration is the long-run cost over the prospective period of employment, of which the short-run cost is only a part. Thus, temporary employment subsidies will at best move forward hirings that were contemplated anyhow, and stimulate casual employment (Phlips, 1978). Desirable as they may be, these effects remain limited in scope.

2.2. Short-run fluctuations

2.2.1. Sources of fluctuations. The short-run equilibrium between supply and demand for regular jobs is subject to numerous hazards – as we know only too well from recent experience. There are several independent factors affecting either the supply or the demand for regular jobs. To begin with the supply of jobs (the demand for labour), four main factors should be listed as exerting macroeconomic influences. (These factors may of course affect specific labour markets differently; the point of interest here is that when these factors affect many specific labour markets in a given country, or set of countries, in the same direction, then macroeconomic implications become noticeable.) First, the demand for output may be slack, due to an excess of savings over investment, a fall in the demand for exports, a contractionary fiscal policy, or a combination of these. Second, labour-saving technological progress may reduce the demand for labour at given levels of output. Third, relative factor prices may induce substitution of capital for labour, or substitution of production elsewhere for production in the home country. Fourth, the capital stock physically available, or open to profitable use, may become insufficient to offer an adequate number of jobs. In a given country at a given time, the first three factors may set in exogenously while the response of fiscal policy is basically an endogenous factor – but that does not guarantee the proper response! Further a self-perpetuating force sets in when public deficits originating in the reduced levels of employment and activity are deemed unbearable and fought through reduced public expenditure. Most significantly, as the demand for domestic output slackens, investment is discouraged, plants are scrapped, and the capital stock is brought down to the level warranted by current output. While the low level of investment further reduces aggregate demand, the fourth factor comes into play: there are no longer enough places of work to generate adequate employment. Reflating the supply of jobs now requires investment in new capacity; the growth of employment is bound to be slow, even in the face of a demand upheaval and demand management is discouraged by the fear that insufficient capacity leads to inflationary pressures.

Turning to the demand for jobs (the supply of labour), the main factors operating in the short run are demographic and migratory movements, and changes in participation rates. In some European countries, female participation rates have gone up steadily over recent decades, resulting in significant increases in labour supply through the recession. There is frequent reference in the literature to the so-called 'discouraged worker effect', but it may also be the case that unemployment discourages some workers, especially married women, from *quitting* jobs which they would otherwise have given up temporarily; at the same time, unemployment may induce others to register as job seekers, even though they might otherwise have postponed entry into the labour force. In this way, unemployment becomes subject to self-perpetuation.

2.2.2. Implications for regular and casual jobs. Because regular jobs entail an initial investment, prospective fluctuations favour casual jobs. In particular, at times of high *uncertainty* about demand, technology and real wages in the future, one may expect a temporary increase in casual employment. Unfortunate as this development may be given the well-founded preference of employees for regular jobs, it is to some extent unavoidable, and still compatible with efficiency. In particular, it may be desirable to postpone investment in a new hiring until it can be directed more effectively. This calls for the development of casual jobs during a recession, while waiting for signs of recovery before incurring the tolls of regular job creation. There is indeed superficial evidence that the private sector relies more intensively on casual employment (including sub-contracting and contracting *ad interim*) in times of recession and uncertainty like the present. In the public sector special employment programmes – especially those providing casual jobs for the young – make sense given the relative ease and speed with which they can be set up, their low net costs, and the social value of the associated output.

Because the supply of regular jobs is inelastic with respect to labour costs in the short-run, relying on wage flexibility to clear the markets for regular jobs is not a realistic prospect. Indeed, market clearing wages could drop to very low levels in response to a conjunction of adverse shocks. Market-clearing wages could even drop to a level where a sizeable part of the unemployment becomes voluntary (although the unemployed may still register as seeking work in order to collect benefits)! There are two compelling reasons why that kind of flexibiltiy is undesirable. The first, of a microeconomic nature, is that it would generate excessive income uncertainty for workers holding regular jobs. That argument is taken up in Section 4.1 and extended to a discussion of wage discrimination between workers under contract and new recruits. The second, of a macroeconomic nature, is that a major drop in labour incomes would depress aggregate demand further, leading to an 'equilibrium' with very low levels of output and employment. The fact that the resulting unemployment is labelled 'voluntary' provides little solace. Given our imprecise estimates of the wage elasticity of labour demand and of the income multiplier, not to mention our near ignorance of the implications of wage moderation for government budgets, it is safer to look at incomes policy as a long-run instrument and not to rely on it as a short-run stabiliser of employment.

2.3. Labour contracts and market failures

2.3.1. The theory of implicit contracts. How does one reconcile the idea that most people want to have a regular job and stable income with the prospect of recurrent fluctuations in the demand for labour? This very question is taken up in recent theoretical work on 'implicit' labour contracts. (Azariadis, 1975, Baily, 1974 and Gordon, 1974, are the seminal contributions; Drèze, 1979a, gives a non-technical presentation of the main ideas; more recent accounts appear in the *Quarterly Journal of Economics*, Supplement, 1983, or in the surveys by Azariadis, 1979, Ito, 1982, Rosen, 1985, and Hart and Holmström, 1989). The main implication of this theory is that *efficient labour contracts will embody an element of risk-sharing*, protecting labour incomes from the vagaries of supply and demand shocks to a sizeable extent. If wages were allowed to vary widely in response to these shocks, the resulting income uncertainty would be costly to workers unable to diversify their labour supply, who therefore will be more risk averse than firms whose shareholders can hold diversified portfolios; hence the possibility of welfare improving risk-shifting arrangements, where the *labour contracts include a form of income insurance through reduced wage flexibility*. The insurance premium should be paid partly through lower wages during the early period of employment (explaining to some extent the practice of seniority bonuses), and partly through reduced upward wage flexibility (to an extent compatible with maintaining incentives). An optimal arrangement would combine an efficient degree of risk-sharing (in particular labour incomes become immune from firm-specific risks and bear a less-than-proportional share of economy-wide risks)[1] with privately efficient levels of employment (the marginal value product of labour equals its opportunity cost for workers at all times).

The combination of downward rigid wages and efficient levels of employment implies that wages do not correspond to the marginal value product of labour at all times, but only do so *on average*. In particular, during a recession, wages in many firms will exceed the marginal value product of labour; these firms practise 'labour hoarding' and will not hire new workers, *even at wages lower than those which they currently pay*. New hirings will start only at wages lower than the marginal value product of labour and with all contracted employees working full hours. For these firms (which could well be a majority during a deep recession), the elasticity of employment with respect to wage reductions is zero. This statement applies only to new hirings, however. Retention of workers under contract will be enhanced by wage cuts in firms facing bankruptcy, which can also

---

[1] Violation of this condition is a major drawback of the otherwise attractive profit-sharing scheme advocated by Weitzman (1984). Firm-specific risks should not matter to holders of diversified portfolios. That argument does not apply to privately owned firms, however.

be numerous in a deep recession – see for instance Sneessens and Drèze (1986b).

Another consideration of interest here is that the optimal (Pareto-efficient) level of unemployment is the level which would have occurred with flexible wages: at that level, the marginal value product of labour would equal the reservation wage of workers and all unemployment would be voluntary. With downward wage rigidity, the marginal value product of labour should not fall below the reservation wage of the workers, but should at least fall that far! The difference is that unemployment *appears to be involuntary* – and is definitely perceived as such by the individual worker. Efficient arrangements again call for work-sharing among employees under contract, who should preferably be laid off on a part-time basis at times of slack employment, to the extent compatible with incentives and organisation of work. In practice, that approach seems applicable only to blue collar workers; temporary layoffs, whether on a part-time or full-time basis, are practically unknown among white collar workers (that seniority bonuses are more significant for white collar workers than for blue collar workers is consistent with this observation). And part-time layoffs for blue collar workers are often discouraged by the rules governing unemployment compensation, which is not always available on a flexible, part-time basis.

There is very little hard evidence on the practical relevance of implicit contract theory, beyond the easy observation of widespread downward rigidity of wages, either real (as in most European countries) or nominal (as in the US). An early study by Abowd and Ashenfelter (1981) provided some indication that a higher probability of temporary lay-off is partly compensated by a higher wage when employed – a finding whose interpretation in the contract framework is not entirely straightforward. Further studies by Ashenfelter and Brown (1982) and Card (1985), quoted by Hart and Holmström (1989), apparently suggest little support for the hypothesis that employment levels can be explained by opportunity costs rather than wages, yet numerous macroeconometric studies corroborate the widespread belief that firms practise 'labour hoarding' during recessions. A study by Oswald (1984) of the written terms of actual labour contracts again finds little corroboration of the theoretical predictions. Neither do we know precisely how reductions of labour inputs are distributed over workers under contract – a subject on which some evidence should now be available in Europe. Collecting and analysing that evidence would seem worthwhile, if only for the light it could throw on the related issue of including the unemployed in work-sharing schemes.

2.3.2. Present and future contracts. The theory of implicit contracts asserts that efficient risk-sharing between risk-averse workers and less risk-averse firms justifies some degree of wage rigidity *for holders of regular jobs.* But that argument has not been extended to the market for regular jobs – although the extension is implicitly suggested in an example of Holmström (1981). The question of interest is whether the terms of new contracts should be flexible enough to clear the market for regular jobs at all times under all conditions, or whether efficient risk-sharing between firms and *prospective job-seekers* calls for some degree of rigidity *in the terms of new contracts*, with the associated implication of some unemployment.

It has been known for a long time that keeping wages above the market-clearing level may raise a worker's expected utility (computed with a probability of unemployment equal to the resulting unemployment rate): a sufficient condition is that the wage elasticity of labour demand be small in relation to the risk aversion of workers (see Appendix to chapter 13). That observation is the starting point of the so-called 'union models' of unemployment, surveyed for instance by Oswald (1985), Pencavel (1985) and Lindbeck and Snower (1985). In these models, however, wages are chosen *ex post* so as to maximise a worker's expected utility and are enforced through the market power of unions. The resulting unemployment is inefficient, as could be expected from a monopoly solution. The question raised here is one of *ex ante* efficiency, in an economy with incomplete insurance markets.

In order to address that question, one must introduce explicitly successive generations of workers, and consider *ex ante* the conditions that will be faced by a new generation entering the labour market. The difference with the implicit contract model is that *ex ante* considerations are not exploited in the design of contracts, because workers and firms do not engage in *forward* labour contracts. The contracts come *ex post*, after a new generation joins the labour force. That simple observation has two important implications.

First, future generations are not present when current generations negotiate labour contracts. Therefore, *the allocation of work between successive generations is not covered by the market.* That inescapable market failure introduces a major asymmetry between holders of regular jobs enjoying contractual pre-emptive employment and newcomers, who face a residual labour demand. There is scope for intervention to correct that market failure, for instance through incentives for work-sharing.

Second, because workers do not engage in forward labour contracts, they do not have access to insurance against the possibility of low wages when they enter the market for regular jobs, yet there are other, less risk-averse, agents (the firms and their shareholders) who could supply such insurance on mutually advantageous terms. Downward wage rigidity is a substitute for such insurance – an inferior substitute, to be sure, but sometimes the only available substitute.

Whether or not downward wage rigidity at less than full employment is justified *on efficiency grounds* depends primarily upon the range of feasible alternatives for income maintenance available to workers – both employed and unemployed – when labour market conditions are unfavourable. To see this, consider a generation of workers that will enter the labour market next 'year', under conditions ('states') that may be either 'good' (high market-clearing wages) or 'bad' (low market-clearing wages). Assume for simplicity that workers are risk-averse but firms (shareholders) are risk neutral. If the government could implement a transfer in favour of the workers (whether employed or not) *in the 'bad' state and only in that state*, then it would be optimal to announce such a transfer, and let wages drop to the market-clearing level. Wage rigidity would be inefficient. The *state-contingent* transfer performs for newcomers the insurance function which is embodied in the labour contracts of the earlier generations.

At the other extreme, assume that such state-contingent transfers are not feasible. In that case, wage rigidity in the bad state is the only feasible insurance for newcomers. It is an inferior form of insurance, however, due to the associated loss of output. But when the loss of output is 'small' relative to the insurance gain, then *some degree of downward wage rigidity becomes an efficient second-best policy; the resulting unemployment is individually involuntary, though socially efficient* (the condition that the loss of output be small enough is given in the Appendix to chapter 13). An essential feature is that the wage rigidity is decided before the state is known, whereas the employment decision is taken after observing the state.

An interesting intermediate case arises when the only transfers actively considered take the form of unemployment compensation – financed, say, from a lump-sum tax on profits. In the absence of additional constraints related to incentives, it is then efficient to set the unemployment compensation at a level such that, in 'bad' states, the unemployed are just as well off as the employed newcomers. Thus *unemployment becomes 'voluntary', but the wage is downwards rigid, resulting in less than full employment* (with a marginal product of labour equal to the reservation wage of idle workers collecting unemployment compensation, which thus exceeds the social opportunity cost of labour: see the Appendix to chapter 13). The special cases provide preliminary insights in a largely uncharted and difficult area, the exploration of which goes beyond the scope of the present paper. They suggest that a form of work-sharing among the newcomers (for instance through part-time jobs) would be desirable when less than full employment is second-best efficient. It would dominate the alternative (full-time work for some, full-time idleness for others), by improving the allocation among newcomers of both regular jobs and hours worked: work-sharing would then be 'first-and-a-half-best'. On that ground alone, it deserves attention.

2.3.3. Wage discrimination and insider-outsider theories. The intriguing stylised fact about downward wage rigidity for new contracts is that we seem to observe little wage discrimination between employees under contracts and new recruits; indeed casual empiricism suggests that wage discrimination *by hiring dates* is not a widespread phenomenon. Of course, some degree of wage discrimination by hiring dates is consistent with the available evidence. Thus teaching assistants hired today by Belgian Universities earn 10% less (at given seniority levels) than those hired a few years ago, whereas bank clerks earn 7% less. In the US, the practice of 'two-tier contracts', introducing explicit wage discrimination between previously employed workers and new recruits, seems to have spread recently, affecting some 25% of union workers outside construction covered by contracts signed in 1983–85 – see Dewatripont (1986) for additional data and analysis. And it is known that the quality of new recruits for given job characteristics improves during recessions and deteriorates during booms – see Okun (1981) and the references given there. Yet in general wages for new workers display little discrimination *vis-à-vis* those of workers already under contract.

It could well be that such discrimination is regarded as impractical by firms and as undesirable by firms and workers alike. Wage settlements, including differentials by occupation and seniority, are complex enough already, and increasing that complexity by adding an extra dimension might be simply impractical. Further, it certainly goes against the grain of accepted ethical norms to accentuate pay differences for equal work. Thus, it could be that wage discrimination by hiring dates has an implicit cost, with the result that the wage rigidities, introduced for the justified sake of risk-sharing in the existing contracts, lead to inefficient involuntary unemployment among newcomers.

An alternative explanation is offered by the so-called 'insider–outsider' theories of unemployment (see Lindbeck and Snower, 1985, for a very useful survey of a growing literature). The point of departure of these theories is 'the observation that, in general, a firm finds it costly to exchange its current, full-fledged employees (the "insiders") for workers outside the firm (the "outsiders") ... The turnover cost generates economic rent ... The insiders raise their wage above the entrant wage, *but not by more than the relevant turnover cost*' (Lindbeck and Snower, 1985, p. 47; italics added). This is a sensible explanation which suggests some interesting links between insider–outsider and implicit contract theories.

Thus existing theories of labour contracts typically assume that markets for new contracts at future dates will be competitive. If, as suggested by insider–outsider theories, the wages of employees under contract (insiders) cannot exceed those of new recruits (outsiders) by more than the turnover costs, then it would be in the interest of insiders to keep the wages paid to outsiders as high as possible, i.e. to impose downward wage rigidity for new contracts. In particular, if it could be stipulated that new recruits must be paid the same (or nearly the same) wages as insiders, then the latter would be protected against competition by outsiders. Conversely, implicit labour contracts typically stipulate that insiders will not be laid off and replaced by outsiders. However, such a stipulation could be of limited effectiveness, because it does not prevent expanding firms and new firms from hiring newcomers at lower, market-clearing wages. The position of these firms *in product markets* would thereby be strengthened, whereas the output and employment prospects of the labour hoarding firms would be weakened further. An extreme but suggestive example is offered by the building industry, where new firms are easily organised. If new firms could hire labour at a fraction of the cost applicable to workers under contracts, established firms would have to lower their bids for new building projects commensurately. Thus, insiders in the established firms would face the competition of outsiders *through product prices*; the stipulation that they could not be laid off and replaced by outsiders is ineffective.

It is thus in the joint interest of established firms and their employees to prevent, if they can, the wages specified in new contracts from falling appreciably below the wages of insiders. Of course, this requires market power. That unions in Europe have market power over wage determination is generally accepted. Two additional and new considerations are proposed here. First, union activity on the market for new contracts is not a matter of concern to newcomers only; it is also of direct concern to insiders seeking protection from competition by outsiders via product markets. Second, that very protection is also valuable to established employers.

The resulting coincidence of interests helps to explain the observed practice of industry-level wage settlements, which are binding on new firms and seem to introduce little wage discrimination between insiders and outsiders.

The absence of market mechanisms leading to wage discrimination between workers under contract and new recruits has led to a number of proposals for *marginal employment subsidies* (see e.g. Dornbusch *et al.*, 1983 or Steinherr and Van Haeperen, 1985). As I have noted above, such subsidies should be substantial and durable in order to affect significantly the long-run cost of a regular job, and hence employment. In addition, the argument presented in this section suggests that existing firms, and their employees, may object to such subsidies as generating unfair competition in the product markets.

2.3.4. Summary and implications. Workers seeking employment during a recession (new entrants, and those who have lost their jobs) face two kinds of firms, those engaged in labour hoarding (which are not hiring), and those hiring new workers (including new firms). The former, which may well be a majority during a severe recession, operate at a marginal value product of labour less than the wage costs and equal to the reservation wage of their employees. Routine demographic replacements, which will normally absorb all new entrants in stationary conditions, are not taking place. Newcomers are excluded both from the labour hoarding and from whatever work-sharing is organised among employees under contract. And these firms will not respond to wage cuts by new hirings, until the gap between wage costs and the marginal value product of labour has been bridged: competition between workers under contract and newcomers is shut off. Expanding firms and new firms hire labour to the point where its marginal value product covers wage costs, but not beyond. And they practise little or no wage discrimination between workers under contract and newcomers.

We thus have three groups of workers: first, those under contract in firms which are not hiring, where they are employed at a marginal value product below their wages; second, those employed in new and hiring firms, with a marginal value product equal to their wage; and third, the unemployed. There are two sources of inefficiency in this situation. First, employment should increase in the expanding firms, to the point where the marginal value product of labour is equal to the reservation wage of the unemployed. It is not clear how this can be achieved without some form of wage discrimination between workers under contract and newcomers. Second, the distribution of jobs and hours worked between the employed and the unemployed is inefficient. Indeed, I have presented some quite compelling arguments to the effect that *some* newcomers at least will place a higher value on finding a regular job than *some* workers under contract attach to keeping theirs. (In particular, young workers may be more eager to start a career than workers close to retirement are to bring their own to an end.) Hence, some redistribution of regular jobs between workers under contract and newcomers would be desirable – but will not be naturally forthcoming. In addition, the supply of *hours* being definitely upward sloping, it would be desirable to increase the number of employees and redistribute aggregate hours among them – a standard argument. Thus, whether we look at jobs (valued positively) or at hours of work (valued negatively), we conclude that the allocation of work between newcomers and workers under contract is inefficient. Finally, it is easy to understand why little or no work-sharing takes place among newcomers, in the form of part-time jobs. With firms facing fixed costs of screening and training, and half the newcomers prepared to work more than full-time (as must be the case if standard working time corresponds to median worker preferences), there is ample scope for mutually agreeable contracts on a full-time basis.

The upshot of these arguments is precisely what we observe today in Europe! Namely, a prolonged spell of deeply depressed demand for labour, with employment declining in many firms (especially in the manufacturing sector which is exposed to international competition), downward rigid wages and a modest degree of work-sharing among workers under contract, with very high unemployment rates among the young (and older workers who have lost their previous jobs), and a fair degree of wage rigidity even on new contracts. The resulting allocation of work among all workers is definitely inefficient both because little or no work-sharing takes place between workers under contract and newcomers, and because little or no work-sharing takes place among newcomers finding employment. More efficient work-sharing thus requires special measures.

2.4. The scope for intervention

Market failures provide a motivation for public intervention aimed at correcting inefficiencies. In the case under discussion, that motivation is enhanced by the existence of a social externality. Unemployment is not only a burden on individuals, who are frustrated in their desire to work and to enjoy a stable employment relationship. It also entails additional real burdens for society – for instance when prolonged inactivity leads to delinquency or health deterioration. Of course, the most immediate externality comes from the existence of unemployment compensation schemes. In the light of the arguments reviewed above, it is obvious 'that public unemployment compensation schemes are important and should be maintained, in spite of some obvious drawbacks'.[2] Unemployment compensation accrues to the unemployed at no private cost but it is paid out of public funds which entails a social cost. Any measure resulting in less unemployment also results in less public expenditure on unemployment compensation. More positively, the money spent on unemployment compensation could be spent more profitably on reducing unemployment. *One way is to subsidise work-sharing, thereby providing financial incentives to overcome market failures.*

There are two additional reasons why public measures aimed at promoting work-sharing could *possibly* be effective. First, in most European countries the social security system has become very complex, introducing additional distortions into an already imperfectly functioning labour market. An obvious example arises when ceilings or other regressive formulae for social security contributions (employment taxes) impose a penalty on part-time jobs as compared with full-time jobs. Eliminating those distortions which discourage work-sharing, possibly even creating distortions which favour it, offers scope for public intervention. Second, the organization of working time is a complex social phenomenon, involving coordination of all kinds of activities, with numerous externalities; it falls largely outside the sphere of market allocation. To take again an obvious example, think back to the transition from the 6-day week to the 5-day week. Although 5 days became the norm for blue collar workers shortly after World War II, it took nearly twenty years before that schedule became universal, and it is probably fair to say that consumption patterns are still adjusting to a universal 5-day week. With further reductions in working time below 40 hours per week now emerging here and there, a number of alternative patterns of work are possible. The coordination aspects and externalities provide scope for public initiative in sorting out the costs and benefits *for society* of these alternative patterns, and for public leadership in promoting that which is most desirable.

---

[2] The most fashionable of these drawbacks, namely the negative impact on job search, is of little consequence during a deep recession, when employment is only very weakly linked to labour supply. The possible impact on wages is a more serious matter.

3. Interlude (sorbet)

Before turning to consider specific measures aimed at promoting work-
sharing in Europe, it is illuminating to speculate how a substantial
temporary decline in the demand for regular labour would be handled in
a cooperative environment – like a kibbutz, a network of cooperatives (as
in Mondragon in Spain) or an integrated set of family businesses. For
concreteness think about a hypothetical kibbutz where the major use of
labour (entirely supplied by the members) goes into manufacturing some
gadget sold outside. Normally, young members are taken up into the
factory work force and trained to replace retiring older members. Assume
now that a non-negligible decline in the need for labour input occurs –
say due to a major accidental plant destruction, a shortage of raw
materials, a sudden fall in the demand for the gadget, the introduction of
a new labour-saving technology, or a combination of these. This decline
was not perfectly foreseen, although it may perhaps have been contemplated. Also suppose the decline is expected to last for some time, with
progressive elimination over a period of months or years at a highly
uncertain rate. (That is, long-term corrective action is under way, but will
only become fully effective after a while.) How would the kibbutz
community react to such an event?

Most likely, a whole set of measures would be combined; diverting
some labour to other uses previously endowed with lower priority, such
as improving the grounds or repainting the buildings; excusing from work
in the factory the older, less able or less motivated workers, or some with
high productivity alternatives (like young mothers, or members with
valuable personal projects); reducing across the board effective working
times, through shorter hours, longer vacations, or occasional days off;
calling some of the young workers into the work force on a part-time
basis, with the rest of their time devoted to continued education, or to
the other work already mentioned.

The list could be extended. The point I wish to make is that various
forms of work-sharing would *naturally* be introduced; and it is highly
unlikely that a large number of young members would remain totally
inactive for prolonged periods.

4. Experience

The digression of Section 3 provides a useful background against which
to evaluate the alternative forms of work-sharing which have been
considered recently by European policy-makers. I will group them under

three headings: *trading jobs*, i.e. replacing a worker under contract by a newcomer; *sharing jobs*, i.e. filling a single working post by more than one person; and *trading hours for jobs*, i.e. reducing working time for workers under contract to create new jobs.

4.1. Trading jobs (early retirement)

Trading jobs between workers under contract and unemployed persons is the simplest, and in a way the most natural, form of work-sharing. In particular, it *does not interfere at all with the organisation of work*. Because the value to individuals of regular jobs varies from one person to the next, there is scope for mutually advantageous trading.[3] By definition, the holders of regular jobs place a non-negative value on their jobs – otherwise, they would quit. But that value could be small – in which case a small 'bribe' would induce the holder to give up the job. If the 'bribe' per year falls short of the level of unemployment compensation, the state can 'buy' the job for an unemployed person, at no net cost (the compensation paid to the quitter is no longer paid to the new employee); this generates a positive externality, namely the value of the job to the new employee. Also, the value of a job is often blown up artificially by social legislation. For instance, some statutory pensions are proportional to average salary over the last five years prior to retirement age; consequently, quitting during these five years entails a cost far in excess of the salary itself (see Hart, 1984). The state could step in to correct the externality – say by neutralising the effect of early quitting on the pension.

These two ideas are combined in early retirement schemes, as introduced in several European countries over the past decade (namely, in the Netherlands and Belgium in 1976, in the UK in 1977, in France in 1981 as a supplement to earlier measures, and in Germany in 1984). Workers close to retirement are natural candidates for giving up jobs, under moderate financial incentives (but subject to suitable adjustments in

---

[3] Could such trading be organized through markets? In exceptional cases, something resembling a private market for individual jobs exists; but closer scrutiny reveals that the 'jobs' in question are in the nature of independent practice or casual jobs, and lack the dimension of a lasting employment relationship. For regular jobs, the presence of a third party, the employer, complicates the trading: the employer must accept (recruit) the 'buyer' of a job; and if jobs in a firm had positive market values this might provide incentives for the firm to reduce wages and capture the 'rent'. I am not aware of any serious work on this topic. It should also be realised that our complex social legislation does not facilitate market trading of individual jobs. Would a seller be eligible for unemployment compensation? Would a buyer inherit the seniority rights of the seller? Basically, social security rights are not transferable.

pension rules). All the schemes under consideration permit early retirement, at no loss of pension rights after the normal age of retirement, and with an income allowance over the intermediate years. The level of that transitory income, and its source, vary from scheme to scheme; typically, the basic component corresponds to unemployment compensation, with an additional allowance sometimes provided by the firm or by the state. In several schemes, the retired workers must be replaced by a member of the unemployed (a young one, in Belgium), or else, the firm must make a case that it operates with excess labour, so that early retirements are a substitute for dismissals. Although most schemes provide incentives for *voluntary* retirements and none make it compulsory across the board, there are undoubtedly many cases where the worker's hand is forced by the prospect of an unappealing alternative (being laid off, transferred, etc.). And there are undoubtedly cases where the employer's hand is forced towards entering a programme with mandatory replacements.

I have not seen a systematic account and analysis of early retirement programmes at the European level. But the fragmentary country data which I have come across indicate clearly that these programmes can involve substantial numbers of people.

4.1.1. The United Kingdom. Introduced in 1976, the Job Release Scheme offers a weekly allowance to older workers retiring early, provided their employer agrees to replace them by unemployed persons. The allowance is paid until the age of normal retirement, and varies (from £48 to £61 per week) with family and health status. The age of eligibility has varied over time from 64 to 62 years of age for men; it is 59 for women and 60 for disabled men. Participation in the programme is entirely voluntary. According to Davies and Metcalf (1985) there were 272,100 entrants into the programme over the period 1976–1984, with a stock of participants totalling 75,000 persons in 1985. They also quote a replacement ratio (new hirings per entrant) of 92% and claim that 'the Job Release Scheme has the lowest net cost per person off the (unemployment) register' of all the Special Employment Programmes implemented in the UK (namely, £1,650 per person-year in 1985, obtained from a gross cost of £3,250 after netting out the savings in unemployment benefits). They also claim that the scope of the programme could be more than doubled, by extending eligibility to all men aged 60–64.

4.1.2. France. Several early retirement programmes have been implemented. The 'Contrats de Solidarité' were introduced in 1981 and required mandatory replacements. Other programmes without mandatory replacement had been introduced in the past. According to Marchand (1984), by the end of 1983 there were some 700,000 beneficiaries of early retirement programmes, namely 180,000 under 'Contrats de Solidarité', 284,000 in early retirement due to dismissal and 230,000 under voluntary early retirement. According to data presented by Baruh (1986), actual participants in the earlier programmes represented a substantial proportion of potential participants. For 36 sectors, Baruh relates the number of actual participants in 1980–82 to the number of employees at the 1975 census in the relevant age group. He finds the number of actual beneficiaries equal to 51.5% of the 1975 stock, with figures between 40 and 70% in 24 sectors (out of 36), and figures below 40% in only 5 sectors, all of them services. These are crude calculations, but they indicate unambiguously that participation rates for these programmes were high. The replacement ratio is known only for the 'Contrats de Solidarité', where it is reportedly close to 95%. It is of course nil in the case of dismissals, and believed to have been relatively low under the previous schemes which did not require mandatory replacement. The gross cost of these programmes, as estimated from the national accounts, seems to be of the same order of magnitude as in the UK (around £3,200 per beneficiary per year). As of April 1983, the 'Contrats de Solidarité' programme was discontinued; instead, voluntary retirement was offered to all workers aged 60 or more with 37.5 years of labour force seniority. Apparently mandatory replacement is not required.

4.1.3. Belgium. A number of early retirement schemes have been implemented since 1977; the age of eligibility has generally been 60 for men and 55 for women. Except in the case of dismissals, replacement by an unemployed person aged less than 30 is mandatory. Observed replacement ratios reach 63% overall and 83% if dismissals are set aside. As of October 1984, the overall number of beneficiaries totalled 138,000 (see Sonnet and Defeyt, 1984). Thus, in both France and Belgium, some 3 to 4% of the total labour force were involved.

Participation rates for the Belgian programmes are very high, confirming the estimates for France, but also pointing to a possible source of bias. Scarmure (1986) has related the number of actual beneficiaries of early retirement schemes to an estimate of the total number of potential beneficiaries in the 'relevant' age group – namely 60–64 for men and 55–59 for women. He finds participation rates that increase steadily from the date when a programme is launched. These are uniformly much higher for men, increasing from 33% in 1977 to 94% in 1981, than for women, for whom the respective figures are 12 and 38%. For both sexes combined, the rates rise from 24% in 1977 to 60% in 1981 and thence to 85% in 1985 (the breakdown by sex is not given after 1981). There are two sources of bias in these figures. First, on a number of occasions involving firms faced with the prospect of bankruptcy or reorganisation, early retirement schemes have been extended outside the official age bracket (I remember one such instance, where men were forced into retirement at 53 and women at 48). Second, the total number of potential beneficiaries has been obtained by multiplying the figures for the labour force *in the relevant age group* by the percentage of wage and salary earners (as opposed to the self-employed) *in the aggregate labour force*. It would seem likely that labour force participation declines more slowly with age in the case of the self-employed than in the case of wage and salary earners. These two sources of bias reinforce each other. The first is probably the more significant and might explain the high rates of early retirement in France as well as in Belgium.

Scarmure (1986) also provides estimates of the net cost to the Treasury of these schemes. His calculations are more detailed, and probably more comprehensive, than those quoted above for the UK and France. Indeed, he assesses separately the loss of revenue resulting from the termination of employment of an older worker (through lost income tax, social security contributions and indirect taxes), the direct cost of early retirement benefits, the savings connected with removing a young unemployed person from the register, and the gain in revenue from the employment of that young worker. He conducts these calculations separately for white collar workers (where seniority bonuses account for 40% of average end-of-career salaries) and for blue collar workers (where seniority bonuses are insignificant). His figures, translated into sterling, are presented in table 17.3. Although rough, these calculations point to the substantial total cost of early retirement schemes for white collar workers *whose employment would otherwise not have been terminated*. Of course, if a person goes into early retirement *instead of being laid off* (for the good), the net cost is minimal (the French data quoted above suggest that the latter case was more frequent than the former).

4.1.4. Conclusion. These data are very fragmentary, and leave unanswered many questions worthy of further investigation. In particular, one would like to know: the proportion of the eligible population which has joined voluntary programmes of early retirement, and how that proportion has varied with age, with sex, with qualifications or occupations and with the income maintenance provisions of the programmes; the net impact of early retirement programmes on labour supply, taking into account natural attrition of the labour force in the relevant age groups; the net impact of these programmes on employment, taking into account normal replacement ratios at the times of normal retirement; the effect of mandatory replacement provisions; and the net budgetary costs of alternative programmes.

Table 17.3. *Net cost per capita of early retirement in Belgium (in £)*

		White collar	Blue collar
Loss of revenue from termination of employment of older worker		14,400	8,700
Early retirement benefits		3,700	4,000
	Subtotal	18,100	12,700
Cost of young unemployed		2,700	2,700
Revenue from employment of young worker		7,900	8,700
	Subtotal	10,600	11,400
Net cost		7,500	1,300

Source: Scarmure (1986).

While awaiting results of further research on these points, it seems safe to draw two conclusions from the British, French and Belgian experiences. The first conclusion is that *a mandatory replacement provision seems to make a crucial difference in terms of job creation.* In contrast to the very high replacement rates quoted above for the UK, France and Belgium, figures as low as 10 or 20% are reported for non-mandatory programmes, for instance in the Netherlands (see Commissariat Général du Plan, 1985). Offhand, early retirement without voluntary replacement may be construed as an indication of labour hoarding. It is not implausible that 80 or 90% of the firms adopting early retirement schemes without mandatory replacements were firms with redundant labour. But these figures may be partly illusory, as one might expect replacements to be staggered over time, with the high mandatory rates concealing some hirings unrelated to the scheme and the low voluntary rates failing to take account of subsequent hirings. The second conclusion is that the potential reduction in the effective labour supply *of workers under contract* through early retirement is definitely substantial, as witnessed by the French and Belgian figures. With state pension schemes largely financed by redistributive taxation rather than from an accumulated fund, the official retirement age is (like standard working time) a 'public good', corresponding roughly to the median worker's preferences. In that case, about half the labour force should have a potential interest in early retirement, at a transitory income close to retirement income, the proportion of volunteers increasing smoothly with the income replacement ratio. Surveys conducted in France and the Netherlands confirm these commonsense observations.[4] In the same way that the attractiveness of early retirement varies across individuals, it also varies across firms. One important aspect is the extent of seniority bonuses, which provide an inducement to replace senior workers by less costly beginners. Another aspect is the extent to which firms try to update the skill composition of their work force: early retirement provides advance opportunities for doing so with constant employment.

4.2.   Sharing jobs (part-time work)

This form of work-sharing occurs whenever a single working post is filled by more than one person. Two separate issues will be considered under this heading, namely early retirement on a part-time basis with replacement on the same basis, and part-time work in general.

4.2.1.   Part-time early retirement. In 1982, the UK introduced a 'Job Splitting Scheme', under which (among other provisions) a worker could retire early on a half-time basis, and be replaced on the same basis by one who was unemployed. After 12 months of operation, the Job Splitting Scheme had covered a mere 578 jobs! In 1983, the French 'Contrats de Solidarité', used by 180,000 persons over a two-year span, were brought to an end, and replaced by a scheme offering incentives for half-time early retirement with replacement. That scheme, parallel to the British Job Splitting Scheme, was equally unsuccessful.[5]

These experiences are definitely sobering, for progressive retirement would seem to convey a number of advantages in comparison with an abrupt end to the working life. Reporting the results of sample polls on the preferences of workers regarding earnings and working time, Van Den Bergh and Wittelsburger (1981) note that diversity of preferences is the

---

[4] According to a survey conducted in France in 1980, 50% of workers would have retired at age 60 instead of 65, if offered the same retirement income. In the Netherlands, when older teachers were given the option of reduced working time in pre-retirement years, 90% of those eligible took advantage of the scheme.

[5] In a sample of 34 firms surveyed in 1984 by a Commission of the French Planning Office, 27 firms had adopted some form of work-sharing or of working-time reduction, but only one case of progressive (part-time) retirement was mentioned; see Commissariat Général du Plan (1985).

rule, with the single exception of German workers who, in a 1979 IFO survey, were 70% in favour of progressive retirement. The apparent failure of progressive retirement schemes in France and the UK should be considered in the light of broader trends concerning part-time work.

4.2.2. Part-time work. The more striking features are the following:

Part-time workers are almost exclusively women and the proportion is rising continuously with age; in the prime age group, it stands uniformly above the average. Although the percentage of men working regularly on a part-time basis has grown somewhat in recent years, the growth is accounted for by older workers or younger workers in special programmes; *there is little or no indication of systematic job sharing among men* (table 17.4).

The percentage of women working regularly on a part-time basis varies substantially across countries, ranging from 40–45% in the UK and Denmark, down to 20% or less in France and Belgium; *variations across countries are much more pronounced than variations over time.*

For women, a high percentage of part-time work tends to be associated with an above average labour force participation rate. When participation rates are adjusted into full-time equivalents as is done in table 17.5, their variability across countries is sharply reduced and adjusted participation rates become independent of the extent of part-time work. This observation suggests that promoting part-time work would increase participation rates, so that the increased employment would not be matched by a commensurate fall in unemployment, nor would it be matched by a commensurate increase in aggregate labour input.

In a country like the UK, where part-time work by women is widespread, the proportion of part-time workers varies substantially with age and family composition (tables 17.6 and 17.7). Also preferences for working time expressed by survey respondents in other countries (like Germany and France), where part-time work is less widespread, imply a desired share of part-time work close to the 40–45% observed in the UK and Denmark (Jallade, 1982). Furthermore, in France with little part-time work, the proportion of part-time workers has increased recently (since 1980), and the increase has been uniform across industries (Drèze, 1986a). On the other hand, in the UK, the percentage of part-time work is stationary. This is consistent with the hypothesis that the extent of part-time work largely reflects the preferences of workers, accommodated by employers, rather than the other way around.

In all countries, part-time work is more widespread in services than in

Table 17.4. Proportion of employees working part-time by sex and age (% of total employment, regular and casual jobs)

	Men						Women					
	1975	1983					1975	1983				
	Total	14–24	25–49	50–64	65 up	Total	Total	14–24	25–49	50–64	65 up	Total
Belgium	1.0	3.8	1.4	1.9	18.8	2.0	13.0	14.7	20.4	23.2	37.5	19.7
Denmark	4.7	20.2	2.7	4.8	20.5	6.6	45.2	30.2	44.5	54.4	46.5	44.7
France	3.0	4.5	1.4	3.0	37.6	2.5	16.7	14.4	19.6	25.2	39.2	20.0
Germany	1.9	1.5	0.9	1.6	39.4	1.7	26.7	6.0	36.7	36.5	55.7	30.0
Greece	—	6.7	2.4	3.3	16.7	—	—	10.1	10.9	13.0	51.4	—
Ireland	2.6	5.8	1.6	2.6	—	2.7	16.9	6.9	19.4	27.3	—	15.6
Italy	3.4	3.7	1.1	3.1	25.3	2.4	12.7	7.8	29.8	13.1	29.9	9.4
Netherlands[1]	2.4	11.0	5.3	7.5	46.6	6.9	28.8	22.0	59.9	66.1	55.6	50.3
UK	2.3	6.0	1.0	2.6	57.9	3.3	41.0	15.9	47.1	51.1	74.5	42.1
Europe 10[2]	2.6	4.6	1.4	2.8	35.8	2.8	26.0	12.1	29.8	34.8	—	27.6

Source: Eurostat, Emploi et Chômage 2, 1985.
Notes: [1]For the Netherlands, a change in definitions occurred between 1975 and 1983.
[2]Europe 9 for data describing all age groups together.

industry: in the 10 EC countries, the percentage of part-time work is 1.3% in industry and 3.4% in services for men, and 18.0% and 30.3% respectively for women (see Drèze, 1986a). In all sectors, it is concentrated in jobs entailing less responsibility and requiring lower qualifications, as hourly earnings of part-time workers are lower than those of full-time workers (see Jallade, 1982).

Table 17.5. *Adjusted labour-force participation rates, women, 1977*

	Gross participation rate	Proportion of part-time employees	Adjusted participation rate	Unemployment rate
Belgium	25.7	16.7	23.3	10.9
Denmark	38.2	46.3	28.6	8.9
France	33.0	17.8	29.9	6.1
Germany	29.5	28.3	25.2	3.8
Ireland	18.6	18.9	16.7	7.4
Italy	19.9	11.9	18.7	7.0
Luxemburg	22.4	14.4	20.8	1.5
Netherlands	17.6	28.3	15.0	3.3
UK	34.7	40.8	27.3	4.4
Europe 9	28.5	26.4	24.5	5.3
Mean absolute deviation (unweighted)	6.63	10.04	4.55	

Definition: Col (3) = Col (1) $\left[1 - 0.5 \dfrac{\text{Col(2)}}{100} \left(1 + \dfrac{\text{Col(4)}}{100} \right) \right]$.

Source: Eurostat, 'Labour Force Sample Survey', *Emploi et Chômage*, 2, 1985.

Table 17.6. *Proportion of women working part-time by marital status and age, UK, 1977*

Age	14–19	20–24	25–34	35–44	45–54	55–59	60–64	65 up	Total
Married	17.2	19.3	51.5	57.5	48.0	49.4	64.7	80.2	50.2
Unmarried	4.1	4.3	14.9	20.7	21.5	33.3	50.0	70.5	21.1

Source: Jallade (1982). *L'Europe à temps partiel*, Economica, Paris.

Table 17.7. *Proportion of women aged 16–59 working part-time, by marital status and age of youngest child, UK, 1977*

Age of youngest child	0–4	5–9	10–15	16–up	No dependent child
Married	78	78	56	52	31
Unmarried	49	52	35	34	6

Source: Jallade (1982). *L'Europe à temps partiel*, Economica, Paris.

Hours worked by part-time workers are largely concentrated at or near the half-time mark (table 17.8). Yet there is a potential supply of part-time work near the 30 hours, three-quarter-time, mark. According to a survey conducted in the EC countries in the Spring of 1985, 'one in six full-time employed workers in Europe has a very keen interest in a significant reduction in working hours, even if this is associated with a corresponding loss of pay. Ideally they would wish to work approximately 30 hours a week rather than conventional half-time employment.'[6] That supply does not seem to be matched by a corresponding demand.

Table 17.8. *Distribution of hours worked by women employees with regular part-time jobs, Europe 9, 1981*

Hours	0	1–14	15–19	20–24	25–29	30–34	35 up
Industry	6.7	12.5	36.7	11.9	23.2	3.7	5.3
Services	7.1	23.1	35.0	11.6	16.6	2.6	4.0

Source: Eurostat, 'Labour Force Sample Survey', *Emploi et Chômage*, 2, 1985.

An attempt was made in 1984 in the Benelux countries to hire public servants on an 80%, four-day week, basis. No systematic report on that experiment is available yet. Casual evidence suggests that it was not very successful, due to insufficient reorganisation of work. That experiment clearly deserves further study.

4.2.3. Conclusion. Job sharing through part-time work has not developed in Europe as a means of work-sharing to alleviate cyclical unemployment. It has not spread among men. The countries where part-time employment of women is growing are the countries where that form of employment is still infrequent, and where one would expect it to spread irrespective of the recession. Although I have not seen hard data, I suspect that part-time work has not been used as a means of work-sharing for workers under contract in firms with declining employment either. The reasons seem to be a natural preference for full-time contracts, shared by firms and male workers, and a lack of flexibility in providing part-time jobs on a more-than-half-time basis. Indeed, if job sharing were to be

---

[6] Quoted from European Economy, Supplement B, No. 10, October 1985, where a summary account of the survey is given. The statement quoted in the text is followed by the following comment: 'In practice, these wishes can generally only be realised if the entire work process is organized more flexibly. Only in this way can discrepancies between company and personal working hours be bridged (e.g. in the form of a rolling four-day week).'

used systematically as a way of absorbing fluctuations in the supply of regular jobs, a natural approach would consist in promoting new hirings on a 75% or 80% basis, combined with reorganisation of work aimed at simultaneously extending the rate of utilisation of capital. The latter measures would be particularly appropriate at times when spare capacity is scarce. Some speculative remarks on this theme are offered in Section 5.

4.3. Trading hours for jobs (the working week)

In the long run, reductions in hours worked have been an important component of welfare gains, accounting for something like 25% of overall gains on a crude estimate (see OECD, 1985, quoting Douglas, 1934). At the same time, these reductions have played an important role in reconciling full employment with productivity gains; see tables 17.1 and 17.2 above. (Of course, the extent to which shorter hours have been permitted by, or have triggered, technological progress is not separately identified.) These are long-run trends. The question of interest here relates to short-run fluctuations. During temporary recessions could employment be stimulated (jobs created) by *anticipating* trend reductions in hours? Off-hand, this is a tempting suggestion. In practice, it seems difficult to implement. It was tried in France in the thirties, with little practical impact on effective working time, and a questionable immediate impact on employment. Over the past decade, the theme of a 35-hour week has been the subject of much controversy, as witnessed by the strike of German metal workers in 1979 or official pronouncements in Belgium in 1978, and France in 1981. As of today, there is no indication that stimulating employment through shorter hours is feasible on a significant scale in the short run, and longer-run effects remain subject to much uncertainty. At best, the nature of the difficulties associated with this approach become progressively better understood. I begin by reviewing the theoretical arguments for and against this approach, and then summarise recent experience.

4.3.1. Theory. The theoretical ground for advocating shorter hours during a prolonged recession is of course the prospect of correcting the inefficient distribution of work between employees under contract and job seekers. If a given number of hours is to be shared more efficiently between the two groups, it seems natural to impose shorter hours on both workers under contract and newcomers (at least, this is more natural than laying off workers under contract to hire newcomers). Hopefully new hirings might occur in the same proportion that hours are reduced.

There is an important qualification, however. The logic of implicit contract theory is that firms should use labour up to the point where its marginal value product is equal to the opportunity cost of workers, which is typically well below the full wage cost to firms in a recession. That logic applies to workers under contract – not to newcomers, who are hired only when their marginal value product covers their full wage cost. Consequently, if the hours of workers under contract are reduced, firms operating at a marginal value product of labour below full wage costs will not hire replacements, unless the reduction in hours is sufficient to bring the marginal value product of labour up to the full wage cost. Put more simply, *firms engaged in labour hoarding will not respond to shorter hours by new hirings*, for the same reason that they do not offset natural attrition of their work force by new hirings (such firms will in any case be willing to reduce hours, since they have excess labour). *Shorter hours will induce additional hirings only in those firms which are already hiring* to offset quits or expand employment. Such firms are a minority during a prolonged recession and they are concentrated in specific sectors. Also, these firms will show great reluctance to reduce hours. In order to increase employment, it might be preferable to create incentives for these firms to hire newcomers on a part-time basis – say on a 75% or 80% basis, with the prospects of switching to full-time work as the pressure of unemployment abates.

Of course, had the newcomers been part of a market clearing process *ex ante*, they would be part of the labour hoarding today, and shorter hours would be an attractive alternative to layoffs. The problem is again one of asymmetry between sharing work solely among those under contract, versus sharing work between those under contract and the unemployed. To overcome that asymmetry (to bridge the gap between the marginal value product of labour and full wage costs), the more radical measure of shorter hours with mandatory new hirings should be considered. That is each firm should be required to increase employment by a fixed percentage, while reducing hours for all. Clearly, measures of that kind entail a high degree of arbitrariness and are difficult to implement. To say that new entrants into the labour force would have a job today, if they had been able to contract yesterday, is not to say that employment *in every firm* would thereby be increased *in the same proportion* (that arbitrariness would be alleviated, but not eliminated, if the hiring obligations were tradable among firms). Also, wages today would be different, and so on. Only if the measure under discussion had been fully anticipated could one claim that it was non-discriminatory[7] and it is clear that if such a measure were announced, it would discourage normal hirings to an extent which could be quite harmful.

Two additional pitfalls of a mandatory general reduction in hours should be mentioned (they are discussed at greater length in Drèze, 1980a, where an attempt is also made to quantify their effects). The first concerns effective hours of plant utilisation. In firms operating one or two shifts for a conventional number of hours, reducing weekly hours is likely to simply reduce plant utilisation and output, with no effect on employment. A typical example is offered by automobile plants working two shifts, with little or no possibility of keeping plant hours constant when weekly schedules of workers are reduced by a few hours. It is only when the number of shifts is simultaneously increased that employment will rise naturally, the limiting case being offered by plants operated on a continuous basis, where shorter hours per worker entail the need for additional employees. The second pitfall concerns effective wage costs. If shorter hours result in higher hourly wage cost, whatever positive effects on employment may be associated with the reduction in work hours must be weighed against the negative effects associated with increased labour costs. These may have two sources. On the one hand, effective wage costs may rise due to the fixed costs of hiring and training, now spread over fewer hours, and due to the capital costs, similarly spread over fewer hours if plant utilisation is linked to the working schedules of employees. On the other hand, workers on shorter hours may attempt to protect their disposable income by claiming higher hourly wages, and a less than proportional reduction in take-home pay. The risk that shorter hours result in higher effective wage costs will be tempered if employment-conscious unions substitute hiring claims for wage claims. The difficult question, ultimately, is to assess the long-run incidence of hours worked on effective wage costs. The instantaneous increases arising from shorter hours at unchanged take-home pay may be partly compensated by smaller wage increases thereafter, whereas the instantaneous wage moderation accompanying demands for more employment may be partly compensated by catching up later. In either case, speculation about future wage patterns is needed to draw firm conclusions. Finally, there is a presumption that many firms are able to offset a gradual reduction in weekly hours by productivity increases without new hirings.

[7] The existence of an equilibrium under rational expectations and proportional quantity constraints is, however, questionable.

4.3.2. Experience. The salient features of recent European experience with hours worked per week seem to be the following:

(i) Over the past 10 years, average hours worked per week have declined (see table 17.9). The main explanation for this decline lies in the near disappearance of overtime work. On the one hand, there was less need for overtime work, due to the depressed demand for output. On the other hand, unions and governments discouraged overtime work, in order to stimulate new hirings.[8]

Table 17.9. *Average weekly hours worked, blue collar workers, manufacturing*

	Belgium	France	Germany	Italy	Netherlands	UK
1972	41.7	45.0	43.2	41.9	43.9	43.0
1982	34.9	39.4	40.0	37.5	40.6	41.4

Sources: Eurostat, *Gains horaires, durée du travail*, 2, 1983.

(ii) In those cases where a reduction in hours with mandatory new hirings has been put forward, it has met with adamant opposition from employers. Thus, a proposal by the Belgian Government in 1979 to subsidise a reduction of the standard working week from 40 to 38 hours with new hirings corresponding to 3% of employment and with some 'wage moderation', was rejected by the employers and some unions. When offered to individual firms on a voluntary basis, the proposal met with negligible success. In 1982 in France, the 'Contrats de Solidarité' offered inducements to encourage new hirings offsetting either reductions in working time or early retirements; out of some 12,500 contracts signed by September 30, 1982, only 4.5% were concerned with a reduction of working time, and 10 times as many new hirings resulted from early retirement as from shorter hours (see Hart, 1984).

(iii) Where a reduction in standard hours was introduced without mandatory new hirings, it seems to have led to very few new hirings in the short run – with one exception mentioned below. At least, *those who have looked for evidence of new hirings do not seem to have found it.* This was the case, in particular, for surveys conducted in Belgium in 1980 and more recently in France (see Quatrième Congrès des Economistes Belges de langue française, 1980, and Commissariat Général du Plan, 1985). The only clear cases of new hirings came from firms operating on a continuous basis with several (typically five) shifts. Shorter hours per shift necessarily

---

[8] Rosen (1985) outlines a simple model of 'returns to hours' in a contracts framework, where firms use overtime in good states, layoffs with constant hours in bad states.

implied some (less than proportional) new hirings.

These findings are sobering, and confirm the theoretical warnings that reductions in hours will not create many jobs in the short run. At the same time, advocates of shorter hours seem to proceed from a *presumption* that shorter hours per week somehow imply more jobs in the long run – other things being equal. The reasoning apparently calls on arithmetic and the analogy with wages is instructive. The short-run elasticity of employment with respect to real wages is generally believed to be small, whereas the long-run elasticity at a given output level should be close to unity given the constancy of factor shares. Similarly, the short-run elasticity of employment with respect to hours per week is apparently small, for the reasons just indicated, whereas the long-run elasticity should be close to unity on grounds of arithmetic. Both arguments of course assume that productivity, technology, and output are unrelated to wages or hours, and departures from these assumptions may well prove significant in the long run. Moreover the presumption rests on the unproven *assumption* that hours and workers are perfect substitutes. This is an area where uncertainties are substantial. Several attempts have been made to throw light on the issue by simulating macroeconomic models (see, for instance, Charpin and Mairesse, 1978, Driehuis and Bruyn-Hundt, 1979, or Plasmans and Vanroelen, 1985). Simulations typically compare employment forecasts with and without a reduction in weekly hours, under alternative assumptions about wages. Sometimes explicit hypotheses about the elasticity of output with respect to hours are also introduced. My own attitude towards these simulations is one of polite scepticism. Too little is known about the elasticity of employment with respect to weekly hours *in a context of general recession* for these simulations to be reliable. Estimates of production functions where hours and number of employees appear as separate arguments, based on time series data covering the past thirty years, are not likely to measure that elasticity accurately, and I have not seen estimates based on recent microeconomic data. Accordingly, I regard the fragmentary information from the surveys mentioned under (ii) above as more instructive for short-run purposes and I refrain from drawing long-run conclusions.

5. Appraisal and policy prospects

5.1. *Appraisal*

Hopefully, this essay may have convinced the reader: first, that some form of work-sharing is called for to efficiently absorb sizeable fluctuations in the demand for labour; second, that market institutions fail to bring about work-sharing between workers under contract and job seekers, or among job seekers themselves; and third, that there is scope for public intervention to correct that market failure during deep recessions. It is thus not surprising that interest in work-sharing as a means of alleviating unemployment should be alive in Europe today and that specific measures have been introduced. The brief review of experience with these measures reveals that early retirement schemes with some form of income maintenance have pulled large numbers of senior workers out of the labour force and have led to roughly commensurate numbers of new hirings when and only when the schemes specified mandatory replacements; part-time work has not spread as a means of sharing work among job seekers, or between job seekers and workers under contract (the total failure of part-time early retirement schemes being particularly striking); and those who have looked for evidence of job creation induced by reductions in weekly hours have not found any appreciable short-run effects, leaving open the question of potential longer-run effects which is subject to related uncertainties over capital utilisation, wage costs and productivity adjustments.

These empirical findings are generally consistent with theoretical considerations, to the extent that the (positive) value of holding a regular job varies substantially across individuals and over an individual's working life, suggesting in particular that a substantial proportion of the members of the older generations could be induced to hand over their jobs to new recruits at little cost. Also the fixed costs of hiring and training deter firms from using part-time labour, except in special circumstances (like peak loads within the week), whereas enough workers eager to work full-time are forthcoming. Finally, firms engaged in labour hoarding, which may well be in a majority during deep recessions, will not respond to shorter hours (or lower wages, for that matter), by new hirings, and firms which are hiring new employees will resist reductions in hours.

There are four immediate implications of this essay for policy purposes. (Since every form of work-sharing has both opponents and advocates, none of these implications is original. My only hope is to have convinced the reader that my own stand is consistent with both theory and recent experience.)

(i) *Early retirement with mandatory replacement stands out as the most promising approach to work-sharing in the short-run.* In several countries that approach has hardly been used, and offers a genuine prospect for some alleviation of unemployment – of youth unemployment especially, if replacements are reserved for the young. More detailed work aimed at quantifying that prospect, both numberwise and costwise, should be encouraged.

(ii) *Shorter weekly hours stand out as the least promising and most uncertain approach to work-sharing in the short run.* At a minimum it should not be used indiscriminately. It will produce positive employment effects in those sectors (including metal working?) where plants are operated on a continuous basis, negative output effects without gains in employment in those sectors where hours of plant utilization are given by the working week, and longer-run effects will be negative if shorter hours imply higher effective hourly wage costs.

(iii) If one accepts the view that firms engaged in labour hoarding will not respond to either lower wages or shorter hours by new hirings, *one should concentrate the promotion of work-sharing on expanding and new firms.* In these firms, part-time work by the new employees may well be the more natural pattern of work-sharing.

(iv) *Part-time work stands out as the most disappointing approach to work-sharing, in the sense that its potential to alleviate unemployment, which could be substantial, has not been exploited at all.* This is all the more disappointing since part-time early retirement would seem so much more natural and appealing than abrupt early retirement. Given the substantial measure of success met by early retirement programmes and the over-whelming desire expressed by workers for gradual retirement, it is doubly disappointing to observe the total failure of the timid attempts in that direction. *Although efforts to promote part-time work are bound to be slow in producing their effects, because they call for substantial reorganisation of work, such efforts are worth undertaking from a long-run perspective.*

5.2. *Policy prospects*

In the longer-run, three interrelated questions must be faced, to which only speculative answers can be given today. First, how long will it take to restore a measure of full employment in Europe (say, with youth unemployment rates of 5% or so)? Second, will the historical trend towards a shorter working week continue itself in the future? Third, how seriously should we take the prospect of other deep recessions, comparable to those of the thirties and the eighties? If full employment will not be restored in Europe for several years to come (and this is my personal reading of the forecasts), and deep recessions may occur again (for the reasons explained in Section 2.2), then one should look seriously at part-time work as a means of sharing jobs during such recessions. In addition since there is no reason why the historical trend towards shorter hours should come to a halt, one should take seriously the issue of maintaining the utilisation of capital and the provision of services. Indeed, as the working week becomes shorter, it is increasingly important to uncouple individual working hours from the period of business activity (over which capital is used and services are provided). Otherwise overhead costs will creep up, and the benefits of additional leisure will be partly offset by the deterioration in availability of services. These two remarks are linked *because uncoupling individual working hours from the period of business activity is bound to open up new prospects for part-time work*, at a gain in overall efficiency as well as in labour market flexibility.

A number of schemes to that effect have been proposed, ranging from the general adoption of half-day shifts six days a week, to rotating vacation periods of up to three months per year (see e.g. Palasthy, 1978, and Van den Broeck *et al.*, 1984). The most appealing scheme to my mind would be a general adoption of the four-day working week with six days of activity. A working post could then correspond to either one full-time and one half-time job, or two three-quarter-time jobs, or three half-time jobs – or one and a half full-time jobs with three full-timers filling two working posts. Aside from the obvious advantages of reducing commuting time for workers by 20% and increasing the use of capital by up to 35% (six days of nine hours versus five days of eight hours), this scheme would generate flexibility in the provision of part-time work especially on a 75% basis. Hopefully, it would also generate flexibility in the provision of part-time early retirement, and facilitate job sharing through part-time work among the new employees of expanding and new firms. A novel perspective would thus be opened for part-time work as a means of work-sharing to absorb fluctuations in the market for regular jobs. Of course, a four-day week with six days of activity is highly speculative as well as controversial. It is speculative, because we lack solid information, beyond the isolated experience of a few firms which have chosen to operate on that basis for reasons of their own.[9] And it is controversial, because six days of activity means Saturday work (typically two weeks out of three) and a reversal of the trend towards longer weekends with less organised activity taking place then. Reversing that trend has an obvious welfare cost, to be weighed against the associated efficiency gains. On the other hand it may be

---

[9] I know of one industrial firm which has adopted the scheme a few years ago to expand capacity by 35% without new investment or multiple shifts; and one savings bank which has adopted the scheme to impose team work on its staff.

indispensable to protect the utilisation of capital, if the working week is to be reduced further as technological progress continues.

I have no particular authority to discuss this speculative proposal. But I may refer back to two points made earlier, which are of relevance here. The first is that, in a world where firms and (male) workers have a common preference for full-time regular jobs, temporary reliance on 75% jobs when there is excess supply of labour will require some inducements. It is a challenging task to think through a coherent approach to this issue. The open questions are numerous, and the answers are not obvious. At a time when only three out of four new entrants into the labour force are employed, if we had a four-day week with six days of activity, should we penalise full-time work, subsidise part-time work, or both? If there is a penalty, should it be levied on the employer or the employee, or is that issue immaterial? Should hours above the average effectively worked, counting the unemployed, carry social security benefits, like rights to pensions and unemployment compensation? A whole set of intriguing questions arise, which require an analysis combining considerations of *ex ante* risk-sharing and incentives. The second point, made earlier in Section 2.4, is that a major reorganisation of work involves numerous externalities and therefore calls for guidelines and coordination from the public sector. In particular, a four-day week with six days of activity requires coordination between production activities, services, leisure activities, schools, etc. Such coordination can only evolve over time, and is facilitated if the new pattern is known ahead of time. It also involves the public sector directly, through the provision of public services. It would certainly make sense for the post office, administrative services open to the public, and the like, to consider six days of activity, with a greater reliance on part-time workers.

18 The two-handed growth strategy for Europe: autonomy through flexible cooperation*

PART I: THE TWO-HANDED STRATEGY

1. The present state of affairs

There is little doubt that over the years 1984–87 economic conditions in Europe have improved. Inflation has fallen to more comfortable levels. Most current account deficits have been reduced, with some countries achieving significant surpluses. Public finances are now sounder in many countries, with the primary budget (i.e. net of interest payments) more often in surplus than in deficit. After a period when the strength of the dollar made European currencies look weak, the much awaited correction has taken place, now raising fears of a hard landing of the US currency. More importantly, the resumption of growth is widespread in contrast to the experience of the early eighties.

Yet there is no room for complacency for at least two reasons. The first one is the unemployment situation. Double-digit unemployment rates are the rule rather than the exception, and no relief seems in sight, in the near future. As of May 1987, there were 16.1 million unemployed (seasonally adjusted) in the 12 countries of the European Community, that is 11.4% of the labour force. Total unemployment has not changed over the last 12 months. Significant decreases in the UK and Portugal have been matched by increases in most other countries. In Germany, while

* *Recherches Economiques de Louvain*, 54, 1 (1988), 5–52. With Charles Wyplosz, Charles Bean, Francesco Giavazzi and Herbert Giersch. This paper appeared as *Economic Papers*, n°60, October 1987, of the Commission of European Communities and as a CEPS paper, n°34, December 1987, of the Center for European Policy Studies. The editors are grateful to both these institutions for their permission to publish this article.

The authors thank Jürgen Kröger for help with the data and Sara del Favero for diligent research assistance.

500

total unemployment has come down by forty thousand, GDP growth has been negative for the last two quarters. Short-run prospects therefore look bleak, with a genuine danger that unemployment may rise once again. Mass unemployment represents a waste of human resources, as well as a major social problem with unpredictable long-run political and economic implications.

The second cause of concern is the disappointingly low rate of private investment, now around 19% of GNP as compared to 22% in the sixties. Although this may be of limited immediate consequence, it bears the seeds of long-term economic stagnation. For some reason Europe is not using and accumulating factors of production as in the past; this is bound to affect future living standards.

This report takes as its premise that Europe still very much needs to enact growth-enhancing policies. We first recall why the present level of utilisation and rate of accumulation of resources are not optimal.[1]

We then consider what corrective actions might be taken. Of course the major reason why these have not yet been carried out is that a certain number of apparent constraints on policy makers stand in the way. It is important to assess the true seriousness of these constraints.

Among these constraints, the question of external balance stands out. Although we regard this concern as largely misdirected, we will consider it in some detail. We stress that the openness of an economy reduces the domestic benefits which a country derives from expanding demand, and conclude that cooperation is a way out of this dilemma. Accordingly, this report's main contribution is to consider how best the EC countries could exploit their differences in size and initial conditions to jointly adopt appropriate policies. In particular, the report highlights the crucial position of Germany, France and the UK in pursuing a set of policies that will enhance growth. It also recognizes that differences in objectives may affect a country's willingness to play the role warranted by the general macroeconomic situation. The result will be a collective loss in overall effectiveness. We believe, however, that the EMS can serve as a focal point for mutually beneficial growth-enhancing policies.

2. Three growth alternatives

One way of understanding why and how Europe fails to adequately exploit its resources is to contrast current forecasts and desirable outcomes.

---

[1] All previous reports of the CEPS Macroeconomic Policy Group have presented similar analysis.

We first review the probable outlook until the end of the decade under existing policies and then consider two alternatives: the EC Commission Cooperative Growth Scenario and the type of performance achieved by Europe in better times during the sixties.

2.1. The baseline

The baseline projection of the EC Commission as presented in its 1986 Annual Report (which is very much in line with forecasts produced by other institutions) is a natural point of departure and is shown in table 18.1. Its main features are slow growth, moderate inflation, sluggish investment and an unacceptably high level of unemployment. Interestingly, given the situation in the rest of the world, such growth rates allow a slight surplus on Europe's overall current account.[2]

Table 18.1. *EC Commission simulations for EC 10*

(Annual average growth rates, 1986–1990, in %)

	Baseline	Cooperative Scenario
1. GDP volume	2.7	3.5
2. GDP deflator	3.3	2.7
3. Employment	0.7	1.2
4. Investment	3.7	6.8
5. Unemployment[a]	10.3	7.1
6. Real unit labour costs	−0.3	−1.3
7. Real wages per head	1.9	1.1
8. Productivity	2.0	2.3
9. Residual[b]	−0.2	−0.1
10. Current account, % of GDP	0.6	0.1
11. Budget deficit, % of GDP[a]	3.4	3.9

[a] 1990 levels.
[b] Residual is (6) − (7) + (8) and is a measure of changes in labour taxes.
Source: *European Economy* n°30, November 1986, p. 44.

However, in many ways the baseline projection must be considered as rather optimistic. The 1987 figures, which define its starting line, have been revised *downwards* in October 1987, relative to the October 1986 forecasts. In every respect, the aggregate revisions exhibited in table 18.2 are for the worse. Detailed member country figures (not shown) indicate

[2] This is quite important given the assumptions made for the rest of the world: rising oil prices, stable ECU/Dollar and ECU/Yen exchange rates, and a reduction of the US budget deficit to 1 percent of GNP by 1990. These assumptions are not favourable from the point of view of the European current account which may exceed the reported forecasts.

that unemployment is expected to increase in five countries, decrease in five, and stay stable for the other two, as well as remaining stable for the European Community as a whole. Furthermore these revised forecasts do not incorporate the latest disquieting trends reported above.

2.2. The Cooperative Growth scenario

In the Cooperative Growth Strategy proposed by the EC Commission, the overall growth rate is raised to above 3%, which will permit a decline in the unemployment rate to 7% by 1990. This growth scenario shares many of the characteristics of the two-handed approach proposed by the CEPS Macroeconomic Policy Group. It rightly emphasizes the benefits of policy coordination which are at the heart of the present report. Its key elements are a decline in real labour costs achieved through wage moderation and decreased labour taxes, a reduction in income taxes and an increase in public investment. According to the Commission's estimates (see table 18.1) this would produce faster growth and lower inflation, at the expense of a worsening of the current account. But even this rather optimistic scenario fails to bring unemployment down to those rates which prevailed in Europe up to the mid-seventies.

The Cooperative Growth Strategy, as designed by the Commission, calls for a cumulative fiscal expansion through additional public expenditures and tax reductions adding up, over the four years 1987–1990, to 3.2% of EC10 GDP. By concentrating the effort in the three largest countries (Germany, France and the UK), which account for 70% of EC 10 GDP, this scenario actually calls for a cumulative fiscal expansion in these three adding up (over the four years) to 4.6% of their own GDP.

Table 18.2. *Revision of 1987 forecasts for EC 12*

(% change p.a. unless otherwise stated)

	October 1986 Forecast	October 1987 Rev. Forecast
GDP in volume	2.8	2.2
Domestic demand	3.5	3.2
Exports of goods and services	3.7	2.0
Imports of goods and services	6.2	4.6
Nominal unit labor costs[a]	2.8	3.4
Real unit labour costs[a]	−0.7	0.1
Unemployment rate (% of labour force)	11.7	11.8

[a] Relative development of labour costs per head and macroeconomic labour productivity (real: deflated by GDP deflator).
Source: E.C. Commission COM(87)77, Table 1, and the Annual Economic Report.

Such an effort is of an altogether different order of magnitude from the programmes currently under consideration in several countries. The fiscal measures decided in Germany for 1988–90 only amount to about 1% of its GDP; similarly, those enacted in the UK for the fiscal year 1987–88 and projected for 1988–89 constitute a cumulative fiscal stimulus of about 1.5% of its GDP. Jointly, these measures amount to 0.5% of EC10 GDP, to which should be added a further 0.2% increase due to various fiscal changes in other countries. So far then, current fiscal plans envisage a stimulus worth only 0.7% of EC 10 GDP, thus falling substantially short of the Commission's proposed Cooperative Strategy 3.2% target.

2.3. The golden sixties

The last scenario that we wish to explore is a return to the kind of economic performance achieved by Europe during much of its post-war years. Its characteristics are well known: an average growth rate close to 5% per year and unemployment between 2 and 3%. Such a GDP growth rate does not necessarily translate into employment growth. One benchmark is provided by the Cooperative Growth Scenario. Its policies imply a short-run marginal employment coefficient of one third, so that a 5% annual GDP growth rate would lead to an annual average growth rate of employment of 1.7%, bringing unemployment down to some 5% in 1990 – an attractive prospect. Another benchmark is the experience of the sixties during which employment growth in Europe was a mere 0.3% per annum. These numbers essentially tell us that growth will have to be more labour-intensive than in the sixties if we wish to reduce unemployment.

Are there real obstacles standing in the way of such a growth pattern? Looking at aggregate unemployment figures, it does not seem to make sense worrying about labour shortages. But aggregate figures are often misleading. Current unemployment is concentrated amongst the unskilled and in particular geographical areas. Youth unemployment is particularly high in all countries except Germany. A reduction in the cost of employing unskilled workers may be necessary to erase such inequalities (see Box 1). We return to this issue below.

BOX 1

One difficult question raised by our hypothetical 'golden sixties' scenario – or by any scenario embodying significant employment growth – concerns the level of skills within the labour force. Unemployment today is largely concentrated amongst the unskilled. There are two ways in which such a situation could have come about. Consider a given decline in aggregate employment – say 8% for illustration's sake – which is accompanied by an increase in unemployment concentrated entirely amongst the unskilled. This could reflect an 8% decline in employment at every skill level, accompanied by a reallocation of some workers to less skilled jobs so that all except the lowest skill groups enjoy full employment, but with a fraction of each group (corresponding to a growing number of people as we move down the skill ladder) accepting employment in less skilled jobs. Thus all the unemployment will eventually be concentrated amongst the least skilled workers. Alternatively, the same *aggregate* picture could emerge if a restructuring of the demand for workers of different skills (possibly induced by inappropriate wage differentials) resulted in a loss of employment at the *lowest* skill level alone, with no reduction in employment at higher levels. The concentration of unemployment amongst the unskilled results from the adaptation of labour supply in the first case, but from the restructuring of labour demand in the second case.

Our illustration is extreme; both labour supply adaptation and labour demand restructuring may take place simultaneously – the relative importance of the two processes is unknown. The supply adaptation (or 'staircase') story is accepted by many as the primary explanation. Recently, our attention has been drawn by Danthine and Lambelet (1987) to the Swiss experience, and in particular to the fact that unskilled migrant workers, numbering some 8% of the Swiss labour force, were repatriated, without this being accompanied by any restructuring of the qualification mix among Swiss workers. That experience lends *prima facie* support to the demand restructuring story. If this is the case throughout Europe a majority of the unemployed in the EC are simply unemployable – unless either their skills are upgraded, or else a reverse restructuring of labour demand is induced, for example by a change in relative prices (i.e., a reduction in the cost of employing unskilled workers).

It matters little whether 'unskilled' is understood in terms of acquired technical skills, or in terms of stable working habits. And it should be clear that putting the long-term unemployed back to work will entail a substantial retraining cost in either case.

Can capital be the binding constraint? It was not in the sixties. But the capital–output ratio has increased in the meantime. With a capital–output ratio as high as 4.5, a growth rate of output at 5% would require a net investment share of 22.5%. With a depreciation rate of 3% this is equivalent to a gross investment share of 36%, which would somehow have to be financed. As an example, the highest gross investment share reached since 1960 for EC10 stood just below 29%. If the capital–output ratio were to drop to 4 (its lowest level was 4.1 in 1973), the required gross investment share would be 32% instead.[3] A traditional savings rate would seem to imply that a 5% growth rate requires either a significant decrease in capital intensity – the kind of decrease which is precisely required for a more labour-intensive growth – or significant borrowing abroad, i.e. current account deficits. It might seem improbable that the trend towards increased capital intensity should be reversed. Such a possibility should not be dismissed outright as fanciful, however. The growth pattern of the sixties was shaped by the short supply of domestic labour (as evidenced by low unemployment rates and the recurrent recourse to immigration). Hopefully, a more balanced growth pattern might emerge naturally in a period of severe unemployment. It would need to be based on capital-widening rather than on capital-deepening investment – hence on relative factor prices more favourable to the adoption of labour-intensive methods employing the categories of workers in the greatest excess supply.

Some reliance on capital imports to finance increased investment would also be justified, despite the implications for the current account. Provided the investment is profitable, it will generate sufficient revenues to finance the increased foreign debt burden. This issue is explored in more detail in Section 3.3.3.

2.4. Assessment

We consider the baseline as a realistic, yet unacceptably pessimistic, forecast. Indeed this report is dedicated to the search for acceptable solutions to avoid its very realisation. The Cooperative Growth Strategy provides a solution which looks satisfactory only when compared to the baseline. Its results are a clear improvement on the current forecast, yet they are quite modest given the size of the unemployment problem. The

---

[3] These calculations are based on data in Mortensen (1984), pp. 62–65. With $K/Y = 4.5$ and $\dot{Y}/Y = \dot{K}/K = 5\%$, the net investment rate is $\dot{K}/Y = (\dot{K}/K)(K/Y)$. With a depreciation rate $d = 3\%$, the gross investment rate is $I/Y = (\dot{K} + d.K)/Y$. The value of d is inferred from the 1984 values as: $d = (I/Y - \dot{K}/Y)/(K/Y) = (22.5 - 9.5)/4.6 = 2.82\%$.

'golden sixties' scenario, on the other hand, looks too good to be true. We fully realize that it may be *politically* unrealistic. What concerns us, however, is whether it is feasible from an *economic* point of view; obviously it requires a different type of growth, but it is not obvious that it is altogether beyond reach. Much depends upon how it is sought. The two-handed approach offers a framework within which policies capable of achieving more ambitious results than the baseline can be developed. It rests on the same logic as the Cooperative Growth Strategy, and may be put to work to pull Europe more forcefully out of its slow-growth, high-unemployment trap.

3. The two-handed approach

3.1. The logical foundation

The two-handed approach, advocated in the previous reports of the CEPS Macroeconomic Policy Group, stresses the need for a simultaneous expansion of supply and demand so as to create additional productive capacity hand-in-hand with the demand for its services.

The logic of the two-handed approach rests on an assessment of the nature of European unemployment and on a parallel assessment of the conditions necessary for job creation. In order for a job to be created, two broad sets of condition must be satisfied. First there must exist a demand for the output generated by that additional worker. Because dismissing a worker is costly, that demand should be sustained long enough to ensure that the additional worker will be required in the foreseeable future. Second, satisfying that demand must be both profitable and physically possible: there must exist spare capacity and the cost of labour (and other inputs) must not be excessive. Keynesian macrotheory stresses the first condition; when that condition fails, unemployment is said to be 'Keynesian'. Classical macrotheory stresses the second condition; when that condition fails, unemployment is said to be 'Classical'. The current European situation requires due attention to both requirements, and the two-handed approach does just that.

The mix of Classical and Keynesian unemployment prevailing at a particular time is of crucial relevance to policy decisions. If unemployment is mostly Classical, then demand policies are useless in the short run, with the stimulus likely to evaporate in price inflation and/or imports. What is called for is an expansion of supply, through increased efficiency and investment. Policy should be 'supply friendly'. If unemployment is mostly Keynesian, then demand stimulation is the required policy, and entails little risk of inflationary pressures. It is thus important to diagnose the relative importance of the two types of unemployment.

Such a classification is always difficult, because it cannot be based on direct indicators, such as the unemployment rate itself, or on national accounts data. Keynesian unemployment is predicated upon the existence of simultaneously unused labour and capital capacity. Classical unemployment would follow either from the absence of physical equipment to be manned by new hirings or from excessive labour costs. Although systematic quantitative analysis along these lines is relatively recent and still fragmentary, the available evidence is entirely consistent in suggesting that European unemployment exhibits *both* Classical and Keynesian features.[4]

We interpret this evidence as indicating that unemployment is Keynesian at the margin, and Classical beyond: a demand expansion would quickly eliminate the Keynesian unemployment component and trigger inflationary pressures as bottlenecks are reached. An indication of the seriousness of the situation is provided by business surveys in industry. Table 18.3 indicates that current use of capacity is slightly below the 1979-80 peak level. The extent to which capacity is reported excessive in relation to demand expectations is much higher (10%) than the 1979 peak level, however, confirming that we currently face a conjunction of low demand and fully used capacity.

This high level of capacity utilisation, despite the low level of demand, is the result of both extensive scrapping and the low rate of new investment which prevailed in Europe over the last decade. Capacity has adjusted to a slow growth environment, transforming a slow growth trap into a capacity trap. Indeed, during a prolonged period of weak demand, it is rational for producers to adjust downwards their capacity to this demand. This constant adaptation of the capital stock to the level of demand is illustrated in figure 18.1: despite continuously growing slack in the use of labour, the degree of capacity utilisation oscillates within relatively narrow margins.

The result is a frustrating situation where no demand stimulus is implemented because of the absence of spare capacity, while there does not exist spare capacity because demand has been, is, and is expected to be weak. *This is the rationale for the two-handed approach: capacity*

---

[4] That evidence arises from a variety of studies based on widely different methodologies: see the special issue of *Economica* (1986, Supplement), *World Economic Outlook* (April 1987), Lambert, Lubrano and Sneessens (1984), Bruno and Sachs (1985), Sachs and Wyplosz (1986). It matters a lot that these studies generally lead to the same conclusion.

Table 18.3. Capacity utilization and expected capacity constraints in manufacturing industry

	Degree of capacity utilization								Expected capacity constraints[a]						
	1973 peak	1975 trough	79/80 peak	82/83 trough	1984	1985	1986	1987 April	1973 peak	1975 trough	79/80 peak	82/83 trough	1985	1986	1987 April
Belgium	85.4	70.4	79.1	74.4	76.0	78.8	79.4	78.2	−12	+58	+35	+53	+29	+26	+27
Denmark											+10	+38	+ 3	+ 8	+20
Germany	88.1	74.8	86.0	75.3	80.2	83.7	84.7	83.8	− 3	+56	+12	+49	+17	+13	+20
Greece				74.4	75.5		77.0	76.8							
France	87.8	76.6	85.3	81.1	81.9	82.8	83.3	83.2	−24	+45	+11	+48	+37	+31	+26
Ireland			68.1	56.8	61.5	67.3	73.0	80.8		+34	+ 2	+40	+25	+18	+19
Italy	78.8	68.0	77.3	69.1	72.0	74.0	75.2	77.2	+ 1	+63	+17	+58	+37	+37	+24
Netherlands	86.0	76.0	83.0	75.8	82.3	83.8	83.4	83.0	− 3	+60	+14	+51	+ 4	+ 4	+ 8
U.K.	90.6	75.5	87.6	73.0	82.5	85.8	85.1	87.0				+63	+23	+28	+17
EC[b]	86.4	75.0	83.9	76.4	79.1	81.6	82.2	82.7	− 7	+54	+14	+50	+26	+24	+21

[a] Balance of respondents expecting to be more than sufficient (+) or less than sufficient (−) in relation to production expectations. Thus (+) indicates excess capacity, (−) capacity too small.
[b] Weighted average of available country data.
Source: European Economy, Sup. B, n°5, May 1987.

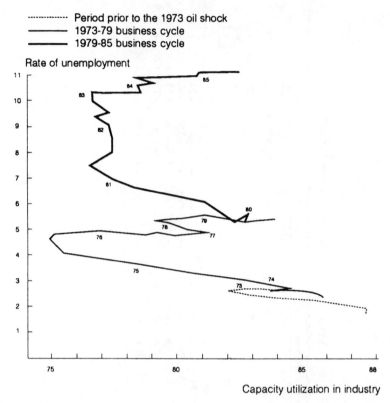

Figure 18.1. Rate of unemployment and capacity utilisation in industry in the Community (Quarterly observations are shown, with the years marked against the first quarter).
Source: *European Economy*, 26, November 1985.

constraints must be eliminated via appropriate supply-side policies while demand must expand to trigger an upward adjustment of productive capacity.

3.2. The agenda

If Europe is to break out of the capacity trap and grow faster, more efficient use must be made of available production possibilities, extended through capacity-widening investment. The profitability of investment and hirings requires a conjunction of adequate profit margins and adequate demand expectations. The policy challenge is to bring about these two conditions *simultaneously*: either of them in isolation would be ineffective.

Ideally, one would like to see capacity expand first, in an anticipation of a growing demand, that could then be satisfied without resistance. It is unlikely that business investors would harbour such confident expectations, however, leaving governments with the option of implementing policies that remove inefficiencies and raise profit margins whilst at the same time raising effective demand in anticipation of the prospective growth of supply.[5] The policy mix is thus bound to be comprehensive. Success is predicated upon determination in using the two hands, and can be further enhanced by selecting measures which have beneficial effects on both supply and demand.

Starting with policies aimed at raising productive efficiency and the profitability of investment, they should consist of the following:
1. medium-run labour cost reductions achieved through a combination of continued wage moderation and cuts in labour taxes;
2. wage differentiation, i.e., a more pronounced reduction in overall wage costs for unskilled workers and for workers in depressed areas;
3. public infrastructure investments likely to raise productive efficiency, especially in regions with high unemployment and a correspondingly high growth potential;
4. elimination of wasteful subsidies and the introduction of measures to speed up the creation of an internal Common Market (deregulation, liberalisation, etc.);[6]
5. measures to enhance the efficient use of capital and labour through more flexible working schedules, hopefully including some uncoupling of worker time and company time.[7]

The first point is essential to generate the medium-run profitability expectations underpining new investment and hirings. Visible progress has been accomplished recently on the front of wage moderation: in every country, except the UK, real unit labour costs have declined – the average decrease in the Community being 2.5% over the past two years (see table 18.4). Continuing wage moderation is essential and, in particular, adverse terms of trade movements should not lead to compensating changes in wages. In some countries this would require altering formal or informal indexation clauses: we do not underestimate the far reaching implications of this measure, yet we wish to stress its importance for the medium-run evolution of labour costs.

[5] The rationale for a demand stimulation that leads the expansion of supply (but not the measures designed to bring it about) has been expounded by Giersch (1987b) under the label of the 'Schumpeter Case'.

[6] See Giersch (1987a).

[7] See Drèze (1986b).

Table 18.4. *Growth in real unit labour costs*[a] *in % p.a.*

	1974–1981	1982–1986	1987
Belgium	1.4	−1.5	0.4
Denmark	0.2	−1.6	3.4
Germany	0.0	−1.3	0.6
Greece	2.6	−0.6	−3.8
Spain	−0.2	−2.5	−0.9
France	1.1	−1.0	−1.6
Ireland	0.7	−2.1	0.3
Italy	0.6	−0.9	0.3
Netherlands	−0.2	−1.6	2.1
Portugal	1.5	−4.8	−0.7
UK	−0.1	−0.1	0.8
EC 12	0.4	−1.2	0.1
USA	0.0	0.0	0.2
Japan	0.8	−0.5	0.0

[a] Wage bill divided by value added.
Source: EC Commission.

However, only so much can be achieved through wage moderation. Fortunately, labour cost reductions can also be achieved through lower labour taxes. The scope for labour tax reductions is best shown by considering the costs incurred when an unemployed worker is hired. The employer will face the full cost, which includes wages and all labour taxes (social security, income). For society as a whole, though, not only do taxes no longer appear as a cost, but in addition there is the extra saving of the unemployment benefits which need not be paid. The size of this divergence between privately incurred costs and their public, i.e. budgetary, equivalent is documented in table 18.5, which gives some numbers based on average labour taxes and social security contributions (we look at the *marginal* cost of moving an *average* worker from the situation of being unemployed to the situation of being employed). Ideally we would like to have comparable figures for unemployment benefits. In the absence of such data for most countries, we have for all countries assumed a replacement ratio (the ratio of average unemployment benefits to average earned income) of 50% based on estimates provided by Layard and Nickell (1985) for the UK.[8] Of course a better measure would use the figures applicable to a marginal worker. Because of such imperfections, table 18.5 should be interpreted with due caution. From table 18.5, we learn that the various taxes which contribute to raise the cost of labour, although

[8] Limited evidence for other countries presented in OECD, *Employment Outlook* 1984, confirms that this ratio is a reasonable number.

Table 18.5. *Costs of reducing unemployment in 1985-% of GDP*

	Net wages and salaries (1)	Social contributions (2)	Income tax paid by labour (3)	Total labour taxes[d] (4)	Total cost faced by employer[e] (5)	Ratio = $\dfrac{\text{Budgetary cost}^f}{\text{Private cost}} \times 100$ (6)
Belgium	41.9	13.5	11.0	24.5	66.4	68.5
Denmark	51.9	1.9	24.2	26.1	78.0	66.7
Germany	29.1	16.9	7.9	24.8	53.9	73.0
Greece	32.8	10.3	2.8	11.1	43.9	64.3
Spain	34.1	12.1			46.2[c]	63.1[c]
France	32.9	21.3	3.4	24.7	57.6	71.4
Ireland	48.9	5.8	10.2	16.0	64.9	62.3
Italy	43.0	12.6	5.1	17.7	60.7	64.6
Netherlands	25.9	25.4	7.2	32.6	58.5	77.9
Portugal	37.8	10.8	2.4	13.2	51.0	62.9
UK	44.9	10.7	8.9	19.6	64.5	65.2
USA	46.0	9.0	10.5[b]	19.5	65.5	64.9
Japan[a]	48.4	15.2	6.5[b]	21.7	70.1	65.5

[a] 1984;
[b] Income tax;
[c] Excluding income taxes;
[d] Total labour taxes include social contributions and labour income taxes (4) = (2) + (3);
[e] The private cost faced by an employer is the sum of net wages and salaries and of total labour costs (5) = (1) + (4);
[f] The budgetary cost is the private cost less labour taxes and less the reduction in unemployment benefits (assumed to be 50% of net wages); hence, (6) = [(4) + 1/2(1)]/(5).
Source: EC Commission.

somewhat different from country to country, are sufficiently large to offer a sizeable room for manoeuvre.

The significance of the wedge between the private and public cost of labour can be expressed alternatively in terms of the wedge between the private and public marginal efficiency of capital, for a capacity-widening investment. In the private calculations, the additional labour employed to operate the new facilities enters at its private cost. From a public viewpoint, part of that cost disappears – namely all labour taxes, plus the unemployment benefits no longer accruing to the newly hired workers. Thus, from a public viewpoint, the marginal efficiency of capital is higher and the private level of investment is too low. Put more simply, *the additional investment draws into use previously unemployed labour resources*, thereby generating a positive externality for the government budget.[9] The full externality is the difference between the private and *social* cost of the labour drawn into use by the additional investment.

Turning to policies aimed at raising effective demand, they should consist of fiscal measures (as detailed below) resulting for Europe as a whole in temporarily larger public deficits. (However this does not mean higher deficits in every country; we discuss at length in Section 7 the country-specific aspects of this general policy.) These temporary deficits are to be financed primarily by borrowing and to be offset by future surpluses with a clear commitment not to resort to inflationary finance. Money growth should only accommodate any anticipated growth in potential output. In what follows, the fiscal expansion is assumed to take this form. We explain in Section 3.3.2 why such a policy of substituting taxes tomorrow for taxes today will indeed be effective in raising demand.

As for the fiscal measures themselves, cuts in labour taxes are probably the most efficient means to reduce the wedge between the private and budgetary cost of labour and to discourage capital deepening, hence our recommendation to focus on them. Although this is not the place to discuss in detail alternative schemes of labour tax cuts, we would favour maximising their employment impact by concentrating their effects on segments of the labour force where the underutilisation of labour is greatest, e.g. the long term unemployed, the young, the unskilled, and the depressed areas.[10] The immediate effect of a cut in labour taxes is to raise

[9] Our reasoning assumes that the added capacity will be used. Otherwise, the investment would not take place. We are thus led back to our previous point that investment and employment require both sufficient profitability and adequate demand expectations.

[10] For instance, the objective of giving priority to the unskilled may be satisfied through an exemption level below which social security contributions are waived or reduced; see Blanchard *et al.* (1985, p. 32) or Drèze (1987b, p. 30).

profits. This affects both consumption and investment. The effect on consumption is indirect via higher dividend income and stock-market wealth. The effect on investment is more direct. Both channels however involve substantial lags. This suggests complementing labour tax cuts with reductions in income taxes. Lower income taxes would, of course, significantly help to promote wage moderation. It is thus comforting to note that both the UK and Germany have recently announced income tax reductions. In addition to these tax cuts, there is scope for increased investment in public services and in the infrastructure, both at the national and European levels. This is an area which has been excessively squeezed in recent years. Any project which yields an adequate social rate of return fits naturally into the proposed fiscal measures. We advocate measures which simultaneously have desirable effects on both supply and demand. We will henceforth refer to this set of measures as a supply-friendly fiscal expansion.

3.3. The risks

In one form or another, the two-handed approach has now been advocated for some time, e.g. the Cooperative Growth Strategy. We cannot therefore avoid asking why progress is so slow. Of course it may be simply that the logic of the two-handed approach is not (yet) readily apparent, but it is likely that other concerns prevent its adoption. The current emphasis on patience is most likely explained by governments' fears of three possible consequences of any fiscal expansion, no matter how supply friendly: (i) a resurgence of inflation; (ii) escalating budget deficits; (iii) a deteriorating current account. We believe that these fears are largely unfounded. Let us briefly sketch our arguments.

3.3.1. Inflation. It is perfectly understandable that governments which have invested so much effort and reputation into the battle against inflation now wish to solidify their success. Emphatically, we share this view. It is important to note that the policies that we advocate rely on supply-expanding and cost-reducing measures, so that by their very design they are unlikely to present major inflationary risks. Quite to the contrary, they have a built-in *anti*-inflationary bias. This is why we believe that the inflationary risks of a supply-friendly fiscal expansion are limited, especially in comparison to the costs of remaining caught in the present slow-growth trap.

3.3.2. Budget deficits. The budgetary picture shares many features with inflation. The process of financial consolidation is still under way in most European countries, so that the time might seem ill-chosen to contemplate measures which will result in heightened deficits. Budget deficits are a natural source of concern, in particular because they result in higher public debts. In the long run, the main issue is the public debt and the ability to meet the required interest payments. To the extent that the proposed strategy generates faster growth and more employment, it will not only generate welfare gains by releasing unused resources, but also additional receipts for servicing the burden of the additional debt.

This is not the place to review the literature on the burden of the public debt. We shall only consider a point which has received limited attention so far.[11] It concerns the question whether raising the debt today serves a useful purpose, given that fiscal policy will have to be eventually tightened in order to honour the debt. This will be the case if aggregate output is currently insufficient so that the deficit serves the useful purpose of inducing an intertemporal substitution in the demand for labour, away from a (future) period of full employment towards a (current) period of unemployment. The net gain is measured by the difference between the private and public costs of labour at a time of underemployment. This argument assumes that when the deficit is later eliminated, the reduction in labour-market distortions will have achieved 'full' employment.[12]

Of course the argument just presented rests upon two important premises. First the fiscal expansion must not be undercut by the crowding-out effect of an interest rate increase or an exchange rate appreciation. Second, it must be credible that the debt will be repaid through a future budget surplus, rather than through the inflation tax. The second condition is not likely to be met in countries where the debt-GNP ratio has already reached very substantial levels. This is why the Cooperative Growth Strategy is right in advocating a fiscal expansion only in those countries where the debt–GNP ratio is lowest – Germany, the UK and France. The relevant data are given in Section 7.

3.3.3. External constraints. The last fear concerns the external balance. As in the case of a budget deficit, the current account feeds into the external debt which is the main external constraint. Upon considering an increase in the external debt the same criterion should apply, namely

[11] Barro (1979), Lucas and Stokey (1983), Persson, Persson and Svensson (1986) discuss the optimal intertemporal pattern of taxes and public debt.

[12] The case under consideration is also one where Barro's (1974) argument, that a fiscal expansion is fully offset by a reduction in private demand, does not apply.

whether the resources borrowed abroad will generate the proper returns. A fiscal expansion accompanied by monetary accommodation is bound to lead to a 'deterioration' of the current account (reduction of an export surplus) so that net foreign indebtedness will increase (capital outflows reduced). To the extent that the current account deficit corresponds to additional investment, the additional foreign debt simply means that the country is relying on the international capital markets to finance its expansion.

A useful benchmark case is one where the government budget remains balanced, but the supply of private domestic savings falls short of domestic private borrowing needs. Then the current account deficit arises because of an increase in private investment as the government budget remains balanced. Rational firms will borrow only if the return on their investment is at least equal to the cost of capital. Much the same applies when investment is carried out by the government, provided that it abides by the same rentability criterion. As long as this condition is satisfied, borrowing abroad actually increases national wealth, and the additional net foreign debt is more than offset by the present discounted value of the stream of future earnings. Because the latter is not measurable, a country's net foreign asset position, which only values its financial assets and liabilities, may be almost as unreliable an indicator as its current account.

Does this imply that if the current account deterioration reflects increased current consumption, the country is 'living beyond its means'? The correct answer is that the country is facing a solvency constraint. There is an important case when there is actually no such constraint: this occurs when the country's growth rate exceeds the real interest cost of the debt so that any fraction of income earmarked for debt repayment, no matter how small, will be sufficient.[13] Otherwise solvency requires that current deficits be matched by future surpluses. If the country's ability to generate sufficient surpluses is in doubt, the main outcome will be a pressure towards exchange rate depreciation, which in some instances may take the form of a speculative crisis. But, whatever the mechanism to establish solvency, what is ultimately required is a reduction in aggregate spending relative to income, and this represents the true external cost of the fiscal expansion.

A simple calculation illustrates the point. Up to the mid-seventies most European countries were running current account surpluses more often

[13] The point is made in Cohen (1985).

than deficits so that it is natural to assume that they then started with little or no net external indebtness. Assuming a real interest rate of 5% and a growth rate of 2%, a current account deficit representing 2% of GNP over ten years amounts to a foreign debt of the size of 23% of GNP. This is the worst situation that we envision for most countries. To consider an extreme case, with deficits as high as 5% for ten years, the debt would represent 58% of GNP. (Only Denmark and Ireland may be in a worse situation.) What is the current account surplus needed to *stabilise* the debt at such levels? For the lower level of 23%, a surplus of 0.7% is sufficient and this figure rises to 1.8% when the debt level represents 58% of GNP. While these numbers are purely illustrative, they suggest that the eventual sacrifice imposed by *continuous* deficits of the size mostly observed in Europe is quite moderate. Several of the arguments of this section are illustrated with a stylised numerical allegory presented in Appendix 18.1.

3.3.4. Deficits or debts? While for both the public budget and the external account, the appropriate constraint is the corresponding debt level (a stock), policy makers typically express concerns about deficits (a flow).[14] What is the proper criterion? In terms of *constraints*, solvency is the correct criterion and the debt level is one way to measure it.[15] But in terms of policy-making the deficit may also be a relevant criterion. The debt is a 'first-order' burden as resources will eventually have to be committed to its service and possible repayment. The deficit is a 'second-order' burden because of the associated macroeconomic adjustment costs of shifting from deficit to balance or surplus. For any target debt level, the wider the present deficit, the larger the needed adjustment will be, and the worse its welfare implications. The deficit is also a more immediate concern and thus attracts the policy makers' attention more forcefully than the debt which cannot be dealt with in anything but the long run.

4. The bottom line

The policy challenge for Europe today boils down to Europe being caught in a low-growth, high-unemployment trap, characterised by: (i) substantial unused labour resources and a correspondingly high growth potential; (ii) production facilities which have adjusted downwards to low

---

[14] See Viñals (1986).
[15] Buiter (1985) discusses these issues in great detail.

levels of effective demand. A return to faster growth requires both an acceleration of growth in supply and a revival of demand expectations. The prevailing uncertainty surrounding the supply responsiveness generates fears in some official quarters that demand stimulation would evaporate in inflation and imports, without any lasting effects on output and employment. These fears breed inaction – and hence low investment.

To break the vicious circle, a two-handed strategy of the kind outlined above, is needed. Unwillingness to follow such a two-handed strategy may reflect a lack of confidence in the prospective effectiveness of the action of either hand. It is inescapable, that confidence in the effectiveness of both the supply-side and the demand-side components is needed today.

The ultimate fear is perhaps that the supply-side measures will be too timid, or the response of supply too slow, to avoid inflationary and exchange rate pressures as the fiscal expansion proceeds. We can only repeat that the more vigorous and productive the supply-side measures, the less likely, and the less severe, such pressures will be.

We do not claim that risks of inflationary or exchange rate pressures are totally absent. We can only repeat that they will depend upon the mix to be chosen and that some of them are worth taking, given the current underutilisation of resources and the danger of a further extension of unemployment in the near future. Each government has to balance its fear of inflation and deficits against its commitment to fight unemployment. As we explain in Section 7, the differences in initial conditions and policy objectives of the European countries will influence both their choice of policy mix and their willingness to expand.

But there is an important additional dimension to the policy challenge, to which we now turn. Due to the high degree of openness of European economies, cooperation in pursuing the two-handed strategy is important to overcome specific constraints on national policies and in internalising some important non-priced externalities.

PART II: AUTONOMY THROUGH FLEXIBLE COOPERATION

5. Openness and the case for cooperation

5.1. Effects of openness on fiscal policy effectiveness

The analysis of Part 1 presented the basis for, and content of, the proposed two-handed growth strategy. This analysis has largely overlooked the fact that some European economies are quite open.

Openness plays a crucial role as it may profoundly affect the cost-effectiveness of the proposed policies. This part considers the role of openness and demonstrates the crucial importance of cooperation for policies designed to enhance demand.[16]

In an economy with unemployment and with a sizeable wedge between the private and public costs of labour, the effectiveness of a fiscal expansion is measured by the additional output and employment resulting from it. Its cost is indicated by the associated increase in the public and current account deficits. The very fact that an economy is open reduces the (domestic) effectiveness and raises the (domestic) costs of the fiscal expansion. Furthermore, the more open the economy, the more pronounced the effect.

5.1.1. Reduced policy effectiveness. The reduced effectiveness results directly from the dampening effect of additional imports, as measured by the marginal propensity to import. A given initial stimulus to demand will produce fewer jobs at home because some of the demand leaks abroad. Although foreigners in turn may spend some of their increased income on domestically produced goods, the feedback will be staggered over time, and will be less than complete if a fraction of the income generated abroad is hoarded. Of course, the import leaks are not lost at the world level – they benefit the suppliers of imports as an externality, if they experience a similar discrepancy between the private and budgetary costs of labour; we shall return to that point.

The fact that the feedback is *staggered* matters when the whole purpose of the fiscal stimulus is to induce an intertemporal substitution in demand,

---

[16] One member of the group (H.G.), while fully supporting the two-handed strategy described in Part 1, wants to take exception to Part 2 to the extent that it deviates from the following position: coordination is not a necessary condition of the strategy. Instead of waiting for others, individual countries can start on their own, e.g. Germany. This country should take the lead, with or without prior coordination, by adopting measures to improve the competitiveness of its domestic locations in the worldwide market for capital and direct investment in order to transform its current account surplus into an additional stock of capital for more permanently productive jobs within its area: in given circumstances, the social returns of investment in Germany would far exceed the rate of interest earned from exporting capital. Even smaller countries could move ahead without time consuming prior coordination. Going alone, however, requires that the measures taken promise as much positive effects on the supply side as they increase demand. The supply-side effects are to improve the competitiveness of domestic producers so that the expanding country captures more of total world demand at the time when part of the domestic demand stimulus leaks out to raise imports. What matters is the balance of demand and supply effects. Coordination takes only care of the demand side. Stressing the coordination issue involves neglect of the supply effects and their importance. It thus runs into the danger of creating a moral hazard problem: a demand expansion may too easily be considered sufficient.

from the future to the present. How staggered the feedback will be, depends on the origin of the imports: Belgian imports from France, which in turn addresses 10% of its own import demand to Belgium, will induce a quicker feedback than Belgian imports from Spain, which addresses less than 2% of its own imports to Belgium. Detailed linked econometric models would be needed to estimate the length of the lags, but the argument that the feedback is less than complete, if part of the income generated abroad is hoarded, is standard. One aspect of that argument is not commonly spelled out, however, yet that aspect is important for our purposes. In Europe, average rates of gross taxation (ratios of public receipts to GDP) are close to 50% in many countries. For a country engaged in fiscal stabilisation, this implies an automatic hoarding of about half of export-led increases in income. For the partner country which contemplates a fiscal expansion, it means that some 50% of the hoped-for feedbacks would be sterilised – at least temporarily. Again, detailed econometric models would be needed to assess the precise magnitude of this effect, but the numbers are bound to be large. Given the current stress in Europe on fiscal consolidation, fears of foreign sterilisation are quite natural and probably go a fair way towards sustaining the expectation that the feedback will be *slow* and *incomplete*, substantially reducing the *effectiveness* of fiscal policy in any single open economy.

5.1.2. Increased costs. The increased cost of the fiscal stimulus derives from the externality corresponding to a private cost of labour in excess of its budgetary cost: the cost of domestic labour to the country is its budgetary cost, while the cost of foreign labour is the full private cost. The difference between the two accrues to the foreign country (with only limited feedback to be expected). To illustrate, if the Belgian government hires formerly unemployed Belgian workers to tend the public parks of Antwerp, the net cost to the Belgian taxpayers is the difference between the net earnings of the workers and the unemployment benefits that they used to receive (labelled budgetary costs in table 18.5). If instead Dutch gardeners are hired the net cost to the Belgian taxpayers is the full gross cost (labelled private costs in table 18.5). Obviously, this increase in cost will be greater the more the increase in demand, the associated increase in employment, leaks abroad, i.e. the higher the marginal propensity to import.

5.1.3. Openness. Thus, as the marginal propensity to import rises, the domestic cost effectiveness of the expansion is affected, reducing the country's incentive to carry it out on its own. The importance of this point has been illustrated vividly by the 'early-Mitterrand' French expansion of 1981–82, the associated current account deterioration quickly leading to a reversal of policy (see Sachs and Wyplosz (1986)). However, if several countries together form a relatively closed area, they can reap the full benefits of an expansion just like a closed economy. We shall argue that this is the case today in Europe, and particularly that it is more reasonable to advocate a simultaneous expansion by France, the U.K. and Germany than to ask Germany to play the locomotive role again while France and the U.K. postpone action until the German expansion takes momentum.

In Appendix 18.2, we explain why import shares, corrected for the import content of exports, provide an operational measure of the degree of openness of an economy, which is well suited for a discussion of the cost effectiveness of fiscal policy. Some figures on import shares, net import shares (imports less import content of exports), and marginal propensities to import are collected in table 18.6. It is clear that openness is inversely related to country size, and directly related to the extent of economic integration with neighbouring countries. EC10 as a whole is about half as open as the least open of its members. In spite of its larger

Table 18.6. *Measures of openness* (*1985*)

	Import Share	Net Import Share	Marginal propensity to import [a]
Belgium	76.1	44.2	53.0
Denmark	36.7	19.8	23.8
W.Germany	28.7	19.8	23.8
Spain	20.2	15.7	18.8
France	24.9	15.6	18.6
Ireland	58.5	40.0	48.0
Italy	28.6	18.9	22.7
Luxemburg	94.4	-	-
Netherlands	59.4	25.0	30.0
Portugal	41.9	25.5	30.6
UK	28.2	18.7	22.4
Greece	32.5	26.0	31.2
EC 10	13.4	-	-
USA	10.1	-	-
Japan	11.4	-	-

Note:[a] (1.2) × (net import share).
Adjustment for import content of exports based on input-output tables when possible.
Source: EC Commission. From country desks, based on national sources.

size, measured by GDP or population, EC10 is still more open than either the US or Japan. In part, this reflects a more limited endowment of natural resources (relative to the US), and in part closer links to former colonies or other non-community European economies. But the degree of openness of Europe as an entity is much closer to that of the US or Japan than to that of a typical member country.

The figures in table 18.6 prompt us to the conclusion that Europe as a whole is sufficiently closed to pursue autonomous fiscal and monetary policies, provided it can define and implement these policies on a cooperative basis. The need for cooperation among European countries derives from their high degree of individual openness, which imposes severe constraints on autonomous policy actions by individual countries.

We thus see openness as a major explanation for the reluctance of European governments to implement the two-handed strategy.

5.2. The case for cooperation

The case for policy cooperation is quite simple and well known.[17] A sufficient condition is that the private and budgetary costs of any factor or commodity (labour for example) diverge at home and abroad. Then, if governments make their policy decisions based only on the effects on domestic welfare, they will ignore any effect on the allocation of resources abroad. In the absence of any wedge between the private and social costs, this does not matter, since the allocation of resources is efficient. However, when, for example, unemployed labour abroad is brought into use by a domestic fiscal expansion, the home country ignores this beneficial effect in deciding how large an expansion to make. The essential point is that there exists an externality which is not properly 'priced'. Hence, we find a strong temptation for each country to act as a caboose in the hope that the other ones will play the role of the locomotive. Thus in assessing the success of the German-led expansion following the Bonn Summit of 1978 – the 'locomotive' experiment – one should take into account the effects of Germany's action on its trading partners. While Germany experienced a deterioration in its current account and some acceleration in inflation, it also raised the level of activity abroad.[18] It should be noted that coordination of policies is emphatically *not* the same as their synchronisation. Thus the

---

[17] Hamada (1976), Cooper (1984), Sachs (1983).

[18] Unfortunately the second oil shock and the contractionary fiscal and monetary policies it engendered prevent any firm conclusion about the overall success of the experiment; see Bean (1985).

worldwide inflation of 1973 was engendered by the simultaneous but *un*coordinated fiscal and monetary expansion pursued by the industrialised economies. The result was chronic overheating.[19]

One natural domain of cooperation concerns the fears of sterilisation through attempts at budget consolidation by trading partners, as explained in Section 5.1. If two countries are both inhibited in their implementation of a desirable fiscal expansion by such fears, it would be natural for them to reach mutual assurance that each country's expansion will not be partly offset by the other country's fiscal stance. Cooperation is then conducive to more successful policies in both countries.

The logic of the case is elementary and widely recognised at different levels. It is the same logic of 'coordination failure' which plays an important role in microeconomic reasoning, to explain why individual firms operating below capacity do not find it advantageous to expand output and employment individually, in anticipation of the demand that would materialise if all firms expanded simultaneously.

The case for cooperation is intimately linked to the two-handed approach. One hand, that directing the supply side, by and large does not require cooperation.[20] The need for cooperation follows from the determination to use the second hand, that of the demand side. Indeed, most of the supply-side measures under consideration can be implemented at national levels by individual countries acting on their own. Not only the measures, but also their effects, are of a primarily domestic nature. The incentives to adopt them are there, whether or not other countries do likewise. Further, these supply-side measures work towards improving competitiveness, so that external considerations reinforce the domestic motivation. (The same cannot be said of measures encouraging market integration or trade liberalisation. These are appropriately approached at the supranational level.)

The fact that macroeconomic policy cooperation is bound to stress the demand element in the policy mix, has a disadvantage. It leads to a rhetoric that neglects the supply side, where a lot of hard work is to be done. This disadvantage is particularly obvious in Section 7 of the present report, which of necessity is devoted almost entirely to demand-side

---

[19] Indeed, it is not generally the case that the lack of coordination leads to over-contractionary policies. It can also result in over-expansionary policies, particularly under a fixed exchange rate regime.

[20] There exist some supply-side measures which would still benefit from cooperation (e.g. when they affect the internal terms of trade, or market liberalisation which spills over abroad), but the magnitude of the gains from cooperation in these cases is likely to be small.

policies. Hopefully, our insistence on the complementarity of the two sides should be clear to the reader from Part 1. For some of us, the anticipatory demand expansion is even viewed primarily as a means of facilitating the removal of supply rigidities, the completion of the internal market and the liberalisation of world trade. However, even though the emphasis placed on the two sides may differ, there is no doubt in our minds that only a two-handed strategy can restore acceptable rates of growth in Europe. There lies the most important message.

6. Europe and the rest of the world

6.1. Little promise for policy cooperation

The income flow measures in Section 5.1 capture adequately the size of the externalities which make the case for cooperation. They reveal clearly that large countries, or country groups, are relatively closed. Table 18.7 summarises the relevant data. As might be expected, the cross-country income multipliers between such areas are quite small. Table 18.8 reports the multipliers from the COMPACT Model – a model yielding results for the European Community as a whole (EC10).[21] The only sizeable entry (0.4) concerns the impact of the US on Japan. Those for Europe are uniformly small (0.1 or 0.2).

Table 18.7. *Trade flows between major countries or groups* (1986)

	USA	EC 12	Japan
Imports as % of own GDP	10.2	9.5[a]	6.6
Exports as % of own GDP	6.8	9.7[a]	11.5
Imports of EC 12 as % of EC 12 GDP	1.9	13.1[b]	1.1
Exports of EC 12 as % of EC 12 GDP	2.6	13.1[b]	0.4

[a] is extra-EC trade
[b] is intra-EC trade
Source: European Economy, July 1987, n°33. Tables 35 and 36.

As a consequence, the need for policy cooperation between such large but closed entities is not great. That conclusion is confirmed by the welfare computations performed by Oudiz and Sachs (1984) reported in Box 2.

---

[21] Where comparable, results from other models (for instance those of the Interlink model used at OECD, or the MCM model used at the Federal Reserve Board, or of the EPA in Tokyo) are not markedly different. See, e.g. Oudiz and Sachs (1984), pp. 20–21.

Table 18.8. *Cross-country income multipliers*

1% of GDP increase in public expenditures (non-wages) with non-accommodating monetary policy

% discrepancy w.r.t. baseline simulation

Country taking action	EC 10			USA			Japan		
	1 year	2 years	3 years	1 year	2 years	3 years	1 year	2 years	3 years
EC 10	1.1	1.3	0.9	0.1	0.2	0.2	0.1	0.1	0.1
USA	0.15	0.2	0.2	1.3	1.2	1.0	0.3	0.4	0.4
Japan	0.05	0.1	0.1	0.1	0.1	0.1	1.1	1.2	1.4

Source: COMPACT Model

┌─ BOX 2: Welfare gains from cooperation ──────────────

The welfare calculations by Oudiz and Sachs (1984) were based on two large models which measure the links between the US, Japan and Germany (the MCM model of the Federal Reserve Board and the Japanese EPA model). Given contemporary forecasts for the three years 1984–86, they looked for the policy actions which would improve the welfare of all three countries, without hurting any of them; welfare is measured in units (percent) of GNP and corresponds to the perceived costs of falling below potential GNP, inflation, and current account imbalances. The striking feature of their results, reported in table 18.9, is how little is achieved through *optimal* coordination: the 0.33 obtained for Germany means that, compared to uncoordinated policy making, full coordination would only improve that country's welfare by an equivalent of 1/3 of one percent higher GNP over the three years period. Clearly, if the best that can be achieved is of this magnitude, there is little incentive in undertaking the kind of elaborate negotiations that full coordination requires.

Table 18.9. *Welfare gains from cooperation*

	USA	Germany	Japan
MCM	0.17	0.33	0.99
EPA Model	0.03	0.03	0.32
MCM Modified	0.54	0.56	2.96

Unit of welfare gain equivalent to a percentage of GNP averaged over three years. Target values are: inflation, zero; current account-GDP ratio, zero for the US, 2% for Germany and Japan.

The last line is based on a modification of the MCM with Germany enlarged three-fold and called 'Europe'.

Source: Oudiz and Sachs (1984).

The scope for coordination is best approached as an exercise in cost-benefit analysis. Small gains may indeed be worth reaping if the cost in obtaining them is minimal, whereas larger gains may sometimes fail to cover their cost. Pending such a quantitative analysis, we feel safe in concluding that the (political) difficulties of coordinating policies at a world level are such that the effort may scarcely be worthwhile.[22]

6.2. A careful exchange rate policy

Another important channel of transmission of policy impacts across countries is the terms of trade. Unfortunately, the effects of fluctuations in the terms of trade are more difficult to capture through econometric models than income effects. Still, in table 18.10, we report cross-country exchange rate multipliers as estimated by the COMPACT Model. The picture emerging from that table confirms our general intuition: the impact of a depreciation of the US dollar against all other currencies exerts less influence at home, and more influence overseas, than a comparable depreciation of the ECU, or even more so of the yen. Presumably, the same conclusion would hold for an appreciation.

Looking at tables 18.8 and 18.10, we note that a 10% change in the value of the dollar has roughly the same medium-term impact on the GDP of EC 10 as a 2.5% change in US national income. But exchange rates are much more volatile than national incomes, so that Europeans are justifiably concerned by the real consequences of the dollar instability. The current situation is dominated by a considerable amount of uncertainty. The sharp appreciation of the dollar from 1980 to 1985 has been mostly undone by its equally sharp depreciation since then. While the full impact of this depreciation remains to be felt, a further sizeable depreciation is seen by some (see Dornbusch and Frankel (1987)) as a distinct possibility. The effects on the exchange rate of an acceleration of growth in Europe must be considered in such a context. If existing macroeconomic models provide any guide to the future (and doubts are legitimate ...), then faster growth in Europe would put downward pressure on its currencies. If current parities are close to their sustainable equilibrium levels (and here too there is ample room for doubt), then it would be desirable to accompany the fiscal expansion with a monetary policy which would avoid significant short-and-medium-term swings.

---

[22] This does not mean that Europe does not stand to benefit from some policy actions in the US. Given the strong linkages between financial markets, a reduction of the US budget deficit would be welcome in Europe. The exchange rate aspect of these linkages is taken up in the following section.

Table 18.10. *Cross-country exchange rate multipliers*

(10% depreciation against all currencies)

Country taking action	EC 10 1 year	2 years	3 years	USA 1 year	2 years	3 years	Japan 1 year	2 years	3 years
EC 10	0.15	0.5	0.8	−0.1	−0.15	−0.2	−0.1	−0.1	−0.2
USA	−0.1	−0.3	−0.5	0.2	0.3	0.35	−0.3	−0.6	−0.8
Japan	−0.05	−0.1	−0.1	−0.05	−0.1	−0.1	0.4	0.7	1.1

Source: COMPACT model.

On the other hand, the experience of the present decade is one where currency movements have been dominated by the dollar and policy initiatives in the US. Under such conditions it is dangerous for Europe to try to stabilise its exchange rates *vis-à-vis* the dollar as it would mean a severe loss of monetary policy independence, an undesirable outcome given the limited gains from transatlantic coordination as shown earlier. Europe should therefore use monetary policy to offset exchange rate pressures caused by its own fiscal actions (this prescription concerns Europe as a whole *vis-à-vis* the rest of the world; internal European exchange rate policies are discussed in some detail in Section 7.2). Our proposed fiscal-monetary mix has precisely that property.

Offsetting exchange rate pressures may not be appropriate, however, in the presence of other shocks. Unfortunately, given the amount of existing uncertainty, we cannot provide succinctly a comprehensive analysis of the appropriate monetary policy responses to the many disturbances which may occur.

6.3. Policy implications: Europe's autonomy

The implications of the discussion so far are clear. It would be futile to aim at finely-tuned coordination of economic policies between Europe, the US and Japan. Our simple, clear conclusion cuts through an issue where the interplay of economics and politics has turned into a complex, confused debate. *We believe that Europe should assume responsibility for its own economic policies and regard itself as an autonomous economic entity.*[23] This conclusion is somewhat at variance with the spirit of efforts initiated at summit meetings of the Group of Seven, and endorsed in

---

[23] To avoid ambiguities: we are not arguing that Europe is more efficient in achieving coordination, rather the gains from coordination within Europe are that much greater due to the more open and interrelated nature of its constituent economies.

particular in Section 4.7 of the EC Annual Report 1986–87 – a point to which we return in Section 7.1.

Being autonomous does not mean disregarding the actions of others, of course. What other countries do is relevant to European policy choices, and must be taken into account. We refer in Box 3 to common responsibilities which Europe shares with others at the world level. Rather autonomy requires accepting one's responsibilities without blaming others for one's difficulties. That is exactly how Europe should approach its severe unemployment problem. The recent experience of a large US trade deficit and an overvalued dollar with its negligible impact on European employment,[24] confirms that we should not expect miracles from increased exports to the US which presently account for only 4% of Europe's GDP.

While world macroeconomic policy coordination does not seem to pass the cost-benefit test, there are nevertheless other areas of cooperation that we wish to mention briefly. One is the international monetary system, a second is trade liberalisation, and the third concerns the LDCs. They are discussed in Box 3.

BOX 3: Three items for world cooperation

The prominent issue is the macroeconomic adjustment required by the LDC debt problem and the US current account deficit. The more developed countries should cooperate actively in improving the growth potential and living standards of the LDCs. Beyond the technical steps needed to organise more realistic terms for the debt and more efficient risk-sharing between rich and poor countries, the main long-run concern should be to promote stable growth of LDC exports. This calls for sustained demand for these exports from the main industrialised areas. As the US attempts to reduce its own external deficit, it is important that the European surplus be reduced and reversed to make room for a surplus by the LDCs, without which their debt situation can only worsen. In this respect the policy mix advocated in this paper – which implies a reduction in the Europe-wide current account surplus, possibly turning it into a deficit – is consistent with Europe's responsibilities in the world economy.

---

[24] Of course, that impact could have been increased, had the supply responsiveness in Europe been greater. That lack of responsiveness in turn was probably influenced by the conviction that the US deficit and overvalued dollar were temporary.

A second area for cooperation is a significant reduction of the role played by the dollar on the international scene. As noted by Oudiz and Sachs (1984, p. 7, table 2 reproduced here in table 18.11): 'The US dollar remains the linchpin of the world monetary system. As shown in table 18.11, the currency of denomination of international reserves, Euro-dollar loans, new issues of Eurobonds, and OPEC portfolio wealth remains to a far higher extent in US dollars than the US share of world GNP would suggest. The special role of the dollar leads to important asymmetries between the effects of US policies on Europe and Japan, and the effects of European and Japanese policies on the United States. Shifts in the value of the dollar can have significant income redistribution effects throughout the world that may also have important demand consequences; changes in the value of the European currencies or the Japanese yen do not have such effects.' With all the prudence called for in this difficult area, we feel that the primary need remains that of developing better alternatives to the US dollar as international instrument of reserves, transactions and liquidity.

The third issue, trade liberalisation, was discussed extensively in the latest report prepared by the CEPS Macroeconomic Policy Group (H. Giersch (1987a)). It would of course be partly self-defeating to work towards smoother trade flows through stabilisation of the dollar, while at the same time accepting other impediments and distortions through tariffs, import restrictions and other barriers. Trade liberalisation can contribute to supply expansion and output growth in all parts of the world. It should be promoted now, and Europe should exercise leadership in that respect. This issue cannot be overemphasised at a time when protectionist pressures are rising on both sides of the Atlantic.

Table 18.11. *The role of the US dollar in international finance*

	Share of US dollars		
	1975	1978	1981
Official reserves	79.4	76.9	70.6
Eurodollar loans	73.7	67.6	70.6
Eurobond issues	47.2	48.2	80.2
US share of world GNP	24.3	25.0	n.a.

Source: Reproduced from Oudiz and Sachs (1984), Table 2.

7. Policy cooperation within Europe

7.1. Cooperation and the EMS

So far, the EMS has brought about some cooperation in monetary, and to a lesser extent, in fiscal policies, but this is not by itself a guarantee that the required policies will emerge naturally. In this section, we briefly review the benefits that member countries have reaped from participation in the EMS, its role in encouraging cooperative behaviour, and the requisite conditions for cooperation in the two-handed strategy.

The primary objective of the EMS is to deliver bilateral exchange rate stability. Trade flows between European countries will be more stable if they are not subject to volatile exchange rate movements. Given the large share of exports in value added, greater stability in trade carries over to greater stability in output and employment. Thus, exchange rate stability helps to insulate the real economy from monetary shocks.[25] In addition, the EMS has been instrumental in enhancing the effectiveness of anti-inflationary policies in the early eighties, when all European countries were sharing the common objective of reducing their excessive rates of inflation. The EMS constraint of maintaining stable exchange rates proved helpful to that end in two ways:

(i) It eliminated the temptation for individual countries, especially the more open ones, to export their inflation through currency appreciation – a policy that obviously could not succeed if pursued by all.[26]

(ii) It also enabled member countries to borrow the anti-inflationary reputation of the Bundesbank to help reduce domestic inflationary expectations.[27]

It was thus important for all concerned to adhere as strictly as possible to the agreed exchange rates. The automatic success of the EMS as an implicit tool of policy coordination resulted from the fact that the tool was ideally suited to the main priority of the day – the elimination of inflation – an objective which was shared by all countries.

---

[25] There is some debate whether these objectives have been met. Rogoff (1985) finds that the EMS has made bilateral exchange rates more predictable, not necessarily more stable. De Grauwe and Verfaille (1987) compare exchange rate variability before and after 1979 and conclude that there is no obvious evidence that the variability of bilateral exchange rates has decreased more inside than outside the EMS.

[26] Giavazzi and Giovannini (1986) show, however, that the EMS has introduced long-run trends in intra-European competitiveness, and suggest that the system has not prevented some European countries – at least Italy – from using currency appreciation to export inflation.

[27] See Giavazzi and Pagano (1988).

To the extent that the system functions as it should (and has done so far), it reduces substantially the leeway for independent interest rate policies in the member states. *Participation in the EMS amounts to a surrender, by all but one country, of domestic interest rates as an unrestricted policy instrument.* It also implies the surrender of the exchange rate as an instrument for equilibrating the current account. Rather, it entails an implicit commitment to achieve long-run external solvency by price adjustment alone. At the same time, the EMS countries retain the option of floating together *vis-à-vis* the rest of the world, thereby achieving external balance in a manner which individual member countries have forfeited by joining the EMS.

The EMS, however, does not enforce automatic cooperation of fiscal policies. It may provide a useful framework for cooperation, but does not substitute for the sort of negotiation required to enact mutually beneficial policies.[28] An important feature of the environment in which cooperation must take place is the fact that the various European countries start from different initial conditions. With different initial conditions, there is still room for cooperation, but it may lead to varied policy actions in the different countries. We call this 'flexible' cooperation. We address this issue in the next section. We shall then consider another aspect which also complicates the matter: the possibility that policy objectives may differ among the various countries.

7.2. Cooperative growth with differentiated initial conditions

7.2.1. The setting. Differences in initial conditions matter because they alter the constraints on policy choices. In the present context, we have identified three such constraints (Section 3.3): inflation, the public debt, and the external debt. We have already stressed that inflation need not be a threat because the two-handed approach incorporates significant contributions to cost and price stability. Looking at the current situation we note that, for the first time in twenty years, Europe's average inflation rate (as measured by the CPI) has receded to its level of the mid-sixties. Yet differences between countries remain substantial, with the four Mediterranean countries well above the European average, the UK close to it, and the remaining countries below it. The inflationary position of the southern countries should thus be kept in mind, while the respite in

---

[28] The EMS merely reduces the possible policy choices of its member countries but does not restrict them completely, leaving room for coordination, or the absence of it. See Begg and Wyplosz (1987).

trend inflation is put to good use. The relevant data are displayed in figure 18.2.

Differences in the state of the public finances amongst the European nations are clearly recognized in the Annual Report of the EC Commission. In particular the Report stresses that budget deficits in several member countries are already so high that they must be reduced rather than increased further – for otherwise the burden of public debt would soon grow beyond control. (Figure 18.3 clearly brings out the association between public debts and deficits.) Hence the Commission's recommendation that fiscal expansion should start in Germany, with France and the UK following.

This internal constraint now has to be connected to the other important one, namely, the external constraint. The two-handed growth strategy should be viewed against the background of figure 18.4, where the twelve EC countries (Belgium and Luxemburg combined) are located in terms of their net government debt/GNP ratio (horizontally) and of their current account deficit/GNP ratio (vertically).[29] Each country is represented by a circle, its size proportional to the country's GNP. Two solid lines are drawn at the (weighted) averages of the ratios for EC 12.

7.2.2. The principles. A supply-friendly fiscal expansion, with monetary accommodation, should lead to a temporary increase of the net debt/GNP ratio and to a temporary deterioration of the current account/GNP ratio. This implies that the EC *averages* in figure 18.4 should move north-east.

The movement of the averages does not, however, require that each individual country moves north-east. Actually, the position of some countries in figure 18.4 is such that they would prefer to move in a different direction. In particular, Italy, Ireland and Belgium are trying to move westward, so as to reduce the weight of their public debt (indeed, the Annual Report of the EC Commission recommends that these countries continue their efforts at budget consolidation). Similarly, Denmark and

---

[29] In principle, we would prefer to measure the external constraint through the net external debt rather than through the current account. However, official figures for net external debt are often lacking, and therefore seldom used, so we use the more familiar figures. On the basis of cumulative current account data since 1960, we have constructed net external debt estimates and used them in figure 18.5. The picture does not differ much from that of figure 18.4 and may be used interchangeably. We have already discussed this issue in section 3.3.4 and will return to it below.

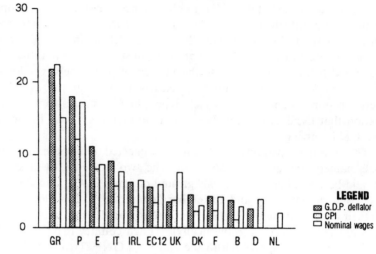

Three Measures of Inflation – 1986

LEGEND
G.D.P. deflator
CPI
Nominal wages

	GR	P	E	IT	IRL	EC12	UK	DK	F	B	D	NL
Unemp.	9.3	7.6	19.8	12.7	17.8	11.4	12.0	7.4	10.6	13	7.8	12.4
Growth 86	-0.4	3.9	2.7	2.7	3.2	2.5	2.6	2.5	2.3	2.0	3.5	1.7

Figure 18.2

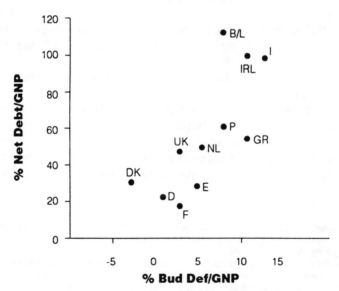

Figure 18.3

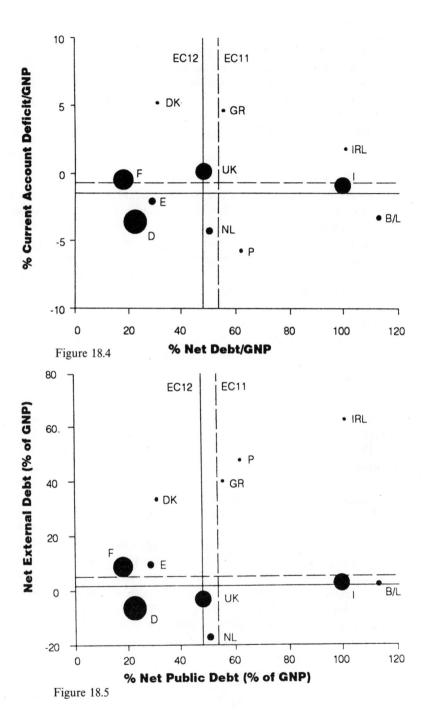

Figure 18.4

Figure 18.5

Greece would like to move southward, to reduce their external deficit. (We return to these specific country tendencies below).

Flexible cooperation, as distinct from policy synchronisation, does not require all countries to move in the same direction. Instead, it tries to define country-specific policies that tend to the common goal, while duly taking into account the differences in initial conditions. What does this mean, in present circumstances?

7.2.3. Flexible cooperation. Countries located in the south-west quadrant need not worry about their debt or external position – Germany is the obvious and well-known instance. It can adopt the two-handed strategy wholeheartedly. As a consequence, Germany moves north-east and pushes the EC average (aggregate) in that direction. As that happens, the remaining countries benefit from an externality (the additional imports of Germany) which would tend to push them in a south-westerly direction if they remained passive, i.e., if they kept their public spending and tax rates unchanged. Indeed, they export more, which improves their current accounts, raises their GNP (by a smaller percentage) and reduces their public deficits. The net effect for EC 12 aggregates is still a displacement north-east, but by less than the initial impulse which is dampened by the externalities.

In order to avoid the dampening, it is desirable that the countries located near the boundary of the south-west quadrant should also follow the two-handed strategy and move north-east of their own initiative. Looking at figure 18.4, we see that France, the UK and the Netherlands fall in that category. Spain is in the same quadrant as Germany and on the surface shares the same degree of freedom; due account should, however, be given to the fact that Spain (as well as Portugal and Greece) is in a difficult transition phase as it gradually integrates its economy into the Community. Together, France, the UK, the Netherlands and Spain account for some 51% of EC 12 GNP. Adding Germany, we now have 77% of the community engaged in the supply-friendly fiscal expansion and unambiguously pushing the aggregate north-east, in spite of some residual dampening from the remaining smaller countries. The two-handed growth strategy for Europe is then definitely under way. It seems clear to us that such cooperative action is far more effective than a repeat of the 'German locomotive experiment'. The bulk of the impact comes from the joint initiatives of Germany, France and the UK which together account for 65% of EC 12 GNP.

What about the remaining countries? If they remain passive, they move south-west. Although their dampening effect on the aggregates is now reduced, it is still there. Could it be avoided? It could indeed, because their antisymmetrical positions relative to the new averages allows for offsetting movements which eliminate the dampening. More specifically, if Denmark and Greece moved south-east, whereas Belgium and Italy moved north-west, the aggregate of these four countries could remain roughly unchanged, allowing the expansion initiated in the other countries to work out its full effects without dampening. Let us look at the implied policies.

The clearest case is that of Belgium. This country is currently engaged in an effort to reduce its budget deficit. Although this effort will be facilitated by the faster growth of neighbouring countries, it should still be pursued. The current account will then display an even larger surplus, whereas the country should move *north*-west. The surplus will naturally be reduced in due time by a currency appreciation. The same policy conclusion holds for Italy, although the implied appreciation would be less marked (both because the initial position involves a smaller surplus and because the smaller degree of openness leads to less pronounced externalities). Conversely, Denmark would see its current account improve under the export pull. This country should adopt a more expansionary fiscal stance, in order to move eastward (contrary to the westward tendency associated with a passive fiscal stance). If the fiscal expansion did more than offset the current account improvement, then a slight currency depreciation would follow. The same applies to Greece, although to a lesser extent. We thus see how Belgium, Italy, Denmark and Greece could play their role by ensuring that no dampening of the initial impulses occurs. The required policies imply some ancillary currency realignments, involving mainly the Belgian franc and the Danish crown. Finally, Ireland could remain 'passive' and move against the tide – but that country accounts for less than 1% of EC 12 GNP or trade.

What remains to be spelled out are the accompanying monetary policies. Given that in each country fiscal policy is set as suggested above, choosing a particular monetary policy is equivalent to the choice of an exchange rate policy, which leads to a consideration of the role of the EMS (assuming that the UK, although not part of the EMS, stabilises the ECU value of the pound). As discussed above, one of the main merits of the EMS is the fact that it provides a credible nominal anchor for price levels across Europe. The system has proven flexible enough to accommodate divergent trends periodically, but it has also penalised (through loss of competitiveness) the more inflation-prone countries in Europe. It has thus provided a credible incentive not to resort to inflationary policies.

All this is crucial for the policies we advocate. A strong commitment to the EMS lends credibility to the announcement that a temporary budget deficit will not be paid for through inflationary finance: it thus reduces the pressures towards exchange rate depreciation that arise whenever the government's ability to generate future budget surpluses is in doubt. Of course the enhanced credibility provided by the EMS cannot eliminate the possibility of speculative attacks: these should be *jointly* resisted by the central banks of the member countries.

In the long run, we cannot rule out the possibility that the fiscal actions necessary to implement the two-handed strategy may require an adjustment of relative prices among European countries. However, the size and even the sign, of these adjustments are difficult to anticipate, as they depend on a number of (often counteracting) factors: the degree of substitutability among debt issued by different governments and denominated in different currencies is, for example, an important one, and one of which we know very little. The flexibility built in the EMS will prove valuable in making these relative price adjustments possible – if and when the time comes.[30]

The foregoing analysis suggests unambiguously that the cooperative growth strategy is feasible, in spite of substantial differences in initial conditions. It also illustrates vividly that cooperation should not be confused with synchronisation.

7.3. *Differences in policy objectives*

The strategy outlined in the previous section assumes common policy objectives among all countries, namely a high priority given to the fight against unemployment. Yet Denmark has recently gone through a period of drastic budget consolidation, and might be reluctant to go into deficit again. More significantly, Germany has a deep-rooted aversion to inflation, and might be reluctant to participate in a strategy where the fiscal expansion anticipates the acceleration of growth in supply. Even though we believe that hesitation is ill-advised, it is nevertheless instructive to discuss its implications. If Germany did not participate in the cooperative growth strategy, the remaining countries would have to choose between

[30] For an analysis of these effects see Sachs and Wyplosz (1984). Needless to say we fully recognize the merits of the relative stability of exchange rates within the EMS. The formulation in the text assumes that our policy recommendations become implemented from a starting situation characterised by sustainable exchange rates. If that was not the case, one should distinguish carefully the consequences of the starting situation from those of the policy actions.

giving up that strategy altogether, or carrying it out on their own. What would the latter alternative look like?

The bulk of the expansion would now come from France, the UK, Spain and the Netherlands. As noted above, these four countries account for 51% of EC 12 GNP, as opposed to 77% with Germany. A rough calculation suggests the extent of the collective loss incurred by carrying out the strategy without active German participation. Using the ratio to GDP of extra-community imports of goods as a rough measure of openness, we get a figure of 13.4% for EC 10. Leaving out Germany, the corresponding figure for the remaining 9 countries jumps to 18.6%, up by a full 5%. In relative terms, the degree of openness of EC 10 goes up by nearly 40% if Germany is left out. The cost to the remaining 9 countries of Germany's failure to participate in the concerted expansion is thus serious, in terms of import leakages and terms of trade deterioration.

Now France and the UK are in the frontline (the dotted lines on figures 18.4 and 18.5 show the EC averages when Germany is left out) and are quite vulnerable with respect to their external position. Furthermore, a fiscal expansion without Germany may well entail some loss of credibility for the monetary authorities and put additional pressure on the exchange rates of the expanding countries. In practice, this amounts to an effective appreciation of the DM. In fact, what is required, is an agreement with Germany to disagree, namely a revaluation of the DM within the EMS; in a sense this would be the German contribution to cooperation. If of a proper magnitude, and if accompanied in the devaluing countries by wage and price moderation – the overriding condition of success in any case – such a realignment would ensure that the collective current account of the expanding countries does not become a source of major concern. Besides this general change, the rest of the recommendations of the previous section apply, except that the fiscal expansion is stronger (even though less effective) wherever it is enacted, and the overall expansion is dampened by Germany's passive fiscal stance.

In addition to being less effective overall, that alternative entails the additional cost of more pronounced currency realignments. And it entails Germany losing competitiveness through appreciation and ending up with increased unemployment. Through that channel, an inflation/unemployment trade-off seems inescapable, even in a country to which the Phillips curve analysis is sometimes considered inapplicable.[31] Thus, not only the expanding countries suffer from the lack of German cooperation, but

---

[31] Phillips curve equations for Germany appear to have been successfully estimated, among others, by Franz (1985), Franz and König (1986), and Bean, Layard and Nickell (1986).

Germany ends up with more unemployment (and less inflation) that in the alternative scenario of the previous section. This confirms the advantages of cooperation, but also suggests that cooperation may arise indirectly: faced with a one-sided expansion elsewhere in Europe, it would still be to Germany's advantage to adopt the two-handed strategy.

8. Conclusion

We have restated the reasons why Europe needs policy actions to extricate itself from its slow-growth, high-unemployment trap. Because of the complex reasons lying behind the underutilisation of the productive resources, and the continuing failure to speed up the accumulation of resources, the required policies must work on both the supply and the demand sides. The two-handed strategy aims at making the economy more efficient in mobilizing its existing resources and readier to increase them. It works on the supply side through a mix of competition enhancing measures as well as cost-cutting fiscal action. It simultaneously works on the demand side through labour tax cuts. Demand feeds into supply by providing the producers with the necessary long-term demand incentives to hire labour and increase productive equipment. Simultaneously, all available opportunities for productive public investment should be seized, both by the EC itself and by member countries. Productive public investments may without reservation be financed by capital inflows. We regard the inflationary risk of this strategy as moderate and well worth taking.

In reviewing the reasons behind the past reluctance to adopt the two-handed strategy, we have emphasised the role of openness, and found it useful to separate the situation of individual countries from the position of the European Community as a whole.

The EC itself is quite closed. The current account constraint, while not to be overlooked, is therefore relatively unimportant. The implication is that the EC should not make the adoption of the two-handed strategy contingent on reaching a cooperative agreement with the US and Japan. Europe should assert its autonomy and adopt the policies that suit it best. This, of course, does not mean that Europe should completely ignore the external effects of these policies, nor that it should renege on its obligations towards the rest of the world. Two important issues emerge in this connection. First, the financial links are important, fast and powerful. This implies that exchange rate management requires considerable caution. However, this is not a one-sided issue and avoiding disruption will require some cooperation with the US and Japan. In particular, a better functioning international monetary system remains a desirable objective. The second important issue concerns the LDC debt problem. At a time when the US must close its external deficit, current account surpluses in the indebted LDCs will require deficits elsewhere, particularly in Europe. The two-handed strategy would bring this about.

Cooperation within the EC is an altogether different matter. An important implication of openness – and all EC countries are very open – is that a fiscal expansion is both less effective and more costly, the more open is the economy. Supply-side policies, on the other hand, tend to become more desirable as the degree of openness rises. The inescapable conclusion is that the external constraint is likely to play havoc with the two-handed strategy: it favours only one hand, supply-side policies. A full commitment to the strategy therefore requires that the external constraint be loosened and that requires fiscal cooperation.

Cooperation is not synonymous with synchronisation. Because economic conditions (chiefly inflation, the public and external debts) differ across countries, policies too will have to differ. Flexible cooperation recognizes this fact and calls for a clear understanding of the role of different initial conditions. Rather than repeating the Bonn Summit approach of staging a fiscal expansion with Germany taking the lead and France and the UK following suit, we think that it would be more effective for the three countries to move simultaneously. The other countries may move less, or not move at all, or use their exchange rates in accordance with their particular initial conditions.

A particularly difficult situation arises when there is disagreement on the policy objectives, especially if a large country is concerned. This would be the case should Germany put a higher weight, relative to other countries, on stabilising its public finances and pursuing disinflation, and a lower weight on resuming growth and reducing unemployment. This would leave much of the burden on the two remaining large countries which can afford to adopt fiscal measures. We think that Europe can resume faster growth even without fiscal expansion in Germany, but this would inevitably cause a significant appreciation of the mark within the EMS, would entail a less favourable outcome on inflation and unemployment in France and the UK, and pose a serious threat of rising unemployment in Germany.

As is often the case, black and white conclusions are deceptive. The choice is not necessarily between a fully coordinated two-handed strategy or the continuation of the status-quo. Each country stands to benefit from the strategy. The more each country expands, the more favourable is the outlook in the remaining countries. The larger is the number of expanding countries, the larger are the gains to each of them individually. Thus, all that is needed is that all, or some of, those countries which can afford it, and fortunately the larger countries can, adopt the two-handed strategy. The others will then either follow, when they can, or simply share in the benefits. How far each country travels the proposed route in the end will depend on its starting position.

Appendix 18.1.   Fiscal expansion in an open economy

In the Island of Flexco, there is an output potential of one mumm per period, controlled by a multinational company and produced with labour alone. The island has two inhabitants, Richard and Mason, and a combined treasury-central bank, the Bank of Flexco (BOF). The local currency, called uce, exchanges for yens one to one. In period 1, Richard holds 100 uces and the central bank's reserves amount to 100 yens. Richard has decided to buy one mumm, which costs 100 uces, in period 2. Accordingly, he deposits his 100 uces at the central bank for one period and will receive an interest of 50%. In what follows his situation will remain unchanged: in period 2 he will own one mumm and 50 uces. The BOF also earns a 50% interest per period on its yen holdings.

Mason would like to buy one mumm as soon as possible but has no money. He has offered his labour services to the company but is not hired in period 1 due to lack of demand. He will be hired in period 2 to produce the mumm ordered by Richard, for which he will get a salary of 100 uces and will then be able to purchase a mumm for himself, but is upset to have to wait. He could borrow from Richard, but they do not know each other. The result is that Mason will order his mumm in period 2 and receive it in period 3. Are there possibilities of improving the island's welfare relatively to the baseline situation just described?

One possibility is for the BOF to give to Mason the 100 uces deposited by Richard as a pure transfer, and announce a tax of 60% on labour income. Mason will then order one mumm at once and will be hired by the company to produce it. Practically, he will pay the mumm upon ordering, will receive his salary at time of hiring, immediately pay a tax of 60 uces and deposit the remaining 40 uces at the BOF. All this happens simultaneously at the beginning of period 1, with interest of 50% accruing at the beginning of period 2. The situation of Mason has now improved. In period 2 he owns a mumm since period 2 plus 100 in cash (his period

1 net earnings of 40 augmented of 20 in interest and his period 2 net earnings of 40). As for the BOF, it has used the 50 yens it earned on its reserve holdings in period 2 to back the creation of 50 uces required to pay back Richard 150 uces in capital and interest, as it only received from Mason 60 in taxes and 40 in deposit. (In period 3 it will use the 60 uces levied as taxes from Mason to pay back his deposit of 40 plus interest of 20.) Relative to the baseline situation, the net addition to the island's assets is the locally produced mumm of Mason. The tax-subsidy mix has raised demand during the slack period, with a balanced inter-temporal budget, and has boosted real income to the same extent.

Suppose however that Mason uses his subsidy to buy yens from the BOF and import a Japanese mumm. The BOF loses its reserves and the associated interest income, which forces it to raise income taxes to 100%. This, of course, allows Mason to order immediately a Japanese mumm which, we assume, he will receive in period 2 (given the remoteness of Japan from the Island of Flexco). On the other hand, Mason is not hired in period 1 to produce his mumm which is imported from Japan, so he foregoes period 1 income and all his period 2 income is taxed away. The BOF ends up with no assets and a liability of 50 uces to serve Richard's interest. One could argue that these uces (the monetisation of the deficit) are worthless – or equivalently that a tax of 100% of interest income would be needed to avoid the liability. The change relative to the baseline is the one-period-ahead mumm of Mason at the loss of the BOF's foreign reserves – i.e. no net gain.

While endless variations of this allegory are possible, it illustrates two important points about a fiscal expansion in an open economy. Firstly, that demand failures offer a prospect for welfare gains. Secondly, that openness, more precisely the marginal propensity to import, works towards cancelling that prospect.

Appendix 18.2. How to measure openness

An economy is open if international trade and financial movements are important for its functioning, and thereby for the welfare of its people. Financial movements affect the interest and exchange rates and may have real effects as well as impose a constraint on policy making. This is an issue that we will consider later on. The importance of trade can take several forms. One of them is the dependence on imports for essential procurements like food or energy. Another is the dependence on exports for marketing domestic resources, like natural resources or labour. An absolute measure of that importance would call for a comparison of welfare levels with and without trade. Such a measure is difficult to construct and its practical significance is limited by the very nature of the question raised – a rhetorical question in most cases since autarky is hardly a realistic option.

Rather, we are concerned with the macroeconomic policy implications of openness. That is a very different, and quite specific question. As shown in the previous section, it arises only in the presence of some disequilibrium which requires, and justifies, the use of macroeconomic policies. In that case, the degree of openness affects the cost and effectiveness of macroeconomic policies through two channels: income flows and the terms of trade. For these specific purposes a rough measure of the degree of openness of an economy is the ratio of imports or exports to national income. That measure is too rough, though, when exports themselves have a significant import content. A corrected measure, the ratio to national income of imports net of import content of exports, coincides with the share of value added which is exported when the trade account is in balance.

To understand how these ratios represent income flows, it helps to consider first the extreme case where exports have a negligible import content, and consist basically of value added. When domestic demand expands, the increment is distributed between imports and domestic output in proportions corresponding to the *marginal* propensity to import. The *average* propensity to import is only relevant in this context because of the *empirical* observation that elasticities of imports with respect to national income are much more similar across countries than marginal propensities to import.[32] Although measures of import elasticities tend to be biased upwards away from unity because of the growing structural independence over the sample period, with the size of the bias likely to vary from country to country, measured elasticities seem to be clustered remarkably around 1.3, implying corrected elasticities around a value of 1.1 or 1.2. Marginal propensities to import dM/dY are then well approximated by a stable (across countries) multiple of import shares M/Y, say $1.2\,M/Y$. The degree of import leakage is thus proportional to the import share.

---

[32] The estimated elasticities of imports with respect to final domestic demand range from 1.2 to 1.8 in the COMET model, and from 1.1 to 1.6 in the DESMOS model, both of which include all major European countries. The COMPACT elasticity for EC 10 as a whole is 1.3. Scattered import equations for individual European countries, that we came across more recently, give similar figures.

Turning now to terms of trade effects, and still neglecting the import content of exports, consider a depreciation which leaves unchanged the value-added deflator. The welfare cost is measured to the first order by the volume of imports times the rate of depreciation. As a percentage of national income, that cost is equal to the import share M/Y times the rate of depreciation. It is thus proportional to the import share for a given rate of depreciation.

This argument would be deceptive if the rate of depreciation needed to correct a given imbalance were itself inversely proportional to M/Y, leaving the product independent of the degree of openness. It is difficult to rule out this possibility generally, in particular without reference to the imbalance to be corrected. An interesting case, of direct relevance to our discussion in the report, arises when the imbalance is a trade deficit generated by an expansion of domestic demand. In such a case, the required rate of depreciation is proportional to the rate of demand expansion, with the factor of proportionality depending upon trade elasticities and being thus, to a first approximation, independent of the degree of openness. Write both exports X and imports M, evaluated in foreign currencies, as functions of (among other things) a 'relative price' variable p, which might be world prices PW divided by the product of home prices (or costs) PH times the exchange rate e. The trade account A is X − M, so that, writing η for elasticities,

$$\frac{dA}{de} = -\frac{X}{e}\eta_{Xp} + \frac{M}{e}\eta_{Mp}, \qquad \frac{de}{e} = \frac{dA}{M\eta_{Mp} - X\eta_{Xp}}.$$

Expansion of domestic final demand D by a given percentage α will affect the current account in an amount αD.(dM/dD). The adjustment in the exchange rate needed to restore the current account balance is thus given by:

$$\frac{de}{e} = \frac{\alpha D \dfrac{dM}{dD}}{M\eta_{Mp} - X\eta_{Xp}} = \alpha \frac{\eta_{MD}}{\eta_{Mp} - \dfrac{X}{M}\eta_{Xp}} \simeq \alpha \frac{\eta_{MD}}{\eta_{Mp} - \eta_{Xp}}.$$

Of course, we need to correct for the import content of exports. The simplest way is to net them out so as to consider net imports. Indeed an increase in domestic demand will not by itself influence the volume of exports, at least if we neglect the feedback effects. (To take into account the feedback effects would require more complex calculations involving matrices of bilateral flows.) Neglecting the feedback effects leads us to understate openness but the bias is not important in the short run, and only marginally related to the degree of openness itself. Neglecting the import content of exports would introduce a severe bias more or less proportional to the degree of openness itself because exports are nearly equal to imports. Actually, the import content of exports is likely to rise with openness, making the bias an increasing function of openness.

References

Abowd, J. and O. Ashenfelter (1981), 'Anticipated Unemployment and Compensating Wage Differentials', in S. Rosen, Ed., *Studies in Labour Markets*, University of Chicago Press, Chicago.

Adams, F. G., Clavijo, F. and R. Orsi (1973), 'A Macroeconomic Model of Belgium: ANELISE', *Recherches Economiques de Louvain*, 39, 303–326.

Allais, M. (1953), 'L'extension des théories de l'équilibre économique général et du rendement social au cas du risque', *Econometrica*, 21, 269–290.

Armstrong, P. J. (1984), *Technical Change and Reduction in Life Hours of Work*, Technical Change Centre, London.

Arrow, K. J. (1953), 'Le rôle des valeurs boursières pour la répartition la meilleure des risques', *Econométrie*, 41–47, CNRS, Paris; translated as 'The Role of Securities in the Optimal Allocation of Risk-Bearing', *Review of Economic Studies* 31, 91–96.

—— (1965), *Aspects of the Theory of Risk-Bearing*, Yrjö Jahnsson Foundation, Helsinki.

Arrow, K. J. and F. H. Hahn (1971), *General Competitive Analysis*, Holden-Day, San Francisco.

Artus, P., Laroque, G. and G. Michel (1984), 'Estimation of a Quarterly Macroeconomic Model with Quantity Rationing', *Econometrica*, 52, 1387–1414.

Ashenfelter, O. and J. Brown (1982), 'Testing the Efficiency of Employment Contracts', mimeo, Princeton University, Princeton, NJ.

Aumann, R. J. (1975), 'Values of Markets with a Continuum of Traders', *Econometrica*, 43, 611–646.

Aumann, R. J. and J. H. Drèze (1986), 'Values of Markets with Satiation or Fixed Prices', *Econometrica*, 6, 1271–1318; reprinted as ch. 6 here.

Aumann, R. J. and L. Shapley (1974), *Values of Non-Atomic Games*, Princeton University Press, Princeton, NJ.

Azariadis, C. (1975), 'Implicit Contracts and Underemployment Equilibria', *Journal of Political Economy*, 83, 6, 1183–1202.

547

548   *References*

(1979), 'Implicit Contracts and Related Topics: A Survey', in Z. Hornstein *et al.*, eds., *The Economics of the Labour Market*, HMSO, London.

Baily, M. (1974), 'Wages and Employment under Uncertain Demand', *Review of Economic Studies*, 41, 1, 37–50.

Balasko, Y. (1978), 'Budget Constrained Pareto-Efficient Allocations', mimeo, Paris.

Banque Nationale de Belgique (1978), 'Politique de change: choix et implications', *Bulletin de la Banque Nationale de Belgique*, avril.

Barro, R. J. (1974), 'Are Government Bonds Net Wealth?', *Journal of Political Economy*, 82, 1095–1117.

(1979), 'On the Determination of the Public Debt', *Journal of Political Economy*, 87, 940–971.

Barro, R. J. and H. I. Grossman (1971), 'A General Disequilibrium Model of Income and Employment', *American Economic Review*, 61, 82–93.

(1976), *Money, Employment and Inflation*, Cambridge University Press, Cambridge.

Barten, A. P., d'Alcantara, G. and G. J. Carrin (1976), 'COMET: A Medium-Term Macroeconomic Model for the European Economic Community', *European Economic Review*, 7, 63–115.

Baruh, M. (1986), 'La réduction du temps de travail en Europe: historique, effets et stratégies d'avenir', Mémoire, Département des Sciences Economiques, Université Catholique de Louvain, Louvain-la-Neuve.

Basevi, G. (1973), 'Commodity Trade Equations in Project Link', in J. Ball, ed., *The International Linkage of National Economic Models*, North-Holland, Amsterdam.

Baumol, W. J., Panzar, J. C. and R. D. Willig (1982), *Contestable Markets and the Theory of Industry Structure*, Harcourt Brace Jovanovitch, New York.

Bauwens, L. (1979). 'Analyse bayésienne d'un modèle d'exportation', Mémoire de Statistique, Faculté des Sciences, Université Catholique de Louvain, Louvain-la-Neuve.

Bauwens, L. and G. d'Alcantara (1983), 'An Export Model for the Belgian Industry', *European Economic Review*, 22, 265–276.

Bean, C. R. (1985), 'Macroeconomic Policy Coordination: Theory and Evidence', *Recherches Economiques de Louvain*, 51, 267–283.

Bean, C. R., Layard, P. R. G. and S. J. Nickell (1986), 'The Rise in Unemployment: a Multi-Country Study', *Economica*, 53, Supplement, S1–S22.

Bean, C. R., Layard, P. R. G. and S. J. Nickell (eds.) (1987), *The Rise in Unemployment*, Basil Blackwell, Oxford.

Beato, P. and A. Mas-Colell (1985), 'On Marginal Cost Pricing with Given Tax-Subsidy Rules', *Journal of Economic Theory*, 37, 356–365.

Begg, D. and C. Wyplosz (1987), 'Why the EMS? Dynamic Games and the Equilibrium Exchange Rate Regime', in R. Bryant and R. Portes, eds., *Global Macroeconomics, Policy Conflicts and Cooperation*, Macmillan, London.

Bénassy, J. P. (1975), 'Neokeynesian Disequilibrium Theory in a Monetary

Economy', *Review of Economic Studies*, 42, 502–523.

(1982), *The Economics of Market Disequilibrium*, Academic Press, New York.

Berckmans, A. and F. Thys-Clément (1977), 'BREUGHEL II, Modèle belge à moyen terme de politique économique', *Cahiers Economiques de Bruxelles*, 76, 475–535.

Bergström, T. C. (1976), 'How to Discard "Free Disposability" at No Cost', *Journal of Mathematical Economics*, 3, 131–134.

Blanchard, O., Dornbusch, R., Drèze, J. H., Giersch, H., Layard, P. R. G. and M. Monti (1985). 'Employment and Growth in Europe: A two Handed Approach', CEPS Paper 21, Brussels.

Blanchard, O. and S. Fischer (1989), *Lectures on Macroeconomics*, MIT Press, Cambridge, Mass.

Blaug, M. (1986), *Who's Who in Economics*, Wheatsheaf, Brighton.

Bleeckx, F., Devuyst, P., Mandy, P. and F. Prades (1978), 'A la recherche des causes du chômage', mimeo, Institut des Sciences du Travail, Université Catholique de Louvain, Louvain-la-Neuve.

Blomme, R. (1978), *Etude des propriétés dynamiques d'un modèle stochastique: application au cas du modèle ANELISE*, Faculté des Sciences Economiques, Sociales et Politiques, Université Catholique de Louvain, Louvain-la-Neuve.

Böhm, V. and H. Müller (1977), 'Two Examples of Equilibria under Price Rigidities and Quantity Rationing', *Zeitschrift für Nationalökonomie*, 37, 1/2, 165–173.

Boiteux, M. (1956), 'Sur la gestion des monopoles publics astreints à l'équilibre budgétaire', *Econometrica*, 24, 22–40.

Bonnisseau, J. M. and B. Cornet (1988), 'Existence of Equilibria when Firms Follow Bounded Losses Pricing Rules', *Journal of Mathematical Economics*, 17, 119–147.

Borch, K. (1960), 'The Safety Loading of Reinsurance Premiums', *Skandinavisk Aktuarietidskrift*, 43, 163–184.

(1962), 'Equilibrium in a Reinsurance Market', *Econometrica*, 30, 3, 424–444.

(1968a), 'Indifference Curves and Uncertainty', *Swedish Journal of Economics*, 70, 19–24.

(1968b), 'General Equilibrium in the Economics of Uncertainty', in K. Borch and J. Mossin, eds., *Risk and Uncertainty*, Macmillan, London, pp. 247–258.

(1976), 'The Monster in Loch Ness', *Journal of Risk and Insurance*, 43, 3, 521–525.

(1985), 'Theory of Insurance Premiums', *The Geneva Papers on Risk and Insurance*, 10, 132–208.

Breeden, D. (1979), 'An Intertemporal Asset Pricing Model with Stochastic Consumption and Investment Opportunities', *Journal of Financial Economics*, 7, 265–296.

Bronsard, C. and E. Wagneur (1982), 'Second rang et déséquilibre', *Cahiers du Séminaire d'Econométrie*, 24, 71–92.

Brown, D. J., Heal, G. M., Khan, M. A. and R. Vohra (1986), 'On A General Existence Theorem for Marginal Cost Pricing Equilibria', *Journal of Economic*

550   *References*

Theory, 38, 371–379.

Brown, D. J. and A. Robinson (1972), 'A Limit Theorem on the Cores of Large Standard Exchange Economies', *Proceedings of the National Academy of Sciences of the USA*, 69, 1258–1260.

Bruno, M. and J. Sachs (1985), *Economics of Worldwide Stagflation*, Basil Blackwell, Oxford.

Buiter, W. (1985), 'A Guide to Public Sector Debts and Deficits', *Economic Policy*, 1, 13–79.

Card, D. (1985), 'Efficient Contracts and Costs of Adjustment: Short-Run Employment Determination for Airline Mechanics', mimeo, Princeton University, Princeton, NJ.

Carré, J. J., Dubois, P. and E. Malinvaud (1972), *Croissance Française: un Essai d'Analyse Causale de l'Après-Guerre*, Seuil, Paris.

Cartter, A. M. (1959), *Theory of Wages and Employment*, Irwin, Homewood.

Champsaur, P. (1975), 'Cooperation Versus Competition', *Journal of Economic Theory*, 11, 394–417.

Champsaur, P., Drèze, J. H. and C. Henry (1977), 'Stability Theorems with Economic Applications', *Econometrica*, 45, 2, 273–294.

Charpin, J. and J. Mairesse (1978), 'Réduction de la durée du travail et chômage', *Revue Economique*, 1, 189–205.

Chetty, V. K. and P. R. Nayak (1978), 'Drèze Equilibria for Polyhedral and Strictly Convex Price Sets', Discussion Paper, Indian Statistical Institute, New Delhi.

Clarke, F. H. (1975), 'Generalised Gradients and Applications', *Transactions of the American Mathematical Society*, 205, 247–262.

—— (1976), 'A New Approach to Lagrange Multipliers', *Mathematics of Operations Research*, 1, 165–174.

—— (1983), *Optimisation and Non-Smooth Analysis*, Wiley, New York.

Clower, R. W. (1965), 'The Keynesian Counterrevolution: A Theoretical Appraisal' in F. H. Hahn and F. Brechling, eds., *The Theory of Interest Rates*, Macmillan, London.

—— (1967), 'A Reconsideration of the Microfoundations of Monetary Theory', *Western Economic Journal*, 6, 1–9.

Cohen, D. (1985), 'How to Evaluate the Solvency of an Indebted Nation', *Economic Policy*, 1, 139–167.

Commissariat Général du Plan (1985), *Aménagement et Réduction du Temps de Travail*, La Documentation Française, Paris.

Cooper, R. (1984), 'Economic Interdependence and Coordination of Economic Policies', in R. Jones and P. Kenen, eds., *Handbook of International Economics*, North-Holland, Amsterdam.

Cornell, B. (1981), 'The Consumption Based Asset Pricing Model: A Note on Potential Tests and Applications', *Journal of Financial Economics*, 9, 103–108.

Cornet, B. and G. Laroque (1980), 'Lipschitz Properties of Constrained Demand

Functions and Constrained Maximisers', Working Paper 8005, INSEE, Paris.

d'Alcantara, G. (1983), *SERENA: A Macroeconomic Sectoral Regional and National Accounting Econometric Model for the Belgian Economy*, Katholieke Universiteit Leuven, Leuven.

d'Alcantara, G. and Associates (1979), 'The International Trade Sector, SERENA Model Report', mimeo, Belgian Planning Bureau, Brussels.

Danthine, J. P. and J. C. Lambelet (1987), 'The Swiss Case', *Economic Policy*, 5, 149–179.

Davies, G. and D. Metcalf (1985), *Generating Jobs*, Simon and Coates, London.

Debreu, G. (1959), *Theory of Value*, Wiley, New York.

(1962), 'New Concepts and Techniques for Equilibrium Analysis', *International Economic Review*, 3, 257–273.

(1972), 'Smooth Preferences', *Econometrica*, 40, 603–615.

Debreu, G. and H. Scarf (1963), 'A Limit Theorem on the Core of an Economy', *International Economic Review*, 4, 225–246.

De Carvalho, F. (1979), *Planning Public Consumption under Restricted Information: A Process-Oriented Contribution*, Facultés des Sciences Economiques, Sociales et Politiques, Université Catholique de Louvain, Louvain-la-Neuve.

De Grauwe, P. and C. Holvoet (1978), 'On the Effectiveness of a Devaluation in the EEC-Countries', *Tijdschrift voor Ekonomie en Management*, 23, 1, 67–82.

De Grauwe, P. and G. Verfaille (1987), 'Exchange Rate Variability, Misalignment, and the European Monetary System', unpublished, University of Leuven, Leuven.

Dehez, P. and J. H. Drèze (1984), 'On Supply-Constrained Equilibria', *Journal of Economic Theory*, 33, 1, 172–182; reprinted as ch. 3 here.

(1988a), 'Competitive Equilibria with Quantity-Taking Producers and Increasing Returns to Scale', *Journal of Mathematical Economics*, 17, 209–230; reprinted as ch. 4 here.

(1988b), 'Distributive Production Sets and Equilibria with Increasing Returns', *Journal of Mathematical Economics*, 17, 231–248.

den Hartog, H. and H. S. Tjan (1976), 'Investments, Wages, Prices and Demand for Labour', *De Economist*, 124, 32–55.

Dermine, J. and J. H. Drèze (1981), 'La Belgique dans la crise et la contrainte de balance des paiements', *Recherches Economiques de Louvain*, 47, 55–76.

Deschamps, P. (1976), *Second-Best Pricing with Variable Product Quality*, Faculté des Sciences Economiques, Sociales et Politiques, Université Catholique de Louvain, Louvain-la-Neuve.

Dewatripont, M. (1986), 'Two-Tier Contracts as Labour Market Adjustment', Working Paper 8603, Université Libre de Bruxelles, Bruxelles.

Diamond, P. and J. Mirrlees (1971), 'Optimal Taxation and Public Production', *American Economic Review*, 61, 8–27, 261–278.

Dierker, E., Guesnerie, R. and W. Neufeind (1985), 'General Equilibrium when Some Firms Follow Special Pricing Rules', *Econometrica*, 53, 1369–1393.

Dixit, A. (1978), 'The Balance of Trade in a Model of Temporary Equilibrium

552   *References*

with Rationing', *Review of Economic Studies*, 141, 393–404.
Dornbusch, R., Basevi, G., Blanchard, O., Buiter, W. and P. R. G. Layard (1983), 'Macroeconomic Prospects and Policies for the European Community', CEPS Paper 1, Brussels; in O. Blanchard *et al.*, eds., *Restoring Europe's Prosperity*, MIT Press, Cambridge, Mass, 1986.
Dornbusch, R. and J. Frankel (1987), 'Macroeconomics and Protection', in R. M. Sterm, ed., *US Trade Policies in a Changing World Economy*, MIT Press, Cambridge, Mass.
Douglas, P. (1934), *The Theory of Wages*, Macmillan, New York.
Dramais, A. (1986), 'Compact – A Prototype Macroeconomic Model of the European Community in the World Economy', *European Economy*, 27, 111–160.
Drazen, A. (1980), 'Recent Developments in Macroeconomic Disequilibrium Theory', *Econometrica*, 48, 283–306.
Drèze, J. H. (1960), 'Quelques réflexions sereines sur l'adaptation de l'industrie belge au Marché Commun', *Comptes Rendus de la Société d'Economie Politique de Belgique*, 275, 3–37; translated as 'The Standard Goods Hypothesis' with a post-scriptum by the author, in A. Jacquemin and A. Sapir, eds., *The European Internal Market: Trade and Competition*, Oxford University Press, Oxford, 1989.
(1964), 'Some Postwar Contributions of French Economists to Theory and Public Policy', *American Economic Review*, 54, 1–64.
(1974a), 'Axiomatic Theories of Choices, Cardinal Utility and Subjective Probability: A Review', in J. H. Drèze, ed., *Allocation under Uncertainty: Equilibrium and Optimality*, Macmillan, London, ch. 1; reprinted as ch. 1 in Drèze (1987a).
(1974b), 'Investment under Private Ownership: Optimality, Equilibrium and Stability', in J. H. Drèze, ed., *Allocation under Uncertainty: Equilibrium and Optimality*, Macmillan, London, ch. 9; reprinted as ch. 14 in Drèze (1987a).
(1975), 'Existence of an Exchange Equilibrium under Price Rigidities', *International Economic Review*, 16, 301–320; reprinted as ch. 2 here.
(1979a), 'Human Capital and Risk-Bearing', *The Geneva Papers on Risk and Insurance*, 12, 5–22; reprinted as ch. 17 in Drèze (1987a).
(1979b), 'Demand Estimation, Risk-Aversion and Sticky Prices', *Economics Letters*, 4, 1–6; reprinted as ch. 9 here.
(1979c) 'Salaires, emploi et durée du travail', and 'Salaires, emploi et durée du travail: Réponse à Paul De Grauwe', *Recherches Economiques de Louvain*, 45, 17–34 and 123–132.
(1980a), 'Réduction progressive des heures et partage du travail' in *Les Conditions de l'Initiative Economique*, 4ème Congrès des Economistes de Langue Française, Commission 3, 2–4 and 57–83.
(1980b), 'Public Goods with Exclusion', *Journal of Public Economics*, 13, 5–24; reprinted as ch. 7 here.
(1981), 'Inferring Risk Tolerance from Deductibles in Insurance Contracts', *The*

Geneva Papers on Risk and Insurance, 20, 48–52; reprinted as ch. 5 in Drèze (1987a).

(1982), 'Decision Criteria for Business Firms', in M. Hazewinkel and A. H. G. Rinnooy Kan, eds., *Current Developments in the Interface: Economics, Econometrics, Mathematics*, D. Reidel, Dordrecht, pp. 27–51; reprinted as ch. 15 in Drèze (1987a).

(1983), 'Stability of a Keynesian Adjustment Process', mimeo, Université Catholique de Louvain, Louvain-la-Neuve.

(1984a), 'Autogestion et équilibre général', *Revue Européenne des Sciences Sociales*, 22, 66, 209–229.

(1984b), 'Second-Best Analysis with Markets in Disequilibrium: Public Sector Pricing in a Keynesian Regime', in M. Marchand, P. Pestieau and H. Tulkens, eds. *The Performance of Public Enterprise: Concepts and Measurement*, North-Holland, Amsterdam, pp. 45–79; and in *European Economic Review*, 29, 3, 263–301, 1985; reprinted as ch. 8 here.

(1985a), '(Uncertainty and) The firm in General Equilibrium Theory', *Economic Journal*, 95, Supplement: Conference Papers, 1–20; reprinted as ch. 16 in Drèze (1987a).

(1985b), 'Aux prises avec l'économique, être chrétien, qu'importe?' *L'Entreprise et l'Homme*, 4, 177–184.

(1986a), 'Work-Sharing: Why? How? How Not …', CEPS Paper 27, Brussels.

(1986b), 'Work-Sharing: Some Theory and Recent European Experience', *Economic Policy*, 1, 3, 561–619; reprinted as ch. 17 here.

(1987a), *Essays on Economic Decisions under Uncertainty*, Cambridge University Press, Cambridge.

(1987b), 'Underemployment Equilibria: From Theory to Econometrics and Policy', *Europen Economic Review*, 31, 9–34; reprinted as ch. 1 here.

(1989a), *Labour Management, Contracts and Capital Markets, A General Equilibrium Approach*, Basil Blackwell, Oxford.

(1989b), 'L'arbitrage entre équité et efficacité en matière d'emploi et de salaires', *Recherches Economiques de Louvain*, 55, 1, 1–31, 1989; English version: 'Wages, Employment and the Equity-Efficiency Trade-Off'; reprinted as ch. 12 here.

(1989c), 'The Role of Securities and Labor Contracts in the Optimal Allocation of Risk-Bearing', in H. Loubergé, ed., *Risk, Information and Insurance. Essays in the Memory of Karl H. Borch*, Kluwer Academic Publishers, Boston; reprinted as ch. 11 here.

(1990), 'Stability of a Keynesian Adjustment Process', to appear in W. Barnett, B. Cornet, C. d'Aspremont, J. Jaskold Gabszevicz and A. Mas-Colell, eds., *Equilibrium Theory and Applications*, Cambridge University Press, Cambridge, forthcoming; reprinted as ch. 10 here.

(1990), 'European Unemployment: Lessons from a Multicountry Econometric Study', *Scandinavian Journal of Economics*, 92, 2, 135–165.

Drèze, J. H. and C. Bean (1991), 'Europe's Unemployment Problem: Introduction and Synthesis', in J. H. Drèze, C. Bean, J. P. Lambert, F. Mehta and H. Sneessens, eds., *Europe's Unemployment Problem*, MIT Press, Cambridge, Mass., ch. 1; reprinted as ch. 16 here.

Drèze, J. H., Bean, C., Lambert, J. P., Mehta, F. and H. Sneessens (eds.) (1991), *Europe's Unemployment Problem*, MIT Press, Cambridge, Mass.

Drèze, J. H. and D. de la Vallée Poussin (1971), 'A Tâtonnement Process for Public Goods', *Review of Economic Studies*, 37, 133–150.

Drèze, J. H. and C. Gollier (1989), 'Risk-Sharing on the Labour Market', mimeo, Université Catholique de Louvain, Louvain-la-Neuve.

Drèze, J. H. and K. Hagen (1978), 'Choice of Product Quality: Equilibrium and Efficiency', *Econometrica*, 46, 3, 493–513.

Drèze, J. H. and M. Marchand (1976), 'Pricing, Spending, and Gambling Rules for Non-Profit Organisations', in R. E. Grieson, ed., *Public and Urban Economics, Essays in Honor of William S. Vickrey*, Lexington Books, Lexington, pp. 59–89, reprinted as ch. 19 in Drèze (1987a).

Drèze, J. H. and F. Modigliani (1972), 'Consumption Decisions under Uncertainty,' *Journal of Economic Theory*, 5, 308–335: reprinted as ch. 9 in Drèze (1987a).

(1981), 'The Trade-Off between Real Wages and Employment in an Open Economy (Belgium)', *European Economic Review*, 15, 1, 1–40; reprinted as ch. 14 here.

Drèze, J. H. and H. Müller (1980), 'Optimality Properties of Rationing Schemes', *Journal of Economic Theory*, 23, 150–159; reprinted as ch. 5 here.

Drèze, J. H., Wyplosz, C., Bean, C., Giavazzi, F. and H. Giersch (1988), 'The Two-Handed Growth Strategy for Europe: Autonomy through Flexible Cooperation', *Recherches Economiques de Louvain*, 54, 1, 5–52; reprinted as ch. 18 here.

Drèze, J. P. (1982), 'On the Choice of Shadow Prices for Project Evaluation', Discussion Paper, Indian Statistical Institute, New Delhi.

Driehuis, W. and M. Bruyn-Hundt (1979), 'Enige Effecten van Arbeidstijdverkorting', *Economisch Statistische Berichten*, 1964, 289–300.

Duffie, G., Shafer, W., Cass, D., Magill, M., Quinzii, M. and J. Geanakoplos (1988), 'Lectures Notes on Incomplete Markets', BoWo Discussion Paper A-192, Universität Bonn, Bonn.

Economie Européenne (1980), *Aménagement du Temps de Travail*, EEC, Strasbourg.

Emerson, M. (1988), *What Model for Europe?*, MIT Press, Cambridge, Mass.

European Economy (1984), *Annual Economic Report 1984–85*, EEC, Strasbourg.

Eyskens, M. (1978), 'Budget: Situation et perspectives', Secrétariat d'Etat au Budget et à l'économie régionale flamande, Bruxelles.

Fair, R. C. (1969), *The Short-Run Demand for Workers and Hours*, North-Holland, Amsterdam.

Fama, E. F. and G. W. Schwert (1977), 'Human Capital and Capital Market Equilibrium', *Journal of Financial Economics*, 4, 95–125.

Fisher, F. M. (1983), *Disequilibrium Foundations of Equilibrium Economics*, Cambridge University Press, Cambridge.

Fontaine, C. (1984), 'L'évolution de la durée annuelle du travail en France depuis 1930', *Chronique d'Actualité*, SEDEIS.

Franz, W. (1985), 'The Past Decade's Natural Rate and the Dynamics of German Unemployment: A Case Against Demand Policy?', *European Economic Review*, 21, 51–76.

Franz, W. and H. König (1986), 'The Nature and Causes of Unemployment in the Federal Republic of Germany since the 1970's: An Empirical Investigation', *Economica*, 53, Supplement, S219–S224.

Gérard, M. and C. Vanden Berghe (1984). 'Econometric Analysis of Sectoral Investments in Belgium (1956–1982)', *Recherches Economiques de Louvain*, 50, 89–118.

Giavazzi, F. and A. Giovannini (1986), 'The EMS and the Dollar', *Economic Policy*, 2, 456–485.

Giavazzi, F. and M. Pagano (1988), 'The Advantage of Tying One's Hands: EMS Discipline and Central Bank Credibility', *European Economic Review*, 32, 1055–1082.

Giersch, H. (1987a), 'Internal and External Liberalisation for Faster Growth', CEC, DG for Economic and Financial Affairs, Economic Paper 54, Brussels.

(1987b) 'Economic Policies in the Age of Schumpeter', *European Economic Review*, 31, 35–52.

Ginsburgh, V. and I. Zang (1978), 'Price-Taking or Price-Making Behavior in Export Pricing', Discussion Paper 7805, CORE, Université Catholique de Louvain, Louvain-la-Neuve.

Gollier, C. (1988), *Intergenerational Risk-Sharing and Unemployment*, Faculté des Sciences Economiques, Université Catholique de Louvain, Louvain-la-Neuve.

Gordon, D. F. (1974), 'A Neo-Classical Theory of Keynesian Unemployment', *Economic Inquiry*, 12, 431–459.

Gourieroux, C., Laffont, J. J. and A. Montfort (1984), 'Econométrie des modèles d'équilibre avec rationnement: une mise à jour', *Annales de l'INSEE*, 55/56, 5–38.

Grandmont, J. M. (1974), 'On the Short-Run Equilibrium in a Monetary Economy', in J. H. Drèze, ed., *Allocation under Uncertainty: Equilibrium and Optimality*, Macmillan, London, ch. 12.

(1977), 'Temporary General Equilibrium Theory', *Econometrica*, 45, 535–572.

(1978), 'The Logic of the Fix-Price Method', *Scandinavian Journal of Economics*, 80, 169–186.

Grandmont, J. M. (ed.) (1988), *Temporary Equilibrium: Selected Readings*, Academic Press, San Diego.

Grandmont, J. M., Laroque, G. and Y. Younès (1978), 'Equilibrium with Quantity Rationing and Recontracting', *Journal of Economic Theory*, 10, 84–102.

Greenberg, J. and H. Müller (1979), 'Equilibria under Price Rigidities and Externalities', in O. Moeschlin, ed., *Game Theory and Related Topics*, North-Holland, Amsterdam, pp. 291–300.

Grossman, S. J. and R. J. Shiller (1982), 'Consumption Correlatedness and Risk

Measurement in Economies with Non-traded Assets and Heterogeneous Information', *Journal of Financial Economics*, 10, 195–210.

Grubb, D., Jackman, R. and P. R. G. Layard (1983), 'Wage Rigidity and Unemployment in OECD Countries', *European Economic Review*, 21, 11–39.

Guesnerie, R. (1975a), 'Un formalisme général pour le "second rang" et son application à la définition des règles du calcul économique public sous une hypothèse simple de fiscalité', *Cahiers du Séminaire d'Econométrie*, 16, 87–116.

(1975b), 'Pareto Optimality in Non-Convex Economies', *Econometrica*, 43, 1–29.

(1977), 'On the Direction of Tax Reform', *Journal of Public Economics*, 7, 179–202.

(1980), 'Second-Best Pricing Rules in the Boiteux Tradition: Derivation, Review and Discussion', *Journal of Public Economics*, 13, 51–80.

(1981), 'Analyse microéconomique normative du modèle keynésien élémentaire', mimeo, CEPREMAP, Paris.

Guesnerie, R. and K. Roberts (1984), 'Effective Policy Tools and Quantity Controls', *Econometrica*, 52, 59–86.

Guesnerie, R. and J. Tirole (1981), 'Tax Reform from the Gradient Projection Viewpoint', *Journal of Public Economics*, 15, 275–293.

Hahn, F. H. (1978), 'On Non-Walrasian Equilibria', *Review of Economic Studies*, 45, 1–17.

Hamada, K. (1976), 'A Strategic Analysis of Monetary Interdependence', *Journal of Political Economy*, 84, 677–700.

Harsanyi, J. (1955), 'Cardinal Welfare, Individualistic Ethics and Interpersonal Comparisons of Utility', *Journal of Political Economy*, 63, 309–321.

Hart, O. D. and B. Holmström (1989), 'The Theory of Contracts', in T. Bewley, ed., *Advances in Economic Theory*, Cambridge University Press, Cambridge, pp. 71–155.

Hart, R. A. (1984), *Shorter Working Time*, OECD, Paris.

Hart, S. (1977a), 'Asymptotic Value of Games with a Continuum of Players', *Journal of Mathematical Economics*, 4, 57–80.

(1977b), 'Values of Non-Differentiable Markets with a Continuum of Traders', *Journal of Mathematical Economics*, 4, 103–116.

(1980), 'Measure-Based Values of Market Games', *Mathematics of Operations Research*, 5, 197–228.

Hellwig, M. and M. Neumann (1987), 'Germany under Kohl', *Economic Policy*, 5, 103–145.

Hendry, D. F. (1982), 'Whither Disequilibrium Econometrics?', *Econometric Reviews*, 1, 65–70.

Henin, P. Y. (1980), 'A Suggestion for Unifying the Theory of Unemployment: A Model of Process Equilibrium under Quantity Rationing', Discussion Paper, Université de Paris I, Paris.

Hicks, J. R. (1932), *The Theory of Wages*, Macmillan, London.

Hildenbrand, W. (1974), *Core and Equilibria of a Large Economy*, Princeton University Press, Princeton.

—— (1981), 'Short-Run Production Functions Based on Microdata', *Econometrica*, 51, 1095–1125.

—— (1982), 'Core of an Economy', in K. J. Arrow and M. D. Intriligator, eds., *Handbook of Mathematical Economics*, Volume II, North-Holland, Amsterdam, ch. 18.

—— (1983), 'On the Law of Demand', *Econometrica*, 51, 997–1019.

Holmström, B. (1979), 'Moral Hazard and Observability', *The Bell Journal of Economics*, 10, 1, 74–91.

—— (1981), 'Contractual Models of the Labour Market', *American Economic Review*, 71, 2, 308–313.

Houthakker, H. (1955), 'The Pareto Distribution and the Cobb–Douglas Production Function in Activity Analysis', *Review of Economic Studies*, 23, 27–31.

Ito, T. (1982), 'Implicit Contract Theory: A Critical Survey', Discussion Paper 82–165, Center of Economic Research, University of Minnesota, Minneapolis.

Jallade, J. P. (1982), *L'Europe à temps partiel*, Economica, Paris.

Kannai, Y. (1966), 'Values of Games with a Continuum of Players', *Israel Journal of Mathematics*, 4, 54–58.

Keynes, J. M. (1936), *The General Theory of Employment, Interest and Money*, Harcourt Brace, New York.

Kooiman, P. (1984), 'Smoothing the Aggregate Fix-Price Model and the Use of Business Survey Data', *Economic Journal*, 94, 899–913.

Kooiman, P. and T. Kloek (1985), 'An Empirical Two-Market Disequilibrium Model for Dutch Manufacturing', *European Economic Review*, 29, 3, 323–354.

Koopmans, T. (1957), *Three Essays on the State of Economic Science*, McGraw-Hill, New York.

Kuipers, S. K. and H. F. Bosch (1976), 'An Alternative Estimation Procedure of a Clay–Clay Type of Vintage Model: The Case of the Netherlands, 1959–1973', *De Economist*, 124, 56–82.

Kurz, M. (1982), 'Unemployment Equilibrium in an Economy with Linked Prices', *Journal of Economic Theory*, 26, 100–123.

Lambert, J. P. (1988), *Disequilibrium Macroeconomic Models, Theory and Estimation of Rationing Models Using Business Survey Data*, Cambridge University Press, Cambridge.

Lambert, J. P., Lubrano, M. and H. Sneessens (1984), 'Emploi et chômage en France de 1955 à 1982: un modèle macroéconomique annuel avec rationnement', *Annales de l'INSEE*, 55–56

Layard, P. R. G., Basevi, G., Blanchard, O., Buiter, W. and R. Dornbusch (1984), 'Europe: The Case for Unsustainable Growth', CEPS Paper 8/9, Brussels; in O. Blanchard *et al.*, eds., *Restoring Europe's Prosperity*, MIT Press, Cambridge, Mass, 1986.

Layard, P. R. G. and S. J. Nickell (1985), 'The Causes of British Unemployment', *National Institute of Economics Review*, 111, 62–85.

Leijonhufvud, A. (1968), *On Keynesian Economics and the Economics of Keynes*, Oxford University Press, Oxford.

Leroy, R. (1962), *Signification du chômage belge*, Office Belge pour l'Accroissement de la Productivité, Brussels.

Lévy-Lambert, H. (1968), 'Tarification des services à qualité variable', *Econotrica*, 36, 564–574.

——— (1969), *La Vérité des Prix*, Seuil, Paris.

Lindbeck, A. and D. Snower (1985), 'Explanations of Unemployment', *Oxford Review of Economic Policy*, 1, 2, 34–59.

Lucas, R. and N. Stokey (1983), 'Optimal Fiscal and Monetary Policy in an Economy without Capital', *Journal of Monetary Economics*, 12, 55–93.

Machina, M. (1987), 'Choice under Uncertainty: Problems Solved and Unsolved', *Economic Perspectives*, 1, 1, 121–154.

Madden, P. (1978), 'Some Results on Drèze Equilibrium', mimeo, Manchester University, Manchester.

Maddison, A. (1982), *Phases of Capitalist Development*, Oxford University Press, Oxford.

Malinvaud, E. (1971), 'Procédures pour la détermination d'un programme de consommation collective', *European Economic Review*, 2, 187–217.

——— (1972), *Lectures on Microeconomic Theory*, North-Holland, Amsterdam.

——— (1977), *The Theory of Unemployment Reconsidered*, Basil Blackwell, Oxford.

——— (1980), 'Macroeconomic Rationing of Employment', in E. Malinvaud and J. P. Fitoussi, eds., *Unemployment in Western Countries*, Macmillan, London.

——— (1982a), 'An Econometric Model for Macro-Disequilibrium Analysis', in M. Hazewinkel and A. H. G. Rinnooy Kan, eds., *Current Developments in the Interface: Economics, Econometrics, Mathematics*, D. Reidel, Dordrecht.

——— (1982b), 'Wages and Unemployment', *Economic Journal*, 92, 1–12.

Malinvaud, E. and Y. Younès (1977a), 'Une nouvelle formulation générale pour l'étude de certains fondements microéconomiques de la macroéconomie', *Cahiers du Séminaire d'Econométrie*, 18, 63–112.

——— (1977b), 'Some New Concepts for the Microeconomic Foundations of Macroeconomics', in G. C. Harcourt, ed., *The Microeconomic Foundations of Macroeconomics*, Westview Press, Boulder; Macmillan, London (1978).

Mangasarian, O. L. (1969), *Nonlinear Programming*, McGraw-Hill, New York.

Marchand, M. (1973), 'The Economic Principles of Telephone Rates under a Budgetary Constraint', *Review of Economic Studies*, 50, 507–515.

Marchand, O. (1984), 'L'emploi en 1982–83: simple répit dans la divergence entre demande et offre', *Economie et Statistique*, 166, 25–38.

Marshall, A. (1920), *Principles of Economics*, 8th edition, Macmillan, London.

Martin, C. (1986), 'Disequilibrium Modelling of the Demand for Corporate Borrowing in the UK: An Application of Linear Disequilibrium Estimation', mimeo, Birkbeck College, London.

Mas-Colell, A. (1977), 'Competitive and Value Allocations of Large Exchange Economies', *Journal of Economic Theory*, 14, 419–438.

Mayers, D. (1973), 'Non-Marketable Assets and the Determination of Capital Asset Prices in the Absence of a Riskless Asset', *Journal of Business*, 46, 258–267.

McDonald, I. and R. M. Solow (1981), 'Wage Bargaining and Employment', *American Economic Review*, 71, 5, 896–908.

McKinnon, R. (1969), 'Portfofio Balance and International Payments Adjustment', in R. A. Mundell and A. Swoboda, eds., *Monetary Problems of the International Economy*, Chicago University Press, Chicago, pp. 189–234.

Meade, J. E. (1982), *Wage Fixing*, Allen, London.

Mertens, J. F. (1980), 'Values and Derivatives', *Mathematics of Operations Research*, 5, 523–552.

(1988), 'The Shapely Value in the Non-Differentiable Case', *International Journal of Game Theory*, 17, 1, 1–65.

Mifflin, R. (1976), 'Semi-Smooth and Semi-Convex Functions in Constrained Optimization', RR–7621, International Institute for Applied Systems Analysis, Laxenburg.

Modigliani, F. and T. Padoa-Schioppa (1977), 'La Politica Economica in Una Economia con Salari Indicizzati al 100 o piu', *Moneta e Credito* 117.

(1978), 'The Management of an Open Economy with 100% plus Wage Indexation', *Essays in International Finance*, 130, Princeton University Press, Princeton.

Morishima, M. (1976), *The Economic Theory of Modern Society*, Cambridge University Press, Cambridge.

Mortensen, J. (1984), 'Profitability, Relative Factor Prices and Capital/Labour Substitution in the Community, the United States and Japan, 1960–1983', *European Economy*, 20, 33–67.

Mossin, J. (1966), 'Equilibrium in a Capital Asset Market', *Econometrica*, 34, 768–783.

(1977), *The Economic Efficiency of Financial Markets*, Heath and Co, Lexington.

Muellbauer, J. (1978), 'Macrotheory vs Macroeconometrics: The Treatment of Disequilibrium in Macromodels', Discussion Paper 29, Birkbeck College, London.

Negishi, T. (1961), 'Monopolistic Competition and General Equilibrium', *Review of Economic Studies*, 28, 196–201.

Neyman, A. and Y. Tauman (1979), 'The Partition Value', *Mathematics of Operations Research*, 4, 236–264.

Nyssens, A. and E. Wittman (1976), 'Comparaison internationale des salaires et de la productivité', *Les Dossiers Wallons*, 3–4–5, 165–255.

Oates, W. E. (1966), 'Budget Balance and Equilibrium Income: A Comment on the Efficacity of Fiscal and Monetary Policy in an Open Economy', *Journal of Finance*, 21, 489–498.

OECD (1983), *Employment Outlook*, Paris.

560   *References*

(1984), *Employment Outlook*, Paris.

(1985), *Employment Growth and Structural Change*, Paris.

Oi, W. Y. (1962), 'Labour as a Quasi-Fixed Factor', *Journal of Political Economy*, 70, 538–555.

Okun, A. (1981), *Prices and Quantities: A Macroeconomic Analysis*, The Brookings Institution, Washington; Basil Blackwell, Oxford.

Oswald, A. (1984), 'Efficient Contracts are on the Labour-Demand Curve: Theory and Facts', mimeo, Oxford University, Oxford.

(1985), 'The Economic Theory of Trade Unions: An Introductory Survey', *Scandinavian Journal of Economics*, 82, 2, 160–193.

Oudiz, H. G. and J. Sachs (1984), 'Macroeconomic Policy Coordination among the Industrial Economies', *Brookings Papers on Economic Activity*, 1, 1–75.

Palasthy, T. (1978), 'Six heures de travail par jour', *Les Dossiers Wallons*, 6, 3–40.

Pencavel, J. (1985), 'Wages and Employment and Trade Unionism: Microeconomic Models and Macroeconomic Applications', *Scandinavian Journal of Economics*, 87, 2, 197–225.

Persson, M., Persson, T. and L. Svensson (1986), 'Time Consistency of Fiscal and Monetary Policy', IIEP Seminar Paper 331, Stockholm.

Phelps, E. S. (1963), 'Substitution, Fixed Proportions, Growth and Distribution', *International Economic Review*, 4, 265–288.

Phlips, L. (1974), *Applied Consumption Analysis*, North-Holland, Amsterdam.

(1978), 'Selective Manpower Policies in Germany, with Special Reference to Wage-Cost Subsidies', in *European Labour Market Policies*, National Commission for Manpower Policy, Washington.

Picard, P. (1982), 'Prix fictifs et déséquilibre en économie ouverte', mimeo, Centre de Mathématiques Economiques, Université de Paris-I, Paris.

Pigou, A. C. (1928), 'An Analysis of Supply', *Economic Journal*, 38, 238–257.

Plasmans, J. and A. Vanroelen (1985), 'Arbeidsuurverkorting: Een Mogelijke Oplossing voor (Jeugd) Werkloosheid?', mimeo, UFSIA (SESO), Antwerp.

Pratt, J. (1964), 'Risk Aversion in the Small and in the Large', *Econometrica*, 32, 127–136.

Quandt, R. E. (1986), *Bibliography of Quantity Rationing and Disequilibrium Models*, Mimeo, Princeton University, Princeton, NJ.

Quatrième Congrès des Economistes Belges de Langue Française, (1980), *Réduction Progressive des Heures et Partage du Travail*, Commission 3, CiFOP, Charleroi.

Ramsey, F. P. (1927), 'A Contribution to the Theory of Taxation', *Economic Journal*, 37, 47–61.

Roberts, K. (1982), 'Desirable Fiscal Policies under Keynesian Unemployment', *Oxford Economic Papers*, 34, 1–22.

Rockafellar, R. T. (1970), *Convex Analysis*, Princeton University Press, Princeton.

(1979), 'Clarke's Tangent Cones and the Boundary of Closed Sets in $\mathbb{R}^n$', *Non-Linear Analysis, Methods and Applications*, 3, 145–154.

Rogoff, K. (1985), 'Can Exchange Rate Predictability be Achieved without

Monetary Convergence? – Evidence from the EMS', International Finance Discussion Paper 245, Federal Review Board, Washington.

Rosen, S. (1985), 'Implicit Contracts: A Survey', *Journal of Economic Literature*, 23, 3, 1144–1175.

Roth, A. E. (1977), 'The Shapley Value as a von Neumann-Morgenstern Utility', *Econometrica*, 45, 657–664.

Rowthorn, B. and A. Glyn (1987), 'The Diversity of Unemployment Experience since 1973', Applied Economics Discussion Paper 40, University of Oxford, Oxford.

Roy, R. (1942), *De L'Utilité – Contribution à la Théorie des Choix*, Hermann, Paris.

Sachs, J. (1983), 'International Policy Coordination in a Dynamic Macroeconomic Model', NBER Working Paper 1166.

Sachs, J. and C. Wyplosz (1984), 'Real Exchange Rate Effects of Fiscal Policy', NBER Working Paper 1255.

(1986), 'The Economic Consequences of President Mitterrand', *Economic Policy*, 2, 261–321.

Sandmo, A. (1974), 'Two-Period Models of Consumption Decisions under Uncertainty', in J. H. Drèze, ed., *Allocation under Uncertainty: Equilibrium and Optimality*, Macmillan, London, ch. 2.

Sargan, J. D. (1964), 'Wages and Prices in the UK: A Study in Econometric Methodology', in P. Hart, G. Mills and J. Whitaker, eds., *Econometric Analysis for Economic Planning*, Butterworths, London.

Scarf, H. (1986), 'Notes on the Core of a Productive Economy', in W. Hildenbrand and A. Mas-Colell, eds., *Contributions to Mathematical Economics, Essays in Honor of Gérard Debreu*, North-Holland, Amsterdam.

Scarmure, P. (1986), 'Réduction, aménagement et redistribution du temps de travail: état de la question et évaluation des politiques en Belgique', Mémoire, Département des Sciences Economiques, Université Catholique de Louvain, Louvain-la-Neuve.

Schmeidler, D. and K. Vind (1972), 'Fair Net Trades', *Econometrica*, 40, 637–642.

Shafer, W. and H. Sonneschein (1975), 'Some Theorems on the Existence of Competitive Equilibrium', *Journal of Economic Theory*, 11, 83–93.

Shapley, L. (1953), 'A Value for *n*-Person Games', in H. W. Kuhn and A. W. Tucker, eds., *Contributions to the Theory of Games*, Volume II, Princeton University Press, Princeton, pp. 307–317.

(1969), 'Utility Comparisons and the Theory of Games', in G. Th. Guilbaud, ed., *La Décision*, CNRS, Paris, pp. 251–263.

Sneessens, H. (1981), *Theory and Estimation of Macroeconomic Rationing Models*, Springer-Verlag, Berlin.

(1983), 'A Macroeconomic Rationing Model of the Belgian Economy', *European Economic Review*, 20, 193–215.

(1987), 'Investment and the Inflation-Unemployment Trade-Off in a Macroeconomic Rationing Model with Monopolistic Competition', *European Economic Review*, 31, 3, 781–808.

Sneessens, H. and J. H. Drèze (1986a), 'A Discussion of Belgian Unemployment, Combining Traditional Concepts and Disequilibrium Econometrics', *Economica*, 53, S89–S119; reprinted as ch. 15 here.

(1986b), 'What, if Anything, Have We Learned from the Rise of Unemployment in Belgium, 1974–1983?', *Cahiers Economiques de Bruxelles*, 110/111, 21–26.

Solow, R. (1962), 'Substitution and Fixed Proportions in the Theory of Capital', *Review of Economic Studies*, 29, 207–218.

Sonnet, A. (1985), 'Valeur ajoutée, contenu en emplois et en travail', *Service de Conjoncture*, IRES, Université Catholique de Louvain, Louvain-la-Neuve.

Sonnet, A. and P. Defeyt (1984), 'Le marché du travail en Belgique', *Bulletin de l'IRES*, 94, 1–99, Université Catholique de Louvain, Louvain-la-Neuve.

Stalder, P. (1989), 'A Macroeconomic Disequilibrium Model for Switzerland with Continuous Regime Transitions and Endogenous Investment', *European Economic Review*, 33, 863–893.

Steinherr, A. (1975), 'Economic Policy in an Open Economy under Alternative Exchange Rate Systems: Effectiveness and Stability in the Short and Long Run', *Weltwirtschaftliches Archiv*, 111, 24–51.

Steinherr, A. and B. Van Haeperen (1985), 'Approche pragmatique pour une politique de plein-emploi: les subventions à la création d'emplois', *Recherches Economiques de Louvain*, 51, 2, 111–151.

Stigler, G. J. (1942), *The Theory of Price*, Macmillan, New York.

Sweezy, P. (1939), 'Demand under Conditions of Oligopoly', *Journal of Political Economy*, 47, 568–573.

Tauman, Y. (1981), 'Value on a Class of Non-Differentiable Market Games', *International Journal of Game Theory*, 10, 155–162.

Thys-Clément, F., van Rompuy, P. and L. De Corel (1973), *RENA, Un modèle économétrique pour l'élaboration du plan 1976–1980*, Belgian Planning Bureau, Brussels.

Tobin, J. (1952), 'A Survey of the Theory of Rationing', *Econometrica*, 20, 4, 512–553.

Van Den Bergh, R. C. and H. Wittelsburger (1981), *Working Time Reductions and Unemployment*, Conference Board in Europe, Brussels.

Van den Broeck, J., Hendericks, E. and L. Coenaerts (1984), *Roterende Vakantie*, RUCA, Antwerp.

Van der Laan, G. (1980), 'Equilibrium under Rigid Prices with Compensation for the Consumers', *International Economic Review*, 21, 63–74.

(1982), 'Simplicial Approximation of Unemployment Equilibria', *Journal of Mathematical Economics*, 9, 83–97.

(1984), 'Supply-Constrained Fixed Price Equilibria in Monetary Economies', *Journal of Mathematical Economics*, 13, 2, 171–187.

Vandoorne, M. and W. Meeusen (1978), 'The Clay–Clay Vintage Model as an Approach to the Problem of Structural Unemployment in Belgian Manufacturing: A First Exploration of the Theoretical and Statistical Problems', Working Paper 7808, Faculty of Applied Economics, State

University Centre, Antwerp.

van Moeseke, P. (1965), 'Stochastic Linear Programming: A Study in Resource Allocation under Risk', *Yale Economic Essays*, 5, 196–254.

Viñals, J. (1986), 'Fiscal Policy and the Current Account', *Economic Policy*, 3, 711–744.

Vohra, R. (1988), 'On the Existence of Equilibria in Economies with Increasing Returns: A Synthesis', *Journal of Mathematical Economics*, 17, 179–192.

Waelbroeck, J. and A. Dramais (1974), 'DESMOS: A Model for the Coordination of Economic Policies in the EEC-Countries', in A. Ando, R. Herring and R. Martson, eds., *International Aspects of Stabilisation Policies*, Federal Reserve Bank, Boston.

Weddepohl, C. (1979), 'An Equilibrium Model with Fixed Labour Time', *Econometrica*, 47, 921–938.

Weitzman, M. L. (1984), *The Share Economy: Conquering Stagflation*, Harvard University Press, Cambridge, Mass.

Wilson, R. (1968), 'On the Theory of Syndicates', *Econometrica*, 36, 119–132.

Younès, Y. (1975), 'On the Role of Money in the Process of Exchange and the Existence of a Non-Walrasian Equilibrium', *Review of Economic Studies*, 42, 489–501.

Index